Scotland's Books

Robert Crawford was born in 1959 in Lanarkshire and grew up there. He studied at the universities of Glasgow and Oxford. He has published six collections of poetry and a *Selected Poems* (2005). With Mick Imlah he edited *The New Penguin Book of Scottish Verse* (2000), now published in Penguin Classics as *The Penguin Book of Scottish Verse* (2006). His other books include *Devolving English Literature* (1992; Second Edition, 2000) and *The Modern Poet* (2001). He is Professor of Modern Scottish Literature at the University of St Andrews and a Fellow of the Royal Society of Edinburgh.

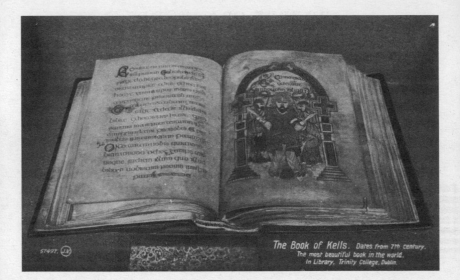

The Book of Kells. Dates from 7th century.
The most beautiful book in the world.
In Library, Trinity College, Dublin.

57497. J.V.

'The most beautiful book in the world'. An early twentieth-century postcard published by the Dundee firm of J. Valentine and Company illustrates the medieval Book of Kells. Thought to have been begun in the monastery on the island of Iona in the eighth century, the manuscript was later taken to the monastery at Kells in Ireland at the time of Viking raids on Iona, and is now in the Library of Trinity College, Dublin. The postcard shows the book open at St Matthew's Gospel. (St Andrews University Library, Valentine Collection JV-57497)

ROBERT CRAWFORD

Scotland's Books

The Penguin History of Scottish Literature

PENGUIN BOOKS

PENGUIN BOOKS

Published by the Penguin Group
Penguin Books Ltd, 80 Strand, London WC2R ORL, England
Penguin Group (USA) Inc., 375 Hudson Street, New York, New York 10014, USA
Penguin Group (Canada), 90 Eglinton Avenue East, Suite 700, Toronto, Ontario, Canada M4P 2Y3
(a division of Pearson Penguin Canada Inc.)
Penguin Ireland, 25 St Stephen's Green, Dublin 2, Ireland
(a division of Penguin Books Ltd)
Penguin Group (Australia), 250 Camberwell Road, Camberwell, Victoria 3124, Australia
(a division of Pearson Australia Group Pty Ltd)
Penguin Books India Pvt Ltd, 11 Community Centre, Panchsheel Park, New Delhi – 110 017, India
Penguin Group (NZ), 67 Apollo Drive, Rosedale, North Shore 0632, New Zealand
(a division of Pearson New Zealand Ltd)
Penguin Books (South Africa) (Pty) Ltd, 24 Sturdee Avenue, Rosebank,
Johannesburg 2196, South Africa

Penguin Books Ltd, Registered Offices: 80 Strand, London WC2R ORL, England

www.penguin.com

First published 2007
1

Copyright © Robert Crawford, 2007
All rights reserved

The moral right of the author has been asserted

Set in 9/12.25 pt PostScript Adobe Sabon
Typeset by Rowland Phototypesetting Ltd, Bury St Edmunds, Suffolk
Printed in England by Clays Ltd, St Ives plc

ISBN: 978-0-140-29940-3

www.greenpenguin.co.uk

Penguin Books is committed to a sustainable future
for our business, our readers and our planet.
The book in your hands is made from paper
certified by the Forest Stewardship Council.

To Alice, Lewis and Blyth
with love

Gente Scotus, Anima Orbis terrarum Civis

Scottish by Nationality, in Spirit a Citizen of the World

– inscribed by the radical Scottish republican Latin poet Thomas Muir of Huntershill inside a book which he presented to the monks of Rio de Janeiro when he was being transported as a political prisoner to Botany Bay in 1794

Contents

List of Illustrations

The Illustrations in This Book

With the exception of the last photograph, all the plates in *Scotland's Books* are drawn from the collections of what can claim to be Scotland's oldest continuously functioning library, that of the University of St Andrews. Founded in 1411, Scotland's first university evolved from earlier schools attached to St Andrews Cathedral, which had its own substantial collection of manuscript books. The collections of St Andrews University were used by some of Scotland's greatest medieval writers, including William Dunbar and Gavin Douglas. Later, during the Renaissance, the University Library was enhanced by gifts of books from poets including King James VI, George Buchanan and William Drummond of Hawthornden. The King James Library was established in 1611, and redeveloped in neoclassical style in 1764 when its readers included the poet Robert Fergusson; it is still in use today. From 1710 until 1837 the Library was a Copyright Library, which allowed it to claim a copy of any book published in Britain, and in the nineteenth century it began to develop its unique photography collections. The Library's modern manuscript collections continue the tradition of acquiring manuscripts by gift and purchase, and include many of the papers of the novelist and writer on feminist issues, Willa Muir. Among the manuscripts is also the Library's fine Muniments Collection, the University's institutional archive. The present-day main library building was built in the later twentieth century and is now expanding, with a substantial collections development programme. For permission to reproduce copyright illustrative material in this book special thanks are due to the Librarian, Jon Purcell, and to Dr Norman Reid, Head of Special Collections. If you would like to support the work of the Library, please write to The Secretary, Friends of St Andrews University Library, University Library, North Street, St Andrews, Fife, Scotland KY16 9TR.

Acknowledgements

Scotland's Books: The Penguin History of Scottish Literature has been over six years in the making and has led me to incur more debts than I can acknowledge. I have tried to build on the work of generations of scholars. Many of the most important among these are cited in the notes to this book. In addition, I gratefully acknowledge specific advice from the individuals named below, several of whom were kind enough to read chapters in draft form.

When this book was first proposed, it was the first time anyone had tried to encompass the extended history of Scottish literature in all the languages of Scotland. Its gestation has been long – rather longer than it might otherwise have been because for three years during its composition I was labouring in the administrative vineyards as Head of the School of English at the University of St Andrews. Thanks are due to Anna South at Penguin who bravely commissioned the volume as a follow-up to *The New Penguin Book of Scottish Verse*, to David Godwin who convinced me it was possible for one person to embark on such a venture, and to Helen Conford who became my editor in the final stages. Helen Campbell copy-edited the typescript with meticulous patience and Dr Rosalind MacLachlan cleverly constructed the index. I am grateful to my students and to all my St Andrews School of English academic and secretarial colleagues for their staunch support; grateful to the Arts and Humanities Research Board (as it then was) for a semester's research leave in 2001 during which I worked on the early medieval section of the book; and grateful to my university for two more recent semesters' research leave during which *Scotland's Books* was completed.

For advice, comment, conversation and rescue in person and in their published works, I thank especially Dr David Allan; Professor Robert Bartlett; Dr Meg Bateman; Professor Priscilla Bawcutt; Professor

Thomas Clancy; Professor Cairns Craig; Dr Alice Crawford; Dr Barbara Crawford; Professor Lewis Dabney; Professor Ian Duncan; Professor Douglas Dunn; Professor Douglas Gifford; Professor Stephen Halliwell; Professor Stephen Harrison; Professor Seamus Heaney; Professor W. N. Herbert; Mr Mick Imlah; Dr Ian Johnson; Dr David Kinloch; Dr Christopher MacLachlan; Professor Dorothy McMillan; Mr Phillip Mallett; Professor Susan Manning; Dr Sally Mapstone; Professor Roger Mason; Professor Edwin Morgan; Dr Andrew Nash; Dr Tom Normand; Professor Murray G. H. Pittock; Dr Rhiannon Purdie; Mr Robert N. Smart; the late Dr Iain Crichton Smith; Dr Fiona Stafford; Professor Derick Thomson. None of these people is responsible for any mistakes in this book; all of them helped to reduce the list of errata.

Much of the work for *Scotland's Books* was done in the Library of the University of St Andrews, particularly its Special Collections Department. I would like to thank all the staff there for their cheerful helpfulness, and am especially grateful to Dr Norman Reid and his colleagues Ms Pam Cranston, Dr Alice Crawford, Mrs Rachel Hart, Mrs Elizabeth Henderson and Ms Moira Mackenzie. Salutes are due also to the National Library of Scotland (especially to Mr Kenneth Dunn); to BBC Scotland (especially Mr Dave Batchelor, Dr David Stenhouse and Dr Louise Yeoman); to Edinburgh University Library; to the Mitchell Library, Glasgow; to Innerpeffray Library, Perthshire (a hidden jewel); in Oxford to the Bodleian Library, the library and archives of Balliol College and the archives of Christ Church.

Over a number of years I have been able to combine invitations to give poetry readings or lectures, or to hold short-term visiting appointments outside Scotland, with intensive bursts of research work in library and archive collections and the chance to get a different view of Scottish culture. Thanks to the Master and Fellows of Balliol College, Oxford, and the organizers of the Smithies Lectures for their kind invitation to deliver the lectures and for their generous hospitality; to Corpus Christi College, Oxford, where I paid homage to James Legge; to the Beinecke Library, Yale (and especially to Professors Sandy Welsh and Ruth Yeazell of the Yale English Department); to the British Council, especially in Budapest and Prague; to the Emory University Manuscript and Rare Books Library, Atlanta (especially to Dr Stephen Enniss there, and Professor Ron Schuchard of the Department of English and the Richard Ellmann Lectures in Modern Literature at Emory); to the Universities of Guelph, Ontario, Mainz at Germersheim, Nantes and Tübingen; to Harvard University Library and Princeton University Library; to Washington University, St Louis (especially to Professor Marina Mackay, Department of English); and at the University of Wyoming at Laramie and Caspar where I relished holding the L. L. Smith Visiting Professorship in 2004 warm thanks are due to Professors Caroline McCracken-Flesher and Paul Flesher, to Professor Lewis Bagby, and to Professor Bruce Richardson and Ms Susan Stanford who, among many other things, drove the Crawford family on a route once taken by John Muir (as well as on many routes which he did not take), and discussed Muir and his work in situ among elk and bison at Yellowstone National Park.

Copyright and scholarly debts are acknowledged in the main text and endnotes to this book. New translations or versions made for *Scotland's Books* remain the copyright of the translator. In addition, where substantial parts of works, or in some cases whole poems, are quoted, the following acknowledgements are due. To Anvil Press Poetry: 'Forgive Me, Sire' by Norman Cameron, from *Norman Cameron: Collected Poems and Selected Translations*, ed. Warren Hope and Jonathan Barker (Anvil Press Poetry, 1990), reprinted by permission of the publisher. To Birlinn Ltd: 'Horse Hymn' and 'Poem against Julius II' by George Buchanan, tr. Robert Crawford, from *Apollos of the North: Selected Poems of George Buchanan and Arthur Johnston*, ed. Robert Crawford (Polygon, 2006), reprinted by permission of Polygon, an imprint of Birlinn Ltd (www.birlinn.co.uk); from 'Summer Farm' and 'Patriot' by Norman MacCaig, from *Collected Poems* (Chatto & Windus, 1990), reprinted by permission of Birlinn Ltd. To Canongate Books: from 'Arran' (Anon.), tr. Thomas Clancy; 'The Attributes of a Gentleman' by Earl Rognvald Kali, tr. Paul Bibire; from 'Elegy of Mael Mhedha, his Wife' by Muireadhach Albanach Ó Dálaigh, tr. Thomas Clancy, all from *The Triumph Tree: Scotland's Earliest Poetry AD 550–1350*, ed. Thomas Clancy (Canongate Books, 1998). First published in Great Britain by Canongate Books Ltd, 14 High Street, Edinburgh EH1 1TE, reprinted by permission of the publisher. To Carcanet Press: 'The Watergaw', 'Empty Vessel' and from 'On a Raised Beach' by Hugh MacDiarmid, from *The Complete Poems of Hugh MacDiarmid, 1920–1976*, two volumes, ed. Michael Grieve and W. R. Aitken (first published by Martin Brian and O'Keeffe, 1978); from 'An Roghainn'/'The Choice', tr. Sorley MacLean, from *From Wood to Ridge: Collected Poems in Gaelic and English* (Carcanet Press, 1989); from 'Two Girls Singing' by Iain Crichton Smith, from *Collected Poems* (Carcanet Press, 1992), all reprinted by permission of the publisher. To Faber and Faber: 'The Blue Jacket' by Marion Angus, from *The Turn of the Day* (Faber and Faber, 1931); 'Waking with Russell' by Don Paterson, from *Landing Light* (Faber and Faber, 2003), reprinted by permission of the publisher. To Tom Leonard: from 'Unrelated Incidents – 3' by Tom Leonard, from *Intimate Voices: Selected Works 1965–1983* (Etruscan Books, 2003), reprinted by permission of the author. To Pan Macmillan: 'The Wishing Tree' by Kathleen Jamie, from *The Tree House* (Picador, 2004), reprinted by permission of Macmillan, London. Thanks are due also to Nick Wetton for his work on clearing permissions.

The dedication of this book expresses my greatest debt. Without the love, cartwheels, humour and wisdom of my wife, son and daughter I could never have written it.

R.C., St Andrews, 2006

Web Resources and Further Reading

Readers may find that this book is usefully complemented by *The New Penguin Book of Scottish Verse* (2000), edited by Robert Crawford and Mick Imlah and published in the Penguin Classics series, and by the web companion to that anthology. The anthology itself was retitled *The Penguin Book of Scottish Verse* in 2006. The web companion is part of the Poetry House, the most authoritative guide to poetry on the internet, and can be found either through its host site at the University of St Andrews,

http://www.st-andrews.ac.uk/english/

or by going direct to

http://www.thepoetryhouse.org

and clicking on the Projects Archive for 2005. As Projects Archive for 2007 there may be at the same site a similar web companion to the full *Scotland's Books: The Penguin History of Scottish Literature*. In the meantime, however, while individual searches on the net for Scottish authors or topics will often yield worthwhile results, the most helpful gateway site for information on the web is the site of the National Library of Scotland:

http://www.nls.uk/

This site gives access to a variety of information sources, including the Bibliography of Scottish Literature in Translation (BOSLIT) project, which lists a huge range of Scottish texts translated into other languages. Further Scottish institutions, such as the Scottish Poetry Library, also maintain valuable electronic resources with useful links pages, and most institutions associated with literature in Scotland, such as the National Theatre of Scotland, have their own websites.

Readers seeking a good modern history of Scotland which covers the same period as *Scotland's Books* may find it helpful to consult *The New Penguin History of Scotland* (2001), edited by R. A. Houston and W W J Knox, or *Scotland: A History* (Oxford University Press, 2005), edited by Jenny Wormald. Both are readable and attractively illustrated. The most extensive scholarly history of Scotland is the ten-volume one now progressing under the general editorship of Professor Roger Mason of the University of St Andrews under the title *The New Edinburgh History of Scotland* and being published by Edinburgh University Press (2004–).

In the notes to this book I have listed sources, including many helpful secondary works. The only A–Z dictionary of Scottish literature remains Trevor Royle's very helpful *Mainstream Companion to Scottish Literature* (1993), but readers who want more extended scholarly treatments of the subject as a whole (including topics outside the area of imaginative writing) may wish to consult the lengthy three-volume *Edinburgh History of Scottish Literature* (Edinburgh University Press, 2007), which has been written by an international team of scholars under the general editorship of Ian Brown. Of similarly extended dimensions will be the four-volume, multi-authored *Edinburgh History of the Book in Scotland*, which is planned to detail the development of manuscript, print and mass media culture in Scotland, and is being produced under the general editorship of the publishing historian Dr Bill Bell of the Centre for the History of the Book, University of Edinburgh. These larger-scale, more specialist works began after the present volume and have not been published at the time of writing, so I have been unable to consult them, but they are likely to be of considerable use to those seeking further reading.

The fold-out 'elegant map' from the second edition of the Gazetteer of Scotland *published in Edinburgh and London in 1806 by two of the most famous Scottish publishing houses, Archibald Constable and Company, and John Murray. (St Andrews University Library, sDA869.S8)*

Introduction

Scotland's books belong to the world and the world disproportionately enjoys them. More than twenty thousand works of Scottish literature have been translated into a range of over seventy languages, from Albanian to Yakut. From 'Auld Lang Syne' to Sherlock Holmes, the imaginings of Scottish authors are part of international currency. *Treasure Island*, Jekyll and Hyde, Peter Pan are familiar reference points of twenty-first-century culture. To most people they matter not because their origins lie in earlier centuries of Scottish literature, but because of their sheer imaginative sparkle.

Yet the fact that these works were nourished by Scottish literary history only adds to their staying power. The ability of even apparently arcane Scottish writing to communicate across centuries and cultures is remarkable. When Sylvia Plath in 1950s Massachusetts recited in her American accent a lament made four and a half centuries earlier by William Dunbar, it is unlikely she pronounced it all correctly, or that she could have identified the dead Scottish poets it lists. Even though Plath would have known that its Latin refrain means 'The fear of death disturbs me', she may not have understood every Scots word in this poem that begins,

> I that in heill wes and gladnes   *health*
> Am trublit now with gret seiknes
> And feblit with infirmité:
> *Timor mortis conturbat me.*[1]

Like most readers, Plath could feel and hear this Scottish poem's grip before she came closer to its meaning. Where the American Plath in the twentieth century was attracted to William Dunbar, the Irishman Seamus Heaney in the present century has gravitated towards the slightly earlier

Scottish medieval poet Robert Henryson and has even presented one of his own poems as if it is a translation from the work of another long-dead Scottish writer – the early seventeenth-century Latin poet Arthur Johnston.[2]

Examples like these indicate that it is not only modern Scottish fiction's urban danse macabre that exercises a powerful gravitational pull on the writerly imagination; nor is it just Scottish verse written in Scots or in English or in Latin. Scotland's books contain much material composed for performance – from plays and lectures to ballads and songs in several languages. One would need to be immune to the allure of poetry not to respond to the graceful Gaelic longing of the seventeenth-century Mary MacLeod to go back to the Isle of Skye:

Do Uilbhinnis	*To Ullinish*
A' chruidh chaisfhinn,	*of white-hoofed cattle*
Far an d'fhuair mi	*where I grew up,*
Gu h-òg m'altrum,	*a little girl*
Air bainne chìoch	*breast-fed there*
Nam ban basgheal,	*by soft-palmed women,*
Thall aig Fionnghail	*in the house of brown-haired Flora,*
Dhuinn nighean Lachainn,	*Lachlan's daughter,*
Is ì 'na banchaig	*milkmaid*
Ris na martaibh	*among the cows*
Aig Ruairidh mór Mac	*of Roderick Mor*
Leòid nam bratach.	*MacLeod of the banners.*[3]

Mary MacLeod's poem attracted the Australian poet Les Murray when he read it as a Sydney student, hunting in his university library for Gaelic verse. Some foreign visitors in search of a taste of Scottish literary history are delighted to find what they want – often material linked to Gaelic culture or to Scotland's great national poet, Robert Burns. Others bring Scottish literature with them, as if to recharge it at source. When the Argentinian writer Jorge Luis Borges (who grew up in Buenos Aires reading Walter Scott, R. L. Stevenson and Thomas Carlyle) spent a week in St Andrews in 1971, he recited Scots ballads to his hosts who knew, like Borges, that the ballads are among the great treasures of Scottish literary history. Yet when the Peruvian novelist Mario Vargas Llosa travelled to Kirkcaldy a few years later, eager to see sites associated with that Fife town's most famous son, the philosopher Adam Smith, he could find almost nothing. In that era many Scots, vaguely associating Adam Smith with the policies of Margaret Thatcher, wished almost to deny he was Scottish.

Scots often undervalue literary or cultural history, occasionally treating it with rancour, and more often with a kind of casual abandon that simply lets it get lost. There is, after all, a lot of it, as both locals and tourists are aware. When Mario Vargas Llosa drew a blank in Kirkcaldy, he simply went to the literary and religious pilgrimage site of St Andrews instead ('beautiful'), then to the home of Sir Walter Scott at Abbotsford in the Scottish Borders. Scott's *Ivanhoe* is the first historical novel the ten-year-old Vargas Llosa read – 'Scott was read all over Latin America then'.[4] If the Scottish author who made such an impression on the Spanish-speaking world was often a Walter Scott retranslated into Spanish from French translations of the originals, that is only another sign of the energy with which Scottish writing can surge across national borders.

There are times when writers realize that literary history is just too important to lose. Robert Burns and Walter Scott both sensed that they lived at such moments. They collected earlier examples of Scottish literature, and they wrote their own, sometimes linking that to work from the past. Other, less celebrated writers have done likewise, feeling an urge both to guard and to glorify the hoard, as well as trying to add to it. This impulse continues today. During a period in Scotland's history when the nation has a fresh sense of democratic control over its own affairs, when its literary spectrum is wide as well as deep, and when from Berkeley to Beijing there are signs of a new interest in Scotland's books, it is time for a fresh history aimed not just at academics but at readers generally – readers who may one day follow in the footsteps of Borges or of Vargas Llosa.

For just as Scottish literature belongs to the world, so does Scottish literary history. However much it helps the local tourist industry, Scotland's literary history also matters to a wider international public. Poetry may be Scotland's oldest and greatest art form, but Walter Scott, a poet and dramatist who defected to prose fiction, is the single most influential writer in the worldwide history of the novel. Like Sappho, Catullus and

Ovid, Robert Burns is one of the world's great love poets. James Boswell laid the foundations of modern literary biography. In no instance was these Scottish writers' Scottishness incidental, though in each case the writer's work is about more than the local complexities of Scotland.

A small northern country with a present-day population of five million, Scotland, through its authors, has played an improbably large part in world literature. From the music of Mendelssohn and Donizetti or the paintings of Turner to contemporary Hollywood and independent cinema, other media have furthered the impact of Scottish writing, as histories of those other media often record. From *Trainspotting* to Harry Potter, works from Scotland continue to attract a mass audience, often through translation into other languages and into other media such as music or cinema. Yet the basis of these works is in the power of the written word, and it is as writing that they are considered in this history of Scottish literature.

While some literary works from Scotland are globally celebrated, bid for, argued over, hyped and hurra'd, others are forgotten or condemned to dusty respect. Yet the international prominence of a substantial number of Scottish writers is all the more surprising because almost none of the world's schools, colleges or universities teaches courses in Scottish literature – even in Scotland itself. There are no Scottish embassies or even Scottish literature bureaux devoted to disseminating knowledge of the country's literature abroad. Although outside Scotland a few enthusiasts teach Scottish literary history, for instance at the universities of Oxford and Wyoming, and there is a small scattering of Scottish Studies Centres around the globe, generally, from Cambridge, Mass., to Cambridge, England, and from Hong Kong to Toronto, Scottish literature stays institutionally marginal. Where Irish literary studies, cannily and energetically promoted by Ireland's government, are prominent in curricula everywhere and Irish books canonical, Scottish poetry, fiction and drama rely far less on institutional muscle than on sheer enthusiasm for their dissemination. Most people read Scottish literature just because they like it, not because they have to. Any university student of English in New York or Melbourne is likely to be required to read English, American and Irish texts. But when was the last time a student in New York or Melbourne was forced to read a Scottish book?

There are advantages to reading books purely for fun, rather than under the beady eye of a teacher. Sometimes, though, without any advice from a literary map, other people's pleasure, their fun, their enthusiasm can seem incomprehensible or at least demandingly obscure. Readers round the world may well understand why in her teens in 1980s Inverness, just like readers of the *New Yorker* magazine decades earlier, the contemporary Scottish writer Ali Smith so relished *The Prime of Miss Jean Brodie*, that masterpiece by Scotland's greatest twentieth-century novelist, Muriel Spark; not so many readers may understand why the ten-year-old Canadian Margaret Atwood 'read all the Andrew Lang folk-tale collections I could find' or was later suspicious of 'Carlyle's blimp-like Great Men'; and very few modern readers will know much about the man whom many in Renaissance Europe, including in France the essayist Montaigne, who was his eager pupil, knew as 'the great Scottish poet'.[5]

Scotland's Books: The Penguin History of Scottish Literature exists to give readers a convenient overview of the landscape of Scottish imaginative writing. It is the first book to present to the general reader the extended history of Scottish literature in a single volume. It aims to provide a narrative that is readable, nuanced and informative. In many ways the book's design follows that of *The Penguin Book of Scottish Verse* which the present writer edited with Mick Imlah in 2000 and which remains the first and only general anthology to present in the original language and in translation fifteen centuries of work by writers linked to the small part of the planet we now call Scotland. Belonging to no transcendent, unchanging national identity, but simply constituting a marvellous inheritance enjoyed by today's Scotland, these fifteen centuries of work include much prose and some drama as well as verse. Earlier anthologies and older histories of Scottish literature cover only around half that historical sweep. Those histories tend also to oversimplify (some might say censor) Scotland's linguistic complexity. Like a good deal of Scottish literature in a period of struggle to reassert political authority in Scotland, they were bound up with asserting or contesting the validity of the Scottish nation. The most ambitious recent multivolume histories of Scottish literature, sometimes involving vast teams of specialist contributors each of whom writes a detailed essay on a relatively narrow topic, have tended to follow the historical design of *The Penguin Book of Scottish Verse*, but have been published by academic presses at a cost and in a style that suggest they are aimed principally at university libraries.

Although I cannot claim to be a specialist in all the material discussed, I hope that there are advantages in having a continuous narrative voice running throughout a single paperback book which sees Scottish literature as a whole. Aimed at the general reader, *Scotland's Books* certainly contains new research which may be of interest to a university audience, but it aims most of all to be helpful, jargon-free and clear. Anyone can read this book, which is at least as much a labour of love as a pedagogical product. If it contains some material which enhances the academic consideration of Scottish culture, that is to the good; but better still if it adds to the simple enjoyment and understanding of a literature much of which remains to many people – including most Scots – obscure, hard to map, even in some cases vanished. Deliberately, for the sake of entertainment as well as enlightenment, I have tried to quote a good deal of lively illustrative material by the writers whose work I discuss.

I take the validity of the Scottish nation for granted, but assert that Scottish literature is both older and more expansive than that nation. If this sounds paradoxical, the point is simply that Scottish literature should never be confined to Scotland. The present-day nation is the inheritor of earlier cultural traditions and literary works associated with the territory we now call 'Scotland', and Scottish literature for many centuries has circulated abroad, influencing as well as being influenced by other literatures. All literatures are porous; 'one's own language', as Mikhail Bakhtin puts it, 'is never a single language'.[6] Scottish writers write about everything, and all literatures, like all writers, exist in dialogue. Inheritors of their literary history, other nations are in a position similar to that of Scotland, whether or not they choose to acknowledge it: the literary history of Spain involves Latin and Arabic as well as Spanish, for instance; *Beowulf* in Old English, late medieval writing in French, and Bede or Milton in Latin are splendid parts of England's literary history. As a confident modern nation, Scotland can take pride in the many, sometimes ancient linguistic and cultural traditions which have nourished it and which, through writerly imaginations, are part of its literary glories. Most Scottish writers have been aware of literature in more than one of the languages of Scotland.

All Scotland's languages are international, though, and the literary imagination, however fascinated with local topography and limits it may be, also likes to hop over borders. Just as the earliest surviving Scottish literature, attributed to the Gaelic-speaking Irish immigrant

St Columba, is written in the international language of Latin, so later Scottish poems are made in languages – Gaelic, Welsh, Norse, French, English, Scots – which also link Scotland to elsewhere. In different centuries great literary capitals such as Paris and London have been crucial for Scottish imaginations, even if some of the finest Scottish writers, most notably Robert Burns, never went there. Literature in English is one of Scotland's greatest glories, and one of the country's furthest-reaching exports. Yet today the struggle to maintain Scottish Gaelic as an international language, through attempts to keep it alive in Canada's Nova Scotia, is perhaps the most poignantly fragile reminder that none of Scotland's literary languages belongs to Scotland alone, but all make Scotland a participant in wider communities of the imagination. This is not a *History* of the literature produced by Scottish-descended communities abroad, nor is it about all the writings which feature Scotland or the Scots, but it is a book alert to the fact that all literatures travel, and often call readers far from their own lives and locations. Many more people have travelled to Scotland, Greece or Japan in the pages of books than have ever gone there in person.

Those witty and moving words spoken by Dr Winifred Ewing in May 1999, 'The Scottish Parliament, adjourned on the 25th day of March in the year 1707, is hereby reconvened', brought Scotland into a new political era which many twentieth-century Scottish imaginative writers had dreamed into being in their works before, eventually, it was delivered by a democratic vote.[7] The (re-)establishment of a Scottish Parliament in Edinburgh was part of a sometimes confident, sometimes anxious political reassertion of Scottish national identity. Many Scottish literary works – ancient and modern – have played their part in defining and redefining that identity. Robert Burns loved to read an eighteenth-century English-language version of Blind Hary's Scots medieval poem about the freedom fighter William Wallace, and Burns in the age of the French Revolution would incite his countrymen as 'Scots, wha hae wi' Wallace bled' to throw off 'Chains and slaverie'; Burns, Mel Gibson (star of Hollywood's Wallace movie, *Braveheart*), and many others have ensured that Wallace has remained across the centuries an international icon of freedom, admired alike by the nineteenth-century Italian patriot Garibaldi and by Scotland's most ardent and most internationally-minded twentieth-century poet, Hugh MacDiarmid, one of the founders of what became the pro-independence Scottish National Party.

Some people in the twentieth century thought that around the world both nationalism and religion were waning as cultural forces, but from the viewpoint of the twenty-first century such an attitude seems misguided. Concerns about environmental change and a huge increase in travel encourage us to see our planet as one complex organism, but this has not resulted in a loss of commitment to local or national traditions. If it is valid to try to see literature in terms of one worldwide republic, it is as valid to view it in terms of national traditions – these angles are not mutually exclusive. Today's Scotland is driven neither by the religious fundamentalism that convulsed the nation in the sixteenth century, nor by the British nationalism that sent so many nineteenth-century Scots across the Empire. While Scotland's books belong to the world, not just to Scotland, a significant number of writers have been eager Scottish nationalists; at different times authors have wished to see Scotland united with an assortment of countries, including variously Ireland, Norway, France and England; other writers have had little interest in national or international politics. 'Scottish literature' does not just mean books about Scotland, or books published in Scotland, or books by men and women born north of the Border. There are many ways to be associated with literature from this small country, and the present *History* tries within the limits of space, judgement and inclination to be generous in its inclusiveness. If in the eighteenth and nineteenth centuries Scottish writers championed ideals of Britishness that never appealed much to the more Anglocentric writers of England, few Scottish writers today find Britishness imaginatively engaging. Nor, however, do they wish their work to be seen exclusively in terms of its Scottishness.

Literature is porous, unpredictable, resistant to pigeonholing. No one could have foreseen that the greatest work of Scots prose would be written not in the Middle Ages but by a late twentieth-century retired St Andrews professor of Greek, whose translation of *The New Testament in Scots* has Christ 'Ae day . . . gaein alangside the Loch o Galilee' in a countryside where only the Devil speaks English.[8] *Scotland's Books* is primarily a history of imaginative writing – rightly the hardest sort to pin down. Although I do include, for instance, some of Scotland's greatest philosophers, I am most interested in their importance for Scottish creative writers. Rather than attempting a history of Scottish thought, or a publishing historian's survey of print culture, I have tried to present the most imaginatively compelling creative writing and writers.

Perhaps in part because I write poetry as well as literary history and criticism, and because I am used to working among creative writers as well as literary critics, theorists and historians, this *Penguin History* presents writers as individuals with their own relevant biographies rather than simply as coordinates on a cultural grid.

Considerable space has been devoted to Scotland's most compelling authors, and some to areas which have been neglected or misunderstood, such as the seventeenth century and the literary arguments around political union with England in 1707. Allocation of space usually implies value judgements, which some modern academics avoid, or at least pretend to avoid. Though I have nowhere followed the late Norman MacCaig, who once gleefully described to me a (still) living poet's work as 'thirteenth-rate', I have included only a smidgen of historically illustrative rubbish. In showing patterns and presenting arguments about cultural structures, while I have often linked writers together, I have attempted to retain some sense of their individual stylistic differences. About a third of this book is given over to literature before 1700, and a third to work produced since 1900: modern Scottish imaginative writing is thriving in its range, its liveliness and its quality.

Many readers may approach *Scotland's Books* from a standpoint of familiarity with English literature and culture. This is not the place to set out all the differences and similarities between Scotland and England, but readers should be alert to the fact that these exist. Sometimes, especially in recent times, their consequences are overlooked. English literature has been loved in Scotland for many centuries. However, if Wordsworth, Keats and other English poets were often markedly Scotophile, English novelists and dramatists were generally the reverse: *Macbeth* is hardly a paean to Caledonia, while the only major English novel set in Scotland is Virginia Woolf's impressive *To the Lighthouse*. The strangeness of Woolf's Hebrides is in part explained by the fact that until several years after she wrote that novel she had never set foot there. When at last she travelled north in 1938, in the Borders at Dryburgh Abbey she 'glutted my passion for Scott on his tomb – like chocolate blanc-mange', and she wrote to her sister from the Flodigarry Hotel in Portree that Skye was 'on a level with Italy, Greece or Florence'. Woolf loved the beauty of the Highland light, 'very subtle, very changeable, running over my pen, as if you poured a large jug of champagne over a hairpin'. But she noted with shock that being on a Hebridean island felt 'like the South Seas – completely remote, surrounded by sea, people speaking Gaelic, no railways, no London papers, hardly any inhabitants'.[9] Woolf is far from the first southern visitor to be struck by the sheer cultural difference of Scotland, then to fall in love with it and over-exoticize it.

A more subtle and sober example of cultural cross-Border difference is the structure and significance of the Scottish universities whose traditional four-year undergraduate degree courses remain broader-based than the three-year degrees of even the most ancient English universities. In England literary texts in English were not taught at university until relatively late in the nineteenth century; in Scotland literary texts in English (including poetry, drama and the novel) were taught at the four ancient Universities of St Andrews, Glasgow, Aberdeen and Edinburgh from the mid-eighteenth century, a fact that markedly conditioned several writers. However, whereas the leading English poets of the Romantic period and after have often been the products of public schools and/or universities, several of Scotland's finest poets – such as Robert Burns, Hugh MacDiarmid and Don Paterson – studied at no university, and very few Scottish writers have attended public schools in the English sense of that expression. On the other hand, none of England's greatest novelists before the twentieth century was university-educated, whereas Scottish novelists of earlier centuries were often highly schooled in the university system; this perhaps conditioned the intellectual inflection of Scottish fiction, which in the eighteenth and nineteenth centuries, for instance, is often bound up with Scottish philosophy, theology and even science. Another related factor is that, until the nineteenth century, Scotland had several more (albeit smaller) universities than its much more populous southern neighbour. The Scottish universities were distributed across their country, whereas the relative proximity of Oxford and Cambridge encouraged the dominance of a southern English elite. The separate educational, legal and ecclesiastical systems of the two countries are indicative of substantial differences in their cultures, even in the years 1707–1999 when their internal affairs were governed to a considerable extent by a common, London-based Parliament.

Again, cultural differences within Scotland and within England can be greater than cultural differences between the two countries. While William Drummond in the early seventeenth century was the first Scottish poet to use English with real and repeated assurance, in modern times the two countries have had English as a shared literary language. Scotland, though, has always been keen on other tongues, and the continuing polylingual inflection of Scottish literature is the most obvious feature that sets it apart from conventional ideas of English literature – and even from some older academic ideas of Scottish literature. Until recently it was taken for granted that general anthologies of Scottish literature simply omitted work in Gaelic and Latin. Historically, the difference between Gaelic-speaking areas of Scotland and Scots-speaking areas is unparalleled in England, but involves the sort of linguistic and literary issues familiar in other countries such as Switzerland and Canada.

It is sometimes tempting for commentators to regard all Scottish writers as imagining the nation, but this can be dangerously reductive. While there are countries who have employed their writers as official ambassadorial representatives – George Seferis from Greece and Octavio Paz from Mexico being twentieth-century examples – few writers, particularly perhaps Scottish ones, relish being portrayed simply as part of a national team. As Salman Rushdie puts it, 'The nation requires anthems, flags. The poet offers discord. Rags.' As Rushdie knows, both the demands of national politics and the pressures of ideology manifested through 'isms' and tramlined critical attitudes, while they can be usefully illuminating, can also be reductive both for readers and for writers:

Beware the writer who sets himself or herself up as the voice of a nation. This includes nations of race, gender, sexual orientation, elective affinity. This is the New Behalfism. Beware behalfies!

The New Behalfism demands uplift, accentuates the positive, offers stirring moral instruction. It abhors the tragic sense of life. Seeing literature as inescapably political, it substitutes political values for literary ones. It is the murderer of thought. Beware![10]

Although there is a difference between writers who come to be identified with particular territories or positions and those who set themselves up simply as national or political spokespersons, Rushdie's note of caution is helpful. So is his mention of literature as apparently 'inescapably political' in the widest sense of that word. Imaginative writing, even if it seeks to be hermetic, is inflected by politics and by wider history.

In writing literary history, I have supplied a necessary minimum of wider historical signposting, but readers who need a fuller account of historical events may wish to turn to recent accounts of Scottish history from the earliest times to the present, such as those which are mentioned in the 'Web Resources and Further Reading' section of this book. Literary history and national history are not always coincident. Alert to ideas like those of Homi Bhabha, and of Benedict Anderson, whose *Imagined Communities* (1983) was an influential book for several Scottish critics, I have engaged in some of the theoretical debates about Scottish literature in my earlier book, *Devolving English Literature* (1992, 2000) and elsewhere. Introducing this present, much more wide-ranging *History*, I would like to point towards the work of differently-oriented thinkers such as Pascale Casanova. Casanova's 1999 *La république mondiale des lettres*, precisely because it is only glancingly and imprecisely keyed to Scottish matters, is stimulating and helpful in thinking about how to present literary history – especially that of small nations – in our globalized era. In Casanova's 'world republic of letters',

national literary space must not be confused with national territory. Taking into account every one of the positions that characterizes a literary space, including those occupied by exiled writers, and regarding them as elements of a coherent whole, helps resolve the false questions that are posed in connection with small literatures. For it is through the interplay between established national literatures and the emergence of autonomous literary positions, which are necessarily international, occupied by writers who are often condemned to a sort of internal exile (like Juan Benet and Arno Schmidt) or to actual exile (like James Joyce in Trieste and Paris, Danilo Kiš in Paris, and Salman Rushdie in London), that the full complexity of a national literary space appears.[11]

Within the limits of this volume, I aim to suggest the rich complexity of Scotland's 'national literary space', while remaining aware that Scottish literature is both much more ancient and much more extensive than many of the literatures which Pascale Casanova discusses – and at least as complicated as any of them.

The plural nature of Scotland's linguistic heritage and the importance of Empire have reinforced that complexity. If some of the earliest Scottish poems were made in Latin by Gaelic speakers, in later centuries speakers of Gaelic and Scots had to learn English as they had once learned Latin. Though sometimes language communities were at war with one another, aspects of bilingualism and/or biculturalism are characteristic of Scottish authors from St Columba to Kathleen Jamie and from Mary, Queen of Scots, to Robert Burns. Writers as different as Walter Scott, Thomas Carlyle and James Kelman have sometimes been attacked by Anglocentric critics for what were perceived distortions of 'correct English' language: Scott was accused of writing 'Anglified Erse', Carlyle of producing 'Allgemeine-Mid-Lothianish', and Kelman of writing in 'lumpenproletarian'.[12] While such accusations reveal kinds of national and class bias, they also show an alertness to a recurring tendency among many Scottish writers to rejoice in heterogeneous linguistic possibilities. Although the bilingual twentieth-century author Iain Crichton Smith considered himself a 'double man' unable fully to commit to Gaelic or to English, writers who move between or mix Scots and English have often done so happily. The strength of the tradition of Scottish Latin, the prominence of Gaelic culture and the popular affection for Scots have all contributed to a sense of plenitudinous variety in the possibilities of Scottish literary expression which is as apparent in the early Middle Ages as it is in our age when Scottish poets may publish collections which mix work in English and Scots and when the range of linguistic possibilities for drama runs from Liz Lochhead's energetic Scots *Tartuffe* to Douglas Dunn's decorously Englished Racine.

Once upon a time writers such as Hugh Blair or Edwin Muir anxiously maintained that a national literature had to be written in a single, homogeneous language. The long history of Scottish literature proves them wrong. Individual writers may be committed to a language, but many like to listen in to as wide a linguistic spectrum as they can. This is not a faddishly postmodern attribute of Scottish writing, but something that draws on the resources of a centuries-old multilingual inheritance which, at once foreign and native to today's Scottish writers, has shaped our ways of reading and writing.

Without concealing struggles between different language communities, *Scotland's Books* crosses between languages, rather than quarantining each of Scotland's literary tongues. I have tried to do justice to the linguistic spectrum, without suggesting that every Scottish author is polylingual, well read in all Scottish predecessors, or corresponds to some one-size-fits-all paradigm. In the medieval period especially, struggles between Scotland's language communities could be bloody, though then as later the quarrels might be cultural, religious and intellectual too. Whereas in the early Middle Ages Gaelic might have been heard across all the land later termed Scotland, today it is spoken and read fluently by perhaps 1 per cent of the population. The medieval Norse language of the Viking-settled Northern Isles and parts of the mainland survives only in place names and in a small, distinguished corpus of literary texts. Little remains in the modern Lowlands of the Welsh and French once associated with ruling elites in parts of medieval Scotland. If the Old English language of the splendidly carved Ruthwell Cross in what is now south-west Scotland indicates that English too is one of Scotland's ancient languages, then in Scotland it evolved into what we call the Scots tongue, whereas in England it became what we now call the English language.

Linguistically, modern Scots and English are branches growing from a common tree. English speakers often regard Scots as a dialect of English – arguments over such terminology can go on too long, and can too readily tend towards the belligerent or the comatose. Latin, one of the most persistent of Scotland's ancient languages, remained a (and often *the*) medium of instruction in schools and universities until the mid-eighteenth century; it has played a crucial role in Scottish literature, and the present book argues that it has mattered not just in poetry but also in drama and in the development of the novel.

If there are signs of Latin and Gaelic holding different kinds of authority in early Scotland, then in more recent times Gaelic and Scots were repressed by the English-language state-educational apparatus. In the twenty-first century there are several Gaelic-medium schools, and several universities teach Gaelic language, literature and culture; Scots is paid at least lip service, and sometimes more, in many schools and is studied in academia. The state-educational apparatus in our own day is more intent on repressing Latin, though the great Scottish tradition of the Classics, however officially sidelined, has been a significant component in the work of poets from Norman MacCaig, Ian Hamilton Finlay and Edwin Morgan to several younger writers. Almost every eighteenth-century Scottish schoolchild could have named Scotland's greatest Latin author, but today it is hard to find anyone in Scotland who even knows his name, or the names of others once regarded as 'Apollos of the north'.[13]

Self-harm is part of Scottish culture, and Scottish educators, for all their brilliance, often have a talent for cultural repression. If book-burning and even writer-burning were vigorously pursued by some

Catholic authorities in medieval and early Renaissance Scotland, then the Protestant John Knox, whose Reformation did wonders for English prose, was a determined iconoclast and smasher-up whose work has at times been viewed as even more damaging. Schooling, indoctrination and cultural repression have routinely gone together in Scotland, as writers as different as the eighteenth-century Robert Fergusson and the twenty-first-century A. L. Kennedy have testified. Scotland's Gaelic, Scots, Latin, English and other literary communities have at different times and in different ways felt the effect of this. Scottish literature is no freer from bigotry, misogyny, sectarianism and other vices than any other literature – and arguably has a more virulent line in invective than most. The tradition that nourished medieval 'flytings' – verbal-insult competitions between poets – is far from dead.

Sometimes, however, repressors get their comeuppance. Feminist scholarship has redrawn the map of Scottish literature in ways which have certainly benefited the present book but which would have horrified alike John Knox and the medieval Blind Hary. In presenting feminism as more important than nationalism or party politics in contemporary Scottish literature, I do not mean to suggest that all women writers have been or are committed exclusively to its cause, but that the strength of recent writing by women surely owes something to a growing, sometimes belated awareness of gender politics in Scotland – a consciousness present not only in writing by or about women. The opening of higher education to women in Scotland in the late nineteenth century was part of a social change which was felt even by those who did not go to university or live to see the advent of universal suffrage. Margaret Oliphant's late Victorian story 'The Library Window' is moving not least for its image of a nineteenth-century girl gazing and gazing into a university scholar's room from which she seems forever excluded.

Distinguished eighteenth-century Scottish academic men – Adam Smith, Hugh Blair and others – pioneered the teaching of English literary texts and initiated the export of 'Eng. Lit.' to the world's universities. Yet no sooner had these Scottish professors, who were anxious for their ambitious students to write 'proper English', pronounced distinctively Scots language virtually extinct than Robert Burns (an educated man with little patience for college classes) established himself as the greatest poet ever to use the Scots tongue in literature. For every thousand people today who know the name of Robert Burns, there is perhaps one who knows the name of Professor Hugh Blair. Repeatedly, attempts by Scottish authorities to repress aspects of Scotland's own cultural, linguistic or literary heritage have (thank God) failed miserably. I remember at school being told by a teacher never to say 'aye' or 'uhuh' when I meant 'yes'. That teacher has since met his match in the work of a host of contemporary Scottish writers who delight to deploy forms of often urban Scots language once regarded as fit only for the gutter.

Yet to treat writing in Scots, or Latin, or Gaelic, or English as somehow more 'authentically Scottish' than writing in other languages of Scotland is misguided. No single language has a monopoly on authenticity, virtue or resentment. The sophisticated English prose of Spark or of A. L. Kennedy is as much part of Scottish literature as the Gaelic of Sorley MacLean or the Scots-inflected fiction of Irvine Welsh. There are many kinds of Scottish literature. Though I am most attracted to some tones of Scottish voice which, however complexly, seem to articulate a democratic impulse, this book also tries to do justice to work produced by sometimes royal or lairdly men and women whose mindsets were far from those of Robert Burns or Janice Galloway or James Kelman or Kathleen Jamie.

Elements of Scottish literature are certainly enjoyed around the world, with or without the swish of a kilt, but there are still very few places on earth where you can get a good education in the subject. As someone who managed to go through two university degrees in English (one in Scotland, one in England) without ever formally studying the literature of my own country, I know what it can mean to grow up deprived of what might have been an inheritance. I have tried to do some work to regain and make available that inheritance, which can belong to anyone who wants it. *Scotland's Books* aims to supply in manageable bulk the beginning of an education in its subject. Sometimes the works quoted or discussed can be hard to locate. For people who wish to track them down, I have supplied endnotes giving the sources: sensible notes are about sharing knowledge, not about pedantry. Where space and narrative flow allowed, I have given original quotations the dignity of standing in their own language, with English translations or glosses supplied when needed. This is one of several ways of reminding readers of the multiple traditions which make up Scotland's literature, even if it also reminds linguistically challenged readers like me that Scottish literature is sometimes complexly ravelled and unravelled.

There is often a journalistic temptation to airbrush away the sheer plenitudinous multiplicity of imaginative writing by all the stay-at-homes, incomers and outgoers, all the royals, rebels and radicals who through their artistry in several languages have contributed over so many centuries to the literary history of Scotland. I hope that, without sacrificing readability, this book escapes such a temptation, and is alert to the risk of a lazy perception that to be Scottish is somehow to be wild, barbaric and macho. Some Scots can even feel nostalgic for this lazy perception, as if Scotland meant only loud past glories and doomed-to-fail aboriginal virtue. It is easy to construct, through nostalgic mists, a vaguely noble, distant Scottish hero, pure, aboriginal, uncorrupted, male and barbarian, a subject for lament in the north.

For much of this Tacitus is to blame. In his account of his father-in-law, Agricola, which dates from AD 98, the Roman historian produced a work which marked not the first mention of the northern part of the island of Britain, but certainly the first sustained literary account of the territory and inhabitants of the land we now call Scotland. In writing about Roman campaigns in 'Caledonia', Tacitus also created literature's first Scottish hero. One of the world's earliest noble savages, this protagonist is 'virtute et genere praestans nomine Calgacus' (a man of outstanding valour and nobility named Calgacus). The name Calgacus may mean 'The Swordsman' (or possibly just 'Shaggy'); it seems to have a genuine northern accent, perhaps being connected with the modern Gaelic 'calgach' – bristly, sharp-pointed, ardent. Calgacus's address to his Caledonian troops as they prepare to fight the Romans is entirely Tacitus's invention, and the Roman historian uses this noble northerner to criticize his own culture's greed and excess. Following the traditions of Greek historiography, Tacitus creates for Calgacus a ringing piece of oratory, destined to be remembered for two millennia:

When I think hard about what makes us fight at this decisive moment, I am convinced that your united front today will be the dawn of liberty for the whole of Britain. All of you are mustered, all of you are free [. . .] and we, the noblest people of all Britain, have stayed in her remotest parts, out of sight of subject shores, our eyes uncontaminated by contact with tyranny. Until today our very remoteness and obscurity have protected us. Ours are the last lands, and we are the last of the free [. . .] The Romans [. . .] are the world's pillagers. Now they have scoured the land indiscriminately, they are turning their attention to the sea. A rich enemy makes them greedy; a poor one makes them hunger for power. Neither the East nor the West is enough for them. They alone hunger after riches and poverty alike. Looting, slaughter, and pillage are what they absurdly term 'empire'; and where they make a desert, they call it peace.[14]

These last words ('atque ubi solitudinem faciunt, pacem appellant') still feature in dictionaries of quotations, and surely comprise the most famous apothegm in Tacitus. The passage remains disturbing as a critique of any dominant imperial power, and we may reasonably imagine that it had such an effect not just on its original audience, but also on later readers, such as those in the crushed post-Culloden eighteenth-century Scottish Highlands. Under different names, Calgacus would be rewritten by James 'Ossian' Macpherson and Walter Scott in Scotland, by James Fenimore Cooper in America, and by many others around the globe. As presented by Tacitus, Calgacus has already internalized some Roman imperial values; enunciating his thoughts in elegant Latin, he thinks of himself and his people as remote and obscure, peripheral. Yet he also stands against Roman imperialism, defending an ideal of freedom. Worthy of the scrutiny of the late Edward Said, Calgacus is all the more a noble savage because he loses to the Romans at the battle of Mons Graupius, whose very name, thanks to a later typographical error, gives us the topographical word 'Grampian'.

Tacitus is responsible, then, not just for the modern designation of a northern area of the Scottish mainland but also for the stereotype of the Caledonian as a male noble savage, a virtuous, remote aboriginal whose ancient conduct represents something far better than the dominant ideology of modern life, but who, defeated, lost and admirably eloquent, can attract our often nostalgic admiration. William Wallace, Ossian and other Scottish heroes may be mapped on to Tacitus's Calgacus. During and after the European Enlightenment era of Rousseau, noble savages were all the rage. Like James Boswell and numerous contemporaries, Walter Scott was aware of Calgacus as well as of Macpherson's Ossian. Scott winks at both in, for instance, his novel *The Antiquary*.[15] The Renaissance Scottish poet George Buchanan, like many others proud that the Romans had never conquered all Scotland, celebrated that fact in his wedding hymn for Mary, Queen of Scots. There have been countless examples of Scottish martial valour, but the wild noble savage of Tacitus can also at times become an ignoble savage, an emblem of Scottish masculinity at its worst. So, in our own era, we have both the noble Wallace of *Braveheart* and the insanely violent, ignoble 'heidbanger' Begbie of Irvine Welsh's *Trainspotting*. Each one – the noble and the ignoble savage – is the flipside of the other. It is no accident that, eighteen centuries after Tacitus, both Jekyll and Hyde belong to the history of Scottish literature.

What we need now, though, is neither a survey of the line of Calgacus – a nostalgic procession of doomed and hirsute Scotsmen with their womenfolk abused, lost, or siphoned off from history – nor an attempt to excoriate Scotland's 'national pastime' of nostalgia by trying (as some recent Scottish writers have attempted to do) to forget about history entirely, and banish literary history to the remoter recesses of the university seminar room.[16] Instead what is needed is a wide-angled view of Scottish literary history that understands alike the riches of medieval writing, the sixteenth-century origins of the Scottish novel, the importance of ecological thought in more than one Scottish literary tradition, and the polylingual glories and longevity of what is now our literary inheritance. What all who care about Scottish literature need is a sense of the full confidence of cultural memory, that confidence of memory which is essential not least to the art of poetry and to the art of any flourishing culture. I hope *Scotland's Books* contributes to that end.

A detail from the lower shaft of the eighth-century Ruthwell Cross. Now housed in the parish church of Ruthwell, Dumfriesshire, the Cross originally stood out of doors nearby. It carries runic inscriptions which present the earliest surviving passages from a version of one of the greatest poems in Old English, 'The Dream of the Rood'. (Photograph by Hamish Brown from the Hamish Brown Collection, St Andrews University Library, HMB-N-RuthwellCross-24A)

I

Praise

Hungry mice, fires, insects and critical judgement have all played their part in the transmission of Scotland's earliest literature – the work produced in the seven centuries or so before the 1320 Declaration of Arbroath asserted Scottish independence. Sometimes stones have preserved individual words or pieces of poetry, and manuscripts have been guarded with cunning.[1] At other times, though, lines of oral or written transmission have come to an end; not just individual works but entire languages have vanished. Parts of Scotland have been settled for over ninety centuries. Beautiful stone monuments such as those of Neolithic Orkney have survived for five millennia, but the earliest extant written materials were produced by immigrants nearly 2000 years ago. From prehistory onwards all communities in Scotland began as immigrant communities. The Roman invasion of mainland Britain brought to the middle of the island not only Mediterranean and Germanic Europeans, but also Syrians and Africans as part of the military forces stationed along Hadrian's Wall. There they built shrines to Mithras, Ashtoreth, Jupiter and the Roman pantheon of gods, as well as to local deities. As conquerors, they made overtures to the surrounding population. Inscribed documents, wooden tablets of hollowed-out Scots pine filled with wax, were discovered wonderfully preserved in water-logged pits near Hadrian's Wall in the 1970s. These include shopping lists, personal letters, and material about a recruitment drive aimed at attracting members of the Anavionenses. Recruiters wanted this tribe, who lived around the River Annan in what is now southern Scotland, to join the Roman army.[2]

Some of the Roman forces moved northwards up the island, fighting and bribing the tribes of 'Caledonia', a Latin name which later came to be applied to what we now call Scotland. In AD 142–3 the Romans erected the Antonine Wall. Built of turf on a sandstone base, it ran for thirty-seven miles between the Firths of Forth and Clyde. Parts of it can still be seen. Never occupied for long, it was designed, like Hadrian's Wall, not as an absolute barrier but as a series of portals to control the movements of native peoples. This resulted in many kinds of contact between the locals and the incoming forces, who were sometimes from distant parts. We know from stone inscriptions, for instance, that the large, wet and windy Roman fort at Bar Hill near Kilsyth in the Scottish Lowlands was garrisoned by Syrian archers, then by soldiers from the Rhineland. Sometimes the incomers recorded their susceptibility to the place around them. One of five nearby altars erected by a Roman centurion is dedicated 'GENIO TERRAE BRITANNICAE' ('To the Presiding Spirit of the Land of Britain').[3]

Inscriptions like this – written by foreign conquerors in their imperial language – are scanty at best. Nothing we could regard as imaginative writing survives from Scotland before the sixth century, though occasionally a short inscription affords a glimpse of the people who passed across the landscape. Standing within the perimeter of Edinburgh airport is the (?fifth-century) Catstone of Kirkliston with its dedication to 'VETTA'.[4] In south-west Scotland, at Whithorn, St Nynia or Ninian (who trained in Gaul) was reputedly part of a very early Scottish Christian community. A local inscription dating from the very late fifth century consists of a monogram made up of the intertwined Greek letters *chi* and *rho* (the first two letters of Christ's name), then some Latin words which can be translated as,

We praise thee, Lord. Latinus, aged 35, and his daughter, aged 4 years, made [this] sign here. [He is the] grandson of Barrovadus.[5]

These few words by a Romanized Briton are the oldest written record we have of an act of Christian worship in Scotland. Articulated on behalf of both male and female, bringing together three generations, they preserve a moment when father and daughter stood by the Solway Firth. It makes it all the more attractive to know that 'Barrovadus' was a British name meaning 'Mole-Head'.

Drawing on several cultures, and fusing Greek and Latin with native elements, this Christian inscription is a suitable early emblem of poly-lingual Scottish literature. Christianity and monastic culture nourished the production of most of the early masterpieces of Scotland's written art. Between them, the Romans and the Christians established Latin as Scotland's most ancient literary language. There appears to have been vigorous oral composition going on in a rich brew of languages across the terrain of Scotland in this early medieval period, but for much of the Middle Ages hardly anyone other than Church personnel could read or write. As far back as we can go, and throughout Scotland's literary history, works have been produced in this country in several tongues, sometimes operating independently, at other times influencing one another. Then as now, virtually all these languages have involved a considerable degree of interaction with oral or written literatures outside Scotland. Some, like Latin and in more recent times English, have been written across the known world of their day; others, such as Gaelic or Welsh, have had their closest links with other parts of the British Isles. Scotland's literary works splendidly and not infrequently celebrate independence; yet even when they do so they also articulate through vocabulary, form, and content kinds of interdependence with many other countries and cultures.

So it should be no surprise that a lot of the early literary works associated with Scotland are written in the international language of Latin. Some of these poems and other written texts were probably produced on Í, better known as Iona, a three-mile-long Hebridean island to which the monk Columba sailed from Ireland in 563, and where he established a monastery. Although in the Middle Ages places accessible by boat were among the most easily reached, getting to Iona still takes time. Today, even after they get to Oban on the West Coast of the Scottish mainland, visitors must take a ferry, then travel thirty miles across the island of Mull to Fionnphort from where they sail over the Sound of Iona. If their timing is good, they step off the lowered bow of the landing craft when a wave has just receded. That way they arrive on Iona with dry feet.

Much of it rebuilt in the 1930s, the modern Iona Abbey is a reconstruction of substantial late medieval stone buildings. Columba's monastery, with its wooden church, *magna domus* (communal building), and farmed plots bounded by a 400-metre-long earth rampart, looked very different. Nevertheless, on top of the rocky mound in front of the present-day Abbey's western facade, archaeologists have unearthed what may well be the base of the small, raised wooden hut or *tegorium* where Columba worked during the day. Born the cousin of an Irish king, then trained as a monk, he appears to have gone into exile in his early forties, shortly after a battle in 561 which involved his family and their allies. Although Columba made periodic visits to Ireland, it is his activities on Iona where he wrote, worshipped, and guided a community of monks, which made him the most celebrated of Scottish saints. The work of his monastery nurtured a Columban family of other Christian foundations from the nearby island of Tiree to a constellation of Scottish and more distant, continental locations including Salzburg and present-day Switzerland. Even today on the shores of Lake Zurich there are small settlements called Stafa and Iona.

The community Columba founded soon became a substantial centre of literary production. On Iona, long before the invention of printing, manuscripts were copied by hand for study and dissemination. Although its handwritten originals are long lost or dispersed, the monks had a library of manuscript books. They kept these in chests to protect them from the elements and wildlife. There is evidence not just of a thorough knowledge of Latin texts on Iona, but also some interest in Greek lettering and vocabulary. Columba was recalled as powerfully busy, constantly attending to prayer, reading and writing. His example inspired a group of writers, poets and thinkers over several hundred years. An early eighth-century Iona manuscript survives in modern Switzerland, while it has been suggested that the seventh-century Latin text of the Gospels now known as *The Book of Durrow* was made on the small Hebridean island. The later, more celebrated *Book of Kells* with its magnificently complex ornamentation was probably begun on late seventh-century Iona, then taken from the island to Kells in Ireland by Columban monks fleeing Viking raiders. This would explain its being described in 1007 as 'the great Gospel of Colm Cille [Gaelic for Columba], the chief relic of the Western World'.[6]

Complex and rich in its symbolism, the gospel *Book of Kells* (now in the Library of Trinity College, Dublin) manifests the Christian Word of God and celebrates that Word's incarnation in flesh; it sings of the harmonious and diverse divine creation, its illustrations ranging from stylized, thick-bearded saints to rats, cats, proud hens and a cockerel. One of the treasures of early medieval European manuscript culture, the *Book of Kells* has been described as the world's most beautiful book and is a two-dimensional counterpart to Iona's later, splendid carved stone crosses. The exact origins of many of the early works linked to

Iona are uncertain, but there is overwhelming evidence for the island as a crucial source for some of Scotland's first surviving Christian writings. Pre-eminent among these is the Latin poem known by its opening words, 'Altus prosator'. Magnificently translated by Edwin Morgan in the early 1990s, this is a poem to set beside the *Book of Kells*. It now stands at the head of several anthologies of Scottish verse.[7] Although it possibly dates from the seventh century, modern commentators have regarded its attribution to Columba as defensible.[8]

The 'Altus Prosator' is a rich and intricate hymn of Christian praise. Far older than the great medieval cathedrals of St Andrews or Glasgow, it nevertheless carries their sense of amplitude and awe. An abecedarian poem, its six-line stanzas begin in turn with each of the twenty-four letters, from A to Z, of the Latin alphabet. This work, attuned to the God who is 'alpha and omega, the beginning and the end', and to the twenty-four hours that measure the human day, speaks through its form of God's power over time and space.[9] Running from the creation of the universe and the ensuing Fall of Man to the Apocalypse and the final Day of Judgment, it is the product of an imagination richly nourished by that *lectio divina* ('holy reading') recommended to monks by St Augustine and others as a way of attuning the reader to the guiding movement of God's Holy Word.

Such an internal attunement to scripture can be heard from the poem's very first line, 'Altus prosator vetustus dierum et ingenitus' ('Ancient exalted seed-scatterer whom time gave no progenitor'). The phrase 'vetustus dierum' ('Ancient of Days', as the Authorized Version of the Bible has it) comes from a Latin version of the Old Testament Book of Daniel. Throughout the poem revoicings of biblical phrases manifest a union with God's Word. The acoustic of the 'Altus Prosator', its sound-patterning, reinforces a sense of bonding, of unity. Every line is made up of two half-lines of eight syllables, and the conclusion of each half-line rhymes with the end of the whole line, as 'vetustus' rhymes with 'ingenitus' above. So a sense of divine wholeness persists through this panoptic, alphabet-shaped work, despite its harsh accounts of evil, hellish torments, and demonic battles where 'aeris spatium constipatur satellitum' ('the airy spaces were choked like drains with faeces'). What the poem calls 'world harmony' ('mundi . . . harmoniam') is articulated through its own structure. If it praises a God who is a 'prosator' ('seed-scatterer') and follows His words, then it also partakes of His power in its creation and dissemination of new words in a way that, though less extreme, suggests the 'Hisperic Latin' which proliferated in seventh-century Irish Latin poetry, rejoicing in neologisms and strange vocabulary. Highly intellectual when it draws on early Christian authorities such as the fifth-century St John Cassian (born in what is now Romania), or when it relishes Greek-derived lexis, the poem is also very accessibly beautiful to a modern audience, not least in its celebration of God's power over the world's climate:

> LIGATAS aquas nubibus frequenter cribrat Dominus
> ut ne erumpant protinus simul ruptis obicibus
> quarum uberioribus venis velut uberibus
> pedetentim natantibus telli per tractus istius
> gelidis ac ferventibus diversis in temporibus
> usquam influunt flumina nunquam deficientia.

> *Letting the waters be sifted from where the clouds are lifted*
> *the Lord often prevented the flood he once attempted*
> *leaving the conduits utterly full and rich as udders*
> *slowly trickling and panning through the tracts of this planet*
> *freezing if cold was called for warm in the cells of summer*
> *keeping our rivers everywhere running forward for ever.*[10]

Cosmic in its scope, the magnificent 'Altus Prosator' goes on to speak of the movements of planets. Its interest is not in empirical astronomy but in seeing how the workings of the universe act as a token of the power and nature of divine order. So the whole cosmos is drawn into this hymn to its Creator.

The 'Altus Prosator' is the greatest of the poems associated with early Iona, but is only one of an impressive group of Latin and Gaelic works linked to Columba's name. Another of these is the Gaelic 'Amra Choluimb Chille' ('Elegy of Columba') attributed to the Gaelic poet Dallán Forgaill, who flourished around the year 600. The poem announces that it was commissioned by Columba's cousin Áed, King of Tara in Ireland. Using some Latin vocabulary and many Irish borrowings from Latin, this long, richly alliterative work often rearranges words in a surprising order to celebrate Columba's guardianship, learning, asceticism and ascent to heaven. The Saint's death has left the world disconsolate:

Is crot cen chéis,
is cell cen abbaid.

It is a harp without a key,
it is a church without an abbot.[11]

In the years that followed, a cult of Columba developed, encouraging such fine and adoring Gaelic poems as those attributed to Beccán mac Luigdech. A professionally trained Christian poet from Ireland, he died in 677 and may have lived for a considerable time on the Hebridean island of Rhum. In work such as Beccán's, Columba is a source of light, a candle, a sun, a bonfire, a flame; but also a tough, heroic wanderer on his *peregrinatio*, his physical and spiritual journeying. Where the Desert Fathers who so influenced these early Celtic Christians travelled across North African sands, Beccán's Hebridean Columba in the 'Tiugraind Beccáin' ('Last Verses of Beccán') voyages over rough and changeable seas:

Cechaing tonnaig, tresaig magain, mongaig, rónaig,
roluind, mbedcaig, mbruichrich, mbarrfind, faílid, mbrónaig.

He crossed the wave-strewn wild region, foam-flecked, seal-filled,
savage, bounding, seething, white-tipped, pleasing, doleful.[12]

In the body of poems associated with Iona, not only are there many links with the ancient poetry of Ireland, but there is also a sense at times of the mutual interlacing of Gaelic and Latin. The modern Gaelic scholar John Lorne Campbell has called attention to Scottish Gaelic verse 'conventions inherited from Middle Irish and based ultimately upon early medieval Latin hymn poetry'.[13] Sometimes Gaelic may have influenced Scottish Latin. Certainly work in both languages is attributed to several of the Columban poets. One of these poets is Cú Chuimne ('Hound of Memory'), a learned Iona monk who, with an Irish colleague, compiled the *Collectio Canonum Hibernensis*, an influential anthology of rules for the religious life. Cú Chuimne's Latin hymn to Our Lady makes use of distinctively Irish kinds of *aicill* or binding rhymes where the sound at the end of one line is echoed during the course of the next; the same poem of praise to the Virgin also employs the ornamental alliteration which characterized poetry in Irish Gaelic. In their elaborate loopings and interweavings, Iona's manuscript interlacings and later carved stone crosses are a visual counterpart to these poems with their elaborate binding together of sounds.

The Iona crosses preserve some of the earliest icons of Mary in the British Isles. Apparently written for choral singing, the thirteen stanzas of Cú Chuimne's hymn to the Virgin bond together a religious community of voices as part of a larger ritual which, like rhyme itself, sounds a division in order to proclaim a unity:

> Bis per chorum hinc et inde
> collaudemus Mariam
> ut vox pulset omnem aurem
> per laudem vicariam.

> *Through two-part chorus, side to side*
> *let our praise to Mary go,*
> *so every ear hears our praise voiced*
> *alternating to and fro.*[14]

Praise of the divine, of religious leaders or of heroic secular lords is the great motivation of most of the early poetry associated with early medieval Scotland. As explained in the Introduction to the present book, across the area we today designate 'Scotland' at least five languages were spoken in the early medieval period. In the surviving literature praise predominates, whether the work is composed in Latin, in Gaelic, in Welsh (which was once spoken in southern areas), or in the distinctive form of Old English used in that Kingdom of Northumbria whose territory included parts of the area now known as the Scottish Borders and extended as far as the Forth.

Praise is also important in the early prose written by monks to glorify God and His saints. Prominent here is the learned Adomnán, ninth Abbot of Iona, who was born in Ireland around 628 and died on Iona in 704. Adomnán is remembered as a great Gaelic legislator. He initiated that Irish *Cáin Adomnáin* (Adomnán's Law) which protects non-combatants and asserts their rights. Its preamble, written later, calls it 'the first law in heaven and on earth which was arranged for women'.[15] During the 680s Adomnán also wrote in Latin his *De Locis Sanctis* (*About the Holy Places*), a sacred travelogue offering detailed accounts of biblical sites. He had never visited these, but his text is presented as drawing on the eye-witness testimony of the Gaulish Bishop Arculf, whose ship has been blown off course to the western coast of Britain. Adomnán seeks to use Arculf's descriptions to enrich the reading of scripture, explaining how the world articulates God's glory, and how apparently diverging accounts actually 'speak together in harmony'.[16] Rich in biblical and liturgical phrasing, this theological work was later abridged by the Venerable Bede in England. Like the 'Altus Prosator', it is a product of much 'holy reading'.

It is a testimony to the intellectual achievements of Adomnán's far western community that, for all its remoteness, it generated such a commentary on Jerusalem. A similar reflection resounds at the culmination of Adomnán's most substantial work, the *Vita Columbae*, his account of his kinsman Columba's life. This was written on Iona in the 690s, by which time the island had a considerable influence on culture elsewhere in Scotland. The ninth abbot, who clearly considers himself an Irishman, delights that, although the earlier saint

lived in this small and remote island of the Britannic ocean, he merited that his name should not only be illustriously renowned throughout our Ireland, and throughout Britain, the greatest of all the islands of the whole world; but that it should reach even as far as three-cornered Spain, and Gaul, and Italy situated beyond the Pennine Alps; also the Roman city itself, which is the chief of all cities.

The three sections of this *Life* seek to demonstrate Columba's power and blessedness through accounts of his prophetic insight, his powerful miracles and his engagement with angelic visions. All these are fused with details of monastic life on Iona – singing, reading, writing, building barns, transporting milk. Although the island at this time appears to have been an all-male community, Columba is presented as sharing and validating Adomnán's concern with the protection of women.

The *Vita Columbae* manifests a political imagination. It is designed to bolster the strength of the developing Columban family of monasteries, not least on the north-eastern Scottish mainland. There Columba's miraculous powers defeat Pictish magicians. His prayers also subdue 'a certain water beast' lurking in the depths of the River Ness which suddenly surfaced 'with gaping mouth and with great roaring'. From this, the first written account of the Loch Ness Monster, to Adomnán's story of Columba expelling a devil from a milk churn, the *Vita Columbae* is full of engaging narratives and vignettes. It is also a didactic work which demonstrates its saint as strong, often austere, and purposefully unbending. Writing with engagement and emblematic vigour, Adomnán aims not to make Iona a place of pilgrimage but to enhance its ecclesiastical power and to portray a spiritual leader who knew and embodied 'the fear of God'. While the name Iona arises from a misreading of the Latin phrase 'Ioua insula' – the Í-ish island – Adomnán explains that it is divine patterning which gives this saint the name Columba (which, like the Hebrew word 'Iona', means 'Dove'), linking him to the emblem of the Holy Spirit. Like the 'Altus Prosator', the *Vita Columbae* speaks of terror and danger, yet also carries a sense of enduring lyrical beauty, as when Iona's monks, returning across the middle of the island 'towards the monastery in the evening after their work on the harvest', all sense 'a fragrant smell, of marvellous sweetness, as of all flowers combined into one', and realize slowly that it is Columba, coming 'not . . . in the body to meet us', but sending his spirit to refresh the harvesters as they walk.[17]

As well as this Latin prose, Adomnán may have written verse in Gaelic. It was his native language, but he maintained that others throughout the Latin-reading world might consider Gaelic a poor ('uilis') tongue.[18] His account of Iona makes it clear that the Columban community contained people who would have spoken several other languages, including Pictish and Old English, though no literature in these tongues is mentioned. Latin was the language of the Church, but the vernacular speech of the kingdom whose ruler granted Iona to the monks, Dál Riata, was what is now called in Ireland Irish and in Scotland Gaelic. Dál Riata was a northern Irish kingdom which had expanded across the sea to western Scotland. When Adomnán writes of 'nostram Scotiam' he means 'our Ireland'. Only centuries later did the word 'Scotia' come to be used of the northern part of the British mainland. Adomnán and the Columban tradition remind us just how Irish are the early surviving literary works of the country we now know as Scotland.

Although the geological outline of the islands of Britain and Ireland has remained virtually unchanged throughout historical time, the tribal territories, kingdoms and national identities projected on to the terrain have altered considerably. It is the nature of such identities to be dynamic, reconfiguring over the years. So, if seventh-century Dál Riata spanned the Irish Sea, then seventh-century Northumbrian power encompassed what is now Dumfriesshire and Galloway. At Ruthwell in modern Dumfriesshire are preserved the earliest surviving parts of a version of the untitled poem known from Victorian times as 'The Dream of the Rood'. This 'Vision of the Cross' is written in a Germanic language which we call Anglo-Saxon or Old English, and which would later evolve into both the English and Scots tongues. Although the poem's rather German-sounding language is far removed from modern Scots or English, it contains some words which today's readers may recognize: the dreamer, for instance, dreams 'to midre nihte' (after midnight) about a marvellous 'treow' (tree). The full Old English text is reprinted with a facing modern English translation in *The Penguin Book of Scottish Verse*.

At Ruthwell sections of four extracts from this ancient poem survive incised in runes on a magnificent carved stone cross. The cross also carries Latin quotations from the Gospels and from accounts of early Christian saints; some of these are identifiable, others shattered or eroded. So, for instance, above the relief carving of John the Baptist holding up the Lamb of God only one word can be read: '... ADORAMUS ...' (... we praise ...). The figurative and decorative carvings clearly allude not only to other biblical texts such as Christ's declaration 'I am the true vine', but also to older, pagan emblems like the Tree of Life in Germanic mythology. In this way the Ruthwell Cross bonds Christianity to older native religious traditions. Its focus on a tree allows it to tap into pre-Christian resonances at the same time as expressing an orthodox Christian viewpoint in a remarkable way that mixes allegory with impassioned personal testimony. It is possible that this cross may once have carried as many as fifty lines of the poem associated with it. The four preserved extracts all come from the middle of 'The Dream of the Rood' as that poem survives in its most expanded version, found in a tenth-century manuscript now in the Cathedral Library at Vercelli, northern Italy. The Ruthwell Cross has been called a 'lapidary edition' of the poem, and its existence probably implies that the local audience had knowledge of a larger work from which these extracts were quoted.[19] While part of the Vercelli Book's text may be a later addition, the northern character of its language marks it out as Northumbrian, and the Ruthwell Cross gives this poem a strong connection with the land we now call Scotland.

Written in the alliterative verse of Old English poetry, in which each line is divided into two halves, each containing (usually) two stressed syllables, the work begins in the early hours of a morning when the speaker dreams a great dream, seeing a huge, scarred, jewelled 'tree of glory' shining like a beacon in the sky 'on lyft laedan leohte bewunden' (held high in heaven, haloed with light). The word 'cross' ('rode') is not mentioned until well into the poem, giving the work a hint of almost riddling allure. However, as my modern English version suggests, it becomes evident as the poem develops just what lies at its heart.

> I lay a long time, anxiously looking
> At the Saviour's tree, till that best of branches
> Suddenly started to speak:
>   'Years, years ago, I remember it yet,
> They cut me down at the edge of a copse,
> Wrenched, uprooted me. Devils removed me,
> Put me on show as their jailbirds' gibbet.
> Men shouldered me, shifted me, set me up
> Fixed on a hill where foes enough fastened me.
> I looked on the Lord then, Man of mankind,
> In his hero's hurry to climb high upon me.
> I dared not go against God's word,
> Bow down or break, although I saw
> Earth's surface shaking. I could have flattened
> All of those fiends; instead, I stood still.
> Then the young hero who was King of Heaven,
> Strong and steadfast stripped for battle,
> Climbed the high gallows, his constant courage
> Clear in his mission to redeem mankind.[20]

Presenting Christ as a 'young hero', the poem draws on secular ideas of the Lord as warrior and protector, but some of its power comes also from the brilliantly imagined talking tree which is forced to share, yet also accepts, Christ's suffering. Violently united with the Son of God as the nails are driven in, the wooden cross is then 'dumped in a deep pit' after the Crucifixion. After its ordeal, the holy tree ascends to heaven as a shining cross with the power to heal all who fear it in faith. It speaks of the heavenly glories that await believers in the hall of their Lord. With its richly measured visionary brilliance, this is a magnificent poem. It tells of intense suffering, but also of triumph and praise.

As the crow flies, the 'ADORAMUS' of the Ruthwell Cross is about

forty miles north-east of the stone recording the praise offered up by
Latinus and his four-year-old daughter at Whithorn two centuries
earlier. The name Whithorn is an Old English one meaning 'white house'
(a reference to St Nynia's church there); the name 'Ruthwell' probably
means 'well of pity'. Both attest to the Northumbrian Christian presence
in this area, one strongly connected to the heroic and visionary literature
of that kingdom. The Northumbrian Bede would praise both Nynia and
Columba in his Latin *History of the English Church and People* (written
in 731), and Latin poems in praise of Nynia may also date from the
same period.

In the early seventh century the Northumbrians had expanded their
territory northwards as far as the Forth, and had come into conflict with
the people of Dál Riata. Adomnán went to central Northumbria in the
680s. There he studied the practices of Anglian monks and secured the
release of Irish prisoners. In 685 Northumbria's King Ecgfrith led his
armies north into Pictish territory, but the Pictish victory at Nechtans-
mere or Dunechtan, now Dunnichen, near Forfar in eastern Scotland,
resulted in the death of Ecgfrith and many of his men. The Northumbrian
Angles were driven south, making possible the eventual establishment
of a Scottish nation. Such recurring bloody conflicts over several hundred
years in this early 'Dark Age' period had literary consequences, nourishing poems in praise of military, rather than spiritual, heroes.

Greatest among these poems is the Welsh-language *The Gododdin*,
which celebrates in complexly rhyming syllabic metre an attack made
around the year 600 by a northern war-band, the Gododdin, from
Din-Eidin (Edinburgh) against a southern enemy force at Catraeth –
Catterick in modern Yorkshire. Comprising a cluster of elegies praising
heroes who fell in the battle, and existing in two incomplete texts, *The
Gododdin* has been called 'the oldest Scottish poem', though it seems to
postdate the 'Altus Prosator' and survives in a thirteenth-century Welsh
manuscript.[21] At the core of this substantial work is archaic material
attributed to the poet 'Aneirin' who is said to have lived in the second
half of the sixth century. Composed for oral bardic recitation, but
perhaps written down in the eighth century, it appears to have been
transmitted though the Welsh-speaking Kingdom of the Britons in
Strathclyde (Strat Clut) which withstood the encroaching Angles in the
sixth and seventh centuries. A fragment interpolated into the *Gododdin*
manuscripts celebrates the victory of the Strathclyde Britons from

Dumbarton in 642 against the ruler of Dál Riata; he is left slaughtered, his corpse's head pecked by crows. Like 'The Dream of the Rood', but in an almost completely secular context, *The Gododdin* (which contains one of the earliest mentions of King Arthur) tells repeatedly in woven, musical language of the sacrificial suffering of a heroic lord:

> Mynog Gododdin traethiannor;
> Mynog am ran cwyniador.
> Rhag Eidyn, arial fflam, nid argor.
> Ef dodes ei ddilys yng nghynnor;
> Ef dodes rhag trin tewddor.
> Yn arial ar ddywal disgynnwys.
> Can llewes, porthes mawrbwys.
> Os osgordd Fynyddog ni ddiangwys
> Namyn un, arf amddiffryt, amddiffwys.

> *A lord of Gododdin will be praised in song;*
> *A lordly patron will be lamented.*
> *Before Eidyn, fierce flame, he will not return.*
> *He set his picked men in the vanguard;*
> *He set out a stronghold at the front.*
> *In full force he attacked a fierce foe.*
> *Since he feasted, he bore great hardship.*
> *Of Mynyddawg's war-band none escaped*
> *Save one, blade-brandishing, dreadful.*[22]

Relentlessly, movingly elegiac in its account of the warriors of the Gododdin, that tribe which the Romans had called Votadini, *The Gododdin* is not a narrative poem but a gathering of laments, sometimes dealing with individual named heroes, and at other times with the whole war-band. On their thick-maned stallions, with blue blades flashing over gold-bordered clothing, these gold-torqued, ferocious comrades charge before the reader in terms of splendid praise. Riding far from their down pillows, mead and drinking halls, they gallop towards violent extinction.

The Gododdin exalts military masculinity, courage, lordly generosity. It makes use of repeated heroic understatement. Confusion surrounding the surviving texts only adds to a sense of that heroic swirl which gives the poems a cumulative elegiac power. While the constant use of proper

names propels hero after loyal hero into the foreground, hymning lar-
gesse and prowess in battle, the omnipresent past tense of lamentation
relegates every man to an irretrievable past:

> Iôr ysbâr llary, iôr molud,
> Mynud môr, göwn ei eisyllud,
> Göwn i Geraint, hael fynog oeddud.

> *Glorious lord of the spear, praiseworthy lord,*
> *The sea's benevolence, I know its nature,*
> *I know Geraint; you were a bountiful prince.*[23]

The sense of loss so strikingly present in *The Gododdin* is shared
with the Welsh Urien cycle of poems which, with their memorable
lament over a severed head and a nettle-strewn hearth, record the bloody
conflicts and mid-sixth-century collapse of Urien's earlier Kingdom of
Rheghed or Reget around the Solway Firth. Alluring among the interpolated materials found in *The Gododdin* manuscript is the short
Welsh-language poem known as 'Dinogad's Coat', which is presented
as sung to a little boy whose father has gone hunting; Thomas Clancy
suggests that, though not obviously connected to Scottish territory,
it may 'be the earliest poem by a woman to have been preserved in
Britain'.[24]

If 'The Dream of the Rood' and the surviving Columban works owe
their origins to the relative peace of monastic communities, *The Gododdin* is a reminder that early Scotland was frequently convulsed by the
sort of warfare that led Adomnán to develop his laws protecting women,
non-combatants and children. Among the heroic warriors of the Dark
Ages, the Picts, who defeated that Anglian force at Dunnichen, and were
themselves defeated by the Scots of Dál Riata, have left such splendid
artworks as Christian and pre-Christian stones carved with Z-rods,
combs, mirrors, beasts, and other symbols, but no extant literature.
Their words survive only in a later Gaelic list of kings and in place
names concentrated around Fife, Perthshire, Angus and the north-east.
Occasionally there survives a personal name: Bliesblituth; Canutu-
lachama. These alluring samplings come from a lost language which
succumbed late in the first millennium to the greater cultural power of
Gaelic. For all their military and artistic feats, the Picts have been silenced
more effectively than the men of Gododdin. The English historian Henry

of Huntingdon, in the 1120s, regarded the disappearance of the Pictish tongue 'which was one of those established by God created at the very beginning of languages' as truly 'amazing'.[25]

So it is that the annotations in the *Book of Deer* from a north-eastern Columban monastery in Buchan are in Gaelic, not in Pictish. This version of the Latin Gospels, ascribed largely to the ninth century, has an Old Irish tailpiece or colophon. Its notes, written in the margins and other blank spaces, provide the earliest known example of continuous written Gaelic in a manuscript in Scotland. Among the notes is a legendary account of the monastery's foundation which culminates with a characteristic Irish and Scottish literary genre, the *Dindshenchas* or legend of how a place got its name. The founding of the monastery is attributed to Columba and one of his disciples who has a Pictish name, Drostán, though his father's name is Gaelic, Coscrach.

Iar sen do-rat Collum Cille do Drostán in chadraig-sen, 7 ro-s benact, 7 fo-rácaib i[n] mbréther, ge bé tísad ris, ná bad blienec buadacc. Tángator déara Drostán ar scarthain fri Collum Cille. Ro laboir Colum Cille, 'Be[d] Déar [a] anim ó [s]hunn imacc.

Thereupon Columba gave Drostán that monastery, and blessed it, and left the curse that whoever should go against it should not be full of years or of success. Drostán's tears [déra] came as he was parting from Columba. Columba said, 'Let Deer be its name from this on.'[26]

There are some other indications of Pictish/Gaelic crossover, but these notes from north-eastern Scotland testify to the written pre-eminence of the literary dialect of Gaelic, with some vernacular influence. For more sustained literary works we must return to Iona where the poet Mugrón, Abbot from 965 until his death in 981, has left several Gaelic poems. Iona had suffered at the hands of Viking attackers, losing sixty-eight monks in a massacre by raiders in the year 806, and had been partly eclipsed by the prestige of the monastery at Kells. However, by Mugrón's time some of the Norse visitors were more friendly, and regarded Iona as a sacred site; Olaf Cuaran travelled to Iona as a pilgrim in the year 980, and died there peacefully. One of Mugrón's poems is in praise of Columba, recalling the saint as, among other things, an eager author. Another, incantatory twelve-stanza poem by Mugrón draws, like 'The Dream of the Rood', on the cult of the cross. Instead of emphasizing the cross's suffering, Mugrón presents it as a potent emblem of protection. His ritualistic repetitions generate a verbal interlacing which binds the cross to the poem's speaker:

> Cros Chríst tar mo láma
> óm gúaillib com basa.
> Cros Chríst tar mo lesa.
> Cros Chríst tar mo chasa.
>
> Cros Chríst lem ar m'agaid.
> Cros Chríst lem im degaid.
> Cros Chríst fri cach ndoraid
> eitir fán is telaig.
>
> *Christ's cross across my arms*
> *from my shoulders to my hands.*
> *Christ's cross across my thighs.*
> *Christ's cross across my legs.*
>
> *Christ's cross with me before.*
> *Christ's cross with me behind.*
> *Christ's cross against each trouble*
> *both on hillock and in glen.*[27]

Physical as well as spiritual protective clothing remained desirable on tenth-century Iona. Mugrón's successor as Abbot was killed along with fifteen monks on Christmas Night 986 by marauding Danes from Dublin. Gone were the days when Adomnán's *Laws* protected non-combatants. Spreading terror through Hebridean communities with treasure to steal, the Vikings had begun their raids about two centuries earlier. With them they brought the Norse language when they began to settle in Orkney (conquered in the ninth century), Shetland, some of the Hebrides, and, later, Caithness. The King of Scotland would take possession of the Hebrides in 1266, but it would be 1468 before the northern isles came under the power of the Scottish throne. The celebrated prose *Orkneyinga Saga* records in Old Norse much of the heroic military and domestic history of Norse Orkney and Caithness. Composed in thirteenth-century Iceland, it was not translated into English until 1873, but has had a considerable impact on modern writing about Orkney, especially that of George Mackay Brown. The

Orkneyinga Saga is full of factional fighting and power-play, typified in the reported words of the tenth-century Olaf Tryggvason, King of Norway, to the Earl of Orkney:

'I want you and all your subjects to be baptized,' he said when they met. 'If you refuse, I'll have you killed on the spot, and I swear that I'll ravage every island with fire and steel.'

The Earl could see what kind of situation he was in and surrendered himself into Olaf's hands . . . After that, all Orkney embraced the faith.[28]

Sometimes it can sound comically abrupt, but the sparely written *Orkneyinga Saga* is complex enough to epitomize its intricately ordered, remarkably cosmopolitan Orcadian world. Written in prose with many interpolated verses, it has at its heart an account of the martyrdom and miracles of Orkney's St Magnus as well as the pilgrimage to the Holy Land made by Magnus's nephew, the Orcadian warrior-poet Earl Rognvald Kali, and his men. Poems referring to Orkney and Caithness heroes and history recur in the *Orkneyinga Saga* and in the late thirteenth-century *Njal's Saga*. Among them are verses attributed to the Icelander Arnor Thordarson, the 'Jarlaskald' (Earl's Poet) who served as court bard to Orcadian rulers, elegizing Thorfin of Orkney, who died around 1065. He is recalled as a hard fighter.

These accounts are preserved in Icelandic sagas – we possess a relatively small number of Norse poems from Scotland itself. The earliest are small fragments by Orm Barreyjarskald, whose nickname 'Poet of Barra' indicates that he was probably one of the Norse settlers in the Hebrides. In these fragments we hear the sea crash on the shingle, and detect a note of Christian praise poetry as the speaker appears to look forward to being welcomed by God, 'ruler . . . of the cart-way'.[29] These atmospheric shards belong to the tradition of Norse skaldic verse which originated in Scandinavian Viking rulers' courts. Professional poets, skalds, were employed to praise their brave, generous lord, and to entertain his followers, sometimes by hymning the noble dead. A Norse lay in memory of Eric Bloodaxe, King of the Norse settlement of York, is thought to have been composed in tenth-century Orkney, where Eric's widow had fled after his death in battle in 954. As skaldic forms developed, they came to deal with a variety of subjects, including love, the heroic past, and Christian pilgrimage. Most of the Norse poems surviving from Scotland are written in variants of the court metre, the *dróttkvætt*, whose stanza contains eight six-syllable lines laced together by means of a complex pattern of alliteration and rhyming syllables. Half-rhyme as well as full rhyme is used within the lines and the language of these Norse poems is highly elaborate. Not only are the poetic metaphorical constructions known as 'kennings' employed, but there are also many *heiti* – periphrases for mundane objects.

All this speaks of a highly sophisticated literature whose flowering in the territories that belong to modern Scotland comes with the work of Earl Rognvald Kali. A Norwegian nobleman with 'light chestnut hair' who claimed the northern isles in the 1130s from his cousin, he commanded the building of the impressive cathedral in Kirkwall, in memory of his uncle, St Magnus. Murdered in Caithness in 1158, Rognvald is remembered as St Ronald of Orkney, and his relics are still in St Magnus Cathedral. A poet and patron of poets, he is celebrated at length in the *Orkneyinga Saga* – 'a many-sided man and a fine poet'.[30] To Rognvald is attributed the *Háttalykill*, or 'Key of Metres', a verse text that exemplifies all the metres of Norse poetry. A lot of his surviving poems in the *Orkneyinga Saga* deal with the pilgrimage to the Holy Land which he made between 1151 and 1153. On his way there, for a time he stayed at Narbonne in the south of France and addressed poems to its female ruler, Ermengard. These works, admiring the lady's cascading hair and white arms, reveal the first datable Troubadour influence on Norse writing. A sense of Rognvald's aristocratic sophistication is clearly communicated by the *dróttkvætt* piece (reprinted in the original Norse and in translation in *The Penguin Book of Scottish Verse*) in which he outlines the attributes of a gentleman:

> Chess I'm eager to play,
> nine skills I know,
> I scarcely forget runes,
> book and handicrafts are my custom,
> I can glide on skis,
> I shoot and row as well as serve,
> I know how to consider
> both harp-playing and poetry.[31]

Rognvald's poems communicate not just a superb technical and emotional assurance, but also lyricism and humour. Mocking Irish monks on a windy island whom he sees as womanly in their monks' clothing, he deploys elaborate language to draw attention to their tonsured heads, then concludes with a well-prepared, yet still striking punchline which complains how these 'girls . . . out west' are all 'bald'.[32] Acute and versatile, leader of a circle of poets, the Norwegian Rognvald, this ruler of Orkney who learned from the Troubadours in his devotion to the Lady Ermengard, stands as one of the most remarkable early named poets of Scotland.

About Ermengard Scottish sources have far less to say than they do about Queen Margaret (d. 1093), the first woman in Scotland of whom a detailed biographical account survives. Written in Latin around 1105 by Turgot, Margaret's confessor, this *Vita* (Life) dates from about half a century before Rognvald's poems. Although Turgot became Bishop of St Andrews at the end of his life, and may have spent time in Norway and in Scotland as a younger man, he probably belonged to a Norse-descended family and lived much of his life in Durham, where he helped found the cathedral in 1093. Writing the life of Margaret at the request of her daughter Matilda who had become Queen of England, Turgot produces an elegant biography. Margaret was the wife of a Scottish King, Mael Coluim III (Malcolm Canmore), who was often in armed conflict with the rulers of England in a series of bloody incursions and counter-raids. Turgot's *Life*, though, largely avoids this material. It makes no mention of Margaret's Hungarian birth, or of Malcolm's first wife, Ingibjorg, widow of Thorfinn, Earl of Orkney. Instead, the biography's political and ecclesiastical underpinnings suggest ways in which Margaret, who had grown up as a princess in England, offers an example of an Englishwoman devoted to the service of God, Scotland and Scotland's king, yet at the same time promoting English Church government and customs.

The Margaret of this *Life* is generous to victims of poverty and war, such as English slaves in Scotland, whose ransoms she pays. Turgot's writing is politically motivated, but in a complex way – one designed to appeal to an English queen while celebrating a Scottish saint of the Church who is a learned woman, thoroughly well read in scripture and constantly meditating on God's word. Ascetic, Margaret eats disturbingly little, but radiates domestic and spiritual power. With impressive results, she instils God-fearing and rod-fearing behaviour into her offspring, instructing their governor 'to curb the children, to scold them, and to whip them when they were naughty, as frolicsome children will often be'. Yet, demonstrating personal kindness to rich and poor alike, Margaret exemplifies the shining, pearl-like virtue which, Turgot points out with a characteristic medieval fondness for the meaning of names, goes with the word 'Margaret' (*margarita* means 'pearl' in Latin). Her veneration of the cross leads eventually to the founding of Edinburgh's Holyrood Abbey; she was directly responsible for other foundations, such as that of Holy Trinity in Dunfermline. Like Columba and most medieval saints, she meditates constantly on 'the terrible day of judgment'. She is also portrayed as encouraging her husband's wisdom and piety. In prayer she teaches the warlord how to cry. As a nineteenth-century Scottish translation of the medieval Latin indicates, Turgot presents the bookish Queen Margaret and her husband as devoted to each other, but quite different in their attitudes to culture:

There was in him a sort of dread of offending one whose life was so venerable; for he could not but perceive from her conduct that Christ dwelt within her; nay, more, he readily obeyed her wishes and prudent counsels in all things. Whatever she refused, he refused also; whatever pleased her, he also loved for the love of her. Hence it was that, although he could not read, he would turn over and examine books which she used either for her devotions or her study; and whenever he heard her express liking for a particular book, he also would look at it with special interest, kissing it, and often taking it into his hands. Sometimes he sent for a worker in precious metals, whom he commanded to ornament that volume with gold and gems, and when the work was finished, the king himself used to carry the book to the queen as a loving proof of his devotion.[33]

Margaret is presented as a source of wise advice, learning and kindness; her illiterate husband here seems charmingly naive. Yet the linguistically adroit Malcolm, who had spent his formative years in English exile, and who ruled an unruly kingdom for longer than any other eleventh-century Scottish monarch, was clearly more than a charming naif. His native language was Gaelic, a foreign tongue to Margaret and to Turgot, neither of whom seems to have learned it. Where the culture of Latin scripture was very much a textual one, poetry in Gaelic was still in the main orally transmitted, and would continue to be so for most of the following millennium. Turgot's beautiful *Life* is very much a politically and aesthetically shaped work; its account of Margaret on her deathbed receiving news of the killing of her husband is psychologically dramatic. Its earlier vignette, typical of saints' lives, records the

miraculous preservation of Margaret's Gospel Book when a priest let it
fall into a river. A Scottish Latin poem, added to the volume in Margaret's lifetime, concludes,

> Saluati semper sint Rex Reginaque sancta,
> Quorum codex erat nuper saluatus ab undis.

> *Eternal salvation to the King and holy Queen*
> *Whose book was only now saved from the waves.*[34]

Generously, the poet's use of the plural 'Quorum' (whose) indicates
that the book in question belongs to both Margaret and Malcolm.
Remarkably, this Latin lectionary still survives, suitably dried out, in
the Bodleian Library in Oxford.

That Scotland, or parts of it, around the time of Margaret's death
could be perceived as a place of culture is implied by a Gaelic poem, the
Duan Albanach, dated to around 1093. Probably made by an Irish poet,
this work begins by addressing the Scots as 'you learned ones of Alba'.[35]
From the late ninth century 'Alba' was used as the Gaelic name for
Scotland north of the River Forth, an area to which the word 'Scotia'
was applied in the eleventh century, before in the 1200s 'Scotia' came
to designate all of mainland Scotland. Surviving poetry attests to the
way Columba's memory continued to be venerated in the Scotland of
Margaret's son, King Alexander I, who furthered the work of English
Augustinian canons at Scone and elsewhere. During the reign of Alexander's brother Edgar, who ruled before him and whose ostentatious
royal seal bore the words 'Imago Edgari Scottorum Basilei' ('Emblem of
Edgar, High King of Scots'), sealed Latin writs had been introduced into
the country, further developing the written authority of the Scottish
monarch.[36] Yet the most beautiful writing of the twelfth century to deal
with a Scottish theme is not a Latin, but a Gaelic work. 'Arann', whose
author may have come from Scotland or Ireland, rejoices in the natural
richness of the large island of Arran in the mouth of the Firth of Clyde.
The seven rhyming quatrains of this packed and delightful lyric begin,

> Arann na n-oigheadh n-iomdha,
>   tadhall fairrge re a formna;
> oiléan i mbearntar buidhne,
>   druimne i ndeargthar gaoi gorma.

Ard ós a muir a mullach,
   caomh a luibh, tearc a tonnach;
oiléan gorm groigheach gleannach,
   corr bheannach dhoireach dhrongach.

Oighe baotha ar a beannaibh,
   mónainn mbaotha ina mongaibh,
uisge uar ina haibhnith,
   meas ar a dairghibh donnaibh.

Arran of the many deer,
   ocean touching its shoulders;
island where troops are ruined,
   ridge where blue spears are blooded.

High above the sea its summit,
   dear its green growth, rare its bogland;
blue island of glens, of horses,
   of peaked mountains, oaks and armies.

Frisky deer on its mountains,
   moist bogberries in its thickets,
cold water in its rivers,
   acorns on its brown oak trees.[37]

Celebrating a heroic ideal, this poem shows a delight in the mountainous natural environment and its inhabitants that will recur in much later
Gaelic poetry and which, however refracted, will condition Romantic
poetry in English and other languages. Yet it would be wrong to read
these verses only in terms of what they appear to anticipate. They are
part of an interlacing of traditions and literatures in early Scotland
where, however terrible the movements of warfare across the landscape
(and this poem with its 'troops . . . ruined' is alert to these), there are
also moments when a sensuous beauty – whether of Arran's mountains
or of scents on Iona – can be relished both for itself and as part of a
larger, divinely ordered harmony. 'Fine at all times is Arran.'[38]

In this period when even kings might be illiterate, when much composition was for oral recitation, and when reading and writing were arts
largely belonging to monks or other clerics, writers tended to be in holy
orders. There were as yet no universities in Scotland, though learned men

such as the twelfth-century philosopher Adam Scot, Abbot of Dryburgh Abbey, may have given classes.[39] Not until 1411 would Scotland's first university be established at the ecclesiastical capital, St Andrews. Scots wanting a university education in the twelfth century had to travel to Europe to the newly founded Schools of Paris or Bologna, the first of their kind. A number of distinguished twelfth-century Scottish intellectuals gravitated towards these growing continental centres of thought. One such man was Richard Scot (c. 1123–73), remembered in France as Richard de St Victor because he became Prior of the Abbey of St Victor in Paris. As a philosopher he followed St Anselm of Canterbury in viewing love as a crucial feature of the universe. He influenced the Franciscan order (established in the early thirteenth century), and not least its leading philosopher, his countryman Duns Scotus.

Occasionally, surviving manuscripts offer us detailed glimpses of the work of these Scottish writers and thinkers in continental Europe:

Perfectus est liber Auen Alpetraus, laudetur Ihesus Christus qui uiuit in eternum per tempora, translatus a magistro Michaele Scoto Tholeti in 18° die ueneris augusti hora tertia cum Abuteo leuite anno incarnationis Ihesu Christi 1217.

Praise be to Jesus Christ who lives for ever in eternity, the book of Alpetraus [Al-Bitrûjî] is completed, translated by Master Michael Scot with the Levite Abuteus at Toledo at the third hour on Friday the 18th day of August in the year AD 1217.[40]

No early written work produced by a Scot can be placed or dated more precisely than this translation of *De Motibus Celorum* (*On the Movements of the Heavens*) by the twelfth-century Spanish Aristotelian Al-Bitrûjî, last of the major Arab astronomers whose work reached the West from Islamic culture in Scholastic times. Perhaps because of the help of Abuteus, Scot's syntax closely tracks that of the Arabic as it expounds matters of spherical trigonometry. Michael Scot (c. 1160–1235) followed this work with translations of the twelfth-century Arab philosopher Averroes's commentaries on Aristotle as well as texts about animals by Aristotle himself. Such endeavours gave Scot access to an advanced synthesis of Greek and Arabic philosophy, preparing the way for his own encyclopedic writings in Latin. These established him as the leading early thirteenth-century Western European intellectual.

Scot worked in Toledo, Bologna, and at the court of Frederick II at Palermo. Translating into Latin from the Arabic of Islamic authors as well as from Hebrew, Scot, in the words of Maria Rosa Menocal, 'was himself a sort of translation' and became 'the most famous of medieval translators'.[41] Praised by the Pope for his remarkable learning, he was elected Archbishop of Cashel in Ireland, but did not reside there, and resigned because he knew no Irish. His great, unfinished work in three parts – the *Liber introductorius* (Introductory Book), its supplementary *Liber particularis* and the *Liber physiognomae* – is dedicated to Frederick II. The first two parts especially are full of the digressions and encyclopedic wanderings that characterize Scot's writings as he discusses such matters as the twenty-eight mansions of the moon, or the centre of the earth as an infernal prison for damned spirits.

Scot's work is full of curiosities. He informs his readers that in many parts of the world eggs are not put under hens but carried by women next to their breasts until the chickens hatch. Yet elsewhere he demonstrates an impressive knowledge of anatomical dissection and close observation. A scientist preoccupied with astronomy and astrology at a time when the two were deeply intertwined, Scot wrote stylishly. Fascinated by names and etymologies, he uses a wide Latin vocabulary spiced with new coinages. Though at times rhetorically elaborate, he often deploys clear, simple illustrative examples. So the universe is whole and round like an apple, filled with seeds for future development. God made and makes the world's marvels, delighting in them like a juggler. A passage from the Latin *Liber introductorius* describing the character of a man born under the influence of the planet Mercury has been regarded in modern scholarship as a possible self-portrait:

A mercurial person naturally delights in an easy, honourable and peaceful occupation, albeit unprofitable at certain times of the year. He is serious and a great reader, notes important questions, and wants to know all the answers. He is interested in miniatures, painting, sculpture, school-teaching and wants to be able to instruct scholars or disciples in white magic, to engage in business, and to perform tricks and subtleties which give pleasure to others.[42]

Though praised by the Pope, and generally orthodox, Scot's amazingly wide-ranging learning brought him a posthumous reputation as a magician. His writings, while condemning necromancy, do display a knowledge of books of magic. There is no evidence that he practised any.

In the following century, however, rumours earned him the singular distinction of becoming the only Scot whom Dante placed in Hell:

> Michele Scotto fu, che veramente
> delle magiche frode seppe il gioco.

> *The late Michael Scot, who truly*
> *Knew every trick of the magician's art.*[43]

Scot's works were influential in medieval Europe. The *Liber physiognomae* was printed in no fewer than twenty editions before 1500, and other works (some concerning magic) were falsely attributed to him. Supposedly a son of Kirkcaldy who lies buried in Melrose Abbey, he is remembered as a medieval man of supernatural knowledge, and still enjoys a remarkable range of afterlives, featuring in novels, poems, and even as a hero in a Canadian children's television series. In the land of his birth he was remembered not least by that later Scott, Sir Walter, who rejoiced in his own soubriquet as 'Wizard of the North'.

The posthumously accredited wizardry of Michael Scot was matched in Scotland by the miraculous prophetic powers attributed to the thirteenth-century poet remembered as Thomas the Rhymer. Sometimes this poet is also styled 'Thomas of Erceldoune', taking his name from a village in Berwickshire. A surviving late twelfth-century legal deed associated with Melrose Abbey is recorded as being witnessed by 'Thomas Rymor de Ercildune', but no literary works by this shadowy figure survive in their original form. What we have is a three-part poem of about 700 lines in a number of fifteenth-century manuscripts, all presenting the story of how Thomas of Erceldoune meets a mysterious fairy woman. The poem opens in the first person with the speaker 'In a mery mornynge of Maye,/ By huntle bankkes my self allone', listening to birds singing. Other parts of the poem present this figure in the third person, making it clear that he is Thomas of Erceldoune, and that a 'lady gaye' who says she is 'of ane other countree' takes him away for a year underground 'at Eldone hill' where he sees marvels and hears many prophecies before his return.[44] The story of Thomas involves an older narrative attached to a very specific Scottish location at Huntly Bank, near Melrose, and containing popular Scottish prophetic materials. In written form it has survived only in later English redactions, though there is plenty of evidence that the story circulated in Scotland through oral ballads and, a good deal later, in printed versions. Throughout the ensuing centuries Thomas and his prophecies attracted many Scottish authors, not least Walter Scott who wrongly attributed to him the northern English metrical romance *Sir Tristrem*, which begins, 'I was at ertheldoun/ With tomas spak y thare.'[45] Posthumously Thomas, like Michael Scot, would acquire the powerful allure of a literary magus.

Equally potent, and with a more tangible physical presence in twelfth-century Scotland, was the impact of the Norsemen. A contemporary Latin poem by a Glaswegian named William attributes to St Kentigern, patron saint of Glasgow where he is also known as St Mungo, the strength to defeat an 'immense army' of rampaging 'Norsemen and Argyllsmen' at the Battle of Renfrew in 1164. In this fight Somerled (Somairlid mac Gille-Brighde), Lord of Argyll and the Isles, was killed – much to the poet's relief. Somerled clearly terrifies the Glaswegians of William's poem, though they do fight back. A cleric chops off the Norse lord's head and places it in the outstretched hands of the Bishop of Glasgow. Earlier in his poem William builds up a sense of vigorous suspense as Somerled's armed fleet approaches up the Clyde.

> Debachantur et vastantur orti, campi, aratra;
> Dominatur et minatur mites manus barbara.
> Glasguensis ictus ensis laesus fugit populus.

> *Gardens, fields and plough-lands were laid waste and destroyed;*
> *the gentle, menaced by barbarous hands, were overwhelmed.*
> *Wounded, Glasgow's people fled the blows of swords . . .*[46]

The Norse wielders of violent weapons celebrated their exploits in poems such as the *Krakumal*, which probably dates from the mid-twelfth century and may have been composed on Orkney or in the Hebrides. Ostensibly the final utterance of the ninth-century Ragnar Lothbrok (Leather Breeches), who has been flung into a snake-pit by King Ælla of Northumbria, this extended poem works variations on the *dróttkvætt* stanza. Its speaker dies with defiant laughter on his lips, and the poem articulates with relentless, controlled aggression the raids of a Viking crew. Each stanza starts with a war-whoop of sword-swinging self-praise, then goes on to chronicle savage attacks on locations in continental Europe, the Hebrides, and 'far and wide in Scotland's firths'.[47]

In this twelfth- and thirteenth-century period the Norse presence in the

Western Isles, Ireland and the north and west of the Scottish mainland is strong. The Gaelic Raghnall, King of Man and the Isles (1187–1229), has a name which comes from the Norse 'Rognvald', and is praised in a substantial Gaelic poem, many of whose nautical and military terms are derived from Norse. Such works both draw on and add to a literature of heroic praise, but a note closer to parody creeps into the Norse 'Song of the Jomsvikings' attributed to Bjarni Kolbeinsson, Bishop of Orkney from 1188 until 1223. Though some of this work is lost, its surviving forty-five stanzas in the *munnvorp* metre (a kind of *dróttkvætt*) show evidence of an imagination that likes to play with and even subvert skaldic conventions. Where at the start most poets might be expected to demand silence for their poem, this poet seems determined to press on with his performance whether or not 'the noble/ knights will listen to me', and later on he addresses 'those not listening'.[48] A sense of a parodic or ironic sensibility continues as the poem mixes the expected materials of Norse heroic exploits with repeated asides about the poet's longing for another man's wife. Aspects of this are reminiscent of Rognvald Kali's Troubadour-influenced work. Though Kolbeinsson's poem can be heroically harsh, it is shot through with flickers of po-faced humour. Like Rognvald Kali's verse, its tonal sophistication can appeal to a modern audience.

The attraction of mixed comic and heroic tonalities is also strong in a remarkable early thirteenth-century work linked to southern Scotland. This is the Norman French *Roman de Fergus* which survives only in continental manuscripts, but whose detailed knowledge of the topography and customs of Scotland suggests an author who had spent time in that country. In 1991, the scholar of medieval French D. D, R. Owen argued that its author, known only as 'Guillaume le Clerc', was probably William Malveisin. This Frenchman appears to have come to Scotland in the 1180s, becoming by 1190 Archdeacon of Lothian before going on to serve as Bishop of Glasgow from 1200 until 1202 when he was made Bishop of St Andrews, a position he occupied until his death in 1238.[49] At just under 7000 lines, the Old French romance of Fergus is both a tale of derring-do in octosyllabic rhyming couplets and a sophisticated spoof of the sort of Arthurian chivalric metrical tale made classic by Chrétien de Troyes, greatest of the French medieval poets, who died in the 1180s.

Fergus is not quite the model Arthurian hero. For a start, he comes from Galloway, an area decried by outsiders for its backwardness, and troublesome to both Scottish and English kings. Serlo, a thoroughly biased mid-twelfth-century English Latin poet, had written of the Gallo-vidians (whom he called 'Picts'), 'Et quas prius extulerunt caudis nates comprimunt' (They use their once-raised tails to shield their arse) and he mocked their supposed preference for raw meat.[50] Fergus, whose ancient name is also that of a twelfth-century King of Galloway, is presented by Guillaume as the son of 'Soumillet' (Somerled), which makes him doubly barbarous. Comically, he first appears as a knight wearing a rusty old suit of armour and carrying a smoke-blackened lance. Dressed like this, he travels to Arthur's court where he is mocked by Sir Kay. Replying with an appropriate oath, 'Par Sai[n]t Mangon qui'st a Glacou' (By St Mungo of Glasgow), Fergus sets off to prove himself a worthy knight, and to win the hand of the beautiful Galiene at Liddel Castle – Castleton in modern Roxburghshire.[51] Galiene first of all throws herself at Fergus, only to be rebuffed, and the poem continu-ally sends up not just the conventions of romantic love but also well-known episodes and motifs from Old French Arthurian romances. A mixture of heroism and ineptitude makes Fergus all the more appealing. Nowhere is this more pronounced than in the way he accomplishes the most demanding of his tasks, vanquishing the north-eastern supernatural forces ranged against him near modern Stonehaven at Dunottar. There, below the spectacular ruined seaside castle, you can still see Fergus's dragon's cave. Doing battle with his formidable Dunottar dragon, our hero falls over:

> A Fergus desplot molt ceste uevre
> Et saciés que molt li anuie.
> Uns autres fust mis a la fuie;
> Mais mius velt morir a honnor
> Que vivre et faire deshonnor
> Et que li tornast a reproce.
> Li sans li saut parmi la boche
> Et par orelles et par le nés
> Que tos en est ensanglentés.
> Et quant il aperçut le sanc
> Qui li arousse l'auberc blanc
> Lors a tel dol, a poi ne font.
> La targe lieve contremont,

Si fiert, iriés comme lion,
Del branc le serpent a bandon
Sor le hance qu'ot hirechie,
Que en travers li a trenchie
La teste et le col a moitié.

Mick Imlah's modern verse translation of this passage is a free one, yet catches something of the tone of the original:

As if in a Highland melodrama,
Fergus cursed through fractured armour.
His only comfort where he lay,
That chevalier of Galloway,
Was joining, since he hadn't fled,
The ranks of the heroic dead.

For so much blood had spouted out
Of his face from the first round of the bout
That when his eyes fell on the hue
Of the tunic he had put on blue,
He almost fainted in distress
At the ruined state of his warrior dress.

Instead, provoked by the red rag,
He sprang up like a cornered stag
And lashed out with his wounded pride
At the tough scales of the serpent's hide: –
Then slicing up at the shocked head,
Severed the neck and dropped her dead.[52]

After many further trials Fergus wins his lady and is recognized as a true hero by all the Arthurian court. A product far less of 'holy reading' than of a mischievous literary imagination steeped in a fashionable Arthurian canon, *Fergus* takes us through a Scotland that is enjoyably suspended between the endless forests of knightly questing and the precisely realized topography of northern Britain. As well as meeting giants and dragons, our praiseworthy hero endures a stormy crossing from Queensferry as he travels north along the recognizable pilgrims' route to Dunfermline. Relying on the supposed barbarousness of the Gallovidian Scot and appealing to the sophisticated taste of an audience

used to secular romances, *Fergus* is an outstandingly polished performance from a period when heroic deeds and literary conventions might
be viewed through the eye of parody, yet still relished for their genuine
excitement and gusto. This is praise with a wink in it.

At a time when different political and linguistic communities in Scotland might view one another with terror, interest and occasional amusement, the great, measured, beautiful music of Gaelic poets active in the
west and in Ireland sounds a more traditional note of praise uncorroded
by irony. Gille-Brighde Albanach, whose bardic career was at its height
in the first three decades of the thirteenth century, was a poet from
the 'lovely yellow woods' of Scotland who composed according to the
metrically strict rules of classic bardic poetry and who wrote in praise
of Irish monarchs such as Cathal Crobhdherg ('Redhand'), King of
Connacht. His praise-poem links the king's strength and justice to the
good health of the terrain he rules over, with its green, nut-rich woods
and 'luscious turf'.[53] This poem of thirty-six quatrains summons up
epithets and terms of praise familiar from six centuries earlier. Where
Beccán of Rhum in the 600s had called Columba 'Caindel Connacht'
(Connacht's candle), so these later verses hymning an early thirteenth-
century King of Connacht style him 'choinnle Tuama' (Tuam's candle).[54]
The elaborate variations of praise are vivid as they bond the king to the
landscape and pursuits of his kingdom. So his 'sure hand' is 'Whiter
than a shirt on washing day', while in Connacht 'struck with a mallet,
each white hazel/ will pour down the fill of a vat'.[55] Although Gille-
Brighde tells us that he was Scottish, his heart seems to have been
in Ireland. Another poem for the same king, written from Scotland,
remembers with tears of longing Ireland's 'land of round, wooded hill-
ocks,/ wet land of eggs and birdflocks'.[56]

As they had done for the best part of a millennium, Gaelic poets
continued to move between Ireland and Scotland. If Gille-Brighde was
a Scot working for Irish patrons, then his contemporary Muireadhach
Albanach Ó Dálaigh was a poet from Ireland's principal poetic family.
He had been bard to the ruler of Tir Conaill, Domhnall Mór Ó
Domhnaill, but had fled to Scotland after a quarrel. Spending about
fifteen years in Scotland, this poet acquired the epithet 'Albanach' (Scotsman) and, settling in his new homeland, is said to be the ancestor of the
most famous Scottish family of Gaelic bards, the MacMhuirichs. Two
surviving early thirteenth-century poems by him praise the rulers of

Lennox whose territorial headquarters was at Balloch in Dumbartonshire. Their descent from a noble Irish family is made much of. In comparison with the substantial amount of work surviving from Ireland, only a small amount of Scottish bardic poetry now exists, and Wilson McLeod points out that Muireadhach Albanach's poem for Alun, first Earl of Lennox (who died around the year 1200), is 'the earliest extant bardic poem composed for a Scottish chief'.[57] Like Gille-Brighde, Muireadhach Albanach participated as a pilgrim in the Fifth Crusade. Beginning in 1217, this involved the temporary capture of the Egyptian fort of Damietta the following year. Muireadhach made a Gaelic poem 'Upon Tonsuring', about having his head shaved. It probably dates from his time as a crusader. His shorn curls are a sacrifice to God: 'This fair hair, Maker, is yours.'[58] Damietta was lost again in 1221 and its siege resulted in severe casualties among the crusading army. A homesick poem made by Muireadhach at Monte Gargano records some of the losses, and exclaims with longing that it would be 'Like Heaven's pay, tonight, to touch/ Scotland of the high places'.[59]

Compiled much later, in sixteenth-century Perthshire, the *Book of the Dean of Lismore* is now one of the treasures of the National Library of Scotland. It includes selections from Scots poets like Henryson and Dunbar but is famous as the most precious of early Scottish Gaelic manuscripts. Brought to the attention of eighteenth-century antiquaries by James 'Ossian' Macpherson, it contains unique transcripts of many earlier poems by Scottish and Irish poets. Among these is what modern readers may consider the most moving work by Muireadhach Albanach, his 'Elegy on Mael Mhedha, his Wife'. Its intricately rhyming quatrains communicate with remarkably sustained lyricism a sense of love, hurt and sundering:

> Do bhí duine go ndreich moill
> ina luighe ar leith mo phill;
> gan bharamhail acht bláth cuill
> don sgáth duinn bhanamhail bhinn.
>
> Maol Mheadha na malach ndonn
> mo dhabhach mheadha a-raon rom;
> mo chridhe an sgáth do sgar riom,
> bláth mhionn arna car do chrom.

Táinig an chlí as ar gcuing,
   agus dí ráinig mar roinn:
corp idir dá aisil inn
   ar dtocht don fhinn mhaisigh mhoill.

There was a soft-gazed woman
   lay on one side of my bed;
none like her but the hazel's flower,
   that dark shadow, womanly, sweet.

Mael Mhedha of the dark brows,
   my cask of mead at my side;
my heart, the shadow split from me,
   flowers' crown, planted, now bowed down.

My body's gone from my grip
   and has fallen to her share;
my body's splintered in two,
   since she's gone, soft, fine and fair.[60]

A poet of emotional power and utterly convincing thematic range, Muireadhach Albanach also wrote a beautiful and erotically charged poem addressed to the Virgin Mary, longing for her 'young round sharp blue eye' and 'soft tresses':

A ÓghMhuire, a abhra dubh,
   a mhórmhuine, a ghardha geal,
tug, a cheann báidhe na mban,
   damh tar ceann mo náire neamh.

O Virgin Mary, O dark brow,
   O great nurse, O garden gay,
of all women the most beloved,
   give me heaven despite my shame.[61]

In terms of its extensiveness, the high point of Gaelic culture in Scotland was around the late ninth century when the court appears to have been an important centre of literary patronage. Although much later, in 1249, King Alexander III had his genealogy read to him in Gaelic by a King's Poet as part of his coronation at Scone, from the late eleventh century the royal court became de-Gaelicized so that the professional literary men known as *filidh* who had been attached to kings and major local rulers turned their attention elsewhere. A lower order of poets, the *baird* or bards (among whom the Ó Dálaighs were prominent), went on developing and making poems, particularly in western and Highland areas. By the twelfth century the Scottish court and the agriculturally rich lands of Lowland Scotland were only vestigially Gaelic. That language was increasingly identified with the less agriculturally productive Highlands and with western areas, especially the Hebrides. As the *filidh* declined and the *baird* developed, praise-poetry in vernacular Scottish Gaelic began to break free of older classical Irish models. Still, making genealogically alert poems and serving just a few families, Scottish bardic poets may have continued to look and listen to Ireland for at least part of their training, even when, like Gille-Brighde Albanach, they were not Irish by birth. Scottish bardic poets liked to emphasize Irish connections, whereas Irish poets paid relatively little attention to Scotland, and most of the medieval prose that survives in Gaelic is clearly Irish rather than Scottish in origin. The major prose works written by Scots in the Middle Ages, from the records of the early Scottish Parliament to elaborate philosophical treatises, are in Latin, not in Gaelic.

Gille-Brighde Albanach's richly imaged Gaelic praise-poetry is very far indeed from the academic Latin prose of John Duns Scotus, greatest of Scotland's early philosophers. Yet Duns Scotus's work, like that of Muireadhach Albanach Ó Dálaigh in his hymn of praise to Mary, is grounded on the assumption that the Christian faith is what makes sense of the cosmos and our being in it. Defending his belief in Mary's immaculate conception, Duns Scotus too argued that 'what is most excellent should be attributed to Mary'.[62] Born around 1266, apparently to a family linked to Duns in Berwickshire, the philosopher is thought to have been educated in Haddington, then ordained a priest at Northampton in 1291. A Franciscan, Duns Scotus was teaching at Oxford in 1300. Soon afterwards he studied and taught in Paris before moving to Cologne where he was lecturing in 1308, the year of his death. The elaborate catafalque containing his remains, now in the Minoritenkirche, Cologne, bears the inscription 'Scotia me genuit, Anglia me suscepit, Gallia me docuit, Colonia me tenet' (Scotland bore me, England reared me, France taught me, Cologne holds my remains). Michael Scot enjoyed a similarly peripatetic career, but where the earlier Scottish thinker's prose is crammed with odd facts, digressions and entertaining images, the writing of Duns Scotus is unsparingly abstract, brilliantly analytical. Aspects of it have appealed to literary imaginations (notably that of Gerard Manley Hopkins), but Scotus is read today mostly by theologians, philosophers and the occasional historian of science.

The form of Duns Scotus's works reflects his academic training which involved rigorous ritualized arguments. He took part in one such *disputatio* in Oxford around 1300; a thirteenth-century manuscript from Balliol College there contains an illuminated initial showing a scholarly disputation in which two groups of learned men face each other.[63] Their body language is controlled but confrontational. Several of the gowned, bearded figures are using both hands to gesture. The right hand of each man is raised, its index finger wagging at the opponents, while the palm of the other hand is open in a gesture of explanation. Duns Scotus's voluminous and acute prose, subjecting his opponents to relentless, often sceptical interrogation and rebuttal before offering his own explanations, operates in a similar manner.

In the Middle Ages Scotus was known as 'Doctor Subtilis', the subtle, learned doctor. His preoccupations include metaphysics (whose goal is God), the nature of knowledge (and how we can know God), God's existence and the immortality of the soul. One of the greatest of medieval philosophers, he reacted strongly against both Aristotle and Aquinas. Arguing for the freedom of the individual will, he had an interest in what it was that made concepts distinctively individual – their individuating difference or 'haecceitas' (thisness), to use a word popular with his followers. Where a poet might have tried to approach such matters through arresting imagery, the philosopher proceeds to attempt to articulate the essence of difference through demanding argument. An extract from Duns Scotus's great *Ordinatio*, a formal revision of his lectures commenting on the *Sententiae* or gathered theological opinions of the twelfth-century theologian Peter Lombard, gives a flavour of his elaborately punctuated, intellectually pugilistic, exhausting prose as it circles, jabs at and sometimes engorges phrases and ideas:

Et si quaeras a me quae est ista 'entitas individualis' a qua sumitur differentia individualis, estne materia vel forma vel compositum, – respondeo: Omnis entitas quiditativa – sive partialis sive totalis – alicuius generis, est de se indifferens 'ut entitas quiditativa' ad hanc entitatem et illam, ita quod 'ut entitas quiditativa' est naturaliter prior ista entitate ut haec est, – et ut prior est naturaliter, sicut non convenit sibi esse hanc, ita non repugnat sibi ex ratione sua suum oppositum; et sicut compositum non includit suam entitatem (qua formaliter est 'hoc') in quantum natura, ita nec materia 'in quantum natura' includit suam entitatem (qua est 'haec materia'), nec forma 'in quantum natura' includit suam.

And if you ask me, What is this 'individuating entity' from which the individual difference is taken? Is it matter or form or the composite? I give you this answer: Every quidditative entity – be it partial or total – of any sort is of itself indifferent as a quidditative entity to this entity and that, so that as a quidditative entity it is naturally prior to this entity as just this. *Now just as, in this natural priority, it does not pertain to it to be this, neither is it repugnant to its essential nature to be other than just* this. *And as the composite does not include qua nature its entity whereby it is this matter, nor does its form qua nature include its entity whereby it is this form.*[64]

Although his fascination with constituting 'differentia' might interest modern academic poststructuralists preoccupied with what Jacques Derrida calls '*différance*', Duns Scotus's relentless method of analytical argument is likely to appeal to a scholarly minority. His works generated much heat in theological arguments. Across Europe the Scotists or Realists were ranged against the Thomists or Nominalists. In English his followers were known as the 'Duns men' and sometimes seen as pedants, but by the sixteenth century around the time of the Protestant Reformation the English language attacked this great Catholic man of Duns by making his name a synonym for 'a hair-splitting reasoner' or even a 'blockhead' – a dunce.[65]

While the huge, penetrating and dry intellect of Duns Scotus was at work abroad, Scotland was going through a long period of troubles and conflicts whose hopes and political growing pains increasingly shaped thirteenth- and fourteenth-century literature. A beautiful Latin song made for the 1281 wedding of Margaret of Scotland and King Eirik of Norway survives along with its music in a manuscript now in Uppsala.

> Ex te lux oritur
> O dulcis Scocia
> Qua vere noscitur
> Fulgens Norwagia.

Que cum transvehitur
Trahis suspiria
Tui subtrahitur
Quod regis filia.

From you, sweet Scotland,
A light arises,
A light whose brightness
Shines clear in Norway.
How you will sigh
When your king's daughter
Is taken from you
Across the sea.[66]

Within two years this Queen was dead; her daughter Margaret (later called 'the Maid of Norway') died in Orkney in 1290, and a royal succession crisis followed. In the thirteenth century the word 'Scotland' had come to be used regularly to describe the whole country, but it was a country whose sense of itself was quickened by danger. Sudden deaths and political violence are the themes of poems of the period. This can be heard in various Latin verses praising the Scottish freedom fighter William Wallace, victor of the Battle of Stirling Bridge in 1297 ('England groans'), or exalting in the death of the violently rapacious 'Hammer of the Scots', England's King Edward I ('Scotland, clap your hands').[67] These times of violence helped cement a stronger sense of a single, independent nation, a Scotland whose population had grown in number to perhaps about half a million people.

From around this era of the Wars of Independence dates what is probably the oldest poem surviving in the tongue we now call 'Scots', though that form of language was then called 'Inglis' in Scotland and was the northern development of that Old English language carved in runes on the Ruthwell Cross about 600 years earlier. Preserved in a later chronicle, these famous lines of anonymous verse date from around 1300 and lament the state of the land in the wake of the accidental death of the Scottish King Alexander III, who was thrown from his horse. It is the first Scottish poem in this present book which can be read by most readers with the aid of a glossary, rather than a translation. Its sense of political distress is urgent, but it continues a note of Christian prayer that harks back to some of the earliest writings preserved in what is now identified by the poet as the nation of 'Scotlande':

Qwhen Alexander our kynge was dede,

That Scotlande lede in lauche and le   *led; law; protection*

Away was sons of alle and brede,   *abundance; ale; bread*

    Off wyne and wax, of gamyn and gle.   *play; pleasure*

Our golde was changit in to lede.   *lead*

    Christ, born in virgynyte,

Succoure Scotlande, and ramede,   *cure*

That stade is in perplexite.[68]   *stood*

The poetry of early fourteenth-century Scotland is a poetry of heroic struggle. A short Latin verse advocates that the troops of Robert the Bruce (who would decisively defeat the English at Bannockburn in 1314) use such difficult terrain as marshy ground and woodlands to aid them; a Gaelic *brosnachadh catha* (incitement to battle poem) by Artur Dall Mac Gurcaigh on 'Eoin Mac Suibhne's Voyage to Castle Sween' records the efforts of the English-supported MacSweens to win back their lands from Bruce's supporters. Praising MacSween's fleet, the poet refers to its crew as 'Lochlannaigh is ármuinn' ('Norsemen . . . nobles').[69] The first of these Gaelic words means Scandinavians, especially Norsemen, while the term 'ármuinn' is a Gaelic loanword from the Norse word for steward. The fleet's ships in this vigorous poem praising military virtues are Norse warships, with shields hanging along the sides. They are involved, though, not simply in a local territorial feud, but in larger struggles between the nations of Scotland and England which resound throughout the literature and oratory of the age.

At governmental level, Latin, the international language of diplomacy, was harnessed in extensive submissions to Pope Boniface VIII by the Scottish lawyer Baldred Bisset of Kinghorn and St Andrews in Fife who as professor of law at Bologna convinced the papal curia in 1301 to take seriously the 'name of Scotia with the race of the Scots', rather than paying too much attention to the Anglocentric propaganda of England's King Edward I.[70] 'Scotia', the Scots claimed, was a name that came from Scota, daughter of an ancient Egyptian Pharaoh. As would later Scottish chroniclers, Baldred set out Scota's lineage and descendants in elaborate, improbable detail, successfully countering the equally ornate and improbable propaganda of English chroniclers and the English king.

Such an origin narrative and plea for national independence may have been fiction, but it was empowering, mythic fiction, drawn on again in a 1309 Latin declaration issued by Robert the Bruce's first parliament in St Andrews, and underpinning a good deal of the celebrated 1320 Declaration of Arbroath. The Arbroath document, redolent of the Scottish struggle to assert and maintain independence from English control, is really a letter drafted by Bernard, Abbot of Arbroath, who since 1311 had been Chancellor to Robert I (Robert the Bruce), crowned King of Scots at Scone, Perthshire, in 1306. Bernard had experience of international negotiations, having helped agree a treaty with the Norwegians in 1312. It was in 1320 that he drew up what eventually came to be known as the Declaration of Arbroath, one of several letters addressed (with some success) to Pope John XXII in April of that year in the names of many of the nobility of Scotland.

Although this sonorous work, composed in the high-flown Latin prose rhythms known as *cursus* used in formal papal documents, acquired in the mid-twentieth century its now familiar title 'Declaration of Arbroath', it might better be styled the 'Declamation of Avignon'. For it was carried there by three envoys (two Scots and a Frenchman) to be read aloud to the Pope by Master Alexander Kinninmonth, a Church lawyer and papal chaplain. What we have is in a sense the script of a great piece of political oratory, addressed to an audience of one. Like most political speeches, this one relies at least as much on aspiration as on achievement. Several of the nobles who endorsed it were soon accused of treason to Bruce, and the speech articulated that king's wish to bind 'the whole community of the Kingdom of Scotland' together, rather than his complete success in doing so.

The Declaration draws on phrasing from the Latin Vulgate Bible and from the Roman historian Sallust.[71] Some of its layout is based on the Irish Remonstrance sent to Pope John around 1318 by Donal O'Neil. Where the Irish appeal included a list of 197 native kings, the Scots could muster a genealogy of just 113.[72] As was customary in this era, there is a good deal of proud mythologizing as the Pope is told how the Scots originally came from Greater Scythia and were converted by Christ's first apostle, St Andrew, before they reached Scotland. The Scots' appeal to the Pope catalogues the atrocities – massacres, burnings, slaughter of monks and nuns – which Edward I has visited on Scotland. A bludgeoning note also surfaces. If His Holiness believes instead the rival English accounts, then 'we must believe that the Most High will lay to your charge all the blood, loss of souls, and other calamities that shall follow on either hand betwixt us and them'. This may sound an unsubtle way to address God's Vicar on Earth, but there are earlier examples in Scottish writings of successful attempts to bully saints such as Columba or Mungo into giving assistance. However, it is one central passage which turns this work into what remains Scotland's most ringing piece of political oratory. As well as a paean of praise to Robert the Bruce as a paragon of endurance and the defence of liberty, the 'letter' contains a magnificent middle section:

Quem si ab inceptis desisteret, Regi Anglorum aut Anglicis nos aut Regnum nostrum volens subicere, tanquam Inimicum nostrum et sui nostrique Juris sub-uersorem statim expellere niteremur et alium Regem nostrum qui ad defensionem nostram sufficeret faceremus. Quia quamdiu Centum ex nobis viui remanserint, nuncquam Anglorum dominio aliquatenus volumus subiugari. Non enim propter gloriam, diuicias aut honores pugnamus sed propter libertatem solummodo quam Nemo bonus nisi simul cum vita amittit.

Yet if he should give up what he has begun, and agree to make us or our kingdom subject to the King of England or the English, we should exert ourselves at once to drive him out as our enemy and a subverter of his own rights and ours, and make some other man who was well able to defend us our King; for, as long as but a hundred of us remain alive, never will we on any conditions be brought under English rule. It is in truth not for glory, nor riches, nor honours that we are fighting, but for freedom – for that alone, which no honest man gives up but with life itself.[73]

This assertion of the right of Scots to choose their own ruler, and this determined praise of the interlinked virtues of personal and national freedom is of huge importance in Scottish history and literature. Its sentiments of resolute self-determination and liberty will be sounded again in the most celebrated lines of John Barbour's medieval epic *The Bruce*, in the sixteenth-century work of George Buchanan, and, in the eighteenth century, in Robert Burns's 'Scots, wha hae'. Yet its importance is not only applicable to Scotland. Designed to appeal to a national community, it is very much a political speech addressed to the earthly head of the huge international community of Christendom, and its reverberations run far beyond the local. The specific wording of the

Declaration of Arbroath was largely forgotten for some time. The only surviving copy lay locked away in Edinburgh Castle; it got damp. But an English translation was published in Edinburgh in 1689 and in the eighteenth century its praise of freedom began to be quoted once again. The influential Enlightenment figure Lord Hailes wrote about it, and James Boswell used the ringing last sentence from the extract quoted above as the epigraph to his celebrated 1768 *Account of Corsica*, whose modern fight for liberty was a focus of much interest to his contemporaries. Today the Declaration is the most treasured document in the National Archives of Scotland. There are holes in it, and from its text dangle the intricate ancient seals of the earls and barons of the nation. Recently it has been suggested that the Declaration of Arbroath is a forerunner of the 1776 American Declaration of Independence whose principal author, Thomas Jefferson, certainly had Scotland in mind as he wrote.[74] The 1215 Magna Carta was an English document very different in tone, and one of which the Scots were rightly wary since its fifty-ninth clause made it clear that their king was to be treated by the English monarch 'in the same way as our other barons of England'.[75] Scotland's struggle against being treated as a mere region of its larger neighbour to the south would continue throughout the centuries, conditioning the political outlook of many authors. More immediately, bringing together the divine and the secular, the locally- and internationally-oriented Declaration of Arbroath anticipated some of the great themes of the literature that would follow. Not least among these were Scotland itself, kingliness, community and vigorously asserted independence.

Two great medieval posts matriculate as students at the University of St Andrews. Upper picture: William Dunbar enters his second year in 1477; Dunbar's name is in the middle of the first column. Lower picture: Gavin Douglas heads a list of students enrolled during the Rectorship of Robert Bosuel in 1490. Bosuel had lectured at the University during Dunbar's time and it is likely that both poets had several of the same teachers. (St Andrews University Library, Muniments, UY411/1 and UY305/1)

2

Liberty

Praise continued. Its ecclesiastical administration, though, had long since shifted eastwards. From the western island of Iona through Dunkeld in Perthshire, Church government in Scotland gravitated to the east coast of Scotland, and specifically to the emerging ecclesiastical centre of St Andrews in Fife. Here, to an ancient, growing church beside the North Sea, St Rule was said to have brought relics of Scotland's patron saint. A monastic site since the eighth century, St Andrews seems to have become the seat of Scotland's most powerful bishop before the end of the first millennium. One of the finest medieval Scottish views can still be experienced if you climb the narrow stone spiral staircase to the top of the eleventh-century St Rule's Tower. Thirty-three metres high, this landmark for pilgrims predates the surrounding St Andrews Cathedral. From the top of St Rule's square tower, looking out over the great sweep of St Andrews Bay and the ancient streets of the town centre, you get a good sense of how, 'imminent itself above the sea', St Andrews was, in Robert Louis Stevenson's words, 'the light of medieval Scotland'.[1]

Still magnificent, but now a ruin, St Andrews Cathedral dates from the twelfth and thirteenth centuries. Before the establishment of an Augustinian priory there in 1144, married clergy received pilgrims; the hereditary priests of the Céli Dé (Clients of God), a Scottish and Irish reform movement with strong links to Iona, oversaw the Cathedral church. Later, St Andrews Cathedral suffered over the centuries from storm, fire, and abandonment after the sixteenth-century Protestant Reformation, but with an internal length of 109 metres it was by far the largest cathedral in Scotland and became an important medieval European pilgrimage site. Its development made St Andrews a hub of religion and learning even before Scotland's first university was founded there in 1411. Indications of St Andrews as a medieval cultural centre range from the carved lion hunt on the eighth-century Pictish St Andrews Sarcophagus, a sculptural masterpiece still displayed in the Cathedral museum, to the Scots verse *Original Chronicle* of Scottish history written in the early 1420s by Andrew of Wyntoun (a former St Andrews Augustinian canon), and the so-called St Andrews Music Book (now in Wolfenbüttel, Germany) which preserves treasures of twelfth- and thirteenth-century music from the Cathedral. Among these are the polyphonic 'Kyrie Virginitatus Amor', celebrating the Virgin Mary.[2]

Thirty miles south of St Andrews is an island in the Firth of Forth whose Gaelic name, Innis Choluim, means Columba's Isle. There in a monastery plainchants were sung to 'Columba, spes Scotorum' ('Columba, hope of the Scots').[3] The *Inchcolm Antiphoner* in which these chants are recorded dates from the fourteenth century. Containing music as well as lyrics, it is our best guide to the song culture of the Columban church. Yet, as some of the poems mentioned at the end of the previous chapter suggest, a new, more secular cult was growing up around another leader who could be portrayed as the hope of many Scots. This was Robert the Bruce, King Robert I, whose great victory against the English at Bannockburn in 1314 became the stuff of history and heroic amplification.

Bruce was present at the consecration of the completed St Andrews Cathedral in 1318, but he was more an astute, ruthless fighter and ruler than a holy man. He died in 1329, a year after securing England's formal acknowledgement of Scottish independence. Over four decades later a Scotsman born around the year of Bruce's death composed the greatest work celebrating the King's achievements. John Barbour studied in England and France, serving as archdeacon of Aberdeen from 1356 until he died in 1395. His twenty-book poem *The Bruce* was probably written under the patronage of Robert Stewart, who ruled Scotland as King Robert II from 1371 until 1390; Stewart's father is favourably presented in Barbour's vast, rather sprawling work. Unique at this date in being a historical-biographical Scots romance rather than a verse chronicle, *The Bruce* comprises 14,000 lines of octosyllabic rhyming couplets, though extra syllables in the lines are common. This was a metre favoured in Old French romances (such as *Fergus*) and in English romances like the early fourteenth-century *Sir Orfeo*; but to modern ears it can become unduly monotonous, quickening an understanding of why Milton in *Paradise Lost* avoided what he called 'the jingling sound of like endings'.[4]

The Bruce is in many ways an aristocratic work. Its being composed in Scots rather than Latin or French adds to its novelty as a courtly romance and makes it a foundation stone of the Scots verse tradition. Written for a royal patron and celebrating a king, it records heroic deeds of chivalry carried out by titled men. Although the presence of the common people – 'The small folk' – is recorded from time to time, the focus stays on aristocratic endeavours.[5] Praise is given to the codes of chivalry, especially to 'Leawté' (Loyalty), the vital bond which attaches a man to his superiors in peacetime and in battle.[6] Offering the great example of Bruce, Barbour's work is in the long tradition of 'advice to princes', a genre comprising how-to-rule manuals for kings which goes back at least as far as Xenophon's ancient Greek *Cyropaedia*, and which includes more modern Renaissance works such as Machiavelli's *Il Principe*. Bruce's exploits are compared to those of older, sometimes Classical heroes. There are allusions to other romances, to biblical precedent, and to history. King Robert I is presented as a paradigm of endurance, strategic wiliness, courage and inspirational leadership. He is the king that Scotland needed.

At the heart of Barbour's poem is a lengthy description of the Battle of Bannockburn. But the flow of the narrative takes in much more than that, moving from Bruce's involvement in Scottish civil wars to his campaigning with his brother in Ireland. Later the King raids England, and even goes on a posthumous excursion to the Crusades where his heart is carried into battle. Hunted along a stream by enemy bloodhounds, talking in disguise to a housewife, or avoiding attempted assassination, Bruce shows an escapological brilliance which makes him at times appear a heroic emanation from those romances that give Barbour's poem its form and some of its details. The King emerges as a lover of such narratives. Being rowed across Loch Lomond in difficult times, he reads 'meryly' to his knights the chivalric French 'Romanys off worthi Ferambrace', whose heroic tale of a small force standing against a more numerous enemy foreshadows Bruce's own victories.[7] Yet while Barbour calls his *Bruce* a 'romanys', and several times links the King's exploits to daring deeds of other romances, he also makes clear from the start that while his poem may be compared with 'auld storys' of 'chevalry' it is full of 'suthfastnes' (truth).[8] Part romance, part history, part military manual, *The Bruce* teems with biographical and societal details which have attracted historians keen for the nitty-gritty of siege engines, strategy, or aristocratic attitudes. Sometimes it seems too baggily constructed. Buttressed by sophisticated allusions to the Bible, Cato and St Margaret of Scotland, as well as to King Arthur and Thomas of Ercildoune, *The Bruce* celebrates a leader's 'hardyment governyt with wyt' (courage ruled with intelligence).[9]

Bruce's friendship with Sir James Douglas is central to the poem. When these two heroes are reunited, all their attendant lords weep with joy. Such chivalric flourishes remind modern readers that Barbour's attention is focused on the nobility, and that his valorizing of 'fredome' is not at all the product of a democratic sensibility. Nonetheless, with its wistfully longing 'A!', the poem's most famous passage has appealed to readers of very different complexions in later centuries:

> A! Fredome is a noble thing
> Fredome mays man to haiff liking.   *allows; contentment*
> Fredome all solace to man giffis,
> He levys at es that frely levys.[10]   *lives; ease*

These lines describe the sentiments of 'a noble hart', the word 'noble' here invoking aristocratic assumptions. However, Barbour portrays a king capable of reaching out to 'Bath mar and les commonaly' (Highborn and low, all together), as he does in his powerful oration before Bannockburn.[11] Uniting the frequently warring factions of Scotland through his force, his rhetoric and his canniness, Bruce leads them to victory against the superior forces of an oppressive neighbour. In so doing he becomes a national celebrity – 'Quharever he raid all the countré/ Gaderyt in daynté [Gathered with pleasure] him to se.'[12]

The Bruce is unflinching in its lengthy descriptions of battle and slaughter. Barbour has an eye for telling dramatic details, as when Bruce's men make their own shoes out of animal hides, or Douglas mixes discarded foodstuffs with enemy corpses to produce the appalling 'Douglas lardner' (larder).[13] In classic medieval style the poem celebrates how 'fortoun' turns her wheel, yet sees all the action as taking place subject to the steering 'grace off God that all thing steris'.[14] Barbour's action is very much male-dominated, and earlier ages clearly delighted in the extended detailing of manly military slaughter. Yet contained in the over-long descriptions of the Bruces' Irish campaigns is an incident in Limerick that, while emanating from male experience, sounds a note arresting not just for its demonstration of Bruce's generous chivalry, but also for its vignette of lower-class female travail:

The king has hard a woman cry,	*heard*
He askyt quhat that wes in hy.	*happening*
'It is the laynder, schyr,' said ane,	*laundress; sir*
'That hyr child-ill rycht now hes tane	*[gone into labour]*
And mon leve now behind us her,	*must stay; here*
Tharfor scho makys yone ivill cher.'	*unhappy cry*
The king said, 'Certis, it war pité	
That scho in that poynt left suld be,	
For certis I trow thar is no man	
That he ne will rew a woman than.'	*pity; [in such a case]*
His ost all thar arestyt he	*host; stopped*
And gert a tent sone stentit be	*pitched*
And gert hyr gang in hastily,	*made her go in quickly*
And other wemen to be hyr by.	
Quhill scho wes deliver he bad	*while she gave birth he stayed*
And syne furth on his wayis raid,	
And how scho furth suld caryit be	
Or ever he furth fur ordanyt he.	*before*
This wes a full gret curtasy	
That swilk a king and swa mychty	*such*
Gert his men dwell on this maner	*made*
Bot for a pouer lauender.[15]	*poor*

Barbour's couplets sound effortless here. Though unusual in some regards, this passage is only one of many that ensure his poem continues to be valued, visited and read (as it was meant to be) aloud.

Some of Barbour's sources were used also by Walter Bower (1385–1449), Augustinian Abbot of Inchcolm and one of Scotland's senior churchmen. Though nibbled by rodents in later centuries, an early working copy of Bower's great Latin *Scotichronicon*, a prose history of the Scots, survives in the library of Corpus Christi College, Cambridge. Its fine illustrations show the mythical Scota and others on board ship sailing westwards from Egypt, as well as depicting more historically-based scenes such as Bannockburn. Opening with a short prayer to the Virgin Mary, the manuscript's preface makes it clear that the *Scotichronicon* was begun as a transcription of the 'famous historical work' of John of Fordun, a fourteenth-century Aberdonian churchman whose own five-book Latin prose *Chronica Gentis Scotorum* (*Chronicle of the People of the Scots*), compiled in the 1380s, is the first surviving attempt at a complete history of the Scottish people and is based on many documents now lost.[16] As Bower's 'laborious work' developed, though, he made marginal additions to Fordun, and eventually took over as author, producing a huge history of Scotland up to his own time which occupies nine volumes in D. E. R. Watt's modern edition.[17] The memorable concluding lines – 'Non Scotus est Christe cui liber non placet iste' (Christ! He is not a Scot who is not pleased with this book) – are in keeping with Bower's spirited account of Scotland's heroic struggles.[18] Impressed by Fordun's 'elegant style', Bower produces a wordy patchwork of earlier sources, digressing in the capacious learned medieval Latin style of the day, familiar to such earlier Latin thinkers as Michael Scot, rather than writing in the more Classically-oriented Petrarchan Renaissance Latin which did not reach Scotland until around 1500.[19]

Regarded by historians as among the most valuable records of late medieval Scotland, Bower's full-bodied work in its earlier sections abounds in curiosities: St Kentigern meets Merlin in an episode informed by ancient Celtic beliefs and tropes; Macbeth threatens to crush the neck of the thane of Fife 'under the yoke like an ox's in a wagon'.[20] Yet it is in the later books of the *Scotichronicon*, where Bower appears to be drawing not only on older sources but also on personal experience, that his work has most literary bite. When he departs from Fordun we get a sense of his strong patriotic bias: 'Anglicus est prodiciosus socius, bonus servus, sed insufferabilis magister sive dominus' ('an Englishman is a treacherous associate, a good servant, but an intolerable master or lord').[21] Bower chronicles the bloody struggles of the 'lion-like Scots' against England, but also details the development of ecclesiastical and other intellectual culture. He gives what may be an eye-witness account of the reception of the papal bulls granted to Scotland's first university, St Andrews, Bower's own alma mater.

Quibus in conspectu omnium perlectis 'Te deum laudamus' canora voce procedentes usque ad magnum altare clerus et conventus decantabant. Quo cantato et omnibus genua flectentibus, episcopus Rossensis versiculum de Sancto Spiritu cum collecta 'Deus qui corda' pronunciabat. Reliqum vero huius diei transigerunt cum inestimabili jocunditate et per totam noctem fecerunt per vicos et plateas civitatis ignes copiosos bibentes vinum in leticia.

When the bulls had been read out before everybody, the clergy and convent processed to the high altar singing Te Deum laudamus in harmonious voice. When this had been sung and everyone was on bended knee, the bishop of Ross pronounced the versicle of the Holy Spirit and the collect Deus qui corda. They spent the rest of this day in boundless merry-making and kept large bonfires burning in the streets and open spaces of the city while drinking wine in celebration.[22]

One of those who associated themselves with the petition to the Avignon Pope Benedict XIII to grant bulls of foundation for St Andrews University was King James I of Scotland (1394–1437), then a prisoner of the English in Nottingham Castle. When he was eleven it had been decided to send James to St Andrews to be educated under the charge of Bishop Henry Wardlaw, later first Chancellor of the university. However, James was captured at sea, and would spend eighteen years in thrall to his English captors. The royal prisoner received a thorough education, reading the works of the recently deceased English poets Chaucer and Gower, as well as those of the still living John Lydgate. Though a Latin obituary mentions James's 'Carmina' (songs), only one work attributed to him survives.[23] It is contained in a fragile late fifteenth-century manuscript made for important aristocratic literary patrons, the Sinclair family of Fife and Roslin. Now in the Bodleian Library, Oxford, this manuscript includes a number of substantial poems by Chaucer and other English poets as well as constituting the first sizeable anthology of Scottish verse. King James I's work in it is *The Kingis Quair* (The King's Book), a beguilingly stylish 1400-line vision poem born out of the King's captivity, though apparently composed in 1424 when on his release he married the English noblewoman Joan Beaufort. Written in the seven-line rhyming iambic pentameter stanza form used by Chaucer in *Troilus and Criseyde*, *The Kingis Quair* is formally very different from Barbour's *Bruce*. It makes no mention of Scotland or England. Yet it too is preoccupied with kinds of 'libertee' and enthralment. What we know of James's life suggests that these were complex issues for him. The English King held him incarcerated (sometimes in the Tower of London), but at other times allowed him considerable freedom and treated him as a useful bargaining counter in negotiations with Scotland and France. James was part of Henry V's English army in its wars against Scotland's allies, the French, and was a chief mourner at Henry's funeral in 1422. The Scottish King married Joan, whose brother, John Beaufort, Fourth Earl of Somerset, had been captured in France in 1421 by Scottish troops and was not released until 1438. James was surrounded by a complex, ironic geometry of 'thraldom' and 'libertee'.[24]

Apparently written when he was twenty-nine, his poem is partly autobiographical, partly a courtly love poem celebrating his meeting with his wife (it may have been composed for St Valentine's Day); it meditates throughout on the workings of Fortune and the will of God. Initially its speaker lies 'in bed allone waking' and starts to read Boethius's early sixth-century Latin *De Consolatione Philosophiae*.[25] After the Bible, *On the Consolation of Philosophy* was probably the most widely read book in medieval Europe; Chaucer translated it. Written in prison by an exiled nobleman, it sets forth the ups and downs of Fortune's Wheel. James's speaker enjoys Boethius's 'poetly' prose work. Then, asleep, he is woken by a matins bell which seems to command him through 'ymagynacioun' to begin his own story. He writes of being captured by 'inymyis' (enemies) and 'led away' to 'thair contree'.[26] He can find no reason why Fortune has treated him so, and he bewails his fate:

> The bird, the best, the fisch eke in the see,
> They lyve in fredome, euerich in his kynd.
> And I a man, and lakkith libertee.[27]

Then, looking out of his prison window, he sees the beauty of spring, hears a nightingale, and catches sight of a beautiful girl, becoming in that instant 'hir thrall/ For euer, of free wyll'.[28] Later, with his head laid against the 'colde stone' of the room in which he is held, the speaker has a vision:

> Me thoght that thus all sodeynly a lyght
> In at the wyndow come quhare that I lent,   *where*
> Of quhich the chamber wyndow schone full bryght,   *which*
> And all my body so it hath ouerwent
> That of my sicht the vertew hale iblent;   *blinded*

And that withall a voce vnto me saide:

'I bring thee confort and hele, be noght affrayde.'   *health*

And furth anon it passit sodeynly   *away; at once*

Quhere it come in, the ryght way ageyne;

And gone, me thoght, furth at the dure in hye   *in haste*

I went my weye, nas nothing me ageyne, –   *[there was nothing against me]*

And hastily by bothe the armes tueyne

I was araisit vp into the air,

Clippit in a cloude of cristall clere and fair.²⁹

So the speaker moves upwards through the spheres until he meets Venus, Minerva, Good Hope and Fortune. Like Boethius, he comes to understand the nature of Fortune's Wheel. Venus advises him to 'Abyde and serue', and to reprove those who have 'broken loose' from her laws; Minerva, representing reason, counsels that all his conduct must attend to God 'That in his hand the stere has of you all', and quotes the biblical advice of Ecclesiastes: 'wele is him that his tyme wel abit' (abides); finally, Fortune, in a walled enclosure, shows the speaker how on her Wheel those 'on hye/ Were ouerthrawe in twinklyng of an eye'.³⁰

After this, the speaker awakes agitated, unsure if he has had only a disturbed dream or a genuine vision. In through the window flies a chalk-white dove which alights on his hand bearing a message of love that reassures him all will be well – as indeed all is, through love, when the prisoner is released. So the 'goldin cheyne' of love gives the poet liberty from the 'thraldom' of imprisonment, and he gives thanks too for the powerful ordering of

. . . him that hiest in the hevin sitt.

To quham we thank that all oure lif hath writt,

Quho couth it red agone syne mony a yere   *could it read many years long ago*

'Hich in the hevynnis figure circulere'.³¹   *high*

This last line quotes the first line of the whole poem, elegantly suggesting how both the Divine Maker and the individual maker – the poet who has accepted the painful shaping of his own life – have eventually become attuned. In God's will is our peace, as Dante (whom James I probably had not read) puts it in his *Paradiso*.

The Kingis Quair is the greatest poem written by any monarch. It is also the first substantial work produced in Scots (or English with a slight Scots inflection) by a poet who was not a clergyman. Its shapely construction provides a reminder that the medieval Scots word for poet – makar – is consonant with the ancient Greek word *poietes*, which also means 'maker'. The major late medieval Scots poets are still called 'the Makars', and King James I's making in *The Kingis Quair* is superb. Blending autobiography and vision, the erotic and the religious, James's work has a much more complex attitude to 'libertee' than has Barbour's *Bruce*. It is rich in incidental beauties such as precise catalogues of animals ('The lytill squerell full of besynesse') and delight in birdsong.[32] Its speaker travels to earth in a beam of light, and his muses, accompanied by a Fury (for this is also a poem of suffering), carry 'bryght lanternis' in a work marvellously alert to physical as well as spiritual illumination.[33] As a king, James I was remembered as wise, tough-minded, energetic and cultured; the splendid Linlithgow Palace was built at his command. But he lived in an age of ruthless political killings and in 1437 he was murdered. Ironically, given the design of the *Quair*, Latin verse epitaphs in the *Scotichronicon* lament Fortune's eventual cruelty to him.[34] None of this detracts from the just and hopeful beauty of his poem. Treasured for centuries, perhaps its most remarkable legacy takes the form of the delicate nineteenth-century mural painted at Penkill Castle near Girvan in Ayrshire by the Scottish Pre-Raphaelite artist–poet William Bell Scott who depicted the visiting English poets Christina Rossetti, Algernon Charles Swinburne and William Rossetti as characters from James's great poem of changing fortunes.

Vicissitude and hurt, longing and conflict are presented by Robert Henryson (c. 1420–90), using the stanza form of Chaucer's *Troilus and Criseyde*, in his own *Testament of Cresseid*. About thirty years younger than James I, Henryson is another of the great Scottish medieval Makars sometimes (though not before the twentieth century) called Scottish Chaucerians. Henryson was a university graduate, but we do not know where he studied. On 10 September 1462 a 'venerabilis vir Magister Robertus Henrisone' (distinguished man, Master Robert Henryson) was admitted for a time to the academic community of the new University of Glasgow, which had been founded in 1451. This 'Henrisone', who already held MA and Bachelor of Decreets (canon law) degrees, is probably identical to the 'Master Robert Henrysoun' who was remembered as a schoolmaster in Dunfermline, Fife.

Henryson's clear-headed literary genius never went too far. Though he can make use of musically elaborate rhymes, usually his poetry channels passion, using no superfluous word, and often has a possibly ironic, tight-lipped quality. It is unlikely that he knew James I's work, which had little influence on later medieval poets. However, like *The Kingis Quair*, Henryson's masterly *Testament* presents a journey towards self-knowledge and a Boethian acceptance of fate. Seeking comfort from bitter weather, the poet takes 'ane quair . . . / Writtin be worthie Chaucer glorious,/ Of fair Creisseid and worthie Troylus', then proceeds to another book where he finds an account of Cresseid's life after she was abandoned by her lover Diomeid.[35] Once the beloved of Troilus, Henryson's Cresseid is now in despair. Returning to her father, she curses Venus for having encouraged her to trust in her good looks. In an ensuing vision the gods, presented in a tragicomic pageant, find her guilty of blasphemy. Now cursed with leprosy, she becomes a beggar to whom Troilus gives alms, but the former lovers fail to recognize each other. Later, when Cresseid realizes that it was Troilus who showed her charity, she sends him the ring that was his first gift to her. After her death, he raises a tomb to her memory.

Henryson's *Testament* has appealed to several centuries of very different readers. Without attribution, it was printed in some early English editions of Chaucer from 1532 onwards. The seventeenth-century Englishman Sir Francis Kinaston translated it into Latin, hoping to ensure its immortality. More recently, Seamus Heaney has made a number of modern English versions of works by Henryson, including the *Testament* in 2004. Heaney hears in the poem 'the pared down truth of heartbreak rather than the high tone of the pulpit' and admires in Henryson 'a unique steadiness about the movement of his stanzas, an in-stepness between the colloquial and the considered aspects of a style that is all his own'.[36] Henryson's narrator lets the reader sympathize with Cresseid, yet the poem ends with a curt one-line sentence: 'Sen scho is deid [Since she is dead], I speik of hir no moir.'[37] Tonally, this abruptness may indicate a pained desire to avoid dwelling on the awfulness of Cresseid's fate for longer than necessary; or it may sound a brassily sharp dismissal of a foolish blasphemer. Perhaps it represents both.

Such uncertainties pervade the poem, infusing it with an uneasy power as Henryson's narrative moves along its fated course. That this course will be tragic is made clear in the opening lines:

Ane doolie sessoun to ane cairfull dyte   *dismal season; sorrowful poem*
Suld correspond and be equivalent . . .[38]   *should conform*

The *Testament* opens in the middle of spring, conventionally the time for romantic love, but the word 'spring' is not used. Instead, we are told it is the period of 'lent', the season of giving up, and we sense only a harsh, purifying northern wind 'Fra Pole Artick come quhisling loud and schill', which makes the narrator retreat 'aganis my will'.[39] Henryson nowhere mentions Scotland, but, like the other Makars, he can make dramatic use of its climate. A sense of progressing against his will characterizes the narrator's approach at times, though he realizes his story must go on. While he speaks of his 'pietie' (pity) for Cresseid, there is something unflinchingly judgmental in his saying that he shall excuse her as 'far furth as I may' (as far as I may).[40] The set-piece procession of gods who come to judge Cresseid is presented in terms of conflicting emotions. So Jupiter, 'richt fair and amiabill' precedes angry, foaming-at-the-mouth Mars who is followed by 'fair Phebus', while Venus alternates between being 'gay' and suddenly 'Angrie as ony serpent vennemous'.[41] This atmosphere of changeability bodes ill for Cresseid, whose 'mirth' will be changed into 'melancholy' as she discovers the vicissitudes of Fortune. Waking, she weeps, and 'ane chyld come[s] fra the hall/ To warne Cresseid the supper was reddy'.[42] When her father sees her he is shocked that she now has the face of a leper. Like Chaucer, Henryson has the artistic confidence to earth the cosmic awfulness of pain precisely in a domestic world where children call their elders through to eat. Such homely details intensify the bruise of the humiliated Cresseid's determination to move away to a leper house, wishing 'not' to 'be kend' (recognized).[43] Just such a failure of recognition lends stinging pathos to Troilus's later encounter with her where she sits begging:

Than upon him scho kest up baith hir ene –   *cast; eyes*
And with ane blenk it come into his thocht   *blink*
That he sumtime hir face befoir had sene.
Bot scho was in sic plye he knew hir nocht . . .[44]   *plight*

Nevertheless, something about this leper makes him think 'Of fair Cresseid, sumtyme his awin darling', so he throws her a purse. When, later, she realizes what has happened, Cresseid collapses, confronted by 'the greit unstabilnes' in herself that led her earlier to scorn the 'lufe . . . lawtie, and . . . gentilnes' (love, loyalty and gentleness) of Troilus when she abandoned him.[45] Ultimately, this is an undeflectably moral poem aimed at 'worthie wemen' for their 'instructioun' (and, no doubt, at sagely nodding men).[46] Yet it is complicated by signs that its own narrator may be flinching from his subject matter. In the final stanza, as well as the abrupt last line the poem uses the word 'schort' twice as it hurries as quickly as possible towards its 'schort conclusioun', moving away from a disagreeable topic. Although his work seems imbued with the common medieval perception of the female as dangerous, Henryson's concluding address to 'worthie wemen' is indeed brief, makes no attempt to class all women with Cresseid, and has the sound of an abrupt piece of moralizing designed to wind things up as quickly as possible after the discomfiture of the narrative.

Troilus recalls with sadness Cresseid's 'amorous blenking' (glancing or blinking). His phrase links her to the changeable goddess Venus who is 'Provocative with blenkis amorous'.[47] While we now know it is an anatomical fact that women blink more frequently than men, it is typical of Henryson that in poems where issues of visual recognition are so crucial he should effectively deploy such a small, telling, erotic phrase. This 'blinking' characteristic is also shared by the heroine of Henryson's *The Tale of Orpheus and Erudices his Quene* where Eurydice 'With wordis sweit and blenkis amorus' asks Orpheus to marry her.[48] Eurydice is again a woman of strong physical appetites who meets a dreadful fate. Fleeing a lustful shepherd, she is bitten by a serpent and ends up in the underworld, not as a leper but

Lene and dedelike, pitouse and pale of hewe,	*pitiful*
Rycht warsch and wan, and walowit as a wede,	*sickly; withered*
Hir lily lyre was lyke unto the lede.[49]	*skin; lead*

Leading her out of the underworld, the musician Orpheus can only exclaim over the terrible change that has befallen her once 'cristall eyne with blenkis amorous'.[50] So full of love for 'his wyf and lady suete' and 'blyndit . . . in grete affection', he looks back at her.[51] This breaks his promise to Pluto, King of the Underworld, who immediately reclaims her. Orpheus weeps over his loss: 'Bot for a luke my lady is forlore'.[52] Those words 'Bot for a luke', repeated in the poem, have a stinging ordinariness that is characteristic of the schoolmaster Henryson.

Retelling this story, he follows not only Ovid and Virgil, but also the Boethius of *De Consolatione Philosophiae*. As in *The Testament of Cresseid*, a sense of tragic inevitability underscores the story, and there are elements of harsh moral judgment as well as pity and sympathy. Eurydice follows her sensuous nature, yet is a loyal wife; having searched and searched for her, Orpheus fails in self-control when he glances back at his beloved. His act is a small private one, but the outcome is sudden and catastrophic. Henryson presents it in a few words, again using the characteristic adjective 'schort':

> In schort conclusion,
> He blent bakward and Pluto come anone,   *glanced*
> And into hell agayn with hir is gone.[53]

Henryson's gift for plain, functional language, his sense of sharp retribution, and his emphasis on the need to discipline what Burns would later term 'fleshly lust' – all these might make him seem to prefigure the often dour milieu associated with the Scottish Reformation. But this level-headed, often humorous poet was dead years before John Knox's birth. Modern readers may be tempted to read older Scottish poetry in the context of later vernacular culture, but in its day it was mostly made by men in a culture where the main medium of literature and education was Latin. Medieval Scottish literature is frequently an offshoot of Latin models. Henryson was a learned man with a sophisticated knowledge of Latin as well as a liking for vernacular registers, and for legal matters. His fascination with morality tales is of a piece with works produced in many parts of Catholic Europe, and his interest in Providence has recently been aligned with that of the later John Ireland (d. 1496) whose work in Latin and Scots made that prose writer, author of *The Meroure of Wyssdome*, 'the most significant Scottish theologian of his and Henryson's generation'.[54] The verse *Moralitas* (or moral explanation of the story) which is the concluding section of Henryson's poem *Orpheus and Erudices* draws heavily on a Boethian commentary by the English Dominican Nicholas Trevet, and warns repeatedly against letting 'warld-lie lust and sensualite' get the better of reason.[55]

While alert to tenderness, eloquent and idiomatic in its fluent handling of verse, Henryson's is at times a grave sensibility. Even his *Testament*, however, can wink at the reader, as it does when the poet comments on bad-tempered Saturn's 'meldrop' (snot) which runs 'fast' from his nose.[56]

A gentler comedy of minute attention occurs more frequently in *The Morall Fabillis of Esope the Phrygian* where 'Maister' Henryson, retelling fables by Aesop and others in a wise Scots voice rich in immediate appeal, presents himself both as a moralizing teacher and as a pupil offering his work to be marked in a Latin class:

> Of this authour, my maisteris, with your leif,
> Submitting me in your correctioun,
> In mother-toung of Latyng I wald preif   *from; try*
> To mak ane maner of translatioun . . .

In using Aesop, Henryson draws on one of the eight authoritative authors – the *auctores octo* – whose work was standard fare in the medieval European Latin schoolroom. Henryson's fables also follow patterns present in the tradition of the widely read Latin *Esopus* by the fifteenth-century German Heinrich Steinhöwel. In one sense, the *Morall Fabillis* are bookish, even schoolbookish; but at the same time, as animal fables should be, they are utterly accessible. Like James I's 'lytill squerell full of besynesse', but in a more fully realized way, Henryson's feral and domestic creatures go about their business. Their presentation is fully anthropomorphic, yet still sensitive to the creaturely pursuits of the natural world.[57] Relished in an age closer than ours to the smell, blood and pelt of beasts, these *Fabillis* are at once quintessentially medieval (akin to *fabliaux* and such popular tales as 'Reynard the Fox') and full of allure for a modern audience. The town mouse, 'Bairfute, allone, with pykestaf in hir hand', sets off like a pilgrim to visit her country cousin:

> Furth mony wilsum wayis can scho walk,   *across; wild*
> Throw mosse and mure, throw bankis, busk, and breir,   *bog; moor*
> Fra fur to fur, cryand fra balk to balk,   *furrow; ridge*
> 'Cum furth to me, my awin sister deir!
> Cry peip anis!' With that the mous culd heir   *once*
> And knew hir voce, as kinnisman will do   *kinsfolk*
> Be verray kynd, and furth scho come hir to.[58]   *[naturally]*

Although each fable comes with its *moralitas* (some more predictably appropriate than others), there is far more jauntiness and humour here than in Henryson's other major works. In the fable of the two mice forms of the word 'blyith' (happy) recur. The moral of that story, which teaches thrift and the wisdom of being content with a modest sufficiency of worldly goods, is that

> Of eirthly joy it beiris maist degré, *[holds the highest place]*
> Blyithnes in hart, with small possessioun.[59] *possessions*

Canniness and a wish to avoid excess permeate Henryson's work. A well-schooled university graduate, this schoolteacher–poet can cite learned texts with the best of them. But, moving easily between Classical foundations and vernacular artistry, the Latinist Henryson writes in a way that, while building *gravitas* and *auctoritas* (that sense of foundational authority beloved of medieval authors), never detracts from his quality of direct address. When, for instance, he makes an accurate reference to Aristotle, Classical polysyllables modulate immediately into common language:

> In Metaphisik Aristotell sayis
> That mannis saull is lyke ane bakkis ee . . .[60] *soul; bat's eye*

In this fable, 'The Preiching of the Swallow', Henryson unusually quotes a whole line of Latin (appropriate in such a clerical work), but the entire story itself, like many of Christ's parables, is placed familiarly in the common world of agricultural life. Details of linseed and flax processing are effortlessly integrated. The swallow's feathered congregation ignore his advice to eat flax seeds, and so end up caught in the flaxen nets men make, while the swallow, a migratory bird, simply leaves. In its cadences and sudden, vertical-takeoff conclusion, the last line of this narrative recalls the final line of the *Testament*. There the narrator ended 'Sen scho is deid, I speik of hir no moir'; in 'The Preiching' we have 'Scho tuke hir flicht, bot I hir saw no moir.'[61] Each of these one-line sentences, abruptly bringing down the curtain, exemplifies Henryson's ability to make dramatic the functionality of language. Without sacrificing the possibilities of subtlety or emotional balance he savours cunningly crafted plain speaking.

Henryson's protagonists are not explicitly Scottish. His poems almost never mention Scottish places. Yet his works are informed by their location. His account of flax production is technically accurate in its Scots terminology. Cresseid's route to her leper house may follow the geography of medieval Dunfermline, and one famous Scottish manuscript records a work whose English title would be 'Master Robert

Henryson's Dream on the Firth of Forth'.[62] Nevertheless, if there are Scottish aspects to Henryson's work, they lie principally in the language, sensibility, and the nature of the terrain in which many of his poems are so firmly earthed. That landscape is one where rough weather is felt as a markedly alliterative presence:

> The wynter come, the wickit wind can blaw;
> The woddis grene wer wallowit with the weit;
> Baith firth and fell with froistys wer maid faw,   *uneven*
> Slonkis and slaik maid slidderie with the sleit . . .[63]   *Hollows and dells*

Descriptions of winter would be developed with gusto by Henryson's fellow Latinist and Makar, Gavin Douglas, and by later Scottish poets. Yet Henryson's lack of proclaimed Scottishness makes him very different from the rumbustiously patriotic Blind Hary (c. 1450–93) whose vast, eleven-book poem on the early fourteenth-century Scottish freedom fighter William Wallace was produced around the same time as the *Testament* and the *Morall Fabillis*. Hary's account of the illustrious and valiant champion of his nation bears the full title *The Actis and Deidis of the Illustere and Vailyeand Campioun Schir William Wallace Knicht of Ellerslie* and dates from about 1477. Circulating in manuscript, it later became one of the first books printed in sixteenth-century Scotland, and enjoyed lasting popularity, going through more editions than any other Scots book before Burns. In the eighteenth century, when many Scottish authors began to worry that some of their upwardly mobile countrymen looked down on the Scots language, Hary's *Wallace* was loosely translated into English couplets by William Hamilton of Gilbertfield. In this form it spurred Burns, James Hogg, Tobias Smollett, and other writers in Scotland and beyond. In his autobiographical poem *The Prelude* Wordsworth enthuses about

> How Wallace fought for Scotland; left the name
> Of Wallace to be found, like a wild flower,
> All over his dear Country; left the deeds
> Of Wallace, like a family of Ghosts,
> To people the steep rocks and river banks,
> Her natural sanctuaries, with a local soul
> Of independence and stern liberty.[64]

Throughout the nineteenth century, when Scotland was playing its full part in British imperialism, a cult of Wallace grew and resulted most strikingly in the erection of that crowned stone tower, the Wallace Monument, which still stands as a national phallus on a hill near Stirling. In the late twentieth century Hamilton's version of Blind Hary's poem formed a principal source for the screenplay of *Braveheart*, the Hollywood epic starring Mel Gibson and scripted by the American Randall Wallace. In this way the popular patriotic fifteenth-century poetry of Blind Hary has been channelled into the international popular culture of our own day.

The Latin historian and philosopher John Mair (sometimes called John Major), who taught at St Andrews University in the early sixteenth century, wrote of Hary's poem that its poet was 'a master' ('peritus') of the vernacular.[65] The *Wallace* could appeal to a highly educated as well as a popular audience. Of Hary himself almost nothing is known except his evident learning. It is possible that he dictated his poem to the John Ramsay whose name is appended to the manuscript, dated 1488. Appropriately, that manuscript is bound together with a copy of Barbour's *Bruce*, which is in a sense its great spur and companion poem. Composing about 160 years after Wallace's death, Hary is further removed from his subject matter than Barbour, and may rely more on popular oral traditions, though he claims some now lost written sources. Chronology is unreliably treated, and Thomas of Ercildoune makes an appearance. Running to 300 pages of rhyming ten-syllable couplets (which can sound awkward to a modern ear tuned mainly to blank verse), the poem is often dramatic, graphic and very bloody. Characteristic is the scene at rocky Dunottar (where Fergus of Galloway had killed his dragon) when Wallace exterminates fleeing Englishmen who have sought sanctuary in a church:

Wallace in fyr gert set all haistely,	*[set all on fire]*
Brynt wp the kyrk, and all that was tharin,	*therein*
Atour the roch the laiff ran with gret dyn.	*around; remainder*
Sum hang on craggis rycht dulfully to de,	*miserably*
Sum lap, sum fell, sum floteryt in the se.	*leapt; floundered*
Na Sotheroun on lyff was lewyt in that hauld,	*[was allowed to live]; refuge*
And thaim with in thai brynt in powdir cauld.[66]	*ashes*

Wallace is simply exacting revenge on his country's oppressors, but that revenge, prolonged over many thousand lines, can become oppressive in itself. Blind Hary helped make Wallace a Scottish superhero, combining martial prowess with hints of underdoggery in a way that would influence both foreign perceptions of the Scots and (especially male) Scots' perceptions of themselves. This poem has a heroic tale to tell; sometimes it tells it like a comic-strip or a rant. It has dramatic sweep and boundless narrative energy but, while giving thanks that 'Wallace . . . has maid all Scotland fre', we may wish to skip some of the atrocities.[67] Wordsworth's conversion of Wallace's legacies into 'wild flowers' and 'natural sanctuaries' is seductively disingenuous in its camouflaging of the much mythologized slaughter on which Scotland, like most other nations, was founded. Burns, an enthusiast for Wallace, is more accurate in the verb he chooses for that famous opening line, 'Scots, wha hae wi Wallace bled . . .'[68]

Whether considering the popular work of Blind Hary or the versions of French manuals of chivalry produced for a knightly elite by Sir Gilbert Hay (fl. 1450), it is as well to remember that, just as twentieth-century military technology underlies aspects of the development of computing, so the business of killing nourishes the codes of medieval heraldry. When the highly educated Hay, who had served at the French court of Charles VII, writes of how 'thare is gevin to the knycht his lytill schort suerd . . . his lang suerde his polax' and so on, he is describing a chivalric killer at the height of his efficiency.[69] Small wonder that Hay in *The Buke of the Gouernaunce of Princis* emphasizes that 'wisedome is the begynnyng of all gude gouernement' and that the passions must be reined in.[70] Henryson, in a different way, stresses the same teaching. Relying on French sources, but sometimes transforming them considerably, Hay in his advice to princes tells them that they are 'of the samyn nature with symple men' and 'how thai suld delyte thame in bukis of stories of vertues and vicis'; they should also be particularly wary of women's advice 'ffor quhen a womman tretis thy gouernaunce traist wele thy persone is in perile'.[71] Hay's versions of these knightly texts are among the first examples of Scots prose. They often cite the heroic example of the protagonist of Hay's long, long poem *The Buik of King Alexander the Conqueror*. In an age of constant military strife extended narratives of campaigning – whether of Bruce, Wallace or Alexander – attracted noble patrons. Across medieval Europe Alexander narratives were in fashion, and Hay's Alexander poem complements an older Scots verse translation from French, *The Buik of Alexander*, which survives in a manuscript dated 1438. Often based on French (and sometimes Latin) originals, such works are hardly exact translations in the modern sense. Like Hay's prose, they belong to a time when translators frequently added to, adapted or embellished their originals, hoping to provide yet more material for audiences eager to hear of 'mony hardie knycht of gret renoun'.[72]

Alexander is also mentioned in Gaelic literature, where in a heroic age 'Battle-loving warriors' were celebrated at least as much as in Scotland's other languages.[73] Classical Gaelic was used as a lingua franca among the nobles and literati of Ireland and much of Scotland from around 1200 until the start of the seventeenth century; vernacular Gaelic dialects had been developing since at least 1100, but do not appear widely in manuscripts until the end of the Classical period. Although its authenticity has been disputed, what is perhaps the most arresting surviving poem in the developing vernacular form is the Harlaw Brosnachadh, an incitement-to-battle chant. Like the works of Barbour, Blind Hary, Hay and others, this Gaelic poem encourages lethal martial valour. It is attributed to Lachlann Mór of the bardic MacMhuirich family whose descendants would make Gaelic verse over many generations until at least the mid-eighteenth century. Lachlan Mór MacMhuirich's poem is dated to the eve of the Battle of Harlaw in 1411, making it an exceptionally early example of vernacular Gaelic verse. Alphabetically structured, it lists adjectives appropriate to the warriors of the Clan Donald, and has a strikingly urgent pattern of syntax and sound, using strong alliteration which can be detected even by the non-Gaelic speaker:

> Gu h-àirneach, gu-arranta,
> Gu h-athlamh, gu h-allanta,
> Gu beòdha, gu barramhail,
> Gu brìoghmhor, gu buan-fheargach . . .[74]

Derick Thomson points out that it deploys an archaic seven-syllable metre with three-syllable line endings, and that it may be the last poem written in that metre.[75] I have made a version of this poem which, though free in vocabulary, reproduces much of the metre and form of the original in a way that may suggest something of the artistry and force of the Gaelic:

You Clan of Conn, remember this:
Strength from the eye of the storm.
Be at them, be animals,
Be alphas, be Argus-eyed,
Be belters, be brandishers,
Be bonny, be batterers,
Be cool heads, be caterans,
Be clashers, be conquerors,
Be doers, be dangerous,
Be dashing, be diligent,
Be eager, be excellent,
Be eagles, be elegant,
Be foxy, be ferrety,
Be fervid, be furious,
Be grimmer, be gralloching,
Be grinders, be gallopers,
Be hardmen, be hurriers,
Be hell-bent, be harriers,
Be itching, be irritants,
Be impish, be infinite,
Be lucky, be limitless,
Be lashers, be loftiest,
Be manly, be murderous,
Be martial, be militant,
Be noxious, be noisiest,
Be knightly, be niftiest,
Be on guard, be orderly,
Be off now, be obdurate,
Be prancing, be panic-free,
Be princely, be passionate,
Be rampant, be renderers,
Be regal, be roaring boys,
Be surefire, be Somerleds,
Be surgers, be sunderers,
Be towering, be tactical,
Be tip-top, be targetters,
Be urgent, be up for it,
In vying be vigorous

In ending all enemies.
Today is for triumphing,
You hardy great hunting-dogs,
You big-boned braw battle boys,
You lightfoot spry lionhearts,
You wall of wild warriors,
You veterans of victories,
You heroes in your hundreds here,
You Clan of Conn, remember this:
Strength from the heart of the storm.

Even though its date may be in doubt, the Gaelic 'Clan Donald's Call to Battle at Harlaw' seems to me at least as great in its way as Blind Hary's vast *Wallace*. Yet the tonal range of Gaelic verse in this period goes far beyond such warsongs to include delicate lyrics like Fearchar Ó Maoíl Chiaráin's richly worked love poem 'The Blackthorn Brooch', or the moving extended lament for a lost son (probably the poet of 'The Blackthorn Brooch') by an author whose first name has been lost, but who is known as Ó Maoíl Chiaráin and for whom the killing of his child in Ireland has meant that 'My son is my own death'.[76] Of particular interest is another lament, the earliest datable poem attributable to a female Gaelic author. This is 'A phaidrín do dhúisg mo dhéar' (O rosary that recalled my tear) by Aithbhreac Inghean Corcadail, widow of Niall Óg McNeill of the island of Gigha. Composed in the 1460s in a Classical Gaelic syllabic metre, it is attuned to the traditions of bardic elegy. The poet produces a work of strong, direct emotion which images her keening to the rosary beads that once belonged to her husband. This device builds from the start a sense of loved, lost intimacy:

A phaidrín do dhúisg mo dhéar,
    ionmhain méar do bhitheadh ort:
ionmhain cridhe fáilteach fial
    'gá raibhe riamh gus a nocht.

Dá éag is tuirseach atáim,
    an lámh má mbítheá gach n-uair,
nach cluinim a beith i gclí
    agus nach bhfaicim í uaim.

O rosary that recalled my tear,
dear was the finger in my sight,
that touched you once, beloved the heart
of him who owned you till tonight.

I grieve the death of him whose hand
you did entwine each hour of prayer;
my grief that it is lifeless now
and I no longer see it there.[77]

Often using traditionally Irish adjectivally-enhanced Gaelic 'kennings' – image-rich phrases which can link a person to a place ('lion of Mull of the white wall') – this lament goes on to hymn the dead man's qualities, particularly his generosity to poets, but its emphasis falls not on military deeds but on the loss of both intimate and societal happiness. For the poet this man is 'mo leathchuing rúin' ('my darling yoke-fellow') rather than simply a hardy knight on the battlefield.

Although they shared many of its martial values, Lowlanders writing in Scots scorned this richly varied Gaelic culture which rarely mentioned Lowland Scotland and which was becoming confined increasingly to the Highland regions. Such an attitude of scorn is found as early as John of Fordun, who writes in his fourteenth-century Latin chronicle of how the Lowlanders are 'domesticated and cultured, trustworthy, patient and urbane, decent in their attire, law-abiding and peaceful', while High-landers are 'a wild and untamed people, rough and unbending, given to robbery ... comely in form, but unsightly in dress'.[78] Sir Richard Holland, whose *The Buke of the Howlat* is roughly contemporary with Aithbreac Inghean Corcadail's lament, probably worked for some time at Abriachan near Loch Ness where he would have been surrounded by Gaelic speakers. Yet his substantial and lively alliterative poem presents a Gaelic poet very much as a figure of fun.

The Buke of the Howlat (a 'howlat' is an owl) is an allegory whose protagonists, as in Chaucer's *Parlement of Foules*, are birds. Holland's Howlat goes to elaborate lengths to seek more splendid plumage. Into the story are built accounts of Robert the Bruce's crusading friend Sir James Douglas, and of a great feast at which the Rook, a Gaelic bard, appears. Lines three and five of the following stanza are alliterative quasi-Gaelic gobbledegook, and may indicate that the speaker likes alcohol and (like many Gaels) declaiming his genealogy. Afterwards, in a common Lowlander's mockery of Gaelic-language constructions, the bard is made to speak of himself as 'hir' (her) and 'scho' (she). The Rook threatens to aim a poem at the audience, and the repeated 'O's of Irish names come out like cries of pain. Linguistic cavorting mixes with mocking energy which Sir Richard Holland both finds in and applies to the music of Gaelic:

Sa come the Ruke with a rerd and a rane roch,	*Rook; shout; rough rant*
A bard owt of Irland with 'Banachadee!'	*God bless you!*
Said: 'Gluntow guk dynyd dach hala mischy doch;	
Raike hir a rug of the rost, or scho sall ryme the.	*Reach; bit; roast; flyte you*
Mich macmory ach mach mometir moch loch;	
Set hir downe, gif hir drink; quhat Dele alis the?'	*Devil ails*
O Deremyne, O Donnall, O Dochardy droch;	*?evil*
Thir ar his Irland kingis of the Irischerye:	
O Knewlyn, O Conochor, O Gregre Makgrane;	*(chiefs or learned families)*
The schenachy, the clarschach,	*Gaelic genealogist-bard; Scottish harp*
The ben schene, the ballach,	*playing woman(?); servant*
The crekery, the corach,	*reciter(?); lamentation (?)*
Scho kennis thaim ilkane.[79]	*knows; each one*

Whether writing in Latin like the philosopher and historian John Mair or in Scots like Sir Richard Holland, most Lowland writers in the late Middle Ages and early Renaissance characteristically treated the Highlands and Gaelic with disdain and mockery. For Scotland's greatest poetic virtuoso, William Dunbar (c. 1456–c. 1513), the word 'bard' is a term of abuse associated with 'Ersche' or Gaelic. Although Scottish monarchs in this period may have given gifts to bards when in the Highlands, Dunbar clearly looks down on them. He wants to avoid their culture, one whose traditions include poems of cursing denunciation as well as praise. In Dunbar's own famous 'flyting' or stylized verse quarrel with his fellow poet the Gaelic-speaking Walter Kennedy, the two men take it in turn to hurl abuse at each other. Conventionally in flytings no punches are pulled, and, relishing elaborate alliterative insults, Dunbar has a genius for going for the jugular:

Iersche brybour baird, vyle beggar with thy brattis,	*Gaelic vagabond bard;*
	torn clothes
Cuntbittin crawdoun Kennedy, coward of kynd;	*cunt-bitten; poxed; [by nature]*

Evill-farit and dryit as Densmen on the rattis,	*ill-favoured; withered; Danes;*
	wheels
Lyk as the gleddis had on thy gulesnowt dynd;	*as if; kites; [yellow nose]; dined*
Mismaid monstour, ilk mone owt of thy mynd,	*[mad once a month]*
Renunce, rebald, thy rymyng; thow bot royis;	*renounce, rascal; [you only*
	talk nonsense]
Thy trechour tung hes tane ane heland strynd –	*treacherous tongue; [has caught*
	a Highland accent]
Ane lawland ers wald mak a bettir noyis.[80]	*a Lowland arse*

Dunbar's carnival of vocabulary here heads rollickingly from 'Iersche' (Gaelic) to 'ers' (arse). Although we may allow for rhetorical exaggeration (Dunbar wants to win this poetic contest), the verse shows among other things a perceived chasm between the languages of Gaelic and 'Inglis', the term Dunbar uses for what we now call Scots. These same lines give a taste of Dunbar's elaborate language of vitriol. Throughout his work, he delights in a wide spectrum of vocabulary, making use of plain-speaking but also of the enriched formal diction termed 'aureate'.

Clearly a learned poet, Dunbar may have come from the Lothians. His name appears on a 1477 document at St Andrews University where a William Dunbar graduated MA in 1479. Although relatively little is known of his life, he seems to have visited England at least once, and celebrates Aberdeen, but it is with Edinburgh that he is most strongly connected, having spent the years 1500–13 (or perhaps longer) there. In 1500 King James IV awarded him an annual salary as a member of the Royal Household. Dunbar produced a number of poems, some respectful, some not, about court affairs. Like that of Robert Henryson, Dunbar's poetry reveals a substantial legal knowledge, and records show him acting occasionally as a court advocate. Valued in his own day, his work was forgotten for much of the sixteenth and seventeenth centuries before it began to be republished (and even rewritten) by Allan Ramsay and others in the early eighteenth century. In the late nineteenth century the literary historian J. M. Ross saw Dunbar as second only to Burns and as exhibiting a distinctively Scots national character; the twentieth-century poet Hugh MacDiarmid read Ross's *Early Scottish History and Literature*, and championed Dunbar rather than Burns as a model for modern Scottish poets. Today, along with Henryson, Dunbar is regarded as the greatest of Scotland's late medieval or early Renaissance Makars.

Dunbar offers remarkably beautiful poetic craftsmanship along with the most dartingly varied themes and forms. Some poets sound the same note repeatedly and with assurance. Since being able to write well is what matters most, this is surely enough, and readers nurtured by the assumptions of Romanticism may admire consistency of voice. Yet this can easily slip into monotony, and there will always be audiences who love the riches of variety, savouring a poet who can be hilariously bawdy as well as producing poems of solemn celebration or of religious glory. 'Formal' in the best sense, Dunbar takes poetic forms and makes each resonate to the maximum. For those who rejoice in poetic biodiversity, his marvellously performative oeuvre is palatial and welcoming. It uses all the instruments of the verbal orchestra. Dunbar's poems are magnificently carved out of sound.

This poet can generate awe through a sense of glory most apparent in his handling of acoustics and vocabulary. Dunbar learned from the music of elaborate medieval Latin (and probably French) poetry. Woven together out of internal rhymes and so filled with delicate reverberation, his poem to the Virgin Mary sings to itself, to us, and to its addressee. It moves into Latin for an internal refrain '*Ave Maria, gracia plena*' (Luke 1:28 – 'Hail, Mary, full of grace') so that these verses celebrating the glory of the Virgin are themselves bonded to the Holy Writ that so musically interrupts them:

Hale, sterne superne, hale, in eterne,	*hail; star [on high]; eternity*
In Godis sicht to schyne!	*God's sight; shine*
Lucerne in derne for to discerne,	*lantern; darkness; by which to see*
Be glory and grace devyne!	*by*
Hodiern, modern, sempitern,	*[for this day and for this age and for ever]*
Angelicall regyne,	*queen of angels*
Our tern inferne for to dispern,	*darkness; hellish; disperse*
Helpe, rialest rosyne.	*most royal rose*
Ave Maria, gracia plena:	
Haile, fresche floure femynyne;	
Yerne us guberne, virgin matern,	*diligently; govern; mother*
Of reuth baith rute and ryne.[81]	*pity; root; bark*

Celebrating a realm and person of ultimate beauty – 'peirles pulchritud' – this is a poetry of appropriate magnificence, in keeping with the sense of glory splendid in medieval Scottish Catholicism. The eloquent fifteenth-century Prior of St Andrews, James Haldenson, was recalled by Walter Bower as adorning his church 'mera et specabili pulcritudine' ('with sheer beauty of outstanding quality'), while William Bower added a rood altar to St Andrews Cathedral that was 'ymaginibus sumptuosis adornatum' ('adorned with costly statues').[82] Dunbar's astonishingly altitudinous word-music in a poem such as his hymn to the Virgin belongs to this rich Scottish Catholic culture and might be heard along-side the sophisticatedly intercrossing voices in the *Mass for Six Voices* (c. 1515) and other works by his near contemporary, the great Scottish composer of often rapturous religious music, Robert Carver.

His sense of glory and his preternatural ear make Dunbar a superb religious poet, as the strong dunts of the 'd' and 'b' sounds that open his poem on Christ's Resurrection – 'Done is a battell on the dragon blak' – affirm.[83] That poem modulates effortlessly from the pugilistic consonants of its first line to the blessing-like assurance of its sibilant Latin refrain; yet in that refrain the dunting 'd's remain audible: 'Surrexit dominus de sepulchro' ('The Lord has risen from the tomb'). Drawing on the Latin Mass for Easter Day (which echoes Luke 23:34), Dunbar has his own Scots language interrupted by the alien yet familiar, 'other' yet internalized language of scripture. His technique of using Latin materials in vernacular verse, though used with unique skill, was a common one in medieval writing and is related to that 'lectio divina' (holy reading) so thoroughly practised centuries before by the Columban writers who wanted to make the Holy Word shine through their words.

Yet Dunbar has also a wonderful, often riproaring sense of humour. Sometimes this can manifest itself in ecclesiastical garb. In 'The Dregy of Dunbar', the poet in 'hevins glory' (i.e., Edinburgh) petitions King James IV, praying that he and his court will return from 'purgatory' (also known, Dunbar somewhat unfairly suggests, as Stirling). 'Dregy' comes from the Latin 'Dirige', the opening word of the initial antiphon of the Catholic Office of the Dead. Winding through its elaborate parts, Dunbar's poem draws on a medieval tradition of liturgical parody, but sounds its own confident and distinctive note – in Latin as well as Scots:

> Et ne nos inducas in temptationem de Strivilling:
> Sed libera nos a malo illius.
> Requiem Edinburgi dona eiis, Domine,
> Et lux ipsius luceat eiis.

89

And lead us not into the temptation of Stirling,
But deliver us from its evil.
The peace of Edinburgh grant unto them, O Lord,
And let its light shine upon them.[84]

The aureate diction of Dunbar's religious verse is of a piece with his more secular word-pageants or formal verse-tapestries such as 'The Golden Targe' which, among other things, blends a paean to the dawn – 'Wp sprang the goldyn candill matutyne,/ With clere depurit bemes cristallyne' – with praise of Chaucer as the 'rose of rethoris all' whose supreme rhetorical skill with 'fresch anamilit [enamelled] termes' makes him the greatest 'lycht' of 'oure Inglisch' poetry. The Anglophile Dunbar also relishes the 'tongis aureate' of the English poets John Gower and John Lydgate.[85] At the same time, his own Scots verse abounds with verbal confidence. If his terms of praise are enamelled and aureate, then the same technique generates elaborately outlandish insults. The internal music of such flyting lines as

Lene larbar loungeour, lowsy in lisk and lonye;   *lean; impotent idler; groin; loin*
Fy, skolderit skyn, thow art bot skyre and skrumple . . .[86]   *scorched skin;*
creased; wrinkled

is the flipside of the interwoven rhymes and terms in Dunbar's great praise-poetry. Dunbar likes nothing better than dance-poems where he can have words and rhymes circling elaborately round one another. This happens in his formal pageant, 'The Dance of the Sevin Deidly Synnis', where the conventional vices are accompanied by devils with such good Scots names as 'Blak Belly and Bawsy Brown' until the culminating appearance of a Highlander (conjured up by the Devil as the ultimate wicked act) leads to such a 'schout' and 'Ersche . . . clatter' that the Devil smothers them 'in the depest pot of hell'.[87] Virtuoso-like, and with a characteristically self-aware sense of dramatic performance, Dunbar propels himself across the dance floor in another poem with the words

Than cam in Dunbar the mackar;
On all the flure thair was nane frackar . . .[88]

'Frackar' means 'nimbler' or 'more energetic', and a nimble energy characterizes Dunbar's verse. He can mix the aureate with the mischievously satirical, starting a poem with the high-flown line, 'As young

Awrora with his cristall haile', before going on to chronicle the crash-landing of an eccentric alchemist and birdman, John Damian, who attempted to fly from Stirling Castle to France with a great pair of feathered wings.[89] Dunbar has good fun with that one.

His pyrotechnics in shorter poems in no way render this spectacular poet unfit for working in longer forms. His 530-line narrative poem 'Apon the Midsummer Evin, Mirriest of Nichtis', also known as 'The Tretis of the Twa Mariit Wemen and the Wedo', manages to be a tour de force without exhausting the reader, who is provided with constant entertainment. Dunbar likes to make poetry that adapts official rituals or documents – whether Church liturgy, court pageants or a formally drawn-up last will and testament. In his 'Tretis', as Priscilla Bawcutt points out, he reshapes the courtly game of 'demande d'amour', a ludic discussion of love through questions and answers. Dunbar's provocative poem has a narrator who overhears a widow (medieval widows were conventionally randy) interrogating two wives about their sex lives in a garden of 'sueit flouris' associated with courtly love. The women confess their intimate secrets as if the widow were a sexual guru or priest who might absolve them. Their attitude to their husbands lets Dunbar unloose some more of his flyting vocabulary as the men's failings are rounded on by their wives, while the poet also takes some delight in the scandalous secrets of these 'gay ladeis'. One, for instance, always charges her husband for sex:

> ... leit I nevir that larbar my leggis ga betuene   *impotent man*
> To fyle my flesche na fummyll me without a fee gret ...[90]   *nor fumble; great*

The other wife hates her man as a lecherous waster. Offering its readers the delights of voyeurism, bizarre scandal, and outrageous comedy, Dunbar's poem reveals the women as superbly appalling sisters of Chaucer's Wife of Bath, but their husbands sound less than saintly. Playing off low actuality against the decorous setting and formal Latin divisions of the 'Tretis' adds to its scandalous gusto. Whatever Dunbar does he does with superlative brio, and the 'Tretis' is among his most ambitious works.

The poem for which he is best known makes use of several techniques deployed elsewhere – the refrain, the pageant-like listing, the mixture of Scots and Latin. Yet it relies generally on a plain language supplemented by the occasional aureate flicker. Commonly known as 'The Lament for the Makars', this work is a sustained memento mori, a poem on the transitory, brittle nature of existence. This is made clear from the early verses, each ending with a refrain (also used by other poets) which translates as 'The fear of death terrifies me'. The refrain's tolling repetition throughout takes up 25 per cent of the poem.

> The stait of man dois change and vary;
> Now sound, now seik, now blith, now sary,
> Now dansand mery, now like to dee:
> *Timor mortis conturbat me.*[91]

What makes this poem unforgettable is the way it moves like a great funeral procession, bearing its extended catalogue of occupations and designations – from renowned rulers to babies – and then its list of individually named poets, all of whom death claims. Yet, the poem suggests with a certain ironic wit, the fame of poets' names can outlast even death. Modern readers often feel both the shock of recognition on hearing familiar names, and a sense of loss on encountering unfamiliar ones. Time and the erosion of memory have complicated and increased the power of Dunbar's lament. For while some of the names, such as 'The noble Chaucer of makaris flour', remain well known, others are now totally unrecognized. Among these are the names of some older Makars of 'this cuntre', i.e., Scotland. The 100-line poem can be heard as a dignified bibliography of loss. Certainly its litany of names has an incalculable cumulative impact. All the verbal variety of names – individual, occasionally echoic – is reduced to the sameness of the Latin refrain that ends each stanza, and whose acoustic inevitability the reader or hearer recognizes from early on, so that its heard inescapability is part of the poem's disturbing, stately power. Death gathers Makar after Makar in an anthology of loss and (occasionally for us) of literary immortality:

He has tane Roull of Aberdene,
And gentill Roull of Corstorphin –
Two bettir fallowis did no man se:
Timor mortis conturbat me.

In Dunfermlyne he has done roune
With Maister Robert Henrisoun;
Schir Johne the Ros enbrast has he: *embraced*
Timor mortis conturbat me.

And he has now tane last of aw,

Gud gentill Stobo and Quintyne Schaw   *[John Reid of Stobo]*

Of quham all wichtis has peté: *persons*

Timor mortis conturbat me.

Gud Maister Walter Kennedy

In poynt of dede lyis veraly –   *[on the point of]*

Gret reuth it wer that he suld de: *pity*

Timor mortis conturbat me.[92]

The inclusion of the almost dead Kennedy, Dunbar's doughty Gaelic-speaking antagonist in their famous flyting, makes the lament all the more moving, though it might just be a sly joke (Dunbar elsewhere wrote a spoof last will and testament for a Kennedy). As the names are read out, a movement is felt that advances towards the poet's own death and hopes of a literary as well as a heavenly afterlife. It also advances towards the death of any reader whose voice comes to intone the lines, and so to embody the Latin '*me*' which is the last word of the refrain, and, eventually, of the poem as a whole: '*Timor mortis conturbat me.*'

Some critics feel melancholy suffuses a lot of Dunbar's work. It is hard to date many of his individual poems, but there may be a sense of gloom that impressively clouds parts of his oeuvre. Still, this is counter-pointed by such a vivacious, precisely detonated humour, and by such a variety of other emotional tones, from glorious exaltation to court intrigue, that it would be wrong to emphasize any one aspect of this poet's writings at the expense of others. If poetry is an art of enriched expression, then very few poets have been able to express to so convincing a degree the range of human experience. We know comparatively little of this early Renaissance poet's life; he seems to know a remarkable amount of ours.

No one can be sure exactly when Dunbar died, but he vanishes from official records after 1513. That year was cataclysmic for the courtly and noble life of Scotland. For on 9 September King James IV, during whose reign the country had prospered, was killed fighting the English at the Battle of Flodden. With him died many of his courtiers, churchmen and other leading subjects. James had been a learned man and a distin-guished patron of letters. He was reported by the Spanish ambassador to speak seven languages (including Italian). To this polylingual king the probably Scottish-born poet Alexander Barclay (c. 1484–1552) addressed six stanzas of praise in his 1509 translation (via Latin) of the German *Ship of Fools*; a Latinist who had been 'a scoler longe, and that in dyvers scoles', Devon-based Barclay wrote the first substantial pastoral poems in English, his five *Eclogues*.[93]

Barclay's work shows the influence of the European Humanist impulse to rediscover Classical culture and to take learning out of the monasteries and into the wider world. This Humanist influence was felt in James IV's Scotland where newer Latin books such as the Italian Humanist Lorenzo Valla's *Elegances of the Latin Language* (1440) began to circulate. Archibald Whitelaw's 1484 Ciceronian oration delivered to the English King in Nottingham testifies to the oratorical power of a St Andrews- and Cologne-educated Scottish cleric whose Humanist tastes are clear. In Paris in 1495 the Scottish historian Hector Boece had been an early patron and admirer of Erasmus, and that great Dutch Humanist lamented the death of his own former pupil, James IV's son Alexander, killed at Flodden. In the early sixteenth century Erasmus saw the Scots (along with the Irish and Danes) as exemplifying a new devotion to literature as a calling. The Montrose-born Latinist Patrick Paniter was admired in later centuries for the 'Corinthian glitter' of his prose.[94] Though not all of it was Humanist, there was certainly an upsurge in Scottish Latin poetry at the time. James Foulis (c. 1490– c. 1549) dedicated his 1511 collection of Latin verse to Erasmus's friend Alexander Stewart, Archbishop of St Andrews. A verse from Foulis's poem to St Margaret of Scotland indicates his elegant accomplishment:

> Inter ingentes aquilonis iras
> Floribus leuem et zephyri sussurum:
> Scotia est naui penetranda, toto ab
> Orbe remota.

> *Between the angry blasts of the North Wind*
> *And the West Wind's zephyr-whisper among flowers,*
> *Scotland must be reached by ship, cut off*
> *From all the world.*[95]

Yet the international language in which Foulis writes so confidently demonstrates that James IV's Scotland was far from cut off from the world. That same Latin language and literature underpin Henryson's work, are vital to some of the greatest moments in Dunbar's, and are central to translations as different as those of Alexander Barclay and Gavin Douglas. Although modern readers may be tempted to think of the later Middle Ages as the era when vernacular Scots won its liberty from 'thraldom' to learned Latin, frequently it makes more sense to see the two languages as rewardingly intertwined. Latin was not only the great language of the European past, it was also a language of the Scottish present, whether for the Scottish authors who wrote in it, or for those Latin-educated Scottish poets who wrote in Scots. At the start of the sixteenth century the magnum opus of Scottish literature is a translation of Virgil's *Aeneid*; in the mid-sixteenth century the greatest Scottish poet of the age, George Buchanan, wrote his verse entirely in Latin. In an era when a town clerk of Perth could be christened 'Dionysius', Latin was both a medium of international exchange and a local language at the heart of Scottish culture, particularly literary culture.

James IV's reign had seen the establishment of a new university in Aberdeen (which became a beacon of Latin Humanism), and the arrival of printing when the King's Clerk Walter Chepman and the bookseller Andrew Myllar established Scotland's first, if short-lived, printing press in Edinburgh in 1508. In the 1490s Paris-educated James Liddell (author of an arcane Latin treatise on semiotics) had become the first Scottish author to have his writings printed during his lifetime; perhaps the first Scots poem to be printed (in London) was Father William of Touris's *The Contemplacyon of Sinners* (1499), a work based on Latin models and annotated in that language. Though enormous in its implications, printing was only one of the great changes in James IV's Scotland. Legal reforms, artistic patronage, architecture and music burgeoned along with literature during the reign of this King who both won the support of Highland chieftains and seems to have tolerated Dunbar's views about them. At James's court the first recorded Africans in Scotland worked as paid musicians and entertainers; the chivalric Tournaments of the Black Lady, held in 1507 and 1508, are alluded to by Dunbar who compares 'My ladye with the mekle [big] lippis' to 'an tar barrell' in a poem that could be called racist, though its rudeness is mild compared with this poet's flyting invective elsewhere.[96] James IV strengthened Scotland militarily, commanding the building of the *Great Michael*, the largest warship of its day, and he renewed the 'Auld Alliance' with France which had linked the two nations since the thirteenth century. Flodden bloodily interrupted a golden age of Scottish culture. In the words of a famous later lament for the dead in that battle, it seemed that 'The Flowers of the Forest' were 'a' wede [all withered] away'.[97]

Yet printing helped quicken the developing literary culture, even as courtly patronage faltered. Chivalric vernacular popular romances in verse and poems by Henryson and Dunbar were among the earliest of the texts Chepman and Myllar published, while, encouraged by the Aberdeen Humanist Bishop William Elphinstone, such printed works as the *Aberdeen Breviary* and the two-volume *Legends of the Saints* (1510) disseminated hagiographies of Scottish as well as foreign Christian heroes and heroines. While Flodden was an undeniable blow to Scottish culture, an increasingly confident set of institutions – ecclesiastical, educational and commercial – now existed to nurture a literature that was both confidently Scottish and internationally alert. James Foulis, a Latin 'poet to his fingertips', returned to Scotland from France in 1513 and enjoyed a successful legal career, as did his colleague the Latin poet Adam Otterburn whose work (now lost) was admired by Scotland's greatest Latin Renaissance poet, George Buchanan.[98] Central to the Scottish literary culture of the age, Latin was the language which let Scottish writers mix with their European contemporaries. Moving among Cambridge, Glasgow, St Andrews and Paris, George Buchanan's teacher, the philosopher and historian John Mair, produced his Latin *Historia Majoris Britanniae* in 1521. Where Buchanan in a famous poem would favour Scottish union with France, Mair (who shrewdly critiqued the superlatively ropy patriotic origin myths of both England and Scotland) controversially favoured a union with England; he shared with Buchanan and many earlier and later Scottish writers the view that a people could legitimately get rid of a bad king. Mair's Latin history was followed in 1526 by the Parisian publication of the *Scotorum Historiae* of Hector Boece (c. 1465–1536), then Principal of King's College, Aberdeen. Boece's work would soon be translated into Scots by John Bellenden, and published in Scotland by Thomas Davidson in 1536. Bellenden dedicated his very free translation to James V, urging him to respect 'thi commoun wele', and he responded enthusiastically to the strong narrative imagination of Boece whose long account of early Scottish kings was in line with the Declaration of Arbroath; Bellenden's Boece also delights in how the Romans were resisted by 'the Scottis and Pichtis, quhilkis wer ane pepill full of chevelry and impacient of seruitude', fighting bravely in their land of 'montanis, mossis, and fludis'.[99]

Although the divisions between some of its linguistic cultures could be substantial, Scotland was a small country and many of the most active Latin scholars knew one another. So, for instance, John Mair was an acquaintance of Gavin Douglas, the learned, St Andrews-educated Bishop of Dunkeld, whose version of *The XIII Bukes of Eneados of the Famous Poete Virgile Translated out of Latyne Verses into Scottis Metre* is one of the earliest full translations of a Classical epic into a European vernacular language, and was thought by Ezra Pound to excel its original. Douglas's great translation was completed on 22 July 1513, six weeks before Flodden. The carnage of the battle was bad news for the nascent Scottish printing industry, and Douglas's poem was not printed until 1553 when it appeared in London. Yet its subsequent publication, when taken along with other works such as those just mentioned, demonstrates a continuing efflorescence of Scottish writing at a time when literary activity in England was relatively unspectacular. Before the Protestant Reformation England was Scotland's greatest enemy, yet Scottish poems circulated and were printed there, and Scottish poets were not so narrow-minded as to despise English verse. Not only did they admire and learn from Chaucer and other medieval English poets; they might even write in praise of England's capital city. An attractive Scottish paean, sometimes wrongly attributed to Dunbar (who hymned 'Blyth Aberdeane' instead), begins,

London, thou art of townes *A per se*.   *[tip-top]*
   Soveraign of cities, semeliest in sight . . .[100]

This was composed to serve the ends of a 1501 Scottish diplomatic mission, but it reads with pleasing conviction, and is written in a century when some Scots, such as John Mair, began to think of a united Britain. They were, however, in a minority. Able to look in many directions, Scotland's literature, at least in Latin and in Scots quickened by Latin, flourished at this time as it had never done before. The work of Gavin Douglas added to its grandeur.

Douglas pursued honour. Scotland's greatest vernacular Renaissance Humanist was born around 1474, third son of the Earl of Angus. He matriculated at St Andrews University in 1490, just eleven years after William Dunbar (whom Douglas admired) graduated there. They seem to have had some of the same teachers. Douglas got his St Andrews MA in 1494 (perhaps going on to study in Paris), and composed his first substantial poem in 1501. It is called *The Palice of Honour*. Rooted in medieval culture, yet alert to such modern figures as Petrarch and other Italian humanists, it is an allegorical poem whose speaker journeys to the palace of the title. Dedicated to James IV, and wishing him 'renoun of cheualrie', it apologizes in a conventional way for its author's 'vulgair ignorance'. *The Palice of Honour*, though, is a poem awash with knowledge, drawing fluently on Douglas's rhetorical education. Its three sections all delight in catalogues – whether of kinds of music, admired poets (Classical, English and Scottish), countries, astronomical lore, virtues, or (as in this stanza) learned men:

> Ptholomeus, Ipocras, Socrates,
> Empedocles, Neptenabus, Hermes,
> Galien, Auerroes, and Plato,
> Enoch, Lameth, Job and Diogenes,
> The eloquent and prudent Vlisses,
> Wise Josephus, and facund Cicero,   *eloquent*
> Melchisedech with vther mony mo.
> Thair veyage lyis throw out this wildernes,   *journey*
> To the Palice of Honour all thay go.[101]

Douglas was eager to follow them. His poem celebrates courtly virtues and, dedicated to the King, seems designed to appeal to an audience with a taste for lists, learning, courts and palaces. 'Honour' is 'The michtie prince' of Douglas's palace where the 'chancelair . . . Conscience' also resides along with such courtiers as the 'fine menstraill' (minstrel) 'Gude hope'. Conscious of his elders, the pushy twentysomething poet makes it clear that 'To papis, bischoppis, prelatis and primaitis,/ Empreouris, kingis, princes, potestatis / Deith settis the terme and end of all thair hicht.'[102] Virtue is hymned with aureate diction in a poem full of learning, life and ambition. It handles a difficult verse form (only two rhymes per nine-line stanza) with brio. It is full of heroes – from Ovid to Robert the Bruce – and a good deal of it is given over to honouring poets. The literary work to which most attention is paid is the *Aeneid* by 'the greit Latine Virgilius', whose epic is summarized over several stanzas telling of 'knichtis' and their 'cruell battellis'.[103] Shortly after this summary Venus gives the narrator 'ane buik' which she commands him to 'put in ryme'.

Although none of his works appears to have been printed in his lifetime, Douglas's later printers took this to be a reference to his sub-sequent translation of Virgil. It may not be, but an interest in Virgil in the context of poetry, honour and chivalry is certainly evident in *The Palice*. A corresponding love of honour resonates through the 'Conclusi-oune' to his later *Aeneid* translation where, drawing on a famous passage from Ovid's *Metamorphoses*, he becomes probably the first poet in the English-speaking world to claim that his verse would make his name immortal, so that, when dead,

The bettir part of me sal be vpheild	
Abuif the starnis perpetualy to ryng,	*stars*
And heir my nayme remane, but enparing.	*without diminution*
Throw owt the Ile ycleipit Albioune	*called Britain*
Red sall I be, and sung with mony one.[104]	*Read*

Yet this announcement in 1513 also marks a turning away from poetry on Douglas's part, and the writings which survive from the later part of his career show his preoccupation with ecclesiastical ambitions and management. His subsequent career would see him advanced to the position of Bishop of Dunkeld, although, as his family lost out in struggles amongst Scotland's ruling nobles, it would also involve exile and incarceration, some of it in 'the wyndy and richt vnplesand castell and royk of Edinburgh'.[105] There are occasional further hints of Douglas the patriotic writer of verse and pursuer of honour, as when he defends the kind of mythological genealogy of the Scottish kings which the Declaration of Arbroath had invoked. But it is sad to see such a gifted ex-poet spending his later years intriguing with the Church and state authorities over 'my promotioun'.[106]

Still, the unusual amount of surviving documentation covering his later career should not blind us to the buoyant, generous mixture of tradition and innovation, translation and origination that is Douglas's *Eneados*. This monumental translation of Virgil's Latin epic appears to date in the main from an eighteen-month period in 1512–13 when, among other things, Douglas was appointed one of several men 'to assist and counsel' the rector of his alma mater, St Andrews University.[107] The erudition of Douglas's Virgil is not in doubt, but it is a poet's learning, with poetry rather than dry scholarship as the driving force. Although a good deal of Douglas's version is 'almaiste word by word' accurate, nonetheless 'Sum tyme the text mon haue ane expositioun, / Sum tyme the colour will caus a litle additioun, / And sum tyme of ane [one] word I mon [must] mak thre.'[108] So, for instance, Douglas will draw effortlessly on the matter of a Latin note in Ascensius's 1501 printed edition of the *Aeneid* (which the Scot used) to make it clear that among those in the underworld lives 'Inordinat Blythness of peruersit mynd', but most of the time he moves directly from Virgil's Latin to a Scots that can sound grandly Miltonic ('Placis of silence and perpetuall nycht'), but more usually makes surefooted use of Scots idiom, as when a fire's 'furyus flambe' is running along thatched roofs, 'Spreding fra thak to thak, baith but and ben'.[109] 'But and ben' means 'the outer and inner parts of a house' and is a common Scots expression; 'flambe' looks towards French, while terms like 'perpetuall' and 'Inordinat' are clearly Latinate. The flavour of Douglas's language is exactly as he describes in his Prologue to Book I of the translation. On the one hand, he protests his own failings in working with his native 'bad, harsk speche and lewit barbour tong [low, barbarous language]'; on the other hand, he's really proud to produce this epic 'Writing in the language of Scottis natioun', as opposed to the perverted, incomplete prose version by 'Williame Caxtoun, of Inglis natioun' on which Douglas flytingly spits.[110]

Yet even as the Scottish poet proclaims the Scottish purity of his translation, he happily praises Chaucer and confesses that he has augmented his own vocabulary from other sources as Latin writers themselves took terms from Greek. Douglas's translation is regarded as a masterpiece of the Scots-language tradition, but it should also be seen as a milestone in the tradition of Scottish Latin; that language, as much as Scots, is crucial to the work. The scansion of Douglas's lines can be unsure at times. Like Blind Hary he uses a sometimes alliterating ten-syllable line which had replaced octosyllabics as a metre for heroic narrative; like his medieval predecessors, he keeps to rhyming couplets. Perhaps only someone who has tried to translate a long work into a strictly rhyming form can fully appreciate how easy Douglas makes it sound. He writes with an energetic confidence, making his couplets carry the action forward so that it can move quickly from urgency to pathos, as it does here when Aeneas recalls searching for his wife through the sacked city of Troy:

And I also my self so bald wox thair,	*so bold grew*
That I durst schaw my voce in the dirk nycht,	*voice*

And cleip and cry fast throw the stretis on hycht	*call*
Full dolorouslie, Creusa! Creusa!	
Agane, feil sise, in vane I callit swa,	*many times; so*
Throw howsis and the citie quhar I yoid,	*went*
But outhir rest or resoun, as I war woid;	*without; mad*
Quhill that the figour of Creusa and gost,	
Of far mair statur than air quhen scho was lost,	*earlier*
Before me, catife, hir seikand, apperit thair.	*wretch*
Abaisit I wolx, and widdersyns start my hair,	*I grew dismaid; on end stood*
Speik mycht I nocht, the voce in my hals sa stak.	*throat so stuck*
Than sche, belife, on this wise to me spak,	*at once*
With sic wourdis my thochtis to assuage:	*such*
O my suete spous, into sa furious raige	
Quhat helpis thus thi selfin to turment?	*yourself*
This chance is nocht, but goddis willis went . . .[111]	*the course of God's will*

Although Douglas is hard for the modern reader unused to Scots, he has such a sense of drama, love of language, and dedication to his poetic calling that his work maintains its power to compel and beguile. When the spirits at the underworld's River Styx, in a famous Virgilian passage, stretch out their hands with longing 'to be apon the forther bray', the use of 'brae' rather than 'shore' is an indication of how confidently Douglas has brought the Classical Latin poet into his 'rurale' vernacular.[112] He is aware that as a busy Christian churchman in his thirties he has devoted a considerable part of his life to translating a pagan poem. Yet though he sees a potential tension here, he seems relatively unworried by it. After all, not only Virgil but Christ is a 'prince of poetis' (since etymologically the word 'poet' means 'maker'), and Douglas has invoked Christ and Christ's mother as his 'muse'.[113] Some might be startled when, in one of his original Prologues, Douglas equates the Sibyl of Cumae with his beloved Virgin Mary. This is just an indication of Douglas's enthusiasm for his poem, and an indicator of Douglas's participation in a longstanding tradition in which the matter of pagan antiquity could be annexed and 'translated' to Christian ends.

A 1510 dialogue by John Mair put into Douglas's mouth impatience with the obfuscatory arguments of medieval schoolmen, and a wish to return to the text of the Bible. In making available in 1513 a vernacular version of the *Aeneid*, a 'wlgar Virgill', Douglas was writing primarily for a courtly, aristocratic audience of men like his Fife patron, Henry, Lord Sinclair. Such men, like Douglas, might value the *Aeneid* for its 'DOUGHTY CHIFTANYS FULL OF CHEVALRY'.[114] The *Eneados* might help guide aristocrats along the paths to the 'palace of honour'. Yet, though he does not envisage the work being printed, there are indications that Douglas sees it reaching a wider audience that is female as well as male, and that extends perhaps beyond the 'gentill':

> Now salt thou with euery gentill Scot be kend,
> And to onletterit folk be red on hycht,
> That erst was bot with clerkis comprehend.[115]

This wish to move a great text from Latin into the vernacular might seem related to the later Reformers' impulse to make the Vulgate Bible available in readers' native tongues. Within a decade of Douglas's translation, legislation would be passed in Scotland banning the importing of Lutheran texts. Douglas's wordplay poem 'Conscience' laments how 'halie kirk' is eroding away, first from 'conscience' to mere 'science' (learning), then just to 'ens' (material stuff).[116] Yet such suggestions should be set in the context of a poet who longed to be a Bishop, and who intrigued to gain ecclesiastical 'promociones'.[117] Douglas was an imaginative and ambitious pre-Reformation Scottish Catholic, not a Reformer. His achievement lies in his fusing of medieval and Renaissance modes. As a great Humanist Latinist he produces a Scottish Aeneas whose chivalry might stand beside that of an idealized Bruce, whose battles might captivate readers alongside those of a heroic Wallace, and whose poet's language might take Scots writing into new areas of vision and expression.

Douglas's work of Latin translation seems to have raised his game as an original poet. Indeed, since each of its books is accompanied by a substantial prologue authored by Douglas, his *Eneados* is also an anthology of his own work. Boccaccio had done something similar in his *Genealogy of the Gods*, a work Douglas admired, but it was an unusual way to proceed. The Scottish poet's poems, grafted on to Virgil's, are not uniformly good but they signal admirable ambition. They set out the development and method of translation, turning Douglas's writerly task into a heroic labour of its own, and are at times absolutely outstanding. Nowhere is this clearer than in the Prologues to Books VII and XII, dealing respectively with winter and with May. Priscilla Bawcutt points out the remarkable fact that 'No other poet writing in English before Douglas devotes so much space to the continuous description of the natural world.'[118] Douglas's celebration of May draws on literary conventions as well as observation to present its cornucopious world of 'amerant medis' (emerald meadows), heat, foliage, singing and dancing beside the sea; he delights in an ecology of abundance. Although it is unlikely that he knew anything about Gaelic poetic treatments of nature, Douglas in his description of winter does owe something to northern alliterative romances, and perhaps to such passages as that on the 'doolie sessoun' at the start of Henryson's *Testament of Cresseid*. Yet no poet in the British Isles had so concentrated on the season as the Douglas who describes with intensifying alliteration in his 'tristis prologus' (sad prologue) that time when the air is 'penetrative and puire' (pure):

The soill ysowpit into wattir wak,	*soaked; boggy*
The firmament ourkest with rokis blak,	*clouds*
The ground fadyt, and fauch wolx all the feildis,	*yellow-brown*
Montayne toppis sleikit wyth snaw ourheildis	*smoothed; [snow-covers]*
On raggit rolkis of hard harsk quhyne stane,	*harsh crags; whinstone*
With frosyne frontis cauld clynty clewis schane:	*surfaces; stony cliffs shone*
Bewtie wes lost, and barrand schew the landis,	*bare showed*
With frostis haire ourfret the feildis standis.	*hoar frost covered*
Soure bittir bubbis, and the schowris snell,	*sore; squalls; biting*
Semyt on the sward ane similitude of hell,	*turf*
Reducyng to our mynd, in every steid,	*place*
Goustly schaddois of eild and grisly deid,	*[old age]; death*
Thik drumly scuggis dirknit so the hevyne.	*gloomy clouds*
Dym skyis oft furth warpit feirfull levyne,	*threw; lightning*
Flaggis of fyir, and mony felloun flawe,	*flashes; fearful squall*
Scharp soppis of sleit, and of the snypand snawe.[119]	*showers*

This Prologue appears to have been sparked off by translating accounts of the journey to the Underworld in Book VI of Virgil's *Aeneid*. The 'hard flint stane' in Douglas's translation of Book VI becomes in his wintry Prologue to Book VII 'hard harsk quhyne stane', while translating the Latin poet's 'skuggis dirk' (dark clouds) at the entrance to 'hell' encourages the subsequent Prologue's wintry 'similitude of hell' where 'scuggis dirknit'.[120] With a poet's instinctively acquisitive ear,

Douglas the original writer draws on Douglas the translator, collaborating with him to develop new, original work. Although later in the sixteenth century the poet Alexander Hume would relish a Scottish summer's day and King James VI would address sonnets to the seasons, not for centuries would another Scottish poet find such sustained inspiration in weathered landscape; shortly after the major republication of Douglas's work in Edinburgh in 1710, James Thomson (a student at Edinburgh University in the ensuing decade) would begin his own poetic career with a similarly spirited account of winter, then would go on to become famous as poet of *The Seasons*. Using a gardening image, Douglas images himself as bonded to Virgil's text as if it were 'a staik'; Virgil's example and range nurtured in the Scottish cleric possibilities which allowed his own creative gifts to burgeon.[121] Two centuries after his death, Douglas's work still opened up possibilities for others.

Douglas had a highly educated imagination, but also a taste for popular culture. Gazing into a mirror in *The Palice of Honour*, the speaker sees not just such English folk heroes as Robin Hood and 'Peirs Plewman', but also the Irish 'Greit Gowmakmorne and Fyn Makcoul'.[122] This reference to the Gaelic heroic cycle of ballads about Finn MacCoul (Fionn MacCumhail) is a reminder that 'Heland bardis' as well as Italian minstrels and Lowland Scottish poets were patronized by James IV, and that bards' subject matter could be well known in a Scotland where Gaelic was still widely spoken in the north and west.[123] Probably Gaelic-Scots bilingualism flourished in areas where the Highlands and Lowlands met. Although John Mair was scornful about the Highlands, his fellow early sixteenth-century Latinist Hector Boece (in Scots translation) wrote of 'Ffyn Makcoul' as 'of huge stature, havyng sevin cubittis in hicht . . . ane crafty huntare and to all man ferefull for the strang quantite of his persoun'. Recording that there were popular stories and poems about 'Ffyn', as there were about King Arthur, this Scots Boece adds a little sniffily that they circulated 'amang the vulgare pepill, mare than amang apprisit authouris'.[124]

In *The Book of the Dean of Lismore*, the great manuscript treasury of Gaelic verse which was compiled mainly between 1512 and 1526, there are about two dozen poems from the Fionn cycle. Collected largely in Perthshire, often from packmen and *lorgánaigh* or wandering Gaelic bards, the poems in this substantial anthology contain much material from the heroic world later designated 'Ossianic'. We glimpse a male 'hunter of magical stags' and a female 'slender foot, a heel white and pointed' as heroic nobles do battle and relax.[125] *The Book of the Dean of Lismore* contains Gaelic work which, even in a modern English version, can have immediate appeal:

> Honey in the call of any bird;
> Honey a human voice in the Land of Gold;
> Honey a crane's song, and there is a heard
> Honey Bun Da Threoir's waters hold.
>
> Honey in the calling of the wind;
> Honey the cuckoo's voice above Caise Con;
> Honey in uncluttered, random sunlight,
> Honey blackbirds' songs till sunset's gone.
>
> Honey the eagle's cry at the Red Falls
> Way above the Bay of Morna's Boy;
> Honey the cuckoo's call beyond the thickets,
> Honey is that pause in the crane's cry.
>
> My father Finn MacCoul had in his war-band
> Seven squadrons ready to fight any
> Man or beast; when we unleashed the deerhounds
> They leapt ahead, their baying pure wild honey.

My English version here tries to catch some of the musical repetition, the lexical and syntactic patterning of the Gaelic original. There are several short lyrics like this in *The Book of the Dean of Lismore*. Often, though, its poems are more extended. The poets in the collection like to hymn great Gaelic families and chieftains. Irish and Scottish works, some by professional (often named) Classical Gaelic poets writing in syllabic metres, mingle with work by amateurs. In addition to the heroic poems, a wide range of forms is represented – from religious work to sophisticated erotic lyrics, bawdy poems, and the sort of verse denunciations that gave rise to the Scots expression 'to playe the baird' (to write scathingly) and may have nourished the 'flyting' tradition in the Lowlands:

> Ní h-iongnadh a bheith i bpéin:
> fada ó b'ionchrochtha Ailéin;
> ná luaidh ar láthair an fhir
> chuaidh go a mháthair 's go a phiuthair.

No wonder he is in torment,
Allan, over-ready for hanging;
say nothing of the manly strength of a man
who slept with his mother and sister.[126]

So Fhionnlagh Ruadh (Finlay, the Red Bard) execrates the son of the chief of Clan Ranald, who died in the first decade of the sixteenth century, and is accused of desecrating Iona. The manuscript contains much older poems, such as those attributed to 'great Ossian, the son of Fionn' and to Muireadhach Albanach, as well as more recent works such as a tailor's denunciation of a 'grey, bristly, surly pack' of Highland wolves and an anonymous battle-incitement addressed to the Earl of Argyll, urging him to fight the English who threaten to divide Scotland, and to burn their 'ungentle' women and children.[127]

Very different in tone in *The Book of the Dean of Lismore* is Aithbhreac Inghean Corcadail's 'O rosary that recalled my tear' (discussed above), or Isabel of Argyll's hurt, courtly love lyric about a secret passion. In the early sixteenth century some poets, not least women, moved from the syllabic Classical Gaelic metres to stress-based verse in vernacular Gaelic, as heard in 'The Lament for Mackintosh', whose author complains that, because her husband was killed on her wedding day, she was 'Am bhréidich, am ghruagaich/'S am bhantraich 's an aon uair ud' ('A kerched woman, a maiden/ And a widow all in that one hour').[128] *The Book of the Dean of Lismore* includes work by the earliest known women writers in Scottish Gaelic, as well as a strain of misogyny. 'I hate a band of poets that includes a woman,' writes Felim MacDugall in a poem listing his detestations.[129] This manuscript, written mostly in Gaelic and containing a chronicle in Latin, represents a multifoliate flowering of Gaelic poetry, though there are occasional signs of a language coming under pressure. 'It is not good to travel on Sunday', begins another poem by Felim MacDugall, sounding a still recognizable note; the same poet also points out that 'ní math iarla gan bhéarla' ('not good is an earl lacking English').[130]

In the areas where 'Inglis' (or what we would now call the Scots tongue) reigned, the spectrum of verse was at least as wide, but attitudes towards Gaelic culture were mostly hostile. Gavin Douglas may have known about Finn MacCoul, but in *The Palice of Honour* he also mentions two popular anonymous works of the late fifteenth century, the northern poem 'Rauf Coilyear' and the absurd piece 'auld Cowkew-

yis sow', where 'a bard' is classed with 'Ane vsurar' and 'a lolard' in a
catalogue of good-for-nothings.[131] 'Colkelbie's Sow' is an absurd and
sometimes heavy-handed freewheeling Scots tale of the sale of a pig;
suspended between oral rhyming and textual culture, the poem is intoxi-
catingly fixated on absurd lists, and mocks the moralizings of more
serious writers. 'The Taill of Rauf Coilyear', on the other hand, shows
what happens when a 'collier' (or charcoal-burner) meets a king; Charle-
magne, in this Scots version of a common European story, seeks shelter
in Ralph's house, is not recognized, and is called 'uncourteous' by the
tetchy Ralph, who boxes the King's ears, but the comedy turns out
happily when, eventually, the collier goes to court and achieves a knighthood. Like the popular, Scottish-inflected Arthurian *Knightly Tale of
Golagros and Gawane*, and like Douglas's writings, 'Rauf Coilyear'
looks back to medieval chivalric codes, but it also carries hints of a
carnivalesque note sounded more uproariously in 'The Gyre-Carling'
with its rock-shitting witch or, less scatologically, in 'King Berdok'
whose Babylonian monarch spends his summer in a cabbage stalk.

These works may sound more enticing in summary than in full, but
there is a more convincingly sustained music in the folk festivities of
'Peblis to the Play', a Beltane romp, and in 'Christis Kirk on the Grene'.
The latter's title may sound as if it belongs to a religious work, but the
solemn-sounding refrain that supplies the title is played off throughout
against the goatlike bleats, bruising fisticuffs and reproachful yells of
vying holidaymakers out for a wild spree on the village green. Some
mischievous 'damysellis' who are 'licht of laitis' (light of manners) set
things going, then men with names like 'Heich Hucheon' (Big Hedgehog)
take centre stage for a full-scale brawl.

The millar wes of manly mak;	
To meit him wes na mowis;	*no joke*
Thair durst nocht ten cum him to tak,	
So nowit he thair nowis.	*knocked; heads*
The buschment haill about him brak	*[whole ambush]*
And bikkerit him with bowis.	*attacked*
Syne tratourly behind his bak	*then treacherously*
Thay hewit him on the howiss	*hacked; calves*
Behind,	
At Christis Kirk of the grene.[132]	

These ten-line stanzas thrive on acoustic belt-tightening – there are only two rhymes in the first eight lines of each. Iambic tetrameter alternates with iambic trimeter until each ninth line hops on a single foot. This is the tiny line, a two-syllable hiccup, called the 'bob', which usually rhymes with nothing else and can be used for comic effect before the refrain that follows. The ram-stam of such stanzas would appeal to later Scottish poets who picked up on variations of this stanza form as well as on the hurly-burly of its contents. The popular tumbling of 'Christis Kirk on the Grene' would have a special appeal in the eighteenth century for Allan Ramsay, Robert Fergusson and Robert Burns when they rejoiced in Scots verse that spoke of a popular milieu. Yet in the early Renaissance much of the finest poetry remained courtly or associated with great aristocratic families like the Sinclairs of Fife. Dunbar and Douglas were followed by their admirer Sir David Lyndsay, who held a court position as a herald.

Born around 1486, Lyndsay had strong family connections with Fife, but by 1511 he was active as part of James IV's royal circle in Edinburgh where he lived close to Gavin Douglas during the time of the *Eneados* translation. After Flodden, Lyndsay was well liked by the young King James V and the two remained friends until the King's death in 1542, by which time Lyndsay had been knighted. Lyndsay's poetic output ranges from dream-vision to flyting, narrative to occasional verse. The King, with whom he flytes, is flattered conventionally one moment, only to be upbraided the next for 'fukkand lyke ane furious fornicatour'.[133] In 'The Dreme' Lyndsay's monarch is warned that the common people are 'raggit, revin, and rent', while Scotland is divided, and must have 'ane gude auld prudent king'.[134] Drawing on the established international genre of 'advice to princes', Lyndsay's work repeatedly touches on such themes, warning against 'For commoun weill makand no cair' even as the author relishes the ups and downs of court life.[135] In 'The Testament and Complaynt of Our Soverane Lordis Papyngo' (1530) a near-dead parrot (papyngo) warns the courtiers,

Traist weill, sum men wyll gyf you laud, as lordis,   *Trust*
Quhilk wald be glaid to se yow hang in cordis.

The parrot then bids a lengthy, high-toned farewell to the royal dwellings ('Adew, Edinburgh, thow heych tryumphant toun') while warning against popular resentment of 'degenerit' churchmen whom the King must control.[136] One such churchman holds forth in 'The Tragedie of the Cardinall' (c. 1547). Written after James V's death and at a time when Lyndsay's poetry seems less narrowly focused on court life, this poem presents, largely in his own supposed words, the life and deeds of the devious figure of Cardinal David Beaton who became Chancellor in 1543 but was assassinated in St Andrews in 1546. Although Beaton ends by preaching virtue, parts of the poem come close to a dramatic monologue as the 'aboundantlie bledyng' Cardinal, boasting of his own 'princelye prodigalytie', celebrates his enthusiasm for 'banketting, playng at cartis and dyse'. Yet the allure of the poem comes less from what Beaton unwittingly reveals about himself than from what he openly declares. We seem to be listening to his last confession as this burner of Protestant heretics recounts how he planned to kill 'Sum with the fyre, sum with the sword and knyfe/ . . . And purposit tyll put to gret torment/ All favoraris of the Auld and New Testament.'[137] The Protestants Beaton martyred are not named, and the poem's focus is all the stronger for its almost Browningesque concentration on Beaton's proclamation of his own domination and violence.

Towards the end of his life, Lyndsay turned towards a more companionable biographical poem. Written in the early 1550s, his warm account of a family friend, 'Squyer Meldrum', presents an actual military and amorous career in the octosyllabic couplets and literary armature of Arthurian romance. William Meldrum from 'the schyre of Fyfe' serves 'nobill Lowes, the king of France' and has many adventures likely to gladden the hearts of a Scottish audience:

Thair was slane, of Inglis band,   *English*
Fyve scoir of men, I understand,
The quhilk wer cruell men and kene,
And of the Scottis wer slane fyftene.[138]

Although he never marries, Meldrum enjoys passionate lovemakings, retires to Fife, and dies of old age after a regretful farewell to his lovers. So the military knight of the Middle Ages is transformed into a Renaissance country gentleman. This warm blend of biography and rerouted chivalric romance allowed Lyndsay both to accommodate and sweeten recent history. He is a poet who touches excellence only unevenly; most of his works are stronger in part than as wholes. Although he wrote of Scotland, his imagination was hardly confined to it. In 'The Dreme', when the figure of Remembrance shows the poet 'the devisioun of the Eirth' there is an impressive international roll-call, an acoustic of amplitude and vision in which Lyndsay may enjoy looking away from Scottish politics:

> Secundlie, we considderit Africa,
> With mony fructfull famous regioun,
> As Ethiope, and Tripolitana,
> Zewges, quhare standis the tryumphant toun
> Of nobyll Cartage, that ciete of renoun;
> Garamantes, Nadabar, Libia,
> Getulia, and Maritania.[139]

Lyndsay had never seen these places, but clearly enjoys escaping into the high-falutin litany of their names. Yet some of Lyndsay's strongest verse is about taking scripture to a common audience without the mediation of Church or courtly hierarchies. Alert to the cultural links that went with 'the weill keipit Ancient Alliance' with France, to the intonations of the Latin Mass, and the 'cairfull corrynogh' or Gaelic funeral lament, Lyndsay, in paying tribute to the 'eloquence' of the great translator Gavin Douglas, could also remind his audience that 'our vulgare toung' had been consecrated for poetic use.[140] Respectful of rhetorical training, and loyal to his Scots and English precursors, Lyndsay at the end of his career grows increasingly concerned about 'lawis' which are 'Inventit be mennis traditioun,/ Contrair to Christis institutioun'. He turns away from the Classical muses ('I did never sleip on Pernaso' (Parnassus)) to take 'God to be my muse'.[141] In 'Ane Dialog Betwix Experience and Ane Courteour' (1554) he produces a kind of vernacular retelling of Bible stories. Like Gavin Douglas, Lyndsay was interested in cultural, not just linguistic, translation. Lyndsay argues that Christ spoke to his people in their native tongue, and that, while Latin may be appropriate for doctors, learned poets and others, there is a need both for the laws to be translated into 'vulgare language' and for scripture in the vernacular:

> Bot lat us haif the bukis necessare
> To commoun weill and our salvatioun,
> Justlye translatit in our toung vulgare.[142]

The use of 'us' and 'our' here by this courtly poet is a gesture of identification with the wider community which was by this time con-

vulsed by the energies of the Reformation. Alert throughout his career
to the abuses of Church privilege, Lyndsay probably continues to speak
from within the Catholic Church, but his writings show how close some
Catholics at this time might be to some of the Protestant Reformers and
champions of vernacular scripture. Lyndsay, as he matured, became
more and more of a bridge between Catholic and Protestant impulses,
and between courtly and 'common' culture.

This is most evident in his major dramatic work, *Ane Satyre of the
Thrie Estaitis* (1552). Lyndsay's play mixes advice to the monarch with
direct appeals to the populace. It stages for mid-sixteenth-century
Scots the contemporary and sometimes violent social conflicts in their
midst. Burgh records show that there were Corpus Christi plays and
other religious dramas acted throughout fifteenth- and early sixteenth-
century Scotland. Little survives. Lost too are other kinds of drama,
ranging from Robin Hood frolics to clerks' plays performed at the
Universities of St Andrews, Glasgow and Aberdeen. We know earlier
playwrights' names and the titles of their works, but Lyndsay's *Satyre*
is the oldest substantial extant dramatic text written in Scotland. Drawing on French *sotties*, or fools' plays, with their daft sermons, as well
as on older French and English morality plays and moralizing farces,
Lyndsay's sophisticated drama operates in dangerous territory. At its
heart is the social unrest surrounding the struggle for 'reformation' in
a land whose king is being told to curb the power and abuses of
Churchmen.

The play was designed for performance in Cupar, just ten miles from
the St Andrews which had become the epicentre of the Scottish
Reformation and scene of notorious sectarian killings, from the burning
and torture of several university students, teachers and preachers who
campaigned for vernacular scripture and Protestant reforms, to the
recent assassination of Cardinal Beaton in 1546. Lyndsay had some
involvement with John Knox in St Andrews, where Knox (an ally of
English Protestantism) had studied at the University under John Mair,
and where Knox preached in 1547 before being captured and enslaved
by the French. To author a play which related to the violent ideological
struggles and social problems which were developing was a perilous
exercise in a Scotland worn down by almost ten years of war against
England. Just a decade before in Dundee, about twelve miles by foot
and ferry from St Andrews, a friar had been burned when his drama

was deemed heretical. Lyndsay may have essayed some contentious contemporary topics earlier. Now, in his mid-sixties, he produced his most ambitious work, operating in a medium which could reach out to literate and illiterate audiences.

In two substantial parts separated by an interlude, this verse drama uses allegorical characters with names like 'Divyne Correctioun', 'Pauper', 'Dame Sensualitie' and 'Rex Humanitas' (King Humanity). It starts with Diligence talking about God in rather aureate-sounding language. 'The Father and founder of faith and felicitie,/ That your fassioun formed to His similitude.' But soon there is a pause, and Diligence begins again with a much more demotic accent, familiarly asking the audience to pay attention and shut up – 'Tak tent to me, my friends, and hald yow coy!'[143] Throughout the play kinds of verse, language and conduct are juxtaposed as Lyndsay both demonstrates dramatic flair and draws on his poetic versatility, transferring elements of poetic form to the stage. So listeners hear about 'Ane perle of pulchritude' as well as taking in the flyting talk of 'Ane fistand flag, a flaggartie fuffe' (A belching slag, a sluttish tinker).[144] The action advances from a land where Sensuality, Wantonness and other vices (often in clerical garb) have got the better of the King, to a state where, thanks to the intervention of 'Divyne Correctioun' and the voices of the country at large, the King calls a Parliament which issues laws to reform the Church and set the state in order. This Parliament comprises the three 'Estates' in the (unnamed) country – the secular aristocracy, the spiritual leaders and the merchants; yet its deliberations also involve John the Commonweal, who represents the whole population, and an unruly Pauper who is on his way to St Andrews in search of justice.

This extension of the Parliament so that it comes to speak for the whole people is only one way in which Lyndsay dramatizes struggles against established authority. More obvious are his characters' repeated denunciations of Church abuses and corruption. Many quote scripture, not only in Latin but also in 'the New Testament, / In Englisch toung', as part of their sometimes knockabout disputations.[145] In an act of cultural translation Lyndsay takes the ecclesiastical and academic genre of the formal public arguments or 'disputations' held in Latin by scholars and, by staging them in the vernacular while including often bawdily funny dramatic flytings of his own, he appeals to the people at large. In Cupar his play was performed in 1552 in front of James V. Clever dramatic use is made of the real King's presence alongside that of Rex Humanitas. But the play was also performed before a general audience likely to sympathize with Gude Counsall's plea:

> Wee came nocht heir for disputatiouns;
> We came to make gude reformatiounis . . .[146]

The King in the play is warned by Correctioun that unless he behaves better he 'sall be ruttit out', as Tarquin was by the Romans. The Pardoner with his fake holy relics who denounces reformers such as 'That Martin Luther, that fals loun', is presented in as unsympathetic a light as is the Flatterie who cries 'Heresie, heresie!' and demands burnings.[147]

This play can be starkly violent. After the Parliament has issued its acts, the figures of vice, who have an appealingly awful vitality, are hanged in front of the audience. Some aspects of *The Thrie Estaitis* are closely attuned to contemporary Reformers' practice. Calvin and, later, Knox would draw up legal frameworks for the reform of Church and society while appealing to the populace for support. Yet *The Thrie Estaitis*, while staging these convulsive contemporary debates, concludes less with theology than with comedy as the figure of Folly denounces warring Christian factions. John the Commonweal may speak a vernacular Scots creed that omits the word 'catholic', but the last words of the play are addressed to God in Latin. Later writers of varying persuasions would claim Lyndsay as one of their own. His play gives voice and body both to rebellion and to conservatism. In its advice to the King and its sense of the monarch as guided by his people, Lyndsay's drama can be aligned with the Declaration of Arbroath, with the 'advice to princes' tradition, and with the political philosophy of George Buchanan whose verse satire on the Franciscans had led him to flee Cardinal Beaton's Scotland at the end of the 1530s. Set beside the work of Shakespeare, who was born twelve years after the play was performed in Cupar, Lyndsay's work looks and sounds medieval. Yet in its very direct engagement with contemporary politics and its unflinching portrayal of social and religious upheaval, it operates in territory Shakespeare avoided. Authored by a nobleman who was for much of his life a courtier, and apparently advocating strict, reforming government, Lyndsay's play has an energy closely bound up with its energetic contentions about several kinds of political, religious, personal and linguistic 'libertie'.[148]

IOANNES CNOXVS.

The image of the iconoclastic author and preacher John Knox, as
presented in the 1580 Icones compiled by the French poet and
dramatist Theodore Bèze ('Beza'), who succeeded John Calvin as
protestant pastor in Geneva. (St Andrews University Library,
Typ SwG.B8oLB)

3

Reformation

Although it came to a head in 1560, the Reformation in Scotland was less an event than a process. It extended over many decades and was closely bound up with the written word. Throughout Europe Protestant Reformers used the new technology of printing to disseminate vernacular translations of the Bible. In polemics, catechisms, confessions of faith and regulations, they also published their own arguments, whose origins predated printing. In fourteenth-century England, for instance, the Oxford academic and author John Wyclif had contested papal supremacy. His stress on the authority of scripture encouraged translation of the Bible into English so that people could read it and decide its significance for themselves. Wyclif's followers were called Lollards and some of his ideas nurtured the related theology expounded by Jan Huss in Bohemia. Subjected to Church persecution, Lollards, Hussites and other Reformers were branded heretics.

Although heresy in fifteenth-century Scotland was relatively rare, a few followers of Wyclif and Huss were put to death. The Bohemian Paul Craw was burned alive in St Andrews in 1433. Over a century later John Knox recorded that a brass ball was jammed in Craw's mouth as he blazed, to stop him protesting his faith to the onlookers. Certainly there are signs that the Church authorities were concerned about dissident student opinion. From 1417 St Andrews Arts students had to swear to oppose Lollardy, but it was the best part of a hundred years afterwards that Lollards in Ayrshire were reproached (a mild punishment) by King James IV. Only after Lutheranism began to take hold on the continent did Reforming ideas become a serious threat to the Scottish ruling elite. In 1525 the Scottish Parliament legislated against the importation of heretical literature from mainland Europe. By 1527 the English ambassador at Antwerp was reporting that copies of William Tyndale's English translation of the New Testament were being transported by ships, some bound for Edinburgh, but more for St Andrews. Vessels with attractive names like *The Lyoun, Sheir the Wind, The Mary Grace* and *The Grace of God* sometimes also carried works by continental Reformation writers. Whatever else it was in Scotland, the Reformation was a battle of books. Long before the 1551 act of the Scottish Parliament requiring the strict control, examination and licensing of printed 'bukis, ballatis, sangis, blasphematiounis, rymes or Tragedeis outher [either] in Latine or Inglis toung', to publish could mean to risk death.[1] Patrick Hamilton, the man whom John Knox saw as the Scottish Reformation's first principal martyr, burned at St Andrews in 1528, was not only a preacher. He was also, like Knox, an author.

This era of Reformation in which authorship could be so dangerous also saw in Scotland a huge expansion of possibilities for writers. Lyndsay's *Satyre* established itself as the cornerstone of Scots drama. The Reformer George Buchanan wrote in Latin prose the first Scottish treatise on poetry, while his pupil King James VI, when still in his teens, published a comparable rulebook for verse written in Scots. Renaissance Humanism, which had been acknowledged by Gavin Douglas, impinged increasingly on Scottish culture, encouraging the development of such courtly forms as the pastoral and the sonnet. The Reformation quickened the growth of artistic and polemical prose writing in both Scots and English. Previously almost all prose by Scots had been confined to Latin, though Acts of Parliament had been in Scots since 1424 and court proceedings were recorded in that tongue. John Gau (c. 1495–1553), a Lutheran convert who was born in Perth and matriculated at St Andrews in 1509, wrote in Malmo, Sweden, what is probably the first Scots prose work, translating from Danish and German to produce his *The Richt Vay to the Kingdom of Heuine* (1533). Much of it is a straightforward version of scriptural passages, but it also hopes that 'neyne sal put thair hop in the virgine Maria or trow that schw cane saiff [believe that she can save] ony man', and it commemorates the Scot 'patrik hammiltone quhom thay pat creuellie to the deid'.[2]

John Knox, in work of rather more imaginative interest, became the first Scot to write prose in English, or at least in a Scots-accented English. Violent, virulent and iconoclastic, the Reformation was also powerfully creative in Scotland. It introduced and harnessed new popular as well as elite modes of expression, often published through the proliferating technology of print. The court remained a centre of literary patronage, but the emerging Protestant movement became a rival encourager of writing, much of it directed against the ruling authorities. Such was Protestantism's impact that this period in Scottish literary history tends to be termed the Reformation, rather than the Renaissance. While the impetus of the Renaissance is evident in Scottish culture from architecture to the burgeoning of the vernacular sonnet, the forces of Reformation develop modern Scottish prose and convulse much of the verse of the time. Scotland's universities play a full and dangerous part in this. It is no accident that Patrick Hamilton was burned right in front of the entrance to St Salvator's College, St Andrews. Much later, his initials were set into the cobbled street there, and it is still regarded as unlucky to walk on them.

Hamilton's short religious treatise was written in Latin prose and published in Antwerp. Soon after the author's burning in 1528, it was translated into English as *Patrick's Places*, and considered 'pithy' by Knox.[3] Some of its contentions, argued from Christian scripture, seem unexceptionable: 'Charity is the love of thy neighbour. The rule of charity is to do as thou wouldst were done unto thee: for charity esteemeth all alike; the rich and the poor; the friend and the foe; the thankful and the unthankful; the kinsman and stranger.' Other parts were far more controversial, as when Hamilton argued that faith in Christ was more important than good deeds in themselves: 'For how is He thy Saviour, if thou mightest save thy self by thy works?'[4]

This doctrine of 'justification by faith' became a tenet of the Scottish Reformers, but in some ways as important was their powerful emphasis on direct access to God's Word through the availability of vernacular Bibles. Alexander Alane ('Alesius'), born in 1500 and educated at St Andrews, opened his 1533 Latin *Epistle* with a stylishly bolshie flourish, assuring the Scottish monarch that this 'nefarious and impious edict' was issued without royal authority. Addressed to James V, Alane's work's full title translates as *An Epistle of Alexander Alesius, against a certain Decree of the Bishops of Scotland, which forbids to read the books of the New Testament in the vernacular tongue*. It champions the need 'at home to read or hear the books of the Gospel'.[5] The Classically learned Alane's work was the first to argue publicly for the availability of vernacular scripture in Scottish households. Its author's contentions were seen as a direct challenge to the regulatory power of the Catholic

Church. By the time of his *Epistle*'s publication, Alane had fled the country. In Germany he wrote his *De auctore et utilitate Psalmorum* (On the Authorship and Use of the Psalms). Praising the music of divine verse, this work helped make the Psalms the cornerstone of an emerging Protestant poetics.

Alane was a Latinist who championed the vernacular. Such a stance became an increasingly common one, but possession or dissemination of vernacular scripture was dangerous in early sixteenth-century Scotland. Around 1540 Murdoch Nisbet, associated with a group of Ayrshire Lollards, 'digged and built a vault at the bottom of his own house'. Literally an underground intellectual, hidden in his vault Nisbet could concentrate on reading the Scots version of the New Testament which he had made in exile during the preceding decades. Based largely on John Purvey's revision of the English version ascribed to Wyclif, Nisbet's text Scoticizes spelling and grammar but otherwise follows the Wycliffite Bible very closely. So Purvey's 'thei felden doun, and worschipiden him' becomes in Nisbet's Scots 'thai fel doun and wirschipit him'.[6] Including portions of the Old Testament as well as all of the New, Nisbet's version remained in manuscript until the twentieth century. This meant that as the Reformation developed Scottish people read the Bible in imported English rather than in Scots. Only when read aloud might the Word to some extent become the Wurd.

Before 1610 only one edition of the Bible had been printed in Scotland. The 1579 Bassendyne Bible was, as Graham Tulloch points out, 'merely a reprint of the second edition of the Geneva Bible which had been first published, in English, in 1560'.[7] So, as a desire for a widely understood version of the sacred scriptures increased in Scotland, it encouraged the use of English, not Scots, as the language of worship. On the page at least, God acquired a southern accent. Gradually, written English came to carry a commanding authority. A printed, widely adopted Bible in Scots might have helped produce a prestigious, standard form of that tongue. Instead, the use of Bibles in English and growing contacts with English Reformers boosted the employment of the southern tongue as a literary language in Scotland.

Few movements have been more mythologized than the Scottish Reformation and its most brassily successful protagonist, John Knox (c. 1513–72). In the nineteenth century, when Thomas Carlyle and others hymned Knox as a Scottish liberator to be hero-worshipped, the

Reformation was presented by influential Protestant Scots as a golden age of Presbyterian saints; in the twentieth century, when Edwin Muir's Knox was one of those men of 'desolation' who 'bundled all the harvesters away', the long-bearded prophet and his age became dour grotesques, targets for newer kinds of oppression as well as for emancipatory mockery.[8] Few today have read a word Knox wrote. Yet write he certainly did, and in a way that can be scandalously quotable:

To promote a woman to bear rule, superiority, dominion or empire above any realm, nation or city is repugnant to nature, contumely to God, a thing most contrarious to His revealed will and approved ordinance, and finally it is the subversion of good order, of all equity and justice.[9]

Knox seldom pulls his punches. This knock-out blow comes from *The First Blast of the Trumpet against the Monstrous Regiment of Women* (1558), one of the most memorably titled Scottish works, though also one whose title is usually misunderstood. Knox uses the word 'Regiment' in its Latin sense of 'Rule', not to mean serried ranks. Still, he just about means what he says. Like his teacher John Mair and his contemporary the Latinist George Buchanan, Knox is making the radical point that the people can get rid of their monarch. More particularly, his pamphlet is hurled against 'that wicked Jezebel of England', the Catholic Mary Tudor, and against the expectation that women might normally rule kingdoms.[10] Such anti-feminist sentiments were widely shared, and had been articulated earlier by good Scottish Catholics like Sir Gilbert Hay who had warned that princes should not be governed by women. Knox's polemic can have a flyting energy to it. His Reformation emphasis on freeing religion from monarchical control was a frequent source of conflict with rulers to whom he insisted 'that in the religion of God only ought His own Word be considered. That no authority of man nor angel ought in that case to be respected.'[11] Scottish monarchs detested this. James VI later complained that a Scottish presbytery 'as wel agreeth with a Monarchy, as God and the Deuill. Then *Jack & Tom & Will, & Dick*, shall meete, and at their pleasures censure me and my Councell and all our proceedinges.'[12] This was hardly the first time in Scottish culture that popular opposition complained against a king; yet the Reformation's backing of such democratic voices would have profound effects on Scottish culture from Knox through Burns to James Kelman.

'Democracy' was a new word in English, and usually a bad one. For most writers it was associated with such things as 'the Democratie of base and vulgar actions'.[13] In this era it is hard to overestimate (for men at least) the radically democratic, potentially empowering nature of the Reformed Kirk. Presided over by leaders like the prose writer Knox and the poet Buchanan, the Church of Scotland emerged with Europe's most democratic system of Church organization. Its egalitarian values would be part of the vital inheritance of later Scottish thought. A note of powerful independence is sounded in *The Book of Discipline* (1560) drawn up by Knox and others for their newly founded Kirk; this rulebook makes it clear that 'It appertaineth to the people, and to every several congregation, to elect their Minister.' Institutionalizing such a democratic principle was potentially dangerous in an authoritarian state. Yet as its title suggests, *The Book of Discipline* was very much an attempt to establish and police new controlling institutions. Its regulatory voice, whose aspirations and timbre were so crucial to the shaping of subsequent Scottish culture, mixes empowerment and stern, often theocratic regulation. About a quarter of *The Book of Discipline* deals with education. It emphasizes 'the necessity of schools' throughout the land, so that 'every several church have a Schoolmaster appointed', and sets out in detail the administrative codes of the universities. The aim of education is seen as the development of virtuous Christians, but knowledge of areas from Mathematics to Rhetoric, Divinity, Law, Ethics, Philosophy, Politics and Languages is encouraged. Though these aims remained in many cases aspirations, their direction is clear. The rich must educate 'their sons . . . of their own expenses, because they are able', but the poor too must have access to knowledge:

The children of the poor must be supported and sustained on the charge of the Church, till trial be taken whether the spirit of docility [aptitude for learning] be found in them or not. If they be found apt to letters and learning, then may they not (we mean, neither the sons of the rich, nor yet the sons of the poor), be permitted to reject learning; but must be charged to continue their study, so that the Commonwealth may have some comfort by them.[14]

Emphasizing socially useful, rather than pure knowledge, this certainly smacks of the Protestant work ethic, but it is also about affording a near-democratic equality of opportunity. It is, in modern parlance, socially inclusive. This text set out ideals which powered the institutions that would be seen as characteristic of Scotland in centuries that followed, and which underpinned what has come to be known as the Scottish Enlightenment.

Associated with the eighteenth century, Scottish Enlightenment values were made possible by the much earlier development of the Scottish universities, boosted in the sixteenth century by the work of St Andrews-educated Andrew Melville (1545–1622). Melville was a determined writer. As an old man imprisoned by James VI in the Tower of London, he scraped Latin verses on the walls of his cell. But he was an even more determined administrator; his Humanist reforms to the universities swept aside the older scholasticism and introduced the pedagogy advocated by the French Latinist Pierre de la Ramée (Ramus) whose first British translator was the St Andrews scholar Roland MacIlmaine. An accomplished Latinist like Alane before him, MacIlmaine in 1574 argued for the Ramist development of 'arte' in 'the Scottyshe or Englishe tongue'.[15] With Melville's backing, Ramist and other Humanist teachings were introduced at Glasgow and St Andrews Universities, while at the new University of Edinburgh in the 1580s Robert Rollock, the St Andrews-educated pioneer of Scottish 'covenant' theology (which saw the nation as bound by a covenant to God), developed applications of Ramism.

Almost unread today, and thought of (if at all) as an arcane ecclesiastical tome, *The Book of Discipline* sought to extend the power and surveillance of the new Protestant Kirk throughout society – from universities to parish meetings – at least as far as the authority of the pre-Reformation Catholic Church had reached. *The Book of Discipline* was more important for the development of Scottish society and culture than the Declaration of Arbroath, though its plainer constitutional prose is less ringing. Prescriptive, strict, and subscribed to by a group of Scottish noblemen and landowners, it states straightforwardly that 'To Discipline must all Estates within this Realm be subject if they offend, as well the rulers as they that are ruled'. It is theocratic as well as ungivingly absolute in its obsessively alliterative insistence that 'idolatry, with all monuments and places of the same, as abbeys, monasteries, friaries, nunneries, chapels, chantries, cathedral kirks, canonries, colleges, other than presently are parish Kirks or Schools . . . be utterly suppressed'.[16] Yet in its emphasis on equality, on direct access to the Word, on work, awareness of the good of the community (or 'Commonwealth'), and the development of education, it gave voice to a developing Scotland. Authoritarian even as it resists authority, sharply repressive as it trumpets equality and freedom, its spiritual and social engineering are characteristic both of Knox and his Reformation Kirk.

So polemically controversial are *The Book of Discipline* and Knox's other writings that it is easy to miss the simple fact that they are written in clear, Scots-accented English prose. Although the 1566 manuscript of his *History of the Reformation in Scotland* (published in 1586–7, but suppressed and seized) is written in several hands, varying between Scots and English forms of words, Knox's intimate letters, written in his own hand, use English forms with few distinctive Scoticisms. This is why it is fair to present his work (as above) in modernized English form, and also why Knox stands as the first Scot to achieve literary mastery over English prose.

This achievement could make him seem a cultural traitor. Probably born in Haddington and educated at St Andrews, where he later sided with Cardinal Beaton's killers, Knox had been forced to become a French galley slave in 1547. Later he sought refuge in Reformation England, then in the English church at Frankfurt. Short, bushy-eyebrowed, his beard 'a hand and a half long', he was in his mid-forties when he returned to Scotland from Calvin's Geneva in 1559 and preached a violent sermon which roused Protestants to destroy Catholic churches.[17] He became minister of St Giles Church, Edinburgh, in July 1560, and the Reformed Church of Scotland was instituted. Though clearly committed to Scotland, Knox looked to England for spiritual and linguistic sustenance. His shrewd contemporary Scottish Catholic adversary Ninian Winzet accuses him of having forgotten 'our auld plane Scottis quhilk zour mother lerit zou'.[18] Knox uses the occasional Scots word, but his stinging sense of drama, passion and narrative lives mainly in English. He writes well. Both his own accounts and the speeches he presents are constantly enlivened with detail. Here is Knox remembering his friend and mentor George Wishart (burned in St Andrews in 1546) whose followers have been barred from an Ayrshire church:

But the said Master George withdrew the said Hew, and said unto him, 'Brother, Christ Jesus is as potent upon the fields as in the kirk; and I find that he himself often preached in the desert, at the seaside, and other places judged profane, than that he did in the Temple of Jerusalem. It is the word of peace that God sends by me: the blood of no man shall be shed this day for the preaching of it.' And so withdrawing the whole people, he came to a dyke in a moor edge, upon the south-west side of Mauchline, upon the which he ascended. The whole multitude stood and sat about him (God gave the day pleasing and hot). He continued in preaching more than three hours.[19]

When he writes of the siege of St Andrews Castle Knox can be pacily exciting, but here his tone is warmly hagiographical. He dramatizes Wishart's words effortlessly. Knox's plain prose is quickened by biblical phrasings, spiced by local and temporal details like the dyke at the edge of the moor and the pleasant sunshine. In such vignettes Knox writes like a proto-novelist. His wish to manipulate history seems to prepare the soil for the historical novel which would take strong root in Scotland centuries later in the age of Walter Scott. Elsewhere, as Knox delights in flourishing long transcripts of his own arguments and speeches, the reader is soon wearied by his hectoring egotism and realizes that for this man a three-hour sermon might have been on the short side.

The French Reformer Jean Calvin was one of the major influences on Knox and his Kirk. Calvin's *Institutes* encouraged the Christian to imagine himself dramatically as part of biblical narratives. This is the sort of imagination Knox applies to his own times; the reader of his *History* is at once in the Old Testament and in Scotland where the prophet Knox holds forth. The work is hot-headed, yet eclectically crammed with lengthy contemporary documents and speeches. The author argues the rightness of his manipulation of history. Knox wrote as events unspooled, rather than with much later reflection. Like Caesar, he presents himself in the third person. He is cast as protagonist in a land whose Protestants are threatened by 'faggot, fire, and sword'. As a later student of Knox's prose, Robert Louis Stevenson, put it, Knox 'had a grim reliance in himself, or rather in his mission; if he were not sure that he was a great man, he was at least sure that he was one set apart to do great things'.[20] Knox's *History* deals much with its author's public struggles, but conceals his private life; he says little about his experience of conversion to Protestantism, and records his sorrow over the death of 'his dear bedfellow, Marjory Bowes', his English first wife, in a parenthesis.[21] Centuries later, Virginia Woolf uses a similar device in *To the Lighthouse* to mark the death of her character Prue Ramsay.

One section of Knox's *History* is set out like a dramatic dialogue. Other parts draw on such forms as the medieval *disputatio*. Widely read not just in the Bible but also in Classical and Church sources from Tertullian's *De cultu feminarum* to Plato's *Republic*, Knox writes as an educated man as well as a fiery partisan. He records in detail his conversations with his Catholic adversary and monarch, Mary, Queen of Scots – she speaks little, he a great deal. Though Knox yields not an inch in argument with Mary, 'that Roman harlot', there seems a strange, perhaps sexual chemistry between them. One senses *hauteur* and outrage, but also a note of mockery when, after a long, 'amazed' silence, the young Queen (who was roughly of an age with the teenage second wife whom Knox later married) retorts to the Reformer, ' "Well, then, I perceive that my subjects shall obey you, and not me; and shall do what they list, and not what I command: and so must I be subject to them, and not they to me." '[22]

Knox's *History* is written to prove the rightness of his own cause. It asserts his centrality to his time. Structurally, it is a huge collage. The whole of *The Book of Discipline*, Patrick Hamilton's *Places*, a catechism, a confession and other texts are embedded in it, so that, like the Bible, it seems more a library than a book. It is an anthology of key documents with Knox and the Reformation at their core. Yet, intentionally or not, part of Knox's success as a writer lies in his affording keyhole glimpses of his most harshly detested adversaries so that, as in a novel, the reader may feel their human hurt. Knox writes 'merrily' of the stabbing of the heretic-burner Cardinal Beaton who at his end 'sat down in a chair and cried, "I am a priest; I am a priest: ye will not slay me." ' As a detester of 'immoderate dancing', Knox recounts of Mary, Queen of Scots, that 'Her common talk was, in secret, she saw nothing in Scotland but gravity, which repugned altogether to her nature, for she was brought up in joyousity.'[23]

'Joyousity', a quality relatively rare in literature, is in scant supply in the writings of Reformation Scotland, including Mary's own. Yet if the locally inflected forces of European Reformation spurred Knox to become the father of English prose in Scotland, they also produced a major Latin poet in the person of George Buchanan. Born in 1506 in Killearn, Stirlingshire, Buchanan was taught by John Mair at the Universities of St Andrews and Paris. Buchanan became a professor in Paris for a decade before returning to Scotland. In the late 1530s, to help appease anticlerical sentiments in his kingdom, James V encouraged Buchanan to develop some poems satirizing the Franciscans. The first of these, the 'Somnium' (Dream) begins by imitating the opening stanzas of a poem by William Dunbar. Buchanan's later *Franciscanus* (published in revised form in 1567) became his longest poem. It fizzes with satiric energy as its Franciscan friar reveals how to hoodwink the common people, seduce girls, and go in for the sort of antics Buchanan ascribes to the Franciscan William Lang, energetically conducting an exorcism at Dysart in Fife:

> nunc tollere vultus
> In coelum, nunc figere humi, nunc plangere pectus
> Langius, et sacra templum conspergere lympha . . .

> *One moment bowing to the dirt and beating*
> *His chest, the next his eyeballs rolling round,*
> *Lang goes for broke and hoses holy water*
> *All night . . .*[24]

Because Buchanan wrote largely in Latin, his poetry is frequently sidestepped in a way that distorts the history of Scottish literature, though the increasing availability of translations may stop this happening in future. A master of the international language of his day, he had a Europe-wide reputation. Throughout the Renaissance among all the writers from the British Isles – Shakespeare included – it was Buchanan who enjoyed by far the greatest international admiration. Fleeing Scotland after an accusation of heresy, he later worked in Bordeaux, in Italy, and as a teacher at the University of Coimbra in Portugal, before returning to Scotland in 1561. Buchanan produced verse of sustained energy and variety. Montaigne, whom he had taught at Bordeaux, calls him in his *Essais* 'the great Scottish poet'.[25] The first Scot to write a treatise on poetry, Buchanan had served as a soldier and had been imprisoned by the Inquisition in Portugal. He went on to become Moderator of the Church of Scotland, and served as a tutor to the Catholic Mary, Queen of Scots. For her wedding to the French Dauphin Buchanan wrote a magnificent Latin wedding poem or 'Epithalamium' which includes his celebration of a brave, cultured Scotland and a wish for union between Scotland and France. As this and other works like 'Adventus in Galliam' (Coming to France) show, Buchanan was the most Francophile of all major British poets:

Jejuna miserae tesqua Lusitaniae,
Glebaeque tantum fertiles penuriae,
Valete longum. At tu beata Gallia
Salve, bonarum blanda nutrix artium,
Coelo salubri, fertili frugum solo,
Umbrosa colles pampini molli coma,
Pecorosa saltus, rigua valles fontibus,
Prati virentis picta campos floribus . . .

Badlands of Portugal, bye-bye
For ever, starving crofts whose year-round crop
Is lack of cash. And you, fair France, bonjour!
Bonjour, adoring sponsor of the arts,
Your air's to die for, and your earth's so rich
Vineyards embrace your warm, umbrageous hills,
Cows crowd your meadows, glens gabble with burns,
Broad, open meadows fan out fields of flowers . . .[26]

In Scotland Buchanan tutored Mary's son, James VI; to James he later addresses his Latin prose *Rerum Scoticarum Historia* (*History of Scotland*) (1582); perhaps as a caution to James, Buchanan also wrote the republican-accented 1579 political treatise *De Iure Regni apud Scotos Dialogus* (A Dialogue on the Law of Kingship among the Scots) which defended a theory of popular sovereignty and gave the people the right to get rid of tyrannical queens or kings. An English translation of the *De Iure* was reprinted in Philadelphia shortly before the American Revolution as part of arguments about the nature of liberty; the book was also relished by Donald Dewar at the time of the re-establishment of the Scottish Parliament in 1999. Written by a man who is a republican in that he believes the *res publica* – the common weal – is more important than unquestioned royal authority, the *De Iure* is a product of the Scottish Reformation. It should also be aligned with the Declaration of Arbroath, with histories such as that of Buchanan's teacher John Mair, and with the great poems about Bruce and Wallace which had made Scottish debates about the selection of a monarch popular around the country. The *De Iure* shares a good deal with the democratization of the pan-European 'advice to princes' tradition in *Ane Satyre of the Thrie Estaitis* by Buchanan's reform-minded Catholic acquaintance and fellow poet, Sir David Lyndsay.

Buchanan's wide life experience nourishes not just his political thought but also his verse. Sometimes bawdy and often vitriolic, his poetry is hugely impressive in its range and learned vivacity. Immediately attractive, for instance, is his 'De Equo Elogium' or 'Horse Hymn' which draws in part on the entry for 'equus' in a Renaissance reference book:

Caetera rerum opifex animalia finxit ad usus
Quaeque suos, equus ad cunctos se accommodat unus:
Plaustra trahit, fert clitellas, fert esseda, terram
Vomere proscindit, dominum fert, sive natatu
Flumina, seu fossam saltu, seu vincere cursu
Est salebras opus, aut canibus circundare saltus,
Aut molles glomerare gradus, aut flectere gyros,
Libera seu vacuis ludat lascivia campis.
Quod si bella vocent tremulos vigor acer in artus
It, domino et socias vomit ore et naribus iras,
Vulneribusque offert generosum pectus, et una
Gaudia, moerores sumit ponitque vicissim
Cum domino. Sortem sic officiosus in omnem,
Ut veteres nobis tam certo foedere iunctum
Crediderint mixta coalescere posse figura,
Inque Pelethroniis Centauros edere silvis.

God manufactured every other beast
For just one job. Only the horse
Does everything. He hauls great wagons,
Lugs pack-saddles, draws chariots, ploughs fields,
Carries his master, swimming river-crossings,
Leaping each ditch, traversing stony ground,
Coursing round woods with hounds, slow-trotting, wildly
Galloping back, or cantering for fun
On open grassland. Then, if war demands,
Vigour kicks in, nervous excitement builds
Till horse and master snort together, angry,
Charging into battle, sharing highs
And disappointments, finding, losing each.
The horse is so loyal that the Ancients dreamed

He could be one with humans, could just fuse
Into a mixed horse-man, man-horse – hybrid
Centaurs in the Pelethronian woods.[27]

Energetic in its syntax, this poem celebrates the ability to do many things well – something we often associate with Renaissance culture. Buchanan, born thirteen years before the death of Leonardo, is himself a true 'Renaissance man'. His poetry encompasses stinging epigrams, the magnificent, Scotland-hymning epithalamium for Mary, Queen of Scots and a genial verse letter to one of Queen Elizabeth's English courtiers, as well as the much admired Latin paraphrases of the Hebrew Psalms, which the poet worked on while a prisoner of the Inquisition in Portugal. In his translations from Hebrew, he seems to have been encouraged by the Elgin-born Scottish Latin poet and commentator on the Psalms, Florence Wilson ('Volusenus') (d. c. 1551). Wilson's prose dialogue *De Animi Tranquillitate* (On the Tranquillity of the Soul) (1543) was admired across Europe for its acceptance of passion as well as reason in human nature, not to mention its dream-vision qualities and account of a walk beside the River Lossie near Elgin. Buchanan's Latin Psalms are often arresting; his version of the twenty-third (which usually begins in English 'The Lord is my shepherd') starts, 'Rabid dogs, why waste your time on me?' Probably Buchanan was thinking of his Portuguese Inquisitors. The ups and downs of his career may also allow him to sound a note of vulnerable trepidation, as heard in 'To Henry Darnley, King of Scots'. This short, beautifully cadenced poem was written around the time Buchanan was appointed Principal of St Leonard's College, St Andrews, and before Darnley, husband of Mary, Queen of Scots, was murdered in 1567:

Ad Henricum Scotorum Regem

Caltha suos nusquam vultus a sole reflectit,
    illo oriente patens, illo abeunte latens:
nos quoque pendemus de te, sol noster, ad omnes
    expositi rerum te subeunte vices.

The marigold nowhere turns from the sun.
Opening at dawn, it closes in the dusk.
We too depend on you, our sun. To all
Your turns of fortune we are left exposed.[28]

Whether longing for Paris, denouncing an academic colleague in Portugal, or writing a remarkable elegy for Jean Calvin, Buchanan is, like Dunbar before him, a poet of committed craft and eloquence. In his Calvin elegy, he addresses the radical theologian,

> Astra tenes, propiusque Deo, quem mente colebas,
> Nunc frueris, puroque vides in lumine purum
> Lumen . . .

> . . . *Your home is in the stars.*
> *In heaven you see up close the selfsame God*
> *You saw here with your inner eye, pure light*
> *Housed in pure light.*[29]

True to its subject and to Buchanan's sometimes fiercely Protestant imagination, this poem goes on to catalogue the vices and fates of an array of Popes, from 'No-clemency Clement' to 'crazy Julius'. In the next world, they will all shudder at Calvin's name. Since the Scottish Reformation is often associated with kinds of vernacular language, it may seem ironic that its greatest poet should have written in Latin. Yet Latin, the language of the Catholic Church in which Buchanan had grown up, was as vital to the Reformers as to the rest of Scottish culture at the time. Certainly Buchanan, like his vernacular brethren, was capable of powerful anti-Papal invective. A fine example is his sectarian poem against Pope Julius II:

> Genua cui patrem, genitricem Graecia, partum
> pontus et unda dedit, num bonus esse potes?
> Fallaces Ligures, et mendax Graecia, ponto
> nulla fides. in te singula solus habes.

Daddy a Genoan, Mammy a Greek,
Yer a fushionless son o' the sea.   *no good*
Tallies, Greeks, an the Med are full o lyin cheek.   *Italians*
You, pal, are full o aa three.[30]

The range of Buchanan's achievements, though, shows him to be far more than a cleg-like Protestant epigrammatist. Early in his career he translated Simonides as well as Euripides' *Alcestis* and *Medea* from Greek into Latin. In Reformation Scotland his dramatic writings (with the exception of some Latin material for masques) went unperformed, but in England his *Alcestis* was presented in front of Queen Elizabeth, and the Classically-educated Protestant Queen asked for a repeat performance. Buchanan's two original plays, written in Latin in Bordeaux in the early 1540s, are significant contributions to European (particularly French and Portuguese) drama as well as being the earliest surviving substantial plays authored by a Scot.

Drawing on the Bible, Euripides and Seneca, Buchanan's *Jephthes* and *Baptistes* (first printed in London in 1577) oppose hypocrisy, tyranny and idolatry. Admired by Sir Philip Sidney, their drama is stylized, rhetorical, rather operatic; they were probably written for schoolboys to perform as exercises. Nonetheless, they are emotionally disturbing. Jephtha is tormented to find himself trapped in a vow that necessitates the sacrifice of his daughter, a fate that she eventually and courageously accepts. Preaching and 'crying on the distant ridges of the mountains', John the Baptist moves to his death 'on the road established since the beginning of the world'.[31] Dramas of predestined inevitability and struggling human conscience, these plays' rhetorical power may be sampled in part of a choral speech from *Baptistes*, translated into Scots by Robert Garioch in 1959:

> qualis Aetnaeis vapor e caminis
> saxa convolvit celeri rotatu,
> qualis arentem coquit in favillam
>   flamma Vesevum,
> talis hunc caecus furor ultionis
> cogit in vatem ruere innocentem,
> ut truci nudam male veritatem
>   crimine vexet . . .[32]

> *Just as the vapour-blast frae Aetna's craters*
> *birls huge boulders, rowinin its caldrone,*
> *just as Vesuvius lowes in flaman grieshoch*   blazes; fire
>   *brenning in fury:*   burning
> *sae is yon dirk and deidlie rage for vengeance*
> *garring him on to kill the skaithless prophet*   forcing; harmless
> *and by the bludie wurk to straik the seelie*   strike; blessed
>   *sooth aa in ruins . . .*[33]   truth

For Buchanan, the major Scottish intellectual of his age, poetry was bound up with a passionate concern for mission and education; yet it was also a powerful imaginative act. In its Senecanism, his drama anticipated the Seneca-gorged drama of Elizabethan and Jacobean England. However, towards the end of his life, Buchanan tells us, he was encouraged to move away from the ear-delighting work of poetry to the more soberly educative labours of history. His *Rerum Scoticarum Historia* surveys Scotland's past and present. Although it would go through many editions as a standard, wholeheartedly Protestant school text, it is often unreliable. Like Knox's *History*, it is strong on partisan details when the author's own engagement with the affairs of his age becomes felt. So Buchanan describes how Cardinal Beaton and his associates surround themselves with silks and tapestries at St Andrews Castle while bags of gunpowder are attached to George Wishart's condemned, still-living body. Such details were grist to the Reformation mill.

Buchanan's mother tongue may well have been Gaelic. Surveying Scotland's cultures, he admitted in Latin that the songs of Hebridean Gaelic bards were 'non inconcinne' (not inelegant) but, alluding to more recent Celtic researches, he drew the line at investigating the history of his country's ancient speech:

As for myself, I would rather choose to remain ignorant of the barbarous dialect of the ancient Britons, than unlearn that knowledge of the Latin tongue which I acquired, when a boy, with great labour. I can perceive without regret, the gradual extinction of the ancient Scottish language, and cheerfully allow its harsh sounds to die away, and give place to the more harmonious tones of Latin. For if, in this transmigration into another language, it is necessary that we yield one thing or another, let us pass from rusticity and barbarism, to culture and civilization, and let our choice and judgment, repair the infelicity of our birth.[34]

Reading Buchanan's translated words in an age when Gaelic still survives, while Latin is increasingly suppressed within the Scottish state-education system, we may hear several layers of unintended irony. Many Scottish writers in the eighteenth century would regard English as Buchanan did Latin. Although he did champion popular access to vernacular scripture, Latin was the language of Buchanan's powerful literary imagination and of fellow Scottish poets like the Humanist Thomas Craig (c. 1538–1608), whose Latin prose work on legal theory would later impact on the Scottish Enlightenment. The foremost among a myriad of European Latin poets, Buchanan taught or mentored several of the Scottish Latin poets of the age. Among these was the St Andrews-educated prodigy James (later nicknamed 'the Admirable') Crichton (1560–82) who went on to hymn republican virtue and wrote an arresting Latin poem about his arrival in Venice. Buchanan also taught the Latinist Hercules Rollock (c. 1546–99) who made poems for royal public occasions, and the Latin poet-historian David Hume of Godscroft (1558–c. 1630) who championed a union between Scotland and England. Buchanan is regarded as the greatest European Latinist of his era; yet for most readers now his work can live only through some sort of 'transmigration'. A new selection of his finest poems (in Latin with facing modern English verse versions) was published in Edinburgh in 2006, to celebrate his 500th birthday. An understanding of Buchanan's poetry helps not least in restoring a sense of the richness and spiky complexity of Scottish Reformation writing, with the result that, as Edwin Morgan puts it, 'one further element of the great jigsaw of Scotland falls into place'.[35]

If Knox and Buchanan were Protestant historians of the Scottish Reformation, deeply involved in its events, then their views were countered by the Catholic historian John Leslie, Bishop of Ross (c. 1527–96). Leslie served as Mary, Queen of Scots's chief representative at Queen Elizabeth's English court. His *De Origine, Moribus, et Rebus Gestis Scotorum* was published in Rome in 1578, then translated into Scots by Father James Dalrymple of the Scottish Cloister in Regensburg in 1596 as *The Historie of Scotland*. Unsurprisingly, Leslie's perspective is very different from that of his Protestant counterparts. For him, for instance, Patrick Hamilton, so revered by the Reformers, is the 'Abbat of fferne' who 'venum verie poysonable and deidlye in Germanie had souked out of Luther, and otheris Archheretikis', with the result that 'for his obstinacie and wickednes committed, he is burnte'. Leslie's Cardinal Beaton is 'ane wyse man of a gude courage and stout spirit' who is 'cruellie' killed, 'his claithis not yit on', and 'full of blodie woundes, be [by] cutthrotis hung furth at the windok [window]'. Where the Protestant historians linger on such scenes, Leslie passes over them relatively quickly. He is astonished at the success of 'Knox, and vtheris apes or messenis [dogs] of Calving, vtterlie haueng na lerning'; celebrating Catholic pamphleteers such as Ninian Winzet, he concludes that Catholicism has not been 'excludet be rasoune [by reason] out of Scotland, but schot out be force'. What James Dalrymple translates here simply as 'Scotland' is in Leslie's Latin original 'our Scotland' ('nostra Scotia').[36] One senses in the work of this orthodox Catholic exiled from his native land the indignant trauma of loss.

In Scotland itself, though, history was being written by the victors. A flurry of historiographical works dealing with the country's past and with very recent events may be explained by the Reformers' urgent desire to take ideological control of the past, bonding it to a Presbyterian present. As earlier saints' lives had served as icons for the faithful, so now accounts of the martyrs in Protestant historiography confirmed the Reformed community. Fife historian Robert Lindsay of Pitscottie (c. 1532–85) was a relatively unlearned Protestant sympathizer who did not play a public role like Knox or Buchanan. He sets out in the form of a dramatic dialogue the interrogation of Patrick Hamilton by 'ane blak freir callit Campbell' who steps forward confidently to arraign the heretic:

The Accusar

'Arratick, thow said it was lesum [lawful] to reid the word of god and in spetiall the new Testament.'

So begins 'this cruell act of persecutioun'. Lindsay's *Historie and Cronicles of Scotland*, written in Scots as a continuation of Hector Boece's work, contains many lively details – from the denuding of the Fife woods so that James IV's flagship the *Great Michael* may be built to the performing of Sir David Lyndsay's pageant to welcome Mary, Queen of Scots to St Andrews; the latter drama features an angelic figure in a cloud who presents Her Majesty with the keys of the nation. Though Lindsay of Pitscottie's *Historie* nods to non-Scottish events such as the death of Petrarch, its strength lies in a journalistic nose for a good story. Lindsay's stories might have delighted a medieval as much as a Renaissance audience. So the historian records the interest taken by James IV in a 'munsture' (monster) born during his reign. This is a child with one lower body but two torsos and two heads. 'They' grow up as 'tuo bodyis in ane personage', and become

in schort tyme werie ingeneous and cunning in the art of musick quhairby they could pleay and singe tuo pairtis, the on the tribill [one the treble] the wther the tennour quhilk was werie dulse [sweet] and melodious to heir be the common pepill quho treatit thame wondrous weill. Allso they could speak sindrie and dyuerse langagis, that is to say, Latine, Frinche, Italieans Spanis Dutch Dens [Danish] and Inglische and Earische.

This figure might seem in some ways indicative of the divided polymathic and polylingual Scotland of Lindsay's lifetime. When one of the two bodies dies, the other protests, 'How cane I be merrie that hes my trew marrow as ane deid carieoun wpoun my bak.'[37] That also sounds like a true voice from the often grim Scottish Reformation in which on each side the body of a Church attended to its martyrs and persecutors. Yet Lindsay's bizarre 'munsture' figure, who eventually prays for death, is for him an image of mortality, and so at one with that older Christian note of memento mori that sounds repeatedly even through the work of such a frenetic poet as Dunbar.

On both sides the Reformation in Scotland mixed absolute spiritual convictions with secular political rivalries. It was so bitter because of the smallness of the country where neighbour could turn against neighbour, but also in part because of the vehemence of the rhetoric employed. If Knox, attacking his 'harlot' Queen and others, most spectacularly carried the Scots flyting tradition into English prose, then that tradition burned on in hectic pamphleteering, popular ballads, satirical poems and denunciatory claims of right. So the Catholic polemicist James Tyrie in his *Refutation of ane Ansver Made be Schir Iohne Knox* (Paris, 1573) classes Knox with those 'fals prophetis, heretikis, and seducears of the people quhilkis ar the ministers of Sathan'.[38] For Reformers the Pope was the Antichrist. Catholics, on the other hand, inveighed against Knox and 'his Maister the Deuil', complaining of their imprisonment simply for professing 'the treu and Catholik Religion'.[39] Only from the 1560s was more than one printer active in the whole country, but this written warfare between the two sides went on in print as well as manuscript, sermons as well as spoken debates, verse as well as prose. At least one of the signatories of *The Book of Discipline* was a poet, the fourth Earl of Glencairn, whose mock 'Epistle Direct fra the Holye Armite [Hermit]' draws on the flyting tradition in having its Catholic speaker inveigh against 'Cankcarit corruptars of the Creid'.[40]

In some ways the energies of the flyting tradition had passed into prose. Yet there are still signs that its spirit continued to animate verse with commendable virulence. It could be harnessed to attack theological

or personal enemies. This short poem by Sir Thomas Maitland (1522–
c. 1572) seems purely personal, but has acquired a title which encourages
us to read it as Reforming propaganda:

*Sir Thomas Maitland's Satyr upon Sir Niel Laing who was a Priest
and one of the Pope's Knights about the time of the Reformation*

Canker'd, cursed creature, crabbed, corbit kittle,	*crooked whelp*
Buntin-ars'd, beugle-back'd, bodied like a beetle;	*plump-arsed; crookbacked*
Sarie shitten, shell-padock, ill shapen shit,	*badly; tortoise*
Kid-bearded gennet, all alike great:	*mare*
Fiddle-douped, flindrikin, fart of a man,	*scraggy-bummed; twit*
Wa worth the, wanwordie, wanshapen wran![41]	*[woe on you]; unworthy;*
	misshapen; wren

Maitland came from a poetic family. His courtier brother, Sir Richard
Maitland of Lethington (1496–1586), compiled a famous manuscript
collection of older verse in which Dunbar, who might have applauded
Thomas's 'Satyr', features prominently; Richard Maitland's daughter
Marie developed the family collection, now known as the Maitland
Manuscripts. Richard Maitland's own verse hankers after the pre-
Reformation milieu, and just because Thomas's 'Satyr' savages a Papal
Knight it should not be assumed that he was an admirer of the Reformers.
His tract *The Pretended Conference* (c. 1569) moves Scots prose in the
direction of imaginative writings in its invented conversations between
Reformers. Knox is portrayed speaking 'with ane stur [harsh] and krok-
ing voce' as he describes a new book he has written which argues that
birth alone entitles no man, king or otherwise, to govern.[42] Knox was
infuriated by this piece – unsurprisingly, since the views attributed to
him might have got him executed – but its parody of his self-important,
vigorous preaching style is accurate. A St Andrews student, the early
diarist and autobiographer James Melvill (1556–1614) noted how the
ageing Knox was 'very weak' but when he preached 'was sae active and
vigorus that he was lyk to ding that pulpit in blads [i.e., to smash it],
and fly out of it!'[43]

In full flight many of the Reformers wrote verse, as did their opponents. Across Scotland numerous minor poets 'lay/With paper, pen, and
inke in hand', as Knox's friend Sir William Kirkcaldy put it in his 1571

'Ane Ballat of the Captane of the Castell'.[44] Such poets' works range from the sometimes effortlessly bawdy ballads of Robert Sempill (c. 1530–95) to the zealous writings of John Davidson (1549–1604), whose oeuvre included a now lost play 'playit in Mr Knox presence; wherin, according to Mr Knox doctrine, the Castell of Edinbruche was besiged, takin, and the Captan with an or twa with him hangit in effigie'.[45] Whatever its historical interest, it is hard to find much imaginative excitement in all this verse. The great majority of the popular black-letter broadsides printed by the penurious Robert Lekprevik, who acted as printer to the Reformers in Edinburgh and St Andrews in the 1560s and early 1570s, are of mainly antiquarian interest. With singular exceptions, such as Buchanan's contributions, most of the campaigning verse produced on both sides in the Reformation struggle is tedious stuff. Occasional verbal felicities (as when a Catholic poet terms the Reformed Kirk the 'Deformit Kirk of Scotland') drown in a whirlpool of poetic mediocrity. From time to time a good line surfaces – 'The Subiect now commandis the Prince, and Knox is grown a king' – only to be swept away in the mêlée.[46]

Initially the energies involved in these ideological struggles were substantially those of titled persons and churchmen, such as the elegant Latin poet and clerical polemicist Patrick Adamson (1537–92) who defended episcopacy and was deferential towards the monarchy. But popular vernacular literature was also very much a channel for the controversies of the time. Far more readable than most of the learned polemical prose pamphlets are the *Gude and Godlie Ballatis*. This collection of poems and songs was gathered by three Dundonian brothers, James (d. 1553), John (d. 1556) and Robert (d. c. 1557) Wedderburn. They had all studied at St Andrews University, the educational establishment most closely linked to the Reformation in Scotland. James died in Rouen, banished for his making of Protestant plays which were performed in Dundee but have not survived. One, like Buchanan's *Baptistes*, was about John the Baptist; another was a comedy called *Dionysius the Tyrant*. John Wedderburn met Martin Luther in Wittenberg, and had been a St Andrews contemporary of Patrick Hamilton and George Buchanan. Robert, a priest and scholar, seems to have been with John in Germany where they became familiar with German translations of Latin hymns. The brothers' collection of vernacular religious songs, ballads, hymns, translations, satirical Reforming poems and secular verse appears to have circulated widely in Scotland before it was eventually published in 1567, after their deaths. Eschewing the aureate and arcane, many of the poems exude a plain-spoken confidence:

> God send euerie Preist ane wyfe,
> And euerie Nunne ane man,
> That thay mycht leue that haly lyfe,
> As first the Kirk began.[47]

The Church politics of the collection are unmistakable ('The Paip, that Pagane full of pryde,/ He hes vs blindit lang'), but the didacticism at its best courses with a stylish energy:

With huntis vp, with huntis vp,	
It is now perfite day,	*perfect*
Jesus, our King, is gaine in hunting,	
Quha lykis to speid thay may.	*succeed*
Ane cursit Fox lay hid in Rox,	*rocks*
This lang and mony ane day,	
Deuoring scheip, quhill he mycht creip,	
Nane mycht him schaip away.	*scare*
It did him gude to laip the blude	
Of yung and tender lambis,	*young*
Nane culd he mis, for all was his,	
The yung anis with thair dammis.	
The hunter is Christ, that huntis in haist,	
The hundis ar Peter and Paull,	*hounds*
The Paip is the Fox, Rome is the Rox,	
That rubbis vs on the gall.[48]	

These are preaching poems, songs that draw on conventional imagery of the time, and often on the words of scripture, so that Holy Writ may be disseminated with all the vernacular force of the ballads. Their plainness might eventually become an aesthetic limitation, but it is also their strength. They avoid theological minutiae and concentrate instead on the articulation of central tenets, taking in a wide emotional range from delighted wonder at 'The Conceptioun of Christ' to the grimly democratic levelling power of death:

Thocht thow war neuer of sa greit degre,   *Though*
In riches nor in dignitie,
Remember, man, that thow mon die,   *must*
   And downe sall cum, down ay, down ay.

Thair is na King, nor Empreour,
Duke, nor Lord of greit valure,
Bot he sall faid as lely floure,
   And downe sall cum, downe ay, downe ay.[49]

In its uncluttered emphasis on educating the people in Reformed Christian beliefs, *The Gude and Godlie Ballatis* corresponds to *The Book of Discipline*. Both spell out clearly the Reformers' emphasis on providing direct access to the Word of God and denouncing those who are seen to stand in the way of this. The Genevan order of service introduced by the Church of Scotland in 1560 required a metrical version of the Psalms for congregations to sing. Translations of the Psalms and of biblical passages were made by many Reformation poets across Europe. The first Scottish Psalter appeared in 1564. Most of its versions of Psalms are English and only two Scots, Robert Pont and John Craig, contributed new versions. Homely rather than exalted, this Psalter contains, for instance, the Scotsman William Kethe's famous translation of Psalm 100, 'All people that on earth do dwell, / Sing to the Lord with cheerful voice'. This version had originally been published in Geneva in 1561, though refreshingly (some might say surprisingly) in the Scottish Psalter Kethe's Genevan 'Him serve with fear' has become 'Him serve with mirth'.[50]

The Reformation affected written culture throughout all Scotland, frequently with little mirth. The Protestant *Book of Common Order* was translated into Gaelic by John Carswell (c. 1520–72), and a poem by Athairne MacEoghain, probably dating from around 1560, survives in a 1631 Gaelic translation of Calvin's Catechism. Its opening stanza signals its stern tone:

> Is mairg do-ní uaille as óige,
>   as iasachd deilbhe, a deirc ghlais,
> a cruth séimh, a suidhe aoibhinn,
>   a céibh bhuidhe chaoimhfhinn chais.

> *Woe to the one who takes pride in youth,*
> *in a borrowed form, in a grey eye,*
> *in a graceful figure, in comely face,*
> *in shining, soft, yellow, curling locks.*[51]

Even in denouncing these things, the poet lingers over them. Beyond translations of the Psalms, the pressures of Protestantism led to a plain aesthetic, purged of much of the sort of glorious aureate imagery so treasured by William Dunbar at the start of the century. Instead, it nourished the dissemination of what were considered facts – biblical and historiographical, rational.

It would be wrong, though, to think that Scottish writing in this time had no sense of loveliness. Fact can have its own dignity and beauty. Nor does all the verse written in later sixteenth-century Scotland insist solely on a dour avoidance of such matters as erotic love or non-theological passion. Mary, Queen of Scots, was the subject of formal Latin and Scots praise-poems, epithalamia, welcomes, celebrations by poets Protestant and Catholic, including Buchanan and the beautiful lyricist Alexander Scott (c. 1515–83). A trained Augustinian musician, Scott sounds resounding peals of welcome in the opening of his 'Ane New Yeir Gift to the Quene Mary, quhen scho come first Hame, 1562'. The start of this work carries on something of the aureate tone perfected by the Dunbar who praised the Virgin Mary two or three generations earlier:

WELCUM, illustrat Ladye, and oure Quene!	
Welcum, oure lyone with the Floure-delyce!	*[fleur-de-lys]*
Welcum, oure thrissill with the Lorane grene!	*thistle; Lorraine*
Welcum, oure rubent roiss vpoun the ryce!	*ruby; rose; twig*
Welcum, oure jem and joyfull genetryce!	*[mother]*
Welcum, oure beill of Albion to beir!	*shelter*
Welcum, oure plesand Princes maist of pryce!	
God gif the grace aganis this guid new yeir.[52]	

This poem goes on to speak rather anxiously of 'erronius questionis' and the 'trew Kirk', but Scott was one of a number of Scottish poets who were able to write convincing verse for public events, as well as moving love lyrics that are at once formally decorous and inhabited by a developing sense of revealed personal voice.

Poetry was not only the preserve of professors like Buchanan or of popular Reforming balladeers. It remained a vital part of court life, and the arrival of Mary brought to the Scottish throne a monarch who was, like several of her Stewart predecessors, both a poet and a friend of poets. In France she had known Ronsard; in Scotland poems and poets circulated round her. A number of works have been credited to Mary; some, such as the beautiful Latin 'O Domine Deus!', said to have been composed on the morning of her execution in 1587, are very dubious attributions, but a number of French sonnets may be her work. Of these, perhaps the most complexly moving is the ninth sonnet addressed to James Bothwell. Though they are at times technically uneasy, these sonnets, translated anonymously into Scots, speak of both physical and emotional damage:

> Pour luy aussi ie iette mainte larme.
> Premier quand il se fist de ce corps possesseur,
> Duquel alors il n'auoit pas le coeur.

> *For him also I powrit out mony teiris,*
> *First quhen he maid himself possessor of this body,*
> *Of the quhilk then he had not the hart.*[53]   which

That last line may be connected to a rumour that Bothwell had raped Mary, though the two of them married in a Protestant service just three months after Mary's husband, Darnley, was murdered. This led George Buchanan to turn decidedly against the Mary he had praised; through his prose writings, Buchanan played a part in her eventual downfall.

Born at Linlithgow in 1542 and sent to France when she was aged five, Mary grew up there as a Catholic. Before his premature death, she married the French Dauphin. Mary came back to Scotland in 1561 but spent less than a decade there. She fled to England after the Scottish Protestant lords rebelled against her, and was imprisoned by Queen Elizabeth for nineteen years prior to her execution in 1587. Exotic, beautiful, doomed, Catholic, and unlucky in love, the regnant yet apparently abject Mary remains the most famous Scottish woman who has ever lived. She became an icon for a country in which women were often downtrodden, not least by the trumpet-blasting Reformers who so vigorously opposed Mariolatry. Sometimes considered foolish, her conversations as recorded by Knox and others suggest that Mary in her twenties was a shrewd, strong-spirited woman. As Queen she had access to educational opportunities denied to most of her sex, and at Holyrood Palace in Edinburgh she had a library of European sophistication. It included such books as *Dante en Italien* (mentioned in 1573, this is the first recorded copy of Dante in Scotland) and other Italian poets, as well as such works as a French version of *The Travels of Marco Polo*.[54]

At Mary's court sonnets began to circulate. While French seems to have been the language in which she was most fluent, Mary knew (and wrote) Latin as well as Italian and, later, Scots. She was reviled by the stern Knox as a lover of dancing and light pleasures, but the poems attributed to her are downcast in tone. This fact might be linked to her treatment by the Reformers and her tragic fate, but it predates her arrival in Scotland. Representative is 'En mon triste et doux chant' (In my sweet and sad song), which has been dated to 1560 and probably relates to the death of Mary's first husband, the Dauphin. Its fourth stanza reads,

> Ce qui m'estoit plaisant
> Ores m'est peine dure;
> Le jour le plus luisant
> M'est nuit noire et obscure,
> Et n'est rien si exquis,
> Qui de moy soit requis.
>
> *He who was my delight*
> *Now is my hard pain*
> *The brightest day*
> *Is dark night to me;*
> *There is no fine thing*
> *Which I desire now.*[55]

At once personal and rhetorical, Mary's articulation of female desire is remarkable throughout her work and arresting for its time. In the seventh sonnet to Bothwell, which asserts her independent-mindedness in the face of male assumptions ('Vous me pensez femme sans jugement' ('You imagine me a woman without iugement')) the lover, as Sarah Dunnigan puts it, 'desires not to be effaced into female archetype'.[56] Mary's supposed last poems, as published by John Leslie in Paris in 1574, are religious. Yet while their speaker may seek 'la ioye infinie' ('infinite joy') rather than that 'joyousity' in which (according to Knox)

Mary was brought up, the tone is deeply abject as the speaker constructs a self beyond physical desire:

> Je ne suis fors qu'un corps priue de cueur
> vn ombre vayn vn obiect de malheur
> Qui n'a plus rien que de mourir enuie

> *I am but a body whose heart's torn away,*
> *A vain shadow, an object of misery*
> *Who has nothing left but death-in-life.*[57]

The plaintive tones of this verse sound far, far removed from the fulminations of Knox, but just as Mary's loyalties may have been complexly divided at times, so there are instances where several Scottish Reformation poets' divided allegiances can be sensed in their verse, giving it at times a rescuing power. One of Cardinal Beaton's murderers, Knox's old ally and later adversary the pro-Protestant William Kirkcaldy, had once resisted attempts to compel him to attend Mass during his imprisonment in Mont St-Michel. Nonetheless, he was loyal to Mary as his sovereign, and held Edinburgh Castle on her behalf for three years after she had been imprisoned in England. When the castle fell to a combined English and Scottish force, Kirkcaldy was hanged for his loyalty. His poem 'Ane Ballat of the Captane of the Castell', speaks of 'our Congregatione', indicating his Protestant adherence, yet it also rounds indignantly on Mary's persecutors:

These wicked vaine venerianis,	*profligates*
Proud poysoned Pharisianes	
With thair blind guydis but grace,	*without*
Hes caused the puire cuntrie	
Assist vnto thair traitorie,	
Thair prince for to displace:	
For teine I can not testifie	*grief*
How wrangouslie they wrocht,	
When thai thair Prince so pitiouslie	
In prisone strong had brocht,	
Abused hir, accused hir	
With serpent wordis fell	
Of schavelis and rebellis,	*tonsured rogues*
Like hiddeous houndes of hell.[58]	

Kirkcaldy's use of what seems a masculine form 'Prince' reinforces his sense that Mary is as rightful a monarch as any man, and flies in the face of his former friend's attack on 'the monstrous regiment of women'. Kirkcaldy's melancholy at the state of the times allies this Protestant writer with the Catholic Richard Maitland who complains in his 'Satire on the Age' that 'All mirriness is worne away' thanks to 'kirkmen cled lyk men of weir [war]'.[59] Before the start of Mary's reign the Reformer Robert Wedderburn, using 'domestic scottis langage, maist intelligibil for the vlgare pepil', had set forth in *The Complaynt of Scotland* (c. 1550) a vision of Dame Scotia as a woman making a 'melancolius cheir . . . vitht mony salt teyris distillant doune fra hyr piteous ene [eyes]'.[60] This much abused lady urges patriotism against the English in her address to the three estates. Drawing on the French of Alain Chartier's *Quadrilogue Invectif* (1422), the enthusiastic, hyperdetailed, often Latinate allegory of *The Complaynt* is arguably the first sustained imaginative achievement in Scots prose. Yet its image of the sad Dame Scotia in some ways prefigures Mary, Queen of Scots, 'the margareit ande perle of princessis' to whom the work is dedicated. This does not seem to be Wedderburn's aim – he delights instead in encyclopedically listing flowers, animal cries and all sorts of quirky acoustic effects – but the weeping woman who shows that 'al realmis that ar diuidit vitht in them selfis be discentione and contentione, sal be left desolat' emblematizes an important aspect of sixteenth-century Scotland where a sometimes fugitive sadness accompanies the Reformers' zealous energy.[61]

The royal welcoming poem of Alexander Scott (c. 1515–83), perhaps the finest Scots-language poet of Mary's reign, regretfully coils into a theological account, but Scott had inherited something of Dunbar's formal virtuosity. He produced a scornful verse attack on 'wantoun Wemen'. His account of 'the Justing [Jousting] and Debait vp at the Drum betuix Wa. Adamsone and Johine Sym' is a romping poem in the 'Christis Kirk on the Grene' stanza and is written in a mock-jousting tradition developed by Dunbar and Lyndsay. Like Dunbar before him and William Montgomerie after him, Scott held a salaried court position as a poet laureate; no such appointment yet existed in England. Sophisticated and metrically adept, he is an appropriate voice for Mary's reign. Scott's delight in exploiting very different poetic forms propels his work in several directions. Yet his more purely lyric pieces are suffused with a grief that seems to exceed the mere conventions of courtly love and Renaissance erotic lyrics:

> To luve unluvit it is ane pain:
> For sho that is my sovereign,
> Some wanton man so he has set her,
> That I can get no luve again,
> Bot breaks my heart, and nocht the better.[62]

Scott's true métier was erotic sadness.[63] Very little is known of his life, though there is a story that his wife left him. An early poem is his lament for Robert Erskine, killed in battle in 1547. Most of his love poems have a note of lamentation, lyrically alert to the musical and emotional possibilities of 'panis smart'.[64] His poems predominate in the love lyrics section of the famous 1568 Bannatyne Manuscript and he is probably the finest love poet to write in Scots before Robert Burns two centuries later.

Mary's 'regiment' may have encouraged a taste for a poetry of courtly love, so different in ethos and acoustic from the aesthetics of the Reformers. In 1575 John Rolland's *The Court of Venus* was published in Edinburgh. Rolland had been part of the circle of court poets gathered around James V. His *Court of Venus* was written in 1560, but its Troubadour-influenced presentation of eroticism and royalty may have appealed to some in an Edinburgh which had known Mary, Queen of Scots. In part an imitation of Gavin Douglas's *The Palice of Honour*, Rolland's poem is addressed 'to Nobill men and gude' and is urged by its author to 'fle the sect of Rurall folke and rude'. Written in the same year as *The Book of Discipline*, when many Reformers sought to address and convert the whole population, Rolland's rather woodenly rhymed allegory harks back to the courtly rhetoric of an earlier age. Nevertheless, there are also ways in which it looks forward. One of its interpolated poems is of considerable metrical interest, as may be heard in the opening stanza:

> Venvs, the well of worthynes,
> Ground of all grace, and greit Goddes,
> Of Quenis Quene, and eik princes,
> > That now dois ring.
> > To our louit condigne Maistres,
> Nemesis constitute but les,
> Our Shiref in that part expres,
> > Dewlie greeting.[65]

This hints at how the Troubadour-derived stanza form which will evolve within a century into 'Standard Habbie' (later called by some the 'Burns Stanza') is establishing itself in Reformation Scotland. Used occasionally in Scotland since the fifteenth century, the stanza form which Burns would make his own is not yet culturally dominant. Rolland's stanza is not a Habbie, but the omission of lines 6 and 7 would produce the Habbie form. Though it is usually very much associated with popular (often rural) vernacular culture, this stanza's origins lie in a high, courtly style, as both T. F. Henderson and Douglas Dunn pointed out in later centuries.[66]

The powerful tone of erotic lament sustained by Mary Stewart in French and by Alexander Scott in Scots is matched in Gaelic by Marion Campbell (fl. 1570) in her 'Cumha Ghriogair MhicGhriogair Ghlinn Sréith' ('Lament for MacGregor of Glenstrae'). Where Mary Stewart and Alexander Scott produce lyrics purged of precise names and events, Mrs MacGregor of Glenstrae is very particular about the fate she wishes for the Campbells who have beheaded her husband. He met his death at Balloch Castle, Taymouth, in 1570 when he failed in his struggle to preserve his clan's independence. His widow's poem combines elements of classic bardic syllabic verse with the concreteness and attention to place typical of Gaelic folksong.

> Chuirinn Cailean Liath fo ghlasaibh,
> Is Donnchadh Dubh an làimh;
> Is gach Caimbeulach th' ann am Bealach
> Gu giùlan nan glas-làmh.

> *White Colin I would lock in jail,*   [Colin Campbell of Glenorchy]
> *Black Duncan I'd arrest;*   [eldest son of Colin Campbell]
> *and every Campbell now in Balloch*
> *I'd padlock by the wrist.*

The poem gains its impact from a sense of the speaker's powerlessness, and the powerlessness of the fatherless baby son to whom the lament is addressed. Yet, however personally detailed, it is also a potent piece of rhetorical construction. Veering in a single stanza from the soaring of a lark to the ground-level of a plummeted stone, it articulates the extremities and compulsions of grief. Words and phrases are obsessively repeated, and the poem ends on a crooned note that is at once angry, tender and hopelessly chastened.

Ba hu, ba hu, àsrain bhig,
  Cha'n 'eil thu fhathast ach tlàth:
Is eagal leam nach tig an latha
  Gun dìol thu t'athair gu bràth.

O lullaby my little child
  you are yet but small:
I fear the day will never come
  when you'll destroy them all.[67]

Ironically but predictably, just as Gaelic verse was beginning to enter its great age of song, and shortly before the production of such sophisticated, Troubadour-influenced Gaelic love lyrics as Niall mór MacMhuirich's 'Soraidh slán don oidhche a-réir' ('Farewell for ever to last night'), there are signs of continuing Lowland scorn of Gaels and their culture. The sixteenth century saw the gathering-up of earlier Scots verse in several important manuscript collections, the Scots counterparts of the Gaelic *Book of the Dean of Lismore* (1512–26). These include the Asloan Manuscript (1515), the Maitland Manuscripts and, most importantly, the Bannatyne Manuscript begun by the Edinburgh merchant George Bannatyne in 1568. It is as if in the midst of ideological and other convulsions lovers of poetry desired to preserve what was best in the vernacular verse heritage of an older, Catholic Scotland now reviled by some of the loudest voices in the community. 'Writtin in Tyme of Pest [Plague]', the Bannatyne Manuscript snatches poems literally from the jaws of death. But these Scots-language collections do not include any work in Gaelic. It would be almost two centuries before Lowland Scots began to take a substantial literary interest in transcribing Gaelic poetry. Instead, in the Bannatyne Manuscript among a treasure trove of earlier work including poems by Dunbar, Henryson and their contemporaries, we find one of the funniest and most characteristically prejudiced Lowland poems ridiculing Highland life. In 'How the first Helandman of god was maid of Ane hors turd in argylle as is said' not only is the Highlander made of shit, but his first words to his Creator are 'I will doun in the lawland lord/ and thair steill a kow'. He then goes on to appropriate God's knife. The characteristic sound emitted by the Highlander in this short, lively poem is the sub-verbal 'Humff', but his speeches also have a provocative exclamatory power, and he gets the self-condemning last word in the concluding couplet:

Vmff qwod the helandman & swere be yon kirk   *[I swear by yon Kirk]*
Sa lang as I may geir gett to steill / will I nevir wirk.[68]   *things*

This poem obviously appealed to Lowland taste enough for George Bannatyne to collect it in his 'maist godlie, mirrie and lustie Rapsodie' of work 'maide by sundrie learned Scots poets'. In an age where there seems to have been some Scots–Gaelic bilingualism in areas like Perthshire, its inclusion indicates something of the continuing perceived gulf between Highland and Lowland culture. This seems ironic when Gaelic, Scots, Latin and English-language poets were all drawing, for instance, both on the convulsive torsions of the Reformation and on aspects of older Troubadour-derived lyric. However, inter-clan strife and Catholicism which persisted in the Highlands may have made that area seem all the more remote from the centralizing powers of Lowland Scotland.

Born in 1566, King James VI may have had little interest in Gaelic, but he was certainly devoted to poetry. Descended from the author of *The Kingis Quair*, James came from a family of poets whose number included both his grandfather and his mother, Mary. Poets hymned his arrival. In his Latin 'Genethliacon Jacobi Sexti Regis Scotorum' ('Birth-Ode of James VI, King of Scots'), George Buchanan expressed the hope that

> Iam neque Saxonidae Scotos, nec Saxona Scotus
> Intestus premet, & cognato sanguine ferrum
> Polluet . . .
>
> *Now neither shall the Saxon's sons the Scot*
> *Nor hostile Scot the Saxon shall oppress*
> *And stain with kindred blood the deadly steel . . .*[69]

When the Scottish and English Crowns were united in 1603, with James becoming the monarch of both countries in Great Britain, these hopes were in a sense fulfilled. However, James the writer-king was far more a Scottish than a British phenomenon. Most of his published works date from his time in Scotland where he was crowned as James VI in 1567. While he grew to maturity during conflicts between Kirk and Crown, he encouraged a group of 'sacred brethren' to develop around him. Some of these were the poets later twentieth-century scholars termed the 'Castalian Band' – the name comes from a Latin-derived term used in one of the teenage King's sonnets but does not seem to have been used by the poets themselves.[70] Like Buchanan, many of the poets who addressed the King from his own circle and beyond wrote in Latin. Even when they did not, their work was often underpinned by Classical tradition, as is evident in John Burel's 1590s Scots translation of an early twelfth-century Latin Ovidian verse drama about rape, *Pamphilus speakand of Luve*.

Given the centrality of Latin to the literature of the age, it is unsurprising that even the group of vernacular poets around King James VI was given a Classical name and emblem by later commentators. The Castalian Spring on Mount Parnassus, sacred to the Classical Muses, furnished an appropriate emblem for this companionable group of what one of them called 'Poets laureat'. This phrase was used by John Stewart of Baldynneis in Perthshire in his sonnet written 'At Command of his Maiestie in Praise of the Art of Poesie'. Born to James V's mistress, Stewart of Baldynneis (c. 1550–1605) was among the senior poets of James VI's court. Though constantly deferring to the talent of his young master, he helped set the tone of court verse in his admiration of poets who were 'laureat scholers' of a 'leirnit muse'.

Highly educated, Stewart of Baldynneis wrote poetry of assurance and metrical experiment, often for court events. His work shows a taste for nature in the guise of 'floras tapestreis', and a genuine love of poetry itself, even if for its makers 'perfume of candill is thair greatest gaine'.[71] Usually Stewart's own fluent verse lacks the power to be verbally arresting, but when he has the assistance of a greater text, he can rise impressively. His overlong 'Ane Schersing [Searching] ovt of Trew Felicitie' is a spiritual journey poem which expresses admiration for Sir David Lyndsay's work. It contains fine versifications of scriptural passages, most notably Christ's beatitudes. Stewart's most assured achievement, fuelled by his learning and spurring his writerly facility, is his Scots abridgement made from French versions of Ariosto's early sixteenth-century chivalrous epic, *Orlando Furioso*. Simplifying the Italian poet's 'moir copius' poem and drawing on a linguistic arsenal built up by earlier Scottish poets, Stewart is at his best in the eleventh and longest of his twelve cantos. There he portrays heroic rage and inveighs against 'crewall fortoune' who 'guid desert in to the dust dings doune'. A shorter passage about swordplay from the third canto illustrates Stewart's gift for verbal choreography:

Quhyls hiche, Quhyls low, The skelping sourds did bend,	*Sometimes high; hitting*
Quhyls thay rebat, And quhyls thay scharplie schair,	*rebound; sheer*
As quhan Vulcanus dois his force extend	*when; does*
Vith hammer flasting fyrflacht in the air,	*flashing like lightning*
Vp hich to Iowe making the thunder rair,	*Jove; roar*
So stronglie strak the steitlie chiftans stout,	*struck*
Quhyls schort, Quhyls long, And quhyls thay seime to spair,	*seem*
Quhyls thay auance, And quhyls thay lychtlie lout,	*advance; bow*
Quhyls couerit close, And quhyls thay stretche tham out,	*hidden*
Quhyls heir, Quhyls thair, Thay skip from part to part,	
Quhyls stif thay stog, And quhyls thay bent about	*thrust*
To schaw tham maisters of the fensing art.[72]	

One of Stewart of Baldynneis's more experimental poems acknowledges 'guid Rob steine'. This seems to have been James VI's nickname for Alexander Montgomerie (c. 1555–98), an Ayrshire poet who travelled widely in Europe on the King's behalf, and was one of the poets associated with the court until he was outlawed in 1597 for his part in a Catholic plot. Impressive in his formal and thematic range, Montgomerie was the most metrically accomplished of these court poets. Grounded in older Scottish forms, he wrote a flyting with a fellow poet called Polwart, though the latter, mocking Montgomerie's Highland links, is the one who tends to go for the jugular. Montgomerie's ear seems more attuned to almost plangent circulations of sound than to scurrility when he opens his attack with

> Polwart, yee peip like a mouse amongst thornes;
> Na cunning yee keepe; Polwart, yee peip;
> Ye look like a sheipe and yee had twa hornes:
> Polwart, ye peipe like a mouse amongst thornes.[73]

This Catholic poet's deepest concern is with kinds of rather Baroque musicality. His superb ear made him the leading poet of James's Scottish court. His long allegorical poem *The Cherrie and the Slae* moves from an encounter with Cupid to the need to choose between Catholicism (the cherry) and Protestantism (the sloe). Formally, the poem is written in the elaborately woven fourteen-line stanza that would come to bear Montgomerie's name. It takes 113 such stanzas before the speaker eats his cherry, and the poem is overlong for most modern readers. Yet its

individual sections manifest a remarkable concern with word music, and
with the technicalities of sound:

Through routing of the river rang	*roaring*
The roches, sounding like a sang,	*rocks*
Where descant did abound.	
With treble, tenor, counter, meene,	*intermediate part*
An echo blew a basse between	
In diapason sound,	*musical harmony*
Set with the C-sol-fa-uth cleife	*[staff notation]*
With long and large at list,	*at one's pleasure*
With quaver, crotchet, semi-breife	
And not a minim mist;	
Compleetly and sweetly,	
She firdound flat and sharp,	*warbled*
Than Muses, which uses	
To pin Apollos harpe.[74]	*strike*

Montgomerie's accomplished sonnets sometimes echo the English
sonneteer Thomas Wyatt. They can achieve a teasing lightness, as when
his mistress asks the speaker in a dream, ' "Art ye on sleip," quod sche,
"o fy for schame! / Haue ye nocht tauld that luifaris takis no rest?" ' Yet
as a sonneteer he can also write ringingly, as when he begins, 'The royall
palice of the heichest hewin [heaven], / the staitlie fornace of the sterrie
round . . .'[75] Though court and ecclesiastical politics sometimes spun
poets far beyond the King's orbit, there was clearly a courtly community
of skilled and educated writers able to draw both on older rhetorical
models and on the new rhetorical codes of post-Petrarchan Renaissance
culture. As a group these poets conversed both in person and in their
verse. 'My best belouit brother of the band' begins the first of Montgomerie's series of sonnets to Robert Hudson, a northern English
musician at the Scottish court; 'My best belovit brother of the craft, / God
if ye knew the stait that I am in!' opens a sonnet 'To Alexander Montgomerie' by his friend Hew Barclay, a fellow Catholic exiled to the sticks:

If ye bot saw me in this winter win	*wind*
With old bogogers hotching on a sped,	*leggings; jumping; spade*
Draiglit in dirt, whylis wat evin to the skin . . .[76]	*bedraggled; wet*

Playful, sometimes virtuosic in manner, these poets were and sought to be a Scottish literary powerhouse. At their height in the mid-1580s, they kept Scotland in touch with modern European high culture through such translations as Stewart of Baldynneis's *Roland Furious*, Thomas Hudson's version of the French Huguenot poet Du Bartas's *Historie of Judith* (1584), James VI's 'The Uranie, or Heavenly Muse' (more Du Bartas) and the 1587 translations of Petrarch's *Trionfi* by William Fowler (1560–1612). In 1587 the King, who not only translated works by Du Bartas but had his own verse translated by him, brought the French poet to Scotland. The first translation of Du Bartas's work into another modern language had been published in Edinburgh in parallel text in 1584 as part of James's *The Essayes of a Prentise, in the Divine Art of Poesie*; James took Du Bartas to St Andrews University, where he enjoyed talking with the staff and partaking of 'a banquet of wat and dry confectiones, with all sortes of wyne'.[77] As part of their own cultural feast, all the members of the supposed 'Castalian Band' practised that most Renaissance of forms, the sonnet. Sonnets had been written in England in the earlier sixteenth century by Wyatt and Surrey, but the French use of the sonnet appears to have been more influential in Scotland where a distinctive sonnet shape evolved. The earliest datable example of this was published in 1584. The form has the rhyme scheme *ababbcbccdcdee*, so that, as James Craigie put it, 'they retained the five rhymes of the Petrarchan sonnet, but arranged them differently.'[78] This was also the form taken up in England by Edmund Spenser.

For the last ruler to sit on an independent Scottish throne, poetry was a ruling passion. To excel as an author demonstrated his royal authority. In 1586 an English agent reported about James VI to the London government:

Generally hee seemeth desirous of peace, as appeareth by his disposition and exercises – viz.: 1. His great delight in hunting. 2. His private delight in enditing poesies, &c. In one or both of these commonly hee spendeth the day, when hee hath no publique thing to doe.[79]

Two years earlier James had published his *Essayes of a Prentise*, which contained, as well as his first Du Bartas translation, several sonnets (on the seasons and other topics), a long poem, *Phoenix*, a translation of Psalm CIV, and 'The Reulis and Cautelis to be Observit and eschewit in Scottis Poesie'. This last is the earliest treatise on Scottish vernacular poetry; its length is comparable with the little Latin treatise on verse written by James's mentor George Buchanan. A thoroughly schooled lover of 'Rhetorique', James knew and admired Horace's *Ars Poetica* and other poets' manuals of their art. A catalogue of the well-read young King's 600-volume library survives. It includes such works as Seneca's tragedies (donated by Buchanan) and Buchanan's *De Iure Regni* (detested by James). As a teenage versifier, James doffs his crown to Virgil, Demosthenes and Du Bartas, but also to 'Dauid Lindsay' in 'His *Papingo*'.[80] James's treatise on poetry draws examples from Montgomerie and other Scottish poets as it sets out several kinds of verse such as sonnets – useful 'for compendious praysing of any bukes, or the authouris thairof' – and irregular '*Tumbling* verse' (James's own term for flyting).[81] The King champions 'Inuentioun' – originality – and warns his readers to avoid political 'materis of commoun weill' as 'to[o] graue materis, for a Poet to mell in'.[82]

James took the lead in his circle of court poets. He gave them rules, named poetic forms, and even drafted a 1588 court masque. Aspects of court life, not least the King's homosexual affair with his French kinsman Esme Stuart d'Aubigny, horrified the Reformers. James's 'metaphoricall invention', *Phoenix* is a loving tribute to his exotic friend, written by one too used to 'this countrey cold,/ Which not but hills, and darknes ay dois beare'.[83] Still, James's translation of a Psalm in his first book was of a piece with the Reformers' wish for vernacular scriptures, and he would later have many more such versions made. His band of court poets might just have included women as well as men. To Christian Lyndesay is attributed an accomplished sonnet addressed to Robert Hudson, accusing him of disloyalty to Alexander Montgomerie ('Thoght not bot kyndnes he did at the[e] craiv / He finds thy friendship as it rypis is rotten').[84] This is Lyndesay's only attributable poem, and it may be that 'she' is simply a persona invented by another poet in an environment that relished courtly games and literary impersonations. Whether or not she was a flesh-and-blood female, this Lyndesay was regarded as not quite one of the lads of the 'Castalian Band'. A sonnet to Robert Hudson by Montgomerie himself treasures the 'daffing' (fooling about) of the group, and insolently delegates more sober stuff to Lyndesay: 'Quhen we ar dead, that all our dayis bot daffis,/ Let Christian Lyndesay wryt our epitaphis.'[85]

Though very few poems by women associated with James's circle survive, the superb calligraphy of the Edinburgh Frenchwoman Esther Inglis (1571–1624) is redolent of the rich Renaissance culture of the age, while a sonnet attributed by Sarah Dunnigan to Elizabeth Douglas, Countess of Erroll (fl. 1585), sums up the wish on the part of the King's Classically-alert poets to develop a vernacular literary culture of European eminence. It prefaces 'her friend' William Fowler's translations of *The Triumphs of Petrarke* (1587):

> The glorious greiks dois praise thair HOMERS quill,
> And citeis sevin dois strywe quhair he was borne;
> The Latins dois of Virgill vant at will,
> And Sulmo thinks her Ouid dois adorne;
> The Spanzoll laughs (sawe Lucan) all to scorne,
> And France for RONSARD stands and settis him owt;
> The better sort for BARTAS blawis the horne,
> And Ingland thinks thair SURRYE first but dout.
> To praise thair owen these countreis gois about:
> Italians lykes PETRARCHAS noble grace,
> Who well deserwis first place amangs that rout,
> Bot FOULAR, thow dois now thame all deface,
>   No vanting grece nor Romane now will strywe;
>   Thay all do yeild Sen foular doith arrywe.[86]

Elizabeth Douglas comfortably displays her learning. James VI, fluent in Italian, joins her in praising Petrarch's 'sugred style' and several other 'Castalians' add their own sonnets to preface Fowler's book.[87] Sadly, its workmanlike fourteen-syllable iambic couplets never quite live up to this hype.

From a prosperous Edinburgh family, William Fowler studied at St Andrews University, then in Paris, where he is said to have been beaten up as a Protestant. After serving for a time as an English agent, he joined the Scottish court. Fowler rose to become Secretary to James VI's Danish wife, Queen Anne, and moved to London with the court in 1603. This poet began his published literary career in 1581 as a sometimes lively Protestant pamphleteer. He opposed the Parisian Scot John Hamilton who, acting along with another French-based Scot, John Hay, sought to trigger a Scottish Counter-Reformation by means of Scots vernacular tracts. Fowler complains that Hamilton (whose tract has not survived) 'brags bosts and threatnis, that I sal be the last protestant, that euer sal lycht a candil in Paris'.[88] Fowler went on to make a late sixteenth-century translation of Machiavelli's *Il Principe* before taking an interest in the fashioning of James VI's own kingly treatise, the *Basilicon Doron* (1599).

Proud of his writerly activities, Fowler wrote a list of 'My Works', which is probably Scotland's first literary CV. He is at his best as a sonneteer, though nothing quite matches the Italianate splendour of the title he gave his sonnet sequence: *The Tarantula of Love*. Fowler could sculpt fine individual lines, but seldom first-rate poems. The sea excites his imagination. A religious sonnet opens, 'Lord quha did marche vpon the stormye sees' and in the sonnet sometimes given the title 'In Orknay' he writes 'Upon the utmost corners of the warld' about 'seing roring seis from roks rebound'.[89] The rhotacism of a Scots accent gives that line extra power. Fowler can make good use of northern locutions like 'firthe', but his language is generally of a piece with some of James's other court poets in signalling for the first time in Scotland a confident handling of English verse, albeit with Scots spellings.

Knox fathered English prose in Scotland. A thousand years after the earliest Scottish poems, the poetry of James's court marks the dawning of English verse. Eventually, English would take over from Latin as Scotland's international language. Were it not for the amazing riches of the poetry written in England during this period by Spenser, Shakespeare, Marlowe and others, the 'Castalians' would have received more attention. With the partial exceptions of Montgomerie and Alexander Scott (whose work spans the reigns of Mary and James VI), they have been regarded as figures of more historical than literary interest. Yet their legacies are to all poets who use English in Scotland. In their own day their literary grouping was more than the sum of its parts. When that day had passed, they left a sustaining Scottish inheritance to William Fowler's nephew, William Drummond of Hawthornden. Although the poets in the King's circle often had their works printed in Edinburgh by Thomas Vautrollier and Robert Waldegrave, it is in Drummond's manuscript collection that many of their poems survive.

There was a marked growth in Scottish publishing in the seventeenth century, but relatively few books were printed in Scotland before 1600. A good number of the sonnets of the time may have been lost. Only one in Scots is attributed to the impressive Latin, Greek and French poet and poetic theorist Mark Alexander Boyd (1563–1601), but that one has kept his reputation bright. An Ayrshireman, Boyd studied law in several French and Italian universities as well as fighting in the French civil war army of Henry III. This Scottish poet wrote Ovidian Latin verse published in the early 1590s, as well as an unfinished treatise on the education of a poet. As soon as he learns to read, Boyd's 'poeta' must read Ovid, and before puberty he should have mastered most of Latin and Greek literature. What appears to be Boyd's sole vernacular poem, sometimes called 'Venus and Cupid', is simultaneously learned, homely and rich in erotic disturbance. It is probably the finest Scottish Renaissance sonnet.

Frae bank to bank, frae wood to wood I rin   *run*
Owrhailit with my feeble fantasie,   *overwhelmed*
Like til a leaf that fallis from a tree,
Or til a reed owrblawin with the wind.
Twa gods guides me: the ane of them is blin,   *blind*
Yea, and a bairn brocht up in vanitie;
The nixt a wife ingenerit of the sea
And lichter nor a dauphin with her fin.   *lighter than; dolphin*

Unhappie is the man for evermair
That tills the sand and sawis in the air;
But twice unhappier is he, I lairn,
That feedis in his hairt a mad desire,
And follows on a woman throu the fire,
Led by a blin, and teachit by a bairn.[90]

Like many writers from Duns Scotus to Muriel Spark, the Latinist Boyd is an example of the 'wandering Scot' whose distinguished contributions to Scottish literature are made substantially from outside the country.

It should not be assumed, though, that the court in this period was the only source of remarkable verse. One of the most beautiful works of James VI's reign was penned by a poet who wrote in Scots English and had only a brief connection with court life. Probably educated at St Andrews and Paris, Alexander Hume (c. 1556–1609) came from a well-connected Border family. He trained in the law, but disliked that profession. His predicament (he 'partely spitted bloud') and the encouragement of the King led him to spend some time as a courtier. Hume, though, had little taste for what in Scotland's first vernacular Horatian epistle he called 'The purpos vaine, the feckless conference, / Th' infor-mall reasons, and impertinent / Of courtiours'.[91] So, while several promi-nent members of his family remained Catholics, he went on to leave court life and become a Church of Scotland minister.

Hume's parish was at Logie in Stirlingshire. Though there are records in his presbytery of men who profane the Sabbath by 'thair playis' and by piping and dancing, the poet appears not to have been a fiercely repressive Calvinist.[92] His prose works, such as the beautiful *A Treatise of the Felicitie of the Life to Come* (1594), confirm English as the pre-eminent language of Scottish prose. The title of Hume's *Treatise* may make it appear yet another rock on the great stony cairn of Reformation tracts, but the work has its own aesthetic appeal. This is strongest in the section called 'A Rehearsall of the Pleasures which we shall inioy in the World to Come'. These pleasures are many, and Hume asks his readers if it is not indeed pleasant

to beholde from the top of an high mountaine, in the time of Sommer, or of Harvest, while the ayre is cleare and purified, the noble & faire Cities adjacent about, the green hilles and dales, the faire woods and forests, the cornes, wines, and fruits of the ground, the fresh Loches and rivers, and the sapheir firmament, the bright Sunne and Moone, and the glistering starres arrayed in good order?

Among Hume's enumerated delights are music and 'To heare the merry interloquutors of facetious Dialogues, pretty and quicke conceits, and rancounters of Comediens, in their comedies, and stage plaies'.[93] This does not quite correspond with the supposed tastes of a caricature Reformation Kirk minister. Hume's *Hymnes, or Sacred Songs, wherein the right use of Poesie may be espied* were published in Edinburgh in 1599. They are dedicated to Elizabeth Melville, Lady Cumrie, whose own poem 'Ane Godlie Dreame' draws on the conventions of older vision poems, infusing them with a scriptural voice: 'I am the way, I am the treuth and lyfe, / I am thy spous that brings thee store of grace'.[94] The title page of Hume's book carries an epigraph from Ephesians 5:18. His use of this passage about 'making melodie to the Lord' indicates that poetry might be consonant with correct religion. His opening letter addressed to 'the Scottish youth' urges that rather than singing 'prophane sonnets, and vaine ballats of loue', one ought to 'Imitat the ald Hebrew Dauid in his Psalmes, as a paterne of all heavinly poesie'.[95] Where Buchanan and others had made poetry founded on the Psalms, Hume recommends them as models; this counsel might not benefit all poets, but it works for Hume at his best. 'The Triumph of the Lord', celebrating the defeat of the Spanish Armada, can be both amplitudinous and nimble:

> Let cities, kirks, and euerie noble towne,
> Be purified, and decked vp and downe,
> Let all the streets, the corners, and the rewis,
> Be strowd with leaues, and flowres of diuers hewis,
> With birks, and lawrell of the woddis wild,
> With Lauendar, with Thime, and Cammamild . . .[96]

Hume's poems shine when they cut against the Petrarchan conventionalism of some of the court poets and attend instead to precise, gleaming details. His 'Of the Day Estivall' contemplates in ballad stanzas the sights and sounds of a midsummer day with its 'perfite light'. Drawing at times on the diction of the Psalms, it rejoices in a lovely purified clarity which calmly catalogues a panorama of human and animal life from dawn to dusk.

The maveis and the philomeen,	*thrush; nightingale*
The stirling whissilles lowd,	*starling*
The cuschetts on the branches green	*wood-pigeons*
Full quietly they crowd.	*coo*

Kindly and panoptic in its beauty, Hume's poem is far removed from the bitterness of the Reformation's polemics, yet its spiced plainness, attuned at times to the Huguenot Du Bartas, and at other moments to the Catholic Montgomerie, gives its fifty-eight stanzas a lyrical attractiveness all of their own, and one fully consonant with one kind of Protestant emphasis on vernacular directness. The conclusion reads:

With bellie fow the beastes belive	*full; quickly*
Are turned fra the corne,	
Quhilk soberly they hameward drive,	
With pipe and lilting horne.	

Throw all the land great is the gild	*clamour*
Of rustik folk that crie,	
Of bleiting sheepe fra they be fild,	
Of calves and rowting ky.	

All labourers drawes hame at even,
And can till uther say,
Thankes to the gracious God of heaven,
Quhilk send this summer day.[97]   *sent*

Hume celebrates divine harmony as well as the ecology of the parish. As a literary voice of the Scottish Reformation, he is much quieter than Buchanan or Knox, and often more appealing if less influential. Like that of Buchanan in Latin, Hume's vernacular work is a reminder that the Reformers' aesthetic need not be hostile to all verse, however suspicious of some it may have been.

Hume lived relatively obscurely. The most successful Scottish book of the age was written by a man always in the public glare. Curiously, this widely translated prose work was first published covertly in a single-figure print run; its Classical title, which means 'kingly gift', was printed in Greek characters, suggesting that it was aimed at a tiny audience. King James's *Basilicon Doron* (1599) was a manual of kingship written for his son Henry. Republished in a new, public edition in 1603, it became the first (and for a long time the only) prose work in English to be translated into French, German, Dutch and Danish at the time of publication; other foreign-language versions soon followed. What made James's book so alluring was that people wanted to know the views of this northern writer-monarch who had taken over the famous English throne of Queen Elizabeth. At the head of James's book stands his finest poem, 'The Argument'. This sonnet elegantly sums up the author's politics. In asserting the Divine Right of Kings, it presents a summary of the argument of his volume.

> God giues not Kings the style of *Gods* in vaine,
> For on his throne his Scepter do they swey:
> And as their subiects ought them to obey,
> So Kings should feare and serue their God againe.
> If then ye would enioy a happie raigne,
> Obserue the Statutes of your Heauenly King;
> And from his Lawe, make all your Lawes to spring:
> Since his Lieutenant heare ye should remaine,
> Reward the iust, be steadfast, true, and plaine:
> Represse the proud, maintaining ay the right,
> Walke alwaies so, as euer in his sight

Who guardes the godly, plaging the prophane,
And so ye shall in princely vertues shine.
Resembling right your mighty King diuine.[98]

Like his ancestor James I, James VI unites makar and Maker, but here he is more conscious of bonding king to King. Following the conventions of many an earlier kingly manual, including that of Xenophon which it mentions, James's 'kingly gift' to his son is often shrewd. It can even be moving, as when he discusses loyalty to parents and cites the tragic case of his own mother. James wrote his book in Scots; a manuscript in his own distinctive handwriting survives. The work was published in Scots English in Edinburgh in 1599, then in a revised form using more southern English in 1603 in London. So, as the *Basilicon Doron* evolves, James's original 'I ame na papist' becomes in both print versions 'I am no Papist', while his manuscript's 'I haue not spaired to playe the bairde against all the estaitis of my kingdome' survives intact in the 1599 Edinburgh edition, but in the 1603 London one becomes 'I haue not spared to be something satyrick, in touching wel quickly the faultes in all the estates of my kingdome.'[99] These moves from Scots to English, reduplicated many times throughout the work, are emblematic of a shift of literary power from Scots to English prose. Whether or not James was responsible for every minute act of translation (probably he was not), he allowed the process. In none of the texts does he disguise his Scottish identity. Indeed, as far as the English are concerned, he makes it clear that he has never 'bene among thaime'. Yet in the 1603 edition his language is as English as can be managed. James seems to have seen no great gulf between the Scots and English tongues. He writes of Britain as 'all bot ane yle, & allreaddie ioined in unitie of religion, & langage'.[100] The very fact that his own work went through significant stages of translation on its way to an English audience complicates this kingly assertion.

Fascinatingly, James gives us a survey of Scotland from its ruler's point of view. The mainland Highlanders, though 'barbarouse', are 'yett mixed uith sum shau [show] of ciuilitie'. Those of the isles, however, are 'alluterlie barbares' and to be thought of simply 'as of uolfes [wolves] & uylde boaris'. James's solution is to plant 'colonies' of loyal subjects among them, a strategy that would be pursued throughout the developing British Empire. He writes with monarchical revulsion about the 'populaire tumulte & rebellion' of the Reformation in Scotland

which has led 'sum of our fyrie ministers' to begin 'to fantasie to thame
selfis a democratike forme of gouuernement'.[101] However much modern
readers may sympathize and identify with this, for King James such
things are not to be tolerated. While he advises his son to learn from the
work of historians, he warns the prince off 'sicc infamouse inuectiues
as buchananis or knokisis croniclis'. The law should be used against
rebellious authors. James's warning against 'deuiding . . . Kingdomes' is
of a piece with *King Lear*, but, oddly for the patron for whom Shakespeare (one of the King's Men) would write such masterpieces, he warns
his son 'not to keepe ordinairlie in youre cumpanie comoedians or
balladins [dancers], for the tirans [tyrants] delyted maist in thaime &
delyted to make comoedies & tragedies thaime selfis'.[102] *Basilicon Doron*
is written relatively late in James's career as an original author. His
move to England largely confined his writing to official correspondence.
Yet James's kingly manual does reveal a continuing interest in poetry,
albeit one less strong than it had been in the 1580s. A final quotation
from the 1603 London version will indicate the taste of this Renaissance
monarch, writer, and companion of poets:

> If ye would write worthelie, choose subjectes worthie of you, that be not full
> of vanitie, but of vertue; eschewing obscuritie, and delighting euer to be plaine
> and sensible. And if ye write in verse, remember that it is not the principall parte
> of a poëme to rime right, and flowe well with many prettie wordes: but the chiefe
> commendation of a poëme is, that when the verse shall be shaken sundrie in
> prose, it shall be founde so riche in quick inventions, & poëticke floures, and in
> faire and pertinent comparisons; as it shall retaine the lustre of a poëme, although
> in prose. And I would also aduise you to write in your owne langauge: for there
> is no thing left to be saide in Greeke and Latine alreadie; and ynewe [enough] of
> poore schollers would matche you in these languages; and besides that, it best
> becommeth a King to purifie and make famouus his owne tongue . . .[103]

So, as he moved from the Scots to the English tongue and throne,
Scotland's last writer-king advised his son. James's words suggest that
much of his own literary career may have been formed in reaction
against that of his Classicist mentor, Buchanan. His advice also suggests
that James's sponsorship of poets, begun at his Scottish court and concluded with poets of England, may have been part of a calculated plan
to glorify the national language. Politics meant that James's considerable
administrative skills helped nurture the glories of the English, not the

Scots tongue. He authored other prose works, including his *Daemonologie* (1597); he was, like the Kirk, a great persecutor of witches. In *A Counterblaste to Tobacco* (1604) he attacks a substance also ridiculed by Buchanan. The majestic publication of James's *Workes* in 1616 signals in its title and splendid title page a continuing literary as well as territorial ambition. Crowned with a crown, it proclaims 'THE MOST HIGH AND MIGHTY PRINCE, IAMES' to be 'Kinge of Great Brittaine, France & Ireland'. It was unusual for a vernacular author to publish his writings under such a title; James's court poet Ben Jonson also published his *Works* in 1616, and the King may have wished not to be outdone.

James was not an author of genius, but he stands as the greatest ever Scottish patron of English literature. Shakespeare, Jonson and a galaxy of other luminaries wrote for his court, and some of the most celebrated English literary institutions have their origin in this Scottish author who headed south for a better job. In granting Jonson a royal pension in 1616, James followed the Scottish custom of having salaried court poets, and initiated what later became the official position of Poet Laureate to the London monarch. Furthermore, the King James Bible or Authorized Version, published in 1611, owes its being to James's authorizing in 1604 at the Hampton Court ecclesiastical conference 'one more exact Translation of the Holy Scriptures into the *English Tongue*' to give a Bible which avoided both Papistical errors and the misinterpretations of 'self-conceited Brethren'. For this the translators thanked God who had dispersed 'thick and palpable clouds of darkness' by giving them James to shine on England like 'the *Sun* in his strength'.[104] However, the original spark for James's enthusiasm for Bible translation came from his participation in a meeting of the General Assembly of the Church of Scotland at Burntisland in Fife in 1601. At that gathering the principle of commissioning a new biblical translation was agreed. The decision was then taken to begin with the Psalms, and James's own Psalm translations, which eventually numbered about thirty, were part of this drive, though his Psalter never achieved public success. So, though the King James Version was translated by a team of English translators under the chairmanship of Lancelot Andrewes, the impetus behind it came in an important sense from James's Scottish background. At an often misunderstood remove, this Scottish author stands behind what became for centuries the world's best-selling book.

The Aberdeenshire Latin poet and physician Arthur Johnston, as presented in Volume II of the Musa Latina Aberdonensis, edited by William Duguid Geddes in 1895. The portrait is attributed to the seventeenth-century Scottish artist George Jamesone, to whom Johnston addressed a poem. Johnston wrote what is arguably the most attractive series of poems about places in Renaissance Britain – his 'Encomia Urbium' – and assembled the delights of Scottish Latin verse in his anthology, the Delitiae Poetarum Scotorum (1637). (St Andrews University Library, per DA840.N3S8[15])

4

The Staggering State

Post-Reformation enmities, the removal of the court from Scotland and the dispersal of northern court poets damaged literary culture. It progressed uneasily, often outside a Scotland whose condition might be summed up in a phrase used by the mid-seventeenth-century man of letters Sir John Scot – a 'staggering state'. In politics as in literature, opportunities came from the King's move south in 1603, but there were also drawbacks. The Renaissance polymath Thomas Craig had hymned James VI's birth in 1567; now he wrote a long, enthusiastic poem about the 1603 coronation. His fellow Scottish-Latin poet John Leech, however, tearfully lamented the King's departure in his *Lachrymae*. In literature as elsewhere, 1603 was a time of uncertainty for many Scots. For King James it was a moment of triumphant royal assertiveness, but not all of his northern subjects felt a comparable surge of confidence.

Anxiety surfaces in 1604 in the *Poetical Essayes of Alexander Craige ScotoBritane*, published in London. A Banff poet educated at St Andrews, Craig (1567–1627) wrote in Latin as well as in the emergent modern literary language of English. He addressed 'To the Kinges Most Excellent Maiestie' an 'Epistle Congratulatorie' celebrating James VI and I's

> happy chaunce,
> Since thou art King of England, Ireland, Fraunce,
> Besides that famous and vnmatch'd renowne
> Of thy vnconquered olde and Scottish Crowne.

Craig even has Queen Elizabeth's ghost deliver a monologue in the seven-stressed iambic lines known as 'fourteeners', assuring Elizabeth's former subjects that 'The Thirsel [Thistle] now defends & guards the red Rose & the white.' Yet in 'Scotlands Teares' Craig worries about an

English takeover: 'Now riuall *England* brag, for now, and not till now /
Thou has compeld vnconquered harts & sturdy necks to bow.'[1]

Craig fears Reformation Scots have hastened Scotland's glories on
their way. In a short poem 'To the Frontispiece of Abakuk Bissets
Booke, Of the Olde Monuments of Scotland', he notes the 'Wrackes,
and Ruines' of religious buildings and concludes *Thy Booke doth shew,*
that such, and such things were,/ But would to GOD that it could say,
They are.'[2] Defending his native Scots tongue as pithy, Bysset wordily
enumerated Scotland's laws and history in his *Rolement of Courtis*
(1622). For Craig, trying to perfect English verse, Bysset's antiquarianism seemed a shoring-up of fragments.

A Protestant poet loyal to the newly crowned James I, Craig is one of
a number of 'Boreo-Britan [North British] *Poets*' unsettled by what
has been happening in Scotland, but clearly determined to flatter that
'*accomplished Archi-Monarch*', the London-based Scottish king.[3]
Whatever his reservations, Craig wants to make Britain work as a United
Kingdom, yet one in which Scotland is not submerged; hence he styles
himself a 'Scoto-Britane'. English poets of the day felt no need to term
themselves 'Anglo-Britons'. Nor, like the Scots grammarian Alexander
Hume (1558–1631), did they term their language 'the Britain Tongue'.
For Shakespeare, indeed, in the second act of *Richard II* 'this sceptred
isle' could be readily synonymous with 'this England'. Like some modern
black British writers, though, Alexander Craig, even as he writes in
English and publishes a good deal of his work in London, wishes to
assert his distinctive cultural identity.

He was not alone. Sir David Murray of Gorthy (1567–1629), a
learned senior official of James VI in Edinburgh and a minor poet, also
styles himself 'Scoto-Brittaine' in his 1611 narrative poem *The Tragicall*
Death of Sophonisba, published in London. This work was dedicated
to King James's son, Henry, for whom Murray then worked. *Sophonisba*
uses the same seven-line stanza as Shakespeare's *The Rape of Lucrece*
and is set in the era of Hannibal. It has no Scottish references, but the
figure of Sophonisba (who would appeal to the Classically-inclined
Scottish poet and dramatist James Thomson in the eighteenth century)
had attracted Scottish-Latin poets, and Craig's story of a foreign queen
who dies a tragic captive may have been chosen to appeal to the grandson
of Mary, Queen of Scots. Unaware she is about to die, Sophonisba puts
on dark clothes

In which her heart-bereauing beauty shin'd,
Like faire *Diana* in the sable night,
Or like a polisht Diamond of Ind,
Set in blacke Iet, to giue a glance more bright . . .[4]

Like Craig, Murray is a poet educated in the Classics. His English-language work shows competence rather than distinction. Both men continue the Scottish tradition of sonneteering, but in a somewhat dutiful vein; 'Write vp each sigh, each plaint, each teare, each grone', urges Murray the lover-accountant. Latin thrives, but gone are the Scots-language fireworks and much of the panoply of an earlier Scotland. Instead we have the frequently undistinguished Renaissance verse of displaced Scots courtiers who wrote often stiffly in English. In Elizabethan and Jacobean England the Scottish-Latin tradition of Buchanan was respected, but Scottish writing in English was not regarded as glorious. Nevertheless, Scottish works continued to circulate in court circles and beyond. It is striking that of the small amount of Scottish material Shakespeare appears to have read, the concentration is on Latin and Scots works: Hector Boece, Buchanan's *Historia*, Douglas's *Palis of Honoure*, Henryson's *Testament of Cresseid*, John Leslie's 1578 *De Origine Scotorum*.[5]

Although the companionship of the northern court poets was ended by death and dispersal, at least one or two of them, the King himself and William Fowler, continued to meet in London. Commendatory verses in which poets wished one another other good luck with their new books indicate that there persisted among the Scottish poets at the southern court a sense of fellowship which extended to other writers still in Scotland; several of the courtier writers moved not infrequently between London, Scotland and the continent. 'I. M.' (probably the Scottish court poet John Murray (d. 1615)) links Craig to '*sweet Castalian streames*' while the London Scottish courtier poet Sir Robert Ayton addresses English and Latin poems to Craig, his 'dear friend, and fellow student' at St Andrews.[6] Simon Graham, author of *The Anatomie of Humors* (Edinburgh, 1609) and other works, adds a flattering sonnet to *Sophonisba*, while its author sends a sonnet celebrating '*Fiction's Ore*' to the Scottish poet William Drummond of Hawthornden.[7] A network of poets, several connected with James's court, developed a Renaissance Scottish poetry in English as well as continuing to write in Latin. James's

Latin Secretary from 1618 was the Aberdeen-loving poet Thomas Reid, an ancestor of his later namesake, the Enlightenment philosopher. Other influential Scots like Alexander Craig, Sir Robert Ayton and Sir William Alexander seem to have known one another well, and to have been in contact with a range of writers within and beyond court circles. For the Latinists, their friends and fellow poets stretched across the European continent.

Robert Ayton (1570–1638) is the best among the Scottish poets who made their living in London. Born in Kinaldie Castle, Fife, then educated at St Andrews, this rich man spent time in Paris and travelled in Europe on diplomatic missions for the King. He was knighted in 1611 and served as secretary to Queen Anne. He knew the English poets Samuel Daniel and Ben Jonson, who influenced his work. Ayton's 'Sonnet: On the River Tweed' opens with the most elegant tribute to the Union of the Crowns: 'Faire famous flood, which sometyme did devyde, / But now conjoynes, two Diadems in one . . .'[8] His best poems flow in an apparently easy conversational style:

> The other night from Court returning late,
> Tyr'd with attendance, out of love with state,
> I mett a boy who ask't if he should goe
> A long to light mee home, I told him noe.[9]

At his best, 'Ayton, Scoto-Britannus', as John Aubrey called him, could write fluent English.[10] His earliest poems appear to have been in Scots and his Latin poetry shows accomplishment. Most impressive, though, is how London literary and court life (where, Ben Jonson told William Drummond, 'Sir R. Aiton loved him dearly') helped Ayton write English unbothered by the sort of 'sindrie other falts' that worried many of his aspiring literary countrymen, unsure what to do about 'Scots words'.[11] Given his English fluency, it is a pleasant irony that Ayton has been suggested as the author of a poem underpinning the world's best-known Scots song. First published by James Watson in 1711, it may be attributed to the 'School of Ayton' (and perhaps to Francis Sempill) rather than to the poet himself. Certainly it runs smoothly, but its English would have been forgotten had it not been given fresh expression in Scots by a later poet:

> Should old Acquaintance be forgot,
>   And never thought upon,
> The Flames of Love extinguished,
>   And freely past and gone?
> Is thy kind Heart now grown so cold
> In that Loving Breast of thine,
> That thou canst never once reflect
> On Old-long-syne?[12]

Though they circulated in manuscript, Ayton's English poems were not published until after his death. During his lifetime a substantial body of his Latin verse found its way into print. This trilingual poet was clearly part of a continuing Scottish Renaissance Latin culture. He was the dedicatee of Robert Fairlie's *Naulogia* (?1635) where Ayton's Fife roots are celebrated and he is linked extravagantly with Virgil and Catullus. In a Latin and Greek poem John Leech suggests 'Aytonius' is '*aei tónos*', always tuneful.[13] Scottish Latinity was still buoyant. Far from confined to James's court, it did thrive there, encouraging contacts between Scots and non-Scottish writers, and supplementing French as the principal influence on Scottish high-literary culture. The Scottish Latinist Thomas Murray translated some of James's own poetry into the Classical tongue. In Latin the Scots could engage with their contemporaries on an absolutely equal footing, using the prestigious international language of learning, whereas in English many felt themselves learners. English for them was the new Latin.

This may be one reason why recourse to the Classics seems such a marked strategy in the work of court Scots who chose to write in English. Best known among these is Sir William Alexander (1577–1640), Earl of Stirling. His Senecan *Monarchicke Tragedies* (1607) come larded with English poems of praise from John Murray, Ayton, Drummond and others, along with Latin verses by John Dunbar ('Megalo-Britannus'), Andrew Ramsay, Arthur Johnston and further Scottish Latinists. Despite the hype, Alexander's dramas are well-nigh unreadable. Written for the library and never performed, they deploy wordy, static speeches to present the careers of ancient monarchs in *Croesus* and *Darius*. These were followed by *The Alexandraean Tragedy* and *The Tragedy of Julius Caesar*. Though scholarship might connect them to the Classical and French rhetorical traditions developed by George Buchanan in his Latin tragedies, when set beside Shakespeare, or even beside Ben Jonson's classicizing *Catiline*, Alexander's tragedies deflate like elephantine dirigibles. Equally vast and windy is this author's 1637 *Dooms-day, or, The Great Day of the Lords Iudgement*, an apocalyptic twelve-book religious epic of around 10,000 lines. In comparison with *Paradise Lost*, whose development may owe debts to Alexander, *Dooms-day* seems sucked dry of convincing detail, phrasing or imagery. In their place is a banally learned facade full of 'vigorous souls', 'great kingdomes' and 'mortall strength'.

The Latinist Arthur Johnston may have perceived what Alexander wanted when he asked,

> Confer Alexandros: Macedo victricibus armis
> Magnus erat, Scotus carmine: major uter?[14]

> *Compare Alexanders: the Macedonian by might*
> *Grew great, the Scot by song: who is the greater?*

As if driven by his own surname, Sir William Alexander of Menstrie longed for glory and tried many ways (from tax-collecting and mining to poetry and drama) to achieve it. He failed. A proud Scoto-Briton and a friend of poets, he may be at his poetic best in his sonnets. One begins impressively, 'Great God that guides the Dolphin through the deepe', but very few are consistently good.[15] Alexander was chief among the poets whom the King recruited to join him in translating the Psalms; King James was keen to be regarded as a successor to the Bible's Psalmist-King David. Like James, Alexander wrote an essay on poetic theory. He was also alert to the possibilities for imperial expansion which his 'matchless Monarke' might offer his subjects:

> It seems this Ile would boast, and so she may,
> To be the soueraigne of the world some day.[16]

Such an imperial vision links Alexander's classical tragedies to some of his writings on contemporary topics, and is most strikingly expressed in his prose. In 1624 he published in London *An Encouragement to Colonies*. The King had granted Alexander vast Canadian territories. Opening his *Encouragement* with a learned history of ancient and modern colonization, Alexander presents the allure of his 'Plantation' of New Scotland to his 'owne Countreymen' in terms of his wish for glory: 'Where was euer Ambition baited with greater hopes than here, or where euer had Vertue so large a field to reape the fruites of Glory . . .' Nova Scotia, he explained, was the ideal territory for 'aduancing the Gospel of Iesus Christ' and seeing 'many thousands of Sauage people (who doe now live like brute beasts) conuerted vnto God'.

Alexander was a lover of Sidney's *Arcadia*. Now in his own Arcadian realm 'those that are so disposed, without making a Monasticall retreate (free from a multitude of troubles) may inioy the pleasures of contemplation'.[17] Sir William never set foot on any of the 60,000 square miles of his Canadian territories, but they took in not only the modern Nova Scotia, Prince Edward Island and Cape Breton Island, but also tracts of the mainland and terrain as far south as Long Island – to be renamed the Isle of Stirling. Alexander's preoccupation was less the actual nitty-gritty of colonizing than the *writing* of it. So on the map appended to his *Encouragement to Colonies* appeared such rivers as the Tweed (now the St Croix), separating New Scotland from New England, and the Clyde (now the St John) as well as the Firth of Forth, which, predictably enough, issued from Alexandria.

All this turned into its own 'Alexandrian Tragedy' when Sir William lost control of his territories, but if Alexander the author was part of a network of court-connected Scottish poets, then Alexander the imperialist was also part of a group of Scottish writers committed to the opportunities offered by colonization. These authors did not visit the colonies of which they wrote, but scripted them for the imperial imagination. As James VI, who had once written of his own remote plantations on Lewis, became an absentee monarch who ruled Scotland by his pen, so these men sought to emulate him with regard to their territories. To Alexander is dedicated Sir Robert Gordon's 1625 *Encouragements* to settlers in '*the new plantation of CAPE BRETON, now New Galloway in America*'. Another of Alexander's circle, 'his most affectionate friend' William Lithgow, had Scotland herself speak approvingly of 'My *Nova Scotia*; where nothing can want'.[18] With no mention of snow or ice, this is the Arcadian never-never land of 'a second *Alexander*', Scotland's great American dream.

William Lithgow, though, was no mere colonial fantasist. Born around 1582 and dying about 1645, he wrote the splendidly titled and illustrated *Totall Discourse, Of the Rare Aduentures, and painefull*

Peregrinations of long nineteene Yeares Trauayles, from Scotland, to the most Famous Kingdomes in Europe, Asia, and Affrica (1632). Earlier Scots like the Latin poet and Catholic Orientalist George Strachan of the Mearns (fl. 1592–1634), who travelled to Baghdad and made pioneering Latin manuscript translations (now in the British Library) from Persian texts, had left occasional records of their travels. Lithgow, however, is a new phenomenon: a compulsive Scottish travel writer. Sometimes jejune and bigoted in his views but always readable, he went first to the northern isles of Orkney and Shetland while still a young man, then began publishing accounts of his travels in 1614. A staunch Protestant, Lithgow gives a graphic account of being put on the rack in Spain, and inveighs against both Catholics and followers of 'Mahomet'. Yet at the same time he is clearly fascinated by Islamic civilization, devoting considerable space to his time in Turkey and North Africa. His prose style is characterful, and, in his introductory remarks, hints at some of the later baroque prose splendours of Sir Thomas Urquhart. So the grizzled Lithgow denounces flatterers:

To such bellowing caves winded with the borrowed rags of patch'd up Commedies, clouted complements, stolne Phrases, and lip-licked labours, of lamp-living spirits, to such hollow Tombes, I say a tush for their kindnesse, and I justly hold it a manifest idolatry to honour, or do homage to any of them.[19]

Lithgow is tough. 'Forc'd to drinke my pisse' in the Libyan desert, he is several times attacked and robbed during his travels across the known world from Ireland to Hungary, from the Holy Land to Ethiopia. Modern readers may smile when Cretan fortifications remind him of Dumbarton, or the River Jordan makes him think of Falkirk, but Lithgow is alert to cultural difference as well as similarity. Using the term 'science' in a way that draws on its Latin sense of *scientia* (knowledge), he goes far towards setting out a theoretical basis for his travels. After detailing the various acknowledged branches of learning, he argues for what he calls 'the science of the world':

This science is onely acquisted by conversation, and haunting the company of the most experimented: by divers discourses, reports, by writs, or by a lively voyce, in communicating with strangers; and in the judicious consideration of the fashion of the living one with another. And above all, and principally by Travellers, and Voyagers in divers Regions, and remote places, whose experience confirmeth the true Science thereof; and can best draw the anatomy of humane condition.[20]

This 'Science' which helps 'draw the anatomy of humane condition' will later be called anthropology. Though it has not yet arrived, it is well on its way towards the Scottish Enlightenment 'science of man'. It can be distorting to read older works only in terms of modern academic categories, but anthropology and sociology are just two of the disciplines to whose formation Scottish writers would contribute substantially in the eighteenth and nineteenth centuries. There would be considerable cross-fertilization between Scottish anthropological writing about society and Scottish fiction. Yet the roots of this strand in Scottish literature may be traced back into the work of seventeenth-century theologians, travellers and imaginative writers. Such roots are in evidence at least as far back as the sometimes commonplace Lithgow. His picaresque *Peregrinations* are written up in the mixture of prose and verse familiar to readers of Elizabethan and Jacobean English-language or Latin romances.

Lithgow deserves to be read not because he is yet another Renaissance traveller, nor because he is a Reformation Presbyterian bigot for whom the Irish, other than 'our collonizd plantators there', live more miserably than 'the Divelish-idolatrous Turcoman, or the Moone-worshipping Caramines'.[21] He should be read for the good reason that he writes with gusto. Sometimes he relishes his own eccentricity. If Hugh MacDiarmid in the twentieth century had a taste for 'whaur extremes meet', then this seventeenth-century Scot seems to have anticipated him:

> Extreamely doe I live,
> > Extreames are all my joy,
> I find in deepe extreamities,
> > Extreames, extreame annoy.[22]

Yet Lithgow also has a sense of humour and a readiness to record small acts of kindness, as when 'one Ellinor the Cooke, an Indian Negro woman, attended mee' during his tortures in Spain. All this means that readers feel a certain regret when this author ends his book with the words 'And so farewell' – after computing that his 'paynefull feet' have walked for 'thirty six thousand and odde miles, which draweth neare to twice the circumference of the whole Earth'.[23]

Lithgow's interest in comparing societies and reporting on other cultures was scarcely unique in the period. Nor was its expression confined to works of fact. 'Fiction' was often a term of abuse in the early seventeenth century, but it was beginning to be used with approval of the literary imagination – as exemplified by Murray of Gorthy's celebration of '*Fiction*'s Ore'. Although the first Scottish novel in English dates from 1660, it is in the early seventeenth century that Scottish prose fiction began. Arguably the most interesting prose writer of the period, John Barclay (1582–1621) helped translate work by King James into Latin and travelled on the King's behalf in France and Germany along with Robert Ayton. Barclay spent about a decade at James's court before moving to Rome in 1615 where he associated with other Scottish exiles. He was the son of a Scottish Catholic jurist, the stylish, Aberdeen-educated William Barclay, a Latinist (and namesake of a minor Scottish Latin poet) who had got out of Reformation Scotland around 1571, becoming a Professor of Law at the newly established French Jesuit university of Pont-à-Mousson in Lorraine. There William Barclay wrote his *De Regno* (1600), a book on monarchic power that attacked Buchanan and (as its reader John Locke would put it) asserted the authority and sacredness of kings. Although William Barclay's son John was born to a French mother and educated in France, the young man seems to have considered himself and to have been regarded by those close to him as a Scot. He was strongly loyal to his exiled Scottish-Latinist father whose *De Potestate Papae* (On Papal Authority) he edited for London publication in 1609. That book argued against papal authority over kings, and John Barclay wrote a congratulatory Latin poem celebrating the accession of James VI to the English throne in 1603. John seems to have travelled to London with his father that year, carrying the poem as an introduction to James's court. To James the younger Barclay dedicated the substantial part of his lengthy Latin prose romance *Euphormionis Lusinini Satyricon* (known in English as *Euphormio's Satyricon*) in 1605.

This freewheeling romance has been called 'the first major *roman à clef*' and 'the most important work of prose fiction published in Europe in the first decade of the seventeenth century', if one excepts Cervantes's *Don Quixote*.[24] Barclay was an innovative Latinist, the first Renaissance Latin writer to choose Petronius's first-century prose-and-verse Latin romance, *The Satyricon*, as a model. Like *The Satyricon* (and a bit like Lithgow's *Peregrinations*), Barclay's work belongs to the genre of 'Menippean satire', mixing prose and verse as its first-person narrator Euphormio moves through a succession of picaresque adventures in several European lands. A foreigner from Lusinia (which some early commentators identified as Scotland), Euphormio is enslaved, meets with witches, falls in love, comes into conflict with the Acignians (Jesuits) and visits several royal courts. In the second (1607) part of the work, the questing hero learns to be a writer. He is educated by the Jesuits, rejects them, then, after further adventures, travels to the court of King Tessaranactus (James VI and I). This second part uses a developed satirical allegory for the first time in prose fiction, and early readers clearly enjoyed trying to decipher the identities of the characters and countries involved. The protagonist of the tale, which may be regarded as the first Scottish novel, articulates in the opening pages a fascination with cultural differences and relative identities which runs through Barclay's work and which will become a major preoccupation in Scottish fiction.

Quod hic religiosum est, alibi profanum esse nihil prohibet. Nempe quaelibet regio non magis suo aere aut terminis, quam suis moribus definitur . . .

What is religious observance here may well be profane elsewhere. For every region is bounded by its customs as surely as by its atmosphere and its frontiers.[25]

This proto-anthropological notion that regions, nations and ages had their own special character would be developed in the Latin essays that make up Barclay's *Icon Animorum* (The Mirror of Minds) (1614). It contains accounts of customs in France, Britain, Germany, Italy, Spain, Turkey, Hungary and other lands, in addition to essays on dispositions and professions. The work's incidental pleasures include a panoramic view of contemporary London from Greenwich and what seems like a record of a private conversation with King James about frostbite. In the *Icon Animorum* Barclay is concerned with the way 'Nature hath granted, besides the Genius of their native Country, something proper [i.e., individual] to every man.' So Barclay seeks, as his seventeenth-century English translator renders it, to 'examine' the various 'rankes of men' so that each reader 'may finde himselfe, and see as it were in a sequestered mirrour, what himselfe would eyther wish or feare to bee'.[26]

The idea of the book offering a mirror to its readers also lies at the heart of Barclay's fiction. He writes with a curious and striking imagination, letting his Euphormio encounter, for instance, marble statues whose heads are made of butter and replaced daily. *Euphormio's Satyricon* contains a good deal of discussion of writing itself, and of the relationship between poets and the academy. However, there are also plenty of vivid vignettes, as here when Euphormio's master, Callion, visits a magistrate:

At Dictator postquam diurna publici officij munera impleuerat, ad domesticas statim curas traduxerat impigrum corpus. Igitur diutius in limine cunctatus Callion, tandem assiduis pulsibus lassauit audientem, qui vxore iussa aperire vrgentibus, ipse non segnius iuuenco ex scalis appenso detrahebat viscerum molem; cruentis adhuc manibus, quibus paulo ante illius iugulum resoluerat. Sed vt insuetum intrantium splendorem aduertit, cultellum in reseratos inserit dentes, manusque in praecinctam pellem tergens, nocturnum capitis tegmen extremis aliquantulum digitis mouit.

The energetic magistrate, after fulfilling the daily chores of his office, had immediately passed on to domestic concerns. So Callion waited for a longish time at his doorstep. Finally assiduous knocking exhausted the man's patience, and he told his wife to open to such insistent visitors. He was standing on a ladder pulling the insides out of a young ox that was hanging from the ceiling. His hands were still bloody, for he had just finished slitting the animal's throat. But when he noticed the unusual splendor of his visitors, he stuck the knife between his clenched teeth, wiped his hands on the piece of fur he was wearing about his waist, and slightly tipped his nightcap with his fingers.[27]

Although John Barclay was a lively writer who wrote poems, theological works and an account of the Gunpowder Plot, his forte was the emerging literary genre ('scribendi nouum genus') of prose fiction.[28] His long Latin novel *Argenis* (1621) was a favourite book of King James, who asked Ben Jonson to translate it; the book was eventually Englished by Kingsmill Long in the 1630s. Frequently republished and read across seventeenth- and eighteenth-century Europe, its later admirers included Cardinal Richelieu, the philosopher Leibniz, and the poet Coleridge who thought its Latin style as concise as Tacitus and as perspicuous as Livy. Recently it has been called 'without a doubt the best novel written in Latin'.[29] A new edition appeared in 2004.

Argenis is set in pre-Roman Sicily and Africa. Its subject is the love of the high-born Poliarchus and Argenis. The story involves chases, disguises, shipwreck, caves, woods, pirates, giants' bones, human sacrifice, rebellion, treason and (after almost 1000 pages) a happy ending in the form of a marriage. *Argenis* also contains much discussion of how to rule a kingdom, lawsuits, authorship, astrology and diplomacy – matters likely to appeal to a courtly audience. Among the more unusual incidents is a pitched battle in which thirteen elephants run amok and destroy an army. As well as poems, this prose text contains transcripts of letters sent between its characters, anticipating later developments in the epistolary novel. Encoded in its narrative of supposedly ancient deeds are many references to recent history. The name of one character, for instance, is an anagram of 'Calvinus' (John Calvin), and an account is given of his followers:

Nihil illorum furori relictum est. Calcare aras Deorum, euertere templa, foedare oppida incendijs, & ciuili sanguine suam furijs consecrare nouitatem. Post tot annos adhuc veluti truncas vrbes excisis Numinum tholis aspicias, in quibus saeuierunt.

Nothing escaped their furie. They trampled on the Altars of the gods, overthrew Temples, fired Houses, and with their owne Countrey-mens bloud, consecrated their Novelties to the Furies. After so many yeeres, you may yet see, as it were, maymed Cities, the Tabernacles of the gods cut downe; upon which, they used most crueltie.[30]

All this is supposedly happening in pre-Roman Sicily. Yet it is hard not to relate it to the family background of the Barclay whose Catholic father had fled Reformation Scotland. Again, when Barclay satirizes a magistrate, we may remember he was a jurist's son; when in the *Icon Animorum* he praises France's generosity to foreigners and readiness to make them feel at ease, a personal note surely nurtures his words.

An awareness of cultural difference is certainly present in the third-century romance *Aethiopika* by the Syrian Greek Heliodorus, a work influential in Latin translation across sixteenth-century Europe. *Argenis* is the first extended Latin romance of its kind and clearly draws on Heliodorus's Greek work in settings and technique. Yet Barclay, this 'Caledonius Gallicus' (Scottish Frenchman) at the London court of King James and then at the Papal Court in Rome, has reasons to compare and register cultural distinctions which come from his own experience as well as from a literary inheritance.[31] He is a sophisticated, entertaining and successful novelist, even if the form of fiction he produces seems as odd to us as Sidney's *Arcadia* – a work which the early seventeenth-century Scottish Latin poet Thomas Reid contrasted unfavourably with Heliodorus. In Barclay's *Argenis* a surrogate author figure, Nicopompus, theorizes about the delights of fiction which can give pleasure and improve without heavy-handed moralizing. He speaks of how 'I will compile some stately fable, in manner of a Historie' ('Grandem fabulam historiae instar ornabo') which will offer readers, as it were, 'a Map of places' so that 'they will love my Booke above any Stage-Play, or Spectacle on the Theater'.[32] Here, five years after the death of Shakespeare, we hear the ambition that will eventually make the novel (still termed a 'fictitious history' in the eighteenth century) the dominant narrative form. Barclay has been forgotten by historians of Scottish literature. Yet, however problematic his 'Scottishness', there is a strong case for seeing this imaginative Catholic Latinist not just as a pivotal figure between the Classical and modern versions of the European novel, but also as the first Scottish novelist.

There was clearly interest in prose fiction among several of the Scottish members of James's court. While Barclay was at work, Sir William Alexander was authoring his thirty-page prose supplement to Sidney's *Arcadia*. Alexander's piece was published in 1621, so it may claim to be the first piece of Scottish prose fiction written in English. Its English, though, sometimes reads as if translated from Latin, and, while Alexander tries to imitate the cadences of Sidney's often mannered prose, in an age when writers from Lithgow to Barclay liked to write 'copiously', his own characteristic orotundity tends to get in the way:

> The place appointed by fortune to be famous by the famousness of this combat was a back court, which they found out at that time emptied of habitants; the stronger being gone to pursue others, and the weaker run to hide themselves; mediocrity being no more a virtue, where all was at height to make excellency eminent in extremity.[33]

Sent to William Drummond in Scotland, Alexander's critical essay, the *Anacrisis*, which probably dates from 1634, is the first such Scottish-authored work to discuss prose fiction. It begins by asserting that modern poets are as good as ancient authors. As well as considering prose and drama, it discusses imaginative prose in several languages, including

Greek, Latin, English, Italian and Spanish. Its scope extends from Heliodorus to that 'most excellent Work', the *Arcadia*, and culminates with praise of 'my Country-Man *Barclay's Argenis*' which is seen as an exemplary modern fiction that successfully combines 'Matters of State, War and Love'.[34]

Barclay, Ayton, Alexander, Drummond and their peers all belonged to the international community of Latin writers and readers, even though they also wrote in other tongues. That community included Thomas Dempster (c. 1579–1625), a Catholic polymath from north-eastern Scotland who served briefly as James I's Historiographer Royal. Dempster was the first person to hold this prestigious English appointment, but he spent most of his life on continental Europe where he was a professor at the University of Bologna. Author of the first Scottish biographical dictionary, as well as poems, tragedies, antiquarian, topographical and other works (some in Greek), the irascible Dempster was a prodigiously learned Latinist, though no great stylist. His *Historia Ecclesiastica Gentis Scotorum: sive De Scriptoribus Scotis* (*Ecclesiastical History of the Scottish People: or Concerning the Scottish Writers*), published in Bologna in 1627, assembles short biographies of Scottish authors from prehistory to Dempster himself. Embracing writers as various as St Columba, William Malveisin and George Wishart, it casts its net improbably wide to include a brace of Irishmen, Boadicea (credited with six literary works), Alcuin of York and many other scarcely Scottish figures. It is easy to mock Dempster's quirky, unreliable directory; in his own engaging autobiographical entry he tells us that he was one of triplets, the twenty-fourth of twenty-nine children born to one mother. Dempster's book attempts to bind together a historically and geographically far-flung community of Scots who wrote in several languages, and who held different religious beliefs. Authored by a Catholic who is fiercely Scottish, yet who has spent most of his life outside his substantially Protestant homeland, Dempster's *Scottish Writers* dates from a time when Scotland's very monarch now lives outwith the country. Viewed from this angle, Dempster's strange-seeming book is redolent of an age full of migrant and wandering Scots, an age which produced not only Dempster himself but also that ultimate contradiction John Barclay, a Scot who may never have visited Scotland.

The Latinist Dempster wishes to demonstrate not just to the Scottish people but also to a much wider Latin-reading audience the complex worth of his supranational Scottish community. He bonds himself to it, even though he feels he has lost much of his own inheritance. Dempster's stance and material would condition the best original prose work by Sir Thomas Urquhart, an equally proud exiled Scot writing in English some three decades later in a southern jail. Urquhart pays tribute to Dempster's 'pretty bulk [book], written in the Latine tongue', just as he admires his 'compatriot Barclay, the author of *Argenis*, *Icon Animorum* and other exquisite treatises, translated out of Latine into the languages almost of every country where use is made of printing'.[35] Far-flung and exotic as these Scoto-Latin writers may appear today, in their time they were seen as part of a Scottish literary community whose disruptive ecclesiastical and political history had dispersed it across several lands, yet which remained a proud and porous network.

In Scotland James VI's court had enjoyed elaborate theatrical spectacles. In 1594 at the baptism of Prince Henry an elaborately choreographed procession had involved an 'artificiall, and wel proportioned ship' forty feet high, captained by Neptune.[36] Men dressed as Amazons, a Moor, and many emblematic figures participated; the poet William Fowler wrote up the proceedings in the most detailed contemporary account of a Renaissance Scottish court spectacle. After James's move south, however, drama suffered more than any other genre. Poetic effusions and pageants greeted Scotland's King in 1617 on his only return visit, but the court was gone, and the Kirk was scarcely minded to sponsor play-acting. In 1599 James had forced the Church of Scotland to accept public performances by a company of English actors in Edinburgh, but with the King away there was little scope to play.

Curiously, in the very year of James's departure a Scots-language drama was published. *Philotus* comes again from the Scottish-Latin tradition. It was closely based on the Roman comedies of Terence and Plautus. Cross-dressing, mistaken identity, a mock-exorcism full of saints' names, and a complex but well-handled plot leave two pairs of young lovers married but the rich, eighty-year-old suitor Philotus still single. *Philotus* is written in eight-line rhyming stanzas, like a poem, but (perhaps like John Burel's earlier *Pamphilus*), it appears to have been designed for performance. The play's authorship and date of composition are unclear. Though it ends with a prayer 'for our king', some of its material may date from as early as the reign of Mary, Queen of Scots. Its publication in 1603 suggests that there were still elements in Scottish society ready to enjoy hearing fourteen-year-old Emilie complaining that she has no wish to marry the 'deid auld' Philotus since she would have nothing to do in bed except fight off the advances of 'Ane auld deid stock [stick], baith cauld and dry'.[37] The verse of *Philotus* is physical and sophisticated, Emilie's 'toung micht mak Demosthenes agast'. The play's language as well as its content occasionally recall the word-world of Dunbar.

By 1603, though, a comic drama whose revels include a minister and a whore was clearly at odds with Kirk-sanctioned discourse. Official public performance in Scotland had shifted from court and theatres to pulpits. In front of large, responsive congregations the sermon developed into a powerful form of performance art. Preachers like Zachary Boyd (1585–1653) in Glasgow, convinced that 'Gods pipes are the ministers mouthes', delivered orations which, within a single sermon, moved from having hearers' 'hearts leape for ioye' at God's saving word to urging all to 'prepare our selues for lamentations', since 'It is farre better to be at the crosse of Christ weeping with good Marie then [sic] to be dancing in King Herods hall with the daughter of that vile strumpet Herodias.'[38] A highly educated Calvinist, Boyd preached in colloquial plain English (not Scots) on scriptural texts. He eschewed rhetorical elaborateness yet aimed to move his congregation through a variety of sometimes dramatically conflicting emotions within a reasoned structure. In this he was typical of most Scottish Protestant preachers, tending to avoid using his sermons 'as a vehicle of "humane learning" ' or imaginative display.[39] Expounding biblical passages and mixing original material with biblical cadences and phrases, Boyd's might be termed a democratic style of address on the part of a community leader. Boyd also wrote poems on biblical themes, but he had a tin ear for verse. His Kirk was not opposed to poetry. After all, its early elected Moderator had been George Buchanan. Many of its ministers wrote original verse, while translation of the Psalms was a recurrent form of Scottish Protestant expression. But like would-be poets in all ages, most Kirk ministers lacked real literary talent and gave their best energies to other pursuits.

Ecclesiastical polemic and historiography flourished and, as in Knox's *History*, grew intertwined. Works such as the *Historie of the Kirk of Scotland* by John Row (1569–1646) chronicle the development of a Church whose concern for its own independence increasingly brought it into conflict with southern authorities. Row's *Historie* contains several

Latin poems, some by Andrew Melville, who was eventually arrested and imprisoned by King James. Zachary Boyd could write Latin as well as English orations, and minor Latin poets like John Johnston (c. 1565–1611) celebrated Protestant martyrs such as Patrick Hamilton:

> Ergo omnis in unam,
> Fraude, odiis, furiis, turba cruenta coit.
> Igne cremant. Vivus lucis qui fulserat igne,
> Par erat ut moriens lumina ab igne daret.

> *So, all against one,*
> *With lies and anger they scapegoated him,*
> *Burned him alive. A shining light in life,*
> *In his death too he brought enlightenment.*[40]

Light, arrestingly deployed by writers as different as George Buchanan, Alexander Hume and the royal educator, alchemist and theologian Patrick Scott (author of the 1623 *The Tillage of Light*), would be fundamental to the imagery of the Protestant culture which would help nourish later forms of Scottish Enlightenment thought. While often aware that 'Scotia' seemed like a pun on 'skotos', the Greek word for darkness, Reformation and Renaissance Scots Protestants saw themselves as shining light on to matters long kept obscure; today the emblem of the Kirk is still the Old Testament burning bush. These presbyterians wrote with as much application as the fiercely Protestant Stevenson family would apply in later times to lighthouse building, or Scotland's nineteenth-century scientists such as David Brewster or Lord Kelvin would bring to the physics of light.

While English was the dominant pulpit language of seventeenth-century Scotland, the country's literary productions remained resolutely polylingual. Poets made work in Scots, Gaelic and English, with Latin remaining a powerful language of the educated Scottish imagination. From George Thomson (who wrote poetry about a heroine from Heliodorus) to David Kynloch (writing about sex, gynaecology and anatomy) or Peter Goldman who hymned Dundee, a great array of Renaissance Scottish poets wrote in the ancient Latin language of their land and continent. Several also wrote in English, but Latin, like Scots, was more familiar to them. Though not all the poets were polymaths like George Strachan, John Barclay, Thomas Dempster, James Crichton, George

Buchanan or Andrew Melville, they all crossed between or among languages. When James Melvill wrote that the poet, polemicist and cleric Patrick Adamson excelled in tongue and pen, he meant in Scots (the language Adamson spoke and preached in) and in Latin (the language in which Adamson wrote and published).

Latin was not just an ancient language; it was also a vehicle for literary innovation. Born in Montrose, the Aberdeen-educated poet and traveller John Leech (fl. 1610–24), brother of another Latin poet, pioneered the British use of the short-lined erotic verse known as 'Anacreontic'. In English this form would be developed by England's Robert Herrick, while in Scotland the aristocratic Sir James Balfour translated Leech's Latin *Panthea* into Scots ('in Metrica Scotica') in the early 1620s.[41] Leech, an admirer of Catullus as well as Buchanan, is the most erotic of Scottish Renaissance poets, and calls some of his poems 'erotica'. He addresses verses to female lovers, real or imaginary, as well as to a circle of friends that includes the Scots Latinists Alexander, Ayton, Dempster, Arthur Johnston, Scot of Scotstarvit and others, as well as continental writers such as Hugo Grotius. Leech may have been influenced by the English poetry of William Drummond. He also learned from modern European Latinists and, like many of the Scottish poets he knew, he was linked to the circle that revolved around Sir Philip Sidney and his sister. Leech's 'Somnium' (Dream) was addressed to Drummond. Its wee Anacreontic lines ('Iam nox tenebricosis / Terram super iacentem') were translated by the nineteenth-century Scottish polymath John Leyden. The translation is very free but catches something of the spirit of the original:

> Ere night's bright wain her course had run,
> Venus to me and Venus' son,
> Descending in a radiant car,
> Rapt from the earth, and bore me far.
> Billing sparrows twittering clear
> Drew us from our swift career;
> The lovely goddess all the while,
> Glow'd with pleasure's wanton smile . . .[42]

The dedicatee of John Leech's 'Somnium' was William Drummond of Hawthornden (1585–1649), the most accomplished poet to write English in seventeenth-century Scotland, and one whose ideals are often close to those of the Scoto-Latinists. In an age when William Alexander defended a British poetic language 'mixt of the English and Scottish Dialects', Drummond strove to eliminate Scottish locutions as he perfected his style, but his rhymes show he retained a Scottish accent.[43] The laird of Hawthornden was the writer whose skill and assurance in verse and prose did most to give Scottish imaginative writing access to the increasingly international language of English. Yet Drummond was also closely connected to Leech, Ayton, Alexander and the network of Scottish Latinists who continued to operate in the older international lingua franca of high culture. Drummond's brother-in-law Sir John Scot of Scotstarvit in Fife (1585–1670) was instrumental in the production of the great anthology of Scottish-Latin verse, the *Delitiae Poetarum Scotorum* (1637). That book's principal editor, Arthur Johnston (c. 1579–1641), was a friend of Drummond's with whom he discussed poetry and poetics.

The son of an official at James VI's Scottish court, Drummond was educated at the new Edinburgh University, graduating in 1605. He then spent time in London, at the University of Bourges (where, one of a substantial number of Scots, he studied some law and relished playgoing) and in Paris. The rest of Drummond's life was spent in Scotland but, drawing on his travels, as a young man he began to amass a superb library of literature in Latin, French, Italian, Spanish and English. Drummond read voraciously. Publishing his plangent *Poems, Amorous, Funerall, Diuine, Pastoral, in Sonnets, Songs, Sextains, Madrigals* in 1614–16 and his *Flowres of Sion* in 1623, he was the best-read poet of his time in Britain. His own work frequently imitated such favourite authors as the Italian poet Marino, the Englishman Sidney, the French Du Bellay and the Spaniard Garcilaso. Here was a Scot who in his early twenties had read John Knox alongside *Romeo and Juliet*, had read Dante as well as Ronsard, and modern French romances as well as 'Jhone Done's Lyriques'.[44] In addition to studying many continental and some southern works, the young Drummond knew what his countrymen were writing in English. He perused such recent publications as Alexander's sonnet sequence *Aurora* and Murray's *Sophonisba*. An inventory of Drummond's library made in 1611 when the poet was just twenty-six years old shows 267 works in Latin, 120 in French, 61 in Italian, 50 in English, 35 in Greek, 11 in Hebrew and 8 in Spanish. These figures come from Drummond himself, a privileged bibliophile who loved everything to do with writing. Over his lifetime he amassed a great collection of manuscripts, including many works by his uncle, the Scottish court poet William Fowler, but also a cornucopia of other materials ranging from eye-witness accounts sent back from Sir William Alexander's Nova Scotia to a plethora of anagrams (IOHN SMITH = SHIT ON HIM) and records of his own literary conversations with Ben Jonson, who came north to visit Drummond in 1618.

Drummond was yet another Scottish-Latinist polymath. Like Leonardo da Vinci, he invented a machine gun and other weapons of war, patenting sixteen. Yet he is best remembered as a mellifluous poet in English, living in pastoral retreat south of Edinburgh by the River Esk as laird of Hawthornden Castle. Drummond, who loved images of flowers and gardens, inherited this noble pile from his father in 1610 and later rebuilt it. It is now an international retreat for writers. Karl Miller describes Hawthornden as 'a vertiginous cottage castle which stands on a rock in whose entrails is a prehistoric cave dwelling, and which has a terrace that looks out over the all but touchable tops of very tall trees, down into a glen crowded with the sepulchral greens of their foliage and threaded by the River Esk ... The place is both large and small, both astonishing and endearing.' Here, 'both on top of the world and well out of it', the Stoical Drummond lived and wrote 'in honest ease' as he put it in a Latin inscription on one of the walls.[45] He wrote diaries, a history of Scotland, madrigals, sonnets, noble religious poems. He wrote a beautifully cadenced prose meditation on death, A Cypresse Grove, which draws on Montaigne as well as other French and Italian models; he wrote letters to many poet correspondents; having transcribed an account of '2 savages in a Canou' in Nova Scotia, he tried to rework the material as a short essay in which a 'Trogolodite song' is heard as having 'a sweet meltone [honey-tone]'.[46] Drummond's own poems often involve reworkings of foreign models, yet accomplish their work so idiomatically that 'a sweet meltone' is what results.

'Sleepe, Silence Child, sweet Father of soft Rest' begins a sonnet with Drummond's characteristic music, one that draws not just on the vowels or even those sibillant consonants, but also on the lulling *l*-sounds in the first three words. Still, however mellifluously toned this poem about sleep may be, its charm is energized by a note of disturbance. When the speaker complains, 'And yet o're me to spred thy drowsie Wings / Thou spares (alas) who cannot be thy Guest', then below the continuing soft music runs a strain of melancholy insomnia, a restlessness under the rest.[47] Drummond is a sensuously musical poet. Nothing illustrates this better than the adverb in the second line of his sonnet 'The Oister', a poem that discusses how pearls are formed:

> With open shells in seas, on heauenly due
> A shining oister lushiouslie doth feed.[48]

This poet's best work has a luscious verbal pearlescence that draws on Petrarchan and continental traditions, rather than on the harsher music of that contemporary English poetry which Drummond may have been the first to term 'Metaphysicall'. Petrarchanism continued to captivate Scottish poets of the earlier seventeenth century, as shown by the learned and accurate English-language translations of Petrarch's *Triumphs of Love* (1644) by Drummond's admirer Anna Hume. The Drummond whom Hume praises is opposed to any mere search for novelty. In the letter to Arthur Johnston where he uses the term 'Metaphysicall', Drummond, probably writing in the 1630s, tells his Latinist friend that poets are not 'Transformeres of evrye thing'. Rather, they should write in accord with 'the matteres, manners, Rules of former ages'.[49] In this he sounds more like Buchanan than like John Donne. His conservative aesthetic means that most of Drummond's finest poems are in some sense elaborations or variations on earlier texts, whether profane or, increasingly in his later career, sacred. Although he rejoiced in giving it expression in longer, often elaborate structures, his combination of formal balance, detail and stately magnitude is evident in 'The Angels for the Natiuitie of our Lord'. Full of internal balances and circulations of repeated words, this echo-chamber poem's stressed first syllable kicks the sonnet energetically from its starting-block, though, revealingly, a re-echoed incitement is needed by line 9, and the poem concludes not with vigorous running but with the more fluid motions of swimming and echoing.

> Rvnne (Sheepheards) run where Bethleme blest appeares,
> Wee bring the best of newes, bee not dismay'd,
> A Sauiour there is borne, more olde than yeares,
> Amidst Heauens rolling hights this Earth who stay'd;
> In a poore Cotage Inn'd, a Virgine Maide
> A weakling did him beare, who all vpbeares,
> There is hee poorelie swadl'd, in Manger lai'd,
> To whom too narrow Swadlings are our Spheares:

Runne (Sheepheards) runne, and solemnize his Birth,
This is that Night, no, Day growne great with Blisse,
In which the power of Sathan broken is,
In Heauen bee glorie, Peace vnto the Earth.
    Thus singing through the Aire the Angels swame,
    And Cope of Starres re-echoed the same.[50]

Drummond is usually seen as a solitary, a self-image he cultivated. It should also be said that he fathered twelve children (nine by his wife), corresponded voluminously, and, as John Kerrigan points out, wrote poetry that grows anxiously and sharply political about 'the British Problem'.[51] Still, Drummond's highly developed sense of leisured melancholy led him to brood in the prose of *A Cypresse Grove* on such topics as how 'The halfe of our Life is spent in Sleepe', and critics have found it too easy to oversimplify the range of his work.[52]

Very different from such dreamy musings is the macaronic Latin-and-Scots poem attributed to Drummond, the 'Polemo-Middinia' or 'Midden Battle between Lady Scotstarvit and the Mistress of Newbarns in Fife'. Written in a reeling mixture of Scots and Latin, full of 'Pypantes arsas, & flavo sanguine breickas/ Dripantes' (Piping arses, and breeks dripping with yellow blood), this substantial carnivalesque, even Rabelaisian poem in which Lady Scotstarvit lets fly 'a baritone fart . . . such as would have cracked Mons Meg [Edinburgh Castle's most famous cannon]' frequently operates in the territory of the older Scots 'Christis Kirk on the Green'. But more than that, it is emblematic of Scottish Latinity. Learned and local, scurrilous and sly, clarted with dung and 'Nympharum Cockelshelleatarum', it is daftly and deftly calculated to appeal to an audience for whom Latin might be as alive as Scots.[53]

Just such an audience rejoiced at the appearance of the 1637 *Delitiae Poetarum Scotorum* (Delightful Productions of the Scottish Poets). Earlier occasional anthologies had been produced when poets had contributed work on a particular topic. So *The Muses' Welcome to King James VI* was edited by Edinburgh University Principal John Adamson to celebrate the King's visit to Scotland in 1617. However, it is testimony to the enduring strength of Latin in seventeenth-century Scottish culture that the *Delitiae*, the first ever printed national anthology of Scottish poetry, was in Latin, not in English, Scots or Gaelic. Printed by John Blaeu in Amsterdam, it was initiated by the lawyer-poet Sir John Scot of Scotstarvit, who visited Holland to correct proofs and who paid Blaeu 'a hundred double pieces for printing the poets'.[54]

Scot, the 'Scots star of Scotstarvit', was a poet and patron of poets who gave money in 1620 to support Latin teaching at St Andrews University where a professorship still bears his name. He collected the works of the Scottish Latin poets at his tower-house, now owned by Historic Scotland, at Scotstarvit near Cupar in Fife. In a poem 'On the Bees Making Honey in the Temple of the Muses of Sir John Scot of Scotstarvit', John Leech writes of honey bees following their leader who

> Delegit certam sibi Scoti in culmine sedem,
> Servat ubi vates bibliotheca sacros.

> *Chose a place on Scot's tower's topmost storey*
> *Where his library holds sacred singers' songs.*[55]

Another splendid poem was addressed to Scot by the principal editor of the *Delitiae Poetarum Scotorum*, Arthur Johnston, the foremost Scottish Latin poet of his age. Drummond assisted in the anthology project, which published the work of thirty-seven Scottish poets, though, curiously, it omited George Buchanan, perhaps because his work was already widely available. This, the major Scottish anthology of the age, celebrated not only an inheritance of Scottish verse but also a living tradition of which Johnston was part.

Proud to have been born near Inverurie in rural Aberdeenshire, Arthur Johnston went to school there in Kintore.

> Hic ego sum, memini, Musarum factus alumnus,
> Et tiro didici verba Latina loqui.

> *Here I remember being made the Muses' pupil,*
> *A wee boy learning to speak the Latin words.*[56]

From Kintore he progressed to King's College, Aberdeen, a great centre of north-east Scotland's (often Episcopalian) Latin culture, and met his lifelong friend the Latin poet and dominie David Wedderburn. Johnston left Scotland in 1608 at the age of twenty-one to study at the Universities of Padua and Sedan. Although he visited London on various occasions, he did not return to live in Scotland until 1622. He was appointed a 'medicus regius' (physician to the king) and in 1637 became Lord Rector of his alma mater but he died four years later on a visit to Oxford. As Wedderburn put it,

> Gallia Melvinum, Buchananum Scotia cepit,
> > Anglia Ionstonum, Mantua Crichtonium:
> Scilicet heroum claris decorare sepulchris
> > Orbem omnem laus est propria Scotigenum.

> *France held Melville, Scotland held Buchanan,*
> > *England held Johnston, Mantua held Crichton:*
> *It seems the special glory of the Scots*
> > *To deck the whole wide world with heroes' graves.*[57]

Collecting work by poets who worked inside and outside Scotland, the *Delitiae* of Johnston and Scot, like Dempster's biographical dictionary, makes a statement about the strength of Scottish culture (especially Scoto-Latin culture), placing it alongside that of the other nations who were represented in the series of national anthologies of which the Scottish one was part.

Johnston's Mount Parnassus was Benachie in Aberdeenshire. He wrote on topics from a Paduan anatomical dissection to the praise of George Buchanan, but his best poems are often set in the Scottish landscape. Among the most attractive is a verse epistle to the Aberdeen academic Robert Baron, written with Ovidian flourish as if from a Donside crofter who describes the sheer slog of his existence:

> Pars messis torrenda focis, frangendaque saxo est,
> > Pars mihi flumineis mersa domatur aquis.
> Aestibus in mediis, hiemis memor, ignibus apta
> > Pabula suffosa quaerere cogor humo.
> Viscera dum rimor terrae, prope conspicor umbras,
> > Ignotum nec me Manibus esse reor.
> Ingeminant curae, ceu tempestate coorta,
> > Cum prior urgetur fluctibus unda novis.
> Vix intempesta clauduntur lumina nocte,
> > Excitor, ut cecinit nuncia lucis avis.

> *Some of the harvest's scorched, ground down,*
> *Some of it's in the Gadie burn.*
> *Through the hot summer I prepare*

For snow, cutting and banking peat.
Excavating the earth's bowels
I just about see spooks and think
The dead peer back. What makes it worse,
As when a storm first hits and then
Wave after wave pounds in, my head's
Just touched the pillow in pitch dark
When I'm awoken by the lark.[58]

For all he could write as an exiled Ovidian crofter, Johnston was part of a cultured Aberdeenshire circle which included the portrait painter George Jamesone, many poets, and William ('Willie the Merchant') Forbes whose beautiful tower-house at Craigievar is a classic work of Scottish Renaissance art. Admired by Samuel Johnson in the eighteenth century, by Hugh MacDiarmid in the twentieth, and republished in 2006, Johnston's own poetry is another such treasure. While the Latin culture of his work gives it an erudite and international tone, evident in his Psalm translations and poems on continental affairs, it is his most locally inflected poems which are among his strongest. His series of paeans to Scottish towns, 'Encomia Urbium', celebrates not only larger cities such as Glasgow and Edinburgh, but also smaller places, including Haddington, Elgin, St Andrews and Inverurie. These poems owe debts to Ausonius, Julius Caesar Scaliger, and Johnston's Dutch friend Caspar Barlaeus who had similarly treated a group of Dutch towns, but more immediately they were written in a spirit of competitive emulation of the poems Arthur's kinsman John Johnston had written on Scottish towns and published in the 1607 edition of William Camden's *Britannia*. Arthur Johnston's poems surpass John's. Only he could have set Dundee beside the pyramids of Memphis, or looked for pyramids in Inverurie. Confidently mixing local knowledge with Classical learning, the 'Encomia Urbium' pull no punches:

Sacred St Andrews, the whole wide world
Saw you as the burgh of God.
Jove, eyeing your great Cathedral,
Blushed for his own wee Tarpeian kirk.
The architect of the Ephesian temple,
Seeing yours, felt like a fake.[59]

Johnston is Scotland's last major Latin poet and his 'Encomia Urbium' is the finest series of poems of place produced in Renaissance Britain. Friends who admired each other's work, he and Drummond wrote much of the most expressively sophisticated Scottish verse of their time. Johnston praised Drummond in Latin verse; Drummond made an English version of Johnston's celebration of Edinburgh in the 'Encomia Urbium'. These two men's sheer talent raises them above other Scottish poets of the period such as (in Latin) the north-eastern Ovidian religious poet and Kirk Moderator Andrew Ramsay (1574–1659), or (in the vernacular) Patrick Hannay (c. 1594–c. 1650) and Alexander Garden (c. 1590–c. 1642) whose conservative, imitative aesthetic is not accompanied by Drummond's panache and fluency. Patrick Gordon (d. 1650) took Spenser as a model and attempted to celebrate Scotland's medieval patriotic inheritance in his 8000-line *Famous and Valiant Historie of the Renouned and Valiant Prince Robert Surnamed the Bruce* (1615). Gordon's more fancifully Spenserian *Firste Booke of the Famous Historye of Penardo and Laissa* (1615) was admired by Drummond who thought its author's 'Jewellis . . . his oune' and wrote of its Laissa that 'whilst fair Iuliett, or the farie quene/ Doe liue with theirs, thy beautie shall be seene.'[60] Drummond loved imaginative beauty, and sought it largely in retirement from a world whose ecclesiastical and political concerns were increasingly bitter and divisive. Yet towards the end of his life even he wrote a poem portraying 'A Character of the Anti-Couenanter, or Malignant' which sets out ironically his position.

Religious tensions between Church and state increased towards the end of King James's reign, much to the King's annoyance. The efforts of the group of Scottish poets he had mustered to join him in translating the Psalms were rejected by the Kirk and by the Church of England. After James's death in 1625, worsening religious and political tensions led to the signing of a Scottish National Covenant in 1638 which pledged Scotland to the service of the Church of Scotland's God. But the Kirk itself was often divided over issues of its own government – should it for instance distance itself from upper-class cliques or allow the appointment of bishops? Not only did conflicts develop between Scottish Presbyterians and the London-based authorities; there was also factional infighting among Scottish Protestants. A 1637 riot in St Giles Kirk in Edinburgh against the royal imposition of a new Prayer Book led in time to wholesale military clashes between King Charles I and the Scots. Such conflicts sometimes uneasily intersected with revolts against absolute monarchical authority in England, and with an uprising in Ireland in the late 1630s and 1640s. Almost half a century after Robert Rollock had expounded 'covenant' theology in Scotland, the Scottish Wars of the Covenant (named after the patriotic National Covenants signed by Scottish Presbyterians in defence of their faith, and often against royal interference in their Church government) tore the country apart until 1651.

Even Drummond, a moderate and Episcopalian, felt the impact of these struggles in his last years. 'Kirke and not church, church and not kirke, O shame!' he exclaimed in a short, sharp satirical poem about internecine ecclesiastical wrangles.[61] His slightly younger contemporary, Alexander Montgomerie's nephew the 'pios & learned' Sir William Mure of Rowallan (1594–1657), served in Covenanting armies and became a Member of the Scottish Parliament in 1645, but mostly lived peacefully on his estate near Kilmarnock, enjoying a lengthy writing career. Mure too subscribes to the Petrarchan aesthetic that continued to hypnotize early seventeenth-century Scottish vernacular poets, though his later work registers something of the conflict of his times. A good Latinist, he translated part of the *Aeneid* to retell the story of Dido and Aeneas. Moments of disturbance can energize his best religious sonnets. In 'O three times happie', using imagery that sends a tremor of surprise through his generally conventional diction, he longs for the divine grace that would change 'Sinnes menstruous rags' into 'pure transparent laune'.[62]

A sometimes troubled longing to know and accept God's will runs throughout much of the Scottish literature of the time, irrespective of language. In Gaelic Donnchadh MacRaoiridh (d. 1630) prays for the forgiveness of his sins and in his 'Four Verses Made by him the Day he Died' seems eager to depart.

> Bho is tu as fiosraich mar a tàim
> Beir mise leat tràth is beir.

> *since You can see the truth in me,*
> *Christ, take me with You – now.*[63]

It was an age of holy dying. Outstanding among its violent theological and physical conflicts is the small body of poems by James Graham,

Marquis of Montrose (1612–50). A supporter of the National Covenant who later defected to the side of King Charles I and won several victories, including the 1645 Battle of Inverlochy, Montrose was eventually executed in Edinburgh in 1650. Educated at St Andrews, well travelled in Europe, a brave master of disguise and, eventually, a heroic fugitive, he acquired increasing posthumous allure as one of Scotland's superb noble failures – a kind of male Mary, Queen of Scots. The learned Marquis's army camp was described by one of his followers as 'an Academy, admirably replenished with discourses of the best and deepest sciences'.[64] The tiny corpus of verse attributed to him, especially the poem 'On Himself, upon hearing what was his Sentence', is electrifying in its movingly enforced formal aplomb and elegantly courageous resolution:

> Let them bestow on ev'ry Airth a Limb;   *part*
> Open all my Veins, that I may swim
> To thee my Saviour, in that Crimson Lake;
> Then place my purboil'd Head upon a Stake;
> Scatter my Ashes, throw them in the Air:
> Lord (since Thou know'st where all these Atoms are)
> I'm hopeful, once Thou'lt recollect my Dust,
> And confident Thou'lt raise me with the Just.[65]

A fierce sense of justice burns through much of the polemical prose of the time, such as the splendidly titled *Lex, Rex* (Law, King) of Samuel Rutherford (c. 1600–61), a leading Protestant theorist who argued that kings should be elected. Rutherford's apparent championing of liberty was also a defence of a theocratic Protestant state. Educated at Edinburgh University, he became an academic at St Andrews. In *Lex, Rex* he expounded the idea that governments rely on a covenant between king and people, so that the people 'measure out, by ounce weights, so much royal power, and no more and no less'. This stress on popular authority countered any absolute notion of royal rule; for Rutherford a monarch 'is made by God and the people king, for the church and people of God's sake'. Although he realized that 'the succession of kings by birth with good limitations' might be beneficial since it avoided 'bloody tumults, which are the bane of human societies', ultimately Rutherford asserted that 'no nation can bind their conscience, and the conscience of posterity, either to one royal line, or irrevocably to monarchy'.[66]

Royalists in England at Oxford University and elsewhere regarded *Lex, Rex* as one of the age's 'pernicious books'.[67] It draws on the work of George Buchanan (whose works were burned in Oxford along with Milton's) as well as Classical thinkers. In some ways Rutherford seems protodemocratically modern; in others, as when he inveighs against 'the Pope's foul tail', he is hotly of his time.[68]

William Drummond, a sometimes splenetic monarchist who worried that 'where equalitye is, a monarchie is hardlye maintained', wrote in his anti-Covenanting *Skiamachia* (Shadow-fighting) (1643) with its elitist Greek title that 'Amongst all the sortes of people upon the face of the earth, christianes should be of the most mild, peaceable disposition.'[69] Few Scots lived up to this ideal, and high passions are reflected in some striking writings. With the Leuchars minister Alexander Henderson, the Edinburgh lawyer Archibald Johnston of Wariston (1611–63) was one of the authors of the 1638 National Covenant, and experienced religion as 'exstasie'. So Johnston's diary records how in his bedroom during the early hours of the morning of 23 April 1637,

> quhyle I was walking al alone and meditating on the nature, essence, naimes, attributs, words, works of a Deitie, my quhol body took a schuddring, and extream coldness seased on al my joints especyaly on the roots of my haire, quhilk stood al steave, bent up fra the croun of my head; my eies stood brent open, never closing, albeit rivers of tears ran doun my scheaks; my tounge strokin dumb; my hands at will now reatched out as it wer to receive a Deitie, nou glasped in as it were to inclose and imbraice a Deitie receaved. This was the temper of my body, quhyl in al this tyme my saul was transported out of myselth and fixed upon the immediat vision and fruition of ane incomprehensible Deitie, lyk lightnings glauncing in at a windou . . .[70]

As David Reid has pointed out, such a powerful account of private rapture counterpoints Wariston's account of the public rapture of all those who 'with many sobs, tears, promises and voues' committed themselves to his National Covenant.[71]

Whilst some might dismiss all this as individual and mass hysteria, to do so is to deny the spirituality of the people involved, and to misunderstand the intensely emotional, even erotic, charge that was often present in Reformation Calvinism – by no means always a dry and sober creed. To scorn sensations like those of Johnston of Wariston is also to demean the sometimes weirdly powerful writing which such sensations and perceptions might trigger. Few other than specialist historians will wish to read the arguments of works such as Wariston's *The Causes of the Lord's Wrath* (1653) or Rutherford's *Lex, Rex*. Yet at times in the writings of each man, as in several of their contemporaries, rhetoric and passion produce an idiom that remains arresting. Often addressed to women, Rutherford's Presbyterian letters contain oddly ecstatic passages that seem suffused with what Burns in 'Holy Willie's Prayer' calls 'fleshly lust'. But the way Rutherford writes of longing to 'eat and suck the honeycomb' of Christ's love and maintains that 'One night's rest in a bed of love with Christ will say more than heart can think, or tongue can utter' speaks of an urgent search to find a viable vocabulary and form for the articulation of passionately felt religious experience.[72] To do this was not easy in a milieu where Protestants like Rutherford had rejected as idolatrous the panoply of the Mass and saints, while seeming suspicious of rich, non-biblical imaginative imagery. Yet they too knew they had souls and wished to speak of them, often deploying powerful biblical language. Some, as Rutherford does here, drew on the erotic poetry of the Song of Songs. Whether reasoned, or enthusiastic, many of the sermons of the day were clearly effective as performances of public oratory, though they may appeal less to modern readers.

In a belligerent age, *Monro, His Expedition with the Worthy Scots Regiment Called Mac-Keys* (1637) by the St Andrews-educated Scottish soldier Robert Monro (c. 1595–c. 1675) gives a good sense of 'Colours fleeing, Drummes beating, horses neying'. By turns bare and ornate, its sometimes platitudinous prose was enjoyed by Scott and Monro's book has been called by the historian Geoffrey Parker 'the first history of a regiment ever written, in any language', but it is a curiosity rather than an artistic treasure.[73] From an aesthetic point of view far more rewarding than Rutherford or Monro is the eccentric, full-bodied prose of Sir Thomas Urquhart of Cromarty (c. 1611–60), a northern Episcopalian laird. Educated at Aberdeen University and well travelled in Europe, Urquhart fought for Charles I against the Covenanters. After Charles II was crowned at Scone in Perth-shire in 1651, Urquhart again joined the Royalist cause. Captured at the Battle of Worcester in 1651, he wrote energetically to demonstrate that he was far too important and promising to be left languishing in prison. His *Pantochronochanon; or, a Peculiar Promptuary of Time* (1652) traces the lineage of the Urquharts as far back as the third millennium BC. Urquhart clearly enjoyed parading ancestors who included not only the familiar Adam and Eve but also the less well-known Molin, Lutork and Spectabundo on the male side (153 generations of Urquharts), with Emphaneola, Stranella and Zaglopis among the females of his line. His *Ekskubalauron* of 1652 – another Greek title, this time meaning 'gold out of dung' – carries the full-throated subtitle *The Discovery of a most exquisite Jewel, more precious then Diamonds inchased in Gold, the like whereof was never seen in any age; found in the kennel of Worcester-streets, the day after the Fight, and six before the Autumnal Aequinox, anno 1651. Serving in this place, To frontal a Vindication of the honour of Scotland, from that Infamy, whereinto the Rigid Presbyterian party of that Nation, out of their Covetousness and ambition, most dissembledly hath involved it.* As John Knox had done, Urquhart writes about himself in the third person, but he uses the editorial pseudonym 'Christianus Presbyteromastix' (Christian Presbyterian-eater), and makes no secret of which side he is on. His earlier, often awkward epigrams (many still unpublished in the Beinecke Library, Yale) had spelled out his views:

> By knocking down of Churches, Knox gave edge
> t'opinions, fuller of blind zeal, then doubt:
> Which hardly can be curbed in our age,
> if some new Knocks come not, and knock them out.[74]

But Urquhart's *Ekskubalauron*, his *Jewel*, is much more than an attempt to aim a knock-out punch at his ecclesiastical and secular enemies. It is a straightfaced, strongly felt lexicographical flourish on the part of a writer determined to demonstrate the importance of his own schemes, especially for a universal language. In addition, following in the footsteps of one of his exemplars, the pugnacious polymathic Catholic Latinist Thomas Dempster, Urquhart writes 'as a patriot' to trumpet forth the glory of the Scottish nation.[75] Eager to demonstrate to his captors that he is a catch to be treasured, not left to languish, he presents himself as the architect of a universal language which, so long as he is given time and freedom to develop it, will benefit all mankind. Noble soldier in exile, he reminds readers also of his ancestry and of the martial valour of the Scottish nation, principally by narrating with spirit the remarkable career of the fifteenth-century soldier-polymath, poet–linguist and exiled Scot 'the Admirable Crichton'. Lastly, Urquhart urges Scots towards 'a close union' with their southern neighbours.[76] Urquhart demonstrates that he can write mathematically, as he had done in his almost impenetrably learned trigonometrical tour de force of 1645, *The Trissotetras*. He shows too that he can write poetically, historically or biographically. He can narrate: his account of Crichton reads almost like a short novella; but he can also argue with his 'logerheadistick' enemies, emblazon, and entertain with what the modern editors of this would-be Admirable Crichton call an 'autoeulogistic style'.[77]

Urquhart is exhaustingly irrepressible. His *Logopandecteision* of 1653 sets out a universal language plan, and is one of several mid-seventeenth-century treatises on such topics by continental and British writers, including the Oxford-based Aberdonian George Dalgarno. It has been pointed out that aspects of Urquhart's thought anticipate the workings of a thesaurus and even principles used in machine translation. Urquhart himself was an enthusiast for the mathematical writings of the inventor and Protestant polemicist John Napier of Merchiston (1550–1617), another Scottish polymath who is best remembered as the inventor of logarithms (set forth in his 1617 *Rabdiologiae*) as well as of an early calculating machine which used ivory rods nicknamed 'Napier's Bones'.

Urquhart the mathematician can be detected often in the prose style of Urquhart the author, but this remarkable man found his métier in the early 1650s when he translated the first two books of Rabelais's *Gargantua and Pantagruel*. The Scot's *Works of Rabelais* (1653) is one of the great classics of English-language translation. Urquhart's queer-pitched, megalolexicographical learning burnishes Rabelais's already carnivalesque narrative to produce the one book in English which most nearly prefigures some of the more exuberant passages of James Joyce and Alasdair Gray (both of whom surely learned a good deal from Urquhart). While Rabelais is certainly a hyperbolic writer, sometimes Urquhart's deep and arcane infatuation with words magnificently outdistances the Frenchman. So, for instance, when the infant Gargantua's governesses and nurses play with the giant's penis, Rabelais lists some thirteen of their nicknames for it. Urquhart goes superabundantly further:

One of them would call it her little dille, her staff of love, her quillety, her faucetin, her dandilollie: Another her peen, her jolly kyle, her bableret, her membretoon, her quickset imp: Another again, her branch of coral, her female adamant, her placket-racket, her Cyprian sceptre, her jewel for ladies: and some

195

of the women would give it these names, my bunguetee, my stopple too, my busherusher, my gallant wimble, my pretty boarer, my coney-burrow ferret, my little piercer, my augretine, my dangling hangers, down right to it, stiff and stout, in and to, my pusher, dresser, pouting stick, my honey pipe, my pretty pillicock, linkie pinkie, futilletie, my lusty andouille and crimson chitterlin, my little couille bredouille, my pretty rogue, and so forth . . .[78]

Urquhart was born to translate Rabelais. At once faithful and free, his is the greatest Scottish translation since Gavin Douglas's *Eneados*. Letting him give full voice to his remarkable talent, Urquhart's *Rabelais* extended rather than suppressed his Scots pride, allowing him for instance not only to contend that 'of all torcheculs, arsewisps, bum-fodders, tail napkins, bung-hole cleansers, and wipe-breeches, there is none in the world comparable to the neck of a goose', but also to have Gargantua confirm that 'such is the opinion of Master John of Scotland, alias Scotus'.[79]

Urquhart's Rabelaisian muse arose partly through reaction against the 'pharasaical superciliosity' of extreme presbyterianism.[80] The imaginative promise of fiction might appeal to people impatient with endless Church feuding, orthodox discipline, and writings about those. The biblically-sanctioned eroticism and enthusiasm evident at times in the writings of legalistic Covenanters like Rutherford or Wariston was a kind of imaginative safety-valve. Yet fiction itself was less than respectable, and remained so. A late seventeenth-century Kirk minister would write in his diary that part of the corruption of prostitutes was that they 'read romances'.[81] Such accusations against the novel would still be heard in the eighteenth century.

Prostitutes were not the only ones interested in new prose fictions. Thomas Sydserf, son of a Scottish bishop, had probably spent some of his youth in Paris with his exiled father. The young man produced one of the first English-language translations of Cyrano de Bergerac in his 1659 prose fantasy *Selenarchia, or the Government of the World in the Moon*. A follower of the executed Montrose, Sydserf made other translations from French, and based his 1667 comedy *Tarugo's Wiles: or, The Coffee-house* on a Spanish play; its English was judged so good when it was performed in London that the Scot Sydserf was hailed as able through his protagonist to 'teach ev'n *English* men the *English* tongue' – a remarkable achievement for the time.[82] Something of a one-man cultural movement, Sydserf was also fascinated by 'eloquence', an interest he shared with some among the clergy in an age when eloquent preaching might win arguments, save souls, advance causes and bad preaching might give rise to books with ironic titles like *Scotch Presbyterian Eloquence* (1692). In the eighteenth century such interests would encourage the Scottish Enlightenment preoccupation with eloquence, rhetoric and belles lettres, but in the seventeenth some of Thomas Sydserf's other interests found less favour with presbyterians. He was the impresario behind Scotland's first regularly established theatre, in Edinburgh. Plays performed there included *Macbeth*, but there were few Scottish dramatists. The Scottish-born poet, printer and maker of *Road Books* John Ogilby had run Ireland's first theatre in the 1630s, but went to England to translate the works of Virgil (1649) and Homer, then write verse *Fables of Aesop* which look more to Ovid and Virgil than to Henryson.

In Edinburgh Sydserf came under attack – literally. He was assaulted at sword-point by a gang of rowdies during a 1669 rehearsal at 'his hous in the Canongate, quher he keeps his theater for acteing his playes'.[83] Sydserf beat them off. A splendid three-quarter-length portrait of him by John Michael Wright shows the wigged playwright standing proudly, hand on hip, and dressed in a rich striped robe with cane and sword.[84] In 1661 Sydserf had launched his *Mercurius Caledonius*, an Edinburgh newspaper with digests of foreign news, praise of the late Marquis of Montrose, and denunciations of 'Antimonarchicall Vermin'.[85] It ran for only one issue, but sixty years later Sydserf's Latin title was Englished to grace the important Edinburgh newspaper the *Caledonian Mercury*. Sydserf could be dismissed as a literary hack, but his example as playwright, newspaperman, impresario, Francophile and English-language purveyor of new imaginative fiction showed what might happen if the grip of the Covenanting Kirk could be relaxed. With Barclay's *Argenis*, William Alexander's continuation of the *Arcadia*, Urquhart's Rabelais, and Sydserf's Cyrano all in circulation, the time was ripe for the emergence of home-grown Scottish prose fiction in English. The unsettled period around the Restoration of Charles II in 1660, a return of the royal repressed, seems to have provided a window of opportunity.

The first Scottish novel in English was authored by the Dundee-born Sir George Mackenzie of Rosehaugh (1636–91), a young man in his twenties who had been a student at the Universities of St Andrews, Aberdeen, then (like Drummond before him) Bourges, where he studied law. Mackenzie went on to become a highly successful judge, legal theorist and essayist. In court this Royalist prosecuted the Covenanters, earning the nickname 'Bluidy Mackenzie', and a splendidly respectable folio edition of his *Works* appeared after his death. But that edition omitted *Aretina, or the Serious Romance*, Mackenzie's 1660 novel, and its omission signals a triumph of Scottish respectability over imagination. Few copies of *Aretina* survive, but there is one in the National Library of Scotland. Published anonymously in Edinburgh, this third-person narrative with epistolary interludes is dedicated with a cavalier flourish 'To all the LADIES of this Nation ... *this is my first born ... let it be admitted to suck the breasts of your favour*'. Significantly, *Aretina* is not only aimed at a female (rather than the more respectable male) audience, it is also subtitled 'The Serious Romance' and prefaced by an 'Apologie for Romances'. Mackenzie's 'Apologie' is a fascinating defence of fiction, and the first Scottish theoretical writing on the art of the novel. It shows that Mackenzie is aware of English, French and Latin romances: '*Sidney, Scuderie, Barkley*'. All these contribute to his work, and he argues 'that where Romances are written by excellent Wits, and perused by intelligent Readers, that the judgement may pick more sound information from them, then [sic] from History, for the one teacheth us only what was done, and the other what should be done'.

With its heroes Monanthropus, Philarites and Megistus, the 'Son to the King of *Ethiopia*', *Aretina* follows closely the classical tradition of romances as developed by such earlier Renaissance authors as John Barclay out of Heliodorus's *Aethiopica*.[86] His education in law gave Mackenzie a fine knowledge of Classical culture and, like much Scottish verse of this period, his novel owes a good deal to Latin precedents, including Barclay's *Argenis*. Where Barclay's cyphered fiction can seem clever-clever, an enormous, over-elaborate puzzle waiting to be decoded, *Aretina* can strike today's readers as arcanely remote. A pastoral romance set in Egypt and Persia, it contains in its third book a coded history of Scotland from James VI up to Mackenzie's own day. So, like Barclay, Mackenzie can write simultaneously about a Classical never-never land and about his own age. The story presents two knights, Megistus and Philarites, who fall in love with Aretina and Agapeta, becoming involved in the politics of Persia and Egypt which involve rebellion, kidnapping and execution. At times Mackenzie's prose may be influenced by that of Sir Thomas Browne, but the unsurprising, often discursive writing of his romance achieves narrative competence, if little more. Local vignettes may be the most entertaining aspect of *Aretina*, as when the polished author sketches how 'A young Country Gentleman, accustomed at home to whistle following the plough, to domineere amongst a great many Countrey Clowns, and to feed a kennel of dogs, was by his friends brought to the City to court a young Citizen.'[87] At times the preface seems more interesting than the story which follows it, but there is no doubt that Mackenzie in 1660 was a literary pioneer in Scotland. It would be some time before other Scottish novelists followed him, and his decision not to republish *Aretina* under his own name suggests that the Kirk-dominated climate remained unpropitious for 'romances' aimed at the ladies. Still, a cultural change was in process and there is evidence that book-hungry Scottish male readers were developing some taste for fiction. In 1652, for instance, Walter Dalgleish, Factor to the Earl of Dunfermline, catalogued his own library of 157 books; it included Sidney's *Arcadia* and a translation of Heliodorus as well as Knox's *History of the Reformation*, theological works and poetry.

Mackenzie's later prose is less imaginative. His argument against 'the strictness of churches' in *Religio Stoici, The Virtuoso or Stoick* (1663) and his contention that 'The body of the visible church must (like all other bodies) be compounded of contrary elements' read like recognitions of cultural difference which align Mackenzie with the more perceptive aperçu of William Lithgow, or even Sir Thomas Urquhart.[88] In his *Jewel* Urquhart had argued,

> Nor shall we think it strange that in the world there are so many different religions, if we consider that the divers temperaments of our bodies alter our inclinations, from whose disparity arise repugnant laws which long obedience makes it seem a sacriledge to violate. In my opinion, truly, there is nothing more natural than variety; yea, and that sometimes with opposition.[89]

Alert to the national and cultural differences between his Egyptians and Persians – and, in the coded narrative of *Aretina*'s third book, among societies closer to home – Mackenzie investigates those differences through romance. Within a century Scottish novels would deal far more confidently and subtly with intersocietal prejudice. Essayed earlier by John Barclay, this theme would evolve into one of the great subjects of Scottish fiction. Mackenzie, though, deserves recognition as the initiator in Scotland of a new vernacular genre. An aristocrat like Drummond, he nevertheless showed how it was possible for a Scottish author to succeed in a remunerative profession and to write. In the absence of the court, increasingly professions such as academia, the law and medicine would provide both income and a measure of stability for middle- and upper-class Scottish writers. Writing about forensic 'Eloquence', Mackenzie defended the Scots tongue as appropriate for pleading in court since 'the *Scotish* Idiom of the *British* Tongue' lends itself to a 'Pronunciation [which] is like ourselves, fiery, abrupt, sprightly and bold'; though he wrote his literary works in English, he claimed not to, asserting that he did not deploy 'the *English* language' since 'I love to speak as I think, and to write as I speak.'[90] These works included *A Moral Essay Preferring Solitude* and *The Moral History of Frugality* (1691), a sober topic for a Stoical Scottish judge.

Seventeenth-century Scottish literature developed not only through the work of individual writers or even through new genres, but also through new institutions. Sir Thomas Urquhart had expressed the wish 'that in every parish of Scotland there were a free schoole and a standing library in the custody of the minister'.[91] Such a design appears a development of the aims in the Kirk's Books of Discipline, though their authors would not have liked Urquhart's warning that ministers might embezzle the libraries' stock. In works such as the Reverend James Kirkwood's 1699 *Overture for Founding . . . of Bibliothecks in every Paroch* the Kirk encouraged the development of parish as well as other communal libraries. Today the jewel among surviving seventeenth-century Scottish community libraries is surely Innerpeffray. Beautifully situated in the fields of Perthshire, this community library was founded in the 1680s, at around the same time as the St Andrews graduate William Baikie bequeathed his books to form the nucleus of a public library in Kirkwall, Orkney. Still housed on site, Innerpeffray's (largely non-fiction) volumes have been read over the centuries by farmers and flax dressers, teachers and ministers. Walter Scott's tutor borrowed books here, and the library remains open to visitors. To stand in the book-lined first-floor room that overlooks the surrounding fields at Innerpeffray is to sense the ancient vitality of Scotland's democratic book culture, and to realize how the availability of learning in seventeenth-century Scotland helped to fuel the much better-known achievements of the Scottish Enlightenment.

Community libraries were relatively common in England and Scotland. North of the Border they multiplied rapidly in the eighteenth century, and academic libraries expanded considerably, but this growth was founded on earlier, seventeenth-century developments. To the city of Aberdeen and Urquhart's alma mater the Latin poet Thomas Reid, Latin Secretary to James VI, willed his books and manuscripts in 1624 'for the Scholars and Clergy to have the use of'. This, one contemporary wrote, 'was the best Library that ever the north pairtes of Scottland saw', and, in one of many indications of the way in which seventeenth-century Scottish culture nurtured the Enlightenment, this library would be used and added to by Reid's younger kinsman Thomas Reid, the philosopher of 'Common Sense'.[92] Latin literary culture remained particularly strong in north-east Scotland where the St Andrews-educated James Philp of Almerieclose near Arbroath worked on his Jacobite Latin epic *The Grameid* at the close of the seventeenth century. The Classical holdings of St Andrews University Library, to which George Buchanan and King James VI had donated books, had been augmented by Sir John Scot of Scotstarvit and by William Drummond, who donated to the students his copy of Aristophanes; the St Andrews King James Library still survives as one of Scotland's most splendid book rooms. When George Mackenzie became Dean of the Faculty of Advocates he furthered the establishment of a scholarly library in Edinburgh. In 1689, towards the end of his life, he presided over the formal opening of the Advocates' Library which had developed out of an earlier 'Bibliothecq' of the 'fynest Lawers and other Raire Bookes' bought by the Advocates since the 1670s.[93] This library was to form the nucleus of the National Library of Scotland.

Private libraries of wealthy Scots in this period were often extensive, ranging far beyond Classical and ecclesiastical tomes. The advocate and diarist John Lauder, Lord Fountainhall, had a collection of books well in excess of a thousand in addition to many manuscripts. His book hoard included French and contemporary English 'comoedies' in addition to plays by Shakespeare and that rare thing, a published mid-seventeenth-century Scottish drama, the rather awkwardly constructed tragifarcical *Marciano* (1663) by William Clerke, a fellow advocate. Clerke's play makes clear in its preface that some people think drama 'abominably abominable'. Written in English but set in Italy, it alludes to recent

British politics and was performed in Edinburgh, then clearly considered by some Scots a worthwhile addition to their libraries.[94] Mackenzie's speech at the official opening of the Library of the Faculty of Advocates on 15 March 1689 emphasized that the volumes should be 'solis Jurisconsultorum scriptis, Jurisprudentiaeque inservientibus' (only books by and of use to lawyers). However, like Thomas Sydserf, Mackenzie had a professional interest in the study of eloquence. He wrote about that topic in Latin, and he emphasized the importance of literature in general for the legal profession.[95] Very soon the Advocates' Library included imaginative writings by Boccaccio, Molière and King James VI in addition to more immediately relevant tomes. Within sixty years the Library's Keeper would be the Enlightenment philosopher David Hume.

The seventeenth century is not the richest period of Scottish imaginative writing, but its middle and later years did see important developments in literary culture. These range from the thoroughgoing use of English prose for fictional as well as argumentative ends to the setting-up of libraries and the production of significant legal, antiquarian and other professional texts. The growth of the professional classes spurred this developing culture. If earlier in the century the Latin poet Arthur Johnston had earned his living as an academic and Royal Physician, by 1681 Edinburgh had a Royal College of Physicians which developed its own specialist library. Its early President and founding member Sir Robert Sibbald (1641–1722) wrote in Latin and in English on antiquarian and medical topics, as well as producing his questionnaire-based survey *Scotia Illustrata* (1685) and writing about George Buchanan. Like medicine and the Church, the law was a distinctive area of Scottish society with its own cultural productions. John Skene compiled the *De Verborum Significatione* (1597), Scotland's first legal dictionary, while the same period saw the publication of the Latin lawyer-poet Thomas Craig's humanist *Ius Feudale* (Feudal Law). This outlines and justifies the practices of Scottish law in the wider context of nature and national traditions. In some ways anticipating the thinking of Hugo Grotius, Craig's magnum opus influenced later works examining Scottish legal customs by such authors as James Dalrymple, Lord Stair (whose *Institutions of the Law of Scotland* circulated for some time in manuscript before being published in 1681) and Sir George Mackenzie, who wrote the first Scottish book about criminal law. These legal texts developed a proto-Enlightenment interest in reasoned systematization, and in Scotland's cultural history. Mackenzie, for instance, is the first person to print the Declaration of Arbroath, in his *Observations upon the Laws and Customs of Nations as to Precedency* (1680). The comparative and wide-ranging approach of these works also furthered that proto-anthropological strain in seventeenth-century Scottish thought, and linked the thinking of Reformation and Renaissance Scotland to the Scotland of the Enlightenment.

Already present at times in such writings as those of Alexander, Lithgow, Drummond, Urquhart and Mackenzie, this proto-anthropological strain is thoroughly evident in the work of Alexander Ross (1591–1654) whom his fellow northern polymath Urquhart places at the head of his list of Scottish writers as a 'most indeared minion of the Muses'.[96] Writing prose and verse in Latin as well as English, the Episcopalian Ross had studied divinity at Aberdeen University, then headed south to England while still in his twenties, working as a teacher and preacher in Southampton. The twenty-first-century intellectual historian David Allan has shrewdly presented neo-Stoicism as a philosophical movement in Scotland which, in troubled times, expressed scepticism about court and urban life, often championing reasoned moderation, even isolation. Neo-Stoic ideals run from Buchanan through a network of seventeenth-century authors including Leech, William Alexander, William Drummond and the George Mackenzie of *Religio Stoici* (1663), before being taken up by David Hume, Adam Smith and other Scottish Enlightenment thinkers. For David Allan, Alexander Ross is 'Scotland's only really substantial neo-classical philosopher of the seventeenth century, producing Stuart Britain's most energetic contribution to the European revival of ancient Stoicism'.[97] Ross's works include *Mystagogos Poeticus, or the Muses' Interpreter* (1647), a 400-page companion to Classical poetry and mythology with alphabetically arranged articles on such topics as ADONIS, MUSES, ORPHEUS, PRIAPUS and SPHINX, followed by explanations that draw on a wide range of mythological and cross-cultural learning. Author of the 1653 *Pansebeia or, a View of all Religions in the World*, the encyclopedically-minded Ross advanced into territory that would fascinate later Scottish anthropologists, most famous of whom would be J. G. Frazer, author of *The Golden Bough*. Ross also published a continuation of Sir Walter Raleigh's *History of the World*, but his surest claim to fame may be that as a devout Christian he became the first person to translate the *Koran* into English. His *Alcoran of Mahomet* relied on a French version and was published in 1649. Its title page declares that it is 'newly Englished for all that desire to look into the Turkish vanities' and is followed by Ross's own 'needful Caveat or Admonition'.[98]

Although he was part of the Scottish neo-Stoic tradition, Ross spent much of his career outside the native institutions of Scottish culture. As Scotland's legal, medical and ecclesiastical establishments developed without the Scottish court, so imaginative writing continued, albeit sometimes uncertainly. In its way the Kirk, though no friend to drama, made ongoing contributions to Scottish verse. In 1650 a Committee of the General Assembly, continuing that Scottish preoccupation with the Psalms that goes back at least to Alexander Alane and George Buchanan and which had been transmitted through the Latin versions of Arthur Johnston, oversaw the adoption of new translations for use in Scottish churches. These translations had been drawn up by the Westminster Assembly in London. With much militancy the Kirk had already rejected the translations made by a group of Scottish poets coordinated by King James and headed by William Alexander. However, the newly approved translations often incorporated earlier work by Scottish writers, and the Synod of Argyll commissioned a translation of the first fifty metrical psalms into Gaelic. Called the Caogad, it was the first Gaelic translation of its kind and was published in 1658. Metrical psalms came to be associated with Scotland because of their widespread use throughout the land. Psalms such as 'I to the hills will lift mine eyes' seemed like native emanations and became part of the culture of generations of Scots. The familiar text of the twenty-third psalm in the Kirk-approved *Psalms of David in Metre* takes its first line from a version by Zachary Boyd, while much of the rest draws on a 1639 translation by Sir William Mure of Rowallan:

> The Lord's my shepherd, I'll not want.
>   He makes me down to lie
> In pastures green: he leadeth me
>   the quiet waters by.
>
> My soul he doth restore again;
>   and me to walk doth make
> Within the paths of righteousness,
>   ev'n for his own name's sake.[99]

If such classic English-language texts began to circulate in a mid-seventeenth-century Scotland where ordinary Scots-speaking or Gaelic-speaking people might be puzzled by the 'hard English tearmes' of some psalms, then they were also ghosted by other, more fugitive pagan survivals.[100] The shamanistic Scots verses of Isobell Gowdie, accused of witchcraft in 1662, articulate her shapeshifting power:

I sall goe intill ane haire	*hare*
With sorrow, and sych, and meikle caire;	*sighing; great*
And I sall goe in the Divellis nam	
Ay whill I com hom againe.[101]	

At her trial Gowdie spoke of her visionary experience, a kind of alien abduction that would have been familiar to admirers of Thomas of Ercildoune, and which may be the pagan counterpart of those accounts of rapturous union with the supernatural found in contemporary Christian writings. As recorded in a transcript of her trial proceedings, her words open a small window into seventeenth-century Scots oral culture and folk belief:

I was in the Downie-hillis, and got meat ther from the Qwein of Fearrie, mor than I could eat. The Qwein of Fearrie is brawlie clothed in whyt linens, and in whyt and browne cloathes, &c.; and the King of Fearrie is a braw man, weill favoured, and broad faced.

This otherworld of witchcraft had obsessed James VI in his *Daemonologie* just as it had the King's Man, William Shakespeare, in *Macbeth* (1606), a play angled to appeal to the Scottish monarch at the same time as confirming English prejudices about the barbarous nature of Scotland. Witchcraft continued to fuel such learned works as *Satan's Invisible World Discovered* (1685) by George Sinclair (c. 1618–96), a physicist, pioneer of underwater exploration and Glasgow University Professor of Mathematics. Sinclair collected reports of such supernatural occurrences as the appearance to King James IV of a mysterious 'ancient man' with 'amber hair hanging down upon his shoulders' who warns the King to delay his expedition to Flodden.[102] All this may sound utterly anti-scientific, but the union of science and the supernatural familiar to the sixteenth-century St Andrews-educated Protestant John Napier (who invented logarithms and published in 1593 his *Plaine Discouery of the Whole Reuelation of Saint John*) would continue strongly at least into nineteenth-century Scottish culture when the Dundee astronomer the Reverend Thomas Dick catalogued the populations of other planets, and the influential mathematician and pioneering topologist Peter Guthrie Tait co-authored *The Unseen Universe*, presenting energy as a spiritual force.

The supernatural, so thoroughly imbricated both in Scottish ballad culture and Gaelic lore, found eloquent written expression in a manuscript essay by Robert Kirk (1644–92). Written in 1691–2, it was published much later as *The Secret Common-wealth of Elves, Fauns, and Fairies*. Originally an Episcopalian, Kirk was a Church of Scotland minister at Aberfoyle who had published in Edinburgh in 1684 the first full translation of the Psalms into Gaelic. Educated at Edinburgh and St Andrews, as a Gaelic speaker Kirk had special access to the world of Highland folk beliefs. One of the very few writers who bridge Highland and Lowland cultures in this period, he was said to be a seventh son who possessed second sight, but he was also a well-liked, respectable son of the manse. The dedicatory note in English that prefaces his *Psalma Dhaibhidh An Meadrachd* (Psalms of David in Metre) in 1684 describes Gaelic-speaking Scots as 'our sagacious *Scottish Irish* people', but in private Kirk complained about 'lack of devout and rousing society' among 'this most illiterat people'.[103] He learned Gaelic ('the Irish tongue') to assist his ministry in a Gaelic-speaking area, but his Psalm translations were considered over-Episcopalian and too influenced by literary Irish, rather than Scottish Gaelic, which had developed considerable differences from its Irish cousin. In 1694 another Gaelic version of the Psalms, approved by the Synod of Argyll, was published. Kirk transliterated from Irish script a Classical Gaelic translation of the Bible by the Dublin-based Englishman Bishop Bedell, so that it might be used in Scotland; its London publication was supervised by Kirk in 1689–90, but it was viewed by Scots Gaels as 'too Irish' and hard to understand. Kirk's time in London and conversations he held there quickened his interest in Celtic folklore and supernatural belief. When he returned north he wrote his essay on 'sith's or Fairies' who 'are said to be of a midle nature betwixt man and Angell' and whose bodies 'somewhat of the nature of a condens'd cloud' were often 'spungious, thin and defecate'.[104] Treasured by modern writers such as Marina Warner (whose insightful edition of *The Secret Commonwealth* was published by the New York Review of Books in 2006), Kirk's account of the supernatural involves as much physicality as Isobell Gowdie's vision, and is much more sympathetic than that of the demonologist King James. Kirk offers a full social survey of his commonwealth of beings:

They remove to other Lodgings at the begining of each quarter of the year, so traversing till doomsday, being impatient of staying in on place, and finding som ease by sojourning and changeing habitations, Their Chamaeleon-like bodies swim in the air, neer the Earth with bagg and bagadge . . . They are distributed in Tribes and Orders; and have children, Nurses, mareiages, deaths and burials, in appearance even as wee . . .[105]

Rich in imaginative stimulation and proto-anthropological in nature, Kirk's essay affords many of the pleasures of fiction as it supplies an account of his 'secret commonwealth' that includes topics which would later preoccupy Scottish and other Romantic writers – topics such as what came to be known as the 'doppelgänger'. Kirk's 'Reflex-man' is 'a *coimimeadh* or Co-walker, every way like the man, as a Twin-brother and Companion, haunting him as his shadow'.[106] Kirk himself was a double-man. Mediating between the realms of the *sidh* and the Church – for him forms of spiritual belief that might reinforce each other – he also mediated between Gaelic and English-language culture. He intended to go beyond his essay to produce what he terms 'a larger discourse, of the Ancient customs of the Scotish-Irish, their nature, habit, manner of warr, husbandry, the air and productiones of their countrey &c'.[107] Such large-scale surveys would follow in the century to come. Collecting Gaelic vocabulary as well as lore, Kirk may be set beside the Edinburgh- and Leyden-educated Skyeman Martin Martin (c. 1660–1719) who worked as a tutor at Dunvegan on his native island in the 1680s and wrote in English both *A Description of the Western Isles of Scotland* (published later in 1703) and *A Late Voyage to St Kilda* (1697).

Where at the start of the century the heroic traveller William Lithgow had begun by visiting Scotland's most northern islands, so these writers developed an interest in Gaelic-speaking areas on the part of Scots- and English-speaking Scottish people which marked a significant move away from the sheer scorn of medieval Lowlanders or the administrative frustration of King James VI. Although there was still plenty of prejudice, some Lowland Scots and others began to view the Highlands and their culture as alluringly different, not just contemptible. By 1710 the Edin- burgh physician, admirer of Newton and author Archibald Pitcairne was making a note to 'write about gallik' and corresponding with the Reverend Colin Campbell of Ardchattan near Oban about druids and bards. Pitcairne was proud to call himself a Highlander, 'one of those from father to sone who beat the Picts', and to send Campbell information gleaned from another 'Mr Campbel advocat' about 'our language'.[108] Not until the mid-eighteenth century would the first Gaelic ballad be published in English translation, but Kirk's *Secret Commonwealth* remains one of several indications in the later seventeenth century of an interest in translating material from Gaelic culture for publication in English.

The sort of folk beliefs that fascinated Kirk were probably linked to some of the originally pagan charms and oral poems collected by folklorists in later centuries. Often this material has been Christianized and may be Catholic in tone – all the more suspect to Reformation Protestants. While some areas of the Highlands vehemently embraced Protestantism, others remained committedly Catholic or returned to the old faith as a result of later Catholic missions. Today it is not hard to find neighbouring islands or mainland villages, one predominantly Catholic, its neighbour adhering to fundamentalist Protestantism. It is often difficult, even impossible, to date the origins of material collected by Highland ethnographers, but a prayer to Christian guardian spirits to watch over the embers of a 'smoored' or smothered peat fire so that it will not go out entirely by morning may serve as representative of a much larger body of verse. A version of this prayer may date to the seventeenth century:

> Smàlaidh mise nochd an teine,
> Mar a smàladh Muire 'n t-aingeal.
> Có bhios air an fhaire nochd?
> Muire gheal 's a Mac,
> 'S aingeal geal an dorus an taighe
> Gus an dig a' là màireach.

> *I shall smoor the fire tonight,*
> *As Mary would smoor the fire.*
> *Who shall be on watch tonight?*
> *Bright Mary and her Son,*
> *And a white angel at the door of the house*
> *Until tomorrow comes.*[109]

Very little first-rate poetry in English was written in Scotland during the second half of the seventeenth century. It was, though, a healthy time for Gaelic verse, much of which was neither written down nor published until significantly later. While not officially a clan bard, Eachann Bacach, a poet loyal to the Macleans of Duart Castle on the Inner Hebridean island of Mull, composed poems praising his clan chieftain in the late 1640s. Using a variant of an old Gaelic metre, and drawing on traditions of folksong, his elegy for Sir Lachlan Maclean, who died in 1648, presents a world of harpsong, chess and gambling, as well as heroism and Bible-reading at the chief's court. Formal elegy with praise of the valour and generosity of local leaders continued to be a mainstay of Gaelic verse. Its practitioners were less affected than their Lowland counterparts by the removal of the royal court, but Highlands as well as Lowlands were involved in religious and political warfare. Not all were combatants, however, and some of the most distinguished Gaelic poets of the time were women.

Though little is known about the life of Màiri Nighean Alasdair Ruaidh (Mary MacLeod) (c. 1616–c. 1706), tradition has it that she was born in Rodel at the south end of Harris, and is buried in the beautiful church there. She was employed for a time as a nurse in the MacLeod chief's family at Dunvegan on Skye where the blind Jacobite harper Roderick Morison (c. 1656–c. 1714) praised, then execrated, the household. Mary MacLeod apparently lived to a great age and composed her poetry late in life. Some of it gave offence, causing her to be banished for a time to another island. Many of the most substantial works in her small corpus are formal court elegies. Nevertheless, they use popular diction and verse forms, elevating common language to deal with noble subjects in stressed metre. Mary MacLeod worked in a period when the local Classical Gaelic court poets were dying out, but her work carries something of their spirit while containing at times what seems a markedly personal note. Surely her most appealing poem is the nimble and pellucid song 'Tuireadh' (Lament), composed during a period of exile in which she recalls the happiness of her youth. I present it here with an English version which, though lower in register, tries to catch something of the fluent lyricism of the original:

| Ma dh'fhaodas mi | *If I can* |
| Théid mi dhachaigh; | *I'll get back home,* |

Ni mi an t-iomramh	*making the journey*
Mar as fhasa,	*right away*
Do Uilbhinnis	*to Ullinish*
A' chruidh chaisfhinn,	*of white-hoofed cattle*
Far an d'fhuair mi	*where I grew up,*
Gu h-òg m'altrum,	*a little girl*
Air bainne chìoch	*breast-fed there*
Nam ban basgheal,	*by soft-palmed women*
Thall aig Fionnghail	*in the house of brown-haired Flora,*
Dhuinn nigheàn Lachainn,	*Lachlan's daughter,*
Is ì 'na banchaig	*milkmaid*
Ris na martaibh	*among the cows*
Aig Ruairidh mór Mac	*of Roderick Mor*
Leòid nam bratach.	*MacLeod of the banners.*
'S ann 'na thaigh mór	*I have been happy*
A fhuair mi am macnas,	*in his great house,*
Danns' le sunnd air	*living it up*
Urlar farsaing,	*on the dance floor,*
An fhìdhleireachd 'gam	*fiddle music*
Chur a chadal,	*making me sleepy,*
A' phìobaireachd	*pibroch*
Mo dhùsgadh maidne.	*my dawn chorus.*[110]

As her twentieth-century editor points out, Mary MacLeod composed her work at a time when Gaelic vernacular was largely 'unaffected by English', though the presence of a few English words in her Gaelic are an indication that this state of affairs was coming to an end.[111] Increasing use of the vernacular in poetry at a time when a degree of older bardic learning continued to circulate gave Gaelic verse a flexibility and an amplitude which raised it above the achievements of later seventeenth-century Scottish poets who published in English or Scots.

Like their Lowland counterparts, Gaelic poets sang of the Wars of the Covenant. Diorbhail nic a Bhriuthainn (Dorothy Brown) (c. 1620–

c. 1690) from the island of Luing praised one of Montrose's comrades, the brave Irishman Alasdair mac Colla, as 'my lute, my harp, my fiddle, / Wherever I go, my string of music', and sent to him in prison in a song which draws on Troubadour tradition 'A kiss from the brown-haired girl of the mountain'.[112] Around the same time an anonymous Campbell woman wrote of the ruin caused by the Battle of Inverlochy near Fort William in 1645 when Montrose and Alasdair mac Colla 'devastated' the Campbells.[113] Yet the long, complex lullaby composed by his nurse for Donald Gorm of Sleat in Skye around 1650 attests to the variety and oral richness of kinds of Gaelic verse. Its incantatory rhythms range across 'piping and harping' to 'football' and offer charms that invoke the 'might of sweet Ossian and valiant Oscar' to protect the infant.[114]

The most celebrated Gaelic poet of the seventeenth century, Iain Lom (John MacDonald) (c. 1620–c. 1710), began to compose verse in the early 1640s when he worked in quite a formal bardic style. Soon he developed a more personal and pithy mode of address, as in his poem on the Battle of Inverlochy with its vitriolic conclusion. Several decades before the 1692 massacre of Glencoe, this MacDonald poet delights that the blood of his Campbell enemies has dunged the battlefield before he ends with the cruel bravado of a curse:

> To Hell with you if I care for your plight,
> as I listen to your children's distress,
> lamenting the band that went to battle,
> the howling of the women of Argyll.[115]

Iain Lom has a vituperative muse, but he is also preoccupied with the texturing of an often densely woven verse, so that emotional punch and technical mastery reinforce one another. Iain Lom could not write, but composes in a variety of styles and over a long period. To him has been attributed a hard-hitting denunciation of the 1707 Union of the Scottish and English Parliaments. Iain Lom attacks the corrupt state of Scotland's avaricious nobles, as does Sir John Scot of Scotstarvit in *The Staggering State of Scots Statesmen*. The Gaelic poet, though, is more bitter than Scot, the Director of Chancery. The Gaelic poem on the 1707 Union blames bribery for Scotland's loss of its Parliament. It savages Lord Queensberry, a great supporter of the Act of Union, and has his fellow Unionist Lord Dupplin shit himself in anticipation of English gold. A note of hostility towards 'Tha Sasannaich' is not new in Iain Lom's poetry. His 'Lament for the State of the Country' bemoans the fate of the executed Montrose, 'the lion valiant and mighty'. The Catholic Royalist poet draws on Covenanting imagery of the Scots as God's chosen people, in bondage to their foreign neighbours, though the tension involved may be between Highlander and Lowlander, Protestant and Catholic, as well as between Scots and English:

> Tha Sasannaich gar fairgneadh,
> Gar creach, gar murt 's gar marbhadh;
> Gun ghabh ar n-Athair fearg ruinn –
> Gur dearmad dhuinn 's gur bochd.

> Mar a bha Cloinn Israel
> Fo bhruid aig rìgh na h-Èiphit,
> Tha sinn air a' chor cheudna:
> Chan èigh iad ruinn ach 'Seoc'.

> *We are plundered by the English,*
> *despoiled, slain and murdered;*
> *we must have caused our Father anger –*
> *for we are neglected and poor.*

> *Like the children of Israel*
> *in bondage to the King of Egypt,*
> *we have the same standing:*
> *they call us only 'Jock'.*[116]

Although he could make elegiac poetry in vernacular Gaelic which drew much from the tradition of bardic verse, Murdo MacKenzie of Achilty (Murchadh Mór Mac Mhic Mhurchaidh), who died around 1689, was also author of the much jauntier poem 'An Làir Dhonn' (The Brown Mare). Composed in the three-line stanza which became fashionable in seventeenth-century Gaelic song, this poem presents a lively picture of the poet's boat, contrasting it with his horse:

> It needed no chaff,
> or straw or mash,
> but the clash of the waves on its prow.[117]

Quick and alert in his rhythms, MacKenzie also provides scenes of life on Lewis involving seal-hunting, deer-hunting and revelry. That he was a poet's son as well as a poet emphasizes how much poetry was handed down from generation to generation within Gaelic families and communities, even after the decline of the formal hereditary structures of the Classical era.

The Gaelic traditions of elegy remained strong, heard in the poems of Sìleas na Ceapaich (Julia – or, sometimes, Cicely – MacDonald) who was born around 1660 and who seems to have begun composing verse at about the age of forty; she died in 1729. Daughter of the chief of the Catholic MacDonalds of Keppoch near Arisaig, she moved east to Tomintoul on her marriage to Alasdair or Alexander Gordon about 1685. Her elegy for her husband and daughter is at once formal and moving. Her incantatory lament for the clan chieftain 'Alasdair á Gleanna Garadh' (Alasdair of Glengarry) lists the dead man's attributes like a Gaelic blazon:

> Bu tu 'n lasair dhearg gan losgadh,
> 'S bu tu sgoilteadh iad gu 'n sàiltibh,
> Bu tu guala chur a' chatha,
> Bu tu 'n laoch gun athadh làimhe,
> Bu tu 'm bradan anns an fhìor-uisg,
> Fìor-eun ás an eunlainn as àirde,
> Bu tu 'n leòghann thar gach beathach,
> Bu tu damh leathann na cràice.

> *You were the red torch to burn them,*
> *you would cleave them to their heels,*
> *you were a hero in the battle,*
> *a champion who never flinched;*
> *a fresh-run salmon in the water,*
> *an eagle in the highest flock,*
> *lion excelling every creature,*
> *broad-chested, strong-antlered stag.*[118]

Some details in this poem, as when Glengarry is called 'a capercailzie in the pine-wood', have an exotic charm for the non Gaelic-speaking reader. Within the Gaelic tradition Sìleas na Ceapaich's images were both familiar and formally appropriate. Her output ranges from intimate family poems to hymns, including one to the Virgin Mary. She composed several religious poems towards the end of her life. At times these make use of English loan-words as they rework gospel stories. The rejection of Robert Kirk's transliterated Irish Gaelic Bible, and the apparent failure of the Reverend Dugald Campbell to complete his biblical translations for the Synod of Argyll meant that not until 1767 was a Scottish Gaelic New Testament published, followed by an Old Testament in four parts which appeared between 1783 and 1801. Highland preachers tended to produce extempore translations of scripture as they preached, often basing their words on the King James Version, so that the ultimate authority for Gaels in the seventeenth century remained an English-language God.

Covenanting times, like the Civil War period in England, were repressive and bloody. Scot of Scotstarvit's Covenanter son George, author of *The Model of Government of the Province of East New Jersey, in America* (1685), was held with other religious and political prisoners on the Bass Rock in the Firth of Forth, then died aboard ship to America, without ever seeing New Jersey. More than a century would pass before Scottish fiction dealt with the dislocating violence of the Covenanting era, but few documents are more redolent of the struggles of the age, its lasting martyrology and its adamantine convictions than the handwritten family letter kept in the small 'Cargill Bible' which belonged to a former student of Samuel Rutherford at St Andrews. Donald Cargill became a republican Protestant 'field preacher and insurgent'. He preached against the King before being hunted down by British government troops. In 1681 he was hanged and his severed head displayed on Edinburgh's Netherbow gate. Cargill

bore this *Bible* to the Scaffold as his last best friend and handed it therefrom as his last sad legacy to be carried to his oldest sister Anne Cargill with these memorable words – 'I am as sure of my salvation being complete in Jesus Christ as I am of the *truth* of all that is contained in this holy this inestimable book of God!'[119]

Then as now, though, not everyone liked God. It was dangerous to be seen as an atheist in this society where religious differences might readily provoke conflict. Thomas Aikenhead, an unfortunate student, was hanged for blasphemy in Edinburgh in 1698. A respectable judge like Sir George Mackenzie of Rosehaugh might inveigh against 'the madcap zealots of this bigot age', but to attack or deny God was to risk one's life.[120] One could of course enjoy some superior sniping. The

Episcopalian Gilbert Burnet (1643–1715) who spent his childhood in Edinburgh, then studied at Aberdeen and Amsterdam, wrote elegant English which would be commended by Scottish university teachers of rhetoric in the century to come. Heading south, Burnet spent time at court before becoming Bishop of Salisbury; he was responsible for the deathbed conversion of the libertine poet Rochester. In 1679 Bishop Burnet published his best-selling *History of the Reformation in England*, a cheeky topic for a Scot to choose. His strategy anticipated that of a number of ambitious eighteenth-century Scots like David Hume who would produce large-scale studies of English history – a highly marketable commodity. Burnet had learned much from the Classically-learned Edinburgh minister James Nairn, whom in a word that looks forward to the Enlightened Kirk of the eighteenth century he calls 'moderate'.[121] However, from the 1680s onwards Burnet wrote his polished memoirs in which he says unfairly that the Presbyterian ministers (often fine Latinists) 'had little learning among them' and that 'the reformers were the ancientest authors they read'.[122] As an English Bishop at a safe distance, Burnet could call these men's plain sermons 'very dull'; it was more insolent for the atheist Edinburgh surgeon Archibald Pitcairne to author an anti-Kirk play called *The Assembly*. Probably Pitcairne wrote this work in the 1690s, encouraged perhaps by rights and liberties promised by the Glorious Revolution, though his play was not published until 1722. He was an accomplished poet in Latin and English, whose Latin work was published after his death by Thomas Ruddiman and became part of the cultural climate that nourished the Scots poetry of Allan Ramsay, who elegized him in 1713 and learned from him – just one of many ways in which the Scottish Latin tradition nourished Scots vernacular verse. The cultured Pitcairne had once considered becoming a Church minister, and, despite his atheism, was not entirely unsympathetic to those who defended the religious causes of the age.

Pitcairne wrote a long poem, *Babell*, satirizing the Kirk's General Assembly. In his play *The Assembly* he brings to the stage characters who would have been recognized not just as contemporary types but as actual individuals. 'Salathiel Little-sense' is based on the Principal of Edinburgh University; 'Brother Turbulent' was a well-known Covenanting minister who was imprisoned for his beliefs; the play's 'Moderator' personified the actual Moderator of the General Assembly in the early 1690s. Drawing rather crudely on the conventions of Restoration comedy, *The Assembly*, subtitled *Scotch Reformation*, mocks the sort of mystical eroticism that surfaces in such Presbyterian writings as Rutherford's letters. The play's ministers are clearly randy. 'What a hideous thing is it for a christian Protestant woman for her breasts to be strutting out thus', the Covenanting Solomon tells young Laura after fondling her bosom.[123] Had this drama been staged, it would have scandalized the Scotland of its age, but Pitcairne wisely kept it in manuscript. Published in several editions in the eighteenth, nineteenth and twentieth centuries, yet kept off the stage, it has become a historical curiosity which nonetheless retains a subversively satirical gusto. Its existence signals that the tight control of Scottish society by a repressive Kirk was not without its critics.

Observant, writerly criticism of the vagaries and absurdities of official Scotland in the second half of the seventeenth century came from a number of voices in its midst. One was that of Covenanter Sir John Scot of Scotstarvit, the man who helped initiate the *Delitiae Poetarum Scotorum*. He wrote in English a biographical directory of Scottish officials, including 'Directors of Chancery' of whom he was one. Its form is a little like Thomas Dempster's Latin biographical dictionary, but it is more catty and carries the impressive title *The Staggering State of Scots Statesmen from One Hundred Years, from 1550 to 1650*. An often critical account of the Scottish nobility, like *The Assembly* it lay some time in manuscript; eventually it was published in 1754. Scot sees the nobility to whom he belonged as corrupt. One man is 'A noble spendthrift, exquisite in all manner of debauchery' while the ill-gotten gains of another go 'melting like snow off a dyke'. As in his use of the last phrase, the Latinist Scot can show an eye and ear for popular Scots culture, even folklore. He likes to mention great families' dealings with witches and warlocks, tells how Montrose as a baby 'ate a toad', and recalls how a noblewoman 'being in a coach at night in the streets of London got her ear rent by a rogue who pulled the diamond forth thereof, and with fright the lady died'.[124] Thomas Carlyle enjoyed Scot's often ironically tinged mini-biographies, but like so much other English-language Scottish writing of the period they constitute a fleetingly attractive minor work, sparking into life only when they yield the sort of precise or weird detail that might be found in a ballad.

The ballads, a treasure trove of oral poetry, were the truly world-class body of vernacular work evolving in this period, though most were not written down until later. In origin, many predate the seventeenth century, but it was at this time that they began to be valued by writers, their form settling into the shape we now recognize. A lot of ballads were not collected until the eighteenth century and after, but an important indication that the ballads could be seen as a national resource comes in the form of a remark endorsed with amazement by the patriotic writer Andrew Fletcher of Saltoun (1653–1716): 'if a man were permitted to make all the ballads, he need not care who should make the laws of a nation'.[125] This is a revealing assertion for it signals a shift away from the notion of a poet as courtly Makar, advising or siding with established authority, to the concept of poets as what Shelley in the early nineteenth century would call 'unacknowledged legislators' who might transmit an authority that ran quite counter to that of the ruling powers.[126]

Written down by Fletcher in 1703 at a time when Scotland was about to lose its Parliament to Westminster, his remark about ballads (though he thought them full of 'lewdness') indicates the way Scots might begin explicitly to look to vernacular folk tradition as a bastion of cultural, even national, identity. If the Lord of Session Sir John Scot and the royal physician Arthur Johnston thought the Scoto-Latin corpus might articulate a Classically-learned national tradition, then the prizing of Scots ballads shows that there were quite different modes of conceiving of Scottish heritage. The ballads, while frequently fascinated with the doings of titled folk, spoke of such people from the perspective of the '*Jack* & *Tom* & *Will*, & *Dick*' whose voices King James VI had so despised.[127] More than that, since ballads were often transmitted orally by female ballad singers, they might even sing from the perspective of Jean or Anne or Mary or Gill.

Who wrote the ballads? A good answer is no one. Like so much Gaelic poetry, including the many ballads in Gaelic, the Scots-language ballads were composed orally, not written, and their composer is Anon. As with the rich ballad traditions of England and continental Europe, some Scottish ballads date from the late Middle Ages, a good number from the sixteenth century, and others are later. Increasingly in the late seventeenth century they were distributed in print through popular chapbooks and broadsides sold by pedlars, as well as circulating through oral recitation. Later, in the eighteenth century and after, some of the broadsheet ballads were collected into books along with versions based on recitations. The editors of these books were not the ballads' authors, though often they were themselves poets. Their number included Robert Burns, James Hogg and Walter Scott, all of whom frequently recast the ballads and used them in their 'original' writings.

The word 'ballad' once meant 'song', but is now associated with mid-length narrative poetry. A ballad is more a performance process than a fixed text. One performance may differ from another in details of content, length and tone. When ballads are transcribed from oral to print culture they often acquire a fixed form, existing primarily for a literate audience to read rather than for a community, literate or not, to hear sung. Print preserves but confines a ballad, though the ballad may continue to evolve orally even after it is written down. As the Romantic poets in particular realized, what is stunning about the Scottish ballads is that they carry a peculiar truth-telling power. All tell stories, or have some narrative element; yet, even when encountered silently on the page, they are also lyrical.

Their lyricism sings in their form and details. Sometimes the form chooses the detail. Ballads fix a shape, a sound pattern on the inner ear which both narrator and hearer come to predict. Usually, but not always, this shape is so-called 'ballad metre', an iambic pattern whose four-line stanzas have alternate four-stress and three-stress lines with a rhyme between lines two and four:

> The king sits in Dumfermline town,
>   Drinking the blude-red wine:
> 'O whare will I get a skeely skipper,   *skilful*
>   To sail this new ship of mine?'[128]

So begins the ballad of 'Sir Patrick Spens', a ballad which harks back dramatically to events of 1290. Like other ballads, it mixes almost casual tragedy with a sense of the unavoidable. The King asks in an offhand manner who might be suitable as captain for his latest vessel, and the chance reply of an old man seals Sir Patrick Spens's fate. On occasion, ballads may use a different stanza form, but what is constant is that each stanza is self-contained. Verse forms such as iambic pentameter encourage long, trailing sentences; ballad stanzas forbid them. The longest ballad sentence lasts four lines. If there are two sentences within a stanza, each is extremely short. Ballads speak pithily because they have to. Every printed stanza ends with a decisive punctuation mark – a full stop, question mark or exclamation mark. The syntax never links two stanzas together. If a speech extends over several stanzas, as happens in 'Sir Patrick Spens', it must always be divided up into short sense-units.

Such moulding of syntax makes for a formal inevitability. The ear always expects a sense of closure as each stanza concludes, and the way ballad rhymes normally occur in the second line and at the very end of each stanza heightens this. When a refrain is used as the fourth line of each stanza, the effect is even stronger. In extreme cases there may be two refrains within each short verse. This emphasizes the ballad's status as song, so that the ear, perpetually expecting the chorus and the forward drive of any narrative, is held in a musical suspension by constantly repeated elements that can be grim or jauntily daft, or perhaps both. That combined effect occurs in a poem about wife-beating, 'The Wee Cooper of Fife', where a husband thrashes a sheepskin which he puts over his wife's back. Like Shakespeare's *Taming of the Shrew*, this ballad is lively and unsettling, carried away with its own energy in the unusually extended refrain which, on the page, occupies the inset lines:

> There was a wee cooper who lived in Fife,
>> Nickity, nackity, noo, noo, noo,
> And he has gotten a gentle wife.
>> Hey Willie Wallacky, how John Dougall,
>> Alane, quo Rushety, roue, roue, roue.[129]

Whether waiting for a chorus or a refrain, or simply for the conclusion of each stanza, the ballad-trained ear hears the music of inevitability. Fate and fatality are great ballad themes. Ballads speak of particular events. Yet, handed down from generation to generation, their inevitable rhythms claim a more general authority: 'A' ye wha hae gotten a gentle wife/ Send ye for the wee cooper o Fife' advises that ballad's universalizing conclusion, trying to make sure its work will never be done.

There is a practical purpose to the fact that no sentence in a ballad lasts longer than one stanza. This makes it easy for a performer to add or delete stanzas in performance. Within the tight turning-circle of the stanza there is no room for elaborate trailing clauses or parentheses. Ballads say what has to be said, mixing lyricism with gusts of violence:

> The moon was clear, the day drew near,
>> The spears in flinders flew,   *splinters*
> But mony a gallant Englishman
>> Ere day the Scotsmen slew.[130]

So says 'The Battle of Otterburn', with an extra, binding internal rhyme. Ballads' unremitting acoustic sounds fatalistic because, in terms of poetic technique, it is. The fatalism is heightened because, like Greek tragedies, ballads often tell what were familiar stories. Calling together old and young, as in a group Bible reading, they assemble a community of dead and living around the shared vernacular word. In so doing, they came to be treasured by Scotland's predominantly Protestant post-Reformation society. The ballad form is notable in the Wedderburns' *Gude and Godlie Ballatis*. Yet often the origins of ballads lie in Catholic Scotland. Repeated from age to age, as carriers of popular wisdom, ballads acquired their own authority dependent on neither Church nor state. Though we rely on it absolutely, our own culture of new technologies tends to denigrate the notion of inherited wisdom, not least wisdom passed down by women. Our expression 'old wives' tales' sums this up, but old wives' tales have been of great importance in Scottish literature, not least in the work of male writers such as Robert Burns and James Hogg. In most cases, we cannot be certain whether ballads were authored by women or men, but often in being passed down through female lines of transmission they acquired the status of insistent old wives' tales. That is their strength, not their weakness. Ballads have a knowing ability to speak about issues such as domestic violence, parent–child relationships, and intimate betrayal. They access areas of experience which were once gendered as feminine, as well as the experience of manly warriors whose 'spears in flinders flew'.

Ballads can move quickly. The space between one stanza and the next may indicate a passage of years. Yet they can also accumulate several stanzas given over to a single speech or focusing on one event of short duration. This heightens their sense of often tragic inevitability. 'Edom o' Gordon' is unusual because it survives in a sixteenth-century manuscript almost contemporary with the events it relates; it deals with incidents in Aberdeenshire but, in its best-known version, transposes them to the Borders; the north-east and the Borders are the areas most celebrated for Scots ballads. Using an almost freeze-frame technique, 'Edom o' Gordon' directs the hearer's attention to an awful incident where a girl is wrapped in 'a pair o shiets' and thrown over a castle wall to escape her enemies.[131] She lands, though, right on the point of an enemy spear. In one stanza we hear her ask to be flung over; in another she falls; in several more the protagonist, Edom o' Gordon, reacts with horror to her fate. The ballads' ability to move rapidly across time or to slow right down is sometimes called their 'leaping and lingering' facility. A braking device can be applied within a single stanza so that one word is taken hold of and repeated, echoed and re-echoed like something inevitable that just will not go away:

> 'To Noroway, to Noroway,
> To Noroway oer the faem:
> The king's daughter of Noroway,
> 'Tis thou maun bring her hame.'[132]

So Sir Patrick Spens 'walking on the strand' reads the message that will seal his fate, and the word 'Noroway', signalling the destination of his difficult voyage, tolls like a bell. Ballads not infrequently halt on a single word to emphasize it, then accelerate ahead. Vocal creations themselves, they like to let us hear voices within them, giving listeners dramatic access to the participants' direct speech. So in 'Get Up and Bar the Door' we hear the quarrelsome voices of thrawn husband and stubborn wife.

As Burns, the English poet John Gay and others realized when they strove to make 'ballad operas' or 'cantatas', the ballads were *dramatic* poems, songs staged for a live audience. While the tradition of Scottish stage-plays is a thin one, the tradition of performative drama in Scottish verse is as strong in the ballads as in Dunbar, Fergusson, Burns, and more recent poets. So 'Sir Patrick Spens', like many other ballads, contains conflicting voices:

> 'Make ready, make ready, my merrymen a',
> Our gude ship sails the morn:'
> 'Now, ever alake! my master dear,
> I fear a deadly storm!
>
> 'I saw the new moon late yestreen,
> Wi the auld moon in her arm;
> And if we gang to sea, master,
> I fear we'll come to harm.'[133]

Yet even in the midst of conflicting emotions that image of the moon is lyrical, perhaps tenderly erotic, a strange focus for respite before the fatal dark storm to come. 'Sir Patrick Spens' ends with images that speak of overthrow, of drowning, but also form an ironic tableau of hierarchical order that could never have been witnessed by a human eye:

> O forty miles off Aberdeen
> 'Tis fifty fathoms deep,
> And there lies gude Sir Patrick Spens,
> Wi the Scots lords at his feet.[134]

The 'Scots lords' who earlier in the poem were loath to wet 'their cork-heeld shoon [shoes]' are overwhelmed by the North Sea. There is no escape. The 'silken claith' with which the sailors try to stop the sea flooding into Sir Patrick's ship is as hopeless as the 'goud kaims [gold combs]' in the hair of the women who wait 'lang, lang' for the sailors' homecoming. These details add ironic point and glancing detail to the narrative. Sometimes we may be unsure how to take them: is it intentionally ironic that cork (as in 'cork-heeld shoon') is a substance that normally rises to the surface of water? Or is that just an accidental thought? The details can seem incidental, but they are subtly functional. The ballad structure, with its need for fixed sound patterns and formulaic phrases, summons them up. They come unflinchingly to their places. The story of Sir Patrick Spens is one of accident as well as design. A mixture of these two elements goes into the finest ballads.

By the late sixteenth century even one of the most sophisticated intellectuals in the British Isles could pay tribute to the ballads, albeit with some embarrassment. Sir Philip Sidney wrote, 'I must confess my own barbarousness, I never heard the old song of Percy and Douglas that I found not my heart moved more than with a trumpet; and yet it is sung but by some blind crowder, with no rougher voice than rude style.'[135] Sidney is probably referring to 'The Battle of Otterburn', which tells of a Northumbrian conflict of 1388, and survives, like many ballads, in English as well as Scottish versions. The ballad is a genre that circulates internationally, and many Scottish ballads have analogues in other countries. Yet the strength of Scottish balladry is particularly distinguished. It is as if Scots vernacular tradition, increasingly eschewed by those high-cultural writers seeking to perfect their Latin or English, focused much of its energy on this one particular form and invested it with a compulsive clarity that is the exact opposite of Urquhart's lexicographical brio.

'Mony a one for him makes mane,
But nane sall ken where he is gane;   *shall know*
Oer his white banes, when they are bare,
The wind sall blaw for evermair.'[136]

That last stanza of 'The Twa Corbies', harshly spoken by a crow that is about to peck the eyes from a slain knight's corpse, relies on a weirdly dramatic psychological effect: the narrator of the ballad overhears the crow who tells us where the body is, so that we know – even as we are told no one will ever know – the knight's fate and his corpse's location. The last stanza of this ballad also relies on straightforward antitheses: 'Mony a one' plays off against 'nane' as the human 'mane [moan]' of the first line is balanced and outdistanced by the eternal blowing of the wind. Like Poe's raven repeating 'Nevermore', this crow whose last word is 'evermair' seems eerily full of a more-than-human awareness.

The ballads' ability to go beyond a single human voice, even as they are performed through it, is part of their power. Their often formulaic diction, their fatalism and their shared form all make for the sensation of work that is transmitted by a single individual but comes from beyond him or her. In that apparently sourceless balladic 'beyond' lies a power which can know without there being personal responsibility for the knowledge. 'I am telling you this because the story says so,' says the voice; not 'Here is my new poem.' In this regard the ballads are like a folk version of those medieval literary texts which claim to be copied from earlier books. Or, to put it another way, in the ballads lies that impersonality which T. S. Eliot thought vital to all great poetry.

Ballads may be tethered to particular or dimly remembered historical events, such as the court of Mary, Queen of Scots, in 'The Four Maries'. They can also provide a no-nonsense language for the visionary imagination. When the ballad of 'Thomas Rhymer' takes the ancient figure of Thomas of Erceldoune from 'Huntlie bank . . . by the Eildon Tree' far away to 'fair Elfland', the poem deals with the sort of crossing into an otherworld that would have been familiar to the witch Isobell Gowdie as well as to readers of romance. This ballad's repetition of the words 'True Thomas' stresses perhaps a kind of loyalty in the protagonist, but also his veracity and a more general confidence in the truth of imagination.[137] A later Shetlandic ballad, 'The Great Silkie of Sule Skerrie', deals with an unmarried mother whose child by an otherworldly silkie (half man, half seal) is taken away by that strange creature. The silkie prophesies that when the woman eventually marries the first thing her new husband will do is to 'schoot baith my young son and me'.[138] These last words of the ballad are chilling, but also psychologically accurate in the way they envisage the new husband's wish to reject and eliminate his bride's former family. Ballads' truth-telling perspicacity works through imaginative vision at least as much as through historical chronicling, and the poems can move easily between the two. In them and through them the dead speak to us with the graininess of vernacular voices.

Bits of ballads find their way into books in the seventeenth century. They appear for instance in the 1644 *History of the Houses of Douglas and Angus* by the highly educated historian and Latin poet David Hume of Godscroft (c. 1558–c. 1630) who wrote in Latin about the unification of the island of Britain. The eighteenth century brought a fuller assimilation of the ballads and their Scots voices into print-culture. Usually undated and often undatable, the ballads are considered in this present chapter because, heard together, they are one of the glories of Scotland's literature. They also remind us that in the often uncertain cultural climate of seventeenth-century Scotland a body of work was passed down which upheld imaginative and vernacular continuities with earlier times and which would fuel the most remarkable poetry of the century to come. Undervalued by academic critics, the ballads are among Scotland's greatest poems. Robert Burns, Walter Scott, Jorge Luis Borges and Muriel Spark have recognized this.

While the popular ballad was the great channel through which vernacular Scots verse flowed in the seventeenth century, Scots was also used by named poets, albeit minor ones. They deserve notice not so much for the quality of their individual poems as for the forms they used and passed on to the future. Notable among these poets is Robert Sempill of Beltrees (c. 1595–c. 1665). His father, Sir James, was author of Protestant pamphlets and an English-language satirical poem, *A Picktooth for the Pope*; he had served King James VI as ambassador in London and Paris. So his university-educated son Robert came from a privileged background. Robert Sempill took a stanza form once used by aristocratic Troubadour poets around the eleventh century and brought into English verse by the thirteenth. By the fifteenth century this high-cultural verse form had reached Scotland and there are a good number of examples of its use among sixteenth-century writers; it occurs for instance at one point in Lyndsay's *Satyre of the Thrie Estaitis* as well as in *The Gude and Godlie Ballatis*, which suggests it was becoming less aristocratic, more popular. What Robert Sempill did was to deploy this stanza form in a seriocomic elegy for a local Renfrewshire piper. 'The Life and Death of the Piper of Kilbarchan, or the Epitaph of Habbie Simson' presents the 'skirl and skreed' of a popular folk musician; it is, as Douglas Dunn points out, 'jaunty, mock, perhaps even condescending'.[139] The predominating four-stress lines in each stanza can be subverted or reinforced by the tail-flicking two-stress lines in ways that are effective, but also sometimes tonally elusive:

> And whan he play'd, the lasses leugh
> To see him teethless, auld, and teugh,
> He wan his pipes beside Barcleugh,   earned
>   Withouten dread!
> Which after wan him gear eneugh;   wealth
>   But now he's dead.[140]

In the century to come this stanza form would be taken up by a wide range of Scots vernacular poets from castles, tenements or cottages, and would acquire the name 'Standard Habbie'. Sempill's poem is no masterpiece, but its frisky music joined to comic-elegiac subject matter hit a cultural nerve in Scotland. If the music of the ballads is one of pithy inevitability, then the tune of Standard Habbie is a laugh–cry melody that veers sometimes vertiginously from solemnity to joking. Here indeed was the rhythm for a staggering state.

Habbie Simson is mentioned also in a lively song about a spirited woman, 'Maggie Lauder', who meets a piper. This poem is attributed to Robert Sempill's son Francis (c. 1616–1682) who may have recast earlier folk material. 'Maggie Lauder' is a poem which hovers on the edge of double entendre and which, like the Standard Habbie stanza, would appeal to Robert Burns:

> Maggie! quoth he; and, by my bags,
>   I'm fidgin' fain to see thee!   excited
> Sit doun by me, my bonnie bird;
>   In troth I winna steer thee;   interfere with
> For I'm a piper to my trade;

My name is Rob the Ranter:

The lasses loup as they were daft, *jump*

When I blaw up my chanter.[141] *pipe*

Other poems attributed to Francis Sempill include 'Fy, Let Us A' to the Bridal' and 'Hallow Fair', works which delight in Scots vernacular language, and in a Scots vernacular cuisine that includes singed sheep's heids and haggis. In the eighteenth century the two great Roberts – Robert Fergusson and Robert Burns – would learn from such work. Another poem, this time essentially in English, 'The Banishment of Poverty by His Royal Highness James Duke of Albany', takes some pleasure in presenting a down-at-heel speaker who can mix educated with demotic locutions in a way that sounds surprisingly modern as he complains of the poverty he can't shake off:

His wink to me has been a law.

He haunts me like a penny-dog;

Of him I stand far greater aw

Than pupill does of pedagogue.[142]

Whether or not Francis Sempill authored all the poems attributed to him, they signal something of the persisting vitality of vernacular verse, even outside the ballads. Sempill is also an instance of a poet who works sometimes in Scots, sometimes in English.

In comparison with the century that followed, the seventeenth century may seem an age of uncertainty, the product of a sometimes staggering Scotland that had lost its court but not quite found its future. Yet in the various languages deployed by its often multilingual writers it laid the basis for the plural literary culture of the modern nation. It also maintained excellence in high as well as low styles. Throughout most of the 1600s these remained separate and, while some traditions of literary language (Scots, English and Latin especially) kept in close contact, others (particularly Scots and Gaelic) stayed resolutely apart. In eighteenth-century poetry there would be greater contact between these different linguistic communities, and between high and low culture. Matters would be complicated by further political change that would deprive Scotland of its own Parliament for almost three centuries. A strong current in much Scottish writing would be the issue of Britishness, though this again was a topic essayed by Scots in the sixteenth and seventeenth centuries. Within Scotland there would be fresh cultural realignments. Latin faded from literary use, but the tradition of Scottish Classical scholarship underpinned the Scottish Enlightenment; more and more the Scots ballads and other older vernacular poems would be collected and prized by the growing and increasingly anglicized polite classes. Gaelic poets would begin sometimes to imitate English-language models. More surprisingly, soon after the traumatic Battle of Culloden a vision of the Gaelic past would capture the European, American and Indian imaginations. And most surprising of all, in an action unthinkable in the staggering state of the seventeenth century, Scotland's greatest Lowland poet would pen the words 'My heart's in the Highlands.'[143]

THE

Ever Green,

BEING A

COLLECTION

OF

SCOTS POEMS,

Wrote by the Ingenious before 1600.

VOL. I.

Published by ALLAN RAMSAY.

Still green with Bays each ancient Altar stands,
Above the Reach of sacrilegious Hands,
Secure from Flames, from Envys fiercer Rage,
Destructive War and all devouring Age.

EDINBURGH,

Printed by Mr. THOMAS RUDDIMAN for the Publisher, at his Shop near the Cross. M.DCC.XXIV.

The title page of the first volume of Allan Ramsay's 1724 Scots anthology The Ever Green, printed in Edinburgh by the great Jacobite Latinist Thomas Ruddiman in 1724. Ramsay, like his admirer Robert Burns, greatly relished the poetry of Alexander Pope, who subscribed to Ramsay's works. (St Andrews University Library, Typ BE.D24RR)

5

Ever Green

In 1707 Scotland and England ceased to exist as nation states. Prominent among the literary reactions are laughter, pride and disgust. A flurry of pamphleteering, preaching and polemic filled the years before and after the Act of Union. The establishment of a London-based Parliament of Great Britain and the loss of a Scottish Parliament in Edinburgh horrified many Scots. As with the 1603 Union of the Crowns, they feared a threat to Scotland's native institutions and traditions. Even writers happy to follow their early seventeenth-century predecessors in stressing their identity as Britons liked to sound a northern patriotic note. The loyal royal physician and plant collector Sir Robert Sibbald (1641–1722) styled his first work *Nuncius Scoto-Britannus* (The Scoto-British Messenger) (1683), but went on to produce surveys of Scottish history and geography with such brassily patriotic titles as *The Liberty and Independence of the Kingdom and Church in Scotland asserted from Ancient Records* (1703). Sibbald also edited a Latin collection of accounts of William Wallace (1705). His late seventeenth-century interest in systematized scientific knowledge, in 'improvements', and in asking questions about what makes people happy are further indications that the preoccupations of Scottish Enlightenment thinkers have Scottish cultural origins that predate the Union of Parliaments. These origins often relate to much earlier seventeenth-century debates around religion, knowledge, finance, and the role of public intellectuals in the Scottish Kirk and state.[1] Sibbald's younger contemporary, the gambler and banking theorist John Law of Lauriston (1671–1729), an advocate of paper currency, discussed exchange in *Money and Trade Considered* (1705), was involved with the Bank of Scotland (founded in 1695), and touched on topics that would be of considerable interest to Scottish economic thinkers in succeeding decades, though the pre-Union Scottish Parliament turned down his overtures.

Around 1707, for most literate Scots political union with England was a matter of immediate and compelling importance. It marked the public extinction of political independence, while offering privileged access to England's burgeoning home and colonial markets. It was a wound and an opportunity. Down south, union with Scotland was certainly an issue, but one less urgent than the ongoing European war. Controlled by the British Crown, English, Scottish and Welsh soldiers under the command of the Duke of Marlborough were playing their part in such decisive continental victories against the French as Blenheim (1704), Ramillies (1706) and Oudenarde (1709). France, not Scotland, threatened English cultural traditions. Nevertheless, there was considerable prejudice against England's northern neighbours, who were often imaged in pretty much racist terms as proud, poverty-stricken, unattractive aliens – whether Scotsmen or Scotswomen:

> The female kind, are a contentious Brood,
> Stubborn, perverse, and not a little proud:
> Addicted to the gossiping infection,
> Rude in discourse and Swarthy in complection . . .[2]

So wrote the anonymous author of *A Trip Lately to Scotland, with a True Character of the Country and People* (1705). Mistrust dogged the negotiations between the two countries, but there was also some enthusiasm – and a flare-up of Scottish political pamphleteering around 1707. Although pre-publication censorship did not lapse until around 1715 in Scotland (where it was partly exercised by local government officials), there seems to have been no intervention to censor pamphlets in the Union debate, perhaps because political opinion was so fragmented. *A Sermon Preached to the People at the Mercat Cross of Edinburgh, on the Subject of the Union* (1706) wooed the Scots with ardour as it serenaded bonding with England:

Dearly beloved countrymen, a generous, a powerful, a victorious nation invites you to an intimate union with themselves, a nation whose laws are more just, whose government is more mild, whose people are more free, easy and happy, than any other in Europe; a nation who by their wealth, wisdom, and valour, have broke the most formidable power that ever threatened Christendom; to whose victorious arms even you yourselves owe your present security.

The nub of this discourse, attributed to the London-based Scot John Arbuthnot, was that it was better for Scots 'to increase our trade, manufacture, and riches by an union with England, than to boast of our sovereignty and starve'.[3] Counter-arguments, however, were equally articulate. In the 1706 Scottish Parliament Lord Belhaven imaged 'our Ancient Mother Caledonia, like Caesar sitting in the midst of our Senate ... breathing out her last with an *Et tu quoque, mi fili*' (and you too have betrayed me, my children).[4] In his *History of the Union of Great Britain* (1709), this speech is reported by Daniel Defoe, who had been sent to Scotland as an English spy while negotiations were being conducted. A particularly detailed Scottish first-hand account of the Union debates in the old Edinburgh Parliament was written by one of its members, George Lockhart of Carnwath (1681–1731) – a sometimes self-interested Jacobite. He curses such 'betrayers of my country' as Lord Queensberry and the 'Judas', John, Earl of Stair, 'author of, the barbarous murder of Glencoe'. Resolutely Lockhart lists the ninety-odd Scottish shires and towns whose representatives protested against Union. He details the riots in Edinburgh, Glasgow and elsewhere that the signing of the Act provoked. He views the 1603 Union of the Crowns as 'the fatal era from whence we are to commence Scotland's ruin', and hymns the way the ancient Scots of Bruce's day fought to maintain their freedom. For Lockhart the Union is shabby, venal, and tragic because the Scottish people represent an ideal of independence:

... show me any country but Scotland that can boast of having defended their liberties so long and so valiantly against a more powerful and numerous people bent upon their ruin, and that frequently without the assistance of allies and having nothing to confide in save their own heroick valour and God's blessing, by means of which they always made good their king's motto: 'Nemo me impune lacesset'.

The quotable detail of his account and the strategic flourishes of his rhetoric may explain why later Unionist apologists have felt a need to defuse or emend Lockhart's writings. Where he denounces England's bribery of Scottish politicians (who might otherwise have impeded the 1707 Union) and reviles an unpatriotic Scottish 'parcel of renegados', Robert Burns will later complain, 'We're bought and sold for English gold,/ Such a parcel of rogues in a nation.'[5] Lockhart's Jacobite passion certainly registers a sense of trauma felt in many sections of Scottish literary society. With horrified incredulity he records the final writing of the Union:

And so the Union commenced on the first of May 1707, a day never to be forgot by Scotland. A day on which the Scots were stripped of what their predecessors had gallantly maintained for many hundred years – I mean the independency and soveraignty of the kingdom. Both which the Earl of Seafield so little valued that when he, as Chancellor, signed the engrossed exemplification of the Act of Union, he returned it to the clerk, in the face of Parliament with this despising and contemning remark: 'now there's ane end of ane old song.'[6]

Lockhart presents these last words as spoken scornfully. Later, others would replay them as resignedly nostalgic, setting them beside that famous remark reported in a different context by another leading literary participant in the Union negotiations: 'if a man were permitted to make all the ballads, he need not care who should make the laws of a nation'.[7] In each case, poetry and legislation are juxtaposed. In Scotland, as in England and, later, Ireland, poetry and literary culture would play a considerable part in articulating national values after the signing away of independent statehood. So poets and other writers often became (in Shelley's nineteenth-century phrase) 'unacknowledged legislators'.[8] For a time Scotland may have mislaid her Parliament; she had not lost her imagination.

The man who wrote down the remark about making ballads was the hero of Lockhart's memoirs, his fellow member of the Scottish Parliament, Andrew Fletcher of Saltoun (1653–1716). Lockhart presents Fletcher as a sort of Admirable Crichton, 'universally accomplished' as well as averse to 'the English and the Union'.[9] Fletcher was friendly with Lockhart, and supported the latter's attempt to have the Union dissolved in 1713. Yet Fletcher, who enjoyed spending time in England and on the continent, was not opposed to any type of British union. Instead, he argued in several lucid speeches and pamphlets for a confederal union which would have seen Parliaments in Scotland and England, operating within a British federation. What Fletcher opposed was the 1707 'incorporating union' which saw much Scottish political power pass to Westminster, and the abolition of the Edinburgh Parliament.

A patrician polymath who disliked over-mighty monarchs, Fletcher had studied under Gilbert Burnet before proceeding to St Andrews

University. He spent about half his life outside Scotland, and wrote his political works in English and Italian. Fletcher learned a good deal from his reading of Machiavelli, but was also alert to the way in which issues of trade increasingly conditioned modern statecraft. A growing concern with commerce and markets would be evident in the work of Hume and Adam Smith, but they would not share Fletcher's Machiavellian leanings. Perhaps more prescient in Fletcher was his concern about the growing dominance of metropolitan centres; his famous remark about ballad-making occurs in a discussion of London. Fletcher is a clear analytical political theorist rather than an imaginative writer. His clarity as well as his openness to modern continental thinkers such as Samuel Pufendorf and the theorist of international law Hugo Grotius continue intellectual currents in seventeenth-century Scottish culture and align Fletcher with some important thinkers in early eighteenth-century Scotland such as Francis Hutcheson. David Hume admired Fletcher, as did Jean-Jacques Rousseau. Republican, patriot and internationalist, Fletcher has been coopted for various causes in his own day and in ours. Works like his 1698 *Two Discourses Concerning the Affairs of Scotland*, his 1701 *Speech upon the State of the Nation*, and his *Speeches by a Member of the Parliament* (published in 1723) remain eminently readable. They also reveal how far Fletcher stands from modern democracy. With an upper-class landowner's predictable indignation he complains about Scotland's itinerant vagabonds and makes a patrician aside about them:

In years of plenty many thousands of them meet together in the mountains, where they feast and riot for many days; and at country weddings, markets, burials, and other the like publick occasions, they are to be seen both men and women perpetually drunk, cursing, blaspheming, and fighting together.

These are such outrageous disorders, that it were better for the nation they were sold to the gallies or West Indies, than that they should continue any longer to be a burden and curse upon us.

Fletcher goes on to propose conditions of enforced service for these 'vagabonds'. Part of his hauteur may be explained by Lowland prejudice against the Highlands – 'an inexaustible source of beggars'; yet this Classically-educated defender of political liberty seems strongly attracted by aspects of personal slavery as practised in the ancient world.[10] While the strong Latin culture of seventeenth-century Scotland may have nurtured such defenders of Scottish national liberty as Lord Belhaven or Fletcher (whom a fellow Scottish Latinist styled 'Cato nostri seculi' – the Cato of our age), it might also channel more oppressive values among patrician elites.[11] No language – whether English, Latin, Scots or Gaelic – articulated only one political position, and even when we understand them it is seldom easy to equate early eighteenth-century political configurations with our own.

The most impressive immediate literary outcome of the 1707 debates was the creation of John Bull. This 'honest plain-dealing Fellow, Cholerick, Bold, and of a very unconstant Temper' was presented as the quintessential Englishman. Soon universally accepted as an English icon, John Bull was a Scottish invention. This may seem paradoxical, but pro-Union Scots were eager to gain access to cultural as well as economic power in the southern heartland of the newly minted British state. In the seventeenth century both the first British monarch and the founder of the Bank of England had been Scots. Now in the eighteenth century one Scot invented John Bull while another penned 'Rule, Britannia'. Bull was seen as England personified, yet he came to be depicted wearing the new British flag, the Union Jack, rather than the English cross of St George. This may hint at how for many in South Britain the terms England and Britain were synonymous, but it also indicates how successful was that maturing ideology of Britishness which many Scottish writers encouraged.

John Bull was the production of John Arbuthnot (1667–1735). Having grown up in the manse beside the beautiful medieval church of Arbuthnott in Kincardine-shire, Arbuthnot could not have avoided an awareness of Scottish history. That small kirk where his father was clergyman is rich in memorials to ancient Scottish families. Yet Arbuthnot's father lost his charge in a late seventeenth-century Presbyterian backlash against Episcopalianism, and the young John headed south, studying at Oxford. In 1696 he returned to Scotland to graduate in medicine at St Andrews. Although the rest of his career was spent in England as a court physician, literary man and friend of writers, Dr Arbuthnot retained an interest in Scottish culture. In 1721, for instance, he subscribed to Allan Ramsay's *Poems*. Arbuthnot's London friends were uncertain how to pronounce his surname; some stressed the second syllable (the Scottish way), others the first (the English), but all regarded him as good company. Alexander Pope addressed to him the celebrated

'Epistle to Dr Arbuthnot', while the Doctor features in poems by his friends John Gay and Jonathan Swift who identified him as 'a Scotch Gentleman'. Arbuthnot seems to have been responsible for the fictional biography *Memoirs of Scriblerus* whose origins lie in London's 1714 Scriblerus Club whose members included Swift, Pope, Gay and Arbuthnot. Eventually published in 1741, the *Memoirs* are a significant early piece of Scottish fiction. They mock pedantry, setting out the birth and career of a German doctor, Martin Scriblerus, who becomes (like Arbuthnot) a celebrated physician. Scriblerus's ridiculous education prefigures aspects of Laurence Sterne's novel *Tristram Shandy* (1759–67), while the device of the absurd, learned German doctor anticipates Thomas Carlyle's Professor Teufelsdröckh in the nineteenth-century *Sartor Resartus*. Arbuthnot's liveliest writing, though, occurs in his letters (later praised by Edinburgh's Professor Hugh Blair) and in his five pamphlets of 1712, collected as *The History of John Bull*. Arising out of the ongoing European war, this allegory satirizes Lewis Baboon (Louis XIV of France), Signora Bubonia (the Catholic Church), and others, but its most vivid material concerns the domestic relations between John Bull and his sister Peg (Scotland):

John look'd ruddy and plump, with a pair of Cheeks like a Trumpeter; Miss look'd pale and wan, as if she had the Green-Sickness; and no wonder, for *John* was the Darling, he had all the good Bits, was cramm'd with good Pullet, Chicken, Pig, Goose and Capon, while Miss had only a little Oatmeal and Water, or a dry Crust without Butter. *John* had his golden Pippens, Peaches and Nectarines; poor Miss a Crab-Apple, Sloe or a Blackberry. Master lay in the best Apartment, with his Bed-Chamber toward the South-Sun. Miss lodg'd in a Garret, expos'd to the North-Wind, which shrevel'd her Countenance; however, this Usage tho' it stunted the Girl in her Growth, gave her a hardy Constitution; she had Life and Spirit in abundance, and knew when she was ill used . . . when he gave her a Cuff on the Ear, she would prick him with her Knitting-Needle.

The gendering of England and Scotland here reflects their perceived status in the Union. Eventually, despite often violent quarrels, Peg is prevailed on to make over her farm to John, provided she 'might have the Freedom of *Jack*'s Conversation', Jack representing Protestant (particularly Calvinist) Christianity. Feisty Peg talks Scots dialect, and her author makes no pretence that her relationship with John is an easy one. During the Scottish Enlightenment Lewis Baboon, John Bull and his sister would be revived in the lively *History of the Proceedings in the Case of Margaret, Commonly called Peg, only lawful sister to John Bull* (a satire sometimes attributed to Adam Ferguson), while the 'Scottish pencil' of Arbuthnot's 'altogether inimitable' John Bull series was much admired by Walter Scott, who edited Arbuthnot's pamphlets in 1814. That was the same year Scott published his first novel, *Waverley*, which examines Scottish–English relations. William Hazlitt's early nineteenth-century *Character of John Bull* 'reads as though it was conceived as a severe but faithful precis of Arbuthnot's original'.[12] Arbuthnot produced what for at least two centuries was recognized as the archetypal Englishman. His achievement is a delicious moment in Scottish literary history.

As had happened with the Union of the Crowns in 1603, so with the Union of the Parliaments in 1707 there was a sense of power drifting southwards. Both the older political theorist Fletcher and the younger wit Arbuthnot were clearly fascinated by London, its coffee houses, clubs, and sheer intimidating size. Arbuthnot also had a taste for the literary milieu of London's Grub Street which would be shared by later Scottish fiction writers like Tobias Smollett. The greatest eighteenth-century Scottish writer, Robert Burns, spent all his life in Scotland, except for a short trip to northern England. Yet other authors, like Andrew Michael Ramsay and David Hume, passed considerable time outside the country. As in the seventeenth century, there was a developed Scottish literary network, some of whose members operated beyond Scotland's borders.

The complexities of such a network involve more than just migration patterns. They include the polylingual currents of Scottish literary culture. Just as several tongues are heard in the Scottish Parliament's Union debates – '*Et tu quoque*', 'ane auld song', 'our Ancient Mother Caledonia' – so in literature Scots, Latin, English and, later, Gaelic, all play their part in arguments over Union. These arguments were accompanied by an increase in learned patriotic publishing. Lockhart of Carnwath mentions with approval Dr Patrick Abercrombie, author of a two-volume survey, *The Martial Achievements of the Scottish Nation* (1711–16), and Dr George Mackenzie whose three-volume *Lives and Characters of the Most Eminent Writers of the Scots Nation* (published by subscription between 1708 and 1722) is an impressive English-language biographical dictionary that includes Scots working abroad as well as home-based authors. Following in the footsteps of such earlier compilers as the seventeenth-century Latinist Thomas Dempster, these works asserted Scottish pride, history and distinctiveness, mustering figures from Scotland's past to bolster and articulate a Scottish identity in an uncertain present. Mackenzie's 'eminent writers' range from familiar names such as Gavin Douglas to figures now forgotten, like the Latinist and Orientalist George Strachan. In a phrase that anticipates a Scottish Enlightenment obsession, Mackenzie catalogues Scots in Europe who have been professors 'of the Belles Lettres'; among his subscribers was Francis Pringle who hoped to place his fellow Classicist Thomas Ruddiman in a Chair of Eloquence proposed at St Andrews University in 1720. This proposal anticipates the later eighteenth-century development in the Scottish universities of the new, French-influenced and Classically-rooted subject of 'Rhetoric and Belles Lettres' which would be exported to American, Indian and (eventually) English universities, then later renamed 'English Literature'.[13]

The development of this subject in the Scottish universities was partly bound up with Scottish anxieties about the need to master the English language. Scots also worried about being able to compete with Anglo-centric Anglophone culture on its own cultural ground within the new Britain, but Scottish uncertainties around 1707 should not be exaggerated. Scotland was hardly powerless. The Union, after all, let her retain her own strong Church, legal, banking and education systems in addition to other markers of cultural difference. The traumatic loss of the Edinburgh Parliament was accompanied by a determination that Scotland's voice should still be heard. If politicians headed for London, then in Edinburgh some educated men looked to Scotland's poets for a renewed sense of cultural self-respect. Where the seventeenth century had seen the appearance of only one major anthology of Scottish verse, the continentally-published Latin *Delitiae Poetarum Scotorum*, the eighteenth century brought several substantial collections of vernacular Scots poetry assembled for patriotic as well as aesthetic purposes. If Scotland the nation state had lost its independence, its political 'auld song' silenced, increasingly poets and singers were treasured as revitalizing national voices. In particular the Scottish Latin tradition might offer sustenance to eighteenth-century writers in Scots and English, especially Jacobites. It is no accident that soon after the Union Thomas Ruddiman was involved in reprinting in 1710 what he regarded as Scotland's greatest work in Scots, Gavin Douglas's translation from Latin in his

Eneados; next, in 1711, Ruddiman brought out the work of the learned Latinist who was then rightly regarded as Scotland's greatest English-language poet, William Drummond; lastly, in 1715, Ruddiman followed with the work of Scotland's greatest Latin poet, George Buchanan, for whose work (and for whose language) he was an outspoken propagandist. Just as later Enlightenment historiographers and social theorists were able to build on debates begun by their pre-Union Scottish predecessors from Buchanan onwards, so poets and imaginative writers were quickened by an awareness of the strength of earlier Scottish poetry. Such patriotic republication asserted the polylingual, Latin-inflected strengths of Scottish literature even as Scotland itself continued to exist as a nation but ceased to exist as a nation state.

Ruddiman did not work alone. Like David Hume after him, he became Keeper of the Library of the Faculty of Advocates (one of Edinburgh's great centres of Latinity and Scots) as well as printer to the young University of Edinburgh. As a librarian, Ruddiman, along with the great Scottish Classicist intellectual and judge Henry Home, Lord Kames, made the Advocates' Library one of Britain's most important repositories of literary learning. It nurtured books such as Kames's own works of legal and cultural history. Written from the 1720s onwards, these advanced Kames's 'stadial theory' of history: society evolved in stages, from hunter-gathering to pastoral-nomadic, and then through organized agriculture to modern commerce. In a more schematic and hard-edged form this four-stage theory of human development would later be applied to European history by William Robertson and used by other Scottish Enlightenment thinkers.

With his brother Walter, with the Latinist Robert Freebairn, and later with his nephew Walter Ruddiman (*Weekly Magazine* publisher and friend of the poet Robert Fergusson in the 1770s), Thomas Ruddiman was part of a growing Edinburgh publishing network. Another of its early members was the patriotic Edinburgh printer James Watson (d. 1721), responsible for one of the most prominent among several vernacular anthologies, *A Choice Collection of Comic and Serious Scots Poems Both Ancient and Modern*, produced in three substantial volumes in 1706, 1709 and 1711. Watson had been jailed in Edinburgh in 1700 for printing a pamphlet called *Scotland's Grievance regarding Darien*. This pamphlet dealt with the ill-fated Scottish Central American colonial venture whose failure may have hastened pressures for political Union.

A mob stormed the prison and released Watson. Eloquent and energetic, he was at the forefront of the developing Scottish press. He published the *Edinburgh Gazette* and printed the *Edinburgh Courant*. The leading Scottish printer of his day, Watson urged fellow printers to join him in a patriotic mission. As he put it in 1713,

since our Native Country has at present as many good Spirits, and Abundance of more Authors than in any former Age; we may make it our Ambition, as well as it is our Interest and Honour, to furnish them with Printers that can serve them well, that they need not, as many of our former Authors have been forc'd to do, go to other Countries to publish their Writings, lest a learn'd Book should be spoil'd by an ignorant or careless Printer.[14]

While the Latin *Delitiae* of the previous century had been the first printed anthology devoted to Scottish verse, Watson's *Choice Collection* proclaimed itself '*the first of its Nature which has been publish'd in our own Native Scots Dialect*', and strove to be '*Correct*' in its texts.[15] Its main importance lies in those last words of its title: '*Both Ancient and Modern*'. For the first time it brought together in print vernacular poetry produced before the Union of the Crowns and verse written more recently. Opening with the boisterous 'Christis Kirk on the Green' and including all of Montgomerie's 'The Cherry and the Slae', it contained a good number of poems by Sir Robert Ayton and Montrose alongside work by living writers such as William Hamilton of Gilbertfield. Scottish forms like the flyting and the Standard Habbie elegy are represented. From a modern standpoint, Watson's omissions may be as striking: no Dunbar, no Henryson. Yet the *Choice Collection* was vital in initiating a published national collection of verse outside the Latin corpus. It did not, though, represent an abandonment of that corpus. Often regarded simply as an anthology of poetry in Scots, Watson's volumes also contain work in Latin and English. While in 1711 Watson and Thomas Ruddiman produced their edition of William Drummond's works, Drummond is also represented in the *Choice Collection*. Indeed, that anthology carries an English version of George Buchanan as well as such Scots poems as 'The Life and Death of the Piper of Kilbarchan' and 'The Blythsome Wedding'. Archibald Pitcairne's Latin appears in the *Choice Collection* as a parallel text beside an English-language poem 'On the King of Fairy', which demands from Watson use of a Greek font. The *Choice Collection* marks not only a patriotic revaluing of the Scots tradition but also a perception of the heritage of Scottish verse as confined to no one tongue.

Recent cultural arguments in England, France and elsewhere had set the ancients against the moderns. Yet there was a strong sense in Scottish writing – from poetry to historiography and social thought – that looking to the ancient might be a way of empowering the modern. Certainly the strong traditions of Scottish Classicism might be drawn on to temper the more zealous objurgations of the Kirk. To be fair, in aligning learning and education with social virtue and the need for general eloquence in arguments over conduct, Covenants, theology and history the Kirk had encouraged open debate and quickened a need for public intellectuals which would grow with the eighteenth century. The more liberal world of London coffee houses and Addison's *Spectator* may have attracted John Arbuthnot after his father was found wanting by stern Scots Presbyterian standards, but the rigorous, fissile Presbyterian tradition produced thinkers in Scotland who argued for a more liberal philosophical standpoint. Some of these thinkers were well-read professors like the Glasgow University Presbyterian divine, John Simson, whose 'knotty case' was argued over by eighteenth-century Kirkmen and serves as a prelude to the emerging Scottish Enlightenment.[16]

Others of these thinkers were students. At Glasgow University the young Scots-Irish poet James Arbuckle wrote Addisonian verse for fellow undergraduates who began to perform English plays such as Nicholas Rowe's *Tamerlane*. Several of these young men's Presbyterian professors turned a blind eye, but since the play involved boys taking female parts it led to a row and, for the time being, student drama was suppressed by the University Principal who considered it depraved.[17] In *Snuff* (1717) and elsewhere, Arbuckle wrote in support of light-hearted fun, and he sided with his fellow student protesters. Classically-grounded in that Christian Latin Stoic tradition familiar from seventeenth-century Scottish writing, Arbuckle's work gives a good sense of student vernacular culture at the time.

Often, even as English replaced Latin as the language of cultural prestige in Scotland, this involved a relishing of those Classical traditions so strong in the Scottish educational tradition. At Glasgow University Gershom Carmichael followed earlier seventeenth-century Scottish poets and thinkers in his engagement with the continental thought of Hugo Grotius; reading aloud his lectures in Latin, Carmichael examined human nature and ideas of moral laws. A Latinist in the Scottish tradition championed by Ruddiman (a great defender of spoken Latin), Carmichael was also one of the first Scottish academics to bring Newtonian thinking into the early eighteenth-century classroom, and so supplemented his Presbyterian orthodoxy with both modern science and Classical learning.

Even in Glasgow Carmichael was not an isolated figure. Also studying divinity at Glasgow University in the second decade of the century was the Irish philosopher Francis Hutcheson. He sat in on Carmichael's Newton-inflected lectures, and delighted in reading ancient secular authors. Like about half his class at Glasgow that year, Hutcheson matriculated as a 'Scotus Hibernus' (Scots-Irishman) in 1711. His Presbyterian upbringing and university training allowed him room to relish Horace, Cicero, Virgil and Terence in addition to the Greeks Xenophon, Homer and even the bawdily carnivalesque Aristophanes. Such a Classical training would be important for the orientation of Hutcheson's own philosophical writings (many authored in Dublin in the 1720s) which deal with laughter and beauty as well as with moral philosophy, liberty and religion. Here was a Presbyterian who enjoyed *Hudibras* and *Don Quixote*; in such tastes he was hardly unique, though some Kirk elders might frown. At Glasgow one of Hutcheson's favourite divinity professors, John Simson, had been censured by the Church of Scotland for his heterodox views. Hutcheson went on to argue that a Protestant understanding of original sin need not conflict with his own ideas about man's social nature and natural benevolence; some have seen such Hutchesonian ideas as underpinning the ideals of American independence later in the eighteenth century.

Hutcheson took up a Chair of Philosophy at Glasgow in 1730. The title of his Latin inaugural lecture, *De naturali hominum socialitate* (On the social nature of man), hints at why Hutcheson's teachings would be so important to his Glasgow student Adam Smith and to his younger correspondent David Hume, who would go on to study what Hume called 'the science of man'.[18] Emerging both out of and in reaction to the rectitudinous scrutiny of the democratically managed Kirk and its often eloquent public intellectuals, Hutcheson's philosophy drew on his Glasgow Classical learning. It develops, though, relatively late in the flourishing Scoto-Latin tradition. As a young man David Hume read widely and intensively in Latin and Greek. He praised Hutcheson as a

Latinist, but Hume produced all his work in English. Hutcheson loved Latin, but was one of the first in the Scottish universities to move to lecturing in English, the language of almost all his published texts. He learned from the English philosophers Locke and Shaftesbury and, like many Scots, enjoyed the essays in Addison's *Spectator*; like Fletcher of Saltoun, Hutcheson read the modern continental theorists of law and morality Grotius and Pufendorf with profit; but the title page of his 1725 *Inquiry into the Original of Our Ideas of Beauty and Virtue* makes plain his siding with 'the antient *Moralists*'. Like his fellow Glasgow student Archibald Campbell, who became a liberal St Andrews professor and wrote *An Inquiry into the Original of Moral Virtue* (1733), Hutcheson nurtured a more open and moderate presbyterian intellectual climate in Scotland which encouraged the growth of philosophy and the literary arts.

When the neoclassical Hutcheson (writing about poetry) argues that rather than being imaginatively impressed by images of total perfection 'we are more nearly touched and affected by the imperfect characters, since in them we see represented, in the persons of others, the contrasts of inclinations, and the struggles between the passions of self-love and those of honour and virtue which we often feel in our own breasts', he helps open up a philosophical space which will welcome more imaginative writing as well as more discussions of poetry and fiction.[19] Adam Smith took up a Chair of Philosophy at Glasgow two decades after his old teacher, Hutcheson. Significantly, Smith chose to teach a special class on Rhetoric and Belles Lettres which drew on modern, but mainly on Classical, authors for its examples. Smith went beyond Hutcheson in the attention he paid to Rhetoric and to literature in our modern sense of that word, and Smith's class is a clear indication of the entry into the university curriculum of the subject that throughout the world's universities would become 'Eng. Lit.' However, the Classical component of Smith's lectures also indicates how far the practically applied culture of the Classics, so strong in Buchanan's Scotland and after, would underpin what later came to be called the Scottish Enlightenment.

During the earlier eighteenth century in works such as his posthumously published *System of Moral Philosophy*, Hutcheson tapped into Scottish ideas of popular resistance so that, as Arthur Herman puts it, 'it is through Hutcheson that the old doctrines of right of resistance and popular sovereignty, espoused by Knox and Buchanan, merge into the mainstream of the Scottish Enlightenment'.[20] The potent appreciation of a Latin inheritance was something which Hutcheson, writing mainly in English, shared with Scottish contemporaries as different as James Watson (with his taste for Scots) and with the Latinist Episcopalian Jacobite Thomas Ruddiman (1674–1757). Ruddiman had been educated at Aberdeen where the Scoto-Latin tradition remained strong. Having participated enthusiastically in a 1709 edition of Aberdeen-educated Arthur Johnston's Latin verse paraphrase of the biblical Song of Solomon, Ruddiman went on to work on another work reconnecting the eighteenth century with Scotland's Scots and Latin past and in 1710 produced his splendid edition of Gavin Douglas's Scots *Aeneid* translation. Ruddiman's glossary for this was in effect the first ever 'Dictionary of the old Scottish Language'. Ruddiman, who wrote a famous 1714 Latin grammar, makes it plain that to him there was a clear link between the 'old Scottish Language' and contemporary spoken Scots: 'It was found necessary also to converse with People of the several Shires and Places, where some of the old Words are as yet used. This seem'd the best method for discovering their true Meaning, next to the Comparing of Translations with the Originals.'[21] The great Classicist's tone here is distant and scholarly. He sounds most at home with Augustan Latin. One would hardly think that he had grown up on a Scots-speaking north-eastern croft.

Yet Ruddiman's insight both typified and spurred the realization that Latin, older Scottish literature and contemporary writing might be reconnected. Works by Buchanan and other Renaissance Scottish Latinists such as Florence Wilson were often reprinted and relished in eighteenth-century Scotland. When the twenty-seven-year-old Allan Ramsay (1684–1758) joined with some friends to found Edinburgh's Easy Club in 1712, he and the members hoped to learn 'Improvement in Conversation' by reading the *Spectator*, regarded in Scotland as a model of correct and stylish metropolitan English. Initially Ramsay and his friends chose pseudonyms drawn from English authors. Soon, though, they switched loyalties to Scottish literary figures and Ramsay styled himself 'Gavin Douglas', after the old Scots Latinist. One of Ramsay's first publications, *A Poem to the Memory of the Famous Archibald Pitcairne* (1713), paid tribute in English to Ruddiman's Latinist mentor. Not long after, however, Ramsay achieved a reputation for such works as *Scots Songs* (1718). His *Christ's Kirk on the Green* (also

1718) was an energetic Scots continuation of the poem that opened Watson's *Choice Collection*. Fusing native ancient and modern with pleasure, Ramsay pointed out that his own cantos were written 'about 300 Years after the first'.[22] The republished poetry of Scotland's past was coming to be viewed as a power source.

Born in the bleakly beautiful upland settlement of Leadhills, Lanarkshire, in 1684 and brought up by his farmer stepfather, Ramsay went to school until the age of fifteen. He attended no university, and so did not pass through the higher-education system still largely under the rigorous management of Kirkmen. Earning his living as a successful wigmaker, then as a bookseller, in the mid-1720s Ramsay had a shop in Edinburgh's Luckenbooths 'at Hawthornden's and Ben Johnson's [sic] Heads'. These English and Scottish emblems are indicative of the catholicity of Ramsay's taste. Translating Horace and Fables by La Fontaine and Fénelon, he admired such English poets as Edmund Waller and Alexander Pope (the latter subscribed to Ramsay's *Poems*), but Ramsay's greatest service was to the Scots tradition. His Scots, especially in Standard Habbie, has both panache and demotic kick. In the dramatic monologue 'Lucky Spence's Last Advice' an Edinburgh bawd blesses 'good doers,/ Who spend their cash on bawds and whores'. The rhyme demands that we pronounce 'whores' as the Scots 'hoors'. Ramsay is cheekily confident enough to take the scarcely respectable English word 'gonorrhoea' and set it dancing to a Scots tune as he has Lucky Spence pronounce

> My malison light ilka day   *curse*
> On them that drink, and dinna pay,
> But tak a snack and rin away;
>   May't be their hap
> Never to want a gonorrhoea,   *lack*
>   Or rotten clap.[23]

Ramsay's 1721 *Poems* was published by Thomas Ruddiman's own press – yet another indication of the empowering interface between Latin and vernacular culture. Half of its poems in English, half in mixed Scots and English, the book comes with decorous English-language footnotes, explaining to polite readers the local Scots references: 'Auld Reeky. A Name the Country People give *Edinburgh* from the Cloud of Smoak or Reek that is always impending over it'.[24] Clearly this volume is aimed at a wide audience that does not understand (or perhaps does not wish to confess to understanding) local references, and an audience that may require some assistance with the Scots language; Ramsay supplied a glossary. Yet for him Scots has a classic, quasi-Classical status. As if to emphasize this, Ramsay transliterates a couple of lines of Gavin Douglas's Scots into Greek lettering. As an author Ramsay was no linguistic purist, but like some seventeenth-century Scots before him he could write of a 'British' language that might include both Scots and English words, providing poets with a richly extended linguistic palette. So he explains how the pronunciation of 'our' Scots language '*is liquid and sonorous, and much fuller than the* English, *of which we are Masters, by being taught it in our Schools, and daily reading it; which being added to our own native Words, of eminent Significancy, makes our Tongue by far the completest*'.[25] Perhaps Ramsay seems a little over-assertive in stating how the Scots have now mastered English. The same preface to his 1721 *Poems* shows an awareness that some readers might feel awkward about the poet's 'Scotticisms'. Yet Ramsay is confident about the attractiveness of the way he writes. He may protest that '*I understand* Horace *but faintly in the Original*', but actually he relished Horace just as much as Francis Hutcheson, and points out that he has included '*Imitations of* Horace' in his *Poems*. In the best of these Ramsay, nurtured by the Scottish Latin tradition of Pitcairne and others, easily fuses Latin and Scots sensibilities. Just to show he knows what he's about, he supplies a Horatian epigraph before launching into his own relaxed imitation. He addresses Edinburgh's 'Phiz' drinking club and moves a Classical mountain to resituate it gracefully in the Pentland hills just south of Scotland's capital:

To the Phiz an Ode

Vides ut alta stet nive candidum	*See how high the white snow shines*
Soracte (Horace)	*On Mount Soracte*

Look up to Pentland's towering taps,
Buried beneath great wreaths of snaw,
O'er ilka cleugh, ilk scar and slap,   *every hollow; cliff; valley*
As high as ony Roman wa'.

Driving their baws frae whins or tee,   *gorse bushes*
There's no ae gowfer to be seen,   *golfer*
Nor dousser fowk wysing a jee   *more prudent; bending to one side*
The byas bouls on Tamson's green.[26]   *bias bowls*

Ramsay can hymn the glories of Scotland in English with a swanky Latin title ('Tartana, or the Plaid'), but he writes best in Scots with an English admixture, a 'British' language in which he can be sly, bawdy and satirical as well as elegant. Ramsay was among the first modern literati to see an energizing potential in the musical heritage of popular Scots songs, even if his 'The Kind Reception. To the Tune of *Auld Lang Syne*' fizzles out after a first line ('Should auld Acquaintance be forgot') which would have to wait several decades for its true poet. Ramsay is closer to prefiguring his later admirer, Robert Burns, when he is at his least high-falutin, as in the simple fling of the chorus to 'Nannyo':

> *My bonny, bonny* Nanny-O,
> *My loving charming* Nanny-O,
> *I care not tho the world do know*
> *How dearly I love* Nanny-O.

To the modern ear, the rhythms of this anticipate Burns's early song 'Green grow the rashes, O'. Revealingly but sadly, in the body of his own song Ramsay spoils things by introducing such rhymes as the Classical '*Danae*-O' and the awkward but topical '*Britannio*'.[27]

Ramsay's quickened taste for modern Scots verse went hand in hand with his enthusiasm for the Scots tradition. In *The Ever Green* (1724) he edited *A Collection of Scots Poems, Wrote by the Ingenious before 1600*. This anthology's epigraph (from Ramsay's admired Pope) is deployed on its first volume's title page to suggest how the Scots verse of three centuries earlier might be prized as a classic inheritance:

> *Still* green *with Bays each ancient Altar stands,*
> *Above the Reach of sacrilegious Hands,*
> *Secure from Flames, from Envys fiercer Rage,*
> *Destructive War and all devouring Age.*

While paying tribute to the English master poet, Pope, Ramsay presents his own Scottish poets with a patriotic flourish. His preface applies to them the term 'bards', a word once associated with the Gaelic tradition, but which would find more general currency in the eighteenth century:

When these good old Bards *wrote, we had not yet made Use of imported Trimming upon our Cloaths, nor of foreign Embroidery in our Writings. Their Poetry is the Product of their own Country, not pilfered and spoiled in the Transportation from abroad: Their* Images *are native, and their* Landskips *domestick; copied from those Fields and Meadows we every Day behold.*[28]

Although this makes medieval Scottish poetry sound far more insular and less internationally sophisticated than it was, it does connect the past to the present. Like Watson, Ramsay begins with the 'Christis Kirk' poem; like Ruddiman, he supplies a glossary for his whole book. Here, for the first time, is a published anthology that brings together work by Dunbar, Henryson, Douglas, Montgomerie, Alexander Scott and Anon. The ballads are also represented. Apparently alert to oral culture, Ramsay writes about his version of 'Johnie Armstrang', 'This is the true old Ballad, never printed before . . . [which] I copied from a Gentleman's Mouth of the Name of *Armstrang*.'[29] *The Ever Green*, as its title suggests, asserts and demonstrates the enduring worth of poetry from the age of the Makars, which had been in danger of being forgotten. Ramsay gave to post-Union Scotland a much fuller sense of Scottish poetic traditions. In his own verse, he showed how this might be fused with a knowledge-able and wide-ranging vernacular voice.

Most of the poems in *The Ever Green* came, as Ramsay acknowledges, from the Bannatyne Manuscript. Along with Watson's *Choice Collection*, *The Ever Green* would provide Burns with a great deal of his knowledge of older Scottish poetry. These *Ever Green* volumes, with their footnotes explaining antique spelling conventions, were hardly best-sellers, but they were loved by Scottish poets. In the anthology Ramsay presented some of his own works as if they were ancient poems. So we have in 'The Vision' a piece signed 'AR. SCOT.', supposedly composed in Latin by '*a most lernit Clerk*' around 1300, then '*translatit in* 1524'. In such productions Ramsay shows his wish to bond with rediscovered Scottish traditions. Ostensibly dating from the era of Robert the Bruce, 'The Vision', with its references to such things as 'Trade', '*Scottish* Peirs' and '*Saxon* Gold', clearly winks towards the events surrounding 1707.[30]

A number of patriotic modern Scottish poets identified with Scotland's rediscovered poetic heritage. Alexander Pennecuik (1652–1722), a loving describer of Tweeddale in his prose, wrote verse in English and Latin, translating from Ovid and George Buchanan; his Englishing of parts of Guarini's *Pastor Fido* perhaps encouraged Allan Ramsay's pastoral *The Gentle Shepherd*; none of Pennecuik's poems lives up to the title of his 'Upon the Marriage of a Crazy Old Presbyterian Divine with a Brisk Young Virgin. Epithalamium'.[31] His namesake Alexander Pennecuik, Burgess and Guild-Brother of Edinburgh (d. 1730), a lover of Arthur Johnston's verse and a minor poet, is livelier, not least in his patriotically Scottish English-language *Historical Account of the Blue Blanket: or Crafts-Man's Banner* (1722) which celebrates the virtues of tradesmen and 'the singular Sanctity of Mechanicks'.[32] Also enthusiastic for Scotland's heritage, Lady Elizabeth Wardlaw (1677–1727) presented her ballad 'Hardyknute' (1719) as a genuine 'Fragment' found in Dunfermline. It dealt with ancient Scottish valour in a way that cultivated an emerging polite taste for balladry. Moreover, in the wake of the 1715 Jacobite rebellion, 'Hardyknute' foregrounded aspects of Highland as well as Lowland Scottish culture as distinctive, proud and alluring:

> To join his King adoun the Hill
> In Hast his Merch he made,
> Quhyle, playand Pibrochs, Minstralls meit
> Afore him stately strade.[33]

Ramsay snapped up 'Hardyknute' for his *Ever Green* anthology. A cultural entrepreneur as well as a poet, he sought to encourage a taste in Scotland for literary culture in general, and for Scottish poetry in particular. If *The Ever Green* sold slowly, Ramsay was more immediately successful with his politely presented four-volume *Tea-Table Miscellany* (1724, 1726, 1727, 1737) of Scots songs and ballads. Often the contents are faithful printings of traditional works, but many are modern 'improved' versions censored of 'all Smut and Ribaldry', or completely new lyrics written to traditional tunes, so that the culture of common folk may occasion no blushes in refined households. Ramsay wanted his 'sangs' to 'steal . . . into Ladies Bosoms' and circulate '*wherever the Sun shines on the free-born chearful* Briton'.[34] While developing vernacular culture, these volumes also played their part in Scottish aspirations for 'refinement' and 'improvement' which became fashionable terms of the day, and often signalled a wish on the part of the middle and upper classes to distance themselves from the milieu of the ordinary people, even as they collected or refashioned their songs. Lady Grizel Baillie (1665–1746), a talented Scottish noblewoman who had grown up in Utrecht, contributed to Ramsay's *Tea-Table Miscellany* her song 'Werena my heart licht I wad die'. Like many writers of this period who learned that kinds of Scottishness might be a marketable asset, Lady Grizel was financially canny. Her *Household Book* (published much later) is meticulous as it tots up the expenses of a noble family devoted to such things as London satin and 'linins for the bairens's shifts' (children's gowns). Her jotted-down menus ('orange pudine . . . Larks rosted . . . sillibubs') show that, as well as a taste for Scots songs, Lady Grizel had a fine sense of haute cuisine.[35]

As the vogue for Scots songs developed, Ramsay, who argued that they were '*so chearful, that on hearing them well play'd or sung, we find a Difficulty to keep our selves from dancing*', was piqued to discover that a London-based Scot, William Thomson, had taken fifty of the best from *The Ever Green* without acknowledgement and published them in London with music under the splendidly Latinate title *Orpheus Caledonius* (1726). So it was that the Princess of Wales, young princesses and top-drawer English noblewomen in metropolitan ballrooms came to tap their toes to such Caledonian exotica as 'The last time I came o'er the Moor' and 'The Gaberlunzie Man'. From Edinburgh and London to Virginia and beyond Scots songs were regarded as charming. Their collection and dissemination continued throughout the century and into later times, reaching its apogee in the work of Robert Burns.

There were also other ways of sounding Scottish and of rediscovering an older Scottish literary heritage. In Edinburgh Allan Ramsay's publisher, Thomas Ruddiman, worked on his great edition of the complete works of George Buchanan. He aimed to present the Renaissance Latinist as his country's national poet. To twenty-first-century readers such an enterprise might appear quixotic, but from an early eighteenth-century standpoint, and given the enduring strength of Buchanan's reputation as poet, historian and public intellectual, it was not. In the seventeenth century Milton admired Buchanan, and later in the eighteenth century Samuel Johnson would still speak of him with awe. Ruddiman's 1715 production of Buchanan's *Opera Omnia* has been called 'the weightiest piece of literary editing ever undertaken in Scotland'; the force of gravity has taken its toll. Yet Ruddiman was passionate in his view of Buchanan along with Milton as 'the two greatest Genius's for Poetry that ever appear'd in this Island'.[36] This fondness for Latin and the Latinate in Scottish poetry may help explain Milton's importance for other eighteenth-century Scottish poets such as the hugely influential James Thomson. In effect, Ruddiman's patriotic editing, positioning Buchanan as Scotland's national poet, developed a role which would be played later in the century by James Macpherson's Ossian, then, soon afterwards, by Robert Burns. That Ruddiman's Buchanan represented the Scottish-Latin tradition, Ossian presented Gaelic rendered as 'sublime' English, and Burns excelled in vernacular Scots with a strong English admixture indicates the rich assembly of different poetries that could be hailed as speaking for Scotland. Each of these poetries received international acclaim. Where the Scottish-Latin tradition may have been in decline, Ruddiman, influential Keeper of Edinburgh's Advocates Library, is the most prominent of several writers and scholars who ensured that it continued to be a living presence. Like many cultured book collections in eighteenth-century Scotland and England, Ruddiman's included John Barclay's Latin fiction, *Argenis*. The fact that Ruddiman had no fewer than nine editions of that Franco-Scot's novel in his personal library emphasizes just how much some Scots still felt part of a Classical as well as a modern culture.

Latin, a language which would underpin the Scottish Enlightenment, was central to early eighteenth-century Scottish education. 'My youngest brother wants a latin dictionary and our people have writ to see if I know where ours was. You mind you have it.'[37] So wrote John Stevenson to his childhood friend Andrew Michael Ramsay in 1709. The two had been fellow pupils at Ayr Grammar School, but Ramsay (1686–1743), after studies at Edinburgh, Glasgow and Leyden, became a Catholic convert and a Jacobite exile in France where he was briefly tutor to the young Prince Charles Edward Stuart and was invested a Chevalier of the Order of St Lazarus. Although this Ramsay does not seem to have been related to Allan Ramsay, they shared an interest in the Catholic author and thinker Fénelon, some of whose *Fables* Allan translated and whose biography Andrew Michael Ramsay published in French in 1723. Andrew Michael, the Chevalier Ramsay, was, with David Hume whom he taught to love France, the greatest Scottish Francophile between George Buchanan and Robert Louis Stevenson. Ramsay also wrote a discourse on epic poetry and an essay on civil government, but became most famous for his Classical *Les voyages de Cyrus* (1727).

Immediately translated into English, this novel's form is based on Fénelon's *Les Aventures de Télémaque* (1699), a prose continuation of Homer's *Odyssey*. The Chevalier Ramsay thought this tale of Telemachus as good as Homer or Virgil, and it would be admired not just by the Scottish Enlightenment rhetorician Hugh Blair but by numerous Scots who read it in French or in English translations such as Tobias Smollett's 1767 *Telemachus*. As a prose epic, it prepares the way for the Ossianic epic prose poems, but more immediately in the 1720s it inspired Ramsay's *Travels of Cyrus* which, also calling on Xenophon's ancient Greek *Cyropaedia* and other Classical works, presents the adventures of the ancient Persian prince Cyrus as he goes from Ecbatan to Sparta, Crete, Babylon, and elsewhere. Though Ramsay's Francophone bestseller now appears a curiosity, it was hugely popular and is a link in Scottish literature between those Classically-oriented fictions, Barclay's *Argenis* and Mackenzie's *Aretina* in the seventeenth century, and the more familiar travel fictions of Smollett and other Scottish novelists in the eighteenth. In *The Travels of Cyrus* the Catholic Ramsay's interests in religious universalism, quietism, prejudice and tolerance are evident. So, allusively, is his Jacobitism. More obvious is a taste for exoticism and, on occasion, the kind of landscape that would later be called sublime: in 'a solitary place upon the frontiers of Persia' we find a garden where

The lofty mountains, which appeared at a great distance all around, and with their craggy tops seemed to touch the sky, served as a barrier against the winds. Through the middle of a garden, less beautified by art than nature, ran a crystal stream, which, falling on a bed of pebbles, formed a cascade, whose agreeable murmur soothed the soul to sweet musing. Not far from hence a wild vine interweaving its branches with many odoriferous shrubs, afforded all the day long a cool and refreshing shade.[38]

Dauntingly learned, this Scoto-French Catholic author, preoccupied alike with modern philosophical arguments and with pagan Zoroastrian Persia (Ramsay was nicknamed by his Franco-Scottish wife 'mon cher Zoroastre'), was accused, like his admirer Walter Scott after him, of making his hero too bland, passive and malleable. But that – as Scott knew – is the point of this kind of Classically-derived fiction about the education of a traveller who functions as a lens through which the reader can examine different societies and systems of belief. Drawing on the Classical novel as mediated by Fénelon, Ramsay kept Scottish fiction alert to the proto-anthropological themes of social comparison which were present in the *Argenis* and which, quickened by Jacobite and Anglo-Scottish tensions in the decades after the 1707 Union, would emerge as important to works authored later by Macpherson, Smollett and Scott.

In English literature, books such as Samuel Johnson's 1759 *Rasselas, Prince of Abyssinia* may owe a debt to the travels of Ramsay's Persian prince. Certainly the author of the *Travels of Cyrus* was widely celebrated. In England he was made a Fellow of the Royal Society in 1729 along with Montesquieu, author of the *Lettres persanes* (1721), and awarded an honorary doctorate by Oxford University in 1730; in France he came close to becoming the first Scot to be elected to the Académie Française; in America Benjamin Franklin's 1751 design for the curriculum of an 'English school' in Philadelphia includes 'the best Translations of Homer, Virgil and Horace, of *Telemachus, Travels of Cyrus*, &c.'[39] Walter Scott was still impressed by Ramsay in the following century, and the *Travels* were republished in New York in 1814, the year of the publication of Scott's novel of Jacobitism, *Waverley*. While he wrote in French, Ramsay, who used French, Scots and English in his letters, was a forerunner of later, much greater Scottish novelists, as well as a reminder that Scots, like other Europeans, still felt close to Classical as well as to more modern literatures.

This was easy to do. Dominant literary genres such as epic verse and pastoral had self-evident Classical affiliations. Allan Ramsay wrote eclogues (short pastoral dialogues of a kind favoured by Virgil), then developed them into his five-act comedy *The Gentle Shepherd* (1725), based on neoclassical pastoral dramas but set in the fields near Edinburgh. Three years later the addition of Scots songs let Ramsay turn this work into a marketably Scottish ballad opera which was performed repeatedly, and is still occasionally revived. '*Gentle*' in its title means 'genteel'. In the eighteenth century Classically-educated critics compared this pastoral play with works such as the Renaissance Italian playwright Giovanni Guarini's *Il Pastor Fido* (1585), another drama with a Classical pedigree, and one which had attracted Alexander Pennecuik before Ramsay. To modern audiences Ramsay's play is a mixture of charm and

stiltedness. Patie and Peggy, its hero and heroine, turn out to be aristocrats under their smocks – which may explain their sometimes awkwardly high-flown English diction. More attractively earthed in this
'green kail-yard' (cabbage-patch) world are the Scots-speaking shepherd
characters of the sub-plot. Bauldy, for instance, memorably describes
the activities of a witch in language that would appeal to the Burns of
'Tam o' Shanter':

> At midnight hours, o'er the kirk-yards she raves,
> And howks unchristened we'ans out of their graves;
> Boils up their livers in a warlock's pow,
> Rins withershins about the hemlock low;
> And seven times does her prayers backward pray,
> Till Plotcock comes with lumps of Lapland clay,
> Mixt with the venom of black taids and snakes . . .[40]

Scots passages like this have an imaginative spark, and the addition
of music and song helps parts of the play canter along in performance.
Too often, though, it panders to a polite tea-table audience, piously
reminding them in rather vapid English about the value of 'Education'
and 'the Arts'. As the Preface to Ramsay's *Poems* mentions, English was
now the language of Scottish education – a revolutionary development
which saw Latin give way to English not just in schools but in universities
too. The Scots tongue came to be heard increasingly as coarse, appropriate only to vulgar subjects. Shepherds might mouth it; but *gentle*
shepherds would readily gravitate towards the emergent international
lingua franca, the language of the British Empire, English.

Ramsay, the poet who presented 'gonorrhoea' as a Scots word, could
revel in coarseness; but he was also attuned to that longing for refinement
which had led the Easy Club to read the *Spectator*. In 1725, when *The
Gentle Shepherd* was first published, Ramsay set up in Edinburgh what
has been viewed (with more Scottish patriotic fervour than accuracy) as
Britain's first circulating library. Circulating libraries had existed in
England from the mid-seventeenth century, but Ramsay's work in
Edinburgh was significant. At least as much as Francis Hutcheson's
lectures, this marked a move towards cultural liberalization that
extended beyond the narrow sphere of the upper classes. The library
roused controversy for lending out English novels and plays which some
regarded as obscene. Similar outrage led to the rapid closing of the

Edinburgh playhouse which Ramsay opened in 1736. Like Thomas Sydserf before him, Ramsay found elements of Edinburgh society markedly resistant to the drama. From 1738 he retreated from public life into his octagonal house, the Goose Pie, built on Edinburgh's Castle Hill.

Ramsay's work encouraged several Scottish institutions: historically-aware anthologies that nourished a new generation of poets; a circulating library that let readers borrow new and old English works; a theatre; and an art college he helped found. His son, also called Allan Ramsay, became a superb portrait painter whose subjects included Hume and Rousseau as well as his own father. Ramsay the poet relished older forms such as Standard Habbie, putting them to modern use in urban as well as rural contexts; he encouraged the taste for Scots songs, and defended the use of Scots language at the same time as reading and writing much English verse. Where in Glasgow Hutcheson argued the case for man's social benevolence, Ramsay in Edinburgh attracted a warm community of writers with whom the poet corresponded and conversed. This sense of community is strong in the Standard Habbie verse epistles Ramsay exchanged with his pal and fellow-poet William Hamilton (c. 1665–1751) of Gilbertfield in Lanarkshire. Where the seventeenth-century Scottish poets had addressed Latin epigrams to one another, now, in the age of the Popean 'Epistle', several poets exchanged verse letters in Scots. Pope the Poet with a capital 'P' did not expect his addressees such as Dr Arbuthnot to reply in verse. These Scots poets often did anticipate replies, and their work was very much part of a vernacular community of poet-equals. Ramsay showed how one might be a Scottish man of letters and a fine poet responsive to both the English and Scots tongues. Though he can be portrayed as a patron saint of Scots vernacular, he is at his best when he writes in the two languages tangled together. The very messiness and blur of relations between Scots and English provides a constant source of literary vitality. This is recognized in Ramsay's 1721 Preface, which also indicates some awareness of how the Latin tradition, even as it faded, might remain a quickening presence.

Two decades after Sir Robert Sibbald's Latin collection of Wallace material, Ramsay's friend William Hamilton of Gilbertfield published a version of Blind Hary's medieval Scots *Wallace* translated into English couplets. Interestingly, the 1722 title page of this most patriotic of Scottish works manages to avoid the word 'English' when describing the language into which Hary's poem has been recast. Yet this poem of epic amplitude, which for a time 'became the most commonly owned book in Scotland, next to the bible', represents in its form a recognition that English, albeit with a Scots infusion, is the dominant language of modern Scottish literary culture. This in no way prevents it from hymning a spirit of Scottish independence and martial valour. Pacy, stirring and popular, this post-Union version of Scottish medieval freedom fighting appealed to many writers who felt a pulse of excitement beating beneath the often awkward Augustan diction:

> Now all is death and wounds; the crimson plain
> Floats round in blood, and groans beneath its slain.
> Promiscuous crowds one common ruin share,
> And death alone employs the wasteful war.
> They trembling fly by conquering Scots oppress'd,
> And the broad ranks of battle lie defac'd;
> A false usurper sinks in ev'ry foe,
> And liberty returns with every blow.[41]

Burns, revolutionary nationalist poet of 'Scots wha hae wi' Wallace bled', quoted that last couplet in a letter, and wrote of how tales of Wallace had 'poured a Scottish prejudice in my veins which will boil along there till the flood-gates of life shut in eternal rest'.[42] Later he would invoke the 'sacred Song' of Wallace's exploits in an English-language poem that praised George Washington and American independence. In the 1760s Burns's favourite Scottish poet, Robert Fergusson, began a tragedy about Wallace, a figure also important to the novelist Tobias Smollett. Repackaged by Hamilton, Wallace also went on to inspire the libertarian souls of later English Romantic poets including Southey and Wordsworth, as well as the novelist Jane Porter in her international best-seller of 1810, *The Scottish Chiefs*. Even the modern American work of Randall Wallace, on which the film *Braveheart* is based, owes a debt to Hamilton of Gilbertfield's poem of 1722.

Those lively verse epistles which Hamilton and Ramsay exchanged in 1719 established a precedent for Burns. Most were written in Standard Habbie, the stanza form adopted by Hamilton in his 'Last Dying Words of Bonnie Heck, A Famous Greyhound in the Shire of Fife'. Hamilton admired how Ramsay could make fresh, sharp verse from a 'Dictionary/ Of ancient Words' – another hint that while jaunty vernacular Scots was living currency for these poets, they might also relish a dash of the antiquarian. Hamilton's praise for Ramsay hints at some awareness of a tradition of Gaelic verse:

> O Fam'd and celebrated ALLAN!
> Renowned RAMSAY, canty Callan,   *boy*
> There's nowther Highlandman nor Lawlan,
>   In Poetrie,
> But may as soon ding down *Tamtallan*   *an ancient fort*
>   As match wi' thee.[43]

Living through the rebellion of 1715 which sought (with notable Highland as well as Lowland support) to install the exiled 'Old Pretender' monarch James Stuart on the now Hanoverian British throne, Ramsay was a Jacobite nationalist. He liked to celebrate the virtues and distinctiveness of a 'Highland Laddie' and his 'Highland plaidy' in a way that signals affection for a milieu traditionally spurned by Lowland authors.

Ramsay's work also attracted younger writers whose finest achievements were of quite a different complexion. Though at his best in Scots, he demonstrated that competent neoclassical English verse might emanate from north of the border – even from a Jacobite nationalist patriot. James Thomson (1700–1748) was born in Roxburgh-shire and began to publish verse in Edinburgh around 1720, along with fellow Scot David Mallet and Francis Hutcheson's Glasgow University student friend and literary ally James Arbuckle whose Latin-titled poem *Glotta* (The Clyde) (1721) takes its Latin epigraph from George Buchanan and supplies a Popeian view of Glasgow life and surroundings. Thomson admired Ramsay's similarly Latin-titled 'Tartana', an English-language poem dealing not only with 'Caledonian beauties' but also with changing weathers and geographies. The younger poet had imitated in Scots one of Ramsay's 1718 elegies, but, with an educated Scottish fondness for the Latinate, he went on to develop an English so ornate that one of the professors at Edinburgh University (where Thomson studied divinity) warned him that he would need to 'express himself in language more intelligible to an ordinary congregation'.[44] For a Scottish divinity-student poet with a taste for Latin, Milton was an obvious model, and Ruddiman's editions of Gavin Douglas (1710) and of Buchanan (1715) significant milestones. The Latin Buchanan showed how a Scottish poet might achieve greatness in the international language of his day. The great Protestant poet Milton had shown how English blank verse, best known as a form for the stage, might also suit a book-length poetry of epic sweep and majesty; in the age of the heroic couplet, his older example offered a potent alternative model. While he did write in early sixteenth-century couplets, the rediscovered Scots Catholic Makar Gavin Douglas had also produced impressive extended visions of winter and summer 'landskip' (to use Ramsay's word) that accompanied his Classical translation. Thomson, writing in English blank verse, published his own extended descriptive landscape poem, *Winter*, in 1726. In the following years he developed his cycle *The Seasons* whose extended treatment of landscape and weather, while drawing on Classicism, would be a huge incitement to the European Romantic imagination.

Thomson had gone to London in 1725, encouraged by Lady Grizel Baillie, and worked as a tutor for her son-in-law, the Scottish nobleman Lord Binning. In October 1725, writing to William Cranstoun, a friend left behind in Scotland, Thomson mentions *Winter* for the first time. He juxtaposes its composition with his longing for the rugged Scottish landscape, and his imagining his friend 'in the well known Cleugh [narrow glen]' back home.[45] Thomson spoke all his life in a broad Scottish accent, but the language of *Winter* is post-Miltonic, somewhat Latinate English. Rhythmically energetic, its fine 'Surge after Surge' of elemental energy would be hailed as sublime by a culture just beginning to develop an enthusiasm for the torrential forces of nature:

> At last, the muddy Deluge pours along,
> Resistless, roaring; dreadful down it comes
> From the chapt Mountain, and the mossy Wild,
> Tumbling thro' Rocks abrupt, and sounding far:
> Then o'er the sanded Valley, floating, spreads,
> Calm, sluggish, silent; till again constrain'd,
> Betwixt two meeting Hills, it bursts a Way,
> Where Rocks, and Woods o'erhang the turbid Stream.
> There gathering triple Force, rapid, and deep,
> It boils, and wheels, and foams, and thunders thro'.
> Nature! great Parent! whose directing Hand
> Rolls round the Seasons of the changeful Year,
> How mighty! how majestick are thy Works![46]

Passages like this helped develop a taste for the mountainous terrain of the Highlands, the Lake District and Snowdonia, places Thomson probably never visited. He also hymned gentler English landscapes. Yet his imagination encouraged in others a 'muse' which, as he put it in *Autumn*, 'sees CALEDONIA, in romantic View'.[47] Republished many times, in cheap as well as splendid editions, and widely translated, *The Seasons* fanfares what will become Romantic taste. Much of the work has little or nothing explicitly Scottish about it, though Thomson in London was certainly part of a Scottish network. He found *Winter* hard to publish. Eventually it was taken on by the London-based Scottish publisher John Millan, who used another Scot, Archibald Campbell, as his printer.

Scots who headed south in search of literary success tended to mask their Scottishness, or to channel it into such emerging niche markets as Scottish songs. Thomson's fellow immigrant David Malloch (1705–65) even changed his distinctively Scottish surname to Mallet. Just as Scottish traders sought access to the commercial opportunities of the whole island and the former English colonies, so did ambitious Scottish poets who used English. Writing to Mallet in 1726, Thomson hints at how as a post-Union Scottish poet working in London he might appeal to a Britain-wide readership. He proposes in his poem *Summer* 'a Panegyric on Brittain, which may perhaps contribute to make my Poem popular. The English People are not a little vain of Themselves, and their Country. Brittania too includes our native Country, Scotland.'[48] Thomson's tone here is one of the incomer eager to make his mark. As an immigrant he found his 'broad Scotch accent' mocked. His 1730 play *Sophonisba* recalls in its title a queenly figure used by earlier Scottish Latinists, and was the first of Thomson's several ventures into the drama. Its London success was attributed by one hostile critic to 'Scotchmen with tuneful hands and many feet' who clapped and stamped their approval in the playhouse.[49]

Yet in print Thomson's Scottish accent was not heard, and he succeeded in wooing his host community. 'HAPPY BRITANNIA!' trumpets the original version of his *Summer*, before listing an all-English team of patriots and sages as part of its 'Panegyric on Brittain'. *Summer* presents a very English landscape of 'Guardian-Oaks', 'Meadows' and '*Villas*'. True, there is a cameo part for the Caledonians – portrayed as Buchanan once portrayed them as 'A gallant, warlike, unsubmitting

Race!/ Nor less in *Learning* vers'd' – but Thomson has a canny awareness of where his principal market lies.[50] He was part of London's
growing, often prosperous Scottish literary network. He befriended
writers from John Arbuthnot to John Armstrong, the patron Duncan
Forbes, the journalist Andrew Reid (whose periodical the *Present
State of the Republic of Letters* puffed Thomson's *Spring*) and the
Strand-based publisher Andrew Millar who would go on to publish the
histories of David Hume and William Robertson, becoming 'the generous patron of Scotch authors'.[51] Though this may seem a Caledonian
mafia, it was not a ghetto. Whereas earlier Scottish Latinists had been
part of a much wider European community, these London Scots now
mingled with English authors, publishers and patrons. Just as Arbuthnot
was a close confidant of Swift and Pope, so Thomson became a friend
of Pope and the English poet William Shenstone. As the eighteenth
century progressed, an increasing number of English tourists began
to visit Scotland. However, before 1750 the only two major English
writers to have visited the country were Ben Jonson and Daniel Defoe.
The former went on what was essentially a holiday, the latter travelled
as a foreign spy. For Scottish authors the way to meet their English
counterparts was to go to London, capital of the now politically united
kingdom.

Educated fellow Scots might be proud of their countrymen's success,
even if, like Allan Ramsay's polymathic patron, the 'improver' Sir John
Clerk of Penicuik (1676–1755), they worried about a southward slipp-
age of talent. A pro-Union Scottish patriot, Clerk was delighted to meet
in London in 1727 'Mr Maloch and Mr Thomsone two young Lads of
my Country & justly esteam'd at present the best poets in Britain'.[52]
Thomson in his twenties was indeed an impressive poet. He spent much
of his later career revising *The Seasons*, a poem which became far the
most popular work by a Scottish author in English libraries before the
1770s. Its sometimes aureate and Latinate English diction includes,
however, a good number of coinages and other locutions which Dr
Johnson later considered unsuited to correct English. Neither Thomson
nor Mallet returned to Scotland. Thomson relished his success. As part
of a masque about Alfred the Great, co-authored with Mallet in 1740,
he penned a poem which, taken out of its Old English context, became
the best-known celebration of Britishness:

When Britain first, at Heaven's command,
Arose from out the azure main,
This was the charter of the land,
And guardian angels sung the strain –
'Rule, Britannia, rule the waves;
Britons never shall be slaves.'[53]

The trope of the unconquered nation was a familiar Scottish one, but most of Thomson's original London audience may well have unthinkingly regarded England and Britain as synonymous. Few today recall that the talismanic words 'Rule, Britannia' were dreamed up by a Scottish member of London's immigrant community. Thomson received a royal pension and became a comfortable British imperialist; he was awarded the sinecure of Surveyor-Generalship of the Leeward Islands, on which he never cast eye. Where contemporary poets in Scotland had hymned the Caledonian 'liberty' in Wallace's 'every blow', Thomson took the same grand term and brandished it with a Union Jack. James Sambrook, his modern editor and biographer, has shown that 'the newly united kingdom provides a unifying idea for much of the *Seasons*'.[54] The poet hymns the 'all-enlivening Trade' of a Britain which can 'reign the Mistress of the Deep', though there may be a slight subterranean tremor as Thomson hopes anxiously that Britain may be 'in Soul united as in Name'.[55] Not all Scots and English people felt a strong mutual affinity in this period. Thomson, however, spoke eloquently for those who did, and united his eloquence with a panoptic vision of nature. He retired from public life at the age of forty, and lived in style at Richmond, Surrey. He celebrated his retreat allegorically in his last poem, *The Castle of Indolence* (1748), which deploys Spenserian stanzas containing self-consciously 'obsolete words'. Among other things, this strange work includes an unsettling description of a lepers' hospital and of gaunt impenitents. Full of 'horror deep-displayed' and 'living catacombs', it sounds a note of disturbance at the end of a remarkable career.[56] Thomson died at the age of forty-eight. His sense of natural sublimity, later so crucial to Wordsworth and the Romantics, makes him the first, and perhaps the only, Scottish poet of whom it can be said that he changed the course of English verse.

The sense of mortality in *The Castle of Indolence* is in some ways attuned to that in *The Grave* (1743) by Robert Blair (1699–1746). The

Scottish Presbyterian minister of Athelstaneford in East Lothian, Blair had studied Divinity at Edinburgh University at the same time as Thomson. His 767 obsessive lines of blank verse meditate on 'The Grave, dread thing,/ Men shiver when thou'rt named.'[57] The same could be said today of Blair's poem. This morose work was part of a Britain-wide vogue for 'graveyard poetry' that led also to Thomas Gray's famous 'Elegy'. However unfashionable in our century, Blair's work was loved by Robert Burns and is an indication that, even when based in Scotland, Scottish poets writing in English might be at the forefront of new literary movements. Painting candle-lit tombs and weeping mourners, in 1804 William Blake would make magnificent watercolour illustrations (rediscovered in 2003) to accompany *The Grave*, whose impact persisted into the nineteenth century.[58] Earlier eighteenth-century Scottish religious literature continued a preoccupation with such matters as the lives and deaths of Protestant martyrs (chronicled by Patrick Walker (1666–1745)) and *The History and Sufferings of the Church of Scotland from the Restoration to the Revolution*, detailed by Glasgow minister Robert Wodrow in 1721. Yet Blair is an example of how Church of Scotland clergy might produce imaginative work that appealed to wider literary taste. Though Allan Ramsay thought that it made people 'laugh & sleep', the Northumberland-born Fife minister Ralph Erskine (1686–1752) also wrote popular religious verse and published a paraphrase of the Song of Solomon in 1738.[59] Like the older Latinate Scottish tradition, the Kirk's littérateurs might nurture the emergent Scottish Enlightenment. Within a few decades Robert Blair's relative, the moderate Edinburgh clergyman and academic Hugh Blair, would become a best-selling moralist and one of the eighteenth century's greatest arbiters of literary taste.

To separate those Scottish writers who went south to London from those who remained in Scotland is as misguided as it is to see an absolute dividing line between composition in Scots and in English. Like Allan Ramsay, minor poets such as Robert Crawford (1695–1733), and the Jacobite William Hamilton of Bangour (1704–54), lyricist of 'The Braes of Yarrow', could compose songs and poems in an English shaded with Scots rhymes and locutions. Crawford's 'The Bush Aboon Traquair' and 'Cowdenknowes' are among many songs that illustrate a growing taste for polite Scottish pastoral, and an emerging sense of the allure of 'lonely wilds'. David Mallet picked up on this when he wrote of 'woods and ye mountains unknown,/ Beneath whose dark shadows I stray'.[60] In London, where Mallet spent most of his unhappy life, such mountains were certainly 'unknown', but, like other Scottish poets, Mallet could encourage a taste for popular forms strong in Scotland. His ballad 'William and Margaret' and his English-language song with a Scots-accented title 'The Birks of Invermay' both do this. Yet Mallet also attempted verses that any London poet might have liked to claim as his own. He is at his most observant in the acutely focused vignette 'On an Amorous Old Man':

> Still hovering round the fair at sixty-four,
> Unfit to love, unable to give o'er;
> A flesh-fly, that just flutters on the wing,
> Awake to buzz, but not alive to sting;
> Brisk where he cannot, backward where he can;
> The teasing ghost of the departed man.[61]

Mallet died aged sixty, so he may have been spared this fate. Probably written in London, this sharply judged poem makes no effort whatsoever to articulate Scottishness, yet is no less a part of Scottish literature. The work of the London Scots went on to play its part in conditioning the literary climate of their native country where later in the eighteenth century 'The Birks of Invermay' became the favourite song of the poet Robert Fergusson, and where Thomson's *Seasons* influenced the Gaelic poet Alasdair Mac Mhaighstir Alasdair in his 'Oran t-Samhraidh' (Song of Summer).

'Oeconomics' (Francis Hutcheson's contemporary spelling of the word emphasizes its Classical roots) continued to exert practical pressures on literary culture, even as it became a subject of serious study for Scottish intellectuals. Those economic migrants, the Scots who prospered in the south, also made their mark on English poetry. None was more peculiar than James Thomson's fellow Roxburgh-shireman Dr John Armstrong (1709–79) who had studied medicine at Edinburgh in the early 1730s before setting up his practice in London. Literary histories tend to mention Armstrong for *The Art of Preserving Health* (1744), his long blank-verse lifestyle guide. Its four didactic books – 'Air', 'Diet', 'Exercise', 'The Passions' – sought to exalt nature while imparting medical lore. In a curious way, hymning natural vigour in sometimes Miltonic tones, Armstrong parallels Thomson. Like Thomson's, his Scottish voice has found its way into what is often viewed as a quintessential articulation of Englishness. Armstrong's earliest sustained poem, *The Oeconomy of Love* (1736), should be remembered as the first popular Scottish-authored sex manual. Though widely read in the eighteenth century, it was later omitted from reprints of Armstrong's works. At once high-flown and explicit, it celebrates heterosexual love and warns young men against masturbation:

> Hold yet again! e'er idle Callus wrap
> In sullen indolence th' astonish'd Nerves;
> When thou may'st fret and teize thy sense in vain,
> And curse too late th' unwisely-wanton hours.
> Impious, forbear! thus the first general Hail
> To disappoint, *increase and multiply*,
> To shed thy Blossoms thro' the desert air,
> And sow thy perish'd Off-spring in the winds.[62]

Although no one has noticed, this second last line about masturbatory release underpins one of the most famous passages written by Thomas Gray in his famous 'Elegy' of 1751. Gray writes of where 'Full many a flower is born to blush unseen, / And waste its sweetness on the desert air.' While Gray's beautiful elegy (Margaret Thatcher's favourite poem) is often viewed as a celebration of Englishness, a good deal of its vocabulary is attuned to Armstrong's, suggesting perhaps a concealed expression of sexual anxieties on the part of the eighteenth-century homosexual Cambridge don Gray. This secret presence of the Scottish physician's words in what is often thought of as a touchstone of Englishness is no more surprising than the Scottish creation of John Bull or 'Rule, Britannia'. Armstrong, the often risible poet who also authored a prose history of venereal disease, is hard to forget completely, if only because he is always reaching into his doctor's bag for an emergency supply of medical terminology. He is at his most uneasily buoyant in his verse epistle to the Scotophobic John Wilkes, 'A Day',

> Now for the weather – This is England still,
> For aught I find, as good, and quite as ill.
> Even now the ponderous rain perpetual falls,
> Drowns every camp, and crowds our hospitals.[63]

Like Arthur Johnston and John Arbuthnot before him, and the traveller-novelists Tobias Smollett and John Moore later, Armstrong was a successful doctor, familiar with English life. As in the seventeenth century, medicine, the Church, academia and (to some extent) the law generated education and income which allowed Scottish men without inherited wealth to launch and sustain literary careers. Patronage and pensions played a part in developing Scottish literary culture, but many male writers belonged to a profession that provided a regular income in addition to their literary earnings. For women, barred from university and the professions, this was not an option. In well-off noble families ladies such as Grizel Baillie might be authors as well as patrons of writing; with some (principally Gaelic) exceptions, lower-class female poets and ballad singers, along with many of their male counterparts in service or manual labour, remained anonymous. They seldom published their own work. Even those lower-class males who became literary figures without passing through university or a learned profession normally earned money from sources other than writing, such as wig-making, bookselling, farming, or being an exciseman.

In London the eccentric Aberdonian Alexander Cruden was allowed to style himself 'the Queen's Bookseller' in 1735 and was congratulated by Queen Caroline in 1737 for producing his great *Concordance* to the Bible. Elsewhere in the British capital the growing phenomenon of Grub Street, which fascinated Scottish authors from Arbuthnot to Smollett and beyond, encouraged the employment of professional journalists and hack writers. Scots were often involved in London critical journals. Kirkcudbright-born Thomas Gordon (c. 1690–1750), translator of Tacitus and Sallust, wrote frequently for the *Independent Whig*. James Elphinston, a quirky spelling reformer, saw through the press an Edinburgh edition of Samuel Johnson's *Rambler*, then moved to London in 1753 where he became a translator of Fénelon and other French authors while running a school and writing his long poem *Education* (1763). Though there were comparatively few such opportunities in Scotland, in Edinburgh James Watson and Thomas Ruddiman are examples of a maturing printing, editing and publishing fraternity which developed alongside institutions like the circulating library, literary and social clubs, periodicals and, increasingly, newspapers such as *The Scots Magazine* (founded in 1739). To modern ears the word 'writer' tends to mean someone who lives off literary work. In eighteenth-century Scot-

land a 'writer' was a lawyer or other man of business; this sense of
the word survives in the expression 'Writer to the Signet'. Aspiring
professional people, some of whom were also authors, might be lured
away by the wealth and employment opportunities of London, site not
only of the royal court but also of the new British Parliament with all
its officials and hangers-on. By 1741, when he was writing mainly in
neoclassical English, Allan Ramsay was also complaining about the
power which the southern metropolis could exercise on culture in Scotland itself:

> London, alas! which aye has been our bane,
> To which our very loss is certain gain,
> Where our daft Lords and Lairds spend a' their rents,
> In following ilka fashion she invents . . .[64]

These lines are addressed to the Scottish musician James Oswald, who
had just headed south where he would become known as the man who
introduced into England the Aeolian harp. This little musical instrument,
hung in trees and played on by the wind, delighted poets and became
an emblem of inspiration for the Romantics. Ramsay knows it was the
hope of 'gold' that tempted Oswald to London. Yet, as was typical of
these migrant Scots, Oswald continued to be part of the Scottish network. Soon he set to music verses by the young medic Tobias Smollett,
who had just come down from Glasgow to seek his fortune and try to
get his first play performed. London, like the growth of the professions,
helped remunerate Scottish writers, a function it still continues to perform. Yet the wealth of London did not lead all Scots towards anglicization. Sometimes it actually spurred a keener examination of what it
meant to be Scottish. In Scotland, understandably, the very growth
of professionalism and commercial specialization led to a developing
Lowland interest in the Highland role of 'bard' – at once a 'primitive'
figure and a trained professional poet. But to live as a professional
author was not an option for most people. As Scottish writers had done
for centuries, and as many would continue to do in the future, authors
pursued both a regular paid job and a literary vocation – work alongside
work. Conceivably this gave them a special feeling for the labouring
society around them. Throughout the period which we now call the
Scottish Enlightenment, this 'work ethic' prevented neither the development of advanced aesthetic theory nor the making of erotic lyric verse.

It is as evident in the career of David Hume as it is in that of Robert Burns, and it is still present in aspects of twenty-first-century Scottish culture.

The effects of the 1707 Union on literary culture were energizing in two quite different ways. Shock caused by loss of political independence spurred a recovery of and reconnection with older Scottish literary traditions – from the Latin of Buchanan to the Scots of the ballads sold in broadsheets and increasingly collected in books in the rapidly expanding print culture of eighteenth-century Britain. Often, though not always, this was accompanied by an attraction towards Jacobitism or nationalism. On the other hand, increased economic access to the markets of England and her colonies across an emerging English-speaking world combined with the growing cultural prestige of written and spoken English in Scotland. This combination alerted ambitious Scottish writers to the greater opportunities now available. Many, but not all, English-language writers subscribed to a Hanoverian and Unionist politics. Scotland's Latin heritage might be called on by a range of new cultural developments, even if there was a decline in significant new Scoto-Latin work. Jacobite rebellions in the 1690s, in 1708 and 1715, then most traumatically in the British civil war of 1745–6, heightened an awareness of Highland culture and of Gaelic poetry. Though Gaelic in the early eighteenth century was still substantially isolated from the rest of mainland Britain as a literary culture, elements of cross-fertilization with Scotland's other literary languages were beginning to emerge.

Snap judgements about these several literary languages should be avoided. It might seem obvious that to write in English was the way to win a wide audience. Yet Samuel Johnson, the most influential English literary man to visit eighteenth-century Scotland, thought that country's poetic excellence lay in Latin. A little later, Robert Burns, regarded internationally as Scotland's national bard, uses a marked admixture of Scots. In the short term, no Scottish work had a greater impact in Europe, North America and beyond than those poems of Ossian which were an outgrowth from Gaelic culture. In English the novelist Tobias Smollett and the philosophers David Hume and Adam Smith (both highly educated in Classical literature) wrote in a way that impressed audiences across several continents and centuries. Just as the political consequences of the Union spurred nationalist as well as unionist impulses, so in complex ways they nurtured the several, increasingly overlapping literary cultures of Scotland. If the 1603 Union of the Crowns had a considerably negative impact on literary culture in Scotland, and perhaps also on the wider Scottish literary network, then for at least two centuries the effects of the Union of Parliaments were both more energizing and more complicated. In each case, Scottish writers had to scrutinize what it meant to be Scottish and what it meant to be British. In neither case, though, were the intellects and imaginations of Scottish authors confined solely to those subtly nuanced topics associated with 1707. Scottish literature was rediscovering its 'ever green' past even as it entered an age when its writers would have their work argued over, sung and relished across all the known world.

11. An robh T. M. Torquatus ceart ann a mhac a mharbhadh air son cogadh an aghaidh an namhaid gun ordughsan?

12. Cia ac is sona an t-Innseanach almhara no an Rinuorpach modhail?

13. Am bheil bardiachd Oisan firinneach no air a sgriobhadh air tus le Mc Fersan?

14. Cia is mo a rinn do dh'fheum de Bhratain Nelson no Wellington?

15. Cia oilean is fearr do dhuine - Mineachd fheumail no Mathematics?

16. Cia ac is truaigh an Struthan no an Spiocaire ga..n garlach?

17. Am bheil e ceart gu 'm bitheadh na cainnt Laidinn air an teugadh ann a chlann og ann an sgoiltibh?

18. Cia is sona leanabitheachd no sean aois?

19. Cia 's mo rinn a choire don traighfhal luchd leanmhuinn eaglais na Roimhe no Mahomet?

20. An ..o an ceudchordadh eadar Sasunn agus Albain gabharach do dh'Albain?

21. Cia is feumail do Bhratain Saighdeara no Seoltara?

22. Am bheil laighean dlighe gabharach do mhodhana?

23. Cia ac is sona duine posta le moran cloinne no duine posta gun neach sam bith?

24. Cia is mosa do dhuine barail as ard no is iosal bhi aige dheth fein?

25. Co ac is buadhach air inntin an duine eisiumplair no teagasg?

26. Am bu choir tochara thoirt maille ri maighdianibh dol a phosadh?

Potential topics for discussion set out in the Gaelic 'Minutes of the St Andrews University Celtic Society' in the early nineteenth century. Clubs and discussion groups were vital to the culture of Enlightenment Scotland, and the repercussions of Enlightenment intellectual life permeated society for generations. Here Gaelic-speaking students consider such topics as the authenticity of the poems of Ossian, western and non-western cultures, and relations between the Christian Desert Fathers and Islam. (St Andrews University Library, Muniments, UY911/Celtic/1/1)

6

The Scottish Enlightenment

'This enlightened age' is a phrase used of her own time by Miss Gauntlet in Tobias Smollett's novel *Peregrine Pickle* (1751).[1] She is being ironic. The term 'Enlightenment' is more slippery than it appears, and some nineteenth-century writers used it pejoratively to refer to eighteenth-century philosophy. Though 'Enlightenment' functions as an English translation of Immanuel Kant's German 'Aufklärung', the phrase 'The Scottish Enlightenment' is not an eighteenth-century one, but a label given currency in 1900 by W. R. Scott, a St Andrews historian of philosophy.[2]

This label has become a sort of intellectual marketing tool. It has stuck because it is an appropriate way to highlight the remarkable contributions made at the time of the Enlightenment by Scottish scientists, historians, economists, philosophers and others. Modern views of these contributions were shaped by the Edinburgh philosopher Dugald Stewart (1753–1828) who had studied with the literary critic Hugh Blair and the philosophers Adam Ferguson and Thomas Reid. Stewart was the influential teacher of Walter Scott and many other men of letters. He wrote biographical memoirs of the philosopher Adam Smith, the historian William Robertson, and Thomas Reid. Stewart's widely read *Dissertation Exhibiting the Progress of Metaphysical, Ethical and Political Philosophy*, written for the *Encyclopaedia Britannica* and eventually published in 1824, stressed among other things the distinctively Scottish formation of Scottish metaphysics. Stewart emphasized the 'science of man', 'conjectural history', 'common-sense philosophy', the culture of the universities and the publishing infrastructure as among the central elements of what we now call the Scottish Enlightenment. He also set this intellectual movement in the wider context of European philosophy. More recently, in the twenty-first century, alert, pacily written surveys like that of the American Arthur Herman present 'The Scottish Enlightenment' as 'The Scots' Invention of the Modern World' and foreground eighteenth-century Edinburgh as what the English intellectual historian James Buchan calls (to the certain chagrin of Glaswegians, Parisians and others) the 'Capital of the Mind'. This Edinburgh was a 'sort of antique Manhattan' which 'Changed the World' and 'stamped the West with its modern scientific and provisional character ... created a world that tended towards the egalitarian and, within reason, the democratic'.[3] We are all, such narratives argue, children of the Scottish Enlightenment.

Sometimes, projecting this Scottish Enlightenment either as almost inexplicably remarkable, or else as too conveniently explained by post-1707 Union Jack-waving British nationalism, modern commentators, like many Enlightenment luminaries, are tempted to sketch earlier Scottish culture as a hopelessly pre-British Dark Age. From a literary point of view, this makes little sense. The measured work of intellectual historians such as Roger Mason and David Allan suggests that it is similarly misleading in terms of historiography, learning and theology.[4] The very word 'Enlightenment', often associated with European rationalist opposition to religion, is a complex term in English. It is underpinned by older notions of spiritual illumination that were strong for England's John Wyclif and for the translators of the 1611 Authorized Version of the Bible, as well as for Scottish Protestant poets like Buchanan who had elegized Calvin in terms of 'in lumine purum/ Lumen' (light/Housed in pure light).[5] Eighteenth-century Scottish thought has roots in an older Scotland, but only a fool would dispute the distinctive international importance of the Scottish Enlightenment, or try to reduplicate here in a literary history the extended, often complex work of specialist historians of philosophy.

This chapter relates Scottish Enlightenment thought to what we now call creative writing. Just as 'creative writing' is a modern, relatively elastic term, so what we now call the 'Scottish Enlightenment' is something of a movable feast. If its origins lie in the seventeenth-century metaphysics that formed part of the intellectual make-up of men like Francis Hutcheson, then its impact also extends well into the nineteenth century. It moulds the work of writers as different as the man of letters Walter Scott and the philosopher James Frederick Ferrier who coined the word 'epistemology'. Perhaps the impetus of Scottish Enlightenment ideas may be detected even in such ground-breaking Victorian scientists as Lord Kelvin and James Clerk Maxwell. Especially in Scottish culture the designations 'Enlightenment', 'Romantic' and 'Victorian' are richly overlapping, and sometimes awkwardly misleading. The misty poems of Ossian were admired by the clear-headed Adam Smith; Walter Scott's Romantic novels, like those of many of his successors, grew out of Enlightenment thought.

At the head of the Scottish Enlightenment's luminaries stand two young men encouraged by Francis Hutcheson – David Hume from Berwickshire and Adam Smith from Kirkcaldy. Hume (1711–76) corresponded in his twenties with Hutcheson. He wanted both Hutcheson and Hutcheson's Glasgow student Smith to read his first book. Ambitious and philosophically revolutionary, this was published in London in three volumes in 1739–40. Its title is *A Treatise of Human Nature: Being an Attempt to introduce the experimental Method of Reasoning into Moral Subjects*, and few reviewers bothered with it. Disappointed by its reception, Hume turned towards the essay form made popular by English writers like Addison. In Edinburgh he published his two volumes of *Essays, Moral and Political* (1741–2). As an essayist there and in his later *Four Dissertations* (1757) Hume treated such topics as literary tragedy and taste, but he concentrated on political and philosophical matters. His 1748 *Philosophical Essays Concerning Human Understanding* (revised in 1756 as *An Enquiry Concerning Human Understanding*) dealt controversially and sceptically with subjects that included miracles and the notion of a Supreme Being. In any history of Scottish literature philosophers such as Hume and Adam Smith demand consideration for their singular importance, their stylish perspicuity, and for the connections between their thought and other, more obviously imaginative literary productions. Too often 'the Scottish Enlightenment' has been viewed in ways that sideline imaginative literature. Including work in Gaelic and work by Lowland Scots based inside as well as outside Scotland, this chapter adopts a more holistic, less sectarian approach.

'A passion for literature . . . has been the ruling passion of my life,' wrote Hume in an age when the word 'literature' took in learned as well as imaginative productions.[6] For Hume as for other Scots, from David Watson, the translator of Horace, to James 'Ossian' Macpherson, the Classics were a reservoir of practical as well as imaginative possibilities; so the young scholar, who would go on to hold various salaried posts, read not just Herodotus and Thucydides but also such works as Lucian's *On Salaried Posts in Great Houses*. It was to Lucian that the Scot Archibald Campbell would turn when he attacked the often Scotophobic lexicographer Samuel Johnson in *Lexiphanes* (1774). Like other well-educated Scots, Hume had a taste for *Don Quixote* and the ballads, for Virgil and Milton, as well as for modern French, English and Scottish writers. He once suggested that in an ideal state 'Music, poetry, and contemplation' would be the 'sole business'.[7] Educated at Edinburgh University (where, not unusually for the times, he had matriculated at the age of ten), Hume rejected a career in law and, after suffering a nervous breakdown from which he recovered in 1734, spent substantial periods in France and in England before becoming for a time a private tutor, then Keeper of Edinburgh's Advocates' Library. He used his income and knowledge to give practical help to such literary men as the blind poet, translator of Buchanan's verse and Kirk minister Thomas Blacklock (1721–91), who in turn championed Robert Burns. Hume was not a poet, but he sometimes writes like one: 'We have other earths. Is not the moon another earth . . . ?' asks one of the speakers in his controversially sceptical, posthumously published *Dialogues concerning Natural Religion* (1779).[8] Even on his deathbed, having penned the short essay 'My own Life' which was, as he wryly put it in the last line, his own 'funeral oration', Hume quoted Lucretius and parried James Boswell's intrusive grilling about the probability of an afterlife. If he personified scepticism, Hume also embodied good-natured sociability. Stylish, clear and imaginative, he was lionized in the mid-1760s by the French intellectuals with whom he partied in Paris, and was admired among the swelling ranks of Scottish literati. His scepticism about miracles and, indeed, Christianity itself, disturbed many, but, while his views cost him professionally in failed candidacies for university chairs, he was not made into a pariah.

Hume's background, like that of Adam Smith, appears strictly Presbyterian. Aged twelve, in his third year at Edinburgh University he was obliged to attend lectures on philosophy delivered in Latin by a stern, old-fashioned Calvinist. The word 'reformation' often carries a positive charge in his prose, even if he was wary of the Scottish Reformers; though in France he was friendly with the Jesuits of Descartes's old Anjou college, his deployment of such terms as 'monkish' and 'priestcraft' is clearly pejorative.[9] When Hume asks Hutcheson in 1739, 'What is the end of man?' he draws on the words of the Kirk's catechism, even as he manoeuvres away from such an 'endless' question.[10]

A tendency towards intense self-scrutiny developed among Calvinists anxiously searching for signs of grace. When Hume scrutinized the self, he did so with such characteristic intensity that it disintegrated under the effort. In the first book of his *Treatise* he wrote that 'For my part, when I enter most intimately into what I call *myself*, I always stumble on some particular perception or other, of heat or cold, light or shade, love or hatred, pain or pleasure. I never can catch *myself* at any time without a perception, and never can observe any thing but the perception.' So, for all that people may treasure the notion of 'selves' as essential and individual, 'they are nothing but a bundle or collection of different perceptions, which succeed each other with an inconceivable rapidity, and are in a perpetual flux and movement'.[11] This sense of apparently haphazard 'rapidity ... flux and movement' at the core of what we think of as a person may be hinted at in the rhotacistic title of Smollett's pacy first novel, *Roderick Random* (1748). The seemingly 'random' narrative structuring of such novels as *Don Quixote* and its eighteenth-century picaresque descendants may have conditioned philosophers' narratives of the self. Certainly philosophy fed the novel. If the Humean self split or dissolved into discrete, random perceptions, then memory might gather these into something like a continuous history, while imagination might envision a self out of the fragmented sense data. Imagination was essential to this view of knowledge and the self. In its implications Hume's most radical and vertiginous critique of the self was encouraging for novelists and historians. Generations of critics have detected dramatically divided selves in Scottish fiction: those selves are Hume's children. Smollett, who wrote history as well as fiction, regarded Hume as the finest writer of the age. Concluding Book I of *A Treatise of Human Nature*, Hume maintained that 'in all the incidents of life we ought still to preserve our scepticism'. As deeply sceptical about cause and effect as he was about the self and aspects of the imagination, Hume was nevertheless a novelists' philosopher. For the self to survive it needed both the pleasures of society and of imaginative reconstruction; it required to be valued as fiction. What life needed was writing.

Novelists such as Smollett and Henry Mackenzie, both of whom knew Hume, scripted the eighteenth-century self as well as eighteenth-century society. When Hume's sometime tenant and intrusive interviewer James Boswell researched and collected documents, anecdotes, testimonies and accounts relating to Samuel Johnson, he was weaving together a literary self out of scattered perceptions and experiences. In his remarkably frank private journals Boswell tried and perhaps failed to do the same for his own variorum of a life. As a biographer (that word means 'life-writer') Boswell has no equal in the English language. Hume's influence on biography and fiction extended well beyond his lifetime. Crucially, Walter Scott's protagonists are noteworthy much less for their own strength of character than for their registering a succession of experiences and perceptions by which they are sympathetically swayed. In this they are Humean in design, even if they also owe something to the fictional Cyrus created by Hume's one-time mentor Andrew Michael Ramsay. Of sympathy Hume at the start of Book II, Section XI of his *Treatise* wrote that 'No quality of human nature is more remarkable.' He saw 'communication' within society as made possible because 'we never remark any passion or principle in others, of which, in some degree or other, we may not find a parallel in ourselves'.[12] Hume's Hutchesonian emphasis on benevolence and the importance of the passions and sympathy over unalloyed reason also encouraged the 'sentimental' school of novelists headed by Edinburgh's Henry Mackenzie. Though it was not his principal intention, the literature-loving Hume did much to encourage imaginative writing. Thinly disguised, he even became a character in a celebrated short story by Mackenzie.

In many ways, though it was in the twentieth century that Hume came to be regarded as one of the greatest of all philosophers, his preoccupations were attuned to eighteenth-century literary culture. Where Alexander Pope in 1733 had written at the start of Epistle II of his verse *Essay on Man* that 'The proper study of mankind is Man', Hume in the introduction to his 1739 *Treatise* sought to develop what he called 'the science of man'. He saw this as doing 'honour to our native country' since 'So true it is, that however other nations may rival us in poetry, and excel us in some other agreeable arts, the improvements in reason and philosophy can only be owing to a land of toleration and of liberty.'[13] Hume, like his Scottish Enlightenment contemporaries, had not just a passion for 'liberty' but also a yearning for 'improvements' in areas as diverse as language, agriculture and justice. We may think of him today as a 'philosopher', but Hume was really a 'man of letters', as were Smollett, Mackenzie, Smith, and so many other Scottish Enlightenment figures. Convenient modern shorthand, which styles Smollett 'novelist' and Smith 'economist', risks straitjacketing these writers according to much later, narrower specializations of authorship. Hume wrote essays on topics such as 'Of Love and Marriage' and on Ossian as well as his extended philosophical analyses. He followed Hutcheson in writing about artistic taste and literary composition, as well as other subjects from national characteristics to government and commerce. While he was fascinated by specific local and temporal beliefs and prejudices, he held a strong belief in a shared, universal human nature. This is evident, for instance, when he writes 'Of the Standard of Taste':

It is evident that none of the rules of composition are fixed by reasonings *a priori*, or can be esteemed abstract conclusions of the understanding, from comparing those habitudes and relations of ideas, which are eternal and immutable. Their foundation is the same with that of all the practical sciences, experience; nor are they any thing but general observations, concerning what has been universally found to please in all countries and in all ages. Many of the beauties of poetry and even of eloquence are founded on falsehood and fiction, on hyperboles, metaphors, and an abuse or perversion of terms from their natural meaning. To check the sallies of the imagination, and to reduce every expression to geometrical truth and exactness, would be the most contrary to the laws of criticism; because it would produce a work, which, by universal experience, has been found the most insipid and disagreeable. But though poetry can never submit to exact truth, it must be confined by rules of art, discovered to the author either by genius or observation.[14]

Modern concerns about cultural relativism may erode some of Hume's universal certainties. However, a passage such as this suggests why his work appealed so widely, and encouraged advanced literary culture.

As it gained in momentum, quickened by the work of men of letters who not only authored but edited, reviewed, and liaised with a developing Lowland publishing infrastructure, Scottish literary culture grew increasingly alert not just to the productions of London, but also to those of France. The countrymen of the Francophile Buchanan and of Hume's mentor the Ayrshire Frenchman Andrew Michael Ramsay, Hume and Smith enjoyed fruitful periods of residence among French intellectuals, and were hardly the only Scots to do so. Smollett was in

Paris in 1750, shown around by his relation and fellow Glasgow medical alumnus Dr John Moore, later author of a proto-Byronic novel *Zeluco* (1789) which was much admired by Moore's correspondent Robert Burns. Smollett (who played a significant part in supervising an English edition of Voltaire's works) drew on his visit to Paris's Scottish colony in *Peregrine Pickle*. Montesquieu in particular, but also Diderot and the French Encyclopedists, fuelled Scottish Enlightenment thought, and many French and Scottish intellectuals conversed or corresponded with one another. William Smellie, Burns's Edinburgh printer and one of the authors of the *Encyclopaedia Britannica*, translated the natural historian Buffon. As well as corresponding with the influential legal theorist Montesquieu, Hume, a sociable correspondent, knew and aided Rousseau, while the latter's *Julie* helped trigger Henry Mackenzie's third and last novel, *Julia de Roubigné* (1777), set in France. This intellectual recasting of the 'auld alliance' operated in both directions. Such was the impact of Scottish thinking on French culture that Voltaire not only wrote a play about a Scotswoman but marvelled at the strength of Scottish culture. David Hume, lauded in France as 'le bon David', might well have given a tasteful smile.

By the late 1740s Hume's younger friend Adam Smith (1723–90) was giving his lectures on 'Rhetoric and the *Belles Lettres*', after an education at Glasgow and Oxford. When he was appointed to the Chair of Logic at Glasgow University in 1751, Smith lectured in English on modern as well as Classical literature, concentrating more on prose than verse. 'Belles Lettres' was a term from French academia where Charles Rollin lectured on the subject in Paris. The fashionable modern equivalent of 'Belles Lettres' might be 'Theory, Criticism and Creative Writing'. Rollin's works were soon translated and read by eager Scottish students. The 1734 English-language title page explains that his lectures are 'An Introduction to Languages, Poetry, Rhetoric, History, Moral Philosophy, Physics, etc., with Reflections on Taste, and Instructions with regard to the Eloquence of the Pulpit, the Bar, and the Stage, the Whole Illustrated with Passages from the most famous Poets and Orators, ancient and modern, with Critical Remarks on them, Designed most particularly for Students in the Universities'. That vast subtitle indicates just why such a subject might appeal to young Scottish students ambitious to advance professionally, and why Adam Smith's development of Rhetoric and Belles Lettres seemed so useful and important.

Smith's work helped encourage in Scotland, then around the globe, the development in universities of the subject we now call English Literature.

If it seems odd that university English Literature is a 'Scottish invention', then this is partly explained by the Scots' anxiety to purify their language of those markers of cultural difference known as 'Scoticisms' so that they might compete with the English on the latter's cultural ground.[15] The way to do this was to study models of 'proper' English and so avoid the fate of William Duff, Ossian-praising author of *An Essay on Original Genius* (1767) and writer on female culture, whose 'Oriental tale' *The History of Rhedi* (1773) was ticked off in London's *Modern Review* for the 'defects' of its 'few Scotticisms'.[16] Hume and others anxiously made lists of 'Scoticisms', as did the Aberdeen poet and philosopher James Beattie, who published in 1787 his list of prohibited *Scoticisms Arranged in Alphabetical Order, Designed to Correct Speech and Writing*. When Beattie complained that 'We who live in Scotland are obliged to study English from books, like a dead language', he highlighted the way learning good English in Belles Lettres classes seemed as important as learning the international language of Latin had been for Scots in earlier centuries.[17] Now aspiring students had to learn not just Latin but English as well. In an era when school pupils might still talk to one another and to their teachers in Latin, the English-language textual culture of Enlightenment Scotland was gradually built upon and came to overshadow the older culture of Scottish Latin. Scots as a spoken (and, in verse, written) language continued in fairly rude health, though often avoided by many Belles Lettres professors and ambitious young Britons as lacking in prestige. Concerns about competing with the English on their own cultural ground and worries about linguistic correctness were soon exported to America where the Scottish academic the Reverend John Witherspoon, an educational pioneer at Princeton, coined the word 'Americanism' by analogy with the term 'Scoticism'. Questions of cultural imperialism are bound up with 'English Literature' as a discipline, and always have been. The pioneers of the subject, though, were not Wicked English Imperialists but, like the Scots-speaking, English-writing Lord Kames, Scottish Enlightenment patriots anxious to teach themselves and their students how to get on in an Anglocentric Britain and British Empire.

In Scotland's universities, this new subject flourished. By 1758 Professor Robert Watson was telling St Andrews students that the old subject of Rhetoric had become the modern one of Criticism, since to his lectures 'you may give the Name of Rhetorick, or Criticism as you please; if they deserve the one they will deserve the other also'.[18] Works like the 1762 *Elements of Criticism* by Henry Home, Lord Kames (1696–1782) developed the subject's appeal. In his Rhetoric and Belles Lettres lectures Adam Smith emphasized clarity and simplicity ('the most beautifull passages are generally the most simple') and almost completely sidestepped works in 'the old Scots Language'.[19] In some ways Smith was rooted in that seventeenth-century Scottish Latin tradition whose poets had so admired the Stoicism he regarded as 'the best school of heroes and patriots', but he was also fascinated by modern 'improvements'.[20] While he admits that 'Poetry is cultivated in the most Rude and Barbarous nations, often to a considerable perfection,' the important point is that such nations 'make no attempts towards the improvement of Prose'. For Smith, prose, improvement and commerce were all bound together: 'Tis the Introduction of Commerce or at least of opulence which is commonly the attendent of Commerce which first brings on the improvement of Prose ... Prose is naturally the Language of Business; ... No one ever made a Bargain in verse . . .'[21] Smith relished poetry. As an old man he planned a 'sort of Philosophical History of all the different branches of Literature, of Philosophy, Poetry and Eloquence'.[22] Yet his youthful eagerness for prose, commerce and improvement were of a piece with his wish to theorize how societies might advance in *An Inquiry into the Nature and Causes of the Wealth of Nations* (1776), and with his concern for kinds of personal and social exchange in *The Theory of Moral Sentiments* (1759).

If *The Wealth of Nations*, published in the year of the American Revolution, is now Smith's best-known work, it was his *Theory of Moral Sentiments* which most impressed Kant in Germany and Voltaire in France. Smith revised both these masterpieces throughout the rest of his life. The 1776 book provided one of the first full commentaries on the workings of a market society. Written in part to praise liberty, that topic loved alike by the Wallace-wielding Hamilton of Gilbertfield and the canny James Thomson, *The Wealth of Nations* can be aligned with the emergence of the novel; the word 'novelist' in the sense of 'writer of novels' was new in eighteenth-century English, but increasingly English-language novels, newly manufactured by a specialized kind of authorial labour, were being consumed by the university students and other readers who were Smith's Scottish contemporaries.[23] As an economist Smith outlined how the division of labour can massively increase productivity. Taking the example of pin manufacture, he points out that one untutored workman 'could scarce, perhaps, with his utmost industry, make one pin in a day'. However, if the work is broken down into separate tasks, so that 'One man draws out the wire, another straights it, a third cuts it, a fourth points it, a fifth grinds it', and so on, then a small number of men equipped with 'machinery' can make thousands of pins in one day. Hence 'The division of labour, . . . so far as it can be introduced, occasions, in every art, a proportionable increase of the productive powers of labour.'[24] Smith is defining and describing the modern world.

He is the greatest explainer and defender of market economics, on which Hume, who commended *The Wealth of Nations* on his deathbed, had written too. Yet Smith is no blind ideologue but a man of foresight. Even before the American Revolution he predicted that an American 'extensive empire' might well become 'one of the greatest and most formidable that ever was in the world'.[25] Working in Glasgow, he was part of a city that was growing rich from trade with the American colonies. However, as a Lowlander from Fife, he realizes, for instance, that his model of specialized, divided labour will not suit all cultures equally: 'In the lone houses and very small villages which are scattered about in so desert a country as the Highlands of Scotland, every farmer must be a butcher, baker and brewer for his own family.' Smith also warns that governments 'in every improved and civilized society' must encourage widespread education, otherwise the division of labour will mean that 'The man whose whole life is spent in performing a few simple operations . . . becomes as stupid and ignorant as it is possible for a human creature to become.'[26]

Smith, who can be seen as an Addisonian moralist, cared for the 'human creature' more than he cared about pure economic theories. His concerns with language, literature, commerce and social interaction are all related. In each sphere, he focuses on kinds of exchange. So literature for him is a social rather than an isolationist pursuit, since we appreciate what we read through imagination and 'sympathy'. In a Scotland where Newtonianism held sway in the universities, Smith was soon imaged as a Newton of the moral arena, with 'sympathy' his 'one general principle, like that of Gravity in the natural world'.[27] Writing about sympathy,

Smith contended that 'As we have no immediate experience of what other men feel, we can form no idea of the manner in which they are affected, but by conceiving what we ourselves should feel in the like situation.' So when we see someone in pain, Smith goes on to argue in *The Theory of Moral Sentiments*, 'it is by the imagination only that we can form any conception of what are his sensations'. Literature may exemplify, even develop this ability. 'Our joy for the deliverance of those heroes of tragedy or romance who interest us, is as sincere as our grief for their distress, and our fellow-feeling with their misery is not more real than that with their happiness.'[28] Our sense of 'fellow-feeling' with fictional and actual other people is made possible because we have a propensity for 'sympathy' – sympathetic imaginative understanding.

A substantial May 1759 review of Smith's work in Tobias Smollett's London-based magazine the *Critical Review* was probably written by Smollett himself. It commends Smith's sense of 'sympathy' and 'the force of imagination', quoting Smith on how 'by changing places in fancy with the sufferer', we come to feel what he feels.[29] The *Critical Review* piece shows how Smith's theory may lead to sympathy overcoming fixed prejudices – a major topic of Smollett's fiction. Like Hume's, Smith's philosophy fuelled Scottish literary culture. As eighteenth-century Scots eager to acquire 'proper' English read Addison's *Spectator*, so Smith proposed that we imagine a spectator in our own breast that provided a less partial view of our own actions. The prose of Section III of *The Theory of Moral Sentiments*,

If we saw ourselves in the light in which others see us, or in which they would see us if they knew all, a reformation would generally be unavoidable

was recast with a theological accent by Robert Burns,

> O wad some Pow'r the giftie gie us
> *To see oursels as others see us!*[30]

Developed perhaps from the Classical novel and its inheritors in French and English, the theme of sympathetic understanding breaking down mutual prejudices is central not only to Smollett's last novel, *The Expedition of Humphry Clinker* (1771), but also to the whole of Scott's Waverley Novels, published in the early nineteenth century. More immediately, that emphasis on 'sentiments' and on 'sympathy' which

Smith developed from Hume's work provides the philosophical under-pinning for Henry Mackenzie's *The Man of Feeling* – Robert Burns's favourite novel.

Hume and Smith were not only outstanding philosophers. With their theories of split selves, imaginative sympathy and with their sheer love of literature, they were also great nourishers of imaginative writing. Through a growing network of convivial literary clubs in Glasgow, Edinburgh and elsewhere, philosophers met other writers. With his friend the portrait painter Allan Ramsay (son of the poet of the same name), Hume had helped found Edinburgh's Select Society in 1754, but it was only one of many formal and informal gatherings of which he was a part. In a small country, authors' influence was personal as well as textual. What we now call 'networking' was at the heart of the Scottish Enlightenment: scientists met poets, historians met inventors, printers met theologians – and, in a society where one might be both a scientist *and* a poet, a painter *and* an inventor, cultural incest, a feature of literary communities everywhere from Medici Florence to 1900s Vienna, could be positively beneficial.

Not just conversation and correspondence, but actual kinship linked a number of Scottish Enlightenment intellectuals. So, for instance, the Adam family of architects (whose young star, Robert, pioneered a neo-classicism that was, Arthur Herman argues, 'the first truly international style in the modern West', and who became 'the spiritual father of American public building') had their roots in Adam Smith's Kirkcaldy and were friendly with Smith. The architect William Adam's wife, Mary, was the sister of Edinburgh University's Principal William Robertson, a remarkable historian, close friend of David Hume and of the historian Adam Ferguson, and academic boss of Hugh Blair.[31] Such networks rewardingly entangled a brilliant constellation of philosophers, poets, critics, scientists, essayists, doctors, novelists, architects, editors, pub-lishers, historians and others, almost all of whom had several strings to their bow. As the Scottish Enlightenment developed, the networks encompassed both Lowland and, to a lesser degree, Highland families. Although Scotland was at the heart of these groupings, their activities and contacts extended not just to the new Union capital, London, and the old ally, France, but across Europe and the British imperial territories. St Andrews University awarded an honorary degree to Benjamin

Franklin, admirer of many Scottish intellectuals; Adam Smith chatted to Glasgow merchants who made much of the hugely expanded opportunities in overseas trade since the Union; in Edinburgh William Robertson worked on the history of India and America.

The network of Scottish kith and kin extended to such figures as Charlotte Lennox (c. 1729–1804), widely read author of *The Female Quixote* (1752), translator from French, and sometimes styled 'the first American novelist'. Born a Ramsay, she spent part of her teens in New York, before moving to London where she married the Scotsman Alexander Lennox, who worked for the great London-Scottish printer William Strahan. Translator of Voltaire, friend of Samuel Johnson, and describer of American colonial life, Charlotte Lennox writes of both the comedy and bleakness of women's experience. Though she is as much an English or an American as a Scottish author, some features, such as the surname of the eponymous heroine of her first novel, *The Life of Harriot Stuart* (published in 1751, just five years after the final defeat of Prince Charles Edward Stuart at Culloden), suggest that her Scottish connections were significant to this Scotsman's daughter.

Central to the intellectual life of Scotland itself, Smith and Hume were the most commanding, globally influential Scottish Enlightenment thinkers. Yet to suggest they were solitary eminences would be to distort both history and the spirit of their own work. Literature for them was a social as well as an imaginative phenomenon. Several of the forms used to construct great Scottish Enlightenment works took an explicitly dialogic turn, whether they were epistolary novels, conversation poems, translations, versions, reference books compiled from questionnaire returns, periodicals, or the many other works born out of intellectual chat and exchange. Hume's questioning of the self, of religion, and of assumptions about cause and effect might have disturbed himself and others; but he managed to live a genial and generous life. As his friend Smith put it, 'Society and conversation . . . are the most powerful remedies for restoring the mind to its tranquillity.'[32]

The intellectual 'centres' of Enlightenment Scotland were so tiny as to seem peripheral by twenty-first-century standards. 'Auld Reekie', smelly old Edinburgh, was about to drain its principal loch and embark on a huge neoclassical public building programme. Yet, despite having doubled in size in fifty years, it was only about a tenth of the size of London, and in 1755 had a population of under 60,000 people. Of these only a small percentage of the males (and none of the females) went on to higher education. Few travelled far afield; it took a day and a half to ride by coach to Glasgow. Yet surrounding Smith and Hume was a remarkable array of men and women whose society let the Scottish Enlightenment burgeon. In an age when the intellectual emphasis on social exchange meant that society gatherings and polite conversation were highly valued, women were more often enablers and hostesses, private diarists and correspondents than published authors. Among the lower classes women were at the heart of ballad transmission and song, but their work survives often as that of the genderless Anon. Some of the finest eighteenth-century songs by Anon sound a hurt and outspoken note in their treatment of women's experience, as in the instance of 'Jenny Nettles':

I met ayont the Kairny,	
Jenny Nettles, Jenny Nettles,	
Singing till her Bairny,	
Robin Rattles' Bastard;	
To flee the Dool upo' the Stool,	*punishment; Kirk penance stool*
And ilka ane that mocks her,	*each*
She round about seeks Robin out,	
To stap it in his Oxter.[33]	*stick; armpit*

In another, comparable anonymous song, 'Waly, Waly,' a forsaken pregnant girl longs for death, 'For of my life I am wearie.'[34] Even those non-aristocratic women poets who made it into print might find success came with a bitter taste. Jean Adam (1704–65), a Greenock shipmaster's daughter orphaned at an early age, published a collection of her verse and won fame after her death when the Edinburgh accountant David Herd included in his anthology of *Ancient and Modern Scottish Songs* (1776) her poem 'There's Nae Luck about the House'. Its stanzas are vivid, but speak also of a loving need for male protection. Jean Adam was a strong woman She founded a school for girls in Greenock. But she also died in the poorhouse.

And gie to me my bigonet,	*linen cap*
My bishop-satin gown;	
For I maun tell the baillie's wife	
That Colin's come to town.	

My turkey slippers maun gae on,
  My hose o' pearl blue;
It's a' to please my ain gudeman,
  For he's baith leal and true.
    For there's nae luck about the house,
      There's nae luck at a'
    There's little pleasure in the house,
      When our gudeman's awa'.[35]

Often the women who transmitted ballads and songs were great characters, but they are usually seen in the shadow of some 'gudeman'. Margaret Laidlaw, James Hogg's mother, recited to her son a beautiful version of the 'Corpus Christi Carol', which begins 'The heron flew east, the heron flew west'. He wrote it down and it was published. Margaret Laidlaw also furnished the obsessive ballad-collector Walter Scott with materials, though she emphasized to him with undaunted spirit that they were 'made for singing, an' no for reading'.[36] Female-transmitted oral culture was a part of the Scottish Enlightenment that was preserved, if at all, by male authors and editors. But there is no doubt of its power. Emblematic is Burns's unconcealed debt not just to his mother's songs but to

an old Maid of my Mother's, remarkable for her ignorance, credulity and superstition. – She had, I suppose, the largest collection in the county of tales and songs concerning devils, ghosts, fairies, brownies, witches, warlocks, spunkies, kelpies, elf-candles, dead-lights, wraiths, apparitions, cantraips, giants, inchanted towers, dragons and other trumpery. – This cultivated the latent seeds of Poesy; but had so strong an effect on my imagination, that to this hour, in my nocturnal rambles, I sometimes keep a sharp look-out . . .[37]

It might be thought that such 'trumpery' was fine for old women and poets, but unsuitable for Enlightenment gentlemen. The reverse may have been true. The questionnaire that produced *The Statistical Account of Scotland* (completed in 1799) inquired after such things as 'traditions', while there was an increasing fascination with ethnographical information and folk beliefs. As Burns knew, old wives' tales might now become the stuff of literature.

Among upper-class women, the aristocratic Alison Cockburn (1712–94) produced a celebrated version of the song 'The Flowers o' the Forest' and wrote private letters whose alert wit at times suggests what helped her organize a fashionable, rather French-style Edinburgh salon. Her friends included Hume and the young Walter Scott. Though an impressive generation of Scottish women of letters was born in the 1750s and 1760s, and will be considered later, a good deal of their predecessors' writings were produced in the form of private journals, coming to public notice only much later, if at all. They spoke in discussions at salons and parties, but scarcely a word of that survives. The English dramatist and intellectual Catharine Cockburn (1679–1749) lived in Scotland from 1726 until 1737 while her husband was an Episcopalian minister in Aberdeen. Lord Monboddo and his daughter subscribed to her 1741 *Works*, as did Thomas Reid, but she seems to have published little or nothing during her Scottish years. More visible to us is Janet Schaw (c. 1737–c. 1801), whose travel journals of the mid-1770s were published under the title *Journal of a Lady of Quality* in 1921. That very title echoes the 'Memoirs of a Lady of Quality' which form part of Smollett's *Peregrine Pickle*, and is indicative of how women's private writings tend to be viewed, deliberately or not, through a lens shaped by men.

Taking in travels in the Caribbean, America and Portugal, Schaw's journal is detailed, often spirited in its response to scenic grandeur, and sometimes revealingly prejudiced; it is 'negroes' rather than slavery which Schaw finds disgusting. The young Maria Riddell's 1792 *Voyages to the Madeira and Leeward Caribbean Isles* is another striking publication. On the whole, though, the writings of named Lowland women in this period are less impressive than the poems and songs of Highland women composing in Gaelic. Modern scholarship, most notably that of Dorothy McMillan, has drawn attention to some often neglected writings by Scotswomen. Gender codes were shifting subtly in the Enlightenment, and were most easily defied by those at the very top or bottom of the social hierarchy. Nevertheless, social expectations confined most women to the role of enabler, whether as household administrator, mother or hostess. Women like Adam Smith's mother (who ran his household) or William Robertson's sister, or David Hume's housekeeper, or Robert Burns's remarkable and resilient wife Jean Armour were essential to the life of the Scottish Enlightenment. They conversed regularly with its best-known luminaries. Literary history, though, tends to think of those luminaries' social and intellectual interlocutors as uniformly and exclusively male.

Among these discussion-hungry men was Thomas Reid (1710–96), a

Church of Scotland minister and university teacher in Aberdeen. A former student of Aberdeen's Thomas Blackwell and George Turnbull, Reid published *An Inquiry into the Human Mind on the Principles of Common Sense* in 1764, then succeeded Adam Smith as a professor at Glasgow. It is striking how many of the leading figures of the Scottish Enlightenment were university staff, at once internationally well connected and closely attuned to their local communities. Respectfully but resolutely critical of Hume, Reid rejected that thinker's extreme scepticism, arguing that 'As there are words common to philosophers and to the vulgar, which need no explication, so there are principles common to both, which need no proof, and which do not admit of direct proof.'[38]

Championing the 'self-evident', Reid's more moderate philosophy was accessible, friendly to religion, and appealed to many in Scotland, Europe and revolutionary America; it is at the root of what came to be called the Scottish 'Common Sense' school of thinking. Some have suggested that the American Declaration of Independence whose 'truths are held to be 'self-evident' owes a debt to Reid.[39] He also worked on developing a new, perspicuous rhetoric appropriate to the discourse of science, and wrote on aesthetic philosophy. Reid was a founder (in 1758) of the Aberdeen Philosophical Society, nicknamed the 'Wise Club', whose members came to include Alexander Gerard who penned a 1759 *Essay on Taste* and, fifteen years later, an *Essay on Genius*. Other members of this circle included the poet-philosopher James Beattie and the author George Campbell, who wrote about miracles, then produced in 1776 his *Philosophy of Rhetoric* before surveying translation issues in *Four Gospels* (1789). All these men were Church of Scotland ministers – another factor which bound them as public intellectuals to the wider society. Their prominence in Aberdeen's literary life was emblematic of a wider pattern in Scottish culture. As the eighteenth century developed, an increasingly moderate faction in the Kirk made it a major player in literary life. Zealots persisted, but even by 1723 Adam Smith's deeply religious mother, Margaret Douglas, was happy to have an image of the Virgin Mary and the Eastern Kings in her dining room, and a likeness of 'Calvin the Reformer' in her kitchen; Smollett, who in 1751 has a character 'snore like a whole congregation of Presbyterians', by 1771 has a fictional Welshman write credibly that 'Even the kirk of Scotland, so long reproached with fanaticism and canting, abounds at present with ministers celebrated for their learning, and respectable for their moderation.'[40]

Moderate clergymen might even go to the theatre. The poet and dramatist of *The Gentle Shepherd*, Allan Ramsay, had supported a theatre company in Edinburgh in the 1730s, but the British government's 1737 Licensing Act had put an end to most theatrical activity. In the 1740s plays were performed in Edinburgh as part of the programme at musical concerts – this got round the Licensing Act – and dramatic performances revived. Though it is easy – and sometimes necessary – to indicate the Kirk's opposition to drama and other aspects of the express-ive arts, it is also vital to register how many of the literary and intellectual designs of Scottish Enlightenment culture had a base *inside* the Kirk. The 1750 publication of an English-language prose version of Renaissance Latinist George Buchanan's *A Tragedy of Jephthah, or, The Vow* by William Tait, 'School-master in Dummelzier' hints at an awareness that men of the Kirk (whose Moderator Buchanan had once been) need not oppose drama. In 1754 the moderate Kirkman the Reverend Alexander Carlyle, who had shown an interest in drama as a Glasgow University student, wrote a prologue to Samuel Hart's *Herminius and Espasia* as performed in Edinburgh and, as Richard Sher points out, 'turned it into a patriotic plea for the "*Scotian* muse" to find a home after long years of wandering'. Carlyle's prologue concludes,

> The muse once cherish'd, happier Bards shall rise,
> And future SHAKESPEARS light our northern skies![41]

From the 1750s until the 1770s, to the discomfiture of some in the Kirk who denounced the 'fatal Influence' of drama, Edinburgh's the Reverend John Home, a Church of Scotland minister of the Moderate party, published his plays. Home was a trained Classicist; his first play, *Agis*, completed in 1749, was set in ancient Greece; it was initially rejected by David Garrick in London, as was his second drama, *Douglas*. Like many another Scottish Enlightenment writer, Home in his second play turned from the Classical world to Scotland in what became the best known of his works. *Douglas* celebrated northern heroism, Highland mountains, and the tragic fates of a mother and her long-lost son.[42] Based on the ballad 'Gil Morrice' ('An Ancient Scottish Poem' republished in January 1755 by the Foulis Press in Glasgow) and performed in December 1756 in the Canongate Theatre in Edinburgh's Royal Mile, this verse-play was hailed as a milestone in Scottish drama.[43] It also caused a Kirk scandal, which helped to make it by far the most famous play of the Scottish Enlightenment.

In the row over *Douglas* Moderate ministers argued with their less liberal, play-hating brethren. Mocking the play-haters, who included the future leader of the College of New Jersey at Princeton, John Witherspoon, the Reverend Alexander Carlyle (who later authored lively recollections and a published *Autobiography*) issued anonymously a spoof *Argument to prove that the Tragedy of Douglas ought to be Publickly burnt by the hands of the Hangman* (1757). More solemnly, the Reverend Adam Ferguson in *The Morality of Stage-Plays Seriously Considered* thought dramas might be good for commerce as well as virtue. In an age when such works as the Aberdeen philosopher George Turnbull's *Treatise on Ancient Painting* (1740) and *Treatise Upon Liberal Education* (1742) had stressed a link between the arts, education and public virtue, more and more Scots, including ministers, were ready to commend literary pursuits – even drama. Although the ambitious Home's later plays were produced in London, *The History of the Sieges of Aquileia and Berwick* (1760) aligned Classical and Scottish history, celebrating Scotland's medieval struggle for independence. David Hume, a relative of John Home and a man unlikely to side with Kirk hard-liners, thought *Douglas* better than Shakespeare; Hume, Adam Ferguson and others had acted parts in the play's rehearsals. *Douglas* entered the eighteenth- and nineteenth-century repertoire, and crowds of lay and clerical fans flocked to see Mrs Siddons (who had taken over the heroine's role from Mrs Sarah Ward) star in it in Edinburgh in the 1780s. Nowadays Home's verse-drama, rarely performed, seems tarnished, characterized by a certain Caledonian Rhetoric and Belles Lettres alliterative strut that sounds as if it were designed for elocution lessons: 'My name is NORVAL: on the Grampian hills/ My father feeds his flocks . . .'[44]

Yet the cultural excitement around *Douglas* in Edinburgh in 1756–7 is hard to overstate. 'Whaur's yer Wullie Shakespeare noo?' one audience member is reputed to have called out. The controversy surrounding the play brought to the surface tensions in Scottish intellectual life, and led to the eventual triumph of the Moderate party in the Kirk to whose views many leading Scottish Enlightenment figures subscribed. Although there are major collections of documents and campaigning pro- and anti-*Douglas* pamphlets in the National Library of Scotland and in the Folger Library, Washington, no document better captures the intellectual and patriotic excitement felt on the day of the first performance, 14 December 1756, than the manuscript prologue (its hype perhaps written for an advertising flyer) now in St Andrews University Library. It has been overlooked by the many scholars who have written about the *Douglas* controversy, and is here reproduced for the first time:

A   *1756, Decer. 14*

Prologue
To the
Long Expected
Tragedy of Douglas
As it is to be acted this Evening at the Theatre in the head
of the Canongate, Edinburgh –

Foretold by* C[arly]le, now the time is come –
When Scotia bears the Palm from Greece & Rome,
When the learn'd Youth, Wits of the present Age,
No more need form their Taste on the translated page,
When Beauxs & Belles old Shakespear shall deride,
And *Bucks & Bloods* cast Rochester aside –
When Levi's sprightly sons shall quit the Chair
And on the more instructive Stage appear
Successfull Preachers to the Youthfull Crowd
That all that pleasure is, is also good.

To thee, great H[o]me these happy days we owe –
And Such the Gifts thy Douglas will bestow;
Douglas! who comes a thousand hearts to chear,
Who wept for† Agis' Death & fate Severe.

*The production referred to will be found in the Prologue to Herminius & Espasia, supposed to be wrote by the Reverend Mr C[arly]le.
†Great were the Expectations of the publick from this performance of the Author, which we are told in the Ecclesiastic Characteristicks, carried dramatick poetry to the Summit of perfection, So that had it been published, it was believed that never one would have presumed to have wrote a Tragedy after it. But, as that ingenious Writer imagined, the knowledge of this Effect, And the Compassion thence arising to future Authors, determined the humble and benevolent theatrick Divine to suppress it's publication: And we are told by the Advertisement in the Edin[burg]h Ev[ening] Courant that the same humble & self-denied temper had almost smothered the present production – Even after the two Journeys the Author made to London, & Sollicitations to Mr Garrick to receive it.[45]

Now shall the English curse their Garrick's Name
Who banished Douglas far from Drury-Lane
Nor would thy humble earnest Prayer regard
But void of Merit the great Work declared

Not so fair Ward, She well to Churchmen known
This Night in publick will thy Merit own
And if some modest ffriends the favour Claim
Place is prepared for these behind the Scene

For all the anxieties surrounding the first night and the subsequent struggles over *Douglas*, after its performance Scottish intellectual life surged ahead with a remarkable confidence. Having rehearsed the part of the maid Anna ('have I distress'd you with officious love . . . ?'), Home's friend the Reverend Hugh Blair became not only the minister of St Giles, Edinburgh's grandest civic kirk, but also the first Professor of Rhetoric and Belles Lettres at Edinburgh University, where he joined the faculty in 1759.[46] Ranging from Homer to James Thomson, Blair's university lectures, hot on the heels of such works as John Miller's partly French-derived *A Course of the Belles Lettres* (1761), instilled literary taste into generations of students. They learned how to read closely, and how to manage 'correct', Anglocentric English. Eventually Blair's *Lectures* were published in book form in 1783 and exported round the globe. A standard text at late eighteenth- and early nineteenth-century Yale and Harvard, Blair's work, along with that of other Scottish teachers of literature, set the agenda for the international development of English Studies. Like the *Lectures*, Blair's *Sermons* (1777) were long-term best-sellers. Their wise moderation is polished, perceptive, and bland:

Disappointed hope is misery; and yet successful hope is only imperfect bliss. Look through all the ranks of mankind. Examine the condition of those who appear most prosperous, and you will find that they are never just what they desire to be. If retired, they languish for action; if busy, they complain of fatigue. If in middle life, they are impatient for distinction; if in high stations, they sigh after freedom and ease.[47]

Such cadences were reassuring – the sound of moderation rather than Knox's earlier pulpit-thumping fervour.

As a man of letters, Blair supervised a huge forty-four-volume Edinburgh edition of *The British Poets* (1773–6), published by Kincaid, Creech and Balfour. The definite article in the title of this edition is crucial, a mark of confidence in critical and entrepreneurial judgment. Such an edition was but one instance of an increasingly healthy Scottish printing and publishing industry. Edinburgh was second only to London in the expanding universe of British publishing, and there were both links and rivalries between the two. After his short novel *The History of Sir Launcelot Edgevile* failed to make much impact in the *Court Magazine*, Edinburgh-born John McMurray (1737–93) headed south, dropped the 'Mc' from his name, and founded in 1768 what became a hugely successful London-Scottish publishing dynasty, with shares in the publishing of Smollett, John Millar, Gilbert Stuart and many other writers. Seven generations of John Murrays at the family firm would go on to make their mark, early on cooperating with the Edinburgh house of Constable to publish Scott. That writer first met Byron, another Murray author, in the Murray house at 50 Albemarle Street, and he became an advisor to the powerful, Murray-published *Quarterly Review*, which ran from 1809 until 1967. In the nineteenth century the house of John Murray published Jane Austen, Charles Darwin and David Livingstone, yet, for all that London was their base of operations, the Murray family retained a sense of their Scottish roots. Having published authors from Scottish Enlightenment physicians to the modern refugee novelist Ruth Prawer Jhabvala, John Murray became the world's oldest independent, family-run publishing house before it was sold to Hodder Headline in 2002. Shortly afterwards, in Britain's largest ever purchase of literary manuscripts, John Murray's magnificent archives, valued at £45 million, were bought by the National Library of Scotland in Edinburgh thanks to strong support from the Murray family, from the recently established Scottish Executive and from other funding bodies. So, due to an unusually maintained loyalty and a bravely decisive government intervention in favour of Scottish literature, the archives of one of the greatest Scottish names in publishing were made available to scholars in the Scottish capital in 2006, almost two and a half centuries after the first John Murray had left Edinburgh.

Although Murray and his heirs helped maintain London as a crucial site of Scottish publishing, north of the border during the Enlightenment entrepreneurial luminaries included the brothers Robert and Andrew

Foulis, whose Glasgow-based Foulis Press printed 'English Poets' along-side Classical and other texts. In Edinburgh William Creech printed the short-lived magazines *The Mirror* (1779) and *The Lounger* (1785–7), edited by Henry Mackenzie. Creech also bought the copyright of the Edinburgh edition of Burns's poems. Edinburgh publishing in the late eighteenth and early nineteenth centuries was exciting, sometimes combative, and thriving. It simply did not operate on the same scale as publishing in the British capital south of the Border.

The press set up by the Foulis brothers, seen by James Boswell as the Elzeviers of Scotland, is worth examining as the most distinguished Scottish Enlightenment printing house. From 1740 until the 1780s it produced around 700 titles. It is symptomatic of the importance of Latin and Greek to the Scottish Enlightenment that, after being encouraged in business by Andrew Michael Ramsay, Robert Foulis's first published *Catalogue of Books Imported* (1740) begins by advertising 'the scarcest Editions of almost all the Greek and Roman authors'. In the eighteenth century a Classicist like Brechin's John Gillies, who succeeded William Robertson as Historiographer Royal for Scotland, might launch *An Inquiry, whether the study of the ancient languages be a necessary branch of modern Education* (1769), confidently expecting an affirmative answer. Encouraged by Glasgow academics like Francis Hutcheson and the Classicist James Moor, the Foulis Press was proudly Classical, but avoided a 'new' genre like the novel. In 1745, when Bonnie Prince Charlie's troops marched on Glasgow, the Foulises not only published Hutcheson in Latin, but also declared '*In the Press, and will Speedily be publish'd*' George Buchanan's Latin epithalamium for Mary, Queen of Scots, with its fervent prayer for Scotland to be united with France. Buchanan's Latin Psalm paraphrases were republished by the Foulis Press in 1765, nine years after the brothers had been awarded a medal by the nicely named Edinburgh Society for Encouraging Arts, Manufactures and Agriculture for their state-of-the-art edition of Homer's *Iliad*. Scots-language work was also part of the international list of these printers to the University of Glasgow. Their 1748 miscellany, *Poems in the Scottish Dialect* may have spurred the title of Burns's 1786 *Poems, Chiefly in the Scottish Dialect*, just as the Foulis subtitle, *An Ancient Scottish Poem* (used twice in 1755), may have encouraged the Ossianic *Fragments of Ancient Poetry* (1760). In 1753 Robert Foulis, with help from Adam Smith and others, set up a Glasgow School for the Art of Design; the first institution of its kind in Britain, it ran until 1775. Though Robert Foulis died the following year, Scottish authors as different as Andrew Michael Ramsay and James Boswell had benefited from the attentions of the meticulous Foulis Press, and had appeared as part of a publisher's list that ran from John Milton to Aristophanes.[48]

If the Classically-minded Foulis brothers were in some ways Scottish Enlightenment successors to Thomas Ruddiman, they were in turn followed by the later eighteenth-century Classicist John Hunter whose press was based in St Andrews and Cupar. Other publishing ventures were important but small in scale. Only two issues of the eighteenth-century *Edinburgh Review* appeared, in 1755; those issues, though, contained the first published works of Adam Smith and William Robertson. While papermaking was a substantial Scottish Enlightenment industry and Edinburgh printing houses increased in number (from six in 1763 to sixteen in 1790), Edinburgh's best-known publishing enterprises came into being in the early nineteenth century, when the *Edinburgh Review* was refounded as a Whig journal by Archibald Constable in 1802; soon hugely influential, it was joined by the Tory *Blackwood's Edinburgh Magazine* in 1817. William Blackwood, like Archibald Constable, learned his trade working for an eighteenth-century Edinburgh bookseller. The roots and authority of Edinburgh publishing are sunk deep in the Scottish Enlightenment, that period when Blair might marshall *the* British poets, and did not hesitate to use his authority to caution Robert Burns against impropriety.

Grand arbiter of taste, Blair knew poets, but was more at home with other literary ministers and academics such as the historian William Robertson (1721–93). Principal of Edinburgh University and friend of David Hume, Robertson too was a member of the 'Select Society'. This exclusive-sounding Edinburgh club, founded to encourage philosophy and public speaking, was one of many such male clubs, some sober, some drunken and bawdy. As well as founders Allan Ramsay and David Hume, its members included Adam Smith and James Burnett, the distinguished Classical scholar Lord Monboddo (1714–99) who published his survey *Of the Origin and Progress of Language* over a twenty-year period from 1773. Monboddo's work achieved notoriety when it claimed orang-utans as non-speaking members of the human species, but its fascination with progress and improvement was typical of Scottish Enlightenment concerns.

In his Glasgow lectures on jurisprudence, Adam Smith, like Lord Kames, stated that 'There are four distinct states which mankind pass thro: first, the Age of Hunters; secondly, the Age of Shepherds; thirdly, the Age of Agriculture; and fourthly, the Age of Commerce.'[49] Substantially borrowed from such continental thinkers as the Dutchman Hugo Grotius, the German Samuel, Freiherr von Pufendorf, and the French physiocrats, such a four-stage model of social development was deployed by other Scottish Enlightenment thinkers like Smith's fellow Glasgow professor, the radical democrat John Millar (1735–1801) whose *Origin of the Distinction of Ranks* (1771) introduced ideas about what we now call class conflict. Edinburgh's the Reverend Professor Adam Ferguson (1723–1816) also followed the four-stage theory. Roman historian and philosopher, he was author of *An Essay on the History of Civil Society* (1767) which examined the progress of civilization and was much admired in Germany by Herder, Schiller and Hegel, then, most significantly, by Karl Marx. In such writings lie at least some of the origins of modern sociology and anthropology, as well as the deployment of a technique which the later, hugely influential Edinburgh philosopher Dugald Stewart (1753–1828), describing Smith's history of astronomy, would christen 'conjectural history'. This relied on common-sense speculation about what humans might have done in remote cultures; it assumed a basic unchanging human nature and encouraged the comparison of ancient and modern less-developed societies (in the Americas or, very rarely, in the Scottish Highlands, for example) with those regarded as sophisticated.

The European Enlightenment of Rousseau and the French *philosophes* relished and often idealized whatever was perceived as 'savage'. The Scottish Enlightenment too delighted in primitivism and accounts of supposedly primitive societies even as it embraced commercial sophistication. So the publisher of Edinburgh's 1770s commercial and social *Directory*, 'Indian' Peter Williamson, was also the autobiographer whose *French and Indian Cruelty* (1757) recounted his own kidnapping, enslavement and subsequent torture by Native Americans. Projects as different as the eloquent, academically footnoted yet also 'primitive' Ossianic poems, Tobias Smollett's novel *Humphry Clinker* (set in modern Britain, but with a character who is tortured by Native Americans), or the elegant histories of exotic societies by Robertson and others fed this craving for the primitive at the heart of modern commercial society.

As it had been to Robert Sibbald and earlier seventeenth-century Scottish writers, so surveying societies and their cultures was central to many Scottish Enlightenment authors. Demography was a British and European obsession of the age. Using a standard questionnaire sent out through the General Assembly of the Kirk to its parish ministers, the agriculturalist Sir John Sinclair (a former student of Adam Smith) brought out in the 1790s *The Statistical Account of Scotland*. This parish-by-parish national survey sought to present 'with anatomical accuracy and minuteness, *the internal structure of society*'.[50] It is vital to appreciate, though, that the outlook of these Enlightenment writers was international. Not just Scotland but the whole world was advancing, and they knew it:

The great alteration in the affairs of Europe within these three centuries, by the discovery of America and the Indies, the springing up of industry and learning, the introduction of trade and the luxurious arts, the establishment of public credit, and a general system of taxation, have entirely altered the plan of government every where.[51]

So wrote the recently returned Jacobite exile Sir James Steuart in *An Inquiry into the Principles of Political Oeconomy* (1767). The polylingual Steuart had spent much of his exile travelling in Europe and his view is strikingly international. When Aberdeen's James Dunbar writes of 'that enlightened people' in his *Essays on the History of Mankind in Rude and Cultivated Ages* (1781), he means not the Scots but the Chinese.[52] In Edinburgh William Robertson examined much more of the world's culture than that small part covered in his fine history of Scotland (1759). His 1769 account of Emperor Charles V was translated into French (1771), German (1770–71), and Russian (1775–8). Robertson's history of America (1777) was translated into French, German and Italian in its year of publication. He followed up in 1791 with a study of religious belief in a comparative Classical and Indian framework. The works of Hume, Smith, Blair and others may have had a Scottish accent and provenance, but the topics addressed were of as much international import as the contemporary work of Scottish scientific writers. Among this latter group the talents were remarkable. Especially after his ideas were promoted by others, James Hutton (1726–97) fathered modern geology with his *Theory of the Earth* (1795): 'With regard to human observation,' he wrote, 'this world has neither a beginning nor an end.' This was profoundly unsettling for those committed to the literal truth of the Bible. More reassuring was the way the Gregory dynasty of physicians and the Monro family of anatomists consolidated Scotland's reputation for medical excellence. Everywhere there were discourses, new theories, improvements. At Glasgow University the chemist Joseph Black theorized latent heat, while his associate the inventor James Watt modified the steam engine so crucial to the Industrial Revolution. A team headed by Edinburgh printer and natural historian William Smellie (1740–95) produced between 1768 and 1771 that greatest of emblems of Scottish Enlightenment learning, the *Encyclopaedia Britannica*.

Even minor Scottish Enlightenment works may have had major international consequences, not least across the Atlantic. Thomas Jefferson's Scottish tutor at the College of William and Mary in Virginia taught Rhetoric and Belles Lettres to his young pupil. Jefferson went on to include that subject in his own later plans for higher-education institutions – though he also speculated as to whether Americans should not, like Robert Burns, have their own dialect.[53] In his lectures on Rhetoric and Belles Lettres between 1774 and 1824 George Jardine continued Adam Smith's work at Glasgow University. Jardine's resulting *Outlines of Philosophical Education* (1818), argues Arthur Herman, 'became one of the most popular textbooks in American higher education. It explained how to create a stimulating intellectual atmosphere in the classroom and lecture hall. It created a system of "writing across the curriculum", as it would later be called, with compositions, essays and research papers assigned in every class and at every level, which taught students how to think for themselves, but also how to write clear, incisive, original English prose.'[54]

The wellsprings of the remarkable outpourings of Scottish Enlightenment thought are several. They include the early adoption of Newtonianism and the shift to English-speaking lecturing in the geographically widely distributed Scottish universities, where student numbers trebled between 1720 and 1840. Use of the medium of Scots-accented English rather than Latin indicated the closeness of the classroom to the pulpit, to commerce, and to the surrounding society, even if there was friction between English and the Scots tongue. Another engine of Enlightenment was the growing moderation of Scottish Protestantism, which went some way to temper anti-Catholic ranting but left a strong, distinctively

Scottish emphasis on widespread access to vernacular knowledge. Scottish prospects were boosted by the wealth made available through access to British imperial markets. Culture was quickened by immersion in Addison's *Spectator* magazine, by international links (not least with France), and by the urgent, sometimes anxious wish to scrutinize national, social and individual identities. There was also an impetus that came from the desire to say and do at least as well as the English, who still had only two universities in their entire, much more populous country, and whose centres of learning (if we are to believe Adam Smith and Edward Gibbon on Oxford) were comparatively moribund. Before the twentieth century, for instance, none of England's great novelists attended university. Throughout the eighteenth century and after, many of Scotland's did.

Its Enlightenment flowering put Scotland at the forefront of the invention of modernity, whether the modernity of industrial production or of the taste for wild, mountainous scenery. Where scientific and technological inventions moved Scotland into the vanguard of the Industrial Revolution, this was complemented, not contradicted, by a counterbalancing fascination with the past. 'This is the historical age, and this the historical nation,' declared Hume, who cheekily wrote the history of the nation next door. His *History of England*, authored in the late 1750s and early 1760s, started with the accession of the Scottish King James VI to the English throne, though the account was later extended backwards to the time of Julius Caesar. Clear, crisp, and unafraid to censure anti-Scottish prejudice on the part of the 'barbarians on the banks of the Thames', it became a standard work. Hume's *History* explained the English to themselves and others.[55] It also made Hume rich. It was such a best-seller that in 1771 when the London Scot William Strahan reprinted it, Strahan could afford not only to have new type cast but to send the proofs to Hume in Scotland in five-sheet batches, keeping a great amount of type committed to the project until Hume's corrections and revisions were eventually returned by the sixty-year-old author in distant Edinburgh – then still a week or more away from London by coach. Correcting his proofs, Hume was now one of a galaxy of Scottish historians, producing a plurality of histories. The vital Scottish Enlightenment interest in history and in conjectural history helps explain why so many Scottish critics like Blair treated the less respectable genre of the novel under the category of 'fictitious histories'. It also explains why Scotland proved such an encouraging culture for the growth of the historical novel. That genre was practised by Walter Scott, James Hogg and others like John Galt, who liked to term his own novels 'theoretical histories'.

Scotland's national past and present further incited Enlightenment interests in improvement and history. Having lost their independent Parliament in 1707, many ambitious Scots, increasingly worried about 'provincialism', strove to develop an ideology of Britishness. They did this through energetic participation in the new British state and empire. They sought to match the English in trade, industry, politics and, not least, literature. Though Scottish literary scholarship from a 1750s edition of Shakespeare (Scotland's first) to Henry Mackenzie's essay on *Hamlet* flourished outside the classroom, nowhere are improving, Scoto-British ambitions clearer than in the university teaching of Rhetoric and Belles Lettres described earlier. Here is Professor William Barron of St Andrews, briefly discussing 'the literary history of Scotland' in his later eighteenth-century lecture hall:

While she remained a separate kingdom, the remoteness of her situation from the seat of politeness and power, was accounted an insuperable obstruction against all attempts to compose in the language of England. Her writers, of course, either confined their compositions to the imperfect dialect of their own country, or undertook to express their sentiments in the language of ancient Rome. Even posterior to the union, when intercourse between the kingdoms became easy and frequent, it was long thought impossible that a North-Briton should produce any work, which could be relished or applauded by an Englishman of taste. A few eminent examples have invalidated every opinion of this sort, and have demonstrated that Scotland, by proper culture, is qualified to furnish English compositions, not less pure and correct, perhaps, than England herself. Let not, then, our situation discourage us in the study either of speaking or writing. Let us remember, that industry is certainly sufficient to surmount every obstacle or inconvenience.

To modern ears, there is an embarrassing note of 'cultural cringe' here. Even as Barron, a staunch defender of imperialism and an opponent of the American Revolution, seeks to strengthen an Anglocentric British identity for Scotland, he sounds like a remote colonial anxious about metropolitan prejudice. Revealingly, in the same lectures he points out that English may be written well even 'in India or America'.[56]

Scots did encounter prejudice, especially when they appeared powerful as the dominant 'Scots Scourge' in the London government. By the mid-eighteenth century they might be stereotyped in English pamphlets and on English stages as 'Sawney', the immigrant beggar, come from a 'scabbie land' to spread 'Caledonian Poison'.[57] All this helped fuel Scots' anxieties about language and literary voice. Many literati, including some of the most stellar, like Smith, Hume and Blair, were convinced that a committed mastery of English was vital for Scottish improvement. They believed their country's greatest opportunities lay in fostering Britishness. In London Tobias Smollett edited a magazine called simply *The Briton*. By 1773 the English novelist Horace Walpole had come to despise the word 'Briton' precisely because it included the Scots.

'What language is principally spoken in it?' asked the questionnaires of *The Statistical Account of Scotland* with regard to each parish. Sometimes the answer was Gaelic. About a quarter of the Scottish population spoke Gaelic, but few could read it. That tongue and its attendant culture also set Scotland apart from monolingual England. If Scots in the south might be denounced as 'bare ars'd *Caledonian* Rogues', it was because of the image of the kilted Highlander.[58] The Jacobite risings of 1715 and 1745 were not exclusively Highland, or even Scottish rebellions. However, they could be perceived that way, making all Scots seem potential traitors. The option of returning to a Stuart monarchy represented the restoration of a history which most Scots and Britons wished repressed, and which threatened Hanoverian Britishness. Smollett, in London with his countryman the Reverend Alexander Carlyle, at the time of Culloden, felt threatened by a backlash against Scottish immigrants there. The two men walked with swords drawn, fearful of attack. Carlyle remembered how Smollett warned him 'against speaking a word, lest the mob should discover my country and become insolent, "for John Bull", says he, "is as haughty and violent to-night as he was abject and cowardly on the Black Wednesday when the Highlanders were at Derby"'.[59] Carlyle had seen Highland soldiers close up and thought them 'of low stature and dirty, and of a contemptible appearance'.[60] Many Scottish Lowlanders might have shared that view of their contemporary northern neighbours, and did not want to be associated with them. Just as Adam Smith was aware that the 'desert' country of the Highlands had a culture unsuited to the improvements in industrial productivity promised by 'civilized' division of labour, so many 'North Britons' seem to have sensed that questions of improvement and comparison between societies at different stages of development were particularly pressing for the Scots.

When the historian of 'civil society' Adam Ferguson, possibly the only fluent Gaelic speaker among the principal luminaries of the Scottish Enlightenment, uses the word 'clans', he is usually referring to Arabs, ancient Gauls, or to native American 'savages'. Fascinated by honour and warriors, Ferguson served for a decade as a chaplain to the Black Watch Highland regiment. He wrote in English and, as a trained Classicist, thought Gaelic might be represented in print using a Greek font. This implies a classic status for the language, but also presents it as dead. Ferguson's entombing gesture clashes with the title of the first collection of secular poetry to be published in Gaelic, *Ais-eiridh na Sean Chánoin Albannaich (The Resurrection of the Ancient Scottish Tongue)* (1751). Its author, Alasdair Mac Mhaighstir Alasdair (Alexander Mac-Donald) (c. 1695–c. 1770) came from a distinguished Gaelic family, and appears to have studied at Glasgow University before becoming a schoolteacher in Moidart. Influences on his poems include the Bible, Catullus, Allan Ramsay, and James Thomson's *Seasons*. In some senses this poet is a Gaelic Enlightenment figure. While Lowlanders investigated such topics as the origin and progress of language, and compiled encyclopedic reference works, Mac Mhaighstir Alasdair compiled his *Leabhar a Theagasc Ainminnin* (1741). Published by the Scottish Society for the Propagation of Christian Knowledge (SSPCK), this was the first secular book printed in Scottish Gaelic; it preceded the Ossian scholar the Reverend William Shaw's 1780 full-scale *Gaelic and English Dictionary*. Mac Mhaighstir Alasdair's own poetry collection was the second secular printed work in Gaelic and carried a preface in English clearly designed to assert the importance of the language to a non-Gaelic audience, most immediately the literati of Edinburgh where the book was published. In the short term at least, the literati were indifferent or hostile; *The Resurrection of the Ancient Scottish Tongue* is said to have been burned by Edinburgh's public hangman.

Its author, cousin of the famous Flora MacDonald who helped Bonnie Prince Charlie escape after Culloden, was a Jacobite rebel. He helped rally the Jacobite clans for the 1745 Rising and claimed to have taught Prince Charlie Gaelic. The fiercely anti-Hanoverian MacDonald may have written an English-language account of the 1745 rising. After working for the Protestant SSPCK, he converted to Catholicism and is

buried in the beautiful graveyard of the Catholic church at Arisaig. If
there is a sense in which this poet was a man of the Scottish Enlightenment, then he fought on the wrong side, wrote in the wrong language,
and converted to the wrong religion for the fact to be recognized by his
Lowland contemporaries.

For all his knowledge of other literatures, Mac Mhaighstir Alasdair
had schooled himself thoroughly in Gaelic verse. He possessed a number
of old Gaelic manuscripts and, teaching himself to read and write their
insular minuscule script as a way of giving himself access to the tradition,
he developed an orthography which imitated that of ancient Gaelic texts;
though to the uninitiated Sassenach this looks almost like something
invented by a Hobbit, the poems written in it by this master poet are
among the finest in all Gaelic. Mac Mhaighstir Alasdair is a poet of
range as well as brilliance, strong feeling as well as intelligence. A lyrical
masculine eroticism is present in the early, hypnotically repetitive 'Song
to his Bride', Jane MacDonald of Dalness, a poet's daughter:

> Fhuair mi mòran, mo thoil mhòr leat,
> Fhuair mi òr na h-Asia.
>
> Fhuair mi òg thu, fhuair mi 'd òigh thu,
> Fhuair mi bòidheach àlainn thu.
>
> *I got a great deal, had great pleasure with you,*
> *I got the gold of Asia,*
>
> *I got you young, I got you as a maid,*
> *I got you beautiful and lovely.*[61]

Sure, sharp and glancing are the observation and physicality that
characterize Alexander MacDonald's 'Òran an t-Samhraidh' (Song of
Summer):

> Bidh bradan seang-mhear nam fioruisg
> Gu brisg, slinn-leumnach, luath,
> 'Na bhuidhne tàrr-ghealach lannach,
> Gu h-iteach, dearg-bhallach, earrach,
> Le shoillsean airgid da earradh
> 'S mion-bhreac lainnireach tuar.
> 'S e fèin gu crom-ghobach ullamh
> Ceapadh chuileag le cluain.

Lithe brisk fresh-water salmon,
lively, leaping the stones;
bunched, white-bellied, scaly,
fin-tail-flashing, red spot;
speckled skin's brilliant hue
lit with flashes of silver;
with curved gob at the ready,
catching insects with guile.[62]

There may be some influence of Thomson's *Seasons* discernible in Mac Mhaighstir Alasdair's work, but Thomson might well have described these fish simply as a 'finny tribe'. The Gaelic poet, on the other hand, was a man fascinated by and able to articulate the precise dart and glitter of salmon.

The modern Gaelic poet and scholar Derick Thomson styles Mac Mhaighstir Alasdair's poetry 'the most overtly nationalist in Gaelic in the eighteenth century'.[63] That aspect surely appealed to Hugh MacDiarmid who produced a twentieth-century version of Alexander MacDonald's masterpiece, 'Birlinn Chlann Raghnaill' (Clanranald's Galley), a long, complex poem full of the energy of living with the sea. MacDonald had a firm sense of the antiquity of Gaelic ('Adam spoke it, / even in Paradise'), and knew it had once been spoken over much of Scotland.[64] Just as he can hymn the natural abundance of an Ardnamurchan village and the 'Sugar Brook' that flows through it, or sing the berries of a beloved corrie, so he can also compose a battle incitement and inveigh against the Hanoverian throne. While it draws on the linguistic energies heard elsewhere in his verse, 'Clanranald's Galley' immerses itself in a sea-world that is its own delight:

Ràimh mhìnlunnacha, dhealbhach,
   Shocair, aotrom,
A nì 'n t-iomramh toirteil, calma,
   Basluath caoirgheal;
Chuireas an fhairge 'na sradan
   Suas 's na speuran –
'Na teine-sionnachain a' lasadh,
   Mar fhras éibhlean.

Oars smooth-shafted and shapely,
  Graceful for gripping,
Made for lusty, resolute rowing,
  Palm-fast, foam-whipping;
Knocking sparks out of the water
  Towards Heaven
Like the fire-flush from a smithy
  Updriven.[65]

This rich, warring incitement to the rowers of a Hebridean galley is a late work by MacDonald. It probably dates from the 1750s. 'Clanranald's Galley' sets the capstone on his oeuvre, a body of work that marks him out as one of the great Scottish poets of the natural environment as well as a learned patriot and scholar who is perhaps the most exuberant user of the Gaelic language.

Several facets of Mac Mhaighstir Alasdair's work link him to his fellow eighteenth-century Gaelic poets. He is said to have appropriated two songs by the North Uist poet John MacCodrum (Iain Mhic Fhearchair) (1693–1779) and printed them as his own. MacCodrum's work has a stinging wit, and often stings those close to him. In one, 'Complaint about his Wife', he makes clear his displeasure that, though his wife is alive, he is the person who has to buy cloth and work with thread. Where Mac Mhaighstir Alasdair could celebrate the beauty of a Highland village, MacCodrum, first of those Gaelic 'village poets' whose work survives, laughingly detailed the doings of the local population. Singing of weddings, drinking, illness, bad bagpiping and tailoring, he could also compose praise-poems and elegies. He was a learned oral historian, a *seanchaidh*. As an older man he made a 'Song to the Fugitives' which lamented 'the exile of the Gael' and how the people were being moved off their land to make way for sheep in the notorious 'Clearances' which followed Culloden.[66] Hugely popular among Gaelic speakers, his work survived orally, not in written or printed form, and much of it was not collected until the 1930s.

In the eighteenth century a succession of Gaelic poets lamented the defeats inflicted on their culture, especially after the failed Jacobite risings of 1715 and 1745. Mairead nighean Lachlain, at the height of her powers around the '15, focused on the Macleans of Duart on Mull, to whom she was connected. She hymns heroism, but among her most haunting lines are those which lament in 1716 not just the death of Sir John Maclean of Duart Castle, but also the loss of hereditary lands and the damage done to her homeland:

> Fhrois gach abhall a h-ùbhlan,
> Dh' fhalbh gach blàth agus ùr-ròs,
> 'S tha ar coill' air a rùsgadh de 'h-àilleachd.

> *Every apple tree has dropped its apples,*
> *Every blossom and fresh rose has gone,*
> *And our wood is stripped of its beauty.*[67]

After the 1745 Rising, terminated near Inverness by the Battle of Culloden the following year when the English General 'Butcher' Cumberland destroyed the Highland infantry with his ordnance, many more laments ensued. Christina Ferguson's beautiful song, 'Mo rùn geal òg' (My Young White Love), has been used to supply the epigraph to the collection of stories *Indelible Acts* by the twenty-first-century Scottish writer A. L. Kennedy. Ferguson's song asserts her continuing devotion to her husband, William Chisholm, whose death in battle on Culloden Moor has left her 'alone / With nothing in the world but a shirt'.[68]

Christina Ferguson was only one among many Gaels who felt bereft. Iain Ruadh Stiùbhard (John Roy Stewart) (1700–47), who had served in the British Army, then fought against it in France and Scotland, left several post-Culloden poems rich in lamentation and baffled pride. Others, like Iain Mac Mhurchaidh (John Macrae), who died around 1780, made sad songs recalling from afar a way of life filled with lively Highland cattle, herring boats in full sail, and tanned sailors. All gone.

> Gur ann an Ameireaga tha sinn an dràsd,
> Fo dhubhar na coille nach teirig gu bràth.

> *It's in America that we are now,*
> *in the shade of the wood that is there for all time.*[69]

In many ways the experience of Culloden and its aftermath, however mythologized, remains the defining experience of Gaelic culture over the last three centuries. It is a Gaelic apocalypse with whose consequences poet after poet has struggled to come to terms. Some aspects of eighteenth-century Gaelic poetry seem almost to anticipate it. The

Perthshire evangelical poet Dughall Bochanan (Dugald Buchanan) (1716–68), born just after the '15, experienced in early childhood 'terrible visions . . . I always dreamed that the day of judgment was come'.[70] His poems extolling the Christian warrior appealed to many Highlanders. 'La a' Bhreitheanais' (The Day of Judgment) (1767) is more than 500 lines long and in some ways complements the work of the English-language 'graveyard' school of poets; Buchanan was well read in English verse. Yet 'La a' Bhreitheanais' may also speak indirectly of the sense of overwhelming convulsion experienced by Gaelic-language culture in the period.

> An cùrtain gorm tha nunn on ghrèin,
>   'S mun cuairt don chruinne-chè mar chleòc,
> Crupaidh an lasair e r'a chèil'
>   Mar bheilleig air na h-èibhlibh beò.

> *The blue drape spread out from the sun,*
>   *cloaking the universe entire,*
> *is wrinkled up by that red flame*
>   *like a birch-tree bark in living fire.*[71]

Though it was felt most strongly there, a sense of the awfulness of Culloden and its aftermath was not confined to the Gaelic-speaking world. In London the Lowlander Tobias Smollett, no Jacobite but a man who had grown up close to the Highland Line, wrote in 1746 'The Tears of Scotland':

> Mourn, hapless Caledonia, mourn
> Thy banished peace, thy laurels torn.
> Thy sons, for valour long renowned,
> Lie slaughtered on their native ground;
> Thy hospitable roofs no more
> Invite the stranger to the door;
> In smoky ruins sunk they lie,
> The monuments of cruelty.[72]

This is a striking example of an Anglophone Scottish writer responding sympathetically to what was principally a calamity for the Gaeltacht. There are other, less obvious instances of the same phenomenon. Though ostensibly it may be about Flodden and about more recent financial reverses, the continuing popularity of the song 'The Flowers of the Forest', reworked by David Hume's friend the shrewd Edinburgh Enlightenment memoirist and poet Alison Cockburn (1712–94), surely gives voice to the sadness of many post-Culloden Scots in its dying fall: 'The Flowers of the Forest are a' wede away.'[73]

The shock of the Jacobite civil war was something many Scots wished to repress through silence or over-compensatory protests of loyalty to the London King. Yet links between Highlands and Lowlands were on the increase during the Scottish Enlightenment. Isaac Newton's staunchly Hanoverian friend Colin Maclaurin (1698–1746), scientific author and Professor of Mathematics at Aberdeen, was one of the greatest European mathematicians of the age. He was also a Highlander whose father had helped with the Gaelic metrical translations of the Psalms issued by the Synod of Argyll in 1694. Enlightenment novelist Henry Mackenzie was of Highland descent, married a Highlander, and eventually chaired an investigation into the Gaelic culture of the Ossianic 'Erse poetry' commended by Adam Smith, Hugh Blair and others.[74] Gaelic culture both fed and was fed by the Scottish Enlightenment.

However, centuries of Lowland prejudice meant that no Gaelic was taught in Scottish universities. Despite this, interest in the smashed Highland culture grew and grew. The Reverend Alexander Pope of Caithness had begun to gather Gaelic lays in the 1730s and in Perthshire the Reverend James McLagan (later one of James 'Ossian' Macpherson's informants) made a substantial collection which fuelled the first printed volume of Gaelic lays in Scotland, produced by the Perth bookseller John Gillies in 1786. Earlier, the young St Andrews alumnus Jerome Stone (who seems to have signed himself Stones), a Lowlander from Fife, also worked in the bilingual territory of Perthshire and began to collect Gaelic poems in the 1750s, writing them down in a notebook. Encouraged by the Principal of St Andrews University, Stone approached the Highlanders with a typical Scottish Enlightenment fascination for comparative cultural and linguistic study. 'There is no people in the Globe of the Earth, whose Language may be proven to have undergone less Change,' wrote Stone, and he found among the Highlanders a remarkable lack of such modern preoccupations as 'Commerce'.[75] In 1756 Stone published in *The Scots Magazine* the first ever English translation of a Gaelic ballad. 'Albin and the Daughter of Mey' is a literary landmark, if only because it marked the first time such Gaelic verse had been brought into direct contact with an audience of English-speaking readers. Set among cairns and mountains, rich in 'tears', 'mourning' and heroic bones, it establishes from the start the note which, for all Stone's neoclassicism, came to characterize Gaelic poetry to Enlightenment and Romantic audiences.

> Whence come these dismal sounds that fill our ears!
> Why do the groves such lamentations send![76]

Such tones of lamentation were part of Gaelic verse, present not least (as the twenty-first-century scholar William Gillies points out) in older poems of 'farewell and elegy'.[77] Just a few years after Jerome Stone published his Gaelic ballad, the elegiac note would be heard as characteristic of the supposedly millennia-old 'primitive' Gaelic poems of Ossian in James Macpherson's English translation when, with Hugh Blair's professorial blessing, they coursed and insinuated their way around the globe. These Ossianic works are by far the most influential outgrowth of Gaelic verse. However distorted, they represent a strange post-Culloden consonance between Highland and Lowland authors, each having much to offer the other, each reaching a point of sympathetic understanding which resulted in tearful regret.

Gaelic poetry came to be channelled to wider audiences largely through the tear ducts of Enlightenment sentimentalism and later Romanticism. Ossian fuelled both these cultural movements. Yet this represented a substantial reduction of the tonal range of Gaelic verse. The lamented Highland heroes of Ossianic lore initiated what eventually became the later nineteenth-century Celtic Twilight movement. 'They went forth to the Battle, but they always fell' was a misquotation from Ossian beloved of both Matthew Arnold and W. B. Yeats who between them did so much to equip the Celtic Twilight with its glimmering dimmer-switch.[78] But eighteenth-century Gaelic poetry could be satirical, stinging and frolicsome as well as sincerely tearful. In 'Briogais Mhic Ruaraidh' (MacRory's Trousers) Rob Donn MacAoidh (Robert Mackay) (1714–78) articulates the loss not of Culloden but of a pair of much-missed breeks. Explicitly at least, anxiety in this poem centres not around cultural collapse but around the danger of a trouserless man being nipped by a water shrew.

Like John MacCodrum, Rob Donn ('Brown Robert') was deeply rooted in oral culture. A Protestant Jacobite sympathizer, born in

Sutherland where he lived most of his life, he could neither read nor write. Print was impinging on Gaelic culture. Rob Donn had heard a good deal of English poetry, including that of Pope, read from books, but Gaelic was still strong in its orality. Among Rob Donn's great gifts was the ability to present a full picture of popular life in a Gaelic community. This again aligns him with John MacCodrum, but he has an impressively wide range, moving from an almost obligatory attack on the Hanoverian monarch whose laws have banned the wearing of the kilt, to reflective spiritual elegies that surely owe something to the Protestantism that influenced Dugald Buchanan. If Buchanan seems evangelical, Rob Donn is moderate. His work can display the ethical perspective of moderatism, and its moral and reasonable assumptions signal that in his way he too is a product of Enlightenment Scotland. There is a rather tight-lipped appraising gaze in Rob Donn's fine poem, 'The Rispond Misers', about three skinflints all of whom have just died in the same week. After presenting the selfishness and ungenerosity of their lives, the poem ends with an incisive wisdom:

> An dèidh na rinn mi rùsgadh dhuibh –
> Tha dùil agam gun lochd –
> 'S a liuthad focal firinneach
> A dhìrich mi nur n-uchd,
> Tha eagal orm nach èisd sibh
> Gu bhith feumail don a' bhochd
> Nas mò na rinn na fleasgaich ud
> A sheachdain gus a-nochd.

> *In spite of this straight talking –*
> *and I feel it's only right –*
> *and all the words of truth I've put*
> *directly in your sight,*
> *I fear you will not listen,*
> *or give the poor a bite,*
> *any more than these did*
> *a week ago tonight.*[79]

Dugald Buchanan, helping to produce a New Testament in Gaelic for the SSPCK, had seen his own poems through the press in 1767; he represented Gaelic poetry's turn towards print textuality, and his writings influenced many later Gaelic evangelical hymns. Influenced by, yet still removed from textual culture, Rob Donn's work would be transmitted orally throughout his own and other Gaelic communities with both respect and glee.

Jauntiness, so associated with the Scottish songs collected by Allan Ramsay and others, could sometimes form part of the non-Gaelic response to Highland affairs. In 'Johnnie Cope' East Lothian farmer and occasional Scots songwriter Adam Skirving (1719–1803) cheers on the Jacobite forces that defeated the Hanoverian army of Sir John Cope at Prestonpans in 1745:

> Fy now, Johnnie, get up and rin;
> The Highland bagpipes mak a din;
> It's best to sleep in a hale skin,
> For 'twill be a bluidy morning.[80]

Such jauntiness, though, soon passed. In response to the Jacobite risings military roads were driven through the Highlands and great government barracks established at such sites as Ruthven near Aviemore and Fort George near Inverness. Fort George took sixteen years to build and is one of Europe's largest military fortifications. This infrastructure and architecture of subjugation eventually made the Highlands safe for tourism. In the shorter term, it was accompanied by attempts to dominate or dismantle the clan system, and rechannel the martial valour of Highland troops into the imperial British army. When England's General Wolfe (who had fought at Culloden) mounted his heroic 1759 attack on the French forces of Montcalm at the Heights of Abraham in Quebec, he sent his Highland soldiers first into the battle, remarking that it was 'no great mischief if they fall'.[81] Over two centuries later those first three words would form the title of the great Scots-Canadian novel by a writer nurtured by the Gaelic-speaking community of Cape Breton, Alistair MacLeod.

Dying falls seemed what Highland culture was for. Seeing the Highlanders not as a modern threat but as a curious ancient remnant made them a cynosure of fascination rather than a source of menace. Rendered comparatively harmless after Culloden, they were viewed as objects of study and a topos of Enlightenment-Romantic cultural pleasure. Only a century and a half earlier, the word 'bard' had been a Lowlanders' term of abuse. Now bards were good for business. Well schooled in the

Classical tradition of the north-east, in 1735 the Aberdeen philosopher Thomas Blackwell in his *Enquiry into the Life and Writings of Homer* had presented the great Greek epic poet as a '*Stroling Bard*', something that helped spur an interest in Highland bards.[82] By the 1740s Adam Ferguson was discussing Gaelic poetry with the dramatist John Home, and the English poet William Collins was suggesting to Home that the Highlands might be a repository of 'Strange lays' by 'Old Runic bards'.[83] So when Home, who knew no Gaelic, met a young Highlander called James Macpherson in the Dumfries-shire town of Moffat in 1759, he persuaded Macpherson to make for him a version of a Gaelic poem. Home, whose *Douglas* had already pronounced him an enthusiast for the culture of the 'Grampian hills', carried this back to Hugh Blair, then about to start lecturing on Rhetoric and Belles Lettres at Edinburgh. As he prepared his lectures, Blair also worked with Macpherson on assembling a slim volume called *Fragments of Ancient Poetry* (1760). These 'fragments' were short bits of English prose. The use of the word 'ancient' in the title echoes such earlier phrasing as 'Ancient Scots Story', used on the 15 December 1756 poster for Home's *Douglas*.[84] It is the new book's subtitle that makes clear the fragments' peculiar fascination. Here was the first ever published volume of work *Collected in the Highlands of Scotland and Translated from the Gaelic or Erse Language*. What matters most about these *Fragments* is their tonality of the dying fall:

I sit by the mossy fountain; on the top of the hill of winds. One tree is rustling above me. Dark waves roll over the heath. The lake is troubled below. The deer descend from the hill. No hunter at a distance is seen; no whistling cow-herd is nigh. It is mid-day: but all is silent. Sad are my thoughts alone. Didst thou but appear, O my love, a wanderer on the heath! thy hair floating on the wind behind thee; thy bosom heaving on the sight; thine eyes full of tears for thy friends, whom the mist of the hill had concealed! Thee I would comfort, my love, and bring thee to thy father's house.[85]

Born at the heart of the Scottish Enlightenment, just as Edinburgh began extending and replacing itself with magnificent neoclassical construction projects that were among the largest in Europe, this is the emerging tonality of Romanticism – lonely, agitated, on a windblown heath. It was a tonality that appealed also to the sympathy-fuelled ethic of sentimentalism, 'eyes full of tears for thy friends'. The incomprehensible, ancient language of Gaelic, so long considered barbarous, has been recast in decorously alluring, sometimes biblical cadences, done into a polite English with just a dash of exotic translatorese. Whatever else he was, James Macpherson was a great translator of taste who encouraged a far-reaching re-imagining of Scottish identity. Did this Highland Classicist, who went on to translate *The Iliad* and enjoy a lucrative career as a British imperialist (he is buried in Westminster Abbey), betray Gaelic culture? Or, in shoring together his post-Culloden *Fragments* and spurring interest in Gaelic literature, did he grant aspects of it an unexpectedly influential future? Without the Ossian controversy and the ensuing investigations into the 'genuineness' of ancient Gaelic poems, works such as the great medieval anthology *The Book of the Dean of Lismore* might have been lost. But Macpherson's work also reinforced very old imaginings about the Caledonian north. Though sentimentally adapted, his Highlanders can be seen as Enlightenment versions of Tacitus's Calgacus, that nobly wild warrior-orator whose speech (scripted by a writer at the heart of the empire) comes as a reproach to 'progressive' Roman imperialism in Tacitus's first-century *Agricola*. Macpherson's mentor Hugh Blair commended Tacitus for being at once 'The Philosopher, the Poet, and the Historian'.[86] The Latin historian was translated between 1728 and 1731 by the Scot Thomas Gordon. Tacitus was popular among the Scottish literati and Calgacus a familiar figure to writers like James Boswell. Unsurprisingly, the first wave of Ossianic epics were joined by a new English translation of the *Agricola*, published in Glasgow by Robert Urie in 1763.

Certainly the elegiac, epic 'translations' which Macpherson developed under Blair's guidance captured imaginations far and near. *Fingal* (1761) and *Temora* (1763) were presented as originally composed by the Gaelic bard Ossian, Son of Fingal, in the third century, and transmitted orally in the Highlands ever since. Gaelic tradition did have an Ossian, and there were ancient Irish accounts of Finn, but these were not quasi-Homeric epic poems. Macpherson collected oral and some written materials which he embellished in full-blown Belles Lettres style. He worked just as European interest in oral cultures was developing, and has been seen in the twenty-first century as pioneering 'the field trip as we know it today'.[87] Modern Gaelic scholarship, especially that of Derick Thomson, suggests that Macpherson took material from genuine Gaelic ballads which still circulated. He mixed this with other matter to produce

his 'epic' works. Some critics, such as Dr Johnson who had little understanding of oral tradition, denounced these as forgeries. Others hailed
them as triumphs of primitive genius that could be connected both to
the Classical epics and to an emergent Belles Lettres canon of great
books. Urged on by Professor Blair, who sang their praises in his lectures,
the Ossianic epics were products of both 'barbarity' and 'exquisite
sensibility'.[88]

At once primitive and sophisticated, these epics were published from
the start with a full scholarly apparatus. They appear as the product of
a convergence between wilderness and classroom. Blair published *A
Critical Dissertation on the Poems of Ossian* in 1763. In the same year
the epics were translated into Italian. They were translated into German
in 1764, and into French within a decade. Their admirers ranged from
Adam Smith to Goethe, from David Hume (who came to doubt their
authenticity) to Thomas Jefferson and Madame de Staël, both of whom
thought Ossian better than Homer. Robert Burns delighted in Ossian,
and Napoleon commissioned a series of Ossianic paintings. For Scots
Ossian's supposed antiquity circumvented the recent humiliations of
Culloden; yet Ossian's mixture of lament and fallen heroes spoke
indirectly of what had happened – and was still happening – in the
modern Highlands. Though best read in small doses, and often scorned,
Macpherson's work became one of the most globally influential Scottish
literary productions. It enthused Goethe and Herder, then brought
Mendelssohn to Scotland, triggering the music of *Fingal's Cave*; it fascinated and empowered Blake, Wordsworth, Byron, Coleridge and many
later poets, including the American Joel Barlow (whose 1807 *Columbiad*
has an Ossianic twitch), Whitman, Longfellow and Whittier. The young
Walter Scott studied it assiduously, and learned from Macpherson's
example. So did James Fenimore Cooper. As Blair explained in his
Critical Dissertation, Ossian was not only characterized by 'tenderness
and sublimity', but also presented 'the scenery throughout, wild and
romantic'.[89] Ossian spurred that shift in sensibility which turned the
'desert' landscapes of northern Britain into Romantic tourist destinations, and let Sassenachs of all persuasions happily sing Burns's refrain
'My heart's in the Highlands'.

Macpherson made the 'fragment' crucial to the Romantic imagination. Ossian, like the Humean self, was pieced together out of fragments
and seemed most alive as a channel for others' perceptions. Making his

short, cadenced prose pieces, Macpherson was a pioneer in English of what we now style the prose poem; he influenced the 'episodic' prose of Henry Mackenzie which, in turn, was bound up with the very early development of the short story. Most of all, the primitive-sophisticated, classroom-wilderness amalgam that was 'Ossian' conditioned assump tions that we still hold about the nature of 'the modern poet'. Such a figure is, in T. S. Eliot's words, 'more *primitive*, as well as more civilized, than his contemporaries'. Poets as different as Wordsworth, Byron, Eliot, Ted Hughes, Seamus Heaney and Don Paterson are all heirs of Ossian's legacy.[90]

Macpherson, though, was only one of the many Enlightenment Scots who bequeathed a potent literary inheritance. Tobias Smollett (1721–71) wrote a brace of novels which would be loved and at times imitated by Dickens, Thackeray and other giants of Victorian fiction. These books established Smollett not as the first Scottish author of prose fiction, but as his country's first novelist of genius. Though there is plenty of evidence that English-language novels were read eagerly by women and students in eighteenth-century Scotland, the genre was still relatively young. In the 1770s around thirty novels per annum were published in Britain and Ireland.[91] Only about forty book-length works of prose fiction were published in Scotland before 1800, and one of the earliest of these, the anonymous 1776 *Select Collection of Oriental Tales*, hints on its title page that its contents are 'Calculated to Form the Minds of Youth to the Love of Virtue and True Wisdom'. Such hints are among many indications that prose fiction had to be defensive about any claims to respectability. Tobias Smollett was not always the most polite of novelists, and like many of his successors he published his novels in London, but he helped strengthen Scottish fiction and English-language fiction generally through work that was ambitious, contemporary, intelligent and funny.

Smollett was born near the Clydeside burgh of Dumbarton, whose etymology, he proudly explained, links it to the ancient kingdom of the Britons from whom 'I would fain derive myself'.[92] The young writer addressed William Wallace in verse and studied George Buchanan's *Rerum Scoticarum Historia* at school. A good deal of Buchanan's writings had been Englished in late seventeenth- and early eighteenth-century Scotland, so that in English as well as in Latin he influenced writers of the period. Buchanan's history furnished Smollett with material for a verbose early play, *The Regicide*, set in the age of James I of Scotland. Smollett's Scotland had a total, scattered population of about 1.2 million people, and very few theatres. After medical studies at Glasgow University, Smollett the ambitious Briton left his small nation and headed south to the Great British capital, hoping to get his play performed. He soon got to know such London Scots as Armstrong, Mallet, Thomson, Andrew Millar and James Oswald. For a time Smollett edited a pro-Scottish London magazine called *The Briton*; its pro-Scottishness was mocked when his English political opponents called their mag *The North Briton*. Smollett liked to socialize with Scottish and English friends at London's *British* coffee house. He wrote his first novel, *The Adventures of Roderick Random* (1748), while he was translating from French Le Sage's *Gil Blas* on which to some extent Smollett modelled his own tale. The opening words of Chapter I of *Roderick Random* indicate both Scottishness and Britishness: 'I was born in the northern part of this united kingdom,' writes Roderick, a first-person narrator schooled in 'the *Belles Lettres*'.[93] Random comes to London as an ingénu, but is helped by fellow Scots there and elsewhere when his adventures on board ship take him as far as the West Indies. This pioneering naval fiction by an author who had himself worked as a ship's surgeon is also a book alert to tensions and prejudices within Britain. 'You Scotchmen have overspread us of late as the locusts did Egypt,' Roderick is told by one English patriot.[94] Eventually, our hero returns to Scotland with an English bride. Such a marriage, emblematizing both personal and political British union, is a device which would be used later by Scott and other Scoto-British novelists. Intriguingly, where forty years earlier John Arbuthnot had gendered Scotland as female – sister to John Bull – Smollett showed how Scotland could be the male partner in a marital union. In Walter Scott's *Waverley* marital union would again emblematize Britishness, but Scotland's would be the female part.

Energy, vigorous satire and splendid detail characterize Smollett's sometimes deliberately masculine fiction, though its author can also display an effortless range of learning. As well as producing a *Universal History*, Smollett made or assisted in an impressive array of widely read and often reprinted translations ranging from Fénelon's *Adventures of Telemachus* (a work beloved of eighteenth-century Scottish student readers among many others) to Cervantes. His own fiction learned from his translations and vice versa. Smollett's prefatory note to his 1755

Don Quixote announces the translator's aim 'to maintain that ludicrous solemnity and self-importance by which the inimitable Cervantes has distinguished the character of Don Quixote', and the Scot's translation is admired alike today by the novelist Carlos Fuentes and by the Yale academic Roberto González Echevarría.

As regards Smollett's own novels, some audiences in succeeding centuries have thought him indecorous or politically incorrect. His is a fictional world in which the hero delights 'to shoe cats with walnut shells, so that they made a most dreadful clattering in their nocturnal excursions', terrifying puzzled insomniacs. An admirer of 'the inimitable Hogarth', Smollett creates such memorable characters as Commodore Hawser Trunnion. Bellowing oaths ('you porpuss-fac'd swab!'), Trunnion steals the show from the eponymous hero of *The Adventures of Peregrine Pickle, in which are included Memoirs of a Lady of Quality* (1751).[95] A caricature of a naval fighter, trapped in his own aggressive, homosocial maleness and clueless about how to behave towards women, Trunnion mentors but is displaced by the less macho Peregrine. In a book which contains a substantial section narrated by a woman and which is playfully alert to gendered behaviour, the Englishman Peregrine, like the protagonist of Smollett's first novel, is a young man finding his way at home. Abroad among prostitutes, artists, homosexuals and soldiers he is 'initiated in the beau monde'.[96] With a knowing authorial wink we are told that Peregrine has read and enjoyed *Roderick Random*. He progresses through a world crammed with incident, if sometimes attended by longueurs. Yet generally there is no shortage of peculiar entertainment in a fictional universe where, ending a 'dissertation' on carnivory, one of Smollett's many eccentric characters assures us that 'in the course of his studies, he had, for the experiment's sake, eaten a steak cut from the buttock of a person who had been hanged'.[97]

Smollett attractively mixes the high-toned and the coarse – cat swallowing and French literary criticism. Like Charlotte Lennox and David Hume, he was a great admirer of *Don Quixote*. His picaresque fictions explore Britishness, sexuality, crankiness and travel in an increasingly mobile commercial society. Historian, magazine editor, translator, and (some said) hack, the multi-talented Smollett wrote a lively account of his *Travels through France and Italy* (1766), sensitive alike to the smell of garlic and the 'spirit of commerce'.[98] While much of his career was spent in London, Smollett too may be viewed in the glow of the Scottish

Enlightenment. Occasionally, as when he uses an expression such as 'disinterested love', there is a hint of his philosophical awareness.[99] The long review of Smith's *Theory of Moral Sentiments* which appeared in Smollett's magazine *The Critical Review* has already been mentioned. Smollett's last, greatest novel, *The Expedition of Humphry Clinker* (1771), seems to take its cue from Smith's thought as it explores through fiction the way in which sympathy may be generated in order to ensure that people achieve 'expedition' (in the older sense of 'liberation') from prejudice. Smith had written of the personal and cultural differences that can occasion prejudice:

> The different situations of different ages and countries are apt, in the same manner, to give different characters to the generality of those who live in them, and their sentiments concerning the particular degree of each quality, that is either blameable or praise-worthy, vary, according to that degree which is usual in their own country, and in their own times. That degree of politeness, which would be highly esteemed, perhaps would be thought effeminate adulation, in Russia, would be regarded as rudeness and barbarism at the court of France. That degree of order and frugality, which, in a Polish nobleman, would be considered as excessive parsimony, would be regarded as extravagance in a citizen of Amsterdam.[100]

With regard to Britain, one of the Welsh characters in Smollett's last novel makes it clear that 'What, between want of curiosity, and traditional sarcasms, the effect of ancient animosity, the people at the other end of the island know as little of Scotland as of Japan.'[101]

Humphry Clinker takes a party of Welsh tourists through England to Scotland. An epistolary novel, it creates strong characters that range from the middle-aged valetudinarian Matthew Bramble and the clever-clever Oxford student Jery Melford to the lively Welshwoman Win Jenkins, who prays for 'God's grease' and is a forerunner both of Sheridan's Mrs Malaprop and, less directly, of Joyce's Molly Bloom. As the Welsh protagonists with their Methodist servant Humphry Clinker pass through Wales, England and Scotland, they learn to interact more sympathetically. 'We are the fools of prejudice,' remarks Jery, and each traveller learns that lesson on the journey north.[102] *Humphry Clinker* has a didactic aspect; English novelist Horace Walpole said it was written by 'the profligate hireling Smollett . . . to vindicate the Scots'. Yet the novel bubbles over with epistolary fun:

I desire you'll clap a pad-luck on the wind-seller, and let none of the men have excess to the strong bear. Don't forget to have the gate shit every evening before dark . . . I know that hussy, Mary Jones, loves to be rumping with the men.[103]

In the concluding sections, as the travellers approach Scotland, they encounter Lieutenant Lismahago, whom Jery regards as a 'Caledonian . . . self-conceited pedant, aukward, rude, and disputacious'; Lismahago discourses about 'war, policy, the belles lettres, law, and metaphysics'. However, this Scottish Enlightenment adventurer's learning outstrips Jery's, while the well-travelled Scot's anecdotes about North American natives who saw off fingers with rusty knives make Scotland seem a reassuringly unprimitive prospect. 'From Doncaster northwards', notes Jery, 'all the windows of all the inns are scrawled with doggerel rhimes, in abuse of the Scotch nation.' As Matt Bramble's Welsh party encounters Scotland, though, such prejudicial abuse is found to be just that – prejudicial abuse. The actual Scotland is awash with 'improvement'. For Bramble, Loch Lomond (near Smollett's boyhood home) is 'romantic beyond imagination', while 'Edinburgh is a hot-bed of genius'. Viewing the country like Enlightenment investigators of 'civil society', the party glimpse David Hume, William Robertson, Hugh Blair and others. Even Jery finds himself converted into an explainer of Scotland to 'The English, who have never crossed the Tweed'. He comes to relish 'the Scotch accent . . . a sort of Doric dialect', hears Gaelic, and becomes eager for an alluring Highland view: 'I feel an enthusiastic pleasure when I survey the brown heath that Ossian was wont to tread.'[104]

Smollett's articulation of sympathetic Britishness stops on the fringes of the Ossianic Highlands. Enthusiasm for Ossian did not usually translate into a knowledge of contemporary Gaelic verse, though it did prompt within and beyond the Gaelic community vigorous collection, investigation and preservation of Gaelic poems and traditions that could be considered ancient. Not far from where Jery Melford surveyed the Ossianic 'brown heath' was Ben Dorain, the mountain so beloved of Smollett's Gaelic near-contemporary Donnchadh Bàn Mac-an-t-Saoir (Duncan Bàn Macintyre) (1724–1812). The first edition of Macintyre's poems had appeared in Edinburgh in 1768. He seems to have enjoyed some success with the beau monde as a 'bard'. In the 1780s he was encouraged by the London Highland Society (whose very name signals a significant shift in attitudes towards Caledonian culture) for whose competitions he composed songs praising the bagpipes and the Gaelic language. He served both in the Hanoverian military and, between 1766 and 1793, in the Edinburgh City Guard, the 'Geard Dhun Eideann' as the Gaels called it. This was the same police force known to the young reveller poet Robert Fergusson and other Lowlanders as 'that black banditti'.[105] Though he spent a good deal of his life in the city, hymned an Enlightenment Edinburgh banker and lamented Highland chieftains, Duncan Bàn is most distinguished as a poet of the natural environment.

He learned from Alasdair Mac Mhaighstir Alasdair, whose work at times he came close to imitating. But in Duncan Bàn's best verse there is a remarkable feeling for what we would now call an 'ecosystem' – a working partnership between landscape, animals and the people who sometimes go hunting. The beautifully detailed 'Oran Coire a' Cheathaich' (Song to Misty Corrie) celebrates the biodiversity of a glen near Crianlarich; it is what Jonathan Bate terms, in another context, a 'song of the earth', and should be read in the light of recent ecocriticism as well as from the standpoints of poetic excellence and Gaelic tradition.[106] Language, its fullness, variety and maintenance, are crucial concerns of this poet; so are land, its management, mismanagement, forfeiture and restoration. In more familiar Scottish Enlightenment terms, Duncan Bàn is a great poet of what Burns termed 'Nature's social union'.[107] Like Burns, he can show the disastrous consequences of breaking that union. 'Cumha Coire a' Cheathaich' (Lament for Misty Corrie) revisits the earlier terrain during an era of bad land management in the wake of Culloden. Some Scottish Enlightenment land managers naively hymned 'improvement'; Sir John Sinclair wanted to 'Kentify Caithness'.[108] Macintyre, however, highlighted ecological disaster. Ironically composed to the tune of 'The Flowers of Edinburgh', his rural keening details the harm visited on flora and fauna. A once fruitful landscape is now characterized by rot, scummy water and choked drainage channels. The poet laments,

> 'S e 'n coire chaidh an dèislaimh,
> On tha e nis gun fhèidh ann,
> Gun duin' aig a bheil spèis diubh
> Nì feum air an cùl.

How the corrie has gone to ruin,
since now it has no deer,
nor any man who loves them
and is efficient on their trail.[109]

Above all, Duncan Bàn was a man who loved deer. He was a poet, not
a philosopher, but just as Adam Smith achieved a remarkable insight
into the workings of human society, so this Enlightenment Gaelic police-
man-poet articulated a vision of harmony and disharmony between
human and natural cycles in his resonant, richly loaded word-music.

Macintyre's masterpiece, 'Moladh Beinn Dòbhrain' (Praise of Ben
Dorain), is a series of complex variations based on the patterns of the
Highland bagpiper's pibroch music. It can be chanted to this music and
fits the piping rhythms exactly. Macintyre's long poem draws on his
experience as a forester and gamekeeper in Glen Lochay, on Ben Dorain,
and in Glen Etive between 1746 and 1766. Lovingly it presents the deer
and their home ground:

Ach caochlaideach curaideach
Caolchasach ullamh,
An aois cha chuir truim' orra,
    Mulad no mìghean.
'S e shlànaich an culaidh,
Feòil mhàis agus mhuineil,
Bhith tàmhachd am bunailt
    An cuilidh na frìthe . . .

Coquettes of the body,
slim-leggèd and ready,
no age makes them tardy,
no grief nor disease.

Their coats get their shimmer –
fat flesh of their glamour –
from their rich local summer
in the store of the moor.[110]

Macintyre's sense of the moor as 'store' – both fruitful place of preservation and larder – is in keeping with the poem's extended verbal
fecundity. In the twentieth century this poet's work was especially prized

by Iain Crichton Smith, and in earlier times it won Macintyre the impressive monument which still stands above Loch Awe in the West Highlands. On nearby Ben Dorain imported sheep displaced deer in Duncan Bàn's lifetime, and his boyhood house is now a sheep-fank, but a fresh sense of the links between poetry and ecology should help restore Duncan Bàn Macintyre to his position as a commanding voice in Scottish verse. Though the Cuillin mountains of Skye and the higher Ben Nevis may be better known today, Duncan Bàn made Ben Dorain the iconic summit of Highland poetry – the Mount Fuji of the Gaelic imagination.

''S i mo dhùthaich a dh' fhàg mi' – ''tis my homeland I deserted' – sings this poet who lived so long in Edinburgh where not Gaelic but 'harsh English/ has assailed our ears daily'.[111] Probably Duncan Bàn in Edinburgh had a better knowledge of 'cùnnradh 's le fasan' (commerce and fashion) than most of those around him had of Gaelic. Yet that did not prevent a taste for Highland culture becoming fashionable, and even commercial in the years that followed the publication of the Ossianic poems. As poetry and music were closely bonded for Duncan Bàn Macintyre, so they were for many Lowland poets. 'Gie's *Tulloch Gorum*,' demanded Robert Fergusson, referring to a fashionable tune with a Gaelic title that was soon celebrated in a poem of the same name by the Aberdeen Episcopalian Church historian and Jacobite sympathizer, the Reverend John Skinner.[112] Skinner, like Fergusson, defended Scottish tunes against a perceived threat from foreign competition in the increasingly sophisticated marketplace of Enlightenment Scottish culture:

What needs there be sae great a fraise	*gush*
Wi' dringing dull Italian lays,	*droning*
I wadna gie our ain Strathspeys	
For half a hunder score o' them;	
They're dowf and dowie at the best,	*dull and sad*
Dowf and dowie, dowf and dowie,	
Dowf and dowie at the best,	
Wi' a' their variorum;	
They're dowf and dowie at the best,	
Their *allegros* and a' the rest,	
They canna' please a Scottish taste	
Compar'd wi' Tullochgorum.[113]	

The song enthusiast Burns, who pinched the word 'variorum' from this and used it as a definition of life, pronounced Skinner's 'Tullochgorum' 'the best Scotch song ever Scotland saw', and it grew fashionable with other Lowland writers and editors, including Walter Scott.[114] That it should have a Gaelic-sounding title, yet be composed in Lowland Scots, hints at the possibilities for cultural fusion now emerging in an Enlightenment Scotland where sympathies, even between cultures formerly antagonistic, were being encouraged by literary developments.

If *Humphry Clinker* is a sometimes rumbustious Scottish Enlightenment classic, powered by the philosophy of sympathy, then *The Man of Feeling*, which appeared in the same year, 1771, is its more soft-centred cousin. Burns relished Smollett, but Henry Mackenzie's *Man of Feeling* was for the poet in his mid-twenties 'a book I prize next to the Bible'.[115] Mackenzie, who came to be known by the title of his most famous book, was born in the eventful year 1745 to a Highland mother and a Lowland father. As a baby he was kissed by Bonnie Prince Charlie. Throughout his life, he retained a feeling for Highland culture. In old age he noted sadly how a particular Highland landscape he prized as 'beautiful' had 'long since changed its possessor, and ... lost more than half its beauty.'[116] Attending school and university in Edinburgh, he became a successful lawyer, working briefly in London before returning to the Scottish capital. Mackenzie married the daughter of the Chief of Clan Grant and would later help investigate the Ossianic poems. In his youth he authored romantic ballads ('Duncan. A Fragment' and 'Kenneth') which blended Scots ballad form with Highland flavouring. He achieved huge success in his mid-twenties with *The Man of Feeling*, a short novel of the 'Sentimental' school which was quickened by the admired French fictions of Prévost, Rousseau, Marmontel and other writers, by the virtuous fiction of Samuel Richardson, by Laurence Sterne's *A Sentimental Journey* (1766), by Smithian 'sympathy', and by the David Hume who, emphasizing the importance of the passions, wrote in his *Treatise of Human Nature* that ' 'Tis not solely in poetry and music, we must follow our taste and sentiment, but likewise in philosophy.'[117]

Mackenzie authored his Sentimental *Man of Feeling* in London, where much of its action takes place. None of his major fictions is set in Scotland, and the Scottishness of their author is not initially apparent. Yet Mackenzie is very much a novelist of the Scottish Enlightenment. In form *The Man of Feeling*, as a 'bundle of little episodes' (several of which carry the title 'A Fragment'), is presented, like the Ossianic poems and like other work by Mackenzie, as collected, edited, incomplete, and so all the more alluring. Starting off by plunging *in medias res*, with the initial section numbered 'Chapter XI', Mackenzie's editorial narrative method is self-conscious. The lawyer-writer pieces together his book like a textual scholar out of the documents of the case. Yet the writing, for all its self-reflexive aspect, is immediately engaging. The book's very first words may be calculating, but, with their bloodsport chattiness (Mackenzie, like Duncan Bàn, was a keen hunter), they have a stylishly casual quality:

My dog had made a point on a piece of fallow-ground, and led the curate and me two or three hundred yards over that and some stubble adjoining, in a breathless state of expectation, on a burning first of September.

It was a false point, and our labour was vain: yet, to do Rover justice, (for he's an excellent dog, though I have lost his pedigree) the fault was none of his, the birds were gone; the curate shewed me the spot where they had lain basking, at the root of an old hedge.

I stopped and cried Hem! The curate is fatter than I; he wiped the sweat from his brow.

This is not a momentous opening, but its very mundanity is part of its charm. The label 'sentimental', once Mackenzie's selling-point, became his curse. Particularly, he suffered at the hands of twentieth-century male critics, wary of 'feminization' and rigorously schooled in the notion that real men never cry. Mackenzie writes with aplomb. If his hero Harley owes something to Smollett's provincial innocents abroad in London, and is too prone to bursting into sympathetic tears or savouring 'romantic melancholy', then the narrator also has what Walter Scott (who in *Waverley*'s 'Postscript, Which Should Have Been a Preface' called Mackenzie 'Our Scottish Addison') acutely identified as Mackenzie's sense of 'fun'.[118] Told to ingratiate himself with a rich elderly relative, the unfortunate Harley gets it all wrong, looking peculiarly po-faced 'when the old lady told the jokes of her youth', then having 'the rudeness to fall asleep, while she was describing the composition and virtues of her favourite cholic-water'.[119] Sociable, consciously feminized ironic humour mixes with essayistic or philosophically motivated speculation and outbursts of sympathetic feeling. Where Smollett's naive lads were duped, then learned to be men of the world, in Mackenzie's fiction the worldly-wise, even as they achieve mastery or success, are shown as shallow in comparison with more sensitive, sympathetic souls who can comprehend others' suffering. Prepared to burst into tears, Harley is a feminized man, not a go-getter or a stentorian Hawser Trunnion, and is presented as all the more admirable for that. In Mackenzie's second novel, *The Man of the World* (1773), partly set among the wilds of America, readers are led, like readers of Ossian, to sympathize with a defeated victim, and to see just what is wrong with 'men of the world'. In *Julia de Roubigné* (1777), Mackenzie's third and last novel, set in France and influenced by Rousseau, the 'little philosopher' heroine Julia is the first woman to take centre stage throughout a Scottish novel.[120]

In this Mackenzie may have been encouraged by the prominent parts for Scottish women in male-authored plays such as Smollett's *Regicide*, Home's *Douglas* and Voltaire's *Le Caffé, ou l'Ecossaise* (1760), but Mackenzie was far from alone among male Scottish writers in being alert to the changing social circumstances of women. An increasing male interest in 'feminization' and female culture is a significant aspect of the Scottish Enlightenment. It produced, among other things, the 'enlightened' reasoner and Kirk Moderator Robert Wallace's unpublished account of 'the Commerce of the 2 Sexes', then later John Millar's 1771 discussion 'Of the Rank and condition of Women'. William Robertson wrote an extended account of the rivalry between Mary, Queen of Scots, and Queen Elizabeth in his *History of Scotland* (1759), while William Alexander's large-scale *History of Women* (1779), like fictions by Smollett, Mackenzie, and others, is alert to the conditioning of 'sexual difference'.[121] The sophisticated, woman-centred novel *Julia de Roubigné* provides a critique of what Mackenzie's friend, sometime literary collaborator and fellow Edinburgh lawyer, William Craig, called in one of Mackenzie's magazines, *The Mirror*, the 'dangerous extreme' to which sentiments, however virtuous, might be taken.[122] This hothouse epistolary novel of love is as much a critique of the sentimental as an exercise in it.

Julia also shows its usually conservative author's radical side in its attack on slavery. Here Mackenzie disagrees with the pro-slavery Hume, but follows the lead of Francis Hutcheson, Adam Smith, John Millar, James Beattie and other Scottish Enlightenment intellectuals who had denounced the slave trade – an abomination also scorned by such conservatives as Edmund Burke and Dr Johnson. To this day Scottish historians tend to gloss over Scotland's participation in profiteering from slavery. Even as the Glasgow 'Tobacco Lords' and other sectors of Scottish society grew rich from imperial trade in such commodities as tobacco and sugar from the West Indies and America, leading Scottish men of letters denounced slavery and attempted to defend the human dignity of its victims. Conscious of the distance between 'improved' and 'primitive' or 'savage' peoples, Smith had written in *The Theory of Moral Sentiments* that

contempt of death and torture prevails among all other savage nations. There is not a negro from the coast of Africa who does not, in this respect, possess a degree of magnanimity which the soul of his sordid master is too often scarce capable of conceiving. Fortune never exerted more cruelly her empire over mankind, than when she subjected those nations of heroes to the refuse of the jails of Europe, to wretches who possess the virtues neither of the countries which they come from, nor of those which they go to, and whose levity, brutality, and baseness, so justly expose them to the contempt of the vanquished.[123]

The presentation of the evils of slavery in *Julia de Roubigné* is at least as spirited. On the one hand, Mackenzie is a lawyer, editor of Edinburgh's *Mirror* and *Lounger*, poet, dramatist. A man of letters rather than a mere novelist, he is a fashionable establishment figure in a Lowland Scotland whose elites were growing rich after the Union of Crowns and Parliaments, profiting from the British Empire. On the other hand, a child of 1745 married to a Highland wife, Mackenzie is author of 'sentimental' writings that show a feeling for the 'vanquished', for ruined men, subject peoples and 'silent, unroofed, desolate homesteads'. In 1770, two years after the publication of Duncan Bàn Macintyre's poems, the Edinburgh-educated Irishman Oliver Goldsmith had published his influential poem 'The Deserted Village', but there were plenty of deserted villages to be seen in post-Culloden Scotland. Mackenzie's sympathy for the defeated is furthered by his 'sentimental' aesthetic, and deserves more than patronizing attention from modern readers. True, his tearfulness, along with Smollett's caricaturist's love of eccentricity, prepared the way for Dickens, but that tearfulness was only part of Mackenzie. His pioneering, sometimes clear-eyed, sometimes emotionally charged questioning of a society's core assumptions surfaces in a remarkable, ironically titled passage when '*The Man of Feeling talks of what he does not understand*':

'I have a proper regard for the prosperity of my country: every native of it appropriates to himself some share of the power, or the fame, which, as a nation, it acquires; but I cannot throw off the man so much, as to rejoice at our conquests in India. You tell me of immense territories subject to the English: I cannot think of their possessions without being led to enquire, by what right they possess them. They came there as traders, bartering the commodities they brought for others which their purchasers could spare; and however great their profits were, they were then equitable. But what title have the subjects of another kingdom to establish an empire in India? to give laws to a country where the inhabitants received them on the terms of friendly commerce? You say they are happier under our regulations than the tyranny of their own petty princes. I must doubt it, from the conduct of those by whom these regulations have been made. They have drained the treasuries of Nabobs, who must fill them by oppressing the industry of their subjects.'[124]

Here, in his disquisition on 'purchasers', 'traders', 'commerce' and 'industry', the Man of Feeling uses language that anticipates that of *The Wealth of Nations*, published five years later. Yet Mackenzie's work, so alert to the idea that 'man is naturally a social animal', and that in a sense 'we are all relations', so keen to provide a 'mirror' for inner and for social life, is also close to the philosophy of *The Theory of Moral Sentiments*.[125] Like Smith, Hume and, in their different ways, the ecologically sensitive Duncan Bàn Macintyre and the socially alert Robert Burns, Mackenzie is preoccupied with 'the science of man'. His modernity matters as much as his faded fashionable appeal. In the introduction to her 1999 edition Susan Manning has drawn attention to the way in which the psychological extremism examined in *Julia de Roubigné* ('It was my own figure in the mirror that stood at my back. – What a look was mine! – Am I a murderer? – Justice cannot murder . . .') points the way towards James Hogg's *Private Memoirs and Confessions of a Justified Sinner* half a century later.

Mackenzie can be the most surprising of innovators. He wrote a remarkable 'story' based around the life of David Hume in France and presented as 'a translation from the French'. This 'Story of La Roche' was published in the *Mirror* in 1779. It shows that, though in title and format Mackenzie's journal depended on *The Spectator*, the magazine let its editor evolve a form of writing that moved decisively away from the essay towards the short story. In his early thirties Mackenzie ceased to be a novelist, but he continued to be a writer. His achievement has not been fully recognized; if his lawyerly propriety led him to stick to polite, Addisonian English, his presence in Edinburgh also asserted that successful novelists might live there. Though it is usually the last word which is stressed in Scott's description of him as 'Our Scottish Addison', the other two words are as important. Mackenzie's 1779 'Story of La Roche', moving beyond, and fusing elements from his Highland-flavoured ballads, essays and the 'bundle of little episodes' that are his novels, is, in effect, one of the first consciously shaped literary short stories in the English language. James Hogg, another Edinburgh periodi-cal writer nurtured like Mackenzie by a ballad-composing apprentice-ship, would develop this form, as would other members of the circle grouped round Hogg's later magazine *The Spy*. So would Walter Scott, who knew he owed Mackenzie a literary debt and who is sometimes presented as the originator of the short-story genre. Not for nothing did Scott admire the 'unexampled delicacy' of Mackenzie's 'fine tale'.[126]

The Scottish Enlightenment is usually treated in terms of its philos-ophy and science, with literature seen either not at all, or else as a minor appendage. Some may have felt that the creative work of the period, with its Romantic and proto-Romantic filiations, fits awkwardly with the reasoned, moderate, neoclassical tone of the philosophers. This view is wrong-headed. Henry Mackenzie is not as great as Adam Smith. Nonetheless, the preoccupation with social interaction and development in Hume, Smith, *The Statistical Account*, Adam Ferguson and elsewhere is closely bound up with the development of Scottish fiction. It is comple-mented by the work of such different poets of 'Nature's social union' as Alasdair Mac Mhaighstir Alasdair, Duncan Bàn Macintyre and Robert Burns. Smith lectured on Belles Lettres as well as economics; Mac-pherson was both bard and profiteer; even Mackenzie wrote a poem called 'Poetry and Business'. A peculiar relationship between taste, sym-pathy and hard cash underpins not only *The Theory of Moral Sentiments* and *The Wealth of Nations*, but also the productions of Ossian and of professional writers such as Smollett. The 'primitive' and 'sophisticated', so much analysed by historians and conjectural historians, were fused by Ossian, Burns and others to produce the cultural space – at once sophisticated and marginal or 'primitive' – occupied by the modern poet ever since. The Scottish Enlightenment invented modern geology, but was also the crucible of the short story. Scottish Enlightenment philosophers at their best wrote with stylish clarity; poets and novelists wrote not as philosophers, but were attuned to modern as well as older ways of thinking, hearing and dreaming. The fascination with a fragmented self is matched by the episodic fictions of Mackenzie and others in this age of the literary fragment. If the world we know is, in Hume's phrase, 'the universe of the imagination', then who better to explore it than imaginative writers?[127]

The frontispiece to the 1787 edition of Robert Burns's Poems,
published in Edinburgh by William Creech. Based on a portrait by
Burns's friend Alexander Nasmyth, the engraving is by John Beugo.
On 24 February 1787 Burns wrote to a friend in his native Ayrshire,
'I am getting my Phiz done by an eminent Engraver; and if it can be
ready in time, I will appear in my book looking, like other fools, to my
title page.' (St Andrews University Library, Sal PR4300.D87E4)

7

The Age of Burns

Writers, particularly poets, are competitive and jealous. So, at least, thought Adam Smith:

They are very apt to divide themselves into a sort of literary factions; each cabal being often avowedly, and almost always secretly, the mortal enemy of the reputation of every other, and employing all the mean arts of intrigue and solicitation to preoccupy the public opinion in favour of the works of its own members, and against those of its enemies and rivals.[1]

This view of literature as a dirty-tricks marketplace, or even battlefield, is a reminder that in 'sympathetic' eighteenth-century Scotland books and literary reputations were an important commodity. Smith's view suits the action of the student poet Robert Fergusson, fighting back against those who had written against him, and neatly penning in a library book the couplet,

> The man that wrote these cursed lines on me
> he now is damned and ever more shall be.[2]

Scottish Enlightenment trade in intellectual property could be hard-headed. Even the author of *The Man of Feeling* was a successful, prosperous lawyer, and it is unlikely that William Robertson became an internationally significant historian – let alone Principal of Edinburgh University – by being commercially naive or soft-hearted. Ambitious authors from Robert Burns to James Boswell helped establish elaborate networks to assist in the distribution and promotion of their works. In an age when many books (like those of Burns) were published by subscription, authors, their friends and supporters, canvassed for subscribers. Writers wanted patrons, allies, review coverage and bookshop sales. An increasingly complex market of literary property developed.

Coffee houses, publishers' offices like that of Burns's Edinburgh publisher William Creech, clubs, societies and literary salons gave writers and would-be writers room to joust.

In 1751 the Glasgow-based Smith's Circulating Library was founded. Soon it became John Smith and Son bookshop. This firm still survived until the start of the twenty-first century, long enough to be hailed as the world's oldest continuously trading bookseller. Burns corresponded with John Smith Jr, whose firm acted as an agent distributing copies of books to subscribers. The shrewd poet is said to have remarked, 'You seem a very decent sort o' folk, you Glasgow booksellers; but, eh! they're sair birkies [sour meanies] in Edinburgh.'[3] Preserved in the Glasgow bookshop's corporate history, this may be as good an example as any of the kind of literary 'intrigue' highlighted by Adam Smith.

The increasing strength of literary institutions – from shops, circulating libraries and publishing houses to university Belles Lettres courses, energetic periodicals or discussion groups – fuelled both alliances and rows. Though originally modelled on the London *Gentleman's Magazine*, the Edinburgh-published *Scots Magazine* (1729–1826) had as one of its aims 'That the Caledonian muse might not be restrained by want of a publick echo to her song'.[4] Sometimes the echoes could be deafening.

The biggest Scottish literary row was over Ossian. When *The Scots Magazine* eagerly published several of the first Ossianic *Fragments*, many of the literati were in ecstasy. Others, not least in England, called Ossian's poems forgeries. In 1773 Samuel Johnson, who directed the anti-Ossianic ordnance, made a tour of the Highlands with his Scottish Sancho Panza, James Boswell, determined to sniff out the stink of Ossianic deceit. Eventually, almost half a century after the *Fragments* had first appeared, Henry Mackenzie, the lawyer and writer, chaired a grand Highland Society Committee '*Appointed to Inquire into the Nature and Authenticity of the Poems of Ossian*'. Its lengthy *Report*, which finds (like modern scholars) that Macpherson greatly elaborated on a smallish amount of genuine original material, reads like a government document, or an attempt at a literary peace treaty.

Bookish quarrels could reach the House of Lords. This happened with the 1774 case of *Donaldson v. Becket* in which the Edinburgh bookseller Alexander Donaldson (whose legal team included James Boswell) defeated a group of London booksellers who claimed perpetual copyright over the Scottish poet James Thomson's *The Seasons*, as well as the works of many other celebrated English poets. Linked to this high-profile legal wrangle were competing editions of canonical writers, often produced by English and Scottish commercial rivals. *The British Poets*, edited by Hugh Blair for Creech and others in forty-four volumes between 1773 and 1776, may be the first full national corpus that people with enough money could buy and set out in their library like a national standing army: Britannia rules the bookshelves. Rival English editions famously included a gang of London booksellers' *The Works of the English Poets with Prefaces Biographical and Critical by Samuel Johnson* (1779–81) – an attempt to reassert metropolitan authority. Grand, competing multivolume editions of the poets went on appearing in Scotland and England for more than a century, with Hugh Blair's influence felt long beyond his death.[5] The *Donaldson v. Becket* case was a milestone in publishing history and the marketing of books.

So strong was the power of Scottish Enlightenment literary culture that some English literary institutions came to be reshaped by it. Most strikingly, perhaps, Shakespeare, who had never presented himself as a 'bard', but who began to be treated in the eighteenth century as a national poet, came to be restyled as 'The Bard'. England's anglophone, monarchist 'Bard' whose successes were metropolitan ones, could be deployed as an antidote to those proudly Caledonian bards, the Gaelic Ossian and, later, Ossian's admirer the radical Scots republican Robert Burns. Burns's triumphs were neither metropolitan nor, as many ears heard them, in the King's English. Hugh Blair presented Burns with a copy of Shakespeare – a significant gesture. Since that day the term 'The Bard' has meant very different things north and south of the Border. Scottish-English bard wars were incited further in the nineteenth century by such a provocatively back-to-front title as Byron's *English Bards and Scotch Reviewers*, and in the twentieth century by that would-be 'Voice of Scotland', Hugh MacDiarmid, proud to list his hobby in *Who's Who* as 'Anglophobia'. To this day in English culture and education Burns is frequently sidelined; Shakespeare is loved in Scotland, but not as Scotland's bard.

Literary fisticuffs are never confined to the level of institutions. They can also be virulently individual. If Henry Mackenzie, that sharp-eyed, well-heeled 'Man of Feeling', could be lauded as a literary lion, he could also be attacked as a *'feeling swine'*. 'The Sow of Feeling' by Robert Fergusson (1750–74) ridicules Mackenzie's best-known character (one often identified with Mackenzie himself) by translating him into a girly pig. The Sow of Feeling lives in fear of butchers and poetically laments her lot, 'With heavy heart, I saunter all the day,/ Gruntle and murmur all my hours away!'[6] Mackenzie was affronted, and tried to get his own back on Fergusson by dismissing him after his early death as 'dissipated and drunken', a bard of 'blackguardism'.[7] Politically and personally divided, Scottish Enlightenment literary life was far from one great round of Olympian sympathetic high-mindedness. It was livelier, and more complicated, than that.

Yet if Adam Smith's remark that poets could be 'enemies and rivals' offers one version of the writer's life, there were other models on offer. The most obvious was the Sentimental-Romantic one of the poet as doomed misfit. We may tend to think of this figuration of the poet in later Romantic terms, calling to mind Keats, or Shelley, or Byron, but the trope was shaped in the tearful Sentimental era. It should not be seen as contradicting Smith's poet as 'mortal enemy', but as complementing it. After all, as the blind Scottish poet Thomas Blacklock (1721–91) put it, 'wrap my heart in tenfold steel,/ I still am man, and still must feel.'[8] In *The Theory of Moral Sentiments*, just before outlining poets' rivalries, Smith writes of poets in terms of 'extreme sensibility' in the face of 'the public', and of their 'hurt' and 'pain'.[9] This is not an image of the poet that would have fitted Henryson, Dunbar or Buchanan; instead, it related to the new commercial culture of 'refinement' and to a growing perception of individual psychological complexity and vulnerability. Mackenzie, deriving his aesthetic of sensibility in considerable measure from Smith's philosophy, had his characters in *The Man of Feeling* discuss the idea that 'the poetical inclination' can lead to 'unfitness for the world'.[10] Robert Burns, who once pronounced *The Man of Feeling* his favourite novel, yet whose favourite Scottish poet seems to have been Robert Fergusson, exclaimed in one of three English-language poems addressed to Fergusson's memory,

> With tears I pity thy unhappy fate!
> Why is the Bard unfitted for the world,
> Yet has so keen a relish of its Pleasures?[11]

Burns's view of being a 'Bard' was shaped in considerable measure by Sentimentalism, and by the fates of some of his younger contemporaries. Earlier Scottish poets had been successful churchmen, academics, courtiers, even monarchs. Often their poetry had been purposefully formal, foregrounding a public voice and only occasionally hinting at the individual that might lie behind that voice. Now in the eighteenth century poets worked as ministers, policemen, gamekeepers, teachers, farmers, even excisemen, yet, as Lowland commercial society developed apace, a notion of the poet as somehow useless, 'unfitted for the world', grew in Ossian's wake. This was only one version of the role of poet, but its influence was marked.

One doomed poet whose work Burns read attentively was Michael Bruce (1746–67). Burns sympathized with Bruce as one who, Hamlet-like, had 'felt, the many ills, the peculiar ills, that Poetic Flesh is heir to'.[12] Bruce was a victim of rivalry. Another poet tried to appropriate much of his work. More obvious is Bruce's suffering: he died of tuberculosis at the age of twenty-one. If the human infant for Bruce in one poem is 'born to weep', then for Burns, more famously, confidently, and alliteratively, 'Man was Made to Mourn'.[13] Bruce's paean 'To Paoli', the Corsican nationalist hero, with its lines 'Thy sons shall lay the proud oppressor low,/ And break the head of tyrant kings', nourishes Burns's Robert Bruce poem popularly known as 'Scots Wha Hae' with its 'Lay the proud usurpers low!/ Tyrants fall in every foe!'[14] More surprisingly, Michael Bruce's mock-Homeric 'The Musiad' (whose Latinate title's meaning would be clearer if it were Englished as 'The Mousiad') deals with an encounter between a farmer and a mouse that will be completely transmuted into Burns's 'To a Mouse, On Turning Her up in Her Nest with the Plough'. The poems are very different, but Bruce's English-language notion of 'evil fortune' as 'The foe of mice as well as men' underpins Burns's celebrated Scots reflection that

> The best laid schemes o' *Mice* an' *Men*,
>> Gang aft agley,   *awry*
> An' lea'e us nought but grief an' pain,
>> For promis'd joy![15]

The university-educated, Ossian-inspired Bruce was a teacher from Kinross in central Scotland. He was no genius. Yet, though he wrote in English rather than Scots, he was a significant precursor of Fergusson, Burns and even (in Bruce's long poem 'Lochleven') Wordsworth. His short life and career helped establish a pattern on to which the lives of such later 'genius' poets as Fergusson, Burns, Thomas Chatterton and

Keats came to be mapped – the figure, to use Wordsworth's term, of the doomed 'marvellous boy'.[16] Like Fergusson's, Michael Bruce's life was blighted by tragedy, and, again like Fergusson, Bruce moved from writing Classical pastoral eclogue to paraphrasing the Book of Job. As did the farmer Burns (who occasionally signed himself as Bruce's admired rural 'Agricola'), Bruce hailed his native land, and, delighting in local rivers and country life, mapped himself on to 'ancient Bards', while maintaining a pained sense of his own mortality.[17] Some lines of Bruce's 'Lochleven' ghost the conclusion of Burns's last song, 'O, Wert Thou in the Cauld Blast', written as Burns was dying.[18]

Poetry's link to 'ruin' was reinforced by William Falconer in *The Shipwreck* (1762). Before he drowned at the age of thirty-seven, the sailor-poet Falconer (1732–70) wrote with an insider's knowledge of 'fated wretches trembling' on a 'fatal shore'.[19] Cultivating a potential patron, Burns, who would die at the same age, pitied Falconer as 'the son of obscurity & misfortune', and was sympathetically impressed by 'that dreadful catastrophe he so feelingly describes in his Poem'.[20] Son of a tenant farmer destroyed by debt, Burns always had an eye open for 'dreadful catastrophe' and, writing poems with titles like 'To Ruin' and 'Despondency: An Ode', he worried about his own fate. Nowhere is this more evident than in his identification with his most important precursor, Robert Fergusson, whom Burns never met but whom he addressed as

> O thou, my elder brother in Misfortune,
> By far my elder Brother in the muse . . .[21]

In some ways Robert Fergusson was very different from Robert Burns. Edinburgh-born and Dundee-schooled, Fergusson was essentially an urban poet. Today, just outside Edinburgh's Canongate Kirkyard where he was buried, there is a bronze statue of him striding out along the Royal Mile. Fergusson was recognized in his own short lifetime as the 'laureate' of Scotland's capital city, whose daytime and night-time streetlife he celebrates in his unfinished long poem *Auld Reikie*. However, for all his love of urban biz, Fergusson went to university in the countryside. As a student at St Andrews in the 1760s, he was probably the first significant poet in the English-speaking world to study English literary texts as part of his university curriculum. In some ways he reacted against the experience, though he did pay tribute to one academic mentor, the St Andrews professor and poet the Reverend William Wilkie (1721–72) who wrote not only the *'new old'* English heroic couplets of *The Epigoniad* (1757), but also essayed a somewhat antiquarian beast fable, 'The Hare and the Partan', in Scots.[22] A professor and farmer who was once said to like nothing better than to sleep in dirty sheets, Wilkie taught Natural Philosophy (physics). The Classically-educated Fergusson wrote a fine Scots pastoral eclogue in Wilkie's memory, and saw his old mentor as inspiring future 'scholars and bards', among whom he might have numbered himself.[23] Certainly 'the Scottish Homer', as Wilkie came to be known, rescued Fergusson from expulsion from the university after a student riot. Fergusson was a lively but not universally popular student. One St Andrews contemporary called him 'a damned eternal Puppy a stinking fairy' and 'a snake in human form stain'd with infamy and wickedness'. Yet the young poet wrote with fondness of the St Andrews students in their *'red gowns'*, sinking pints with the University porter. Less affection is shown towards most of the academic authorities; Fergusson remarks on the Principal's 'canker'd snout'.[24] He seems to have drawn on student lore in what may be his first surviving poem, an 'Elegy' for a maths professor:

> He could, by *Euclid*, prove lang sine   *long ago*
> A ganging *point* compos'd a line;   *moving*
> By numbers too he cou'd divine,
> > Whan he did read,
> That *three* times *three* just made up nine;
> > But now he's dead.

What at first sight sounds ritualistically solemn dissolves into cheekiness; the poem balances between affectionate mockery and assured insolence. Surely the first piece of verse in any variety of the English language to use the expression 'surd roots', it effortlessly outlines Euclidean geometry in Scots, while elegizing a professor in the Standard Habbie form which, until Fergusson came along, was associated with familiar verse epistles or poems memorializing beasts, bagpipers and bawds.[25] Learned yet carnivalesque, at ease in formal English but possessing a frolicsome and fraternal love of Scots vernacular speech, Fergusson is an exemplary poet of physical and intellectual vivacity. When Dr Johnson and James Boswell were sycophantically feasted by the St Andrews profs in 1773, Fergusson, in Edinburgh, wrote an address 'To the Principal and

Professors of the University of St Andrews, on their Superb Treat to Dr Samuel Johnson'. Johnson was notorious in Scotland for having defined oats in his great 1755 English *Dictionary* as 'A grain, which in England is generally given to horses, but in Scotland supports the people'. Taking revenge, Fergusson delivers a mock verse-lecture in Scots with Latin headings to the Doctor and Professors, setting out all the distinctively Scottish, often oat-rich foods *he* would have fed to 'Sam, the lying loun', making him eat his words. '*Imprimis*, then, a haggis fat', begins Fergusson's menu, which goes on to heap up other delicacies such as 'bloody puddins' and 'a gude sheep's head'. Burns's festal address 'To a Haggis', celebrating that oatmeal apogee of Scots cuisine as 'Great Chieftain o' the Puddin-race!', takes up where Fergusson's superb feast-poem leaves off.[26]

Fergusson seems to have regretted Scotland's Union with England. At St Andrews he started a tragedy about William Wallace, but it does not survive. Most of his extant work comes from his Edinburgh years when local fresh ('caller') oysters were a favourite on the menu:

> Auld Reikie's sons blyth faces wear;   [Edinburgh's]
> September's merry month is near,
> That brings in Neptune's caller chere,
>   New oysters fresh;
> The halesomest and nicest gear
>   Of fish or flesh.[27]

Fergusson loved Edinburgh, even if it didn't always love him back. Walter Ruddiman (1719–81), nephew of the great Latinist Thomas Ruddiman, published many of Fergusson's Edinburgh poems in the town's popular *Weekly Magazine or Edinburgh Amusement*, founded in 1768. Ruddiman's lively paper also published Michael Bruce, James Boswell, James Beattie and other Scottish poets. It was one among a number of flourishing Edinburgh periodicals, so that by 1779, in a poem about the terror spread by the Scottish-American revolutionary 'pirate' John Paul Jones as he menaced the coast of Fife, an anonymous versifier could write,

> You've heard what amazement has fill'd all the coast,
> Since the tidings of Jones by the last Wednesday's post,
> When the Mercury, Courant, and Ruddiman's Gazette,
> Made the bravest to tremble, and the leanest to sweat . . .[28]

Ruddiman also published Fergusson's work in book form. In *Auld Reikie* (1773; 'Printed for the Author; and Sold at OSSIAN'S HEAD'), just as Edinburgh's elegantly neoclassical New Town was being built, Fergusson notes both the attributes of the Old Town and recent novelties with an eye, ear and nose for telling detail:

On stair wi' tub, or pat in hand,	*pot*
The barefoot housemaids looe to stand,	*love*
That antrin fock may ken how snell	*wandering; sharp*
Auld Reikie will at morning smell:	
Then, with an inundation big as	
The burn that 'neath the Nore Loch Brig is,	*stream; North Loch Bridge*
They kindly shower Edina's roses,	
To quicken and regale our noses.[29]	

'Edina's roses', by the way, are the contents of Edinburgh's chamber pots. Fergusson knew the pong as well as the aromatic side of Edinburgh life. Changeable as the Scottish weather, *Auld Reikie* can veer vertiginously between darkness and light, as can Fergusson's oeuvre as a whole. Poet of such celebratory town-life pieces as 'The Daft-Days' and 'Leith Races', he can sum up the carnivalesque jollity of rural life in 'Hallow-Fair' with its 'chapman billies [pedlar men]', and in 'The Farmer's Ingle' where his presentation of domestic rural life both outshines and heralds Burns's less certain version of the same in 'The Cotter's Saturday Night'. By day Fergusson slogged at his work as a clerk copying legal documents; by night he enjoyed theatre, concerts, companionship. His friends included the artist Alexander Runciman (who painted his portrait), the Italian singer Giusto Ferdinando Tenducci (though Fergusson once called Italian songs 'A bastard breed!'), and the great ballad and song collector David Herd, whose *Ancient and Modern Scottish Songs* (1776) would later inspire both Robert Burns and Walter Scott.[30] Fergusson drank with Herd and other pals – writers, clerks, tradesmen – in the all-male Cape Club which met in various Edinburgh pubs and whose members or 'Knights' enjoyed quasi-Masonic rituals and regalia, delighting in 'Mirth, Music' and drink to rid themselves of 'Cares and Poortith [poverty]'.[31]

Cares, though, caught up with nimble Robert Fergusson. Perhaps a manic depressive, he turned to writing poems with titles such as 'Ode to Disappointment' and 'Ode to Horror'. Like Michael Bruce, he gravitated towards the biblical Book of Job: 'Perish the fatal Day when I was born' begins his terrifying 'Job, Chapter III Paraphrased', with its chilling last line, 'New trouble came, new darkness, new controul.'[32] Fergusson died raving on a bed of straw in Edinburgh's madhouse. He was twenty-four. Syphilis? Manic depression? No one knows.

Fergusson, like Burns after him, is most celebrated as a poet who wrote in Scots. But English too was of great importance to both poets. Using it on its own, and in combination with Scots words, these writers were linked to a growing community in Scotland scripting decorous English verse. Fergusson's fellow Cape Club member, the sophisticated Thomas Mercer, wrote poetry about Arthur's Seat and drew on his admired Rousseau for *The Sentimental Sailor, or St Preux to Eloisa* (1772), an elegy whose plot comes from Rousseau's *Nouvelle Eloïse*. Mercer's account of the terrors of drowning in a whirlpool ('Wretch, hope no more! but tremble and obey!') might companion Falconer's *Shipwreck* or some of Fergusson's darker work.[33] Just as Fergusson was recalled discussing Greek in an Edinburgh drawing room, so Mercer's notes to his verse range effortlessly from Ariosto to Dante, from Boileau to George Buchanan. An academic tone at times constrains the work of the Reverend James Beattie, the Aberdeen philosopher who censured Hume and published in 1778 his list of forbidden *Scoticisms*. Yet Beattie's poem 'To Mr. Alexander Ross at Lochlee, author of The Fortunate Shepherdess and other poems in the broad Scotch dialect' was itself in Scots, and its jocular portrayal of the 'poor hizzie' muse 'Scota' gave Burns the idea for his own local muse of Kyle, Coila.[34] Like Hugh Blair and William Wordsworth, Burns admired 'immortal' Beattie's *The Minstrel* (1771–4), an English-language verse account of someone Beattie terms a 'heaven-taught' poet.[35] This wild Edwin, a 'visionary boy', dreams of 'long-robed minstrels' and is advised to 'Flee to the shade of Academus' grove'.[36] Beattie himself had fled in that direction, becoming probably the first academic to publish an edition of a living poet (Thomas Gray), but this did not stop Burns enjoying the professor's work and learning from it.

Poet, philosopher and leading university teacher, Beattie was part of the Scottish Enlightenment's sophisticated network of literati. Connections between Church and literature included not just prominent figures such as Hugh Blair and John Home, but also men like Blacklock and Robert Burns's friend Dr William Greenfield. Blair's Belles Lettres assistant and successor at Edinburgh University, Greenfield became Moderator (i.e., elected head) of the Church of Scotland, and developed an interest in aspects of Scottish literature, but was expelled from his posts for what seem to have been homosexual acts.[37] Academia nurtured the authors of such works as the first full-scale treatise in English on the theory and practice of translation. This *Essay on the Principles of Translation* (1791) was written by Alexander Fraser Tytler, Lord Woodhouselee (1747–1813), and developed from papers read to a group of scientists and creative artists, the Royal Society of Edinburgh, founded in 1783 and still going strong today. Tytler was a judge who taught 'universal history' at Edinburgh University and influenced Walter Scott, who took his course in 1789–90. Much more wide-ranging than his earlier *Essay on the Life and Character of Petrarch* (1784), Tytler's translation *Essay* ranges from Homer and Ovid to Arthur Johnston, Smollett as a translator of Cervantes, and Voltaire as a translator of Shakespeare. Tytler codifies laws of translation:

I. THAT the Translation should give a complete transcript of the ideas of the original work.
II. THAT the style and manner of writing should be of the same character with that of the original.
III. THAT the Translation should have all the ease of original composition.

Discussing these, the twenty-first-century critic Matthew Reynolds points out that analysing extremes of translational practice lets Tytler 'anticipate the poles set up by later theorists'.[38] Tytler gives detailed close readings as well as often wise general observations: only a 'true poet . . . should attempt to translate a poet'.[39]

Tytler's own translation of Schiller's drama *The Robbers* (1792) followed in the wake of the 1784 Foulis Press printing of a translation of Swiss Salomon Gessner's heroic prose poem *The Death of Abel* 'attempted from the German', and Henry Mackenzie's 1788 essay on German theatre read to the Royal Society of Edinburgh. Such activities and a 1794 Edinburgh reading by the English writer Anna Barbauld spurred early translations of German drama and verse by Walter Scott in the mid-1790s. Enthusiasm for German literature would be developed in England by Coleridge, and would remain strong in nineteenth-century Scottish literature at least as far as Carlyle, but its growth was just one aspect of a burgeoning of Scottish translations. These ranged from the nine-volume version of Count de Buffon's French *Natural History, General and Particular* made by Burns's future printer, the encyclopedist William Smellie in 1780–85, to *The Lusiad: or, The Discovery of India*, a translation of Camoëns's Portuguese epic published in 1775 by the Langholm-born William Julius Mickle (1735–88). In touch with the Islamic and Indian worlds, *The Lusiad* is an epic of 'commercial Empire' which nonetheless demonstrates how 'The dreams of bards surpass'd the world shall view,/ And own their boldest fictions may be true.'[40] Scottish translations of the period ranged beyond the European languages, from a late 1780s version of 'the Hedaya, or Code of Mussulman Laws' (translated by Charles, brother of the novelist Elizabeth Hamilton) to John Leyden's pioneering *Malay Annals* (1821) with their accounts of Sumatra and other distant lands.[41]

Empire reinforced Scotland's internationalism. The Borderer Mungo Park (1771–1806) oscillated between being a Peebles doctor and friend of such literary men as Adam Ferguson and Walter Scott to adventuring as an African explorer and great travel writer. Park's *Travels in the Interior Districts of Africa* (1799) record in plain but vivid detail his contacts with Islamic and African cultures. The later eighteenth century was an age when the glories and cruelties of Empire reached right to the heart of the Scottish intellectual and artistic establishment. In the 1770s, for instance, the distinguished Edinburgh University Greek Professor Andrew Dalzel had as his brother the bookseller, pirate and slave-trader Archibald Dalzel (1740–1811) whose 1793 *History of Dahomy*, with its pro-slavery prose, may be one of the curiosities of eighteenth-century Scottish writing, but should not be considered merely a wild aberration; with regard to slavery among Africans, Mungo Park argued that, given 'the present unenlightened state of their minds', the effect of its discontinuation 'would neither be so extensive or beneficial, as many wise and worthy persons fondly expect'.[42] Into this Scotland enlightened and unenlightened, cosmopolitan and thrawnly local, was born the poet whom many might regard as the greatest bard of human brotherhood.

Robert Burns was born in Alloway, Ayrshire, on 25 January 1759, and grew up on several local farms. His father, a tenant farmer and a committed Christian proud of the relatively democratic traditions of Presbyterian Church government, made sure Robert was well schooled; from his mother's side of the family he absorbed a wealth of often supernatural Scots-language folktales. Growing up with Scots talk and song alongside English book-learning, Burns was bicultural from the start. As a boy he studied works such as the Belles Lettrist Arthur Masson's *Collection of Prose and Verse from the Best English Authors*, and learned French. In his early twenties, the young poet watched his father work himself to death and face financial ruin. Burns's earliest heroes in books – Hannibal and Sir William Wallace – were heroic freedom fighters whose lives ended in disaster. Idealizing independent-mindedness, but lacking financial independence, the republican demo-crat Burns had a strong streak of libertine rebelliousness – made clear in his liking for Milton's Satan. In his late twenties, writing a fascinating autobiographical letter to the London-based Scottish travel writer Dr John Moore, author of the proto-Byronic novel *Zeluco* (1786), Burns exhibits his own proto-Byronic streak. He considered *Zeluco* 'A glorious story!'[43] His own relationship with his long-suffering wife, Jean Armour, was a stormy one, and he enjoyed a succession of mistresses.

Highly conscious of the Sentimental conception of the poetic tempera-ment as 'unfitted for the world', Burns feared personal ruin.[44] Much of his life was spent slogging at farmwork, a job he once summed up as 'the unceasing moil of a galley-slave'.[45] Then, after he became famous in 1786, he was lionized in Edinburgh and toured Scotland, but returned to the south-west to work, often out of doors in foul weather, as an exciseman. Doing this job made Burns the servant of a Crown and system of government with which, especially after the 1789 French Revolution, he had little sympathy. Eventually, broken by ill health, he died in 1796 at the age of thirty-seven.

Burns's sympathies lay with his native rural community, its men, women, children, rivers and beasts. He was happy to introduce himself in print as a local 'obscure, nameless Bard'.[46] But he made sure his name was on the title page of his first book, the 1786 *Poems, Chiefly in the Scottish Dialect*. Just a year later, when he was being hailed as a celebrity, he presented himself in the first Edinburgh edition of his work to '*the illustrious Names of his native Land*' as '*A Scottish bard, proud of the name, and whose highest ambition is to sing in his Country's service*'.[47] Operating in the wake of 'Ossian, prince of Poets', and toasted by his fellow Edinburgh Freemasons as 'Caledonia's Bard, brother B—', Burns did not have bardhood thrust upon him; it was part of his script from the start.[48]

Similarly, Burns Suppers and the whole panoply of bardolatry are rooted in the culture of which this poet was part. A form of secular communion conducted in remembrance of our Bard, Burns Suppers and Burns Clubs began in the western Lowland towns of Greenock and Paisley only after the poet's death. But those enthusiastic fellow Masons who toasted their 'brother', and the lads of several all-male fraternities to which Burns belonged are significant precursors of modern Burns Supperers. Convivial clubs like Fergusson's Cape had toasted dead bards such as James Thomson and William Shakespeare before Burns achieved fame. At twenty-one, Burns helped draw up the rules of the all-male Tarbolton Bachelors Club in Ayrshire, whose members each had to be 'a professed lover of one or more of the female sex'.[49] This young men's debating club, meeting in a pub room, was the public cousin of the later, more clandestine 'Court of Equity' invented in verse by the poet who 'takes the chair' and joins with local male pals in a ritual examination of sexual scandals. Parodying the courts of Kirk and state government, Burns's Court with its 'Fiscal' and 'Clerk' scrutinizes such matters as 'a hurly-burly/ 'Bout JEANY MITCHEL'S tirlie-whirlie [vagina]'.[50] Whether as a Mason or, later, a member of the Edinburgh radical male drinking club, the Crochallan Fencibles (a mock regiment for whom he collected such bawdy songs as 'Nine Inch will Please a Lady'), Burns relished various fraternities with their rites and rituals. Membership of several helped his literary career, but, more than that, he just liked them, laddish fraternity shading at times towards French revolutionary *fraternité*.

In a mock-monarchic proclamation of 1786 sent with an improper poem to two Ayrshire male confederates, Burns writes as 'We, ROBERT BURNS, by virtue of a Warrant from NATURE, bearing date the Twenty-fifth day of January, Anno Domini one thousand seven hundred and fifty-nine, POET-LAUREAT and BARD IN CHIEF' of his locality. Signing off 'GOD SAVE THE BARD!', however jocularly, the irrepressible Burns, egalitarian lad, tips the wink to a million Burns Suppers at which he and the lasses will be ceremonially toasted by Scots and their friends each 25 January for centuries to come. Though modern intellectuals and poets have often decried Burns suppers, they are in some ways true to the nature of their subversively clubbable subject. Thanks to the eighteenth-century media and thanks to word of mouth, Burns was the first Scottish poet to become a national celebrity in his own lifetime; eventually, this may have narrowed his gift. Nowadays we take celebrity culture for granted, but Burns Clubs lose touch with Burns's greatest achievements if they see Burns only as a 'star', a Scottish pin-up with a fascinating sexual and political life, who was only incidentally a poet.

As poet Burns had more control over the contents of his first book, the 1786 *Poems*, than over any later publication of his work. As his fame flared after the publication of this book in Kilmarnock, Ayrshire, more and more people wanted to 'advise' Burns and reshape his verse for their own ends; he published only about one-eighth of his poems in his own books, and (especially in the 1790s when Scottish democrats were being hanged or transported by order of the Crown) he had to be increasingly careful lest his words be regarded as scandalous or treasonable. Even early on, a degree of self-censorship conditioned the Kilmarnock *Poems*. Burns left out, for instance, his biting dramatic monologue 'Holy Willie's Prayer' which mocks the Calvinist doctrine of predestination, according to which God has chosen from the start of creation who will be damned, and who will be saved. Holy Willie is a Kirk elder whose hypocrisy is satirized as readers are allowed to overhear his 'Spiritualized Bawdry' and 'Liquorish Devotion':

> O Lord! yestreen, thou kens, wi' Meg –   *yesterday; knows*
> Thy pardon I sincerely beg –
> O may't ne'er be a living plague
>   To my dishonor!
> An' I'll ne'er lift a lawless leg
>   Again upon her.[51]

Burns would also hold back from publication 'Love and Liberty. A Cantata' whose singers concluded,

> A fig for those by law protected!
>   *Liberty*'s a glorious feast!
> Courts for cowards were erected,
>   Churches built to please the priest.[52]

Such poems, circulating informally, caused excitement and consternation. Yet self-censorship did not obscure the design of Burns's first book which, though expanded in its 1787 Edinburgh edition, was the only book of his verse published in his lifetime.

Cornucopia is what Burns aims for, a startling polyvocality. Dialogue, epistle, address, elegy, vision, lyric, ode, prayer, dirge, epigram and epitaph are all present in the 1786 Kilmarnock *Poems*. Predominantly, this is a Scots cornucopia, but there are English poems too. The very titles signal a daft sense of humour; the first poem is called 'The Twa Dogs, a Tale'. But there is clearly a darker side: 'Despondency, an Ode'. A similarly extensive spectrum had characterized the posthumous, 1782 edition of Robert Fergusson's *Poems* which Burns had read (probably in 1784) at a time when he had almost 'given up' making poems. He told Dr John Moore how on 'meeting with Fergusson's Scotch Poems, I strung anew my wildly-sounding, rustic lyre with emulating vigour'.[53] The result was a remarkable crop of Scots poems, including many of Burns's best known, such as 'Holy Willie's Prayer', 'To a Mouse', 'To a Louse', and several of the vividly intelligent verse epistles. Though there are also marked debts to Allan Ramsay, a number of the Kilmarnock *Poems* very directly 'emulate' Fergusson, about whom Burns was still enthusing in 1785 as he began to contemplate his own first collection. Three of the four opening poems in Burns's debut volume rework Fergusson originals: 'The Twa Dogs, a Tale' depends on Fergusson's dialogue, 'Mutual Complaint of Plainstanes and Causey'; 'Scotch Drink' draws on Fergusson's 'Caller Water'; 'The Holy Fair' rewrites Fergusson's 'Hallow-Fair', as, to an extent, does another Burns poem of folk festivity, 'Halloween'. Such debts are manifold. Eighteenth-century readers versed in Scottish poetry could not fail to map Burns's noonday brilliance on to 'the glorious dawnings of the poor, unfortunate Ferguson [sic]'; just to make sure his readers did so, Burns nudged them in his 'Preface'.[54]

Burns often learned through emulation. 'The Death and Dying Words of Poor Mailie, the Author's only Pet Yowe [Ewe]', Burns's first use of the 'Standard Habbie' stanza form, was an imitation of a poem by Hamilton of Gilbertfield, 'The Last Dying Words of Bonnie Heck', a famous greyhound. Today's readers unfamiliar with older Scottish poetry may miss just how inspiredly kleptomaniac and imitative Burns can be, or else we may hear only the usually less convincing Miltonic or Sentimental revoicings in his English-language poems. Burns's heartfelt tribute to his own father ends by quoting a line from the Edinburgh-educated Irish poet Oliver Goldsmith; in his epitaph for Robert Fergusson Burns quotes a line from Gray's 'Elegy'. Determinedly, Burns paid for the erection of a tombstone on the older Robert's unmarked Edinburgh grave. Like most great poets – Shakespeare, Milton and T. S. Eliot come to mind – Burns had a superbly acquisitive ear. In a good deal of his early work that talent allowed him to recast Ramsay or Fergusson, or to Miltonize; later it underpinned his collection and remaking of many old Scots songs so that the original and Burns's 'improvements' are sometimes hard to unpick. In each case Burns is bonding himself to admired exemplars – to 'the excellent Ramsay, and the still more excellent Fergusson', to England's great republican poet Milton, or to the popular heritage of Scots song.[55] For all his energetic and individual genius, Burns likes to sing as part of a chorus. His literary sympathies are wide and eloquent, and crucial to his polyvocality.

Burns's many-voicedness is as bound up with 'sympathy' as is Smollett's *Humphry Clinker* or Mackenzie's Sentimentalism. In his early twenties Burns was already commending 'that extraordinary man' Adam Smith for his *Wealth of Nations*, but probably Burns's favourite passage of Smith came from *The Theory of Moral Sentiments*.[56] This was the section '*Of the sense of Justice, of Remorse, and of the consciousness of Merit*' which nourished in early 1783 some feverishly Shakespearian lines on guilt, and to which Burns returned two years later when he wrote those famous lines of 'To a Louse',

> O wad some Pow'r the giftie gie us
> *To see oursels as others see us!*

As noted in my previous chapter, these lines are a versification of Smith's contention with regard to 'our neighbour' that 'We must . . . view ourselves not so much according to that light in which we may naturally appear to ourselves, as according to that in which we naturally appear to others.'[57] At the end of the poem 'To a Louse' (set in a church) Burns may glance towards God – 'some Pow'r' – not least because Smith's words sound like an Enlightenment gloss on Christ's commandment to 'love thy neighbour as thyself'. The poet knew his Bible intimately, and likes to quote it, often to discomfit Kirkmen. Burns's sympathies lay with the more liberal 'New Light' wing of the Kirk in Ayrshire which, while different from Edinburgh's 'moderate' caucus, sought to modify the stern old-style Calvinism of the 'Auld Lichts'. The exact nature of Burns's own religious beliefs is hard to perceive, but just as it is evident

that Fergusson's work and example helped 'kindle' Burns's verse, so the
poet's knowledge of scripture and of Scottish Enlightenment philosophy
nourished his imagination.[58]

Burns was very well read. He realized that the philosophy of sympathy
not only offered a way of letting him move beyond his own immediate
viewpoint to inhabit the views of others, but also held a radical, democratic potential. In his lifetime, when less than 1 per cent of the Scottish
population was allowed to vote, 'democracy' was a bad word: Burns's
exact contemporary the Scottish novelist Robert Bisset calls it 'the con-
summation of human misery' in his *Sketch of Democracy* (1796).[59] But
Burns had strong, sometimes dangerously democratic instincts. In 1786,
signing himself 'saint or sinner,/ RAB THE RANTER', he sent to a
local miller friend

> Twa sage Philosophers to glimpse on!
> Smith, wi' his sympathetic feeling,
> An' Reid, to common sense appealing.
> Philosophers have fought an' wrangled,
> An' meikle Greek an' Latin mangled,
> Till with their Logic-jargon tir'd,
> An' in the depth of science mir'd,
> To common sense they now appeal,
> What wives an' wabsters see an' feel . . .[60]

Potentially such philosophy put women and 'wabsters' (weavers – a
working-class group often noted for their political radicalism) on a
democratic level with university-educated toffs. Burns liked that. No
one had a monopoly of feeling or of common sense. Contemporary
philosophy, like Sentimentalism, might seem the preserve of belletristic
polite society, but could also have a radical edge. Tears, along with
sympathy, humour and the ideals of the French Revolution, made all
men brothers, and could even be shared by womenfolk. Whereas Henry
Mackenzie, that Sentimental Man of Feeling, might attack imperialism
and slavery, so in Burns Sentimentalism, sympathy and political radicalism went hand in hand. If Fergusson offered a range of tones and topics,
a formal nimbleness and a Scots-accented range of voices that was not
confined to Scots, then the principle of sympathy, with its philosophical
and imaginative concomitants, encouraged the full exploration of these
through the medium of poetic art.

The art is crucial. In terms of sheer finesse it is what sets Burns apart from a myriad of imitators. The sympathetic flexibility of his poetic language seems breathtakingly effortless. Powered by a knowledge of Scots folklore from his mother's side of the family, Burns, after a high-toned Miltonic epigraph, can buttonhole even the devil with flaunted casual aplomb:

> O THOU, whatever title suit thee!
> Auld Hornie, Satan, Nick, or Clootie![61]

In the same first collection Burns has voices for everyone, whether muse, mouse or louse. He moves easily from tones of sympathetic address – 'Wee, sleeket, cowran, tim'rous beastie' ('To a Mouse') – to confident invective: 'Yon ill-tongu'd tinkler, *Charlie Fox*' (referring to the Leader of the Opposition in the British Parliament).[62] Generations of Scottish mothers have sent their children to meet strangers, headmasters, royalty and public transport officials with the words 'You've a guid Scots tongue in yer heid'. Burns's ability to speak for and to anyone may seem the apotheosis of this wish for fearlessly democratic powers of address.

The opening poem of the 1786 Kilmarnock *Poems* is spoken by a narrator and two dogs. This wry use of animal chat would have been recognized alike by Henryson or the William Hamilton who penned words for the greyhound Bonnie Heck. One of Burns's 'Twa Dogs' is a Newfoundland, Caesar, 'the *gentleman* an' *scholar*'. The other is the Ossianically named Luath, 'A rhyming, ranting, raving billie' of a '*ploughman's collie*'. This is Burns's way of demonstrating from the start of his book that he can do different voices, and that different voices are crucial to what he does. The poem embraces markedly diverse social classes. Doggily down-to-earth, it also jokes about Ossianic scholarship. It takes in '*Mill* or *Smiddie* [smithy]' as well as 'VIENNA or VERSAILLES'. It does not stereotype its speakers. Rather Luath, while admitting that the poor '*Cotter* howckan in a sheugh [digging in a ditch]' is hard pressed and on the brink of economic ruin, makes it clear that family and ale provide real delight. Caesar, on the other hand, presents the gentry as rich but decadently discontented, psychologically fragile and so cut off by 'pomp an' art' that 'joy can scarcely reach the heart'.[63] 'The Twa Dogs, a Tale' balances with knowing wit between presenting the economic exploitation of one class by another, and presenting a

SCOTLAND'S BOOKS

sympathetic appraisal of rich *and* poor. If ultimately it stands up for honest but simple plainness, then it suggests through language and tone, rather than through stereotype, which side it is on.

Burns's word-brew in his best work is usually made up of linguistic 'intermingledoms of . . . the pure & impure'.[64] Like Shakespeare in Elizabethan England, Burns lived at a time and in a country of great linguistic fluidity. He mixes words from several dialects of Scots, and spices English with a zestful Scots admixture. He flits with pinpoint fluency between the two languages, using one to ignite the other. When he writes purely in English, the imitator in him tends to work at the expense of (rather than reinforcing) the sparkily original poet. There is elocutionary eloquence in the republican sentiments of the 1794 'Ode [For General Washington's Birthday]', a poem celebrating a successful freedom-fighting rebel at a time when Britain was violently at odds with republican revolutionary France,

> . . . come, ye sons of Liberty,
> Columbia's offspring, brave as free,
> In danger's hour still flaming in the van;
> Ye know, and dare maintain, The Royalty of Man.[65]

However, this English-language work lacks the kick, fluency, frolic and intelligence of the deservedly better-known 1795 Scots lines,

> Ye see yon birkie ca'd a lord,   *twit*
> Wha struts, and stares, an' a' that:
> Tho' hundreds worship at his word,
> He's but a coof for a' that.   *fool*
> For a' that, an' a' that,
> His ribband, star, an' a' that,
> The man o' independent mind,
> He looks an' laughs at a' that.[66]

As he grew into his thirties Burns developed the democratic note of Scottish republican radicalism that was part of his gift from his teens onwards. Reshaping traditional songs to articulate the sentiments of post-1707 Scots who felt 'bought and sold for English gold', at the same time as looking forward to a day when 'man to man the world o'er,/ Shall brothers be for a' that', Burns combined anti-Unionist nationalism with republican internationalism.[67] In so doing he established himself as the master poet of Scottish republican democratic radicalism, and as the greatest ever collector and fashioner of Scottish songs. Neither his politics nor his Scottishness functioned as a limitation. Quite the opposite. Over 2000 editions of his work exist in more than fifty languages and round the globe there are more than 1000 societies and clubs formed to sing his praises. Burns is a niftily learned poet of popular song, popular music. Yet, prompted by the Scottish musician George Thomson, the classical composer Haydn alone made over 200 arrangements of Burns song melodies. Many other internationally renowned composers from Beethoven and Weber to James Macmillan and Arvo Pärt have arranged Burns songs, which still form a vital part of the body of Scottish folk-music from which they sprang. No other Scottish poet has so held the ear of the world.

If there was a strain of Jacobitism in Burns, it offered him an image of a fidelity to older Scottish ideals rather than something to cancel out his pro-French Jacobinism. As a young man Burns had met the radical Lord Daer. Towards the end of his life one of his friends was the physician William Maxwell, who had been a member of the guard at the revolutionary execution of the French King and Queen. Maxwell was branded Britain's most dangerous Jacobin by the *Sun* newspaper. Expression of his political beliefs became both more urgent and more risky for the exciseman Burns in the 1790s when treason trials and the repression of the Friends of Liberty grew intense in England, Scotland and Ireland. The re-presentation of traditional songs, and the production of pseudonymous poems, were among the bardic strategies Burns adopted for these dangerous times. Scotland's national bard is a radical, anti-Union republican, though many Unionist, monarchist and imperialist critics have tried to play this down. Burns himself, fearful of endangering his family, several times made protestations of loyalty to the Crown, but tended to slyly undercut such faithful flourishes; as he put it at the end of what seems his loudest public assertion of loyalty to the British monarchy, 'But while we sing, GOD SAVE THE KING, / We'll ne'er forget THE PEOPLE!'[68]

The Robert Burns championed by Edinburgh's literati in the mid-1780s, though, was not the denouncer of Unionism in 'A Parcel of Rogues in a Nation'. He was the 'genius' and 'Heaven-taught ploughman' (Henry Mackenzie's words) whom the Enlightened literati could patronize and, they hoped, mould to their design.[69] When the

Kilmarnock *Poems* appeared, Burns, hard-pressed and in trouble with Jean Armour's family, was about to emigrate, as a number of his Scottish friends had done, to the slave-owners' plantations of Jamaica. Some of the poems towards the end of his first book, with titles like 'On a Scotch Bard gone to the West Indies' or 'The Farewell to the Brethren of St James's Lodge, Tarbolton', call attention to this. Concluding the volume with 'A Bard's Epitaph', Burns signals more than a touch of self-conscious anxiety over his own plight.

If this was a strategy to attract sympathy and support, it worked. Immediate and resounding success brought Burns influential admirers and fame. As he rode to Edinburgh farmers left their houses to hail and admire him. Soon he was in the Scottish capital, preparing a new, expanded edition of his *Poems*. This was printed for the author by William Smellie and sold by the famous Edinburgh bookseller–publisher William Creech, who bought Burns's copyright from the poet for 100 guineas, and then grew rich on it. However lauded, Burns was always something of a stranger in the metropolis. He was no street-wise city boy like Fergusson, and 'Edina! *Scotia*'s darling seat!' is his most risible opening line.[70] Nevertheless, as a resilient 'man o' independent mind', he held his own in Edinburgh's drawing rooms.[71] In his teens Walter Scott met the twenty-eight-year-old Burns at a literary party in the Scottish Enlightenment philosopher Professor Adam Ferguson's house. Later Scott recalled that Burns 'actually shed tears' over a print depicting a family's ruin.

His person was strong and robust; his manners rustic, not clownish; a sort of dignified plainness and simplicity . . . I would have taken the poet, had I not known what he was, for a very sagacious country farmer of the old Scottish school . . . There was a strong expression of sense and shrewdness in all his lineaments; the eye alone, I think, indicated the poetical character and temperament. It was large, and of a dark cast, and glowed (I say literally *glowed*) when he spoke with feeling or interest. I never saw such another eye in a human head, though I have seen the most distinguished men in my time.

His conversation expressed perfect self-confidence, without the slightest presumption. Among the men who were the most learned of their time and country, he expressed himself with perfect firmness, but without the least intrusive forwardness; and when he differed in opinion, he did not hesitate to express it firmly, yet at the same time with modesty . . . I have only to add that his dress corresponded with his manner. He was like a farmer dressed in his best to dine with the laird . . . I was told, but did not observe it, that his address to females was extremely deferential, and always with a turn either to the pathetic or humorous, which engaged their attention particularly.[72]

Scott, the insightful Tory lawyer, is highly conscious, as were most of Burns's Edinburgh hosts, of the farmer–poet's lower-class position. Scott also recognizes Burns's uniqueness, while presenting the poet as a kind of model of what we might now call democratic address. The Edinburgh Common Sense philosopher Professor Dugald Stewart (1753–1828), a man sympathetic towards some of the ideals of the French Revolution, and someone who saw 'the political philosophy of the eighteenth century' as attuned to the republican ideals of George Buchanan, remembered Burns as always 'simple, manly, and independent' in manners, with a gift for 'purity' of English rare among eighteenth-century Scots.[73] 'Nothing, perhaps, was more remarkable among his various attainments than the fluency, and precision, and originality of his language, when he spoke in company . . .'[74]

The superbly assured prose of Burns's letters allows us to sense something of this discursive ability. With protean sympathetic adaptability, he could suit his tone to his correspondent. Most letter writers do this, but Burns does so to a striking degree. Writing to a male friend, he could give a shocking account of rough sex with the heavily pregnant Jean Armour:

I have given her a guinea, and I have f—d her till she rejoiced with joy unspeakable and full of glory . . . and I took the opportunity of some dry horse litter, and gave her such a thundering scalade that electrified the very marrow of her bones. Oh, what a peacemaker is a guid weel-willy p[int]le! It is the mediator, the guarantee, the umpire, the bond of union, the solemn league and covenant, the plenipotentiary, the Aaron's rod, the Jacob's staff, the prophet Elisha's pot of oil, the Ahasuerus' Sceptre, the sword of mercy, the philosopher's stone, the Horn of Plenty, and Tree of Life between Man and Woman.[75]

Yet this same domineering bard of linguistic exuberance and phallic force could discuss philosophy in measured tones with titled correspondents. Distinctions between the polyvocal epistolary prose and the poetry blur since several of Burns's verse epistles were actually sent as letters. To his early Edinburgh encourager, the blind divinity scholar and poet

Dr Thomas Blacklock (1721–91), who heard in his 'brother' Burns 'Nature's voice' and who was the author of 'Happy Marriage', Burns could write,

> To make a happy fireside clime
> To weans and wife,
> That's the true *Pathos* and *Sublime*
> Of Human life. –[76]

Nourished by Sentimentalism, these lines may sound to modern ears cosily compromised, but, showing off a knowledge of modern aesthetic criticism, they come from a poem also filled with self-reproach. Burns explains to Blacklock that he has 'turn'd a Gauger' (exciseman) since he has 'a wife and twa wee laddies' to support. For all his infidelities, Burns, after his fashion, loved them dearly, and worked hard for them. His poem protests how difficult it is to create that longed for 'happy fireside clime' without compromising both poetry and principles. As often, fraternity in this verse letter is a highly charged concept:

> Lord help me thro' this warld o' care!
> I'm weary sick o't late and air!   *early*
> No but I hae a richer share
>   Than mony ithers;
> But why should ae man better fare,   *one*
>   And a' Men brithers!

Signed 'ROBT. BURNS, Ellisland, 21st Oct., 1789', this poem-letter to an Edinburgh gentleman is sent from Burns's farm. Sentimentally hymning the family fireside, it also manages to keep faith with revolutionary *fraternité* just a few months after the Fall of the Bastille.[77] It shows something of the complexity and flexibility of tone in Burns's writing, a quality which, along with musicality and verbal dash, has made for almost universal appeal.

The 'eternal swervin' and complex 'zig-zag' of Burns's sympathy are caught also in the 'Second Epistle to Davie', a much more energetic work sent not to an Edinburgh divine but to a fiddle-playing Ayrshire grocer and 'Brother Poet', David Sillar.

> For me, I'm on Parnassus brink,
> Rivan the words tae gar them clink;   *wrenching; sound well*

Whyles daez't wi' love, whyles daez't wi' drink,   *sometimes stupefied*
    Wi' jads or masons;   *women*
An' whyles, but aye owre late, I think
    Braw sober lessons.

Ultimately, here, Burns urges loyalty to the poetic impulse – 'Haud [Hold] tae the Muse' – above all else. 'Let's sing our Sang' was his great credo.[78] For all Burns's famous picture of farmfolk's piety in 'The Cotter's Saturday Night', his God has less of a sense of the Kirk observances of 'the Unco Guid, or the Rigidly Righteous' than of vital inner music:

Who made the heart, 'tis *He* alone
    Decidedly can try us,
He knows each chord its various tone,
    Each spring its various bias . . .[79]

Burns's greatest triumph is tonal, musical. He lets the sound of 'Each spring, its various bias' be heard in words, whether frisky, solemn, loving, satirical or, often, complex mixtures of these. His phenomenal control of verse movement, frequently in stanza forms inherited from earlier Scottish poets such as Fergusson and Alexander Montgomerie, and his gift for the mot juste is powered by that sympathetic understanding which lets him make songs in women's voices as well as men's.[80] 'John Anderson My Jo', turned by Burns from a bawdy song into a wife's paean to married love, is as moving as the love song 'A Red, Red Rose'. The latter is lyrically aware of the kind of modern geological theory discussed in the 'History and Theory of the Earth' section of William Smellie's Buffon, or by the Enlightenment Scot James Hutton in his 1785 *Theory of the Earth*, on which modern geology depends. Yet Burns's lyric is also a fluent recasting of a traditional song:

Till a' the seas gang dry, my dear,
    And the rocks melt wi' the sun!
And I will luve thee still, my dear,
    While the sands o' life shall run.[81]

Collecting songs for such Edinburgh anthologists as James Johnson (c. 1750–1811), editor of the compendious *Scots Musical Museum* (1787–1803), Burns in some ways subdued his own virtuosity to the simpler trajectories of popular lyric. On the other hand, fusing his own words with the tunes and verses of earlier, often anonymous songwriters, he extended his gift for sympathetic many-voicedness. Without the accompanying music, Burns's songs may be incomplete, but in many cases they have a very vital word music that sustains their life on the page and makes them suitable both for individual reading and communal use. None more so than 'Auld Lang Syne':

Should auld acquaintance be forgot
  And never brought to mind?
Should auld acquaintance be forgot,
  And auld lang syne!   *[long since]*

    For auld lang syne my jo,   *dear*
      For auld lang syne,
    We'll tak a *cup o' kindness yet,
      For auld lang syne.

And surely ye'll be your pint stowp!   *flagon*
  And surely I'll be mine!
And we'll tak a cup o' kindness yet,
  For auld lang syne.

    For auld lang syne my jo,
      For auld lang syne,
    We'll tak a cup o' kindness yet,
      For auld lang syne.

We twa hae run about the braes,
  And pou'd the gowans fine;   *pulled; daisies*
But we've wander'd mony a weary fitt,   *foot*
  Sin auld lang syne.

    For auld lang syne my jo,
      For auld lang syne,
    We'll tak a cup o' kindness yet,
      For auld lang syne.

We twa hae paidl'd in the burn,   *paddled; stream*
  Frae morning sun till dine;   *dinner-time*

*Some sing, Kiss in place of Cup. [RB]

But seas between us braid hae roar'd,
  Sin auld lang syne.

    For auld lang syne my jo,
      For auld lang syne,
  We'll tak a cup o' kindness yet,
    For auld lang syne.

And there's a hand, my trusty fiere!   *comrade*
  And gie's a hand o' thine!
And we'll tak a right gude-willie-waught,   *[hearty drink]*
  For auld lang syne.

    For auld lang syne my jo,
      For auld lang syne,
  We'll tak a cup o' kindness yet
    For auld lang syne.[82]

The emphasis here is on almost hypnotic repetition, a kind of infinite acoustic recall as the phrase 'auld lang syne' keeps leaving the poem only to be recalled and re-called. Partly taken down 'from an old man's singing', partly remembering a verse of Allan Ramsay, and with analogues in popular chapbooks, this is a tender memorial poem, a song that celebrates recall and re-calling as a bond which outdistances distance.[83] It is a song of communion based around intimate shared memory, a poem whose acoustic body extends an offered hand – 'And there's a hand, my trusty fiere!/ And gie's a hand o' thine!' – so that, in an interactive gesture, the audience becomes part of the poem's memory system, pulled into it. One might set that offered, vernacular hand beside the most famous outstretched hands in Classical literature, '*Tende-bantque manus ripae ulterioris amore* [Their hands stretched out in longing for the further shore]'.[84] These hands belong to the dead in the Underworld of Virgil's *Aeneid*; yet one of the most moving aspects of Burns's poem, and the use it has fulfilled in Burns's own and in other national cultures, is that the hand of the living poem stretches out both to and from the dead. The song may spring from a particular erotic encounter; it also goes beyond it. Those words 'auld lang syne' carry us back to all their previous utterances, not just in earlier, different versions of the song, but to previous occasions when the same song was sung. They transport us beyond individual memory to a collective memory that is supra-individual. The way the poem mixes that great collective pull towards 'lang syne' with the peculiar details of particular engagements gives it a power to reach forward, back and across not just its own culture but also other cultures which might have very little sense of what on earth a 'gude-willie-waught' might be. Music can heighten the effect of this song, but the lyric, written to a traditional tune, also builds its own purposeful word-music of constant re-calling. The poem's recollection of a community takes place first in a distinctively nuanced Scottish linguistic context; it also exemplifies poetry's power to cut across and go beyond national memory. The power in it is the power that makes Burns not only a great poet of calling and re-calling, collecting and recollecting, but also, along with Sappho and Shakespeare, one of the world's greatest love poets.

Love had been a sharp spur to Burns's muse from the start. As he put it with a Calvinistic wink, he 'first committed the sin of RHYME' when working a field with a girl in harvest time.[85] His many sexual liaisons both fuelled and were fired up by his gift for passionate lyric. This is evident in Burns's relationship with Mrs Agnes McLehose, the 'Clarinda' with whom in Edinburgh 'Sylvander' Burns had a steamy erotic correspondence that might have been scripted by the Sentimental Mackenzie of *Julia de Roubigné*. For Clarinda Burns wrote 'Ae Fond Kiss' with its exclamatory yet lingering tensions between coupledom and loss:

> Had we never lov'd sae kindly,
> Had we never lov'd sae blindly,
> Never met – or never parted,
> We had ne'er been broken-hearted . . .
>
> . . . Ae fond kiss, and then we sever;
> Ae fareweel, Alas! for ever!
> Deep in heart-wrung tears I'll pledge thee.
> Warring sighs and groans I'll wage thee.[86]

While giving him a channel of popular expression for his political views, as in 'Scots, Wha Hae', Burns's song-making and song-collecting also let him explore erotic love through the voices of men and women, faithful and forsaken, predatory and vulnerable. His last song, made (probably for his nurse) at a time when he was enduring immersion in the freezing waters of the Solway Firth in a mistaken attempt to cure his fevers, uses his own experience of appalling cold, but, with tender eroticism, projects it on to a suffering girl:

> Oh, wert thou in the cauld blast,
>> On yonder lea, on yonder lea;   *pasture*
> My plaidie to the angry airt,   *plaid; [direction of the wind]*
>> I'd shelter thee, I'd shelter thee . . .[87]

The hugely sympathetic body of song which Burns produced is a glorious exploration of human love. Its frequent tenderness is counterpointed by the uproarious celebration of masculinity and the treatment of sexual psychology in his late masterpiece, 'Tam o' Shanter', Burns's only extended narrative poem.

'Tam o' Shanter. A Tale' presents the Ayrshire story of a young husband who stays out late boozing with his cronies at the pub, then has to ride home through a storm in which he witnesses a dance of witches and warlocks at '*Alloway*'s auld haunted kirk'. After Tam yells at her, a short-skirted witch chases and almost catches him as he crosses a bridge, but ends up simply clawing off his horse's tail. Deeply rooted in Burns's schooling (his earliest favourite poem concerned a bridge), as well as in the Scots folklore inheritance which had 'cultivated the latent seeds of Poesy', this poem was written for Burns's friend Captain Grose, an English antiquarian and lexicographer of '*the Vulgar Tongue*' who had a taste for pornography.[88] 'Tam o' Shanter', ranging across formal English and racy Scots, is a tale about 'tail' (slang for the genitals). The poem's protagonist is punished for his glimpse of tail, but it is the female tail of Tam's grey mare which is exacted as the penalty. Males have a good time, but females pay the price.

The poem makes fun of the conventionally feminine. Its mimicry of Tam's wife Kate haranguing him – 'She tauld thee weel thou wast a skellum [scoundrel]/ A blethering, blustering, drunken blellum [fool]' – wins over sympathies for Tam.[89] Burns's narrative is in part one for men who enjoy 'getting off' on the sight of naked female flesh, but it is much more than that in its verbal exhilaration and affirmative fun. Perhaps unexpectedly at one point Burns's storyteller seems to address female listeners:

> Ah, gentle dames! it gars me greet,   *makes; weep*
> To think how mony counsels sweet,

> How mony lengthen'd, sage advices,
> The husband frae the wife despises!

Gendering the audience, these lines are clearly mocking, designed at least as much to entertain men as to speak to women. Such 'gentle dames' are soon passed over as we move 'to our tale' and to a pub setting which is predominantly masculine, a place where the male bonding of true brotherhood is achieved:

> But to our tale: Ae market night,   *one*
> *Tam* had got planted unco right;   *settled*
> Fast by an ingle, bleezing finely,   *fireside; blazing*
> Wi' reaming swats, that drank divinely;   *frothing beers*
> And at his elbow, Souter *Johnny*,   *Cobbler*
> His ancient, trusty, drouthy crony;   *thirsty*
> *Tam* lo'ed him like a vera brither;
> They had been fou for weeks thegither.   *drunk; together*

From this snug space of fou fraternity, warm in Ayrshire alcohol culture, Tam must leave to go out into the stormy night, heading for his hame and his dame. Drunkenly dependent on the female ('his gray mare, *Meg*'), Tam rides further and further from the 'bleezing' ingle of the pub towards the much less convivial 'bleeze' of the satanic convention at Kirk Alloway. He travels into more and more frightening, hellish, and eventually dangerous female territory. He becomes a voyeur at a secret ritual with its own satanic regalia and dreadful rites.

Tam watches excitedly as the witches strip off and cavort in their underwear. In a passage which might have delighted Burns's laddish fraternity, the Crochallan Fencibles, even the warning narrator fantasizes about himself in trouserless excitement watching beautiful young near-naked women dancing:

> Now *Tam*, O *Tam*! had thae been queans,   *girls*
> A' plump and strapping in their teens,
> Their sarks, instead o' creeshie flannen,   *greasy flannel*
> Been snaw-white seventeen hunder linnen!   *[finely woven]*
> Thir breeks o' mine, my only pair,   *those*
> That ance were plush, o' gude blue hair,   *once*
> I wad hae gi'en them off my hurdies,   *buttocks*
> For ae blink o' the bonie burdies!

The narrator, though, keeps his breeks on because this passage is a male sexual fantasy which the poem refuses to realize in full. Instead, its dancing 'hags' offer an 'auld and droll' female sexuality of a kind normally taboo for men to see. 'I wonder [it] didna turn thy stomach,' girns the narrator, speaking to his fellow onlooker, Tam. But Tam is as yet in control of the situation, for he even manages to find one of the witches whose physique is attractive. This, though, leads him into danger and a loss of male control. Like the Satan who 'fidg'd fu' fain' [fidgeted excitedly] at the sight of the female body, Tam grows 'like ane bewitch'd' to the extent that, having 'tint [lost] his reason a' thegither', he ejaculates. His ejaculation takes the form of a yell to the attractive witch, 'Weel done, Cutty Sark' (Well done, Short Shirt!). With this yell Tam turns her from sex object into fiendish pursuer as she, Nannie, becomes the foremost of a hellish legion of witches who chase him.

Tam is now at the mercy of the female in two ways. He risks being caught by Nannie, and only his mare Meg can save him. This makes him doubly ridiculous as he has to seek protection from the female by the female. The climax of this furiously energetic poem is a moment of parodic sexual climax, spiced with the horrors of *vagina dentata*, when Meg's

> Ae spring brought off her master hale,   *safe*
> But left behind her ain grey tail:
> The carlin claught her by the rump,
> And left poor Maggie scarce a stump.

Ouch! This isn't really a castration, though, for it marks the reassertion of male power: Tam is saved. What happens is a kind of joke castration visited on the female who, for a moment, took the dominant part, the mare who became the active protector of her supposed 'master'. Tam triumphs over his wife's prophecies of doom and over Nannie's hellish pursuit. The taboo female sexuality of the witches is banished, thanks to Maggie's 'mettle', and it is she who has to pay the price: 'Remember Tam o' Shanter's mare' warns the abrupt mock moral of this mock-heroic poem, which is itself chopped short after Maggie's sudden amputation. It is the female who suffers in the tale's end, not the brotherly Tam.

'Tam o' Shanter' hints at the kinds of sexual licence relished in song (and sometimes otherwise) by the sort of boozing, fraternal male clubs Burns knew and liked. It also makes fun of secret rituals, satanic parodies of Christian forms, and bawdy wordplay, presenting a mischievous public face that almost – but not quite – subverts decorum. The work is a teasing triumph of masculinity, but one so well paced, so full of linguistic brio and sheer fun that it can win over even the most ideologically hostile audiences. If some might see it as standing for a masculine domination that has remained unusually strong in Scottish society, the poem presents this phenomenon not as solemnly phallic, but as ludically daft.

It has been suggested that the best line in all of Burns's verse is the one that, in a well-known song, sighingly canonizes a belovedly ordinary name, ' "Ye are na Mary Morison." '[90] Yet I'd contend his most emblematic voiceprint is heard in that line that describes the witches dancing in 'Tam o' Shanter', 'They reel'd, they set, they cross'd, they cleekit.' Protean in its change of direction, energetically nimble in its verbs, quick yet entranced in its repetitions, the line encapsulates not just Burns's amazing dexterity, but much of his poetic personality. That personality's sympathetic ability to inhabit other voices and bodies is its saving grace. In his life Burns may have been spectacularly inconsistent, but in his poetry all that is transformed into breadth of sympathy, variety of expression and perspective. Burns's great English admirer John Keats came up with the notion of the poet as a chameleon; Burns's version of this was the Scottish Enlightenment philosophical principle of sympathy applied to poetic art. A mature appreciation of his work involves not a narrowing focus only on its sentimentalism, its radicalism, its eroticism or its satire, but a way of seeing the poetry as an expansively rewarding whole. Ever eager to recruit Scotland's bard for their own causes, too few readers are prepared to go that sympathetic distance.

Where Robert Fergusson had several imitators, Robert Burns had many. Some of these poetic emulators had talent. John Mayne (1759–1836) was a Dumfries poet whose 'Glasgow: A Poem', first outlined in the *Glasgow Magazine* in 1783 and praised by the radical poet Alexander Geddes, tried to do for that city what Fergusson had done for Edinburgh in 'Auld Reikie':

> Hence, Commerce spreads her sails to a'
> The Indies and America:
> Whatever makes ae penny twa,
>   By wind or tide,
> Is wafted to the Broomielaw,
>   On bonny Clyde!

Glasgow's 80,000 citizens might have relished this celebration of their trade, 'Clean-keepit streets' and 'piazzas'.[91] Mayne's over-long Standard Habbie celebration of a Dumfries shooting contest, 'The Siller Gun' (begun in 1777 and revised throughout the poet's life) draws on Fergusson and seems a bit like a worthy pedestrian trying to keep up with Burns's hop, skip and jump. Mayne wrote in Scots, but his wish to make a poetry rooted in West of Scotland localities can be related to such earlier English-language works as James Arbuckle's 1721 *Glotta* (Latin for the Clyde) and *The Clyde* (1764), an extended proto-Romantic descriptive poem in couplets by the Greenock Grammar School dominie John Wilson (1720–89).

A number of writers tried to cash in on Burns's success, publishing their own *Poems, Chiefly in the Scottish Dialect*, but simply copying the bard's title was no way to rival his talent. It is a predictable but unfortunate aspect of late eighteenth- and early nineteenth-century Scottish minor poetry that a lot of it is unexcitingly sub-Burnsian. Major talents, such as Scott and Byron, sound confidently unBurnsian, but too many ventriloquize. Some of the poets who were Burns's contemporaries achieved greater fame in other fields. Paisley's Burns-admiring Alexander Wilson wrote Scots verses, including a 1791 debate poem, 'The Laurel Disputed', about the relative merits of Ramsay and Fergusson, before his poetry's political radicalism led to his arrest in 1793 and he emigrated the following year. In the United States he wrote his long poem *The Foresters* (1809–10), but found his true métier as the great author and illustrator of the nine-volume *American Ornithologist* (1808–14). The editor of the *Encyclopaedia Britannica*, James Tytler, who wrote pleasant enough Scots lyrics, remade his name as 'Balloon Tytler' when he became the first person in Scotland to fly in a fire balloon; he too ended his days in the United States, in Massachusetts, though he did not travel there by balloon; Tytler's 'The Bonnie Bruckit Lassie' probably helped supply the title for one of Hugh MacDiarmid's most famous early twentieth-century Scots lyrics, 'The Bonnie Broukit Bairn'. Another generally under-inspired poet and novelist, Hector MacNeill (1746–1818), wrote in English (his Ossianic 'The Harp' is set on 'Kilda's dark and dismal shore') and in Scots ('Come under my plaidie'), but his most interesting works for modern readers are likely to include his semi-autobiographical novel, the *Memoirs of the Life and Travels of Charles Macpherson, Esq., in Asia, Africa, and America* (1800).

MacNeill was one of several Scottish writers who had direct experience of the slave trade. Burns imagined death in the Caribbean, and could sometimes be dismissive of 'half-starv'd slaves'.[92] A prospective emigrant, he must have considered that he might 'herd the *buckskin kye*' [American cattle, i.e., slaves].[93] He had also imagined, in a Scotland which had over sixty anti-slavery societies, what it might mean to sing 'The Slave's Lament'. As Burns knew, many of his countrymen had headed for 'The Indies and America' to make their fortunes as part of that British imperial 'Commerce' in which John Mayne's Glasgow and Scotland as a whole were increasingly confident players. In 1764 the Duns-born, Edinburgh-educated doctor, Latinist and man of letters, James Grainger (c. 1725–66), was living at St Kitts in the West Indies where he had married a rich sugar-planter's daughter. That year Grainger published *An Essay on the More Common West-India Diseases*, which also contained *Some Hints on the Management, &c., of Negroes*. This work (re-edited in 1802 by the Physician to His Majesty's Forces) discussed such matters as 'the method of seasoning new Negroes'. It was opportune, and opportunistic 'at this time, when the demand for Negroes, on account of our new acquisitions in America, must become annually greater'.[94]

Recalled by a bishop friend as 'generous, friendly, and benevolent', Grainger is in some ways enlightened.[95] The first page of his Preface makes it clear that he aims to treat the 'management' of 'these useful people' in 'a more scientific manner than has hitherto been generally practised', but he nowhere questions the justice of the slave system. 'Mighty Commerce hail!' exclaimed Grainger in his 'West India Georgic', *The Sugar Cane*, published in 1764, the same year as his *Essay*. This lengthy poem, modelled on Virgil's agricultural *Georgics*, was hailed by London's *Critical Review* as a work in which 'A new creation is offered, of which an European has scarce any conception: the hurricane, the burning winds; a ripe cane-piece on fire at midnight; an Indian prospect after a finished crop, and Nature in all the extreme of tropical exuberance.'[96] Among most writers, though, *The Sugar Cane* provoked guffaws and titters. James Boswell recalled a story of how 'assembled wits burst into a laugh, when, after much blank verse pomp, the poet began a new paragraph' with the words ' "Now, Muse, let's sing of *rats*." '[97] Re-edited in 2000, Grainger's note-larded poem, in which Nymphs and Muses alternate with 'Blacks' and 'swains' (i.e., slaves), is a revealing curiosity whose lush diction sparkles with peculiar exoticism 'On the mangrove-banks of Guayaquil'.[98] Yet Grainger's attempt to blend the Classical and the Caribbean is in tune with the black Latin verse-culture of the eighteenth-century West Indies, and set an enduring pattern still enacted in such modern works as Derek Walcott's *Omeros*. When this Scottish poet who had fought on the Hanoverian side at the Battle of Culloden replaced his infelicitous 'sing of *rats*' passage with the supposedly improved lines,

> Nor with less waste the whisker'd vermin race
> A countless clan despoil the lowland cane[99]

he shows how easily the old Lowland prejudice against bearded Highland clansmen could be transposed to the slave-owning Caribbean.

When the full story of Scottish culture's engagement with slavery comes to be written, a more honourable place will be found for Thomas Reid's student and lifelong friend, the far-travelled Reverend James Ramsay (1733–89) from Fraserburgh, who was driven out of Grainger's St Kitts and other Caribbean livings for his efforts to alleviate slaves' sufferings. In his *Sea Sermons* Ramsay made popular the military phrase 'band of brothers', but more important was his 1784 *Essay on the Treatment and Conversion of African Slaves in the British Sugar Colonies*.[100] He followed up with such works as his *Inquiry into the Effects of putting a Stop to the African Slave Trade* (1784) and his *Reply to ... Invectives* (1785), but organized opposition to this friend and inspirer of William Wilberforce destroyed his health. Ramsay was subjected to intense character assassination, collapsed, and died in 1789 but his work was the intellectual lynchpin of the anti-slavery movement in Britain which led to the eventual ending of the British slave trade in 1807. Hector MacNeill's pro-slavery *Observations on the Treatment of the Negroes* added to this debate, as did *The Sorrows of Slavery* (1789) by the lexicographer the Reverend John Jamieson (1759–1838) whose *Etymological Dictionary of the Scottish Language* (1808–9) was the first full lexicon of Scots. The twenty-first-century historian of 'Scottish Empire', Michael Fry, has drawn attention to a range of other anti-slavery publications including the 1824 *Horrors of Slavery* by Robert Wedderburn, son of the white James Wedderburn of Inveresk and a black mother. The modern Scottish poet Douglas Dunn in his 1980 radio play *Wedderburn's Slave* and the Scottish novelist James

Robertson in *Joseph Knight* (2003) explore the famous case of an escaped black slave, Joseph Knight, who was freed by the Court of Session in Edinburgh in 1777 when Lord Kames and the other Scottish judges ruled that the slave laws of Jamaica were abhorrent, unjust, and should not be supported by a Scottish court. James Boswell in Edinburgh was 'well entertained' by the pleading of Knight's defence lawyer, and got Samuel Johnson to dictate an argument in favour of Knight's liberty, but Boswell thought slavery vital to Britain's commercial interest. His poem 'No Abolition of Slavery' is hardly one of his most glorious productions.[101]

'The slave trade' is seen as something that 'debases the understanding, and degrades the moral character of the natives of Africa' in John Leyden's striking synthetic work, *A Historical & Philosophical Sketch of the Discoveries & Settlements of the Europeans in Northern & Western Africa, at the Close of the Eighteenth Century* (1799).[102] Leyden (1775–1811), a remarkable polymath, drew on an international range of literature, including the work of Mungo Park, Alexander Dalzel, and the Abyssinian narratives of James Bruce (1730–94) from Stirlingshire, author of *Travels to Discover the Source of the Nile* (1790). Continuing to sound that anthropological note heard strongly in such Enlightenment writers as Adam Ferguson, the twenty-four-year-old Leyden had never been to Africa, but wrote of that continent's sacred groves as an Edinburgh armchair anthropologist, a precursor of Helensburgh's J. G. Frazer a century later. Scottish Enlightenment philosophy underpins Leyden's impressive, vivid survey of African tribes: 'By contemplating their manners and customs, we may discover the simple and unmixed operation of those principles which, in civilised society, are always combined with extraneous circumstances.' Contesting 'the supposed inferiority of the negro to the white', Leyden's book introduces to English-language Gothic culture (with its fictions of vampires and other horrors) such notions as driving a stake through the body of a cursed man. Leyden likens African secret societies to 'masonic fraternities' and compares the historical poems of Dahomy with the legends of Ossian.[103] His book, which launched a spectacular career, has been undeservedly overlooked. One of its rhetorical high spots is when Leyden quotes the impassioned speech of John Henry Naimbanna of Sierra Leone:

If a man rob me of my money, I can forgive him; if a man should shoot at me, or try to stab me, I can forgive him; if a man should sell me and all my family to a slave-ship, so that we should pass all the rest of our days in slavery, in the West Indies, I can forgive him; but, (added he, rising from his seat with much emotion), if a man takes away the character of the people of my country, I can never forgive him.[104]

Leyden, who went on to help Walter Scott collect ballads, wrote some good poems, and produced a grammar of Malay, cared much about the character of his own country, as well as about such international issues as African slavery. He was an idealist, with some sympathy for the ideals of 'the French Revolution'.[105]

The kind of moral passion which Leyden foregrounds, and which lies behind several of the anti-slavery writers, may be related to types of ethical fervour heightened by Scotland's religious struggles. This social and moral energy relates not so much to the hypocritical and oppressive policings of the Taleban-like Auld Licht faction of the Kirk against which Burns railed. It may be tied more to struggles to maintain a sense of individual and corporate liberty of doctrine and Church government. Clearly such struggles conditioned Burns's own democratic instincts. As he once put it with reference to the seventeenth-century Solemn League and Covenant, which preserved the Presbyterian order of the Church of Scotland,

> THE Solemn League and Covenant
> Now brings a smile, now brings a tear.
> But sacred Freedom, too, was theirs;
> If thou 'rt a slave, indulge thy sneer.[106]

Some Scots, including David Hume, seemed content with the slave trade. Others held Christian anti-slavery views that went hand-in-hand with Scottish ideals of liberty moulded by Reformation struggles. While reported to be at ease in the company of Catholics, Episcopalians and others, the lexicographer Jamieson, for instance, belonged to the Seceder Church which disagreed with landlords' power of patronage over Kirk ministers, and his Church's marked emphasis on independence and freedom may have conditioned Jamieson's opposition to slavery. In Mackenzie and others Sentimentalism could also nourish a sympathetic feeling for oppressed people; so, in unpublished 1788 correspondence,

William Russell (1741–93), the historian of America and Europe who was author of *Sentimental Tales* (1770) and the epistolary poetic romance *Julia* (1774), as well as being the translator-expander of the Frenchman Thomas's *Essay on the Character, Manners, and Genius of Women* (1772), expressed his interest in 'the bill for abolishing the slavery of the Negroes'.[107] Russell's is an interestingly complex case, since he probably benefited from family money made in Jamaica.

Whether or not they were writing about slavery, eighteenth-century authors such as the prose writer John Howie (1735–93) in his *Scots Worthies* (1774) and the poet James Grahame (1765–1811) kept alive the traditions of independent-mindedness associated with the Reformers and Covenanters. Celebrating those hard-pressed Covenanters who had had to worship out of doors in fear of persecution, the liberal Whig Grahame in *The Sabbath* (1804) hymned how

> Thy persecuted children, SCOTIA, foil'd
> A tyrant's and a bigot's bloody laws . . .[108]

Such passions for liberty can be related to Burns's more revolutionary opposition to tyranny, and to the anti-slavery movement of which Grahame was a supporter. Political radicalism, however, was not exclusive to Scottish Protestant writers, as is demonstrated by the remarkable career of the Latin, Scots- and English-language poet and biblical scholar Alexander Geddes (1737–1802). Like Burns, Geddes praised the French General Dumourier, and feared British 'political Inquisitors'.[109] Geddes's radical activities ranged from scriptural translation and innovative German-influenced biblical textual scholarship to addressing a 1792 Latin 'Carmen Saeculare' (Song of the Era) to the French Revolutionary National Assembly. Geddes was a farmer's son from Banffshire. He trained at a Highland seminary, then at the Scots College in Paris before working for a time as a priest and farmer at Auchinhalrig, Banffshire. His bolshie opinions led to his attending a Protestant service and to his being deposed by his Bishop, although as the admired translator of *Select Satires of Horace* (1779) he was awarded an honorary Doctorate of Laws by Aberdeen University. Volume I of his translation of the Holy Bible, containing Genesis to Joshua, appeared in 1792. Defender of Catholic rights, friend of Coleridge and inspirer of William Blake, during his life Geddes was in dispute with his Catholic Church and with the

Crown. Geddes published *An Apology for Slavery* (1792), yet the inscription on his tomb in the cemetery of St Mary's Church, Paddington, in London suggests both eloquence and generosity of spirit:

> Christian is my name and Catholic is my surname,
> I grant that you are a Christian as well as I,
> and embrace you as my fellow disciple in Jesus,
> and if you were not a disciple of Jesus,
> still I would embrace you as my fellow man.[110]

The wording of this inscription is taken from *Dr Geddes's General Answer* (1790). Its opening draws on the Latin of St Pacianus, fourth-century Bishop of Barcelona; its ending is at one not just with Burns's 1790s 'A Man's a Man for a' That' but also with the Latin Horatian Sapphics of Geddes's own 1790 *Carmen Saeculare pro Gallica Gente tyrannidi aristocraticae erepta* (Song of the Era for the French People Snatched from the Tyranny of Aristocracy).

Publishing this work in London and Paris, Geddes in the 1790s sounds the last trump for Scottish Latinity. In the Boswell papers now at Yale there is a passage where Boswell, writing of his 1773 Scottish tour, speculates that it is through Ruddiman's work that 'a knowledge of the Roman language must be preserved in Scotland, if it can be preserved at all – or revived'. Even as the study of the Classics underpinned the Scottish Enlightenment Boswell sounds uncertain if Scottish Latin is still breathing. Geddes demonstrated in some style that it was. Yet the most remarkable lines of later eighteenth-century Scottish Latin verse were written at Rio de Janeiro in 1794 by the young Scottish republican radical Thomas Muir of Huntershill (1765–99) while he was being transported to Botany Bay as a political prisoner. Muir, a democrat and (like Geddes) a supporter of the French Revolution, was one of the 'Scottish political martyrs' the British government wished to get rid of as it crushed dissent in the 1790s. As far as most literary histories go, the British government seems to have succeeded, but Muir's short occasional poem written in a book he presented to the monks of Rio, and linked to quotations from Virgil and Horace, is one of the most remarkable documents produced by an eighteenth-century Scottish writer. Describing himself as 'Thomas Muir de Hunters hill/ Gente Scotus, Anima Orbis terrarum Civis' (Thomas Muir of Huntershill/

Scottish by Nationality, in Spirit a Citizen of the World), the well-read
Glaswegian lawyer laments in heartfelt Latin his nation's fate and his
own:

> O Scotia! O longum felix longumque superba
> Ante alias patria, Heroum sanctissima tellus
> Dives opum fecunda viris, laetissima campis
> Uberibus!
> Aerumnas memorare tuas summamque malorum
> Quis queat, et dictis, nostros aequare dolores
> Et turpes ignominias et barbara iussa?
>
> Nos patriae fines et dulcia linquimus arva.
>
> Cras ingens iterabimus aequor.

which may be freely translated,

> *O Scotland! proud, long blessed above all others,*
> *My sacred country, rich, broad-meadowed, strong,*
> *Who could spell out your many grievances*
> *And wounds, then find the words to match our own*
> *Hurts* in extremis *under barbarous laws,*
> *As now, sailing still further from the frontiers*
> *Of our own land with all its lovely farms*
> *I take up Horace –*
>   Cras ingens . . .
>   *Tomorrow*
> *We put out once again on the great deep.*

Muir was transported across the ocean to become Australia's first political prisoner, but he escaped and eventually joined other Scottish radicals
in Paris such as Robert Watson who urged the 'patriots of Scotland' to
rise and 'recover liberty'.[111] Though Muir died in Chantilly in 1799,
Latin, democracy and republicanism all managed to survive in Scotland
– if sometimes only just.

Nowadays Scottish poets continue to translate from Latin, and some
(most notably Ian Hamilton Finlay) have used fragments of the language
in their work, but after the eighteenth century Latin virtually ceased to
be used outside academic or Church contexts for extended literary
compositions. In the later twentieth and early twenty-first centuries

Latin, the language of George Buchanan, Alexander Geddes and so many other Scottish writers from St Columba to the Enlightenment, has been subject to considerable government-backed repression in the Scottish state-school system; today only three of Scotland's universities (St Andrews, Glasgow and Edinburgh) have Classics departments. Even as Geddes's revolutionary *Carmen Saeculare* salutes democratic modernity, like Muir's 'O Scotia!', it marks a spirited farewell to the composition of significant poetry in one of the two most ancient languages of Scottish literature.

Less controversially, while Alexander Geddes translated sacred scripture and authored secular songs, the Kirk encouraged the making of metrical psalms for use in worship. A Committee of the General Assembly of the Church of Scotland oversaw the production of the 1781 *Translations and Paraphrases, in Verse, of Several Passages of Sacred Scripture*, while individual poets including Michael Bruce and Robert Burns produced poetic versions of biblical texts. Some contributors to the 1781 *Translations and Paraphrases* were not principally poets, but brought to the challenge a sense of clarity and conviction which paid literary dividends. This might be said of the work by the Aberdeen University graduate the Reverend John Morison (1750–1798), minister at Canisbay, who produced some of the most widely sung versions of scripture, including his paraphrase of Hosea VI: 1–4:

> Come, let us to the Lord our God,
>   With contrite hearts return:
> Our God is gracious, nor will leave
>   The desolate to mourn.
>
> His voice commands the tempest forth,
>   And stills the stormy wave;
> And though His arm be strong to smite,
>   'Tis also strong to save.[112]

These plain, stately words have been sung frequently over the centuries. Something of the range of religious expression in eighteenth-century Scottish poetry is evident if they are set beside the intense religious eroticism of the near-contemporary 'Luinneag Anna Nic Ealair' ('Anna Nic Ealair's Song') which dates from around 1800 and, perhaps as a result of the Evangelical Revival, presents a woman's love for Christ in ecstatic terms:

Is millse leam do ghaol na'm fion,
    Seadh am fion, 'nuair is treis' e,
'S 'n uair a thug thu dhomh do ghràdh
    'S ann a dh' fhàilnich mo phearsa.

Sweeter to me your love than wine,
even wine at its strongest;
when you showed me your esteem
it made my body falter.[113]

All we know of this song's composer is her name, but the work stands as a strong Scottish fusion of physical and religious passion in its longing for the risen Christ.

Anna Nic Ealair's name survives because of a single lyric. The same can be said about Jean Glover (1758–1801), who sang a lively, very different song. Glover's 'O'er the moor amang the heather' was transcribed by a Robert Burns delighted to have discovered a singer who was 'not only a whore, but also a thief'.[114] Most women had to struggle hard to make their mark in a male-dominated environment. Lower-class girls often received little schooling, and so were illiterate. 'My learning it can soon be told,/ Ten weeks, when I was seven years old,' recited Isobel Pagan (1741–1821), whose works were written down and brought to publication in 1805 by her friend the tailor William Gemmel.[115] Pagan, who ran an Ayrshire pub, sang a song 'Ca' the yowes', which was first brought into print by Burns; who its author was is impossible to tell.

Lack of education meant that lower-class women found it hard to enter and make their name in the networks of print culture to which their male counterparts had more ready access. Barred from university, women of all classes had to struggle for advanced knowledge. 'In Scotland, as far as I have observed,' wrote Elizabeth Hamilton around 1802, 'judgment is the only faculty which it is deemed allowable for women to cultivate.' One of the first Scotswomen to make her name as a published novelist, Hamilton had taught herself polite writerly discourse in relatively comfortable surroundings. 'Do I not well remember hiding *Kames's Elements of Criticism* under the cover of an easy chair, whenever I heard the approach of a footstep, well knowing the ridicule to which I should have been exposed, had I been detected in the act of looking into such a book?'[116]

Minor male poets had at least a greater range of options as they tried to make ends meet. The Edinburgh music teacher John Hamilton (1761–1814) contributed alongside Burns to Johnson's *Scots Musical Museum*. Andrew Scott (1757–1839) imitated Ramsay and Fergusson as he served as a young British soldier on Staten Island during the American War of Independence. America loomed increasingly large in the Scottish imagination, not just in such tomes as the histories of America by Robertson and Russell, but also because many Scots had family there. Robert Fergusson's brother Hary (soon to die in Jamaica) wrote from Virginia about capturing a smuggler's sloop 'loaden with coffee and sugar'. By 1775 he found it hard to believe that 'We are now actually at war with the Americans.'[117] William Julius Mickle was convinced that 'To have given a savage continent an image of the British constitution is indeed the greatest glory of the British crown'. In his 1777 history of colonization the St Andrews Belles Lettres Professor and imperialist William Barron argued with regard to the American rebellion that 'No colonies were ever so prosperous and so happy'.[118] However, other Scots from Adam Smith to Robert Burns were more imaginatively understanding, and tended to sympathize with the rebels.

Although Scotland's commercial interests made many Scots on both sides of the Atlantic pro-British, Burns's Washington ode is just one of several notable statements of allegiance to American ideals. Scotland was in Jefferson's mind when he drew up the Declaration of Independence, a third of whose signatories had Scottish or Ulster-Scots backgrounds. Outstanding among them was the Fife-born James Wilson who championed Scottish Common Sense philosophy in America. During his student days at St Andrews University, Wilson had acquired a sense of wider horizons; across the Atlantic, he wrote on political and legal philosophy, was instrumental in setting up the United States Supreme Court, and became one of the most important eighteenth-century Scottish Americans. Wilson's library borrowings as a St Andrews student, his later reading, and the literary quotations in his legal writings show that he was polished in the Belles Lettres. Even though their subject was often bound up with Anglocentric pressures, Scottish pioneers of university Belles Lettres, whether domiciled in America like Paisley's the Reverend John Witherspoon at Princeton, or still safe in Edinburgh like the Reverend Hugh Blair, became celebrities in the emerging centres of American academia. Even as late as the mid-nineteenth century, when

St Andrews became the first British university to teach American literature, Professor William Spalding in Fife maintained that 'In respect to those circumstances which affect style, the position of Americans is very much like that of Scotsmen.'[119]

For some men and women in eighteenth-century Scotland, poetry could bring a patronizing kind of celebrity that marked them out as freaks. Where Burns was Ayrshire's 'heaven-taught ploughman', his ambitious contemporary Janet Little (1759-1813) was promoted as 'The Scotch Milkmaid'. Like Burns, she tries both to exploit and sometimes to complain about her status as peasant poet, but Little's models (often Ramsay, Fergusson, and Burns himself) are less confidently transmuted. Carlisle's 'Muse of Cumberland' Susanna Blamire (1747-94) was one of a good number of northern English poets, some writing in dialect, who can be aligned with Burns. Occasionally seeming to anticipate his work, Blamire made Scots songs with a convincing Highland tincture, frequently visiting her sister who had settled in Stirlingshire. In the twentieth century Hugh MacDiarmid in a 1947 radio broadcast praised Blamire's Scots songs as deserving to 'be set beside the best that have ever been produced by Scotsmen writing in their own tongue'.[120] She published in the *Scots Musical Museum* (1790) and wrote of Nabobs as well as Highland scenes.

Not everyone, though, liked the Highlands. If ongoing arguments over the genuineness of the Ossianic poems continued to be a focus for those sympathetic to Highland culture, they also generated hatred. In his *Origins and Progress of the Scythians and the Goths* (1787) Edinburgh-born, London-based Scottish historian John Pinkerton (1758-1826) tried to prove that the Celts were degenerate Gothic aborigines, racially inferior to the Lowland Scots. Pinkerton's arguments were contested virulently by the County Durham Scotophile and ballad collector Joseph Ritson. Ritson published several works on Scottish literature, and in 1785 compiled an anthology, *The Caledonian Muse*, eventually published in 1821. However hostilely intended, Pinkerton's Gothicizing of the Highlands may have had imaginative benefits (especially for women readers and writers) at a time when Gothic literature was coming into vogue; an Ossianic Highland setting is important to the famous English Gothic writer Ann Radcliffe in her first novel, *The Castles of Athlin and Dunbayne* (1789) and a stream of Scottish-set novels followed in the next few decades, with titles like *The Castle of Caithness*

(1802). Pinkerton's bias is really just a continuation of a much older Scottish topos: the Celtic peoples of Britain are and have always been 'mere radical savages ... and if any foreigner doubts this, he has only to step into the Celtic part of ... Scotland, and look at them, just as they were, incapable of industry or civilization'.[121] Pinkerton got his comeuppance when he was forced by Ritson to admit he had passed off traditional ballads as his own compositions. It was an age when 'genius' and 'originality' were hotly debated; Aberdeen's Alexander Gerard published his *Essay on Genius* in 1774, after his 1759 *Essay on Taste*. A would-be genius revealed as a thief, Pinkerton was not alone in his larcenies. A number of writers, from James Macpherson to the playwright and poet John Logan (dramatist of *Runnamede* (1774)) were accused of plagiarism. Logan stole from the dead Michael Bruce. If poets were to be pitied, wept over sentimentally as 'unfitted for the world', they were also to be traded and pillaged. As elsewhere in Enlightenment Scotland, there prevailed a mutual relationship between sympathetic imagination and hard cash.

The Gaelic version of the doomed poet apparently 'unfitted for the world' is Skye-born Uilleam Ros (1762–90). After Robert Burns, he is Scotland's greatest eighteenth-century love poet. Like Burns, the Jacobite William Ross sometimes reworked existing songs. A schoolmaster in Gairloch, Wester Ross, he seems to have had a short, intense romance with a Stornoway cousin, Marion, who married another man. Dead at twenty-eight, probably from tuberculosis, the unhappy lover Ross is said to have burned his poems – a gesture that runs counter to that Gaelic saying, 'Smeig a loisgeadh a thiompan ria' ('Woe to the one who'd burn his harp for them') which was given fashionable Lowland circulation as the epigraph to Hector MacNeill's *The Harp*, published around the time of Ross's death. Ross, the doomed, tubercular destroyer of his own music, has all the ingredients of the quintessential Romantic poet, and can present himself as such: ' 'S e dh'fhàg mi mar iudmhail air treud' (I'm a fugitive strayed from the flock).[122] Yet his work is also rooted in earlier Gaelic verse, as well as in the work of Mac Mhaighstir Alasdair, John MacCodrum, and the poetry of Burns, Ossian and Classical poets. While Ross can compose jauntily, like Fergusson and Burns he is conscious of ruin as well as delight. A poem in which the poet debates with his opposite – 'the Hag who ruins songs' – shows Ross knew well the balance of his temperament.[123] The Hag wins. Ross's greatest work is a series of pang-ridden love songs. Bleakest of them is 'Oran Eile air an Aobhar Cheudna', its title meaning simply 'Another Song on the Same Theme.' Its first stanza complains,

Tha mise fo mhulad san àm,
Chan òlar leam dràm le sùnnt,
Tha durrag air ghur ann mo chàil
A dh'fhiosraich do chàch mo rùin:
Chan fhaic mi dol seachad air sràid
An cailin bu tlàithe sùil,
'S e sin a leag m' aigne gu làr
Mar dhuilleach o bhàrr nan craobh.

Overburdened with sorrow now
I can drink no dram with joy,
a maggot broods in my mind
telling my secrets to all:
no longer I see in the street
the girl with the gentlest eyes,
and so my spirits have fallen
like leaves from the foliage of trees.[124]

In the twentieth century, writing his own tormented love lyrics, Sorley MacLean admired 'the musical chiselling/ of words, which is a marvel in his [Ross's] poetry'.[125] With the word 'bard' in its last line, 'Oran Eile' ends with a certain Ossianic note of pride, its poet compelled 'to journey to final sleep/ in the hall of the poets who are dead'. Macpherson's impact on Gaelic poetry has been denounced, yet remained ubiquitously perceptible in the century that followed.

Where poets like Fergusson, Burns and Ross were poor and struggling, the most successful songmakers among their published contemporaries were often rich upper-class women whose elite social status had procured them an unusual measure of education, leisure, and access to influential channels of circulation. Among the most talented were the sentimental Jacobites Lady Anne Barnard (1750–1825) and Carolina Oliphant, Lady Nairne (1766–1845), though neither was eager to be celebrated as an author. Kirsteen McCue quotes a revealing passage in which Lady Anne Barnard remembered performing one of her compositions, 'Auld Robin Gray':

Happening to sing it one day at Dalkeith-House, with more feeling perhaps than belonged to a common ballad, OUR friend Lady Frances Scott smiled, and, fixing her eyes on me, said, '*You* wrote this song yourself.' The blush that followed confirmed my *guilt*. Perhaps I blushed the more (being very young) from the recollection of the coarse words from which I borrowed the tune, and was afraid of the raillery which might have taken place if it had been discovered I had ever heard such.[126]

Respectable lady poets and singers did *hear* songs, but they also read them in such 'tea-table' collections as those of Allan Ramsay, David Herd and the Englishman Joseph Ritson. Often proper and decorous, the aristocratic women's songs are also beautiful and spirited.

> I'll no be had for naething,
> I'll no be had for naething,
> I tell ye, lads, that's ae thing,
> So ye needna follow me.[127]

So sings Lady Nairne's 'The Heiress'. Nairne's version of the Jacobite 'Will Ye No Come Back Again?' is a classic song that mixes plangency with clarity. It names precisely the size of the reward for 'Bonnie Charlie''s capture (£30,000) even as it celebrates with sentimental force how 'Siller canna buy the heart'.[128] Lady Nairne is one of Scotland's greatest songwriters. Her social status did not prevent her from imaginatively identifying with other people in a variety of very different situations, not least those of suffering women: 'I'm wearin' awa', John,/ Like snaw-wreaths in thaw, John,/ I'm wearin' awa', begins her mournful song of loss and endurance 'The Land o' the Leal'.[129] Though she can be tearful, Carolina Oliphant can also portray women of independent mind who may confront, or dance with, Robert Burns's more celebrated male counterparts.

As well as songs like 'Auld Robin Gray', at the start of the nineteenth century Lady Anne Barnard wrote entertaining letters to leading Scottish politicians such as the apparently omnipotent Henry Dundas about her experiences in the Cape of Good Hope. Travelling there with her husband, Lady Anne thought the admired Kaffirs were 'united in Clans exactly like those of the Highlands of Scotland'.[130] Yet the most exciting account of upper-class life written by an eighteenth-century Scotswoman is surely Grace Dalrymple Elliott's *Journal of My Life During the French*

Revolution, produced for King George III in 1801 and conveyed sheet by sheet to its first, excited royal reader. Grace Dalrymple, an Edinburgh lawyer's daughter born in 1758, was educated in France before returning to her native Auld Reikie around 1773. A disastrous marriage led to a series of affairs and a celebrated career as a high-class prostitute in Scotland, England, and in France where she died in 1823. She is said to have seduced the Prince of Wales, the Duke of Orleans and Napoleon; her portrait by Gainsborough now hangs in New York's Metropolitan Museum. Dalrymple's *Journal* says little of her sex life, though there is an extended and excited account of how, as a fervent royalist, she hid a wanted man in her bedroom when French republican revolutionaries entered it. Filmed in the twenty-first century by Eric Rohmer, her account is, at its best, electrifying. In Paris on 13 July 1789, just before the Bastille fell,

I was unfortunate enough to try to go to my jeweller's that evening, and I met in the Rue St. Honoré the soldiers of the French Guards carrying Monsieur de Foulon's head by the light of flambeaux. They thrust the head into my carriage: at the horrid sight I screamed and fainted away . . .

Imprisoned, almost executed, on the run, Mrs Elliott, a proud 'Scotch-woman' who delights to call herself English, is at once shrewd and aristocratically bewildered, whether cast on the straw of a cart, or fleeing along the road near Meudon: 'My feet were covered with blood, having no soles to my shoes or stockings. My shoes were thin white silk, and that road is very stony.'[131]

Grace Dalrymple Elliott did not consider herself a professional author, but her account is still highly readable. The long-lived Joanna Baillie (1762–1851) is important as perhaps the first woman in Scottish litera-ture to regard herself as a fully professional, publishing author. Walter Scott, who liked her plays, may have praised 'our immortal Joanna Baillie', but her writings are now mainly of interest to academics.[132] A minister's daughter from Bothwell in Lanarkshire, Baillie was educated at a Glasgow boarding school. When her father died in 1778 she moved to London where she lived for a time in the care of the great Scottish physician Dr William Hunter. She published her first and finest collection of poems, *Fugitive Pieces*, anonymously in 1790. At her best as a poet Baillie has a (sometimes too) charming sense of detail and an ability to convey the effortfulness of day-to-day life, not least the life of women.

She made Scots songs as well as English verses like 'A Winter's Day' which describes a mother and her young children:

> Their busy mother knows not where to turn,
> Her morning work comes now so thick upon her.
> One she must help to tye his little coat,
> Unpin his cap, and seek another's shoe.
> When all is o'er, out to the door they run,
> With new comb'd sleeky hair, and glist'ning cheeks,
> Each with some little project in his head.
> One on the ice must try his new sol'd shoes:
> To view his well-set trap another hies,
> In hopes to find some poor unwary bird
> (No worthless prize) entangled in his snare;
> Whilst one, less active, with round rosy face,
> Spreads out his purple fingers to the fire,
> And peeps, most wishfully, into the pot.[133]

In her own day Baillie was celebrated for grander things than this vignette. Her verse is frequently competent, but can be jejune or, in the sub-Shakespearian dramas which filled her later career, bombastic. Refined and considered rather solitary at a time when intellectuals were usually supposed to be male, she numbered among her friends Maria Edgeworth, Scott, and the brilliant Jedburgh-born mathematician and memoirist Mary Somerville (1780–1872), who gave her name to an Oxford college. Like Elizabeth Hamilton, Baillie furthered the case for women's educational rights. She was an inspirational figure for the Scottish novelist Mary Brunton and the fiction writer Mary Ann Kelty, both of whom dedicated novels to her. Baillie impressively outlined her dramatic theory in her Introductory Discourse to *A Series of Plays: in which it is attempted to delineate the stronger passions of the mind, each passion being the subject of a tragedy and a comedy* (1798), but on the whole the plays are as unexciting as the title. The underpinning Scottish Enlightenment philosophy exceeds the poetic and dramatic practice. Where Mary Somerville, her pet sparrow on her shoulder, writes with intellectual brio and accuracy, still demanding to be read, Joanna Baillie matters most as a half-forgotten icon of literary professionalism. Too often, her work asks only to be studied.

Yet even the most arcane of eighteenth-century Scottish tomes can yield passages of compelling imaginative vibrancy. The irascible Stirlingshire laird James Bruce (1730–94) published in 1790 his often protracted and eccentric five-volume *Travels to Discover the Source of the Nile*. Bruce was a heroic traveller, annoyed when some of his contemporaries thought he had invented what he saw. Psychologically revealing is his memory of his feelings when he actually reached his distant African goal:

> I was, at that very moment, in possession of what had, for many years, been the principal object of my ambition and wishes: indifference, which, from the usual infirmity of human nature, follows, at least for a time, complete enjoyment, had taken place of it. The marsh, and the fountains, upon comparison with the rise of many of our rivers, became now a trifling object in my sight. I remembered that magnificent scene in my own native country, where the Tweed, Clyde, and Annan, rise in one hill; three rivers, as I now thought, not inferior to the Nile in beauty, preferable to it in the cultivation of those countries through which they flow; superior, vastly superior to it in the virtues and qualities of the inhabitants, and in the beauty of its flocks crowding its pastures in peace, without fear of violence from man or beast. I had seen the rise of the Rhine and Rhone, and the more magnificent sources of the Soane; I began, in my sorrow, to treat the inquiry about the source of the Nile as a violent effort of a distempered fancy:–

> > What's Hecuba to him, or he to Hecuba,
> > That he should weep for her? –

> Grief, or despondency, now rolling upon me like a torrent; relaxed, not refreshed, by unquiet and imperfect sleep, I started from my bed in the utmost agony; I went to the door of my tent; every thing was still; the Nile, at whose head I stood, was not capable either to promote or to interrupt my slumbers, but the coolness and serenity of the night braced my nerves, and chased away those phantoms that, while in bed, had oppressed and tormented me.[134]

Here, plunging to despair at the height of what should be his moment of triumph, Bruce shows a psychological kinship with Fergusson and Burns. His torrential despondency is only momentary, but his recording of it is astute. Quarrelsome at home, he pines for Scotland's comforting beauty when abroad. He quotes Shakespeare, writes in English, publishes in London, but remains passionately, even anguishedly, Scottish.

In all these respects James Bruce approaches the other Scottish author whose large-scale prose work was a literary milestone of the early 1790s.

James Boswell's Nile was Samuel Johnson. Boswell sought, through developing the art of biography, to trace Johnson's course and sources. In so doing he explored not Africa but England. The relations between England, Scotland and Britain are as central to his work as is a preoccupation with those psychological vagaries of 'ambition', 'human nature', 'enjoyment' and 'despondency' highlighted by James Bruce.

Boswell's is a life of hero-worship and displacement. Son of a distinguished advocate, he was born in Edinburgh in 1740. He studied law – and rebelled against it – at the universities of Edinburgh, Glasgow and Utrecht. Aged nineteen, he admired his Glasgow Belles Lettres professor, Adam Smith, not least for the kind of asides that might appeal to a future biographer: 'I remember Dr Adam Smith, in his rhetorical lectures at Glasgow, told us he was glad to know that Milton wore latchets in his shoes, instead of buckles,' Boswell recalled nearly forty years later when approaching his biography of Johnson.[135] Though their relationship was sometimes strained, the young Boswell also came to know David Hume well. At twenty-eight he made his name with *An Account of Corsica* (1768). An admiring study of that island and its nationalist leader, Pascal Paoli, Boswell's book carries as its Latin epigraph what are now the most famous words from the then little regarded 1320 Scottish 'Declaration of Independence', the Declaration of Arbroath:

Non enim propter gloriam, divitias aut honores pugnamus, sed propter libertatem solummodo, quam nemo bonus nisi simul cum vita amittit.

We fight not for the sake of glory, riches, or honours, but for the sake of liberty alone, which no good man relinquishes except with his life.[136]

Fascinated by London where, as an advocate who longed to be a rake, he spent much time, Boswell is not a Scottish nationalist. He is a Briton. Yet he is fascinated by Scottish culture, and his first book at several points maps Corsica on to Scotland. Well travelled in Europe, Boswell cultivated Rousseau and Voltaire as well as Paoli. He wrote an 'Ode to Ambition'. He liked to know and be known by great men. Obsequiousness can be one of Boswell's failings. Yet his autobiographical private journals (published long after his death) reveal an almost Rousseauesque honesty about his own weaknesses, as well as a superb eye and ear for the life around him in London and elsewhere. Owner of the manuscript autobiography of 'Sir Robert Sibbald the celebrated Scottish antiquary',

Boswell admired this as 'the most natural and candid account of himself that ever was given by any man'. He planned for a time to print it 'with additions by myself', and sought to match Sibbald's self-observation.[137] Classically educated, Boswell was familiar with the 'wise counsel' of the Greek 'ancient philosopher . . ., "Know thyself"'. He authored his private journals with fascinated self-scrutiny, maintaining a penchant for autobiographical and biographical minutiae.[138] Even in his early twenties he was being accused jocularly by David Hume of putting private conversations into print. Boswell's work raises the recording of such revealing intimacies into high art.

Entranced by London (where he later became a partner in the *London Magazine*), the twenty-two-year-old Boswell could feel fervently Scottish at a Covent Garden first night:

Just before the overture began to be played, two Highland officers came in. The mob in the upper gallery roared out, 'No Scots! No Scots! Out with them!,' hissed and pelted them with apples. My heart warmed to my countrymen, my Scotch blood boiled with indignation. I jumped up on the benches, roared out, 'Damn you, you rascals!,' hissed and was in the greatest rage. I am very sure at that time I should have been the most distinguished of heroes. I hated the English; I wished from my soul that the Union was broke and that we might give them another battle of Bannockburn.[139]

Yet only a week later, somewhat tongue-in-cheek, he has 'resolved today to be a true-born Old Englishman'. In flight from 'dreary Tolbooth Kirk ideas', embarrassed by Scottish '*hamely* company' in London, and eager to cut a dash as a sophisticate, Boswell delights in bedding a young actress while 'The bells of St Bride's church rung their merry chimes hard by.'[140] In the same spirit, he enjoys walking with the Reverend Prof. Hugh Blair, 'passing under the windows of my first London lady of the town [i.e., prostitute] with an Edinburgh minister whom I had so often heard preach . . .'[141] Anxious to impress himself and others, whether as a buck, a man of the world, or as a man of letters, Boswell can be a joy to read. He notices things. His mob in the theatre isn't just throwing fruit; it's throwing *apples*. At the same time, his observation of his own complexities and instabilities makes him a more sympathetic biographer of other people. Like James Bruce, he knows what it is to be despondent at the height of success:

For here was I, a young man full of vigour and vivacity, the favourite lover of a handsome actress and going to enjoy the full possession of my warmest wishes. And yet melancholy threw a cloud over my mind. I could relish nothing.[142]

However hard he tried to deny it, the depressive Boswell, like Burns and Byron, may have been conditioned by the 'dismal hours of apprehension' and 'infernal horror' he associated with the strict Calvinist doctrine which was familiar to him from around the time of his first sexual experiences.[143] Several members of Boswell's family had suffered from insanity and his brother was confined to a Newcastle asylum. It was after he and Johnson had told each other of their shared 'disorder' – melancholy – that Boswell began to record 'Mr Johnson's *Memorabilia*' in detail.[144] From studying himself in his private writings, Boswell moved to scrutinizing a man with whom he felt a sympathetic, intimate connection, yet who was also sufficiently and dauntingly different – in talent, recognition and, not least, in his Scotophobic Englishness – so that he could be portrayed as fascinatingly and heroically other.

Boswell had been writing about Johnson for almost three decades before, just four years in advance of his own death, he published in 1791 *The Life of Samuel Johnson LL. D.* As early as 1772 he had 'a constant plan to write the *Life* of Mr Johnson'.[145] He made a tour of Scotland (including the Highlands and Islands) with Johnson in 1773, and both men published accounts of their journey. These are rich in vignettes – as when Dr Johnson, England's greatest man of letters, steps out of a Hebridean bed into a muddy puddle. While transcribing his bons mots, Boswell loves to portray Johnson as 'at bottom much of a *John Bull*; much of a blunt *true-born Englishman*'. Boswell records both his subject's anti-Scottish jibes (especially anti-Ossianic ones) and his occasional praise of things Caledonian. 'I now had him actually in Caledonia,' marvels the biographer.[146] Boswell's Scotland lives constantly in the eyes of the great metropolitan spectator, is seen as English others see it. Though Boswell protests at some of Johnson's outbursts, he loves to provoke them and knows they make excellent copy. Boswell's *Journal of a Tour to the Hebrides with Samuel Johnson, LL. D.* (1785), like his full-scale *Life of Johnson*, is not just the portrait of a man but a biography of Britain.

When Boswell and Johnson first met, Boswell apologized for his Scottishness: 'I cannot help it.'[147] A couple of months later he was already recording with entranced admiration one of the most celebrated pieces of Johnson's Scotophobic wit – 'the noblest prospect that a Scotsman ever sees is the road which leads him to England!' – before offering his own paean to the 'wild grandeur' of his 'native country'.[148] Part of Boswell knows that Johnson is just as prejudiced as the apple throwers in the theatre, but he loves the Doctor's aplomb, and, like Arbuthnot before him, reveals the strains within Britain at the same time as rather enjoying a situation in which England comes out on top. The *Life* is the life of a culture, rich in accounts of literary life, not least among the London Scots. It is also a work which constantly takes the temperature of the British Union. Yet, as its title makes clear, it is pre-eminently an account of a singular individual. Drawing not only on Boswell's own voluminous papers (now at Yale University) and personal memoirs, but also on research and editing of other people's accounts, Boswell's great biography was designed to present 'innumerable detached particulars ... with a scrupulous authenticity'.[149] The 'detached' nature of the particulars gives the 'life' a Humean cast. As biographer and autobiographer Boswell learned from Scottish Enlightenment philosophy, from drama, and perhaps from the emergent genre of the novel, how to portray a greater degree of psychological complexity than any prose writer in English had yet managed to communicate. His work would stand as a magnificent example not just to later biographers but also to novelists and examiners of human psychology.

Boswell's Humean Samuel Johnson is constructed out of a myriad of separate anecdotes and detailed moments; he is an amalgamation of fragments, some contradictory or apparently unrelated, rather than a simplistically unified 'self'. The biographer is Hume's friend and Smith's student, who remembered his old professor's curiosity about Milton's shoes. As Boswell puts it, 'Though a small particular may appear trifling to some, it will be relished by others; while every little spark adds something to the general blaze.' He sees his '*Magnum Opus*' as a 'Flemish picture which I give of my friend, and in which, therefore, I mark the most minute particulars'.[150] So we hear of how Johnson on occasion gave 'a half whistle, sometimes making his tongue play backwards from the roof of his mouth, as if clucking like a hen, and sometimes protruding it against his upper gums in front, as if pronouncing quickly under his breath, *too, too, too* ...'[151] Prose like this may have learned from the novel; it also had much to teach. No man had ever been presented in such amazing detail. Even Richard Ellmann, most meticulously stylish of twentieth-century biographers, spoke of Boswell with awe, and in the twenty-first century Bruce Redford presents Johnson's great biographer as 'a bold, imaginative, and scrupulous artist' who produced 'a revolutionary paradigm for biography'.[152]

'Bozzy' left literary legacies to many later writers of fiction and nonfiction, not least to his admirer Walter Scott. The great biographer records equally what Johnson thought of David Hume's Scotticisms, and how much he paid for three pairs of scissors, but his method is humanely comprehensive, rather than undiscriminating. Chronologically ordered, the *Life*, so rich in transcribed letters and conversations, is also honest about gaps and omissions. It is carefully sculpted to convey what it felt like to be with Johnson from day to day as well as year to year. Authentic, it is too a masterpiece of manufacture. Just as 'Rule, Britannia' was penned by a Scotsman early in the eighteenth century, so at its end the greatest ever literary portrait of an Englishman was made with extraordinary attentiveness and architectural ambition by another Scot. Yes, it was the age of Robert Burns. It was also the age of Boswell.

The Scott Monument on Princes Street, Edinburgh, during construction in 1844. This is one of the most striking pictures taken by the pioneering St Andrews photographer Robert Adamson, working with the Edinburgh artist David Octavius Hill. Designed by George Meikle Kemp, the Scott Monument is just one of Edinburgh's public tributes to the great author of Waverley. Nearby Waverley station makes the Scottish capital the only city in the world to have named its principal railway station after a first novel. (St Andrews University Library Photographic Collections, ALB77-8)

8

Volcano, Wizard, Bankrupt, Spy

Chalk Farm, near London, 11 August 1806. Open ground, screened by hedge and large trees. 'What a beautiful morning it is,' says a Scotsman to an Irishman. They have come to fight a duel with pistols. The previous night the Irishman went to a shop in Bond Street and bought enough powder and bullets 'for a score of duels'. Neither man is good with guns. The Scot, a literary critic, has loaded his pistol with difficulty. The Irishman, a poet, is anxious because on his only earlier experience with firearms he almost blew his thumb off. After their nervous conversation about the weather, they walk to their respective positions and level their weapons. Constables rush from behind a hedge. Neither duellist fires. Later, as the newspapers and Lord Byron note with glee, one pistol is found to have no bullet in it. Held for questioning, the two men chat eagerly. The critic stretches out full length on a bench, discoursing elegantly about books. The poet listens admiringly. After their release, both men breakfast together 'most lovingly'.[1]

The Irishman, who had issued the challenge, was Thomas Moore. He would have liked to fight the duel in Edinburgh, but could not afford the fare north. His Scottish opponent was a young, well-off Edinburgh advocate, Francis Jeffrey, who, in a book review, had accused Moore of immorality. Both men wrote about their confrontation, which is also recorded by Jeffrey's biographer Lord Henry Cockburn (1779–1854) whose *Journal* (1874), *Circuit Journeys* (1888), *Selected Letters* (2005) and other writings give an affectionately detailed account of early nine-teenth-century Edinburgh well-to-do literary and social life – all 'Coffee pots', 'sleet above' and 'claggy [thick] cream'.[2]

The aborted duel at Chalk Farm and its happy outcome are both testimony to the forcefulness of Jeffrey (1773–1850), co-founder of 'that mighty arbitrator of the present day', the monthly *Edinburgh Review*.[3]

As an editor, Jeffrey took 'the unquestioned and unlimited power of alteration and rejection of all reviews'.[4] From 1802 his commanding Whig magazine published not just book reviews but new poetry, fiction and articles on topics ranging from India to economics. The early nineteenth century might now appear the golden age of the Scottish novel, yet with an average of under five new novels each year appearing across the country – not just in Edinburgh and Glasgow but also in places like Greenock and Dumfries – Scotland was responsible for publishing only about 6 per cent of book-length fiction in Britain and Ireland between 1800 and 1830. It is true that Scottish novel publishing rapidly increased in the 1820s, to take a larger share of the market. However, though there were spectacular exceptions, notably Walter Scott, many Scottish novelists wanted to publish in London where almost 90 per cent of British and Irish novels first appeared.[5]

The novel was on the rise, but arguably what seemed the most potent Scottish cultural channel was the magazine. Jeffrey claimed his *Edinburgh Review* was read by 50,000 people a month. Certainly in 1813 it had a circulation of 12,000 copies; in our own age literary magazines do well to sell 1000 copies a quarter. As well as studying at Edinburgh and Oxford, the British gentleman Jeffrey, in true Belles Lettres style, had been taught 'the elements of taste and criticism' by Professor George Jardine at Glasgow University.[6] A friend of Dugald Stewart and Henry Mackenzie, Jeffrey was rooted in Scottish Enlightenment thought. His authoritative magazine was hospitable to the writings of academics like Edinburgh's influential philosopher Sir William Hamilton (1788–1856), who carried the liberal, common-sense traditions of the Enlightenment well into what we think of as the era of Romanticism. While fascinated by Romantic poetry, Jeffrey was happy to denounce the 'intolerable prolixity' of 'our modern literature'. He may have argued that his magazine presented 'indulgent criticism'; others felt differently.[7] George Gordon, Lord Byron, Aberdeen's greatest literary export, suggested in his 1809 *English Bards and Scotch Reviewers* that the magazine was characterized by piss, shit and its editor's diseased 'Itch'. For Byron, the Edinburgh Reviewers, who could earn 20 guineas per poet-devouring page, were 'northern wolves' –

> A coward brood, which mangle as they prey,
> By brutal instinct, all that cross their way – ...[8]

Wordsworth and Goethe were among the mangled, but Jeffrey championed Madame de Staël and his early contributor Walter Scott. At Scott's suggestion he started in 1803 a supper club whose thirty members included not just Scotland's great and good, but also ambitious twenty-somethings like Henry Cockburn, poet Thomas Campbell, and Sidney Smith, the Edinburgh-based English wit who had suggested the *Edinburgh Review*. In some ways this networking continued the spirit of earlier Edinburgh 'select societies'; but the club's close links to the *Review* whetted the diners' appetites.

There had been magazines in Edinburgh before, but never like this, never ones that led to London duels or Edinburgh lawsuits and sought to lay down the literary law for the English-speaking world. In a sense the aims of the *Review* and other new Scottish magazines followed the literary law-givings of the university teachers of Rhetoric and Belles Lettres, but the magazines operated outside the classroom and were part of a much wider developing infrastructure of Scottish commercial publishing. The *Review*'s backer was Archibald Constable (1774–1827), a factor's son from Carnbee in Fife who had learned his trade as an Edinburgh bookseller. Earlier Scottish literary entrepreneurs like William Strahan had made fortunes in London, but eighteenth-century Edinburgh's bookseller-Provost William Creech had a reputation for treating authors meanly. Constable offered them respect as well as cash. The year after he launched the *Edinburgh Review* he signed up Walter Scott, later a business associate. Within a decade Constable had bought the rights to the *Encyclopaedia Britannica*. Called by Cockburn 'the most spirited bookseller that had ever appeared in Scotland', Constable like John Murray was among the first of the great modern publishers.[9] He worked with and encouraged Robert Cadell (1788–1849), later his business partner and Scott's publishing mentor. Scott in turn helped his friend the lawyer and journalist James Ballantyne (1772–1833) set up a printing business in Edinburgh, and aided John Ballantyne (1774–1821), James's novelist brother, to establish himself as a publisher and bookseller. These men belonged to a rapidly expanding Scottish publishing network that extended from newspapers (the *Glasgow Advertiser*, later the *Herald*, had begun in 1783) to book-publishing houses across Lowland and north-eastern Scotland. Between 1800 and 1830 there were about fifty imprints publishing or co-publishing novels in Edinburgh and about ten in Glasgow.

In the west, evangelical ex-weaver William Collins (1789–1853) set up in 1819 as bookseller, printer and publisher with Charles Chalmers, whose brother Thomas (1780–1847) was one of the firm's best-selling authors. Powerful preacher, theologian and social reformer, Thomas Chalmers gave much of his attention to urban industrial poverty, one of the most pressing problems of the age; his books ranged from *The Christian and Civic Economy of Large Towns* (1821) to *On Cruelty to Animals* (1826). Along with Collins's publishing protégé the Reverend Edward Irving (1792–1834), Chalmers was one of many Scottish divines who satisfied and fuelled the wish for improving Christian reading. Chalmers's publisher, Collins, tapped into the newly expanding market for school textbooks, and handed on a very successful business to his son, also called William. The firm's name survives in the present-day New York- and London-based multinational company HarperCollins.

The early nineteenth century was the great age of Scottish publishing. On Burns Night 1817 Edinburgh's *Scotsman* newspaper first appeared, founded by two radically-minded Burnsians, exciseman Charles Maclaren and Fife solicitor William Ritchie. Initially a weekly which sold just 300 copies, their paper was perhaps helped by being denounced by a Scottish peer as an enemy of the government. The *Scotsman* became a daily in 1855 and still exists, but its politics have changed. In the same year as the *Scotsman* started another publishing development was announced by William Blackwood (1776–1834), a bookseller who had set up as a publisher in Edinburgh in 1804. In 1817 at 17 Princes Street he established the *Edinburgh Monthly Magazine* – which soon became the Tory *Blackwood's Edinburgh Magazine*, or 'Maga' – to rival Constable's Whig *Edinburgh Review*. Other journals attempted to join in the fray, but *Blackwood's* was outstandingly successful; as an emblem of high literary ambition, the head of George Buchanan portrayed on the magazine's cover proudly proclaimed Scottish internationalism. Under the editorial team of advocates John Wilson and John Gibson Lockhart (soon to be Scott's son-in-law), and with assistance from James Hogg, *Blackwood's* published in October 1817 the 'Translation from an Ancient Chaldee Manuscript'. Allegedly discovered in Paris's Bibliothèque Nationale, this hoax translation, couched in an Old Testament idiom, was a coded attack on writers associated with the *Edinburgh Review*. It generated not just a storm of literary recriminations –

sufficient to ensure the new magazine's success – but also lawsuits for the literary–legal cabal at the heart of Edinburgh's cultural life.

The Scottish capital was now established as a 'hot' place for writing and gossip about writers. Edinburgh's magazines were read in London, in America and throughout the English-speaking world; the rapidly expanding commercial interests of the British Empire made it possible to distribute journals widely within Britain and abroad. American as well as British, European and Indian books were reviewed, so that, as well as having a strong Scottish provenance, these magazines became the first to be conscious of a global audience. Their success prompted English retaliations, some in kind: 1809 saw the launch of London's Tory *Quarterly Review*, set up by John Murray, son of the London-Scottish publisher of the same name. All these magazines paid authors, often handsomely, as might the publishing houses linked to them. They signal how decisive was the move from patronage to commerce as the 'backer' of authors. The aristocratic Byron might scorn 'sons of song' who 'descend to trade', but most writers wanted the money.[10] Increasingly canny, they changed publishers, wrote for rival magazines, and felt the commercial pressures that convulsed a volatile marketplace. The runaway success of Byron's narrative poems helped drive Scott from verse romances to prose ones. Publishers would more and more suggest to novelists what and even how they might write.

Important customers for fiction were the popular circulating libraries, which liked the standard, three-volume novel format. They wanted work that would appeal to their many female members; in the early nineteenth century, as in the eighteenth, the novel was often associated with women readers as well as women writers. The majority of novels published in the British Isles between 1810 and 1820 were by women, and the same may well have been true of the preceding decade. Women writers attracted women readers. Byron's mother, for instance, was an eager novel reader, and two circulating libraries flourished in Aberdeen when she lived there in the late 1790s. Reading of native and foreign books was on the increase; Greenock, a growing Clyde trading port, boasted a Foreign Library founded in the early nineteenth century. If libraries liked three-volume novels ('three-deckers'), several early nineteenth-century Scottish writers with a penchant for Scottish-accented fiction were happy to supply this demand and succeed in a growing market. Publishing in Edinburgh, Grace Kennedy, author of such three-deckers as *Dunallan*

(1825), had her fiction translated into French, while a German edition of her collected works appeared in the 1830s. Sometimes, as in the case of Margaret Cullen's *Home* (1802), Scottish novelists produced works five volumes long, but not all authors liked the multivolume format, or the three-volume norm. James Hogg and John Galt sometimes ignored it, sometimes wrestled with it. Though magazines certainly serialized entire novels (such as George Robert Gleig's popular military story, *The Subaltern* (1826)), shorter tales and episodes favoured by Hogg, Galt and others were often best suited to journal publication, and the magazine format greatly encouraged the growth of the Scottish short story. Tales might be collected and shoehorned into three volumes later, or might be reworked as novels. Writers used and were shaped by new printing and publishing formats. They kept their eyes on the market.

'L[ockhart] also says that [the London publisher] Colburn has completely revolutionized the book trade with regard to all light literature, and that Murray's books have not sold of late because he will not puff and paragraph like Colburn,' worried Thomas Hamilton, unsure if Blackwood in Edinburgh and Cadell in London were the best publishers to sell his semi-autobiographical novel of Glasgow and army life, *The Youth and Manhood of Cyril Thornton* (1827).[11] Increasing awareness of market sectors for such things as 'light literature' (roughly, popular fiction), and of advertising 'puffs' and the machinery of reviewing made many authors opportunistic, wary and mobile, part of a complex British and international marketplace. Elizabeth Hamilton's popular and influential single-volume *The Cottagers of Glenburnie; A Tale for the Farmer's Ingle-Nook* (1808) was printed by James Ballantyne in Edinburgh and marketed by booksellers in London; it reprinted several times in its year of publication when it was also published in New York, and in 1827 it was translated into German. The same writer's 1804 three-volume *Memoirs of the Life of Agrippina* was printed in Bath for different London firms. John Galt, who wrote for a plethora of firms, including Edinburgh rivals Blackwood and Oliver & Boyd, approached publisher Henry Colburn in London when he needed money, but felt Colburn wanted to influence what his author wrote. He complained about publishers who 'give orders, like an upholsterer for a piece of furniture'.[12] Galt felt that in Edinburgh Blackwood (nicknamed by authors the 'man whose name is as ebony') pressured him into happy endings.[13] Constable suggested subjects to Scott for future novels, though

Scott did not always oblige. Richer and more powerful than Galt, Scott came to use John Ballantyne as his literary agent. He may have been the first Scottish writer to enjoy such a luxury, but he found himself deep in debt after the financial collapse of the publishing house of Constable in 1826.

The roots of that collapse lay in London, not Edinburgh. Increasingly able to exploit United Kingdom and overseas markets, many Scottish publishers, magazines and writers also grew more aware of having to appeal to non-Scottish and, not least, London audiences. Walter Scott would make an Englishman the protagonist of his first novel; the influential Mary Brunton chose an Englishwoman as her heroine in *Discipline* (1814). The *Edinburgh Review* and *Blackwood's Magazine* were closely attuned to London literary gossip and publishing, accounts of which were important to their success. The Edinburgh magazines were shipped south so they would reach London for 'magazine day' on the first of every month, and so be available at the same time as London journals were published.[14] Edinburgh's mighty reviews liked to make use of London-based writers, sometimes emigrant Scots. One of the *Edinburgh Review*'s London contributors, for instance, was James Mill, a shoemaker's son from Angus who published his *History of British India* in 1818, and edited several London magazines; a founder of the new London University and of the *Westminster Gazette*, he was a philosopher who fathered a philosopher, John Stuart Mill. The Empire loomed large in Scottish thought. Internationalism – obvious in the writings of Elizabeth Hamilton, Scott, Galt, and others – was a strength, but also a market demand. Eventually, market forces would play a considerable part in luring Scottish writers to the buzz and blur of London.

''Tis distance lends enchantment to the view,' wrote Glaswegian poet Thomas Campbell (1777–1844) in his still quoted success, *The Pleasures of Hope* (1799).[15] The poem greatly appealed to the English artist J. M. W. Turner, who illustrated Campbell's work, then later the works of Scott. In 1803 Campbell moved to London and made poetic capital out of the expanding Anglophone world. His verse narrative *Gertrude of Wyoming* (1808) presented American scenery he had never seen, while his annotated anthology *Specimens of the British Poets* (1819), produced for Byron's London publisher, John Murray, is a forerunner of today's ubiquitous Norton Anthologies.[16] One of Campbell's best poems, 'Lochiel's Warning', offers an enchanting view of a Wizard who declaims about 'Culloden, that reeks with the blood of the brave', but Campbell, making his money as a journalist and biographer, was not alone in selecting the remunerative 'distance' of London.[17] Among many Scottish literary émigrés, Dumfries-shire-born poet, editor, novelist and biographer Allan Cunningham (1784–1842), a friend of Scott and Hogg, moved to the British capital in 1811 and stayed for three decades, writing novels with titles like *Sir Michael Scott* (1828). His best work in verse anxiously claims a Scottish superiority ('The Thistle's Grown aboon [above] the Rose') or frolics, a little antiquely, with Scottish Jacobite dislike for the Hanoverian George I – 'What the deil hae we got for a King,/ But a wee, wee German lairdie'.[18]

Even if they hankered after Scottish culture and language, ambitious Scots often made for London. Like John Home before him, the young Walter Scott tried to succeed as a dramatist there. Fortunately for Edinburgh, he failed. John Galt spent much time in the 'metropolis'; significantly, for Galt that word meant London, not Edinburgh. Both Lockhart and Jeffrey eventually headed south, where Scotland and Scottish culture could be sold, their allure and authority coming partly from Enlightenment legacies. But post-Ossianic Scotland also carried a tincture of exoticism; its attractiveness lay not just in its judgmental Athens-of-the-North-ism, but also in its perceived wildness, its marginality and even quaintness. All could be exploited, as exotically suggested in Scottish-accented titles from Mary Julia Young's *Donalda; Or, The Witches of Glenshiel, A Caledonian Tale* (1805) to Susan Fraser's *A Winter in Edinburgh; Or the Russian Brothers* (1810). Yet with such exploitation went the danger that in a British state whose capital lay hundreds of miles to the south, writers might heighten Scotland's status as part curiosity, part province, part otherworld.

Byron knew and relished this. Born in London in 1788, he was evacuated to Aberdeen in early infancy, so that his Scottish mother could be closer to her depressive Aberdeenshire relatives, the Gordons of Gight, and further from Byron's father, 'Mad Jack'. In Aberdeen Byron imbibed Calvinism and eros in equally strong doses. He obsessed about his cousin, Mary Duff, and read the Old Testament with his Calvinist nurse May Gray, who taught him masturbation. Considering himself predestined to wickedness, he included in his early, voluminous reading *Zeluco*, the novel by Burns's London-Scottish friend, Dr John Moore. Byron loved *Zeluco*'s dark anti-hero, his 'ungovernable' temper, as

Byron put it, 'as inflamable as gunpowder, bursting into flashes of rage at the slightest provocation'.[19] Schooled at Aberdeen Grammar where, like most nineteenth-century Scottish boys, he spoke Scots in the play-ground but English in the classroom, Byron, attended by the promiscu-ous May Gray who regularly took him to bed with her, left Aberdeen at the age of ten to become an English Lord and public schoolboy, but his Scottish childhood and the ensuing sense of displacement remained vital to him. In his teens he wrote of 'When I rov'd, a young Highlander, o'er the dark heath'. Byron is a Harrovian Highlander, but one equipped with a sense of 'Culloden', 'pibroch', gales and mountains which allows him, when he wishes, to distance himself throughout his work not just from Harrow School but from English mores:

> England! thy beauties are tame and domestic
> To one who has roved o'er the mountains afar:
> Oh for the crags that are wild and majestic!
> The steep frowning glories of dark Loch na Garr.[20]

Titles such as 'Oscar of Alva. A Tale' and 'The Death of Calmar and Orla' indicate that Ossian is one of the strongest presences in Byron's early verse. In 1814, after Byron commended Scott's *Waverley* and identified himself to his correspondent James Hogg as 'half a Scotsman', Hogg was urging Byron that 'A review of your native mountains, of their heights of gray sublimity, and their dark woody glens would now inspire you with more noble enthusiasm than all the fertile and classic shores of Greece.'[21] Byron's Romantic taste for mountain roving and wild, stormy landscapes is articulated convincingly in his early poems of Scotland, before being developed much more fully in a work attuned to European Romanticism, *Childe Harold's Pilgrimage* (1812–18). Arguably Byron's residual Ossianism, as well as Scott's example, strengthened his poetry's pan-European appeal. His first fully-fledged long poem, *English Bards and Scotch Reviewers* (1809), written partly in excoriating reaction against Jeffrey and the *Edinburgh Review*, takes Pope as its satiric master. But Byron's finest long poem, *Don Juan* (1819–24), momentarily returns with a pang of affection to 'Dear Jeffrey, once my most redoubted foe', when Byron declares that 'I am half a Scot by birth, and bred/ A whole one'.[22]

Like so many Scottish Enlightenment works and like Walter Scott's first novel *Waverley* (1814), *Don Juan* encourages the reader to compare

and evaluate different kinds of society. Yet where Scott bonded himself
to a nation and culture, Byron made an epic out of the displacement
that sprang from his childhood. Scotland schooled him less in home, love
and country than in loss of them, and in a dark doctrine of predestination
which the club-footed poet took on board as branding him as one of the
devil's own. Like his admired Burns (whose work supplies the epigraph
for one of Byron's best-selling verse tales, *The Bride of Abydos*), Byron
played the part of the poet as erotic star in an emerging literary culture
of celebrity. The memoirs and confessions of his alter ego, Don Juan,
delight in scandal as they move from lyrical love-making to witty displacement and flux. Don Juan's self might be viewed as atomistically
Humean, or as kaleidoscopic. *Don Juan* is the first major literary work
to mention the kaleidoscope. Invented by the Scottish scientist and writer
Sir David Brewster in 1819, the kaleidoscope's constantly shifting bright
displacements offer a visual analogue to the chatty, shifting movement
of *Don Juan*'s verse:

> Some take a lover, some take drams or prayers,
>   Some mind their household, others dissipation,
> Some run away and but exchange their cares,
>   Losing the advantage of a virtuous station.
> Few changes e'er can better their affairs,
>   Theirs being an unnatural situation,
> From the dull palace to the dirty hovel.
> Some play the devil, and then write a novel.[23]

If the success of Byron's earlier poems helped propel Scott from verse
to the novel, then *Don Juan* works partly as brilliantly novelized verse,
a picaresque poem in which narrator and hero blur and vie for the
reader's attention. Byron's favourite *ottava rima* stanza form, used in
his 'Epistle to Augusta' (1816), in *Beppo* (1818) and *The Vision of
Judgment* (1822) as well as in *Don Juan*, may have come from the
fifteenth-century Italian of Luigi Pulci as mediated in English by John
Hookham Frere, but probably Byron saw it first used at length in
post-Renaissance English in the November 1814 *Edinburgh Review*
when Jeffrey quoted substantial chunks of 'Anster Fair' (1812) by the
Fife poet, linguist and St Andrews professor, William Tennant (1784–
1848). Tennant's poem's verve and tone would have appealed to Byron:
'My pulse beats fire – my pericranium glows,/ Like baker's oven with

poetic heat'.[24] James Hogg wrote to Byron (himself a superlative letter-writer) in 1814 about the 'strength of mind' and 'originality of conception' in Tennant's poem – 'you must by all means see it'.[25] Hogg arranged for a copy to be sent to the future author of *Don Juan*. In the era when, helped by poet Walter Scott, the novel became the dominant literary genre, Byron showed that poetry might still compete. Friend of Scott and Galt, Byron may belong to the poetry of England, but, as Hugh MacDiarmid and T. S. Eliot realized last century, he was also Scottish by formation.

Famously described by Lady Caroline Lamb as 'mad, bad, and dangerous to know', Byron lived much of his life on the continent, dying in 1824 at Missolonghi in Greece where he was engaged in Greek struggles for independence from Turkish rule.[26] He was styled a 'great poet' by John Gibson Lockhart's imaginary letter-writer Peter Morris in Lockhart's pen-portrait of early nineteenth-century Edinburgh culture, *Peter's Letters to his Kinsfolk* (1819), and Francis Jeffrey (who stressed poetry's attraction to the primitive) viewed Byron in 1816 as 'a volcano in the heart of our land'. Byronic lava might be problematic, though, where 'the frailty of woman' was concerned, and Jeffrey also thought Byron guilty of 'perversions of morality'.[27] Safe at the foot of its own extinct volcano, Arthur's Seat, Edinburgh and her 'Scotch reviewers', for all they liked to attack the mad, bad Lord and the southern Cockney School of poets, were on the whole unscathed by Byronic eruption. While the city's magazine culture might boil over in lawsuits, and even occasional duels, when it came to sex, in comparison with the notorious Byron, the native northern literati were generally far better behaved.

They were, though, in a state of creative ferment. Imperial economics, a productive meeting of vernacular speech with Belles Lettres education, and a strong publishing infrastructure may all help explain this, but at its heart is the vitally inexplicable: sheer talent. Three decades – the 1810s, 1820s and 1830s – may be called the golden age of Scottish fiction. The subsequent, and now more globally celebrated, achievements of Dickens, Thackeray, the Brontës, George Eliot and other English Victorian novelists have largely obscured the remarkable Scottish contributions to early nineteenth-century imaginative prose. These contributions were multifarious and concentrated in the opening years of a century we may regard as 'Victorian', but which before Victoria came to the throne in 1837 saw the burgeoning of the Scottish novel in the years around Napoleon's 1815 defeat at Waterloo. Particularly between the death of Jane Austen in 1817 and the publication of Dickens's *Posthumous Papers of the Pickwick Club* in 1836–7, Walter Scott established himself as the single most influential writer there has ever been in the global history of the novel.

Though he certainly did not invent the emergent genre of the historical novel, Scott made it the great imaginative and analytical instrument used by later writers from George Eliot to Leo Tolstoy, and from Balzac to Thomas Hardy. At the same time, preparing the way for Pickwick's electioneering, John Galt wrote the first political novels in English. Grounded, like Scott, in Scottish Enlightenment thinking, Galt developed fiction as 'theoretical history' and produced an impressive range of tales that draw on his experiences of America, Canada and England, as well as on his Scottish family background. While Scott and Galt developed the novel in complementary, if different, directions, the sometimes astounding works of Scott's friend James Hogg outdistanced polite expectations. Drawing on oral as well as textual conventions, Hogg produced the most psychologically shocking of all historical novels, *The Private Memoirs and Confessions of a Justified Sinner* (1824).

Sophisticated postmodern critics may shy away from a label like 'golden age'. Yet that term is worth using. It reminds us that this was not only the era of the remarkable Walter Scott but the period when Scottish authors, with Scott at their head, played a major part in making the novel the dominant literary genre. They also demonstrated more fully than ever before the radical and experimental imaginative possibilities of prose fiction. By around 1820 people everywhere wanted to read Scottish work. Books like the unidentified E. H. H.'s 1819 *The Highlander; or, a Tale of My Landlady* and Sarah Green's waspish *Scotch Novel Reading* (1824) testified to the power of Scott and the heady rush of 'Caledonian mania'. By 1827 Scott had one of his narrators state that 'I am informed that Scotch literature, like Scotch whisky, will be presently laid under a prohibitory duty.'[28] He was joking, but only just.

For fiction readers at the very start of the nineteenth century, though, the remarkable success of novel-writing Scotsmen lay out of sight. Around 1800 the most widely admired new Scottish novelists were female. The lawyer and editor Walter Scott had written no novels, but was acquiring a reputation as a poet, albeit one who 'writes so quick

that he must ... be very fond of money'.[29] In prose fiction Scottish
novels had already begun to explore the imperial connections of an
increasingly powerful Britain. Elizabeth Hamilton (1758–1816) began
her career as a novelist with *Translations of the Letters of a Hindoo
Rajah* (1796), published in London and dedicated to Warren Hastings.
The book's supposedly Indian narrator presents Europeans as treating
Indians fairly, but, as well as noting that 'the people of Great Britain
are, at this day, divided into separate Casts [sic]', he can sound critical
notes: 'unhappy negroes are torn from their country, their friends and
families, for no other purpose, but to cultivate the sugar-cane; a work
of which the lazy Europeans are themselves incapable'.[30]

Belfast-born, Hamilton grew up in Stirlingshire, spent 1788–91 in
London, and settled in Edinburgh. Her brother served in India and did
translation work. To her first novel 'is prefixed a preliminary dissertation
on the history, religion, and manners of the Hindoos' – a not unusual
strategy of mixing fiction with improving fact. Though her prose can be
hard going, with all her emphasis on 'Self Denial', Hamilton stands out
as one of the first Scottish feminists. Modern readers may be struck by the
way in her *Letters on Education* (1801) she imagines 'Mrs Shakespeare',
though that lady is William's mother, rather than the sister later presented by Virginia Woolf in *A Room of One's Own*. A decade before
the publication of *Sense and Sensibility*, Hamilton assures us of Mrs
Shakespeare that 'instead of being a woman of *sensibility* . . . she was a
woman of plain good sense'. It is striking too how Hamilton ranges
across cultures investigating '*Associations producing Contempt for the
Female Character*'.[31] Her curiously researched, classicizing, novelized
Memoirs of the Life of Agrippina, the Wife of Germanicus (1804)
presents itself as a 'biography' which will show the effects of education
in tracing 'the progress of an extraordinary mind' of a woman who
might be styled '*the mother of her country*'.[32]

Like Maria Edgeworth and other women novelists of the time, Hamilton was preoccupied with improvements in education. She shares this
with her friend Hector MacNeill whose *Memoirs of the Life and Travels
of the Late Charles Macpherson, Esq., in Asia, Africa and America*
(1800) is notable not least for its 'Particular Investigation of the Nature,
Treatment, and Possible Improvement, of the Negro', though it warns
that 'benevolence' can lead to 'rebellion'.[33] In her often amusing *Memoirs
of Modern Philosophers* (1800) Elizabeth Hamilton is interested in

'*female philosophers*', in 'Rousseau's system of female education', and in Mary Wollstonecraft.[34] These *Memoirs* enjoyed considerable success, partly perhaps as a result of what modern criticism has called their 'stridently feminist anti-heroine', Bridgetina Botherim.[35] Witty, Hamilton sees the novel as a predominantly female domain. Bridgetina (invented as part of a political and literary battle with the writer Mary Hays) runs over a long list of phrases such as '*Moral sensibility . . . congenial sympathy*' and '*melancholy emotions*' before her text supplies a

Note, for the benefit of Novel-writers. – We here generously present the fair manufacturers in this line with a set of phrases, which, if carefully mixed up with a handful of story, a pretty quantity of moonshine, an old house of any kind, so that it be in sufficient decay, and well tenanted with bats and owls, and two or three ghosts, will make a couple of very neat volumes.[36]

This sort of mockery of the Gothic 'descriptive' and 'sentimental' fiction often associated with North British settings would find its counterpart in Jane Austen's *Northanger Abbey*, but several of the very elements which Hamilton associates with 'fair manufacturers' (i.e., women novelists) would be essential to many of the fictions of Walter Scott and a host of other male writers.

Hamilton, who lets her lower-class characters speak idiomatic Scots, achieved most success with *The Cottagers of Glenburnie; A Tale for the Farmer's Ingle-Nook* (1808). With its independent, widowed heroine, Mrs Mason, who educates and improves the inhabitants of a 'wild' Highland village, this book prepared the way for other Scottish village fictions, including those of John Galt, though it sometimes partakes of the sentimentality which Hamilton elsewhere mocked. Moreover, like Ann Radcliffe's first Gothic novel, though with a different tone, it is one of many works which show how, in Ossian's wake, prose fiction might be attracted into Highland surroundings.

The vividly detailed *Letters from the Mountains* (1806) by Ossian's admirer Mrs Ann Grant of Laggan (1755–1838) argued that the traditions of Highland life had 'extended the women's province both of labour and management'.[37] Shrewd and experienced, Grant had been born to Highland parents in Glasgow. She spent her formative years on the Hudson River near Albany in New York State, and writes as sympathetically about Mohawk culture in her *Memoirs of an American*

Lady (1808) as she does about the Highlanders in the *Letters* written after her return to Scotland. Her American memoirs were among a number of Scottish treatments of that country, ranging from Frances Wright's enthusiastic *Views of Society and Manners in America* (1822) to the less impressed Thomas Hamilton's *Men and Manners in America* (1833). Ann Grant's ambition is evident in her *Essays on the Superstitions of the Highlanders of Scotland* (1811) with its defence of Gaelic culture, but she was no feminist. In response to Mary Wollstonecraft, she argued that

Some women of a good capacity, with the advantage of superior education, have no doubt acted and reasoned more consequentially and judiciously than some weak men; but, take the whole sex through, this seldom happens; and were the principal departments, where strong thinking and acting become necessary, allotted to females, it would evidently happen so much the more rarely, that there would be little room for triumph, and less for inverting the common order of things, to give room for the exercise of female intellect. It sometimes happens, especially in our climate, that a gloomy dismal winter day, when all without and within is comfortless, is succeeded by a beautiful starlight evening, embellished with aurora borealis, as quick, as splendid, and as transient, as the play of the brightest female imagination: of these bad days succeeded by good nights, there may, perhaps, be a dozen in the season.[38]

For Ann Grant an image of breastfeeding women 'membresses' of the House of Lords is the height of absurdity, but she wrote with acuteness about her time as a participant in the lives both of Highlanders and of the inhabitants of the American woods.

Grant's *Letters* were among a growing number of works attending to Highland culture. If Ossian and the poet Scott encouraged this, it was predominantly women who began the fashion for Highland prose fictions. Jane Porter (1776–1850) was born in Durham but spent her formative years in Edinburgh where her mother knew Walter Scott's mother. In 1803, the year she moved to London, Porter made her name with one of the earliest historical novels, *Thaddeus of Warsaw*, which dealt with recent events in Warsaw centred round the Polish nationalist Tadeusz Kosciuszko. She followed this European success with *The Scottish Chiefs* (1810), which interested Scott, was loved by Joanna Baillie, and enjoyed an enthusiastic response in Britain and America. Portraying Wallace and Robert the Bruce among craggy mountains, cliffs and a barren landscape loved by a 'grey-haired bard', this eager 'romance' in prose, dedicated to Thomas Campbell and carrying its epigraph from Ossian, suggested what might be done in a Scottish historical novel.[39] In the same year, the theatrically-minded Walter Scott was helping to arrange the Edinburgh premiere of Joanna Baillie's Highland drama *The Family Legend* (whose rehearsals Scott attended), featuring banqueting, a Highland castle and wild mountain scenery. Audiences applauded the lot.

While her anonymously authored first novel, *Self-Control* (1810) had included such excitements as a North American canoe chase, the Orkney-born Mary Brunton (1778–1818) headed for the Highlands in her second novel, *Discipline* (1814). Living in Bolton, then Edinburgh, with her supportive minister husband, Brunton is a determinedly ethical writer, as her novels' titles suggest. She felt, too, a need to stand up for her chosen genre. Reacting to Scott's 1814 *Waverley*, she wrote in a letter to a woman friend,

Why should an epic or a tragedy be supposed to hold such an exalted place in composition, while a novel is almost a nickname for a book? Does not a novel admit of as noble sentiments – as lively descriptions – as natural character – as perfect unity of action – and a moral as irresistible as either of them? I protest, I think a fiction containing a just representation of human beings and of their actions – a connected, interesting and probable story, conducting to a useful and impressive moral lesson – might be one of the greatest efforts of human genius.[40]

Written four years before Jane Austen published her own praise of prose fiction in chapter five of *Northanger Abbey*, Brunton's words are perhaps the most spirited early nineteenth-century defence of the novel. Brunton's fiction is eminently readable and, though readers can find defects in her work, her admirers have ranged from Austen to Fay Weldon. Brunton sets much of *Discipline* in London, where her mother had been a socialite. She is interested in how women, especially isolated women, learn to survive and develop. She enjoyed reading the Scottish Enlightenment Common Sense philosopher Thomas Reid, and the historian William Robertson. Brunton began to study Gaelic and relished what she described to Joanna Baillie as 'melancholy, romantic' Highland scenery.[41] Ellen Percy, the English first-person narrator of *Discipline*, is almost carried off to Scotland by the rakish Lord Frederick. She manages to resist, but feels 'as friendless as the first outcast that was driven forth a wanderer'.[42] Growing in strength of character, but having rejected the advances of the strong, reliable Maitland, a West India merchant, Ellen later struggles to make a living in Edinburgh. She studies some Gaelic, and finds a job as a governess, but is imprisoned in an asylum thanks to a vengeful mistress. Eventually she gravitates to the Highlands where, 'Though I no longer had leisure to pursue my Gaelic studies', Ellen likes to hear Gaelic spoken, sings Gaelic songs, and treasures the Ossianic.[43] Readers encounter Gaelic phrases both in the original and in translation. All ends happily when Maitland is revealed as Henry Graham, Highland hero and brother of the girl who has become Ellen's closest friend. The Highlands in this novel are a place of healing. Its last words are a paean to virtue, but also suggest the virtue of Gaelic:

Having in my early days seized the enjoyments which selfish pleasure can bestow, I might now compare them with those of enlarged affections, of useful employment, of relaxations truly social, of lofty contemplation, of devout thankfulness, of glorious hope. I might compare them! – but the Lowland tongue wants energy for the contrast.[44]

To imply the superiority of Gaelic would have been unthinkable a century earlier, but by 1814 things Highland had acquired a bon ton. Completing *Discipline*, Brunton was disturbed by the publication of Scott's *Waverley*. She recognized that novel's quality, but worried it might make her Highland setting seem merely fashionable.

Scott's novels did confirm the fashionable status of the Highlands, but he was not the first sophisticated male Scottish novelist to do this. As a St Andrews University student, the Highlander Robert Bisset (1759–1805) read Hutcheson, Hume, and Edmund Burke's 1757 *Philosophical Enquiry into the Origin of our Ideas of the Sublime and Beautiful*. Bisset also devoured lots of plays, novels including *Don Quixote* and Sarah Fielding's 1744 inheritance romance *David Simple*, and Englishman James Ray's recent *Compleat History of the Rebellion from its first Rise in 1745; to its total suppression at the glorious battle of Culloden*.[45] In his first, virulently anti-Jacobin novel, *Douglas; or, The Highlander* (1800), which seems partly autobiographical, Bisset summons up the allure of John Home's earlier drama *Douglas* and some Ossianic resonances, but he sends his Highland hero to St Andrews, then to Edinburgh University. In Edinburgh Charles Douglas studies with Dugald Stewart and with Adam Ferguson who encourages him to take up English law. Shifting to London and involving an inheritance plot as well as arguments in favour of Burke's philosophy, *Douglas* deals with Highland, Lowland Scottish and metropolitan English cultures. It shows how a Highlander may still enjoy and be proud of Highland traditions yet at the same time progress in an Enlightened, commercial age.

Written by another law student educated in the academia of the Scottish Enlightenment, Scott's *Waverley* would engage with just such concerns, but would move its hero towards rather than away from the Highlands. Scott's fiction also developed narrative techniques and subjects explored by other earlier writers. If cultural comparison and intersocietal Anglo-Scottish prejudice were major themes for the Smollett of *Humphry Clinker* (1771), they also figured in works such as the English novelist Charlotte Smith's *The Old Manor House* (1793). That book's wandering protagonist goes to America, starts to sympathize with the 'primitive' Native Americans, and begins to question English attitudes towards them. Scott is known to have admired this work, just as he is known to have read *Humphry Clinker*. After the plaintive Ossian and the female-authored Highland prose narratives of Elizabeth Hamilton, Mary Brunton and others, Scott more than anyone else re-masculinized this terrain.

Scott also re-masculinized the entire genre of the historical novel in what might seem a predatory way. Katie Trumpener has pointed out that even the title of *Waverley* comes from the name of a character, Waverly, in Charlotte Smith's *Desmond* (1792), whose name had also been adopted for the wavering Sir William Waverley in Jane West's English Civil War tale *The Loyalists: An Historical Novel* (1812). West's ruined 'Waverley Hall' becomes Scott's 'Waverley Manor' and contributes other details to *Waverley*.[46] Scott did acknowledge a debt to the Irishwoman Maria Edgeworth, whose *Castle Rackrent* (1800) was an early example of a thoroughly articulated regional fiction and has been called 'the first true historical novel in English'.[47] Contributing to the genre of the 'national tale' in which a visiting outsider reveals a local way of life and which is closely bound up with the growth of the 'historical novel', Edgeworth's Irish model was easily exportable as is shown by such titles as *Caledonia; or, The Stranger in Scotland: A National Tale, in Four Volumes. Illustrative of the State of Civil Society and Domestic Manners in Scotland, at the Present Time* (1810). Clearly

Scott is indebted to many precursors in the British Isles and perhaps on the continent, including those Scottish women historical and regional novelists who were his immediate predecessors and contemporaries. Though Scott's authority, productivity and imaginative power tended to 'brand' the Highlands and the historical novel as his own, masculine territories, several Scottish women, most notably Christian Johnstone (1781–1857) and Susan Ferrier (1782–1854), continued the tradition of female-authored Highland novels.

From 1812, when she and her husband took over the *Inverness Courier*, Johnstone, unusually for a woman at this time, worked as a journalist. Eventually, in the 1830s, she became in effect the first woman to edit a major British literary periodical, *Tait's Edinburgh Magazine*. Johnstone was professional, energetic and versatile. As well as editing tales of Ireland and of Edinburgh, she produced educational works, and wrote a popular cookbook. Among her several novels, the best known is *Clan-Albin, A National Tale* (1815). As an Inverness journalist, Johnstone knew Highland life. Her first book was *The Saxon and the Gael: or, The Northern Metropolis: Including a View of the Lowland and Highland Character* (1814). Her fiction blends a journalist's eye for such matters as Highland depopulation and urban squalor with a Gothic imagination in full flight over such spectral northern landscapes as the secluded island of Eleenalin where 'the romantic swell or dying murmur of distant wind instruments were [sic] undulating in every breeze'.[48] With weak interpolated poems supposedly translated from the Gaelic, and some rather stronger female characters, *Clan-Albin* takes its orphan Highland hero to Ireland and Spain, laments a fading Highland culture, and looks askance at Lowland commercial values. Its twenty-first-century editor finds it 'excitingly at odds with the whole concept of union and patriotism' that is seen to predominate in Scott's fiction.[49] It is, though, very heavy going.

Susan Ferrier's Highlands are funnier. With their 'dingy turnip fields ... raw and cold', they are also less Romantically grand.[50] In her first novel, *Marriage* (1818), Ferrier, the very well-connected Edinburgh woman of letters, appears to have learned from the example of her friend Walter Scott. Ferrier, however, angles her fiction from a consciously feminine perspective, concerned with female education and ethical values of the sort prized by Mary Brunton. The Highland scenes of *Marriage* are impressively described, but at least as arresting is

Ferrier's presentation of the absurdly self-preening diminutive Highland laird, the ironically named Sir Sampson Maclaughlan, whose piping is less pibroch than pique when his wife suggests he was born with 'a cradle cough':

'My dear Lady Maclaughlan!' screamed Sir Sampson, in a shrill pipe, as he made an effort to raise himself, and rescue his cough from this aspersion; 'how can you persist in saying so, when I have told you so often it proceeds entirely from a cold caught a few years ago, when I assured his Majesty at —' Here a violent relapse carried the conclusion of the sentence along with it.[51]

So much for heroic Highland masculinity. Ferrier is well aware that she writes from the home of '*belles lettres*', the nation now viewed as 'Scotland, the land of poetry and romance', and she likes to play with that notion.[52] Her characters read Scott, Byron and Thomas Campbell, but their creator is often successful at introducing into their territory something of the eye and ear of Austen. Scott thought *Marriage* 'very lively', and suggested that it would prompt him to 'retire from the field' of novels set in Scotland.[53] *Marriage* can entertain as well as functioning as something of a handbook aimed at young women. Able to deal with modern English as well as Scottish life, Ferrier continued to mix humour and sharp observation in her later novels *The Inheritance* (1824) and *Destiny* (1831). Unlike Scott, she chose the present, not the past, as her customary fictional milieu, and so played to that strength of shrewd, often humorous observation evident in her letters. Though little discussed, they deserve modern attention and provide ready, subtly nuanced enjoyment. It is striking how, even in her late twenties, the quick-witted, unmarried Ferrier in Edinburgh begins to think of herself as 'doomed to doze away my days by the side of my solitary fire and to spend my nights in the tender intercourse of all the old tabbies in the town'.[54]

Ferrier's impact, though, was small in comparison with that of Scott. No other novelist, not even James Joyce, so impressed the world or his own country. Thanks to Scott, modern Edinburgh is the only capital city on the planet to have named its main railway station after a first novel. As you walk up out of Waverley station, one of the first landmarks you see towering over the city centre is the Scott Monument, a Gothic stone space rocket neatly parked off Princes Street. Walter Scott made his mark on nineteenth-century Scotland like no one else. 'After 1814,' writes William St Clair, 'what subscribers to circulating libraries read most were Waverley novels . . . When a ship bringing the first copies of the latest Waverley novel from Edinburgh docked in London, the books would be distributed by noon the next day, even breaking the rules against working on the sabbath.'[55] Scott's fiction colonized the nineteenth century. In the Glasgow suburb of Shawlands street after street is christened after his prose 'romances'. From paddle-steamers to pubs, villas to vistas, he and his works gave names to the substance of his country – to the productions of modern technology as well as to more ancient sights – so much so that by the mid-nineteenth century the poet Alexander Smith suggested that Scotland should be spelled with two *t*'s.

Nor was Scott's impact confined to Caledonia. Even before he turned to the novel, he had a keen sense of an international Scottish audience, particularly a male one, diffused through empire, so that

> thy wild tales, romantic Caledon,
> Wake keen remembrance in each hardy son.
> Whether on India's burning coasts he toil,
> Or till Acadia's winter-fetter'd soil,
> He hears with throbbing heart and moisten'd eyes,
> And, as he hears, what dear illusions rise![56]

Yet if he was alert to the tearful nostalgia of expatriates keen for 'illusions', Scott could also appeal to non-Scots whose knowledge of 'romantic Caledon' might be confined to the pages of Ossian. That earlier Scottish work, as Scott put it in the 1805 *Edinburgh Review*, was so impressive for its power 'to interest the admirers of poetry through all Europe'.[57] Scott's poetry, then, later, his prose fiction, had a similarly international effect, and were designed to do so. Developing the 'national tale' and the 'historical novel', his prose fictions offered a model for the articulation of national characteristics which, in an age of European nationalism, fascinated and influenced writers in France, Spain, Germany, Italy, Russia and elsewhere. Scott's works sold remarkably. His 1810 narrative poem *The Lady of the Lake* sold 20,000 copies in its first year, and was novelized (though not by Scott) within weeks of publication. *Waverley* went through four editions in four months. Scott commanded vast publisher's advances.

Though rightly regarded as a historical novelist, Scott is also a geographical one. Scottish Enlightenment works which he admired, such as David Macpherson's 'excellent historical map' of 1796, *Geographical*

Illustrations of Scottish History, had fused terrain and historiography.[58] So had the writings of Robert Sibbald and Sir John Sinclair's *Statistical Account of Scotland*; in 1804, just before Scott turned his poetic attention to the Highlands, Sinclair published his *Observations on the Proprieties of Preserving the Dress, the Language, the Poetry, the Music and the Customs of the Ancient Inhabitants of Scotland*, a work which encouraged cultural conservation in the Highland region. What Scott did as a poet, and more remarkably as a novelist, was to write a substantial series of fictions which scripted and gave a heightened imaginative identity to a geographical area. Most notably, but by no means always, that area was Scotland. To some extent Edgeworth had essayed such a project in Ireland, but Scott was the first novelist to do this on a grand scale. Soon, though, Dickens would do something similar for London; Fenimore Cooper, known in the nineteenth century as 'the American Scott', did the same for frontier America in his Leatherstocking Tales; Thomas Hardy, towards the end of the century, scripted Wessex. Today we are so familiar with the notion that fiction writers produce a series of works which identify them with and give identity to a particular territory – whether 'actual' (Joyce's Dublin) or 'made up' (Faulkner's Yoknapatawpha County) – that we take the process for granted. Scott started it. In providing the most authoritative impetus for this way of writing – the prose equivalent of being an Ossianic or Burnsian national bard – Scott is of signal importance. Outside the English-speaking world novelists from Manzoni in Italy to Stendhal in France looked to him as their model in their wish to dramatize a national, territorial past with which readers could imaginatively identify.

Scott's novels were translated widely and very, very quickly. Read in their hundreds of thousands, they were also disseminated through other media, particularly the stage. Andrew Hook has pointed out how 'On the same evening in Paris in 1827 the theatre-goer could have chosen to attend one of four Scott plays, all derived from different Waverley Novels'.[59] Many of Scott's best-known titles – such as *Waverley*, *Rob Roy* and *The Heart of Mid-Lothian* – belong to novels set in Scotland. However, he also wrote about the Middle East in *The Talisman*, about India in *Chronicles of the Canongate*, about England in *Kenilworth* and *Woodstock*, and about continental Europe in a number of late works. Producing twenty-six novels and a vast quantity of other writings in a mere seventeen years, Scott was not only the most productive fiction writer of his age but also the first novelist in any language who wrote for a global audience. His imagination is preoccupied by how cultural differences may be maintained in the face of the forces we now characterize as 'imperialism' and 'globalization'. Scott is fascinated by the eras and zones where the tectonic plates of cultures – whether Highland and Lowland, 'wild' and mercantile, Christian and Islamic, or small states and large – grate against one another, producing drama but also the search for reconciliation. Yet, for all that, in what seems a reaction against his enormous Romantic and Victorian popularity, he is little read today.

One reason is the sheer bulk of his work. 'A big book is a bad book,' wrote Callimachus from the ancient library at Alexandria, and many later readers have agreed. Most of Scott's novels are individually large, and, in their revised versions, bulked out with notes and prefaces. In their earliest versions, they were less prolix. Yet his works are so many. Even before Scott began to write novels, Henry Cockburn felt that 'there can be little doubt that ten or twelve presses are groaning to feed the public maw with his crops'.[60] To stockpile the original editions of all the books with which Scott was involved as author, translator, prefacer or editor would fill a barn with several hundred volumes. In addition to his better-known works, he produced (with help) an authoritative nineteen-volume edition of *The Life and Works of John Dryden* (1808); he edited legions of historical memoirs, wrote introductions to the works of most of the male and female writers of note who had preceded him in English; he planned on a megalomaniac scale.

Scott was a compulsive drawer-up of literary projects; proposals for editions of 'at least a hundred volumes, to be published at the rate of ten a-year' seemed to come naturally to him.[61] With financial interests in printing and publishing, he operated on an industrial scale, sometimes treating his collaborators with scant acknowledgement. Yet, though his prose can show the strain, his productions are far from hackwork. While it may not rival Boswell's *Johnson*, John Sutherland suggests, for instance, that 'Scott's life of Dryden is probably the first social–critical biography of any British author.'[62] Scott, an admirer of Boswell, made sure that Scottish literature continued to develop, even pioneer, the art of literary biography. Boswell's recent example may have encouraged in Scott a sense of the self as more psychologically complex, more assembled out of Humean fragments, more negotiated with others than earlier novelists had realized. Boswell, and Scott's own experience as a biographer, may have taught Scott the novelist. Yet such is the huge extent of Scott's work that this biographical accomplishment has gone virtually unnoticed. Repeatedly, oddly arcane aspects of Scott's work turn out to be innovative and fruitful. His interest in Icelandic and northern European translations, for instance, about which he wrote in the 1806 *Edinburgh Review*, not only encouraged a readership for the Scottish antiquary Robert Jamieson's 1806 Danish translations, but prepared the way for later Scottish translators of Icelandic work such as Ebenezer Henderson in 1818, then the later nineteenth-century Mary Gordon and the lexicographer William Craigie. Every interest of Walter Scott can seem both influential and prescient.

Even to focus on Scott's fictional output is a challenge. The most recent, meticulously edited edition of his 'Waverley Novels', the Edinburgh Edition completed in the first decade of the twenty-first century, runs to thirty volumes. It is worth setting out the bare table of contents of that edition. Not only does it show the order and scale of Scott's fictions, most of which run to about 400 pages of modern authorial text; it also makes clear that, with all his other commitments, this Edinburgh lawyer could publish up to three novels a year:

Waverley (1814); *Guy Mannering* (1815); *The Antiquary* (1816); *The Black Dwarf* (1816); *The Tale of Old Mortality* (1816); *Rob Roy* (1818); *The Heart of Mid-Lothian* (1818); *The Bride of Lammermoor* (1819); *A Legend of Montrose* (1819); *Ivanhoe* (1820); *The Monastery* (1820); *The Abbot* (1820); *Kenilworth* (1821); *The Pirate* (1822); *The Fortunes of Nigel* (1822); *Peveril of the Peak* (1822); *Quentin Durward* (1823); *Saint Ronan's Well* (1824); *Redgauntlet* (1824); *The Betrothed* (1825); *The Talisman* (1825); *Woodstock* (1826); *Chronicles of the Canongate* (1827); *The Fair Maid of Perth* (1828); *Anne of Geierstein* (1829); *Count Robert of Paris* (1831); *Castle Dangerous* (1831); *Stories from 'The Keepsake'* (1828); *Introductions and Notes from the 'Magnum Opus' edition of 1829–33* (two volumes).[63]

A 'shopping list' of Scott's novels set out in this way suggests something of the sheer, daunting scale of his achievement in fiction over a mere decade and a half. Though it uses the earlier, barer texts of the novels as its base, the modern edition, running to thirty volumes, is filled with scholarly commentary and notes. As his novels were reissued in the early nineteenth century, Scott added more and more 'paratexts' –

prefaces, afterwords, and notes on history, geography and sources. He clad the fiction with historical commentaries, narratives within narratives and cultural comparisons, almost as if he were turning his novels into postmodern historiography. Playing off both real and fictitious editors, historians and commentators against one another, this author wrote compulsively, unevenly, and, it seems, endlessly. It is hard to know where to start.

The untitled Walter Scott was born in 1771. His father was an Edinburgh lawyer, his mother a well-read professor's daughter. His surroundings were comfortably Edinburgh upper-middle-class. Yet infantile paralysis left Scott permanently lame, and long childhood holidays took him into the very different setting of the rural Borders where his fascination with stories of often violent local conflicts began. To complicate things further, Scott was taken as a young child to Bath where he was entranced by the 'witchery' of a visit to the theatre to see *As You Like It*, and by meetings with the Scottish dramatist John Home.[64] Scott's father's antiquarian friend George Constable developed the boy's Shakespearian and historical enthusiasms. Scott was schooled with Adam Smith's heir at the Edinburgh High School, then briefly at Kelso where he devoured works from the circulating library and enjoyed Thomas Percy's best-selling 1765 three-volume anthology *Reliques of Ancient English Poetry*. Going to Edinburgh University, Scott acquired a Scottish Enlightenment education. His best friend was the son of the comparative historian Adam Ferguson, at whose house the teenage Scott met the young poet Robert Burns.

Scott's admiration for Adam Ferguson's 'classic elegance, strength of reasoning, and clearness of detail' hint at how much he relished Scottish Enlightenment values; for *Guy Mannering* he wrote small 'fragments', pen-portraits of Ferguson, John Home, Monboddo and other Enlightenment luminaries.[65] In Scott's own mature fictions his Enlightenment analytical inheritance would sometimes meld awkwardly with Gothic and Romantic tastes. At Edinburgh University Scott read an essay before Principal William Robertson, the celebrated historian, was 'rivetted' by the lectures of the philosopher Dugald Stewart and, in the year of the Fall of the Bastille, attended the 'Universal History' lectures of Alexander Fraser Tytler. An exponent of German dramatic translation, Tytler in his historical lectures compared different stages of society and included a paean to the British Constitution.[66] More than any other novelist, Scott would propound an ideology of Britishness. In so doing he continued the British enthusiasm articulated by Smollett, as well as by men like Tytler. Britishness hardly interested English novelists. They wrote about England and Englishness instead. But Britishness is a recurrent topic in Scottish fiction until the early twentieth century when Scott's admirer, the imperialist John Buchan, provided its swansong in his works. Scott, like Buchan, was patriotically Scottish, but unswerving in his loyalty to the British state. That loyalty he learned in his youth.

Called to the Bar in 1792 at the start of his twenties, Scott the Scoto-Briton had a long career as an established lawyer. From 1799, thanks to the Duke of Buccleuch whose favour he courted, Scott worked as a sheriff. He sought to make his literary mark first in his late twenties as a translator and dramatist with a special interest in German Romanticism. This might seem to some a long way from the Scottish Enlightenment, but it was the same German Romanticism which had impressed Henry Mackenzie, Scott's teacher Tytler, and other Edinburgh literati rooted in Enlightenment thought. Scott's first book, *The Chase, and William and Helen, Two Ballads from the German* (1796) of Gottfried Bürger, was praised by Dugald Stewart in Edinburgh, but made little headway beyond. Scott translated a series of German Romantic dramas by Schiller, Goethe and others, publishing in 1799 the first English translation-cum-elaboration of Goethe's medievalizing historical melodrama *Götz von Berlichingen*. He wrote his own historical melodrama, *The House of Aspen*. Violent, atmospheric and tinged with the supernatural, despite the encouragement of the Gothic writer M. G. Lewis it failed to reach the London stage.

Although Scott would re-invent himself as editor, poet, critic, biographer and novelist, his early dramatic aspirations and continuing enthusiasm for German and British theatre are a signal part of his make-up. He relished what he called in an 1800 letter to Bishop Percy the 'Dramatis Personae' of Border ballads.[67] His first substantial, best-selling narrative poem, *The Lay of the Last Minstrel* (1805), has, as its title suggests, an Ossianic dimension, but with some sections set out as characters' dramatic speeches, it also contains aspects of historical verse drama in its treatment of violent Borders lore. The *Lay* drew on Scott's editing of *The Minstrelsy of the Scottish Border* (1802–3), an anthology of Border ballads, in three volumes 'humbly following' the plan of Percy's trio.[68] Many of the *Minstrelsy*'s ballads were collected and transcribed for

Scott by John Leyden, James Hogg and others, and a good number written or recast by Scott himself.

A frustrated soldier of Border descent, in 1794 the Tory Scott had cudgelled Republican students in an Edinburgh theatre when they mocked the British national anthem. Fancying himself as an anti-democratic cavalryman, he set up the Royal Edinburgh Light Dragoons in 1797. James Hogg would later comment on Scott's enthusiasm for 'the feudal stile' and on his 'too high devotion for titled rank'.[69] An ardent monarchist, Scott got his baronetcy in 1818, not a moment too soon. He liked the feudal violence and wild allure of Border history, making much of his own family's part in it. In the *Lay* the name 'Scott', even 'Walter Scott', is dropped a lot. *Marmion, A Tale of Flodden Field* (1808) revisits the Borders and, as well as presenting a convoluted, medievalizing Gothic narrative (forged letters, gory deaths, treacherous knights), it acts as a kind of anthology of Scott's own verse. Revealing are two lines from the Highland narrative poem *The Lady of the Lake*, published two years later. There, after a description of romantic Highland landscape, Scott describes it all as

> So wondrous wild, the whole might seem
> The scenery of a fairy dream.[70]

This, in a nutshell, can be the effect of Scott's verse. After the initial exhilaration wears off, many modern readers are left rubbing their eyes. Most of Scott's contemporaries, though, were entranced. Increasingly overshadowed by the wilder and more nimble verse tales of Byron, Scott's poetic dream continued through such long historical poems as *Rokeby* (1813), *The Lord of the Isles* (1815) and *Harold the Dauntless* (1817). In these, as in *The Lady of the Lake*, Scottish landscape with its attendant history is presented in a heightened imaginative state, shading into dramatic fantasy. The words 'scene' and 'scenery', much used in the late eighteenth century, could mean, as they still can, both a theatrical 'set' and a landscape vista. For Scott the two were often fused. Much later, in *The Fair Maid of Perth* (1828), there occurs a passage which draws on his own first visit to the Highlands:

I recollect pulling up the reins without meaning to do so, and gazing on the scene before me as if I had been afraid it would shift like those in a theatre before I could distinctly observe its different parts, or convince myself that what I saw was real. Since that hour, and the period is now more than fifty years past, the recollection of that inimitable landscape, has possessed the strongest influence over my mind . . .[71]

For Scott, landscape and history became theatre. His 1799 version of Goethe's *Goetz of Berlichingen* had gone far beyond the original; the twenty-first-century commentator Kenneth Haynes shrewdly points out that Scott's elaboration of Goethe's drama was formative since Goethe in *Götz*, like Scott in his later fiction, shows how 'in the course of history one way of life, one society, one set of values gives way to another'.[72] Scott and his early audiences loved the kinds of theatrical exaggeration and complication popular in the Gothic tales and melodramas of his youth. The Gothic, when added to history like a fizzy pill, seemed invincibly theatrical.

In a sense, Scott never stopped writing poetic drama. His novels are peppered with sub-Shakespearian epigraphs attributed to many an 'Old Play', but really made up by Scott himself, the unstoppable creator of a theatrical past. If *Halidon Hill* (1822), a dramatic sketch, was a flop, this hardly mattered, since other dramatists made versions of Scott a mainstay of the nineteenth-century Scottish stage. Notoriously, Scott choreographed and costumed 'the King's Jaunt', George IV's 1822 visit to Edinburgh. Everyone sported tartan, including the King, who wore flesh-coloured tights under his kilt; the radical poet Alexander Rodger (1784–1846) mocked the proceedings in Scots verse, while Byron cocked a snook in *Don Juan* and John Galt thought they provoked 'the depths of absurdity'.[73] Having published *Waverley* and its successor novels anonymously, so that the identity of the 'Great Unknown' who was 'The Author of Waverley' became the most celebrated literary mystery of the age, the theatrical Scott revealed his authorship 'at a public meeting, called for establishing a professional Theatrical Fund in Edinburgh' on 23 February 1827, likening himself to the masked Harlequin.[74] At his best, Scott has been called 'the single Shakespearian talent of the English novel'.[75] His works can have Shakespearian amplitude, character, atmosphere, humour and drama, but there is also a staginess at the heart of much of his fiction that can make modern readers uneasy. If early cinema welcomed Scott's work to the screen, it may have been because at times he can operate like Cecil B. De Mille. The Scott of performance loves spectaculars and set pieces – jousts, tournaments, mistaken identities, hidden familial bonds. Landscape, history, national identity and personal relations for Scott can all become kinds of performance. Sometimes, this can make each seem phoney. However, the sense of performance, like Hume's self which, out of discrete perceptions must be imagined into being, makes imagination all the more central. Certainly it is as an imaginative writer, not as a historian, that Scott should be regarded and judged. For him individual selves and even national character are to be imagined and re-imagined, sometimes echoically, re-invented in performance.

The eponymous hero of Scott's second novel, *Guy Mannering* (1815), is viewed in terms of a long quotation from a play by Schiller; to save time, Scott just sent the whole play to his printer, asking him to 'Copy from p. 82 top of page'.[76] A pirate in *The Pirate* (1822) chooses to change his name to that of an actor. The villagers of *Saint Ronan's Well* (1824), Scott's only novel set in the present, put much of their energy into 'theatricals', rummaging their 'circulating library' for plays, before deciding on *A Midsummer Night's Dream*.[77] When the Highland widow in Scott's moving story of that title exclaims over her dead son, 'My beautiful! – my brave!' she speaks 'the language of nature' which 'arose from the heart', but her words, as the narrator points out, are also those of 'my old friend, John Home' in his best-known play, *Douglas*.[78] History and fiction, for Scott, echo the theatre. As in the Gothic fiction of Ann Radcliffe, Shakespeare is often quoted. *The Bride of Lammermoor* (1819), rich in Shakespearian allusions, is in part a Scottish *Romeo and Juliet*, and Scott several times reminds readers of lines from that play.

Like an eager nineteenth-century director, Scott, elaborator of Goethe's *Götz*, has a taste for pageants and tableaux. Many a Waverley Novel reads like an opera waiting to happen, and over a hundred actual operas were made from Scott's prose romances, the most celebrated by Donizetti and Bizet. For good and ill, Scott's fundamental theatricality has reached far beyond him. When at American presidential inaugurations a choir sings 'Hail to the Chief', it uses words from a song in *The Lady of the Lake* 'intended', Scott wrote, 'as an imitation of the *jorrams*, or boat songs of the Highlanders'.[79]

Americans are right to settle for selected extracts from Scott's poetry. Phenomenally fashionable in its own day, when a whole tourist industry developed to take visitors to the scenes of Scott's poems, it is unlikely ever again to achieve a wide readership. The post-Ossianic taste for wild scenery has remained, but Scott's verse, like Ossianic prose, now seems tarnished: too churned out, too samey, too, too long. In extract, though, it represents a classic statement of familiar sentiments, and a ringing formulation of Scotland, one which remains alive, not least abroad.

> Breathes there the man, with soul so dead,
> Who never to himself hath said,
>   This is my own, my native land!
>
> . . . .
>
> O Caledonia! stern and wild,
> Meet nurse for a poetic child!
> Land of brown heath and shaggy wood,
> Land of the mountain and the flood . . .[80]

At his best, Scott touches what he called 'the wizard note'. Nicknamed 'The Wizard of the North', he makes magnificent poetic play with scenery and place names, whether 'the wild heaths of Uam-Var' or 'the bold cliffs of Benvenue'.[81] The Victorian anthologist Palgrave particularly admired Scott for his handling of such names, which often function as a distinctive linguistic marker in Scottish poets' work, carrying like leylines through the verse the embedded music of older etymologies and languages.

In his novels, or prose 'romances' as he called them, Scott's sense of Gothic fairytale, theatrical spectacle and history fused with landscape persists. But they are more strongly underpinned by that Enlightenment sense of comparative history which he had learned in his youth and developed through his own extensive historical researches. This historical reading underwrites the text, and is often quoted, alluded to, echoed or footnoted. At its best, it contributes a densely textured context for the action; at its weakest, the effect is of pedantically reconditioned goods. Scott had an unusually strong sense of his own weaknesses, however, and often makes fun of them, both directly and indirectly.

Begun in 1805 and abandoned; revived in 1810; eventually reworked and published in 1814, *Waverley* is both more and less than an adventure. Less, perhaps, to many modern readers because its learnedly companionable style relies on points of reference which have faded from our compass. Yet more because in addition to narrative surprise the story contains shrewd and sympathetic insights into comparative cultural

history and an ironically humorous awareness of the dangers of roman-
ticizing, as well as the pleasures of adventure and romance. Ossianically,
Edward Waverley is the 'last' of his 'race', the house of Waverley. A
naively bookish young Englishman brought up on the 'romantic fiction'
of Spenser and other poets, he travels north to Scotland during the
Jacobite rebellion of 1745. From the Lowland, Scots-speaking culture
of the decaying village of Tully-veolan and its pedantic laird Baron
Bradwardine, Waverley moves north into the Gaelic mistbound 'heathy
and savage mountains' that surround 'the hold of a Highland robber'.[82]
The third-person narrator prompts the impressionable Waverley (and
the reader) to compare and evaluate these different cultures. Waverley
'wavers' between them like a sympathetic cultural broker. He even
changes sides between the opposing Jacobite and Hanoverian forces. As
the narrative progresses, Waverley has to choose between the alluring
Flora with her Highland minstrelsy, and the more practically-minded
Lowland Rose, whom he eventually marries. The action of the novel
touches on the Battle of Culloden and its aftermath which includes the
execution of Waverley's Jacobite friend and mentor, the Highlander
MacIvor, 'the last Vich Ian Vohr'.[83] That note of Ossianic lastness calls
for sympathy towards the defeated Highland culture, yet views it as
belonging to a romantic past. It is in the Hanoverian commercial present
that Waverley and Rose Bradwardine, Englishman and Scotswoman,
celebrate a personal and political British union. Waverley himself may
have been the last of his race, but unlike MacIvor he has learned to
change, adapt and survive.

Linguistically, *Waverley* is interesting for its sense of moving through
and across different speech communities, drawing on English, Scots,
Latin, Gaelic and French for lexical effects. This was a technique which
Scott would develop, one that is born out of the history of Scottish
literature itself. Neither Elizabeth Hamilton nor Mary Brunton had gone
anything like as far in terms of varying linguistic texture. One English
reviewer of Scott's second novel, *Guy Mannering*, complained the book
was 'too often written in a language unintelligible to all except the
Scotch', but most readers rose to the challenge.[84] Scott wanted to give a
sense of local language, even linguistic exoticism. His characters'
speeches (especially those in Scots, in which Scott delighted) move the
text away from standard English, though the principal narrator's tone
retains the hierarchical authority of an educated English voice. Scott

found a way of using Scotland's linguistic spectrum in fiction, even more widely than recent poets had done in verse. He might be accused by Little Englanders of writing a 'dark dialect of Anglified Erse', but in fact he knew very little Gaelic, and quotes almost none in the original.[85] He had to borrow a Gaelic Grammar while writing *Chronicles of the Canongate* in 1826, but, loving language and variety, he relished un-English accents that let his fiction speak of cultural difference. When writing his 'Eastern tale', 'The Surgeon's Daughter', he applied to friends for 'a little Hindhanee [Hindustani], a small seasoning of curry powder'.[86]

If some modern readers may be uncomfortable about the way Scott cooked up cultures, they may also admire his range and daring. He was fascinated both by cultural minutiae and by wider processes of cultural change which he detected not only abroad but right on his well-swept doorstep. 'There is no European nation which, within the course of half a century, or little more, has undergone so complete a change as this kingdom of Scotland,' wrote Scott in his postscript to *Waverley*.[87] He had a genuine, lingering fondness for recent and distant history; later he wrote accounts of Scotland and of France, aimed primarily at children. Scott encouraged Patrick Fraser Tytler (1791–1849), son of his old history professor, to write a huge *History of Scotland* (1828–43). With the younger Tytler Scott helped set up the Bannatyne Club (1823–61) which republished early Scottish texts, many edited by its secretary, the antiquarian David Laing (1793–1878), Scotland's first thoroughgoing bibliographer. Modern visitors to Edinburgh Castle are regaled with the story of how Scott rediscovered there Scotland's ancient royal regalia.

The anonymously authored *Waverley* was recognized almost as soon as it appeared as among the crown jewels of Scottish literature. It was, Mary Brunton wrote in 1814, 'by far the most splendid exhibition of talent in the novel way which has appeared since the days of Fielding and Smollett'.[88] *Waverley* certainly draws on historiography such as the dramatist John Home's 1802 *History of the Rebellion in the Year 1745*, but the book's inventiveness is what gives it spirit. Edinburgh's eighteenth-century Hugh Blair had viewed novels as belonging to a genre called 'fictitious history'. Developing the historical novel, Scott gave Blair's term a new twist. His fiction has a considerable narrative drive, but also an anthropological dimension in its detailed juxtaposition of different societies and cultures. Like Smollett, Charlotte Smith and others, Scott highlights intersocietal prejudice. Echoing phrasing from the first scene of Shakespeare's *Coriolanus*, *Waverley*'s English Colonel Talbot inveighs against the barbarian Highlanders,

Let them stay in their own barren mountains, and puff and swell, and hang their bonnets on the horns of the moon, if they have a mind: but what business have they to come where people wear breeches, and speak an intelligible language? I mean intelligible in comparison with their gibberish, for even the Lowlanders talk a kind of English little better than the negroes in Jamaica.[89]

Most readers are likely to feel differently, because Scott has given them sympathetic access to Highlanders and Lowlanders. Like David Hume's self, or like the earlier eighteenth-century traveller protagonist created by the writer Scott in 1817 called 'the well-known Chevalier Ramsay', Scott's 'passive' heroes often appear to lack a fixed, core identity. Yet this makes them all the more effective lenses for viewing the societies and dramatic environments they pass through.[90] Scott has a Romantic liking for scapegoated outsiders whose way of life risks being consigned to the past – whether Vich Ian Vohr in *Waverley*, the characterfully Gothic gipsy Meg Merrilees in *Guy Mannering*, or the abbot in the Scottish Reformation novels *The Monastery* (1820) and *The Abbot* (1820). He writes of these people with attraction and imaginative excitement, yet implies that, unable or refusing to change, they must be consigned to what the title of his 1816 novel of Covenanting religious strife calls *Old Mortality*.

In *A Legend of the Wars of Montrose* (1819) Scott quotes Dryden's theatrical lines about 'the noble savage'.[91] He liked to portray noble savages, and exploit them from a historically safe distance. History could be turned into theatre, the dead recast for the entertainment of the present, then allowed to die back into the landscape with eloquent, dramatic gestures. So Ranald, the vengeful Highland leader of the 'Children of the Mist', dies a 'savage' death that pre-empts the farewell speeches of Fenimore Cooper's, and then later Hollywood's, Indians.

The deep frost mist which had long settled upon the top of the mountains, was now rolling down each rugged glen and gully, where the craggy ridges shewed their black and irregular outline, like desert islands rising above the ocean of vapour. 'Spirit of the Mist!' said Ranald MacEagh, 'called by our race our father, and our preserver – receive into thy tabernacle of clouds, when this pang is over, him who in life thou hast so often sheltered.' So saying, he sunk back into the arms of those who upheld him, spoke no further word, but turned his face to the wall . . .[92]

For the Wizard of the North, books were a way of conjuring up the past, giving it for a time a new and living body. As he aged and his fictions ranged beyond Scotland – to the England of medieval and Elizabethan times in *Ivanhoe* and *Kenilworth*, to the medieval France of *Quentin Durward*, or the Constantinople of *Count Robert of Paris* – Scott became increasingly fascinated by the relationship between the power of the imaginative maker, the novelist, and that of the makers of history, both potent historical personages and historiographers. So the historians Philipe Des Comines in *Quentin Durward* and Anna Comnena in *Count Robert of Paris* become characters in Scott's fiction; his Des Comines even lectures the French King on the feudal system.

As well as authoring histories of Scotland and of France (his wife's native country), Scott wrote an enormous biography of Napoleon. Published in 1827, it begins with a full-scale, hostile account of the French Revolution, anticipating the work of Thomas Carlyle. At Abbotsford by the River Tweed Scott developed an impressive Gothic house, characteristically equipped with the gleaming mod con of gas lighting. There Scott, who wrote more about France than any other major British creative writer, collected an array of historical relics, including Napoleon's pen. Abbotsford is one of the most magnificently revealing of all writers' houses open to the public. Planning his own literary campaigns within its walls – part baronial stronghold, part research library – Scott, without losing his sense of humour, sought to exercise over the past the overwhelming power which his near contemporary Napoleon fought to wield in the European present.

Yet Scott, lawyer and literary man of business, lived and worked in gas-lit modernity. Over and again his fictions show that, for all the past is a rich source of imaginative pleasure and nourishment, individuals and societies that wish to survive and develop cannot turn back the clock. Emblematic is his treatment of Baron Bradwardine's mansion at Tully-veolan in *Waverley*. Surely deriving from the fiction of Charlotte Smith, with its stone bear sculptures Tully-veolan is also clearly based on the ancient Scottish Border house of Traquair whose gateposts are adorned with just such creatures. When Bonnie Prince Charlie's forces left Traquair, the gates were closed, never to be reopened until a Stuart was once more on the British throne. They have remained closed to this day. In the twenty-first century the main driveway between the gates and Traquair house is grassed over so that visitors have to make their way in through a side entrance. This makes for an impressive Jacobite anecdote, but it is not the story of *Waverley*. In that novel Bradwardine's dilapidated mansion is restored, all its bears intact, thanks to the increased wealth that comes with a Hanoverian British constitution. Where Burns might have complained about being bought and sold for English gold, Scott, despite his strong sense of Scottish cultural distinctiveness, takes the money and writes. When the re-instated Baron Bradwardine utters the words 'An auld sang' (a phrase associated with the passing away of an older Scotland and its Parliament), he refers not to lost ancient glories but to a modern rent book.[93]

Scott was used to financial calculation. He came to refer to the Waverley Novels as a joint stock company. It was one in which lots of earlier narratives, oral and written, had been invested, grown, and yielded spectacular results. While Scott was a major shareholder in several actual companies with interests ranging from publishing to gas supply, he was also, imaginatively speaking, his own board of directors. Scott the historian, Scott the biographer, Scott the poet, Scott the dramatist, Scott the Gothically-inclined novelist and Scott the editor were only some of those who sat round the boardroom table. Sometimes they divided their imaginative labour, and sometimes they collaborated to manufacture the tales and romances. Often the directors struggled for ascendancy. The company they ran produced fiction, but also versions of Walter Scott. Time after time, from *The Antiquary* to the Dryden-obsessed bard of *The Pirate*, Scott presents parodies of himself, whether as 'dryasdust' antiquarian, or wordy narrator, telling 'such damnable long-winded stories'.[94] Scott tried, not always successfully, through his characters and stand-in narrators, to poke fun at his own weaknesses, thereby turning them into strengths. Readers may lose patience with his bagginess when he anthologizes umpteen supposedly Old Norse prophetic poems in *The Pirate* or conjures up a mysterious female ghost in *The Monastery*. Yet at his strongest, as in *The Heart of Mid-Lothian*, he melds action and historical sweep. With a marked ethical passion Scott pursues a quest to recognize cultural difference as far as is possible in a unified society.

Scott's insight into such topics as childlessness may seem remarkable, but is simply a measure of his imaginative gift. If his world is, on the whole, masculinized, his protagonists tend to be young men who are still a bit wet behind the ears. His strongest characters are often peripheral and doomed, as if the emerging modern world is not quite fit for heroes. Extremes, however imaginatively exciting, are to be renounced; sexuality, while acknowledged, is never dwelt on. Episcopalian son of a Calvinist father, Scott could write both about Scotland's Protestant and its Catholic past with sympathetic engagement, but ultimately he is averse to the fanaticisms of either side. He can use the phrase 'rigidly righteous' (once deployed by Burns against extreme Protestants) in the context of medieval Scottish Catholicism, while writing with some empathy about the Catholic milieu of Mary, Queen of Scots.[95] Meg Merrilees may be his most striking female creation, but Jeanie Deans, the virtuous, determined and resourceful heroine of *The Heart of Mid-Lothian* (a novel set round Edinburgh's 1736 Porteous Riots), is his most convincing, proving that he can do better than crudely naming his female characters after flowers, as he does in *Waverley*. Often Scott's most admired characters have a comic side: the imperial businessman Nicol Jarvie in *Rob Roy*, fully and babblingly conscious of his merits as a Glasgow bailie, is rather taken aback to confront a roguish Highland robber and his equally formidable wife. Yet, however striking Scott's individual characters may be, this novelist's great strength is an ability to incorporate them into a broad canvas. That, most of all, justifies the adjective 'Shakespearian', and is a crucial factor which made Scott's work so influential.

Scott himself had a heroic dimension which went beyond that of Tory cavalryman. He wrote or dictated his novels despite significant periods of illness. Suddenly, in 1826, he faced financial ruin when the publishing house of Constable collapsed. Taking on far more than his share, Scott agreed to shoulder the outstanding debts, calculated at £126,000, a huge sum in the early nineteenth century. Exceptional arrangements were made to protect his lairdly lifestyle. Scott lived on in Abbotsford, keeping his wine cellar of several thousand bottles, yet showed courage in his determination to write himself out of debt: 'I will involve no friend either rich or poor – My own right hand shall do it . . .' With regard to his creditors, the feudally-minded novelist wrote in his *Journal* (published after his death) that 'I will be their vassal for life and dig in the mine of my imagina[tion] to find diamonds (or what may sell for such).'[96] He had sunk in a few days from laird to vassal.

Just months later, in May 1826, Scott's wife, Charlotte Carpenter, died. His published *Journal*, a moving and intimate, though hardly objective work, conveys something of his suffering:

26 FRIDAY A rough morning . . . the clouds seem[d] accumulating in the wildest masses both on the Eildon Hills and other mountains in the distance . . .

Dull, dropping, cheerless the day has been. I cared not to [be] carrying my own gloom to the girls and so sate in my own room dawdling with old papers which awaked as many stings as if they had been the nest of fifty scorpions. Then the silence seemed so absolute – my poor Charlotte would have been in the [room] half a score of times to see if the fire burnd and to ask a hundred kind questions – Well – that is over – and if it cannot be forgotten must be rememberd with patience.

27 SATURDAY A sleepless night – It is time I should be up and be doing and a sleepless night sometimes furnishes good ideas. Alas! I have no companion now with whom I can communicate to relieve the loneliness of these watches of the night. But I must not fail myself and my family and the necessity of exertion becomes apparent.[97]

At that very moment, the worst of his life, Scott began work on a book which, though neglected, may be one of his most appealing to modern readers. *Chronicles of the Canongate* (1827) is not a novel but a number of shorter fictions linked by the connecting narrative of an anxious aspiring writer, Chrystal Croftangry, whose family has faced financial ruin. Rather than living on in a corner of his old country estate, Croftangry now stays in Edinburgh, looked after by his old Highland landlady, the Gaelic-speaking Janet MacElroy, whose own native glen is left 'desolate'.[98] Set in Scotland, England and India in the later eighteenth century, Croftangry's stories, like his own career, speak in the era of British imperial expansion about the need to avoid trying to return to an old way of life. They chronicle, too, efforts made to preserve honour in the face of disgrace. In 'The Highland Widow' a proud mother drugs her son in an attempt to avoid his betraying his father's memory by becoming a British soldier; but the boy dies, executed as a military deserter. 'The Two Drovers', set in the north of England, has a Highland cattleman beaten up by his English friend after a business misunderstanding; humiliated, the Highlander, Robin Oig, stays true to his own traditional code and revenges himself with a knife, even though it leads to his arrest and execution. In 'The Surgeon's Daughter' efforts to maintain old attachments again lead to disaster; the girl of the story is narrowly saved from ruin in India where her devious childhood sweetheart ends up in spectacular disgrace. After all her adventures she is regarded by her imperceptive neighbours back in Scotland as an unremarkable old lady who has spent her life at home spinning wool.

These linked 'chronicles' have a sharp sense of irony. From the spare, fatalistic account of Robin Oig to the more exotic, but still richly realized, presentation of an India which Scott had never seen, the writing has panache. The tales' darkness is offset by Croftangry's accounts of his life. Like Dickens, Scott, once mocked as 'Mar-Mee-Ong, A *Visionary* Arabian Story-Teller', knew and admired the linked, episodic *Arabian Nights*.[99] He often referred to his one-time assistant Henry Weber's 1812 *Tales of the East*. On an even larger scale than that of the *Arabian Nights*, Scott tried to use introductory narrators and series titles such as 'Tales of my Landlord' to link entire novels in strands. In the smaller compass of the 1827 first series of *Chronicles of the Canongate* this device functions more convincingly. As do Oriental story collections, and groups of tales or episodes by some of his Scottish contemporaries, these chronicles work both independently and as an ensemble. None yields quite his full 'Shakespearian' diorama, but the *Chronicles* offer modern readers one of Scott's best and most approachable works. Part of their appeal to a twenty-first-century audience may be related to the fact that they also comprise the book of Scott's which comes closest to the juxtaposed tales of his friend James Hogg.

For two centuries Hogg's works lay in Scott's shadow. Then in the late twentieth and early twenty-first centuries the vast Stirling/South Carolina edition of his writings (many out of print since the early nineteenth century) restored a sense of his protean vitality. Hogg's strength is his unpigeonholeable variety, an alert refusal to be pinned down by conventional expectations. Corpses sit up. Decorum veers into disturbance. The conventions of print narrative are disrupted by the raciness of spoken story. Hogg's energy flares most along and across faultlines. To young writers, his advice, as refracted through his invented 'old French monk', was to 'borrow the fire and vigour of an early period of society, when a nation is verging from barbarism into civilization'. Ossian and Hugh Blair might have approved, but neither ever sounded like Hogg. 'I dislike all fine and splendid writing in prose' was his confident pronouncement. As for those 'Scotticisms' so diligently purged by the would-be arbiters of Scottish Enlightenment taste, 'I never guard against their introduction.'[100]

Yet the same James Hogg delighted in the narrative tricksiness of *Tristram Shandy* and wrote the most telling literary parodies of his time. Like other nineteenth-century working class writers, he learned through mimicry. He can 'do' the voices of Scott, Macpherson, Henryson and others in verse or prose. At its best his mimicry has a subversive note as he unpicks fine writing from the inside, searching for what it might mean to 'sing to please myself alone'. Hogg comes to recognize that his own imaginative 'self' is (again Hume may lie in the background) protean and dynamic rather than fixed:

> Yes I'll be querulous, or boon,   *gracious*
> Flow with the tide, change with the moon . . .[101]

Born in the Borders, in Ettrick Forest, in 1770, Hogg came from a part of Scotland south of Edinburgh whose hills (Hogg liked to call them mountains) are now sites for telecommunications masts. Especially in winter, when the snow lies thick in the glens, the area can seem remote. In comparison with the carpeted literary salons of early nineteenth-century Edinburgh's Georgian New Town, Hogg's bleak uplands and dark 'cleuchs' (ravines) were another world. There, among bare feet and dark, low-lintelled, mud-floored bothies, Hogg grew up as a farm servant. Cows, sheep and shite were his daily work, and he remembered often 'sitting in the bield [shelter] of a craig [crag], wet to the skin, and chumping up my dinner of dry cheese and bread'.[102] As a boy, Hogg learned to write, then forgot the skill, so that he had to relearn several years later how to form the letters of words. He called himself an illiterate, but loved and was nourished by folktales and oral poems. Hogg's grandfather Will Laidlaw (1691–1775) was 'the last man of this wild region, who heard, saw, and conversed with the fairies'.[103] Hogg portrayed his mother, Margaret Laidlaw, as 'a living miscellany of old songs' and a great chanter of ballads, not afraid to reproach Sheriff Walter Scott when in 1801 he came to call and ask her for material which he might publish:

'there war never ane o' my sangs prentit till ye prentit them yoursel', an' ye hae spoilt them awthegither. They were made for singing an' no for reading; but ye hae broken the charm now, an' they'll never be sung mair. An' the worst thing of a', they're nouther right spell'd nor right setten down.' . . . Scott answered with a hearty laugh, and the quotation of a stanza from Wordsworth, on which my mother gave him a hearty rap on the knee with her open hand, and said, 'Ye'll find, however, that it is a' true that I'm tellin' ye.' My mother has been too true a prophetess, for from that day to this, these songs, which were the amusement of every winter evening, have never been sung more.[104]

Here, as oral and textual culture clash, Hogg records the encounter. When his characters speak in dialect they stake a claim to truth, rather than putting on show eccentric comedy or nostalgia. He relishes his mother's resolute, lippy resistance to the Wordsworth-quoting gentleman. Proud of his own background, he has, like his mother, a wariness about how the well-to-do might come and skim off his culture's material just to add colour to their books. Yet Hogg himself wrote down, reworked, published and sold (with limited success) the tales he had grown up with. Helped by William Laidlaw, later Scott's estate manager, Hogg educated himself by using the good library of Blackhouse Farm, where he was shepherding in the 1790s. Hogg was a real Borders shepherd who read Allan Ramsay's *Gentle Shepherd* and joined a rural literary club. He started to publish poems, craving recognition as a writer, while also treasuring the status of 'Nature's unstaid erratick child'.[105]

For lower-class poets without powerful connections, literary life could be unforgiving. Scott may have romanticized the 'wild', blind storyteller Wandering Willie, whose tale is one of the highlights of *Redgauntlet*, but the real partially-sighted Dumfriesshire balladeer Wandering Wull (William Nicholson, 1782–1849), poet of 'Aiken Drum', struggled to live as a travelling rural packman, and died in exhausted poverty. In industrialized Paisley, west of Glasgow, weaver Robert Tannahill (1774–1810) hoped, like Hogg, to become a Burns-like bard. Collecting songs and helping to found Paisley's Burns Club in 1803, he managed to get some of his work printed, but, finding little support, drowned himself in a local canal. Like Hogg, Tannahill wrote well in Scots vernacular about corners where the limelight never reaches,

While dowless Eild, in poortith cauld,   *resourceless Age; poverty*
 Is lanely left tae stan the stoure.[106]   *endure the storm*

Hogg knew his own ambitions made life hard. As a working shepherd, he authored a manual about how to look after sheep. Then he made a hash of things as a farmer. He was spurred as an ambitious poet by hearing 'Tam o' Shanter' recited in 1797, with the result that his *Scottish Pastorals* (1801) and *The Mountain Bard* (1807) were attempts to succeed Burns. Yet there were times when Hogg felt that 'the people of Ettrick ... shun all intercourse with me', and by 1809 he had been rejected by his native community.[107] They distrusted his poetic pretensions, and, knowing he had made a mess of farming, refused him further work as a shepherd. Cold-shouldered by the friends he had grown up among, Hogg at the age of forty was a failure. He had some small literary reputation, but not nearly enough. He urgently needed money, work, company. He had to re-invent himself.

Moving to Edinburgh in 1810, Hogg found no magazine would pay him for his writing. He was trying hard to publish his collection of poems, *The Forest Minstrel*, whose title suggests his eager ear for the market. James Beattie's *The Minstrel* (1771–4), presenting a primitive-sophisticated poet, was still quoted as a Scottish classic, while *The Lay of the Last Minstrel* was a recent best-seller. Hogg's *Forest Minstrel* would win him some patronage, but sold badly. In trying to establish his own magazine, *The Spy*, he sought to set up a significant vehicle for his writing, one whose profits would go directly into his pocket. The journal was at once his outlet and his income stream.

To start with, no publisher or printer would touch it. Hogg hustled. He was told he needed sponsorship from a bookseller. Eventually he found a little-known radical Edinburgh printer, James Robertson, who was willing to produce the small magazine to Hogg's design. Hogg plotted daily with Robertson in 'a dark house in the Cowgate, where we drank whisky and ate rolls with a number of printers, the dirtiest and leanest-looking men I had ever seen'.[108] Robertson thought that the countryman Hogg was simply a go-between used by the real, anonymous editor of *The Spy*, and Hogg was happy to adopt this role. In the magazine itself, he developed his 'Spy' persona. The Spy is presented as an elderly Highland bachelor only recently arrived in Edinburgh. He is a failed preacher, failed farmer, failed poet, whose solution has been to become instead 'a Spy upon the manners, customs, and particular characters of all ranks of people, and all ranks of authors in particular'.[109] More spikily alien than Addison's comfortable Spectator, the Spy is cut off in the metropolis, 'alone in the midst of my species; or rather like a cat in a large family of men, women, and children, to whose joys it bears witness, without being able to partake of them'.[110] The Spy, then, is in some ways close to the provincial Hogg who has just arrived in the capital. Yet he is also sufficiently different (in age, native language and point of origin) to allow Hogg to develop another self that can diverge from as well as interact with his own. *The Spy* ran for exactly twelve months. In so doing, it demonstrated that Hogg was a year-round professional writer. Later, Hogg would run farming and writing careers in tandem. He would go on being patronized, admonished, helped and strengthened, but at the age of forty-one he had come of age as an author, and he knew it.

With the invention of the Spy, Hogg set off on the road that would lead to his greatest work, *The Private Memoirs and Confessions of a Justified Sinner* (1824), a marvellous pas de deux of self and other, whose title, like that of *The Spy*, teeters between concealment and revelation. In its little eight-page issues, *The Spy* plays with points of view and narratives that draw on odd perspectives. In one, to which Hogg would return later in his collection of *Winter Evening Tales* (1820), a preacher is viewed as a devil, the ultimate Bad Shepherd. As the persona of the Spy is played with in his magazine, Hogg discovers what it is to be an author. The figure of the Spy is both familiar and elusive, vitally independent. While anticipating, however distantly, the shape-changings of the *Justified Sinner*, *The Spy* also served a more immediate purpose. Its first issue's epigraph from Burns conjures up that bard's own position as an insider-outsider in Edinburgh society. Hogg, who invited and received the nickname 'The Ettrick Shepherd', still wished to be seen as successor to Scotland's ploughman poet. He plotted a pricey 'anniversary dinner to the memory of Burns in Edin.' and, like Burns, he could play Edinburgh at its own games, while remaining a 'man of independent mind'.[111] As Burns had done, Hogg sought to write in a variety of voices, some bonded to popular oral tradition, others distinctively textual. His development as a writer involves finding not his voice, but his voices. In his polyvocality he belongs with Burns, Dunbar, Drummond, MacDiarmid and many other Scottish writers. *The Spy* was Hogg's sound-box and echo-chamber. Sometimes quietly pious, sometimes boisterously noisy, Hogg's voices greeted and confounded the citizens of Auld Reekie.

Often those citizens were affronted. Several subscribers cancelled after the indelicacy of a story involving a bastard child, while the 'Epitaph on

a Living Character' whose body 'Will scream like a goat at the grand
resurrection' was rightly considered disturbing.[112] Yet Hogg's own
poetry, even in his well-received, medievalizing fantasy narrative *The
Queen's Wake* (1813) with its 'Kilmeny' who mysteriously goes 'up the
glen' and into another world, is often disappointing.[113] At his quirky
poetic best, Hogg trips us into the visionary, as when in a 'Balloon song'
a poet glimpses 'The Witch o' Fife' heading

> Away, away, o'er mountain an' main,
>   To sing at the morning's rosy yett;   *gate*
> An' water my mare at its fountain clear, –
>   But I see her yet, I see her yet.
> Away, thou bonny witch o' Fife,
>   On foam of the air to heave an' flit,
> An' little reck thou of a poet's life,
>   For he sees thee yet, he sees thee yet.[114]

It's hard to know quite what's going on in this short poem of inspiration
from an era which happily mixed ballooning with Gothic superstition,
but its rhythms are lithe and convincing. Hogg collected and reshaped
verse in his *Jacobite Relics of Scotland* (1819–21), whose best-known
song is 'Charlie is my Darling' with its celebration of 'The young
Chevalier'.[115] Murray Pittock points out how Hogg's 'editorial act modified the [Jacobite song] tradition into an accepted corpus of printed
texts.'[116] Following Burns and Scott, Hogg also anthologized Scotland,
bringing together in his oeuvre Highland and Lowland materials as well
as different genres. If Scotland was no longer a nation state, it was
certainly an internationally recognized body of writing, collected,
refashioned, resung.

Some of Hogg's best work lies not in his many imitations but in sheer
spoof. The outsider who went on to write for *Blackwood's Edinburgh
Magazine*, and to number Edinburgh's great and good among his literary
friends, loved hoaxes. He claimed to be behind the publication in *Blackwood's* in 1817 of that 'Chaldee Manuscript' which satirized *Edinburgh
Review* authors, and which caused such uproar that it was later withdrawn from reprints. Just as deadly in its aim was another 1817 work,
Hogg's *Poetic Mirror*, published anonymously in London. According to
its preface, the book was compiled by an editor who had been grateful
to receive work from 'each of the principal living bards of Britain'.[117]

Scott, Coleridge, Byron, Wordsworth, Southey, and (a nice, characteristic touch) Hogg appear among the favoured. Hogg, though, had written
the lot himself. A few aromatically Wordsworthian lines from 'The Flying
Tailor' (supposedly extracted from the Great Man's ever-ongoing long
poem, *The Recluse*) show Hogg's sniper-like attentiveness:

> A pair
> Of breeches to his philosophic eye
> Were not what unto other folks they seem,
> Mere simple breeches, but in them he saw
> The symbol of the soul – mysterious, high
> Hieroglyphics! such as Egypt's Priest
> Adored upon the holy Pyramid . . .[118]

And so on for many more lines of 'wise philosophy'. Scott's son-in-law
J. G. Lockhart, the Irishman William McGinn and Professor John Wilson
(aka 'Christopher North'), luminaries of Edinburgh's literary establishment and supposed friends of Hogg, gave the hoaxer and mimic more
than a taste of his own medicine by running a series in *Blackwood's*
between the early 1820s and the mid-1830s called 'Noctes Ambrosianae'
(Nights in Ambrose's tavern), apparent transcripts of sometimes less
than ambrosial literary get-togethers at which one 'Ettrick Shepherd'
jaws in broad Scots about 'turnips', sheep' and 'colleys'. Surrounded by
an otherwise upper-crust English-speaking company of authors (including Edinburgh resident Thomas De Quincey, Byron, and Christopher
North himself), the often shrewd Shepherd complains of 'universal
plagiarism' and eventually swallows a brown-winged fishing fly.[119] For
Hogg this famous, long-running series meant that he was preceded
everywhere by a doppelgänger – the caricature 'personality' of the *Blackwood's* 'Noctes' – whose exaggerated boorishness a global public took
as a portrait of the real Hogg. Sometimes, set up in this way by middle-
and upper-class contemporaries in the 'Noctes' and elsewhere, the much-
punned-against Hogg felt his second self as an affliction. As early as
1821 his pain is evident in a letter to Scott:

I am neither a drunkard nor an idiot nor a monster of nature – Nor am I so
imbecile as never to have written a word of grammar in my life.[120]

By presenting the spoof conversations of the 'Noctes', *Blackwood's
Magazine* both entertained its readers and let them feel they shared

top-table literary high jinks. Like Boswell's work, the 'Noctes' helped prepare the way for interviews with living writers, a fashion which developed later in the nineteenth century and still persists. The 'Noctes' also alluded to other articles in the magazine, to contemporary events, books and personalities; using the magazine format to the full, this serial was in some ways a precursor of modern soap operas, satirical news round-ups, and chat shows. With mingled admiration and condescension the *Blackwood's* journalists mimicked Hogg the mimic.

Hogg's link to mimicry was his blessing and his curse. Working with and speaking Scots, he could be regarded as a bit of a Burns soundalike; collecting Border lore, he might appear a member of Sir Walter's feudal retinue. The Hoggs and the Scotts were old Border families, but the Scotts had always been the social superiors; for much of his career Hogg's writing conducted a sometimes parodic interrogation of Scott's work. Though he may have worked on it as early as 1813, what has been called Hogg's first novel, *The Brownie of Bodsbeck*, was not published until 1818. Set in the seventeenth century, this historical fiction's sympathetic treatment of the Covenanters was seen in the shadow of *Old Mortality* (1816) where Scott presented Covenanters (in a manner described by Byron as 'exquisite') as fanatical bigots.[121] If Scott ameliorated the violence done by the Royalist Earl of Claverhouse to those Protestant Covenanters who opposed Charles II's Episcopalian polity, Hogg presents 'Bloody' Claverhouse as a persecutor. To Hogg's repressive aristocrat a broad Scots voice might be speaking 'the language of the Moguls'. To Hogg's Romantic imagination the Covenanters, driven on to the moors as they try to live and worship, are personified by the 'Brownie', a being supposed demonic, but eventually revealed as a human refugee when, hiding in his cave, he protests eloquently,

'You see here before you, sir,' said the little hunchbacked figure, 'a wretched human remnant of that long persecuted, and now nearly annihilated sect, the covenanted reformers of the west of Scotland. We were expelled from our homes, and at last hunted from our native mountains like wolves, for none of our friends durst shelter any of us on their grounds, on pain of death.'[122]

If for Scott such a remnant would have to be consigned to the past, Hogg sees it as linked to the present. Where *Old Mortality*, with ironic aplomb, allows its readers a concluding 'glimpse of sunshine', raw hurt pervades Hogg's story to the end.[123] For both writers society and understanding are made dynamic through conflict, but where Scott's imagination makes for reconciliations, Hogg's emphasizes divisions. Neatness for Hogg, like fine writing, seems false.

Sometimes this can make Hogg's work seem wearisome or clumsy. Trying several times to justify the sprawling narrative structure of his medievalizing 'border romance', *The Three Perils of Man: War, Women and Witchcraft* (1822), he writes of there being 'so many truths', but his speechifying lords and ladies sound monotonously false.[124] Better is the treatment of the devilish 'wizard' Michael Scott, surely another of Hogg's many digs at the modern Wizard of the North whose *Lay of the Last Minstrel* partly undergirds Hogg's prose here. In what is probably a riposte to Scott's 1819 *A Legend of Montrose*, Hogg in *Tales of the Wars of Montrose* (1835) ends the long tale 'Some Remarkable Passages in the Life of an Edinburgh Baillie, Written by Himself' by having the protagonist buried 'at the Marquis of Huntly's feet', but it is not clear whether the feet belong to the older Marquis (mentor of the Baillie) or to his son (the Baillie's foe). Though in Hogg's best work radical uncertainties are richly unsettling, on some occasions they just seem careless. Rejected, bowdlerized or uncollected, Hogg's writings suffered at the hands of editors and hostile reviewers who misunderstood his talent. But the reviewers were not always wrong.

Hogg's finest extended narratives are *The Three Perils of Woman; or Love, Leasing, and Jealousy* (1823), and *The Private Memoirs and Confessions of a Justified Sinner* (1824). Though little read in the nineteenth century, the latter is now acknowledged as a masterpiece, and the former as a remarkable book. Neither is easy to categorize, though in different ways each deals with the limitations of the desire for order.

Two quite distinct tales make up *The Three Perils of Woman*. 'Peril First. *Love*' tells the story of Gatty Bell whose repressive sense of decorum leads her to hide and deny her love for the Highlander McIon; thinking himself spurned, McIon becomes engaged to Gatty's cousin Cherubina. When they realize Gatty's true feelings, McIon and Cherubina agree not to marry, but Cherubina pines to death and Gatty, now Mrs McIon, is so upset that she is committed to an asylum. Though she recovers and some measure of domestic harmony returns, the reader is haunted by having seen the heroine as 'a face without the least gleam of mind – a face of mere idiotism, in the very lowest state of debasement'. Addressed by Hogg to 'my beloved countrywomen', the novel borrows considerably from Brunton's *Discipline*, but shows that strict discipline alone does not make for happiness. Part of the process of Gatty's recovery is her perhaps Humean, perhaps Christian acknowledgement that 'My life is a mystery to myself.'[125] Hogg had a strong sense of mystery, treasuring 'not the theory of dreams, but the dreams themselves', as he once put it.[126] He can offer, but prefers to mimic and subvert, neat explanatory frameworks. He likes to rasp the world of Enlightenment rationality against the supernatural. Buoyantly he presents the day-to-day life of a Scottish girl with her 'worsted stockings' and farmer father who talks incessantly of sheep; but the gaiety of household life can veer suddenly into darkness, circling vertiginously from comedy to horror.

> I like that way of telling a story exceedingly. Just to go always round and round my hero, in the same way as the moon keeps moving round the sun; thus darkening my plot on the one side of him, and enlightening it on the other, thereby displaying both the *lights* and *shadows* of Scottish life.[127]

Whatever one thinks of Hogg's astronomy, his prose can seem powerfully and disturbingly lunar as it rings the emotional changes. No doubt the passage just quoted gives an intertextual wink to establishment darling Professor John Wilson's *Lights and Shadows of Scottish Life* (1818), with its often soppy stories of Highlands and Lowlands; Hogg wants something more probing than Wilson's belated sentimentalism.

Hogg's second narrative in *The Three Perils of Woman* deals with 'Leasing' (Lying) and jealousy in eighteenth-century Scotland. The Highland housemaid Sally, servant of a lecherous Kirk minister, thinks she can manipulate local men and events, but she and those dear to her end up dead or ruined in the aftermath of Culloden. Sally cannot order things just as she wishes; nor is history itself, with its attendant 'carnage' and 'devastations', powered by codes of progressive order. Where Scott the lawyer's *Waverley* passes through elegy to reconciliation and progress, the unsettling 'spy' Hogg has a different sense of both personal and historical truth:

> There were many things happened to the valiant conquerors of the Highlands in 1746 that were fairly hushed up, there being none afterwards that dared to publish or avow them. But there is no reason why these should die. For my part,

I like to rake them up whenever I can get a story that lies within twenty miles of them, and, for all my incidents, I appeal to the records of families, and the truth of history.[128]

'The truth of history' in Hogg's work is filled with conflict, frequently hard to fathom. The title page of his great stereoscopic historical novel pronounces it to be *The Private Memoirs and Confessions of a Justified Sinner: written by Himself: with a Detail of Curious Traditionary Facts, and other Evidence, by the Editor*. As that title suggests, the book is split into two principal sections; 'The Editor's Narrative' is followed by the sinner's own 'memoirs'. In a piece of technical daring, each narrative goes over many of the same events, but from a different perspective. Clearly the sinner is a subjective narrator, but the editor's opening words, 'It appears from tradition', hint that he too may be less than objectively reliable. A final coda further destabilizes our interpretation of the 'evidence' presented. 'What can this work be?' it begins. Then, calling attention to an apparently germane letter in *Blackwood's* by one James Hogg, it quotes a respected authority who exclaims, 'God knows! Hogg has imposed as ingenious lies on the public ere now.'[129]

Hogg's novel, arguably the most unforgettable English-language fiction of its age, sold only 500 copies of its first edition at full price. Few understood it. Yet it was written a little after De Quincey's *Confessions of an English Opium Eater* at a time when a writer in *Blackwood's* had claimed 'this is confessedly the age of confession' in literature, and while Hogg's friend Robert Gillies was translating E. T. A. Hoffmann's German Gothic doppelgänger tale, *The Devil's Elixir*.[130] Set before the 1707 Union, Hogg's divided story concerns Robert Wringhim, educated in the tenets of strict Calvinism, who comes to believe that he is one of the 'just', a member of the elect whom God has set aside to be saved. Guided by his mysterious friend Gil-Martin (*gille-martuinn* is Gaelic for 'fox'), Robert commits murder and other crimes, convinced that his divinely 'justified' status sanctions any atrocity. Yet this fundamentalist terrorist ends his life in torment, apparently committing suicide. In Hogg's doppelgänger novel of evil, Robert is told by Gil-Martin, 'I am wedded to you so closely, that I feel as if I were the same person.'[131] For André Gide in his 1947 preface to the Cresset Press edition Hogg's novel had a psychological explanation: Gil-Martin was part of Robert's mind. Yet other characters appear to see Gil-Martin, and there are strong suggestions that he is the Devil. Jailed in a claustrophobic relationship with his mysterious 'friend', Robert grows more and more isolated from normal society. Written before the modern science of psychology was invented, but in a Scotland where '*divided consciousness*, or *double personality*' was beginning to be discussed, the book's power lies not just in its psychological insight, its exploration of fanaticism, its divided structure and stylishly violent narrative, but in its thorough unresolvability.[132] Some readers have tried to neaten its effect by presenting one explanatory 'answer', but the book puts up a productive resistance against being so fixed. A tale not of 'either/or' but of 'both', theology as much as psychology powers it. Its scripturally knowledgeable author became a Kirk elder, and could write about his own 'directing angel'; in a famous portrait, Hogg stands wrapped in his dark shepherd's plaid, not dressed as a scientist or doctor.[133] Brilliantly dreamed and cunningly constructed, *Memoirs and Confessions* is a novel whose editor and readers attempt to sift its evidence. It should be filmed. Fusing logic and satanic nightmare, Edinburgh, Border glens and Hellfire torments, it stands between Gothic fiction and the not-yet-born genre of detective fiction. Its generic oddity could be overstated, but, as usual with Hogg's work, this great crime book triumphs because it does not fit in.

'Memoirs', 'confessions', 'tales', 'romances' – Hogg does not describe his works as novels. Our retrospective use of this now dominant term tends to oversimplify the varieties of early nineteenth-century Scottish fiction. In terms of the genres we recognize today, Hogg's major contribution was to the development of the novella and, especially, the short story. *The Spy* is one of the places where the modern short story was nurtured. Coming out of the ballad tradition, but modified by pamphlets and a Belles Lettres taste schooled on *Spectator* essays, Gothic fiction and *Man of Feeling* sentimentalism, Hogg's writing in *The Spy* includes some of his first published prose stories, such as 'The Country Laird' (later reprinted as 'The Wool Gatherer' in Hogg's 1818 volume *The Brownie of Bodsbeck*). Here Hogg writes not as 'The Spy' but as 'John Miller', a man with an ear for Scots and an attentive eye that notes exactly how 'little George was eating a lump of dry pease bannock, making very slow progress'. 'The Country Laird, a Tale' is distributed over three issues of *The Spy*. Its first part begins not with moralizing, or descriptive scene-setting, but with direct speech: ' "I tell you this will never do George," said the old lady to her son' are the arresting first words.[134] Part One ends on a note of suspense likely to make readers eager for the next issue of *The Spy*.

Cannily experimenting with (and sometimes baiting) the taste of the market, Hogg the short-story writer and Hogg the editor learned their crafts together, helped by a variety of pen-names and personae that allow the development of writerly shape-shifting. Flexibility of form is a recurrent concern of Hogg's writing. *The Spy*'s hotchpotch of genres and voices is springily productive. As he learned on the hoof, Hogg invited others to pitch in. More than half *The Spy* was his own work, but there are other contributors such as the short-story writer Mary Gray (1767–1829), a close friend of Burns's Clarinda, and the widely connected, influential man of letters Robert Anderson (a contemporary and friend of Robert Fergusson, and editor of *The Poets of Great Britain*). Hogg outshines these other helpers, but they enriched his contact with literary life, developing alongside him.

Prose storytelling developed Hogg's deep and tricksy, protean gifts. In tales such as 'George Dobson's Expedition to Hell', one of the 'Dreams and Apparitions' from *The Shepherd's Calendar*, he seems to pre-empt R. L. Stevenson, just as the Justified Sinner may prefigure Jekyll and Hyde. Prophecies, tests and trials underpin many of Hogg's best stories which, as in 'Julia McKenzie' from *Tales of the Wars of Montrose*, rely on clashes between kinds of belief. Even Hogg's taxonomically dutiful grouping of his tales – *The Three Perils* or 'Class Second. *Deaths, Judgments, and Providences*' – plays off against their irregular, disruptive subject matter and style. The title *Winter Evening Tales*, given to the group of novellas, stories, poems and sketches which he published in 1820, is true to the 'folk' origins of several, yet might also align the work with newer 'fireside' English anthologies and magazines as well as with familiar, older literary treasures such as Shakespeare's *Winter's Tale* and the *Thousand and One Nights*; when Hogg published *Winter Evening Tales*, the standard English version of that Arabic work was called *Arabian Winter-Evenings' Entertainments*.

At their best Hogg's *Winter Evening Tales collected among the Cottagers in the South of Scotland* come close to what Ian Duncan calls them, 'a prose equivalent of *Lyrical Ballads*'. Certainly, as some early reviewers recognized, the collection gives vivid, intimate access to working-class life. 'Basil Lee', a story of '*instability of mind*' and self-division, is the tale of a soldier and 'a common street-walking girl from the town of Inverness'. Moving from rural Borders Scotland to revolutionary America and supernatural occurrences on the isle of Lewis, this story treats polite literary conventions as a punchbag and delights in 'a dissipated, confused, irregular sort of life'. Narrated, mainly in prose, by women as well as men, and involving domestic violence, unmarried mothers, 'dreams and apparitions', and landscapes where mountains can be 'grizly' as well as 'sublime', Hogg's stories focus on the two-thirds of the Scottish population who lived in the countryside. His prose ballads show from the inside a world of the Scottish peasantry about which Edinburgh's literati could only sentimentalize. The partly autobiographical 'Love Adventures of Mr George Cochrane' is a sex comedy whose protagonist, 'behoved to appear' as two different people in an elaborate game of deception, is a comic counterpart to the Justified Sinner. When he tries to write about 'waggish lords', Hogg bombs; when he writes of a haunted library or 'the intensity of the frost wind' in a winter storm, he triumphs.[135] Where Scott made terrain his own through a series of novels, Hogg through collections of shorter prose fictions and slanted autobiographies suggests a landscape and mindscape that can never be encompassed completely.

If the first piece of short fiction in English prose may be Sir William Alexander's addition to the *Arcadia*, later, freestanding work was produced by Defoe, and several *Spectator* essays shade towards short stories, then, as Hogg's achievement shows, much of the impetus in the development of the short story came from late eighteenth- and early nineteenth-century Scotland. This is evident not just in eighteenth-century magazine pieces such as Henry Mackenzie's story of Albert Bane and 'Story of La Roche' (much admired by John Galt), but also in the early nineteenth-century pieces which were suited to and nourished by the periodicals. Of the many Scottish short-story writers of the period, including Scott and John Galt, Hogg may be the most distinguished and the one who appeals most to modern taste. As Karl Miller puts it in his subtly shaded 2003 'likeness of Hogg', *Electric Shepherd*, 'Great Scott, once so overshadowing of other nineteenth-century Scots writers, has been challenged, if not replaced, in the affections of some, by poor Hogg.'[136] The very faults – ragged edges, breaches of decorum, mixtures of the rational and bizarre, liberties with the English language – which damned 'poor Hogg' in the eyes of many earlier readers may now seem among his virtues.

Hogg has benefited from extensive modern scholarly editing which has sought to return to us the works as he wrote them. Galt, on the other hand, remains partly submerged by neglect. Hogg met the twenty-five-year-old Galt in Greenock in 1804, laughed at his 'infinitely amusing' stories 'of old-fashioned and odd people', liked his emphatic reasoning, and was sure he was ' "no common youth" '. Though he had not yet written a word worth preserving, Galt the conversationalist – and Hogg the shrewd recorder – had articulated some of the best features of Galt's later prose fictions. As a Greenock youngster Galt liked to cut a dash, as

a tall thin young man with something dandyish in his appearance dressed in frock-coat and new top-boots; and it being then the fashion to wear the shirt collars as high as the eyes, Galt wore his whole of that night with the one side considerably above his ear, and the other flapped over the collar of his frock-coat down to his shoulder.[137]

Born in Irvine, Ayrshire, son of a sea captain and ship-owner, Galt (1779–1839) wanted to appear a man of the world, long before he was one. Brought up by a forceful mother and educated for business, he was in several senses a mercantile writer; the year after meeting Hogg he authored 'An Essay on Commercial Policy'. He read Machiavelli and William Godwin as well as Ann Radcliffe's Gothic novel *The Italian*, which he loved. After several false starts in the Belles Lettres (*The Battle of Largs; a Gothic Poem*, 1803–4, and a string of dud plays), Galt headed south to London, making a full-scale assault on the world of commerce. For all his inveterate mercantilism, Galt's business ventures did him harm. He was bankrupt before he was thirty. Yet almost accidentally prior to leaving Greenock, where he had clerked in the Customs House and helped to found a literary and debating society, Galt had discovered his true literary métier. Thanks to his knowledge of Greenock society, he was asked by John Leyden to write a biographical account of John Wilson, poet of *The Clyde*. Galt knew that when Wilson had been appointed a schoolmaster the magistrates had stipulated that he desist from poetry. In his published account of this, Galt put into the magistrates' mouths an attack on 'the profane and unprofitable art of poem-making' –

I had nothing in view save a fling at the boss-headed baillies, but Dr Leyden took the joke as no jest, and with foot advanced and hand uplifted, declaimed on the Presbyterian bigotry at some length . . .[138]

So convincingly phrased were the words Galt made up for the baillies that they have continued to be quoted as fact in modern accounts. Instead, as fiction, they show the future direction of Galt's best imaginative writing. However, his fictional debut, *The Majolo: A Tale* (1816), set on the continent, made little impact. Grounded in lengthy conversation and anecdote, it has a hero who discovers 'by a mental process' that the man he is talking to is a poisoner. If *The Majolo* is another early nineteenth-century Scottish story that anticipates crime fiction, it also draws uneasily on the Radcliffean Gothic, and on the travelogue, among other genres.

Galt hit his stride in his early forties. In 1820–21 *Blackwood's Magazine* serialized *The Ayrshire Legatees*. This largely epistolary novel reverses the northern journey of Smollett's *Humphry Clinker* and Lockhart's 1819 *Peter's Letters to his Kinsfolk*, and takes instead a party of Ayrshire Scots south to the British capital, letting them describe things in their own words to the folks back home: 'The milk here is just skimm, and I doot not, likewise well watered – as for the water, a drink of clear wholesome good water is not within the bounds of London.'[139] While writing this book, Galt also worked on a series of educational *Pictures . . . from English, Scottish, and Irish History* (1821). *The Ayrshire Legatees* is a light social comedy of cultural difference; set in the present, it appealed to Scottish and English, rural and urban readers. It catches voices and mores, liveliness, pretension, urban isolation. Though published in Edinburgh, it confirms that for Galt and his readers the 'metropolis' is London. Scotland is loved, but provincial. With its clear Scottish accent, Galt's fiction, as much as Scott's, articulates Britishness – that state in which 'the now united British nations have been advancing in a career o [sic] unrivalled prosperity and glory'.[140]

Developing his literary career with a succession of shrewd, post-Boswellian narratives of Scots who head south either naively or with an 'eye on the main chance', Galt draws on his own life, whose lodestones lay in London, Lowland Scotland and North America.[141] As his writing matures, it depends more and more on his wide experiences – his speculative travels in Europe and the Near East around 1810, his work from 1818 onwards as a Westminster political lobbyist, his struggles in the late 1820s and early 1830s as a North American settler. Though he returned to end his days in Greenock, Galt was most proud of his Canadian exploits. He founded cities (most notably Guelph in Ontario in 1827) and managed companies as well as writing novels. Ambitious, he considered himself Byron's friend and, in 1830, became His Lordship's best-selling biographer. Galt's fiction found an audience from Scotland and France (where it was soon translated) to the United States and Australia. Galt was a great Scottish literary export.

Believing that 'after religion, political economy and jurisprudence are the two most interesting branches of human knowledge', Galt wrote practical fictions of empire that showed how people, especially the middle class or 'ordinarily genteel', might emigrate and trade according to 'the commercial circumstances of the age'.[142] Though not without an occasional lyrical beauty, 'Land in Canada' in *Bogle Corbet; or, The Emigrants* (1831) 'is a commodity as vendible as any other merchandize'. Galt is aware of dispossession and displacement, whether of 'the Indians, who have the best right to the land, if anybody has a right', or of the Scottish Highlanders emigrating from a terrain now given over to 'sheep – Men have no business here.' Yet in a novel of Scottish empire, ranging from the radicalism of late eighteenth-century 'democratical' Glasgow to the West Indies, Canada, and the London Colonial Office where, at the heart of 'the Colonial Labyrinth', 'Government conduct themselves no better than decent mercantile folk', trade and practicalities are central.[143] The story in part aims to teach the skills needed to cope with what Margaret Atwood calls the central theme of all early Canadian writing: 'survival'.[144]

Ambitious yet plain, *Bogle Corbet* is an exploration of empire far removed from the Caribbean adventures of Glaswegian Michael Scott's *Tom Cringle's Log*, serialized in *Blackwood's* between 1829 and 1833, but it is one of a clutch of Scottish imperial fictions from the period. So is Galt's other large-scale North American work, *Lawrie Todd; or, The Settlers in the Woods* (1830), whose vivid accounts of everyday settlers' lives in upstate New York State are sharp and convincing; Galt criticized Fenimore Cooper's 1820s accounts of colonial life as fantastical. *Lawrie Todd* opens in the 1790s, at a time when 'New York was then full of Scotsmen.' With its glossed Americanisms and its 'Yankee oddity' Zerobabel L. Hoskins, who would like to see the British monarch 'skinned alive', it has (like *Bogle Corbet*) a young Scottish protagonist who narrates the story and whose radical politics lead him to seek freedom on another continent. For modern readers *Lawrie Todd* is attractive in its pictures of settler life where in the forest 'tin horns . . .

call the workmen to their meals' and, as a new settlement is founded, trees crash to earth, 'banishing the loneliness and silence of the woods forever'. Even in the twenty-first century some touches are more disconcertingly familiar: 'I was rather hurt to see the accommodation of taverns and hotels generally in Scotland so far behind those in America.'[145] Long out of print, these novels, redolent of the emigrant mindset, are the most substantial early Scottish-North American fictions. They deserve new attention, even if they are outshone by Galt's more stylishly written Scottish tales. They should be reprinted as part of a full edition of Galt's fiction and selected prose. Remarkably, there has never been one.

Galt learned from Smollett, but also from Henry Mackenzie. Though he knew that 'the sentimental novel' had 'ceased to be popular', he did essay a 'sentimental tale' of his own, and admired Mackenzie's 'historical sketches' for what Galt called in his 1824 edition of Mackenzie's *Works* their 'episodes' and 'graphic touches'.[146] Many of Galt's best books, like Mackenzie's, are slim, episodic volumes, not the three-deckers publishers and libraries now demanded. Galt liked short works, filled with sly observation of provincial life as revealed by self-important first-person narrators living in Mackenzie's own time, the period from 1760 to 1820. Galt's best-known mercantilist fictions, sometimes grouped together as the 'Tales of the West' (the West of Scotland, that is), chronicle the growing industrialization of rural small towns. These books provide what Galt later called a 'theoretic history' of the dawning industrial age.[147] But what readers enjoy most about them is that they are funny. Sometimes the writing approaches a prose equivalent of the dramatic monologues written by Galt's fellow Ayrshireman, Burns. For all his historical and economic nous, Galt is the most immediately accessible and entertaining of early nineteenth-century Scottish novelists. He is also the greatest ever novelist of the Scottish middle classes. Baillies, provosts, ministers and entrepreneurs are his menfolk; teachers and merchants' widows are among his often impressive female characters. In what he called his 'kind of light writing' Galt presents 'the events of the passing day' rather than grand chivalric epics.[148] His earliest childhood memory involved the shape of a kettle; better than any of his contemporaries he shows us not just the people but also the 'gear' of households.

Burns had made village characters the focus of great comic poetry, and the English poet George Crabbe (admired by Scott, Byron, Hogg,

Austen and Galt) had produced verse tales of village and parish. Elizabeth Hamilton's *Cottagers of Glenburnie* had established village life as a standard subject for extended Scottish prose fiction, but Galt went further. Partly spurred by Oliver Goldsmith's *The Vicar of Wakefield*, he wrote much of *The Pastor* in 1813, but failed to find a publisher. In the year before *Waverley*, William Blackwood obtusely told him there was no market for fiction about Scotland. Following the success of *The Ayrshire Legatees*, Galt's reworked *Pastor* was published by Blackwood in 1821 as *Annals of the Parish*. When Christian Johnstone wrote that this book should be added to *The Statistical Account of Scotland*, she meant not that it was dull, but that it was superlatively accurate; she compared it to the lively paintings of Scottish village life by Sir David Wilkie, an artist then lauded in London and the first Scottish artist to merit a full-scale biography (by Allan Cunningham). Galt, who in 1816 had written the first full-length biography of an American artist – Benjamin West – also admired Wilkie. As the novelist who had published (in 1807, long before he went there) a *Statistical Account of Upper Canada*, Galt had found in Christian Johnstone one of his most sympathetic readers. There were many others. From Byron, Scott and Coleridge to those *Blackwood's* addicts who, like modern soap-opera viewers, regarded his characters as real, audiences relished Galt's work. His characters do sound convincingly, bustlingly full of themselves:

> In the same year, and on the same day of the same month, that his Sacred Majesty King George, the third of the name, came to his crown and kingdom, I was placed and settled as the minister of Dalmailing.[149]

So begins *Annals of the Parish*. Its narrator, the Reverend Micah Balwhidder, reveals his guid conceit of himself from his first words. Like many of Galt's works, and a substantial number of other nineteenth-century novels, the book appeared anonymously. One early reader thought that, though it was amusing, Balwhidder had been foolish to publish it. Galt, who wrote some schoolbooks as 'Rev. T. Clark', delighted in his clergyman's voice. He loved to manufacture first-person narrators, and several of his tales have subtitles such as 'An Autobiography'. The Reverend Balwhidder reveals more than he realizes about himself and his flock, but his words are plainly and stylishly constructed by the unseen Galt. Galt's best prose is sharply calibrated.

In revising the proofs of another of his constructed first-person narratives, *The Provost* (1822), he meticulously honed away 'verbal repetitions'.[150]

Galt often fought publisher's desiderata, and his work could offend. Susan Ferrier thought it unreadably vulgar. Galt's subjects included municipal corruption, illegitimacy, trade and prostitution on the streets of Edinburgh. J. G. Lockhart may have tried to depict the taboo subject of a clergyman's adultery in his novel *Adam Blair* (1822), but Galt took Scottish fiction into new terrains with more convincing economy and aplomb. Few others looked as hard as he did at what was happening to western Scotland, though one who did was the indigent Lanarkshire poet Janet Hamilton (1795–1873) who saw in 'Oor Location' the energy of 'A hunner funnels bleezin', reekin',/ Coal an' ironstane charrin', smeekin'', but also the 'dool [sorrow] an' desolation' of many women in a world of 'dram-shop . . . pawn' and industrial squalor: 'Drink's the King in oor location!'[151]

As in Burns's and Janet Hamilton's work, a sense of community is strong in Galt's writings. He wrote of an entire local town-and-country community, a 'parish', as George Eliot would do, later, in *Middlemarch*. There is in Galt an attentive emphasis on social change – the coming of cotton mills, atmospheric pollution, politics, crockery, dress – whether treated in a comic or a darker vein. His novel of the horrors of excessive materialism, *The Entail* (1822), traces a family over several generations; it is in a sense a 'family saga', probably the first important one in English after Galt's correspondent Maria Edgeworth's *Castle Rackrent* (1800). It is also a book which portrays female resolution. Galt could write well about women and their lives – whether as matriarchs or midwives. 'The Mem', one of the best of his impressive short stories, deals with a highly educated woman reduced to teaching girls housekeeping. Her alertness, once trained in the reading of Hebrew, now manifests itself in detailing the cracks in a bowl; her death comes with a sudden cough. 'For what use was knowledge and instruction given to her? I ponder when I think of it, but have no answer to the question.'[152]

Galt wrote quickly. Between 1820 and 1822, as well as educational books, he published eight novels. Several are among his best. Towards the end of *Sir Andrew Wylie, of that Ilk* (1822) the theme of getting into Parliament is introduced. The machinations of local politics are at the heart of *The Provost*, published the same year. Its narrator, Provost

Pawkie, is an Ayrshire Machiavelli who offers self-made wisdom ('to rule without being felt ... is the great mystery of policy') at the same time as feathering his own nest with what the twentieth-century Galt scholar Ian A. Gordon called 'great decorum'.[153] In the early 1830s Galt returned to politics with a vengeance. His 1832 novels *The Member* and *The Radical*, set around the contemporary debates over the Reform Bill, are unforgiving in their treatment of politicians. In *The Member* the Scot Archibald Jobbry returns from India, buys an English parliamentary seat, then has to ask where his constituency is; in *The Radical* the future Nathan Butt MP begins (at the age of two) a career which will eventually take him to Westminster: he strangles a kitten, then bites his grandmother in token of 'the divine right of resistance'.[154] These sly, cynical and immediately amusing books consolidate Galt's place as the first fully-fledged political novelist in the English language, but *The Member* has been republished only once in the last two centuries, *The Radical* never. Galt's short parliamentary 'autobiographies' deal with principle, cronyism and sleaze. Authored by a shrewd political lobbyist, they are aimed at targets still entirely recognizable.

Deftly and unshowily, Galt also pioneered or helped to develop several genres. An aspiring dramatist, he published one of the earliest English translations of Goldoni in 1814. As well as giving impetus to the political novel, the family saga and the novel of community, he was perhaps the first important Scottish literary author to write fiction specifically for children. He was not, though, the only Scottish author in this area. As 'Mrs Blackford', Lady Isabella Wellwood Stoddart in *The Eskdale Herdboy* (1819), *The Scottish Orphans* (1822), and other works 'calculated to improve the minds of young people', had written children's literature successful enough to be translated into French.[155] Certainly children were an audience valued by Galt's 'Rev. T. Clark' who realized that amid a flurry of school texts

books designed for the leisure reading of youth have been strangely neglected. The ladies, in this respect, have been more attentive: many ingenious and elegant works for girls have been published of late years; – few, however, and those not of any particular reputation, for boys.[156]

As 'Robin Goodfellow' Galt wrote for children *The History of Gog and Magog, The Champions of London* (1819). Fighters for 'prosperity', the eponymous heroes battle the giant Humbug and show 'an invincible animosity against giants, and oppressors of every description'.[157] *The Rocking Horse* followed in 1825. Galt wrote well for 'juvenile readers', and in *The Wandering Jew* (1820) produced a child's history of the world. Presenting there what he called 'a view, as it were, of public history, in connection with the adventures of an individual', he essayed a method which he would soon use in his adult works.[158] Though many of his best writings did not correspond to contemporary expectations of what novels should be, Galt did author a series of Scottish fictions set in eras beyond living memory, books that came closer to the three-decker historical novel as produced by Scott. The best of these is *Ringan Gilhaize; or, The Covenanters* (1823). Here, like Hogg in *The Brownie of Bodsbeck* and like the dour sub-Miltonic poet Robert Pollok (1798–1827) in his livelier 1820s prose fictions, Galt presents the Covenanters in a favourable light, taking issue with their depiction in *Old Mortality*. Published a year after *The Entail*, this book too covers several generations of family life, but, for all its achievement in taking us into an earlier mindset, it is wordier and heavier going than Galt's shorter fictions. Galt is strongest when he occupies more modern ground, rather than those areas explored by Scott and Hogg.

Galt's brilliance lies in a fusion of gifts. He has a Scottish Enlightenment economist's awareness of commercial and political operations in the world of Mr Stipend and the Earl of Clawback – Galt was always good with names. He delights in creating and ironically subverting voices. Titles such as *The Steamboat* (1821) hint that he could relish modernity as much as the past. Galt rejoices in using Scots as well as English, not just for his characters' speeches, but also for his narrators' accounts. Like many Scottish authors before and since, he took pride in 'the fortunate circumstance of the Scotch possessing the whole range of the English language as well as their own', yet his use in those words of the pronoun 'their' rather than 'our' indicates an eye and ear on a non-Scottish market. The fact that Galt's narrators use Scots may make them more amusing, rather than simply more eloquent. In his best work, writing of 'uncarpeted tidiness' and 'pinched gentility' as well as opulence, he allows apparently insignificant details to carry much of the meaning of the tale. So Galt communicates the state of a marriage as the wife recalls an early conversation with her new husband:

'But,' replied he with a smile, 'I am the head of the house; and, to make few words about it, Mrs Thrifter, I will have my shoes warmed anyhow, whether or no.'

'Very right, my dear,' quo' I; 'I'll ne'er dispute that you are the head of the house; but I think that you need not make a poor wife's life bitter by insisting on toasting your shoes.'[159]

If this sounds like Dickens, that is only because Dickens, another close observer of Parliament who began his literary career a few years later, can often sound like Galt. Long afterwards Scottish writers as different as J. M. Barrie and Alasdair Gray would owe debts to Galt's example. Galt, Scott and Hogg constitute the great triumvirate of male writers who made their mark in early nineteenth-century Scottish fiction, but Galt has been the only one denied a full edition of his work. All these three writers, in different ways, were Tories. Scott's sheer influence and Hogg's outsider 'peasant' status have made them unignorable, even in later ages when Toryism was seen as alien to Scottish writing. Galt's subtleties and probings of middle-class lives were often too easily brushed away in the late twentieth-century era of *Trainspotting*. But if we want to appreciate both the quality and plenitude of Scottish fiction, then Galt, with all his range and cool interrogation, needs to be counted in.

Boswell had scribbled copiously and brilliantly about himself in journals, as had Scott, who wrote some unfinished, posthumously published 'Memoirs' in 1808. Galt, though, was the first important Scottish author to publish in his lifetime a really substantial autobiography. Having published so many fictitious 'autobiographies', he indicates some awkwardness about presenting an account of his own 'transactions': 'It is certainly not a very gentlemanly occupation to write one's own life . . .'[160] He also makes it clear that he is writing because, ailing, he needs money. The 1833 *Autobiography* says a good deal about Galt's trading and colonial ventures, but surprisingly little about his inner life or authorial work. The first volume of his *Literary Life*, published in the following year, is more forthcoming, but there is no soul-baring. Instead, in sober, Protestant, mercantile style, Galt offers an 'Estimate of Myself' – 'The love of fame was my ruling passion.' It confirms that the man whose sons would make great imperial careers in Canada was prouder of his colonial achievements than of his books.[161]

Galt had literary disciples, though. Prominent among them was David Macbeth Moir (1798–1851), a Musselburgh doctor who wrote regularly for *Blackwood's Magazine* under the pen-name 'Delta'. To his friend Galt Moir dedicated his first novel, '*The Life of Mansie Waugh, Tailor in Dalkeith, written by himself* and edited by D. M. Moir'. This was serialized in *Blackwood's* from 1824 onwards, prior to book publication in 1828. Later the busy Moir took over from John Wilson much of the *Maga*'s editorial work, and in 1843 he published a biography of Galt. *Mansie Waugh* is partly a soft-centred version of Galt's provincial fictions, though it also looks towards the piously sentimental rural fiction of Wilson, novelist of *The Trials of Margaret Lyndsay* (1823) and *The Foresters* (1825). Although Wilson's 1822 *Lights and Shadows of Scottish Life* did deal with the risky territory of illegitimacy, Hogg (who once called the charismatic Wilson 'an ideot and a driveller') detected in it 'a great deal of very powerful effect purity of sentiment and fine writing but very little of real nature as it exists in the walks of Scottish life'.[162] Some of these points could be made about *Mansie Waugh*. Moir and Professor Wilson were middle-class professionals of moderate literary talent writing about peasant folk. 'Why are Professional Men Indifferent Poets?' asked Moir in *Blackwood's* in 1821; the question may be misguided, but there is a sense in Dr Moir's fiction of a 'professional man' patronizing his subject matter. *Mansie* is amusing and charming but, peppered with underachieved exclamation marks, tries too hard to be cute:

Now and then the birds gave a bit chitter; and whiles a cow mooed from the fields; and the dew was falling like the little tears of the fairies out of the blue lift, where the gloaming-star soon began to glow and glitter bonnily.[163]

Although the story is set during the Napoleonic wars, anticipations of the later 'Kailyard' [cabbage-patch] and Celtic Twilight movements are discernible. Mansie's world often seems like living inside a snow scene. He loves it, but his son heads off to London. What in Galt is sly, analytical, even cynical has been largely saccharined away. Village fictions were not uniquely Scottish at this time; England, for instance, had Mary Russell Mitford's *Our Village* (1832), but Mitford's work is les sentimental, more precise. In an era when (as Galt's work had indicated) Scotland was increasingly industrialized, Moir's nostalgically unsurprising work was a literature of flinching.

Another of Galt's followers, Andrew Picken (1788–1833), can register the 'long straggling suburban streets' of 'the populous manufacturing town of Paisley', Picken's birthplace. 'Minister Tam', a story about a 'sticked minister' (a clergyman who has not found a charge) is one of the first Scottish fictions about urban unemployment, but Picken's prose is usually flat and tired.[164] Although his admired novel *The Sectarian* (1829) makes a strong stab at depicting Christian fanaticism, too much of his work recycles and dilutes aspects of Scott and Hogg. Titles like 'Wee Watty' point towards Kailyard diminution.

Livelier was Michael Scott (1789–1835), no relation of the Wizard, but a well-off boy from Cowlairs in Glasgow who was involved with a Glasgow trading dynasty, the Bogles, who gave their name to Galt's *Bogle Corbet*. Having worked for over a decade in the Caribbean, Scott came back to Glasgow and published anonymous sketches with titles like 'Heat and Thirst – A Scene in Jamaica' and 'Davy Jones and a Yankee Privateer' in *Blackwood's Magazine* during 1829–30. William Blackwood urged Scott to develop these into an adventure novel, *Tom Cringle's Log* (1834). Racing ahead like accelerated Smollett or like a modern Indiana Jones movie, this ripping yarn takes its young midshipman hero through innumerable perils and scrapes. A casual imperial racism and a confusion over whether Tom is Scottish, English or British are both revealing. By the end of the opening paragraph of Michael Scott's second novel, *The Cruise of the Midge* (1836), its hero has already been born, reached the age of twenty-one and made four ocean voyages:

Being naturally a rambling, harumscarum sort of a young chap, this sort of life jumped better with my disposition than being perched on top of a tall mahogany tripod, poring over invoices, daybooks, journals, and ledgers . . .[165]

Just the sort of thing to appeal to other young men – like the post-office clerk Anthony Trollope – who were sick of nineteenth-century ledgers. Though not at first explicitly presented as what Galt had called 'leisure reading . . . for boys', these books paved the way for the tales of Edinburgh's R. M. Ballantyne (a scion of the printing family) and other Scottish purveyors of sea fights and treasure islands.[166]

The Empire and beyond continued to permeate Scottish imaginations. Lewisman Sir Alexander Mackenzie (1764–1820), the first European to cross the breadth of the North American continent, published his *Voy-*

ages in Edinburgh in 1801. John Ross (1777–1856) wrote of Inuit
'Arctic Highlanders' in his *Voyage of Discovery* (1819). Archibald
Campbell's *A Voyage Round the World* (1821) ranges from Alaska to
Hawaii, and includes a Hawaiian–English phrase book. In 1820 John
Crawfurd's *History of the Indian Archipelago* was the first full survey
of Britain's territories in South-east Asia, while the same writer's *Journal
of an Embassy* (1828) reported first-hand on Siam and Cochin China.
Even homely *Mansie Waugh* contains an embedded Oriental tale. To
Moir has been attributed 'The Canadian Boat Song', published in *Black-
wood's* in September 1829 as the supposed translation of a rowing song
sung by Scottish Gaels in Canada:

> Fair these broad meads – these hoary woods are grand;
> But we are exiles from our fathers' land.
>
> . . . .
>
> From the lone shieling of the misty island
>   Mountains divide us, and the waste of seas –
> Yet still the blood is strong, the heart is Highland,
>   And we in dreams behold the Hebrides.[167]

While attuned to a trend in actual early nineteenth-century Gaelic
poetry, this sort of manufactured heartbreak was just the sort of thing
to appeal to *Blackwood's* readers. Few of these readers knew any Gaelic;
the 'Boatsong' did nothing to stop the Highland Clearances, and not
many Scots had access to the contemporary Gaelic work of Iain Mac
GhillEathain (John MacLean) (1787–1848). After publishing a collection of Gaelic poetry in 1818, he left the island of Coll for Nova
Scotia where he wrote in 'Am Bàrd an Canada' ('The Poet in Canada')
about the hard facts of living off nothing but potatoes. He also warned
against the enticements of emigration agents. For more than a century
afterwards Nova Scotia and the Cape Breton area continued to produce
Gaelic poets. Those places still treasure an eroding heritage of Gaelic
verse.

After the great achievements of the eighteenth century, Gaelic poets
in Scotland were often, as Derick Thomson puts it, 'unambitious'.[168]
Still, in soldiers' songs with titles like 'The Battle of Egypt' they too
registered empire's dreams and hurts. If the Lochaber-born Aberdeen
Classicist and Gaelic scholar Ewen MacLachlan (1773–1822) published

in his 1807 *Metrical Effusions* one of Scotland's most polylingual books of verse, unfortunately none of his poems in Latin, Greek, Gaelic and English is thought to have star quality. A lot of minor, sometimes sentimental poets, hymned a land and language from which they were being parted. Iain Gobha na Hearadh (John Morrison) (c. 1796–1852), an evangelical blacksmith from Harris, is outstanding as a prominent religious poet, but his work is hard to appreciate in English.

The Highlands lacked a developed book-publishing infrastructure. Oral transmission continued to matter. In the wake of Scott, though, northern Scotland attracted more and more Lowland literary attention. James Hogg travelled there, and almost moved there to look after sheep on Harris. The early nineteenth century saw the publication of a Latin translation of Ossian, and by 1807 the so-called 'original Gaelic' of the Ossianic poems was published. In 1818 an edition 'for the general good of the people of the Gaidhealtachd' was distributed to every Highland parish school where there was Gaelic teaching.[169] Even as Highlanders were cleared from their land to make way for sheep, their culture was being celebrated in English – not just in *Waverley* but in such historical studies as the *Sketches of the Character, Manners and Present State of the Highlanders of Scotland: with Details of the Military Service of the Highland Regiments* (1822) by ex-Black Watch officer and eager imperialist David Stewart of Garth (1772–1829). In his soldiering novel *The Black Watch* (1834) Andrew Picken contrasts eighteenth-century Highland life where 'poverty itself had the sacredness of virtue' with modern 'southern luxury and Lowland greed [which have] . . . found their way among the mountains, to the fatal corrupting of landlord and clansmen – making all men mercenary'.[170] Two years earlier, though, the same author had edited Galt's Canadian papers to encourage 'Emigrants, Colonists, and Capitalists', among whom were many Highlanders.[171] A hint of the Highlands, as in the title of Thomas Dick Lauder's 1825 historical novel *Lochindhu*, might tempt readers with a seemingly insatiable taste for *Highland Rambles* and *Legends* – here too Lauder obliged. But what readers increasingly wanted was a sentimentalized version of the Highland past and views of picturesque landscape, not details of present-day political or economic problems. Ossianization had laid the road to Balmoral.

Outside fiction, the most attractive early nineteenth-century account of Grampian life is in the posthumously published *Memoirs of a High-*

land Lady by Elizabeth Grant of Rothiemurchus (1797–1885). Well off, lively and alert, Grant never pretends to be otherwise. Sometimes writing 'in spite of Walter Scott', she remembers her activities in 1812, and seems to tell it like (for her) it was:

We never see such inns now; no carpets on the floors, no cushions on the chairs, no curtains to the windows. Of course polished tables, or even clean ones, were unknown. All the accessories of the dinner were wretched, but the dinner itself, I remember, was excellent; hotch potch salmon, fine mutton, grouse, scanty vegetables, bad bread, but good wine.[172]

Grant's remembered Highlands are constructed from selected perceptions, but are not a never-never land.

In London the young Elizabeth Grant acted in *Macbeth* and loved going to Covent Garden. Moir's Mansie Waugh, on the other hand, is portrayed as such a naive theatregoer that he interrupts the performance by talking to the actors. What ensues literally brings the house down – the gallery collapses. 'So much for plays and playactors – the first and last, I trust in grace, that I shall ever see.'[173] By the 1820s Moir did not expect many even among his most resolutely Presbyterian readers to share such an attitude to the theatre, but it is hard to argue that Scottish dramatic writing was in a flourishing state. There was, though, no shortage of performances. As a teenager in 1790s Greenock John Galt could choose between two theatres, offering plays from tragedy to farce; in plays like *The Humours of Greenock Fair* (1789) the prolific Archibald Maclaren presented Highlanders and Lowlanders in comic juxtaposition. Late in life Galt wrote glumly that 'my published Dramas, for number and variety, entitle me to be ranked among the most considerable dramatic authors of my native land, and I have several manuscripts of plays, at least half-a-dozen, lying by me'. No one wanted them. There may be flickers of promise in his lighter pieces, but Galt's plays usually billow with sub-Shakespearian rhetoric. This conventional tendency is the playwriting curse of Baillie and Scott too. Even Hogg succumbed to numbing propriety when he tried to write for the theatre.

Byron's 1821 *Cain* (dedicated to Scott) and his other closet dramas contain some more powerfully disturbing writing, but were not written for performance. Unlike Galt, Baillie found it relatively easy to find publishers and performers for her dramas, but by far the most successful Scottish theatre works were hewn from well-known novels and poems by dramatists aiming for theatrical spectacle, rather than manifesting great literary gifts of their own. Written in 1817, then published in 1867 and again in 1888, William Barrymore's dramatization of *Wallace* concluded with Lady Wallace's on-stage hysterics; H. R. Addison's 1834 dramatization of 'Tam o' Shanter' (one of several) made unBurnsian use of ghosts cavorting in sheets. There were hundreds of stage adaptations of Scott's novels, from William Terry's 'Terrification' of *Guy Mannering* (c. 1817) to Isaac Pocock's *Rob Roy MacGregor* (1818) which was performed before George IV in Edinburgh in 1822 as part of the King's own theatrical 'jaunt'. Even the modern critic Alasdair Cameron, defending Scottish drama of the period, concedes that once-popular plays like *Virginius* (1820) and *The Hunchback* (1832), written by the Glasgow Irishman Sheridan Knowles for the tragedian William Macready, now seem utterly unconvincing in their language.[174] The Scott dramatizations have more vitality partly because (in contrast with most Scottish plays of the time) they retained some vernacular Scots speech. On stage they might also feature songs and dancing, performing an iconic, stylized pageant of Scottishness for their audience. Scott's direct and indirect encouragement of the Edinburgh Theatre Royal, ably managed by the brother-and-sister team of Mrs Henry Siddons and the Scott adapter W. H. Murray, helped that theatre achieve unofficial national status. There was, though, a wide network of playhouses throughout Lowland Scotland, stretching from Dumfries to Elgin. For all its ceilidhs, preachings, village poets and poems of heroism, Gaeldom probably had no theatrical tradition.

In an age when John Wilson ('Christopher North') liked to pontificate in *Blackwood's* about 'a National Character in Literature', Scott adaptations and other stagings of Burns or Wallace-related spectaculars may have performed a costume-drama Scottishness that reinforced but threatened to fossilize national identity.[175] These plays could be loud, colourful, sometimes even provocative, as when they showed Rob Roy's pistol-brandishing wife. It is hard to argue that their literary value was high. More exciting-sounding, if only because she got away and became 'the most notorious feminist radical in America', is Dundee's playwright Frances Wright. Born in 1795, she learned her radicalism from her uncle, James Mylne, before crossing the Atlantic in 1818.[176] Wright was influenced by the Welsh social reformer Robert Owen (1771–1858). His model industrial community, set up at New Lanark outside Glasgow in 1813, included the first ever day nursery and playground and is now a World Heritage Site. Owen's *A New View of Society* (1813) argued that environment was vital to character formation. From Frances Wright's first arrival in America and throughout her transcontinental journey with her sister Camilla, she loved the American environment and the new nation's democratic spirit. Her *Views of Society and Manners in America* praises these, and she later took over from Robert Owen's Scottish-born son the editing of the newspaper at the idealistic Owenite community of New Harmony, Indiana. An energetic writer and lecturer, Wright was admired by Walt Whitman. Her only full-length drama, *Altorf* (1819), was performed in New York and published in Philadelphia, then New York and London. It is dedicated to 'the people of America', but set in fourteenth-century Switzerland where it portrays a romantic liaison against the background of the independence struggle of the early Swiss cantons. Though the modernity of Wright's ideals, which included racial and sexual equality, is admirably striking, her rather operatic drama's exclamatory rhetoric sounds uncomfortable. As political theatre drawing on German Romanticism, *Altorf* is one of the most arresting Scottish-authored plays of its day. But its day has gone.

Arthur Conan Doyle's Sherlock Holmes as visualized by Sydney Paget in London's Strand *magazine in 1891. Conan Doyle in 'A Case of Identity' writes of Holmes 'half asleep, with his long, thin form curled up in the recess of his armchair' beside 'a formidable array of bottles and test-tubes'. This was one of the first Holmes stories which Paget illustrated. His pictures reinforced the image and characteristic body-language of the London detective whom Doyle (as Robert Louis Stevenson realized) had based on his old Edinburgh medical professor, Joseph Bell. (St Andrews University Library, per AP4.S8M2)*

9

Scotland and London

London called. Scottish writers headed there as never before or since. At the age of thirty-one Walter Scott's son-in-law, the lawyer, novelist and journalist John Gibson Lockhart, went to the British capital in 1825 to edit John Murray's *Quarterly Review*; later it was feared that even the *Edinburgh Review* might 'go, and die, in London'.[1] Approaching forty, the Borderer Thomas Carlyle headed for London in 1834; he developed into the Sage of Chelsea. Born on the Isle of Arran and in Irvine in Ayrshire, the Scottish brothers Daniel and Alexander Macmillan in the early 1840s established in London and Cambridge their great publishing house whose list would include English authors from Lewis Carroll to Tennyson and Hardy, as well as such new journals as *Macmillan's Magazine* (founded in 1859) and *Nature* (founded in 1869); thanks to these Scottish entrepreneurs, both Scott and Burns would be written up in London's famous Macmillan monographs as 'English Men of Letters'. Born in Midlothian in 1828, Margaret Oliphant, most productive of the major Scottish Victorian novelists, was taken to England by her businessman father when she was ten, and published her first novel in London in 1849. A decade later the Aberdeenshire man of letters and children's writer George MacDonald accepted a London professorship. The greatest English-language urban poem of the nineteenth century, *The City of Dreadful Night* (1874), is set in a nameless, hallucinatory city, but one that owes much to the London where the poem's author, Scottish-born James Thomson, had grown up in the Royal Caledonian Asylum. *Kidnapped*, Robert Louis Stevenson's splendid Highland tale, was penned in Bournemouth; *The Strange Case of Doctor Jekyll and Mr Hyde* may be underpinned by the geography of Edinburgh, but unfolds entirely in the metropolis of London. 221B Baker Street is late nineteenth-century London's most famous fictional address. Sherlock Holmes, who lived there, was based on an Edinburgh pioneer of forensic medicine, and created by Edinburgh's Arthur Conan Doyle. Yet Holmes is as much a London icon as the Peter Pan of Kensington Gardens.

Fortunately for Scotland, there was some movement in the opposite direction. The English man of letters Thomas De Quincey moved permanently to Edinburgh in 1830. Like George Eliot, Margaret Oliphant sent a good number of her works north to be published by William Blackwood. Edinburgh magazines remained influential in the Victorian age, even if the publishing house of Chambers found it expedient to drop the word 'Edinburgh' from the masthead of its leading periodical. Parts of Scotland, Scott-land, most strikingly the royal retreat at Balmoral, became popular tourist destinations. In 1848 an English poet, Arthur Hugh Clough, published one of the finest Highland poems, *The Bothie of Toper-na-fuosich*. Though he may have been distantly related to the Gaelic poet William Ross (whose beloved cousin Marion married a Liverpool Clough), A. H. Clough knew little or no Gaelic; he felt obliged to change his poem's title when he discovered it referred to the female genitalia.[2] Dealing with a reading-party of Oxford students in the north, his *Bothie* associates the Highlands with democratic ideals and energies.

English, American and other authors could find imaginative stimulus in Scotland, sometimes by misreading it. In 1841 Dickens mistook the wording on a memorial slab in Edinburgh's Canongate Kirkyard. He thought he saw the words 'Ebenezer Lennox Scroggie – mean man', and went on to create the Ebenezer Scrooge of *A Christmas Carol* (1843); actually the Scroggie slab memorialized a 'meal man'.[3] While English writers from Clough to Queen Victoria certainly visited, in an age when so many Scots wrote about London not one major English novelist set a novel north of the Border. As today, so in most of the previous two centuries Scotland was at best part of England's peripheral vision. In contrast, Scots such as Barrie and Conan Doyle produced work which helped define London for the international imagination.

Not all Scottish writers who left Scotland set up house in London. Some, like David Livingstone, simply passed through, en route to mission and empire. Robert Louis Stevenson travelled for his health, and because foreignness excited his imagination. Most of the Scottish writers who worked outside Scotland came back for long or short periods. J. M.

Barrie, Peter Pan's creator, delighted in returning to his native Kirriemuir in what was then Forfarshire; R. L. Stevenson's boyhood author-hero, R. M. Ballantyne, who wrote ripping imperial yarns devoured by British lads, worked for the Hudson's Bay Company in Canada, then returned to Edinburgh in 1848 and stayed there for over a quarter of a century before moving to France, then England. Stevenson himself, after spells in France and America, worked on *Treasure Island* in Braemar in the summer of 1881, but by October he was in Zurich; his sense of mobility is part of his restless modernity. Margaret Oliphant, modern not least in her conception of what it means to be a working woman writer financially reliant on her own ability, worked for short spells in Edinburgh, Elie and St Andrews. Most of her time, though, was spent in southern England with excursions to the continent. David Masson, an Aberdeen stonecutter's son and influential literary critic, took up a Chair of English at London's young University College in 1853; six years later he became the first editor of *Macmillan's Magazine* before moving back from London to the Chair of Rhetoric and English Literature at Edinburgh.

Empire and technologies of travel encouraged a sense of cosmopolitan mobility whose hub was imperial London. Still, some Scots stayed put and did well. Publisher William Chambers wrote observant memoirs of Edinburgh, all 'honest-like bakers, in pepper-and-salt coats' and 'dainty-looking youths, in white neck-cloths and black silk eye-glass ribbons' at the ageing James Hogg's parties.[4] William's brother Robert Chambers, author and publisher, collected the world's first book of urban folklore, *Traditions of Edinburgh* (1824), then edited reference books in the Scottish Enlightenment tradition, and became a pioneer of evolutionary theory. His contemporary, the stonemason Hugh Miller, a courageous, Scottish-based writer, fared less happily. On the whole, in this era of Lowland mass industrialization and rapidly developing modes of locomotion, the more ambitious and adventurous writers left Scotland, for a time if not for good. As with the Latinists of the seventeenth century, these Victorian writers in the imperial language of English were scattered across several countries, though still part of a Scottish network with links to Scotland itself. At home there were pockets of local strength – dialect novels in newspapers, working-class poets and storytellers struggling to articulate a new urban consciousness or remarket an older, rural one. There were collectors of Gaelic songs, and Edinburgh bookmen. But among Scottish-based authors it is hard not to sense a diminution of energy after the era of Byron, Scott, Galt and Hogg. 'Old Scotland', for Robert Chambers, 'now seems to be passing away.'[5]

Scottish literature had been written outside Scotland before. Both 1603 and 1707 had triggered southward authorial migrations. In the eighteenth century Thomson, Smollett, Boswell, Macpherson and others had negotiated between Scotland and the British capital. Burns had avoided London; Scott and Galt had tried their fortunes there. Yet among nineteenth-century Scots a conviction developed that Scotland was somehow on the wane. It was fading, and the financial and cultural dominance of London was to blame. Even the ageing Scott felt this. In 1829 he wrote in his Journal about how 'London licks the butter of[f] our bread.'[6] He knew ambitious Scots were attracted south, but, shrewdly, he realized also that Scotland's distinctive Church, educational and legal systems did keep some talented men north of the Border.

For authors writing in English, however, London offered an incomparably vast marketplace. Despite the power of the *Edinburgh Review*, *Blackwood's Magazine* and Scottish publishers, the imperial capital's literary infrastructure was growing ever larger. In 1852, looking back to the early nineteenth-century heyday of Francis Jeffrey, his biographer Lord Cockburn wrote with astonished resentment of how

all this was still a Scotch scene. The whole country had not begun to be absorbed in the ocean of London. There were still little great places, – places with attractions quite sufficient to retain men of talent or learning in their comfortable and respectable provincial positions; and which were dignified by the tastes and institutions which learning and talent naturally rear. The operation of the commercial principle which tempts all superiority to try its fortune in the greatest accessible market, is perhaps irresistible; but anything is surely to be lamented which annihilates local intellect, and degrades the provincial spheres which intellect and its consequences can alone adorn ... From about 1800, everything purely Scotch has been fading.[7]

Nowadays we distrust searches for national or ethnic 'purity'. Yet Cockburn's language is revealing in its sense of 'a Scotch scene' linked to the 'provincial' and apparently destined to be submerged under those values represented by 'the ocean of London'.

As Lord Advocate and an MP, Francis Jeffrey spent much of the 1830s in London, but that decade's most notable Scottish literary emigrants to the English metropolis were Thomas and Jane Welsh Carlyle. Thomas, the more important though often less appealing of these two writers, was by no means 'purely Scotch'. His authorial manner owed much to German Romantic writing, particularly that of Goethe and the stylistically contorted Jean-Paul Richter; Carlyle translated both men's works. He was a polemical pamphleteer, reforming author, and English-language historian; in all these capacities, despite his Germanism, he does display a strong Scottish streak which may remind some readers of one of his own declared heroes, John Knox.

Carlyle's strict Presbyterian father would 'not tolerate anything fictitious in books'.[8] Carlyle as an adult denounced modern 'Novel-garbage'.[9] Still, he enjoyed fiction from Smollett to the *Arabian Nights* as he grew up in the village of Annandale, Dumfries-shire. In late 1809, aged fourteen, he made a three-day-long slow cart ride to the city of Edinburgh, carrying his mother's gift of a two-volume bible. He was expected to train for the ministry, and did so, but mathematics and the chance to read widely were what he enjoyed most at Edinburgh University. Carlyle preached his first sermon at the Divinity Hall of the National Church in Edinburgh in 1814, but soon lost his sense of full Christian belief. He spent some years working as a teacher in Kirkcaldy and elsewhere. There was a sense, though, in which Carlyle remained a preacher all his life. He relished using the vocabulary of Christianity, and came to believe that 'the writers of Newspapers, Pamphlets, Poems, Books, these *are* the real working effective Church of a modern country', while 'a Collection of Books' was modernity's 'true University'.[10] His sometimes messianic authorial career began in the Edinburgh milieu of encyclopedia-making and book reviewing. One of the first books he received for review was Joanna Baillie's 1821 *Metrical Legends of Exalted Characters*. Throughout his life Carlyle would be attracted by those whom he saw as exalted characters – Goethe, Burns, Cromwell, Frederick the Great of Prussia. He built up a pantheon of heroic males and came to advocate what he termed 'hero-worship' as a form of noble human devotion. By 1832 he saw Johnson's biographer James Boswell as a 'wonderful martyr' to this new faith, a shining example 'that Loyalty, Discipleship, all that was ever meant by *Hero-worship*, lives perennially in the human bosom'.[11]

Sartor Resartus, Carlyle's first authored book, was serialized in *Fraser's Magazine* in 1833–4, then published in book form in America in 1836 before publication in London two years later. Its Latin title means 'the tailor retailored', and its protagonist is in part comical, not quite a hero to be worshipped. With this protagonist Carlyle followed in the wake of John Arbuthnot's eighteenth-century pedantic German Martin Scriblerus, and established one of English-language culture's enduring stereotypes: the earnest German professor. Scottish Enlightenment thought had been so influential in Germany and there were so many translations between Scotland and Germany in the early nineteenth century that for Carlyle to choose to adopt a Germanic guise is understandable. To some extent, the eccentric Professor Teufelsdröckh of the University of Weissnichtwo (a German translation of Scott's Kennaquhair – 'Don't Know Where') is a version of Carlyle himself. With his learned work *Der Kleider, Ihr Werden und Wirken* (On Clothes: Their Origin and Influence), the Professor emerged from the young Scot's experiences writing encyclopedia articles, reviewing, and translating German. At one point Carlyle even began to write a history of German literature, but he never completed it. Instead, after Englishing Goethe's *Wilhelm Meister's Apprenticeship* (1824) and four volumes of *German Romance* (1827), Carlyle, as he knew Scott had done, made German Romantic writings a springboard for his own work. Where Jean-Paul Richter had appointed himself ' "Professor of his own History" ' and written prose crammed with the 'grotesque' and 'ludicrous', overflowing with a 'boundless uproar' of stylistic excess, Carlyle sought to emulate him.[12] Carlyle's was a European rather than an insular view of literature. In 1827, in his early thirties, he argued that 'so closely are all European communities connected, that the phases of mind in any one country, so far as these represent its general circumstances and intellectual position, are but modified repetitions of its phases in every other'.[13] A true Europhile, he drew attention to parallels between German and Scottish literature.

Wildly eclectic, and supposedly pieced together by an English editor working from the voluminous texts of a biblioholic German academic, *Sartor Resartus* is a hybrid work that draws on the genres of novel, sermon and polemical philosophical or theological treatise. Often in absurdist guise, it is precociously Victorian in preaching a doctrine of 'Self-help'.[14] Confused and confusing, it flaunts a calculatedly barbarous Germano-unEnglish style. *Sartor* emphasizes the need to face down despair and negativity – 'The Everlasting No' – and seek instead what is positively worth believing in. This may be a gospel of 'work' or 'a new Mythus' taken over from Christianity, or the 'Fragments of a genuine Church-*Homiletic*' that 'lie scattered' in 'this immeasurable froth-ocean we name LITERATURE'.[15] Carlyle's trumpet-blast idea that literature would replace religion would be sounded again in a more muted fashion by the less volatile Victorian Englishman Matthew Arnold. The notion persists sometimes in our own day, though for many 'the media' and media celebrities rather than literature and its heroes have come to occupy the position of Carlyle's 'working effective Church' to which a society offers devotion.

Sartor Resartus grew out of Carlyle's crisis of religious belief. Urging the need to search for values that were not outdated, he quixotically imagined both a nude House of Lords and a 'dandiacal body' as part of his quest for appropriately modern spiritual and intellectual garb.[16] Praising what he calls 'Natural Supernaturalism', he presents the Book of Nature 'With its Words, Sentences, and grand descriptive Pages, poetical and philosophical, spread out through Solar Systems, and Thousands of Years' as 'a Volume written in celestial hieroglyphs'.[17] Many readers have found Carlyle's own book equally amazing, arresting and baffling. Its restlessness struck a chord with Victorian contemporaries and its exclamatory style remains oratorically exciting. Yet, for all its brilliance, *Sartor Resartus* can sound windy and needlessly, heedlessly exhausting. Carlyle wrote the book towards the end of six years when he and his young wife Jane Welsh lived a demanding life in the remote Craigenputtoch farmhouse on the bleak Dumfries-shire moors. Jane hated the cold there, and Thomas was increasingly attracted by the resources and conversation of London. In 1834 they took up residence at 5 Cheyne Walk in Chelsea.

Carlyle was a driven, compulsive writer. After his death, a controversial biography by J. A. Froude hinted at his sexual inadequacy, and more recent work by Rosemary Ashton scrutinizes the Carlyles' often uneasy marriage. The Great Man's literary tasks dominated the Carlyle household. Shrewd Jane was subjected to claustrophobic pressure. When John Stuart Mill lost much of the manuscript of *The French Revolution*, Carlyle doggedly rewrote the lot. His work was published to acclaim and amazement in 1837. Running to over 900 pages, it plays fast and loose with history in search of rhetorical effect, but also draws on eye-witness accounts. It seems less written than blared – filled with

John-Knoxian din and scorn, though Knox might have had more sympathy than Carlyle with the Revolution's democratic ideals. Carlyle sees the Revolution as a secular apocalypse. It ends an old way of life but leaves confusion and carnage in its wake: 'the Death-Birth of a World!'[18]

Ten years earlier Scott had surveyed this terrain in the opening volumes of his *Life of Napoleon*. Carlyle went further in scope and vehemence. He shows some sympathy for the common people who 'pine stagnantly in thick obscuration', but, almost as much as Robert Bisset forty years earlier, he despises the 'Spectre of DEMOCRACY'.[19] Carlyle's scorn extends not just to the French Revolution but also, despite a strong friendship with his Massachusetts admirer Ralph Waldo Emerson, to the American Revolution. He hears 'on Bunker Hill, DEMOCRACY announcing, in rifle-volleys death-winged, under her Star Banner, to the tune of Yankee-doodle-doo, that she is born, and, whirlwind-like, will envelop the whole world!'[20] Carlyle's French Revolution is volcanically catastrophic, and that sense of catastrophe excites his scalding prose. His Carlylese mocks the Revolution's 'great game'.[21] Sometimes he revoices Old Testament prophecies ('Ye and your fathers have sown the wind, ye shall reap the whirlwind') or borrows the tones of an epic bard; his prose is crammed with clashing dictions as foreign phrases, slang and neologisms ('Strumpetocracies') do battle among exclamation marks and a forest of actual and satirical names – 'Astraea Redux without Cash' is a characteristic chapter title.[22]

For Carlyle the horrific Revolution must never be repeated. Writing of such horrors as 'a Tannery of Human Skins', he perceives that like Original Sin, an appalling 'Madness . . . dwells in the hearts of man'. He views civilization as a mere veneer: 'Alas then, is man's civilization only a wrappage, through which the savage nature of him can still burst, infernal as ever?'[23] That rhetorical question carries as much force in the twenty-first century as it did in the twentieth or the nineteenth, but *The French Revolution* offers more prolonged stylistic convulsions than many modern readers find acceptable.

Carlyle's influence on Victorian Britain was immense. Not least, his own work shaped the Tory party. As others of his countrymen from Gilbert Burnet to David Hume, James Boswell to Walter Scott had done before him, this charismatic and ambitious Scot scripted a version of Englishness. In his state-of-the-nation book, *Past and Present* (1843), Carlyle invokes on the first page the spectre of the Bastille, and seeks a remedy for industrial England's social ills. His work spurred several explorations of the 'condition of England' by novelist (and later British Prime Minister) Benjamin Disraeli, by Elizabeth Gaskell, and by Charles Dickens; Engels, Marx, Nietzsche and others reacted to Carlyle's analyses. Highly influential on English, American and continental writing, Carlyle, for all his Scottishness, presented himself and his country as, in a qualified way, English:

A heroic Wallace, quartered on the scaffold, cannot hinder that his Scotland become, one day, a part of England: but he does hinder that it become, on unfair terms, a part of it; commands still, as with a god's voice, from his old Valhalla and Temple of the Brave, that there be a just real union as of brother and brother, not a false and merely semblant one as of slave and master. If the union with England be in fact one of Scotland's chief blessings, we thank Wallace withal that it was not the chief curse. Scotland is not Ireland . . .[24]

Carlyle's anti-Irish admiration for the 'brave true heart' of Wallace in Valhalla with his 'god's voice' is, like his devotion to Oliver Cromwell whose memory 'is or yet shall be as that of a god', a form of that masculine adulation outlined in his 1841 lectures *On Heroes and Hero-Worship*. There, in an anthropological sweep, the heroes range from pagan gods through Mahomet, Dante, Shakespeare and Luther to Knox, Johnson, Burns, Cromwell and Napoleon. Writing as one of 'We English' in *Past and Present*, and mixing fiction with polemical philosophizing, Carlyle juxtaposes an idealized, medieval pastoral England with modern industrial society subservient to its 'Gospel of Mammonism'. He lambasts the England which seems to have forgotten that '*Cash-payment* is not the sole relation of human beings.' Yet, writing in the age of Samuel Smiles, Carlyle exalts the idea of hard work as something which might unite the old, masculine Catholic medieval England he admires with the modern world he inhabits.[25] Carlyle coined phrases such as 'Captains of industry', and *Past and Present* came to be offered to early twentieth-century students as a work articulating 'authentic manliness' with its 'battle-music' and work ethic: 'All true Work is Religion . . . Admirable was that of the old Monks, "*Laborare est Orare*, Work is Worship." '[26] So a re-imagined medieval English Catholicism is fused with Carlyle's Scottish Protestant work ethic.

Work was Carlyle's refuge and strength. The fun and play present in *Sartor Resartus* turn to scorn and savage irony in his later writings.

Dismissive of the idle, titled rich, Carlyle grew convinced that 'Europe requires a real Aristocracy, a real Priesthood', and his hero-worshipping tendencies led him towards Cromwell (whom he saw as 'authored' by John Knox) and towards Prussia's Frederick II as unflinchingly strong rulers, ironclads of the spirit. Though Engels and others saw in Carlyle a compelling arguer against social ills, his own ideology with its worship of supermannish heroes, 'the select of the earth', takes its bearings from a secularization of the Calvinist idea of the elect, and points towards both Nietzsche and fascism.[27] Perceptively, H. J. C. Grierson identified this proto-Fascist tendency in his 1933 study *Carlyle and Hitler*; a dozen years later, one of the last books with which the Führer was consoled in his Berlin bunker was Carlyle's *History of Friedrich II of Prussia, Called Frederick the Great* (1858–65). Carlyle's hero-worship is a dangerous religion.

This Scottish writer's bitterness against the '*swarmeries*' of modern democracy increased with age.[28] His racism, which may not have been unusual in nineteenth-century Scotland or England, is evident in essays like 'The Nigger Question', with its horror of turning 'the West Indies into a *Black Ireland*'. In 'Shooting Niagara: And After?' the growth of full democracy is likened to plunging over Niagara Falls.[29] Just as Scottish writings for and against slavery should be better known, so Scottish literary racism needs to be more openly discussed. Scots too readily hymn their literature as straightforwardly 'democratic'. It is salutary to hear the patrician tones of 'Shooting Niagara', a piece composed during Carlyle's term of office as democratically elected Rector of Edinburgh University:

One always rather likes the Nigger; evidently a poor blockhead with good dispositions, with affections, attachments, – with a turn for Nigger Melodies, and the
like: – he is the only Savage of all the coloured races that doesn't die out on sight
of the White Man; but can actually live beside him, and work and increase and
be merry. The Almighty Maker has appointed him to be a Servant.[30]

More palatable, and less exhaustingly written than much of the rest of Carlyle's oeuvre, are his posthumously published *Reminiscences* (1881) in which he recalls his father, his friends, and his late wife, Jane. When he writes lovingly about his peasant father, trying to identify with him, yet cut off from him by milieu and religious doubt, Carlyle hints at how readily he moved from the 'elect' of Calvinism to the 'Happy few' who may follow the wisdom of *Sartor*, and from the 'old excessive Edinburgh hero-worship' of his youth to the proto-Fascist devotion to strong men in his later works.[31] His hurt, grieving account of Jane should be supplemented by her own often tart published letters and accounts of their relationship. Clearly written and moving, the *Reminiscences* show a Carlyle who has shifted from the volcanic to the melancholy. Not for nothing did the young, Scots-descended American artist James McNeill Whistler paint him in 1873 as an 'Arrangement in Grey and Black'.

As well as keeping in touch with their relations and literary friends hundreds of miles to the north, the Carlyles in London knew and corresponded with Tennyson, Browning, and many other English and continental luminaries. To them, to her husband, and to such personal friends as the English novelist Geraldine Jewsbury, Jane Welsh Carlyle (1801–66), a doctor's daughter from Haddington, wrote strikingly witty, detailed and sometimes bitter letters which often mentioned her husband:

In virtue of his being *the least unlikable* man in the place, I let him dance attendance on my young person, till I came to *need* him – all the same as my slippers, to go to a ball in, or my bonnet to go out to walk. When I finally agreed to marry him, I *cried* excessively and felt excessively shocked – but if I had said *no* he would have left me and how could I dispense with what was equivalent to my slippers or my bonnet?[32]

The sheer bulk of the ongoing scholarly edition of the Carlyles' correspondence may be offputting, but often the individual letters, especially Jane's, shine out.

Women feature little in Thomas Carlyle's writings. He hymned heroes. Only after Jane's death did he realize that he might have lost if not a heroine, then certainly a woman so important to him that without her his own work faltered. Throughout her married life the well-read, intelligent Jane kept house and tried to mollify her husband's bouts of angry despair; but she and other Scottish women were thinking and writing about their treatment. Continuing that interest in female education which had been so strong in the work of Susan Ferrier, Mary Brunton and Elizabeth Hamilton, Catherine Sinclair (1800–64), daughter and secretary to Sir John Sinclair of Ulbster, embarked on a considerable career as a published author just after her father's death in 1835. Her *Modern Accomplishments, or the March of the Intellect* (1836) is an examination of female education, while the popular and often lively *Holiday House* (1839) was a series of Scottish tales aimed specifically at children. Whether they thought to win greater social freedom for women or to defend the status quo, all writers about women agreed about their influence over children. Often women encouraged other women to read and educate themselves. In 1831 in a manuscript written for a female friend, the elderly Joanna Baillie recalled how seventy years earlier in Bothwell 'My mother took pains to teach me' and how when she was ill her sister 'came to me with Ocean's [Ossian's] poems in her hand and coaxed me in a very persuasive soothing manner to open the book and read some of the stories to myself: I did so and was delighted with them (as far as I can recollect) the first book which I had read willingly and with pleasure.'[33]

An article dealing with 'Woman's Rights and Duties' in the 1841 *Edinburgh Review* appears to have helped incite *A Plea for Woman*, published by William Tait in Edinburgh in 1843 and written by Marion Reid, a Glasgow merchant's daughter living as a married woman in Liverpool. Demonstrating a taste for poetry that ranges from 'the old ballad of the Wife of Auchtermuchty' to William Cowper, and a strong gift for reasoned argument, Reid produced a work 'designed to show, that social equality with man is necessary for the free growth and development of woman's nature', and that it 'belongs of right to woman'. Countering 'female depression' ('subjection' would be J. S. Mill's word in 1869), Reid considers not just education – 'no public care, in short, is taken to provide means for the education of girls, as is done for that of boys' – but also parliamentary voting rights: 'We have no wish whatever to see women sitting as representatives; but, in saying this, we must not be misunderstood; for neither do we think it just to prevent them by law from doing so.'[34] Introducing a modern reprint of Reid's work, Susanne Ferguson argues that

A Plea For Woman is a landmark book as the first to be written by a woman, for women, specifically arguing that possession of the vote is crucial in ending the discrimination against their gender in education and employment, showing that women's condition can improve only when they have a voice in choosing those who make laws.[35]

Certainly the book was several times reprinted and was read on both sides of the Atlantic. In 1844 the Scottish novelist and journalist

Christian Johnstone (who may have had some influence over the work's first publication) reviewed the *Plea* with interest in *Tait's Edinburgh Magazine*, revealing her own knowledge of feminist thinking and her wish for women to acquire greater financial and intellectual 'self-reliance'.[36] Writers such as Reid were beginning to realize that there was now a significant body of work written by modern female authors, some of them Scottish, so that 'woman' might take pride in 'the very respectable figure she has made in modern literature. De Stael, Hemans, Edgeworth, Baillie, Morgan, Martineau, More, Somerville, are names taken almost at random from a host of female writers who have certainly been much above mediocrity, even of manly talent.'[37]

More reassuring to conventional readers would have been the writings of Reid's near contemporary, the little-girl author from Kirkcaldy, Marjory Fleming (1803–11), whose three-volume diary was several times published decades after her death. In an age with a fondness for Little Nells, Fleming's accounts of her dolls and her reading captivated audiences. They remain charming and vivid, especially when shorn of the prettifications introduced by Victorian editors like Dr John Brown (1810–82) who, in a gesture which Marion Reid would not have appreciated, called the dead girl 'Pet Marjorie'. Brown's own pets were dogs and this Edinburgh physician wrote stories about them in such stories as *Rab and his Friends* (1859) and *Our Dogs* (1862). Henryson had written beast fables; Burns and other poets had given voices to dogs; now Brown published some of the first extended and artistically crafted adult prose fictions to have animals as protagonists. From *Black Beauty* and *Lassie* to John Muir's *Stickeen*, Jack London's *Call of the Wild*, Virginia Woolf's *Flush* and Kipling's *Jungle Book*, we take this genre for granted in fiction and in cinema, but Brown's work is important in its development, and should be remembered with his other essays. It was not only Charles Darwin whose Victorian prose investigated the links between humans and other species.

Brown's dog books appealed to the same Victorian taste that relished William Chambers's *Kindness to Animals* (1877). Alert to human suffering and decay, William's brother Robert felt a need to conserve a vanishing Scotland. In his twenties Robert Chambers (1802–71) collected *Traditions of Edinburgh* (1824) and *The Popular Rhymes of Scotland* (1826) as well as editing or writing other folkloric and historical works. With William he ran the publishing house of W. and R. Chambers, producing from 1832 their *Journal* which survived until 1956 and contained popular writing – essays, anecdotes, stories, articles – in Scots and English for a mass readership of over 30,000. The Chambers publishing house also brought out celebrated reference works such as Robert's four-volume *Biographical Dictionary of Eminent Scotsmen* (1832–4) and *Chambers's Encyclopaedia* (1859–68). Authoring books on topics from America to gypsies, the Peebles-born Chambers brothers were great Edinburgh educators whose work fuelled the kind of 'self-culture' encouraged in different ways by Carlyle, Marion Reid and Samuel Smiles. Robert Chambers's pioneering, controversial, and widely-read *The Vestiges of the Natural History of Creation* (published anonymously in 1844) also argued for evolutionary theory. This book was of great importance to the thinking of the Edinburgh-educated Charles Darwin and, looking out along the West Sands at St Andrews from his seafront villa, Robert Chambers went on to ponder the significance of *Ancient Sea-Margins* (1848).

Evolutionary thought developed alongside Carlyle's search for new systems of belief that might replace or reroute Christianity. The 1840s brought, too, not just growing political and industrial unrest, but also the ecclesiastical Disruption of 1843 which saw a breakaway from the Church of Scotland. Over 450 of its ministers refused to accept that landowners and influential patrons had a right to choose clergy for a parish. This choice, the breakaway group insisted, was the democratic entitlement of a congregation. These ecclesiastical democrats formed the Free Church of Scotland under the leadership of Thomas Chalmers, and this division in Scotland's Established Kirk had wide repercussions throughout society. The literary figure in Scotland who best exemplifies many of the upheavals of the time is the largely self-taught polymath Hugh Miller (1802–56), a Cromarty stonemason whose *The Old Red Sandstone* (1841) was partly published in *The Witness*, the periodical most closely identified with supporters of the Disruption. Here and in other geological studies like *Footsteps of the Creator* (1849), Miller eloquently articulated evolutionary thought and pondered the significance of fossils. Reading the biblical Book of Genesis allegorically, he argued that there must have been several stages of divine creation, the last of which produced humans. His works were very widely read, popular with those who struggled to reconcile Christian teaching with modern scientific discoveries. Robert Chambers was one of Miller's supporters, and the two men shared a passion for education. Miller's autobiography, *My Schools and Schoolmasters, or the Story of my Education* (1854), was admired by Carlyle and others for its emphasis on the need for working people to educate themselves, rather than engaging in social revolution.

Many of Miller's contemporaries showed more restless anger. The working-class Aberdeenshire weaver poet William Thom (1798–1848), author of a Disruption poem 'Chants for Churls' as well as of the urban 'Whisperings of the Unwashed', published his *Rhymes and Recollections of a Handloom Weaver* in London in 1844 and complained in prose that 'Starvation to death is not uncommon amongst us; yet we are in the nineteenth century – the pearl age of benevolent societies, charity-schools, and "useful knowledge".'[38] Others, like Thomas Chalmers and the Free Church minister Thomas Guthrie (1803–73) in his *A Plea for Ragged Schools* (1847) and *The City: Its Sins and Sorrows* (1857) were all too aware of such problems, but none wrote of a working man's quest for education more engagingly than Hugh Miller.

Growing up poor in Cromarty, Miller was lucky to be born into rural rather than urban Scotland. 'It seems to be very much the fashion of the time', he wrote, 'to draw dolorous pictures of the condition of the labouring classes', but he knew what it was to struggle. Noting how the dust from stoneworking 'had begun to affect my lungs', Miller mentions almost casually that 'few of our Edinburgh stone-cutters pass their fortieth year unscathed, and not one out of every fifty of their number ever reaches his forty-fifth year.'[39] His title *My Schools and Schoolmasters* is largely ironic. Miller's is not a book about academics, but shows 'that life itself is a school, and Nature always a fresh study'. Whether he writes about the Highland Clearances or about Scottish colliers who had the status of 'born slaves', the well-read Miller, steeped in Burns, presents what is probably the nineteenth century's best auto-biography by a British working man.[40] Its readers should bear in mind that serfdom ended in Scotland only in 1799 and that the eighteenth century associated with the Scottish Enlightenment was also the century which inscribed on a housebreaker's penitential brass collar (now one of the most eloquent pieces of material culture in Edinburgh's National Museum of Scotland) the words 'A PERPETUAL SERVENT'.

Miller's book shows how different were the several Scotlands of his day. Growing up on the edge of a northern, Gaelic-speaking community, the young Miller knew Edinburgh only from books and anecdotes. He came to it as to 'a great magical city' and was 'as entirely unacquainted with great towns at this time as the shepherd in Virgil'. Edinburgh, with its Old Town and New Town, came to impress him as 'not one, but two cities – a city of the past and a city of the present – set down side by side as if for purposes of comparison'.[41] Drawing in part on the doppelgänger motif of German Romanticism, this conscious imaging of division, notable in Hogg and Stevenson, was not uncommon in nineteenth-century Scottish writing; it would be held up by Hugh MacDiarmid in the twentieth century as characterizing a peculiarly Scottish aesthetic. Division, though, belongs to no one nation. Just as much as Hugh Miller's Scotland, nineteenth-century England was seen as just as divided between haves and have-nots, while, later, Laforgue, Yeats, Eliot and other non-Scottish modernist authors would write in ways that hardly suggest that the divided consciousness was uniquely Caledonian. Hugh Miller, stonemason and man of letters, geologist and defender of the Bible, his prose winding from local anecdotes to elaborate descriptions of fossils, might seem a divided personality. Yet his prose is not just based on binaries. It is convincing because it sets out the way in which he is a complex, nuanced person who cannot simply be pigeonholed as 'working-class autodidact' or 'split self'. He discovered in writing the way to articulate his manifest interests and beliefs but, prone to despair, he took his own life. He shot himself in 1856, only two years after completing his autobiography. He was a stonemason who had passed the age of fifty.

Though it is often characterized as an age of stifling respectability, Victorian Scotland, like Carlyle's prose, seethed and veered between excitement and despair. Readers rightly despair when they encounter the work of Dundee's seething and veering celebrant William McGonagall (c. 1825–1902), author of such metrical atrocities as the 'Railway Bridge of the Silvery Tay'. No one has ever proved that the Tay rail bridge tragically collapsed in 1879 simply because McGonagall sang its praises, but the thought is allowable. Still in print and much translated, his verse is so earnestly and elaborately bad that deservedly, despite all naysaying, it has ensured his immortality. Just across the Tay from the jute mills of Dundee, but otherwise far removed, the St Andrews philosopher James Frederick Ferrier in his 1854 *Institutes of Metaphysics* coined the word 'epistemology' – the science of the foundations of knowledge – but he also invented another, more negative-sounding term which failed to catch on: 'agnoiology', the philosophy of ignorance. The chill of abnegation felt in Carlyle's 'Everlasting No' is also heard in the journalist–poet William Anderson's 'I'm Naebody Noo', and resounds most appallingly in James Thomson's later Victorian poem *The City of Dreadful Night*.[42] Despair as well as faith is a marked note in Scottish Victorian writing. The Kelso minister Horatius Bonar (1808–89) wrote some of Scotland's finest nineteenth-century hymns, sometimes showing a tender eroticism ('Beloved, let us love: love is of God'). He also redirected some of the language taken over by Carlyle for his gospel of work, and brought it back into the fold of a Christian hymn:

> Go, labour on while it is day:
>> The world's dark night is hastening on;
> Speed, speed thy work; cast sloth away;
>> It is not thus that souls are won.[43]

Some of this might seem in tune with a drive for greater industrial productivity, but there were times when, even for Carlyle himself, all the hard work could appear pointless:

> What is man? A foolish baby,
>> Vainly strives, and fights, and frets;
> Demanding all, deserving nothing; –
>> One small grave is what he gets.[44]

Revealingly, Carlyle has no time for babies. A sense of doomladen struggle is heard often in the religious verse and hymn-writing of the time. 'Courage, brother! do not stumble/ Though thy path be dark as night', urges Glaswegian evangelist Norman Macleod in a popular hymn, while in Edinburgh the professor–poet William Edmondstoune Aytoun (1813–65), teaching Rhetoric and Belles Lettres (soon renamed English Literature) at the University, wrote of how the Calvinist 'cold Geneva ban' on older Catholic festivities had long since turned 'The ancient Scottish Christmas' into 'A cheerless day! – A gloomy time!' 'Let us all be unhappy on Sunday,' urged Charles, Lord Neaves (1800–76), mockingly rhyming 'frigid' with 'over-rigid'.[45]

Harshness in mid-nineteenth-century Scotland was registered not only by titled after-dinner wits like the stylish Neaves, but also by hard-pressed working-class poets like Glasgow's poverty-stricken James

Macfarlan who, before his death at the age of thirty in 1862, had won the attention of Dickens and Thackeray. Working close to the Lanarkshire coalfields, Macfarlan wrote in 'The Lords of Labour' of how 'Through the mists of commerce ... / ... souls flash out, like stars of God,/ From the midnight of the mine'.[46] Contrasts between illumination and pitch-blackness, riches and poverty, high culture and destitution characterize the general culture of the time and the specific literary productions of a host of significant, often little-researched minor writers. Sir William Stirling Maxwell (1818–78), whose family had grown rich from the horrors of Caribbean slavery, produced his groundbreaking art-historical work *Annals of the Artists of Spain* (1848). The poet–painter William Bell Scott published in 1869 his monograph on Albrecht Dürer, and painted in Northumbria a large-scale industrial scene, *Iron and Coal* (1861). Yet Scott's unoriginal verse is in flight from such a sense of modernity, and his finest paintings are small, luminous landcapes such as the painting of Ailsa Craig now in the Yale Center for British Art.

Scottish writers contributing to the world of European high-art connoisseurship seem far removed from the urban poor depicted in Alexander Brown's documentary prose in 'Shadow''s 1858 *Midnight Scenes and Social Photographs: Being Sketches of Life in the Streets, Wynds, and Dens of the City*. Originally written for a newspaper, Brown's 'sketches' reveal in convincing detail Glaswegian slum life with its 'Rags, poverty, disease and death' – and pubs:

One can scarcely realize the enormous number of these houses, with their flaring gas lights in frosted globes, and brightly gilded spirit casks, lettered by the number of gallons, under the cognomen of 'Old Tom' or 'Young Tom', as the case may be, with the occasional mirror at the extreme end of the shop reflecting at once in fine perspective the waters of a granite fountain fronting the door, and the entrance of poor broken-down victims, who stand in pitiful burlesque in their dirty rags, amid all this pomp and mocking grandeur.[47]

South of the Border, such scenes were the stuff of fiction for Dickens, Elizabeth Gaskell and others. Industrialization and city squalor certainly inform some of Carlyle's writings, but in the mid-nineteenth century these issues feature surprisingly little in the imaginative prose from a Scotland whose Central Belt was one of the world's most rapidly industrializing zones. After the heyday of Scott, Hogg and Galt, Scottish fiction was rather in the doldrums and seldom engaged with the greatest challenges facing the surrounding society.

For all that a series of *Whistle-binkie* anthologies of generally sub-Burnsian verse attracted popular praise, the most convincing attempts to deal imaginatively with the modern city came not in mid-nineteenth-century Scottish fiction, but in poetry. In 1857 Alexander Smith, a twenty-seven-year-old West of Scotland tradesman who eventually became Secretary to Edinburgh University, published *City Poems*. One of these was 'Glasgow' in which Smith rather determinedly discovered 'Another beauty, sad and stern' in the 'streams of blinding ore' of local steelworks, in 'smoky sunsets' and in 'rainy nights, when street and square/ Lie empty to the stars'. This city of flaring lights and darkness is hailed apocalyptically as 'Terror!' and 'Dream!' It is also where the speaker lives, veering between excitement and exhaustion, and where his dead are buried: 'A sacredness of love and death/ Dwells in thy noise and smoky breath'.[48] Accused of plagiarisms from Romantic and other poets, Smith is an uneasy writer of verse. There were great arguments about the way his poetry evolved, but these may tell us more about Victorian anxieties over evolution than they tell us about Smith. Often his poems sound as if they have pinched images from James Macfarlan (or perhaps vice versa). Smith is associated with the 'Spasmodic' school of the 1850s with its liking for rather melodramatic emotionalism, tellingly mocked in W. E. Aytoun's 'spasmodic tragedy' of 1854, *Firmilian*. Nevertheless, contemporaries recognized in *City Poems* and its predecessor, *A Life Drama* (1853), the possibilities of a new urban poetry. Writing about *A Life Drama* in the 1853 *North American Review*, the Oxonian Scotophile Arthur Hugh Clough speculated a little grandly that 'in the blank and desolate streets, and upon the solitary bridges of the midnight city . . . there walks the discrowned Apollo, with unstrung lyre'.[49]

Smith, though, moved east to a different city. 'Edina, high in heaven wan,/ Towered, templed, metropolitan', begins his 'Edinburgh'. Scotland's capital is 'a Cyclops' dream'.[50] Hugh MacDiarmid would rework this in the following century as 'a mad god's dream'.[51] Smith, however, headed more and more towards the rural picturesque. The prose of *Dreamthorp* (1863) idealizes unchanging village life. Yet his charming travel book *A Summer in Skye* (1865) is hard-headed enough to picture a community 'encouraged' to emigrate to Canada by a landlord who sees his land as unproductively 'over-populated':

When we got to Skeabost there were the emigrants, to the number perhaps of fifty or sixty, seated on the lawn. They were dressed as was their wont on Sundays, when prepared for church. The men wore suits of blue or gray felt, the women were wrapped for the most part in tartan plaids. They were decent, orderly, intelligent and on the faces of most was a certain resolved look, as if they had carefully considered the matter and made up their minds to go through with it.[52]

This understated prose about Gaelic emigrants is at least as eloquent as Smith's spasmodic urban exclamations.

Among Gaelic poets, whether emigrants or not, there was resentment against what was happening to their communities. Sometimes this had a political dimension. Eóghan MacColla from Argyll emigrated to Canada in 1849, thirteen years after publishing his first collection of poetry in Gaelic and English. His 'Fóghnan na h-Alba' (Thistle of Scotland) may have a nationalist resonance that attunes it to some of the notes heard in the later 'Na Croitearan Sgitheanach' (The Skye Crofters) by Niall MacLeòid (1843–1924). Now considered too sickly-sweet, but once the nineteenth century's most popular Gaelic poet, MacLeòid looked forward to a time when 'An end will come to oppression'.[53] A similar nationalist strain is detectable in the work of the autodidact Uilleam MacDhun-léibhe (William Livingstone, 1808–70) who was born on the Inner Hebridean island of Islay, worked as a tailor, and emigrated not to Canada but to the Scottish Lowlands. Livingstone spent his latter years in Tradeston, Glasgow, a city that was increasingly a destination for Gaelic speakers seeking work. Absorbing or reabsorbing the epic scale and sustained narrative of Macpherson's Ossianic materials into Gaelic poetic tradition, Livingstone celebrates Bannockburn and battles between Gaels and Norsemen. Sometimes virulently anti-English, he sympathizes with an oppressed Ireland and writes of the Highlands with bleak images of depopulation and resentment – 'nettles sprouting through stones'.[54]

Livingstone began a history of Scotland, and translated from French, Latin and other tongues. If his nationalism can have a bitter streak, he was not small-minded. Perhaps his finest poem, 'Fios thun a' Bhàird' (A Message to the Poet) offers at the start of its fourteen eight-line stanzas an idyllic picture of Islay on a sunny, breezy day. Yet, as the poem develops, it becomes obvious that Livingstone's native island 'has lost her people,/ the sheep have emptied homes.' A refrain,

Mar a fhuar 's a chunnaic mise:
Thoir am fios so chun a' Bhàird.

will you carry this clear message,
as I see it, to the Bard.

gives the poem a sense of insistent urgency, yet also makes the hearer or reader aware that the Bard, the poet to whom the message is addressed, is elsewhere, not on Islay. More than that, if the poem repeatedly insists on the conveyance of a bleakly lyrical message, it is never clear that the message reaches the Bard. Livingstone's figure of the Bard might be taken to represent not just a past or contemporary poet, but also the Gaelic poets of the future who must make something of this poem's message.

Tha'n nathair bhreac 'na lùban
Air na h-ùrlair far an d' fhàs
Na fir mhòra chunnaic mise:
Thoir am fios so chun a' Bhàird.

The spotted adder's coiling
on the floors whereon there grew
the great men that I saw here:
take this message to the Bard.[55]

Such a message would be a heavy burden for Gaels of the future to bear. In the school system, Gaelic was generally banned; none of the Scottish universities had a Chair in the subject. A note of resentful protest against the dwindling of their often oppressed culture can be heard in the work of many of the best Gaelic poets who followed Livingstone. It was, however, not the only note. The international popularity of the English version of a Gaelic carol by Mary MacDonald (1817–c. 1890) of Ardtun on the island of Mull indicated that Gaelic religious song, for instance, could have a powerful appeal outside Gaeldom, albeit through the reshaping medium of translation:

Leanabh an àigh, an leanabh aig Màiri,
Rugadh san stàball, Rìgh nan Dùl . . .

Child in the manger,
Infant of Mary;
Outcast and stranger,
Lord of all![56]

473

The translation is not quite a literal one, yet that English phrase 'Outcast and stranger' might refer not just to Christ but also to many an estranged and dispossessed nineteenth-century Gael.

Among such people might be numbered crofters from Skye, Islay and elsewhere; also, on occasion, lairds. By 1847 the Laird of Islay was forced by his creditors to sell the island where his son John Francis Campbell (1821–85) had grown up mixing with the locals and speaking Gaelic. Well connected, Campbell later worked in London as a leading civil servant who maintained a strong interest in science. A polymathic inventor and traveller with a knowledge of more than two dozen languages, he went on to publish in 1865 his *Short American Tramp* and other travel books including *My Circular Notes* (1876), perhaps the first artistically crafted Scottish literary account of a world tour. A good deal of Campbell's work lies unpublished in over a hundred manuscript volumes in the National Library of Scotland. Whether singing Gaelic songs in Tokyo with local resident Colin MacVean, son of a Mull Free Church minister and head of the Japanese Ordnance Survey, or taking part in a Faroese whale hunt, Campbell emblematizes that internationalism and sensitivity to other cultures which is strong in several of the most fascinating Scottish Victorian writers: from Daniel Wilson whose 1851 survey of Scottish archaeology and prehistory preceded a distinguished educational career in Canada and a study of *The Present State and Future Prospects of the Indians of British North America* (1874) to the much better-known Robert Louis Stevenson, writing with intelligent sympathy about Samoa as well as Scotland. Like these other authors, Campbell had a deep concern for threatened cultures and environments. He was in the Yosemite Valley at the same time as the Scottish-born conservationist John Muir, who would publish his own accounts of life there much later, and who promoted the idea of American National Parks. Where Muir's greatest service was to America, though, Campbell's was to Gaelic Scotland. He was encouraged to collect Gaelic material by the advice of the Reverend Norman MacLeod, the hymn-writer and essayist whose *Leabhar nan Cnoc (Book of the Hills)* (1834) included traditional Gaelic stories, and who published sermons and general prose as editor of the pioneering magazines *Teachdaire Gae'lach (Gaelic Messenger)* (1829–31) and *Cuairtear nan Gleann (Pilgrim of the Glens)* (1840–43). Work by his English friend George Dasent in *Popular Tales from the Norse* (1859) also spurred Campbell and several assistants to collect *Popular Tales of the West Highlands* (1860–62), a four-volume selection from a greater body of work which, the Islayman maintained, had been 'hitherto despised by natives and unknown to strangers'.[57]

Here, almost at a stroke, was the prose tradition Gaelic literature appeared to lack. Prose tales which had circulated orally were translated into English and bound between the covers of a book. Campbell urged helpers such as his old Islay tutor Hector MacLean to collect the stories without attempting to embellish them:

Choose rather the least educated parts of the Highlands . . . where Gaelic only is spoken . . . Do not trouble yourself to go to ministers and schoolmasters except for information as to the people. The educated generally know nothing of the amusements of the people and the Highland Ministers sometimes strive to put them down. I think they are wrong . . .[58]

Here the highly educated Campbell, writing to a tutor, recognizes the dangers of the largely Anglocentric education system for Gaelic culture. Like many translators from minority into majority languages, Campbell may at times appear a double agent, an imperial civil servant with primitivist tastes and sometimes suspect aversions. Yet there is a sense in which, wanting Gaelic and English materials 'side by side', Campbell performed a great service to the knowledge of Gaelic literature.[59] He corresponded with Gaelic poets like William Livingstone, and encouraged younger collectors including Alexander Carmichael (1832–1912). He brought Gaelic stories to a wider, non-Gaelic audience increasingly alert to comparative folklore and traditional tales. In 1872 Campbell published his *Leabhar na Féinne*, a major work on Gaelic heroic ballads that had been linked to Ossian. Whether at Balmoral or on the grouse-moors, Queen Victoria and others made sure the Highlands held a place in the Victorian imagination. Although there were important Scottish Celtic and Gaelic scholars such as William Forbes Skene in his co-translation of the medieval Gaelic *Book of the Dean of Lismore* (1862) and in *Celtic Scotland* (1876–80), Campbell was none too sympathetic towards the attempts in 1870 of Archibald Clerk to publish *Poems of Ossian in the original Gaelic* with a parallel English text. Ossianic enthusiasm remained strong in Victorian Scotland, sometimes frustrating Campbell's more scholarly projects; on reading P. Hately Waddell's *Ossian and the Clyde*, Campbell rewrote the author's name as 'Hateful

Twaddle'. However, conscious that there was now in Norway a professor of the Lapp language, Campbell joined in campaigning against the 'extraordinary and culpable neglect' of Gaelic studies in Scotland.[60]

Such vehemence led eventually to the establishment of a Chair of Celtic Language and Literature at Edinburgh University, and the appointment of a professor of that subject in 1882. Better late than never, but by this time there were clear indications that Gaelic was in serious decline. Its heritage was being archived – as in the Reverend Alexander Nicolson's 1881 *Collection of Gaelic Proverbs and Familiar Phrases* – but when Campbell had been a boy on Islay there had been over a quarter of a million Gaelic speakers in a Scotland of around two million people; by the end of the nineteenth century the total number of Gaelic speakers had declined only slightly, but it now represented only about 7 per cent of a Scottish population nearly five million in number. In 1800 there were not far off 300,000 monolingual Gaels; by 1901 there were fewer than 30,000.[61] If the power of London made some Scottish commentators worry that a distinctive Scottish culture was being lost, then in the Highlands and Islands Gaelic was acutely threatened. In the early years of the twentieth century my English-speaking maternal grandfather, a MacLean of Duart, went with his friend Lachie Macintyre to Skye and stayed in the house of an old Gaelic-speaking woman who had no English. A few decades later there were almost no monolingual Gaelic speakers left in the whole country. Even in the nineteenth century it became evident that Gaelic was imperilled.

Often employment prospects and the chance of industrial work drew Gaelic speakers southwards, and even to the ends of the earth. Descended from Gaels on the island of Ulva, the young David Livingstone famously read his way out of a cotton mill in Blantyre in industrial Lanarkshire, trained as a medical missionary, then headed for Africa where the town of Blantyre, Malawi, is one of several tributes to his mission. An evangelist and explorer who campaigned against African slavery, he published vivid English-language accounts of his travels. Livingstone wrote about having to drink water swarming with insects, putrid with rhinoceros urine and buffalo dung. His narratives dealt with wrestling with a lion, and with the horrors of chained slave gangs. *Missionary Travels and Researches in South Africa* (1857), which chronicled his journeys across Angola, Zambia and Mozambique, found an eager Victorian public for whom Livingstone embodied courage and muscular Christianity.

'Discoverer' of the Zambesi River, he relished Africa and his fame was far from confined to Britain. When Livingstone, ill at Tobora, lost contact with the outside world in 1871, it was the *New York Herald* which sent its correspondent, Welsh-born H. M. Stanley, to find him. Stanley and his heavily armed team took four months to locate their man. Their success brought about a decorously amazing, half-embarrassed meeting – 'Dr Livingstone, I presume?' – which gave Stanley an international scoop and became one of the great tales of Victorian exploration. Joseph Conrad's *Heart of Darkness* relies for some of its darkly ironic power on readers knowing of this hunt for the great lost liberator, missionary and educator.

Livingstone delighted in his discoveries: a pencil drawing of 'the sanjika', a fish found in Lake Nyasa, swims diagonally across a crammed page of his journal (now in the National Library of Scotland's John Murray archive), surrounded on all sides by a crammed, black-ink account of a kind of potato found in the African 'highlands'.[62] Though they surely convey hardship, there is at times in Livingstone's several published books a sense of heroic gusto which can have a ripping-yarn quality. He communicates not only faith, but also a zest and danger shared by many other Victorian explorers, mountaineers and travellers – usually, but not exclusively, male:

The mere animal pleasure of travelling in wild unexplored country is very great. When on lands of a couple of thousand feet elevation, brisk exercise imparts elasticity to the muscles, fresh and healthy blood circulates through the brain, the mind works well, the eye is clear, the step firm, and a day's exercise always makes the evening's repose thoroughly enjoyable.

We have usually the stimulus of remote chances of danger either from beasts or men. Our sympathies are drawn out towards our humble hardy companions by a community of interests, and, it may be, of perils, which make us all friends.[63]

Although he seems to have had little taste for novels, Livingstone was well read. Stanley found him quoting long passages of Burns and Byron, as well as more recent British and American poets. His prose is some of the best nineteenth-century Scottish travel writing. Rich in anecdotes, it might be set beside other Scottish Victorian travellers' tales such as *Walk Across Africa* (1864) by Captain James Augustus Grant, a son of the manse from Nairn, or the many writings of the English-born,

Scottish-domiciled Isabella Bird Bishop (1831–1904), whose books dealt with her remarkable travels to America, Persia, China, Japan and Tibet.

Empire, evangelism and emigration provided opportunities for Scots with literary talents. If, early in the nineteenth century, the one-time editor of what became *Blackwood's Magazine*, Thomas Pringle (1789–1834), had written sometimes fascinatingly in his *African Sketches* (1834) effortful poems about the landscapes of South Africa, in the mid-century going abroad was often good for Scottish writers and writing. The international experience recorded in *My Circular Notes* and elsewhere by John Francis Campbell enhanced his awareness of comparative folklore and strengthened his work with Gaelic. Before emigrating, Fife's Thomas Carstairs Latto may have been the minor versifier of *The Minister's Kailyard* (a parish cabbage-patch title that heralds the later nineteenth-century so-called 'Scottish Kailyard' school), but across the Atlantic he grew more ambitious and set up in New York the *Scottish-American Journal* which published material in English, Scots and Gaelic. In Canada, where Scottish fiction would have a strong influence, Scottish-born Margaret Robertson, in *Shenac's Work at Home* (1866), wrote of the struggles and religious turmoils of a determined woman and her Highland family. Descended from Highland Scots, the great John Ross, Chief of the Cherokee Nation, supported his Native American people in developing their own newspaper and educational system while attempting with significant but only partial success to stand against the ethnic-cleansing policy of the Ulster-Scots US President Andrew Jackson.[64] Sometimes internationalization in nineteenth-century Scottish culture has been viewed too simply as a depletion of native talent. In the long run, it may have had a positive side, widening literary horizons and preparing the way for that more sophisticatedly stylish Scottish internationalism articulated by Robert Louis Stevenson.

Certainly an international outlook was opportunistically important to one of Stevenson's boyhood heroes, the novelist Robert Michael Ballantyne, nephew of James Ballantyne, Walter Scott's printer. Born in Edinburgh in 1825, R. M. Ballantyne left for Canada aged sixteen. For seven years he worked as a clerk for the Hudson's Bay Fur Company, then returned to Edinburgh to work for the publisher Thomas Constable. Ballantyne began his authorial career as a travel writer, publishing his journal as *Hudson's Bay* in 1848, but from 1855 until his death in Rome in 1894 he spiritedly manufactured a series of adventure stories for boys. Among his many books are *Snowflakes and Sunbeams; or The Young Fur-Traders* (1855), *The Coral Island* (1857), *The Gorilla Hunters* (1862) and *The Pirate City* (1874). These tales remained hugely popular well into the twentieth century, and girls read them too. My father was awarded two as school prizes in 1920s Aberdeenshire; one was part of the ambitious Glasgow publisher John Blackie's Library for Boys and Girls, the other published by Oxford University Press for Herbert Strang's Empire Library; my own copy of *The Coral Island* was published in 1968 in the Bancroft Classics children's series. These books' appeal is evident from the summary preceding the start of chapter XIV of *Martin Rattler, or A Boy's Adventures in the Forests of Brazil* (1858):

Cogitations and canoeing on the Amazon – Barney's exploit with an alligator – Stubborn facts – Remarkable mode of sleeping.[65]

Mixing strange facts and explorers' lore with death-defying adventures, Ballantyne's yarns with their boy heroes were competently written and offered their young readers a diet of curious foods, lots of smoking, and high-octane, exotic excitement:

Barney groaned again, and the hermit went on to enumerate the wicked deeds of the vampire-bats, while he applied poultices of certain herbs to Martin's toe, in order to check the bleeding, and then bandaged it up; after which he sat down to relate to his visitors the manner in which the bat carries on its bloody operations.[66]

Interestingly, the young hero Martin Rattler is English rather than Scottish. Charles (fifteen) and Kate (fourteen) in *The Young Fur-Traders* are Scots-Canadians, but frequently Ballantyne chooses English protagonists, probably with an eye on likely buyers of his books. Although the English naval author Captain Frederick Marryat had written land-based stories for children such as *The Settlers in Canada* (1844) and *The Children of the New Forest* (1847), the work of the man whom Stevenson in prefatory verses to *Treasure Island* called 'Ballantyne the Brave' is more exciting. The range and speed of Ballantyne's fiction both fed and were fuelled by the Scottish experience of empire. More than anyone else, he helped open up the market for boys' imperial tales that would be exploited by such periodicals as the London-based *Boy's Own*

Paper, and by such chaps as Banffshire-born William Stables whose more than a hundred ripping yarns included *Wild Adventures in Wild Places* (1881). This trend reached its apogee, though not its culmination, in *Treasure Island* (1883) where Stevenson's 'Mr Arrow, a brown old sailor with ear-rings in his ears and a squint' probably owes his unusual name to that of the ship in *The Coral Island*.[67]

Several of the greatest children's classics – *Treasure Island*, *Kidnapped*, *Peter Pan* – were written by Victorian Scots at the forefront of developments in this genre. Although its title was appropriated in the twentieth century by Enid Blyton, *Holiday House* (1839) by Catherine Sinclair moved Victorian children's fiction away from mere moralizing towards lively adventure, even if Sinclair's tales have a pious conclusion. Some of the most atmospheric children's writing was produced by authors who also wrote for an adult audience. Like Thomas Carlyle, George MacDonald (1824–1905) steeped himself in German literature – translating works such as E. T. A. Hoffmann's fantasy *The Golden Pot* – and studied for the ministry. Born in Huntly, Aberdeenshire, then educated at King's College, Aberdeen, he trained at London's Highbury Theological College where many of his friends and mentors came from the Scottish community. Doctrinal problems and serious illness meant that MacDonald's career as a Congregational minister was a short one, though he went on to work as a Professor of English at the recently founded Bedford College for Ladies in London. He also lectured in America and elsewhere, eventually going to live in Italy with his large family. Literature for MacDonald could be a surrogate church from whose pulpit he might sometimes attack Calvinism and at other times offer long, improving homilies. Even a contemporary reviewer used to Victorian moralizing could complain of MacDonald's novels that 'Each succeeding volume has been increasingly didactic . . . there is a lamentable falling off in artistic method and purpose.'[68]

Alongside didacticism in many of MacDonald's more than thirty novels runs a strange, often sensationalist, horrified fascination with sexuality. A naked young wife in *Paul Faber, Surgeon* (1879) urges her husband to 'Whip me and take me again', while the narrator imagines seeing 'the purple streak rise in the snow'; emblems of incest, bestiality and voyeurism contribute to an often claustrophobically dark eroticism that sits very uneasily with the didactic tone.[69] There is a strong sense of barely repressed urges in MacDonald's work, and fantasy – in the sexual as well as in other senses of that word – is bound up with some of his most 'realistic' fictions.

Critics may praise passages in MacDonald's *David Elginbrod* (1863), *Alec Forbes of Howglen* (1865) and *Robert Falconer* (1868) with their strong, sometimes autobiographical north-east Scottish settings and often lively Scots dialogue, but the books are damagingly uneven and their characters can be two-dimensional. MacDonald is at his best when he goes more fully into quite another dimension, as in his early and late fictions *Phantastes* (1858) and *Lilith* (1895). Neither book is aimed at children, but the 'Faerie Romance for Men and Women', *Phantastes*, a quest tale that draws on Novalis and German Romantic forms, offers adults a sense of magical fairytale transformations. One such moment is when the book's twenty-one-year-old protagonist Anodos, part fairy, part human, wakes in his bedroom:

I . . . became aware of the sound of running water near me; and, looking out of bed, I saw that a large green marble basin, in which I was wont to wash, and which stood on a low pedestal of the same material in a corner of my room, was overflowing like a spring; and that a stream of clean water was running over the carpet, all the length of the room, finding its outlet I knew not where. And, stranger still, where this carpet, which I had myself designed to imitate a field of grass and daisies, bordered the course of the little stream, the grass-blades and daisies seemed to wave in a tiny breeze that followed the water's flow . . .[70]

This sense of the domestic becoming the fantastic would appeal to such later fantasy writers as C. S. Lewis and J. R. R. Tolkien. It also powers MacDonald's fairy stories for children such as 'The Golden Key', *At the Back of the North Wind* (1871) and *The Princess and the Goblin* (1872) which helped to establish this author as one of greatest fantasy writers of nineteenth-century Britain, much admired by his friend Lewis Carroll.

With *Lilith* MacDonald's taste for strange sexuality is again apparent alongside his ability to trip the reader into an engulfing otherworld that intersects with the everyday. In that otherworld the bookish Vane finds the leopardess-leech-cat-vampire-princess Lilith, whose name is that of the biblical Adam's legendary first lover. 'Queen of Hell . . . Vilest of God's creatures', Lilith represents *'Life in Death'* and 'lives by the blood and lives and souls of men'.[71] Like Rider Haggard's *She* (1887) and Bram Stoker's *Dracula* (1897), *Lilith* is an exploration of the darker side of sexuality. Unlike those works, though, its centre of gravity lies in semi-allegorical fantasy, a genre which MacDonald did so much to develop in English prose. His fondness for fairies in books like *Dealings with the Fairies* (1867) would be continued in Scottish writing by the man of letters and anthropologist Andrew Lang (1844–1912), some of whose tales and edited collections such as *The Blue Fairy Book* (1889) were more innocently aimed at children. In softer, more folkloric form, the 'adult fairytale' would be part of the phenomenon of the Celtic Twilight. There its presence may have been encouraged by a sometimes soft-focus attitude to the collecting of folklorists such as John Francis Campbell and Alexander Carmichael, but also by writings like Mac-Donald's. MacDonald, like Lang and several of the Celtic Twilight writers, began as a poet, and the verse he produced throughout his writing life has its occasional but relatively rare successes.

Given the amount of time that MacDonald spent out of Scotland, it may seem surprising how many of his novels are set there. Yet memory is a strong theme in his work. His use of remembered scenes, events and dialogue from his youth in Aberdeen, Cullen and other parts of the north-east was often admired. A contributor to the genres of the sensation novel and, like Lewis Carroll, to children's fantasy fiction, Mac-Donald along with his fellow Victorian Scots should be seen against a British as well as a Scottish background. In this imperial era it was not unusual for Scots (including at times such luminaries as Carlyle) to describe themselves as English. If Scotland and Scottish cities gained wealth from the power of the British Empire, they did so as 'provincial' places. Some Scots might write 'N. B.' (North Britain) as part of their addresses, emphasizing a Britishness, but the term 'S. B.' for England was a non-starter. England, especially London, called the shots where Britain was concerned, not least when it came to novels published in book form.

Interestingly, William Donaldson argues that 'Book-fiction had never sold particularly well in Scotland and by 1900 it probably comprised about 3 per cent of the British market.'[72] There were ways round this, however. Some quite impressive novels appeared as serializations in popular Scottish newspapers. Notable here is the fiction of the Liberal Aberdeen journalist William Alexander (1826–1894), especially *Johnny Gibb of Gushetneuk* (1871), with its strong sense of vernacular voice and its sharp examination of capitalism at work. Alexander wrote, sometimes bitingly, of urban as well as rural Scotland. His work demonstrates a journalist's nose for political corruption. Born in Dundee in 1828, Alexander's fellow newspaperman David Pae published in the *North Briton* and other papers often melodramatic fictions such as *Lucy, the Factory Girl* (1860), taking beautiful heroines through urban slums. Pae's widely syndicated work may have enjoyed a broad Scottish readership, but most fiction in newspapers, then as now, was writing to be thrown away. While there was cash in this market, and journalism could be a useful training ground for writers, those with literary ambitions usually hankered after book publication, and the most powerful book-publishing houses were increasingly based in London. To write for them meant producing work which, while it might have a Scottish tang, had to appeal to an Anglocentric market. In a Scottish newspaper William Alexander might be able to present speech in the vernacular grain without apology (though his narrator uses standard English), but George MacDonald, publishing *Alec Forbes of Howglen* in London in 1865, is more self-consciously defensive when he wants to use Scots language:

I do not allow however that the Scotch is a *patois* in the ordinary sense of the word. For had not Scotland a living literature, and that a high one, when England could produce none, or next to none – I mean in the fifteenth century? But old age, and the introduction of a more polished form of utterance, have given to the Scotch all the other advantages of a *patois*, in addition to its own directness and simplicity.[73]

MacDonald's awareness that Scottish literature had flowered during a fallow period in the literature of England might prompt reflection not just on the position of Scots language versus imperial Victorian English, but also on the way in which in the heyday of Dickens, Thackeray, George Eliot and others – the greatest period of English fiction – the novel in Scotland is comparatively disappointing. There is no single explanation for this, but one should be wary about expecting a small culture to 'compete' with its much larger neighbour on quite the same terms, especially at a time when the high summer of the British Empire and the remarkable financial and cultural glow of London were alike attracting Scottish talent. Not so long before, Walter Scott had triumphantly sold Scottish cultural distinction to literary audiences around the globe. In Victorian times, though, the ideology of Britishness which Scott had championed led inevitably to kinds of cultural and economic assimilation. London's magnetic pull may have horrified Cockburn, and there might be attempts to resist it, but even those tended to be muted. The Edinburgh imperial soldier James Grant (1822–87) wrote Scottish-accented historical novels, a large-scale history of *Old and New Edinburgh* (1880), and chronicled imperial *British Battles on Land and Sea* (1873–5). He also founded the National Association for the Vindication of Scottish Rights in 1852, serving as its secretary. However, though it may be seen as an indication of concerns about asserting Scottish political and cultural distinctiveness, the Association did not envisage separation from the British state, monarchy or Empire. Among Grant's late works were studies of clans, tartans and Scottish soldiers. Symptomatically, he died in London.

So did Margaret Oliphant Wilson Oliphant, whose work became for three-quarters of a century a lost continent in Scottish literature. In recent years a small international band of scholars has explored her prodigious oeuvre, but almost all of her 125 or so books are out of print. At the very least, Oliphant is a missing link in Scottish literary history; at her best, she is a brave and hauntingly powerful writer. Born in 1828 in Wallyford, Midlothian, she lived as a child at Lasswade near Edinburgh, then in Glasgow before her family moved to Liverpool when she was ten. Though she later enjoyed sojourns in continental Europe, in Scotland and in the Middle East, most of her life was spent in south-eastern England; she died in Wimbledon in 1897. Margaret Oliphant once wrote of how England had swallowed up her principal publisher, Edinburgh's William Blackwood, 'like a husband with his wife'.[74] England would become her own principal residence, and the setting for many of her novels. But it never swallowed her up.

Oliphant's first published novel, *Passages in the Life of Mrs Margaret Maitland, of Sunnyside, Written by Herself* (1849) is set in Scotland and has a heroine who 'in her firm voice' stands up to her exploitative father: 'I *will not* go with you.' The Scots-tongued first-person narrator lives her life unwed, much to the consternation of an insistent suitor:

> 'Eh me!' cried out the body, mostly like to fall down with wonder and astonishment, 'but I thought a' womenfolk wanted to be marriet!'[75]

Oliphant is far from opposed to marriage; it is simply not for her the be-all and end-all of a woman's life. Her views and several of her future fictional preoccupations are clear in *Margaret Maitland*, published three years before her own marriage to her artist cousin Frank Oliphant in 1852. When Frank died of tuberculosis in Rome seven years later, Margaret was left there in debt, heavily pregnant, and with several young children to support. She never remarried. With the exception of the Queen (whose biography she wrote), she became the Victorian age's most successful single mother, her work read across several continents. For the rest of her life she made enough money from her writing to educate her large family (all of whom predeceased her) and to support an array of male and female relations. Although women were still excluded from the universities, Oliphant wrote pioneering non-fiction in fields as different as modern literary and publishing history, the aesthetics of dress, and Dante. Often working at night while her children slept, she was a biographer, a frequent reviewer (especially for *Blackwood's Magazine*), but most of all a writer of fiction. She may be seen as a feminist heroine; yet she was unsure if she wanted the vote, and often appears to champion quiet, rather conventional feminine manners against outspokenly feminist ones. As a result, male critics have tended to ignore her, while some feminists have found her politically and aesthetically incorrect. Having read many of Oliphant's works, Virginia Woolf, who was financially secure and had no dependants, asked if anyone could avoid deploring 'the fact that Mrs Oliphant sold her brain, her very admirable brain, prostituted her culture and enslaved her intellectual liberty in order that she might earn her living and educate her children?'[76]

There may be some truth in Woolf's stinging, self-interested question; but Oliphant, who had written ten books by the age of twenty-five, was a prolific, fast worker before she needed to earn money or provide for children. Although she later joined the Church of England, she grew up as a staunch supporter of the Free Kirk whose values of independent refusal of patronage are championed in *Margaret Maitland* and elsewhere. Like her friend Thomas Carlyle, Oliphant seems to have had a powerful sense of the Gospel of Work; her obsessive literary work ethic was reinforced, rather than initiated, by her later circumstances. However, where Carlyle gravitates towards heroic, masculine public life, Oliphant is attracted to removed, often feminine spaces. What can sound at times embarrassingly over-sweet or restricted in some of her titles – *Sunnyside*, *Lilliesleaf*, *The Minister's Wife* – is bound up with what spurs her imagination. Great events of history (such as the Disruption in *Margaret Maitland* or slavery in *Kirsteen*) are sensed in her work, but are not the focal point. This gives much of Oliphant's writing a displaced, provincial feeling. Her 'Chronicles of Carlingford' series, popular in her lifetime, is set not in London but in an English provincial town. Its 'pinched' and 'little' Salem Chapel, based on Oliphant's memories of Liverpool's Free Church of Scotland, is set 'on the shabby side of the street . . . in a narrow strip of ground . . . [so that] The big houses opposite, which turned their backs and staircase windows to the street, took little notice of the humble Dissenting community.'[77] *Salem Chapel* (1863), its minister protagonist based partly on her friend George MacDonald and partly on the Carlyles' Scottish evangelical friend Edward Irving (whose biography Oliphant wrote), relies, like her other Chronicles of Carlingford, on the precedent of Anthony Trollope's Barsetshire novels, as critics have noted. Yet aspects of Oliphant's place in Scottish literary tradition have been misunderstood.

The wording of Oliphant's 1849 title, *Passages in the Life of Mrs Margaret Maitland, of Sunnyside, Written by Herself*, echoes the titles of two earlier works. One is the resolutely provincial *The Life of Mansie Wauch, Tailor in Dalkeith, Written by Himself* (1828) by D. M. Moir, who had been Oliphant's childhood doctor and, later, her literary mentor; the other is J. G. Lockhart's 1822 *Some Passages in the Life of Mr Adam Blair, Minister of the Gospel at Cross-Meikle*. Like Lockhart's, Oliphant's book is in part a story about a minister, though where Lockhart concentrates on a man's adultery, Oliphant (who tackled such topics elsewhere) is interested in female attempts at self-definition. Her book's concern with the improvement of the rundown community of cottages at Cruive End, and the setting up of a new working-class 'colony' nearby, develops the interest in improvement in Elizabeth Hamilton's *The Cottagers of Glenburnie*. There are also references to Scott. As a strong female protagonist, Scott's Jeanie Deans is a model for several Oliphant heroines, including that of *Kirsteen* (1890), while the bereaved Oliphant identified strongly with the struggling widowed Scott of the *Journal*. However, Oliphant's work also points forward in Scottish literary history. Towards the end of *Margaret Maitland* we hear of 'the inhabitants of the town of Thrums' who are seeking to call a new Free Kirk minister.[78]

About four decades later in fictions by Oliphant's literary admirer the

London Scot J. M. Barrie, such as *Auld Licht Idylls* (1888), *A Window in Thrums* (1889) and *The Little Minister* (1891), the fictional Thrums would become the quintessential location for what came to be called 'Kailyard' (cabbage-patch) fiction. Barrie's provincial, small-town, restricted, minister-centred, sometimes feminine life of Thrums so enraged later (almost exclusively male) critics in part, surely, because Barrie, like his fellow Kailyarders, was working, sometimes with an element of ironic play, in a feminine genre. Galt and Moir had sketched small-town presbyterian Scottish life, but by Oliphant's time novels of this type had largely passed into the hands of female authors and audiences. Oliphant delighted in small-town stories, though she might write of Glasgow tenements and English life as well. Among her contemporaries was the prolific, best-selling Henrietta Keddie (1827–1914), a Cupar schoolmistress who later moved to London and often wrote as 'Sarah Tytler'. Keddie's novels include the lively depiction of small-town Cupar life in *Logie Town* (1887) as well as the Glasgow industrial fiction *St Mungo's City* (1884) and a sharp-eyed autobiography. When the mature Oliphant was uneasy about the writing of another younger best-selling Scottish author, Annie S. Swan (1859–1943), Swan admitted that her first great success, *Aldersyde* (1883), considered by Prime Minister Gladstone 'beautiful as a work of art' for its 'truly living sketches of Scottish character', was derived from Oliphant's work: 'The story was frankly modelled on the Border stories of Mrs Oliphant, for whom I had passionate admiration, amounting to worship.'[79] The Aberdeen-born London Scot and Free Church minister the Reverend William Robertson Nicoll (1851–1923), one of Oliphant's editors, also edited Swan (principal writer for his magazine *The Woman at Home*) and published the young J. M. Barrie as well as other 'Kailyard' writers in his journal *The British Weekly*. Barrie corresponded with Oliphant, edited a collection of her stories, and spoke at the unveiling of a memorial tablet to her in St Giles Cathedral, Edinburgh. His taking the place name of Thrums (meaning loose ends of thread in a loom) from Oliphant's first published novel represents both a wink and an act of covert homage. For Barrie and the male 'Kailyarders' with whom later critics connected him, to move into Oliphant's feminized territory was partly an act of shrewd commercialism – and partly a piece of gender-bending that over many decades has revealingly enraged many male Scottish writers and critics.

Oliphant, though, is much more than a bridge to the Kailyard. Her *Autobiography*, published in bowdlerized form in 1899, and in full by her biographer Elisabeth Jay in 1990, is the finest nineteenth-century Scottish work in that genre. Written between the mid-1860s and 1890s, its fragmentary form only enhances its power. It has a radiant sense of damage, often quickened by its author's grief over the deaths of her children, and by her sense of the pressures of her work. A number of its most memorable vignettes involve windows: the window of the all-male Royal and Ancient Golf Club at St Andrews through which Oliphant peers in a vain attempt to see her son; in Elie, Fife, in 1860, 'a deeply bowed window in which I worked, and where I remember people spoke of seeing my white cap always bending over the table'; a window in Normandy in 1864 where, after the death of a daughter, she was visited by her Free Kirk close friend Robert Story (whose proposal of marriage Oliphant seems to have refused):

... we went to see Bayeux and the tapestry, jogging along in a country shandry-dan [rickety conveyance] with a huge red umbrella ... and a wonderful thunder-storm there was – which he and I sat at an open window to watch, much to the annoyance and terror of our hosts, who would have liked to shut it out with bolted shutters –[80]

Oliphant is well aware that windows can shut out as well as admit a wider world. 'The Library Window', the finest of her impressive supernatural short stories 'of the seen and the unseen', features a girl who looks through a drawing-room window and sees, through another window across the street, an old scholar working in a room with books and papers in 'the old College Library' opposite.[81] Some see the window across the street as blocked off; to a few it is transparent. Set in a very identifiable St Andrews ('St Rule's') where, as Oliphant knew, there had been much debate about the admission of women to the university, this first-person narrative can be read in terms of a girl's longing for closed-off, male-controlled knowledge and literary power – the old scholar is associated at one point with Oliphant's admired Walter Scott; yet the tale is also about female sexuality, isolation and loss. What makes it perhaps the best Scottish short story about a ghost is its nuanced refusal of any one interpretation, and its fusion of precise local detail with barely discerned supernatural presence. This narrative is in many ways deep-rooted in Oliphant's psyche. Its strange old Lady

Carnbee, who eventually wills to the protagonist her fascinating but threatening ring, takes her name from a hamlet between St Andrews and Kellie, old Oliphant family territory; Oliphants lie buried in Carnbee kirkyard.

Oliphant's best short fictions often involve encounters with representatives of the recent and the long-gone dead. From the first, she had felt an impulse to write in ways other than the straightforwardly realistic. *Margaret Maitland* contains a long inset allegorical piece in which the figure of Hope retreats further and further inside a sunlit fortress surrounded by 'a beleaguering army'.[82] Offering a critique of materialism and making subtle use of multiple narrators, her splendid 1879 tale, 'A Beleaguered City', hints at women's spiritual strengths as it tells how, after the men in French Semur maintain that 'There is no *bon Dieu* but money', the town is taken over by the spirits of the dead.[83] Others among those 'stories of the seen and the unseen' which Oliphant felt compelled to write over a number of years, and with which she took particular stylistic care, engage with hope, despair, longing and scepticism. They also indicate the impact of Dante on her work. The Italian poet is alluded to directly in both 'Earthbound' and 'The Land of Darkness'.

Even as Christianity came under attack, Dante fascinated the Victorians. Carlyle had supplied corrections to the 1844 edition of Englishman Henry Cary's early nineteenth-century translation of *The Divine Comedy*, and regarded Dante as a 'world-voice' in his lecture on 'The Hero as Poet'.[84] In Dundee the poet James Young Geddes (1850–1913), an admirer of Whitman who wrote bitingly about industrial capitalism, invoked Dante in *The New Inferno* (1879). Dante Gabriel Rossetti, Margaret Oliphant and others published studies and translations of the Italian poet, but no writer made more compelling imaginative use of Dante than the poet James Thomson (1834–82) who, though an atheist, came to agree with Ruskin that Dante was 'the central intellect of all this world'.[85] Born in Port Glasgow on Clydeside, Thomson had little time for the Scot who had 'no national fervour', though his mother (a follower of the charismatic Scottish preacher Edward Irving) had removed him to London when he was eight after his father, a seaman, suffered a stroke.[86] Brought up in London's Royal Caledonian Asylum, Thomson recalled obtaining a copy of *Ivanhoe* 'for an heroic sacrifice of fruit or sweeties', and poring over it.[87] Entering the army, then, as alcohol and depression took their toll, living eventually as a struggling freelance writer, he added to his love of Burns and ballads a remarkable knowledge of literature that extended from Heine and Leopardi (whose poems he translated) to Baudelaire and Whitman, subjects of some of his many essays and reviews. Perhaps Thomson's happiest time was spent as secretary to a mining company in Colorado. He wrote vividly of his time in the American West, relishing hailstones in a canyon, 'quite as big as goodsized walnuts'.[88] Better known and more characteristic, however, are his hallucinatory visions of urban life.

With epigraphs from Dante's *Inferno* and from Leopardi, Thomson's masterpiece, the long poem *The City of Dreadful Night* (1874), presents a nameless phantasmal cityscape. An exhausted speaker treks through it, encountering figures such as a vast statue of Albrecht Dürer's *Melancolia* whose significance brings 'confirmation of the old despair'. In this greatest Victorian urban poem, there is a chilling, steely nihilism:

> As whom his one intense thought overpowers,
>   He answered coldly, Take a watch, erase
> The signs and figures of the circling hours,
>   Detach the hands, remove the dial-face:
> The works proceed until run down; although
> Bereft of purpose, void of use, still go.[89]

At its often hallucinatory best, Thomson's work helped propel T. S. Eliot's Dantescan vision of London in *The Waste Land*; Eliot's famous phrase 'memory and desire' comes from Thomson.[90] *The City of Dreadful Night* has also mattered to poets from the Greek Cavafy to the modern Scots Edwin Morgan and Tom Leonard, Thomson's most recent biographer. Among the poets Thomson himself admired were Shelley, another atheist who sought to redeploy Dante in English, and the German Novalis, whose *Hymns to the Night* Thomson translated. Sometimes, in homage to these poetic exemplars Thomson styled himself 'Bysshe Vanolis', or 'B. V.' In 1873, while suffering from an eye infection, he wrote to his sister-in-law from a rented room at 230 Vauxhall Bridge Road, London, and imaged himself, half-jokingly, as tramping the city streets, 'an inverted sleep-walker – eyes shut awake instead of eyes open asleep'.[91] In Thomson's diaries (now in the Bodleian Library, Oxford) his neat black-ink nib-writing every so often becomes jagged and hard to decypher as alcohol overcomes the writer. It is hard not to view this diarist as the suicidal author in Thomson's remarkable poem 'In the Room' where dusty, beetle-ridden household objects discuss the behaviour of the late occupant:

> The table said, He wrote so long
>   That I grew weary of his weight;
> The pen kept up a cricket song,
>   It ran and ran at such a rate:
> And in the longer pauses he
>   With both his folded arms downpressed,
> And stared as one who does not see,
>   Or sank his head upon his breast.[92]

Strictly schooled in religion, Thomson recalled as a young child reading for their imagery Edward Irving's apocalyptic volumes among his mother's books in Port Glasgow. Though Thomson can reveal a sense of humour, doom-laden imagery seldom leaves his poetry. Its intensity is more aesthetically convincing than the uplift of a plethora of minor Scottish Victorian hymn-writers. *The City of Dreadful Night* sits impressively beside such powerful tales as Oliphant's 'A Beleaguered City' and 'The Land of Darkness'.

Thomson very seldom wrote about Scotland. Like Oliphant, he had in England a writerly network in which several Scots were prominent. This is exemplified by the reviews and essays which he wrote for an unusual journal, *Cope's Tobacco Plant*. Edited from Liverpool by John Fraser, this heady mix of nicotine and literature sold through tobacconists, newsagents and railway bookstalls, as well as direct to subscribers. *Cope's* was one of Thomson's most regular literary employers. A London-Scottish bookman friend, William Maccall, put Thomson in touch with Fraser, who also gave work to other England-based Scots such as Gordon Stables (like Fraser, an ex-seaman). The *Tobacco Plant* was by no means exclusively Scottish, but Thomson (who kept his copies, now in Glasgow University Library, marked up with meticulous authorial corrections) wrote there about Hogg and Burns as well as about Rabelais and Meredith. He always tried to find a smoker's angle, reviewing books on his 'smoke-room table' or discussing 'The Tobacco Duties' or 'Charles Baudelaire on Hasheesh'. Such a masculine, 'smoke-room table' milieu was part of the fug of the age. The same era produced the tobacco-ash expert Sherlock Holmes. It led Stevenson in *An Inland Voyage* (1878) to write about a canoe called *Cigarette*. A few years later J. M. Barrie wrote for the *St James's Gazette* ironically playful pieces with titles like 'My Smoking-Table' and 'How Heroes Smoke' which he collected in 1890 as *My Lady Nicotine*.

Barrie's playfulness is alien to much of Thomson's work, though both men were London freelance authors. Scots were responsible for some of the best-known, most durably dangerous versions of London in the later nineteenth century, whether the capital was metamorphosed into the city of dreadful night, or the 'city in a nightmare' of Stevenson's 1886 Jekyll and Hyde, or that other murderscape with its 'ghost-like ... procession of faces' in Arthur Conan Doyle's stories of Sherlock Holmes.[93] As Lord Cockburn had sensed in 1852, London was irresistible. That city, not Glasgow or Edinburgh, was the great metropolis of the late Victorian and Edwardian Scottish literary imagination. The cityscape through which Jekyll and Hyde pass bears the name of the British capital. The Edinburgh surgeon, Joseph Bell, may have been Conan Doyle's model for Sherlock Holmes, but London is where he operates. However much Peter Pan owes to Barrie's Scottish childhood, if he belongs anywhere on earth it is to London's Kensington Gardens. The height of Britain's global power made London the pre-eminent world city. The nation-building impetus in Scottish fiction, so long geared to Britishness, now fed (and fed off) the commercial, political and literary dominance of the British capital.

If James Thomson in London was a kind of *flâneur* of hell, then Robert Louis Stevenson (1850–94), playing truant as a teenage student in the open streets of Edinburgh, sought to be more buoyantly Parisian. Like Thomson, Stevenson admired Walt Whitman, and Whitman's 'loafer' in part underlies Stevenson's early praise of the 'idler', a *flâneur*-like figure developed later by England's Jerome K. Jerome. Raised in a remarkable Scottish family of often sternly Calvinist lighthouse-builders, the sickly Edinburgh child Stevenson delighted in his heroic heritage, but, in an era shaped by Carlyle's gospel of work as popularized by Samuel Smiles, Stevenson made it clear that he had had enough: 'Extreme *busyness*, whether at school or college, kirk or market, is a symptom of deficient vitality; and a faculty for idleness implies a catholic appetite and a strong sense of personal identity.'[94] Stevenson's use of the word 'kirk' in that sentence from his essay 'An Apology for Idlers' (not to

mention his provocative use of the word 'catholic') hints at the
Knoxian solemnity he was reacting against. 'Child's Play', another of
the slightly mannered essays from his early book 'for girls and boys',
Virginibus Puerisque (1881), invoked Paris's Théophile Gautier
(who had used the phrase 'Art for art's sake') and said of children at
play that ' "Art for art" is their motto.'[95] The rarefied Oxford don Walter
Pater had controversially championed 'the love of art for its own sake'
in the conclusion of his 1873 *Studies in the History of the Renaissance*.
Stevenson, writing of ' "Art for art" ' in the context of 'nursery education', made it seem natural and good for all. One of Stevenson's
supporters, the St Andrews educationalist and pioneering translator
of Turgenev Professor John Meiklejohn, was an enthusiast for the
German movement then known in Britain and America as 'Children's
Gardens' – kindergarten, as we now say – which emphasized the importance of parent-and-child play. The poems of Stevenson's *A Child's
Garden of Verses* (1885) revel in playing, though sometimes the
child's play separates offspring from parents, as in 'The Land of
Story-Books':

> At evening when the lamp is lit,
> Around the fire my parents sit;
> They sit at home and talk and sing,
> And do not play at anything.
>
> Now, with my little gun, I crawl
> All in the dark along the wall,
> And follow round the forest track
> Away behind the sofa back.[96]

Such a transformation of the domestic into imaginative wilderness is of
a piece not just with George MacDonald's best work but also with what
happens in the 'boys' stories', *Treasure Island* (1883) and *Kidnapped*
(1886). Stevenson, however, did not begin as a children's writer, but
more as an energetic 'idler'.

Written with studied insouciance, *An Inland Voyage* (1878) follows
in the wake of John MacGregor's highly popular *A Thousand Miles in
the Rob Roy Canoe* (1866) which established its author as a European
celebrity and made canoeing a popular pastime. As his manuscripts
(now in the Beinecke Library at Yale) record, MacGregor canoed solo

to France and back in 1867. Robert Louis Stevenson's 1878 book lovingly details a canoe trip made by Stevenson and his pal Walter Simpson through Belgium and Northern France. Often ordered south for his health, Louis (he pronounced it 'Lewis') was a Francophile as well as one of the mainstays of modern travel writing. Going furth of Scotland brought him far less a sense of cultural diminution than a delight in travel for travel's sake that matches his stylish sense of art for art's sake. As he puts it, on the road in *Travels with a Donkey in the Cevennes* (1879),

For my part, I travel not to go anywhere, but to go. I travel for travel's sake. The great affair is to move; to feel the needs and hitches of our life more nearly; to come down off this feather-bed of civilization, and find the globe granite underfoot and strewn with cutting flints.[97]

Curiously, as it moves among French Catholic and Protestant communities, *Travels with a Donkey* is one of the best Scottish books about sectarianism. Those cutting flints may have appealed to a sensibility shaped by Calvinism, but they also spark and speak of the energetic relish for the physical outdoor world on the part of an 'idle' man often bedridden. On and off the road, *Treasure Island* and *Kidnapped* are full of energetic running and jumping, chases, hide and seek. 'Hide and seek', Stevenson wrote in 'Child's Play', 'is the well-spring of romance.'[98] The playfulness of Stevenson's style often manifests itself in a mixture of sympathetic engagement and ironic humour – a simultaneous involvement and independence that retains a companionable warmth. J. M. Barrie would sometimes attempt something similar.

Stevenson's relations with his father were strained by his liaison with a married older woman, the American Fanny Osbourne, whom the writer met in France and pursued to California. The two married there in 1880. Savouring 'the smack of Californian earth', they lived for a time on the American west coast: 'These long beaches are enticing to the idle man.'[99] *The Amateur Emigrant* (1895) and *The Silverado Squatters* (1883) were written then, though published later. They vividly record Stevenson's interactions with the human and non-human aspects of the American environment. He was happy as a squatter in the high-altitude mining village of Silverado, breathing the resinous forest air. As the first major Scottish writer to be influenced by American literature, Stevenson in his 'healthy' Californian 'glen' draws on impulses in Thoreau and

Whitman; his sensuous love of the American wilderness, however, also links him to his literary contemporary John Muir (1838–1914), the pioneering ecological thinker and 'self-styled poetico-trampo-geologist-bot' who had left Scotland as a boy and whose own love of Californian landscape led him to promote the concept of America's National Parks, and to publish his wilderness discovery books such as *The Mountains of California* (1894), *Our National Parks* (1901) and *My First Summer in the Sierra* (1911).[100] The Muir of *Our National Parks* who encouraged tourists to 'Camp out among the grass' so that 'Nature's peace will flow into you as sunshine flows into trees' would have appealed to Stevenson the energetic outdoor idler.[101]

1880–81 was a crucial time in Stevenson's life. Marriage brought him an eleven-year-old stepson, Lloyd Osbourne. Becoming a father, Stevenson began both *A Child's Garden of Verses* and *Treasure Island*. Father and son made little books together; Lloyd began 'A Pirate story' about 'five . . . villinous [sic] looking men' who are engaged by a Captain and put to sea for a distant island.[102] With Lloyd, Stevenson, the one-time enthusiast for R. M. Ballantyne, re-entered his boyhood world as a participant, not simply as an observer. His stepson recalled how, when the family moved to Braemar in the summer of 1881, he tried to school Stevenson's belletristic literary tastes:

The thing that puzzled me was that he was as fond as I of Mayne Reid, Fenimore Cooper, Jules Verne, and Marryat; it was not as though he didn't appreciate good books; and certainly none of the seven hundred and fifty readers of *An Inland Voyage* could possibly have recognized in him the Indian, or Frontiersman, or Explorer, or Naval Officer (with accompanying Midshipman) landing with Secret Despatches on a Hostile Coast – embellishments which served to give such delight to our walks together, and always brought me home in such a glow of romance. That idolized step-father of mine was the most inspiring playfellow in the world – which made it seem all the sadder that he was unable to write a book worth reading.[103]

Lloyd was able to gain access to the boys' story enthusiast Stevenson which underlay the belletristic littérateur. More than anyone else, his stepson released in Stevenson the man who could play as distinct from the man who simply wrote about play. This was acknowledged by Stevenson in his eventual dedication of *Treasure Island*

To

LLOYD OSBOURNE

An American Gentleman
in accordance with whose classic taste
the following narrative has been designed
it is now, in return for numerous delightful hours
and with the kindest wishes, dedicated
by his affectionate friend

THE AUTHOR

Treasure Island is the product of father-and-son play, play of the kind that returned Stevenson to his own childhood world of 'Skeltery' – cut-out pirates – and of fantastic geographies such as those described in the essay 'Child's Play'. The pace and audience of *Treasure Island* demanded a curbing of Stevenson's 'fine writing', and in that curbing lay liberation. What is sometimes wrong with Stevenson's early work is that it strives too hard for a sophisticated 'Man of Letters' tone. His prose, like his best poetry, is often strongest when its language is both nuanced and most direct. That directness is linked to the author's deepest preoccupations, as in Stevenson's most famous poem, 'Requiem', which dates from early 1880:

> *Home is the sailor, home from sea,*
> *And the hunter home from the hill.*[104]

So it is with Stevenson's prose that around 1880–81 a shift takes place that rescues his writing from an excess of poise, and turns him towards purposeful play.

As a child, Stevenson had loved drawing maps; not to mention painting, dressing up, and playing with pirate figures. As an adult confined indoors by bad weather at Braemar in 1881, he joined Lloyd Osbourne in playing with 'pen and ink and a shilling box of water-colours' and on one occasion drew a map of an island.[105] *Treasure Island* began to emerge. Vital to its emergence was the nurturing collaboration of Stevenson's stepson as playmate, but also the presence of Stevenson's father, Thomas. For *Treasure Island* was not just a way of entertaining Lloyd; it was also a book to cement the reconciliation of Louis with his father, a reconciliation to be achieved through a literary game that made boys of three generations, and in which Stevenson's father 'set himself actively to collaborate'.[106]

Through adventure narrative, Stevenson returns to that bedtime story 'land of counterpane' where exciting tales of voyaging had been crucial to him as a sickly child.[107] He also makes contact with the 'childishness' of his father's 'original nature'.[108] In a sentence that precedes that phrase in his account of the genesis of *Treasure Island*, Stevenson said of the tale, 'It seemed to me original as sin; it seemed to belong to me like my right eye.' There are hints of darkness here, as there were in Stevenson's father's character, and in Stevenson's own, but the story, for all its violence, turns those to collaborative play. In *Treasure Island* sin – murder, maiming – is present, yet is kept at bay through playful proteanness as the pirate Long John Silver changes sides, roles and nature, as magistrate becomes tropical hero, or as the protagonist Jim Hawkins (exact age unspecified) is at one stage a boy to be ordered around, and at another a being mature enough to take charge of a ship. Authority becomes playful. Man rescues boy, boy rescues man. While we are closest to the principal narrator, the story's only boy, the narrative itself is passed between generations, being delivered at one time by Jim, at another by Dr Livesey. So adult readers must see at times from a boy's point of view, and young readers at other times must look on as an adult. It is a book told by different generations of characters and designed to bring together different generations of audience. Pace and stylish constant movement yield a common denominator of excitement which releases playfulness and childishness in child and adult alike, while its speed allows the narrative to avoid lingering moralizing or worry. *Treasure Island* is about a fatherless boy surrounded by many potential fathers who are often grotesque, yet enjoyably grotesque. The adult world may be *amoral* but that makes it all the more like a romance or a game.

Treasure Island is a book not just to read but to play at. It is full of an energy that comes from play; from hide and seek, from boys' toys such as swords and boats, from fancy dress, from chases. Part of its fun and power comes from a knowledge that exoticism and violent voyaging are safely earthed in the domestic and that, equally, the domestic is spiced with danger. The young first-person narrator, Jim Hawkins, finds his home, an English inn, taken over by pirates; he sails to a tropical Treasure Island which turns out to be populated with the local worthies of his home ground. The book's first sentence reassures us that Squire Trelawney, Dr Livesey and Jim all survive the adventure; its last sentence leaves us with the enjoyable frisson of fear that even at home in bed the piratical world can get at us:

Oxen and wain-ropes would not bring me back again to that accursed island; and the worst dreams that ever I have are when I hear the surf booming about its coasts, or start upright in bed, with the sharp voice of Captain Flint still ringing in my ears: 'Pieces of eight! pieces of eight!'

A related movement between domesticity and safety, and a shifting collaboration between child and adult are crucial to *Kidnapped* (1886), a novel set in Scotland where in 1751 the young Lowlander David Balfour, having lost a father and having been betrayed by his own flesh and blood, finds a surrogate father in Highlander Alan Breck Stewart. The roles of adult and child are reversed in this coming-of-age novel, and again rapidity of pace and the adventure story format govern fine writing to the benefit of the book. The familial circumstances which, out of 'childish' collaboration and play, produced both *A Child's Garden of Verses* and *Treasure Island*, marked Stevenson's stylistic maturing. With these works, reconciling generations through imaginative play, he achieves a greatness all the more striking for being founded on accessibility.

All good books kidnap their readers. *Kidnapped* does so with unusual aplomb. When you start reading a novel, you remove yourself a little from your life. David Balfour, the book's first-person narrator, does something similar in the very first sentence when, as he says, 'I took the key for the last time out of the door of my father's house.' David and the reader put their pasts behind them at exactly the same time. They are bonded from the start.

David sets out on a journey through a reality underpinned by folktale and fairytale. Stevenson based Alan on the historical Jacobite Allan Breck Stuart, and carefully marked passages about actual Highland emigration in his copy of Boswell's *Journal of a Tour to the Hebrides* (now at Yale); *Kidnapped* offers a realistic vignette of Highland emigration. It starts, too, by sending its hero to an actual place, to Cramond, near Edinburgh. But with his bundle on his staff's end, David is also a fairytale hero off to undergo his trials. He thinks of himself as being in 'a story like some ballad I had heard folk singing, of a poor lad that was a rightful heir and a wicked kinsman that tried to keep him from his own.'[109] David's story is not just the story of that ballad. He is also like Pilgrim in *The Pilgrim's Progress*, trekking towards his kingdom; having been kidnapped, David is shipwrecked and marooned à la Crusoe; he wanders over the eighteenth-century Highlands like Scott's Waverley. Stevenson has written a novel that steals the best bits from his own favourites. They succeed one another at an accelerated pace that points towards John Buchan's *The Thirty-Nine Steps*, and catapults eighteen-year-old David Balfour into the world of myth. Sometimes he seems much younger than eighteen, a Lowland naif, an innocent abroad in that foreign country north of the Highland line, where he learns about the decencies of community; at other times he is disconcertingly grown up, gunning down enemies, dictating terms to his miserly, slightly Dickensian Uncle Ebenezer, transacting business with lawyers.

If Lowland David is a man-boy, so is his companion, Alan Breck. A Jacobite go-between, Alan has eyes 'as bright as a five-year-old child's'.[110] He looks after David as they flee through the Highlands, but David, at significant moments, has to look after Alan. This is a rite-of-passage novel, about maturing from boy to man. But it is also a novel of reclamation which allows an older reader and protagonist to plug into their own childhoods that seemed left behind. So, clambering and hiding, we join David at night climbing the pitch-black stairs of his uncle's house and seeing by a flash of lightning that he is about to plunge to his doom when the stairs run out; we hide with David and Alan on top of a great boulder, broiling in the noon-day sun while a hostile redcoat soldier stands below, unaware.

David is happy and eager to mature. Yet neither he nor Alan renounces childishness. This makes them immortal, companions of the imagination. There are few women in the book, but it is as much a tale of male parting as of male bonding. Latent differences between David and Alan eventually separate them after David glimpses Catriona, the woman who will become his sweetheart in the admittedly less impressive sequel, *Catriona* (1893). Male bonding plays its part, but not oppressively. David has a gender, but little sex, so that girls as well as boys can identify with him. He is more of a tomboy than a boy.

Muriel Spark, Jorge Luis Borges, Alasdair Gray and Henry James – Stevenson fans all – may have found different things in *Kidnapped*, but an ability to combine magic with mundanity is surely one of them. The book works like a poem. It feeds the reader the accurate surface of the world – place names, recipes, jokes – yet also grants access to a more wildly imaginative realm where men play cards in a house built of living trees, where prince and pauper, adult and child share the same bodies, mercurially shifting in a story which moves with the speed of entrancement through the island of Mull, by Loch Rannoch, and across the Firth of Forth.

The prose may be plain, but it can be subtly parenthetical. Lots of colons help keep up the deftly punctuated hurry. Loyalty matters, and weather – sunlight, singing wind, 'the clearness and sweetness of the night, the shapes of the hills like things asleep'.[111] This is a lyrical as well as an artfully playful book. Its last chapter is called 'Good-bye', and David, who exits a door in the novel's first sentence, enters one in its last, when, a canny Lowland Scot, he goes to the bank. A combination of unobtrusive elegance and pacy excitement makes *Kidnapped* one of the world's most re-readable books, a yarn especially for adults to read to children, or simply to the child in yourself.

Some of Stevenson's sense of stylish play also informs *The Strange Case of Dr Jekyll and Mr Hyde* (1886) which is, as one of its multiple narrators, 'the dry lawyer' Mr Utterson, puts it, a story of 'Hyde' and 'Seek'.[112] In 1880 with his friend W. E. Henley Stevenson had co-authored *Deacon Brodie, or The Double Life: A Melodrama, Founded on Facts* which told the true story of Edinburgh's William Brodie who had managed to be both a respectable town official and a flamboyant criminal. The play failed, but the theme of a man whose 'life was double' (as a cancelled line of *Jekyll and Hyde* has it) continued to preoccupy Stevenson.[113] His later *Strange Case* is a work with a complex textual history, but surviving pages of manuscript in New York and New Haven show that it was carefully revised. Stevenson had grown up reading Poe's 'analytical' sleuth Dupin, as well as knowing that American writer's story of doubles, 'William Wilson'. Like Conan Doyle after him, the author of the *Strange Case* also had a taste for recent French crime fiction. Glancing towards the embryonic detective story and towards Hogg's *Memoirs and Confessions of a Justified Sinner*, Stevenson's *Strange Case* has a darker hue than his 'boys' stories'.[114] He was 'haunted' by Hogg's *Confessions*, which he read around 1881; his own tale, with its multiple narrators, concludes with a sealed 'confession'.[115] Walter Scott's *Saint Ronan's Well* (1824) has a Scottish character called

'Henry Jekyl' and touches on 'fiendish possession', but Stevenson's Dr Henry Jekyll is a London scientist, a Fellow of the Royal Society, who experiments on himself in his laboratory with a consciousness-changing drug.[116] In Edinburgh the obstetrician Dr James Young Simpson, founder of modern gynaecology and father of Stevenson's canoeing friend Walter Simpson, had experimented on himself while researching the properties of chloroform, developing anaesthetics in the face of medical and religious opposition. Jekyll, however, is not just a doctor and scientist, but, long before he discovers his new 'drug', a man 'already committed to a profound duplicity of life' and troubled by the sense of good and evil that 'lies at the root of religion'.[117] *Jekyll and Hyde* can be read as a cautionary tale about scientific intervention in human development and the 'womb of consciousness'. It can be read as an exploration of the bounds and bonds of male homosocial society, and as a book about what Stevenson terms the 'psychological'. But it is also a Calvinist-inflected book about the 'polar twins' of good and evil and the unleashing of original sin.[118] This inherent evil underlies the lab work. His drug releases in Henry Jekyll the libidinous killer Edward Hyde who stalks the streets and 'fogs of London', a city of dreadful night and horror that anticipates the city not just of Jack the Ripper, Sherlock Holmes and modern detective fiction, but also the London of Conrad's *The Secret Agent*.

As Jekyll starts to be taken over by Hyde ('This, too, was myself . . . He, I say – I cannot say, I'), personal pronouns buckle. Stevenson, while writing as a Victorian, anticipates, as he often does, the vertiginous modernist consciousness formulated in Rimbaud's famous phrase of 1871, 'Je est un autre'.[119] Stevenson's masterpiece sits interestingly as a tale of urban crime and punishment beside Dostoevsky's great St Petersburg novel about an experiment in murder; Stevenson enthused about that work around the time he was working on his *Strange Case*. *Jekyll and Hyde* also looks to the explorations of self and other in the French poet Jules Laforgue and in the Irishman Wilde's *The Picture of Dorian Gray* (1890), but, for all its sheer style, it retains a sense of pained alarm and Victorian post-Darwinian fear of moral and social degeneration as it concludes with Jekyll taken over by the 'wonderful selfishness' and 'ape-like' spite of Hyde.[120]

This novella which is so confined to the voices, deeds and writings of men, is dedicated to a woman with a writerly interest in extreme psychological states, Katharine de Mattos, sister of Stevenson's bohemian cousin, Bob. The first line of the dedication, 'It's ill to loose the bands that God decreed to bind', suggests Jekyll's tampering with the human mind, but the three lines that follow imply far more a sense of Stevenson's determination to stay true to his own culture, however estranged from it he seems:

> Still will we be the children of the heather and the wind;
> Far away from home, O it's still for you and me
> That the broom is blowing bonnie in the north countrie.

This may seem a strange poem to place at the beginning of *The Strange Case*, and its presence may signal all the more strongly the text's Scottish filiations – a Calvinist dualism and sense of Simpson's Edinburgh underlying the modern, secular London. Certainly the verse is in tune with some of Stevenson's finest poems such as 'To S. C.' in which the exiled Stevenson speaks with a marvellous tonal precision from the South Sea island world of 'The king, my neighbour, with his host of wives' to the faraway British Museum where Stevenson's friend Sidney Colvin worked among statues of 'island gods':

> So far, so foreign, your divided friends
> Wander, estranged in body, not in mind.[121]

Division was an obsession for this author – whether in the Scottish historical novels *Kidnapped* or *The Master of Ballantrae* (1888), the modern-day *Jekyll and Hyde*, or such late works as the impressive unfinished Scottish historical tale of father-and-son conflict, *Weir of Hermiston* (1896), and Stevenson's South Sea narratives. Yet division is far from the be-all and end-all of Stevenson's art. With their stories of missionaries and devil-work in the tropics, where Stevenson had sailed to Samoa in search of a healthy climate, such late fictions as the masterly novella *The Beach of Falesá* (1892) lend themselves to postcolonial interpretation and show a remarkably sympathetic understanding of aspects of the Samoan clans. Stevenson the 'Tusitala' (Teller of Tales) lived for the last six years of his life at Vailima on the Samoan island of Upolu, where he died and was buried in 1894. He has been seen as a forerunner of the Conrad whose early fictions are set in the Malay archipelago. Yet this academic repositioning of the complex Scottish novelist hides his often sprightly light under Conrad's more bituminous shadow. Conrad could never have written *Treasure Island*; nor could he have dashed off Stevenson's captivating letters, a full edition of which appeared in 1994–5. It is Stevenson's sense of play, as well as the consciousness of psychological and even theological darkness in such tales as 'Thrawn Janet' and 'Markheim', that contributes to his stylish, mobile vitality.

In part the complexity of Stevenson is bound up with the variety of his work – essays, travel books, novels, tales, poetry, drama aimed variously at child and adult audiences. He was admired alike by 'Kailyard' novelists and by the labyrinthine Henry James. Inevitably, as a writer of historical romances, he looked back to Scott whom the young Stevenson linked to 'the birth of Romance'; like Scott, Stevenson restated in his work the internationalism as well as the 'Scottishness' of Scottish literature.[122]

Dealing with, and sometimes juxtaposing, a great range of societies, Stevenson's imagination, ranging across 'many years and countries . . . the sea and the land, savagery and civilization', is in some ways akin to that of his admirer and fellow literary descendant of Scott, the anthropologist J. G. Frazer.[123] Scott's fascination with folklore and cultural comparisons, nurtured by Enlightenment Scotland, had helped spur such diverse works as Hugh Miller's *Scenes and Legends of the North of Scotland* (1835) and Andrew Lang's 1873 essay 'Mythology and Fairy Tales'. Scottish Enlightenment energies encouraged other anthropological studies including *Primitive Marriage* (1865) by the Inverness-born John Ferguson McLennan, a friend of the poet Alexander Smith, and fuelled works of biblical and anthropological scholarship by McLennan's Aberdeenshire admirer William Robertson Smith (1846–94).

Controversial author of *The Religion of the Semites* (1889), Smith joined the St Andrews Professor Thomas Spencer Baynes as editor of the great ninth edition of the *Encyclopaedia Britannica* whose scientific editor was the famous Scottish scientist James Clerk Maxwell. Maxwell was one of a galaxy of distinguished Scottish Victorian scientists and scientific writers including the Glasgow-based Irishman William Thomson (Lord Kelvin) and the topologist Peter Guthrie Tait. While Kelvin and others developed in Scotland a new physics of energy, it was Maxwell's work in Cambridge (published in such epoch-making works as his 1873 *Treatise on Electricity and Magnetism*) which made possible Einstein's research into relativity. In an age when some Scottish scientists stayed in Scotland and others headed south by choice, Robertson Smith was compelled to leave. He was accused of heresy while a professor at Aberdeen's Free Church College, and moved to a Chair of Arabic at Cambridge where he became a mentor of his fellow Scot, J. G. Frazer.

Born in Glasgow in 1854 and brought up in Helensburgh on the north bank of the Clyde, Frazer grew up an avid reader of Scott. The topographical Romanticism and comparative cultural method of *The Golden Bough* (1890–1915), Frazer's great 'anthropological epic', owe a good deal to Scott. *The Golden Bough* was produced during Frazer's long career as a don at Trinity College, Cambridge, where he, Robertson Smith and others were among the university's 'Scotch contingent'.[124] Though most of his published letters are drily, obsessively bookish, Frazer's long, Scottish-accented 1897 letter to John F. White in which he recalls Robertson Smith is, along with Tennyson's *In Memoriam*, one of the great documents of Victorian male friendship.[125]

Revising and greatly expanding *The Golden Bough*, Frazer cites a precedent in Scott when, for aesthetic reasons, he leaves unchanged a telling detail which he knows to be factually incorrect. Nowadays Frazer's work has as much literary as scientific value. A huge, kaleidoscopic catalogue of 'savage' practices, *The Golden Bough* would be raided by imaginative writers, including Yeats, Eliot and other modernists. Frazer's work implied that Christianity too was part of a network of primitive belief systems which its author tended to dismiss as folly. In libraries, Frazer read till he dropped, but he was an 'armchair anthropologist'. He never did any fieldwork; probably he had never seen a 'savage'. Just as ironically, expanding his original two-volume *Golden Bough* of 1890 into the twelve volumes of the 1911–15 third edition, he brought to his labours as much of a Calvinist work ethic as that other rewriter of Christianity, Thomas Carlyle.[126]

If an anthropological impulse can be discerned in Scott and in the Carlyle fascinated by the worship of heroes, it is certainly discernible in a good deal of later nineteenth-century Scottish writing. It features not least in works produced outside Scotland by Robertson Smith, Frazer and others who, like them, owed much to the Scottish tradition of Classical education. Born in Huntly, Aberdeenshire, James Legge (1815–97) was an eager student of George Buchanan and of Classics before he became a Protestant missionary and educator for the London Missionary Society in Hong Kong. His seven-volume translated *Chinese Classics*

(1861–75) is now recognized as 'the greatest single achievement of Western Sinological scholarship during the nineteenth century'.[127] True to the educational traditions of north-east Scotland, Legge translated Chinese in his *Book of Poetry* (1876) not only into English verse but also at times into Doric Scots and Latin. However, when he came back to Britain he returned not to his Aberdeen alma mater but to take up the new Chair of Chinese at Oxford where he produced further translations and studies that, like J. G. Frazer's work, contributed to the comparative scientific study of religions. Among the many Scottish writers in London and Oxford Legge's linguistic skills were matched by those of the lexicographer James A. H. Murray (1837–1915), whose 1873 study *The Dialect of the Southern Counties of Scotland* is a milestone in dialectology, and whose later editorial labours made him not only the greatest ever gatherer of the English language but also the man behind one of the world's most famous books, the Philological Society's *New English Dictionary*, later retitled the *Oxford English Dictionary*; begun in 1879, its final volume appeared in 1928. Legge and Murray were older contemporaries of the Scottish anthropological writer and historian of religion, Andrew Lang (1844–1912). In Oxford, London and St Andrews, this influential man of letters produced work that ranged from *Myth, Ritual and Religion* (1887) to books of fairytales for children such as *The Blue Fairy Book* (1889). In his poem 'Almae Matres' Lang wrote nostalgically about 'St Andrews by the northern sea', but he made his mark in London.

In Europe, America and the South Seas, Lang's friend R. L. Stevenson drew on the local customs and stories of three continents, writing sometimes longingly of Scotland. In Oxford Legge wrote in his unfinished autobiography (now in the Bodleian Library) about his delight in childhood reading in Aberdeenshire. J. G. Frazer might hanker after Scottish 'shores how dear to me!' but is regarded as a Cambridge scholar of exotic cults.[128] It is as if the anthropological sensibility, nurtured by the Scottish Enlightenment impulse towards cultural comparison and spurred by the Scottish tradition of training in the Classics, was quickened at a time when so many Scottish writers were displaced. Some of the most popular fiction about Scotland in the late nineteenth century, even in protesting its Scottishness, also came to have a gently anthropological tinge. It displayed – often to a London audience – the quaint and curious customs of the Scots.

'A work on folk-lore' is one of the few books in the library of one of the inhabitants of 'Thrums' as portrayed by J. M. Barrie (1860–1937). Thrums's Scottish village inhabitants are often presented by their London-based author as having their own comically folkloric, quasi-anthropological interest.[129] If the philosopher Ludwig Wittgenstein censured Frazer for his basic assumption that the actions of 'savages' should be seen as folly, then Scottish critics from Hugh MacDiarmid to Cairns Craig have attacked Barrie for assuming that Scottish small-town life of the recent past existed to provide quaintly exotic entertainment for English and American audiences – and for Scottish readers happy to play along. As soon as Barrie discovered that such materials would make him money, he exploited them, beginning in the mid-1880s with journalistic vignettes written for English periodicals. 'I liked that Scotch thing – any more of those?' asked the editor of the St James's Gazette in 1884, rejecting Barrie's other submissions.[130] In the sketches of Auld Licht Idylls (1888) and A Window in Thrums (1889), as well as in the Thrums-related novels The Little Minister (1891), Sentimental Tommy (1896) and Tommy and Grizel (1900), Barrie drew on his experience of his mother's Kirriemuir. He also applied his newer knowledge of modern London where hack journalism intersected uneasily with literary aspirations. At least as strongly, however, he maintained his couthy engagement with the small-town anecdotes of minister, dominie and characterful parishioners in a 'Thrums' of auld lang syne. By 1885 Barrie was already planning in his tiny notebooks a description of a 'school near Kirrie' where children were 'conveyed in carts' and there was 'contempt for new things'. He sketched ideas for 'Thrums gossip' and even a 'Thrums Odyssey'.[131] To be fair to Barrie, his Thrums is not just a chocolate box. It has single parents in addition to charming infants. It is a location of alcoholism and suicide as well as a repository of homely tales and hearthside gossip. Barrie knew well that the sort of weavers' community about which he wrote had a history of political radicalism and even rioting, but he played that down. The hostile male critic J. H. Millar came to see Thrums as the centre of what he called in the New Review in 1895 the 'Literature of the Kailyard' (Cabbage-patch) school, and this has been much denounced as provincializing the Scottish literary imagination. The term 'Kailyard' has become something of a lazy shorthand, and certainly obscures some of J. M. Barrie's interest to modern readers. It also leads to simplifications of Barrie's character and writing.

For his tenth birthday Barrie's mother gave him an inscribed copy of *Men Who Were Earnest*, a collection of biographies of such figures as 'Dr Arnold, the Earnest, Intrepid Teacher' and 'Dr Chalmers, the Religious and Social Leader'.[132] This was a lot for a boy to live up to. The following year, though, Barrie's sister gave him something more fun: Mayne Reid's *The Castaways: A Story of Adventure*. Torn between earnestness and larking around, in his twenties the diminutive Barrie would plan stories which indicate an anxiety about heroic masculinity: about 'Male Nursery Maids' and a 'Hero frightened at barmaids'; about a man who feels the 'trial of his life is that he is always thought a boy'; about a man who 'used to waken with horror from dreaming he was married'; about a 'Third Sex'.[133] In the era of the 'New Woman', Barrie was very interested in masculinity and femininity, but also in game-playing. The little boy who devoured *The Castaways* went on as an adult to obsessive, even criminal plotting in order to adopt boys of his own. For his young, upper-class Llewelyn Davies boys he assembled and published privately *The Boy Castaways of Black Lake Island* (1901), a precursor of *Peter Pan*.

Denunciations of Barrie are often interestingly gendered. As indicated earlier, this writer took the name 'Thrums' from the work of Margaret Oliphant, whom he considered 'the most distinguished Scotswoman of her time', and who was 'among women novelists' a favourite author of himself and of his mother, Margaret Ogilvy. Barrie maintained that many of his Thrums stories were drawn from his mother's memories of the old days in Kirriemuir, north of Dundee. His 'loving mother' wrote anxiously to her 'dear beloved Jamie' in London to tell him of 'my love no words can say'.[134] Barrie's unique, sometimes cloying, but also revealing tribute to his 'heroine' mother, *Margaret Ogilvy, by her Son* (1896), is the only book-length account of a mother by a male Scottish writer.[135] When Barrie was seven his older brother David had died in an accident; Barrie felt he could never live up to the dead boy's example in the eyes of his mother, though the bereavement drew them closer. Barrie and his mother spoke Scots to each other, and, though his books are written in English they are spiced with 'Doric' words. 'I am as Scotch as peat,' wrote Barrie at the age of fifty-nine, 'but with a mighty regard for England.'[136] Schooled partly in Dumfries (where his 'womanly touches' helped him play female parts in plays), he wrote his first, unpublished novel there, getting 'the best of my love scenes out of the novels by sparkling ladies'; sometimes acting as his mother's 'maid of all work', he sent off his first novel to a publisher who rejected it, assuming its author was female.[137]

Early reviewers related Barrie's Thrums to such works as Moir's *Mansie Wauch*, but Thrums's name and nature came from a substantially feminine tradition of domestic and romantic fiction. Mrs Oliphant praised *A Window in Thrums* for virtues that were 'homely', relishing its 'fun and pathos and tenderness'.[138] Fictionalizing his mother's memories of earlier nineteenth-century small-town life, Barrie was a male writer operating in female territory. He joked about himself as 'the first woman journalist'.[139] For his early readers, Barrie's Thrums tales, in newspapers then in book form, had the appeal of a soap-opera. Today his stories of the 'Auld Licht' Presbyterian sect, quaint even by the 1890s, may offer too much of the diminutively couthy and the restrictedly sectarian – Roman Catholicism in Thrums is the ultimate disgrace. The anecdotes, though, have an impact that goes beyond whimsical pawkiness:

Tammy, who died a bachelor, had been soured in his youth by a disappointment in love, of which he spoke but seldom. She lived far away in a town to which he had wandered in the days when his blood ran hot, and they became engaged. Unfortunately, however, Tammy forgot her name, and he never knew the address; so there the affair ended, to his silent grief.

Much of Barrie's work is semi-autobiographical, and he retells various versions of that story; as a fiction it indicates a wish on the part of the author to subvert readers' expectations about heroic masculinity and male desire. Calling his 1896 novel *Sentimental Tommy* or joking in *When a Man's Single* (1888) about an article called 'Man Frightened to Get Married' has a similar effect.[140]

Although he sent *A Window in Thrums* 'to Robert Louis Stevenson from his friend J. M. Barrie', the ambitious younger writer from Kirriemuir was jealous of Stevenson's panache.[141] Like Stevenson, Barrie, schooled in 'Carlylese', inherited Carlyle's Protestant work ethic and carnivalized it by turning it to play.[142] Barrie also feminized it, and reflected on an artist's often narcissistic engagement with his own work. Where Carlyle welcomed repression of all sorts, Barrie subversively and wittily imagined Carlyle entertaining four-year-olds at a children's party. In Barrie's most successful novel, *The Little Minister*, the Auld Licht preacher Gavin Dishart is mocked for his John-Knoxian first and second sermons against women, then is made to fall in love with a mischievous, gipsy-like girl, though readers are aware too of male bonding 'passing the love of woman'.[143] Homosocial bonds, literary ambition, workaholism, repression and feminized play all dance round one another in Barrie's prose, which repeatedly teases about what it is 'to act the part of a man', whether in lonely London or in snowbound Thrums.[144]

Barrie wrote too much, too quickly. Like Margaret Oliphant, he turned to the well-crafted supernatural tale late in life. One of his finest works is the pellucid novella *Farewell Miss Julie Logan* (1932), about a minister in love with a ghost-woman. In notebooks Barrie collected Scots locutions and in revising this novella he intensified the Scots accent of the text in a way that can be aligned with Scottish modernist ideals.[145] Barrie's oratorical 1922 rectorial address to St Andrews University students on the theme of 'Courage' offers another, more troubled examination of masculinity in the wake of World War I, and demonstrates his power as a rhetorical performer. It is hard not to suspect that his challenge to conventional masculinity, as much as his marketing of Scotland as provincial entertainment, is what has riled many of Barrie's critics. A celebrated Scottish painting of the 1920s, William McCance's 'From another Window in Thrums', shows a man and a woman energetically copulating, as if to reassert 'normal' sexual and gender relations in the face of Barrie's subversions. McCance's picture takes its title from a work by the masculinist Hugh MacDiarmid, who anxiously excoriated Barrie. Sadly, later critics have been insufficiently alert to the subversive genderings and regenderings of his texts.

The prose writer who once wrote, 'Ah, if only it could have been a world of boys and girls!' is the dramatist who authored *Peter Pan*.[146] Other than a number of Shakespeare's plays, *Peter Pan* is the only drama in English whose plot is known around the Western world. This fact is not explained away simply by the work's undeniable whimsicality nor by its Disney adaptation. Written shortly before Freud's work became familiar in English, *Peter Pan*, like Stevenson's writing, engages with deep delights and desires. *Peter Pan* (1904) exists as both a novel and a drama. Like *Kidnapped*, it is a story about abduction: abducted from the adult world of work, urban life and responsibilities, its audience enters into the childhood world of play. *Peter Pan* as well as *Treasure Island* has its pirates and pirate ship – but that name 'the Never Land' shows how much Barrie's art wears its impossibility on its sleeve.

Stevenson's play world is where, temporarily at least, adults may become children and children act at grown-up pursuits; it is a world of protean fluidity. In Barrie's early plays such as *Quality Street* (1902) and *The Admirable Crichton* (1902) time and the fluidity of identity are also recurring themes. Barrie owned a copy of Patrick Fraser Tytler's 1823 *Life of the Admirable Crichton* which drew on Thomas Urquhart's seventeenth-century account of that Renaissance Scottish hero, but the heroic male of Barrie's play is not that of earlier hero-worshippers.[147] Marooned on a desert island, an Edwardian household finds that Crichton, its butler, becomes its patriarch; when the household gets back home, though, the rules of polite English society are reasserted. The assumptions of the class system have been questioned, but only for a ludic interval. In Stevenson we delight in playing; with Barrie, though, there is more of an awareness of the pathos of fixed rules. Peter Pan will never grow up, but other children must. If Stevenson writes about how the play world is forever there to be discovered, Barrie knows it must always be lost.

Barrie's most famous play drew on its author's games with those young boys, the Llewelyn Davies family, whom Barrie, with some sleight of hand, adopted on their parents' death. *Peter Pan* begins in Bloomsbury, where Barrie had lived. It sets the grown-up world of Mr Darling with his talk of 'the office' against the much richer imaginative world of Peter Pan, whose name fuses Christian and pagan. Peter spirits away the Darling children for adventures in Never Land where they do battle with the pirate Captain Hook, his boatswain Smee and their crew. 'Yo ho, yo ho,' sing the pirates. Their 'pieces of eight' and a mention of 'Flint' gesture towards *Treasure Island*; Smee's favourite oath ('you spalpeen') comes from R. M. Ballantyne's stage Irish; but Peter, with his pan pipes and his fairy companion Tinker Bell, is Barrie's own.[148] Peter refuses to return to the world of the Bloomsbury Darlings, despite his attachment to their daughter Wendy. He will not 'be a man' and go 'to an office', but stays instead true to his own ideal: 'I just want always to be a little boy and to have fun.'[149] In part, Peter, with his pipes, is an artist – a bohemian in capitalist London, like Stevenson, or the nascent Bloomsbury Group; this makes Peter emblematic of the imaginative life, and so adds to his appeal. Yet he is also a manifestation of a yearning for arrested development sensed elsewhere in Barrie – whether in *Margaret Ogilvy* or in the quaint Thrums that is islanded by history. Like most of us in some circumstances, but with a peculiar and lasting acuteness, Barrie wanted time to stop.

It is tempting to reduce Barrie's literary achievement by seeing it all as the product of some psychic wound: a refusal to grow up, a mother fixation, some failure of masculinity. His marriage to the actress Mary Ansell was childless, and he later divorced her for adultery. Yet rather than trying to reduce all the writing to some putative original flaw, it is surely fairer to say that what Barrie's psychology and imagination made possible was a remarkable range of work from largely successful fictions to captivating drama. In their hugely elaborate stage directions, Barrie's published dramas show more than any how much the plays of this era were shaped by the dominance of the novel. Among other things, like so many of his contemporaries' artistic productions, from George Mac-Donald's *Lilith* (1895) to Oscar Wilde's *The Importance of Being Earnest* (1895), Barrie's writings explore gender and sexuality in new ways, yet do so within the safe parameters of middle-class art. Unlike Shaw, Barrie, who would receive a knighthood, never had a play banned by the Lord Chamberlain. Yet, while rather relishing the 'Auld Licht' Presbyterian sensibility of his mother's Scotland, he helped free Scottish writing from the dour heaviness of Carlyle and Victorian manliness, letting it frolic in Thrums, in London, and, most of all, in Never Land.

Critics have sometimes berated Barrie for avoiding the realities of history, but he matters for his emphasis on the need for freedom of imagination in an age more and more preoccupied with the capitalist managerialism of 'the office'. He also matters for his willingness to explore the flexibility and restrictiveness of gender. Though on stage he may do this with less assurance than Oscar Wilde, Barrie knew how to entertainingly unsettle his audience. In *What Every Woman Knows* (1908) he presents the boorishly masculine Scot John Shand, 'The Ladies' Champion', whose wife types his speeches, secretly improving them to make them 'so virile'.[150] In Barrie's superb one-act play *The Twelve-Pound Look* (1910), written just before he had divorced his wife, he presents an apparently successful man on the eve of getting a knighthood, whose success is shown as a complete sham by Kate, a typist who arrives at his home and turns out to be the man's ex-wife. What terrifies 'Sir Harry' is that Kate left him not for another man but in order to achieve an independent life of her own: having earned twelve pounds, enough to leave Harry, she left him. This play, like a good number of Barrie's writings, is about gender and 'success'. Emblematically, *Success* became the title of a popular, Scottish-edited London magazine of the 1890s; authors in this period began to be agented, to be increasingly interviewed, to go on regular publicity tours, and to become part of what we would now call 'celebrity culture'. Success, which Barrie moved to London to seek, and which he achieved – success which capitalist society demanded its workers strive for – is shown in Barrie's work as hollow, a sham. So are conventional gender roles:

KATE. ... If only you had been a man, Harry.
SIR HARRY. A man? What do you mean by a man?[151]

Barrie's later plays like *Dear Brutus* (1917) and *Mary Rose* (1920) emphasize the grip of the past. Barrie's Thrums fictions show a tendency on the part of the metropolitan sophisticate to consign Scotland to a past both smiled at and wept over. It is that persistent question, 'What do you mean by a man?' that hints why Barrie, from *The Little Minister* to *Peter Pan*, for all he may seem a 'period piece', retains an insistent modernity.

A good deal of Barrie's best work is in marginal genres such as one-act plays and children's writing. The wider world is right to remember him principally as a dramatist. Yet Scottish criticism is not entirely wrong to pay close attention to his Thrums fiction, since reactions to this kind of writing would be important for the twentieth-century Scottish novel. In Thrums Barrie had his imitators. One reason why Thrums and the 'Kailyard' fictions critics later linked to Thrums enjoyed a huge international success, yet have not worn well, is that they were manufactured rather than written. The young Barrie who reacted to a London editor's liking for 'that Scotch thing' and produced his 'Auld Licht Idylls' was soon followed by John Watson. As 'Ian Maclaren' Watson wrote the idylls of *Beside the Bonnie Briar Bush* (1894) and dedicated to his mother *The Days of Auld Lang Syne* (1895). This latter work is set in the parish of Drumtochty, described somewhat patronizingly by the author as being 'in its natural state'.[152] Watson (1850–1907) had grown up in Perth-shire and was a Liverpool Free Church minister. His Drumtochty idylls were encouraged by William Robertson Nicoll, an Aberdonian in London who edited *The British Weekly*. In that journal's pages Barrie, Maclaren, and another of Nicoll's protégés, Samuel Rutherford

Crockett (1859–1914), were encouraged to publish their sketches of quaint Scottish life. These became fashionable in a milieu more used to what Maclaren coyly called 'Southern culture'.[153]

The Free Church and presbyterianism were prominent factors in Kailyard fiction, not just because they encouraged wholesomeness but also, perhaps, because in an age preoccupied with material success they encouraged a sense of reflective otherworldliness. Church ministry provided writers with a position relatively uncircumscribed by the working routines of capitalist society; in a milieu where sermons were scrutinized by demanding congregations, an important part of a minister's work was to write. S. R. Crockett was another Free Church minister, though he went on to leave his Galloway charge to concentrate on full-time authorship. Where Barrie had his 'Auld Lichts', Crockett had his tiny Presbyterian sect of the 'Marrow Kirk'; where Barrie wrote of 'The Little Minister', Crockett's first (1894) book of stories was *The Stickit Minister*. The title refers to a minister who has been trained but has 'stuck' and failed to progress to a charge. *The Stickit Minister* is dedicated to Stevenson, who wrote Crockett a fine poem and whose Scottish adventure stories the prolific Crockett aped in novels such as *The Raiders* (1894).

Crockett also wrote about Stevenson and Barrie, but where Barrie, on the make, might mock success, Crockett simply craved it. Busy with his several typewriters and his dictaphone, Crockett was professionally represented by Glasgow-born A. P. Watt, the man substantially responsible for the development of modern literary agenting; as the market took more and more account of female readers, Crockett was able to publish in magazines such as the popular *People's Friend* and Nicoll's *Woman at Home* as well as in book form. Fittingly, in 1895 he was even written up by Robertson Nicoll in the journal *Success*. In a letter of the following year Barrie wrote of how 'Crockett was with us for a weekend. "His terms are" – "he sells" – "Watt says" – "his publishers say" – "his terms" – "his sale" –'.[154] Crockett churned out too many books, often carelessly plotted and melodramatically inflected. Yet, writing of 'common men' in rural Scotland, he can show Hardyesque or proto-Lawrentian touches. *The Lilac Sunbonnet* (1894) sold out on publication day, and discernible through the purple prose is a sensuous feel for landscape that matches an erotic charge in the narrative:

The bees in the purple flowers beneath the window boomed a mellow bass, and the grasshoppers made love by millions in the couch grass, *chirring* in a thousand fleeting raptures.[155]

Crockett can deal with urban modernity too; like Barrie he writes about typists. Occasionally he even hints at more radical interests: a character in an early story speaks of how 'there was no doubt that Jesus was a working-man and his followers socialists'.[156] Along with Ian Maclaren, Crockett enjoyed most success as a purveyor of unthreatening 'Kailyard'. J. H. Millar's critical term 'Kailyard' was probably taken from an old Scots song which Maclaren used as an epigraph to *Beside the Bonnie Briar Bush*:

> There grows a bonnie briar bush in our kailyard,
> And white are the blossoms on't in our kailyard.

'Kailyard' became a dismissive term used of sentimental rural Scottish tales, but we should not ignore the great international appeal of such work. In 1895 for the Philomathic Society at Canada's Dalhousie University students wrote papers on the hugely admired fiction of Barrie, Crockett and Maclaren, and in 1897 there was a debate on Kailyard novels at the Oxford University Union. Maclaren died in 1907 on a lecture tour of America; Crockett had earlier turned down an offer of £6000 for such a tour. In Canada L. M. Montgomery admired the way Barrie's *A Window in Thrums* showed an ability to touch 'common places and they blossom out into beauty and pathos'.[157] She was a fan, too, of Ian Maclaren's work, reading or re-reading his Drumtochty novel *Kate Carnegie* (1896) about the time she wrote *Anne of Green Gables* (1908). Montgomery identified Maclaren's Drumtochty with her own Prince Edward Island home: 'The atmosphere of *Kate* is delightful. I seemed to be back in the Cavendish of my childhood. There was the same tang and charm and simplicity in people, place and religion. One had a sense of "time to grow".'[158] Montgomery's enthusiasm sums up much of the nostalgic appeal of Kailyard. Yet where her own Anne books learn from it and address a childhood world, too often Kailyard fiction fails because it presents adults to an adult readership as if they were slightly comical children. Its doing so ensured that it was internationally successful – for a time.

Late nineteenth-century Scotland traded in kail, but also in twilight.

From Ireland W. B. Yeats's 1893 collection *The Celtic Twilight* had whispered in its final poem about 'a time outworn', even as it hoped for a national rebirth. In Scotland too some writers looked towards ancient Celtic lands and traditions as sources of nourishment for a distinctive cultural revival linked to the Highlands. For his lectures *On the Study of Celtic Literature* (1867) Matthew Arnold had chosen an epigraph from Ossian ('They went forth to the war, but they always fell'), and had presented the Celtic as a kind of ethereal, feminized other to modern English literature.[159] This view of the Celtic had some influence on Yeats, and much over William Sharp, foremost of the Scottish writers who contributed to what Yeats in an 1898 essay on Sharp's work called 'Le Mouvement Celtique'.

Born in Lowland industrial Paisley in 1855, Sharp went on to study at Glasgow University, then travelled widely and worked in London in the 1880s, writing poetry as a minor Pre-Raphaelite. In Rome in 1890 Sharp completely regendered himself as Arnold's feminized Celt. He began to write poems and visionary prose fictions set in an ancient Celtic realm, publishing these works under the specially constructed identity of 'Fiona Macleod'. Even more strikingly than the young J. M. Barrie, Sharp became a woman writer. Fiona's first name was Ossianic and her second markedly Highland, perhaps encouraged by the often melodramatic work of best-selling Glasgow-born novelist William Black (1841–98) who exoticized the Highlands in works like *Macleod of Dare* and in a score of other novels with such titles as *The Wise Women of Inverness*. Sharp's exploration of a feminine self, like Barrie's, shows a willingness to play games with gender in line with international fin de siècle culture. Sharp gave Fiona Macleod her own entry in *Who's Who* and 'specially favoured enquirers were shown her portrait, but it never appeared in the Press'.

In a decade when Andrew Lang sold many copies of his charming children's tales in *The Red Fairy Book* (1890), *The Green Fairy Book* (1892) and other volumes, Fiona Macleod was regarded by some as herself 'a Fairy'.[160] A friend of Yeats, Sharp was a considerable literary operator. His enterprises ranged from introducing *Lyra Celtica: An Anthology of Representative Celtic Poetry* (1896) to serving as President of the London Stage Society. That Society produced Fiona Macleod's 'psychic dramas', while *Lyra Celtica* contained a good dollop of her verse, in addition to poems by Ossian, Yeats, Bliss Carman, Villiers de l'Isle Adam and Arthur Quiller-Couch. With Scottish contributors playing a prominent part, *Lyra Celtica* attempts to claim a bewildering variety of writers from Milton to Stevenson as 'Celtic' in an effort to present a swelling international movement fuelled by Arnold, John Francis Campbell, Ernest Renan and others. The anthology's introduction argues that 'A strange melancholy characterizes the genius of the Celtic race' and that a modern 'Celtic Renascence . . . is, fundamentally, the outcome of "Ossian," and, immediately, the rising of the sap in the Irish nation'.[161] Sharp was a writer keen on Gaelic lore, the faery and the gipsy; his book *The Gypsy Christ* was published in America in 1895 and US publication of other works followed. Well read in Turgenev, Baudelaire and Whitman, he wrote 'prose rhythms' (he disliked the term 'prose poems') which seem modern descendants of the Ossianic *Fragments*. Typical of their emphasis on hypnotic, even druggy vagueness is 'The Immortals':

I saw the Weaver of Dream, an immortal shape of star-eyed Silence; and the Weaver of Death, a lovely Dusk with a heart of hidden flame: and each wove with the shuttles of Beauty and Wonder and Mystery.

I knew not which was the more fair: for Death seemed to me as Love, and in the eyes of Dream I saw Joy. Oh, come, come to me, Weaver of Dream! Come, come unto me, O Lovely Dusk, thou hast the heart of hidden flame![162]

However kitschy this may sound, such work was influential. It presented 'the Celtic fringe' as mistily, cloudily and elegiacally alluring. With their absurdly overwritten Hebridean sunsets, William Black's novels appeared in a twenty-six volume collected edition in 1894. Two years later and a century after James Macpherson's death, Sharp introduced 'the Centenary Ossian', praising the Ossianic poems' 'cosmic imagination'.[163] Also announced as part of Sharp's 'Celtic Library' for that November was Fiona Macleod's *From the Hills of Dream: Mountain Songs and Island Runes*. The 1896 Celtic tales in the Inveraray-born Glasgow journalist Neil Munro's *The Lost Pibroch* led to his *Gilian the Dreamer* (1899). Munro could be hard-headed. He wrote enjoyable post-Stevensonian Highland historical novels such as *John Splendid* (1898) and *The New Road*, as well as gently observed modern comic tales about Para Handy, captain of a small Clyde 'puffer' steamboat, in *The Vital Spark* (1906). Yet figures of rather melancholy Highland dreamers recur in his fiction, leading it to be dismissed by the younger,

demanding Scottish novelist George Douglas Brown as 'damned sentimental filigree'.[164]

The early stories of Munro and the books of Sharp reinforced a
perception of the Highlands and Islands as a noble, spiritualized
otherworld. In 1899 the civil servant Alexander Carmichael (1832–
1912) prefaces the first volume of his *Carmina Gadelica* with an introduction that mentions not only W. F. Skene's *Celtic Scotland: A History
of Ancient Alba* and John Francis Campbell but also the island of
Atlantis and Renan's notion of the 'profound feeling and adorable delicacy' of the Celts. Scholars argue about the Gaelic oral prayers, charms,
hymns and invocations collected by Carmichael and later published over
several decades in Gaelic with his verse translations. These works seem
partly genuine, partly reshaped to fit modern notions of what an ancient
Celtic sensibility ought to be like. Certainly their measured repetitions
speak of a Catholic and sometimes pagan Scotland which has often been
repressed, and which could entrance listeners from Fiona Macleod to
T. S. Eliot.

> Bi Bride bhithe, bhana, leinn
> Bi Moire mhine mhathar, leinn.
> Bi Micheal mil
> Nan lanna liobh,
> 'S bi Righ nan righ,
> 'S bi Iosa Criosd
> 'S bith Spiorad sith
> Nan grasa leinn,
> Nan grasa leinn.

> *The calm fair Bride will be with us,*
> *The gentle Mary mother will be with us.*
> *Michael the chief*
> *Of glancing glaves,*
> *And the King of kings*
> *And Jesus Christ,*
> *And the Spirit of peace*
> *And of grace will be with us,*
> *Of grace will be with us.*[165]

Such verses came to be far better known than the untranslated, often angry Gaelic poetry of Iain Mac a' Ghobhain (John Smith, 1848–1880) who complained about the conditions of poor people in the Highlands and saw Scotland becoming a playground for imperial hunters, shooters and fishers. After Carmichael's *Carmina Gadelica*, later collectors such as Marjory Kennedy Fraser in *The Songs of the Hebrides* (1909) further blurred the seldom policed boundary between scholarship and romance. Where the Kailyard presented an often elegiac ideal of small-town community spirit, the Celtic Twilight offered something similar for Highland culture generally. Both sounded distinct Scottish notes that caught the international imagination. Implicitly or explicitly, they also defined Scottishness as other than urban modernity. This may have made urban readers all the more eager to turn to Kailyard and Celtic Twilight works for escape and consolation in what was now one of the world's most industrialized countries.

Both these literary movements were encouraged by one of the pioneers of urban modernity. The polymathic Scottish town planner Patrick Geddes invented the word 'conurbation' and wrote *Cities in Evolution* (1915). He not only published the 'Celtic Library' but brought together the Kailyarder Crockett with William Sharp and Alexander Carmichael in his short-lived 1895 magazine, *The Evergreen*. This journal aimed 'to pass through Decadence, towards Renascence'.[166] At the Camera Obscura on Edinburgh's Castlehill Geddes had set up his 'Outlook Tower', which has been called the world's first sociological museum, and which had exhibitions on different floors linking the local to the universal, connecting Edinburgh to Scotland, Scotland to Europe and the world, while stressing language as a vital link.

In *The Evergreen* Geddes looks back to Allan Ramsay's *Ever Green* anthology of older Scottish literature, and hopes that a new view of Scotland as 'one of the European Powers of Culture' may help quicken what he calls 'The Scots Renascence'. Geddes censures what he saw as an anglicization of Scottish culture and society:

Never before indeed, not even in the interregnum of the War of Independence, not after the Union of the Crowns or Parliaments, not after Culloden, has there been so large a proportion of Scotsmen conscientiously educating their children outside every main element of that local and popular culture, that racial aptitude and national tradition, upon which full effectiveness at home, and even individual success elsewhere, have always depended, and must continue to depend. But to this spoiling of what might be good Scots to make indifferent Englishmen, natural selection will always continue to oppose some limit.[167]

Such talk of the 'racial' and of 'natural selection' is worrying to modern ears, but Geddes was far more interested in cultural productions than in the sort of eugenic ideas fashionable at the time. He emphasizes Scottish distinctiveness and internationalism. Longing for a synthesis of the arts and sciences, he brings together artists with writers working with English, Scots and Gaelic materials to develop a Scots Renascence. In 1895 this was a commendable failure. Yet in the longer term such ideas would be brought to fruition by Hugh MacDiarmid, an admirer of Geddes and a much more gifted writer. Though MacDiarmid, born in 1892, liked to adopt a hostile pose towards turn-of-the-century Scottish culture, he was undeniably nourished by it. A Scottish Renaissance may have been delayed, but it would come.

Meanwhile, though, nothing from the Kailyard or Celtic Twilight could compete for excitement or evergreen readability with the adventures of Sherlock Holmes. Their author, Arthur Conan Doyle (1859–1930), was in some ways a product of the sort of upbringing Geddes had denounced. Born in Edinburgh, Doyle was sent south at the age of nine. He attended Stonyhurst, an English Jesuit public school, before returning to Edinburgh to train as a doctor at the University. There he encountered Joseph Bell, Consulting Surgeon to the Edinburgh Royal Infirmary, pioneer of forensic medicine, and the dedicatee of *The Adventures of Sherlock Holmes* (1892). The character of Holmes is, as Doyle put it, 'a bastard between Joe Bell and Poe's Monsieur Dupin (much diluted)'. The Edinburgh connection was soon recognized by the writer Doyle most admired, Robert Louis Stevenson: 'can this be my old friend Joe Bell?' Stevenson wrote from Samoa praising Doyle's 'very ingenious and very interesting adventures of Sherlock Holmes'.[168] Doyle had written a long article on 'Mr Stevenson's Methods in Fiction' in 1890, and sought to follow Stevenson in such historical novels as *The White Company* (1891). Several of Doyle's early fictions, including *The Firm of Girdlestone* (1890), are set in Edinburgh, while later, more popular novels like *The Lost World* (1912) draw on their author's experiences as an imperial adventurer from the Arctic to Africa. Now several times filmed by Hollywood, *The Lost World* takes its hero Professor

Challenger to a previously unknown jungle area where dinosaurs have survived and rule. Though Doyle was desperately eager to emulate Stevenson as a historical novelist, his true talent was for well-paced modern best-sellers. He knew Stevenson had written about London and the 'detective', and his favourite Stevenson story seems to have been 'The Pavilion on the Links' – a mystery tale about pursuit and murder. Stevenson had presented London criminal mysteries in *The Strange Case of Dr Jekyll and Mr Hyde*, and stories like 'The Adventures of the Hansom Cab'. Though Doyle failed as a historical novelist, the adventures of Sherlock Holmes, his strange cases, may still owe something to Stevenson.

Much to his chagrin, Doyle came to be known not as Stevenson's successor in the historical novel, but as the creator of the Sherlock Holmes stories. The first of these, *A Study in Scarlet*, appeared in 1887, serialized in *The Strand Magazine*. All the Sherlock Holmes adventures are narrated by Dr John Watson, a well-travelled Empire medical man who graduated from the University of London around the same time as Dr Doyle finished his studies at Edinburgh. In the very first instalment, readers of *The Strand* entered a laboratory. There, meeting a man to whom Watson is a total stranger, they shared the good doctor's surprise:

'Dr Watson, Mr Sherlock Holmes,' said Stamford introducing us.

'How are you?' he said cordially, gripping my hand with a strength for which I should hardly have given him credit. 'You have been in Afghanistan, I perceive.'

'How on earth did you know that?' I asked in astonishment.[169]

So begins Watson's career as the baffled 'Boswell' to Holmes's 'Bohemian soul'. The story soon progresses to 'The Science of Deduction' and to 'No. 221B, Baker Street', the great detective's famous London address.[170] Holmes later criticizes Watson's 'small brochure', *A Study in Scarlet*, for making 'Detection . . . an exact science' and proceeding to 'tinge it with romanticism', yet this is exactly the appeal of these stories. They cloak minute observation and exaggerated reasoning with adventures among 'all that is bizarre and outside the conventions and humdrum routine of every-day life'.[171] Holmes is at once artist and scientist, rebel and upholder of the law. In an era when willed decadence confronted defenders of morality, the drug-taking, zealous investigator might appeal to both sides at once: 'I suppose that I am commuting a felony, but it is just possible that I am saving a soul.'[172] Later to become one of Scottish literature's many legacies to the cinema, Holmes is the best-known fictional character in 1890s writing. He possesses a universal appeal. Among such classes of modern fiction as romances, 'slum novels' and 'detective stories', Andrew Lang felt that the last category were recognized as ' "not literature" ', but could certainly be among the most readable.[173] Conan Doyle's stories have become classics, still eminently readable and a cornerstone of crime fiction, now the dominant fictional genre of our age.

In December 1893 when Doyle let Holmes plunge to his doom over the Reichenbach Falls along with his arch-enemy the criminal mastermind Professor Moriarty, public outcry forced the author to resurrect his character. In *The Return of Sherlock Holmes* (1904) the polymathic great detective reveals that he saved himself through his knowledge of 'baritsu, or the Japanese system of wrestling, which has more than once been very useful to me'.[174] From *The Hound of the Baskervilles* (1902) to *The Casebook of Sherlock Holmes* (1927), Holmes sleuthed his way into the world's imagination, coming to occupy a place at least as secure as that of Peter Pan. Dr Jekyll's London *Strange Case* had drawn on detective story elements, but Dr Watson followed Holmes to even stranger cases, bringing 'savage' poison darts to civilized modernity and solving riddle after riddle in the modern metropolis. Though unfazed by muddy fields, Holmes is predominantly the Theseus of the urban labyrinth. Where the Kailyarders and Celtic Twilight writers let readers escape from the evolving conurbations theorized by Patrick Geddes, Holmes confronted and solved the city's riddles. He showed that the necessary counterpart to proliferating modernity was a precisely monitored flow of information. His answers remain alluring in our information age. Ultimately, Holmes's solutions may be as absurdly constructed as the escapist fictions of Kailyard or Celtic Twilight, yet they are more consoling since they provide a sense of closure rather than merely the illusion of escape. Holmes's fog-bound London may appear at times a city of dreadful night, even a heart of darkness, but it is one where hope, reason and security rather than despair win out.

London continued to attract Scottish writers, whether to success or ignominy. If Doyle's first story had appeared in the Edinburgh *Chambers's Journal*, his literary triumphs were in London periodicals and with London publishers. Part of the group of London Scots, Doyle co-wrote a book with Barrie in 1893. In Edinburgh *Blackwood's*

Magazine retained the prestige and editorial acumen to begin to publish in its thousandth issue Conrad's masterwork *Heart of Darkness* in 1899, but, despite vigorous flourishes in Edinburgh and Glasgow, publishing was increasingly dominated by London houses. The newer firm of Thomas Nelson, for which John Buchan went to work in 1907, may have had its nominal headquarters in Edinburgh's Dalkeith Road, but was effectively run from London. New and smaller Scottish imprints such as 'Patrick Geddes & Colleagues' might publish Ossian with art nouveau decoration, but ambitious modern writers like the Kailyarders, Doyle and Stevenson worked with larger London – and, increasingly, American – firms in an expanding, internationalizing mass market.

So, for example, the poet, novelist and dramatist John Davidson (1857–1909), a minister's son who fled from 'the Philistinism' of his native Greenock, began his publishing career in Glasgow but, fed up with schoolteaching in Scotland, moved to London in 1888.[175] There, in search of literary and journalistic success, Davidson attended the Sunday parties at William Sharp's house in Hampstead. This led to Davidson's meeting Yeats through the Celtic Rhymers' Club. Although the young author from Greenock could appreciate 'everything fairy like and romantic', he developed a poetry often attuned to modern city life.[176] Almost all the poems of *In a Music Hall* (1891) had been written in Scotland, but the *Fleet Street Eclogues* (1893) were new. Conflictedly articulate, Davidson put into verse more convincingly than anyone else the struggles of the urban clerk:

> For like a mole I journey in the dark,
>   A-travelling along the underground
> From my Pillar'd Halls and broad Suburbean Park,
>   To come the daily dull official round;
> And home again at night with my pipe all alight,
>   A-scheming how to count ten bob a pound.[177]

As here in 'Thirty Bob a Week', Davidson's verse articulates not just the daily struggles of city workers to make a living, but also their inner anxieties and ennui, a wish to escape from a seemingly inane world since 'It is better to lose one's soul,/ Than never to stake it at all.'[178] Such a tone and subject matter would attract the young T. S. Eliot to Davidson as an exemplary poet. In the 1890s he may have been valued most for his more conventional lyrics, but later poets including Hugh MacDiarmid and Edwin Morgan have responded to his use of modern scientific ideas and terminology. Davidson had not only a muscular sense of rhythm, apparent in poems like 'A Runnable Stag', but also a liking for adventurous subjects, rhythms and diction, readily audible in 'The Crystal Palace':

> Contraption, – that's the bizarre, proper slang,
> Eclectic word, for this portentous toy,
> The flying machine, that gyrates stiffly, arms
> A-kimbo, so to say, and baskets slung
> From every elbow, skating in the air.[179]

Able to write about the crystal structure of snow, about suburban housing, and Fleet Street, Davidson admired Burns but rejected the language of post-Burnsian Scots, committing himself to English. Many of his ballads and lyrics are lingeringly Romantic, yet his poetry often draws on encyclopedia articles, dictionaries, and prose works of non-fiction – including his own. He was, in a term used of some Scottish poets a century later, an 'informationist'.

Freelancing in London, doing all sorts of literary work from acting as a publisher's reader to translating Montesquieu's *Lettres persanes*, Davidson maintained a circle of friends which included Conan Doyle, but he remained intellectually lonely. In an age when Scottish translators such as Sir Theodore Martin and the Glasgow University translator of Kant and Hegel, the Reverend Professor William Hastie (1842–1903), as well as the Greenockian Edward Caird, a highly influential Hegelian philosopher who also taught at Glasgow University, championed German thought, Davidson responded with enthusiasm to Nietzsche. He saw his own father as 'the last of the Christians' and, sure that 'All poets are fanatics', wanted to 'come out of Christendom into the Universe'. As a boy in Greenock, Davidson 'on Sundays . . . generally made some blank verse about the universe'.[180] Later, in his forties, he began to write ever-longer blank verse, materialist, anti-Christian 'Testaments' and grew increasingly isolated. 'I never go anywhere. I never see anyone. I am not like other men,' Davidson in London told a nonplussed visitor from Greenock, before closing the door in his face.[181] 'Be haughty, hard,/ Misunderstood', he counsels the soul in 'The Outcast'.[182] Described by a friend as 'a cross between Khubla Khan and a bank manager', the depressive poet suffered mental health problems. Eventually, it appears, he killed himself. But Davidson would be looked back on as a brother in the muse by the Nietzschean Hugh MacDiarmid.[183] MacDiarmid was seventeen when Davidson's disappearance was widely discussed in the international press. Eventually the poet's body was washed ashore at Mousehole in Cornwall, badly decomposed but still clad in a dark overcoat. Paying tribute to Davidson, MacDiarmid would later recall that 'small black shape by the edge of the sea' as 'A bullet-hole through a great scene's beauty,/ God through the wrong end of a telescope'.[184]

Today Davidson seems essential to modern Scottish verse. At the end of the nineteenth century, though, far more marketably Scottish were such poetic productions as the Scots language pastorals, *Horace in Homespun* (1885), by the Edinburgh schoolteacher James Logie Robertson ('Hugh Haliburton' (1846–1922)), or the newspaper verse of fellow schoolteacher Walter Wingate (1865–1918), writing not without irony about 'The Dominie's Happy Lot'. Quietly inturned were the poems of John Gray (1866–1934), but only when the modernity of Davidson would be linked to a fresh imaginative investigation of the Scots tongue would a 'Scottish Renaissance' truly arrive. Until then, there would be rows of books with titles like *For Puir Auld Scotland's Sake* and *Thistledown: A Book of Scotch Humour*. More discerning readers might choose, perhaps, translations of Theocritean peasants into 'Twae collier lads frae near Lasswade'.[185]

The aspiring poet who followed Andrew Lang's advice to Scotticize Theocritean pastoral, and who kept up a marked interest in Scots verse, was John Buchan. Like Davidson (whom he met in London), Buchan was a minister's son. Born in 1875, he grew up in a Free Church manse in Glasgow, but spent boyhood summers tramping and fishing near the Tweedside Borders homes of close relatives. At Glasgow University one of Buchan's teachers was Andrew Lang's friend 'our Tweeddale neighbour' Professor John Veitch, author of *The History and Poetry of the Scottish Border* (1878). Buchan too loved Border lore. He was 'born and bred under the shadow of that great tradition' of Walter Scott, whose biography he wrote.[186] Although a good deal of his life would be spent serving the British government in England and Canada, when ennobled Buchan chose the Scottish title Lord Tweedsmuir. His first novel, *Sir Quixote of the Moors* (1895), written while he was a Glasgow student, is a historical fiction which opens in Galloway. Buchan's first essay collection, *Scholar Gipsies* (1896), carries an Arnoldian title but includes overworked prose about the Vale of the Upper Tweed. *Grey Weather: Moorland Tales of My Own People* (1899) might hint in its title at a Kiplingesque or even a Kailyard filiation, but by that time Buchan was an Oxford student who had spoken at the University Union, supporting the motion that 'this House condemns the Kailyard School of Novelists'.[187] Buchan pronounced Kailyard narrow, parochial. Yet he too published in the magazine of one of its staunchest supporters, Nicoll's *British Weekly*, when seeking to win a place in London literary life. Cannily, Buchan also contrived to write for the Decadents' *Yellow Book* and for the folks back home who read the unyellowed *Glasgow Herald*.

At Glasgow University Buchan had been encouraged to go to Oxford by his Australian-born professor, Gilbert Murray. This sophisticated young Oxford-trained Classicist alerted his student to wide literary horizons. Driven by a Presbyterian work ethic, yet also attracted towards a Stevensonian freedom, Buchan was hugely ambitious. By the age of twenty-three he was already in *Who's Who* where he stated his profession as 'undergraduate', and listed five book-length publications. Two years earlier he had written out a long 'List of Things to be Done'. This occupied four columns designated '*Literary, Academic, Prob. Income, Practical*'. Another list from around that time is headed 'HONOURS GAINED AND TO BE GAINED'. Buchan's plans for his twenty-sixth year include mention of a job ('Professorship of English at the University of Edinburgh') and a planned book, *The Borderers*; he also lists the sums of money he has won for university literary prizes.[188]

The title of Buchan's best-known book, *The Thirty-Nine Steps* (1915), suggests he had a head for figures. So does the title of his least-known, *The Law of Tax relating to the Taxation of Foreign Income* (1905). The author of the latter gave his name on the title page as 'John Buchan, Esq., . . . Barrister-at-Law', but the younger Buchan also enjoyed several other careers: as secretary to the High Commission for South Africa in the Cape, as essayist for the *Spectator*, as London man-about-town, and as literary adviser to the publishing firm of Nelson. Workaholic, staunch imperialist and, in due course, MP, he published poetry, essays, journalism, histories, biographies and historical novels (like the fine *Witch Wood* (1927)), as well as the thrillers for which he is best remembered. As a Glasgow undergraduate Buchan had praised Stevenson as 'one Admirable Crichton in days when narrowness is a virtue, and a man of many interests and capacities is thought to be in a fair way to destruction'.[189] Stevenson's example had a considerable influence on Buchan's prose style and career. Though *The Thirty-Nine Steps* is presented by its author as a '"dime novel"' or '"shocker"', its theme of pursuit over rugged Scottish terrain harks back to *Kidnapped*, while the ability of its hero, Richard Hannay, to adopt a variety of disguises owes something to the adventures of Sherlock Holmes.[190] Again in *Huntingtower* (1922) the Scottish coastal setting with a house besieged by foreigners recalls Stevenson's 'The Pavilion on the Links' while the working-class lads who help out the protagonist, the Gorbals Diehards, are a Glaswegian version of Conan Doyle's Baker Street Irregulars. Buchan worked phenomenally hard, yet his best books seem imaginative sanctuaries, pacy escapes from the routines of careerist labour.

Ambitious for himself, Buchan, who would be cultivated by Hugh MacDiarmid and who would preface MacDiarmid's work, was also ambitious for Scottish culture. In 1907 he tried to make the *Scottish Review* a sort of internationally-oriented Scottish magazine, the 'centre of a Scottish school of letters such as Edinburgh had a hundred years ago'.[191] Among his contributors were the elderly Andrew Lang, Edinburgh's impressive literary professor George Saintsbury, and Neil Munro. Topics ranged from the future of the Scots tongue to Flaubert and the Ibsen whose work was translated and championed by an influential polylingual London-Scottish playwright and critic, the Perth-born William Archer (1856–1924) who campaigned from 1873 for a British National Theatre. Like Patrick Geddes a decade earlier, Buchan sought to use a magazine to encourage a Scottish-international literary renaissance, but the magazine failed and London, rather than Edinburgh, remained the powerhouse of Buchan's world.

Still, the Scotland of his childhood, his parents and his siblings was as crucial to Buchan as to Barrie. It gave him his values and goals, as well as a presbyterian distrust of the very success he sought. Buchan disliked Barrie, but had a marked liking for the work of another exalter of childhood, Kenneth Grahame (1859–1932). That writer's earliest years had been spent in Edinburgh and Inveraray before his father's death occasioned a move to England. Grahame, another author with a head for figures, worked in London for the Bank of England. In *Pagan Papers* (1893) his work shows a clear debt to Stevenson's essays. Grahame's *The Golden Age* (1895) and *Dream Days* (1898) idealize early childhood. His fondness for Pan and childhood was scarcely unique, but surely encouraged *Peter Pan*, while his Arcadian visions enthused the Buchan whose *Scholar Gipsies* (1896) has Pan on its cover. Grahame's appealing children's book *The Wind in the Willows* (1908) again features Pan; its riverbank animal protagonists, Mole and Ratty, adventure in the Wild Wood where Badger's den with its cigars and armchairs is rather like an Edwardian gentlemen's club. Celebrated aspects of *The Wind in the Willows*, such as chases involving high-performance cars and the siege of a country house, would reappear in Buchan's adult fiction. In books like *The Thirty-Nine Steps*, for all the cinema-friendly engagement with technologies of modernity, a vital sense of Arcadia persists. Grahame, whose novel would become a Disney film, helped give birth to that great set-piece of modern entertainment, the car chase. Buchan, whose most celebrated novel would inspire a Hitchcock masterpiece, was the first writer to sense how the car might make Scottish landscape more exciting, yet, for the moment, no less Arcadian. Less than forty years after Richard Hannay wrestled with a codebook, donned disguises, and drove 'that 40 h.p. car for all she was worth over the crisp moor roads on that shining May morning', Ian Fleming created his Scots-descended spy James Bond.[192]

Though he was instrumental in developing the spy-story 'shocker' whose pace, engagement with technology, and love of chases underpins so much modern popular entertainment, Buchan began his writing life with an attempted epic about hell. He patterned this on the minor Scottish poet Robert Pollok's 1827 dourly sub-Miltonic epic *The Course of Time*. The book Buchan read most as a boy was *The Pilgrim's Progress*, an equally pious if more exciting work. Like John Bunyan, John Buchan writes of conflict-filled journeys towards salvation, with fiendish enemies to be defeated along the way; in Buchan's more secular world it is British imperial civilization that is saved at the end.

Whether the scene is the Middle East, Scotland or Europe, this is the pattern of *The Thirty-Nine Steps*, *Greenmantle* (1916) and Buchan's later spy stories. From the Glasgow grocer Dickson McCunn to the colonial Scot Richard Hannay and the cosmopolitan Sir Edward Leithen, this writer's heroes draw on facets of their author's own career. Each hero enjoys adventures in a separate series of novels. Buchan's baddies are charismatic fiends. In 1895, questioning Kailyard values, Buchan had used an Old Testament phrase to denounce those who go seeking 'after strange gods'.[193] His villains are usually foreign false messiahs, whether the African chieftain in *Prester John* (1905) or the manipulated Muslim prophet in *Greenmantle*. Casual xenophobia, or at least an easily assumed imperial superiority, is present in the plotlines. There are antisemitic moments and a strain of period racism will offend some readers; it was part of the author's world. Buchan *was* an imperialist. An admirer of Walter Scott, he was also the last major Scottish writer to articulate fully an ideology of that generally assured but sometimes anxious Britishness which also characterized the Scot Sir John Reith's British Broadcasting Corporation. This ideological loading, along with the pace, plotting and relish for plain language, gives Buchan's best adventure tales a compulsive period appeal. His is a lost world of jolly good and jolly bad chaps: 'I had just finished breakfast and was filling my pipe when I got Bullivant's telegram', begins *Greenmantle*; the pipe-filling is essential to the milieu. As in most of Stevenson and Conan Doyle, female characters are marginal. They supply a soupçon of love interest or, like Holmes's Mrs Hudson, domestic help. John Buchan's work is as conventionally masculine as that of his sister Anna is conventionally feminine: anyone wanting a sense of the politely circumscribed world of middle-class Scottish female gentility should read works such as Anna Buchan's *The Setons* (1917) or the semi-autobiographical *Ann and Her Mother* (1922), in which Ann aims to 'become the writer for middle-aged women'.[194]

Anna Buchan (1877–1948) admired Barrie and wrote under the pen-name 'O. Douglas'. She was a professional writer who travelled to India. She was also to some extent supported by John, who helped his sister place her work and gave her an allowance of £100 a year which, she wrote, 'made all the difference in the world' to her. There is some mockery of a fellow Scottish popular novelist when Anna Buchan has a book-carrying character announce, 'I've brought you one of Annie Swan's – she's *capital* for a confinement.' Yet Buchan was happy to know that her own novels had been chosen by pregnant women. She chose to address successfully a middlebrow audience, having one of her characters speak rather slightingly of 'Virginia Woolf and other highbrows'.[195] Authors admired in her work include Violet Jacob, Stevenson, and, of course, John Buchan. As a young woman, Anna too kept lists of achievements ('Recited Barrie at Samaritan Hospital,/ Went to Band of Hope'), but though she was a seasoned public lecturer, her sphere is usually much more domestic and interior than that of her brother. She wrote, after all, at a time when many women still lacked the right to vote (a right extended to all British women only in 1928), and when a man such as her brother, as a graduate of a Scottish university, still enjoyed two votes. Women tried to sustain protective domestic spaces 'There is probably nothing a child values so much as a feeling of safety,' Anna Buchan wrote in her 1945 autobiography, *Unforgettable, Unforgotten*. This daughter of the manse presents home as a feminized place of struggled-for safety, a domestic sanctuary.[196]

Her brother too writes of sanctuaries, but his are masculine spaces: safehouses rather than safe houses. His sanctuaries are all-male clubs and, most of all, rugged, generally masculine, wilderness areas. There, as to the Wild Wood in *The Wind in the Willows* or to the mountains of John Muir and Stevenson, men go to prove themselves in their journey towards some kind of salvation. Such an impulse is evident in some of Buchan's early writings. It is certainly present in *The Thirty-Nine Steps*, *John MacNab* (1925) and many of his adventure fictions. In late books, like *The Island of Sheep* (1936) and the spiritually and ecologically alert *Sick Heart River* (1941), the quest for sanctuary is even acutely apparent. *Sick Heart River* is more a pilgrim's progress than a thriller. Its ageing imperialist Sir Edward Leithen encounters in northern Canada both native peoples and a Christian mission where, dying, he senses 'the rebirth of a soul'.[197] Buchan's last, unfinished book was called *Pilgrim's Rest*.

A driven man, Buchan loved nothing better than to impress his very possessive mother with his respectable success. Yet, as with Barrie, essential to his imaginative life was a distrust of the conventional success he pursued. If London was the centre of power for Buchan, it is almost incidental to his best fictions. Most of their memorable scenes take place in wilderness zones. Whether in the ambitious Indian novels of Flora Annie Steel (1847–1929) or in children's fiction such as *The Story of Little Black Sambo* (1899) by Helen Bannerman (one of the first Scottish women writers to graduate from a university), Empire loomed large in the Scottish imagination. It helped reshape what Scotland meant. Richard Hannay's Scotland is a kind of 'veld', a place where the colonial feels at home:

. . . I got out an atlas and looked at a big map of the British Isles. My notion was to get off to some wild district, where my veldcraft would be of some use to me, for I would be like a trapped rat in a city. I considered that Scotland would be best, for my people were Scotch and I could pass anywhere as an ordinary Scotsman.[198]

Buchan himself was proudly Scottish and British. One can argue that his Scotland seems a mere imperial adventure playground, an internal colony, often a kind of Arcadia. Yet, though he took his orders from London, his interest in Scotland never ceased, and, as Kailyard and Twilight waned, he made it again a place for the modern imagination.

Buchan was not the only London Scot to do this. He recognized in George Douglas Brown (1869–1902) an impressive talent. From a very different background, Brown was the illegitimate son of an Ayrshire farm servant, and of a farmer who took little to do with him and whom Brown several times claimed was dead. However, like Buchan, Brown had studied Classics at Glasgow University, had been encouraged there by Gilbert Murray, then had gone to Oxford (which Brown disliked) before moving to London. Writing as 'Kennedy King', Brown tried his hand at imperial boys' fiction. He shared with the Kailyarders an admiration for Burns and Galt, but he detested Kailyard sentimentality. In 1901, the year before Gilbert Murray's first version of a Greek tragedy was performed on the London stage, Brown used Greek drama as a framework for his novel *The House with the Green Shutters*, set in the small fictitious Ayrshire town of Barbie.

Brown had produced a Scots glossary for the 1895–6 Blackwood Collected Edition of John Galt's novels, introduced by S. R. Crockett. A careless reader, Crockett tries to map Galt's fictions on to the Kailyard genre, finding in them 'peace', 'restfulness' and a sort of literary 'oatmeal porridge – with cream'.[199] John Buchan realized many readers might set Kailyard 'Idylls . . . on our shelves not far distant from Galt', but John Hepburn Millar, about to write a history of Scottish literature, perceived in Galt's work a remarkable insight into historical change and a sense of village communities being 'the nation in miniature'.[200] George Douglas Brown came to view his native Ayrshire village of Ochiltree as 'an epitome of all the world', and read Galt attentively. In *The House with the Green Shutters* he presents a book which shows 'antagonism' towards the 'sentimental slop of Barrie, and Crockett, and Maclaren'. Yet Brown's work clearly evolved from a Kailyard milieu. In 1895 David Meldrum, the London Scottish editor of *Success*, encouraged him to submit 'Scottish idylls of a more robust character than was the fashion'.[201] Brown developed a style conscious of the world of 'Auld Licht Idylls', but also able to draw slyly not just on a careful reading of Turgenev's studies of Russian peasant life in *Sportsman's Sketches* and on Balzac, but also on his knowledge of Galt's acute awareness of the coming of economic change to small-town Ayrshire.

Galt represented for Brown not just a Scottish precursor as a novelist but also the 'type' of the Scot richly endowed with 'commercial imagination'.[202] Set, like Barrie's early fictions, in the Scotland of his mother's youth, Brown's novel is different from Barrie's tales in its alertness to and interest in Scottish market forces. In Barbie, where the schoolmaster reads *The Wealth of Nations*, the 'tyrant' businessman John Gourlay fails to move with the times and loses out to an astute commercial rival who sees that money is to be made from the coming of the railway. If John Gourlay senior, exulting in his green-shuttered house, suffers from 'insufficiency as a business man', then his oppressed son John shows some signs of writerly talent. Sent to Edinburgh University, the boy uses his 'uncanny gift of visualization' to win an essay prize, but is warned that he needs a philosophy to sustain him.[203] Instead, in a shocking departure from the 'lad o' pairts' stereotype beloved of the Kailyarders, the depressive younger Gourlay takes to drink and ends up murdering his ruined father before taking his own life. This leads immediately to the suicide of his terminally ill mother and sister.

Brown's sometimes melodramatic plot using motifs from Greek tragedy may owe something to his admired Thomas Hardy, who had essayed the use of a Greek tragic framework in *The Mayor of Casterbridge* (1886), and had scandalized the public with the familial suicides of *Jude the Obscure* in 1896. What makes Brown's writing remarkable, though, is its fusion of Scots vernacular with Classically-inflected English narrative – and its superb precision. A resourceful stylist, Brown planned a textbook on *Rules for Writing* whose strictures might have hinted at the Imagist-like emotive accuracy of his own prose.

The old-fashioned kitchen grate had been removed and the jambs had been widened on each side of the fireplace: it yawned, empty and cold. A little rubble of mortar, newly dried, lay about the bottom of the square recess. The sight of the crude, unfamiliar scraps of dropped lime in the gaping place where warmth should have been, increased the discomfort of the kitchen.[204]

Like the young John Gourlay, the embittered and depressive Brown has a remarkable 'gift of visualization'. As a child he had been fascinated by such details as a baby's toenails; at Ayr Academy his gifted teacher, the Irish Classicist William Maybin (to whom Brown dedicated *The House with the Green Shutters*, and who soon afterwards was a pall-bearer at Brown's funeral) taught the young writer to '*prune*' and to concentrate on 'clear' pictures.[205] The intensity of Brown's vision is maintained through a minutely plotted narrative. Brown's Classical sense of unity is very different from the meanderings preferred by the Kailyard writers whose world he sought to explode.

Like those writers, however, Brown had his centre of operations in London. If the Scottish-American industrialist-turned-philanthropist Andrew Carnegie champions enlightened charity in *The Gospel of Wealth* (1900), Brown presents a community in thrall to money and where charity is dramatically lacking. Galt might have combined commercial and artistic imagination, but Brown, like Barrie, finds the two hard to reconcile. Again, like Barrie, Brown can write of 'the Scots' as if he were an outsider, even an anthropologist. At school, he thought Burns sometimes 'an alien in his own land', yet like Burns he could identify with peasant life 'from the inner and the under side'.[206] As a trained Classicist, Brown must have known the work of J. G. Frazer; his novel investigates the killing of a commercial king. While Brown the Oxonian Londoner can produce a distanced critique of the place he sprang from, Brown the Ayrshireman can write with sharp knowledge of the 'democratic Scotland' where old men's 'slaver slid unheeded along the cutties [clay pipes] which the left hand held to their toothless mouths'.[207] As sometimes in Barrie, a mixing of Scots and English not just in the characters' speeches but also in the narrative voice makes for a sense of shared acoustic between narrator and community. In themes, design and narrative style, *The House with the Green Shutters*, an antidote to the Kailyard mixed substantially from Kailyard ingredients, marked a direction for future Scottish fiction.

In the short term that direction would be taken by John Macdougall Hay (1879–1919) whose Gillespie Strang in *Gillespie* (1914) is a Gourlay filled with destructive ambition. But Hay's novel suffers from melodramatic, impasto, expressionist over-writing: 'The Sphinx face, smileless and bloodless, with cruelty in its stony flesh and a hawk-like craftiness in the single wild, wary eye, was devilish with its faint glitter of pleasure, and fed with the damnable fiery liquid, which he heard gurgling, gurgling.'[208] Brown's fiction would find more distinguished successors in Lewis Grassic Gibbon's *A Scots Quair* in the 1930s and Alasdair Gray's *Lanark* in 1981, both of which examine, among other things, how the sensitive imagination may come to terms with the commercial and technological changes endemic to capitalist society. Like many of Stevenson's and Barrie's stories, Brown's is a historical novel. If his coalfield fiction anticipates D. H. Lawrence in its portrayal of claustrophobic relationships, it does so too in its determination to engage through strong emotion and imagistic style with the structures of industrial modernity. As would many works written by Scots living in nineteenth-century London, Brown's fiction became a resource for writers in Scotland in the century that followed.

CONTENTS

The contents page of the magazine The Modern Scot *for October 1932. Published from Dundee and edited from St Andrews by the American Scottish nationalist James H. Whyte, the magazine championed Scottish nationalism along with Scottish-internationalism, a combination typical of the twentieth-century 'Scottish Renaissance' movement. Whyte developed a theory of Scottish nationalism which did not depend on ideas of race; in 1930s St Andrews his circle included Willa and Edwin Muir as well as other writers, composers and artists. To Whyte Hugh MacDiarmid dedicated his greatest extended poem in English, 'On a Raised Beach'. (St Andrews University Library, StA AP4.M6S2)*

10

Renaissance

'To the memory of the Boys of Form Senior V, Greenock Academy, 1909–1910, most of whom were killed in the First War' reads the dedication to a 1952 book about the Clyde.[1] Often in unexpected places, aftershocks of World War I reverberate through twentieth-century Scottish writing. The conflict's bleak legacy shapes masterpieces as different as Lewis Grassic Gibbon's 1930s trilogy *A Scots Quair* and Muriel Spark's 1961 *The Prime of Miss Jean Brodie*. During the war itself, though, battlefield experience produced relatively little outstanding Scottish literature. Like the later autobiographical writings of the Scottish spy Bruce Lockhart (1887–1970), John Buchan's transcontinental wartime thriller *Greenmantle* (1916) anticipates the dynamics of James Bond fiction, but it is also a propagandist adventure. Buchan lost his brother and many friends in combat. He tried to memorialize them in verse whose conventional diction generally lets him down. More successful in their uneven way are some of J. M. Barrie's wartime Home Front one-act plays. Anxieties about manliness articulately underpin the relationship between a father and soldier son awkwardly attempting to show their love for each other, or an orphan Black Watch fighter eagerly adopting an old woman as a surrogate mother so she may write to him in the trenches. Barrie has a mother and father converse with their dead son, each painfully discovering their own emotions, in *A Well-Remembered Voice* (1918). A more calculatingly ruthless voice is heard in Charles Murray's poem, 'Dockens afore his Peers', in which a man wheedles his way into exemption from military service. From Donside, Murray (1864–1941) wrote his best work in his native Aberdeenshire Scots; as part of his linguistically lively dramatic monologue, Dockens suggests that, rather than him, the kitchen-maid would make a good soldier:

She's big an' brosy, reid and roch, an' swippert as

    she's stoot,   *well-fed; rugged; agile*

Gie her a kilt instead o' cotts, an' thon's the gran' recruit.[2]   *petticoats*

Far from the Donside Home Front, and a world away from the Austrian-born, eruditely witty travel writer Norman Douglas (1868–1952), who had spent his boyhood on Deeside and wrote with hedonistic gusto of a bishop's indiscretions on Capri in *South Wind* (1917), Scots recruits served and died on filthy, miles-long battlefronts in Belgium and France. In Scotland male conscription made it increasingly possible for women to take on what had been men's roles. So, for instance, the Lewiswoman Agnes Muir Mackenzie (1891–1955), later a published novelist and critic, lectured in English at Aberdeen University during the war. To begin with, some men seem to have viewed battle as a marketing opportunity: 'The undoubted supremacy of "Blackwood's Magazine" in obtaining the best material in records of the war is now universally recognised,' a copywriter declares at the back of *The First Hundred Thousand* (1915) by 'Ian Hay' (John Hay Beith, 1876–1952). Manchester-born and Edinburgh-educated, Hay dispatched from the Front jaunty, hugely sanitized sketches of Scots military life: 'The trench system has one thing to recommend it. It tidies things up a bit.'[3] Hay went on to write public school tales and to work with P. G. Wodehouse. Others, though, told a different story.

Rain, clay, mud, boredom and 'Àileadh cianail an tine' (The acrid stench of fire) characterize such songs as 'Air an Somme' (On the Somme) by Dòmhnall Ruadh Chorùna (Donald Macdonald, 1887–1967). This North Uist poet never learned to write Gaelic; his work was later recorded and published. Macdonald's songs of poison gas and of marching at Arras towards 'na h-uaigh/ Far nach fhuasg'lear barrall' (the grave/ Where no bootlace is untied) represent a folk tradition of Gaelic singing coming to terms with trench warfare. These songs are less innovative than the heroic elegy of Iain Rothach (John Munro, 1889–1918), a Lewisman seen as a pioneeer of modern Gaelic free verse. Few of his poems have survived.

Thoroughly read in English literature, Munro graduated from Aberdeen University in 1914, then served with the 4th Seaforth Highlanders. In his poetry corpses lie stretched out like pointing fingers, directing successive waves of fighters. For all its sense of twentieth-century warfare, this acoustically rich work draws on traditions of the Gaelic 'call to battle' poem that go back at least to Lachlann Mor Mac-Mhuirich's fifteenth-century battle incitement to Clan Donald at Harlaw. In combat Munro, awarded the Military Cross in 1918 and killed three days later, invokes not the honour of Britain but something smaller-scale, more tribal:

> 'n-sin cuimhnicheam Leódhas, m' àit-àraich,
> is gléidheadh mo làmh a clì.

> *then may I remember Lewis, where I was reared,*
> *and may my hand keep its strength.*[4]

One of the best-known poems of World War I is 'In Flanders Fields' by the Scots-Canadian doctor, John McCrae (1872–1918): 'In Flanders fields the poppies blow/ Between the crosses, row on row . . .'[5] From Scotland itself there are moments in poems by forgotten poets which are suddenly redolent of European wartime, as when a group of soldiers in Shetlander John Peterson's 'Billets' slump upstairs in the attic of an old chateau, 'Box-respirators dropped among the straw.'[6]

Undoubtedly, though, other than those who wrote in Gaelic, Scotland's finest battlefront poets were English public schoolboys. In each case their Scottishness was deflected, yet proudly and consciously adhered to. Born to an academic family in Aberdeen, Charles Hamilton Sorley, killed at the Battle of Loos in 1915 at the age of twenty, was schooled at Marlborough in southern England. There he wrote essays on Burns and Scott, and befriended a multilingual Scottish 'bard'. Sorley aimed to go to Oxford University, then become a social worker. Immediately before the outbreak of war, he had been studying in Germany, a country he loved. In the trenches he read Goethe's *Faust* in the original, used German phrases, and showed marked heroism, carrying a fatally injured comrade like 'a piece of living pulp'.[7] Sorley's prose descriptions of battle conditions – 'a quickfirer . . . pounding away . . . like a cow coughing' and machine guns firing like 'thousands of motor-cycles tearing round and round a track, with cut-outs out' – are hard to forget.[8] He sensed his voice being matured by the experience of war, which let him escape from predictable, privileged existence:

Sorley is the Gaelic for wanderer. I have had a conventional education: Oxford would have corked it. But this has freed the spirit, glory be.[9]

Indubitably a public school 'chap', Sorley nevertheless rejected Rupert Brooke's war poetry as too clothed in 'fine words' and a 'sentimental attitude'.[10] Some of his own best verse fuses body and soul as he sings of the physical exaltation of running, or of being at one with the earth in battle. For Sorley the German troops are simply 'blind like us'.[11] One of his last poems is a verse letter to his Scottish friend John Bain, praising Homer, and there is probably an allusion to *The Iliad* in the tenth line of his magnificently uncompromising final sonnet, found in his kit when it was sent home from France after Sorley had been shot in the head by a sniper:

> When you see millions of the mouthless dead
> Across your dreams in pale battalions go,
> Say not soft things as other men have said,
> That you'll remember. For you need not so.
> Give them not praise. For, deaf, how should they know
> It is not curses heaped on each gashed head?
> Not tears. Their blind eyes see not your tears flow.
> Nor honour. It is easy to be dead.
> Say only this, 'They are dead.' Then add thereto,
> 'Yet many a better one has died before.'
> Then, scanning all the o'ercrowded mass, should you
> Perceive one face that you loved heretofore,
> It is a spook. None wears the face you knew.
> Great death has made all his for evermore.

Strongest in using the word 'mouthless' in its great opening line, this poem counterpoints its rhetorical alliterations and repetitions with short, flat sentences. Its awkward 'heretofore' is just about rescued by the word 'spook'. Like other impressive war poems, this is an attempt on the part of someone intimate with slaughter to communicate to others the banal workings of carnage. There is a moving effortfulness when Sorley in that letter about the noise of gunfire attempts to explain to his philosopher father what it sounds like to be in the midst of trench warfare.

A similar sense of principled, sympathetic engagement and pained

separation powers the best poem by Ewart Alan Mackintosh (1893–
1917). Born to Highland parents in Brighton, Mackintosh won scholar-
ships to St Paul's School in London (where he edited the school magazine), then read Classics at Oxford. John Murray, his tutor at Christ
Church, recalled him studying Gaelic and the pipes, rather than distin-
guishing himself as a Classicist; Mackintosh rowed competitively,
belonged to Oxford University's Fabian and Caledonian Societies, and
numbered several Scots with Highland surnames among his closest
student friends. At war, he served with the 5th, then later the 4th
Seaforths, the same battalion as the Gaelic poet John Munro. Mackintosh wrote a number of English poems with Gaelic titles or phrases in
them. He relished Oxford, but early works written there, such as a
verse drama about tensions between the Old Gods and Christianity in
Highland Morvern are too misted over by the Celtic Twilight; in Sussex
in 1912 he complains of being 'sickened of the south' and of being
'weary for the islands and the Scuir that always frowns,/ And the sun
rising over Mallaig Bay.'[12] Visits to Brora and Golspie in Sutherland
before and during the war strengthened Mackintosh's sense of Highland
Scottishness. His first book, *A Highland Regiment*, appeared in 1917, a
thistle on its cover. In *War, the Liberator* (1918) the poem 'Recruiting'
scorns 'Fat civilians' and 'blasted journalists' with their patriotic posters,
preferring the 'honest men' of the trenches who simply ask soldiers to
'Come and die'.

War, the Liberator includes songs and parodies that 'Tosh' wrote for
his men to sing. His prose 'Studies in War Psychology' mention 'hysteri-
cal rage' and the odd sense of theatricality some soldiers felt at the Front.
Accounts of a raid with grenades on a German position and other
military operations include a sense of the understated casual banter
among men with little chance of survival. Mackintosh won a Victoria
Cross at the Battle of the Somme in 1916. In the photo of him that is
the frontispiece to his second collection he looks thin. Dressed in a kilt,
hand on hip, the young man leans on his walking stick. Probably that
picture was taken after he had been gassed and invalided home, where
he got engaged and planned to emigrate to New Zealand. However,
Mackintosh turned down the chance of 'peace and easy living' in Cambridge where he was teaching bombing to military cadets.[13] Instead, he
opted to return to the Front. Written two days before he was killed, his
last letter to his sister was scribbled on a small fragment of paper.

Reproduced in his twenty-first-century biography, it remains moving in its heartfelt, iconic scrappiness:

> *4th Seaforth*
>
> 19/11/17
> My darling Muriel
> We're going
> over to-morrow so I'm
> leaving this in case I
> don't come back Goodbye
> No time for more
> Your loving
> Alan[14]

Mackintosh's finest poem, 'In Memoriam, Private D. Sutherland, Killed in Action in the German Trench, May 16, 1916, and the Others who Died', has an eloquent, conflicted clarity. Addressing the 'you' of the Highland father, then moving to the 'you' of the son, it draws on and tries to connect the poet's treasured familial knowledge of Highland life with the self-lacerating responsibilities of the officer class into which he had been educated:

> So you were David's father,
> And he was your only son,
> And the new-cut peats are rotting
> And the work is left undone,
> Because of an old man weeping,
> Just an old man in pain,
> For David, his son David,
> That will not come again.
>
> Oh, the letters he wrote you,
> And I can see them still,
> Not a word of the fighting
> But just the sheep on the hill
> And how you should get the crops in
> Ere the year got stormier,
> And the Bosches have got his body,
> And I was his officer.

You were only David's father,
But I had fifty sons
When we went up in the evening
Under the arch of the guns,
And we came back at twilight
O God! I heard them call
To me for help and pity
That could not help at all.

Oh, never will I forget you,
My men that trusted me,
More my sons than your fathers',
For they could only see
The helpless little babies
And the young men in their pride.
They could not see you dying,
And hold you while you died.

Happy and young and gallant,
They saw their first-born go,
But not the strong limbs broken
And the beautiful men brought low,
The piteous writhing bodies,
The screamed 'Don't leave me, Sir,'
For they were only your fathers
But I was your officer.[15]

Ewart Alan Mackintosh died fighting with the 4th Seaforths at Cambrai on 21 November 1917. Some of his lines appear on the Scottish-American War Memorial in Edinburgh's Princes Street Gardens.

Mackintosh was not the only young Scottish poet with an interest in war psychology. 'For the soldier the rush of impressions had been tremendous, beyond the possibility of assimilation', wrote Christopher Murray Grieve (1892–1978), whose closest schoolfriend had been killed, like C. H. Sorley, at the Battle of Loos in 1915.[16] Born and schooled in the Borders village of Langholm, Grieve had spent a year in Edinburgh at Broughton Higher Grade School. He had worked in Wales and Scotland as a local journalist before enlisting in the Royal Army Medical Corps in 1915. Posted to Salonika from 1916 to 1918, he caught malaria and was invalided home, before serving later at a military hospital near Marseilles. Grieve's first collection of poems, *A Voice from Macedonia*, found some favour with John Buchan, but secured no publisher. Only several years later, and particularly after 1922 when he began to write poetry in Scots under the name 'Hugh MacDiarmid' did this author fully realize his gifts.

At the beginning and end of his writing life, MacDiarmid was an unpromising poet. In mid-career he could be magnificent. His verse and often incendiary polemical prose scorched twentieth-century Scottish intellectual life. 'My job', he wrote to the poet and broadcaster George Bruce in 1964, 'has never been to lay a tit's egg, but to erupt like a volcano, emitting not only flame, but a lot of rubbish.'[17] Almost half a century earlier, World War I letters to his old schoolteacher and mentor, George Ogilvie, give a similar impression. Grieve's war service seems almost wholly taken up with reading and planning books. In Salonika he discusses with excited admiration Wyndham Lewis's Vorticist avant-garde magazine, *Blast*, but also speaks in praise of the immortal memory of Robert Burns at a Burns Supper, plots 'the formation of a "national" school' of Scottish art, and intends to return home to 'enter heart and body and soul into a new Scots Nationalist propaganda'.[18] This Grieve certainly did. Throughout his career, he would attempt to fuse ideas of national language, culture and Scottish independence with an intense enthusiasm for the international modernist avant-garde and for radical socialism.

In the hot summer of 1919, demobbed, newly married and recently returned to Scotland, Grieve was living in St Andrews in a 'wee house' (now demolished) at 65 Market Street.[19] Here he sought to realize his dream of placing himself at the heart of a vigorous new Scottish literary movement. A year later he presented the eleven poets in the first of his three *Northern Numbers* anthologies as participating in 'an experiment in group-publication' following 'the "Georgian Poetry" series'. England's Georgian Poetry series was hardly avant-grade, and nor were Grieve's contributors (mostly 'close personal friends') who included John Buchan, Neil Munro, Will H. Ogilvie, Grieve himself, and Violet Jacob – the only female contributor.[20] Later volumes of *Northern Numbers* would be just about as unadventurous, though they would include work by the worthwhile polylingual poet, translator and economist Alexander Gray (1882–1968). Gray's verse ranged from poems in Mearns dialect to 1920 versions of Heine and the English-language poem 'Scotland' with its felicitously phrased praise for a native land and people 'Kissed by the wind/ And caressed by the rain'.[21]

In 1920, all too familiar with East Coast wind and rain, Grieve took a job in Montrose. There, on the coast north of Dundee, he worked for the *Montrose Review*, an Angus local newspaper, a good deal of which he is said to have written himself. By the early Twenties its readers were being reminded that 'It is not generally known that one of the most consistent and interested patrons of Montrose Library is Mrs Violet Jacob, the well-known poetess and novelist, and acknowledged to be Scotland's greatest exponent of the Doric.'[22] Violet Jacob (1863–1946) writes not only in 'the Doric' (Scots), but also in English. She crafts fine short stories and her historical novel *Flemington* (1911) impressively continues the Stevensonian theme of divided identity which would also preoccupy MacDiarmid. Jacob's best poetry is contained in the wartime *Songs of Angus* (1915) and *More Songs of Angus* (1918). With their evocations of local people and places such as 'Craigo Woods, wi' the splash o' the cauld rain beatin'' these, along with some of Charles Murray's work, were some of the most confident poems in Scots since Stevenson.[23] Though MacDiarmid rather scorned Murray, the Aberdeenshire poet's God's-eye view of the earth in 'Gin I Were God' probably made an impact on him. So did the sometimes antique Scots language of the nationalist poets Pittendrigh MacGillivray (1856–1938) and Lewis Spence (1874–1955). The many publications of the Scottish Text Society (founded in 1882) had helped call attention to older work in Scots, but the young newspaperman Grieve was impatient that Scots-language ('Braid Scots') poetry was not in touch with the work of modernist writers like Woolf, Eliot or Joyce. Publicizing his *Northern Numbers* to the Montrose YMCA Literary and Debating Society in 1921, Grieve admitted that 'Even the merely linguistic influence of the great genius of Burns is unexhausted', but argued strongly that 'the hand of the clock could not be put back, and that Scotland, having evolved tremendously in all human directions since "Braid Scots" ceased to be used, "Braid Scots" was no longer an adequate vehicle for the thoughts and feelings' of most Scottish people.[24]

So, rather than spending much time on the belatedly Pre-Raphaelite if occasionally beautiful verse of Rachel Annand Taylor (1876–1960) or the emergent Scots charm of poet W. D. Cocker (1882–1970),

MacDiarmid looked further afield. The names of Joseph Conrad, Aldous Huxley, Virginia Woolf and Dorothy Richardson surface surprisingly among accounts of cattle shows and council meetings in the 1920s *Montrose Review*. As early as February 1920 C. M. Grieve was lecturing on Lenin to the local branch of the Independent Labour Party. In 1922, the year of their first publication, Grieve reacted enthusiastically to Joyce's *Ulysses* and to T. S. Eliot's *The Waste Land*. By 1924 he was enjoying Wallace Stevens's *Harmonium*. While writing energetically for the *Montrose Review*, he was also warning, in London's *New Age* and in other periodicals, against 'provinciality of outlook'.[25]

A wish to blend modern internationalism with well-nurtured adherence to local tradition is something MacDiarmid shared with his friend the Orkney-born poet, critic and autobiographer Edwin Muir (1887–1959). In *We Moderns* (1918) Muir argued that 'The true modern is a continuator of tradition.' Adopting a Nietzschean pose, he saw art as bound up with clashing opposites, or at least with 'the conflict – an eternal one – for his [the modern's] tradition against its opposite'.[26] Around the same time, in this era of European battles a markedly conflictual view of Scottish literature was being developed by the Belfast-based Scottish critic, Professor G. Gregory Smith, whose *Scottish Literature: Character and Influence* (1919) sees its subject as characterized by 'a zigzag of contradictions'. For this supposed hallmark of Scottish writing Smith coined the phrase 'the Caledonian antisyzygy'.[27] Increasingly determined to be 'whaur extremes meet', MacDiarmid eagerly adopted this phrase and much of its accompanying theory. He argued with gusto that Gregory Smith's was 'the first text-book I would like to place in the hands of any young Scot likely to play a part in bringing about a National Renaissance'.[28]

Such a 'National Renaissance' soon erupted. Orchestrated by Mac-Diarmid, it played a crucial part in making Scotland rather than London the focus of Scottish writers' activities, though there were certainly authors such as the remarkable London Scot David Lindsay (1876–1945) who operated outside MacDiarmid's parameters. In Lindsay's spiritual-quest novel *A Voyage to Arcturus* (1920) a crystal torpedo is fired from north-east Scotland to a distant planet where strangely named characters experience fantastic adventures. Lindsay's weird imagination had been prefigured in the work of George MacDonald, and would find successors in writings by C. S. Lewis and Alasdair Gray. It seems, though, far from the Renaissance which MacDiarmid, with his eye on the Irish literary revival, was trying to launch from Montrose.

Not without self-interest, MacDiarmid later wrote of Montrose as 'the cultural centre of Scotland' in the 1920s.[29] Energizing and shaping a Renaissance involved this poet in his own zigzag of contradictions. Characteristically, he would dismiss something as impossible, then do it. So, in 1921, the *Montrose Review* showed great interest in 'Group publication' and in the example of 'The Liverpool Chapbook':

The essence of such an undertaking lies in having a sufficiently good little group of local writers and artists capable of an expression of themselves on a certain level, and with such a significance in their work as is distinctively local, or at least regional. How many provincial centres in Great Britain can even attempt this? What would be the fate of such a project in Montrose? The Biblical test of the essential ten just men would fail. No writers of any ability at all exist even in Glasgow or Edinburgh – let alone Montrose.[30]

No sooner had this been asserted than, with a typically confident backflip, Grieve launched his magazine *The Scottish Chapbook* in Montrose on 26 August 1922. The following month he did something more surprising. Having completely scorned the sort of revival of 'Braid Scots' then being championed by the Vernacular Circle of the London Burns Club, he went as representative of Montrose Burns Club to the annual conference of the Burns Federation, held that year in Birmingham. He cultivated the Burnsians, and on 30 September 1922, having leafed through a book on the Scots tongue, he published his first poems in Scots. One of these is clearly sub-Burnsian. The other, 'The Watergaw' (whose title means 'the fragmentary rainbow'), is a minor miracle:

Ae weet forenicht i' the yow-trummle	*one wet evening; [cold spell during sheep-shearing]*
I saw yon antrin thing,	*strange*
A watergaw wi' its chitterin' licht	*chattering*
Ayont the on-ding;	*beyond; downpour*
An' I thocht o' the last wild look ye gied	
Afore ye deed!	*died*
There was nae reek i' the laverock's hoose	*smoke; lark*
That nicht – an' nane i' mine;	
But I hae thocht o' that foolish licht	

Ever sin' syne;   *since then*
An' I think that mebbe at last I ken   *know*
What your look meant then.[31]

The language of this poem is in part familiarly vernacular, in part synthetic. 'Yow-trummle', for instance, came from the book on Scots, while the rainbow owes something to Burns's 'rainbow's lovely form/ Evanishing amid the storm' in 'Tam o' Shanter', and something more to a hymn sung at MacDiarmid's father's funeral in which the Victorian hymn-writer George Matheson seeks to 'trace the rainbow through the rain'.[32] To have drawn in an almost collage-like way on earlier texts is typical of MacDiarmid, but his lyric has its own distinctive life. Like an Imagist poem, it fires clues at the reader, who must make of them what he or she can. The final meaning of that 'last wild look' is not explained; it may be beyond explanation. Set at the meeting-point of two extremes – life and death – the poem is a template for MacDiarmid's subsequent work. Its mixture of rhythmical vernacular speech and form with strange, even estranging vocabulary enhances its sense of oddly angled perceptions, something developed in MacDiarmid's other Scots poems of the period, such as 'The Innumerable Christ' or 'The Bonnie Broukit Bairn', where the poet adopts a consciously eccentric yet revelatory viewpoint.

At a time when many go-getting Scots still headed for London or emigrated overseas, MacDiarmid was conscious of what seemed the perversity of a commitment to Montrose and to ambitious poems in Scots. He regarded the idea of the 'canny Scot' as a stereotype which encouraged the Scots to be dutiful servants of British capitalism. He scorned such a Scot as John Reith (1889–1971) who, as influential Director General of the BBC, set that Corporation's establishment tone. While Reith was said to be able to detect the exact provenance of Scottish accents with uncanny precision, he nevertheless encouraged the notion of a standardized, proper-sounding 'BBC English'. Most Scots found, and find, such English alien. Although he did not write in Scots, and regarded his own knowledge of English as 'almost idiomatic', the middle-class dramatist James Bridie, a contemporary of MacDiarmid, maintained humorously yet revealingly that,

In conversation with the English I find myself unevenly balanced between what we call Kelvinside English, which I despise, and Music Hall Scots, which I do not speak very well. I cannot talk Well Off for more than two or three sentences at a time. This dilemma makes it hard for me to concentrate on what the English are saying to me. I have to cover my wandering attention by talking too much.[33]

Hugh MacDiarmid wrote and talked a lot. His first authored, published book, *Annals of the Five Senses* (1923), gathered English prose sketches and poems, some from his World War I days. This work is inferior to MacDiarmid's Scots lyrics, though both share his love of quotation, textual collage, and psychological restlessness. MacDiarmid's first collection of Scots verse appeared in 1925 and was called *Sangschaw* – the Montrose Burns Club held an annual 'songshaw' or song festival. MacDiarmid's second Scots collection, *Penny Wheep*, was published in 1926. Its title means 'small beer' and comes from Burns's 'The Holy Fair' where the poet praises drink. Though these books sold in small numbers, MacDiarmid publicized them aggressively. In part thanks to his own machinations, in part through his remarkable talent, he was soon hailed as 'a new Burns' as well as the leader of a 'Scottish renaissance'.[34] In 1926, writing as C. M. Grieve, he edited a short selection of Burns's poems, explaining that in choosing them 'my ideas generally coincide with his, especially where these are at odds with conventional opinion', and emphasizing the reader's need for 'a thorough knowledge of Scots'. It is this Scots-language aspect of Burns's work, Grieve contends, which is 'to-day ... stimulating the most vital Scots poetry for over a century'.[35]

As early as 1923 his friend Edwin Muir had written to MacDiarmid suggesting that 'a long poem in the language you are evolving would go tremendously'.[36] In the following summer and autumn Muir and his novelist wife Willa were living in Montrose where Willa's mother, Mrs Anderson, had a draper's shop. Willa Muir, wary of MacDiarmid, was writing *Women: An Inquiry* (1925) for Leonard and Virginia Woolf at the Hogarth Press. Later she followed this with the lively feminist study *Mrs Grundy in Scotland* (1936) and her shrewd novel *Imagined Corners* (1931) which deals especially with the circumscribed lives of women in the provincial East Coast Scottish town of 'Calderwick', based on Montrose. Willa Anderson had been an outstanding student at St Andrews University. She went on to become the principal English-language translator of Kafka. To Montrose the Muirs brought their commitment to internationalism and aspects of modernism. Edwin's

1926 book of essays, *Transition*, its preface signed 'E. M., Montrose, Scotland', deals with Joyce, Lawrence, Woolf, Eliot and others.

While the Muirs lived at 81 High Street, MacDiarmid worked in Review Close at 97 High Street, Montrose. His immediate response to Muir's suggestion of a long poem had been to begin work on 'Braid Scots', dedicated to Muir, part of which was later reworked as 'Gairm-scoile' (Singing School). There MacDiarmid argues, *'It's soon', no sense, that faddoms the herts o' men'*.[37] That commitment to sound highlights MacDiarmid's sheer delight in the acoustic of Scots, and his belief in the power of its peculiar vocabulary. He wanted to link these with avant-garde modernist writing. His 1923 *Scottish Chapbook* 'Theory of Scots Letters' argues that there is a remarkable resemblance 'between Jamieson's *Etymological Dictionary of the Scottish Language* and James Joyce's *Ulysses*'. Claiming with characteristic bravado that 'The Scottish Vernacular is the only language in Western Europe instinct with those uncanny spiritual and pathological perceptions alike which constitute the uniqueness of Dostoevsky's work', MacDiarmid invokes Lawrence, Proust and others. He asserts that 'The Scots Vernacular is a vast store-house of just the very peculiar and subtle effects which modern European literature in general is assiduously seeking.'[38]

Looking both towards that older Scottish European polymath, Patrick Geddes, and across the Irish Sea to the example of the Irish Literary Revival, MacDiarmid provided a theory, publication outlets, publicity and a focal point for a Scottish Renaissance. He also trumpeted a politics which sought to combine Scottish nationalism with radical socialist internationalism. An active town councillor, in 1922 he campaigned in the *Montrose Review* 'for a Scottish Free State'; in 1928 he became a founder member of the National Party of Scotland, which later became the Scottish National Party.[39] Often considered eccentric, MacDiarmid's noisy politics could be insightful and far-seeing, but came to grate with the Muirs and others. Determinedly anxious about people who were 'uprooted and out of touch with national traditions', MacDiarmid wrote in 1923 that a 'Programme for a Scottish Fascism' of the left is *'the only thing that will preserve our distinctive national culture'*.[40] In the following decade he wrote Hymns to Lenin.

Yet for all MacDiarmid's flaunting of his Communism, it is hard not to feel that the work of the Fife dramatist Joe Corrie (1894–1968) is closer to the grain of working-class experience around the time of the

1926 General Strike; Corrie's best play, *In Time o' Strife* (1927), gives a keen sense of a mining community 'fightin' a losin' fight' while sensing 'It's a revolution that's needed here.'[41] MacDiarmid too wrote about the Strike, but seems more intellectually aloof. In 1934, having been expelled by the Nationalists, he joined the Communist Party of Great Britain, only to be expelled from that four years later for nationalist deviation. He rejoined the CPGB after the 1956 Hungarian uprising, to show his solidarity with Stalin. It may be possible to see a good deal of consistency in MacDiarmid's long-standing support for radical Scottish republicanism alongside full-blooded international socialism, but it is worth remembering that he liked to quote Walt Whitman: 'Very well then I contradict myself,/ (I am large, I contain multitudes)', and many people sensed in him just one contradiction too many.[42] He loved to provoke. If he thought it good for Scotland or for himself (two entities not always seen as distinct), he adopted a position of strategic extremism. As soon as he was included in *Who's Who*, he listed his recreation as 'Anglophobia'.

In his lifetime, many who found MacDiarmid's poetry hard to understand knew him mainly as a stridently eccentric political agitator. Today, when support for left-wing Scottish nationalism seems far less eccentric, and when a devolved Scotland has a strong sense of its own distinctive identity, his political outspokenness may be seen to have paid off. During the mid-twentieth century, thanks not least to MacDiarmid's efforts, Scottish nationalism was bound up with cultural life rather than narrowly with economics. MacDiarmid helped shift the Scottish cultural climate away from London-centred Britishness. He had no time for the London-based J. M. Barrie, for instance. The *Montrose Review* argued that 'the "Window in Thrums" would be smashed aside . . . by anyone determined to have a clear view today.'[43] Yet when, with his amazing cosmological imagination, MacDiarmid ends one of his finest Scots lyrics, 'The Bonnie Broukit Bairn', by imagining planet earth as a baby among other, more splendid-looking planets, and exclaims

> *– But greet, an' in your tears ye'll droun*   *weep*
> *The haill clanjamfrie!*[44]   *[whole rabble of them]*

he is using a striking Scots phrase deployed in its English guise by that son of Kirriemuir, Barrie, who wrote of 'the whole clanjamfry' in his preface to a 1917 play.[45] Typically, MacDiarmid seeks to make explicitly and acoustically Scottish what in Barrie is presented in an apparently anglicized British guise.

MacDiarmid was far from the only younger writer negotiating with the legacy of 'Barrie the dear old "whimsical" bastard'.[46] Far from her native north-east village of Strichen, the Hollywood scriptwriter Lorna Moon (1886–1930) both inveighed against 'Barrie blah' and wondered if Barrie might be approached 'about a preface' for her short-story collection *Doorways in Drumorty* (1925).[47] Its title suggests the strong Kailyard filiations evident in the stories, but not the way they attempt to break out of Kailyard conventions. Moon was a woman of the era of Marie Stopes whose 1916 *Married Love* and other books championed women's sexual freedom. 'It is revolting to me,' wrote Moon, 'that in a civilized world a woman's virtue rests entirely upon her hymen.'[48] Her stories emerge from Barrie's Thrums and Ian Maclaren's Drumtochty but go beyond them as Moon aims especially to depict women's lives from the inside. 'Wantin' a Hand' puns aggressively in its title on the need for domestic help and on the situation of the resolute, spurned Jean who has lost her arm in a farming accident and whose face is 'pouchy with drink'.[49] Sometimes the writing in this story veers towards melodrama, a tendency more evident in Moon's novel *Dark Star* (1929). Set in north-east Scotland, it uses the trope of a visiting carnival to explore a young woman's sexual awakening in a constricting community. Published in America's *Century Magazine* from 1921 onwards, Moon's stories became known in Scotland after the publication of *Doorways in Drumorty* by Jonathan Cape in London. They mapped out the north-eastern territory with which Lewis Grassic Gibbon would come to be most closely associated. Moon's tales both depended on and burst out of Kailyard values. Thanks to a modern biography and twenty-first-century republication, California-based Helen Nora Wilson Low or 'Lorna Moon' can be seen as an effective contributor to Scottish literature in the era of the Scottish Renaissance.[50]

Often commentators have tended to accept MacDiarmid's view of that literary Renaissance as an all-out male attack on Barrie and Kailyard values. In fact there are some marked continuities between Kailyard writing and the small-town-based Renaissance. One unlikely link is A. S. Neill, the pioneering educationalist, a friend of the Muirs and of MacDiarmid, who worked in Forfar around 1920 and later founded

Summerfield School. In a series of books beginning with *A Dominie's Log* (1915) Neill wrote sketches that were Kailyard in structure. At times his magazine schoolroom pieces come close to the couthy charm of J. J. Bell's Glaswegian waif in *Wee MacGreegor* (1902). While the prolific Neill was an admirer of *The House with the Green Shutters* and planned a biography of its author, he also knew and relished work by Barrie. His often charming observations of the children he taught served as his focus for discussing Nietzschean ideas and 'the Guild Socialism of *The New Age*' from the standpoint of a self-proclaimed 'Socialist . . . doubter' and 'heretic'.[51] On the one hand, Neill maintained in 1920, 'Barrie proved himself a genius when he created Peter Pan,' but on the other hand Neill argues that 'The genius who will help man to look forward instead of backward must not return to boyhood; he must go forward to superman. To put it psychologically, Barrie's genius comes from the unconscious, but what the world needs is a man whose genius will come from the superconscious, the divine.'[52]

Lorna Moon did not aim to be such a superman; writing in America and mixing Kailyard with Hollywood genres, she sought to reveal the constraints and needs of women's lives. In Scotland, however, Hugh MacDiarmid aimed to be just the sort of 'man . . . genius' his friend Neill had outlined, and the poet's magnum opus of the 1920s articulates several of the problems involved. Anglicization, Scottishness, emblems of nationhood and sexuality are all deconstructed and reconstructed in the 2685-line poem MacDiarmid produced in 1926 as a cornerstone for his Scottish Renaissance movement. In *A Drunk Man Looks at the Thistle* Burns and T. S. Eliot feature repeatedly, either through direct invocation or through allusion. This strange combination of exemplars hints at something of the poem's largely successful ambition to fuse Scots vernacular language and culture with the shifting, fragmented consciousness and perceptions of modernism.

Reeling from satire to lyricism, from the tender to the bawdy, the native to the translated, the synthetic to the warmly idiomatic, this long poem in Scots uses the trope of a drunken speaker to license its rollercoasting shifts of perception and attitude. *A Drunk Man Looks at the Thistle* broods on Scotland's national flower and on ideas of cultural rootedness. It explores Scotland's national spirit, in the alcoholic and soulful senses of that word. It examines national and sexual development, as well as the relationship between Scotland and modernity. Contemporary Scotland in the poem is seen as a waste land, 'Eliot's . . . Land o' Drouth'; false, too readily marketable versions of Scotland are mocked as the productions of 'Croose London Scotties wi' their braw shirt fronts' at Burns Suppers.[53] In tone and subject matter MacDiarmid draws on aspects of Burns's drunk man poem, 'Tam o' Shanter', even as he inclines towards the modernist sensibility of *The Waste Land*. His poem shifts its metrical form many times, though there is a gravitational attraction towards balladic and pentametric rhythms. Verse by Russian and French poets is incorporated through Scots translation into a text which is sometimes densely allusive, sometimes rollicking or metaphysically speculative. *A Drunk Man* strives to see Scotland not just as peculiarly moribund but as capable of being re-energized through bonding with the rest of the created universe; Scotland must come to serve simultaneously as a focus for universal as well as local ideas and sensations:

> I wad ha'e Scotland to my eye
> Until I saw a timeless flame
> Tak' Auchtermuchty for a name,
> And kent that Ecclefechan stood
> As pairt o' an eternal mood.[54]

Soaring and ambitious, like *The Waste Land* MacDiarmid's poem heads towards a kind of peace that passes understanding, a sublime 'Silence'. Yet this is also splendidly undercut by the final deflationary remark of the drunken speaker's wife:

> O I ha'e Silence left,
>
> > 'And weel ye micht,'
> > Sae Jean'll say, 'efter sic a nicht!'[55]

A Drunk Man Looks at the Thistle retains clear elements of a 'folk' acoustic, but is also aware of the dissonant music of Schönberg. Like the same poet's shorter Scots lyrics, it can draw on arcane vocabulary, though it does not always do so. When MacDiarmid in his early Scots work uses an odd word like 'how-dumb-deid' (silent depth), the likelihood is that he had found it by trawling through a Scots dictionary; he loved in particular to search through John Jamieson's 1808–9 *Etymological Dictionary of the Scottish Language*, seeking vocabulary that excited him. Many poets find that poems come from a sense of individual words or a few words combined in a rhythm, so this practice is readily understandable. On a larger historical level MacDiarmid was also aware of the great tradition of Scottish lexicography which involved not only Jamieson, and Sir James Murray's *New English Dictionary* (1879–1928), later called the *Oxford English Dictionary*, but also the lexicographical labours of Murray's assistant Sir William Craigie. Craigie's work led to the instigation of the *Scottish National Dictionary*, edited by William Grant and David Murison between 1929 and 1976, and afterwards to the production of the *Dictionary of the Older Scottish Tongue* (1936–2002). MacDiarmid's dictionary-trawling could spur his imagination to the point of verbal kleptomania. At times he worked into his poems lexicographers' illustrative citations – whole lines of earlier verse, traditional sayings. The technique of building fragments of older work into a new text was a common modernist practice, used by Pound, Joyce, Eliot and others, but, as in the case of Eliot, so with MacDiarmid this collage technique could bring charges of plagiarism. Later he would take long passages of other people's prose, and, often with a very fine feel for line-breaks and verse movement, realign them as verse.

Sometimes MacDiarmid's efforts strike readers most for their lexical oddity. His practice and persona were both inspiring and offputting for younger writers. The poet Kathleen Jamie, who was sixteen when MacDiarmid died in 1978, remarked in the early 1990s that

I was being told in this loud but subliminal way 'You must read MacDiarmid and take those ideas on and espouse his ideas', I was told there was this poem that I had to read; it was called *A Drunk Man Looks at the Thistle*. Drunk? Men? Thistle? What? This was what we'd been striving to get away from for umpteen years. This is the smoky darkness of those pubs that you weren't allowed into because you were a woman. Yes? No. No, not for me.[56]

MacDiarmid, however, is such a protean poet that it would be unfair to view him only in this light. His early lyric 'Empty Vessel' treats the topic of a mother who has lost her child. Its allusive title – referring to the saying that an empty vessel makes the most noise – may have a certain modernist harshness to it, but the poem itself appears to have a Wordsworthian simplicity. It relies on a folk voice, but not a whit on arcane vocabulary:

I met ayont the cairney	*beyond; cairn*
A lass wi' tousie hair	*tousled*
Singin' till a bairnie	
That was nae langer there.	

Wunds wi' warlds to swing	*winds*
Dinna sing sae sweet.	
The licht that bends owre a' thing	*over everything*
Is less ta'en up wi't.[57]	

Yet this beautiful lyric about a mother grieving for a baby she has lost also has a subliminal signature of modernity. It was written not long after Einstein's early 1920s visit to Britain when the national press was full of reports of his theories, including talk of 'Light Caught Bending', as Rose Macaulay puts it.[58] A poem about absolute concentration and focus, 'Empty Vessel', like several of MacDiarmid's other Scots lyrics, sees human emotions as more important than the vastness of the universe. It is all the more moving for its simple diction. Its image of light indicates too that right from his early career this poet had a keen interest in 'Science and Poetry' – the title of one of his 1922 poems in English. This interest became increasingly dominant in his later work.

In 1920s Montrose MacDiarmid gathered round him a group of friends, fellow artists and correspondents who either lived nearby or kept in regular touch. They published in a series of magazines MacDiarmid edited, using the facilities and contacts offered by his experience as a journalist. This group included Edwin and Willa Muir, Violet Jacob, the Highland novelist and nationalist Neil Gunn, A. S. Neill, and the future novelist Thomas Macdonald (1906–75) who went on to write as 'Fionn MacColla'. Macdonald's boyhood home was in Links Avenue, the street of council houses where the Grieves lived. MacDiarmid did much of his writing in his garden shed. He designated his address at number 16 'The Scottish Poetry Bookshop'.

The ambitious poet maintained a lively awareness of international writing. He loved to invoke not only Joyce or Eliot but also less familiar figures such as the politically active Icelandic poet Jonas Gudlaugsson ('Ah, Gudlaugsson, my cry is e'en as thine') who had been influenced by Nietzsche.[59] MacDiarmid's radical views, outspokenness, hard drinking and often abrasive manner made him enemies in the local community. In 1929 he moved to London where the English-born extrovert Scottish nationalist novelist Compton Mackenzie helped him secure the editor-ship of *Vox*, a magazine based around radio.

This move initiated a period of deep unhappiness in MacDiarmid's life. He published *To Circumjack Cencrastus* in 1930, but that long poem lacks the sustained achievement of *A Drunk Man*. In London his wife left him, taking their children; *Vox* failed. Heavy drinking led to a breakdown that required hospitalization, and MacDiarmid worried he had caught syphilis. By 1933, attempting to dry out after his alcohol problems, he and his second wife, the Cornishwoman Valda Trevlyn, went to live on Whalsay in the Shetland Isles in conditions of great poverty. At times they ate gulls' eggs and used furniture made from driftwood. Deploying some Shetlandic vocabulary, MacDiarmid wrote poems about his experiences with the local fishermen, but on the whole, though his advocacy of the Scots language remained fierce, he gravitated towards writing most of his poetry in English.

On Whalsay MacDiarmid was isolated, but not cut off from the currents of modern culture. The outstanding artist John Quinton Pringle had painted on Whalsay in the 1920s, while the influential Edinburgh literary professor Herbert Grierson (dedicatee of several MacDiarmid poems) had family connections with the island, but, like Thomas Carlyle at remote Craigenputtoch a century before, MacDiarmid relied princi-pally on magazines, correspondents and his own imagination. As he wrote to Ezra Pound in 1933,

I am, of course, a fraud as you will see from my address. I still contrive by a species of magic to maintain an appearance of being au fait with all that is happening in welt-literatur ... But it must become increasingly difficult for me to produce these occasional effects of omniscience.[60]

The dictionary, though, remained MacDiarmid's best friend. He con-tinued to draw on lexicographical, scientific and other informational prose sources to nourish his work. This tendency is very pronounced in the opening of 'On a Raised Beach', arguably his most remarkable long poem, published in his 1934 collection *Stony Limits*. Its first lines are written in the English language, but not as most of us know it:

> All is lithogenesis – or lochia,
> Carpolite fruit of the forbidden tree,
> Stones blacker than any in the Caaba,

Cream-coloured caen-stone, chatoyant pieces,
Celadon and corbeau, bistre and beige,
Glaucous, hoar, enfouldered, cyathiform,
Making mere faculae of the sun and moon . . .[61]

Most of the poem is not written in this style, but its opening paragraph piles up a wall of stony words in front of the reader. Like 'The Watergaw', 'On a Raised Beach' is fascinated by the confronting of life by death. Stones, the things on the planet furthest from human vitality, are scrutinized and meditated on in detail. MacDiarmid, who once told David Daiches that he considered people to be 'one of God's mistakes', seems to wish to move into an inhuman arena.[62] 'There are plenty of ruined buildings in the world but no ruined stones', reads one of the most memorable lines of 'On a Raised Beach' – a line which just happens to be adapted from another source.[63] MacDiarmid's later poetry often deals with scientific topics. It may work most effectively at lyric length, as in 'To a Friend and Fellow-Poet', which likens a Guinea worm giving birth to the 'suicidal art' of poetry.[64]

This poet had something of an instinct for martyrdom. Certainly there is a self-aggrandizing egotism in 'To a Friend and Fellow-Poet'. More striking, though, is MacDiarmid's delight in the way scientific vocabulary and the factual account of an unusual process can be recast as poetry through deft use of enjambement, punctuation, rhythm and, not least, vocabulary. 'To a Friend and Fellow-Poet' is surely the first poem in English to use the word 'musculocutaneous'. Though no scholar has yet located the source of it, this adventurous poem appears to be based closely on a scientific article. Like John Davidson before him, and like his own earlier, dictionary-trawling self, MacDiarmid delights in using reference books and informational texts as bases for poetry. His literary kleptomania could get him into trouble, as happened in the case of his 1930s lyric, 'Perfect', which turned out to be a brilliantly judicious relineation of a passage from a Welsh short story. Yet not the least of MacDiarmid's strengths is his restlessly shape-shifting imagination. He became more and more interested in long, scientifically inflected poems in English, epic achievements which may be a Scottish counterpart to Ezra Pound's *Cantos*. He did continue to work with Scots language – as in 'Harry Semen', which broods on evolution. He also produced other short English-language lyrics, best known of which is 'The Little White

Rose'. There, addressing a Jacobite symbol, the poet protests that he wants not the rose of the world as a whole but 'Only the little white rose of Scotland/ That smells sharp and sweet – and breaks the heart.'[65]

MacDiarmid's aspirations for Scotland often seemed to involve lost causes. He liked to present himself as the voice of a nation, but, for all his polemics in prose and broadcasting, he was hardly a popular voice. 'The highest art at any time can only be appreciated by an infinitesimal minority of the people – if by any', he wrote in 1926. His modernist elitism was no doubt heightened by a sense of the elect nurtured by that youthful Calvinism against which the atheist MacDiarmid ostensibly reacted.[66] At the outbreak of World War II he and his family were still living in Shetland, but by 1941 he had been conscripted, and went on to work in a Clydeside engineering firm producing materials for the war effort. This is one of the many ironies in MacDiarmid's career. For, though he once characterized Hitler as a man 'who would chop up a Stradivarius violin/ To grill a steak', in 1940 he wrote, but did not publish, a treasonable poem 'On the Imminent Destruction of London, June 1940' in which the speaker maintains he does not care about the blitzing of a city that has been a centre of all that is reactionary.[67]

War made it impossible for MacDiarmid to publish the long poem on which he had been working in the late 1930s. Extracts from it were published as freestanding poems, but not until 1955 did the extended work appear under the title *In Memoriam James Joyce*. Published in Glasgow by William McLellan, and numbering Edwin Muir among its subscribers, this poem was at once remarkable and hard to read at length. A paean to human knowledge, especially linguistic and scientific knowledge, it incorporates versified bibliographies as well as MacDiarmid's signature tune of unusual vocabulary. Its engagement with science may be related to the ideal of 'generalism' championed by the poet's philosopher friend George Davie. It was exemplary for younger poets such as Edwin Morgan. MacDiarmid's central assertion of the fusion of poetry and science as forms of discovery was both valid and exciting at a time when in England very different assumptions about what C. P. Snow called the 'two cultures' of the humanities and sciences came to prevail.[68] Still, for many readers short extracts from *In Memoriam James Joyce*, such as the celebrated lyric, 'Scotland Small?' ('Scotland small? Our multiform, our infinite Scotland *small*?') are more poetically convincing.[69]

MacDiarmid's later career saw many volumes appear under his name

– from a selection of the poems of William Dunbar, that poet of aureate diction whose example he greatly championed, to a *Selected Essays* and an edited book on John Knox. Knox's fiery polemic had something in common with MacDiarmid's own. Yet this great poet wrote very little great poetry in the last three decades of his life. He and Valda lived frugally near Biggar in a small cottage loaned to them by the Duke of Hamilton. Lauded by Communist countries during the Cold War era, MacDiarmid made various visits behind the Iron Curtain, meeting dignitaries from Chairman Mao to the Russian poet Yevtushenko. More familiar at home were his heroic alcoholic exploits and public protests. Photographs show him standing beside placards with slogans like 'Demand a Scottish Government Now' as well as 'Scots Beef for Scots Shops'.[70] He continued to act as friend, mentor and spur to a constellation of mainly male writers including the Gaelic poet Sorley MacLean, the English-language poet Norman MacCaig, and Scots poets like Sydney Goodsir Smith, Douglas Young and Robert Garioch. Stylistically, most of these writers were markedly different from MacDiarmid, but all acknowledged his pre-eminent achievement. They understood too his enduring need to be viewed (in words he once suggested for his epitaph) as 'a disgrace to the community'.[71]

MacDiarmid's prose, especially his earlier prose, can be splendidly disgraceful.

Scottish literature, like all other literatures, has been *written* almost exclusively by blasphemers, immoralists, dipsomaniacs, and madmen, but, unlike most other literatures, has been *written about* almost exclusively by ministers . . .[72]

Committed absolutist intelligence and verbal exuberance add fizz to his style. Yet in order to get advances of much-needed cash MacDiarmid churned out too many prose volumes, and promised to write even more. His autobiographical writings in *Lucky Poet* (1943) and *The Company I've Kept* (1966) indicate what he was and wanted to be. Like his first prose book, and so many others, they rely on vast amounts of quotation from other writers and, sometimes, from himself. Engaging throughout is the panoptic *Scottish Scene, or the Intelligent Man's Guide to Albyn* (1934), co-authored with James Leslie Mitchell (1901–35) who wrote his best books under the name Lewis Grassic Gibbon.

As the Scottish Renaissance gathered steam and that new Scottish political phenomenon, the National Party, made an impact, an increasing number of publications reflected on Scottish culture and on Scottish/English differences. As well as writing detective stories, A. G. Macdonnell (1895–1941), an Aberdeen-born novelist, authored both the satirical *England, their England* (1933) and the fond *My Scotland* (1937). Edwin Muir produced his thoughtfully disillusioned *Scottish Journey* (1935). MacDiarmid's supporter the nationalist Glasgow journalist William Power published *My Scotland* (1934), *Scotland and the Scots* (1935) and *Scotland and Oatmeal* (1935). In *Scottish Scene* MacDiarmid and Gibbon present a personal account of the nation written at a time when, thanks largely to the work of Scottish film-maker John Grierson (1898–1972), documentary was becoming an increasingly important genre. *Scottish Scene* includes 'Newsreels' – assemblies of flavoursome newspaper extracts – as well as essays, poems, one-act plays, and short stories by the book's two incisive authors. MacDiarmid emphasizes that *'modern Scotland will never be understood until its desire to resume an identity distinct from that of England is appreciated.'*[73] He flies the flag of the Scottish Renaissance alongside banners of political and economic nationalism. Both authors use the phrase 'the new Scotland' and sense a renewed struggle for cultural identity. Sympathetically interested, though not committed to Scottish nationalism, Gibbon contributes much of the best literary material, including his stories 'Smeddum' and 'Clay' as well as splendid essays on topics such as Aberdeen – 'an Eskimo's vision of hell'. In 'The Land' he declares himself 'a jingo patriot of planet earth' and writes with profound ecological feeling for the terrain and communities of north-east Scotland where he had grown up, 'this land and its queer, scarce harvests, its hours of reeking sunshine and stifling rain'.[74]

MacDiarmid typed his contributions to *Scottish Scene* in Shetland. Gibbon wrote his in Welwyn Garden City, a southern English new town founded as an ideal community, a garden city. Their essays aimed to deliver what the book's characterful dustjacket calls a 'slashing indictment' of Scotland. Gibbon works from an anti-Christian perspective, reserving special venom for the Free Kirk. He also writes with a deep, sometimes primitivist feeling for landscape, at the same time as recognizing that many young people, like modern civilization as a whole, have a craving to escape from the back-breaking slog and limited horizons of farm work; so, inevitably, the rhythms of agriculture and peasant communities are being left behind.

Gibbon's best writing is powered by just such a perception, and the sensuous, troubled, lyrical consideration of it. Born James Leslie Mitchell in Aberdeenshire in 1901, he came of farming stock. At beautiful, harsh Arbuthnott in Kincardineshire he was recognized as a gifted young writer by his schoolteacher, Alexander Gray. Like MacDiarmid, Gibbon hacked in local journalism – in Aberdeen and Glasgow – before entering the armed forces. With the Royal Army Service Corps, then with the RAF, he did tours of duty in the Middle East. Several novels written under his own name are set there, and his work draws on interests in worldwide archaeology, exploration, and 'Diffusionism' – an anthropological theory which posited a primitive, tribal golden age destroyed by the growth of so-called civilization. Mitchell set novels in Egypt, South America, Scotland and England. He wrote rapidly on topics from ancient Roman slave revolt in *Spartacus* (1933) to time travel in *Gay Hunter* (1934). His best novels, though, are the trilogy posthumously collected and published as *A Scots Quair*. Written by 'Lewis Grassic Gibbon', the three constituent volumes of the 'Quair' or 'literary work' are *Sunset Song* (1932), *Cloud Howe* (1933) and *Grey Granite* (1934). These centre on Chris Guthrie and her family as they engage with the hard north-eastern farming life of the Mearns. After the local community is decimated by World War I, Gibbon traces a movement away from the land towards urban life during a postwar climate of radical political unrest that draws on his own experience as a socialist and 'a revolutionist'.[75]

The 'song' of *Sunset Song* is 'The Flowers of the Forest', that old Scots lament for the dead at the Battle of Flodden. Gibbon includes its music in his text, where the song is applied to those slaughtered in World War I. Modern visitors to Arbuthnott may be struck by the number of names on the war memorial in this tiny hamlet. Names on gravestones in Arbuthnott churchyard feature in Gibbon's trilogy. Earthed in a tough fidelity to the local, his work records the passing of a pre-war community and way of life. He once wrote with some irony of 'my Kailyard literary forerunners', and *Sunset Song*, like Lorna Moon's work, is clearly aware of that tradition.[76] But Gibbon is also alert to the example of George Douglas Brown; an unflinching, nuanced presentation of incest, suicide and other darker aspects of community life, combined with a feel for the persistent pull of the land, gives Gibbon's work a seasoned tang of its own. This flavour is strong not least in the language and rhythms of the narrative voice.

And then a queer thought came to her there in the drooked fields, that nothing
endured at all, nothing but the land she passed across, tossed and turned and
perpetually changed below the hands of the crofter folk since the oldest of them
had set the Standing Stones by the loch of Blawearie and climbed there on their
holy days and saw their terraced crops ride brave in the wind and sun.[77]

Beginning with 'And', then accented with Scots ('drooked' means
drenched), this sentence slips away from formal English towards a more
distinctively Scottish style of narration. Often the narrator's voice comes
close to that of the protagonist, Chris, and to the Scots-tongued dialogue
of the characters. At his best Gibbon is a much more assured prose
stylist than Lorna Moon, though in his choice of characters he sometimes
seems to follow in her footsteps. He uses relatively little direct speech in
the *Quair*, and avoids inverted commas. Yet a sense of direct speech is
often part of his storytelling voice, placing narrators and characters on
the same linguistic level, rather than having a third-person English-
speaking narrator hierarchically elevated as the voice of authority over
the Scots-speaking folk of the story. This style lets Gibbon move towards
solving a technical problem which had interested George Douglas
Brown, Lorna Moon and others: how to balance English and Scots in
the novel to give a sense of cultural distinctiveness. Gibbon's solution –
to bring the narrative voice closer to the voice of the community being
written about – would be taken further by James Kelman in the later
twentieth century in the context of working-class Glaswegian speech.

Gibbon writes in English, but with a marked Scots inflection. His
Quair shows a rural society disintegrating and an urban society
attempting through radical politics to come to terms with capitalist
industrialism. Though her son plays a more prominent part in the
trilogy's urban third book, *Grey Granite*, Chris Guthrie is throughout
the *Quair* a remarkably convincing female character scripted by a male
author. Gibbon the historical novelist disliked the historical fictions of
Walter Scott. The twentieth-century author shows a much fuller concern
with a woman's life than that shown by Scott or Stevenson; it is notable
that in common with some of the fictions of Moon and other contemporary women writers Gibbon's finest story, 'Smeddum', also creates a
resolute female protagonist. Unlike Kailyard tales or so many earlier
Scottish books, these fictions do not flinch from male and female sexuality. Gibbon's writing was influenced by Hardy, Lawrence and Russian

novelists, but is immediately Scottish in tone. Ironically, given its author's attitude to Scott, *A Scots Quair*, like *Waverley*, offers the reader several different versions of social organization which may be compared in an almost anthropological way. Yet *A Scots Quair* has remained one of the best-loved works of Scottish literature because of its rhythms, characterization and sense of weathered landscape, rather than because of its philosophical underpinnings.

Overwork became second nature to Gibbon. He died suddenly of a perforated gastric ulcer and ensuing peritonitis in 1935. His synthesized Scots 'art speech' makes him the novelist most closely comparable with MacDiarmid. Like Brown and Moon, he is a writer of clear achievement who died disconcertingly young, but he is not the sole eminence in earlier twentieth-century Scottish fiction. He learned from and may be grouped with several immediate predecessors and contemporaries able to write with resourcefulness and authority about Scottish women's experiences. Moon was one of these, but more prominent in Scottish literary life was Nan Shepherd (1893–1981) who came, like Moon and Gibbon, from Aberdeenshire, and studied at Aberdeen University. In her novels *The Quarry Wood* (1928) and *The Weatherhouse* (1930) Shepherd writes strongly and insightfully about the lives of young women in north-eastern rural Scotland. Her female protagonists are torn between their sense of being part of a place and their longing for 'air, space, widened horizons' beyond the constraints of small-town respectability.[78] Shepherd records the impact of World War I on this local community. Though the texture and rhythms of her prose are less distinctively compelling than Gibbon's, she registers a deep sense of surprise and delight at the sometimes paradisal plenitude of her native environment

with chickens newly broken from the shell, ducks worrying with their flat bills in the grass; with dark, half-known, sweet-smelling corners in the barn, and the yielding, sliding, scratching feel of hay; with the steep wooden stair to the stable-loft and the sound of the big, patient, clumsy horses moving and munching below, a rattle of harness, the sudden nosing of a dog . . .[79]

Shepherd has a developed ecological awareness, a sense not of disembodied spirituality but of the rich weightiness of working with nature: there is, as she puts it in a letter to Neil Gunn, a part of her 'that weighs the wind of the spirit with the weights of corn and potatoes and things'.[80] Late in life, Shepherd's environmental imagination led to her prose

paean to the Cairngorms, *The Living Mountain* (1977); it is present also
in her poems. Like the work of many twentieth-century Scottish writers,
Shepherd's is ecological in its attention to the relationship between the
human community and the land; she seeks 'a society', as MacDiarmid
puts it, 'itself in proper ecological balance'.[81] Such interests are shared
by Ian Macpherson (1905–44) who had presented, just before *Sunset
Song*, an account of Mearns life in *Shepherds' Calendar* (1931) where
the young male protagonist leaves the land for a new life at university;
a similarly strong sense of north-eastern land-love is present in John
Robertson Allan's *A New Song to the Land* (1931) and *Farmer's Boy*
(1935).

All these books prompt the thought that Gibbon worked with well-
tilled literary soil. More than that, they indicate a strong interest in 'the
land' as well as in nationalism among 1930s Scottish intellectuals. The
land mattered to intellectuals in other European countries, not least
Germany, yet this Scottish interest is generally benign. There has been a
tendency to emphasize urban material in overviews of modern Scottish
writing and to see treatments of rural life either as backward-looking or
as representing just some dim afterglow of post-Walter Scott Romanticism. Many twentieth-century rural writers from Grassic Gibbon to
George Mackay Brown have disliked Scott, however, and their work
may be viewed at least as fruitfully in the light of a strong ecological
turn of thought in Scottish culture. This runs from John Muir and
Patrick Geddes through such thinkers as Frank Fraser Darling (1903–
79), author of *Wild Life Conservation* (1934), *The Natural History of
the Highlands and Islands* (1947) and *Alaska: an Ecological Renaissance*
(1953). If it is present in Gibbon, Shepherd, Macpherson and others in
the 1930s, it is also manifestly strong in mid-twentieth-century writers
like Neil Gunn, Naomi Mitchison and Sorley MacLean. Today it attracts
John Burnside, Kathleen Jamie and others, including the present writer.
Where nineteenth-century Scotland was the terrain of the sublime, much
of twentieth-century Scotland became through its writers the landscape
of the ecological. Literary artists sought to investigate imaginatively how
people, creatures, crops and landscape might co-exist in balance.

This concern is prominent in some of the best work by Edwin Muir
(1887–1959). Poet, novelist and critic, Muir was a leading figure in the
Scottish Renaissance movement of the 1920s and early 1930s before he
and MacDiarmid fell out in a bruising disagreement over the use of the

Scots tongue in modern verse. Like MacDiarmid, whose most extreme investigation of ecology is 'On a Raised Beach', Muir came from a rural hinterland. Literary modernism in Scotland, with its headquarters in such places as Montrose and St Andrews, was a markedly rurally-based phenomenon, for all that Scottish modernist writers including MacDiarmid, Edwin and Willa Muir, and Catherine Carswell had clear links with London and other urban centres. Edwin Muir's criticism is strongly cosmopolitan. A ready lightning conductor, he sensed the electricity of writers as different as Proust, Woolf, Hermann Broch and Wallace Stevens. Both MacDiarmid and T. S. Eliot, who became Muir's publisher and editor, regarded his criticism as among the best of the age. Sometimes reviewing three or four books a week, Muir might write, for example, about Hölderlin for MacDiarmid's Montrose-based *The Scottish Nation*, while maintaining his long association with A. R. Orage's influential London journal, *The New Age*. Muir did not go to university; nor did MacDiarmid. Unlike MacDiarmid, the shy Muir led a respectable literary life: in the later 1930s he lived in St Andrews, and during the 1940s he worked for the British Council, first in wartime Edinburgh, then in Prague and Rome. In the Fifties he was Warden of the Scottish adult education college, Newbattle Abbey; in 1955 he became the only Scot to deliver the Charles Eliot Norton Lectures at Harvard.

The imaginative core of Muir's writing owes comparatively little to such cosmopolitanism, except, perhaps, in being intensified by contrast with it. Muir's roots were deep in a micro-world. His early boyhood was spent on the tiny, low-lying, roadless Orkney island of Wyre where his father farmed. Aged eight, Muir moved with his family to live near Kirkwall on Orkney's 'mainland'. Thereafter his life was a series of displacements and migrations – the most traumatic to industrial Glasgow where Muir arrived at the age of fourteen. Several of his family soon died there. Horror at this experience darkens Muir's novel *Poor Tom* (1932) and conditions his view of Central Belt Scotland in his social survey *Scottish Journey*. Evoked in her novel *The Road Home* (1932), the move to Glasgow of Muir's fellow cosmopolitan Orcadian the Scottish nationalist F. Marian McNeill (1885–1973) was largely happy, and encouraged the compilation of her ground-breaking study, *The Scots Kitchen* (1929), then her four-volume work on Scottish folklore, *The Silver Bough* (1937–68). Edwin Muir, however, associated Glasgow with pain. Reacting against that, his *Autobiography* presents

Wyre as Edenic. Muir writes superbly, with intimate detail about his childhood there – about how, for instance, a little boy

is closer to things, since his eyes are only two or three feet from the ground, not five or six. Grass, stones, and insects are twice as near to him as they will be after he has grown up, and when I try to re-create my early childhood it seems to me that it was focused on such things as these, and that I lived my life in a small, separate underworld, while the grown-ups walked on their long legs several feet above my head on a stage where every relation was different. I was dizzily lifted into that world, as into another dimension, when my father took me on his shoulders, so that I could see the roof of the byre from above or touch the lintel of the house door with my hand. But for most of the time I lived with whatever I found on the surface of the earth: the different kinds of grass, the daisies, buttercups, dandelions, bog cotton (we did not have many flowers), the stones and bits of glass and china, and the scurrying insects which made my stomach heave as I stared at them, unable to take my eyes away.[82]

Muir's sense of his childhood ecosystem on Wyre is arresting, but not Peter Pan-ishly arrested. Modern visitors to Orkney marvel at its World Heritage Site neolithic structures. Muir makes no mention of the islands' prehistory, but his perception of the importance of light to Orcadian life is remarkably in tune with what we know of neolithic culture there. His childhood on Orkney predates the publicizing of its ancient sites, and takes place within a geography so circumscribed that a journey of a few miles would mean deracination. The smallness of the young Muir's farm habitat makes all the creatures there important and gives his whole environment a sense of archetypal justice.

Often Muir tried to catch that sense of archetype in his poetry. Sometimes in the 1930s and 1940s his verse suffers from the distorting influence of T. S. Eliot's cadences, but he produced a clutch of excellent poems that usually involve moments of hypnotic fascination. Repeatedly these poems touch on material from his Orkney years. Purged of people's names and place names, 'Childhood', from *First Poems* (1925), has its small boy protagonist lying among rocks and grasses, watching islands and a passing ship in a world where 'time seemed finished', until in the last line the spell is broken, yet also securely renewed when 'from the house his mother called his name'.[83] At best, Muir's poetry finds a dreamlike world in the heart of the actual, 'Deep in the diamond of the day', as one of his surest lines puts it.[84] In his *Autobiography* he writes about a boyhood sensation familiar to Robert Burns and many, many pre-twentieth-century generations, but now alien to most of us: the feeling of closeness to horses. 'The Horses' is deservedly Muir's best-known poem. Aware of the Cold War as well as of ecological anxieties, this 1955 work presents a world in which, after an unspecified techno-logical catastrophe, horses return 'Stubborn and shy, as if they had been sent' to renew their 'long-lost archaic companionship' with people.[85]

Muir's ecological Christian sensibility and sometimes dreamlike pre-cision make it tempting to align some of his work with the poetry of the Elgin-born Reverend Andrew Young (1885–1971) who spent much of his life in England and who wrote prose on botany as well as acutely observant English-language lyrics about the natural world. Young was a stern, selfish man. He ruled with a rod of iron and is said to have summoned his gifted wife by ringing a handbell. Still, his often depopu-lated poems have a clear beauty, whether a mole's body lies above ground 'Buried within the blue vault of the air' or 'slow black slugs' are 'Making soft shameless love on the open road'.[86] Young is at his most assured as a pinpoint miniaturist, but ultimately Muir's poetic range is wider. Muir was prone to depression; in 1941 in St Andrews 'his health and heart collapsed' as a sympathetic observer put it.[87] 'Scotland 1941' presents the country in 'desolation', viewing Presbyterianism in terms of oppressive 'iron', and seeing Scotland's greatest writers, 'Burns and Scott', only as 'sham bards of a sham nation'.[88] Though not always so pessimistic, Muir had written in 1936 of the position of the Scottish writer as 'both unhappy and unique'. In *Scott and Scotland*, published that year, he bemoaned Scotland's 'confusion of tongues' and the 'scat-tered fragments' of its past, insisting that 'The prerequisite of an auton-omous literature is a homogeneous language.' For Muir, since dialect led to 'provincialism' and 'regression to childhood', the language for Scotland had to be standard English.[89] Hugh MacDiarmid reacted furi-ously to what he saw as Muir's attack on his work and his Scottish Renaissance. MacDiarmid retaliated in various ways, most effectively perhaps in his *Golden Treasury of Scottish Poetry* (1940) which, for the first time in a general anthology, brought together a heterogeneity of poetry in Scots and English alongside (albeit only in translation) Scottish poems originally written in Gaelic and Latin.

MacDiarmid was correct to emphasize the plural linguistic inherit-ances of Scottish literature as a strength. Yet Muir too was right in his insistence that Scotland had to renegotiate terms with a world where English was the lingua franca. Many poets of the time, including Muir, MacDiarmid, William Soutar and others, wrote, as the title of A. D. Mackie's first (1928) collection has it, *Poems in Two Tongues*. To insist on a monoglot Scotland, or on all Scottish writers working *only* in English or in Scots or in Gaelic seems absurdly blinkered. What Mac-Diarmid had detected in the usually mild-mannered Muir was an absolutism that clashed head-on with his own.

Muir took his cue from T. S. Eliot's view of Scottish culture as possessing no continuous autonomous tradition, 'no concurrence of bone', and from Eliot's notion of a 'dissociation of sensibility'.[90] For Muir, Calvinism in Scotland had driven 'a wedge' between 'thought and feeling'.[91] It is ironic that his lament over fragmentation comes in the modernist period when the fragmentary is often fundamental to artistic technique, and iconoclasm (that Reformation hallmark) is de rigueur. For much of the twentieth century, though, Scottish writers and readers had to choose between two literary myths: the MacDiarmid-sponsored Caledonian Antisyzygy of clashing opposites and the Scots tongue as sources of strength, and the English-language-based Muir view of endemic division as utterly enfeebling. Only in the late twentieth century did a more inclusive, more mobile sense of 'Scotlands', of multiple, once largely separate but increasingly cross-fertilizing literary and cultural strands, come to replace these older, one-size-fits-all models.[92] In the short term the Muir–MacDiarmid clash skewed accounts of the Scottish Renaissance, casting Muir as its enemy. In retrospect, one may suspect it was the cosmopolitan Muir's links with such figures as Glasgow University French academic Professor Denis Saurat or the composer Francis George Scott, not to mention A. R. Orage and A. S. Neill, which helped MacDiarmid in the 1920s ally such figures to 'his' Renaissance.

That Renaissance had many participants, from the poet William Soutar, whose best early Scots work in *Seeds in the Wind* (1933) was written for children, to the novelist Compton Mackenzie, a West Hartlepool-born author and spy. Soutar (1898–1943) served in the Royal Navy during World War I, then studied English at Edinburgh University. Spondylitis caused the bones of his spine to fuse solid, and rendered him increasingly bedridden in his home town of Perth. His Scots poetry has a shrewd clarity, and, at its finest, a rare lyricism, evident in 'The Tryst' where a love poem becomes a dream of death,

Sae luely, luely, cam she in   *softly*
Sae luely was she gaen
And wi' her a' my simmer days   *summer*
Like they had never been.[93]

Soutar had a gift for companionship. His friends ranged from literary figures such as the poets Helen Cruickshank and Hugh MacDiarmid (who edited Soutar's posthumous *Collected Poems*) to the local Kirk minister, Donald Cubie. His *Diaries of a Dying Man* (1954) were written over more than a decade when he was bedridden. They can be eloquent in their clearsighted acknowledgement of suffering and their author's refusal to be defined wholly by his illness. So, in September 1939, Soutar remembers with honesty how in 1916 at his school sports practice he reacted to news of Lord Kitchener's death by

leaping and running and shouting, 'Hurrah! Kitchener's dead!' Then, on joining the staring party, I picked up the weight and gave it a mighty heave, outdistancing all the previous throws. I suppose the unconscious thought expressing itself in such a display of animal boisterousness is: 'Look, Death, look; here is somebody alive and very much alive.'[94]

That sense of vitality was shared by MacDiarmid and by Compton Mackenzie (1883–1972). Born and educated in England the son of Edward Compton, this remarkable man proudly added 'Mackenzie' to his name to stress his Scottish ancestry. He enjoyed considerable success with his 1913 novel *Sinister Street*. Scott Fitzgerald felt his later work 'had gone off', but that Compton might still have become one of early twentieth-century England's most noted authors.[95] However, in a turn of events which even his admirer Henry James could not have predicted, Compton re-invented himself and came to be photographed shoulder to shoulder with Hugh MacDiarmid at the first public meeting of the National Party of Scotland in Glasgow in 1928. That same year, as 'Compton Mackenzie', the novelist settled on the Hebridean island of Barra and published his MacDiarmid-sounding *Extremes Meet* – actually a lively account of its author's experiences as 'Z', a spy, in Greece. Several of Mackenzie's England-based tales, and his later Scotland-based ones, were best-sellers; some warmly humorous fictions set on Barra, especially *Whisky Galore* (1947, later splendidly filmed), have tended to overshadow his more ambitious series of novels *The Four Winds of*

Love (1937–45) and his ten-volume autobiography (1963–71). The latter sets out a spirited life that wheels from bohemian parties on 1920s Capri to trial at the Old Bailey ('a bit of an ordeal') and romps with the Home Guard on Barra.[96] Edmund Wilson recognized that 'For years' Mackenzie had 'been trying in his work to plead for the rights of small nations and cultural minorities, as against all the forces which are driving us in the direction of centralized power that tries to process or crush them'.[97] Fittingly, in the 1928 photograph taken at the National Party of Scotland meeting, Mackenzie stands beside one of MacDiarmid's heroes, the ecologically-minded Robert Bontine Cunninghame Graham (1852–1936), another larger-than-life Scottish figure committed to cultural and national minorities. Nicknamed 'Don Roberto', Cunninghame Graham wrote fictional and historical accounts of life in Paraguay, Morocco and elsewhere which were the product of a life in which among other distinctions he served as first president of the Scottish Labour Party, then president of the National Party of Scotland, then of the Scottish National Party.

The presence of such men in the nationalist camp helps indicate both that Scottish nationalism in the period was closely enmeshed with artistic production, and that it was far from provincial. Muir had at best tepid nationalist sympathies; Gibbon was no nationalist; yet like all other Scottish writers and intellectuals of the period, they were quickened by an engagement with nationalist arguments. The cause of nationalism was not popular at the polls. It was regarded as improbable by the wider public, and by a Scottish media which, then as now, was strongly biased towards monarchist unionism. Yet nationalism's intellectual ferment was the clearest sign that, though Scottish writers continued to engage with London and more and more to publish their books there, it was a distinctly Scottish culture with which they identified. Wilder flights of fancy or of unionist scaremongering ranged from John Connell's 1935 thriller *David Go Back*, which features a Dublin-style Scottish rebellion with a pitched battle in central Edinburgh ('a brief spit of fire from the North British Hotel') to W. H. Auden's lines, written while he was living in Helensburgh on the Clyde in the early 1930s,

> Scotland is stirring: in Scotland they say
> That Compton Mackenzie will be king one day.[98]

Scotland *was* stirring. The left-wing Scottish republican and Bolshevik John Maclean had died in 1923, worn out after several terms of imprisonment for sedition, yet nationalism remained remarkably non-violent. If in the 1920s MacDiarmid (who admired Maclean's example) assembled many nationalist and other writers in the pages of his Montrose journals, in the 1930s the leading nationalist literary periodical was *The Modern Scot*. This impressive magazine was edited from St Andrews by the young bisexual Jewish-American Scottish Nationalist James H. Whyte, to whom MacDiarmid dedicated 'On a Raised Beach'. Publishing authors from MacDiarmid, Mackenzie and Muir to Auden, Kafka and Hermann Hesse, *The Modern Scot* became, in Tom Normand's words, 'the principal forum for Scottish intellectual debate in the 1930s'.[99] In its pages Whyte articulated a theory of inclusive Scottish nationalism which stressed 'pluralism' and aimed to be 'acceptable to a good European, whether Socialist or Conservative, Catholic, Protestant, or Pagan'. Conscious of European nationalisms of the 1930s, Whyte is careful to reject essentialist nationalism founded on 'worship of race', and warns against 'the fanatic insularity of the Fascists or the Hitlerists'.[100]

Although, as in MacDiarmid's more polemical flytings, it could sound strategically Anglophobic, the nationalist impetus which did so much to restore and develop an awareness of the value of Scotland's linguistic, cultural and political distinctiveness was far from narrow-minded. Like almost all other movements of the time, it was very much male-led, and none of the principal female Scottish writers of the earlier twentieth century is close to its heart. Women such as the poet Helen Cruickshank (1886–1975) supported the literary Renaissance, but scarcely challenged its masculinism. Cruickshank served from 1927 to 1934 as the secretary of the Scottish branch of PEN (the international association of Poets, Playwrights, Editors, Essayists and Novelists), founded by MacDiarmid with the religious novelist and children's writer Marion Lochhead and others in 1926. More marginal was another early member, the poet Marion Angus (1865–1946). A daughter of the manse, she spent most of her life in the north-east and wrote in the 1920s and 1930s some extremely beautiful and subtle poems, rich in implication. Her best work has a clear Scots inflection and sometimes deals with love between women. She writes acutely about the isolated brilliance of Mary, Queen of Scots in 'Alas! Poor Queen', but perhaps her finest poem is her lyric

'The Blue Jacket', which is all the more carrying for its understatement and apparent simplicity:

> When there comes a flower to the stingless nettle,
>   To the hazel bushes, bees,
> I think I can see my little sister
>   Rocking herself by the hazel trees.
>
> Rocking her arms for very pleasure
>   That every leaf so sweet can smell,
> And that she has on her the warm blue jacket
>   Of mine, she liked so well.
>
> Oh to win near you, little sister!
>   To hear your soft lips say –
> 'I'll never tak' up wi' lads or lovers,
>   But a baby I maun hae.   *must have*
>
> 'A baby in a cradle rocking,
>   Like a nut, in a hazel shell,
> And a new blue jacket, like this o' Annie's,
>   It sets me aye sae well.'[101]   *suits*

Marion Angus published two collections of poems before MacDiarmid and knew the value of the ballad tradition, on which he too came to draw. Though her work was long out of print, its republication in 2006 should ensure that her singular, feminine talent is not submerged.

Marion Angus was a supporter of PEN, and Helen Cruickshank its secretary. It is hard to imagine Willa Muir providing administrative support for any of MacDiarmid's schemes. The poet had an almost pathological dislike of her, and this may well have been reciprocated. Willa Muir was the most important female literary intellectual active in early twentieth-century Scotland. Born and educated in Montrose, then a student at the University of St Andrews, she writes in *Women: An Inquiry* (1925) about creative power and the need for women 'to carry their womanhood with them into all occupations, otherwise the advantage of their entry into public affairs will be entirely lost'.[102] However, Muir's arguments sometimes lack the feminist vigour of Dot Allan (1886–1964) whose Glasgow novel *Makeshift* (1928) features an aspiring female writer confronting entrenched notions of feminine limitation. Muir has a strong interest in psychology, but lays too much emphasis on women's essential role as mothers and on their being closer than men to the unconscious for her to sit easily in the development of fully-fledged mid-twentieth-century feminism. Still, in such works as *Mrs Grundy in Scotland* (1936) she wrote incisively about the often oppressive demands made of women in her own country. She feels particularly strongly about the scorning of women as mothers, writing in 'Women in Scotland' (1936) that 'a mother should become also a political comrade, with an economic status of her own and a "say" in public affairs. I suggest that Scotsmen accustom themselves to this idea, and do their utmost to enlarge the environmental circle within which their women are cramped.'[103]

Highly educated and widely travelled, Muir made this theme of the cramped lives of women in Scotland central to her novels *Imagined Corners* (1931) and the adventurously provocative *Mrs Ritchie* (1933). In the former she takes from J. M. Barrie the name Shand (given by Barrie to one of his most boneheadedly masculine characters) and looks at the domestic life of the Shand family in small-town, East Coast Calderwick. Eventually, female friendship and escape to continental Europe are seen as remedies for crushing Scottish patriarchy and small-mindedness. Muir's *Imagined Corners* may be compared with Lorna Moon's *Dark Star* (1929), but to regard Muir only as a writer about the situation of Scottish women is wrong. She took the leading role, assisted by her husband Edwin, in the English translation of Kafka's *The Castle* and several other important works of modern literature in German, while later in life she also authored her study *Living with Ballads* (1965). For all their interest in modernism, the ballad form was as important to Edwin Muir and MacDiarmid as it was to Marion Angus, while William Soutar in 1943 regarded 'the qualities of the ballad' as 'the most appropriate for the poetry of our time'.[104] Willa Muir's *Living with Ballads* (1965) is an account of 'the Ballad world' which is as astute as her memoir of married life, *Belonging* (1970).[105] On occasion the characters in her fiction seem too programmatically plotted, as if they were part of some psychological experiment, but *Belonging* is compellingly sharp.

A sense of a sometimes troubled life is signalled by the title of Catherine Carswell's unfinished autobiography, *Lying Awake* (1952). Born in Glasgow in 1879, Carswell studied English at Glasgow University and music at the Frankfurt Conservatorium. After her first husband tried to kill her and was committed to a mental hospital, she worked as a reviewer for the *Glasgow Herald* while bringing up her daughter; her successful proceedings to annul her marriage made legal history, but Carswell was sacked from the *Herald* in 1915 for praising her friend D. H. Lawrence's novel *The Rainbow*. Her Lawrence review is less than adulatory. Its worry that Lawrence displays an 'increasingly mannered idiom' that relies on the 'repetition of certain words', especially in 'the more emotional passages', could be applied to her own first novel, *Open the Door!* (1920), which Lawrence read in manuscript.[106] Semi-autobiographical, it tells the story of Joanna Bannerman as she searches for love and fulfilment. With its strong sense of female 'erotic rhapsody', this book, like *Imagined Corners*, articulately presents the situation of a young Scotswoman growing up in circumscribed middle-class respectability and longing to escape it.[107] In her diary-like novel *The Camomile* (1922), seven years before Virginia Woolf addresses the same issue in *A Room of One's Own*, Carswell has her Glasgow musician Ellen Carstairs ask the question,

Don't you agree that there must be something radically wrong with a civilization, society, theory of life – call it what you like – in which a hard-working, serious young woman like myself cannot obtain, without enormous difficulty, expense, or infliction of pain on others, a quiet, clean, pleasant room in which she can work, dream her dreams, write out her thoughts, and keep her few treasures in peace?[108]

Simple, radical questions like this one, a strong sense of vocation, and an interest in sexual as well as intellectual and economic emancipation give Carswell's fiction a range and accomplishment beyond that of, say, Anna Buchan. They also condition her 1930 *Life of Robert Burns* which shocked readers with its forthright comments on the Scots ('Probably no other peasantry the world over has been so exuberant in lewdness') and its shrewd examination of Burns's sexuality: 'The love of women was necessary to him, but equally necessary his absolute domination as the male.' To be Burns's first female biographer was itself an act of daring in earlier twentieth-century Scotland. With his 'dark sinewy beauty', Carswell's Burns has a Lawrentian aspect. To her second husband, the Glaswegian critic and biographer Donald Carswell (1882–1940), Lawrence wrote that he would 'like to write a Burns life' and had long harboured such an idea.[109] Catherine Carswell published a memoir of Lawrence, 'this non-Christian saint', in 1932; *The Savage Pilgrimage* still reads well, and is the first biography of the English novelist, though it lacks the intimacy of *Lying Awake*, the fragmentary autobiography in which Carswell records her childhood in a Glasgow of 'sirens and steam-whistles on foggy days' and writes of travelling with 'mother in her grey alpaca dustcloak' carrying 'the large cage containing our green parrot' on holiday in Tayside.[110]

The work and example of D. H. Lawrence were important to Scottish writers from Catherine Carswell and Lewis Grassic Gibbon to the philosopher John Macmurray (1891–1976) and the novelist Elizabeth Hyde. Educated in Aberdeen, Glasgow and Oxford, Macmurray argued in books such as *Reason and Emotion* (1935), *The Self as Agent* (1951) and *Persons in Relation* (1961) that 'Reason itself is not a private but a mutual possession; and our personality is not in us but between us. The principles of morality are the laws of personal relationship.'[111] Preoccupied like Lawrence, Carswell, Moon, Grassic Gibbon and many older Scottish novelists with the relationship between individual and community, Macmurray contended that 'I apprehend myself as a self, that is to say, as a person, only in and through the apprehension of other persons in the world who are not myself.'[112] Emphasizing Christianity as leading to a full sense of community for all people, his philosophy has roots in the democratic traditions of Scottish presbyterianism and has impressed later thinkers as different as R. D. Laing and Tony Blair, who prefaced a selection of Macmurray's writings shortly before becoming British Prime Minister in 1997.[113]

In 1930 Macmurray was 'profoundly moved by the work of D. H. Lawrence', a man 'conscious of life in a way which' Macmurray 'was not'. Lawrence's writing made even more of an impression on Macmurray's novelist wife who described herself as a 'female Lawrence' and whose work has been eclipsed by that of her husband.[114] Born on Deeside in 1891, Elizabeth Hyde Campbell studied English at Aberdeen University with her lifelong friend the novelist Nan Shepherd who would base her character Luke in *The Quarry Wood* (1928) on John Macmurray.[115] At 5 Mansfield Road, Oxford, and elsewhere Campbell lived with the bookish philosopher in a complex open marriage, an experimental 'social unit' in which several partners sought sexual and intellectual satisfaction. This experience informs *Out of the Earth*, the novel she published as 'Elizabeth Hyde' in 1935. Starting in the Highlands, the story deals with sexual frustration, an unfulfilling marriage to a don in Oxford (a place the author loathed), and the wish of the protagonist Agnes for a child. This novel about a married woman who has a child by a man who is not her husband is a Lawrentian fiction of 'Defiant life! bursting through rough tweed and winceyette'.

Elizabeth Hyde's partly autobiographical novel would have been particularly shocking in the presbyterian Scotland she came from, but that, surely, is one reason she needed to write it. In London one of her female characters sees ahead of her

the Peter Pan statue. She had always disliked it, but now she hated it. The gay indifferent boy piping a carefree song belonged to another world of sexless beings, where joy had no value because pain was unknown. A silly make-believe! An escape from reality! She wanted to take a hammer and smash it to bits. She had been duped too long by her sexless fancies.[116]

Considering the novels of Hyde, Gibbon, Carswell, Willa Muir, and such other novelists as Nancy Brysson Morrison (1903–86) might suggest that Scottish fiction in the 1920s and 1930s is, for the first time, more remarkable for heroines than for heroes. Morrison, whose work was popular in America, presents the Highland Clearances from the perspective of dispossessed crofters in *Breakers* (1930) and writes spiritedly about Highland women in *The Gowk Storm* (1933). Another heroine of that decade's fiction is the determined Jean Ramsay in *The Land of the Leal* (1939) by James Barke. Like Gibbon's Chris Guthrie, Jean moves from peasant country Scotland to the industrial city. While male as well as female writers created strong women characters, women did not write only about other women. Elizabeth Mackintosh (1896–1952), who wrote as 'Gordon Daviot' and as 'Josephine Tey', authored several historical dramas as well as novels. In the Highland adventures of Inspector Grant of Scotland Yard in *The Man in the Queue* (1929) and in a range of mainly England-based crime novels that followed – best known of which is *The Franchise Affair* (1948) – she produced some of Scotland's finest contributions to the golden age of detective fiction.

If heroines may seem to outnumber heroes in the fiction of the period, the reason lies less in the literary energies of the Scottish Renaissance than in social changes bound up with women's suffrage. Scottish suffragettes are less celebrated than their English sisters, but there was considerable suffragette activity in areas such as East Fife – where Willa Muir as a St Andrews student may have taken part in clandestine suffragette ploys. Conscious reactions to patriarchy permeate novels throughout the era, and several women writers such as Muir, Carswell and Hyde draw on their experience of continental or London life as less constricting than the mores of their native country.

The Scottish Renaissance was inflected by differences of gender, but not fissured by them. Nan Shepherd knew the Macmurrays, and Elizabeth Hyde Macmurray knew both the Muirs. Catherine Carswell was a friend of MacDiarmid, and an admirer of his work, while her *Open the Door!* was relished by the Highland novelist Neil M. Gunn (1891– 1973). Nan Shepherd was a perceptive supporter of Gunn with whom she shared a spiritual and ecological awareness of land and community. Responding to Gunn's *Wild Geese Overhead* (1939) and *Second Sight* (1940), she wrote to him in 1940 about something more instinctive than Macmurray's 'persons in relation':

To apprehend things – walking on a hill, seeing the light change, the mist, the dark, being aware, using the whole of one's body to instruct the spirit – yes, that is a secret life one has and knows that others have. But to be able to share it, in and through words – that is what frightens me . . . It dissolves one's being. I am no longer myself but a part of a life beyond myself when I read pages that are so much an expression of myself. You can take processes of being – no, that's too formal a word – *states* is too static, this is something that moves – *movements* I suppose is best – you can take movements of being and translate them out of themselves into words . . .[117]

Shepherd here characterizes something essential to Gunn's fiction and essays, though sometimes problematic. Gunn was born and spent his early childhood in Dunbeath, Caithness, though education and employment took him south for several years before he became a Customs Officer in Inverness, then (from 1937) a freelance writer based in the far north-east of Scotland. Almost all his work deals with the Highlands, and several novels with Highland history or prehistory. *Butcher's Broom* (1934) follows Nancy Brysson Morrison's *Breakers* in its engagement with the Highland Clearances; *Sun Circle* (1933) deals with Pictish and Viking Caithness.

Revealingly, one of Gunn's early essays, 'At the Peats' (1923), describes, with an allusion to Yeats's Celtic Twilight poem 'The Lake Isle of Innisfree', how around a Highland peat fire peace will ' "come dropping slow" ', though the same essay also goes on to discuss peat smoke in the context of 'ammoniacal smoke' and presents a geologically accurate account of peat deposits.[118] A mixture of physical accuracy and sometimes awkward dreaminess characterizes much of Gunn's writing. At the time of his first novel, *The Grey Coast* (1926), his editor at Cape warned him about 'fine writing' and asked for 'simple, direct English'. Gunn, however, had a taste for what he several times called the 'arabesque'; he later complained that 'what the Englishman calls Celtic Twilight is to us something as natural as a plate of porridge'.[119] Gunn liked his porridge. A strain of mysticism underpins his writing, leading him eventually towards an interest in Zen: 'Extraordinary the arabesques the intellect can weave about a moment of illumination'.[120] But Gunn's best writing tends to rely on a sharp, subtly weighted sense of the material world in order to signal spiritual awareness. This is clear in his first fully successful novel, *Morning Tide* (1930), with its account of a Highland boy's upbringing on the north-east coast. From its first sentences about 'ware' (drift seaweed), the book creates an animated sense of illumined, illuminating presence in the natural world:

The boy's eyes opened in wonder at the quantity of sea-tangle, at the breadth of the swath which curved with the curving beach on either hand. The tide was at low ebb and the sea quiet except for a restless seeking among the dark boulders. But though it was the sea after a storm it was still sullen and inclined to smooth and lick itself, like a black dog bent over its paws; as many black dogs as there were boulders; black sea-animals, their heads bent and hidden, licking their paws in the dying evening light down by the secret water's edge. When he stepped on the ware, it slithered under him like a living hide. He was fascinated by the brown tangled bed, the eel-like forms, the gauzy webs. There had been no sun to congeal what was still glistening and fresh.[121]

Many of the most alert passages in Gunn's writing concern physical perceptions which hint at spiritual insight. His novels, though, are in no sense plotless. Like Gibbon (whose work he admired), Gunn wrote poor poetry but infused an attentive lyricism into prose attuned to the cycles of nature and their interaction with the workings of human community – what Gunn called 'the old Highland earth life'.[122]

The great bulk of Gunn's writing is about the Highlands. While

Gibbon and Muir wrote about the regions in which they had grown up, recognizing that modernity was consigning many aspects of their agricultural life to the past, Gunn deals with an area whose values he wishes to defend. He is not opposed to modernity, but wants to assert what is valuable yet imperilled in his region and its ecology. In so doing he maintains a strong, generous nationalism: 'The more varied and multiple your nationalism,' he wrote in 1931, 'the richer and profounder your internationalism.'[123] Yet in producing a body of work where regionalism, not nationalism, is to the fore, Gunn both succeeds Gibbon and Shepherd and precedes more recent writers such as George Mackay Brown. Gunn's longest novel, *The Silver Darlings* (1941), follows *A Scots Quair* in presenting a family saga that moves across generations and takes its protagonists from one form of community to another. Alluding in its title to herring ('the silver darlings'), this is a historical novel of well-nigh epic sweep, set in the nineteenth century. In the wake of the Clearances, Catrine and her son Finn move from crofting to fishing and come to terms with the harsh demands of the sea. The 'grey lichened stones', which give Finn 'a feeling of immense time on whose threshold he lay', parallel the standing stones of which Chris Guthrie is so fond in *Sunset Song*.[124]

In common with MacDiarmid, Gibbon, Muir and others, Gunn confronts the great expanses of time revealed by Victorian science as well as the ancientness of Scotland. He reveals those Scotlands – Pictish, Viking, Neolithic – which both predate and underpin the modern nation's sense of itself. His interest in the past did not preclude an engagement with hydro-electric schemes and motorized transport. In *Highland River* (1937) the boy Ken journeys further and further inland through country once occupied by Picts and Vikings. He is conscious too of a world of modern physics textbooks and the horrors of World War I, so that the novel tries to find what T. S. Eliot (with whom Gunn enjoyed a long friendship) called in *Four Quartets* 'The point of intersection of the timeless/ With time'.[125] Late in life, Gunn was regarded by some as twentieth-century Scotland's greatest novelist, but readers often detect a strain of the fey in his prose. It makes some sense to view him as an ecological writer, along with Shepherd, Gibbon and that admirer of *Morning Tide*, the John Buchan of *Sick Heart River*. Gunn could use popular forms, such as the family saga novel or the detective thriller in *Bloodhunt* (1952), as convincing vehicles for his more mystical insights. His writing about Highland life, not least in his non-fiction, can have a telling precision as well as a transcendental glint. Some of his short essays, collected in books like *Highland Pack* (1939), contain his sharpest writing.

Gunn was the greatest twentieth-century novelist of Highland culture, but not all his work has lasted well. In over thirty books he chronicled the social and economic pressures felt by remote communities largely reliant on the rhythms of nature. This appealed greatly to his friend Edwin Muir, whose account of his own Orkney childhood in *An Autobiography* sits fruitfully beside Gunn's accounts of Highland boyhoods. Muir was convinced that 'No one else has evoked so sensitively the atmosphere of Highland life.'[126]

This may have been true, but it is striking that though Gunn wrote much about the Gaelic world, he knew little Gaelic. He recalled his father as having the language, and made some efforts to learn it himself, but was no authority. Not long after Gunn's death in 1973 the once Gaelic-speaking region of East Sutherland just south of his birthplace became the subject of a classic study of 'language death'.[127] Fictions such as Gunn's *The Green Isle of the Great Deep* (1944) engage with modern technologies of extinction such as the 'concentration camp'.[128] They also seem concerned with how one might create or re-create a Gaelic ideal, even a literature of the Gael, without Gaelic.

In this Gunn was not alone. 'It's a dead language that's in the Gaelic. The young people of to-day will see it under the ground,' says one of the Gaels in *The Albannach* (1932) by Thomas Douglas Macdonald (1906–75). Writing as 'Fionn MacColla', he grew up as a Montrose neighbour of Hugh MacDiarmid, who championed his work. Trained as a teacher in Aberdeen, Macdonald worked for a time in Wester Ross, studied Gaelic at Glasgow University, and later became a Hebridean headmaster. Perhaps ignoring Gunn, he saw *The Albannach* as 'the first novel to treat life in the Gaidhealtachd in a realistic manner'. MacColla's book deals with a young man resolved to escape the stern Free Presbyterianism of Wester Ross where his parents are 'unthinking as cattle'. Going to university in 'dirty' Glasgow, Murdo Anderson is disgusted by slummy squalor and religious sectarianism.[129] Eventually, he comes to love his native Gaelic culture, and returns home to learn the classical music of the bagpipes. This English-language novel incorporates an amount of Gaelic, and has a clearly polemical purpose to defend that language and its culture, especially against the stultifying repressions of Calvinism. Modern readers may be struck too by its treatment of sexuality. In what is probably the first Scottish novel to feature masturbation, the protagonist is unable to come to terms with fatherhood, seems prepared to leave his baby to die, and patronizes his wife.

MacColla seems less concerned about this than about the state of Gaelic culture. A quality of scorn in *The Albannach* is also present in his later writings, best known of which is *And the Cock Crew* (1945), which deals bitterly with the Highland Clearances. There is something uneasy about this 1945 nationalist presentation of the Clearances as a Scottish holocaust, and the book's obvious antipathy towards what MacColla's character Fearchar the Poet calls 'England, our Enemy'.[130] MacColla had been a Presbyterian missionary, but converted to Catholicism and wrote with a convert's fervour. A gentler comedy pervades Bruce Marshall's investigation of how Catholicism might deal with contemporary issues; Marshall's writing career extended from the 1920s to the 1980s and included *Father Malachy's Miracle* (1931) and the middle-class Edinburgh family saga *The Black Oxen* (1972). Sectarianism was strong in Scotland (especially western Scotland) in the 1920s and 1930s, with ministers of the established Protestant Church of Scotland warning of the dangers of Catholic Irish immigration, but among the intellectuals of the Scottish Renaissance there were strong Catholic sympathies. These led not just to denunciations of Presbyterianism by Muir and MacColla (most stridently in *The Ministers* (1979)), but also powered such works as Compton Mackenzie's *Catholicism in Scotland* (1936). The intellectual orthodoxy of the Scottish Renaissance was that Protestantism had stifled the nation's arts, whereas these had flourished in an older, independent Catholic Scotland. Surely there is some truth in such a view; Calvinist-nurtured writers such as Burns, Byron or Stevenson may have shared it. However, it ignores much of the work of the era of George Buchanan; it sidelines the strong links between Kirk 'moderates' and Enlightenment culture; it ignores the assertive moral independence Protestantism may have nurtured among Gaelic poets from Rob Donn to Sorley MacLean and beyond; it seems to deny the importance of radical presbyterianism to nineteenth-century fiction from Hogg and Oliphant to George MacDonald and J. M. Barrie. Broad-brush intellectual sectarianism was strong in twentieth-century Scotland. The Scottish Renaissance movement was not immune to this, even as it championed the rights of minority languages, whether Scots or Gaelic.

For all their wariness of it, Gunn, MacColla, and others like the poet 'Adam Drinan' (Joseph Macleod, 1903–84) inherited something of the Celtic Twilight urge to 'whisper in Gaelic;/ for the dead have the Gaelic, and the birds of the air,/ and the saints hear Gaelic prayers'.[131] Long after James Macpherson's Ossian, these writers aimed to produce an English-language representation of a fading Gaelic culture. Lacking Gaelic, Compton Mackenzie worked with the young English public school-educated Gaelic scholar John Lorne Campbell (1906–1996) on The Book of Barra in 1936. Campbell went on to collect Gaelic literary materials from Barra and the wider Highlands and Islands, most notably in Highland Songs of the Forty-Five (1933) and other anthologies. With his American wife the Gaelic folklorist Margaret Fay Shaw, Campbell built up a notable collection of Gaelic recordings on Canna. He wrote an authoritative study of that Hebridean island. His co-authored pamphlet Act Now for the Highlands (1939) proposes practical plans for rural infrastructure, while Shaw's beguiling autobiography From the Alleghenies to the Hebrides (1993) gives an eager account of her life as a song collector in the 1920s and after.

The English-language education system and a lack of any Highland university were continuing problems for Gaelic, but there was also a growing infrastructure designed to provide support. An Comunn Gaidhealach (The Highland Association) had been founded in 1891 with the aim of supporting the language and its associated culture, including the economy of the Highlands and Islands. From 1892 it organized an annual Mod, a festival of literature, oral performance and music based on the Welsh Eisteddfod, which continues today. The first Gaelic novel Dùn Aluinn no An t-Oìghre (Dunaline or The Banished Heir) was written by John MacCormick and published in 1912; a few other similarly undistinguished historical novels followed it, but novel-length Gaelic fiction had to wait more than fifty years to establish itself successfully. Language activists campaigned hard, though. In 1929 an all-Gaelic sub-committee of An Comunn was founded and from 1933 there was a growing movement to organize regional branches and summer camps, increasingly in liaison with regional local committees. The periodical Scottish Gaelic Studies appeared from 1926 onwards, and was followed in 1934 by the establishment of the Scottish Gaelic Texts Society. 1928 saw the reprinting of the first two volumes of the Carmina

Gadelica in Gaelic and English, and further volumes followed in succeeding decades.

Yet for the greatest Gaelic poet of modern times, Somhairle MacGill-Eain (Sorley MacLean, 1911–96), the early twentieth century was a bleak period for Gaelic verse. Born on Raasay, an island which had suffered dreadfully in the Clearances, MacLean was schooled at nearby Portree on Skye. From 1929 until 1933 he studied English at Edinburgh University. One of his professors was the pioneering anthologist of Metaphysical poetry, Herbert Grierson, whom MacLean remembered as 'outstanding'.[132] Though he continued to read and began to write poetry in Gaelic, MacLean chose not to study the language at university, fearing it would hardly help him find a job; but he rejected Grierson's encouragement to pursue postgraduate work in English at Oxford, choosing instead to return to teach English on Skye where, he wrote, 'The Radical tradition was strong enough to make the teaching of Marxism unnoticed.'[133] From 1938 until the start of his war service MacLean taught on the greatly depopulated island of Mull. After the war he went on to become headmaster at Plockton in Wester Ross.

In 1933 MacLean's close student friends the polylingual James Caird and George Elder Davie (afterwards a historian of Scottish philosophy) introduced him to the Scots poetry of MacDiarmid. He soon made contact with that poet and in the later 1930s supplied MacDiarmid with English translations of Gaelic poems on which MacDiarmid, who knew little Gaelic, based his own versions. MacLean was excited not least by his new friend's enthusiasm for the eighteenth-century Gaelic poet Alexander MacDonald, and helped MacDiarmid translate his work. He later regretted that MacDiarmid did not give him the chance to check the results, but, MacLean told me in conversation, 'I would have forgiven him anything.' He thought MacDiarmid had written 'some of the greatest European poetry of the century', and the Scots poet's work served as an incitement to MacLean's own verse in Gaelic.[134]

The student MacLean was schooled in the English Romantic poetry of Wordsworth and Shelley, as well as in Gaelic verse. He wrote poems in English while under the influence of Pound and Eliot, but Professor Grierson's beloved Metaphysical poetry and the work of Yeats are surely the strongest English-language influences on the Gaelic work he produced from the early 1930s onwards. Around 1930 he wrote the first lyrics of what became the sequence *Dàin do Eimhir* (1943). Most of this work was written in the late 1930s and early in the following decade. These 'Poems to Eimhir' are addressed to a compound female lover and muse. Hurt and passionate, they draw on several of MacLean's love affairs, though they are not straightforwardly autobiographical.

Sunderings – between lovers, between reason and emotion, reality and ideal, erotic longing and political commitment, present and past – power much of MacLean's strongest poetry.

> Choisich mi cuide ri mo thuigse
> a-muigh ri taobh a' chuain;
> bha sinn còmhla ach bha ise
> a' fuireach tiotan bhuam.
>
> *I walked with my reason*
> *out beside the sea.*
> *We were together but it was*
> *keeping a little distance from me.*[135]

The speaker of *Dàin do Eimhir* is torn between his wish to fight against Franco in the Spanish Civil War and his love for a woman. Elsewhere he is appalled by a 'Dead stream' in his love's 'tortured body'. As in some of Yeats's lyrics, the speaker articulates kinds of internal civil war, so MacLean conveys a sense of 'a hook stuck in the throat of rapture', as Seamus Heaney memorably puts it.[136] At a time when MacDiarmid was hymning Lenin, MacLean wrote with disgust of the 'poison' of the bourgeoisie in a 'dismal Scotland'. With savage clarity he complained in his poem 'Ban-Ghàidheal' (A Highland Woman) that Christ had never seen in 'the distant vineyard' the sufferings of an old Highland woman struggling to carry a deadweight of seaweed on her back. Instead, Christ's Church preached 'about the lost state of her miserable soul', ignoring the conditions that make existence for her 'like a black sludge' ('mar shnighe dubh').[137]

MacLean's attacks on Free Presbyterian Christianity are as intense as that in MacColla's *The Albannach*, which he read closely in the 1930s. Yet his sense of lyrical beauty and the power of love takes the poems beyond – and even makes them tease – his Marxist political commitment. While in *Dàin do Eimhir* 'Am Boilseabhach' (The Bolshevik) pronounces himself heedless of king or queen, and longs for a free Scotland, he concludes by promising his lover,

dh' èighinn 'nad bhànrainn Albann thu
neo-ar-thaing na Poblachd ùir.

I would proclaim you queen of Scotland
in spite of the new republic.[138]

Where Yeats, infatuated with Maud Gonne, writes of how love 'hid his face amid a crowd of stars', MacLean detects 'soillse cruinne an lasadh t' aodainn' ('lighting of a universe in the kindling of your face').[139] MacLean, though, far more than Yeats, has an intimate knowledge of Gaelic communities and their heritage. He may address a poem to the Irish poet, and even quotes from Yeats's earlier verse in *Dàin do Eimhir*, but he denounced the Celtic Twilight writers for their production of 'very little else but a "foziness with infinity", a vague, misty, cloudy romanticism' which attributed 'to Gaelic poetry the very opposite of every quality which it actually has'.[140]

Readers without Gaelic will miss the intricate word-music of MacLean's verse, though recordings of him reading are available and preserve something of his remarkable acoustic presence. Though he came from a family distinguished for its Gaelic singing, and inherited a rich cultural legacy, the poet was tone deaf. He maintained that this had made him a Gaelic singer manqué. In World War II he served with the Signals Corps in North Africa, and almost died when blown up by a landmine at the battle of El Alamein in 1943. Drawing on a heritage of Gaelic heroic poetry at the same time as registering the circumstances of modern warfare, his war poems are among the finest of World War II. Often, as when 'Glac a' Bhàis' (Death Valley) describes a grey-faced dead boy soldier of the Führer lying in the fly-infested, dun sand of the desert, these poems have a declarative clarity which allows for irony as well as registering waste and a grim respect.

MacLean was not a prolific poet. He complained that conditions in the army, and later in schoolteaching, gave him too little 'simmering time'.[141] His collected poems in Gaelic occupy around 160 pages. All that matters, though, is the remarkable quality of his verse. In the 1940 poem 'Coilltean Ratharsair' (The Woods of Raasay) he writes with anguished love of his native terrain which has given him helmets and banners like an army, as well as its 'kiss' of 'unrest'.[142] His poetry is often spurred by hurt. In 'Coin is Madaidhean-Allaidh' (Dogs and Wolves) he imagines his unwritten poems, 'bristles raging, bloody tongued' as they run over the snows of eternity, 'a hunt without halt, without respite'.[143]

In postwar Scotland and, gradually, further afield MacLean established himself as a remarkable public reader of his work. He read, sometimes almost chanted to audiences, using a powerful, lingering intonation captured in several recordings. He looked and sounded an incarnation of his culture, and of the wider European struggles of the twentieth century. Speaking about MacLean's poem 'Hallaig', its twenty-first-century translator Seamus Heaney recalls that first hearing MacLean read aloud had 'the force of revelation . . . This was the song of a man who had come through, a poem with all the lucidity and arbitrariness of vision'.[144] MacLean's work marries a combined European symbolist technique and bleak existentialist outlook to a deeply traditional Gaelic voice which is informed by the Gaelic heroic ethos and 'otherworld'. He demonstrates the unquenchable human spirit through the landscape of Skye, but the vision remains so vulnerable that it is never comforting. For Gaelic writing MacLean's poetry has been of immense importance for its intensity and its openness to an expanding range of subject matter.

After the Second World War MacLean's poetic output dwindled, though he continued to write remarkable poems, including the magnificent 'Hallaig' which evokes with scything clarity the landscape around the cleared, now abandoned village of Hallaig on the east coast of Raasay. MacLean sees there dead and absent generations of men and women processing in an 'endless walk' through the 'dumb living twilight'.[145] The poem ends with a pang of intense lyrical commitment to a loved culture and landscape. Drawing on Raasay's painful history, and treating it with resolute tenderness, 'Hallaig' is at once raw and accomplished in its lyrical blessing. It is an epitome of and a plea for a civilization. MacLean was by no means the only significant Gaelic poet of twentieth-century Scotland, but it seems unlikely that Scottish Gaelic will again be the language of such a distinguished body of verse.

Poetry has continued to be the principal medium for Gaelic literature, with only a limited amount of prose fiction and autobiography. Published in 1912, the awkwardly Ossianic imperial novel *Dùn-Àluinn* (*Dunaline*) by Iain Mac Cormaic (c. 1870–1947), a Mull-born Glaswegian novelist and short-story writer, is little read or admired today. It was followed in 1913 by the confused Jacobite historical romance *An t-Ogha Mór* (*The Big Grandson*) by Angus Robertson. Later came Seumas

MacLeòid's *Cailin Sgiathanach* (*Skye Maid*) in 1923, but not until the 1970s did any significant Gaelic novels or novellas follow. Striking novellas included Iain Crichton Smith's *An t-Aonaran* (*The Hermit*) (1976) and, later, *An Sgàineadh* (*The Split*) (1993) by Tormod Calum Dòmhnallach. For all the heritage of oral song and storytelling, Gaelic drama scarcely exists before World War II, and it would be 1978 before a professional Gaelic drama company was founded – in Tarbert on Harris.

Across Scotland as a whole the twentieth century saw a marked increase in dramatic writing. Between 1900 and 1910 the number of theatres in the country almost doubled, to a total of 53. The year 1909 brought the establishment of the influential Glasgow Repertory Company, founded by Englishman Alfred Wareing who had been influenced by his knowledge of Dublin's Abbey Theatre. Owned by public subscribers, the Glasgow Rep was the Anglophone world's first 'citizens' theatre', and Scotland's first repertory company. Its aim was to begin and develop 'purely Scottish drama ... written by Scottish men and women of letters'.[146] Despite such an aim, plays by Shaw, Ibsen, Galsworthy and Bennett were the mainstays of the first season and World War I put an end to the project. By then sixteen new Scottish plays had been performed, best known of which is J. A. Ferguson's *Campbell of Kilmohr* (1914), set in the Highlands and dealing effectively with betrayal at the time of the 1745 Jacobite rebellion. Between the 1918 Armistice and the start of World War II the number of theatres in Scotland declined to around thirty, partly thanks to the popularity of the country's 600 or so cinemas. Yet alongside ongoing traditions of pantomime and music hall there was a growth in amateur dramatic performance. The Scottish Community Drama Association was founded in 1926 at the time of the General Strike and a decade later there were over a hundred amateur drama clubs across the land, many participating in one-act play festivals. By 1934 a character in John MacNair Reid's *Homeward Journey* exclaims to an upwardly-mobile girl from a lower-middle-class household who acts in amateur dramatics that 'The time's coming when there won't be any audiences at all: nothing but players!'[147] This popular movement continued in strength well after World War II.

By 1922 a Scottish National Theatre Society aimed through a touring semi-professional company, the Scottish National Players, to produce 'plays of Scottish life and character'. The Society wanted to encourage 'public taste for good drama of any type', and 'To found a Scottish National Theatre'.[148] In this last aim the Society failed, but its formation did encourage native dramatic writing, not least by some of their own board of governors. These included two medical doctors, John Macintyre (1869–1947) who wrote plays as 'John Brandane', and Osborne Mavor who wrote most of his plays as 'James Bridie'. In the 1920s one of the producers the Scottish National Players hired was the young Tyrone Guthrie, who went on to direct at London's Old Vic. Later, Guthrie became a guiding spirit in Canadian theatre. Bridie, in particular, was able to make use of such theatrical links outside Scotland, and Guthrie made possible Bridie's 1930 London theatrical debut.

John Brandane's humorously sly if somewhat stereotypical exploration of a clash between tradition and capitalist modernity in Highland life, *The Glen is Mine* (published in 1925), may contain some of his best dramatic writing, but his contribution to Scottish theatre is overshadowed by that of Bridie, to whom he initially acted as mentor. James Bridie (1888–1951) was born into a cultured middle-class family. He spent his early years in what was then the Lanarkshire village of East Kilbride, a few miles south-east of Glasgow. Like the best-selling and widely translated novelist A. J. Cronin (1896–1981), whose readable 1931 anti-Kailyard saga *Hatter's Castle* preceded a popular series of medical tales (some later adapted for 1960s television as *Dr Finlay's Casebook*), Bridie studied medicine at Glasgow University. He wrote plays throughout his time as a medical student and while serving in the Royal Army Medical Corps during World War I. In a 1916 letter to his mother from a Dressing Station on the Somme, Bridie wrote of his surgical work on amputations,

I did two yesterday – one on a Private Geordie Robinson, late of Govan and Fairfield's [Clyde shipyard], and another on a Boche prisoner. I did Geordie's beautifully with no haemorrhage at all. I'm sorry to say that he died and the dirty Boche lived and is going strong.[149]

Here Bridie's professional ethics override a horror and pity controlled by a certain ironic wit, partly directed at himself. Such a mixture of tones and themes is evident in his plays, arguably the most impressive body of dramatic work written in twentieth-century Scotland but one which, though it was internationally successful, has fallen out of fashion.

In some ways Bridie was of his time. He could present historical pageants of Scottish life, as in *John Knox* (1947) where, prefiguring Liz Lochhead's 1987 *Mary Queen of Scots Got Her Head Chopped Off*, he mixes modern characters with the sectarian flyting of Mary and Knox. Yet the major creator of Scottish historical dramas of the period was the Scots-language playwright Robert McLellan. McLellan wrote in naturalistic Scots and his most successful play, *Jamie the Saxt* (1937), engages audiences through its presentation of the monarch James VI as a venal plotter after the British throne. At times, though, as when encountering many of the Scottish historical novels of the mid-twentieth century, one wonders what the point of such costume dramas may be, whereas Bridie's contemporary plays in English avoid the charge of antiquarianism.

Bridie's experience of battlefield surgery was intense, but some of his time during World War I (when he was in Baku in Persia) proved hugely enjoyable. From the Middle East he returned to become a successful doctor in suburban Glasgow, leading a respectable upper-middle-class life: Bridie became surely the only modern Scottish writer who had his own chauffeur. Surprisingly, the dramatist and his wife came from a strong Free Presbyterian religious tradition. Though Bridie described his published play *The Sunlight Sonata* (1930) as 'the last and only survivor of my morality play period', many of his works are morality plays of some sort, often involving ethical, even theological, debates, and some, like *Tobias and the Angel* (1930) and *Susannah and the Elders* (1937), have biblical themes.[150]

Several of Bridie's best plays, such as *The Anatomist* (1930), *Mr Bolfry* (1943) and *Dr Angelus* (1947), involve the temptation of what the last terms a 'Moral Holiday' – a move beyond the rules of conventional morality and professional ethics.[151] The allure of this may be strongest in *The Anatomist* where the doctor-dramatist who returned to Glasgow from the Somme presents Edinburgh's charismatic Dr Robert Knox. Knox's work relies on a supply of fresh corpses from the notorious nineteenth-century murderers Burke and Hare, and the Doctor is uneasily involved with the polite, bourgeois world of the Disharts, a Scottish family whose name comes from Barrie's *The Little Minister*. In Bridie's 1943 play *Mr Bolfry* the title character, who introduces himself as 'Dr Bolfry', turns out to be the devil, summoned up by a bored wartime group of liberal-minded people in the Highlands. Though they joke about Free Presbyterians as 'Devil-Worshippers' and advocates of 'totalitarianism', and though they are attracted by Bolfry's encouragement to 'Honour your Self and set him free', these people are saved only because the religion they mock provides a morality strong enough to withstand the charismatic evils represented by Hitler and Bolfry.[152] In *Dr Angelus* the manipulative doctor of the title murders his patients, including his wife, arguing that 'The realization of oneself is the aim and objective of existence.'[153]

Out of sympathy with the Nietzscheanism espoused by the young MacDiarmid, Bridie emphasizes the limitations of humanity. His work emits more than a whiff of original sin. Working within the theatrical tradition of Barrie and of Shaw (who admired 'such stunners as Bolfry'), Bridie liked to experiment with structure, sometimes awkwardly. He disliked conclusive endings: '*Only God can write last acts, and He seldom does.*'[154] In Bridie's plays themes range from religious sectarianism (one of the major topics in twentieth-century Scottish drama) to the Trojan War. He draws on theatrical traditions as different as those of the well-made play and Punch and Judy. He has a great sense of stagecraft. His confrontations feature engaged, and engaging, dialogue; yet his work is fitful. It is both fuelled by and chafes against the polite Scottish milieu in which the playwright made his home life. The title of his son's revealing memoir, *Dr Mavor and Mr Bridie* (1988), hints at a certain Jekyll and Hyde strain to this respectable citizen who, in *Mr Bolfry*, has the devil lay claim to all art.

True to his emphasis to go beyond the mere 'realization of oneself', Bridie, whose work brought him into contact with Shaw and Laurence Olivier as well as Scottish actors like Alastair Sim, Duncan Macrae and John Laurie, did an enormous amount for Scottish theatre. If his own international success as a dramatist and his local distinction as a doctor made him well off, he was active on behalf of fellow dramatists in an often philistine Scottish culture. As he put it six years before his death, in a 1945 account of British playwriting,

A Scotsman writing in his own language and according to his own way of thinking has a poor chance in London. In Scotland he can get a hearing of a sort but a hearing alone will not buy boots for his children. A week's performance in a local theatre will bring him in, if he is lucky, £25. This is not a very handsome return for six months' work.[155]

Author of over forty plays, Bridie sought to improve such a situation. From 1942 he chaired the Scottish Committee of the Council for the Encouragement of Music and the Arts, which eventually in 1967 became the Scottish Arts Council. Working with the Glasgow novelist and opera enthusiast Guy McCrone, whose 1937 fiction debut, *The Striped Umbrella*, led to his observant popular saga of 'puritan' and 'philistine' middle-class life in *Wax Fruit* a decade later, Bridie was also the moving force behind the setting-up of the now world-famous Glasgow Citizens' Theatre.[156] Based in the Gorbals and founded in 1943, its origins lie in World War II, as do those of the Glasgow Unity Theatre founded two years earlier. Before its demise, the Unity Theatre produced radical new works by Clifford Odets, Sean O'Casey and Maxim Gorki as well as by such socially concerned Scottish dramatists as Robert McLeish, whose *The Gorbals Story* (1946) was very popular. Unity Theatre also produced work by Ena Lamont Stewart (1912–2006), an affluent Glasgow clergyman's daughter whose first play, *Distinguished Company*, was presented in Rutherglen in 1942. Stewart's powerful drama *Men Should Weep* (1947; revised 1982), set in an East End Glasgow tenement during the 1930s Depression and using sharp vernacular Glasgow dialogue, was pioneering in its stage presentation of a working-class woman's perspective on sexuality. It was unflinching in its treatment of how to look after 'a hoose an a man an five weans' in an environment of lice, tuberculosis, rickets, and men who 'canna staun up tae things like a wumman. They loss the heid and shout.'[157] For the programme notes to John McGrath's sharpened 1980s production of *Men Should Weep* Stewart recalled how 'One evening in the winter of 1942 I went to the theatre. I came home in a mood of red hot revolt against cocktail time, glamorous gowns, and under-worked, about-to-be-deceived husbands. I asked myself what I wanted to see on stage, and the answer was life. Real life. Ordinary people.'[158] Stewart's achievement was a milestone in modern Scottish theatre, but her work was not fully appreciated in the 1940s. James Bridie crushingly suggested she 'stick to comedy'.[159] She burnt her next script.

At once of and ahead of its time, *Men Should Weep* presents a loud clamouring for social justice. 'Born intae poverty', its male protagonist feels like 'a human question mark, aye askin why? Why? *Why*?'[160] Like the 1934 novel *Hunger March* by iron merchant's daughter Dot Allan (1886–1964), Stewart's play gives a sharp insight into working-class

Scotland during the Depression. Yet the best-known representation of working-class Glasgow life in the 1930s is neither *Men Should Weep* nor Allan's novel but a story of Gorbals slum life written by a Glasgow baker, Alexander McArthur, then considerably recast by H. Kingsley Long, an English journalist who had written about American gangsters. The book they produced, *No Mean City* (1935), went on to sell around a million copies. In some ways *No Mean City* appealed to the kind of readers who enjoyed the harsh tales of rural and urban working-class life by such writers as Irish-born Patrick MacGill (1890–1963), author of *Children of the Dead End: The Autobiography of a Navvy* (1914) and *The Rat-Pit* (1915). Yet the focus of *No Mean City* is more resolutely urban. Its protagonist, Johnnie Stark, gangleader and 'Razor King', encouraged a view of Glasgow working-class men as monsters and of the town itself as a city of razors and slumland violence. Denounced by critics for its sensationalism, *No Mean City* veers between insider knowledge and patronizing, semi-sociological explanations of its subject: 'Most working-class men can cook for themselves.'[161] This dual perspective dramatizes an uncertainty about class and nationality felt by much more literary novelists, like George Douglas Brown, unsure whether they address a Scottish or a predominantly middle-class English or a wider international audience. *No Mean City* presents some issues – such as childlessness – with surprising insight. In its own time it was succeeded by more nuanced Gorbals narratives such as the 1942 *Growing Up* stories by Edward Gaitens (1897–1966) who was born in the Gorbals. Gaitens was encouraged to publish by James Bridie, and some of the 1942 stories were incorporated in his substantially autobiographical novel *Dance of the Apprentices* (1948). Though many West of Scotland writers have sought to counter or modulate its influence, the 'hard man' novel *No Mean City* with its influential urban Scottish gangsterism did leave literary legacies to later Glasgow authors and to generations of Scottish urban crime writers from William McIlvanney to Ian Rankin, not to mention the Irvine Welsh of Edinburgh's *Trainspotting*.

However, Glasgow gangland had been explored before. Greenock-born George Blake's *Mince Collop Close* (1925) features a female gang leader. Blake (1893–1961) wrote several novels about 1920s radical politics. A Glasgow University law graduate, he had worked in journalism with Neil Munro, then as a London magazine editor before becoming with T. S. Eliot a director of the recently established London publishing house Faber and Faber in 1930. Blake returned to Scotland in 1932 to work with George Malcolm Thomson at Faber's Edinburgh subsidiary, the Porpoise Press. This imprint published for a time work by several novelists including Neil Gunn and John MacNair Reid, as well as volumes of poetry by Marion Angus and many Scottish authors. From *Clyde Built* (1922) through the autobiographical *Down to the Sea* (1937) and a series of 'Garvel' novels set in a fictionalized Greenock, Blake expressed a deep love of and concern for the shipbuilding region of industrial Clydeside. In *The Shipbuilders* (1935) he produced perhaps the finest of a crop of novels about the industrial West of Scotland in the first half of the twentieth century. Against a background of 'economic crime' this Depression novel weaves together the lives of a rich shipyard manager, Leslie Pagan, and Danny Shields, 'a riveter, a specialist in a job outmoded'.[162] As officer and batman the two men have been comrades in World War I. In very different class settings, their families undergo similar experiences of bereavement, marital tensions and work-related stress. *The Shipbuilders* can show signs of middle-class condescension and casual xenophobia, but it is also aware of these problems. Though character development is limited and the style a little flat, the book's dual portrayal of middle-class as well as working-class Glasgow experience makes it all the stronger in showing how economic needs, class conventions and family pressures pull apart men once bonded by a sense of shared purpose. An alertness to the implications of new technologies, to a north–south divide in Britain, and to both sides of a widening class divide give it a perceptive dignity. Dot Allan's story of several generations of a Glasgow shipbuilding family, *Deepening River* (1932), and her mixing of working-class and middle-class narratives in *Hunger March* (1934) anticipate some aspects of Blake's novel.

In the latter stages of World War I, then after the 1922 British general election which doubled the young Labour Party's seats at Westminster, 'Glasgow blazed red'.[163] That is how Gordon Brown, the twenty-first-century Labour politician, puts it in his biography of MP and Glaswegian Labour orator James Maxton (1885–1946). Historians argue over the precise significance of the powerfully mythologized 'Red Clydeside'. Yet there is little doubt that Marxism as well as nationalism convulsed twentieth-century Scottish literary life, from the fiction of Grassic Gibbon to the poetry of MacDiarmid and Sorley MacLean or industrial novels of the 1930s and after. Class concerns became crucial to prose fiction in particular, and grew more insistent as the twentieth century developed.

Frederick Niven (1878–1944), who grew up in Glasgow, then moved to England and emigrated to British Columbia in 1920, wrote in novels such as *The Justice of the Peace* (1914) and *The Staff at Simson's* (1937) about class-divided Glasgow life. Earlier in the century Blythswood Fergus and Patrick MacGill had explored Glasgow slum conditions, but Blake's *The Shipbuilders* ranges from a gangland knifing to the loneliness of managerial decision-making. Its themes of selfishness and duty are shared with Bridie's plays and with contemporary Scottish works like *Homeward Journey* (1934) by *Glasgow Herald* journalist John MacNair Reid. Reid's is a subtle, fastidiously written novel about a liaison between a sexually inexperienced young Glasgow upper-middle-class man and a lower-middle-class young woman who is keen to escape her background. Its familial canvas is much smaller than that of *Deepening River*, *Hunger March* or *The Shipbuilders*, which also pay greater attention to politics and economics, but it is memorably attentive to its milieu. Before he turned to writing a quintet of historical novels centred on Robert Burns, James Barke (1905–58) brought together in his sometimes propagandistic novel *Major Operation* (1936) a hospitalized Glasgow coal merchant and a union leader. Efforts to bridge a perceived gulf between working-class and middle-class Scotland characterized several 1930s Scottish fictions, but later writers largely abandoned the attempt. Where an author like George Blake sought to traverse the widening class divide, more recent and more stylistically convincing novelists such as the shrewdly middle-class Muriel Spark or the committedly working-class James Kelman make almost no sympathetic effort to cross class boundaries.

A recent prevailing assumption that Scottish fiction should deal only or principally with working-class subject matter makes the often stylish and jaunty work of Eric Linklater (1899–1974) appear a curious anachronism. Some of Linklater's fiction also deals with the Depression years of the 1920s and 1930s, but says little about the problems of the Scottish working class. Born in Wales, Linklater grew up in his ancestral Orkney before going to school in Aberdeen. After courageous service in World War I, he studied medicine and English at Aberdeen University, then spent time as a journalist in 1920s India before working as assistant to the Professor of English at his alma mater. This led to the award of a Commonwealth Fellowship which allowed the young author to tour the United States before returning (eventually to Orkney) to become a full-time writer.

As a fourteen-year-old at Aberdeen Grammar, Byron's old school, Linklater read *Don Juan* with glee, and stared from the classroom at the poet's statue: 'Byron, through the window, undid the schoolroom teaching that literature must be a solemn thing.'[164] In 1920 Linklater's first printed poem was an accomplished imitation of *Don Juan*. The fledgling writer was attracted not just to Byron's freewheeling vivacity but also to the very different laconic Norse heroic prose and poetry of the *Orkneyinga Saga*, another work of great literature which he connected with his family background. Linklater's first novel, *White-Maa's Saga* (1929), has an Orcadian title – it means *Seagull's Saga*. This semi-autobiographical book is set in Orkney and Aberdeen ('Inverdoon'), but his second novel, *Poet's Pub* (1929), is predominantly English in location. Wittily if rather indulgently written, it builds slowly and elegantly towards a comical car chase, while possessing for modern readers something of the feel-good glow of an Ealing film comedy. Suspicious of the avant-garde, Linklater, like Yorkshire's J. B. Priestley, wrote for a middlebrow audience, but liked sophisticated literary jokes and allusions. *Poet's Pub* includes a United States fraudster who has grown rich from passing himself off on American lecture tours as a variety of famous English authors; eventually, worldwide reporting of the death of Thomas Hardy in England results in the fraudster's being caught out while posing as that celebrated writer in South Dakota. Linklater's literariness and his affection for America led to his sending a descendant of Byron's hero on a tour of the Prohibition-era USA in his best-selling *Juan in America*. That novel's picaresque gusto is counterpointed by the much barer and much less popular prose of *Men of Ness* (1932), a Viking tale that draws on the *Orkneyinga Saga* and anticipates some of George Mackay Brown's later fiction.

A Juanesque joie-de-vivre characterizes many of Linklater's books, including *Magnus Merriman* (1934) – based on his experiences as a Scottish Nationalist parliamentary candidate in Fife. This mischievous tale portrays Hugh MacDiarmid as Scots poet 'Hugh Skene', and the real-life nationalist activist Wendy Wood as 'Beaty Bracken', who flushes a Union Jack down a toilet; Wood sued, while MacDiarmid, Compton

Mackenzie and most reviewers enjoyed the story. Yet many an individual Linklater book, like his oeuvre as a whole, is uneven. He wrote nearly two dozen adult novels, as well as children's fiction, autobiographies, short stories and verse. When the hedonistic openness of Don Juan and the grimmer, fatalistic ethos of the sagas meet in *Private Angelo*, he produces his finest novel. In one of history's odd balancing acts, World War II brought to Orkney Italian prisoners of war who transformed a nissen hut into the now famous 'Italian chapel' by Scapa Flow; the same conflict took Orcadian novelist Linklater to Italy in 1945 as a war reporter and led him to write a novel which celebrates Italy, survival and love among the bombed ruins of the Italian campaign.

The most intense time in Linklater's life had been his service as a sniper in World War I, during which an enemy bullet tore through his helmet, narrowly missing his brain. His autobiographical *Fanfare for a Tin Hat* (1970) recalls those days. Linklater writes convincingly about war. Its sense of confusion, the topsy-turvydom of a physical landscape without 'stability', is at one with the episodic yet fatalistically plotted benignity of *Private Angelo*. That novel tells the story of a loving, lovable Italian man who variously serves the Italian, German and Allied armies. He comes to generous terms with war's hurt, not to mention with his own impressively extended family. Affording Linklater a vehicle for comment on war, nationality and love, Angelo is his most lasting creation, a sometimes cowardly little man who preserves a dash of Don Juan. His eventful saga has guile as well as gusto. Angelo is shrewd about everything from Renaissance art to what we now call 'friendly fire'. Typical is his conversation with Simon, one of the Duke of Rothesay's guardsmen:

'We do not all carry bombs. To make a private mistake in your own house is one thing, but to make a public mistake with a bomb of two hundred and fifty kilogrammes is different altogether.'

'Year by year,' said Simon philosophically, 'science puts more power into our hands.'

'So that we may throw bombs at the wrong people?'

'Science like love,' said Simon, 'is blind.'

'I prefer love,' said Angelo. 'It makes less noise.'[165]

The globetrotting of Linklater's amused, amusing cosmopolitanism is outdone by the wide-ranging international travels of Naomi Mitchison.

Her books' settings range from Scotland to Africa, from ancient Europe to outer space. Born in Edinburgh in 1897 but brought up in Oxford, Mitchison spent formative time north of the Border with relatives, including her grandparents who had a Scottish castle. She made her home in Scotland in 1947 when she and her husband, the Labour politician Dick (later Baron) Mitchison, bought a big house at Carradale in Kintyre. Naomi Mitchison enjoyed a very privileged upper-class Edwardian childhood. Her favourite reading included Kipling, and Tennyson's Arthurian *Idylls of the King*; she chatted about fairies with Andrew Lang; her grannie introduced her to the Cambridge-based Scottish Classicist J. G. Frazer's great anthropological study of myth and religion, *The Golden Bough*, whose volumes Naomi devoured.

From *The Conquered* (1923) onwards, Mitchison's early novels are regularly set in the Classical world, but, written in a generally colloquial modern idiom, they often involve contemporary issues. An early unpublished play was subtitled 'A Study in Recurrence'; in *The Conquered* the Roman conquest of Gaul is aligned with Britain's later relationship with Ireland through the use of epigraphs from songs like 'The Croppy Boy'. Stories in *When the Bough Breaks* (1924) and other fictions set in ancient times, most ambitious of which is the Frazerian *The Corn King and the Spring Queen* (1931), deal directly with issues of sexuality and women's rights; Mitchison was also the controversial author of *Thoughts on Birth Control* (1930). She had a long-lasting interest in tribal organization, and a special concern with the opportunities (or lack of them) for women in non-Western as well as Western society. Erif Der, ancient 'Spring Queen' of Marob, has supernatural powers in Mitchison's sometimes violent 1931 novel of sexuality, travel and regeneration. Underpinned by Frazer and Freud, *The Corn King and the Spring Queen* is authored with great commitment by a remarkable woman. Mitchison's long life saw her not only observing and praising the place of women in 1930s Russia, but also campaigning for better conditions in the 1950s Highlands, then being adopted in the 1960s as honorary matriarch to a tribe in Botswana.

Unorthodox and courageous in life, Mitchison can be a prescient thinker but is not always sure-footed as a writer. Some readers may find it awkward, for instance, that 'Erif Der' is simply 'Red Fire' backwards. Much of Mitchison's fiction is set in the past or future, yet its idiom is a sometimes flat twentieth-century English. Her first Scottish novel,

The Bull Calves (1947), deals with the upheavals of the 1745 Jacobite Rebellion, but implies a comparison with the convulsions of World War II and its aftermath. *The Swan's Road* (1954) and *The Land the Ravens Found* (1955) are direct, effective retellings of Viking voyages which form part of that modern heritage of Scottish Viking narratives from Linklater's *Men of Ness* to George Mackay Brown's *Vinland* (1992) and fiction by Margaret Elphinstone. Mitchison's *Early in Orcadia* (1987) is set in prehistoric Orkney, while her *Memoirs of a Spacewoman* (1962) is one of a number of science-fiction explorations of topics such as cloning and genetics. This prolific writer's output (she wrote over ninety books) is comparable with that of Margaret Oliphant a century earlier. Mitchison's preoccupation with the life of a community, and not least women's place in it, unifies much of her work. Several autobiographical volumes, such as *Small Talk* (1973), *All Change Here* (1975) and the meticulous World War II diaries that she kept as a result of her participation in the Mass Observation project, are immediately appealing in their precisely registered actuality: in 1941 in Kilbowie Road on bombed wartime Clydeside 'everywhere was the smell of plaster and burning, everywhere this incredible mess, everywhere people trailing about with a mattress or a bundle or a few pots and pans'.[166]

Like a number of her other works, Mitchison's *The Corn King and the Spring Queen* can be related to that preoccupation with 'the land' so strong in the writing of Scottish authors active between the two World Wars. From Muir's *Autobiography* (whose first version appeared in 1940) to James Barke's *The Land of the Leal* (1939) and John McNeillie's *Wigtown Ploughman* (1939), from MacColla's *The Albannach* to Shepherd's *The Weatherhouse* or Gunn's *Morning Tide*, there is a constant awareness of pressures to move from what Barke calls 'the hard insatiable fields' of rural Scotland either to that urban industrial Scotland summed up by countrymen Sorley MacLean and Hugh MacDiarmid as hellish, or to new settlements overseas.[167] These were decades of population movement and emigration, but also of a developing ecological sense. Drift away from the country towards urban centres was not new, but writers used the historical novel and other forms to investigate it more thoroughly than before. Where Walter Scott had developed that genre to examine social changes like those associated with the Jacobite rebellions, novelists like Gibbon and Barke, though they may have admired modern Russian fiction far more than the tomes of Scott, re-imagined the impact of industrialization on the land. In so doing they offered modern city readers a sense of memory that might link them to a familial and national past tied to terrain relatively untouched by technology.

'There must be a harmony between ourselves and our environment – society,' declares Tom, the radical Church minister who is one of the more complexly presented characters in Barke's big historical novel *The Land of the Leal*.[168] Politically aware, that book explores attempts at revolution against forms of slavery, as do Gibbon's *Spartacus* (1933) and *A Scots Quair*. Yet the sense of 'environment' runs beyond political or social environment in the work of Barke, Gunn, Shepherd, Muir, MacDiarmid, MacLean, Mitchison and so many other writers of the time. It extends to a greater sense of communion with or hurt estrangement from 'the land'. Hugh and Terry, the husband and wife in Ian Macpherson's futuristic *Wild Harbour* (1936), literally go to ground, living off the land after they abandon their house for a cave following the outbreak of a war that the author sets in 1944. Though part of the interest in *Wild Harbour* is psychological and speculative, the novel is most memorable for its simultaneously dystopian and Edenic sense of getting back to earthy basics. 'You can't take a man in a town and compare him with country folk of old,' says Terry, but, like the novel as a whole, she shows a fearful relish for attempted self-sufficiency in a situation where as 'knitted things wear through I'll unravel them and reknit them'. As it had been for the Gaelic poet Duncan Bàn MacIntyre in the eighteenth century, the hillside becomes a larder, albeit one with 'an adder, slender and vicious and as full of fat as a pike'.[169] Author of *Shepherds' Calendar* (1931), *Land of Our Fathers* (1933) and other novels, Macpherson (1905–44) grew up in the north-east, close to Grassic Gibbon, then studied English at Aberdeen University. Like many of his Scottish contemporaries, he seeks to re-inscribe a sense of seasonal changes and rhythms in an era and a nation where many worried that 'The countryside's dead. An' a' the young folks are makin' for the towns.'[170]

In *Wild Harbour* there is an assertion that 'this place, this land, is ours, and we, tied to it as the wild creatures are, cannot escape from it by going', but the 'land' is not the nation; it is a specific piece of ground.[171] Ian Macpherson's protagonists try to find how to live close to the land without becoming 'savage'. *Wild Harbour*, though, is not the only 1930s Scottish fiction to look ahead to a wider war. In *The Land of the Leal*, Barke's finest novel, completed in Bearsden in 1938, we see Glaswegians going off to fight Fascism in Spain. The book looks back and discovers or imaginatively constructs a tradition of radical history through fiction. It is also attuned to an apocalyptic future, with its talk of civilians 'systematically bombed to death' and of 'the abominations inflicted on political prisoners in the German concentration camps'.[172] Not so stylish a writer as Grassic Gibbon, Barke may have had a more astute political imagination. At any rate, he knew what was coming.

Muriel Spark, photographed by Peter Adamson just after receiving the honorary degree of Doctor of Letters from the University of St Andrews in 1998. Scotland's greatest twentieth-century novelist, Spark spent much of her life outside the country, living in Africa, England, America, and Italy. (St Andrews University Library Photographic Collections, PGA-D107-4)

I I

Hard-wearing Flowers

'Woke from nightmare' begins the entry for 1 September 1939 in Naomi Mitchison's wartime diary. Later that day, she hears the 'Bad news' about the outbreak of war.[1] A climate of foreboding in the 1930s could make even nature seem different. The American Scot Ruthven Todd (1914–78), whose best work shows occasionally the facility of Mitchison's friend W. H. Auden, wrote of the Spanish Civil War and sensed greater conflicts to come. Todd's poem 'In September 1939' presents a 'tarnished' landscape where even the tiny creatures around seventeenth-century poet William Drummond's idyllic country house are seen as combatants. 'At Hawthornden there is bombardment by dragon-flies/ And the willow-wren warbles like a siren'.[2]

Just before hostilities began, new groupings of Scottish poets were emerging. Emblematic of this is the tiny 1938 anthology, *Albannach*, published in Dingwall, Ross-shire, under the editorship of C. J. Russell and J. F. Hendry. Dedicated to Scottish Renaissance notables – J. H. Whyte, Edwin Muir, Hugh MacDiarmid and Glasgow poet–journalist William Jeffrey – *Albannach* assembles several younger poets whose names would be prominent in the years to come. Contributors include Robert Garioch, G. S. Fraser, Ruthven Todd, J. F. Hendry and Norman MacCaig. Two decades later, in middle age, MacCaig would change his style radically. His clotted and obscure 1930s poems give a sense of the kind of verse that, drawing on Dylan Thomas and Surrealism, grew popular among intellectuals at the start of World War II:

> You whose brow was an oak barn
> of compass winds knelt down on the water
> like a sheep grazing and in the boned ambers

> of eyes I watched myself dancing on a stick
> of smoke . . .

Elements of MacCaig's later poetry are present here, overwhelmed by an effort to project a sort of fantastic dream world. In the young Mac-Caig's verse Moscow is hauled on a sledge and 'teeth are/ kittens'.[3]

An occasionally bathetic flavour of the nightmarish, tempestuous unconscious fills the poetry gathered by Glasgow-born J. F. Hendry (1912–86) in anthologies like *The New Apocalypse* (1940). This 'New Apocalypse' was a 'Celtic' neo-Romantic movement directed against what Hendry called in his semi-autobiographical Bildungsroman, *Ferny Brae* (1947) 'the ruling social neurosis' of modern mechanical civilization.[4] New Apocalyptic poets strove for a sense of disturbed intensity appropriate to their moment in history. The movement included Dylan Thomas, but several of its early leaders were Scots with knowledge of continental European Surrealism. In a group photo taken at London's first exhibition of Surrealist art in 1936 Ruthven Todd stands next to Salvador Dali and the French poet Paul Eluard.[5] Several young Scottish poets were attuned to continental developments. Hendry had studied modern languages at Glasgow University; his fellow Glaswegian G. S. Fraser (1915–80) was interested in André Breton and Giorgio de Chirico, as well as in Yeats and Freud. At St Andrews University a magazine edited by the student Fraser was closed down by the authorities. Sometimes tinged with Surrealism, New Apocalypticism liked to shock polite society and uncover 'fundamental, organic myths'. Its excesses, anticipating and participating in what Hendry calls 'blind war' in his 1940 poem 'London Before Invasion', can seem too lazily won and overblown, with concussed talk of how

> Flood-tides returning may bring with them blood and fire,
> Blenching with wet panic spirit that must be rock.[6]

Striving to communicate a sense of what Norman MacCaig (1910–96) called 'The tiger in words' clothing', too often New Apocalyptic poetry produces an uneasy 'mirror of terror and mimicry of rapture' that seems self-indulgently gaudy.[7] *Far Cry*, MacCaig's first, apocalyptically-accented collection was published in 1943; its title not only indicates remote energy but implies this poet's long-standing interest in perception of likeness and difference. In World War II the strong-minded

MacCaig was a conscientious objector. He spent some time imprisoned as, in Edinburgh, did his fellow Classical scholar, the poet and later translator of Aristophanes, Douglas Young (1913–73), an ardent Scottish nationalist who refused to fight in the British army. In MacCaig's second collection, *The Inward Eye* (1946), there are lucid intervals that signal a fascination with perception, the natural world and the composition of the self which his later poetry will articulate more clearly. Still, it would be almost another decade before MacCaig moved decisively beyond the rhetoric of Dylan Thomas and the New Apocalyptics.

The best World War II Scottish poetry ignored or reacted against such rhetoric. In the North African desert Sorley MacLean wrote a small number of war poems, such as 'Glac a' Bhàis' (Death Valley), all the more magnificent for their combination of declarative clarity and understatement. A remarkable number of Scottish poems emerged from the North African campaign, either at the time or afterwards. Born in Blairgowrie, Perthshire, then educated at Dulwich College and Cambridge, Hamish Henderson (1919–2002) went on to become a great folksong collector, working for the School of Scottish Studies at Edinburgh University. Between 1943 and 1947, spurred by a captured German officer's remark that 'the desert is our common enemy', he wrote *Elegies for the Dead in Cyrenaica* (1948) in which Sorley MacLean's 'Death Valley' is quoted. Both Eliotic and New Apocalyptic tremors are felt in the free-verse accounts of Henderson's 'dead land . . . insatiate/ and necrophilous', though the poems are often rescued by precise observation, whether of 'tent-pegs driven into cracks of limestone' or the 'raucous apocalypse' of Highland bagpipes in the desert.[8] Later Henderson translated Antonio Gramsci's prison letters and composed popular folksongs celebrating political radicalism. From the 1950s onwards, along with Peggy Seager and Ewan MacColl (author of the Spanish Civil War ballad-opera *Johnny Noble* (1946)), Henderson was a prominent figure in the recording of Scottish folk music and the 'folk revival'. Genial and learned, he remained a well-known Edinburgh character throughout the twentieth century, long after the New Apocalyptic tide had ebbed.

Descended from the fierily apocalyptic prose of his novelist father, J. MacDougall Hay, and indebted to that love of storminess in some Gaelic verse, George Campbell Hay's 'Bisearta' suggests in its account of the bombing of the Tunisian town of Bizerta one way in which the

New Apocalypse may have impacted on Gaelic. The poem's talk of 'ochanaich no caoineadh' (weeping and lamentation) and of 'an t-Olc 'na chridhe' (Evil as a pulse) suggests such a possibility. Yet its metre comes from a fifteenth-century Italian religious poem by Savonarola, and its rhythms are described by Sorley MacLean as 'wistful, questioning'.[9] George Campbell Hay (Deòrsa Mac Iain Deòrsa, 1915–84) wrote poetry in Gaelic, English and Scots, as well as translating from other tongues. His Gaelic poems often have a highly elaborate musicality, which some have found overwound. Born in Elderslie, Renfrewshire, Hay grew up in Tarbert, Argyll, where he learned Gaelic as his second language. Then, like several mid-century Scottish poets, he was schooled at what he called 'that piece of Forever England, Fettes College' in Edinburgh, and at Oxford University where he befriended Douglas Young and studied Classics.[10] Hay returned to Edinburgh an active Scottish nationalist. Early in World War II he went to ground in Argyll, and was jailed. Like Young, he objected to fighting in the British army, though he did later serve in North Africa. Becoming a cornerstone in the Gaelic renaissance, he published widely and revived poetic metres more complex than any currently in use. His life in Scotland was dogged by illness, but the post-humous publication of his *Collected Poems and Songs* (2000) made manifest a remarkably protean, if sometimes poetically antiquarian, talent.

Other poems by Scots who fought in the Desert War confirm that those who avoided or freed themselves from New Apocalyptic tonalities wrote best. Much later, Edwin Morgan, some of whose earliest work exhibits a New Apocalyptic strain, writes movingly in *The New Divan* (1977) of how, serving in the Royal Army Medical Corps in North Africa, he 'dreaded stretcher-bearing' lest his fingers 'slip on the two sweat-soaked handles'.[11] Morgan, Hay and others found that time spent in the desert led to a sympathetic fascination with the local people, and with Arabic poetry. Being in North Africa could also clarify thoughts of home. In wartime Cairo G. S. Fraser is at his most impressive writing in *Home Town Elegy* (1944) about springtime Aberdeen's

> Glitter of mica at the windy corners,
> Tar in the nostrils, under blue lamps budding
> Like bubbles of glass the blue buds of a tree . . .[12]

Fraser's opening words provide the title for *Glitter of Mica* (1963) by Jessie Kesson (1916–1994), a north-eastern novelist whose work was encouraged by Nan Shepherd, and whose later tales often draw on memories of the 1920s, 1930s and 1940s. In crystalline prose tanged with snatches of verse Kesson's novellas present memorable accounts of women's lives, not least in wartime. *Another Time, Another Place* (1983) traces the mutual attraction between a Scottish farm girl and an Italian prisoner of war. Its conclusion is less affirmative than that of Eric Linklater's *Private Angelo*, though its female protagonist moves from thinking of herself as 'Wifie, the title that had made her feel old before her time' to learning the true meaning of '*con amore*'.[13]

Kesson's sharply focused novel may be set beside Mitchison's wartime diaries, *Among You Taking Notes* (1985), as part of the documenting of women's and men's experience on a Home Front where the Scots mixed with displaced people of various nationalities. Teaching English to Polish troops quartered in eastern Scotland during World War II, the New Zealand-born professor's son Sydney Goodsir Smith (1915–75), a committed Scottish nationalist who had studied at Edinburgh and Oxford, wrote in a Scots language he had adopted and idiosyncratically adapted. Rhyming 'awa' with the rhotacistic Scots word 'war' in a way that does not sound idiomatically Scottish, 'The War in Fife' from Smith's 'Armageddon in Albyn' complains of how

The foreign war tuims mony a bed	*empties*
But yet seems faur awa –	
Twa hunner years o Union's bled	
The veins mair white nor ony war.[14]	*than any*

While none went as far as the absolutist MacDiarmid who longed for the all-out blitzing of London, Smith, Sorley MacLean and others were among a number of Scottish poets who supported the war against Fascism, but were determined that the issue of Scottish autonomy should not be ignored. In the years after 1945 there would be no immediate dramatic breakthrough for Scottish nationalist politicians. It would be the end of the twentieth century before a Parliament was re-established in Edinburgh. However, postwar development of the welfare state, government grants which encouraged students to study at a rapidly increasing number of universities, and a sometimes patrician cultural impetus supplied by the development of the Edinburgh International Festival, the Scottish Arts Council and other bodies improved social and artistic opportunities in Scotland for several decades. Upward social mobility increased and greater numbers of working-class children born just before, during and after the war were able to take advantage of better health and educational opportunities. Writing would give these new generations different ways of articulating the life of working-class communities.

In World War II, though, as Clydebank and Greenock were blitzed, as conflict raged in Europe, North Africa and the Far East, the prospect of any postwar civilization looked uncertain. For some people, such as Edinburgh's Eric Lomax whose powerful memoir *The Railway Man* (1995) records the sufferings of prisoners of war constructing the Burma–Siam railway, wartime experiences would define their whole lives, and take decades to work through. Much of the best Scottish writing about the war – whether by Muriel Spark or Jessie Kesson, Edwin Morgan or Eric Lomax – appeared long after the conflict ended. The simple fact that many Scottish writers, male and female, young and old, survived the war meant that the literary and cultural energies of the 1920s and 1930s were not entirely dissipated.

A feeling of ongoing Scottish Renaissance was quickened by a 1946 anthology, *Modern Scottish Poetry*, edited by the poet and energetic cultural activist Maurice Lindsay (b. 1918). Alongside MacDiarmid and Muir, Lindsay included younger writers such as Norman MacCaig and Goodsir Smith. Smith's admirers champion his elegies and his celebrations of lovers from Orpheus and Dido to Burns and Smith himself in *Under the Eildon Tree* (1948). For some readers an over-bookish ear for language and rhythm can make Smith's poems seem forced – better in theory than in practice – but he triumphs in the souped-up Rabelaisianism of 'The Grace of God and the Meth-Drinker'. That poem's rhythms reach a literally staggering conclusion as the speaker, stunned by the meths drinker with his toothless gums and drooling mouth, exclaims that there

> But for the 'bunesaid unsocht grace, unprayed-for,   *aforesaid*
> Undeserved
>   Gangs,
>   Unregenerate,
>   Me.[15]

In poetry and person, Smith was part of an overwhelmingly male homosocial Edinburgh literary pub culture of the 1950s, confirming the

MacDiarmidian equation that poet equals drunk man. A generation later, Alasdair Gray has the narrator of his novel *1982, Janine*, recall a typical 1950s gathering 'in a basement in Hanover Street', featuring, in order, MacDiarmid and his cronies MacCaig and Goodsir Smith:

The bar was crowded except where three men stood in a small open space created by the attention of the other customers. One had a sombre pouchy face and upstanding hair which seemed too like thistledown to be natural, one looked like a tall sarcastic lizard, one like a small shy bear. 'Our three best since Burns,' a bystander informed me, 'barring Sorley, of course.'[16]

Absent from this scene, but very much a poet of modern Edinburgh life, is Robert Garioch. More idiosyncratic, less demonstrative than Goodsir Smith, Garioch, in his Scots contribution to the 1938 *Albannach* anthology, celebrates, as Goodsir Smith likes to do, 'the lusts o the flesh', but does so in a way that stresses what happens 'quietlenwise' (quietly).[17] While much of Garioch's work has a sly quality to it, his range is wider than is sometimes admitted. Born and educated in Edinburgh, Robert Garioch Sutherland (1909–81) worked for a long time as a school-teacher but served in North Africa during World War II; with fellow soldier Sorley MacLean he had shared a first, sixpenny book of verse, *17 Poems for 6d*. Published in an era of paper rationing, this was the first-ever joint collection by a Gaelic and a Scots poet. Its appearance in 1940, the same year as MacDiarmid's *Golden Treasury of Scottish Poetry*, indicates a growing wish to celebrate the nation's plural literary traditions. Captured during the war, Garioch wrote about his experience of several 'lousy' prison camps in *Two Men and a Blanket* (1975). 'The Wire', his balladic re-imagining of this experience, is one of the finest Scottish poems to emerge from the war.

Heich in their sentry-posts, the guairds	*high*
wha daurna sleep, on pain of daith,	*dare not*
watch throu the graticules of guns,	*sights*
cruel and persecuted, baith.	
This endless muir is thrang wi folk	*thronged*
that hirple aye aa airts at aince	*limp; everywhere*
wi neither purport nor content	*reason*
nor rest, in fidgan impotence.[18]	*fidgety*

After the war, Garioch became best known as a droll commentator on Scottish, particularly Edinburgh, mores. Repeatedly and effectively he used the sonnet form with unsonnet-like tonalities. His sonnet 'Elegy' for 'heidmaisters' of his youth concludes with the lacerating one-liner, 'Weill, gin [if] they arena deid, it's time they were.'[19] This poet–dominie made Scots versions of Latin plays by George Buchanan. Garioch's later translations of the Roman poet Giuseppe Belli are another part of an Italian thread discernible in modern Scottish literature from *Private Angelo* and Henderson's Gramsci to novels by Muriel Spark, and translations by Edwin Morgan, Douglas Dunn and other poets.

If it was an era when Scots fought in global wars, the twentieth century was also a great age of Scottish literary translation. MacDiarmid translated and encouraged internationalism in Scottish letters. So did the Muirs. Postwar verse translations ranged from Alexander Gray's Danish ballads to Edwin Morgan's dazzling variety of versions made from Russian, Old English, Hungarian, German, French, Italian, Latin, Spanish and other languages. Whatever other results they had, the upheavals of Communism and the Second World War quickened a sense among Scottish writers that contact with other literatures was an antidote to Kailyard stereotyping. The impulse to translate may have been strongest among poets and playwrights. In French drama alone, for instance, the second half of the century saw Scots versions of Molière from Robert Kemp's 1948 *Let Wives Tak Tent* to Liz Lochhead's 1985 *Tartuffe* and beyond; at Glasgow's Citizens' Theatre Robert David Mac-Donald staged the work of Proust; Edwin Morgan translated Rostand's *Cyrano*; Douglas Dunn Englished Racine; Bill Findlay and the Scots-Canadian Martin Bowman made Scots versions of plays by Michel Tremblay from Quebec. The finest work of poet Tom Scott (1918–95) is probably his Scots translations of *Seevin Poems o Maister Francis Villon* (1953). A markedly international consciousness would be developed in the postwar period by such very different authors as Alastair Reid and Muriel Spark, who spent much of their lives abroad and drew on their foreign experiences, and by incomers like the Irish-born, English-educated anthologist and historian of translation Peter France, whose anthology *European Poetry in Scotland* (1989), co-edited with Duncan Glen, gives a taste of many areas of vigorous activity.

Although sometimes they seemed to ignore home-grown literary talent, the postwar development of such institutions as the Edinburgh

International Festival (mocked by Robert Garioch), the Glasgow Citizens' Theatre and other cultural organizations encouraged internationalism. The Scottish Arts Council has furthered this work, though sometimes awkwardly its remit encourages it to focus on Scotland, with such things as foreign tours by Scottish writers being controlled by the British Council headquartered in London. It might be hard to find Scottish poets at the very start of the twentieth century reacting directly to contemporary European painting, but there are several references to de Chirico, for instance, in Scottish poetry of the 1940s. Whether in the work of Sorley MacLean, writing of Tobruk and Vietnam in Gaelic, or Norman MacCaig whose Scotocentric English-language poems nonetheless take in Moscow, Italy and New York, or the assertively internationalist Edwin Morgan who, endorsed by MacDiarmid, translated Mayakovsky from Russian into enthusiastic Scots, Scottish writing developed in tandem a strong nationalist impulse and a corresponding cosmopolitanism.

Not that all the cosmopolitans were nationalists. Translating from Greek, Latin, Czech, French and German, Norman Cameron (1905–53) wrote few poems, but some are near perfect. Born in Edinburgh, he was taught at Fettes College by Sutherland-born Walter Sellar, a minor poet best known for co-authoring the irreverent romp through English history, *1066 and All That* (1930). After studying Classics at Oriel College, Oxford, Cameron globetrotted, spending time in Nigeria, Mallorca (where he lived with Robert Graves and Laura Riding in the 1930s), then in North Africa during World War II. Later employment as a London advertising copywriter may have heightened his sense of the epigrammatic. Surely concision works for good in the four lines of one of his finest poems,

> Forgive me, Sire, for cheating your intent,
> That I, who should command a regiment,
> Do amble amiably here, O God,
> One of the neat ones in your awkward squad.[20]

Another of the 'neat ones' was Cameron's friend John Innes Macintosh Stewart (1906–94) who had gone from Edinburgh Academy to study at Oriel College, and who eventually taught at Christ Church, Oxford. As 'Michael Innes' he published from 1937 onwards many successful, if patchy, detective stories featuring the English Inspector

Appleby. As J. I. M. Stewart he authored literary criticism as well as fiction that included five novels about Duncan Pattullo, a Scot who goes to Oxford as 'a kind of half-foreigner'.[21] Published in the 1970s, though featuring a generation that came of age during World War II, these novels are interesting for their momentary alertness to issues of Anglo-Scottish cultural difference. A Scot writing at the educational heart of the English establishment, Stewart gives as redolent an account of his Oxford milieu as his very different contemporaries Fionn MacColla and Ena Lamont Stewart do of theirs. Stewart's fellow Oxonian, the London West End playwright William Douglas Home (1912–92), held pro-appeasement views, was court-martialled in World War II, and did time in Wormwood Scrubs. Born in Edinburgh, brother of Scotland's only twentieth-century Tory Prime Minister, Home wrote successful dramas over six decades from *Great Possessions* (1937) and his prison play *The New Barabbas* (1947) through his class comedy *The Chiltern Hundreds* (1947) to *The Secretary Bird* (1967) and later works. At times execrated by the Angry Young Men of 1950s London, Home, like Stewart, represents an upper-middle- and upper-class strand of Scottish culture. Several writers in this strand were as attracted by Oxford and London society as John Buchan had been half a century earlier. Though downplayed by commentators, this line of writers (whose twenty-first-century representatives might include William Boyd and Candia McWilliam) deserves recognition and deeper investigation. Economic and employment prospects lured Scots south, but there were other reasons too. Like the Carswells and Willa Muir before them, women of all classes and some middle- and upper-class men may have found London liberating. A number reacted against Scotland's residual Calvinism and philistinism, not to mention its male-dominated, pub-centred, left-wing nationalist intellectual culture. With the partial exception of Eric Linklater's work, fiction written in Scotland in the years after World War II seldom dealt successfully with middle- or upper-class life.

Popular writers working north of the Border could still find a ready international market for historical material or village fictions, though even the latter began to take on a more cosmopolitan feel. 'Jane Duncan' (Elizabeth Jane Cameron, 1910–76) wrote novels of Jamaica as well as Highland tales, and dealt with racism, marital failure and alcoholism in addition to friendship and nostalgia. The heartily indefatigable Nigel Tranter (1909–2000) campaigned for a Scottish Parliament, and wrote scores of novels with such durable heroes as Wallace and Bruce, as well as works on Scottish architectural history; Orcadian Robert Kemp (1908–67), who worked for the BBC as a radio producer, made a modern version of Sir David Lyndsay's *Satyre of the Thrie Estaitis* which was a hit at the 1948 Edinburgh Festival. Kemp also wrote a number of historical plays, including one about Burns, *The Other Dear Charmer* (1951). In a period when little Scottish literature or history was part of the school curriculum, and when Scots or Gaelic was still frowned on in many classrooms, imaginative writing played its traditional, substantial part in keeping national narratives familiar. Scottish history and folklore were also important to the dramatist Alexander Reid (1914–82) who wrote plays in Scots such as the ballad-derived *The Lass wi' the Muckle Mou*, performed at Glasgow's Citizens' Theatre in 1950.

These novelists and dramatists could make a living off their writing and other related work. Poets in Scotland generally required 'day jobs'. Here substantial postwar investment in schools and universities provided opportunities for writers, though not yet as teachers of creative writing. Education was the employment option favoured by poets of the generation of MacLean, Garioch and MacCaig. Younger contemporaries including the bilingual Gaelic–English writer Iain Crichton Smith and the Gaelic poet–professors Derick Thomson and Donald MacAulay also taught. Before the war, poets like MacDiarmid, William Jeffrey and the Scots poet–playwright A. D. Mackie (1904–85) had lived as newspapermen; by the 1950s, other options were open. In 1959 Norman MacCaig brought together twenty-seven contemporary Scottish poets in English, Scots and Gaelic for his Burns Bicentenary anthology, *Honour'd Shade*. All these poets are male. At least eight either worked or had worked as schoolteachers and a further nine held university appointments. In an era when there was often much less managerial form-filling, and when university arts academics were under no great pressure to publish scholarly research, the long holidays that went with teaching were conducive to the production of poetry. MacCaig spent decades as a primary school teacher in Edinburgh before in 1967 at Edinburgh University he became the Scottish Arts Council's first university writer in residence. Later, from 1970 until 1978, he was Lecturer, then Reader in Poetry at the new University of Stirling.

Throughout the 1950s the dominie was still a respected figure in Scottish society. In ensuing decades this position altered. The change is signalled in the career and work of Glasgow's schoolteacher–novelist George Friel (1910–75). From the 1950s onwards he wrote with an insider's knowledge of working-class life. His most memorable, if sometimes awkward and reactionary, novel is the bleak *Mr Alfred M. A.* (1972). This chronicles the downfall of an alcohol-dependent, paedophile teacher. Bitter about proliferating vandalism and gang warfare in a tough urban area, and horrified by disregard for high culture, Mr Alfred is soured by official adherence to a failing idea of comprehensive education built around 'the child-dominated classroom'. Like the book's author who parades odd words like 'kyphosis' and 'strabismic', and seems dismissive of 'creative writing', Mr Alfred is among other things a failed poet.[22]

Working as a rural headmaster, Sorley MacLean used to complain that as soon as he had begun to clear his mind of his schoolwork and felt ready to turn to poetry, it was time to go back to school. For others, though, the combination of poetry and education was less oppressive. Charismatic to adults and children alike, the primary teacher and academic Norman MacCaig (1910–96) changed from being the obscure, Surrealist-influenced 'McCaig' of his never reprinted first two books to the much-loved, wittily accessible 'MacCaig' of *Riding Lights* (1955) and over a dozen subsequent collections. Yet common to both McCaig and MacCaig are a concern with elusive self-image, self-perception, perception of the world, and fluidity of metaphorical language. 'Summer Farm' from *Riding Lights* has MacCaig's signature wit in the lines 'A hen stares at nothing with one eye,/ Then picks it up.' This same poem includes an apparently dreamy poet lying in the grass. It ends with an image that seems self-revelatory, but is more about sly multiplicity, the final word emerging only as an elusive item of vocabulary rather than as a concrete, clearly discernible entity:

> Self under self, a pile of selves I stand
> Threaded on time, and with metaphysic hand
> Lift the farm like a lid and see
> Farm within farm, and in the centre, me.[23]

The slyness that made MacCaig hard to interview and led to his complex private life, contributes to the sense here of a pronounced but playfully elusive personality. What makes him Scotland's finest twentieth-century writer of short poems in English is a continuing

nimbleness and verbal precision, a pinpoint, unafraid accuracy which
leads to unusual but just combinations of language: male pigeons are
'wobbling gyroscopes of lust'; a basking shark is a 'roomsized monster
with a matchbox brain'.[24] MacCaig is a miniaturist, but one often
fascinated by large issues. Comparing the expanse that light from a
distant star traverses to reach the human eye with the distance it then
travels between eye and brain, he asks in 'Instrument and Agent', 'And
which is star – what's come a million/ Miles or gone those inches
farther?'[25] He likes selves and perceptions that are simultaneously precise
and unstable. Son of a Lowland chemist and a bilingual (Gaelic/English)
mother from Scalpay in the Outer Hebrides, MacCaig lived in Edinburgh
but summered in the West Highlands near Lochinver. 'Aunt Julia', a
1960s poem about his 'flouncing' Scalpay aunt who 'wore men's boots/
when she wore any' is one of many which record his loving fascination
with Gaelic culture, and his sense of being cut off from the Gaelic
language: an increasingly common sensation for Scottish poets.[26] Mac-
Caig writes very well about his native Edinburgh, but many of his poems
spring from his affection for the rural Gaidhealtachd. 'Praise of a Collie'
does so clearly, and celebrates a certain elusiveness:

> Once, gathering sheep on a showery day,
> I remarked how dry she was. Pollóchan said, 'Ah,
> It would take a very accurate drop to hit Lassie.'[27]

It is hard to stop quoting MacCaig, a testament to his genius with
plain words in an era when people often thought of poetry as hard to
understand. He was a mischievous, hugely popular reader of his work.
Seamus Heaney, one of the poets he influenced, rightly locates in it an
appealing 'mixture of strictness and susceptibility'.[28]

Disliking authority, MacCaig was court-martialled during World War
II. He went on to become that ultimate 1950s authority figure, a classroom teacher. An atheist who wrote of and with grace, he was a brilliant
conversationalist. His university training in 'Classical writing [which]
. . . keeps to the fact' was important to him, as was his love of pibroch
and fiddle-tunes; MacCaig's poems are exquisitely bowed.[29] He was a
close friend of MacDiarmid and of Sorley MacLean whom he liked
teasing. When asked if he enjoyed a filial relationship with MacDiarmid,
a man two decades his senior, MacCaig replied, 'Yes, in a way he was
my son.'[30] I remember sitting beside MacCaig when his almost exact

contemporary MacLean was reading to a live audience; MacCaig (who was due to read next) muttered and sat looking ostentatiously at his watch while MacLean at the microphone recounted ever-lengthening Gaelic genealogies. Each poet twinkled at the other. Such a sort of teasing pernickitiness enhances much of MacCaig's poetry. A lover of Bach and Haydn, he favoured short, wittily lyrical poems. His style, though, changed twice – in his forties when he sloughed off his New Apocalyptic skin, then again in his fifties when he moved away from rhyming forms towards free verse.

Sometimes there are disturbing undertones to MacCaig's teasing. In his eighties he spoke to me about his commitment as a nationalist voter, but in his verse he is suspicious of politics. A poem from the early 1970s, 'Patriot', declares that

> My only country
> is six feet high
> and whether I love it or not
> I'll die
> for its independence.[31]

MacCaig liked independence, and hated totalitarian authority. Relishing Eastern European poetry, he read Zbigniew Herbert and Miroslav Holub as well as the lusher American Wallace Stevens. But 'Patriot' can also be heard as selfish, or at least as highly self-aware. The poet who tried to suppress his own first books and who liked to display his rapier wit to acolytes was clearly conscious not just of his imagery but of his image.

At the same time, MacCaig was highly sociable, with a close circle of Highland friends, especially Angus MacLeod with whom he loved to fish and talk. There is something of the finesse – the just-rightness – of the fly fisherman about this poet's work. In Edinburgh, after the deaths of cronies like MacDiarmid and Goodsir Smith, he and his wife Isabel, a lexicographer, played host at their Leamington Terrace flat to groups of younger writers such as the poet–novelists Ron Butlin, Andrew Greig and Alan Spence; MacCaig had a fund of stories about Scottish authors, from the most distinguished to those whom he called in conversation 'thirteenth-rate'. His sense of mischief and conviviality recalled a fraternal Edinburgh literary life that harks back to the era of Fergusson and Burns. Nowadays several social changes – not least in attitudes towards gender roles, childcare and public smoking – have led to a shift away from that lively if sometimes exclusive sense of literary brotherhood so strong in Rose Street pubs, in The Abbotsford or Milne's Bar, or at the MacCaigs' flat.

In 1950s Edinburgh the Orcadian poet and fiction writer George Mackay Brown (1921–96) sat shyly watching 'that famous huddle' of MacCaig, Goodsir Smith and others at the smoky counter of The Abbotsford: 'I drank my beer but dared not go near them.'[32] Though later invited to join their company, Mackay Brown was not really part of the Edinburgh literary scene. He was very much a voice of Orkney. He had studied as a mature student at Edwin Muir's Newbattle Abbey before progressing to Edinburgh University, but all the rest of his life was spent in Stromness. Muir praises the 'grace' of Brown's first, Orkney Press collection of poems, *The Storm* (1954), and Brown much later edited a selection of Muir's prose. The two writers share interests in 'Orkney, past and present', in Christianity (Brown became a Catholic convert), in ecology and in the permeability of time.[33] As Brown's work develops he strives for and achieves a honed if sometimes mannered style. Like Eric Linklater before him, he read and tried to imitate Norse sagas. He was also attracted to the historical and regional fiction of Neil Gunn. At its best the music of Mackay Brown's poetry is resonantly convincing. Kathleen Jamie argues that 'If you care to take a pencil and map through any Brown poem the placing of vowel and consonant sounds, the half-rhymes and occasional full rhymes, what is revealed is a dense web wherein no sound is left alone and unsupported, unless for good reason.' Jamie contends that 'Brown's music enacts the ecology it describes, it's the soundscape of an interconnected, secure community.'[34]

Brown's short stories in books like *A Calendar of Love* (1969) and *An Orkney Tapestry* (1969) are intimately suffused by the seasons, weather and people of his islands. The ecological theme so strong in mid-twentieth-century Scottish prose had been maintained by the popular nature writer and troubled autobiographer Gavin Maxwell (1914–69), who came from an aristocratic family of amateur and professional natural historians and whose *Ring of Bright Water* (1960), an account of living with otters opposite Skye, became a beguiling film. Today, to visit Maxwell's last home on the tiny island of Eilean Bàn (now overshadowed by the concrete span of the Skye Bridge) or to stand outside Brown's house just off the spindly main street in Stromness on Orkney is to confront questions about the relationship between land, small communities and modernity. These questions pervade the writings of both Maxwell and Muir. Differently expressed, a deep concern with ecological balance is present in Maxwell's work and in George Mackay Brown's novel *Greenvoe* (1972). Greenvoe's island community, with its horse-cult representing ancient wisdom, is menaced by the industrial technology of the Black Star project. Though the book is not directly about the discovery of North Sea oil, it is hard to separate from a reading of *Greenvoe* the Scottish environmental issues raised by a rapidly developing late twentieth-century petrochemical industry. The environmentalist resonances of *Greenvoe* have strengthened and widened since the decade in which it was written.

As part of his Orkney stories, Brown likes to write of meetings between representatives of different cultural and racial groups, intercutting antiquity with modernity. He does this in his novel of World War II sacrifice and medieval Orcadian martyrdom, *Magnus* (1973). In his prose and verse Brown aims for a kind of heraldic, stylized plainness enlivened by accurate, richly musical phrasing: the speaker in his poem 'Kirkyard' comes 'to sip the finished/ Fragrance of men'; in 'Taxman' short declarative sentences chronicling the celebration of a successful harvest end with the more menacing, emblematic statement, 'Then between stubble and heather/ A horseman rode.'[35] If Brown's work can seem repetitive, that is also an index of its fidelity to Orkney and its history. Characteristically, 'For the islands I sing' is the first line of the first poem in his first book, and also the title of his posthumous autobiography published over forty years later. Towards the end of a life in which he struggled at times with tuberculosis, depression and alcohol dependence, Brown enjoyed a late flowering in the novels *Beside the Ocean of Time* (1994), which melds short stories into a traditional account of Orkney, and the valedictory *Vinland* (1992). Set in politically-riven Norse Orkney, *Vinland* chronicles from youth to withdrawn old age the life of a man who once participated in the Norse 'discovery' of North America.

Mackay Brown was young enough to avoid being much influenced by the Scottish New Apocalyptics, though his early poems contain overeffortful phrases such as 'the praying sea' or 'Swung me in fluent valleys' which reek more of Dylan Thomas than of the G. M. Hopkins whose work Brown studied as an Edinburgh postgraduate.[36] Thomas's vocabulary and rhythms are manifestly present in the work of several Scottish poets of the period, most notably W. S. Graham (1918–86). Graham's books of the 1940s and even 1950s, beginning with *Cage without Grievance* (1942), are thumb-printed with the Welsh poet's surging obscurity. Like Mackay Brown, Sydney Graham, born and brought up in shipbuilding Greenock, writes a lot about the sea. Both poets studied at Newbattle Abbey, then lived much of their lives in comparative remoteness. Published by T. S. Eliot at Faber, Graham spent a year (1947–8) lecturing at New York University and passed (stumbled might be a better word) through the bohemian London of Fitzrovia, but largely avoided the Edinburgh of Milne's Bar. He spent most of his adult years with his Scottish wife Nessie Dunsmuir in Madron, Cornwall, enjoying links with the artists of nearby St Ives. Determined, spirited and difficult, he wrote letters (many now collected) which are a testament to the art of poetry. Like Norman MacCaig, he also sloughed off the style of his first books. This process is underway in *The Nightfishing* (1955), which uses trawling dark seas as a trope for poetic creation, but that long poem can still be tortuously difficult and Dylanish.

Throughout his work Graham writes of the problematic nature of communication. He alerts readers to the structure of a poem's making or discovery, how 'the song sleeps to be wakened'. Graham does this best once his poetry evolves a clearer diction, doing what it urges the reader to do, 'Listen. Put on morning.'[37] The manifest unusualness of Graham's language and his continuing constructional sense of verse are fused with a lyric talent. This means he can ask his structuralist question, 'What is the language using us for?' but also give an urgent sense of how each poem, each human speaker, wants 'to be telling/ / Each other alive about each other/ Alive.'[38] In *Malcolm Mooney's Land* (1970) it is not the sea but a frozen icescape which has to be traversed as part of the struggle to communicate, to find voice. Drawing on the journals of the heroic polar explorer Fridtjof Nansen, Graham produces a work which, like passages of Eliot's *Four Quartets*, presents language cracking and breaking as it tries to operate on 'the edge of earshot'.[39] Graham is sometimes regarded as a poet's poet, but his concern is with the universal urgency of human communication. Alongside more philosophical work, a series of moving late poems in *Implements in their Places* (1977) present in obviously autobiographical terms and with characteristically quirky syntax his sense of intimacy with and estrangement from the Greenock geography of his youth,

> And I am here with my mammy's
> Bramble jam scones in my pocket.
> The firth is miles and I have come
> Back to find Loch Thom maybe
> In this light does not recognize me.[40]

As a young man Graham befriended Edwin Morgan (b. 1920), whose work he encouraged. The two men shared enthusiasms for Dylan Thomas, Clydeside, and a sense of poems as constructed, almost ship-built. They also admired Ezra Pound's translation of the Old English poem *The Seafarer*. In 1936 Morgan's first published poem was a 'Song of the Flood'; he then went on to make his own version of *The Seafarer* and other Old English poems, most notably *Beowulf* (1952). 'Lands end, seas are unloosed' begins *The Cape of Good Hope* (1955).[41] Voyages fascinate Morgan – not just early embarcations but also later space odysseys in *From Glasgow to Saturn* (1973) and after. In 1952 financial problems at his publisher prevented the launch of what would have been his first collection, *Dies Irae*, with its 'Mortal voyager in the far flood of the north/ When growling berg became his acre and burgh'. Such language from a 'throat choked hoarse in the raw haul of the waves' pronounces Morgan in debt to Pound's *Seafarer* and to medieval poetry, but also shows him a poetic kinsman of W. S. Graham.[42]

A sometimes bookish but engaging post-Poundian medievalism is present in Morgan's *The Vision of Cathkin Braes*, which did find a publisher in 1952. However, it was not until 1968 with the Edinburgh University Press publication of *The Second Life* that Morgan, at the age of nearly fifty, published his first fully-assured collection. He had found not so much his voice as his voices. Opening with 'The Old Man and the Sea' and closing with 'many waters', *The Second Life* too is a book of voyages. Its contents range from a Whitmanesque elegy for Marilyn Monroe to poems in which Morgan takes on the identity of a computer working through arrangements of words, as in 'The Computer's First Christmas Card'. Such poems 'were simulated and not actual computer poems'. Morgan had been collecting information about 'Cybernetics' since 1949 and he wrote articles and gave talks on what relations there might be between artistic creativity and high-speed computing. But when it came to poetry itself, I started off with pencil, pen, or typewriter, and made the poems a bridge, as it were, between traditional methods of composition and adumbrations of a future where human brain-circuits might be challenged.[43]

Also including several poems tracing the grain of Glasgow urban life, and hoaching with liberated variety, *The Second Life*, this book of 1968, is the collection of Scottish poetry most redolent of the Sixties. Though its plenitude could not have been predicted, in retrospect it is evident that Morgan sought in his own work the range of voices 'from fantasy to ethics, from ethics to satire, and from satire to stately elegy and eulogy' which he had praised in his astute 1952 essay on 'Dunbar and the Language of Poetry'.[44] Translating from Old English, Italian, Russian and other languages in the 1950s and early 1960s encouraged such polyvocality, as did Morgan's insightful critical examinations of Mac-Diarmid. Morgan's work as a translator later extended to the theatre. His stylish version of *Cyrano de Bergerac* (1992) preceded his own less assured plays about the life of Christ, *A. D.* (2000), which grew from his characteristic hunger for 'state-of-the-universe plays and not merely state-of-the-nation ones'.[45]

Some of Morgan's most striking poems function as translations or decodings, searching for a 'Message Clear' concealed in another form of words.[46] His work has a restless, adventurous curiosity and formal dexterity that are immediately winning. The poems celebrate and embody metamorphic energy, mercurial vitality. Using English and an invented language, 'The First Men on Mercury' presents a dialogue between earthmen and Mercurians in which each, through verbal encounter, is translated in the direction of the other.[47] In Glasgow Morgan delights in the 'endless ... interchange' of the city, whether examining religious sectarianism in 'King Billy' ('Deplore what is to be deplored,/and then find out the rest') or hymning new motorway systems. His 1972 *Glasgow Sonnets* show a marked preference for technological innovators over 'Environmentalists, ecologists'.[48] Unlike many earlier and later Scottish writers, the 1970s Morgan, in common with Muriel Spark in her 1976 novel *The Takeover*, regarded ecology as faddish. For all his medievalism, Morgan succeeds John Davidson and Hugh MacDiarmid as a poet of modern science as well as *scientia* – knowledge.

His substantial 2006 essay on this topic sums up a lifelong preoccupation, but Morgan is also attracted to the rebelliously new.[49] A very early poem speaks of a wish 'to change/ the unchangeable', and decades later Morgan declares in 1974 that 'CHANGE RULES is the supreme graffito.'[50] Yet in a 2004 poem his protagonist 'Old Gorbals' indignantly sprays on a wall the words 'DONT FORGET'.[51] Where George Friel's schoolteacher Mr Alfred sees Glasgow graffiti as the ruination of culture, Morgan, the innovator who spent much of his long-memoried life teaching in the Department of English Literature at Glasgow University, accepts it as grist to his mill.

If Morgan is very conscious of earlier literatures and histories, he is also, throughout the Cold War period, attracted not just to Soviet and Eastern European socialist poets like Hungary's Attila József but also to the apparent wildness of the American Beats. Receptiveness to change and to kinds of experimentation – from Beatles songs to concrete poetry – makes Morgan a very different poet from Mackay Brown or MacCaig. Though he lacks MacCaig's remarkable sense of the precisely finessed mot juste, he is a much more ambitiously adventurous poet whose openness made him a generous source of encouragement to younger writers. The elderly MacDiarmid became something of an aesthetic reactionary, with no time for Beat poetry or concrete poetry. Mac-Diarmid loathed the work of Morgan's one-time student, the drug-fuelled Alexander Trocchi (1925–84), an admirer of Camus, whose Paris-based career produced such scandalous Scottish novels as the sexually explicit *Young Adam* (1954). Morgan, though, tended to ally himself with such outrageous Scottish innovators.

Although his homosexuality was not publicly declared until 1988, in his poetry Morgan shows a clear interest in gay assignations. He dedicated his finest collection to a lorry driver, and his *Poems of Thirty Years* to his lover John Scott. The loved one in his erotic lyrics has a 'breast' rather than 'breasts', while other poems feature gay rape and a meeting in a public toilet; generations of Scottish schoolteachers were untroubled by this in the classroom, though Morgan's later gay poems have fared less well there.[52] His coming out was part of a more open sexual climate slowly developing in later twentieth-century Scotland. It was followed by the account of his own forty-three-year 'homosexual marriage' written by the distinguished Edinburgh-born short-story writer and anthologist Fred Urquhart (1912–95), and Morgan along with other openly gay or lesbian writers such as Christopher Whyte, Carol Ann Duffy, Jackie Kay, Ali Smith and David Kinloch, has played a significant part in finding new ways of 'gendering the nation'.[53]

Morgan's enthusiastic drive 'to change/ the unchangeable' may be linked to his sexuality, but his sexual orientation should not be seen as the defining feature of his work, any more than sexuality defines the verse of Dunbar or Burns. Like those earlier poets whose protean gifts he so admires, Morgan shows a freeing humour in his verse, whether sounding 'The Loch Ness Monster's Song' ('Sssnnnwhuffffll?') or inventing the speech of an anaesthetized Egyptian mummy.[54] Late in life and at the instigation of the Scottish Poetry Library, Morgan was selected by the devolved government at Holyrood as Scotland's National Poet; he wrote a poem, 'Open the Doors', for the inauguration of the new Parliament building at Holyrood. At the same time, however, he declared his support for 'an independent Scottish republic built on the principles of liberty, equality, diversity and solidarity'.[55]

A celebrant of virtuosity and a resolute yet accessible virtuoso, Morgan reveals his poetic self in one of his best poems, about the juggler 'Cinquevalli':

> Cinquevalli is practising.
> He sits in his dressing-room talking to some friends,
> at the same time writing a letter with one hand
> and with the other juggling four balls.
> His friends think of demons, but
> 'You could all do this,' he says,
> sealing the letter with a billiard ball.[56]

Morgan's own love of juggling, shape-shifting and change, as well as his sense of fun, were important aspects of his participation in the international concrete poetry movement during the 1960s. He and Ian Hamilton Finlay were active from very early on in this worldwide avant-garde grouping. Though verse whose physical layout is part of its meaning has a history that extends over two millennia, modern concrete poetry was given its impetus in the 1950s by the Brazilian brothers Haroldo and Augusto de Campos and by the Swiss Eugen Gomringer whose Eugen Gomringer Press in Frauenfeld published Morgan's *Starryveldt* in 1965.

In Britain *Starryveldt* was distributed by the small Wild Hawthorn

Press, founded in 1961 by Jessie McGuffie and Ian Hamilton Finlay. Born in Nassau but brought up in Glasgow and Orkney where, after service in World War II, he worked as a shepherd, Finlay (1925–2006) became friendly with George Mackay Brown. Brown thought Finlay's 1950s short stories 'beautiful' and shared his early 'enthusiasm for the literature of the north, particularly Scandinavia'.[57] Still, as early as 1948 Finlay rejected 'Northern Romanticism' for what he then termed 'East Coast Classicism'.[58] In the *Glasgow Herald* newspaper and in his 1958 book *The Sea-Bed and Other Stories* Finlay published finely observed small-scale stories: 'His toes made polite, thoughtful movements,' he writes of a boy on a beach, while fishing boats are likened to circus ponies performing tricks.[59] A similarly individual quirkiness using diction that ranges from Orkney dialect to children's rhymes is evident in the *faux naif* small formal verses of *The Dancers Inherit the Party* (1960). That book's poems owe something to the Robert Louis Stevenson of *A Child's Garden of Verses* and *Moral Emblems*. Finlay moved further in the direction of emblems with his 1961 *Glasgow Beasts, an a Burd* where small animal woodcuts accompany phonetically presented Glaswegian poems that in some ways anticipate the work of Tom Leonard: 'aa sayed ah wis a GREAT fox/ aw nae kiddin'.[60] Finlay's next step was to fuse emblem and words in the form of concrete poems. These draw on images from his earlier work – fishing boats, the sea, circus performance – but their designs are more playfully risk-taking. In touch with like-minded experimental poets in America, continental Europe and Scotland, Finlay began to produce small-press booklets of his poems and to publish them in his magazine *Poor. Old. Tired. Horse.*, which ran from 1962 until 1968. Uniting visual art, poetry and conceptual art, over the following decades Finlay combined clarity with arresting angles of vision to produce one-word poems and, usually working with collaborators, sculptures, pictures and installations. The most famous of these is his internationally important garden at 'Little Sparta' (formerly Stonypath) in the Southern Uplands of Scotland.

Much of Finlay's work highlights links between culture and authoritarianism. Often it focuses on the military power which accompanies and is an unacknowledged part of civilizations. So his 'garden temple' at Little Sparta is inscribed 'TO APOLLO HIS MVSIC HIS MISSILES HIS MVSES', and is situated not far from a 1972 bird table in the shape of an aircraft carrier from whose flight-deck sparrows take off and

land.[61] Finlay's work with French Revolutionary and with Nazi iconography led to his being accused of Fascism, but it is truer to say that
(like MacDiarmid, whose work he knew well) he is fascinated with
authority, rebellion, and areas where extremes converge. Many of
Finlay's works are made by 'collaborators' who 'executed' his ideas,
giving them three-dimensional form. In his Arcadia Finlay sets army
tanks and groves of guillotines; he knows that the original speaker of
the words 'Et in Arcadia ego' is Death. Finlay's single-minded commitment to his work led him into sometimes acrimonious disputes, not least
with the Scottish Arts Council and his regional council; he designed
campaign medals to commemorate such Little Spartan wars. Like any
original artist, Finlay is unique. At the same time, he shares a number
of concerns with Scottish poets who were his contemporaries. Like
Mackay Brown and Morgan, he loves the sea. He lists fishing-boat
names, writes of steering by the stars, meditates on driftwood and waves.
Some of his most beautiful works have a classic simplicity. His 1967
one-word poem 'THE CLOUD'S ANCHOR' reads simply 'swallow'
– referring to that bird's shape as it drifts like a little anchor below a
cloud.[62] Like Morgan, though unlike MacDiarmid, Finlay had a strong
sense of the playful as well as an adventurous formal and thematic
imagination.

Extending from MacCaig to Finlay, from Sorley MacLean to Morgan,
the range of Scottish poetry in the second half of the twentieth century
is outstanding. Merely to set traditionalists against an avant-garde would
be misleading. MacLean is a modernizer as well as a transmitter of
Gaelic culture. The Classically clear-headed MacCaig began as an avant-
garde New Apocalyptic; the 'experimental' Morgan wrote many more
sonnets than did MacCaig. Mackay Brown and Finlay shared not dis-
similar preoccupations in the 1950s. A belief in intellectual breadth and
shared contacts was championed by George Elder Davie (1912–2007),
the long-standing friend of MacDiarmid, MacLean and other Scottish
writers. In his studies of Scottish philosophy and educational tradition,
The Democratic Intellect (1961) and The Crisis of the Democratic
Intellect (1986), Davie defended the generalist tradition of university
education which made philosophy a core concern, bridging arts and
sciences and providing unity for students studying a portfolio of subjects.
Davie speaks up for the older tradition of a 'metaphysical Scotland' but
sees this as weakened by an increasingly dominant Oxbridge model of

academia which emphasizes specialization. For thinkers of the Scottish Renaissance and beyond Davie gave a fresh intellectual focus to the ideal of the 'lad o' pairts' once admired by Kailyard writers. He provided in Scotland an alternative intellectual model to that of C. P. Snow's 'two cultures' theory in England, which viewed the arts and sciences as irreconcilably distinct. Though they did not always agree with Davie's intellectual historiography, poets from MacDiarmid through Morgan to W. N. Herbert and the 'Informationists' have been strengthened by engagement with his intellectual ideals.[63] Such poets like what Thomas Carlyle called in *Sartor Resartus* the study of Things in General.

Where Davie championed generalism and contacts between disciplines, his fellow Edinburgh philosopher John Macmurray argued that action and contact with the Other rather than individual spectatorship or imagination constituted the identity of the self: 'the Self exists only in dynamic relation with the Other'.[64] This sense of the 'heterocentric' self as communally defined, bound up with others and with the Other, also encourages contact among individual disciplines, genres, social groups and forms of thought. Like Davie's work, Macmurray's stress on the need for an identity bound up with engagement with the Other sits easily beside recent readings of Scottish cultural identity; these foreground the idea of Mikhail Bakhtin that 'It is only in the eyes of *another culture* that foreign culture reveals itself fully.'[65] More immediately and more darkly, Macmurray's thought had an impact on the Scottish thinker R. D. Laing (1927–89). Laing's critique of psychiatry, *The Divided Self* (1960), criticizes the pretensions of science to present a 'reality' which is in fact a constructed discourse; instead, Laing stresses the perceptual value of off-centre, disordered states of mind. Working in Glasgow, then at London's Tavistock Clinic, Laing fuelled through his writing the 1960s counterculture that attracted Alexander Trocchi and, to a lesser extent, the professor–poets Edwin Morgan at Glasgow University and at the Sorbonne the younger French-based Scottish writer Kenneth White. Born in 1936, White, whose *Collected Poems, 1960–2000* were published with the title *Open World* (2003), likes to champion shamanism, 'geopoetics', border-crossing and intellectual 'nomadism'.[66]

As White often points out, there is a tradition of the Scot as intellectual nomad, which goes back at least as far as Duns Scotus. Nineteenth- and twentieth-century migrations have also played their part, producing alongside Scotland's linguistic communities of English, Scots or Gaelic speakers other groups who participated in or interacted with these, and whose members in turn went beyond Scotland. David Daiches (1912–2005) was arguably Scotland's most formidable twentieth-century literary critic. Working in America, England and Scotland, he authored studies of topics from Moses and Milton to Burns and Virginia Woolf, as well as playing a crucial role in the development of the internationally influential *Norton Anthology of Poetry*. Daiches writes shrewdly in his autobiographical *Two Worlds* (1956) of his Edinburgh-Jewish childhood after World War I. Son of Edinburgh's Chief Rabbi, he felt that 'the two cultures of my childhood did not fight each other but dove-tailed into each other', though he is also aware that in some ways the Jewish culture of the 1920s and 1930s 'golden years of Scots-Yiddish' may have been undervalued, its speech going unrecorded, so that, even by 1956, 'it was too late now'.[67]

The modern Glasgow Jewish community in particular has produced a striking number of accomplished writers. They range from the Polish-born novelist Chaim Bermant (1929–98) who celebrates Glasgow in *Jericho Sleep Alone* (1964), and his exact contemporary C. P. Taylor (1929–81) whose many plays such as *Bread and Butter* (1967) and *Good* (1981) explore Jewishness and evil in the century of the Third Reich, to the very different poet Ivor Cutler (1923–2006) whose surreal humour animates both his verse and his prose sketches of Scottish life. American-born James Hyman Singer ('Burns Singer') (1928–64) studied in Glasgow and wrote carefully-cadenced poetry that reveals his admiration for the work of W. S. Graham. Among younger generations A. C. Jacobs (1937–94) translated Hebrew poetry as well as writing his own verse, and the twenty-first-century Glasgow-educated novelist Michael Mail (b. 1959) set his impressive, tightly plotted fictional debut *Coralena* (2002) in postwar Germany. The outstanding literary energy of the Glasgow Jewish community with its own newspaper, educational and religious networks has not been fully investigated; perhaps pressures to seek and present a unified Scottish identity have blocked such examinations. However, it seems hard to dispute that in Edinburgh the greatest writer born into Scotland's Jewish milieu was also Scotland's finest twentieth-century novelist. As a child Muriel Spark (1918–2006) played with the Rabbi's son David Daiches, and she presents in her autobiography *Curriculum Vitae* (1992) an awareness of Scotland as 'historically rich in sects'. Spark conveys too a sense of religious and cultural variety in her officially Presbyterian girls' school, James Gillespie's in Edinburgh, where

Many religious persuasions were represented among the pupils. There were Jewish girls in practically every class. I remember one Hindu Indian named Coti whom we made much of. There were lots of Catholics. Some girls were of mixed faiths – mother Protestant, father Jewish; Irish Catholic mother, Episcopalian father. It meant very little in practical terms to us. The Bible appeared to cover all these faiths, for I don't remember any segregation during our religious teaching, although in other classes some pupils may have sat apart, simply 'listening in'.

While the young Muriel Camberg mixed easily with these other children, she was conscious of kinds of segregation, not least because she had her own marked gift for 'listening in'. She recalls, for instance, how she 'nearly died' because one day outside the school her English mother used the phrase 'I have some shopping to do', rather than saying in the Scottish idiom, 'I've got to get the messages'. Her Edinburgh Jewish father spoke like the other fathers, 'So he was no problem.' Schooled in a milieu where children regularly played a game called 'Scotch or English?' Spark became in her fiction a brilliant mimic with a gift for shifting tone and for showing how one individual or group might appropriate another's register and replay it for their own ends.[68] An ear for and awareness of differences that set people apart in racial, national or religious groups, as well as a ready cosmopolitanism nurtured by her Edinburgh childhood – all would be crucial for her fiction.

She began, though, as 'the school's poet'. Her English lines about how inhabitants of other planets look up and say, 'The Earth twinkles clearly tonight' sound like a recasting of MacDiarmid's more obviously Scots-accented 'Earth twinkles like a star the nicht' in 'The Innumerable Christ'.[69] Her charismatic primary teacher, Miss Kay, a lover of Italian Renaissance painting, encouraged her to be an author, as did the nationalist poet Lewis Spence, with whom, at the age of thirteen, she took tea. 'Of course you will write as a profession,' he told her. By her teens one of Spark's favourite novels was Eric Linklater's *Poet's Pub*, with its comically interwined plots, detective story elements, and search for elusive truth in an upper-class setting. She admired its tone, its 'throwaway quality of liberty and humour . . .; at the same time it was a serious book'.[70] Perhaps in search of liberty, Muriel Camberg at nineteen went to Southern Rhodesia (now Zimbabwe), married Sydney Oswald Spark, then had a son by him; but the marriage veered towards disaster when 'S.O.S.' showed signs of mental instability. It is typical of Muriel Spark that she should ironically convey and compress the pain of the relationship through presenting her husband's initials.

Spark wrote poetry intensively around this time – about such African sounds as the haunting cry of the 'Go-away bird'. Africa decisively matured her writing. In 1948 she imaged a creator God as 'like Africa' in his blazing, plenitudinous opulence and because (as, perhaps, with 'S.O.S.') 'The dangerous chances of his mind' resemble the precipices and 'Perpetual waterfalls' of the Zambesi.[71] Spark went on to write prose with a poet's sense of phrasing. She likes to quote poetry in her novels. Material from her own verse, some of which was published as *The Fanfarlo and Other Poems* (1952), crops up in her early fiction. This happens in her first, prize-winning short story, 'The Seraph and the Zambesi', which made Spark's name as a writer when it won the *Observer* newspaper's Christmas story competition in 1951. By then Spark had been back in Britain for some considerable time, mixing 'Detailed truth with believable lies' during wartime Political Intelligence work for MI6, then editing the magazine of the Poetry Society in London from 1947 to 1949.[72]

Spark went on writing beautifully crafted short stories for much of her career. Her first published tale is remarkable not least for the way it establishes patterns which much of her later fiction builds on. 'The Seraph and the Zambesi' is set in Africa in 1946. Breaking the laws of what we usually consider reality, it features Cramer, an apparently middle-aged man who has nonetheless featured in the nineteenth-century writings of Baudelaire, along with his one-time dancing partner, 'Le Fanfarlo'. Cramer attempts to stage a Christmas Eve Nativity Masque, but is interrupted by a grotesque-looking winged 'true Seraph' who disputes with him, before flying off into the waterfalls of the Zambesi:

' – this is my show,' continued Cramer.

'Since when?' the Seraph said.

'Right from the start,' Cramer breathed at him.

'Well, it's been mine from the Beginning,' said the Seraph, 'and the Beginning began first.'[73]

Frequently Spark's elegant, ingeniously plotted fiction features bizarre incidents and the notion of a deeper, older pattern or script (often a religious one) which underlies present-day actions. In the 1950s Spark may have drawn sustenance from her published studies of earlier women writers including Mary Shelley (1951) and the visionary Emily Brontë. Spark's first novel, *The Comforters* (1957), relates not just to her conversion to Anglicanism, then to Catholicism in 1954 prior to co-editing Cardinal Newman's letters, but also to her work on an unfinished study of T. S. Eliot. Preoccupied with the thought that what we perceive may be 'Unreal' and that 'human kind/ Cannot bear very much reality', the Anglo-Catholic Eliot presented in poetry and in plays like *The Confidential Clerk* (1953) topics and ideas which obsess Spark in her fiction.[74] She reviewed the Edinburgh Festival premiere of *The Confidential Clerk* with insight and enthusiasm, and Eliot corresponded with her. Often her novels operate in the sort of upper-class environment found in Eliot's drama, in Linklater's *Poet's Pub*, in the Anglo-Catholic fiction of Evelyn Waugh and – sometimes – in Graham Greene's fiction. Eliot characteristically overlays a modern situation on a much older narrative pattern or ritual; during a breakdown which Spark underwent in 1954 she became convinced that there was a code built into Eliot's work and that, if she tried hard enough, she could crack it.

In *The Comforters* Spark's protagonist Caroline Rose, wrestling with writing a piece about fictional realism, becomes aware she is part of a novel which is being written, and which eventually becomes *The Comforters*. In an anxious, complexly plotted comedy, Caroline tries to reconcile herself to the tenets of Christianity at the same time as sensing she is acting in accordance with an underlying script. Such a sense of a hidden supporting story is also present in *Robinson* (1958), set on a desert island. An awareness of earlier texts such as *Robinson Crusoe* and *Swiss Family Robinson* ghosts the narrative pattern. In *Memento Mori* (1959) the words 'Remember, you must die', translating the Latin of the title, are spoken down the telephone to members of a group of people associated with the ward of a modern London hospital. A sense of ancient words, stories and rituals – a deeper underlying truth – breaking through the complexly intersecting surfaces of contemporary life recurs in Spark's palimpsest-like novels. In *The Ballad of Peckham Rye* (1960) a Scotsman, Dougal Douglas, appears a reincarnation of the devil; 1970s events in *The Takeover* (1976), set in Nemi, Italy, depend on the ancient worship of Diana as explained by J. G. Frazer. This account of struggles for priestly power features an expatriate who considers himself a descendant of the Classical goddess and refounds her cult, setting up an alternative religion to Christianity, but one which in turn comes to be overcome and absorbed into Catholic practice. For Spark there are not just fictions within fictions, but imaginings are inseparable from what her characters and readers may think of as realities. In *Curriculum Vitae* she presents imagination as offering knowledge unobtainable through customary channels.

Spark returned to Scotland regularly, but most of her life was spent in southern Africa, England, then Rome, New York, and latterly Tuscany where she died. She used each of these locations in her work. She wrote too about the Middle East in her longer novel of division, evil and authority, *The Mandelbaum Gate* (1965), an ambitious exploration of Jewishness. Usually her fictions deal with restricted environments – sects, tightly-knit social units, or circumscribed bodies such as companies, hospital wards, schools, nunneries, hostels or family circles – rather than operating on a more panoramic scale. Spark likes to telescope, to compact, to compress. This makes for an intense focus and allows her to present in marvellously nuanced, trustworthy prose economically structured fictions that are closer to novellas than novels. Still, these books are so deftly plotted and verbally close-woven that they envelop the reader. The stories can be read in terms of postmodern literary theory, but their interest reaches beyond academia. Spark's characters are often tempted to impose their own narrative patterns on the lives of others, but find themselves part of a pre-scripted narrative over which they lack ultimate control.

Nowhere is this more apparent than in *The Prime of Miss Jean Brodie* (1961). Spark's short masterpiece is set in an Edinburgh girls' school. Aspects of it are clearly based on her own experience of Miss Kay and James Gillespie's. Much of the story happens in the 1930s, but the book also uses flashbacks and flashes forward. These let readers see and judge the actions of the charismatic teacher, Miss Brodie, not just according to the standards of that decade (when many, like Miss Brodie, admired the efficiency of Mussolini's Fascists), but also in the light of World War II. Regarding her girls as her 'vocation', Miss Brodie is beguiling and manipulative. She separates off her special 'set' of girls in the school and grooms them as her 'crème de la crème'. The book's first paragraph begins with the words 'The boys', its second with 'The girls'; then we hear of 'the Brodie set'. Early mentions of boys' bicycles as a 'protective fence . . . between the sexes' and of 'hatlessness' as 'an offence' alert us to the stylistic perfection of the writing. 'Hatlessness' is a comical version of words like 'carelessness'; but repeatedly in this book comical details appear less innocent when re-read. Protective fences and the segregation of specially selected groups seem more troubling when we realize that this story is about Fascism. It is about the idea of the Calvinist elect, and about the manipulation of language to control impressionable minds.

The Edinburgh school setting with its 'hard-wearing flowers' is superbly realized.[75] Spark's story is full of such sly, unique phrases. Yet when Miss Brodie's teaching encourages one girl to go off and lose her life in the Spanish Civil War, and another to sleep with a male teacher with whom Miss Brodie is fascinated, it becomes evident that the novel is about much more than just Edinburgh. As Miss Brodie knows, her surname pronounces her 'a descendant' of that city's William Brodie, a respectable 'man of substance, a cabinet maker and designer of gibbets' by day and a burglar by night who eventually died 'on a gibbet of his own devising'. As if preordained to do so, Miss Brodie too will help devise the instrument of her own destruction. She schools as a leading member of her 'set' a girl called Sandy Stranger. However, with her significant surname, Sandy establishes her own independence. Early in the book she too leads a 'double life', conducting a conversation in her own head while listening to Miss Brodie reading aloud her beloved dream-poem, Tennyson's 'The Lady of Shalott',

> Down she came and found a boat
> Beneath a willow left afloat,
> And round about the prow she wrote
> *The Lady of Shalott.*

'By what means did your Ladyship write these words?' Sandy inquired in her mind with her lips shut tight.

'There was a pot of white paint and a brush which happened to be standing upon the grassy verge,' replied the Lady of Shalott graciously. 'It was left there no doubt by some heedless member of the Unemployed.'[76]

Sandy's sceptical question destroys the spell of Miss Brodie's treasured Tennysonian dream-world. Sandy also takes from that dream-world a tone which lets her project the Lady's voice with pinpoint accuracy. Her imagined Lady speaks 'graciously' with poetical words such as 'grassy verge', 'upon', and that choice phrase with its capital 'U', 'some heedless member of the Unemployed'.

Later, realizing that the manipulative Miss Brodie 'thinks she is the God of Calvin', Sandy Stranger becomes the instrument of Miss Brodie's 'betrayal', the Judas to her pseudo-Christ. Having betrayed Miss Brodie, Sandy goes on to commit herself to the vocation of being a nun. She authors a book of psychology whose title speaks exactly of Miss Brodie's gifts as a teacher, 'The Transfiguration of the Commonplace'.[77] Rich in references to tales of enthralment, from 'The Lady of Shalott' to Stevenson's *Kidnapped*, *The Prime of Miss Jean Brodie* enacts ultimately a mischievous but profoundly ethical variation on the story of Christ and his disciples, and on the pattern of Calvin's chosen few, the elect. Not just the psychological insightfulness and complexity of the writing, but its nuanced humour makes *The Prime* at once a constantly amusing and a profound, disturbing read. Muriel Spark and Sandy Stranger have more than their conversion to Catholicism in common. Spark writes that

In fact, it was the religion of Calvin of which Sandy felt deprived, or rather a specified recognition of it. She desired this birthright; something definite to reject.[78]

In a moving and revealing essay about her own birthplace, birthright and vocation, Spark recalls returning to her 'native city' in the 1960s. This short article is called 'What Images Return' and its title comes from T. S. Eliot's father-and-daughter poem 'Marina'. In 'What Images Return' Spark writes about the time when her father was dying and when she felt 'an outpouring of love for the place of my birth, which I was aware was psychologically connected with my love for my father'. Characteristically, in this same piece Spark the lover of apparent contradiction sees her whole fiction as pivoting around the word 'nevertheless'. That word is for her 'the core of a thought-pattern' she particularly associates with Edinburgh where the word is pronounced with 'heartfelt' emphasis and sounds approximately like 'niverthelace'. She goes on to state that 'Edinburgh is the place that I, a constitutional exile, am essentially exiled from'. Exile for her 'has ceased to be a fate, it has become a calling'.[79]

At once native and foreign, Scottish by formation, Spark, like her characters Miss Brodie and Sandy Stranger, remained true to her vocation. Her later fictions such as *The Public Image* (1968) often deal with issues of self-image, celebrity, survival, and the truth that lies beneath sculpted ideas of personal identity. Elements of these themes are also inherent in the earlier books, whether *The Prime of Miss Jean Brodie*, or *The Girls of Slender Means*. This 1963 novel presents not so much a spiritual elect as a physical one; only those girls slim enough to escape through a hatchway are saved from the inferno that destroys a wartime London women's hostel. Increasingly through the 1970s and after Spark writes a fiction which is itself slimmed down. When she chooses, she can evoke settings superbly, as she does with the Edinburgh of *The Prime of Miss Jean Brodie* or the stifling Manhattan of *The Hothouse by the East River* (1973), but conventional realism is seldom her aim. Sometimes her settings, whether the Geneva of *Not to Disturb* or (in a rare return to Scotland) the St Andrews of *Symposium* (1990), are so minimally presented that we might almost be reading a witty philosophical dialogue.

Although her last novels show a falling-off, Spark's courageous duel with realism makes her fiction imaginatively liberating and daring. In *The Hothouse* we learn well into the story that most of the characters died long before its start. Yet they seem destined to continue their purgatorial afterlife in modern New York. Like Graham Greene, Spark loves puzzles and paradoxes, and enjoys drawing on the machinery of the detective story; like that other novelist in exile, Henry James, her plots are often about plots. In *The Abbess of Crewe* (1974) the Watergate scandal is transposed to an abbey, producing the sort of strange juxtapositions between ancient practices and modern behaviour that Spark relishes. So, campaigning for her faith, 'By river, by helicopter, by jet and by camel, Sister Gertrude covers the crust of the earth, followed as she is by photographers and reporters.'[80]

Though not overtly feminist, Spark's novels repeatedly feature strong, even dominating female characters whose presence is registered with minute calibration. Not infrequently these appear to draw on aspects of Spark herself. It is tempting to use a gendered adjective to describe her wit, and say it is unflinchingly feline. Her formidable intelligence developed outside academia, and usually far from Scotland – 'It was in Africa that I learned to cope with life.'[81] Yet when Spark has Miss Brodie link Hitler to Thomas Carlyle, she follows a connection made by the 1930s Edinburgh professor Herbert Grierson. Spark may share with another Edinburgh professor, John Macmurray, a fascination with the self as agent formed through decisive interactions with and reactions against other selves. In common with R. D. Laing she is preoccupied with insights gained through unusual psychological states, with true or supposed versus manufactured realities, and even with 'the divided self'. While Spark is often and rightly viewed against the background of Anglo-American cosmopolitan fiction, it also makes sense to see her in terms of Scottish literary, religious and cultural history. When we perceive, for instance, how far Sandy and Miss Brodie are indissoluble, we may relate them not just to Laing, but to works by Stevenson and Hogg, as well as to the historical William Brodie.

For all she was Scottish by formation, Spark seems to have had little to do with other Scottish writers of her generation. Though alert to Edinburgh life in the 1930s, she showed scant sympathy for the ideals of the Scottish Renaissance. Eric Linklater, admiring the Scoto-European Byron and writing sophisticated, often high-society comedies about America, Italy and Scotland, is far closer to Spark than the atheistical Communist and nationalist MacDiarmid. The predominantly masculine, cronyish world of 1950s Edinburgh letters offered Spark little. She felt too that 'the Caledonian Society aspect of Edinburgh ... cannot accommodate me as an adult person'.[82] She had a focused, even ruthless commitment to her art which might have been acceptable for a man in mid-twentieth-century Scotland, but was much less acceptable in a woman. Fused assimilation and rejection power Spark's work.

Nevertheless, even among writers who spent most of their lives in Scotland a certain cosmopolitanism was enforced by the experience of war. Born in 1920, James Allan Ford wrote a semi-autobiographical novel about the 1941 Japanese capture of Hong Kong. In the occasionally melodramatic but readable prose of *The Brave White Flag* (1961) the tentative Lieutenant John Morris, an Edinburgh law student, goes to his death as a 'reluctant leader' among the 'reluctant led' of a Scottish regiment. Learning the lethal 'accountancy of battle', and falling in love with a Chinese woman, Morris is a world away from his background. 'Careful people, sheltered by their lack of money and their Presbyterian training from high adventure and uninhibited joy, suspicious of everyone unlike themselves, they would never understand . . .'[83] Colonel Barrow, Scottish battalion commander in the tragic first novel, *Tunes of Glory* (1956) by the upper-class Perthshire Scot James Kennaway (1928–68) has also experienced a Japanese prisoner-of-war camp; Kennaway, a London publisher, probes regimental and class rivalries with a psychological acuteness which he went on to develop in several later novels and screenplays before his early death in a car crash. Perhaps the most impressive Scottish literary attempt to make a readership understand the horrors of the war in the Far East is Eric Lomax's 1995 account of his efforts to heal the lifelong psychological wounds of his experience of torture there. Far more popular, though, in the years that followed the Second World War, were Gaelic-speaking Alistair MacLean's widely published, best-selling, cinema-friendly English-language thrillers about wartime heroics in Europe such as *HMS Ulysses* (1955), *The Guns of Navarone* (1957) and *Where Eagles Dare* (1969). These furnished escapist reassurance, but impatience with that confiningly 'careful' Presbyterian Scotland summed up by J. A. Ford can be sensed in writers as different as Muriel Spark and Alastair Reid (b. 1926). Working in America for the *New Yorker* while translating Borges and Neruda, the poet Reid longs in his essay 'Digging up Scotland' for a time when the cobbles of Market Street in his old university town of St Andrews will be 'crisscrossed with singing waiters – Italians or, better, Brazilians, carrying laden trays, sambaing, animating the place, rescuing it from its prim residents'.[84] The desire for wider horizons and the sense of internationalism which took Spark and Reid abroad was shared at home by Edwin Morgan, Ian Hamilton Finlay and others just as keen that Scotland should not lapse into a Kailyard mentality. Significantly, a new magazine launched in Edinburgh in 1968 by its editor Bob Tait was called *Scottish International*.

For postwar writers there was a perceived lack of female role models in Scotland. Marion Angus and Violet Jacob both died in 1946. Long-lived authors as individually different as Nan Shepherd, Helen Cruickshank and Ena Lamont Stewart had largely fallen silent, while Catherine Carswell, Willa Muir, Jessie Kesson and Muriel Spark were all examples of writers who had left the country. Though very different from the poetry of Spark or the much more vatic verse of the Englishwoman Kathleen Raine who enjoyed a period of residence in Scotland, poems by Airdrie-born Elma Mitchell (1919–2000) show that she shared these women's interest in religion. Mitchell's voice has a measured exactness, but she had moved to London in her youth and did not feature on the maps of Scottish verse circulating in the 1960s or 1970s. The title of her book *The*

Human Cage (1979) might stand for a continuing sense of restriction articulated in the short stories and novels – such as *Winter's Traces* (1947) – of Dorothy K. Haynes (1918–87) or the more experimental plays of Joan Ure (1918–78), like *Something in it for Cordelia* and *Something in it for Ophelia*, which try to liberate their characters from the roles of victims in dramas where women move centre-stage. A similar impulse lies behind the powerfully concentrated feminist first novel *At Home* (1969) by Naomi May, born in Glasgow in 1934. *At Home* subjects to ironically plotted examination several women's relationships with one another and with an absent but dominant man. Set in upper-class Hampstead, this book has been undeservedly excluded from con-siderations of modern Scottish fiction. It was published in London by the Scots-born avant-garde publisher John Calder, but has long been out of print. Among the very different women writers of Spark's genera-tion who spent most of their lives in Scotland, Maureen McIlwraith ('Mollie Hunter', b. 1922) enjoyed success as an actress, popular histori-cal novelist and children's author of magical Scottish-based tales, while painter and novelist Dorothy Dunnett (1923–2001) wrote from the 1960s onwards both crime novels with a female detective and best-selling historical sagas about a sixteenth-century Scottish mercenary.

In Scotland some of the most impressive, though less commercial, imaginative prose of the period was produced by the subtle and cour-ageously experimental Edinburgh short-story writer and novelist Elspeth Davie (1919–95), a Kilmarnock minister's daughter who studied and taught art. Like Naomi May, Davie published fiction with John Calder whose cornucopious list also included such adventurous writers of fiction as Samuel Beckett, Jorge Luis Borges, William Burroughs and Marguerite Duras. Davie's strangely comic first novel *Providings* (1965) features trapped people observed at times almost as if they were things. Peter Beck, who like David Hume before him 'could scarcely believe in his own identity', has his life dominated by the endless supply of jam sent to him by his mother.[85] In the era of Existentialism Peter seems unable to accept let alone embrace freedom, but his life is defined by material objects. Elspeth Davie had studied philosophy and was married to the philosopher George Davie. Too often her characters talk as philosophers, but there is an oddly angled precision in her writing and in her ideas about human interactions with the material world. Like her novel *Creating a Scene* (1984) and her novelistic celebration of

Edinburgh, *Coming to Light* (1989), her stories sometimes draw on her experience of the visual media. Davie's intellectually demanding fiction can read like the script for a piece of conceptual art. She was reputedly a rather silent person, but her devotion to her work and her persistence as a Scottish-based female avant-garde writer make her a precursor of later generations of novelists. Her best writing is now undervalued.

After the 1967 establishment of the Scottish Arts Council, there was a growing impetus to teach Scottish literature in schools and universities. Encouraged by such men as the Glasgow University poet–academics Edwin Morgan, Alexander Scott (1920–89), and Ruaraidh Mac-Thòmais (Derick Thomson, b. 1921), the institutional appreciation of Scottish writing matured. Strikingly, in 1963 the first journal devoted to the study of Scottish literature, called appropriately enough *Studies in Scottish Literature*, came not from Scotland but from America where it was edited by the Burnsian Professor G. Ross Roy. In Scotland itself many of the members of the Association for Scottish Literary Studies, founded in 1970, were schoolteachers, and the Association's *Scottish Literary Journal* (now *Scottish Studies Review*) was the first Scottish-published magazine devoted entirely to critical essays on Scottish writing. This academic periodical was soon accompanied by an annual anthology of creative work, *New Writing Scotland*, and complemented a generation of emerging literary magazines. Callum Macdonald's *Lines Review* began in 1952 and ran for almost half a century, while another poetry magazine, *Akros*, was edited between 1965 and 1983 by the poet, critic and book designer Duncan Glen, a most generous encourager of younger writers. To some extent *Akros* was succeeded by *Chapman* (1973–), edited by Joy Hendry, and, later, by the revived *(New) Edinburgh Review*. The Gaelic Books Council was founded in 1968 at Glasgow University, from whose Celtic Department Derick Thomson also edited the Gaelic creative writing magazine *Gairm* (1952–2002).

Active as a scholar from the 1950s, the Lewis-born Thomson helped disseminate knowledge of Gaelic literary history to a wider world still largely ignorant of it. His *Introduction to Gaelic Poetry* (1974) and his *Companion to Gaelic Culture* (1983) remain unsurpassed. Thomson's heroic endeavours as scholar, editor and publisher were accompanied by a prolific career as a poet championing the cause of Gaelic, though some of his best-known poems, like 'Cisteachan-Laighe' ('Coffins') record a Gaelic world that is passing away, being buried under the

'English braid' and 'Lowland varnish' of its home-produced coffins. As lyrically strong, but more positively accented, is his poem of 'Clann-Nighean an Sgadain' (The Herring Girls), 'Their laughter like a sprinkling of salt'. The lives of these women fish-gutters have made them 'slaves' following the fishing fleet round Britain's coast, but they have a pride that is moving as it hints at the sexuality as well as the enduring sexism of their world:

> agus bha obair rompa fhathast
> nuair gheibheadh iad dhachaigh,
> ged nach biodh maoin ac':
> air oidhche robach gheamhraidh,
> ma bha siud an dàn dhaibh,
> dhèanadh iad daoine.
>
> *and there was work awaiting them*
> *when they got home,*
> *though they had no wealth:*
> *on a wild winter's night,*
> *if that were their lot,*
> *they would make men.*[86]

One such man was Thomson's younger Lewis contemporary Iain Mac a' Ghobhainn (1928–98), best known by his English name of Iain Crichton Smith. Smith's mother belonged to that throng of hard-worked herring girls 'who never had a rose' and about whom Smith too wrote fine poems.[87] Publishing from the 1950s onwards, this bilingual writer studied at Aberdeen University, then worked for much of his life teaching English on Clydeside and at Oban High School. He is perhaps the only poet to have written first-rate original poetry in both Gaelic and English. Remarkably, he was also an accomplished writer of fiction and drama in the two languages. His restless imagination extended from the wry and lyrical haiku-like 'Sgialachdan Gàidhlig' (Gaelic Stories), which beautifully epitomizes a civilization in around 130 words, to novels such as *Consider the Lilies* (1968) which confronts the still open wound of the Highland Clearances. Smith was ready to face up to suffering, whether that endured by his culture generally, or by specific people such as hermits, old women, carers, exiles. Bravely and humorously he drew on his own experience of mental illness. Influenced by Kierkegaard, he repeatedly makes a plea for people not to be constricted in their humanity by power or snobbery, fear or narrow religion. His prose may be inflected by suffering, but it is ultimately optimistic as it shows our human potential to live not less, but more. His poetry also shows a rare gift for accessible and beautiful lyricism, as in 'Two Girls Singing' which concludes,

> So on the bus through late November running
> by yellow lights tormented, darkness falling,
> the two girls sang for miles and miles together
>
> and it wasn't the words or tune. It was the singing.
> It was the human sweetness in that yellow,
> the unpredicted voices of our kind.[88]

One of Smith's poems is titled 'Shall Gaelic Die?' This question obsessed him. Yet his work manifests, too, an immediately beguiling sense of humour. His naive alter ego, Murdo, asks Dante what magazines he first sent his poems to. Smith joked, and thought hard. His shrewd English-language essay, 'Real People in a Real Place', spells out an abiding, clear-headed commitment to his native Gaelic. In an insight shared with W. S. Graham, he argues that 'we are born inside a language and see everything from within its parameters: it is not we who make language, it is language that makes us.'[89]

Smith's ability to write in Gaelic and English seems enviable. But he saw himself as an afflicted 'double man', pulled both between the harsh 'law' of the Calvinist upbringing he rejected and the 'grace' of art, as well as between two languages, to neither of which he could give exclusive commitment.[90] Once, in the late 1980s, asked to say something in Gaelic before a monoglot English-speaking audience at an Aberdeen University conference, he reacted with determined embarrassment, replying only in English and sensing that he was being treated as a kind of rare survival or exhibit. Still, he joked that around the place where he then lived, Taynuilt in Argyll, the surviving Gaelic speakers were all on lung machines. Smith's commitment to and sometimes deep pessimism about a way of life that seemed to be inexorably on the wane has something in common with the English-language work of the poet and memorialist Alasdair MacLean (1926–94). MacLean was born in Glasgow to Highland parents. His *Night Falls on Ardnamurchan: The Twilight of a Crofting Family* (1984) mixes his father's journal with his own attempts to come to terms with the loss of parents and a way of life that has suffered 'a bad attack of history'. Detailing practices now unfamiliar – such as hand-scything a field of hay – this book is a wise testament to 'ecological principles'. Yet, though it contains Gaelic proverbs and occasionally notes on a word or custom derived from 'the dregs of Gaelic culture', it never once remarks on the way that the Gaelic language would at one time have been the native speech of the community.[91]

In areas where Gaelic remained relatively strong, such as the Western Isles, though some such as Skye poet and hymn-writer Catriona NicDhomhnaill (Catriona MacDonald, b. 1925) might movingly express their faith, many writers, following Crichton Smith and his older friend Sorley MacLean, were in conflict with the strict Free Presbyterian mentality. Domhnall MacAmhlaigh (Donald MacAulay, b. 1930), who grew up on Lewis and taught Gaelic at Aberdeen and Glasgow Universities, writes in 'Soisgeul 1955' ('Gospel 1955') of the distinctive tradition of Gaelic psalmody and of the 'liberating, cascading melody' of Church prayer – 'my people's access to poetry' – but reacts against the dominant sermonizing and self-righteousness he perceives in Church and community. Like Smith and many other Gaelic poets active in the postwar period, Macaulay produces English verse translations of some of his own work, which deploys in the original what Meg Bateman calls 'a rhythmically subtle free verse'.[92] However, other Macaulay poems remain untranslated, and to an extent untranslatable, since, influenced perhaps by e. e. cummings, he was intrigued by the word-play specific to a particular language. Undeterred by concerns about readership, his poetry upholds the integrity of the poet to speak out, even in the face of a community who took as dim a view of agnosticism as of free verse. He has been critical of a later generation of poets whose verse is more informed by English than by Gaelic, but an increasing problem for Gaelic poets who published books in this period was the small size of their Gaelic readership. The worry grew that some might be tempted to write as much for readers of the English translations as for the sometimes less liberal native Gaelic-speaking audience, few of whom might have an interest in risk-taking modern verse.

Potentially the audience for English-language Scottish fiction was much larger. In his 1979 novel *Fergus Lamont* Robin Jenkins

(1912–2005) has the eponymous poet-hero mock the 'disastrously unprofitable' publishing of Scottish literature.[93] Jenkins's own fiction came and went from the lists of so many publishers – from Penguin to Balnain Books of Nairn – that his output of over thirty novels across six decades since the 1950s is hard to keep track of. Born in Cambuslang, Lanarkshire, in 1912 and educated at Glasgow University, from 1936 he taught English in Scotland, Afghanistan, Spain and British North Borneo until his retirement to Toward on the Firth of Clyde. He drew on the cultures of all these places in his writing. Publishing his first novel at the age of thirty-eight, throughout his career Jenkins examined and re-examined struggles between extremes of good and evil. These conflicts are set in locations as different as a Scottish pine forest in *The Cone-Gatherers* (1955) and the troubled Afghanistan of Christian–Muslim conflict in such undervalued novels as *Dust on the Paw* (1961) where Abdul Wahab encounters 'problems ... so complicated that even if he were able to describe them intelligibly, God might not be able to follow'.[94] Jenkins's ability to empathize with other cultures is a marked strength in his fiction, even if his Scottish-based novels are his best known. In Scotland he often deals with tensions between rural and urban life, whether in his story about wartime evacuees, *Guests of War* (1956) or in *A Very Scotch Affair* (1968) where a Scot formed by Calvinism tries to leave his wife for a hedonistic life in Spain. In *Fergus Lamont*, published a decade later, a Hebridean idyll is balanced against a Clydeside working-class town. Life-changing moral choices and compulsions fascinate Jenkins, from early novels like *The Cone-Gatherers* to *Matthew and Sheila* (1998); though over forty years apart in publication, both these books deal with murder and are written in the plain prose rich in implication which is the hallmark of Jenkins's best work.

The Cone-Gatherers is in part an Edenic eco-fiction set during World War II. It is also a novel about the kind of irreducible evil represented by Hitler's extermination of the weak. Gathering cones in a pinewood with his protective brother Neil (who sings 'in Gaelic, although his knowledge of that ancestral language was grown meagre and vague'), the retarded Calum is killed by the gamekeeper, Duror, driven by an ultimately inexplicable hatred. Wartime anxieties of the landowner Lady Runcie-Campbell and the local presence of conscientious objectors anchor the story in a particular time. Yet, as Iain Crichton Smith argues in his introduction to a 1983 reprint, the story has 'bell-like harmonies' of a 'fairy-tale . . . a lean, spare, classical, inevitable quality as visible as the pines themselves'.[95] *The Cone-Gatherers* may be Jenkins's finest novel, but it is not his only powerful one. His oeuvre is distinguished by its commitment to examining Scottish working-class life at a time when this was much less fashionable. *The Thistle and the Grail* (1954) deals with saints, martyrs, and communion rites of Scottish football as it traces the fortunes of Drumsagart Thistle Junior Football Club; surprisingly, it is unusual in the attention it pays to football, an institution so important to many Scottish men, yet seldom well treated in fiction. Jenkins has received less attention than his style or subject matters merit. As one of the characters warns the poet in an attack on book reviewers in the sophisticatedly tribal *Fergus Lamont*,

'If you had written about Greek peasants, or Australian aborigines, these critics would have shown some interest and sympathy; but no section of the whole human race is less congenial to them than the Scottish working-class.'[96]

Whether or not this was so, the 1960s saw several attempts to write about working-class West of Scotland urban life. These were usually made by male novelists with, unsurprisingly, a male-centred view. In Archie Hind's *The Dear Green Place* (1964) Glasgow's 'foundries, steel-works, warehouses, railways, factories, ships' move the protagonist Mat Craig 'in a way that art could only be secondary to'. Yet, working in a brutally described city slaughterhouse and talking about creativity, Mat is unable to find an art adequate to his experience. Perhaps part of his problem is that, though he writes about 'the gutter patois into which his tongue fell naturally when he was moved by a strong feeling', neither Mat nor his author can harness that language. At times Gordon Williams, born in Paisley in 1934, does so in his bleak, ironically titled coming-of-age novel about damaged, 'hard as nails' working-class West of Scotland masculinity, *From Scenes Like These* (1968).[97] Williams is best known as the author of the novel *The Siege of Trencher's Farm* on which Sam Peckinpah based his violent 1971 movie, *Straw Dogs*. At times these 1960s fictions share with Alexander Trocchi's writing a wish to shock, comparable with the treatment of incest in the Greenock novel *A Green Tree in Gedde* (1965) by Alan Sharp, which suffers from strain in the sub-Joycean writing ('She smoked one of her seldom cigarettes. From it rose lithe smoke, fluting inflections, blue aubade').[98] Sharp went to Hollywood and became a screenwriter.

More than once a tendency to overcolour his language in an unnecessary attempt to dignify his subject matter also tinges the prose of William McIlvanney (b. 1936). McIlvanney grew up in Kilmarnock, studied English at Glasgow University, and worked as a schoolteacher from 1960 until 1975 when he became a full-time writer. His is a humane fiction rooted in West Coast working-class life. *Docherty* (1975), set in the mining community of 'Graithnock', deals movingly with the father–son bond in a close-knit society with conflicting loyalties and aspirations. The characters speak urban Scots; the narrative voice uses standard English. McIlvanney's purposeful and deft detective stories such as *Laidlaw* (1977) represent a Scottish version of the 'hard-boiled' crime novel familiar in America. Focusing on an unhappily married, middle-aged policeman, McIlvanney uses the genre to investigate working-class masculinity; homosexuality and homophobia are part of *Laidlaw*'s plot, and the book is written with a markedly local sense of humour which would be matched by Ian Rankin's detective Rebus in later decades:

'No, wait!' The big man was still trying. 'If you've got to have hostages to conformity, take me. I'm against everything you stand for. I'm a dropout. A hippie. A mystic. An anarchist.'

'I'm a Partick Thistle supporter,' Laidlaw said. 'We've all got problems.'[99]

While *Laidlaw* led to other Glasgow detective novels such as Frederic Lindsay's *Brond* (1983), the tone of Jack Laidlaw's retort just quoted, like other aspects of McIlvanney's crime fiction, also provided something of a template for younger generations of Scottish crime novelists who, encouraged by Rankin's work, enjoyed considerable success in the 1990s and at the start of the twenty-first century.

In McIlvanney's *Docherty* working-class Scots speech is kept in its place by a highly literate narrative voice whose more or less standard English dominates the text. However, in Scottish theatre working-class Scots became for several playwrights the dominant linguistic medium. Often plays presented to 1970s audiences the radical history passed over in Scottish schools. Other dramas were set in contemporary factories and workshops. On the continent the theatre of Brecht, in works like *Mother Courage*, had spurred explorations of working-class perspectives using songs as well as speaking parts; more recently in England the dialogue of Harold Pinter had encouraged a new attention to the grain of everyday voices. The vehemence of a soldier's outburst in the Reformation drama *The Jesuit* (1976) by Donald Campbell (b. 1940) is all the stronger for sounding close to the twentieth-century Scottish working-class sectarianism treated by Roddy Macmillan (1923–79) in *The Sash* (1974):

Papes, they're bastards! Bastards! I'd pit every fuckin pape in Scotland on that fire gin I had my wey; every fuckin pape in Scotland . . .[100]

Campbell's ranting speaker comes to sympathize with the Jesuit martyr John Ogilvie, but Campbell sets Ogilvie unsympathetically apart by having him speak in formal English. As the 'Troubles' in Northern Ireland emerged, Protestant–Catholic sectarianism, a persistent theme in modern Scottish literature, not least drama, came to the fore in milieus very different from that of *The Prime of Miss Jean Brodie*, itself a hit on stage and screen. Beginning with his 1972 television play, *Just Your Luck*, set in sectarian Greenock, the dramatist Peter McDougall (b. 1947) explored violence, deprivation and bigotry. 1970s audiences were coming to trust and relish the contemporary demotic Scots of plays such as *Willie Rough* (1972) by Greenock-born Bill Bryden or Roddy Macmillan's *The Bevellers*. Macmillan's play was directed by Bryden in 1973 at Edinburgh's Royal Lyceum Theatre before Bryden went south to the National Theatre in London. In *Civilians* (1981), *The Ship* (1990) and elsewhere, Bryden has written repeatedly about Clydeside life, dealing with urban working-class subjects in the language of the urban working class. He is part of a striking heritage of Greenock writing that goes back through W. S. Graham and George Blake to John Davidson. Bryden's play *Willie Rough*, like John McGrath's *The Game's a Bogey* (1974) and *Little Red Hen* (1975), draws on the history and iconography of Red Clydeside.

That heritage was given fresh relevance by the 1971–2 work-in at Upper Clyde Shipbuilders when 8000 workers occupied shipyards to try to save what was left of their industry. Decades earlier, plays such as Robert McLeish's *The Gorbals Story* and Ena Lamont Stewart's *Men Should Weep* (revived in the 1970s by McGrath's influential left-wing 7:84 Theatre Company) had used urban Scots speech. Early in his career dramatist and poet Stewart Conn (b. 1936) in *I Didn't Always Live Here* (1967) had dealt with Glasgow working-class history in its own language, but in 1970s theatre demotic urban Scots came decisively centre-stage. Such speech is crucial to the work of Roddy Macmillan, Bill Bryden and Tom McGrath (b. 1940), who collaborated with Glasgow murderer Jimmy Boyle on their 1977 Gorbals drama *The Hard Man*. Urban Scots vernacular is vital too in the work of artist–dramatist John Byrne, best known for his *Slab Boys* trilogy which, like *The Bevellers*, though with nimbler wit, involves uneasy rites of initiation into the male West of Scotland workplace. Plays like Bryden's *Benny Lynch* (1975) and W. Gordon Smith's *Jock* (1973) added to a sense of a male-dominated, often macho ethos, but the sheer liveliness of Byrne's work frolicsomely avoids pigeonholing.

Born in Paisley in 1940, Byrne began his career with *Writer's Cramp* (1977), a play about the spoof Scottish poet Francis Seneca McDade; Byrne's work often contains high-cultural jokes but delights most in a melange of pop culture, following the grain of a Scotland increasingly awash with Americana. In television dramas such as *Your Cheatin' Heart* (1990) this hybrid land stretches from 'a sushi restaurant in East Kilbride' to 'the Radio Kelvin compilation CD, *Country Comes to Calton*'. With all his stylized humour, Byrne maintains the sharpest of ears for vernacular rhythms in a Scots English alive with American twinges:

what'd I do then? Aw, yeh ... saw this advert for a Mobile Librarian in the *Dundee Courier* ... spent the next year an' a half drivin' about Angus in a converted ambulance dolin' out *True Detective* an' cowboy books to the natives ... thought I was gonnae go off ma head ... eventually got the heave for chuckin' fourteen hundredweight of Annie S. Swans into a skip in Forfar ... took to ma bed for a year, read a lotta Descartes ... which is where I got the notion to go to university ... plan was to study French literature but that would've meant learnin' French so I settled for philosophy an' economics ... bought myself a Hofner Senator to replace the one ma old man made into a coffee table ... started goin' wi this knockout doll wi' buck teeth an' a Ferrari, managed to clinch a pretty poor 'second', got myself a job on the *Evening Echo*, spearheadin' their telephone advertisin' department ...[101]

Strong demotic rhythms and a confident articulation of left-wing Scottish politics also characterize works as different as Hector Mac-Millan's historical drama of the 1820 radical weavers, *The Rising* (1973), with its 'plan ... to set up a Scottish Assembly, or Parliament, in Edinburgh', and John McGrath's *The Cheviot, the Stag, and the Black, Black Oil*, first performed in 1973. In the year that saw the establishment of the Scottish Society of Playwrights, McGrath's drama engaged in a Highland setting with the Clearances, nationalism, work-ing-class history, and the contemporary politics of North Sea oil.[102] Following on from Billy Connolly's *The Great Northern Welly Boot Show* (1972), the play drew on popular traditions of community theatre such as music-hall and pantomime as well as agit-prop, which resonated with audiences across Scotland. Unusually for an English-language drama, it included songs and readings in Gaelic; its characters range from 'Andy McChuckmeup, a Glasgow Property-operator's man' to Queen Victoria.[103] Such theatre also contributed to a continuing empha-sis on radical left-wing and nationalist impulses, encouraging a pressure for Scottish devolution or independence. Although, thanks to its awk-ward design, a 1979 referendum in Scotland narrowly failed to yield devolution, this pressure did not go away, especially among writers. Setting plays of the 1970s beside the earlier working-class fiction of, say, Alan Sharp or Archie Hind shows how much more confident was the demotic voice in the burgeoning Scottish theatre than in the novel. Yet the reinvigorated theatre voices of the 1970s helped prepare the way for famous working-class novelists of the 1980s and 1990s like James Kelman and Irvine Welsh. With a wonderful ear for the spoken voice, both these writers have written drama as well as novels and stories.

It would be wrong, though, to think of 1970s drama only in terms of the demotic voice. From 1972 when he joined Giles Havergal and Philip Prowse at the Citizens' Theatre in Glasgow, Robert David MacDonald (1929–2004) worked as dramaturge and director. A former UNESCO interpreter, he authored plays including the Diaghilev drama *Chinchilla* (1977), as well as translating Goldoni, Pirandello and a host of other European playwrights. Visually stunning, *A Waste of Time*, his 1981 adaptation of Proust's *A la recherche du temps perdu*, was regarded by many who saw it as one of the triumphs of modern Scottish theatre. This was also the era of such very different playwrights as C. P. Taylor, the Edinburgh philosopher–dramatist Stanley Eveling, and the poet–dramatist Stewart Conn whose plays include *The Burning*, which deals with King James VI and witch trials. Such a remarkable efflorescence in the drama makes it all the more regrettable that, despite much contem-porary effort and hesitant promising, it took three more decades for a Scottish National Theatre to be established. Before its eventual success, that effort to found a National Theatre would continue in the ensuing decades, by which time new generations of female playwrights were emerging to challenge the masculinism prevalent in 1970s Scottish drama.

An interest in the history of Scottish radicalism shared by Hector MacMillan, Bill Bryden and others was also felt by Alasdair Gray. He worked in the 1970s on plays about the transported eighteenth-century democrat Thomas Muir of Huntershill, and about radical weavers. A remarkable polymath, Gray was already known as a visual artist with an enthusiasm for painting murals. With the publication of *Lanark* in 1981 he became one of twentieth-century Scotland's great novelists. Born in Riddrie, Glasgow, in 1934 and brought up in Glasgow, Perth-shire and Yorkshire, the young Gray 'learned to draw words when four or five'. He thinks of himself as having become a writer in the first year of primary school when 'At the age of five I was confined to a room made and furnished by people I had never met and who had never heard of me.'[104] Confinement and entrapment within bodies, systems or codes of conduct is a theme that permeates Gray's work, as is a search for elusive self-definition.

At Whitehill Secondary School in Glasgow Gray was taught English by Arthur E. Meikle. One of modern Scotland's great dominies, Meikle appears under his own name in *Lanark* and Gray pays tribute to him in *Ten Tales Tall and True* (1993). In his second year at Whitehill Gray wrote and presented in class a story called 'The Wise Mouse'. This features a monster who encircles the earth only to be blown up by a hand-grenade-carrying mouse who with his 'small electric torch' jumps down the monster's throat and explodes its heart.[105] Reading voraciously at school, Gray also drew Theseus battling the Minotaur in its labyrinth, and illustrated the biblical Book of Jonah ('my favourite book in the bible'); at Glasgow School of Art he wrote a puppet play, *Jonah*, and in 1961 he painted a mural on the Jonah theme in a flat in Glasgow's West Princes Street, with the prophet in the whale's mouth.[106]

Some years before this Gray had embarked on what, three decades later, would be published as *Lanark: A Life in Four Books*. True to the Classical custom of leaping *in medias res* (into the midst of things), *Lanark* begins with Book Three. Its doubled narratives splice a semi-autobiographical portrait of Glasgow mural artist Duncan Thaw with the fantastic, constantly inventive account of Lanark, a man who suffers from eczema-like 'dragonhide' and who falls through a giant mouth into a monstrous labyrinthine Institute. There, like Duncan Thaw, Lanark searches for love. Eventually the wandering Lanark meets the book's author who tells him, 'Your survival as a character and mine as an author depend on us seducing a living soul into our printed world and trapping it here long enough for us to steal the imaginative energy which gives us life.'[107]

Entrapment and release, whether of Theseus, Jonah, Thaw, Lanark, or his readers, fascinate Gray. Like all his books, *Lanark* is illustrated. Its layout as well as its contents are designed by the author, with the result that it is a remarkable typographical and artistic object, at once individual and mass-produced. A work of epic scope and protean inventiveness, *Lanark* was hailed from its first appearance not just as the greatest Glasgow novel, but as an encyclopedic epic, alive with the sort of amplitudinousness and fantastic imagination that the young Gray had admired in Victorian classics. *Lanark* fuses Borgesian cunning with the relatively plain style employed by John Galt or Stevenson at their best. This makes the book knowingly 'postmodern' – to use a word Gray dislikes. First appearing from the young Edinburgh publisher Canongate in the wake of the 1979 Devolution referendum disappointment, *Lanark* made confident, masterful use of what Edwin Morgan had called a decade earlier 'The Resources of Scotland'.[108] This not only gave Canongate its reputation for ambitious literary publishing, but also helped establish Gray's book as the cornerstone of modern Scottish fiction. Its publication helped encourage a new cultural and even political confidence.

Repeatedly Gray has recycled or reshaped much earlier work in his books of the 1980s and 1990s. His masterly *Unlikely Stories, Mostly* (1983) includes narratives from the 1950s as well as more recently written tales. One of the earliest 'unlikely stories' is 'The Spread of Ian Nicol' – about a man who splits in two; the finest is Gray's Kafkaesque 'Five Letters from an Eastern Empire', which presents a writer trapped in a social and educational system which seeks to control his writing. Enveloping systems of control loom large also in *1982, Janine* (1984) with its Scottish protagonist Jock McLeish, an installer of security systems who is trapped in his own pornographic fantasies. Like *Something Leather* (1990), *1982, Janine* explores kinds of psychological – and sometimes physical – bondage. Both pornography and the political ideology of contemporary capitalism are seen as cages from which the individual and the national self must seek liberation.

The topic of entrapment and a sense for authentic identity is one
which has attracted many Scottish writers of markedly different styles,
from Muriel Spark to James Kelman. In some but not all cases there
may be a connection with the situation of a late twentieth-century
Scotland struggling to gain greater autonomy and at times obsessively
concerned with its own identity. Such Scottish political concerns clearly
feature in Gray's *1982, Janine*, but entrapping systems and searches
for identity are prevalent in much fiction – from the Dickens of the
Circumlocution Office to the Kafka of *The Castle* or the Don DeLillo of
Underworld. In an age when information technologies and international
intellectual movements such as structuralism, deconstruction and post-
modernism all focused on the way in which great systems of discourse,
ideology and control govern the circulation of words, people, styles and
ideas, it would be foolish to view Gray's fiction or that of other Scottish
writers only in the context of Scottish politics. Equally, it would be naive
simply to invoke Michel Foucault and ignore the specifically Scottish
political and cultural background.

Gray's national politics are set out with convincing wit in *Why Scots
Should Rule Scotland* (1992); his politics of the self may be more complex. Readers often notice that his prose style can be at once plain, even
childlike, and cunningly sophisticated. His 1992 novel *Poor Things*
again involves the monstrous. A Frankenstein story set in Victorian
times, it features Bella, a woman into whose body a child's brain has
been transplanted by the Glasgow surgeon Godwin Baxter (known for
short as 'God'), giving her an identity both youthful and mature. Published less than a decade before the world's first cloned mammal was
produced in Scotland, Gray's novel ranges from imperialism to medicine.
An ambitiously imagined book, it mixes sexual fantasy, energetic pas-
tiche and a sense of entrapment in discourses of sometimes monstrous
control. The novel's continually enlivening humour and arresting inventiveness go hand in hand with a growing awareness of how characters
and readers, minds and bodies, are caught up in overlapping systems of
circulation and replication.

Even to achieve such awareness may be something. Gray worked for
decades on his anthology, *The Book of Prefaces*, eventually published
in 2000. It is an attempt to furnish readers with a way of educating
themselves out of the prisonhouse of the merely 'useful' into a larger,
liberating world of thought and imagination. Ranging from Caedmon

to Wilfred Owen, the gathered, idiosyncratically annotated prefaces form what Gray calls 'a memorial to the kind of education British governments now think useless, especially for British working class children'.[109] Like *Lanark* and Gray's other work, it mixes encyclopedism with a Scottish-accented radical impulse to read, dream, and imagine our way beyond predictable and engulfing labyrinths.

Though it may be strongest in the work of James Kelman, this radical impulse is shared by a number of other Glasgow working-class writers who are Gray's friends. These include Jeff Torrington (b. 1935) in his 1992 Glasgow novel *Swing Hammer Swing!* and Carl MacDougall (b. 1941) in *Stone over Water* and subsequent novels. With Gray and Kelman, Agnes Owens (b. 1926) shared a 1985 collection of stories, *Lean Tales*, the year after the publication of her first novel, *Gentlemen of the West*. There, as in *A Working Mother* (1944), Owens writes in a calculated, deceptively plain and unflinching style about the often bleak lives of working-class men and women whose living is shunted aside in an urban Scotland where gender roles, economics and family circumstances all threaten to restrict their options.

Though Owens shares their awareness of the politics of gender, her work is very different from that of her Scottish-born near contemporaries Emma Tennant (b. 1937), Elspeth Barker (b. 1940), Shena Mackay (b. 1944) and Alison Fell (b. 1944). All these novelists have spent most of their lives in middle-class England. The Gothic 'dream kingdom' girlhood of Barker's 1991 *O Caledonia!* glances at times towards Muriel Spark's prose.[110] The upper-class Emma Tennant also enjoys evoking adolescence in *Alice Fell* (1980). In such works as *The Bad Sisters* (1978) or *Two Women of London* (1989), which rework respectively James Hogg's *Memoirs and Confessions of a Justified Sinner* and Stevenson's *Jekyll and Hyde*, Tennant unpicks patriarchal assumptions. Moving towards experimental fiction, poet and novelist Alison Fell explores the restrictions placed on a woman's life in modern Scotland in *The Bad Box* (1987). Sometimes using fractured narratives, Fell (born and educated in Scotland, though based in London) writes novels that are aware of psychology and feminist theory while calling on aspects of her own biography. It may be that both the more practically-oriented Anglo-American and the more abstrusely theorized French feminist thought of the 1960s, 1970s and even 1980s made a more immediate and thorough-going impact on English society than on most men and women in Scotland. Certainly feminism is a motivating impulse in the sometimes bleak but acute work of Edinburgh-born Shena Mackay, who published her first novella at the age of twenty. In collections like *Babies in Rhinestones* (1983) Mackay is a good, sly, observant short-story writer. At times her usually appropriate prose can slither, as when she has an old poet 'lower his accipitrine head appreciatively into the efflorescence of his cup', but her stories are well plotted.[111] Her impressively panoramic *Dunedin* (1992) – about emigrant Scots in early twentieth-century New Zealand and later London – deals with imperialism and includes a critique of the imperialism of the Scots.

A determinedly far-ranging internationalism characterizes the fiction of Allan Massie (b. 1938) whose historical novels are set in milieus as far apart as ancient Rome, fifteenth-century Scotland, and interwar continental Europe. Massie was born in Singapore, educated at Glenalmond and Trinity College, Cambridge, and lives in the Scottish Borders. Fluent and accomplished, not least in his sense of the political imagination, he began to publish novels at the age of forty. He has been described by Douglas Dunn as 'perhaps the finest of living Scottish novelists', and Muriel Spark (of whose work Massie has made a study) wrote of *Shadows of Empire* (1997) that 'it can be compared to Thomas Mann at his best'.[112] However, for all his astute intelligence, Massie lacks in his prose the kind of individual stylistic signature identifiable in the work of Spark or Alasdair Gray. Massie prefers prose to be 'unobtrusive'.[113] His finest work is the 1989 *A Question of Loyalties*, a father-and-son novel which deals with Vichy France and whose sympathetic portrayal of shifting familial and political allegiances may stand beside similar patterns treated by Massie's admired Walter Scott in *Waverley*. Among modern Scottish writers Massie, a very active journalist, is unusual because his political leanings, like those of Scott, are clearly Conservative. This, along with his tendency to deal with middle- and upper-class life and to set much of his work outside Scotland, may have led to his omission from some too sketchy notions of what constitutes modern Scottish literature.

Recent Scottish fiction can certainly be international in its settings, and it is myopic to assume that 'Scottish literature' means books about Scotland. The era of Edwin Morgan, Muriel Spark and Ian Hamilton Finlay, not to mention Shena Mackay and Allan Massie, has been one when Scottish literature manifested a confident internationalism inside the country as well as outside it. In London the critic, biographer and autobiographer Karl Miller, born in Midlothian in 1931, enjoyed distinguished careers as literary editor of the *Spectator* and *New Statesman* before going on to edit the BBC's *Listener* magazine. Then in 1979, while he was Lord Northcliffe Professor of Modern English Literature at University College London, he became founding editor of the *London Review of Books*. This publication soon became the most important literary periodical set up in postwar Britain. A stylish and wide-ranging writer, Miller drew in his work on his close knowledge of nineteenth-century Edinburgh literary culture as well as on his contemporary contacts in London and elsewhere. With an able team, he spent thirteen years editing the *LRB* so that it 'ran from first to last like the *Edinburgh Review* – in no set thematic order and with very little in the way of segregation'. With a democratic Scottish intelligence, Miller wanted this literary, cultural and political paper to be 'neither highbrow nor lowbrow, to provide a subject-matter that was both popular and abstruse'.[114] Like the great Oxford-based Scottish scholar H. C. G. Matthew (1941–99), historian and founding editor of the *Oxford Dictionary of National Biography* (2004), Miller combined scholarship, intuition and a sense of wide horizons. Though north of the Border magazines such as the refounded *Edinburgh Review*, and more recently the enterprising *Scottish Review of Books*, have attempted something similar on a smaller scale, none has been able to match the intellectual or other resources of the *LRB*.

In Edinburgh, where Miller had been schooled and acquired many of his literary bearings, there were also signs beyond the new *Edinburgh Review* that there was a local internationalism that did not flinch from difficult issues. Joan Lingard (b. 1932) grew up in Belfast before training as a teacher in the Scottish capital. Lingard is a popular and highly accomplished writer for young people. In Ireland and Scotland her 1970s books for teenagers *Across the Barricades* and *The Twelfth of July* – about a love affair between a Catholic boy and a Protestant girl from Belfast – have featured in school curricula designed to confront sectarianism. Lingard's success as a writer for children and young people should not obscure her writing for adults. Early novels such as *The Prevailing Wind* (1964), her study of a middle-class single mother in Edinburgh, use Scottish and Irish settings, while later works feature England, France, Latvia and other parts of continental Europe. Like Massie, Lingard enjoys writing about tensions within families which may be emblematic of wider social or political issues, but her focus tends to be on the women in these families. In *After Colette* (1993) the feline sophistication of Colette's France is aligned with the sometimes tough life of a woman in working-class Edinburgh.

Though Lingard's treatment of working-class Edinburgh life and Edwin Morgan's work as a middle-class Glasgow writer complicate the picture, it is tempting to hear in 1970s and 1980s Scotland a West Coast acoustic of demotic voices playing off against a more refined East Coast voice, so confirming stereotypes about Glasgow and Edinburgh. Certainly from the late 1960s the poems of Tom Leonard (b. 1944), a friend of Gray and James Kelman, explore among other things the implications of a Glasgow working-class accent.

> this is thi
> six a clock
> news thi
> man said n
> thi reason
> a talk wia
> BBC accent
> iz coz yi
> widny wahnt
> mi ti talk
> aboot thi
> trooth wia
> voice lik
> wanna yoo
> scruff.[115]

While Leonard's phonetic examinations are funny, a deeply serious and humane experimentalism underlies his work. Like Ian Hamilton Finlay, and like Edwin Morgan (who encouraged Leonard's postgraduate thesis on the nineteenth-century urban poet James Thomson), this poet wishes to explore the resonances of sound and language, sometimes from oblique angles. Admiring the feeling for vernacular speech in William Carlos Williams and other American writers, Leonard treasures the grain of the speaking voice. Like his novelist friend Kelman, he seeks to do justice to the language and preoccupations of his West of Scotland working-class community and, by implication, to stress the need to do justice to all peoples and their speech. In this spirit, Leonard's 1990 anthology *Radical Renfrew* unearths many forgotten poetic voices. Distrustful of an educational system that sought to demean them, Leonard argues passionately that 'Any society is a society in conflict, and any anthology of a society's poetry that does not reflect this, is a lie.'[116]

Official awareness of linguistic diversity was increasingly quickened by the work of such bodies as the Scottish Arts Council and the Association for Scottish Literary Studies. In 1977 the Edinburgh publisher Canongate brought out a bilingual (Gaelic/English) edition of the poems of Sorley MacLean, though, like so many earlier anthologies, both the 1966 *Oxford Book of Scottish Verse* and the 1970 *Penguin Book of Scottish Verse* omitted Gaelic entirely. Born on Skye in 1942, the Gaelic poet Aonghas MacNeacail studied at Glasgow University. Like his friend Tom Leonard he developed an attraction towards aspects of American free verse. MacNeacail writes poems in English and Gaelic. The number of Gaelic speakers has declined throughout most of MacNeacail's life but he has been a vigorous campaigner for Gaelic at the same time as asserting the rights of other minority languages, including Scots. Proclaiming that 'tha gàidhlig beó' ('Gaelic is alive'), his poem of that title concludes with an incitement:

> 'n aire nach gabh i sùrdag ro bhras
>
> ach dèan dannsa dèan dannsa
> 's e obair th'ann a bhith dannsa
>
> *defend her from too bold a leap*
>
> *but be dancing be dancing*
> *it is work to be dancing*[117]

Although efforts to forge stronger links between Scottish and Irish Gaelic continue, and although there are other, younger Gaelic poets active in Scotland, such 'dancing' takes place on the brink of extinction. It is not surprising that poets of MacNeacail's generation such as the evangelical Christian Fearghas MacFhionnlaigh (b. 1948) explore issues of loss, relative size and authority – as MacFhionnlaigh does in his ambitious long poem *A' Mheanbhchuileag* (*The Midge*) (1982). Recently the Scottish Parliament has lent its support to moves to stabilize the number of speakers of the language, but Gaelic poets cannot rely on many Gaelic-speakers having a strong interest in new collections of contemporary poetry.

Conjuring up the all-male 'parliament' that met on the remote Scottish Atlantic island of St Kilda before the island was evacuated in 1930 at the islanders' request, the poet Douglas Dunn writes of how 'On St Kilda you will surely hear Gaelic/ Spoken softly like a poetry of ghosts'.[118] Dunn's poem 'St Kilda's Parliament: 1879–1979' is voiced by a photographer who 'revisits his picture'; the date 1979 is that of the failed Scottish Devolution referendum. In that year the renewal of a national Scottish Parliament had seemed a possibility, only to vanish. Though there was a majority of 'yes' votes cast, the referendum was lost because of a British government requirement that at least 40 per cent of all those on the Scotland's Voters' Roll had to vote for the Parliament for it to be established. Dunn's fine poem is one of a number of literary reactions to the 1979 referendum. Later his *Faber Book of Twentieth-century Scottish Poetry* (1992) became the first general anthology of Scottish verse to give full and equal status to Gaelic work; a decade after that, Dunn was involved in selecting the quotations from Scottish literature to be incorporated into Enric Miralles's new Scottish Parliament building in Edinburgh.

Born in Inchinnan, Renfrew-shire, in 1942, Dunn worked as a librarian in Glasgow and Akron, Ohio, before studying English as a mature student at Hull University where he graduated with first-class honours and went on to work under Philip Larkin in the university library. His first collection of poems, *Terry Street* (1969), is set largely in Hull. Its poems deal humanely both with working-class life there and with the poet's sense of estrangement. As a poem about Clydeside puts it, he wishes to be, but cannot be 'An example of being a part of a place'.[119]

Dunn's rich sense of precise language makes him the leading Scottish poet of his generation. Throughout his career he has shown a profound commitment to the art of poetry, and to the craft of verse. In *Barbarians* (1979) he articulates in formal English a clear left-wing politics, but never sloganeers. Even in his anger or delight a note of elegy can tinge Dunn's work, from *Terry Street* onwards. He has written elegiacally about Scotland throughout his career, but on his return from England in 1981, the year of his first wife's death, he began a profound re-engagement with Scottish culture that (though it is not the subject of the book) coincided with the writing of his most celebrated collection of poems. *Elegies* is dedicated to Lesley Balfour Dunn, who died of cancer. At once loving and tactful, these formal poems dealing with 'the coupledom of us' and with the stunned pain of loss have been compared with the finest elegiac poetry of Tennyson and Hardy.[170] As a volume, *Elegies* has a remarkable cumulative power, mixing tenderness and strong emotion with subtle formal control and a heartbreaking accuracy. Its last poem, 'Leaving Dundee', also marks an opening-out which leads to the happier work of *Northlight* (1988).

Dunn's later poetry develops a feeling for language which has led some critics to align him with his friend Seamus Heaney. After the harsher, caged quality of his long poem about a ship's voyage to destruction, *The Donkey's Ears* (2000), his recent work has a mellower aspect, mixing hedonistic impulses with lyric melancholy. In addition to his poetry, Dunn has published many short stories in the *New Yorker*; his subtle tales are collected in *Secret Villages* (1985) and *Boyfriends and Girlfriends* (1995).

Throughout his career in Hull and in Fife Dunn has been a generous encourager of younger writers. After two years there as Writer in Residence, in 1991 he was appointed Professor of English at St Andrews University where, with the present writer, he designed Scotland's first postgraduate degree in creative writing. He has directed this since 1993 while continuing to produce collections of finely observed poetry, short stories, criticism, translations and other work written in a language judiciously chosen and burnished. If some of his longer poems use a sophisticatedly discursive syntax, his finest work is strikingly clear and lingeringly resonant.

> A builder is repairing someone's leaking roof.
>
> He kneels upright to rest his back.
> His trowel catches the light and becomes precious.[121]

Using a lyrically-charged standard English, Dunn has managed to keep faith with his sense of working-class community in a way that is strikingly different from the demotic urban writers of contemporary Scotland. His wise, quieter work attuned to 'secret villages', to 'tidal aviaries' and 'sprawled potatoes' as well as to the urban unemployment of 'Clydeside Street' is as much part of recent Scottish literature as the subtly 'hard-wearing flowers' of Muriel Spark or the more loudly celebrated junkies of *Trainspotting*.[122]

*The poet Kathleen Jamie was born in Renfrewshire and lives in Fife.
Like many contemporary Scottish writers, she has spent some time
outside Scotland, but chose to return. Jamie's first collection of poems
appeared in 1982. She has published prose accounts of her travels to
Baltistan, northern Pakistan, and other parts of Asia, though much of
her work in verse and prose draws on her experience of a Scotland
'alive – in fact, in bud'. (Photograph by Claire McNamee)*

12

Globalization and a Smirr of Rain

The challenge for Scottish literature today is to engage not just with Scotland but with the world. For Scotland as elsewhere 'globalization' is hastened by travel, by the internet, economics, and awareness of climate change. Reacting to this, literary engagement draws on more than one strand of linguistic inheritance in a country where kinds of language can still represent different sorts of culture and power. Often what seems like a local interaction with words in the period when Scotland achieved political devolution develops into or implies a relationship with transnational issues such as gender, class or ecology. Sometimes, in an age when technology and migration increasingly blur the distinction between the local and the remote, there can be a treasuring of apparently inconsequential Scottish distinctiveness – as in several contemporary poets' liking for the Scots word 'smirr' (fine, soft drizzle) – at the very same time as there is an excited realization of belonging to a wider world, changing it, and being changed by it.

Some people fear the internet is altering patterns of reading and will be bad for literature, but use of the internet makes reading even more central to our lives. As much as the encyclopedism of the Enlightenment, the internet is about extending access to knowledge. In literature, minute acts of verbal selection remain as important as they always were, conditioning as well as conditioned by subject matter. At a time when Scotland has regained a Parliament of its own, if not quite yet a new national vision, what was regarded as marginal, or taken for granted, or beneath notice, may emerge as imaginatively compelling for readers across the world. This has happened when contemporary writers from Scotland have turned their attention to drug addicts in Leith, to fidelity to local speech patterns, to an elderly schoolteacher – even, in an age of impending droughts and inundations, to the scorned national treasure of rain.

This chapter concentrates on writers born since the end of the Second World War who began publishing in the 1980s, 1990s and in the early twenty-first century. To impose too rigid a grid on such recent work would be wrong. The patterns are still developing, and the relationship between imaginative writing and society is frequently oblique. Still, literature is connected to some aspects of recent Scottish history and politics. In Britain throughout the 1980s and much of the 1990s the Westminster government was Conservative, the prevailing English ideology Thatcherite. In Scotland, however, Labour was the dominant power, with the Scottish National Party challenging; north of the Border, Conservative MPs were and are almost extinct. This meant that Scots felt acutely disenfranchised at Westminster. Time after time in recent Scottish writing the most arresting voices come from people who in terms of class, health, gender, nationality, race, language, age or other factors, seem socially marginal, apparently ignored. From James Kelman and Janice Galloway to Ali Smith, from Irvine Welsh to Kathleen Jamie there is a powerful urge to give voice to those apparently sidelined – not just within Scotland but in the global community. The dominant, though not the only, tones and styles of contemporary Scottish writing have been subtly or blatantly oppositional; if the issues at stake were most immediately local, they have a wider resonance too.

Scottish disenfranchisement extended far beyond party politics. It became a state of mind, an accent of imagination which might be a trap as well as a source of energy. Certainly it was reflected in campaigning for a devolved Scottish Assembly or Parliament, but there was also a sense of growing alienation from political processes; where in the decades following World War II there had been a surge in material prosperity and upward social mobility encouraged by factors like the rapid expansion of the university system, in more recent times there has been a marked decline in social mobility. About 50 per cent of Scottish school leavers enter the tertiary education system, but often expectations of what constitutes 'graduate employment' have diminished. In a nation whose latent tendency to conceive of itself as an underdog in Britain was heightened by Thatcherism, many writers have tended to investigate the underclass. The overclass has gone almost unexamined. As, even in a time of apparent prosperity, the gap between rich and poor has widened, this has caused unease in a supposedly egalitarian society. Worry about this goes beyond the politics of elections, and intersects with the politics of gender; if traditions of Scottish egalitarianism were strong, they were often resolutely, even Masonically masculinist. Scotland has found it hard to create a climate of genuine equality for women. Yes, nationalism has been important to modern Scottish literature, but recently feminism has been even more important than nationalism.

Not just ideas about women but also notions of masculinity (once founded around a culture of heavy drinking, heavy industry and heavy-handedness) have been challenged by newer ideologies and technologies impacting on work and home. With the striking exception of the Harry Potter series, books from Scotland by men have more readily attracted mainline cinema treatment, but much of the best contemporary Scottish fiction is by women. Members of groups whose sexuality was repressed in earlier generations – not least openly lesbian and gay writers – now find their historically marginal position allows them to stand outside and so critique society's apparently adamantine assumptions. Scotland and Scotland's writers are readjusting both to more liberated assumptions about sexual and gender identity, and to the capitalist commodification of sexuality in a culture of ruthlessly marketed image and celebrity. Yet just as it would be wrong to see 'class' in contemporary Scottish literature exclusively in terms of working-class fiction, so it is naive to regard sexuality and gender as topics of interest only to writers of any one particular sexual orientation. In recent work by authors as different as Janice Galloway and Ronald Frame, Irvine Welsh and Jackie Kay, the exploration of sexual and gender identity has been intense and sometimes figuratively violent, part of a wider international pressure in some writers' work to re-form or 'queer' conventions of 'standard English'.

Contemporary Scotland is one of the world's most advanced societies. It also has serious health problems in areas from heart disease to mental illness, eating disorders and domestic violence; again, long-cherished myths of egalitarianism have been qualified by the need for a traditionally mixed but white society to face up to racism in its midst. Wider issues to do with globalization have led to a wish for Scottish identities that are at once internationally-oriented and yet distinctive in their local accent. Scotland enjoys a very vibrant contemporary literature, and there are ways in which the new Scottish Parliament has supported the development of literature – from its imaginative use of poetry in its various opening ceremonies to its backing for the National Theatre of

Scotland, launched across the land in 2006. Yet inevitably there are times when writers and politicians seem at loggerheads. Too often in a caricature 'Calvinist' way Scottish politicians at national and local level show a deep distrust of the arts when not used as direct instruments of social, economic or educational policy. At the same time, in a caricature 'anti-Calvinist' stance, artistic excellence is suspect since it sounds as if it smacks of the elite or the elect; access, not access to excellence, is the mantra. In arts policy as elsewhere in Scottish life there is a clash between an ideal of democratic egalitarianism and an anxiety about election or elitism which forestalls aesthetic judgement. Whatever truths Scotland's Parliament holds to be self-evident, they seem not to include any claim that artistic excellence is among the summits of human achievement and as such deserves to be encouraged and enjoyed for its own sake. Scottish politicians take football (at which the national team rarely excels) much more seriously than excellence in literature or the other arts. No phrase is more scorned by Scottish politicians – and even by Scottish arts administrators – than 'art for art's sake'. Twenty-first-century Scottish aesthetes are very, very hard to find.

Where some other societies, such as those of South America, have regarded their writers as international cultural ambassadors, Scotland in recent decades has too readily treated its writers as social workers manqué. Many authors are strongly engaged with their communities; yet there are moments when disengagement is an artistic necessity, an essential breaking of the bounds. Sometimes Scottish writers and artists need to assert vigorously the aesthetic validity of what they do. Art, as Alasdair Gray, and many other writers of earlier generations have signalled, lives uneasily with institutional bureaucracy. Most of the time it lives uneasily, full stop.

Yet there are connections between the recovery of a Parliament in Edinburgh and the ambitious course of modern Scottish literature. While its approach is through imaginative reshaping, selection and honing, this literature is often quickened by substantial problems in society. These difficulties are far from uniquely Scottish, but writers have often looked to markedly Scottish forms of local language – in vocabulary, allusion or structure – in order to articulate them. Though the word is a slippery one, a 'democratic' urge within Scottish writing has grown in strength, going beyond the boundaries of conventional politics, and beyond Scotland itself.

As it often does, literature has operated in advance of political structures, to signal the need to pay attention to the conventionally excluded, then to focus attention on a global community and Scotland's relationship to it. In literature the clearest pressures for devolution were in the 1980s and at the start of the 1990s; thereafter the writerly accent has been on internationalism of several kinds – whether Candia McWilliam writing of Scotland viewed from the Pacific or Don Paterson making his versions of Antonio Machado and Rainer Maria Rilke. The development of e-culture and the growing importance of ecological thought look likely to quicken this internationalism further. At times when the Scottish Parliament, established with such great hopes in 1999, has seemed mired in tawdry arguments about Members fiddling their travelling expenses, it is good to be able to turn to writers whose literary standard is international excellence and who see the need for Scottish people to take a clear-headed global perspective. The nation's Parliament, which sometimes seems to lack the imagination and constitution to think in terms both national and international, will surely catch up. Again, in an age ruled from the shallow end by jargons of 'spin' and 'incentivization', it is impressive to encounter the robust sense of spirituality, love and precisely registered nuance in contemporary Scottish poetry. Its value is incalculable, and so all too often neglected.

The strength and diversity of contemporary Scottish literature is astonishing. At its most exceptional, it could never have been predicted. Early twenty-first-century Scotland, like early nineteenth-century Scotland, is home to the world's best-known living writer. When the unpublished J. K. Rowling arrived 'shell-shocked' in Edinburgh in 1993 she did not expect to stay; she has now written most of her work in her adopted country.[1] Though none has achieved Rowling's universal fame, a growing number of Scottish novelists – including Iain Banks, James Kelman, A. L. Kennedy, Ian Rankin, Ali Smith and Irvine Welsh – are known to many readers around the world both in English and in translation. Poets and dramatists take longer to achieve international recognition, but there is every sign that John Burnside, David Greig, Kathleen Jamie, Don Paterson and others will be seen as among the finest writers of their generation.

The confidence of today's Scottish literature has been achieved thanks to the struggles of several generations; it is also refreshingly unpredictable. What was long imagined throughout the twentieth century – a new

Scottish Parliament giving Scotland democratic control over her own affairs – came into being in 1999 as a result of a successful referendum on devolution set up by the British Labour government under the Edinburgh-schooled Prime Minister Tony Blair. Welsh and Northern Irish assemblies, with lesser powers, were also established through devolution legislation. The Scottish Parliament controls only domestic issues like education and healthcare, not other matters – such as defence and immigration – handled under 'reserved powers' by the United Kingdom Parliament at Westminster, which also deals with England-wide topics; as yet the Scottish Parliament's tax-raising powers are very limited. After the era of British Thatcherite Conservatism, twenty-first-century Scotland already takes its Scottish government – the Scottish Executive – for granted, and girns about its cost. At Holyrood in Edinburgh a great and controversial work of art, the Scottish Parliament building, envisaged as a working democratic village by its Catalan architect Enric Miralles, confronts the royal residence across the road. The word 'Holyrood', which for so long meant a monarch's palace, now means a people's Parliament.

This reassertion of national identity was fuelled not just by political resentment but also by positive developments in intellectual life – by books. In the two decades between the 1979 devolution debacle and the establishment of the Parliament in 1999 substantial cultural histories such as Roderick Watson's *The Literature of Scotland* (1984), Duncan Macmillan's *Scottish Art 1460–1990* (1990) and John Purser's *Scotland's Music* (1992) restated the fact that Scotland was a nation with still vital artistic traditions. In literature particularly this nation-gathering effect was heightened by the appearance of the four-volume *History of Scottish Literature* (1987–8) whose general editor was Cairns Craig, and later by *A History of Scottish Women's Writing* (1997) edited by Douglas Gifford and Dorothy McMillan. Begun in 1987, the series of Canongate Classics (whose editors include Watson, Craig and McMillan) republished over a hundred volumes of earlier Scottish literature. A surge of scholarly and publishing activity that ranges from monumental editions of canonical writers such as Scott, Hogg and MacDiarmid to the far-ranging, Scottish-focused activities of what became Edinburgh's Birlinn group of publishing imprints directed by Hugh Andrew has kept pace, sometimes breathlessly, with imaginative productions. In the wake of 1979 these activities could be seen as a

subtle, measured, and remarkable cultural fightback. Looking now from
the vantage point of an achieved Scottish Parliament, this intellectual
impulse towards consolidation can appear inevitable. It did not always
feel so at the time.

After many decades in windy cold storage, Scotland's capital city has
a new sense of purpose. One thing Edinburgh is for is literature. Each
year it hosts the hugely successful Edinburgh International Book Festival;
it has been designated UNESCO's first World City of Literature; the
elegant Scottish Poetry Library, founded in 1984 by the tenacious Tessa
Ransford, is now housed at 5 Crichton's Close, off the Canongate, near
the Scottish Parliament. The Poetry Library's website, like that of the
National Library of Scotland, is as vital a part of Scottish literary
cyberculture as the Scott Monument is of Princes Street Gardens. Admin-
istered from Glasgow, the powerhouse of 1980s Scottish literature, the
nascent Scottish National Theatre launched its devolved, Scotland-wide
programme in 2006, the result of a century of campaigning. On Skye a
cluster of Gaelic poets and prose writers are associated with the Gaelic
College, Sabhal Mòr Ostaig – another project long in the making. In
St Andrews the Poetry House not only boasts an impressively authoritative website about worldwide Anglophone verse, but proclaims itself to
be the largest building in Britain, excluding libraries, devoted to the
reading and writing of poetry. In an age when literature, like the other
arts, is surrounded by often state-sponsored networks of administration,
marketing, education and funding, Scotland's literary infrastructure
appears to be burgeoning.

As always, however, the position is unstable. The state-supported
Scottish Arts Council, which emerged from the Scottish Committee of
the Arts Council of Great Britain in 1967, operated as a devolved body
at arm's length from government and funded the arts in Scotland for
four decades. It is too early to say what effect new Scottish Executive
funding structures will have on literary institutions, let alone on individual writers – who too often tend to be put at the end of any bureaucratic queue. Poets, novelists and dramatists imaginatively investigated
Scottish identity throughout the twentieth century, and imagined a Scottish Parliament. So far, for all the high expectations that greeted it,
Scotland's devolved government has made little difference to the lives
of writers. Maybe this is a good thing. Early in the actual Parliament's
life an official report into Scottish culture mentioned literature only

once. Even the bookish inaugural First Minister of the Scottish Parliament, Donald Dewar, guiding hand behind much of its constitutional legislation and admirer of aspects of the political thought of George Buchanan, liked to make it clear that he had not read the novel which, more than any other, loudly asserted a cult 1990s Scottish identity. Irvine Welsh's internationally celebrated account of heroin addiction in Edinburgh, *Trainspotting* (1993), was a book he wished to avoid.

Yet in its way *Trainspotting*, like the Scottish Parliament, was a sign of unpredictable new energy. The shape of Scottish literature, like that of Scottish politics, has been shifting. As in earlier centuries, some celebrated Scottish writers live outside the country, but in recent decades a surprising number have left Scotland only to return after a few years – from North America, France or England. They have been joined north of the Border by migrants from America, Australia, England, Holland, Ireland, Pakistan, Sudan, some of whom have settled permanently, others taking temporary residence. In 2005, ahead of his visit to the Edinburgh International Book Festival, Salman Rushdie pointed out to a Scottish interviewer that 'Because of the shrinking planet and the consequences of mass migration and geopolitics and so on, we all live in a world where our stories are no longer separate.'[2] Today's Scottish writers write out of that awareness.

At the start of the 1990s James Kelman (b. 1946), the most influential Scottish novelist of his generation, defended Rushdie's *The Satanic Verses* as a 'good' novel at the same time as deploring racial attacks on Muslims in England and Scotland.[3] African writing by Chinua Achebe and Okot p'Bitek, the fiction of Kafka and the work of Samuel Beckett are all important to Kelman's imagination. While his oeuvre has a markedly Glaswegian accent, its concern with issues of freedom and class oppression is universal. Hot on the heels of Alasdair Gray's magnum opus, *Lanark*, Kelman's work stirred up a Scottish literary scene. Critics had grown used to praising Christopher Rush whose *Peace Comes Dropping Slow* (1983) diluted motifs from George Mackay Brown, and John Herdman (b. 1941) whose more ingenious *Three Novellas* (1987) fitted neatly into notions of literary 'Scottishness', but sometimes owed too much to Herdman's graduate work on James Hogg. Kelman's fiction was more surprising. Its author was wary of any easy assimilation into Scottish literary tradition. Ironically, Kelman's oeuvre can have a protesting absolutism about it that is John-Knoxian in its

undeflectable commitment. His merging of narrative voice and characters' voices, as well as his production of a modified, Scots-inflected
English appears to develop the technique of Grassic Gibbon. At the same
time, Kelman draws on that emphasis on the grain of the vernacular
voice strong in American culture from Twain and Salinger to the Country
and Western music enjoyed by this Scottish author who has spent several
periods in the United States.

Scottish and non-Scottish influences twine in Kelman's work. Translated by the Muirs, admired by so many Scots, and vital to Alasdair
Gray, the Czech Kafka was already almost a native Glaswegian before
Kelman drew on his work. Moreover, around the 1970s several of
Glasgow's professional philosophers were particularly interested in Existentialism, with its emphases on liberating choice and on individual
freedom versus sometimes Kafkaesque systems of control. Brought up
in working-class Glasgow, where he still lives, Kelman studied philosophy as a mature student at Strathclyde University. Existentialism has
been important to his fiction, but a rather Calvinistic sense of predestination rather than liberating choice colours its deployment. Commitment to communal voice sometimes strains against the near-solipsism
of Kelman's male protagonists. Like Gray's, Kelman's work is often
obsessed with entrapment and control. In turn, Kelman's 'existential'
writing can be read alongside later, philosophically inflected consider-
ations of social surveillance, educational formation and punishment of
deviation developed in Britain by R. D. Laing and in continental Europe
by Michel Foucault, Theodore Adorno and Pierre Bourdieu; however,
these issues were also part of pop culture. Singing about the teacher who
is 'just another brick in the wall' and denouncing education as 'thought
control', the rock band Pink Floyd popularized ideas that had obsessed
the Helensburgh teacher W. H. Auden in *The Orators* in the 1930s.
George Friel's Mr Alfred, MA, had pondered such worries decades
before they preoccupy schoolteacher Patrick Doyle in one of Kelman's
best novels, *A Disaffection* (1989).[4]

What sets Kelman's work apart is its highly influential style, embry-
onically present in the opening of the title story of his first book, *An
Old Pub Near the Angel*, published in Maine in 1973:

Charles wakened at 9.30 a.m. and wasted no time in dressing. Good God it's
about time for spring surely. Colder than it was yesterday though and I'll have

to wash and shave today. Must. The face has yellow lines. I can't wear socks either. Impossibility. People notice smells though they say nothing.

Here a third-person narrative voice slips into first-person; conventional punctuation is elided or changed; sentences track shifts of thought and speech. This London story of Charles, who is described by another character, Ahmed, as a 'Scotch dosser', also anticipates Kelman's later work in its close attention to the physical details of daily transactions.[5] However, unlike some of the other stories collected in Kelman's first British volume *Not Not While the Giro* (published by Polygon in Edinburgh in 1983), this tale uses inverted commas and never veers far from 'standard English'. Kelman's debut novel, *The Busconductor Hines* (1984), marks a confident stylistic development:

Hines didnt reply. He walked to the rear of the bus, shaking his head and occasionally snorting. He sat down. He sniffed. Naw, christ naw, no now, definitely, definitely not, bastards, the decision's made and that's it final; hh; fuck it; the bastards, them and their fucking promotion, all I wanted to be was a fucking the Busdriver Hines.[6]

What is new here is less the use of four-letter words – used by Gordon Williams's young men in *From Scenes Like These* – than the approach to vernacular West of Scotland urban working-class speech. Kelman produces not a phonetic transcript with glottal stops, but a cunningly crafted artistic representation of speech which lets him question and even attack the value systems of a society that judges people by their social labels – 'a . . . the Busdriver Hines' – rather than as individuals. As the combative Kelman puts it in an essay, 'For the writer in particular the fight is through language, and subverting the value-system is intrinsic.'[7]

Kelman left school at fifteen to serve an apprenticeship as a compositor in an era when typesetting still involved metal pieces of type. The minute attention to punctuation and individual words required by the compositor's trade surely schooled Kelman's sense of how to present a sentence. As he told the *New York Times* in 1994, 'Every comma in my work is my comma. Every absence of a comma or full stop or semicolon or colon is my absence.'[8] Though not presented conventionally as direct speech, his sentences create the illusion of speech:

Aw aye; naw – well aye, I did earlier on but there was nothing. He yawned again; he placed the cigarette on an ashtray and stretched his arms. Think I will go to bed.[9]

Kelman's style may have been encouraged by his friend Tom Leonard, whose poetry sometimes comes closer to phonetic transcription, and by the often perceptive and pugnacious Englishman Philip Hobsbaum whose Glasgow writing group Kelman, Leonard, Liz Lochhead and others attended. A published poet and Glasgow University teacher, Hobsbaum (1932–2005) was proud to have encouraged the young Seamus Heaney in Belfast; he admired earlier writers like George Crabbe who wrote closely detailed accounts of local circumstances. In Kelman's mature fiction use of local voice occurs not just when characters speak or think, but also throughout third-person accounts. The traditional division between an authoritative third-person standard-English narrative voice, and the subsidiary voices of minor characters who (as in Scott's fiction) speak with a local accent is abolished by Kelman. He shifts the narrative power balance so that the narrator's voice and the characters' voices flow into each other, mixing on one level. The voices of character and narrator belong to the same speech community, joining together to mock the hieratic language of other speech communities whose bureaucratic, sociological or managerial jargons seek to dominate their lives. In Kelman's novels the central drama is linguistic. In *How Late It Was, How Late* (1994), Sammy, an ex-convict, goes blind and navigates the streets of Glasgow, clashing continually with discourses of authority: in speech, in examinations, statements, accounts, whether given to doctors, local government officers, or to the police:

... I know it wasnay the polis's fault they're only doing their bloody job, how did they know what would happen they didnay, they didnay know, I'm no blaming them, no in that way, it wasnay bloody intentional I mean I admit that christ ... Sammy shook his head, then he was aware of the keyboard. Are ye putting that down?

I beg yer pardon?

Christ almighty. Sorry ... Look miss I didnay know ye were gony write all that down, I mean ...

Is there something you'd like withdrawn? Are you asking that I withdraw something?[10]

When Kelman won the Booker Prize for this novel a literary row erupted which revealed a lot about British society and the attitudes Kelman wished to challenge. On the front page of England's *Times* newspaper on 12 October 1994 one of the Prize judges, Rabbi Julia

Neuberger, branded the decision a 'disgrace', while the paper's editorial spoke of the book's 'lumpenproletarian' narrator. It was left to the *Times*'s Scottish journalist Magnus Linklater to explain in this era of UK Conservative government that 'Kelman has sought to capture an authentic voice – the voice of a dispossessed class from the city's housing schemes, a world where few Booker judges would care to step', and to quote Kelman's statement: 'All I want to do is to write as well as I can from within my own culture and community, always going more deeply into it. It's therefore just logical that I should write a novel like this, becoming more at home with these linguistic rhythms.' When Kelman at the same time resisted descriptions of his work as 'vernacular' or 'dialect', he argued that 'To me, those words are just another way of inferiorizing the language by indicating that there's a standard . . . The dictionary would use the term "debased". But it's the language! The living language, and it comes out of many different sources, including Scotland before the English arrived.'[11] Such a defence recalls Tom Leonard's attack on dictionaries and other authorities that aim to patronize Glaswegian working-class speech: 'all livin language is sacred/ fuck thi lohta thim'.[12]

Much of Kelman's often dark but also funny and sometimes tender fiction deals with Glasgow working-class life in an English modified to articulate the experience of the community in something close to local language. His flickeringly brilliant novel *Translated Accounts* (2001) goes further. Set in an unnamed country with a repressive regime, it presents fragmentary first-person reports and ruminations as if they were garbled in translation. In the novel's world of 'wwwdotcom' all language seems incongruously machined. Kelman mixes management-speak – 'All have aims and objectives, targets they must achieve' – with mangled accounts of terrorism, Third World sufferings, atrocities:

> Sexual activity. They would say things, whisper them, fiercely, yes, some if not all. No I do not say unusual, if fiercely. Not what women say, I do not know. I did not go often. Some went often. I know that. I said that I did not.
>
> I did, I said that I did.[13]

Kelman's breaking of so-called 'standard English' here matches a comparable impulse in Ali Smith's more successful *Hotel World* (2001); in different but related ways each of these novelists engages with issues of globalization and with contests for linguistic control. Struggles involving the cultural authority of different languages and kinds of language are as vital to contemporary Scottish literature as they were in the eighteenth century; sometimes these contests grow out of an awareness of distinctively Scottish idioms, sometimes they are universalized. The intellectual ambition of *Translated Accounts* is manifest. Yet as kinds of translation – across languages, media and geography – both engage and disengage readers, Kelman's novel has too much creative-writing-workshop avant-garderie about it. In such books as *The Good Times* (1998) Kelman shows himself a master of the short story, but *Translated Accounts* seems too long, too bulked out, too designed for academic interpreters.

Kelman may have written some of *Translated Accounts* years earlier, then worked on it again while he held a short-term appointment at the University of Texas, shortly before embarking on a not entirely happy spell as a Professor of Creative Writing at the University of Glasgow. In his livelier novel *You Have to Be Careful in the Land of the Free* (2004) he returns to the grain of his trademark Glaswegian voice yet also presents a critique of American politics as his exiled Scots protagonist Jeremiah Brown returns home after twelve years in the United States. Subverting the foundational American dream of the successful immigrant, Kelman's novel mixes American, 'Skarrisch' (Scottish) and other dictions and discourses, drawing on US narrative conventions to portray its 'failed fucking immigrant' in a land now deeply suspicious of outsiders and the downtrodden.

Where Scottish drama of the 1970s had placed urban working-class speech centre-stage, and where Tom Leonard's poetry had made the sound and implications of such speech resound in poems from the late 1960s onwards, Kelman has made this language the lynchpin of his writing. He deploys it in much of his best work with an ethical rigour and a radical political edge. Such ethical and political militancy is usually lacking in the work of the most internationally celebrated of the writers who followed Kelman in using Scottish urban skaz or vernacular language. While so many younger authors learned or borrowed from Kelman that the words 'Scottish fiction' in the 1980s and 1990s were sometimes regarded, not least by lazy journalists, as synonymous with dark accounts of addiction, stalled lives and working-class urban deprivation, it was Irvine Welsh's novel *Trainspotting* (1993) which made far the greatest international impact. Filmed in 1996, it became part of the media culture of globalization. Before Welsh was signed up by Robin Robertson, then James Kelman's Scottish editor at the London publisher Secker and Warburg, sections of the episodic *Trainspotting* had appeared in Scotland in Kevin Williamson's magazine *Rebel Inc* and in the Clocktower Press publications of writer Duncan McLean, then working as a hall janitor in South Queensferry; however, another early published section of *Trainspotting* appeared in the 1991 annual volume of the *New Writing Scotland* anthology produced by the respectably academic Association for Scottish Literary Studies. Operating almost simultaneously in both 'alternative' and more official publications may be characteristic of Welsh. Born in 1958, he grew up in a deprived area – Edinburgh's Muirhouse housing scheme. On the one hand he became head of training for Edinburgh City Council, having completed a Master of Business Administration degree at Heriot Watt University; on the other, his often gleefully graphic accounts of heroin addiction, sodomy, and violence have shocked and excited audiences around the world.

Admitting 'that duality's always been part of my character', and that 'My construction [of Scotland] is in some ways just as false as the Walter Scott construction', Welsh has learned to manufacture his fictions with disciplined care as well as outrageous energy.[14] Writerly crafting is evident in a comparison of the initial published version of 'The First Day of the Edinburgh Festival' section of *Trainspotting* with the section as published in the novel two years later. In 1991 Welsh writes about an addict trying to come off heroin,

Third time lucky. It was like Sick Boy telt us: you've got tae know what it's like tae try tae come off before you can actually dae it. You can only learn through failure, and what you learn is the importance of preparation. He could be right. Anyway, this time I've prepared. A month's rent in advance on this big, bare room overlooking the Links. Cash on the nail! Parting wi' that poppy was the hardest bit. The easiest was my last shot, taken in my left arm this morning.[15]

A careful look shows that by 1993 this had been subtly revised to give it a sense of freer vernacular flow, further distanced from 'standard English', more confidently Scots in its demotic inflection as Welsh lets his writing catch up with his ear for speech:

Third time lucky. It wis like Sick Boy telt us: you've got tae know what it's like tae try tae come off it before ye can actually dae it. You can only learn through failure, and what ye learn is the importance ay preparation. He could be right. Anywey, this time ah've prepared. A month's rent in advance oan this big, bare room overlooking the Links. Too many bastards ken ma Montgomery Street address. Cash oan the nail! Partin wi that poppy wis the hardest bit. The easiest wis ma last shot, taken in ma left airm this morning.[16]

Like Kelman's Glaswegian, this East-Coast-accented prose is a constructed art speech designed to carry a flavour of working-class vernacular. While markedly Scottish, it is close enough to English to be comprehensible to an international audience familiar through hearsay or direct experience with the problems of drug addiction, and possessing some knowledge of contemporary youth culture. In Kelman the drugs tend to be alcohol and nicotine; in Welsh, as in the 'chemical' novelist Martin Millar (b. 1958) who began publishing in the 1980s, they are harder. Through first- and third-person narration, *Trainspotting* tells a darkly comic story of the drug-fuelled antics of Aberdeen University dropout Mark Renton and his Leith cronies who include Sick Boy, Spud and the violent 'heidbanger' Begbie. Many devices, from Welsh's use of the preposition 'ben' (inside) to his characters' philosophizings, mimicry and replaying of high-register phrases in a fiction of jostling discourses, are among the stylistic indications that this author has learned from Kelman's prose.

This is murder. Lesley. Ah'm fuckin useless at these things. Less than useless in this condition. Of negative utility.[17]

As readers encounter the death of a neglected baby, anal suppositories and 'the free market whin it comes tae drugs', they are introduced to the largely amoral world of Welsh's fiction. Often funnier, and much less ethical than Kelman's more stylistically innovative but sometimes dour prose, Welsh's later novels include calculatingly appalling, taboo-breaking behaviour from the cleverly and ironically plotted 'orangutan-like grapple' and 'fuckin Belsen horror' of *Porno* (2002) to the sex scenes between a young man and an eighty-five-year-old woman in *Bedroom Secrets of the Masterchefs* (2006).[18] Though at times he can parade a politically correct awareness of 'zero tolerance', as in *Marabou Stork Nightmares* (1995), Welsh's work frequently appears to encourage laddish voyeurism and to revel in the exploitation of women. In his first, best books, *Trainspotting* and the collection of tales *The Acid House* (1994), there is arguably a fierce, post-Thatcher exposure of rampant freemarket consumerism in a world of 'me, me, fucking ME ... NUMERO FUCKING UNO' where the imperative is to 'sell yirsel'. In *Trainspotting* one of Renton's friends hears an ironically Sean Connery-like voice intoning, '*I admire your rampant individualishm.*'[19] In some of the stories in *The Acid House* total selfishness is revealed through sexual confrontations in a rush of magic realism whose typography and topics owe something to the Alasdair Gray of *1982, Janine*, but not all Welsh's clichés seem ironic and some of his writing is uneasy.

Welsh's impact owes as much to his fiction's scandalous subject matter as to its author's stylishly crafted demotic. In book form, on stage and on screen, this younger writer's work has proved more marketable than that of Kelman because Welsh's scandalous carnival of dark humour is more readily complicit with marketeers' agendas. 'The best book ever written by man or woman ... deserves to sell more copies than the Bible,' pronounced the magazine *Rebel Inc* in what soon became a front-cover blurb for the 1994 paperback of *Trainspotting*. Countercultural outrage and slick marketing were at one. Welsh has a superb ear and a plotter's sense of ironic geometries, but the commercially winning, outrageous formula of his later fictions often takes devices used by Kelman, Gray and others, recasting them for brutal, brutalizing comic effect.

Following Alexander Trocchi, Gray, Kelman, Welsh and others have violently liberated Scottish fiction from the narrowly middle-class, residually presbyterian assumptions that still governed Scottish society of the 1950s and 1960s when these writers were growing up. With the virulence of a backlash they have revealed energies which such a society repressed. In their significantly different, Scottish-accented ways they have engaged with aspects of some of the obsessions of contemporary literature: globalization and gender. In both these areas power relationships in language, violence and sexuality are revealed as brutally exercised. Where Gray and Kelman present their material from the standpoint of an oppositional ethic, Welsh often seems to write with more of a casual acceptance. In all three male writers, there is a focus on men who show signs of addictive or abusive behaviour; masculinity in this contemporary Scottish fiction is bleak, damaged, frequently damaging.

It is tempting to relate this bleak sense of men's predicaments to changes in a society where working-class values were often centred on the masculine manual labour of heavy industry and assumptions about women as home-makers. John Burnside's memoir *A Lie about my Father* (2006) is a classic of modern Scottish autobiography which epitomizes this milieu. Yet other commentators' generalizations about Scottish masculinity and femininity can be exaggerated, and are not always true to patterns of working-class life; in cities like Dundee, for instance, working women were often the family breadwinners, while images of urban Scottish males as noble or ignoble savages are too easily reductive. For all that, public health and domestic violence statistics, changing employment patterns, legislation and ideological changes all suggest that many Scotsmen have found it difficult to adjust to new expectations. Their problems are an obvious part of recent Scottish fiction, and not just fiction by men.

Among many younger novelists influenced by Kelman and Welsh, laddish brutality is taken for granted. Born in Fraserburgh in 1964, son of a pharmacist and a schoolteacher of English, Duncan McLean studied English at Edinburgh University; encountering Kelman and his work led McLean to re-read Grassic Gibbon's *A Scots Quair* and produce his own first novel, *Blackden* (1994), which presents the activities of a male teenager in a modern north-east Scottish village. As well as publishing early work by Welsh, McLean went on to author dark fictions of brutalized masculinity, violence, rape and paedophilia in the award-winning stories of *Bucket of Tongues* (1992) and *Bunker Man* (1995). Accomplished and articulate, author of a play and a Texan travel book, McLean appears to have turned away from the novel. He now works as a businessman in Orkney, but has written for the new National Theatre of Scotland and may yet return to fiction.

McLean is one of the dedicatees of Alan Warner's 1995 novel *Morvern Callar* which presents, as Warner's friend Welsh puts it in his blurb for the book, 'a fearlessly cool and sassy party chick propelled by her own delicious morality around the geographic peripheries and fun epicentres of Europe'. In a poem published the year before and adapted from his own prose, Warner presents several versions of himself, including 'Big Al, 26. Does the biz. Drinks too much: heavy with whisky./ . . . Eats the fatty foods . . . / Awaits cardiac arrest in/ AIDS capital. Seeks likewise females for gigs, laughs etc . . .'[20] Rich in references to raves, favourite tracks, youth culture and addictive substances, Warner's fiction is also, like its author, highly self-conscious. Warner admires the Uruguayan novelist Juan Carlos Onetti who fused fantasy and realism to create a series of novels about a fictional region, and Warner seems to be seeking to emulate that achievement in a series of loosely connected novels that begin with *Morvern Callar*. Written with huge style in a rhythmical prose that admits a wide range of high as well as popular cultural reference, these books show an anarchic sense of humour – most evident in the rampaging 'ladette' schoolgirls of *The Sopranos* (1998). Warner's sometimes hallucinatory linguistic brilliance is illustrated by a passage from *These Demented Lands* (1997):

Higher near ridge-crest, the rondel trees of the valley floor clustered closer into mushy clumps of black with bumpy edges. The whole island seemed to slip down through me like a disc, spread out round, saw otherside from up there, distant mountains lifting up as if explosions of steam, cloud pillars like spring blossom, the mountain range I was named after on the opposite side of the Sound that lay with a wet sun along in dazzling shimmers, up to where the water turned angry black – wide wide ocean that goes forever 'cept maybe for a Pincher Martin rock jutted out the teeth of ocean bed.[21]

Re-imagining the Highland landscape of Morvern and peopling Highland communities with strange figures with names like Nam the Dam and Argonaut, Warner's prose fictions sometimes confusingly swirl with allusions and mythologies. His often cinematic and lyrical imagination moves impatiently into riffs of linguistic inventiveness as he bends English to his will. At times cunningly voyeuristic, his fictions are adventurously presented in both male and female voices. Offering a startlingly new version of contemporary Highland culture, these books strike Frank Kermode as 'sophisticated, baffling and dismaying'.[22] They display a prodigious but sometimes self-indulgent talent. Where Duncan McLean sought to remake Grassic Gibbon's north-east, Warner remoulds the Highlands of Stevenson and Crichton Smith for an educated generation accustomed to drugs, dark humour and often brutal violence, but he is also eager to engage with a wider world beyond Scotland, as in his stylish Spanish novel of rape, HIV and alcohol abuse, *The Worms Can Carry Me to Heaven* (2006).

A decade before the work of Welsh, McLean, Warner and other writers, dark Scottish comedy and shocking brutality had featured strongly in the work of Iain Banks (b. 1954). Banks's first published novel, *The Wasp Factory* (1984), seethes with mutilations. His later novels include gang rape, torture, electrocution and many other kinds of death. Banks revels in cunningly plotted, outrageous imaginings, but it would be wrong to cast him as the standard-English forerunner of Irvine Welsh. Banks's imagination is both more ambitious and more versatile. Following the major early 1980s achievements of Alasdair Gray's *Lanark* and *1982, Janine* whose narratives are split between Scottish actuality and the fantastic, Banks's work, splicing detective story, Gothic thriller, fantasy and other genres, arrived like a power-surge in Scottish fiction of the 1980s. Its shock tactics were accompanied by a go-anywhere internationalism; its imagined worlds had a confident global contemporaneity.

Born in 1954 and brought up in North Queensferry (where he now lives close to the Forth Railway Bridge), then schooled on the West Coast in Greenock and Gourock, Iain Banks was a student at Stirling University. He hitch-hiked around Europe and Morocco at the start of his twenties before working for British Steel, IBM, and as a costings clerk in London. He had written six novels before he revised a seventh, *The Wasp Factory*. Banks's early published books deploy intensely imagined milieus, ranging from *The Wasp Factory*'s Scottish island to the Panama of *Canal Dreams* (1989). Between the middle-class London of *Walking on Glass* (1985) and a realistically presented working-class Paisley in *Espedair Street* (1987) comes the fantastically imagined linear city of *The Bridge* (1986). Alongside these novels, as Iain M. Banks, he has also produced popular, highly regarded science fiction stories or 'space operas' that include *Consider Phlebas* (1987), *Use of Weapons* (1990) and *Feersum Endjinn* (1994). The range of Banks's imagination can seem boundless, but a tight sense of plotting and a pacy prose stop this facility being over-indulged. So arresting were his early novels that, though the *Times Literary Supplement* dismissed *The Wasp Factory* as 'a literary equivalent of the nastiest brand of juvenile delinquency', other reviewers soon hailed Banks as 'a novelist of remarkable talents', and even (in a phrase which came to adorn the jackets of the early twenty-first-century paperback edition of his works) as 'the most imaginative novelist of his generation'.[23]

With a range of reference that extends from 1960s television spy series to *The Waste Land*, Banks offers many things to a substantial international readership. He has acknowledged that his finest novel, *The Bridge*, owes a debt to Gray's *Lanark*; its adventures narrated by a man who turns out to be in a coma, it is in part Kafkaesque in conception; it also fuses science fiction with Scottish scenes. A sly paean to the Forth Railway Bridge, *The Bridge* links apparently casual details with meticulous overall design. This novel is a haunting virtuoso performance – in several senses a landmark work – even if its occasional deployment of Scots vernacular now seems rather arch or patronizing when set beside the writing of Kelman or Welsh.

While Banks's imagination offers at times the laddish James Bond excitements of the cinema blockbuster – raiding a master criminal's lair, making love to exoticized beautiful women, setting up the headquarters of a secret organization – it can also deconstruct and reassemble the elements of such popular culture to expose their shortcomings. The rock music protagonist of *Espedair Street* looks 'like a henchman in a Bond movie', but turns out to be more complex.[24] Set during an imaginary Central American revolution, *Canal Dreams* has missile launchers, kidnappings and spectacular shootouts. In a Bond movie, Banks's Hisako Onoda, a Japanese cellist, might at best be the hero's 'love interest'; Banks, though, places her centre-stage and has her wreak havoc on her American captors. The extreme violence of *Canal Dreams* is linked to the Holocaust and to the Hiroshima bombing which, years earlier, resulted in the death of Onoda's father. Banks deploys the conventions of blockbuster cinema to spectacular effect, but adds a sense of moral complexity that unpicks and moves beyond the restrictions of Hollywood conventions.

As novelists from J. G. Ballard to Günter Grass wrote in the 1960s, 1970s and 1980s work whose violence reflected a postwar awareness of horror, so, in their wake, Banks's fiction from *The Wasp Factory* to *Dead Air* (2002) and beyond is acutely conscious of atrocities. Banks is also part of a generation brought up on increasingly globalized, American-dominated cinema, television and computer technology in a world where 'product' is the 'buzzword of the century'.[25] 'Product' and images from popular global culture – women as eye candy, fast cars, high-octane living – are there to be consumed in Banks's writing, and at times make him seem a latter-day, sexed-up John Buchan, offering a good read rather than a profound one. With all the sophisticated postmodern cleverness that calls a character David Balfour, and likes to be a player of narrative games, goes a not unattractive but sometimes tired re-use of plot elements, suggesting that Banks is at least as in thrall to reassuring narrative conventions as he is eager to subvert them. Protagonists as apparently different as Daniel Weir in *Espedair Street* and Kate Telman in *The Business* have made 'the great working class escape' so that readers can enjoy vicariously a world where childcare is seldom an issue and there are plentiful Porsches, castles, abundant cash and readily available sex and drugs.

Like Gray and Welsh, Banks can present the male Scot as 'a monster, a mutant'. Yet he likes his male protagonist, having sampled life with a dangerous, exotic woman, to choose instead a safer, girl-next-door partner, as happens in *Espedair Street*, *The Bridge* and *The Crow Road*.[26] His novels' endings are sometimes as reassuring as their beginnings are arresting, even though Banks likes to add a late plot twist or revelation that demands a revaluing of what has gone before. Bound up with a liking for narrative tricksiness is a suspicion of deceit. Deceit is a, if not the, recurring obsession of Banks's work: sexual deceit, the deceits involved in manufacturing and marketing 'product', and the deceits we make or buy for ourselves. Astutely linked to the horrors of 9/11, *Dead Air*, for instance, is about the effort to combat extremist lies with extremist lying. Banks throughout his work likes to write about how deceptive dreams and aspirations can require crucial revision. His prose, for all its clever one-liners ('a car plant that withered'), lacks a distinctive verbal texture; highly intelligent structure is his distinctive forte.[27] *The Bridge* is his most haunting, because most poetically dreamed, book, but its poetry is thinner than, say, that of Italo Calvino's *Invisible Cities*, let alone the Kafka admired by Banks and so many other modern Scottish writers.

Deceit, and darkly humorous, married-to-alcohol Scottish masculinity are stock-in-trade to Ian Rankin's Inspector Rebus. Owing not a little to the earlier Scottish urban detective stories of William McIlvanney and Frederic Lindsay, Rankin uses his deftly written Edinburgh crime fiction to investigate aspects of contemporary Scotland without his friend Banks's postmodern tricksiness. Taking his detective's name from a 'favourite picture puzzle' which he recalled from childhood days with 'the family's *Sunday Post*' newspaper – 'The puzzle they call a "rebus"'

– Rankin has produced arguably the most successful detective stories by a Scottish writer since Conan Doyle.[28] Much readier than Conan Doyle to defend the genre, he may also feel limited by it. Born in working-class Fife in 1960, Rankin studied English at Edinburgh University and began, then later abandoned, postgraduate work on Muriel Spark. In an essay on her work Rankin shows a sophisticated interest in the narrative technique exhibited in works like Alain Robbe-Grillet's *The Erasers* which 'deals with the day leading up to a murder'. Rankin argues that Spark's obsession with appearance and reality may be set in a context that includes Stevenson's *Jekyll and Hyde*, Hogg's *Justified Sinner*, Barrie's *Peter Pan*, and the cityscape of Edinburgh itself. He seems particularly attracted to Spark's sense of how, as Rankin puts it, 'The novelist "loiters with intent", this being also, of course, a criminal act: Spark as ever acknowledges the darker side of the creative impulse.'[29]

Rankin's sense of the Sparkian novelist as involved in a 'criminal act' is part of his wish to avoid seeing literary fiction and crime fiction as separate. Although his uneasy first novel *The Flood* (1986) was not crime fiction, and although he has also written spy stories, as early as 1984 'Ian J. Rankin' published a short tale about 'Big Rab', a dour, ageing uniformed police sergeant who, after thirty years in the force, suffers from 'dizzy spells', feels the boredom of his monotonous job, and soldiers on, determined to ignore waning health.[30] The later Rebus character develops Big Rab's dour masculinity into an almost Kelmanesque disaffection. Rebus shares an initial with his creator (whose middle initial is J.), but his surname presents him as different, a puzzle. Rankin's liking for writing as a 'criminal act' may romanticize authorship, but writers, not least freelance or would-be freelance writers like the young Rankin, uncertain in the later 1980s about finding and keeping a publisher, share with criminals a sense of operating outside the usual routines of society. In Rebus – the ageing, disaffected policeman who upholds and operates within society's official systems, yet is constantly bolshie, distrustful of his ambitious colleagues, and dangerously in thrall to alcohol and nicotine – the writer finds a mixture of companion and mirror-image. Where the younger Rankin is an outsider on his way in, the older Rebus is an insider on his way out; the better each is at his role, the more he develops the other. Discussing Spark, Rankin quotes David Lodge on how the author can make 'the reader "*participate* in the aesthetic and philosophical problems the writing of fiction presents, by embodying them directly in the narrative" '.[31] This is what Rebus does for Rankin.

It is also related to what Rebus does for many of Rankin's readers. Particularly for those who work among tangled strands of organizational rules and regulations there is a sympathetic satisfaction in reading about a figure such as Rebus who is so wary of them. Having an affair with the woman who becomes his boss, drinking too much, being awkward and often cynical but also goodheartedly decent, Rebus offers readers at once the solace of rebellion and a grudging acceptance of working within the system. Rebus's dark humour is similarly compliant and disaffected: recording a death occasioned by a plunge from the Forth Road Bridge on to the deck of a vessel below, Rebus describes it as a boating accident. Rankin takes Edinburgh, that supposedly cultured city, and presents not just its historic sites but also its deprived areas, housing schemes and drug problems; although he does so less outrageously than Welsh, and uses a more conservative narrative style than Banks, Rankin too presents a dark, gritty place. Through Rebus's character, and the increasingly prominent presence of his junior colleague Detective Sergeant Siobhan Clarke, Rankin also investigates gender roles in a rather old-fashioned, but not untypically Scottish 'masculinized' environment. The isolated male Rebus seeks not just sex but also mothering; in some ways he is emotionally inept. Yet his pained experience of parenthood, for example, gives him a human dimension sometimes lacking in the characters of Banks and Welsh, though subtly explored by Kelman in *The Busconductor Hines*.

More and more, Rankin has used his crime fiction to explore not just Edinburgh, but Scotland. *Black and Blue* (1997), with its epigraph from Burns about being 'bought and sold for English gold', investigates the state of the nation just before devolution. *The Hanging Garden* (1998), like many of Rankin's novels, takes its inspiration from fact and deals with the issue of war crimes. *Set in Darkness* (2000) discovers an old murder on the building-site of the rising Scottish Parliament, a lingering presence of Original Sin built into the dreams of a new Scotland. *Fleshmarket Close* (2004) deals with the controversial Scottish and international issue of asylum seekers. Yet the politics in Rankin's atmospheric Edinburgh narratives is as much organizational and managerial, seen not from the podia of motivational speakers, but from the scuffed underside. Rankin is no Kafka, but his protagonist's cannily cynical, practical response to bright organizational bluster is at once dourly confirmatory and heartening for readers in an international culture of 'spin':

> Through a landing window, Rebus could see that outside night had fallen prematurely. Scotland in winter: it was dark when you came to work, and dark when you went home again. Well, they'd had their little outing, gleaned nothing from it, and would now be released back to their various stations until the next meeting. It felt like a penance because Rebus's boss had planned it as such. Farmer Watson was on a committee himself: Strategies for Policing in the New Scotland. Everyone called it SPINS. Committee upon committee . . .[32]

At times Rebus sounds like a male version of the Calvinistic woman in Alastair Reid's celebrated poem 'Scotland' who exclaims on a bright, beautiful day, 'We'll pay for it, we'll pay for it, we'll pay for it!'[33] Using the conventions of detective fiction, Rankin produces a sly investigation of the institutional mind and its discontents that stands beside the openly Kafkaesque experiments of Gray, Kelman and Banks. Vestigially religious, Rebus illuminates his darkness principally through music, intuitive reason, humour, and the good sense of his colleague Siobhan. The challenge for Rankin, as for Banks, is to write accessible mass-market fiction without simply ending up in thrall to or boxed in by its internationally recognized conventions. Seeking to develop his individual style in a global marketplace, his situation parallels that of twenty-first-century Scotland.

Rankin, like Kelman, Welsh and Banks, has become a brand. Just how quickly fiction from Scotland can achieve global product recognition is most apparent in one spectacular case. Iain Banks's casually insolent reference to Harry Potter in *Dead Air* in 2002 would have been recognized around the planet; five years earlier almost no one had heard of Harry Potter or his author, a young Englishwoman who had moved to Edinburgh in 1993.

J. K. Rowling's is the most remarkable success story in literary history. For that reason alone she and her work would deserve attention. In the present context, though, she is also the most prominent example of a striking phenomenon in contemporary Scotland: a writer from elsewhere who may write little about the country, but has chosen to settle in it. Today such authors include the Americans Lucy Ellmann, Todd McEwen and Siri Reynolds in Edinburgh, the Dutch Michel Faber in the

Highlands, the Irishman Bernard McLaverty long domiciled in Glasgow; other authors for whom Scotland has provided a long-term or short-term base range from the English-born Kate Atkinson, Charles Palliser and Ruth Thomas to the Glasgow-educated poet Imtiaz Dharker and the Sudan-born Leila Aboulela whose first novel *The Translator* (1999) deals with a Muslim immigrant in Aberdeen. Never before have so many writers from outside the nation chosen to move to Scotland. In an age when Scottish writers live in Italy, Japan and America, globalization and the legacies of empire are only some of the reasons for this; although, unlike the Republic of Ireland, Scotland offers writers no tax breaks, its combination of history, culture and perceived 'remoteness' with advanced, highly literate modernity may hint at other explanations.

Perhaps none of these incoming authors could be described in a phrase of Muriel Spark's cited by Ian Rankin, 'a writer of Scottish formation', but it is appropriate to welcome their presence with glee; like the Edinburgh International Book Festival, their impact enriches the cosmopolitanism of Scottish cultural life, is a good thing for literature, and may even have played a part in encouraging a marked number of Scottish-born writers – from Ian Rankin and A. L. Kennedy to Don Paterson – to return to the country.[34] Authors who have moved to or spent considerable amounts of time in Scotland have produced such distinguished novels as Bernard McLaverty's superb study of an Irish woman composer, *Grace Notes* (1997), and Aboulela's *The Translator*. Both books are set partly in Scotland, but to claim all these migrant and immigrant writers straightforwardly for Scottish literature would be as crude and naively imperial a gesture as to claim James Joyce for Swiss literature. On the other hand, it seems worth looking in detail at by far the best known among the authors who have moved to Scotland relatively recently, with some speculation about how her work might relate to Scottish culture.

J. K. Rowling has written most of her fiction in Scotland and has come to regard the country as her home. Born in Chipping Sodbury in 1965, she grew up near Bristol, then near Chepstow in the Forest of Dean, and enjoyed a middle-class upbringing; favourite childhood books included Elizabeth Goudge's cleverly constructed *The Little White Horse*, and later, in her teens, *Hons and Rebels* by Jessica Mitford, who had left behind a comfortable English background to marry in the dangerous environment of Civil War Spain, before going on to become an American Communist and supporter of civil rights causes. Rowling studied Modern Languages at Exeter University, enjoyed a year teaching English in Paris, and trained in London as a bilingual secretary. She was on a train returning to London from a flat-hunting trip to Manchester when the figure of Harry Potter came into her imagination. Caught without her customary pen and notebook, she began to work out detailed plot ideas in her head.

Hogwarts School of Witchcraft and Wizardry was the first thing I concentrated on. I was thinking of a place of great order but immense danger, with children who had skills with which they could overwhelm their teachers. Logically, it had to be set in a secluded place and pretty soon I settled on Scotland, in my mind. I think it was in subconscious tribute to where my parents had married.[35]

Although, like James Kelman and so many other writers, Rowling may have longed for more imaginative systems of education, at this time she had no intention of moving to Scotland. However, when she did so later she travelled in a direction already signalled by her imagination. The Harry Potter books do not locate Hogwarts in any specific country, but there are hints that the school is in a northern zone; the Hollywood Potter films' use of such Scottish landmarks as the Glenfinnan viaduct, Ben Nevis and other nearby Highland locations for exterior shots has given closer Scottish definition to the location, but that definition is true to Rowling's original conception. She worked on the first book in the series throughout 1991, during temporary jobs in Manchester at a time when she was shocked by the death of her mother from multiple sclerosis. Unhappy and attempting to change her life, Rowling left England to teach in Oporto, Portugal, where she married, had her first child (named after Jessica Mitford) and completed a rough draft of *Harry Potter and the Philosopher's Stone*. When her marriage failed, she came to Edinburgh in December 1993 to visit her sister. Rowling was distressed, and did not intend to stay. She found Edinburgh 'snow-covered, almost dauntingly beautiful and austerely unfamiliar'. Her small daughter enjoyed going round the Museum of Scotland and Princes Street Gardens. Rowling 'stumbled along in her wake', but came to realize 'I can be happy here.'[36] In an interview with Lindsey Fraser, she adds, 'Maybe it was my Scottish blood calling me home.' This, and stories of how she sat in Nicolson's Restaurant nursing a cup of coffee while working on Harry Potter, make Rowling's early Edinburgh experiences sound fairytale. They were not. For three years she lived as a single mother below the poverty line in Leith, where much of *Trainspotting* is set. Her South Lorne Street flat was broken into and stoned. 'Violence, crime and addiction were part of everyday life in that part of Edinburgh,' she has written, despite its proximity to genteel shops and powerful financial institutions just ten minutes away. Rowling felt 'an abyss' separated her from the douce middle-class people she saw in the city centre. Her fiction is alert to dramatic social divisions and, though written in the first instance for children, is often unflinching in its treatment of potentially disturbing subject matter.

With the aid of a £4000 loan from a friend to do a teacher-training course and, following the initial publication of *Harry Potter and the Philosopher's Stone* (1997), a £6000 grant from the Scottish Arts Council's Literature Department, Rowling wrote her way out of poverty. Revised in Edinburgh and rejected by several editors, her first novel eventually found a London publisher – Bloomsbury. It had very little marketing behind it, but received a favourable review in the *Scotsman*, then praise elsewhere, and began to sell better than expected. It won a prize sponsored by a confectionery firm. Its clear prose seems flat: 'Mr and Mrs Dursley, of number four, Privet Drive, were proud to say that they were perfectly normal, thank you very much,' reads the first sentence. But that implied promise of a world of imaginative enfranchisement where 'normal' routines are surpassed holds the allure of much to come. Adults brought up on boarding-school stories such as those of Enid Blyton or Anthony Buckeridge's Jennings series may feel that Rowling recycles aspects of such tales, remixed with ideas from C. S. Lewis and other fantasy writers. Yet, in the first book, and more so as the series develops, Rowling presents an enveloping imaginative world with its own laws, divisions and logic which, like the imaginative worlds of Dickens's novels or the Sherlock Holmes stories, combines the familiar and the remarkable so closely that readers pass immediately from one to the other.

Rowling, admirer of the 'rebel' Jessica Mitford who left her domestic environment for a different, far more exciting one, saw in Edinburgh what can be seen in all cities: the juxtaposition of 'violence, crime and addiction' with a respectable, 'different world'. She offers her readers encounters which move them from the drab 'normal, thank you very much' environment to an amazing, exciting but also dangerous world of witchcraft and wizardry. Her books provide mystery, detective story elements and the routine, calendared, minutely legislated environment of a school as well as the fantastic dreamworld of flying children, dragons and battles with forces of evil as the remarkably gifted boy wizard Harry battles with the powers of the evil dark Lord Voldemort. It's as if *The Lord of the Rings* was being fought out at Mallory Towers or Greyfriars. A global audience of children and adults with a taste for plainly written yet extensively detailed imaginative narrative enjoy this apparently escapist fiction.

As Harry ages, the books deal with growing up; they start as stories of childhood, then become tales of adolescence. They feature school crushes, bullying and rivalries, but also darker matters. If the second book of the series, *Harry Potter and the Chamber of Secrets* (1998), is perhaps the weakest, imaginative interest intensifies in the third, *Harry Potter and the Prisoner of Azkaban* (1999), when Harry and his readers encounter the cloaked Dementors, their hands 'glistening, greyish, slimy-looking and scabbed, like something dead that had decayed in water . . .' On first seeing one of these creatures, Harry catches his breath and feels a sensation of intensive cold 'inside his very heart'.[37] For all their wrap-round detail and imaginative humour, it is these books' ability to deal through their treatment of 'Death Eaters', 'Killing curses', were-wolves and 'Dark Arts' with deep, universal fears and, ultimately, even death, which is the strength of the series. Rowling, a reticent Episco-palian, has been attacked by Christian fundamentalists for glamorizing witchcraft. This is a naive misunderstanding, and one that child readers are unlikely to make. In an interview published in 2006 Rowling argued that 'My books are largely about death.'[38] Even if this is an exaggeration, her best writing and most intense imagining – such as the long account leading up to the death of the paternal Dumbledore, Headmaster of Hogwarts, in the sixth book, *Harry Potter and the Half-Blood Prince* (2005) – centres around mortality.

In an era of sudden, globally communicated violence, yet also an age which regards talk of death as taboo, and at a time when fears about the protection of children are ubiquitous, Rowling has found an access-ible, lively and powerful way to write about death for children and adults. For an author 'depth-charged' by the death of her mother and confronting her own fears in mid-1990s Leith's squalor, the books may represent an imaginative, refracted working-out of often dark experiences; for readers, they provide a structured environment in which to confront fear, pain and grief, as well as somewhere to play and laugh. As Robert Louis Stevenson knew long before Rowling, the ludic, the fearful and the deathly are often closely connected, and nowhere more than in writing that appeals to children. Perhaps Rowling can be understood as an Edinburgh-based writer who in her own way understands, and even at times gravitates towards, a psychology of darkness and violence familiar in the fictions of such very different Scottish contemporaries as Ian Rankin, and even Irvine Welsh.

Living in Edinburgh and Perthshire may allow Rowling to manage the awkwardness of her celebrity status more helpfully than might permanent residence in London or Los Angeles. In terms of her global profile, she is by far the most internationally prominent of Scotland's living literary celebrities – and now by far the wealthiest. Yet Rowling's are only a few among many successful children's novels recently produced by Scottish authors such as Theresa Breslin, Julie Bertagna and (writing for younger children) Mairi Hedderwick whose series of illustrated books set on the island of 'Struay', beginning with *Katie Morag Delivers the Mail* (1984), have found an international audience. It would be inappropriate to give over most of this chapter to best-selling novelists, but mention should be made too of the observant children's writer, Edinburgh University academic and prodigiously versatile author Alexander McCall Smith. Among Smith's books for adults his internationally best-selling Botswana-based detective fictions in books like *The No. 1 Ladies Detective Agency* (1998) offer a near-Kailyard Africa sometimes suspiciously free of fearful facts, so that his work can seem more escapist than Rowling's. In an attempt to block out the terrors of a helicopter flight, one of P. D. James's fictional investigators reads about 'Smith's gentle and engaging Botswanan detective'.[39] Best known for his presentation of an African woman detective, Mma Ramotswe, Smith (who grew up in Botswana) has a good, clear prose style and a wonderful rapport with audiences; he also nicely observes the ethical dilemmas of middle-class Edinburgh in detective stories featuring Isabel Dalhousie. Common-sensically intelligent and enjoyably meandering, McCall Smith's work in its international settings and appeal can be seen as a form of soft globalization. He matters because he shows that happiness, not just horror, is worldwide.

Certainly we live in a great age of Scottish crime fiction. The much tougher sleuths of another internationally best-selling Scottish author, Val McDermid, include Mancunian Kate Brannigan ('No woman is a heroine to her dentist'), criminal profiler Tony Hill and the lesbian detective Lindsay Gordon.[40] Often gritty as well as witty, McDermid's accomplished, feminist-accented detective stories outsell even those of Rankin and McCall Smith in some countries. Born in Fife in 1955, she grew up in Kirkcaldy and now lives in Manchester. One of her novels, *The Distant Echo* (2003), is set in St Andrews, but most of her locations are non-Scottish. Both McDermid and McCall Smith have an interest in literary history, and between them Rankin and McDermid have encouraged the appreciation of older Scottish crime novelists such as Frederic Lindsay and Quintin Jardine. They have also spurred new generations of sometimes experimental authors including Glasgow's hard-hitting Denise Mina, much more consciously literary Louise Welsh, and the energetically popular Christopher Brookmyre – all of whom, though sometimes working in other areas, have produced Scottish urban crime novels looping from the horrific to the humorous in a style that has come to be nicknamed 'tartan noir'. For Scots, as for so many others, crime fiction offers the suggestion that clever use of information can solve problems and provide an assurance of at least partial closure – an appealing promise in an age overwhelmed by proliferating technologies of not always reliable information.

Where earlier Scottish Calvinists searched anxiously for signs of grace, today's Scottish crime writers and readers snap up disgrace wherever they can find it. Frequently they find it in Edinburgh or Glasgow. Crime afficionados should seek out Frank Kuppner's *A Very Quiet Street* (1989), a 'novel of sorts' based around a notorious Glasgow murder case. Kuppner (b. 1951), a Glaswegian poet preoccupied with cityscapes, randomness, patternings and the vagaries of human folly, is known for such superbly quirky volumes of verse as *A Bad Day for the Sung Dynasty* (1984). Layering interpretation on interpretation, hiding parenthesis inside parenthesis, his work raises questions about the relativity of knowledge and interpretation. *A Very Quiet Street*, his best prose book, mixes stylistic vagaries with ethical commitment. It is the oddest of all Scottish detective stories.

In Scottish fiction where crime is of the essence many writers take the opportunity to explore the darker aspects of masculinity, but there is rarely a sense of spirituality, something of which many Scottish novelists now seem wary or frightened. In part again this may be a backlash against an older, theocratic Scotland, or a Scottish fiction overpopulated with ministers. Among the linked, partly autobiographical short stories of *Its Colours They Are Fine* (1977) Alan Spence (b. 1947) presents a sometimes brutalized mid-twentieth-century Glasgow. However, Spence's book culminates in nuanced accounts of a sensitive boy whose upbringing in an environment both of kindness and of harsh Protestant–Catholic sectarianism leads him to turn towards Buddhism. Some of this territory is revisited in *The Magic Flute* (1990), a novel which examines coming of age in a milieu of 'young team boys, loud and raucous . . . looking for *real* trouble, aggravation, bother'.[41] Spence's fiction gravitates towards how people, especially men, can grow in an environment of male bravado accompanied by spiritual and emotional repression. In *Way to Go* (1998) the protagonist and his Indian wife try to move beyond the harsh world of a dour Scottish father who worked as an undertaker and whose communication with his son was always difficult.

A deftly handled relationship between father and son is at the heart of 'The Face', one of the best short stories by Brian McCabe (b. 1951), whose finely observed fiction often deals with male dilemmas and whose poetry images an alcoholic man in a doorway as 'the Buddha in Edinburgh'.[42] Much admired by Irvine Welsh, who described it as 'One of the greatest pieces of fiction to come out of Britain in the 80s', *The Sound of my Voice* (1987), the first novel by McCabe's Edinburgh contemporary Ron Butlin, presents a middle-class male alcoholic careering towards self-destruction while attempting to tune into an inner voice.[43] Masculinity in extremis is also a theme important to Andrew Greig in novels such as *Electric Brae* (1992) and *That Summer* (2000), though Greig's abiding theme is heterosexual love. Spence, McCabe, Butlin and Greig are all poets as well as novelists, their work at its best charged with a lyricism which infuses their fiction with a sense of spiritual questing. For the haiku-writing Spence who runs a meditation centre, for Greig (one of whose books is subtitled 'Adventures with the Heretical Buddha'), and momentarily at least for both McCabe and Butlin, there seems an attraction to an Eastern spirituality which might be the reverse of the macho stereotypes of dour, emotionally stunted Scottish hardmen. Such an attraction, and some of its difficulties for a Glasgow man and his family, are thoughtfully and funnily explored in

Buddha Da (2003), the debut novel by the Glaswegian writer Ann Donovan.

Also modifying 'hardman' stereotypes are the characters of Ronald Frame's fiction. Born in 1953, Frame lived for a long time with his middle-class parents (dedicatees of many of his books) in suburban Glasgow. His highly mannered television programme *Ghost City* (broadcast by BBC Scotland in 1994) features an actor playing a character called 'Ronald Frame' who revisits Glasgow to promote his newest book and feels 'halfway to a ghost'. Resisting the equation of Glasgow simply with working-class fictions, this 'Frame' argues persuasively that 'There is a lost city . . . another Glasgow . . . the middle-class one in which I and all my sort were brought up,' and he contends that 'Now there's one voice where there used to be other voices. It shouted them down,' though the same speaker also asks, 'Am I turning the past into a fable to suit myself?' An immensely sophisticated Scottish writer, Frame is both preoccupied with the need to make fictions of the self and attuned to 'the essence of suburbia', though the locations of his novels range from Borneo to New York and most often involve a fictionalized southern England.

Recurringly Frame's fiction is fascinated by the way identity, not least sexual identity, is both taken and mistaken over time. Often his protagonists are female and several times he presents homosexual men in apparently conventional marriages. Identities are fluid, sometimes washed away. 'When I wrote down in my notepad *"Sometimes I feel I am no one"*, even the writing of it faintly cheered me,' recalls the unhappy diplomat's daughter in Frame's first novel, *Winter Journey* (1984), while a character in *Sandmouth People* (1987) is taking part in Terence Rattigan's play *Harlequinade*: ' "I play an actress playing an actress." '[44] Alert to the globally circulating literary and cinematic fictions of Spark, Robbe-Grillet, Jean-Luc Godard and John Ashbery, but also attached to Proust as well as to an older milieu of the middle- and upper-class anglicized 1950s with their plays by Rattigan, novels by Rose Macaulay, and much-photographed celebrity glamour models, Frame's novels attempt to combine postmodern weavings and unweavings of the self with the conventions of middlebrow, middle-class fiction. Several of his characters change their names repeatedly, often under 'the cover of ignorance and respectability'.[45]

Novelists are part of Frame's novels, most obviously in *Penelope's*

Hat (1989), which turns out to have been written by its protagonist whose 'characters', we are told in 'Appendix B', 'are almost spectral, liquid, sometimes they hardly hold their shape from one page to the next'. The self in Frame's work seems a kind of often-changed garment; Frame writes about women's clothing with almost fetishistic care. This novelist is concerned with the way the self or self-image, uncertain enough for David Hume, seems even more fluid and artificial in our age of media celebrity and 'personalities'. *Sandmouth People* includes a competition to find Miss Modern Personality, while *Bluette* (1990) centres around a model who becomes a media celebrity. Even in youth this woman could look in a mirror and become 'transparent. She saw through herself, and she was transformed . . .' *Bluette*'s characters move 'almost as figures in a film themselves', and references to T. S. Eliot's *The Cocktail Party* raise unanswerable questions about what is 'the real reality'. Imaginative and assured, Frame's work in his hugely productive first decade as a published author can be over-indulgent ('The house was kept tenebrous, aphotic'); he writes of loveless proprieties and often hopeless sexual outbursts.[46] His fiction is nowhere better than in his short stories and novellas in such collections as *A Long Weekend with Marcel Proust* (1986) and *Walking with My Mistress in Deauville* (1992), or in the miniature television drama *Paris* (1987) with its beautifully notated elderly unmarried Glaswegian women longing for the unreachable abandon emblematized for them by Parisian life.

Frequently containing sly Scottish references (in street names, glancing mentions, memories), Frame's stories and novels have included Scottish settings from the start, but his most explicitly Scottish novel is *The Lantern Bearers* (2001) which alludes to R. L. Stevenson, Thomas Mann and others in its subtle presentation of the relationship between a boy and a Scottish composer. More recent books such as the stories of *Time in Carnbeg* (2004), centred around a fictionalized Perthshire town, also make more of their Scottishness. Some of these tales show, though, a dip in imaginative intensity, and a tendency to repeat in politely diluted form the obsessions of earlier work. If Frame's characters are caught repeatedly between respectability and hunger for (often sexual) adventure, his fiction may have become trapped between the conventions of a once popular middlebrow fiction and a more experimental 'postmodern' style where, as an epigraph Frame selects from Godard puts it, 'Seeing is deceiving'. Some of his most recent stories appear to settle for safety rather than risk, though his intelligent, stylish treatment of gender, nostalgia and 'image' align him with Muriel Spark and Elspeth Davie, as well as with younger writers like Andrew O'Hagan.

A male writer who likes to write in a feminine voice, Frame writes confidently about homoeroticism. His 'mimicry' of the female has been followed by very different writers such as Alan Warner, while his interest in gay men's lives anticipates the development of that theme in Scottish fiction by Christopher Whyte, Joseph Mills and others. Where Frame wrote in *Ghost City* of a childhood among Protestant, Jewish and other boys at the then single-sex, brown-blazered, fee-paying Glasgow High School where 'nobody should be apart' but all should take part in 'group activities' in a 'world in which I was being educated to *accept* things', Whyte writes in the wittily scandalous comedy of *Euphemia MacFarrigle and the Laughing Virgin* (1995) a novel that may relate to his own experience at the green-blazered Glasgow Catholic school, St Aloysius College. Whyte too writes in crisp English about the need for people denied identity to construct or reconstruct selves, but does so from an openly gay perspective.

A non-native speaker who learned Gaelic and who has written the first openly gay poetry in that language, the strikingly learned Whyte (b. 1952) is a Scot educated at the Universities of Cambridge, Perugia and Glasgow; he lived in Italy for twelve years, and later resigned from a post at Glasgow University in order to return to the continent. While his most energetic novel is his first, Whyte's second novel, *The Warlock of Strathearn* (1997), is a remarkable re-imagining of the life (or, more accurately, lives) of a seventeenth-century wizard whose outsider's adventures include several kinds of sexual experience as well as time spent as, among other things, a mole, a weasel, an otter, a gnat and a trout. Drawing on his scholarly knowledge of Scottish literature and, perhaps, on such a protean exemplum as Woolf's *Orlando*, Whyte produces in standard English a shape-shifting tale that ranges from Perthshire to Bohemia and wishes to slyly scandalize; his work, like Frame's, includes an energetic discharge of bodily fluids. Yet Whyte's fictions in *The Gay Decameron* (1998), for all their internationalism and engagement with middle-class Scottish life, seem rather linguistically flat, as does the ambitious, rather bookish rendering of Venice in *The Cloud Machinery* (2000). A difficulty for middle-class Scottish fiction writers writing in English has been to find a grain and texture that makes their prose always recognizably individual in terms of style rather than subject matter. The younger authors A. L. Kennedy and Ali Smith may have been most successful in this regard, but of the male novelists born in the 1950s Frame comes closest. In *Ghost City* he argues that middle-class Scots born in the 1950s 'could never be quite sure where we belonged – to ourselves as Scots, or as northern vassals of a southern imperial power'. Oxford-educated Frame is not a writer who fits the 'gritty working-class' label lazily applied to contemporary Scottish fiction. He matters all the more for that reason.

For several Scottish writers, not least middle-class ones, residence in England and integration into the English literary scene may have been as much accident as design. Born in Ghana in 1952, William Boyd was educated at one of Scotland's relatively few public schools, Gordonstoun, but recalled it with astonishment as a place of 'patrician venom' where 'a strong Scottish accent was a real stigma . . . any regional accent was parodied mercilessly', and 'to us the locals were "yobs", "oiks", "plebs", "proles"'.[47] This seems the mirror-image of Kelman's working-class Glasgow where any middle-class accent seems suspect and upper-class accents are nowhere, but what Boyd describes is another version of the theme so often treated by Frame, Kelman, Ali Smith and many other Scottish writers: the suppression or robbery of identity which leads in turn to a new or invented identity. This theme, strong in Walter Scott and older Scottish imaginative writing, remains important in the era of Scottish devolution and the literary imagining of new individual and supra-individual identities.

William Boyd attended Glasgow University, though the effect of most of his education at Gordonstoun, Nice and Oxford was surely to educate him out of any perceptible sense of being a Scot. From *An Ice-Cream War* (1982) with its Scottish doctor in East Africa to his more recent work, Scottish accents or attitudes appear marginal, with the exception of *The New Confessions* (1987) whose title recalls not just Rousseau but also James Hogg's masterpiece, and whose film-director protagonist, Edinburgh-born John James Todd, hangs on to a residual Scottishness, though he has long since left Scotland. It may be that for Boyd, as for Byron and several other Scots in earlier centuries, Scottish upbringing and long-time London residence may have quickened a sense of cosmopolitan displacement rather than any profound articulation of

'Scottishness'. With his Scottish-sounding forename, Lorimer Black in Boyd's London comic novel of transfiguration, *Armadillo* (1998), is actually Milomre Blocj, child of immigrant gypsies, brought up with '*the constant incantation of, "Now you are English boy, Milo. This is your country, this is your home*."'[48] If Boyd's apparently very English fictions deal repeatedly with outsiders, it may be that this is conditioned by the experience of displacement in his own perceived Scottish, unScottish upbringing and education.

Displacement matters too in the work of Candia McWilliam, though some of her best writing shows a much deeper engagement with Scotland and traditions of Scottish literature. Born in 1955 in Edinburgh, she was raised 'to notice every astragal, every stone' in a city where her father Colin McWilliam, an architectural historian, co-authored *The Buildings of Scotland: Edinburgh*. At the start of her teens McWilliam was sent to boarding school in England, then went to Girton College, Cambridge, where she graduated with first-class honours in English before working in advertising and journalism. She has spent most of her adult life in the south of England, but maintains, for instance, admiration for 'James Hogg's great novel, *The Private Memoirs and Confessions of a Justified Sinner*, in which so much Scots writing has its roots', and has written of *The Prime of Miss Jean Brodie* that 'I've read it more than twice a year since I was ten.'[49]

With its 'Scots Calvinist' aristocrat Anne Cowdenbeath who is 'used to the idea of there being unjustified sinners', McWilliam's first novel, *A Case of Knives* (1988), follows Hogg in its presentation of a murder from several narrative points of view. Like Hogg's novel it is also a story about fatal attempts to manipulate identity, though McWilliam splices Hogg's narrative strategies with a rather Oxonian framework of Iris Murdochry. Written with panache, and almost mannered lexical attentiveness, the book can appear a little too neatly contrived. A homosexual London heart surgeon or 'plumber of the heart' locates a young woman whom he 'can train and prune' to become the wife of Hal, the man he loves; the young woman, regarded as a 'Miss Nothing', a kind of doll to be played with, is actually using Hal so she can find a father for the child she is carrying.[50] The characters' attempts at mutual exploitation and control go wrong in a plot whose geometry in some ways recalls the fate of Spark's Willie Brodie who 'died . . . on a gibbet of his own devising', as Spark puts it in a phrase quoted elsewhere by McWilliam.[51]

Like Ronald Frame, McWilliam writes about hidden as well as overt homosexuality, and about the sometimes violent contortions of gender roles in a substantially middle-class or upper-class world where life can appear 'as one unending television advertisement'.[52]

Other themes too interest McWilliam. One is motherhood – a topic given strikingly little attention in modern Scottish fiction, where fatherhood looms much larger – and another is self-image. Written in the era of magazines like *The Face*, and authored by a woman photographed by celebrity photographers including Richard Avedon, McWilliam's books may draw on such experiences and on their author's time in the advertising industry. Her fictions can present doll-like women who are revealed as both troubled and troubling. Easy and commercially-reinforced assumptions about femininity are both acknowledged and upset. In *A Little Stranger* (1989) a lonely, affluent woman watches her nanny who 'resembled a woman in a television advert for chocolate mints' and who 'dressed as though her classical heroes were Berkertex and his legendary protector Aquascutum'.[53] But the nanny turns out to be both dangerous and bulimic, while the neglected mother is trapped in addiction to over-eating.

McWilliam's first two novels are tightly plotted and stylishly written with a kind of reined-in, manicured anger; her third, prompted in part by personal pain that included the death of her father, is a masterpiece of modern Scottish fiction. Set in the South Seas, but obsessively engaged with Edinburgh, *Debatable Land* (1994) is a novel of globalization which takes six characters on a voyage from Tahiti to New Zealand. With its epigraph from Stevenson's poem of longing for his familial Edinburgh which begins, 'The tropics vanish', this cosmopolitan Scottish novel treats of topics which include longing, bereavement, the oppressiveness of the male ego, and the search for love. Like McWilliam's short stories in *Wait Till I Tell You* (1997) it juxtaposes north and south. Its prose shows off less than that of McWilliam's first two novels, but achieves striking verisimilitude as well as lyric beauty:

Under the boat the water divided and remet itself around her keel. The two lappings of the water on each side of the boat were separately audible, and beneath them the deeper licking the sea made at the island's hidden reaches ushered a lower and graver sound over the sea's surface, under the talk and human movement on the boat.

McWilliam's prose is imaginatively attentive and wise, not just about inanimate objects from boats to the cityscape of Edinburgh and the Roslin chapel ('a building that seemed to have been cooked at different temperatures over much time'), but also about human behaviour and emotions. Alec, an Edinburgh artist in flight from his home life, recalls of his alcoholic partner, 'She was happy when she drank for about half a sentence, like a lifted eyelid. Then the eyelid closed again and the dark came down.' Variously paced, this prose has humour and practicality about it, as well as lyricism. Trying to find an old folks' home in Edinburgh for the elderly Muriel, Alec and his partner Lorna inspect several:

> The second place was full of whimpers. There were no men, who make old people's homes smell but also give the old ladies something to live for beyond spite. On the walls were strung messages of Life Beautiful, penned in the prose of girlish serfdom and laminated. The bathroom contained an old woman being washed when they were shown around. When Alec withdrew to save her feelings, the woman sponging her said, 'Don't worry, she doesn't know the difference.' By then Lorna was out too. The confiscation of privacy seemed to kill the old ladies more quickly than widowhood and bitter winters.

These several quotations may hint at how meticulously and humanely written this novel is. Though it was praised, particularly by non-Scottish critics, when it appeared, its publication soon after that of *Trainspotting*, and its sense of 'Anglo-Scots' make it seem very different from what has tended to be defined as 'contemporary Scottish writing'.[54] Posh-voiced, living down south, and focusing often on the well-off, McWilliam has written fiction that is a vital part of the spectrum of recent Scottish literature.

The remarkable range and vivacity of that spectrum can be indicated by setting beside McWilliam's work not just that of Kelman and Welsh but also the poetry and drama of Liz Lochhead. If concerns with gender, with Scotland, and with a critique of nostalgia are common to McWilliam and Lochhead, their articulation in terms of genre, register and style could not be more different. The differences reflect background, but also individual artistry: they are not explained by sociology alone. Born in 1947 and brought up in working-class industrial Lanarkshire, Lochhead treasured stories told by her mother and grandfather; taught by 'maiden ladies' at a school which still had separate entrances for 'Girls' and 'Boys', she felt sometimes in her youth 'too bluff, too braggy'.

She recalls being schooled at Newarthill Primary School near Mother-well by 'Miss Jean Brodies twenty years beyond their prime'.

Lochhead's reference to Jean Brodie occurs in a 1977 memoir written at the end of her twenties, and confirms the powerful impact of Muriel Spark on younger women writers' views of Scotland; at least as striking, though, is the way Lochhead emphasizes differences between her own childhood and the childhoods offered to her by literature – whether *The Prime of Miss Jean Brodie* or the school stories of Enid Blyton. Before welcoming the 'Freedom' of Art School in Glasgow, Lochhead was educated at Dalziel High School in Motherwell where, at the start of the 1960s, she won an essay prize for writing about autumn and 'tea by the fire and toasted muffins'. In the 1970s she wrote more honestly,

I don't think I'd ever tasted toasted muffins and jam in my life but they sounded right, English enough, almost Enid Blytonish. It was not a lie, exactly. Just that it had never occurred to me, nothing in my Education had ever led me to believe that anything among my own real life ordinary things had the right to be written down. What you wrote could not be the truth. It did not have the authority of English things, the things in books.[55]

In terms of working-class upbringing, Lochhead's statement could be set alongside others by English poets like Tony Harrison, but Lochhead's consciousness of being unEnglish aligns her experience more readily with reflections by writers from Australia, the Caribbean, Ireland, or the Scotland of Tom Leonard or James Kelman, who later became her friends. As a gifted female poet in 1960s Scotland, Lochhead developed in a markedly male milieu. Her tragically short-lived Scottish contemporary Veronica Forrest-Thomson (1947–75) was a student in Cambridge, publishing with specialist English poetry presses; Forrest-Thomson's lively, experimental work in *Twelve Academic Questions* (1970) and elsewhere, though it was innovatively alert to structuralist and post-structuralist arguments in literary theory and would have an impact on the developing, sometimes aridly intellectual 'Cambridge School' poetics, was relatively little known in Scotland.

Arguably more than in Forrest-Thomson's work gender was impor-tant in Lochhead's writing; at the same time, her account of 'the auth-ority of English things' might speak for many of her older and younger male contemporaries. While maintaining an independence, Lochhead also learned from their work and was welcomed by them. Alasdair Gray drew Lochhead's portrait for her first book *Memo for Spring* (1970), and a phrase from one of its poems, 'unironic lips', is borrowed from 'King Billy' in the recently published collection *The Second Life* (1968) by Edwin Morgan, whose adventurous way with Glasgow and with gender Lochhead admires.

Still, for all her filiations with Scottish male writers, Lochhead in her first book and ever since has consciously articulated female experience. Ready at times to call on feminist perspectives, she is reluctant to let her writing be pigeonholed by them. Sometimes relishing the jokey mobility of pun, her poetry is mostly written in English and shows a gift for shrewd observation – right from her first book when she notes how a new Glaswegian neighbour in a sari

> . . . has
> a jewel in her nostril.
> The golden hands with the almond nails
> that push the pram turn blue
> in the city's cold climate.[56]

In other poems like 'My Mother's Suitors' Lochhead writes well about the era of her childhood and before. As it develops, in poems such as 'What the Pool Said, On Midsummer's Day', her verse pushes often towards the performative, most obviously in *True Confessions and New Clichés* (1985). From the 1980s, while continuing to produce poetry, Lochhead has invested more and more energy in writing for the theatre. Her work extends from translations and adaptations of Molière, Chekhov, and Greek dramas such as *Medea* (2001) to original plays, best known of which is the impressive *Mary Queen of Scots Got Her Head Chopped Off* (1987).

This last play intercuts past and present as it zeroes in on themes of national identity, chauvinisms, female power and sectarianism. These issues are explored through a presentation of characters from John Knox, Mary, Queen of Scots, and Elizabeth I of England to contemporary schoolchildren. Most of the work is in prose, but the chorus-like speeches of La Corbie, a 'ragged, ambiguous creature' who appears to have flapped straight out of the famous ballad of 'The Twa Corbies' (quoted in full in the play), provide some of Lochhead's most insightfully energized poetry when, in answer to the quesion, 'Country: Scotland. Whit like is it?' the answer is cackled:

National flower: the thistle.
National pastime: nostalgia.
National weather: smirr, haar, drizzle, snow.
National bird: the crow, the corbie, le corbeau, moi!
How me? Eh? Eh? Eh? Voice like a choked laugh. Ragbag o' a burd in ma black duds, a' angles and elbows and broken oxter feathers, black beady een in ma executioner's hood. No braw, but Ah think Ah ha'e a sort of black glamour.[57]

Sometimes 'bluff . . . braggy' and ironized, this play, like Lochhead's other work, exhibits several Scotlands: dour Knoxian masculinity confronts and is confronted by female intelligence, power and beauty. Learning from the theatre of Brecht as well as from the poetry of Burns and the ballads, Lochhead's dramas present female power, critiquing male authority – not just the domineering masculinity of Knox, but also that of Molière's Tartuffe, a Burnsian Holy Willie in the deft 'theatrical Scots' *Tartuffe* of Thatcherite 1985:

> God's guid indeed, that he should grant
> Tae me, a miserable sinner, a' Ah want—[58]

Recasting traditions of popular drama that include the old Scottish favourites, music-hall and pantomime, and fusing these with more classical drama, has resulted in much of Lochhead's best work: a body of plays theatrically ambitious and accessibly vernacular. In the late 1970s when male dramatists dominated Scottish theatre, the work of Marcella Evaristi (b. 1953) introduced a clear concern with women's lives, the need for female independence, and the complex cultural make-up of Scotland, articulated in plays like *Mouthpieces* (1980) and *Commedia* (1983). These themes are also important in Lochhead's work and her influence can be sensed at times in the work of younger writers like the poet Carol Ann Duffy or the poet, prose writer and dramatist Jackie Kay. Lochhead's example has helped empower a new generation of Scottish playwrights from Rona Munro (b. 1959) in such plays as *Bold Girls* (1991) where women confront male violence in contemporary Belfast to Iain Heggie in his aggressively masculine Glaswegian drama *A Wholly Healthy Glasgow* (1988). Lochhead's preoccupations may be compared with the interest in female strength and attempts at liberation in the work of Sharman Macdonald (b. 1951) whose plays such as *When I Was a Girl I Used to Scream and Shout* (1985) and *Shades* (1992) have investigated the constraints of women's lives with humour as well as attack. An ambitious woman writer committed to and usually based in Scotland, Lochhead has worked with theatres from the Royal Shakespeare Company to the Royal Lyceum in Edinburgh, providing through her work and presence much encouragement for younger practitioners.

Glaswegian dramatist Chris Hannan (b. 1958) has investigated the history and mores of his native city in such plays as *Elizabeth Gordon Quinn* (1985), *The Evil Doers* (1990) and *Shining Souls* (1996), but his range extends from original drama set in ancient Rome to a version of Ibsen for the Royal Shakespeare Company. Late twentieth- and early twenty-first-century Scottish drama runs from an ambitious version of Goethe's *Faust* (2006) and the earlier history play *Losing Venice* by John Clifford (b. 1950) to the sharp Scots and English dialogue of Ann Marie di Mambro and the popular drama of working-class women's slog, *The Steamie* (1987) by Tony Roper. Dark and difficult relationships are often explored in the work of David Harrower, dramatist of *Kill the Old Torture their Young* (1998), *Dark Country* (2003) and *Blackbird* (2005) with their focus on abuse, frustrated desire and menial work. Definitions of work, culture and identity are unstable in the often nameless locations of Harrower's dramas, aware of global forces and alert to the uncertain pressures of economic change. Born in Edinburgh and based in Fife, Sue Glover (b. 1943) conducts a sustained dramatic examination of women's lives in a context of rural hardship and large-scale economic forces in such plays as *Bondagers* (1991), about indentured women workers on an 1860 Borders farm, and *Shetland Saga* (2000) which deals with today's international capitalism. In a world of globalization where the pay and conditions of women workers remain sometimes difficult topics, not least in Scotland, Glover in *Bondagers* makes skilful use of historical drama to emphasize that attitudes and behaviour thought of as unchangeable are seldom actually so:

ELLEN: 'Don't be ridiculous, Ellen,' says the maister. 'We can't do away with the bondage. I can't employ a man who hasn't a woman to work with him. One pair of horse to every fifty acre, one hind for every pair of horse, one bondager for every hind. That's the way it's done,' he says. 'I'm all for progress,' he says, 'but I won't do away with the bondage,' he says. 'We need the women. Who else would do the work? . . . Women's work, for women's pay.'[59]

The gathering strength of contemporary Scottish drama was emblematized by the launch of the Scottish National Theatre in February 2006. Events across the land ranged from performers abseiling down an eighteen-storey Glasgow tower-block to a 'multimedia experience' (partly scripted by Jackie Kay and Shetland playwright Jacqui Clark) on board a ferry at Holmsgarth Ferry Terminal, Lerwick. Without its own theatre building, but with a core staff based in Glasgow under the direction of Vicky Featherstone, the National Theatre of Scotland acts as a supporter and developer of theatre work across the country. This makes the NTS affordable (attractive to its Scottish Executive financial backers), and may make it hard to achieve consistent international excellence, but it also offers opportunities. The NTS's first dramaturge, David Greig, is attracted to the way 'We ... the Scots have chosen literally to make the statement that our national identity is without walls.'

Born in Edinburgh in 1967, David Greig was raised in Jos, Nigeria, between the Muslim north and the Christian south of the country, before returning to his native city; he then studied English and Drama at Bristol University, coming back to Scotland at the start of the 1990s when he founded with Graham Eatough the theatre company Suspect Culture in a Glasgow which had recently been designated European City of Culture. Author of nearly thirty plays before the National Theatre of Scotland was launched, Greig is Scotland's most adventurous and accomplished living playwright, his plays honed, poetic, and deeply engaged with stagecraft. Beckett and Kafka are among writers who matter to Greig and several of his concerns – personal and societal identity, spirituality and ecology among them – link him to other Scottish writers of his generation, especially the poets. Although he did not grow up a Catholic, he has spoken of perceiving in his own plays a 'haunted quality that you find in writers from ... a kind of Catholic tradition', and he sees the work of drama as close at times to that of poetry. His plays use prose, with occasional movements towards verse lineation.

Several Greig dramas, such as his wisely impressive study of a domineering workaholic and of family collapse, *The Architect* (1996), and his 1930s drama *Outlying Islands* (2002) are set in Scotland. The architect Leo Black has to learn painfully about 'the human element' and the difference between designing houses and having to 'house people'. Other plays by Greig are set in deliberately indeterminate locations which evoke multiple possibilities. The displaced people in a provincial railway station of *Europe* (1995) are coming to terms with a social order where 'God wears a suit' and 'express trains' go 'so fast they can't even make out the station name as they pass', while minority populations are persecuted.[60] Riskily isolated on a foreign island, a man is taken to represent all the values of his powerful country in *The American Airman* (2005). Greig's wish to investigate 'the constant pull between actually wanting to . . . find something that roots us and is local, whilst at the same time wanting to embrace the global' may be related to his own upbringing, but it is equally present in the work of many contemporary Scottish novelists, playwrights and poets.[61]

Globalization and its economic impact on the local is explored, for instance, not just in many of Greig's plays but also in Gregory Burke's *Gagarin Way* (2001), set in a Scottish factory. Burke (b. 1968) wrote the hard-hitting wartime drama *Black Watch* which was the great success of the National Theatre of Scotland's 2006 programme. In *Gagarin Way* he acutely interrogates through demotic confrontations a world where, as his factory worker Eddie puts it,

Capital comes, capital goes. That's the nature ay capital. Nay cunt's fucking immune ay. Got tay consider the options provided globally for inward investment. There's always some mob ay peasants scratching at the topsoil somewhere whose wildest dream is a shift in here.[62]

All the characters in Burke's *Gagarin Way* are men. All the characters in Glover's *Bondagers* are women. While it is not infrequently the case that works of contemporary Scottish literature can be 'gendered', it would be wrong to ghettoize them, assuming that they have an import only for one sex or gender. More than that, playwrights like David Greig and David Harrower can write strong parts for both sexes while remaining aware of a power struggle against entrenched masculinism. Playwrights including Lochhead, Glover and Sharman Macdonald produce a popular feminist Scottish voice in art that reaches an audience much wider than that reached by Ena Lamont Stewart or Willa Muir or by the novels of Catherine Carswell in earlier generations. In the 1980s and 1990s imprints such as Canongate Classics in Edinburgh and Virago in London committedly reprinted some earlier Scottish women novelists who might appeal to a late twentieth-century sensibility modified by feminism, but it was a younger generation of novelists which made the greatest impact.

Janice Galloway's first novel, *The Trick Is to Keep Breathing* (1989), was signed up by the remarkable Peter Kravitz, editor at Edinburgh's innovative Polygon publishing house, originally an offshoot of Edinburgh University Student Publications Board, and first book publisher of writers as different as Rankin, Kelman and, later, A. L. Kennedy. Galloway (b. 1956) had learned from the syntax, typography, articulation of class position, and struggles with entrapment that permeated the fiction of Kelman and Gray. Her novel, however, was very much written from a female perspective in its fragmented, shapeshifting presentation of a young West of Scotland teacher, Joy Stone. Traumatized by the death of her lover, Stone struggles with an eating disorder and depression in the midst of an environment whose systems of work, healthcare and social services seem geared to depersonalized institutional, masculinist, hierarchical managerialism. This is evident when Stone, here labelled 'PATIENT', visits the man who is her 'DOCTOR':

PATIENT I don't seem to know how I am except bad. There's nothing there but anger and something scary all the time. I don't want to get bitter because it will ruin my looks.

DOCTOR Maybe a hobby would help. Facetiousness is not an attractive trait in a young woman.

PATIENT I know I know. I can't help myself.

DOCTOR OK. We'll try these green ones for a change. And step up the antidepressants. Don't drink or drive. Make an appointment for a few days time and try to be more helpful in future.[63]

A couple of years after her novel's publication Galloway spoke of her own experience as a psychiatric patient and complained of health professionals who 'seemed to spend most of their time trying to retain their rank in the hierarchy'; at this time she was presenting what was styled as a 'consumer guide' to 'different forms of therapy for mental illness' on BBC Radio 4, and she has spoken elsewhere of her alcoholic father (who died when Galloway was five), her mother's attempted suicide, and her own depression.[64]

None of this should obscure the fact that Galloway is most notably a literary artist. Like many writers, she may have drawn on aspects of her life in her work, and she may hold strong beliefs which inform her work, but she is not simply a spokesperson. A comparison of the first, 1988 published version of her short story 'Fearless' with the text of the same story in her sometimes shocking collection *Blood* (1991) reveals small rhythmical alterations to punctuation and paragraphing which confirm the artistry of the prose. Galloway writes as a committed feminist for whom the personal is the political. Her early fiction in particular uses a Scots accent to disrupt the authoritative voice of conventional English prose and her sometimes experimental style may have encouraged the more recent work of Glaswegian Suhayl Saadi in *Psychoraag* (2004). Galloway signals not just class and nationality but more importantly an edgy, female-gendered voice (perhaps what French feminist critics call a kind of *écriture féminine*) which defies both masculinist assumptions and the normative 'feminine' assumptions of glossy commercial journalism aimed at women: 'I have to stop reading these fucking magazines,' reflects Joy Stone.[65]

With its refrain

> Cassie and Rona
> Rona and Cassie

Galloway's second novel, *Foreign Parts* (1994), is again written in fragmented but rhythmically structured prose, deploying a collage-like technique in what the book itself (hinting at a term made fashionable by the anthropologist Claude Lévi-Strauss) calls 'bricolage'. This technique of juxtaposition produces not conventionally 'poetic' prose, but does use some devices more familiar in verse. Invoking 'all female friends' in its dedication, Galloway's story of two women from Scotland driving past the dead men's war graves of northern France seems to emphasize the separateness of men and women in an attempt to move beyond a 'Doris Day' image of femininity where 'Maintaining a fiction about real life was just what you did.'[66] Using sometimes funny, sometimes angry literary art, Galloway nudges readers out of assumptions about national, sexual and gender identity. In the later 1990s when, in the wake of the film of *Trainspotting*, Scottish fiction became 'cool', Galloway complained that 'The word "Scottish" started to mean this media-thing rather than anything else', so that there was a 'danger of being contained, gift-wrapped. We were all "urban and gritty", even those of us who weren't.' She felt she wanted 'to write and say *Excuse me, there are women over here as well, taking only prescribed drugs if any,*' and was tired of a lazily confected image of Scottish writing as 'being blokey – adolescent blokey at that'.⁶⁷

Some years earlier Galloway had written a story, 'Sonata Form', which presents a woman who literally holds the coat of her 'maestro' pianist lover; she is exploited by him but loves him. In 1995 Galloway, who studied Music and English at Glasgow University, wrote a text to be spoken at a concert of music by women, including Clara Schumann; with committed irony Galloway's text presents reasons why women's composition can be seen repeatedly as anomalous. Metamorphosing her relationship with a classical pianist and her own love of music which was encouraged at Ardrossan Academy, Ayrshire, by her music teacher there, Ken Hetherington, Galloway's novel *Clara* (2002) took six years to write. Dedicated to Hetherington's memory, *Clara* presents a fictional version of the intense, pained life of the pianist and composer Clara Schumann and her relationship with her manic husband, Robert.

In this hugely accomplished book, Galloway indicates the arduous servitude of even one of the most ostensibly privileged and gifted women in a masculinist culture and economy. However, her ideological design does not compromise but intensifies a convincingly imagined portrayal of love and mental illness. Galloway's style, at once adventurous and sharp, has a visionary clarity that belies the years of research behind the text. Robert Schumann stands 'rigid as a splint, staring up at the falling snow'; Clara accepts applause after a concert, 'a noticeable tremor in her hands, gooseflesh bristling her arms'.⁶⁸ The European world of the Schumanns is realized with flair, amplitude and pertinacity in a superb tale that burns with the sometimes conflicting passions of love and art.

In writing a historical novel, Galloway also signals a move away from that supposedly 'adolescent blokey' present of some 1990s Scottish fiction which at times, probably out of a wish to escape from the burdens of Scottish history and excoriate what Lochhead terms the national pastime of 'nostalgia', manifests almost a cultural Alzheimer's disease. More recently, ambitious re-imaginings of history by very different twenty-first-century Scottish novelists seem part of a wish to re-engage more closely with the past, as well as with a world wider and deeper than that of the ' "urban and gritty" ' present. Such a re-engagement signals not a retreat into heritage, but a use of the Scottish and non-Scottish past in order to connect with international issues. So, for instance, through novels like *Islanders* (1994) and *Voyageurs* (2004) (the latter set in nineteenth-century North America) Margaret Elphinstone (b. 1948) re-creates in books constantly aware of ecological issues ancient Scottish and non-Scottish communities, or imagines some of the customs of older societies returning to modern Scotland. Raised in Dundee, James Meek (b. 1962), who has lived for some time in Kiev, writes in *The People's Act of Love* (2005) a historical novel of epic scale about religious extremism and persecuted minorities. In a sweeping tale which begins in eighteenth-century Scotland the Glaswegian Alex Benzie (b. 1961) chronicles with panache religious prejudice and technological change in *The Year's Midnight* (1995). James Robertson (b. 1958), an imaginative writer with a PhD on Walter Scott, produces in *The Fanatic* (2000), *Joseph Knight* (2003) and *The Testament of Gideon Mack* (2006) historical and contemporary novels which examine respectively fundamentalist violence, slavery and faith. Slavery and a search for lost identities underlie the poetic envisaging of a nineteenth-century lighthouse community in Alice Thomson's *Pharos* (2002). The coded violence of Edinburgh-based Thomson's experimental novellas is very differently presented from the investigations of endurance in Douglas Galbraith's historical novel about late seventeenth-century Scottish imperialism, *The Rising Sun* (2000). Galbraith also explores Chinese and European history in the 1930s in *A Winter in China* (2005). Attracting too novelists as different as Louise Welsh, Galloway, the sophisticated Jane Stevenson (b. 1959) and A. L. Kennedy, historical fiction is enjoying a resurgence – not as a retreat from, but as a thoughtful and measured engagement with, the pressures of globalization.

A wish for a wider world that nonetheless connects with Scotland is also present in *Trumpet* (1998) by Jackie Kay (b. 1961). Written in pacy prose and using multiple narrators as a way of engaging with point of view and prejudice, *Trumpet* presents a fictional investigation of the public and private lives of a black jazz trumpeter who died in 1997. Eventually, Colman Moody discovers that the person he loved as his adopted father was in fact female. *Trumpet* was published in the same year as Kay's biography of blues singer Bessie Smith. Set in England and Scotland, like Kay's poems in *The Adoption Papers* (1991) and other books, it explores race, sexuality, belonging, and other kinds of identity. The novel is written with a generous intelligence and subtlety that makes it a rewarding and moving read. Although Kay, who now teaches

creative writing at Newcastle University, has lived outside Scotland for
some time, her experience of a Scottish upbringing is vital to her work.
Her writing has been welcomed not least for its complication of sometimes naively cherished assumptions about identity and 'Scottishness'.
Growing up in her part of Glasgow in the 1960s and 1970s, Kay has
written, 'I never saw another black person. There was my brother and
me. That was it.' While sometimes explicitly, sometimes implicitly, she
can write from the standpoint of a black lesbian Scot, Kay has an
imagination which, like the imaginations of Galloway, Gray and Lochhead, aims ultimately at artistic suppleness and excellence. However, a
difficulty for many Scottish writers before and after the achievement
of devolution has been the readiness of some commentators to treat
imaginative writing as if it were straightforward campaigning on behalf
of a particular group identity, whereas the writing often inhabits such
identities only to blur or metamorphose them.

At the same time, Kay's wish to illumine secret histories is something
she shares not just with other gay and lesbian Scottish writers of her
generation such as novelists Louise Welsh and Ali Smith or poets Carol
Ann Duffy and David Kinloch – authors sometimes keen to celebrate
openly aspects of sexuality that would have been concealed in an earlier
Scotland – but also with heterosexual authors such as Andrew O'Hagan.
O'Hagan's first book, *The Missing* (1995), fuses both journalistic and
novelistic abilities of a high order in its investigations of family history
and wider social issues about 'mispers' (missing persons). *The Missing*
contains some of O'Hagan's finest writing, but his alert, thoughtfully
crafted prose shines also in novels such as *Our Fathers* (1999), *Personality* (2003), and his impressive tale of modern Scottish sectarian violence
Be Near Me (2006). Dealing with the destructive pressures of celebrity
culture on a media-manipulated female 'personality', O'Hagan in *Personality* operates in territory explored in different ways by Ronald
Frame, Candia McWilliam, A. L. Kennedy and others, while *Be Near Me*
stylishly and intelligently approaches the theme of Protestant–Catholic
bigotry which several commentators have seen as contemporary Scotland's shame. It is interesting to set David Greig's play *The Architect*
beside *Our Fathers*, which investigates masculine-accented Scottish left-
wing politics and civic ideals. Shrewdly and elegiacally viewing an older
Scotland from the point of view of a generation conscious of being in
the midst of globalization, O'Hagan writes about Hugh Bawn, a fictional

elder statesman of a kind of Scottish urban planning now seen as dubiously outdated:

> Hugh had always looked on Ayrshire and Glasgow as the great world. He had never wanted any other part of the planet. Never a thought of elsewhere. In a way he considered the rest of the world quite small by comparison. And Scotland to him was an entire globe. A full history. A complete geology. A true politics. A paradise of ballads and songs. There was some sort of fullness there for him. And even towards the end of his days, the force of his rejection, his late disappointments, served only to confirm his extravagant rootedness.[69]

Although there could be a danger of younger generations of writers and critics patronizing the perceived 'extravagant rootedness' of earlier generations where Sorley MacLean, Edwin Morgan, Muriel Spark and Ian Hamilton Finlay (to name but four very different authors) were highly conscious of internationalism, there is certainly a powerful wish in the work of contemporary writers as various as Kelman and Banks, Galloway, McWilliam and O'Hagan to write from standpoints where, in the globalization of the third millennium, Scotland is a vital part but not the whole of their vision.

Of no writer is this more true than A. L. Kennedy. For all her love of Hogg, Burns, Spark and other eminences of Scottish literature, Kennedy (b. 1967) is wary of labels that will confine her own and her readers' expectations of her imagination, including the term 'Scottish writer'. A singularly accomplished novelist and a great short-story writer, she has as one of the continuing obsessions of her work the mismatch between a person's inner life and the social roles seen by society as that person's identity. *Paradise* (2004) is an extended monologue by a woman isolated inside her own alcoholism – 'It's ugly in here where *I* live, inside my skin' – but also aware of having achieved freedom from the need to exist only in terms of social roles:

> Most people exist through what they do, they have lost the clarity that once permitted them to *be*. Me? – I'm completely simplified, I am distilled. Washed down to nothing, I remain exactly who I am, no matter where or when. I understand my fundamental sources, my provenance.[70]

Almost fifteen years earlier, Kennedy had written a story, 'Cap o' Rushes', published in her first book, *Night Geometry and the Garscadden Trains* (1990). In this story a woman who feels the rest of her family are 'goblins' and who is treated by her husband as 'wee wifie' takes a job, keeps her first name 'a private thing', and achieves a sense of being 'enough in herself, which made her confident, which made her enough in herself'.[71] Sometimes comically, sometimes horrifically, sometimes in ways which mix violence and dark humour, Kennedy writes repeatedly about characters struggling to live with themselves, seeking to achieve a relationship between a secret inner self and the need for some sort of social persona. The disjunction between the two can be extreme. In a story from *Now That You're Back* (1995) an American mother reveals to her daughter 'Papa's homicidal tendencies'.[72] Like Kelman, Galloway and many other contemporary Scottish authors, Kennedy seeks to reveal the complexity of so-called 'ordinary' lives: 'So many people, if you actually get to know them at any level, are enormous inside and their life doesn't actually permit them to express what they want to.'[73]

Educated at Dundee High School, then in Theatre Studies and Drama at Warwick University, Kennedy now lives in Glasgow; she has written drama, screenplays and poems as well as fiction, while outside employments include working with people with special needs, performing her own stand-up comedy, and teaching creative writing at the University of St Andrews. Since the publication of her first short-story collection and her first novel *Looking for the Possible Dance* (1993), Kennedy has been much interviewed, often by journalists keen to mention her private life; in *On Bullfighting* (1999) she expressed an anxiety about 'having nothing inside' and wrote of a suicidal impulse. Two of her books carry the Gaelic epigraph 'Mo rùn geal òg' (My pure white love) from Christina Ferguson's eighteenth-century poem of lamentation. Yet, however keen interviewers may be to relate Kennedy's often bleak work to her life, it is the imagination and precisely calibrated, brave expressiveness of the writing that give her fiction its distinction. While a 'cartoon' self she presents to stand-up comedy audiences or interviewers may have intensified her fascination with personal identity, this theme was part of her work from its inception. Like all good art, her writing passes personal, observed and imagined elements through the charged, transformative medium of language. While it might be possible to argue, for instance, that the mutually obsessed principal characters in Kennedy's novella *Original Bliss* (1997) may owe something to the Robert Burns and Agnes MacLehose whom she discussed in a 1996 lecture about Burns's 'sexually compulsive side', Kennedy's Mrs Brindle and

Edward E. Gluck in their world of global cybernetics and Bavarian sex shops are some distance from eighteenth-century Auld Reikie.[74]

Emphasizing the role of the crafting intelligence, the distinction between 'to write' and 'to be a writer', Kennedy has written of her sense of being disconnected from her perceived public image: 'A. L. was me, but I was not, it seemed, A. L.' She has also called attention to dangers in the Romantic assumption that 'creativity stems directly or almost solely from present mental anguish' since

> When do I feel like making the huge emotional commitment, the massive leap of faith that writing involves? When my mind is at its fittest. When I am happy and well.[75]

Kennedy's work often explores extremes of mental torment, longing, and the 'indelible acts' that form and re-form the self. Her overlong, though often beautifully written novel *Everything You Need* (2000) scrutinizes the art of fiction and how difficult it is to reveal truths, particularly in close relationships. The remarkably imaginative Glasgow novel *So I Am Glad* (1995) examines related territory but in a startlingly different way. Yet most impressive of all are Kennedy's short stories where, as at the very start of 'Spared' from *Indelible Acts* (2002), minutely nuanced prose and unsettlingly shrewd observation reveal characters to readers and, discomfortingly, to themselves:

> Things could go wrong with just one letter, he knew that now. Just one.
> 'Actually, I moved here ten years ago.'
> He had found it so terribly, pleasantly effortless to say, 'Actually, I moved here ten years ago.'
> There had only been a little thickness about the *m*, a tiny falter there that might have suggested a stammer, or a moment's pause to let him total up those years. Nobody listening, surely, would have guessed his intended sentence had been, 'Actually, I'm married.' In the course of one consonant everything had changed.[76]

This very, very precise listening, and this imagined particularity lie at the root of Kennedy's skill with language. At her best she writes with an assurance comparable to that of the typist in 'Cap o' Rushes', a writer-figure whose sense of not ostensibly being a writer is captured in sharp sentences that catch something of the consciousness of discovery vital to literary art: 'When she was into the flow of it, the words lined across the paper, as if she was rubbing the whiteness away; not putting a blackness on. She was squeezing the words out from where they were already hiding.'[77]

The most astute criticism of Kennedy, Galloway, Kay and the poet Kathleen Jamie appeared in a 1993 article in the long-lived Scottish literary magazine *Chapman* by Alison Smith, then a lecturer in English at Strathclyde University. Two years before publishing her first book as 'Ali Smith', Alison Smith the critic sees Galloway as 'really the first woman to take advantage in her fiction of the pioneering styles of Kelman and Gray'. Admiring how Galloway 'takes apart and ironizes figures and places of supposed authority, the systems and those who make them work', Smith argues that 'Galloway sees gender as inescapable and women as physically defined by their own blood to the point of being silenced by it.' Smith praises how Kennedy 'examines the hard times and lost lives of people, but emphasizes the determination to survive, even possible routes to survival'. Seeing Kennedy as 'a generous novelist', she quotes with approval Kennedy's sentences, 'Go to a place where history is stored and listen. Hold your breath. Hear how still it is . . . It is the sound of nothingness. It is the huge, invisible, silent roar of all the people who are too small to record.' While Smith in 1993 admires Kay as 'one of the few Scottish writers to deal adequately with the subject of gay sexuality', she also notes that Kay's work shows 'a thematic exploration rather than one in form'. In Kennedy's work Smith is excited by the international range as well as the style, arguing that 'There's a democratic basis to her work and this is its Scottishness, its preoccupation with the value of the ordinary.'[78]

In retrospect it is clear Smith was using her academic critical work to pay homage to and kick off from the work of writers she valued. Her criticism also marks out themes and approaches which attract her as a writer of fiction. Born in 1962 in Inverness, she studied English and Scottish literature at the Universities of Aberdeen and Cambridge. The short stories of *Free Love* (1995), and her first novel, *Like* (1997), marked a strong literary debut. The stories are warm but sometimes a little neat, yet, along with those of Kennedy, Galloway, Frame, Dunn, Gray, Kelman and other fine short-story writers including Dilys Rose (b. 1954), they are part of a remarkable flowering of this genre in contemporary Scotland. This phenomenon has not received adequate critical attention, but surely owes something to the rich history of the

short story in Scottish literary tradition. Smith's first novel is more
bravely experimental than her early stories, but maybe not fully
achieved. Motifs that will recur in her work – women who die young,
lesbian relationships, illness and the passage to adulthood – are mapped
out. 'Okay So Far', one of the stories in *Other Stories and Other Stories*
(1999) whose very title hints at the sort of postmodern but unpretentious
wordplay which Smith relishes, essays themes of haunted deracination
which, mixing up the living and the dead, are developed further in *Hotel
World* (2001), her second novel.

Hotel World marks a stylistic advance in Smith's fiction that is as
striking as the stylistic discoveries made in prose by James Kelman two
decades earlier. Like Kelman's, Smith's breakthrough appears technically simple, but has led to profound consequences. Unjustifying the
right-hand margin of her prose, so that her line endings look like those
of poetry, Smith produces a prose texture that is 'freed up', able to
operate like a fusion of traditional fiction with aspects of poetry and
conceptual art.

In this prose the line endings do not matter individually as in verse,
but their layout on the page encourages reader and writer to find kinds
of sometimes litany-like rhythm and forms of imaginative fusion beyond
that of conventional prose. Smith's is at times like a contemporary
version of Woolf's risk-taking writing, and may owe something to
experimental fiction such as that of Christine Brook-Rose and to recent
literary theory, especially French feminist theory, but it is able to keep
a close, democratic, alert purchase on ordinary lives across a wide class
spectrum in a way Woolf and the more rarefied literary theorists of the
later twentieth century failed to manage.

Smith's novels *Hotel World* and *The Accidental* (2005), along with
the shorter fictions of *The Whole Story and Other Stories* (2003), mix
imaginatively liberated, warm, close-grained accounts of daily experience with a cunning-minded engagement with such contemporary
phenomena as globalization, self-conscious media culture and electronic
saturation. Engaging with systems of forms, protocols and types of
surveillance which reduce or degrade the human image, Smith writes of
outsiders and insiders in their pursuit of love and sex, as well as their
compulsive search for pattern or acceptance in the face of loss of bearings, bereavement and randomness. Hugely ambitious, flotational in
texture, these books are also splendidly attentive in their writing. Taking

on in her narrative prose the idioms of her characters, Smith speaks out of a world where a homeless woman watches passers-by who 'hold mobile phones to their ears and it is as if they are holding the sides of their faces and heads in a new kind of agony'.[79] If Smith has learned both from magic realism and from Galloway's experimentally fractured feminist fiction, she has developed her own style, at the same time as being aware, as an epigraph from John Berger chosen for *The Accidental* puts it, that 'Between the experience of living a normal life at this moment on the planet and the public narratives being offered to give a sense to that life, the empty space, the gap, is enormous.' In *Hotel World* the vapid idioms of quality assurance, human resource management and marketing are pitched against individual pain and interior imaginative lives, but this is done with an intellectual ambition and clarity which are sometimes humorously and always winningly accessible.

The full complexity and torsions of Smith's narrative technique work best in her large-scale fictions. Critics may take some time to come to terms with the multiply reflexive play, the makings-up, the replication of images, and the interactions with art in *The Accidental* where a girl takes camcorder footage of surveillance cameras and a philandering Don Juan of a don writes verse in the stanza form of Byron's *Don Juan* about the culture of spin, 'New Labour', and 'the Millennium Dome' where 'a lie/ was at the very centre of belief'. Smith's recent fiction is able to mediate between a keen imaginative scrutiny of contemporary mores and a potentially wide as well as discerning public appeal. Without sacrificing warmth, humanity and plot-driven interest, she has developed a style that breaks new ground and conveys angles of perception that are hard to forget.

When she looks in the mirror above the sink she sees the imprint of her own thumb below her cheekbone where she slept on her hand ! ! She is like the kind of pottery things her mother buys that have been made by real people (not factories), actual artisans working in hot countries who leave the actual marks of their hands in it as their signature i.e. she has signed herself in her sleep![80]

Although the word 'democratic' (used by Smith of Kennedy's prose) is often used naively in Scottish literary history and criticism – as if it were a way of avoiding value judgements – Smith's new style is both aesthetically excellent and democratic in its attentive reach, its imaginative enfranchisement. Aspects of Scottishness are present in perhaps surprising touches – a dedication to Sorley MacLean, an account of St Magnus of Orkney – and sometimes in settings. But more important is the way Smith's deep sense of democratic values and valuings operates without tribalism or pretentiousness as an aesthetically exciting energizer of her distinctively early twenty-first-century prose. There may seem little connection between the 1980s graduate student Smith whom I remember enthusing about Lewis Grassic Gibbon and the novelist Smith who now lives near Cambridge, but as Gibbon sought to interrupt the texture of standard English narrative and bend it to his will, so Smith, having come through the era of deconstruction, has taken English to bits and allowed it to flow in a new channel, learning not least from poetry.

In characteristic prose which is both inside and outside her character's thoughts, Smith writes of the poetry-loving homeless woman Else in *Hotel World*,

She can't be bothered with novels any more. She has read enough novels to last her a lifetime. They take too long. They say too much. Not that much needs to be said. They trail stories after them, like if you tied old tin cans to your ankles and then tried to walk about.[81]

Tin-can-free, honed, and often remarkable, the poetry of Ali Smith's Scottish contemporaries is at its best every bit as imaginatively exciting as modern Scottish prose. Glasgow poet Donny O'Rourke's punningly titled 1994 anthology *Dream State* (revised in 2002) provided, arguably for the first time in Scottish literature, a broad survey of a new poetic generation as it emerged. As editors, contributors or interviewees, a good number of the poets were linked to the international magazine *Verse* which, from its 1984 founding until its move to America after the publication of the book of interviews with poets, *Talking Verse* (1995), maintained a strongly Scottish-international flavour. In a 1994 testimonial letter reproduced in the University of Chicago's exhibition volume *From Poetry to Verse*, Seamus Heaney calls *Verse* 'one of the most valuable poetry magazines published in the English-speaking world' and draws attention to 'the sheer extent and focus of its coverage. Australia, Ireland, Scotland, United States – its attention to poets in these and other areas has been unique'.[82] The founder editors of *Verse* were Henry Hart, David Kinloch and the present writer who were later joined for a time by Richard Price and Nicholas Roe. Among other things, the magazine aimed to publish older and newer generations of Scottish poets in the best international company. Like the highly accomplished poet, critic and anthologist Mick Imlah (b. 1956), several members of the youngest generation of Scottish poets, including the fine poets Kate Clanchy (b. 1965), Roddy Lumsden (b. 1966) and Richard Price (b. 1966) live in England, while others like Iain Bamforth and Peter McCarey are based overseas. Yet in Scotland itself the Scottish Poetry Library, Scotland's annual poetry festival StAnza (based in St Andrews where poetry festivals have been held since the 1980s), state support, and encouragement for poetry through its teaching in the universities have encouraged the health of Scotland's oldest and greatest art form.

A striking number of Scottish poets now work in university departments, often teaching creative writing: the School of English at St Andrews has on its permanent staff the poets John Burnside, Robert Crawford, Douglas Dunn, Kathleen Jamie and Don Paterson, along with prose writers including Meaghan Delahunt and A. L. Kennedy. In Glasgow the poets Tom Leonard and Alan Riach teach at Glasgow University, and David Kinloch at Strathclyde teaches alongside the novelist Margaret Elphinstone. Alan Spence at Aberdeen University teaches and directs the Word literary festival. Edinburgh has had a number of poets attached to its English Department on short-term contracts, including the Shetlandic poet and novelist Robert Alan Jamieson and the poet Valerie Gillies. In England several Scottish-born poets with university positions include Carol Ann Duffy at Manchester Metropolitan University, W. N. Herbert and Jackie Kay at the University of Newcastle, and the experimental poet Drew Milne at Cambridge. Clearly there is a risk that poetry might become academicized, and divisions arise between poets in the classroom and poets and readers outside it, yet the relationship between poetry and academia in Scotland is an old one, and has shaped our expectations about 'the modern poet'.[83] Just as twentieth-century Scottish poets such as Edwin Morgan and Norman MacCaig managed to work in universities, yet reach a wider public, so these contemporary Scottish poets aim to address not just seminar groups but a wider Scottish and international audience.

Among the poets of what might be called the 'Dream State' generation who reached maturity in the years leading up to the achievement of Scottish devolution are John Burnside (b. 1955), Carol Ann Duffy (b. 1955), Robin Robertson (b. 1955), Robert Crawford (b. 1959),

W. N. Herbert (b. 1961), Kathleen Jamie (b. 1962) and Don Paterson (b. 1963). While it may be reasonable to mention that Robert Crawford has published six collections of poetry and a *Selected Poems* (2005), as well as several critical books and anthologies including the *New Penguin Book of Scottish Verse* (co-edited with Mick Imlah in 2000), it would not be appropriate to include discussion of his work here. It is essential, however, at a time when the mass media respond often rapturously to prose but cluelessly or not at all to poetry, to stress the distinctiveness and value of the work of the other poets just mentioned.

Although Carol Ann Duffy was born in Glasgow in 1955, she left as a child and has lived the rest of her life in England. As with William Boyd's, Duffy's Scottishness may be present most obviously in a sense of displacement. Variations on the word 'home' occur often in her early books, but, for all Duffy conveys a sense of modern society and popular culture, the precise sense of home in her work seems elusive, however much she feels at times a 'homesickness' for when, where, what'.[84] In some ways as a caustic, confident feminist Duffy has reacted strongly against her Catholic childhood in Staffordshire. 'For Christ's sake, do not send your kids to Mass' ends 'Ash Wednesday 1984' in her first collection *Standing Female Nude* (1985). Yet Duffy's sense of erotic veneration may have been conditioned by aspects of an upbringing transformed into the eroticism of 'The Laughter of Stafford Girls' High', the longest poem in *Feminine Gospels* (2002), or the ecstatic love poems of *Rapture* (2005) with their excited articulation of desire and the way a lover's name is heard 'rhyming with everything'.[85]

The true 'home' of Duffy's poetry is in the expression of sexual desire, keenest in such works as the intensely phrased lesbian love poem about 'milky stones', 'Warming Her Pearls'.[86] Duffy's papers, now in the Manuscript and Rare Book Library of Emory University, Atlanta, show that this excellent phrase was part of the poem from its inception, though some other, cruder touches were refined away over the course of at least six drafts. The lyric impulse in Duffy's work has often been fused with a political imperative to catch, caricature or denounce attitudes and facets of society regarded as oppressive – tabloid journalism, male oppression of women and homophobia are among Duffy's targets. If her collection *The Other Country* (1990) glances occasionally towards her Scottish origins, it also asserts in the poem 'Originally' that 'All childhood is an emigration', and the book more firmly squares up to the

England of Margaret Thatcher whose era and ideology Duffy sums up in the title of her fourth collection *Mean Time* (1993). There poems like 'Poet for Our Times' ironically contend that 'The poems of our decade' are tabloid headlines such as *'Stuff 'em!'* or *'Gotcha!'* In its sometimes staccato abruptness and subversive use of popular icons Duffy's poetry is itself in search of a way to be popular, and to engage more subtly with populism. 'Queen Kong', 'Mrs Faust', 'Mrs Midas' and other poems from *The World's Wife* (1999) do this in ways that are linguistically alert, yet also have journalistic appeal; at times they may draw on the feminist accents and strategies of Lochhead's *The Grimm Sisters* (1981), but they go beyond such influences, and, as is often the case with poems, they are sometimes the result of an extended process of gestation. It is clear from her manuscripts that Duffy worked on a poem called 'Mrs Freud' as early as 1985. Duffy is a most assured performer of her own work, but its strengths lie in a sure command of traditional technique, a sense of driving, intelligently channelled emotion, and a linguistic finesse often at its best in less public poems such as 'Prayer' where a faithful impulse of love is sensed in the midst of loss and faithlessness – in the litany of shipping forecast which is 'the radio's prayer' or 'in the distant Latin chanting of a train'.[87]

Facets of a Catholic childhood also haunt the very different writing of John Burnside. Born in Dunfermline, Fife, in 1955, Burnside grew up in nearby Cowdenbeath but left Scotland at the age of eleven when his father's work took the family to the Northamptonshire steel town of Corby, later the setting of Burnside's fourth novel, *Living Nowhere* (2003). Burnside recalls how his father demanded everything had a 'twist of machismo'.[88] He has written about the violence of his childhood and youth, and about his experience of drugs and of breakdown in his powerful memoir *A Lie about my Father*. In the 1990s, after working in England in the computer industry as a knowledge engineer, he moved back to Fife to become a full-time writer. Poet, novelist, memoirist and essayist, the prolific Burnside is able to produce arresting and beautifully imaginative work across a range of genres. Like his memoir, his fiction from *The Dumb House* (1977) onwards often centres on obsessive, abusive and violent relationships involving isolated, withdrawn men. The darker aspects of masculinity preoccupy Burnside, most obviously in *The Mercy Boys* (1999) with its focus on emotionally damaged alcoholic Dundonians, and in *The Locust Room* (2002) whose plot revolves around a rapist in Cambridge. Yet if this author's characters swell the ranks of the armies of walking wounded so conspicuous in recent Scottish fiction, his prose style is very much his own, and infuses his fluent writing with precision, assurance, even lyrical beauty. So, for instance, the young woman Alma in *Living Nowhere* digs up fragments of pottery in her garden and with a Wordsworthian intensity creates indoors something 'less like a shrine now than a threshold, a portal into some other world' so that she can glance up from housework and 'imagine herself passing through to another space, like the separate reality of folk-tales'.

Everywhere she looked, there were clues. A flicker of shadow, a shaft of light, the sound of rain at the windows in the small hours when Marc was on night shift: it all added up to something and Alma knew that she was close to that something, that it would take no more than a slight shift of attention to find what she was looking for. It was so close, just a matter of inches, just a heartbeat away.[89]

This sense of something of the earth but beyond everyday attention constantly excites Burnside's writerly imagination. A burning realization of the importance of ecology is vital to his work, though it often makes use of religious imagery. 'Angels', he has said, 'to me are real in the way metaphors are real, in the way imagination is real.'[90] It is in his poetry rather than his prose fiction that Burnside's spiritual insight seems purest, most vividly quickened. From his first collection of poems, *The Hoop* (1988), he has been drawn repeatedly to evanescent effects – rain on glass, light on snow or water, mirrorings and juxtapositions of the insistently physical with the insubstantial, his finely cadenced, frequently pentametric verse always heading towards a 'borderline of substance and thin air'.[91] He has spoken of poetry as 'repair work', a way of trying to 'mend' the human 'relationship with . . . the more than human world', and so, for a moment, make contact with 'the authentic world' that is banished by the language of much everyday life.

If Burnside's early collections, sometimes mixing verse with prose poems, usually present brief lyric glancings towards 'rain-laced windows watching us for years' and achieve a sense of delight in fleeting sensuous moments, his more recent work in collections such as *The Asylum Dance* (2000) and *The Good Neighbour* (2005) often offer more extended meditations or swatches of work in swaying lines which can operate like

                                        pebbles of glass
            made smooth
                        in the sway of the tide.[92]

Open to American and Spanish as well as to Scottish and Irish writing,
and true to his early emphasis on 'acceptance and celebration of the
mystery, of the fact that the world is here . . . for no reason that I can
tell', Burnside has developed one of the most recognizable voices in
modern British poetry; a sense of phrasing, line, and rhythmic flow
presents verse which communicates 'a sine wave of grace and
attunement'.[93]

    Burnside's editor and exact contemporary Robin Robertson was born
in Aberdeen in 1955 and grew up in north-east Scotland; he now works
for the publisher Jonathan Cape in London where he edits a remarkable
list of Scottish authors among whom are Irvine Welsh, Janice Galloway
and A. L. Kennedy. Robertson's energy as a publisher of prose and as
editor of Cape's poetry list along with the slow development of his own
meticulously ambitious poetic style combined to ensure that his first
collection did not appear until he was in his early forties. His precisely
musical verse is subtly evocative, not least of his native Aberdeen and
of 'The sifting rain, italic rain; the smirr / that drifted down for days'.[94]
The powering, rhotacistic repetition in these lines, and the way, for
instance, in this poem of ebb and flow the *i* vowel followed by an *r*
sound in the Scots 'smirr' is then reversed in the *r* followed by an *i* in
the English 'drift' – such acoustic details hint at the craft in Robertson's
verse. His collections *A Painted Field* (1997), *Slow Air* (2002) and
Swithering (2005) show both an uncompromising engagement with
poetic tradition that extends to versions of Classical poetry, and a
darkening sensibility. In Robertson's poetry fascination with heterosexual love is often accompanied by a preoccupation with pain, violence
and despair.

    Robertson's slim volumes of poised English are very different from
the rumbustious collections often unleashed by W. N. Herbert (b. 1961),
the leading Scots-language poet of his generation. In his late teens
Herbert left his native Dundee to study English at Brasenose College,
Oxford, where he wrote a PhD (later a book) on Hugh MacDiarmid.
Dundee is a recurring presence in Herbert's poetry, and the long-running
popular Dundonian Scots comic-strip culture of *The Beano*, 'The

Broons' and 'Oor Wullie' (all of whose origins lie in the 1930s) have nourished his imagination. His risk-taking verse melds a dictionary-quarried, post-MacDiarmidean Scots with pop culture to produce its 'bad shaman blues'. Over two decades in books such as *Cabaret McGonagall* (1996) and *The Big Bumper Book of Troy* (2002) Herbert has produced a substantial body of work in Scots and increasingly English, using lyric, ballad, Standard Habbie, free verse and other forms, sometimes with elaborate glossaries. Ever since his schooldays when he edited a magazine called *Strawberry Duck*, he has been consistently eccentric and highly intelligent, mixing the considered and the throwaway in a manner sometimes inspired, sometimes careless, but continually lively. Among his finest poems are erotic Scots lyrics such as 'Coco-de-Mer' which draws on what remain to the English-accustomed ear the strangeness and intoxicating sound patterns of Scots vocabulary, urging its reader to 'let gae on thi dumbswaul' (silent sea-swell) and be floated ashore like the Molucca bean to the shores of the island of Lewis, 'thi lucky-bean tae thi haunds o thi misk' (coarse grassland).[95]

Part of Herbert's aim is to assert the intellectual and acoustic validity of Scots in an age of many Englishes. He shares this ambition with David Kinloch (b. 1959) whose use of Scots, especially in translations, asserts that 'Whit is rale [real] is the wurd.'[96] In *Paris-Forfar* (1994) and elsewhere Kinloch also writes poetry in English which deals with the situation of the Scots tongue; he often aligns the situations, speech and customs of minority groups – users of Scots, national minorities, gay men – and can see each in terms of the other. An editor of the magazine *Verse*, which published John Ashbery, Les Murray and many other non-Scottish poets alongside work from Scotland, Kinloch, like W. N. Herbert, the Richard Price of *Lucky Day* (2005) and others, has been seen as part of a network of 'Scottish Informationist' poets who emerged in the late 1980s and early 1990s.[97] These poets' commitment to Scotland was twinned with an internationalism and, at a time when the internet was in its infancy, bound up with a liking for scientific, lexical and other kinds of knowledge often lyrically displayed in their poetry. It might be tempting to set their work beside such fictions as *Music in a Foreign Language* (1994) and *Pfitz* (1995) by the scientifically educated novelist Andrew Crumey (b. 1961). However, the 'Informationist' label may have had the effect of over-emphasizing the cerebral dimension of these writers' work, and exaggerating the similarities between the different

styles of a group of friends. Kinloch's own poetry, Scottish and internationally-minded, is at its strongest in his third collection *In My
Father's House* (2005) with its intensely realized presentation of two
seventeenth-century homosexual English medical travellers in the
Middle East:

> we were Zeno's arrow, shaft and quiver,
> barely different, presenting motion
> and then decamping. Out. Elsewhere.[98]

For poets with an interest in a wide spectrum of linguistic expression
it is vital to maintain a connection between the language or languages
of home and the often liberating expansiveness of 'Elsewhere'. In his
book *A Waxing Moon* (2005) a modern 'Gaelic revival' has been presented by the cultural historian Roger Hutchinson as centred on the
Skye Gaelic college Sabhal Mòr Ostaig whose splendid new campus
overlooking the Sound of Sleat was opened at the end of the 1990s. The
literary achievement of writers who have come to be associated with
the college (which hosts Scotland's only Gaelic theatre company) has
attracted praise from Sorley MacLean and A. L. Kennedy who expressed
admiration for the work of Gaelic poet and novelist Angus Peter Campbell. Campbell's work has been encouraged not just by Sabhal Mòr
Ostaig, but also by the Gaelic Books Council's Ùr-Sgeul (New Story)
initiative, launched in 2003 to fill a perceived paucity in Gaelic prose
writing when compared with poetry. In its first three years this scheme
made possible the publication of twelve works, including novels, short-
story collections and biographies whose subject matter is taken from
urban as well as rural Scotland. Gaelic writers, educators and publishers
know it is important to offer worthwhile reading material to a new
generation of Gaelic speakers who, probably unlike their parents, have
acquired literacy skills and maybe even the language itself through the
education system. Gaelic fiction is buoyant, but it is too soon to say if
the writing of the newest authors linked to the Gaelic language, such as
Kevin McNeil (writing in English with a Gaelic undertow), Dublin-born
Rody Gorman, or Meg Bateman (b. 1959), now an academic at Sabhal
Mòr Ostaig, will maintain the literary health of this minority tongue.
These last three writers have all learned Gaelic, rather than being born
into it, and are best known for poetry. In common with poets in Scots,
Gaelic poets write not infrequently about the language itself; for several

generations now they have had to wrestle with 'Sìoladh na Gàidhlig' (the decline of Gaelic). Yet, as in Scots, some of the best work in Gaelic may take the form of intense love lyrics, drawing at times on the precarious hold of the language in which they are written. One such poem is Bateman's 'Aotromachd' (Lightness) with its praise of laughter, a kiss,

> is 's e aotromachd do ghlaic mum chuairt-sa
> a leigeas seachad leis an t-sruth mi.

> *and the lightness of your embrace*
> *that will let me go adrift.*[99]

Like Burnside, Kinloch and other poets of her generation, Bateman is aware of living in a Scotland and a world where the meaning of 'iomal-lachd' (remoteness) is changing. This can have its excitements. Published in 1982 when she was a Philosophy student at Edinburgh University, *Black Spiders* by Renfrewshire-born Kathleen Jamie (b. 1962) has poems that engage with the Arab world as well as a Scotland haunted by guisers who, like ghosts from the past, 'demand/ all the fruit we can give them'.[100] A wish to escape the hauntings of an older Scotland is strong in much of Jamie's early work, as is a nourishing inability to do so completely. The first poem of *The Way We Live* (1987) is resonantly titled 'Clearances', but turns out to be less about grief for the 'depopu-lated' Highlands, and more about the heady promise of leaving as

> an old idea
> returns again, the prodigal friend:
> of leaving: for Szechwan, or Persia.[101]

The title of Jamie's 1993 collection *The Autonomous Region* had a particular resonance for Scottish readers eager for devolution, but the book is about Tibet, and about the kind of inner freedom Burns called 'independent mind'. At times the poems state directly what will become more implicit in Jamie's later work. For instance, in a poem about a miraculous ride by the Panchen Lama the poet presents 'a scented tree/ whose every leaf/ shimmers with the face of the divine'. The last poem of the book, 'Xiahe', mixes a foreign, Tibetan name with Scots speech, so that each becomes both familiar and strange as the realization arrives that 'A'm far fae hame,/ I hae crossed China.'[102]

Fusion of self and other in that attempt to move beyond the self which is so essential to all imagining is enacted geographically in Jamie's writing, but also historically in the World War II poems which maintain a sense of 'country beyond' in *A Flame in Your Heart* (1986), a collection co-authored with Andrew Greig. Like her journeyings to Tibet, Jamie's travels in Northern Pakistan, written up with focused vivacity in *The Golden Peak* (1994), a prose account later reshaped as *Among Muslims*, were crucial to her development. Not least, they let her see Scotland in a new, more intense and broader light. Such a light has been encouraged more generally in Scottish literature by the informed and subtle accounts of other European cultures and of his own country given by Neal Ascherson (b. 1932) and the investigations of Asian, Middle Eastern and Indian cultures by the travel writer William Dalrymple (b. 1965). Both these men, like Jamie, are writers of intelligent, graceful and moving Scottish non-fiction. If it is gender that predominates in some of the poems of Jamie's *The Queen of Sheba* (1994), the foreignness signalled in the book's title is also important. Jamie takes a question (Who do you think you are? The Queen of Sheba?) long used to put down young women in Scotland so they do not become 'too cliver' or above themselves, and turns it into an assertion of power as the 'Presbyterian living rooms' and 'vixen's bark of poverty' in Scotland are subdued by the incoming, energizing arrival of the Queen of Sheba herself, leading her 'great soft camels/ widdershins [contrary to the sun's course] round the kirk-yaird' and shouting her name with 'a thousand laughing girls'.[103]

In its very finely tuned assertions of female identity, *The Queen of Sheba* is the best individual collection of poems by a woman living in twentieth-century Scotland, with the probable exception of Jamie's 1999 collection *Jizzen*, which takes its title from the Scots word for child-bed. In 'Arraheids' Jamie sees the collections of ancient flint arrowheads in an Edinburgh museum as 'a show o' grannies' tongues'; she gives confident voice to women's experience in poems that use Scots, English and mixtures of the two. Aware of a 'demon' in herself called 'WEE WIFEY', she moves beyond a sense of being limited by femaleness or femininity, and instead draws on her personal, national, gender and other identities – some garnered abroad – using them as imaginative resources out of which to build a poetry of precisely judged musicality and clear line.[104]

In *Jizzen* and *The Tree House* (2004) Jamie's lyricism strengthens. She is able to call on traditional religious imagery in 'The Tay Moses' where she dreams of making a 'creel' woven of rushes as a 'gift/ wrought from the Firth' for her child, and elsewhere to write about old women selling flowers in Hungary, come from their 'mild southern crofts' to the bus depots and termini of Budapest. The word 'crofts' gives her poem 'Flower-sellers, Budapest' an almost subliminal Scottish accent, and Jamie's own alertness to Scots, English and other kinds of linguistic variety surely quickens her sense of a culture with 'several languages – / one for each invasion'. Faultlessly lineated, poems like this counterpoint others which explore the history of Scottish migrant and emigrant experience – whether in pioneer Ontario with a wife 'dead, and another sent for' or in present-day Highland Poolewe where rhododendrons have brought with them a settlement of 'Himalayan earth'.[105]

Jamie's poetry has burgeoned not just through engagement with other cultures but also through a reading of older Scottish poets. It is striking that several of the poets of her generation publish books which contain work in both Scots and English, and mix original poems with versions of poems from other languages. Book titles such as *Forked Tongue* and *Other Tongues* hint at this tendency. Jamie admires the earlier Scottish-internationalist Willa Muir's *Living with Ballads*, and a response to the work of Violet Jacob and Marion Angus may have nourished the poetry Jamie has written in her forties. The assured, quick-eared, quick-eyed prose of *Findings* (2005) with its accounts of travels and daily life in Scotland, especially rural Scotland, balances Jamie's earlier prose about Northern Pakistan, but it is as a lyric poet that she does her finest work. In 2005, asked what poetry is for, Jamie spoke of a poem as 'soul work' and of poetry as 'a liminal place' where 'you meet the world and the world comes to meet you'. Although she stated that 'we've lost our religious vocabulary, for good or ill', she affirmed the need to maintain 'the ability to contemplate, to take time out', so that in poetry one can achieve 'a contemplative state ... to reclaim silence and to bring out of that a contact with the authentic world'. Such an almost mystical view of poetry was voiced in the same conversation by John Burnside who emphasized the importance of receptive 'silence', and by Don Paterson who spoke of the poem as 'opening a space' rather than enforcing a closure.[106]

Through precise attention, Jamie presents the physical world as loaded with spiritual meaning. This and her concern for ecological fragility (the balance of the poem – its sounds and shape – aligned with that of nature) link her with John Burnside and several other Scottish poets of her generation, helping that strong sense of spirituality in contemporary Scottish verse – a spirituality often as open to Buddhist, pagan and other beliefs as it is to Christianity. Drawing on Hölderlin and others, *The Tree House* presents in English and sometimes Scots a natural world deliberately shorn of place names and so at once Scottish and universal enough to speak to a global audience at a time when ecological concerns teach us to see our planet as one. Ecology is one of the central concerns of some of the best contemporary Scottish writing, particularly in poetry.

In 'The Wishing Tree', a poem which encapsulates many of the strengths of Jamie's recent poetry, she writes about an old tree into which coins have been hammered by people who hoped this action (akin to throwing coins in a fountain) would bring their wishes true. Like some of Jamie's other work, the poem could be read in terms of recent Scottish politics, or of ecology, but to pursue either reading exclusively would be distortingly reductive. Not the least remarkable aspect of 'The Wishing Tree' is the way that in an age stacked with competing complexities Jamie has found an adequate language in which to articulate hard, hardy experience at the same time as maintaining a clarity of line and verse movement whose superbly paced beauty is self-evident:

> I stand neither in the wilderness
> nor fairyland
>
> but in the fold
> of a green hill
>
> the tilt from one parish
> into another.
>
> To look at me
> through a smirr of rain
>
> is to taste the iron
> in your own blood
>
> because I hoard
> the common currency
>
> of longing: each wish
> each secret assignation.

My limbs lift, scabbed
with greenish coins

I draw into my slow wood
fleur-de-lys, the enthroned Britannia.

Behind me, the land
reaches towards the Atlantic.

And though I'm poisoned
choking on the small change

of human hope,
daily beaten into me

look: I am still alive –
in fact, in bud.[107]

Just as, in different ways, fiction by A. L. Kennedy or Ali Smith presents remarkable survivors of painful experience and aims for a democratic style that speaks for the silenced and 'the common currency/ of longing', Jamie here achieves an inviting yet uncompromisingly nuanced style. Although she has written elsewhere of the struggle for Scotland to have democratic control over its own affairs, and even about the new Scottish Parliament building, it is when she writes work whose resonances may take in such matters, but also sound beyond them, that she is at her finest. The imagination works obliquely, dislikes being tied down. When in 2006 the *Scotsman* newspaper asked various distinguished Scots what they thought of as a wonder of modern Scotland, Jamie selected light and the sky.

The development of Jamie's work seems measured and assured throughout the first quarter-century of her book publications. The sudden rise to pre-eminence of her contemporary (and recently her editor and teaching colleague) Don Paterson, born in Dundee in 1963, is as astounding as it is justly merited. Not since the work of Hugh MacDiarmid in the 1920s has Scottish poetry felt such a remarkable surge of marvellously controlled poetic language. As well as publishing four intense and sophisticated collections of his own poetry in a decade, Paterson, a musician's son and himself a skilled musician who for several years played alongside his close friend the late Irish-American poet Michael Donaghy in the band Lammas, has also edited and co-edited anthologies that range from the surprising *101 Sonnets* (1999) and a heretical 2001 selection of Burns to *New British Poetry* (2004), the standard North American anthology of contemporary verse from England, Scotland and Wales. Paterson's work as poetry editor at Picador in London since the 1990s has seen him edit a strong list of poets including Jamie, Duffy and Kate Clanchy, while as a university teacher at St Andrews he has given unusually insightful lectures based around his own *ars poetica*. None of this has detracted from the outstanding quality of his verse.

That quality is evident from the first pages of Paterson's bleakly titled *Nil Nil* (1993) where the balls on a pool table 'were deposited/ with an abrupt intestinal rumble' and where the pigeonholes in a tourist office are 'a columbarium of files and dockets'. In 'Heliographer' a boy learning to drink from a heavy lemonade bottle raises it towards the sun 'until it detonated with light,/ My lips pursed like a trumpeter's.'[108] Written in English with a Scots and even on occasion a Gaelic infusion, Paterson's poetry brims over with language at once surprising and just. It is also the most intellectually ambitious verse of his generation, at times so densely playful that it is hard to unpack.

Having learned from Douglas Dunn and Paul Muldoon in English, Paterson makes his poems with the obsessive care he once devoted to origami. A working-class boy, Paterson grew up in a Dundee he recalls as so isolated it was almost 'a walled city' or an island with its own myths and 'village mentality'. He has spoken of 'paranoid insecurity about your own intelligence' as a Dundonian trait, and recalls how as a child in a household that was not bookish he became 'obsessed with building a library' and so 'trawled' through local markets for 'strange wee books' which he collected for later reading. Paterson did not go to university but worked for a time for the Dundee newspaper and comic-book firm of D. C. Thomson. Like Burns and MacDiarmid before him, he has the boundless intellectualism of the autodidact, but is also wary of the class and other snobberies that can attend such a term. 'An Elliptical Stylus', a poem from his first book, signals aggression towards any 'cunt/ happy to let my father know his station'.[109] This same Paterson delights in the *Pensées* of his invented philosopher François Aussemain, one of which serves as epigraph to his brilliant but somewhat self-indulgent celebration 'The Alexandrian Library'. Aussemain surely contributes to the evolution of Paterson's clever, engaging and sometimes but not always profound prose collections of aphorisms such as *The Book of Shadows* (2004).

'In some Neanderthal part of me, every husband poses an affront' runs one of these aphorisms, and a display of laddish heterosexual plumage is noticeable in some poems from Paterson's second collection *God's Gift to Women* (1997) and elsewhere.[110] 'No man slips into the same woman twice' ends '*from* Advice to Young Husbands', while 'Imperial' concludes unforgettably with mention of 'the night we lay down on the flag of surrender/ and woke on the flag of Japan'.[111] Paterson's treatment of sexuality can be joyous, but is often unflinchingly bleak, and a disaffected hunger to engage with spiritual experience is perhaps as important in *God's Gift to Women* as the more immediately obvious burning sexuality, self-irony and even self-loathing. The remarkable long poem of body, soul, sex and whisky, 'A Private Bottling', gives a new twist to Burns's Holy-Willie phrases 'Spiritualized Bawdry which refines to Liquorish Devotion'. Paterson details a late-night drinking spree where whisky (as elsewhere in Scottish literature from Burns and MacDiarmid to Candia McWilliam) is a way of presenting something of the spirit of Scotland, and spirituality, as well as being a drowner of sexual sorrows. While various whiskies' 'gold tongues slide along my tongue', the speaker both senses 'the live egg' of his lover's 'burning ass' and recalls how, playing with the far-off stations on an old-fashioned short-wave radio, he once 'steered the dial into the voice of God/ slightly to the left of Hilversum'.[112]

With *The Eyes* (1999), subtitled 'a version of Antonio Machado', Paterson turns to the Spanish poet of 'God and love and memory', re-creating a sense of his work in English poems which, among other things, offer an alternative to the dour Scottish fundamentalist Christianity with which Paterson grew up, yet still allow ways of figuring the self of a traveller as a 'wayfarer, sea-walker, Christ' seen through a sun-flecked Spanish prism.[113] As Paterson's style has developed, it has sought, like Jamie's, ways to engage with other cultures, traditions and beliefs, including Buddhism, which may counterbalance and enrich the cultures of Scotland. Paterson has spoken of poetry as 'primarily a commemorative act' with elegy as its 'default' position, and he locates as 'the tonic and the dominant' in his own work 'the play between . . . being rooted and absolutely breaking out'. In his versions of Machado, Paterson achieves a lyrical directness which sometimes but not always he carries over to his work in *Landing Light*. That splendid 2003 collection shows a formidable intelligence that ranges from Plutarchan Rome to Rilke to the world of 'dials ... EQs and compressors' in the 'departuary, or antiterminus' of 'The Black Box'. But the poems at their best are also full of a sense of physical being, and deeply humanized not least by the poet's relationship with his family.

Though Paterson's work repays and often demands re-reading, few of his poems are more immediately and deeply appealing than a sonnet about one of his sons. 'Waking with Russell' draws on the opening of Dante's *Inferno* where the poet *'mezzo del cammin'* (in the middle of life's journey) feels lost. Paterson rewrites even Dante with aplomb, but preserves a sly complexity, even in his declaration of love:

> Whatever the difference is, it all began
> the day we woke up face-to-face like lovers
> and his four-day-old smile dawned on him again,
> possessed him, till it would not fall or waver;
> and I pitched back not my old hard-pressed grin
> but his own smile, or one I'd rediscovered.
> Dear son, I was *mezzo del cammin*
> and the true path was as lost to me as ever
> when you cut in front and lit it as you ran.
> See how the true gift never leaves the giver:
> returned and redelivered, it rolled on
> until the smile poured through us like a river.
> How fine, I thought, this waking amongst men!
> I kissed your mouth and pledged myself forever.[114]

The 'forever' of Scottish literary history has now lasted for fifteen centuries. With a glance towards some of the finest modern poets, and a plea for Scotland's contemporary poetry to be given as much attention as its prose and drama, it is time for this book to end. In twenty-first-century Scotland, a society blessed and disillusioned with its taste of a renewed democratic Parliament and wrestling with physical and psychological blights, a land whose writers may be more ready than its politicians to explore the consequences of globalization, there is an inheritance of spectacularly rich literary history; there is a literary present which is an impressive part of international contemporary culture; there are signs of a future whose very unpredictability may be an imaginative gift. It is much too soon now for a summing up. It is time both to conclude, and to continue.

Notes

Introduction

1. See *The New Penguin Book of Scottish Verse*, ed. Robert Crawford and Mick Imlah (Harmondsworth: Penguin Books, 2000), 95; since this anthology was given the cover title *The Penguin Book of Scottish Verse* when it entered the Penguin Classics series in 2006, it is hereafter cited as *PBSV*; on Plath's reading of Dunbar's poem see Stephen C. Enniss and Karen V. Kukil, *No Other Appetite* (New York: Grolier Club, 2005), 24.
2. Seamus Heaney, *The Testament of Cresseid* (London: Enitharmon, 2004); Seamus Heaney, 'To the Poets of St Andrews' in Robert Crawford, ed., *The Book of St Andrews* (Edinburgh: Polygon, 2005), 11.
3. *PBSV*, 210–11.
4. Mario Vargas Llosa, conversation with the present writer, April 2006, used with permission.
5. Margaret Atwood, *Negotiating with the Dead* (Cambridge: Cambridge University Press, 2002), 11; Montaigne, *Essays*, tr. J. M. Cohen (Harmondsworth: Penguin, 1958), 82.
6. Mikhail Bakhtin, *The Dialogic Imagination*, ed. Michael Holquist, tr. Caryl Emerson and Michael Holquist (Austin: University of Texas Press, 1981), 66.
7. These words were the basis of the banner headline on the front page of the *Scotsman* newspaper, 13 May 1999.
8. William Laughton Lorimer, tr., *The New Testament in Scots* (Edinburgh: Southside, 1983), 61.
9. Virginia Woolf, *Leave the Letters Till We're Dead*, ed. Nigel Nicolson (London: Hogarth Press, 1980), 247 (letter of 26 June [1938] to Ethel Smyth) and 243–4 (letter of 25 June [1938] to Vanessa Bell).
10. Salman Rushdie, *Step Across This Line* (New York: Modern Library, 2002), 59, 60.
11. Pascale Casanova, *The World Republic of Letters*, tr. M. B. DeBevoise (Cambridge, Mass.: Harvard University Press, 2004), 206.
12. See Robert Crawford, *Devolving English Literature*, 2nd edn (Edinburgh: Edinburgh University Press, 2000), ch. 3; also ch. 12 of the present book.
13. See Robert Crawford, ed., *Apollos of the North* (Edinburgh: Polygon, 2006).
14. Tacitus, *De Vita Agricolae*, ed. H. Furneaux, 2nd edn, rev. J. G. C. Anderson (Oxford: Clarendon Press, 1922), 22–3; my own translation has been helped by that of H. Mattingly and S. A. Handford (Penguin Classics, 1970).
15. See Walter Scott, *The Antiquary*, ed. David Hewitt (Edinburgh: Edinburgh University Press, 1995), 107, 108.
16. Liz Lochhead, *Mary Queen of Scots Got Her Head Chopped Off* (Harmondsworth: Penguin, 1989), 11.

1 Praise

1. In writing this chapter Thomas Clancy's anthology of modern translations of Scotland's earliest poetry, *The Triumph Tree* (Edinburgh: Canongate, 1998) (hereafter *TT*), has been invaluable, as have the other works cited in the notes that follow. These notes provide precise sources for quotations in my text which also draws on the works cited for other details.

2. David Montgomery, 'Lists show life of Romans in Britain', *Scotsman*, 7 March 2001, 5.

3. See Lawrence Keppie, *Scotland's Roman Remains* (Edinburgh: John Donald, 1986), 45.

4. Derick S. Thomson, ed., *The Companion to Gaelic Scotland* (Oxford: Blackwell, 1983), 221.

5. Ibid.

6. Ibid., 194.

7. See Meg Bateman, Robert Crawford and James McGonigal, ed., *Scottish Religious Poetry* (Edinburgh: St Andrew Press, 2000) (hereafter *SRP*) and Robert Crawford and Mick Imlah. ed., *PBSV* (London: Penguin, 2000).

8. See, e.g., Thomas Owen Clancy and Gilbert Márkus, *Iona* (Edinburgh: Edinburgh University Press, 1995), 39–40.

9. Revelation, 21:6 (*Authorized Version*).

10. Translated by Edwin Morgan (*PBSV*, 6–7).

11. Clancy and Márkus, *Iona*, 104–5; tr. Clancy.

12. Ibid., 146–7; tr. Clancy.

13. John Lorne Campbell, Introduction to *Highland Songs of the Forty-Five*, rev. edn. (Edinburgh: Scottish Gaelic Texts Society, 1984), xxix.

14. Clancy and Márkus, *Iona*, 182; tr. Robert Crawford.

15. Gilbert Márkus, tr., *Adomnán's 'Law of the Innocents'* (Glasgow: Blackfriars Books, 1997), 8.

16. Adomnán, *De Locis Sanctis* I. xxv, tr. Thomas O'Loughlin in his article 'Res, tempus, locus, persona: Adomnán's exegetical method' in Dauvit Broun and Thomas Owen Clancy, ed., *Spes Scotorurm, Hope of Scots* (Edinburgh: T & T Clark, 1999), 153; see also Thomas O'Loughlin, 'The Exegetical Purpose of Adomnán's De Locis Sanctis', *Cambridge Medieval English Studies* 24 (1992), 37–54.

17. *Adomnán's Life of Columba*, ed. and tr. Alan Orr Anderson and Marjorie Ogilvie Anderson, rev. edn. (Oxford: Clarendon Press, 1991), 232–3, 133, 5, 69.

18. Ibid., 3.

19. Professor Éamonn Ó Carragáin used this phrase in a 2000 lecture on the poem at the British Academy.

20. *PBSV*, 14–17; tr. Robert Crawford.

21. Kenneth Hurlstone Jackson, *The Gododdin* (Edinburgh: Edinburgh University Press, 1969); see also A. O. H. Jarman, *Aneirin: Y Gododdin* (Llandysul: Gomer Press, 1988) and John T. Koch, *The Gododdin of Aneirin* (Cardiff: University of Wales Press, 1997).

22. *PBSV*, 12–13; tr. Joseph P. Clancy.

23. Ibid.

24. *TT*, 94.

25. Henry, Archdeacon of Huntingdon, *Historia Anglorum*, ed. and tr. Diana Greenway (Oxford: Clarendon Press, 1996), 25.

26. Kenneth Jackson, *The Gaelic Notes in the Book of Deer* (Cambridge: Cambridge University Press, 1972), 30 and 33; tr. Kenneth Jackson.

27. *PBSV*, 24–5; tr. Thomas Clancy.

28. *Orkneyinga Saga*, tr. Hermann Pálsson and Paul Edwards (Harmondsworth: Penguin Classics, 1981), 37.

29. *TT*, 148; tr. Paul Bibire.

30. *Orkneyinga Saga*, 108, 214.

31. *PBSV*, 30–31; tr. Paul Bibire.

32. *SRP*, 32–3; tr. Paul Bibire.
33. Turgot, Bishop of St Andrews, *The Life of St Margaret*, ed. and tr. William Forbes-Leith, 3rd edn. (Edinburgh: David Douglas, 1896), 39–40.
34. Ibid., 88; tr. Robert Crawford.
35. See Wilson McLeod, *Divided Gaels* (Oxford: Oxford University Press, 2004), 125.
36. See Michael Lynch, *Scotland* (London: Century, 1991), 78.
37. *PBSV*, 28–9; tr. Thomas Clancy.
38. Ibid.
39. Alexander Broadie, *The Shadow of Scotus* (Edinburgh: T. & T. Clark, 1995), 2; see also James Bulloch, *Adam of Dryburgh* (London: SPCK, 1958).
40. Al-Bitrûjî, *De Motibus Celorum, Critical Edition of the Latin Translation of Michael Scot*, ed. Francis J. Carmody (Berkeley and Los Angeles: University of California Press, 1952), 150; tr. Robert Crawford.
41. Maria Rosa Menocal, *The Ornament of the World* (New York: Little, Brown, 2002), 193.
42. Quoted in Lynn Thorndike, *Michael Scott* (London: Nelson, 1965), 14–15; tr. Lynn Thorndike.
43. Dante, *Inferno*, Temple Classics edn (London: Dent, 1970), 220 (Canto XX); tr. Robert Crawford.
44. *The Romance and Prophecies of Thomas of Erceldoune*, ed. James A. H. Murray (London: Trübner for the Early English Text Society, 1875), 2–10.
45. *Sir Tristrem*, ed. George P McNeill (Edinburgh: Blackwood for the Scottish Text Society, 1886), 1 and 97.
46. Latin text from W. F. Skene, ed., *The Historians of Scotland, I, Johannis de Fordun, Chronica Gentis Scotorum* (Edinburgh: Edmonston and Douglas, 1871), 449; English from *TT*, 212; tr. Thomas Márkus (emended).
47. *TT*, 223; tr. Paul Bibire.
48. Ibid., 225–6; tr. Judith Jesch.
49. See D. R. Owen, ed. and tr., *Fergus of Galloway* (London: Dent, 1991) and *ODNB*.
50. Quoted in A. G. Rigg, *A History of Anglo-Latin Literature, 1066–1422* (Cambridge: Cambridge University Press, 1992), 53.
51. Guillaume le Clerc, *The Romance of Fergus*, ed. Wilson Frescoln (Philadelphia: William H. Allen, 1983), 56.
52. *PBSV*, 32–5.
53. *TT*, 247, 250; tr. Thomas Clancy.
54. Clancy and Márkus, *Iona*, 146 (cp. *TT*, 248); E. C. Quiggin, 'A Poem by Gilbride MacNamee in Praise of Cathal O'Conor' in *Miscellany presented to Kuno Meyer*, ed. Osborn Bergin and Carl Marstrander (Halle: Max Niemeyer, 1912), 170; both translations by Thomas Clancy.
55. *TT*, 248 and 247; tr. Thomas Clancy.
56. Ibid., 251; tr. Thomas Clancy.
57. McLeod, *Divided Gaels*, 25.
58. *TT*, 265; tr. Thomas Clancy.
59. Ibid., 268; tr. Thomas Clancy.
60. *PBSV*, 36–9; tr. Thomas Clancy.
61. *SRP*, 36–7; tr. Meg Bateman.
62. Duns Scotus in his *Quodlibet*; translation from William A. Frank and Allan B. Wolter, *Duns Scotus, Metaphysician* (West Lafayette: Purdue University Press, 1995), 7.
63. Reproduced as plate C5 in John Jones, *Balliol College, A History: 1263–1939* (Oxford: Oxford University Press, 1988).
64. Text from Frank and Wolter, *Duns Scotus*, 184–7.
65. See *OED* under 'dunce'.
66. Latin text from John Purser, *Scotland's Music* (Edinburgh: Mainstream, 1992), 60; tr. Robert Crawford.

67. *TT*, 298 and 301; tr. Gilbert Márkus.
68. *PBSV*, 42.
69. Derick Thomson, *An Introduction to Gaelic Poetry* (London: Gollancz, 1977), 29.
70. See William Ferguson, *The Identity of the Scottish Nation* (Edinburgh: Edinburgh University Press, 1998), 40.
71. See Edward J. Cowan, *'For Freedom Alone'* (East Linton: Tuckwell Press, 2003), 6.
72. See Ranald Nicholson, 'Magna Carta and the Declaration of Arbroath', *University of Edinburgh Journal*, XXII (1965), 143.
73. Sir James Fergusson, *The Declaration of Arbroath* (Edinburgh: Edinburgh University Press, [n.d.]), 8, 9.
74. On Boswell and Jefferson see Robert Crawford, *Devolving English Literature*, 2nd edn (Edinburgh: Edinburgh University Press, 2000), 77 and 176–7.
75. Nicholson, 'Magna Carta and the Declaration of Arbroath', 140.

2 Liberty

1. Robert Louis Stevenson, 'The Coast of Fife' in *Further Memories*, vol. XXVI of the Skerryvore Edition of Stevenson's Works (London: Heinemann, 1925), 91.
2. See John Purser, *Scotland's Music* (Edinburgh: Mainstream, 1992), 53.
3. Bateman et al., ed., *SRP*, 38–9; tr. Gilbert Márkus.
4. John Milton, *Paradise Lost*, ed. Alastair Fowler (London: Longman, 1971), 39.
5. John Barbour, *The Bruce*, ed. A. A. M. Duncan (Edinburgh: Canongate, 1997), 101.
6. Ibid., 65.
7. Ibid., 133.
8. Ibid., 47.
9. Ibid., 243; tr. A. A. M. Duncan.
10. *PBSV*, 43.
11. *Bruce*, 463; tr. A. A. M. Duncan.
12. Ibid., 617.
13. Ibid., 211.
14. Ibid., 407.
15. *PBSV* 44.
16. Walter Bower, *Scotichronicon*, ed. D. E. R. Watt (Aberdeen: Aberdeen University Press, 1987–98), 9 vols, IX, 3.
17. Ibid., VIII, 337.
18. Ibid., 340–41.
19. Ibid., IX, 3.
20. Ibid., II, 437.
21. Ibid., V, 414–15; tr. Simon Taylor.
22. Ibid., VIII, 78–9; tr. D. E. R. Watt.
23. Ibid., IX, 128.
24. James I of Scotland, *The Kingis Quair*, ed. John Norton-Smith (Oxford: Clarendon Press, 1971), 27 and 46.
25. Ibid., 1.
26. Ibid., 2, 3, 6.
27. Ibid., 7.
28. Ibid., 11.
29. *PBSV*, 46.
30. James I, *Kingis Quair*, ed. Norton-Smith, 27, 29, 33, 34, 41.
31. Ibid., 49.
32. Ibid., 39.
33. Ibid., 5.
34. Bower, *Scotichronicon*, ed. Watt, VIII, 336 and IX, 128, 130.
35. *PBSV*, 56.

NOTES

36. Seamus Heaney, *The Testament of Cresseid* (London: Enitharmon, 2004), 9 and 5.
37. *PBSV*, 73.
38. Ibid., 55.
39. Ibid.
40. Ibid., 57.
41. Ibid., 60–61.
42. Ibid., 64, 65.
43. Ibid., 66.
44. Ibid., 69.
45. Ibid., 69, 71.
46. Ibid., 72.
47. Ibid., 69, 61.
48. Robert Henryson, *Poems*, ed. Charles Elliott, 2nd edn (Oxford: Clarendon Press, 1974), 110.
49. *PBSV*, 73.
50. Ibid., 73.
51. Ibid., 74.
52. Ibid., 75.
53. Ibid., 74.
54. R. J. Lyall, 'Henryson, the Hens and the Pelagian Fox' in Sally Mapstone, ed., *Older Scots Literature* (Edinburgh: John Donald, 2005), 93.
55. Henryson, *Poems*, ed. Elliott, 124.
56. *PBSV*, 59.
57. Henryson, *Poems*, ed. Elliott, 2; James I, *Kingis Quair*, 39.
58. *PBSV*, 48.
59. Ibid., 55.
60. *SRP*, 40.
61. Ibid., 47.
62. Henryson, *Poems*, ed. Elliott, xxv.
63. *SRP*, 46.
64. William Wordsworth, *The Prelude*, ed. J. C. Maxwell (Harmondsworth: Penguin, 1971), 46.
65. Mair, quoted in James Moir, ed., Henry the Minstrel, *The Actis and Deidis* (Edinburgh: Blackwood for the Scottish Text Society, 1889), Introduction, vii.
66. *PBSV*, 76.
67. *Actis and Deidis*, ed. Moir, 362.
68. Robert Burns, *Poems and Songs*, ed. James Kinsley (Oxford: Oxford University Press, 1969), 561.
69. Jonathan A. Glenn, ed., *The Prose Works of Sir Gilbert Hay*, vol. III (Edinburgh: Scottish Text Society, 1993), 35 (*The Buke of the Ordre of Knychthede*).
70. Ibid., 65.
71. Ibid., 54, 83 (*The Buke of the Gouernaunce of Princis*).
72. Sir Gilbert Hay, *The Buik of King Alexander the Conqueror*, ed. John Cartwright (Edinburgh: Scottish Text Society, 1986), 1.
73. Derick Thomson, *Introduction to Gaelic Poetry* (London: Gollancz, 1977), 31.
74. Text from Carolyn Proctor, *Ceannas nan Gàidheal* (Armadale: Clan Donald Lands Trust, 1985), 16.
75. Thomson, *Introduction*, 31.
76. *TT*, 313; tr. Thomas Clancy.
77. *PBSV*, 78–9.
78. Fordun, cited in Priscilla Bawcutt, *Dunbar the Makar* (Oxford: Clarendon Press, 1992), 256.
79. Quoted from Roderick Watson, ed., *The Poetry of Scotland* (Edinburgh: Edinburgh University Press, 1995), 25, with alterations to glosses.

NOTES

80. *PBSV*, 87–8.
81. Ibid., 84.
82. Bower, *Scotichronicon*, ed Watt, III, 436–7, 438–9; tr. Donald Watt.
83. *PBSV*, 86.
84. *SRP*, 60; tr. James McGonigal.
85. *The Poems of William Dunbar*, ed. Priscilla Bawcutt (Glasgow: Association for Scottish Literary Studies, 1998), 2 vols, I, 184, 192.
86. *PBSV*, 89.
87. Ibid., 95.
88. *Selected Poems of Robert Henryson and William Dunbar*, ed. Douglas Gray (Harmondsworth: Penguin, 1998), 229.
89. Ibid., 267.
90. Ibid., 282, 283, 289.
91. *PBSV*, 96.
92. Ibid., 98.
93. See Barclay's entry in the *Oxford Dictionary of National Biography* (hereafter *ODNB*).
94. R. L. Mackie cited in Roger Mason, 'Laicisation and the Law' in L. A. J. R. Houwen, A. A. R. MacDonald, S. L. Mapstone, ed., *The Palace in the Wild* (Leuven: Peeters, 2000), 15.
95. Latin text from John Durkan, 'The Beginnings of Humanism in Scotland', *Innes Review* 4.1 (1953), 8; tr. Robert Crawford.
96. Dunbar, *Poems*, ed. Bawcutt, I, 113.
97. Jean Elliot, 'The Flowers of the Forest', *PBSV*, 266.
98. Giovanni Ferreri, quoted in Durkan, 'The Beginnings of Humanism', 8.
99. John Bellenden, tr., *The Chronicles of Scotland, compiled by Hector Boece*, ed. R. W. Chambers and Edith C. Batho (Edinburgh: Blackwood for the Scottish Text Society, 1938), I, 17, 111 and 171.
100. Dunbar, *Poems*, ed. Bawcutt, I, 64; *The Poems of William Dunbar*, ed. W. Mackay Mackenzie (London: Faber and Faber, 1932), 177.
101. *The Poetical Works of Gavin Douglas*, ed. John Small (Edinburgh: William Paterson, 1874), 4 vols, I, 81 and 12.
102. Ibid., I, 67, 68 and 74.
103. Ibid., I, 61.
104. Ibid., IV, 223.
105. Ibid., I, cvii.
106. Ibid., I, xlii.
107. Quoted in Priscilla Bawcutt, *Gavin Douglas* (Edinburgh: Edinburgh University Press, 1976), 9.
108. Douglas, *Poetical Works*, ed. Small, IV, 225 and II, 14.
109. Ibid., III, 27, 26, and II, 217.
110. Ibid., II, 4, 6 and 7.
111. Ibid., II, 113.
112. Ibid., III, 29 and II, 4.
113. Ibid., II, 17.
114. Ibid., IV, 230 and 232.
115. Ibid., IV, 230.
116. *SRP*, 61.
117. Douglas, *Poetical Works*, ed. Small, I, 36.
118. Bawcutt, *Gavin Douglas*, 190.
119. *PBSV*, 107.
120. Douglas, *Poetical Works*, ed. Small, III, 8 and 26.
121. Ibid., II, 12.
122. Ibid., I, 65.
123. Bawcutt, *Gavin Douglas*, 47.

124. *Boece's History of Scotland in the Mar Lodge Translation*, ed. George Watson, (Edinburgh: Blackwood for the Scottish Text Society, 1946), 2 vols, I, 418.
125. William J. Watson, ed. and tr., *Scottish Verse from the Book of the Dean of Lismore* (Edinburgh: Oliver & Boyd for the Scottish Gaelic Texts Society, 1937), 27 and 121.
126. Ibid., 138 (English version by Robert Crawford).
127. *PBSV*, 125; Watson, ed., *Book of the Dean of Lismore*, 179 and 163; tr. Watson.
128. Text and translation of 'Cumha Mhic an Tòisich' from Anne C. Frater, 'The Gaelic Tradition up to 1750' in Douglas Gifford and Dorothy McMillan, ed., *A History of Scottish Women's Writing* (Edinburgh: Edinburgh University Press, 1997), 2; tr. Anne Frater.
129. Watson, ed., *Book of the Dean*, 245.
130. Ibid., 240–41.
131. Douglas, *Poetical Works*, ed. Small, I, 65; *The Bannatyne Manuscript*, ed. W. Tod Ritchie (Edinburgh: Blackwood for the Scottish Text Society, 1928–34), 4 vols, IV, 284.
132. *PBSV*, 104.
133. Sir David Lyndsay, *Selected Poems*, ed. Janet Hadley Williams (Glasgow: Association for Scottish Literary Studies, 2000), 99.
134. Ibid., 33, 36.
135. Ibid., 45.
136. Ibid., 71, 79, 84.
137. Ibid., 112, 115, 119.
138. Ibid., 130, 146, 152.
139. *PBSV*, 120.
140. Lyndsay, *Selected Poems*, ed. Williams, 104, 82, 58.
141. Ibid., 184, 191.
142. Ibid., 205.
143. Sir David Lindsay, *Ane Satyre of the Thrie Estaitis*, ed. Roderick Lyall (Edinburgh: Canongate Classics, 1989), 1.
144. Ibid., 12, 77.
145. Ibid., 41.
146. Ibid., 101.
147. Ibid., 62, 75, 41.
148. Ibid., 108.

3 Reformation

1. Quoted in James Cranstoun, ed., *Scottish Satirical Poems of the Time of the Reformation* (Edinburgh: Blackwood for the Scottish Text Society, 1891–3), 2 vols, I, lvii.
2. John Gau, *The Richt Vay to the Kingdom of Heuine* (Edinburgh: Blackwood for the Scottish Text Society, 1888), 101, 104.
3. *John Knox's History of the Reformation in Scotland*, ed. William Croft Dickinson (London: Nelson, 1949), 2 vols, II, 219.
4. Ibid., 226, 228.
5. Alane, quoted in George Christie, *The Influence of Letters on the Scottish Reformation* (Edinburgh: Blackwood, 1908), 30, 31; tr. Christie.
6. Quoted in Graham Tulloch, *A History of the Scots Bible* (Aberdeen: Aberdeen University Press, 1989), 4, 6.
7. Ibid., 4.
8. *PBSV*, 403 ('Scotland 1941').
9. John Knox, *On Rebellion*, ed. Roger A. Mason (Cambridge: Cambridge University Press, 1994), 8.
10. Ibid., 177.
11. Ibid., 60.

12. James VI, quoted by William Barlow (1604) in Robert Ashton, ed., *James I by his Contemporaries* (London: Hutchinson, 1969), 183.

13. *OED*.

14. *Knox's History*, ed. Dickinson, II, 284, 295–6.

15. Quoted by Neil Rhodes, 'From Rhetoric to Criticism' in Robert Crawford, ed., *The Scottish Invention of English Literature* (Cambridge: Cambridge University Press, 1998), 25.

16. *Knox's History*, II, 309, 283.

17. Ibid., I, lxxxvii.

18. Ibid., I, lxxix.

19. Ibid., I, 62.

20. Robert Louis Stevenson, *Familiar Studies of Men and Books* (London: Heinemann, 1925 (Skerryvore Edition)), 235.

21. *Knox's History*, I, 149, 351.

22. Ibid., II, 17.

23. Ibid., I, 77 and II, 64, 25.

24. Robert Crawford, ed., *Apollos of the North: Selected Poems of George Buchanan and Arthur Johnston* (Edinburgh: Polygon, 2006), 4–5.

25. Michel de Montaigne, *Essays*, tr. J. M. Cohen (Harmondsworth: Penguin, 1958), 82.

26. Crawford, ed., *Apollos*, 30–31.

27. Ibid., 32–3.

28. *PBSV*, 126–7 and *Apollos*, 62–3; tr. Robert Crawford.

29. Crawford, ed., *Apollos*, 70–71.

30. Ibid., 78–9.

31. George Buchanan, *Tragedies*, ed. P. Sharratt and P. G. Walsh (Edinburgh: Scottish Academic Press, 1983), 151 and 157; tr. P. G. Walsh.

32. George Buchanan, *Tragedies*, ed. P. Sharratt and P. G. Walsh (Edinburgh: Scottish Academic Press, 1983), 106.

33. George Buchanan, *Jephthah and the Baptist*, tr. Robert Garioch Sutherland (Edinburgh: Oliver & Boyd, 1959), 64–5.

34. George Buchanan, *History of Scotland*, tr. James Aikman (Glasgow: Blackie, 1827), I, 9.

35. Edwin Morgan, Foreword to Crawford, ed., *Apollos*, vii.

36. *The Historie of Scotland wrytten first in Latin by the most reuerend and worthy Jhone Leslie Bishop of Rosse and translated in Scottish by Father James Dalrymple*, ed. E. G. Cody and William Murison (Edinburgh: Blackwood for the Scottish Text Society, 1895), 2 vols, II, 215, 245, 290, 464, 472.

37. Robert Lindesay of Pitscottie, *The Historie and Cronicles of Scotland* (Edinburgh: Blackwood for the Scottish Text Society, 1899), 2 vols, I, 308, 312, 233, 234.

38. *Catholic Tractates of the Sixteenth Century*, ed. T. G. Law (Edinburgh: Blackwood for the Scottish Text Society, 1901), 7.

39. Ibid., 162, 109 (Nicol Burne's *Disputation* (Paris, 1581)).

40. Knox, *History of the Reformation*, ed. Dickinson, II, 333.

41. *PBSV*, 135.

42. R. D. S. Jack and P. A. T. Rozendaal, ed., *The Mercat Anthology of Early Scottish Literature, 1375–1707* (Edinburgh: Mercat Press, 1997), 277.

43. Quoted in Robert Crawford, ed., *The Book of St Andrews* (Edinburgh: Polygon, 2005), 53.

44. James Cranstoun, ed., *Satirical Poems of the Time of the Reformation* (Edinburgh: Blackwood for the Scottish Text Society, 1891–3), 2 vols, I, 174.

45. Ibid., I, xlv (quoting the diarist James Melville).

46. Ibid., I, 333, 201.

47. *PBSV*, 130.

48. *A Compendious Book of Godly and Spiritual Songs, commonly known as 'The Gude and Godlie Ballatis'*, ed. A. F. Mitchell (Edinburgh: Blackwood for the Scottish Text Society, 1897), 204; *PBSV*, 128.

49. *SRP*, 76, 79–80.

50. Ibid., 83, 311.

51. Ibid., 72–3; tr. Meg Bateman.

52. *PBSV*, 131.

53. Ibid., 142–3.

54. William Fowler, *Works*, ed. H. W. Meikle, James Craigie, and John Purves (Edinburgh: Blackwood for the Scottish Text Society, 1914–40), 3 vols, III, cx.

55. Jane Stevenson and Peter Davidson, ed., *Early Modern Women Poets* (Oxford: Oxford University Press, 2001), 66–7; tr. Stevenson and Davidson.

56. Sarah Dunnigan, 'Scottish Women Writers c. 1560–c. 1650' in Douglas Gifford and Dorothy McMillan, ed., *A History of Scottish Women's Writing* (Edinburgh: Edinburgh University Press, 1997), 21.

57. Ibid., 25; tr. Robin Bell.

58. *Satirical Poems*, ed. Cranstoun, I, 175.

59. *The Maitland Folio Manuscript*, ed. W. A. Craigie (Edinburgh: Blackwood for the Scottish Text Society, 1919), 2 vols, I, 37.

60. Robert Wedderburn, *The Complaynt of Scotland*, ed. A. M. Stewart (Edinburgh: The Scottish Text Society, 1979), 13, 54–5.

61. Ibid., 1, 131.

62. *PBSV*, 134.

63. Alexander Scott, *The Poems*, ed. James Cranstoun (Edinburgh: Blackwood for the Scottish Text Society, 1896), 19, 9.

64. Ibid., 33.

65. John Rolland, *The Court of Venus*, ed. Walter Gregor (Edinburgh: Blackwood for the Scottish Text Society, 1884), 13, 42.

66. See Douglas Dunn, 'Burns's Native Metric' in Robert Crawford, ed., *Robert Burns and Cultural Authority* (Edinburgh: Edinburgh University Press, 1997), 61–2.

67. *PBSV*, 136–7, 140–41; tr. Iain Crichton Smith.

68. Ibid., 189.

69. Buchanan, *Opera Omnia*, II, 58; tr. J. Longmuir, from his Buchanan's *Silvae* (Edinburgh: Menzies, 1871), 41.

70. *New Poems by James I of England*, ed. Allan F. Westcott (New York: Columbia University Press, 1911), 31; see Priscilla Bawcutt, 'James VI's Castalian Band: A Modern Myth', *Scottish Historical Review*, 80.2 (2001), 251–9.

71. John Stewart of Baldynneis, *Poems*, ed. Thomas Crockett (Edinburgh: Blackwood for the Scottish Text Society, 1913), 2 vols, II, 129, 165, 136, 189.

72. Ibid., 55, 83, 31.

73. Alexander Montgomerie, *Poems*, ed. James Cranstoun (Edinburgh: Blackwood for the Scottish Text Society, 1887), 59.

74. Jack and Rozendaal, ed., *Mercat Anthology*, 293–4.

75. *PBSV*, 146–7.

76. Montgomerie, *Poems*, ed. Cranstoun, 101; Roderick Watson, ed., *The Poetry of Scotland* (Edinburgh: Edinburgh University Press, 1995), 180.

77. *The Diary of Mr James Melvill* (Edinburgh: Bannatyne Club, 1829), 171.

78. James Craigie, 'Introduction' to Thomas Hudson, *The Historie of Judith* (Edinburgh: Blackwood for the Scottish Text Society, 1941), xciv.

79. Ibid., xxii, n. 1 (quoting a document by John Colville).

80. [James I], *The Essayes of a Prentise* (Edinburgh: Vautroullier, 1584), G.iv.

81. Ibid., M.

82. Ibid., M.iij.

83. Ibid., H. ii.

84. Montgomery, *Poems*, ed. Cranstoun, 104.

85. Ibid., 101.

86. Fowler, *Works*, I, 19; for attribution see Dunnigan, 'Scottish Women Writers', 27.

87. Fowler, *Works*, I, 18.
88. Ibid., II, 28.
89. Ibid., I, 229; *PBSV*, 156.
90. *PBSV*, 157.
91. Alexander Hume, *Poems*, ed. Alexander Lawson (Edinburgh: Blackwood for the Scottish Text Society, 1902), 72, 77.
92. Ibid., xxxiii.
93. Ibid., 158.
94. *SRP*, 94.
95. Hume, *Poems*, ed. Lawson, 6, 7.
96. Ibid., 53.
97. *PBSV*, 154, 155.
98. King James VI, *Basilicon Doron*, ed. James Craigie (Edinburgh: Blackwood for the Scottish Text Society, 1944–50), 2 vols, 1, 4.
99. Ibid., I, 35, 94–5.
100. Ibid., I, 72, 200.
101. Ibid., I, 70, 74.
102. Ibid., I, 149, 134, 197.
103. Ibid., I, 185–7.
104. Dedication of the Authorized Version of the Bible.

4 The Staggering State

1. *The Poetical Works of Alexander Craig*, ed. David Laing (Glasgow: Hunterian Club, 1873), *Poeticall Essayes*, 9, 10, 24, 18.
2. Ibid., *Poeticall Recreations* (1623), 22.
3. Ibid., *Poeticall Essayes*, 3.
4. *Poems of Sir David Murray of Gorthy* (Edinburgh: Ballantyne, for the Bannatyne Club 1823), unnumbered pp.
5. See Stuart Gillespie, *Shakespeare's Books* (London: Athlone Press, 2001).
6. Craig, *Poetical Works, Amorose Songes, Sonets, and Elegies*, 166; *The English and Latin Poems of Sir Robert Ayton*, ed. Charles B. Gullans (Edinburgh: Blackwood for the Scottish Text Society, 1963), 175.
7. *Poems of Murray of Gorthy*, last page.
8. *PBSV*, 158.
9. Ibid., 158.
10. Aubrey, cited in Ayton, *English and Latin Poems*, 88.
11. Ben Jonson, *Discoveries, and Conversations with William Drummond of Hawthornden (1619)* (London: John Lane The Bodley Head, 1923), *Conversations*, 8; Patrick Gordon, *The Famous Historie of the Renouned and Valiant Prince Robert Surnamed the Bruce* (Dort, 1615), Errata.
12. Ayton, *English and Latin Poems*, 203.
13. John Leech, *Musae Priores* (London, 1620), Epigrams, 52.
14. Arthur Johnston, 'Comes Sterlini', in *The Poetical Works of Sir William Alexander*, ed. L. E. Kastner and H. B. Charlton (Manchester: Manchester University Press, 1921–9), 2 vols, I, ccxiii.
15. Ibid., 488.
16. Ibid., 536.
17. Alexander, quoted in Thomas H. McGrail, *Sir William Alexander* (Edinburgh: Oliver and Boyd, 1940), 47–8.
18. Lithgow, quoted in McGrail, *Sir William Alexander*, 209–10.
19. William Lithgow, *The Totall Discourse of The Rare Adventures* (Glasgow: MacLehose, 1906), 3–4.
20. Ibid., 329, 300, 301.

21. Ibid., 376, 374.
22. Ibid., 100.
23. Ibid., 414, 439.
24. John Barclay, *Euphormionis Lusinini Satyricon (Euphormio's Satyricon) 1605–1607*, tr. and ed. David A. Fleming (Nieuwkoop: B. De Graaf, 1973), xv and ix.
25. Ibid., 8–9.
26. *The Mirrour of Mindes, or Barclays Icon Animorum*, Englished by T. M. [Thomas May] (London, 1631), 2 vols, II, 3, 4.
27. Barclay, *Euphormio's Satyricon*, tr. Fleming, 122–5.
28. Ioannis Barclaii *Argenis* (1621) (3rd edn, Paris, 1623), 308.
29. See Catherine Connors, 'Metaphor and Politics in John Barclay's *Argenis*' in Stephen Harrison, Michael Paschalis and Stavros Frangoulidis, ed., *Metaphor in the Ancient Novel* (Groningen: Peeters, 2005).
30. *Argenis*, 220; *Barclay his Argenis*, tr. Kingsmill Long, 2nd edn (London, 1636), 135–6.
31. Barclay, *Argenis* (in Latin), frontispiece.
32. Barclay, *Argenis* (in English), 192, 193; (in Latin) 306, 307.
33. 'A Supplement to the Said Defect by Sir W. A.' in Sir Philip Sidney, *Arcadia*, ed. Maurice Evans (Harmondsworth: Penguin, 1977), 600.
34. William Alexander, *Anacrisis*, in William Drummond, *Works* (Edinburgh: James Watson, 1711), 161–2.
35. Sir Thomas Urquhart, *The Jewel*, ed. R. D. S. Jack and R. J. Lyall (Scottish Academic Press, 1983), 92, 155.
36. *The Works of William Fowler*, ed. H. W. Meikle et al. (Edinburgh: Blackwood for the Scottish Text Society, 1914–40), 3 vols, II, 190.
37. *Philotus*, repr. in R. D. S. Jack and P. A. T. Rozendaal, ed., *The Mercat Anthology of Early Scottish Literature, 1375–1707* (Edinburgh: Mercat Press, 1997), 432, 408, 399, 405.
38. *Selected Sermons of Zachary Boyd*, ed. David W. Atkinson (Aberdeen: Aberdeen University Press for the Scottish Text Society, 1989), 88, 95.
39. Ibid., xxxiii.
40. John Johnston from Robert Crawford, ed., *The Book of St Andrews* (Edinburgh: Polygon, 2005), 22; tr. R. Crawford.
41. R[obert] S[ibbald], *Memoria Balfouriana* (Edinburgh: Andrew Anderson, 1699), 5.
42. Leech, *Musae Priores*, Eroticon Lib. I, 70; John Leyden, *Poetical Remains* (London: Longman, 1819), 200.
43. Alexander, *Poetical Works*, I, cxvi.
44. Reading lists reproduced in French Rowe Fogle, *A Critical Study of William Drummond of Hawthornden* (New York: King's Crown Press, 1952), 183.
45. Karl Miller, *Rebecca's Vest* (London: Hamish Hamilton, 1993), 90.
46. Drummond's manuscripts reproduced in McGrail, *Sir William Alexander*, 237, 246.
47. *PBSV*, 190.
48. Ibid., 191.
49. William Drummond of Hawthornden, *Poems and Prose*, ed. Robert H. MacDonald (Edinburgh: Scottish Academic Press, 1976), 191–2.
50. *PBSV*, 190.
51. John Kerrigan, *On Shakespeare and Early Modern Literature* (Oxford: Oxford University Press, 2001), 152–80.
52. Drummond, *Poems and Prose*, 153.
53. *PBSV*, 196, 192.
54. Sir John Scot, *The Staggering State of Scots Statesmen* (Edinburgh, 1754), 163.
55. Quoted in Crawford, ed., *Apollos*, xlix.
56. Ibid., xliv.
57. Ibid., l.
58. Ibid., 126–7; *PBSV*, 202–3.

59. Crawford, ed., *Apollos*, 93.

60. *The Poetical Works of William Drummond of Hawthornden*, ed. L. E. Kastner (Manchester: Manchester University Press, 1913), 2 vols, II, 162.

61. Drummond, *Poems and Prose*, 136.

62. *SRP*, 97.

63. Ibid., 98–9; tr. Meg Bateman and James McGonigal.

64. Thomas Sydserf, preface to *Entertainments of the Cours* (London: T. C., 1658).

65. *PBSV*, 206.

66. Samuel Rutherford, *Lex, Rex* (1644), cited in John Coffey, *Politics, Religion and the British Revolutions: The Mind of Samuel Rutherford* (Cambridge: Cambridge University Press, 1997), 164, 174.

67. 1683 Decree of the University of Oxford, quoted in Coffey, 174.

68. Samuel Rutherford, *Joshua Redivivus* (1664) c. 411, rpt in David Reid, ed., *The Party-Coloured Mind: Prose Relating to the Conflict of Church and State in Seventeenth Century Scotland* (Edinburgh: Scottish Academic Press, 1982), 47.

69. Drummond, *Skiamachia*, rpt in David Reid, ed., *The Party-Coloured Mind*, 83, 80.

70. Wariston's Diary, rpt in Reid, *The Party-Coloured Mind*, 41.

71. Ibid., 44.

72. Rutherford, cited in Coffey, 104.

73. Robert Monro, *Monro, His Expedition*, ed. William S. Brockington, Jr (Westport, Conn.: Praeger, 1999), 14, ix.

74. Urquhart, 'A non covenanters opinion of the violent, and impetuous disposition of some of our Puritans in Scotland' in Peter Davidson, ed., *Poetry and Revolution: An Anthology of British and Irish Verse, 1625–1660* (Oxford: Oxford University Press, 1998), 356.

75. Urquhart, *The Jewel*, ed. Jack and Lyall, 88.

76. Ibid., 124, 191.

77. Ibid., 147, 13.

78. *The Admirable Urquhart: Selected Writings*, ed. Richard Boston (London: Gordon Fraser, 1975), 55–6.

79. Ibid., 159.

80. Urquhart, *Jewel*, 88.

81. Robert Kirk, manuscript diary (1689), quoted in Robert Kirk, *The Secret Commonwealth*, ed. Stewart Sanderson (Cambridge: D. S. Brewer for The Folklore Society), 13.

82. The Earl of Dorset, quoted in *Miscellany of the Abbotsford Club, Volume First* (Edinburgh, 1837), 88.

83. Trial proceedings, rpt in the above, 91.

84. Reproduced in the *Scotsman*, 28 June 2004, 5 (when the portrait was being sold at Sotheby's).

85. *Mercurius Caledonius*, 31 December 1660–8 January 1661, 8.

86. [George Mackenzie], *Aretina* (Edinburgh: Broun, 1660), 3, 6–7, 25–6.

87. Ibid., 208–9.

88. Mackenzie, *Religio Stoici* in Jack, ed., *Scottish Prose 1550–1700*, 165–6.

89. Urquhart, *Jewel*, 180.

90. George Mackenzie, *Works* (Edinburgh: James Watson, 1716), 2 vols, I, *Pleadings* (1673), 17, 10.

91. Urquhart, *Jewel*, 190.

92. *ODNB*, Thomas Reid.

93. 1680 Report of a Committee of the Faculty of Advocates quoted by Thomas I. Rae, 'The Origins of the Advocates' Library' in Patrick Cadell and Ann Matheson, ed., *For the Encouragement of Learning* (Edinburgh: HMSO, 1989), 15.

94. Lauder's library catalogue, quoted in Rae, 'Origins of the Advocates' Library', 13; William Clerke, *Marciano or the Discovery, A Tragi-comedy* (Edinburgh, 1663), 19, quoted by Alasdair Cameron, 'Theatre in Scotland 1660–1800' in Andrew Hook, ed.,

The History of Scottish Literature, volume 2, 1660–1800 (Aberdeen: Aberdeen University Press, 1987), 192.

95. Mackenzie's speech quoted by Brian Hillyard in Cadell and Matheson, ed., *For the Encouragement of Learning*, 25.

96. Urquhart, *Jewel*, 149.

97. David Allan, *Philosophy and Politics in Later Stuart Scotland* (East Linton: Tuckwell Press, 2000), 151.

98. Ross, cited in Peter France, ed., *The Oxford Guide to Literature in English Translation* (Oxford: Oxford University Press, 2000), 142.

99. *SRP*, 101.

100. General Assembly of the Kirk, quoted in Kerrigan, *On Shakespeare*, 171.

101. Verse redacted by Isobel Gowdie, in Jane Stevenson and Peter Davidson, ed., *Early Modern Women Poets: An Anthology* (Oxford: Oxford University Press, 2001), 399–400; the prose quotation that follows is from p. 399.

102. Sinclair, *Satans Invisible World Discovered*, in R. D. S. Jack, ed., *Scottish Prose, 1550–1700* (London: Calder & Boyars, 1971), 184.

103. Kirk, *The Secret Common-wealth*, ed. Sanderson, 8, 6, 7.

104. Ibid., 49–50.

105. Ibid., 51.

106. Ibid., 52.

107. Ibid., 49.

108. *The Best of our Owne: Letters of Archibald Pitcairne, 1652–1713*, ed. W. T. Johnston (Edinburgh: Saorsa Books, 1979), 63, 60.

109. *SRP*, 106–7; tr. Margaret Fay Shaw.

110. *PBSV*, 210–13; English version by R. Crawford.

111. J. Carmichael Watson, ed., *Gaelic Songs of Mary MacLeod* (1934; rpt Edinburgh: Scottish Academic Press for the Scottish Gaelic Texts Society, 1982), xxvi.

112. Diorbhail nic a Bhriuthainn, 'Oran do dh' Alasdair mac Colla' (A Song to Alasdair mac Colla) in Stevenson and Davidson, ed., *Early Modern Women Poets*, 274.

113. Ibid., 284.

114. Ibid., 288–9.

115. Iain Lom, 'The Battle of Inverlochy', tr. Derick Thomson in Derick Thomson, *An Introduction to Gaelic Poetry* (London: Gollancz, 1977), 122.

116. *PBSV*, 214–15; tr. Meg Bateman.

117. Thomson, *Introduction to Gaelic Poetry*, 115.

118. *PBSV*, 218–19; tr. Derick Thomson.

119. Cargill Bible, St Andrews University Library.

120. MacKenzie, *Religio Stoici* (1663), rpt in Reid, ed., *The Party-Coloured Mind*, 142.

121. Burnet quoted in Allan, *Philosophy and Politics*, 188.

122. Burnet, *Memoirs*, rpt in Reid, ed., *The Party-Coloured Mind*, 124.

123. Pitcairne, *The Assembly* (1722), rpt ibid., 199.

124. Scot, *The Staggering State* (1754), quoted in T. G. Snoddy, *Sir John Scot, Lord Scotstarvit* (Edinburgh: T and A Constable, 1968), 218, 206, 216.

125. Andrew Fletcher, *Political Writings*, ed. John Robertson (Cambridge: Cambridge University Press, 1997), 179.

126. Percy Bysshe Shelley, *A Defence of Poetry*, ed. H. F. B. Brett-Smith (Oxford: Blackwell, 1929), 59.

127. James VI, quoted by William Barlow (1604) in Robert Ashton, ed., *James I by his Contemporaries* (London: Hutchinson, 1969), 183.

128. *PBSV*, 160.

129. Ibid., 183.

130. Ibid., 166.

131. Ibid., 170.

132. Ibid., 160.

133. Ibid., 161.
134. Ibid., 163.
135. Sidney, 'An Apology for Poetry' in Edmund P. Jones, ed., *English Critical Essays (Sixteenth, Seventeenth, and Eighteenth Centuries)* (Oxford: Oxford University Press, 1922), 32.
136. *PBSV*, 188.
137. Ibid., 180–82.
138. Ibid., 174.
139. Douglas Dunn, ' "A Very Scottish Kind of Dash": Burns's Native Metric' in Robert Crawford, ed., *Robert Burns and Cultural Authority* (Edinburgh: Edinburgh University Press, 1997), 60.
140. Roderick Watson, ed., *The Poetry of Scotland* (Edinburgh: Edinburgh University Press, 1995), 210.
141. *PBSV*, 207.
142. Ibid., 208.
143. Ibid., 293.

5 Ever Green

1. See David Allan, *Virtue, Learning, and the Scottish Enlightenment* (Edinburgh: Edinburgh University Press, 1993).
2. Anon, *A Trip Lately to Scotland* (1705), 11 (cited in John Arbuthnot, *The History of John Bull*, ed. Alan W. Bower and Robert A. Erickson (Oxford: Clarendon Press, 1976), lxvii).
3. George Aitken, *The Life and Works of John Arbuthnot* (Oxford: Clarendon Press, 1892), 396–8.
4. Defoe, quoted in Douglas Duncan, *Thomas Ruddiman* (Edinburgh: Oliver & Boyd, 1965), 151.
5. Robert Burns, *Poems and Songs*, ed. James Kinsley (Oxford: Oxford University Press, 1969), 511.
6. *'Scotland's Ruine': Lockhart of Carnwath's Memoirs of the Union*, ed. Daniel Szechi (Aberdeen: Association for Scottish Literary Studies, 1995), 6, 58, 245, 244, 248, 204.
7. Andrew Fletcher, *Political Works*, ed. John Robertson (Cambridge: Cambridge University Press, 1997), 179.
8. Percy Bysshe Shelley, *A Defence of Poetry*, ed. H. F. B. Brett-Smith (Oxford: Blackwell, 1929), 59.
9. *'Scotland's Ruine'*, 44.
10. Fletcher, *Political Works*, ed. Robertson, 67, 69.
11. Thomas Ruddiman, quoted in Duncan, *Thomas Ruddiman*, 151.
12. Arbuthnot, *History of John Bull*, xxiii, 49–50, 55, vii.
13. See Robert Crawford, ed., *The Scottish Invention of English Literature* (Cambridge: Cambridge University Press, 1998).
14. Watson, 'The Publisher's Preface to the Printers in Scotland', prefaced to *The History of the Art of Printing* (1713), quoted in Duncan, *Thomas Ruddiman*, 73.
15. *James Watson's Choice Collection of Comic and Serious Scots Poems*, vol. I, ed. Harriet Harvey Wood (Edinburgh: The Scottish Text Society, 1977), Watson's Preface, i and ii.
16. See Anne Skoczylas, *Mr Simson's Knotty Case* (Montreal: McGill-Queen's University Press, 2001).
17. *ODNB*, James Arbuckle.
18. See Frances Hutcheson, *On Human Nature*, ed. Thomas Mautner (Cambridge: Cambridge University Press, 1993), 124–5, 152.
19. Frances Hutcheson, *An Inquiry Concerning Beauty, Order, Harmony, Design*, ed. Peter Kivy (The Hague: Martinus Nijhoff, 1973), 55.
20. Arthur Herman, *The Scottish Enlightenment* (London: Fourth Estate, 2001), 71–2.
21. Ruddiman's 1710 Preface, quoted in Duncan, *Thomas Ruddiman*, 56.

22. *The Works of Allan Ramsay*, ed. Burns Martin et al. (Edinburgh: Blackwood for the Scottish Text Society, n.d.), I, 66.

23. *PBSV*, 228.

24. Ramsay, *Works*, I, 10.

25. Ibid., xix.

26. *PBSV*, 229.

27. Ramsay, *Works*, I, 45, 43.

28. Allan Ramsay, ed., *The Ever Green* (1724; repr. Glasgow: Robert Forrester, 1876), 2 vols, I, vii–viii.

29. Ibid., II, 190.

30. Ibid., I, 220.

31. Alexander Pennecuik, *Works* (Leith: Allardice, 1815), 363.

32. Alexander Pennecuik, *An Historical Account of the Blue Blanket* (Edinburgh: John Mossman, 1722), 87.

33. Ramsay, *The Ever Green*, II, 256.

34. Ramsay, ed., *The Tea-Table Miscellany* (London: J. Watson, 1730), ix.

35. *The Household Book of Lady Grisell Baillie*, ed. Robert Scott-Moncrieff (Edinburgh: Edinburgh University Press for the Scottish History Society, 1911), 203, 283.

36. Duncan, *Thomas Ruddiman*, 62, 64.

37. John Stevenson, 1709 letter quoted in G. D. Henderson, *Chevalier Ramsay* (London: Nelson, 1952), 10.

38. Ramsay, *The Travels of Cyrus*, tr. Anon. (Albany, New York: Pratt and Doubleday, 1814), 55.

39. Benjamin Franklin, cited in Stuart Gillespie and David Hopkins, ed., *The Oxford History of Literary Translation in English* (Oxford: Oxford University Press, 2005), 49.

40. *Poems by Allan Ramsay and Robert Fergusson*, ed. A. M. Kinghorn and Alexander Law (Edinburgh: Scottish Academic Press and Association for Scottish Literary Studies, 1985), 58.

41. William Hamilton of Gilbertfield, *Blind Harry's Wallace*, intro. Elspeth King (Edinburgh: Luath Press, 1998), xvi, 75.

42. Robert Burns, *Letters*, 2nd ed., ed. G. Ross Roy (Oxford: Oxford University Press, 1985), 2 vols, I, 136.

43. Ramsay, *Works*, I, 116, 115.

44. Patrick Murdoch, 'Life', in *The Works of James Thomson* (London: A. Millar, 1762), 2 vols, I, p. vi.

45. James Thomson, *Letters and Documents*, ed. Alan Dugald McKillop (Lawrence, Kan.: University of Kansas Press, 1958), 16.

46. *PBSV*, 238–9.

47. James Thomson, *The Seasons*, ed. James Sambrook (Oxford: Clarendon Press, 1981), line 880.

48. Thomson, *Letters*, 48.

49. Quoted in Douglas Grant, *James Thomson, Poet of 'The Seasons'* (London: Cresset Press, 1951), 181, 91–2.

50. James Thomson, *The Seasons*, ed. James Sambrook (Oxford: Clarendon Press, 1981), Summer (1727), lines 498ff and 563–4.

51. Old *DNB*, 'Andrew Millar'.

52. Grant, *James Thomson*, 73.

53. *The Complete Poetical Works of James Thomson*, ed. J. Logie Robertson (Oxford: Oxford University Press, 1908), 422.

54. James Sambrook, *James Thomson, 1700–1748: A Life* (Oxford: Clarendon Press, 1991), 101.

55. See Robert Crawford, *Devolving English Literature*, 2nd edn (Edinburgh: Edinburgh University Press, 2000), 53.

56. *PBSV*, 240.

57. See David McCordick, ed., *Scottish Literature: An Anthology* (New York: Peter Lang, 1996–2001), 3 vols, I, 892.
58. See Mike Wade, 'The watercolour windfall worth £5m', *Scotsman*, 13 May 2003, 3.
59. Ramsay, *Works*, III, 241.
60. McCordick, ed., *Scottish Literature*, I, 889, 970.
61. *PBSV*, 243.
62. Clive Hart and Kay Gilliland Stevenson, 'John Armstrong's *The Oeconomy of Love*: A Critical Edition with Commentary', *Eighteenth Century Life*, 19.3 (1995), 45.
63. George Gilfillan, ed., *The Poetical Works of Armstrong, Dyer, and Green* (Edinburgh: James Nichol, 1858), 91.
64. Ramsay, *Works*, III, 144.

6 The Scottish Enlightenment

1. Tobias Smollett, *Peregrine Pickle* (1751; rpt London: Dent, 1967), 2 vols, I, 110.
2. Kant used the term in his short 1784 essay 'Was ist Aufklärung'; the phrase 'the Scottish Enlightenment' comes from William Robert Scott in *Francis Hutcheson* (Cambridge: Cambridge University Press, 1900).
3. Arthur Herman, *The Scottish Enlightenment* (London: Fourth Estate, 2001); James Buchan, *Capital of the Mind* (London: John Murray, 2003), 6, 336.
4. See especially David Allan, *Virtue, Learning and the Scottish Enlightenment* (Edinburgh: Edinburgh University Press, 1993).
5. *OED*; Buchanan, 'Elegy for John Calvin' in Crawford, ed., *Apollos of the North* (Edinburgh: Polygon, 2006), 70, 71.
6. David Hume, 'My Own Life' in *Dialogues concerning Natural Religion*, ed. Norman Kemp Smith, 2nd edn (London: Nelson, 1947), 233.
7. David Hume, *Enquiries concerning Human Understanding and concerning the Principles of Morals*, ed. L. A. Selby-Bigge, and P. H. Nidditch, 3rd edn (Oxford: Clarendon Press, 1975), 183.
8. *Hume's Dialogues Concerning Natural Religion*, ed. Norman Kemp Smith (Oxford: Clarendon Press, 1935), 186.
9. Alexander Broadie, ed., *The Scottish Enlightenment, An Anthology* (Edinburgh: Canongate, 1997), 39, 312, 366.
10. Scott, *Francis Hutcheson*, 117.
11. David Hume, *A Treatise of Human Nature*, ed. L. A. Selby-Bigge, 2nd edn rev. P. H. Nidditch (Oxford: Oxford University Press, 1978), 252.
12. See John Mullan, *Sentiment and Sociability* (Oxford: Clarendon Press, 1988), 29.
13. Hume in Broadie, ed., *The Scottish Enlightenment*, 39.
14. Ibid., 249.
15. Robert Crawford, ed., *The Scottish Invention of English Literature* (Cambridge: Cambridge University Press, 1998).
16. Peter Garside, James Raven and Rainer Schöwerling, *The English Novel 1770–1829: A Bibliographical Survey* (Oxford: Oxford University Press, 2000), 2 vols, I, 204.
17. James Beattie, letter to Sylvester Douglas, 5 January 1778, in William Forbes, ed., *An Account of the Life and Writings of James Beattie* (Edinburgh: Constable, 1806), 2 vols, II, 17.
18. Watson (1758), quoted by Neil Rhodes, 'From Rhetoric to Criticism' in Crawford, ed., *The Scottish Invention*, 29.
19. Adam Smith, *Lectures on Rhetoric and Belles Lettres*, ed. J. C. Bryce (Oxford: Clarendon Press, 1983), 33.
20. Adam Smith, quoted in David Allan, *Virtue, Learning, and the Scottish Enlightenment* (Edinburgh: Edinburgh University Press, 1993), 212.
21. Smith, *Lectures on Rhetoric*, 137.

22. Adam Smith, *Correspondence*, ed. Ernest Campbell Mossner and Ian Simpson Ross (Oxford: Clarendon Press, 1977), 287.

23. See Ian Duncan, 'Adam Smith, Samuel Johnson and the Institutions of English' in Crawford, ed., *The Scottish Invention*, 37–54.

24. Broadie, ed., *The Scottish Enlightenment*, 434, 435.

25. Adam Smith, *The Wealth of Nations*, ed. R. H. Campbell and A. S. Skinner (Oxford: Clarendon Press, 1976), 2 vols, II, 623.

26. Broadie, ed., *The Scottish Enlightenment*, 445, 455.

27. James Wodrow (1808), quoted in Ian Simpson Ross, *The Life of Adam Smith* (Oxford: Clarendon Press, 1995), xxi.

28. Adam Smith, *The Theory of Moral Sentiments*, ed. D. D. Raphael and A. L. Macfie (Oxford: Clarendon Press, 1976), 9, 10.

29. Review of Adam Smith, *The Theory of Moral Sentiments*, *Critical Review*, 7, May 1759, 384–5.

30. Smith, *Theory*, 158–9; Robert Burns, *Poems and Songs*, ed. James Kinsley (Oxford: Oxford University Press, 1969), 157.

31. Herman, *The Scottish Enlightenment*, 179–80.

32. Smith, *Theory of Moral Sentiments*, 23.

33. *PBSV*, 247.

34. Ibid., 246.

35. Ibid., 244.

36. Bateman et al., ed., *SRP*, 156; *PBSV*, xix.

37. *The Letters of Robert Burns*, 2nd edn, ed. J. De Lancey Ferguson and G. Ross Roy (Oxford: Clarendon Press, 1985), 135.

38. Broadie, ed., *The Scottish Enlightenment*, 94.

39. Herman, *The Scottish Enlightenment*, 251.

40. Ross, *Life of Adam Smith*, 11; Smollett, *Peregrine Pickle*, I, 277; Smollett, *The Expedition of Humphry Clinker* (1771; rept London: Dent, 1968), 221.

41. Samuel Hart, *Herminius and Espasia* (Edinburgh: The Author, 1754), i; *ODNB*.

42. Presbytery of Edinburgh *Admonition* (1757), quoted by Adrienne Scullion, 'The Eighteenth Century' in Bill Findlay, ed., *A History of Scottish Theatre* (Edinburgh: Polygon, 1998), 104.

43. Philip Gaskell, *A Bibliography of the Foulis Press*, 2nd edn (London: St Paul's Bibliographies, 1986), 303.

44. John Home, *Douglas*, ed. Gerald D. Parker (Edinburgh: Oliver & Boyd, 1972), 35.

45. University of St Andrews Library Special Collections, Manuscript 657, reproduced with permission.

46. Home, *Douglas*, ed. Parker, 29.

47. Broadie, ed., *The Scottish Enlightenment*, 187.

48. Foulis quotations from entries in Gaskell, *A Bibliography*, 65, 100, 126, 303.

49. Broadie, ed., *The Scottish Enlightenment*, 479.

50. Ibid., 560.

51. Ibid., 408.

52. Ibid., 729.

53. See Robert Crawford, *Devolving English Literature*, 2nd edn (Edinburgh: Edinburgh University Press, 2000), 39.

54. Herman, *The Scottish Enlightenment*, 373.

55. David Hume, quoted in old *DNB*, Hume entry, 220.

56. William Barron, *Lectures on Belles Lettres and Logic* (London: Longman, Hurst, Reess, and Orme, 1806) 2 vols, I, 118–19, 131.

57. See Eric Rothstein, 'Scotophilia and *Humphry Clinker*: The Politics of Beggary, Bugs, and Buttocks', *University of Toronto Quarterly*, 52/1 (Fall 1982), 63–4.

58. Crawford, *Devolving English Literature*, 56.

59. Quoted in Lewis M. Knapp, *Tobias Smollett* (Princeton: Princeton University Press, 1949), 58.
60. Carlyle's *Autobiography*, quoted in Richard B. Sher, *Church and University in the Scottish Enlightenment* (Princeton: Princeton University Press, 1985), 39.
61. Text and translation from Derick S. Thomson, 'Gaelic Poetry in the Eighteenth Century: the Breaking of the Mould' in Andrew Hook, ed., *The History of Scottish Literature, Volume 2, 1660–1800* (Aberdeen: Aberdeen University Press, 1987), 180.
62. *PBSV*, 232–3; tr. Derick Thomson.
63. Thomson, *An Introduction to Gaelic Poetry*, 158.
64. 'In Praise of the Ancient Gaelic Language', quoted in Thomson, *Introduction*, 158.
65. *PBSV*, 234–5.
66. Roderick Watson, ed., *The Poetry of Scotland*, 285; tr. William Neill.
67. Text from Anne C. Frater, 'The Gaelic Tradition up to 1750' in Douglas Gifford and Dorothy McMillan, ed., *A History of Scottish Women's Writing*, 7–8; tr. Anne Frater.
68. Ibid., 12.
69. *PBSV*, 254–5.
70. Buchanan's *Diary*, quoted in Thomson, *Introduction*, 205.
71. *SRP*, 124–5; tr. Derick Thomson.
72. McCordick, ed., *Scottish Literature*, I, 1026.
73. Ibid., 1003.
74. Smith, *Lectures on Rhetoric and Belles Letters*, 136.
75. Jerome Stone, 20 Sept. 1755 letter to Thomas Tullideph (Edinburgh University Library MS La.III.251).
76. Quoted in Robert Crawford, *The Modern Poet* (Oxford: Oxford University Press, 2001), 42.
77. William Gillies, ' "Nothing Left but their Mist": Farewell and Elegy in Gaelic Poetry' in Sally Mapstone, ed., *Older Scots Literature* (Edinburgh: John Donald, 2005), 370–96.
78. See Crawford, *The Modern Poet*, 148 and 159.
79. *PBSV*, 250–51; tr. Derick Thomson.
80. Ibid., 252.
81. Quoted as the epigraph to Alistair MacLeod, *No Great Mischief* (London: Jonathan Cape, 2000).
82. Blackwell, quoted in Crawford, *The Modern Poet*, 32.
83. Roger Lonsdale, ed., *The Poems of Gray, Collins, and Goldsmith* (Harlow: Longmans, 1969), 504–5 and 516.
84. This poster is reproduced in Bill Findlay, ed., *A History of Scottish Theatre* (Edinburgh: Polygon, 1998), 102.
85. *PBSV*, 267.
86. Hugh Blair, *Lectures on Rhetoric and Belles Lettres* (London: Strahan and Cadell, 1783), 2 vols, II, 279.
87. Thomas A. McKean, 'The Fieldwork Legacy of James Macpherson', *Journal of American Folklore*, vol. 114, no. 454 (2001), 460.
88. John Bruce, notes transcribed from Hugh Blair's lectures in 1765 (Edinburgh University Library MS Dc.10.6, pp. 205 and 90).
89. Blair (1763) in *The Poems of Ossian and Related Works*, ed. Howard Gaskill (Edinburgh: Edinburgh University Press, 1996), 356.
90. See Crawford, *The Modern Poet*, 23.
91. Statistics here are from Garside, Raven and Schöwerling, *The English Novel*, I.
92. Crawford, *Devolving English Literature*, 62.
93. Tobias Smollett, *The Adventures of Roderick Random* (1748; rpt London: Dent, 1973), 1 and 27.
94. Ibid., 91.
95. Smollett, *Peregrine Pickle*, I, 62, 70, 10–11.
96. Ibid., I, 326.

97. Ibid., I, 243.
98. Tobias Smollett, *Travels through France and Italy* (1766; rpt Oxford: Oxford University Press, 1981), 103.
99. Smollett, *Peregrine Pickle*, II, 55.
100. Smith, *Theory of Moral Sentiments*, 204.
101. Smollett, *Humphry Clinker*, 203–4.
102. Ibid., 48.
103. Horace Walpole, quoted in Wolfgang Franke, 'Smollett's *Humphry Clinker* as a "Party Novel" ', *Studies in Scottish Literature*, 9/2–3 (Oct.–Jan. 1971–2), 97; Smollett, *Humphry Clinker*, 6.
104. Ibid., 181, 188, 235, 221, 213, 211, 228.
105. Robert Fergusson, 'The Daft-Days', in *Poems by Allan Ramsay and Robert Fergusson*, ed. Alexander Kinghorn and Alexander Law (Edinburgh: Scottish Academic Press and Association for Scottish Literary Studies, 1985), 123.
106. Jonathan Bate, *The Song of the Earth* (London: Picador, 2000).
107. Burns, *Poems and Songs*, 101 ('To a Mouse').
108. Rosalind Mitchison, *Agricultural Sir John* (London: Geoffrey Bles, 1962), 27.
109. Angus MacLeod, ed., *The Songs of Duncan Bàn Macintyre* (Edinburgh: Scottish Academic Press for the Scottish Gaelic Texts Society, 1978), 176–7; tr. Angus MacLeod.
110. *PBSV*, 262–3; tr. Iain Crichton Smith.
111. *Songs of Duncan Bàn Macintyre*, 230–31.
112. *Poems by Allan Ramsay and Robert Fergusson*, 122 ('The Daft-Days').
113. Watson, ed., *The Poetry of Scotland*, 413.
114. *The Letters of Robert Burns*, 2nd edn, ed. J. De Lancey Ferguson and G. Ross Roy (Oxford: Clarendon Press, 1985), I, 167.
115. *Letters of Robert Burns*, I, 17.
116. Henry Mackenzie, *Works* (1808; rpt with a new introduction by Susan Manning, London: Routledge/Thoemmes Press, 1996), 8 vols, VIII, 100.
117. Hume, *A Treatise of Human Nature*, ed. E. C. Mossner (London: Penguin, 1985), 311.
118. Henry Mackenzie, *The Man of Feeling*, ed. Brian Vickers (Oxford: Oxford University Press, 1970), 5, 3, 113; Walter Scott, *Journals*, ed. W. E. K. Anderson (Edinburgh: Canongate, 1998), 33.
119. Mackenzie, *The Man of Feeling*, 12–13.
120. Henry Mackenzie, *Julia de Roubigné*, ed. Susan Manning (East Linton: Tuckwell Press, 1999), 7.
121. See Buchan, *Capital*, 260; Millar, *Origin*, ch. 1; and Robert Crawford, 'Burns's Sister' in Douglas Gifford and Dorothy McMillan, ed., *A History of Scottish Women's Writing*, 92.
122. Quoted by John Mullan, 'The Language of Sentiment: Hume, Smith, and Henry Mackenzie' in Andrew Hook, ed., *The History of Scottish Literature, Volume 2*, 281.
123. Smith, *Theory*, 206–7.
124. Mackenzie, *The Man of Feeling*, 102–3.
125. Ibid., 106, 97.
126. Scott on 'Henry Mackenzie' in *The Lives of the Novelists* (London: Dent, 1910), 297.
127. Hume, *Treatise*, ed. Selby-Bigge, 68.

7 The Age of Burns

1. Adam Smith, *The Theory of Moral Sentiments*, ed. D. D. Raphael and A. L. Macfie (Oxford: Clarendon Press, 1976), 125.
2. Written by Fergusson on p. 92 of vol. IV of the St Andrews University Library copy of Jonathan Swift, *Miscellanies in Prose and Verse* (London: Motte, 1727–35) where other students had scribbled abuse of Fergusson.
3. See J. De Lancey Ferguson and G. Ross Roy, ed., *The Letters of Robert Burns* (Oxford: Clarendon Press, 1985), 2 vols, I, 298, 355, and II, 480.

4. Quoted in W. J. Couper, *The Edinburgh Periodical Press*, (Stirling: Eneas Mackay, 1908), 2 vols, II, 72.
5. See Robert Crawford, *The Modern Poet* (Oxford: Oxford University Press, 2001), ch. 2.
6. *The Poems of Robert Fergusson*, ed. Matthew P. McDiarmid, (Edinburgh: Blackwood for the Scottish Text Society, 1954–6), 2 vols, II, 130.
7. *The Anecdotes and Egotisms of Henry Mackenzie*, ed. Harold William Thompson (Oxford: Oxford University Press, 1927), 150.
8. Thomas Blacklock, 'An Hymn to Fortitude' in David McCordick, ed., *Scottish Literature: An Anthology, Volume I* (New York: Peter Lang, 1996), 1010.
9. Smith, *Theory*, 123.
10. Henry Mackenzie, *The Man of Feeling*, ed. Brian Vickers (London: Oxford University Press, 1970), 81.
11. Robert Burns, *Poems and Songs*, ed. James Kinsley (Oxford: Oxford University Press, 1969), 258.
12. Burns, *Letters*, ed. Ferguson and Roy, II, 75.
13. James Mackenzie, *The Life and Complete Works of Michael Bruce* (Edinburgh: Riverside Press, 1914), 296 ('Ode to Sleep'); Burns, *Poems and Songs*, ed. Kinsley, 92.
14. Mackenzie, *Michael Bruce*, 241; *PBSV*, 303.
15. Mackenzie, *Michael Bruce*, 244; *PBSV*, 282.
16. William Wordsworth, 'Resolution and Independence', *Poetical Works* (London: Warne, n.d.), 103.
17. Mackenzie, *Michael Bruce*, 222, 204.
18. Ibid., 211; *PBSV*, 305.
19. William Falconer, 'The Shipwreck' in McCordick, ed., *Scottish Literature*, I, 1122–3.
20. Burns, *Letters*, ed. Ferguson and Roy, II, 6–7.
21. Burns, *Poems and Songs*, ed. Kinsley, 258.
22. Oliver Goldsmith, cited in *James Buchan, Capital of the Mind* (London: John Murray, 2003), 115.
23. Fergusson, *Poems*, ed. McDiarmid, II, 85.
24. See Plate III in Robert Crawford, ed., *Launch-site for English Studies: Three Centuries of Literary Studies at the University of St Andrews* (St Andrews: Verse, 1997); Fergusson, *Poems*, ed. McDiarmid, II, 191–2.
25. Ibid., II, 1.
26. *PBSV*, 275 and 290.
27. Ibid., 268.
28. Anon. *Paul Jones: or The Fife Coast Garland* (Edinburgh, 1779), 19 and 2.
29. *PBSV*, 271.
30. Fergusson, *Poems*, ed. McDiarmid, II, 39.
31. Ibid., II, 113–14.
32. *SRP*, 128–9.
33. [Thomas Mercer], *The Sentimental Sailor or St Preux to Eloisa, An Elegy* (Edinburgh: Kincaid and Creech, 1772), 31.
34. Burns, *Letters*, ed. Ferguson and Roy, I, 256.
35. Ibid., I, 235.
36. James Beattie, *The Minstrel*, in *The Poetical Works of Gray, Beattie and Collins* (London: Warne, n.d.), 188, 203, and 206.
37. See Martin Moonie's chapter on Greenfield in Crawford, ed., *The Scottish Invention of English Literature* (Cambridge: Cambridge University Press, 1998).
38. Matthew Reynolds, 'Principles and Norms of Translation' in Peter France and Kenneth Haynes, ed., *The Oxford History of Literary Translation in English, Volume 4, 1790–1900* (Oxford: Oxford University Press, 2006), 63.
39. Alexander Fraser Tytler, Lord Woodhouselee, *Essay on the Principles of Translation* (1791; rpt London: Dent, n.d.), 45.

40. *The Lusiad: or, The Discovery of India* trs. William Julius Mickle, 3rd edn. (London: Cadell and Davies, 1798), 2 vols, I, xxxvii and 9.
41. *The Memoirs of the late Mrs. Elizabeth Hamilton*, ed. Miss Benger, 2nd edn (London: Longman, 1819), 2 vols, I, 104.
42. Mungo Park, *Travels in the Interior Districts of Africa* (London: Newnes, n.d.), 307.
43. Burns's inscription in a presentation copy, cited in *Letters*, ed. Ferguson and Roy, II, 469.
44. Burns, *Poems and Songs*, ed. Kinsley, 258.
45. Burns, *Letters*, ed. Ferguson and Roy, I, 137.
46. Robert Burns, *Poems, Chiefly in the Scottish Dialect* (Kilmarnock: John Wilson, 1786), iv.
47. Robert Burns, *Poems, Chiefly in the Scottish Dialect* (Edinburgh: William Creech, 1787), v.
48. Burns, *Letters*, ed. Ferguson and Roy, I, 265 and 83.
49. Quoted in James Mackay, *Burns: A Biography of Robert Burns* (Edinburgh: Mainstream, 1992), 82.
50. Burns, *Poems and Songs*, ed. Kinsley, 207.
51. *PBSV*, 279.
52. Ibid., 288.
53. Burns, *Letters*, ed. Ferguson and Roy, I, 143.
54. Burns, *Poems, Chiefly in the Scottish Dialect*, v.
55. Burns's First Commonplace Book, quoted in McDiarmid, ed., *The Poems of Robert Fergusson*, I, 179.
56. Burns, *Letters*, ed. Ferguson and Roy, I, 410.
57. *PBSV*, 287; Smith, *Theory of Moral Sentiments*, 83.
58. Burns, *Poems, Chiefly in the Scottish Dialect*, v.
59. Robert Bisset, *Sketch of Democracy* (London: Matthews et al., 1796), 340.
60. Burns, *Poems and Songs*, ed. Kinsley, 179–80.
61. *PBSV*, 282.
62. Ibid., 281; Burns, *Poems and Songs*, ed. Kinsley, 152.
63. Burns, *Poems and Songs* ed. Kinsley, 110–16.
64. Burns, *Letters*, ed. Ferguson and Roy, II, 143.
65. Burns, *Poems and Songs*, ed. Kinsley, 580.
66. *PBSV*, 304.
67. Ibid., 302, 304.
68. Burns, *Poems and Songs*, ed. Kinsley, 605.
69. Henry Mackenzie, unsigned essay in *The Lounger* (9 December 1786), rpt in Donald A. Low, ed., *Robert Burns: The Critical Heritage* (London: Routledge and Kegan Paul, 1974), 70–71.
70. Burns, *Poems and Songs*, ed. Kinsley, 249.
71. *PBSV*, 304.
72. Scott in 1827, quoted in Mackay, *Burns: A Biography*, 267.
73. Stewart, cited in Liam McIlvanney, *Burns the Radical* (East Linton: Tuckwell Press, 2002), 30.
74. Quoted in Mackay, *Burns: A Biography*, 243.
75. Burns, *Letters*, ed. Ferguson and Roy, I, 251.
76. Burns, *Poems and Songs*, ed. Kinsley, 387, 388, 390.
77. Ibid., 389–90.
78. Ibid., 146; *PBSV*, 289; Burns, *Poems and Songs*, ed. Kinsley, 146.
79. Burns, *Poems and Songs*, ed. Kinsley, 37, 39.
80. On Burns's use of Scottish stanza forms see Douglas Dunn, ' "A Very Scottish Kind of Dash": Burns's Native Metric' in Robert Crawford, ed., *Robert Burns and Cultural Authority* (Edinburgh: Edinburgh University Press, 1997), 58–85.
81. *PBSV*, 303.

82. Ibid., 292–3.
83. See Donald A. Low, ed., *The Songs of Robert Burns* (London: Routledge, 1993), 25–7.
84. Virgil, *Aeneid*, tr. H. R. Fairclough (London: Loeb/Heinemann, 1974), 528–9.
85. Burns, *Letters*, ed. Ferguson and Roy, I, 137.
86. *PBSV*, 301.
87. Ibid., 305.
88. Grose's *A Classical Dictionary of the Vulgar Tongue* appeared in 1785; Burns, *Letters*, ed. Ferguson and Roy, I, 135.
89. All quotes from 'Tam o' Shanter' are from *PBSV*, 294–300.
90. Ibid., 277.
91. John Mayne, *Glasgow: A Poem* (London: Cadell and Davies, 1805), 21 and 11.
92. Burns, *Poems and Songs*, ed. Kinsley, 153.
93. Ibid., 47.
94. James Grainger, *An Essay on the More Common West-India Diseases*, 2nd edn (Edinburgh: Mundell, 1802), i, iii.
95. Dr Percy, Bishop of Dromore, quoted in James Boswell, *The Life of Samuel Johnson* (London: Dent, 1973), 2 vols, I, 621 n.
96. Alexander Chalmers, ed., *The Works of the English Poets* (London: J. Johnson et al., 1810), 21 vols, XIV, 507, 478, 473.
97. Boswell, *Life of Johnson*, I, 621.
98. Chalmers, ed., *The Works*, XIV, 497, 491; see also John Gilmore, *The Poetics of Empire* (London: Athlone, 2000).
99. Boswell, *Life of Johnson*, I, 621.
100. See Ramsay's entry in *ODNB*.
101. Charles Ryskamp and Frederick A. Pottle, ed., *Boswell: The Ominous Years, 1774–1776* (London: Heinemann, 1963), 235; Marcus Wood, ed., *The Poetry of Slavery* (Oxford: Oxford University Press, 2003), 184–94.
102. John Leyden, *A Historical & Philosophical Sketch of the Discoveries & Settlements of the Europeans in Northern & Western Africa, at the Close of the Eighteenth Century* (Edinburgh: Moir, 1799), 95–6.
103. Leyden, *A Historical & Philosophical Sketch*, xi, 29, 115.
104. Ibid., 96.
105. Ibid., 126.
106. Burns, *Poems and Songs*, ed. Kinsley, 634.
107. William Russell, manuscript letter of 24 May 1788, stuck in the copy of David Irving's *Lives of Scotish [sic] Authors: viz. Fergusson, Falconer, and Russell* (Edinburgh: Pillans, 1801) in St Andrews University Library.
108. *SRP*, 145.
109. Geddes, letter of 15 July 1801 to H. E. G. Paulus in Reginald C. Fuller, *Alexander Geddes* (Sheffield: Almond Press, 1984), 146.
110. Quoted ibid., 151.
111. Boswell Papers, M 132, *Journal of a Tour* ms, 144 verso, Beinecke Library, Yale University; Muir's poem is quoted in Latin in Christina Bewley, *Muir of Huntershill* (Oxford: Oxford University Press, 1981, 115–6 (the English version is my own); Robert Watson's words are quoted on p. 182 of Bewley's book.
112. *SRP*, 130.
113. Ibid., 152–3; tr. Meg Bateman.
114. Quoted by Kirsteen McCue, 'Burns, Women, and Song' in Crawford, ed., *Robert Burns and Cultural Authority*, 44.
115. Quoted by Valentina Bold, 'Beyond "The Empire of the Gentle Heart": Scottish Women Poets of the Nineteenth Century' in Douglas Gifford and Dorothy McMillan, ed., *A History of Scottish Women's Writing* (Edinburgh: Edinburgh University Press, 1997), 246.
116. Hamilton, *Memoirs*, II, 203.
117. See Fergusson, *Poems*, I, 97 and 99.

118. Mickle, *Lusiad*, xvi; William Barron, *History of the Colonization of the Free States of Antiquity. Applied to the Present Contest between Great Britain and her American Colonies* (London: Cadell, 1778), 142–3; see also Robert Crawford, ed., *The Scottish Invention of English Literature* (Cambridge: Cambridge University Press, 1998).

119. See Crawford, ed., *Launch-site for English Studies*, 57–9; William Spalding, *The History of English Literature*, 3rd edn (Edinburgh: Oliver & Boyd), 1855), 414.

120. MacDiarmid, quoted in *ODNB* entry for Blamire.

121. John Pinkerton, *A Dissertation on the Origin and Progress of the Scythians or Goths* (London: George Nicol, 1787), 69.

122. *PBSV*, 306–7; tr. Derick Thomson.

123. See Derick Thomson, *An Introduction to Gaelic Poetry* (London: Gollancz, 1974), 211.

124. *PBSV*, 306–7; tr. Derick Thomson.

125. Sorley MacLean, *Spring tide and Neap tide: Selected Poems 1932–1972* (Edinburgh: Canongate, 1977), 108.

126. Quoted by Kirsteen McCue, 'Women and Song 1750–1850' in Gifford and McMillan, ed., *A History*, 66.

127. *PBSV*, 311.

128. Ibid., 312.

129. Ibid., 313.

130. Quoted by Dorothy McMillan, 'Some Early Travellers' in Gifford and McMillan, ed., *A History*, 129.

131. Grace Dalrymple Elliott, *Journal of My Life During the French Revolution* (London: Bentley, 1859), 25, 200, 69. Eric Rohmer's film is called *L'Anglaise et le Duc*.

132. Walter Scott, *The Bride of Lammermoor*, ed. J. H. Alexander (Edinburgh: Edinburgh University Press, 1995), 164.

133. *PBSV*, 310.

134. James Bruce, *Travels to Discover the Source of the Nile*, ed. C. F. Beckingham (Edinburgh: Edinburgh University Press, 1964), 163–4.

135. James Boswell, *The Journal of a Tour to the Hebrides*, ed. R. W. Chapman (1924; rpt Oxford: Oxford University Press, 1974), 171.

136. James Boswell, *An Account of Corsica* (Glasgow: Robert and Andrew Foulis, 1768), title page.

137. Boswell, *Life of Johnson*, II, 165; see also Marshall Waingrow, ed., *The Correspondence and Other Papers of James Boswell Relating to the Making of the 'Life of Johnson'*, 2nd edn (Edinburgh: Edinburgh University Press, 2001), 391, n. 17.

138. *Boswell's London Journal*, ed. Frederick A. Pottle (London: Reprint Society, 1952), 49.

139. Ibid., 78.

140. Ibid., 92, 120, 140–41.

141. Ibid., 232.

142. Ibid., 120–21.

143. Ibid., 107–8.

144. Ibid., 308.

145. See Waingrow, ed., *The Correspondence*, xlix.

146. *Boswell's Journal*, ed. Chapman, 172–3.

147. Boswell, *Life of Johnson*, I, 242.

148. Boswell's *London Journal*, 284–5.

149. Boswell's 'Advertisement' to the *Life*, quoted in Waingrow, ed., *The Correspondence*, xxxv.

150. Boswell quoted in Waingrow, ed., *The Correspondence*, xxxvi and 399.

151. Boswell, *Life of Johnson*, I, 302.

152. I remember this with pleasure from a conversation with Richard Ellmann in the mid-1980s; Bruce Redford, *Designing the 'Life of Johnson'* (Oxford: Oxford University Press, 2002), 13, 54.

8 Volcano, Wizard, Bankrupt, Spy

1. *Memoirs, Journal and Correspondence of Thomas Moore*, ed. Lord John Russell (London: Longman, Brown, Green & Longmans, 1853), 8 vols, I, 204; Henry Cockburn, *Life of Lord Jeffrey* (Edinburgh: Black, 1832), 2 vols, I, 173.
2. Lord Cockburn, *Selected Letters*, ed. Alan Bell (Edinburgh: John Donald, 2005), 20–21, 28.
3. James Hogg, *Collected Letters*, I, ed. Gillian Hughes (Edinburgh: Edinburgh University Press, 2004), 75.
4. Cockburn, *Selected Letters*, ed. Bell, 37.
5. In this chapter statistics about novel publication are drawn from Peter Garside, James Raven and Rainer Schöwerling, ed., *The English Novel 1770–1829* (Oxford: Oxford University Press, 2000), 2 vols.
6. George Jardine, *Outlines of Philosophical Education* (Glasgow: n.p., n.d.), title page; for Jeffrey's debt to Jardine see Cockburn, *Life of Jeffrey*, I, 10.
7. *Jeffrey's Criticism: A Selection*, ed. Peter F. Morgan (Edinburgh: Scottish Academic Press, 1983), 85, 125.
8. Lord Byron, *The Complete Poetical Works*, ed. Jerome J. McGann (Oxford: Clarendon Press, 1980), 7 vols, I, 246, 242.
9. Cockburn, *Life of Jeffrey*, I, 133.
10. Byron, *Complete Poetical Works*, ed. McGann, I, 234.
11. Quoted by Maurice Lindsay, ed., Thomas Hamilton, *The Youth and Manhood of Cyril Thornton* (Aberdeen: Association for Scottish Literary Studies, 1990), xi.
12. John Galt, *Literary Life and Miscellanea* (Edinburgh: Blackwood, 1834), 3 vols, I, 311.
13. Hogg, *Letters*, ed. Hughes, I, 401.
14. Ibid., xxxii.
15. Thomas Campbell, *Poetical Works*, ed. J. Logie Robertson (Oxford: Oxford University Press, 1907), 2.
16. Robert Crawford, *The Modern Poet* (Oxford: Oxford University Press, 2001), ch. 2.
17. *PBSV*, 325.
18. Ibid., 327.
19. Quoted in Benita Eisler, *Byron* (London: Hamish Hamilton, 1999), 27.
20. Byron, *Complete Poetical Works*, ed. McGann, I, 47; *PBSV*, 336.
21. Hogg, *Letters*, ed. Hughes, I, 191 and 194.
22. *PBSV*, 340–41.
23. Ibid., 339.
24. Ibid., 330.
25. Hogg, *Letters*, ed. Hughes, I, 179, 185.
26. Quoted in Eisler, *Byron*, 340.
27. *Jeffrey's Criticism*, ed. Morgan, 86–7.
28. Walter Scott, *Chronicles of the Canongate*, ed. Claire Lamont (Edinburgh: Edinburgh University Press, 2000), 52.
29. Cockburn, *Selected Letters*, ed. Bell, 41.
30. Eliza Hamilton, *Translations of the Letters of a Hindoo Rajah* (London: G. and J. Robinson, 1801), 2 vols, I, 127, 87.
31. Elizabeth Hamilton, *Letters on Education* (Bath: Cruttwell, 1801), 2 vols, I, 258, II, 307 and I, 218.
32. Elizabeth Hamilton, *Memoirs of the Life of Agrippina, the Wife of Germanicus* (Bath: Cruttwell, 1804), 3 vols, I, xiv, xvi, and III, 41.
33. Hector MacNeill, *Memoirs of the Life and Travels of the late Charles Macpherson* (Edinburgh: Constable, 1800), 186, 190.
34. Elizabeth Hamilton, *Memoirs of Modern Philosophers* (Bath: Cruttwell, 1800), 3 vols, I, 57, 194.
35. Carol Anderson and Aileen M. Riddell, 'The Other Great Unknowns: Women Fiction

Writers of the Early Nineteenth Century' in Douglas Gifford and Dorothy McMillan, ed., *A History of Scottish Women's Writing* (Edinburgh: Edinburgh University Press, 1997), 182.

36. Hamilton, *Memoirs of Modern Philosophers*, III, 102.
37. Ann Grant, *Letters from the Mountains* (London: Longman, 1813), 3 vols, I, 123.
38. Ibid., 269–70.
39. Jane Porter, *The Scottish Chiefs*, 3rd edn (London: Longman, 1816), 3 vols, I, 128.
40. Mary Brunton, letter to Mrs Izett, 15 August 1814, quoted in Mary McKerrow, *Mary Brunton* (Kirkwall: The Orcadian, 2001), 132–3.
41. Brunton, autumn 1813 letter to Baillie, quoted ibid., 129.
42. Mary Brunton, *Discipline* (1814; rpt London: Pandora, 1986), 211.
43. Ibid., 261.
44. Ibid., 375.
45. Evidence for Bisset's student reading is from the student borrowings register in St Andrews University Library.
46. Katie Trumpener, *Bardic Nationalism* (Princeton: Princeton University Press, 1997), 139.
47. Margaret Drabble and Jenny Stringer, ed., *The Concise Oxford Companion to English Literature* (Oxford: Oxford University Press, 1987), 173.
48. Christian Isobel Johnstone, *Clan-Albin, A National Tale* (Glasgow: Association for Scottish Literary Studies, 2003), 200.
49. Andrew Monnickendam, Introduction to his edition of Christian Isobel Johnstone, *Clan-Albin, A National Tale* (Glasgow: Association for Scottish Literary Studies, 2003), xiii.
50. Susan Ferrier, *Marriage*, ed. Herbert Foltinek (Oxford: Oxford University Press, 1986), 9.
51. Ibid., 44.
52. Ibid., 414.
53. Walter Scott, *A Legend of the Wars of Montrose*, ed. J. H. Alexander (Edinburgh: Edinburgh University Press, 1995), 183.
54. *Memoir and Correspondence of Susan Ferrier*, ed. John A. Doyle (London: John Murray, 1898), 59.
55. William St Clair, *The Reading Nation in the Romantic Period* (Cambridge: Cambridge University Press, 2004), 245.
56. Walter Scott, *Poetical Works* (London: Ward, n.d., 350) ('Prologue to Miss Baillie's Play of the Family Legend').
57. Scott, review of Henry Mackenzie, *Report*, and Malcolm Laing, *The Poems of Ossian*, *Edinburgh Review*, July 1805, 429.
58. Walter Scott, *Saint Ronan's Well*, ed. Mark A. Weinstein (Edinburgh: Edinburgh University Press, 1995), 1.
59. Andrew Hook, 'Scotland and Romanticism: The International Scene' in Andrew Hook, ed., *The History of Scottish Literature, Volume 2* (Aberdeen: Aberdeen University Press, 1987), 319.
60. Cockburn, *Selected Letters*, ed. Bell, 44.
61. Scott in a letter quoted in John Sutherland, *The Life of Walter Scott* (Oxford: Blackwell, 1995), 128.
62. Ibid.
63. This is the listing that appears on the rear jacket of each volume of *The Edinburgh Edition of the Waverley Novels* (Editor-in-Chief, David Hewitt) (Edinburgh: Edinburgh University Press, 1993–), 30 vols.
64. David Hewitt, ed., *Scott on Himself* (Edinburgh: Scottish Academic Press, 1981), 16.
65. Scott, memorial tablet to Ferguson in the perimeter wall of St Andrews Cathedral, quoted in Robert Crawford, *Devolving English Literature*, 2nd edn (Edinburgh: Edinburgh University Press, 2000), 111.

66. Hewitt, ed., *Scott on Himself*, 31.
67. Scott to Percy, 6 October 1800, in William Ruff, 'Sir Walter Scott and Bishop Percy', *Notes and Queries*, 4 November 1933, 308.
68. Ibid.
69. James Hogg, *Anecdotes of Scott*, ed. Jill Rubenstein (Edinburgh: Edinburgh University Press, 1999), 5, 3.
70. Walter Scott, *Selected Poems*, ed. Thomas Crawford (Oxford: Clarendon Press, 1972), 147.
71. Walter Scott, *The Fair Maid of Perth*, ed. Andrew Hook and Donald Mackenzie (Edinburgh: Edinburgh University Press, 1999), 13.
72. Kenneth Haynes in K. Haynes and Peter France, ed., *The Oxford History of Literary Translation in English, Volume 4, 1790–1900* (Oxford: Oxford University Press, 2006), 16; Haynes is quoting F. J. Lamport, *German Classical Drama* (Cambridge: Cambridge University Press, 1990), 44.
73. Galt, *Literary Life*, I, 240.
74. Scott, *Chronicles of the Canongate*, ed. Lamont, 4.
75. V. S. Pritchett, quoted on the rear jacket flap of the volumes of the Edinburgh Edition.
76. See Walter Scott, *Guy Mannering*, ed. P. D. Garside (Edinburgh: Edinburgh University Press, 1999), 18–19 and 522.
77. Scott, *Saint Ronan's Well*, ed. Weinstein, 183.
78. Scott, *Chronicles of the Canongate*, ed. Lamont, 76.
79. Scott, *Selected Poems*, ed. Crawford, 295.
80. *PBSV*, 321.
81. Scott, *Selected Poems*, ed. Crawford, 140, 141, 143.
82. Walter Scott, *Waverley*, ed. Andrew Hook (Harmondsworth: Penguin, 1985), 64, 48, 145, 139.
83. Ibid., 472.
84. Quoted in Edgar Johnson, *Sir Walter Scott: The Great Unknown* (London: Hamish Hamilton, 1970), 2 vols, I, 478.
85. Quoted ibid., I, 519.
86. Scott, *Chronicles of the Canongate*, ed. Lamont, 453.
87. Scott, *Waverley*, ed. Hook, 492.
88. Brunton in McKerrow, *Mary Brunton*, 133.
89. Scott, *Waverley*, ed. Hook, 387.
90. Scott to William Blackwood, 21 September 1817, in H. J. C. Grierson, ed., *The Letters of Sir Walter Scott 1815–1817* (London: Constable, 1933), 521.
91. Scott, *A Legend*, 171.
92. Ibid., 173.
93. Scott, *Waverley*, 487.
94. Walter Scott, *The Pirate*, ed. Mark Weinstein and Alison Lumsden (Edinburgh: Edinburgh University Press, 2001), 118.
95. Walter Scott, *The Monastery*, ed. Penny Fielding (Edinburgh: Edinburgh University Press, 2000), 105.
96. *The Journal of Sir Walter Scott*, ed. W. E. K. Anderson (Edinburgh: Canongate, 1998), 77, 81.
97. Ibid., 171–2.
98. Scott, *Chronicles of the Canongate*, ed. Lamont, 49.
99. 'Mar-Mee-Ong' appears on one of the early nineteenth-century mock playbills for the Royal Mohock Theatre preserved in University of Guelph Library, Ontario.
100. James Hogg, *Lay Sermons*, ed. Gillian Hughes and Douglas S. Mack (Edinburgh: Edinburgh University Press, 1997), 103, 104; James Hogg, *Queen Hynde*, ed. Suzanne Gilbert and Douglas Mack (Edinburgh: Edinburgh University Press, 1998), 220.
101. Hogg, *Queen Hynde*, ed. Gilbert and Mack, 30.
102. Hogg, *Letters*, ed. Hughes, I, 367.

103. James Hogg, *The Shepherd's Calendar*, ed. Douglas S. Mack (Edinburgh: Edinburgh University Press, 1995), 107.

104. Hogg, *Letters*, ed. Hughes, I, 15; *Anecdotes of Scott*, ed. Rubenstein, 38.

105. Hogg, *Queen Hynde*, ed. Gilbert and Mack, 31.

106. *PBSV*, 324.

107. Hogg, *Letters*, ed. Hughes, I, 1.

108. James Hogg, *Memoir of the Author's Life*, ed. Douglas S. Mack (Edinburgh: Scottish Academic Press, 1972), 20.

109. James Hogg, *The Spy*, ed. Gillian Hughes (Edinburgh: Edinburgh University Press, 2000), 3.

110. Ibid., 165.

111. Hogg, *Letters*, ed. Hughes, I, 219; Burns, *Poems and Songs*, ed. James Kinsley (Oxford: Oxford University Press, 1969), 602.

112. Hogg, *The Spy*, ed. Hughes, 19.

113. *PBSV*, 315.

114. Ibid., 318.

115. Ibid., 317.

116. James Hogg, *The Jacobite Relics of Scotland (First Series)*, ed. Murray Pittock (Edinburgh: Edinburgh University Press, 2002), xxiv.

117. Hogg, quoted in Dwight Macdonald, ed., *Parodies: An Anthology* (London: Faber and Faber, 1961), 69.

118. Ibid., 90–91.

119. J. H. Alexander, ed., *The Tavern Sages: Selections from the Noctes Ambrosianae* (Aberdeen: Association for Scottish Literary Studies, 1992), 109, 95.

120. Hogg, *Letters*, ed. Hughes, I, 174.

121. Byron, *Poetical Works*, ed. McGann, I, 369.

122. James Hogg, *The Brownie of Bodsbeck*, ed. Douglas S. Mack (Edinburgh: Scottish Academic Press, 1976), 63, 161.

123. Walter Scott, *The Tale of Old Mortality*, ed. Douglas S. Mack (Edinburgh: Edinburgh University Press, 1993), 350.

124. James Hogg, *The Three Perils of Man*, ed. Douglas Gifford (Edinburgh: Scottish Academic Press, 1989), 190.

125. James Hogg, *The Three Perils of Woman*, ed. David Groves, Antony Hasler and Douglas S. Mack (Edinburgh: Edinburgh University Press, 1995), 202, 213.

126. Hogg, *The Shepherd's Calendar*, ed. Mack, 119.

127. Hogg, *Three Perils of Woman*, ed. Groves et al., 1, 25.

128. Ibid., 405, 407, 332.

129. James Hogg, *The Private Memoirs and Confessions of a Justified Sinner*, ed. P. D. Garside (Edinburgh: Edinburgh University Press, 2001), 1, 165, 169.

130. Ibid., Introduction, xlvi–xlviii.

131. Ibid., 158.

132. Ibid., Introduction, liii–liv.

133. Hogg, *Letters*, ed. Hughes, I, 91.

134. Hogg, *The Spy*, ed. Hughes, 250, 246.

135. James Hogg, *Winter Evening Tales*, ed. Ian Duncan (Edinburgh: Edinburgh University Press, 2002), xxvi, 4, 28, 73, 499, 145, 220, 284.

136. Karl Miller, *Electric Shepherd* (London: Faber and Faber, 2003), 217.

137. Hogg, *Reminiscences of Some of his Contemporaries*, appended to his *Poetical Works*, 1878 edition, quoted in Jennie W. Aberdein, *John Galt* (London: Oxford University Press, 1936), 26–7.

138. John Galt, *Autobiography* (London: Cochrane and McCrone, 1833), 3 vols, I, 55–6.

139. John Galt, *The Ayrshire Legatees* (1821; rpt Edinburgh: James Thin, 1978), 40.

140. John Galt, *Pictures, Historical and Biographical, Drawn from English, Scottish, and Irish History* (London: Phillips, 1821), 2 vols, I, p. v.

141. John Galt, *The Member: An Autobiography*, ed. Ian A. Gordon (Edinburgh: Scottish Academic Press, 1985), 5.

142. 'Rev. T. Clark' [i.e., John Galt], *The Travels and Observations of Hareach, The Wandering Jew*, 2nd edn (London: John Souter, n.d. [probably 1820]), xii; John Galt, *Bogle Corbet; or, The Emigrants* (London: Bentley, 1831), 3 vols, I, iii.

143. Galt, *Bogle Corbet*, III, 46; II, 220; I, 41; II, 135, 134.

144. Margaret Atwood, *Survival* (Toronto: Anansi, 1972).

145. John Galt, *Lawrie Todd; or, The Settlers in the Woods* (London: Colburn and Bentley, 1830), 3 vols, I, 38, 88, 122; II, 58, 59; III, 8.

146. John Galt, ed., *The Works of Henry Mackenzie* (Edinburgh: Oliver and Boyd, 1824), 3, 4, 8; Galt, *Literary Life*, II, 218.

147. Galt, *Literary Life*, I, 226.

148. John Galt, *Selected Short Stories*, ed. Ian A. Gordon (Edinburgh: Scottish Academic Press, 1978), 49.

149. John Galt, *Annals of the Parish* (London: Nelson, n.d.), 7.

150. Galt's instructions to Blackwood (April 1822), quoted in John Galt, *The Provost*, ed. Ian A. Gordon (Oxford: Oxford University Press, 1982), xi.

151. *PBSV*, 342–3.

152. Galt, *Selected Short Stories*, ed. Gordon, 9.

153. John Galt, *The Provost*, ed. Ian A. Gordon (Oxford: Oxford University Press, 1982), 8 and xiv.

154. John Galt, *The Radical: An Autobiography* (London: Fraser, 1832), 5.

155. 'Mrs Blackford', *The Scottish Orphans* (London: Wetton and Jarvis, 1822), title page.

156. Clark, (i.e., Galt), *Travels and Observations*, x.

157. John Galt, *The History of Gog and Magog* (Whitefish, Montana: Kessinger Publishing, 2004), 40.

158. These words are quoted from the first edition of *The Wandering Jew* in Patricia Wilson's introduction to John Galt, *Ringan Gilhaize or The Covenanters* (Edinburgh: Scottish Academic Press, 1984), ix.

159. Galt, *Selected Short Stories*, ed. Gordon, 22, 23, 12.

160. Galt, *Autobiography*, I, 1.

161. Galt, *Literary Life*, I, 354.

162. Hogg, *Letters*, ed. Hughes, I, 263; 14 June 1822 letter to Blackwood quoted in *The Three Perils of Woman*, xviii.

163. D. M. Moir, *Mansie Waugh* (1828; rpt London: Foulis, 1911), 134–5.

164. Andrew Picken, *The Dominie's Legacy* (London: Kidd, 1830), 3 vols, I, 95.

165. Michael Scott, *The Cruise of the Midge*, A New Edition (Edinburgh: Blackwood, 1845), 1.

166. Clark (i.e., Galt) *Travels and Observations*, x.

167. Roderick Watson, ed., *The Poetry of Scotland* (Edinburgh: Edinburgh University Press, 1995), 420.

168. Derick Thomson, *An Introduction to Gaelic Poetry* (London: Gollancz, 1977), 221.

169. See John Macinnes, 'Gaelic Poetry in the Nineteenth Century' in Douglas Gifford, ed., *The History of Scottish Literature, Volume 3, Nineteenth Century* (Aberdeen: Aberdeen University Press, 1988), 379.

170. Andrew Picken, *The Black Watch* (London: Bentley, 1834), 3 vols, I, 8.

171. Andrew Picken, ed., *The Canadas* (London: Wilson, 1832), title page.

172. Elizabeth Grant of Rothiemurchus, *Memoirs of a Highland Lady*, ed. Andrew Tod (Edinburgh: Canongate, 1988), 208.

173. Moir, *Mansie Waugh*, 170.

174. Alasdair Cameron, 'Scottish Drama in the Nineteenth Century' in Gifford, ed., *The History*, 432.

175. See, e.g., *Blackwood's Magazine* for September 1818.

176. Barbara Taylor, quoted in Adrienne Scullion, 'Some Women of the Nineteenth-century Scottish Theatre' in Gifford and McMillan, ed., *A History of Scottish Women's Writing*, 178.

9 Scotland and London

1. Lord Cockburn to Andrew Rutherford, 14 February 1847, in *Selected Letters*, ed. Alan Bell (Edinburgh: John Donald, 2005), 203.
2. See Robert Crawford, *The Modern Poet* (Oxford: Oxford University Press, 2001), ch. 3.
3. Jim McBeth, 'Revealed: the Scot who inspired Dickens' Scrooge', *Scotsman*, 24 December 2004, 19.
4. William Chambers, quoted in Karl Miller, *Electric Shepherd* (London: Faber and Faber, 2003), 274.
5. *Man of Letters, The Early Life and Love-Letters of Robert Chambers*, ed. C. H. Layman (Edinburgh: Edinburgh University Press, 1990), 20.
6. Scott, *Journal*, ed. W. E. K. Anderson (Edinburgh: Canongate, 1998), 604.
7. Lord Cockburn, *Life of Francis Jeffrey with a Selection of his Correspondence* (Edinburgh: A. & C. Black, 1832), 2 vols, I, 159–60.
8. Fred Kaplan, *Thomas Carlyle: A Biography* (Cambridge: Cambridge University Press, 1983), 21 (quoting Carlyle's *Reminiscences*).
9. Thomas Carlyle, *The French Revolution*, ed. K. J. Fielding and David Sorensen (Oxford: Oxford University Press, 1989), 2 vols in one, II, 335.
10. Thomas Carlyle, *On Heroes, Hero-Worship and the Heroic in History* (1841; rpt Oxford: Oxford University Press, 1963), 213.
11. Thomas Carlyle, 'Boswell's Life of Johnson' in *Critical and Miscellaneous Essays* (London: Chapman and Hall, 1903), 8 vols in three, IV, 77.
12. Carlyle, *Critical and Miscellaneous Essays*, III, 7 and I, 264.
13. Ibid., I, 57.
14. Thomas Carlyle, *Sartor Resartus* (1836; rpt London: Dent, 1984), 87.
15. Ibid., 121, 149, 146, 190.
16. Ibid., 204.
17. Ibid., 194.
18. Carlyle, *French Revolution*, ed. Fielding and Sorensen, I, 223.
19. Ibid., I, 15, 24.
20. Ibid., I, 9.
21. Ibid., II, 224.
22. Ibid., I, 51, 222, 46.
23. Ibid., II, 376–7.
24. Carlyle, *Past and Present*, ed. A. A. M. Hughes (Oxford: Clarendon Press, 1927), 11.
25. Ibid., 130, 132.
26. Ibid., lxi, lxxx (Hughes), and 181 (Carlyle).
27. Ibid., 217; Carlyle, *Essays*, VII, 176, 177.
28. Ibid., VII, 223.
29. Ibid., VII, 83.
30. Ibid., VII, 203.
31. Carlyle, *Sartor Resartus* in *Works* (London: Chapman and Hall, 1897–9), 30 vols, I, 214; Carlyle, *Reminiscences*, ed. J. A. Froude (London: Longmans, 1881), 2 vols, II, 41.
32. Jane Welsh Carlyle, letter to Jeannie Welsh [8 January 1843] in Clyde L. Ryals and Kenneth J. Fielding, ed., *The Collected Letters of Thomas and Jane Welsh Carlyle, Volume 16* (Durham, N. C.: Duke University Press, 1990), 12.
33. Joanna Baillie, 'Recollections' in Dorothy McMillan, ed., *The Scotswoman at Home and Abroad* (Glasgow: Association for Scottish Literary Studies, 1999), 92.
34. Marion Reid, *A Plea for Woman*, with an Introduction by Susanne Ferguson (Edinburgh: Polygon, 1988), 59, ix, 55, 77, 63.

35. Ibid., v.
36. Johnstone, 'Mrs Hugo Reid's Plea' in McMillan, ed., *The Scotswoman*, 137.
37. Reid, *A Plea*, 83.
38. William Thom, Prefatory Note to 'The Overgate Orphan' in *Rhymes and Recollections of a Handloom Weaver*, expanded edition (Paisley: Gardiner, 1880), 'Rhymes', 45.
39. Hugh Miller, *My Schools and Schoolmasters, or The Story of my Education* (Edinburgh: B. & W. Publishing, 1993), 483, 338.
40. Ibid., 301.
41. Ibid., 289, 292–3.
42. *PBSV*, 344.
43. Bateman et al., ed., *Scottish Religious Poetry*, 180, 181.
44. Ibid., 173 (Carlyle, 'Cui Bono?').
45. Ibid., 182, 183, 178.
46. Ibid., 190.
47. Brown, quoted in T. C. Smout, *A Century of the Scottish People, 1830–1950* (London: Collins, 1986), 137.
48. *PBSV*, 351–4.
49. *The Poems and Prose Remains of Arthur Hugh Clough*, ed. his wife (London: Macmillan, 1869), 2 vols, I, 362–3.
50. See David McCordick, ed., *Scottish Literature: An Anthology* (New York: Peter Lang, 1996), 2 vols, II, 987.
51. Hugh MacDiarmid, *Complete Poems*, ed. Michael Grieve and W. R. Aitken (London: Martin Bryan & O'Keeffe, 1978), 2 vols, II, 1204.
52. Alexander Smith, *A Summer in Skye*, ed. William F. Laughlan (Hawick: Byway Books, n.d.), 182.
53. Quoted in Derick Thomson, *An Introduction to Gaelic Poetry* (London: Gollancz, 1977), 228.
54. Ibid., 235.
55. Roderick Watson, ed., *The Poetry of Scotland* (Edinburgh: Edinburgh University Press, 1995), 482–3; tr. Derick Thomson.
56. Bateman et al., ed., *Scottish Religious Poetry*, 185; tr. Lachlan MacBean.
57. Campbell, 1859 letter quoted in Iain F. Maciver, *Lamplighter and Story-teller: John Francis Campbell* (Edinburgh: National Library of Scotland, 1985), 25.
58. Ibid., 26.
59. Ibid., 27.
60. Ibid., 35.
61. Statistics from Donald MacAulay, 'Canons, Myths and Cannon Fodder', *Scotlands*, 1 (1994), 44.
62. This is reproduced in *Quarto, Newsletter of the National Library of Scotland*, 16 (Summer 2004), 5.
63. David Livingstone, *The Last Journals* (London: John Murray, 1874), 2 vols, I, 13–14.
64. See George Rosie, *Curious Scotland* (London: Granta, 2004), 110–28.
65. R. M. Ballantyne, *Martin Rattler* (1859; repr. London and Glasgow: Blackie, n.d.), 102.
66. Ibid., 62.
67. Robert Louis Stevenson, *Treasure Island*, ed. Wendy R. Katz (Edinburgh: Edinburgh University Press, 2000), 57.
68. J. Knight, quoted in William Raeper, *George MacDonald* (Tring: Lion, 1987), 194.
69. George MacDonald, *Paul Faber, Surgeon* (Whitehorn, Calif.: Johannesen, 1992), 243 and 244.
70. George MacDonald, *Phantastes, A Faerie Romance* (Whitehorn, Calif.: Johannesen, 1994), 20.
71. George MacDonald, *Lilith* (Whitehorn, Calif.: Johannesen, 1994), 233.
72. William Donaldson, 'Popular Literature: The Press, the People, and the Vernacular

Revival' in Douglas Gifford, ed., *The History of Scottish Literature, Volume 3, Nineteenth Century*, ed. Douglas Gifford (Aberdeen: Aberdeen University Press, 1988), 206.

73. George MacDonald, *Alec Forbes of Howglen* (Whitehorn, Calif.: Johannesen, 1995), 107.

74. Margaret Oliphant, *Annals of a Publishing House*, 2nd edn (Edinburgh: Blackwood, 1897), 3 vols, I, 4.

75. [Margaret Oliphant], *Passages in the Life of Mrs Margaret Maitland*, 2nd edn (London: Henry Colburn, 1850), 3 vols, III, 229, 280.

76. Virginia Woolf, *Three Guineas* (1938; rpt Harmondsworth: Penguin, 1977), 106.

77. Margaret Oliphant, *Salem Chapel* (1863; rpt London: Virago, 1986), 1.

78. Oliphant, *Margaret Maitland*, III, 282.

79. Annie S, Swan, *My Life* (London: Nicholson & Watson, 1934), 43, 40.

80. *The Autobiography of Margaret Oliphant*, ed. Elisabeth Jay (Oxford: Oxford University Press, 1990), 88, 118.

81. Margaret Oliphant, *A Beleaguered City and Other Tales of the Seen and the Unseen*, ed. Jenni Calder (Edinburgh: Canongate Classics, 2000), 385.

82. Oliphant, *Margaret Maitland*, III, 179.

83. Oliphant, *A Beleaguered City*, 3.

84. Carlyle, *On Heroes and Hero-Worship*, 133.

85. G. W. Foote, 'James Thomson, 1 – The Man', *Progress: A Monthly Magazine*, April 1884, 253.

86. [James Thomson], review of Principal Shairp, *Robert Burns*, *Cope's Tobacco Plant*, September 1879, 384.

87. [James Thomson], review of R. H. Hutton, *Sir Walter Scott*, *Cope's Tobacco Plant*, September 1879, 384.

88. James Thomson, *Shelley, a Poem: with Other Writings* (London: Chiswick Press, 1884), 92–3.

89. *PBSV*, 365, 362.

90. See Robert Crawford, *The Savage and the City in the Work of T. S. Eliot* (Oxford: Clarendon Press, 1987), 37.

91. Quoted in Henry S. Salt, *The Life of James Thomson ('B. V.')*, Revised Edition (London: Watts & Co., 1914), 73.

92. *PBSV*, 356.

93. Robert Louis Stevenson, *The Strange Case of Dr Jekyll and Mr Hyde and Other Stories*, ed. Jenni Calder (Harmondsworth: Penguin, 1979), 48; *The Original Illustrated 'Strand' Sherlock Holmes by Arthur Conan Doyle* (Ware: Wordsworth Editions, 1989), 71.

94. Robert Louis Stevenson, *Virginibus Puerisque* (1881; rpt London: Heinemann, 1925 as vol. XXII of the Skerryvore Edition of Stevenson's *Works*), 66; unless otherwise indicated, other references are also to the Skerryvore Edition.

95. Ibid., 128.

96. Stevenson, *Works*, XX, 118.

97. Ibid., XV, 196.

98. Ibid., XXII, 130–31.

99. Ibid., XVI, 187 (*The Silverado Squatters*) and 141 (*The Amateur Emigrant*).

100. Ibid., XVI, 259; John Muir, *The Eight Wilderness-Discovery Books*, intro. Terry Gifford (London: Diadem, 1992), 18.

101. Muir quoted in Bruce Richardson, 'Thoreau in Yellowstone?' in Edmund A. Schofield and Robert C. Baron, ed., *Thoreau's World and Ours* (Golden, Colorado: North American Press, 1993), 334.

102. See the reproduction of Lloyd's *The Surprise* in George L. McKay, *A Stevenson Library*, Volume I (New Haven: Yale University Library, 1951), plate facing p. 30.

103. Stevenson, *Works*, II, xvii (Lloyd Osbourne's 'Note').

104. *PBSV*, 372.

105. Stevenson, *Works*, II, xxix ('My First Book, *Treasure Island*').
106. Ibid., xxxii.
107. Stevenson, *Works*, XX, 92.
108. Stevenson, *Works*, II, xxxii.
109. Stevenson, *Works*, V, 24.
110. Ibid., 75.
111. Ibid., 175.
112. Stevenson, *Dr Jekyll*, ed. Calder, 43, 38.
113. Folio 76 of Beinecke Library, Yale University's MS Vault Stevenson 6934.
114. *The Letters of Robert Louis Stevenson*, ed. Bradford A. Booth and Ernest Mehew, (New Haven: Yale University Press, 1994–5), 8 vols, I, 113.
115. Ibid., VII, 125.
116. Walter Scott, *Saint Ronan's Well*, ed. Mark Weinstein (Edinburgh: Edinburgh University Press, 1995), 252, 336.
117. Stevenson, *Dr Jekyll*, ed. Calder, 81.
118. Ibid., 82, 87.
119. Ibid., 94, 84; Arthur Rimbaud, letter to Georges Izambard, [13] May 1871, in *Oeuvres*, ed. S. Bernard and A. Guyaux (Paris: Editions Garnier, 1987), 346.
120. Stevenson, *Dr Jekyll*, ed. Calder, 96, 97.
121. *PBSV*, 375 ('To S. C').
122. *Letters of Stevenson*, ed, Booth and Mehew, I, 475.
123. Stevenson, *Works* IX, xxv (Preface to *The Master of Ballantrae*).
124. J. G. Frazer, *Creation and Evolution in Primitive Cosmogonies* (London: Macmillan, 1935), 69; Robert Ackerman, *I. G. Frazer* (Cambridge: Cambridge University Press, 1987), 60.
125. See Robert Ackerman, ed., *Selected Letters of Sir J. G. Frazer* (Oxford: Oxford University Press, 2005), 102–10.
126. See Robert Crawford, *Devolving English Literature*, 2nd edn (Edinburgh: Edinburgh University Press, 2000), ch. 3.
127. *ODNB*.
128. J. G. Frazer, *The Gorgon's Head* (London: Macmillan, 1927), 439.
129. J. M. Barrie, *Auld Licht Idylls* (London: Hodder and Stoughton, 1888), 150.
130. J. M. Barrie, *The Greenwood Hat* (London: Peter Davies, 1937), 7.
131. Barrie notebooks A2/4 and A2/9, Beinecke Library, Yale.
132. Barrie's inscribed copy of this anonymous work, published in Edinburgh by Gall and Inglis, is in the Beinecke Library.
133. Barrie notebooks A/6 and A2/9, Beinecke.
134. Margaret Ogilvy, letter to J. M. Barrie [c. 1892], Beinecke.
135. Barrie, *Margaret Ogilvy* (London: Hodder and Stoughton, 1896), 163.
136. Barrie to Nancy Astor, 20 August 1919, Reading University Library Nancy Astor archive.
137. J. M. Barrie, *The Greenwood Hat* (1930; rpt London: Peter Davies, 1937), 68; Barrie, *McConnachie and J.M.B.* (London: Peter Davies, 1938), 81; *Margaret Ogilvy*, 107.
138. Oliphant in *Blackwood's*, quoted in Barrie, *Auld Licht Idylls*, concluding publisher's advertisement.
139. Barrie, *McConnachie*, 173; 'Tommy', *Auld Licht Idylls*, 13.
140. Barrie, *When a Man's Single* (1888; rpt London: Hodder and Stoughton, n.d.), 269.
141. This inscription on item 7214 of the Beinecke Library's Stevenson collection is reproduced as a plate in George L. McKay, ed., *A Stevenson Library*, vol. VI (New Haven: Yale University Library, 1964).
142. Barrie, *Greenwood Hat*, 37.
143. J. M. Barrie, *The Little Minister* (1891; rpt London: Hodder and Stoughton, 1911), 174.
144. J. M. Barrie, *Tommy and Grizel* (London: Cassell, 1900), 139.

145. See Andrew Nash, 'Ghostly Endings: The Evolution of J. M. Barrie's *Farewell Miss Julie Logan*', *Studies in Scottish Literature*, XXXIII–XXXIV (2004), 124–37.

146. Barrie, *Tommy and Grizel*, 168.

147. Barrie's copy is in Beinecke.

148. *The Plays of J. M. Barrie*, ed. A. E. Wilson, rev. edn (London: Hodder and Stoughton, 1942), 526, 539, 563.

149. Ibid., 574, 554.

150. Ibid., 706, 744.

151. Ibid., 776.

152. Ian Maclaren, *The Days of Auld Lang Syne* (London: Hodder and Stoughton, n.d.), 211.

153. Ibid.

154. *Letters of J. M. Barrie*, ed. Viola Meynell (London: Peter Davies, 1942), 10.

155. S. R. Crockett, *The Lilac Sunbonnet* (London: Fisher Unwin, 1894), 59–60.

156. Crockett, 'In the Matter of Incubus and Co', quoted in Islay Murray Donaldson, *The Life and Work of Samuel Rutherford Crockett* (Aberdeen: Aberdeen University Press, 1989), 43.

157. *The Selected Journals of L. M. Montgomery, Volume I: 1889–1910*, ed. Mary Rubio and Elizabeth Waterston (Toronto: Oxford University Press, 1985), 223.

158. *The Selected Journals of L. M. Montgomery, Volume III: 1921–1929*, ed. Mary Rubio and Elizabeth Waterston (Toronto: Oxford University Press, 1992), 109.

159. Matthew Arnold, *Lectures and Essays in Criticism*, ed. R. H. Super (Michigan: Ann Arbor, 1962), 291.

160. Neil Munro, *The Brave Days* (Edinburgh: The Porpoise Press, 1931), 294–5.

161. William Sharp, Introduction to *Lyra Celtica*, ed. E. A. Sharp and J. Matthay, 2nd edn (Edinburgh: John Grant, 1932), xlix and xxxv.

162. 'Fiona Macleod', *The Silence of Amor*, in *Works*, ed. Mrs William Sharp, 7 vols, VI (London: Heinemann, 1916), 17.

163. William Sharp, Introductory Note to *The Poems of Ossian* (Edinburgh: Patrick Geddes, 1896), xxiv.

164. George Douglas Brown, 1901 letter quoted in James Veitch, *George Douglas Brown* (London: Herbert Jenkins, 1952), 149.

165. *Carmina Gadelica*, tr. Alexander Carmichael et al., 6 vols, I (Edinburgh: Oliver and Boyd, 1928–71), 256–7.

166. Patrick Geddes, Prefatory Note, *The Evergreen*, Spring 1895.

167. Patrick Geddes, 'The Scots Renascence', ibid., 133.

168. *Letters of Stevenson*, ed. Booth and Mehew, VIII, 49–50.

169. Arthur Conan Doyle, *The Original Illustrated 'Strand' Sherlock Holmes: Facsimile Edition* (Ware: Wordsworth Editions, 1989), 13.

170. Ibid., 120, 117, 14.

171. Ibid., 65, 132.

172. Ibid., 213.

173. Andrew Lang, Introduction to Cuthbert Lennox, *George Douglas Brown* (London: Hodder and Stoughton, 1903), 6.

174. Doyle, *Illustrated 'Strand' Sherlock Holmes*, 558.

175. Davidson, 1878 letter to A. C. Swinburne quoted in John Sloan, *John Davidson, First of the Moderns* (Oxford: Clarendon Press, 1995), 22.

176. Davidson, letter to Mrs Menzies McArthur, 29 July [?1879] (Princeton University Library).

177. *The Poems of John Davidson*, ed. Andrew Turnbull (Edinburgh: Scottish Academic Press, 1973), 2 vols, I, 63; *PBSV*, 379.

178. Ibid., I, 22.

179. Ibid., II, 427.

180. John Davidson, 'About Myself', *The Candid Friend*, 1 June 1901, 178; signed letter to

the *Westminster Gazette* enclosed with letter to Grant Richards, 11 May 1906 (Princeton University Library).

181. Munro, *The Brave Days*, 177.

182. *Poems*, ed. Turnbull, I, 147.

183. Grant Richards quoted in Sloan, *John Davidson*, 151.

184. *PBSV*, 411.

185. John Buchan, *Memory Hold-the-Door* (1940; rpt London: Dent, 1984), 315.

186. Ibid., 37; John Buchan, *Sir Walter Scott* (London: Cassell, 1932), 7.

187. Andrew Lownie, *John Buchan: The Presbyterian Cavalier* (Edinburgh: Canongate, 1995), 52.

188. Janet Adam Smith, *John Buchan and his World* (New York: Scribner's, 1979), 27–9.

189. Quoted in Janet Adam Smith, *John Buchan* (Oxford: Oxford University Press, 1985), 33.

190. John Buchan, *The Thirty-Nine Steps* (1915; rept Harmondsworth: Penguin, 1991), 9.

191. Adam Smith, *John Buchan*, 171.

192. Buchan, *Thirty-Nine Steps*, 46.

193. Quoted in Adam Smith, *John Buchan*, 86.

194. O. Douglas, *Ann and Her Mother* (London: Nelson, 1922), 209.

195. Anna Buchan, *Unforgettable, Unforgotten* (London: Hodder and Stoughton, 1945), 102, 131; O. Douglas, *Taken by the Hand* (London: Hodder and Stoughton, 1935), 203.

196. A. Buchan, *Unforgettable*, 69, 10.

197. John Buchan, *Sick Heart River* (1941; rpt Edinburgh: B&W, 1991), 205.

198. John Buchan, *The Thirty-Nine Steps*, 28–9.

199. Crockett, quoted in P. H. Scott, *John Galt* (Edinburgh: Scottish Academic Press, 1985), 118.

200. Buchan quoted in Adam Smith, *John Buchan*, 86; Millar quoted in Scott, *Galt*, 117.

201. Brown quoted in Veitch, *George Douglas Brown*, 181, 153, 85.

202. George Douglas Brown, *The House with the Green Shutters*, ed. Dorothy Porter (Harmondsworth: Penguin, 1985), 98.

203. Ibid., 126, 154.

204. Ibid., 53.

205. Brown, quoted in Veitch, *Brown*, 27, 33, 30.

206. Ibid., 29, 60.

207. Ibid., 156; Brown, *House*, 41.

208. J. M. Hay, *Gillespie* (1914; repr. Edinburgh: Canongate, 1979), 395.

10 Renaissance

1. George Blake, *The Firth of Clyde* (London: Collins, 1952).

2. *PBSV*, 391.

3. Ian Hay, *The First Hundred Thousand* (Edinburgh: Blackwood, 1915), 228.

4. Quotations and translations of these World War I Gaelic poets are from Ronald Black, ed., *An Tuil, Anthology of Twentieth-Century Gaelic Verse* (Edinburgh: Polygon, 1999), 124–5, 122–3, 216–17, 218–19.

5. Reprinted in Brian Gardner, ed., *Up the Line to Death* (London: Methuen, 1964), 49.

6. John Peterson, *Roads and Ditches* (Lerwick: T. & J. Manson, 1920), 31.

7. Letter quoted in Jean Moorcroft Wilson, *Charles Hamilton Sorley: A Biography* (London: Cecil Woolf, 1985), 198.

8. Sorley, letter to his father, 15 July 1915, in Hilda D. Spear, ed., *Poems and Selected Letters* (Dundee: Blackness Press, 1978), 102.

9. Sorley, letter to Arthur Watts, quoted in Wilson, *Sorley*, 215.

10. Sorley, letter to his mother, 28 April 1915, in Spear, ed., *Poems and Selected Letters*, 98.

11. 'To Germany' in *Collected Poems*, ed. Jean Moorcraft Wilson (London: Cecil Woolf, 1985), 70; ibid., 91 ('When you see millions of the mouthless dead').

12. 'Mallaig Bay' in E. A. Mackintosh, *A Highland Regiment* (London: John Lane, 1917), 59.

13. E. A. Mackintosh, *War, The Liberator* (London: John Lane, 1918), 15–16, 138, 31.

14. Reproduced in Colin Campbell and Rosalind Green, *Can't Shoot a Man with a Cold* (Glendaruel: Argyll Publishing, 2004), 205.

15. Mackintosh, *A Highland Regiment*, 40–42.

16. C. M. Grieve, *Annals of the Five Senses* (1923; rpt Edinburgh: Polygon, 1983), 70.

17. *The Letters of Hugh MacDiarmid*, ed. Alan Bold (London: Hamish Hamilton, 1984), 531.

18. Ibid., 9; *The Hugh MacDiarmid–George Ogilvie Letters*, ed. Catherine Kerrigan (Aberdeen: Aberdeen University Press, 1988), 13.

19. MacDiarmid, *Letters*, ed. Bold, 38.

20. [C. M. Grieve, ed.], *Northern Numbers* (Edinburgh and London: T. N. Foulis, 1920), Foreword.

21. Douglas Dunn, ed., *The Faber Book of Twentieth-century Scottish Poetry* (London: Faber and Faber, 1992), 14.

22. 'A Local Poetess and Novelist', *Montrose Review*, 2 January 1920, 5; see also Robert Crawford, 'MacDiarmid in Montrose' in Alex Davis and Lee M. Jenkins, ed., *Locations of Literary Modernism* (Cambridge: Cambridge University Press, 2000), 33–56.

23. *Northern Numbers*, [28].

24. 'Is "Braid Scots" Dead?' *Montrose Review*, 17 June 1921, 6.

25. Hugh MacDiarmid, *The Raucle Tongue*, ed. Angus Calder, Glen Murray and Alan Riach (Manchester: Carcanet, 1996–7), 3 vols, I, 29.

26. Edward Moore [i.e., Edwin Muir], *We Moderns* (London: Allen and Unwin, 1918), 129.

27. G. Gregory Smith, *Scottish Literature: Character and Influence* (London: Macmillan, 1919), 4.

28. Hugh MacDiarmid, *Contemporary Scottish Studies*, ed. Alan Riach (Manchester: Carcanet, 1995), 64.

29. Hugh MacDiarmid, 'The Angus Burghs' in Alan Bold, ed., *The Thistle Rises* (London: Hamish Hamilton, 1984), 220.

30. B. L., 'The World of Books', *Montrose Review*, 3 June 1921, 6.

31. *PBSV*, 407 (Hugh MacDiarmid, *Complete Poems*, ed. Michael Grieve and W. R. Aitken (London: Martin Brian and O'Keeffe, 1978), 2 vols, I, 17).

32. See Duncan Macmillan, *The Life of George Matheson* (London: Hodder and Stoughton, 1907), 195–7.

33. James Bridie and Moray McLaren, *A Small Stir: Letters on the English* (London: Hollis and Carter, 1949), 2.

34. Thomas Amos, 'Secretary's Annual Report', *Burns Chronicle* 24 (1925), 152; Alan Bold, *MacDiarmid* (London: John Murray, 1988), 159.

35. C. M. Grieve, Preface to *Robert Burns* (London: Benn, 1926), iii.

36. MacDiarmid, *Complete Poems*, ed. Grieve and Aitken, II, 1234.

37. Ibid., I, 74.

38. Hugh MacDiarmid, *Selected Prose*, ed. Alan Riach (Manchester: Carcanet, 1992), 22.

39. C. M. Grieve, 'Home Rule for Scotland', *Montrose Review*, 20 January 1922, 5.

40. 'Folk-song Recital', *Montrose Review*, 4 April 1924, 7; MacDiarmid, *Selected Prose*, ed. Riach, 38.

41. Corrie, *In Time o' Strife* in Cairns Craig and Randall Stevenson, ed., *Twentieth-century Scottish Drama* (Edinburgh: Canongate Classics, 2001), 73–4.

42. Walt Whitman, *Complete Poetry and Collected Prose*, ed. Justin Kaplan (New York: Library of America, 1982), 246 ('Song of Myself', 51).

43. 'Book Reviews, A Green Grass Widow', *Montrose Review*, 20 May 1921, 7.

44. *PBSV*, 407 (MacDiarmid, *Complete Poems*, ed. Grieve and Aitken, I, 17).

45. Barrie, preface to *The Old Lady Shows her Medals* in *The Plays*, ed. A. E. Wilson (London: Hodder & Stoughton, 1942), 967.
46. *The Collected Works of Lorna Moon*, ed. Glenda Norquay (Edinburgh: Black and White, 2002), 267 (letter of '5 or 6 January 1929' to David Laurance Chambers).
47. Ibid., 260 and 258 (letters of 20 August 1928 to D. L. Chambers and 9 May 1925 to H. H. Howland).
48. Ibid., 268 (letter as in note 47 above).
49. Ibid., 23.
50. Richard de Mille, *My Secret Mother* (New York: Farrar, Straus and Giroux, 1998).
51. A. S. Neill, *A Dominie's Log* (London: Herbert Jenkins, 1915), 88, 13.
52. A. S. Neill, *A Dominie in Doubt* (London: Herbert Jenkins, 1920), 225.
53. MacDiarmid, *Complete Poems*, ed. Grieve and Aitken, I, 134 and 84.
54. Ibid., I, 144; *PBSV*, 410.
55. Ibid., I, 167; *PBSV*, 411.
56. Kathleen Jamie in Robert Crawford et al., 'A Disgrace to the Community', *PN Review*, 19.3 (1993), 21.
57. *PBSV*, 409 (MacDiarmid, *Complete Poems*, ed. Grieve and Aitken, I, 66).
58. Rose Macaulay, *Potterism* (London: Collins, 1920), 231.
59. MacDiarmid, *Complete Poems*, ed. Grieve and Aitken, II, 1235 ('Braid Scots').
60. MacDiarmid, *Letters*, ed. Bold, 845 (19 December 1933).
61. *PBSV*, 412 (MacDiarmid, *Complete Poems*, ed. Grieve and Aitken, I, 422).
62. David Daiches in Crawford et al., 'A Disgrace to the Community', 19.
63. *PBSV*, 414 (MacDiarmid, ibid., I, 425).
64. Ibid., 423 (MacDiarmid, ibid., II, 1058).
65. Ibid., 422 (MacDiarmid, ibid., I, 461).
66. MacDiarmid, *Selected Prose*, ed. Riach, 39.
67. See Lesley Duncan, 'Secret MacDiarmid', *Glasgow Herald*, 11 April 2003, 18.
68. See Robert Crawford, ed., *Contemporary Poetry and Contemporary Science* (Oxford: Oxford University Press, 2006), Introduction and chapter by Edwin Morgan.
69. *PBSV*, 424 (MacDiarmid, *Complete Poems*, ed. Grieve and Aitken, II, 1170).
70. See photographs in Gordon Wright, *MacDiarmid* (Edinburgh: Gordon Wright Publishing, 1977), 93.
71. Hugh MacDiarmid, *Lucky Poet* (London: Cape, 1943), 426.
72. MacDiarmid, *Selected Prose*, ed. Riach, 3.
73. Hugh MacDiarmid and Lewis Grassic Gibbon, *Scottish Scene* (London: Jarrolds, 1934), 43.
74. Ibid., 241, 305, 303.
75. Lewis Grassic Gibbon, 'Controversy: Writers' International (British Section)' in *Smeddum: A Lewis Grassic Gibbon Anthology*, ed. Valentina Bold (Edinburgh: Canongate Classics, 2001), 739.
76. *Scottish Scene*, 292.
77. Lewis Grassic Gibbon, *A Scots Quair* (1946; rpt London: Pan, 1982), 117.
78. Nan Shepherd, *The Quarry Wood* (Edinburgh: Canongate, 1987), 145.
79. Nan Shepherd, *The Weatherhouse* (Edinburgh: Canongate, 1988), 2.
80. Nan Shepherd, letter to Neil Gunn, c. 1930, quoted in F. R. Hart and J. B. Pick, *Neil M. Gunn, A Highland Life* (London: John Murray, 1981), 90.
81. MacDiarmid, *Complete Poems*, ed. Grieve and Aitken, II, 837 ('In Memoriam James Joyce').
82. Edwin Muir, *Autobiography* (1954; rpt London: Methuen, 1968), 20–21.
83. *PBSV*, 402; *The Complete Poems of Edwin Muir*, ed. Peter Butter (Aberdeen: Association for Scottish Literary Studies, 1991), 3.
84. *PBSV*, 402; Muir, *Complete Poems*, ed. Butter, 80 ('Merlin').
85. Ibid., 406; Muir, ibid., 227.

86. *PBSV*, 398 ('A Dead Mole'), 309 ('A Wet Day') (*The Poetical Works of Andrew Young*, ed. Edward Lowbury and Alison Young (London: Secker and Warburg, 1985), 63, 80).
87. Typed account headed 'Edwin Muir', and dated 5/7/41: probably a letter from Sir David Russell to Principal Irvine of St Andrews University (University of St Andrews Special Collections, Sir David Russell Papers, Box 98).
88. *PBSV*, 403–4; Muir, *Complete Poems*, ed. Butter, 100.
89. Edwin Muir, *Scott and Scotland: The Predicament of the Scottish Writer* (1936; rpt Edinburgh: Polygon, 1982), 1, 6, 90, 7, 111, 42.
90. T. S. Eliot, *The Complete Poems and Plays* (London: Faber and Faber, 1969), 141 ('Landscapes IV, Rannoch'); Eliot, *Selected Essays*, Third Enlarged Edition (London: Faber and Faber, 1951), 288.
91. Muir, *Scott and Scotland*, 44.
92. See Robert Crawford, 'Bakhtin and Scotlands', *Scotlands*, 1 (1994), 55–65; and Douglas Gifford and Alan Riach, ed., *Scotlands* (Manchester: Carcanet, 2004).
93. *PBSV*, 426 (*The Poems of William Soutar*, ed. W. R. Aitken (Edinburgh: Scottish Academic Press, 1988), 209).
94. William Soutar, *Diaries of a Dying Man*, ed. Alexander Scott (Edinburgh: Chambers, 1988), 144–5.
95. Edmund Wilson, *The Fifties*, ed. Leon Edel (New York: Farrar, Straus and Giroux, 1986), 146.
96. Compton Mackenzie, *My Life and Times*, Octave Seven (London: Chatto & Windus, 1968), 98.
97. Edmund Wilson, *The Bit Between My Teeth* (New York: Farrar, Straus & Giroux, 1965), 540.
98. John Connell, *David Go Back* (London: Cassell, 1935), 137; W. H. Auden, *The English Auden*, ed. Edward Mendelson (London: Faber and Faber, 1977), 106.
99. Tom Normand, *The Modern Scot: Modernism and Nationalism in Scottish Art 1928–1955* (Aldershot: Ashgate, 2000), 43.
100. Whyte, quoted in Normand, *The Modern Scot*, 44, 174.
101. *PBSV*, 394; *The Singin' Lass: Selected Writings of Marion Angus*, ed. Aimée Chalmers (Edinburgh: Polygon, 2006), 175–6.
102. Willa Muir, *Imagined Selves*, ed. Kirsty Allen (Edinburgh: Canongate Classics, 1996), *Women: An Inquiry*, 25.
103. Ibid., 'Women in Scotland', 4.
104. William Soutar, *But the Earth Abideth* (London: Andrew Dakers, 1943), 9.
105. Willa Muir, *Living with Ballads* (London: Hogarth Press, 1965), 13.
106. [Catherine Carswell], 'New Novels', *Glasgow Herald*, 4 November 1915.
107. Catherine Carswell, *Open the Door!* (1920; rpt London: Virago, 1986), 35.
108. Catherine Carswell, *The Camomile* (1922; rpt London: Virago, 1987), 41.
109. Catherine Carswell, *The Life of Robert Burns* (1930; rpt Edinburgh: Canongate Classics, 1990), 5, 312, 31, viii.
110. Catherine Carswell, *The Savage Pilgrimage* (1932; rpt Cambridge: Cambridge University Press, 1981), xli; *Lying Awake*, ed. John Carswell (Edinburgh: Canongate, 1997), 22 and 51.
111. John Macmurray, 1944 inaugural lecture at Edinburgh University, quoted in John E. Costello, *John Macmurray* (Edinburgh: Floris Books, 2002), 306.
112. Macmurray, *Freedom in the Modern World* (1932), quoted in Costello, *Macmurray*, 172.
113. Philip Cornford, ed., *The Personal Word* (Edinburgh: Floris Books, 1996).
114. See Costello, *Macmurray*, 190 and 211.
115. Ibid., 411, n. 37.
116. Elizabeth Hyde, *Out of the Earth* (London: Peter Davies, 1935), 62 and 194.
117. Shepherd, May 1940 letter to Gunn, quoted in Hart and Pick, *Neil M. Gunn*, 155.

118. Neil M. Gunn, *The Man Who Came Back*, ed. Margery McCulloch (Edinburgh: Polygon, 1991), 20–21.
119. Neil M. Gunn, *Selected Letters*, ed. J. B. Pick (Edinburgh: Polygon, 1987), 3, 10, 102.
120. Ibid., 241.
121. Neil M. Gunn, *Morning Tide* (Edinburgh: Porpoise Press, 1931), 7.
122. Neil M. Gunn, *The Green Isle of the Great Deep* (1944; rpt London: Souvenir Press, 1975), 158.
123. Gunn, *The Man Who Came Back*, 72–3.
124. Neil M. Gunn, *The Silver Darlings* (1941; rpt London: Faber and Faber, 1969), 583.
125. T. S. Eliot, *Collected Poems 1909–1962* (1963; rpt London: Faber and Faber, 1974), 212.
126. Muir in a broadcast talk quoted on the inside cover of *The Silver Darlings*.
127. Nancy C. Dorian, *Language Death: The Life Cycle of a Scottish Gaelic Dialect* (Philadelphia: University of Pennsylvania Press, 1981).
128. Gunn, *The Green Isle*, 10, 93.
129. Fionn Mac Colla, *The Albannach* (1932; rpt London: Souvenir Press, 1984), 105, 155.
130. Finn Mac Colla, *And the Cock Crew* (1945; rpt London: Souvenir Press, 1977), 121.
131. Adam Drinan, *Women of the Happy Island* (Glasgow: McLellan, 1944), 28.
132. Sorley MacLean, 'Edinburgh Impressions', *Alumni Bulletin, University of Edinburgh Magazine*, 1990, 5.
133. MacLean to MacDiarmid, 27 February 1938, quoted in Christopher Whyte, ed., *Dàin do Eimhir* (Glasgow: Association for Scottish Literary Studies, 2002), 9.
134. Somhairle Mac Gill-Eain, *Ris a' Bhruthaich: The Criticism and Prose Writings*, ed. William Gillies (Stornoway: Acair, 1985), 109.
135. Sorley MacLean, *From Wood to Ridge: Collected Poems in Gaelic and English* (Manchester: Carcanet, 1989), 22–3 ('An Roghainn' / 'The Choice', tr. MacLean).
136. *PBSV*, 445 ('Muir-tràigh'/ 'Ebb', tr. MacLean's; text from Sorley MacLean, *From Wood to Ridge*, 140–41); Seamus Heaney, 'Introduction' to Raymond J. Ross and Joy Hendry, ed., *Sorley MacLean, Critical Essays* (Edinburgh: Scottish Academic Press, 1986), 1.
137. MacLean, *From Wood to Ridge*, 26–9 ('Ban-Ghàidheal'/ 'A Highland Woman', tr. MacLean).
138. Ibid., 136–7.
139. W. B. Yeats, *Collected Poems*, 2nd edn (London: Macmillan, 1950), 46 ('When You Are Old'); MacLean, *From Wood to Ridge*, 16–17 ('Lìonmhoireachd' / 'Multitude', tr. MacLean).
140. MacLean, *Ris a' Bhruthaich*, 20.
141. MacLean to MacDiarmid, 8 March 1941, quoted in Whyte, ed., *Dàin do Eimhir*, 4.
142. MacLean, *From Wood to Ridge*, 179.
143. Ibid., 134–5.
144. Seamus Heaney, quoted in Rosemary Goring, 'Legend in own rhyme', *The Herald*, 16 August 2002, 23.
145. MacLean, *From Wood to Ridge*, 229; *PBSV*, 451.
146. Prospectus, quoted in David Hutchison, '1900–1950' in Bill Findlay, ed., *A History of Scottish Theatre* (Edinburgh: Polygon, 1998), 208–9.
147. John MacNair Reid, *Homeward Journey* (1934; rpt Edinburgh: Canongate Classics, 1988), 62.
148. Quoted by Hutchison in Findlay, ed., *A History of Scottish Theatre*, 221.
149. Bridie quoted in Ronald Mavor, *Dr Mavor and Mr Bridie* (Edinburgh: Canongate and the National Library of Scotland, 1988), 38.
150. Ibid., 63.
151. James Bridie, *John Knox and Other Plays* (London: Constable, 1949), *Dr Angelus*, 4.
152. James Bridie, *Mr Bolfry*, in Cairns Craig and Randall Stevenson, ed., *Twentieth-century Scottish Drama* (Edinburgh: Canongate Classics, 2001), 239, 221, 234, 255.

153. Bridie, *Dr Angelus*, 65.

154. Shaw, 1943 letter to Bridie reproduced in Mavor, *Dr Mavor*, 116; Bridie, *One Way of Living* (London: Constable, 1939), 298.

155. James Bridie, *The British Drama* (Glasgow: Craig Wilson, 1945), 38.

156. Guy McCrone, *Wax Fruit* (London: Constable, 1947), 217, 407.

157. Ena Lamont Stewart, *Men Should Weep*, in Craig and Stevenson, ed., *Twentieth-century Scottish Drama*, 277, 286.

158. Ena Lamont Stewart, quoted in Anna Millar, 'Giving reality a good name', *Scotland on Sunday*, 28 August 2005, 13.

159. Ibid.

160. Stewart, *Men Should Weep*, 306–7.

161. A. McArthur and H. Kingsley Long, *No Mean City* (1935; rpt London: Corgi, 1984), 167.

162. George Blake, *The Shipbuilders* (1935; rpt Edinburgh: B&W, 1993), 134, 221.

163. Gordon Brown, *Maxton* (1986; rpt London: Fontana, 1988), 11.

164. Eric Linklater, *The Man on My Back* (London: Macmillan, 1941), 10–11.

165. Eric Linklater, *Private Angelo* (1946; rpt Edinburgh: Canongate Classics, 1999), 104, 89.

166. Naomi Mitchison, *Among You Taking Notes*, ed. Dorothy Sheridan (Oxford: Oxford University Press, 1986), 133.

167. James Barke, *The Land of the Leal* (1939; rpt Edinburgh: Canongate Classics, 1987), 23.

168. Ibid., 586.

169. Ian Macpherson, *Wild Harbour* (1936; rpt Edinburgh: Canongate Classics, 1989), 25, 83.

170. Barke, *Land of the Leal*, 491.

171. Macpherson, *Wild Harbour*, 148.

172. Barke, *Land of the Leal*, 603, 609.

11 Hard-wearing Flowers

1. Naomi Mitchison, *Among You Taking Notes*, ed. Dorothy Sheridan (1985; rpt Oxford: Oxford University Press, 1986), 32.

2. Ruthven Todd, *Until Now* (London: Fortune Press, 1942), 24.

3. Norman McCaig, 'Poem' in C. J. Russell and J. F. Hendry, ed., *Albannach* (Dingwall: C. J. Russell, 1938), 20–21.

4. J. F. Hendry, *Fernie Brae* in Liam McIlvanney, ed., *Growing Up in the West* (Edinburgh: Canongate Classics, 2003), 262.

5. This photograph was published in John Davidson, 'Painting is an Infinitely Minute Part of any Personality', *Scotland on Sunday, Spectrum*, 16 May 2004, 15.

6. J. F. Hendry in Robin Skelton, ed., *Poetry of the Forties* (Harmondsworth: Penguin, 1968), 24, 93.

7. Norman McCaig, *Far Cry* (London: Routledge, 1943), 11, 9.

8. Hamish Henderson, *Elegies for the Dead in Cyrenaica* (1948; rev. edn Edinburgh: Polygon, 1990), 59, 17, 23, 28.

9. *PBSV*, 458–9 (Hay's translation); see also Michael Byrne, ed., *Collected Poems and Songs of George Campbell Hay* (Edinburgh: Edinburgh University Press for the Lorimer Trust, 2000), 2 vols, II, 46.

10. Ibid., II, 7.

11. Edwin Morgan, *The New Divan* (Manchester: Carcanet, 1977), 56.

12. G. S. Fraser, *Poems*, ed. Ian Fletcher and John Lucas (Leicester: Leicester University Press, 1981), 51.

13. Jessie Kesson, *Another Time, Another Place* (1983), rpt in *The Jessie Kesson Omnibus* (London: Chatto and Windus, 1991), 330.

14. *PBSV*, 456; Sydney Goodsir Smith, *Collected Poems* (London: Calder, 1975), 57.
15. *PBSV*, 458; Smith, *Collected Poems*, 95.
16. Alasdair Gray, *1982, Janine* (London: Cape, 1984), 282.
17. Robert Garioch, 'Quiet Passage' in *Albannach*, 13.
18. Robert Garioch, *Two Men and a Blanket* (Edinburgh: Southside, 1975), 26; *PBSV*, 430; Robert Garioch, *Complete Poetical Works*, ed. Robin Fulton (Edinburgh: Macdonald, 1983), 50.
19. *PBSV*, 434; Garioch, *Complete Poetical Works*, ed. Fulton, 87.
20. Norman Cameron, *Collected Poems and Selected Translations*, ed. Warren Hope and Jonathan Barker (London: Anvil, 1990), 59 ('Forgive Me, Sire').
21. J. I. M. Stewart, *Young Pattullo* (1975; rpt London: Methuen, 1976), 140.
22. George Friel, *Mr Alfred M. A.* (1972); Edinburgh: Canongate Classics, 1972), 139, 4, 62.
23. *PBSV*, 435–6 (from Norman MacCaig, *Collected Poems*, New Edition (London: Chatto and Windus, 1990), 7).
24. *PBSV*, 437 ('Wild Oats'), 436 ('Basking Shark') (from MacCaig, *Collected Poems*, 232, 219).
25. Ibid., 435 (ibid., 3).
26. MacCaig, *Collected Poems*, 189.
27. *PBSV*, 439 (MacCaig, *Collected Poems*, 318).
28. Heaney, quoted on rear jacket of MacCaig, *Collected Poems*.
29. Norman MacCaig, *The Poems* (Edinburgh: Polygon, 2005), xxxix.
30. MacCaig, 1980 BBC Radio Scotland interview quoted in Marjory McNeill, *Norman MacCaig* (Edinburgh: Mercat Press, 1996), 25.
31. MacCaig, *Collected Poems*, 266.
32. George Mackay Brown, *For the Islands I Sing* (London: John Murray, 1997), 122.
33. Edwin Muir, Introduction to George Mackay Brown, *The Storm and Other Poems* (Kirkwall: Orkney Press, 1954), 5.
34. Kathleen Jamie, 'Primal Seam', *Scotsman*, 'Critique', 30 July 2005, 14.
35. *PBSV*, 480, 481; George Mackay Brown, *Selected Poems* (London: Hogarth Press, 1977), 75, 53.
36. Brown, *The Storm*, 13 ('Saint Magnus on Egilshay') and 15 ('The Storm').
37. W. S. Graham, *Collected Poems* (London: Faber and Faber, 1979), 48.
38. Ibid., 192, 'What is the Language Using Us For?'
39. *PBSV*, 463; Graham, *Collected Poems*, 144.
40. Ibid., 466 ('Loch Thom'); ibid., 214.
41. Edwin Morgan, *Collected Poems* (Manchester: Carcanet, 1990), 61.
42. Ibid., 21.
43. Edwin Morgan, 'Virtual and Other Realities' in Robert Crawford, ed., *Contemporary Poetry and Contemporary Science* (Oxford: Oxford University Press, 2006), 38.
44. Edwin Morgan, *Essays* (Cheadle Hulme: Carcanet New Press, 1974), 97.
45. Edwin Morgan, 'Scottish Drama', *ScotLit* 20, Spring 1999, 4.
46. *PBSV*, 470; Morgan, *Collected Poems*, 159.
47. Ibid., 473; ibid., 267.
48. Ibid., 408, 'New Year Sonnets, 4'; 167, 'King Billy'; 'Glasgow Sonnets'; *PBSV*, 472.
49. See Morgan's essay in Robert Crawford, ed., *Contemporary Poetry and Contemporary Science* (Oxford: Oxford University Press, 2006).
50. See Robert Crawford, ' "to change/ the unchangeable" – The Whole Morgan' in Robert Crawford and Hamish Whyte, ed., *About Edwin Morgan* (Edinburgh: Edinburgh University Press, 1990), 10–24; Morgan, *Essays*, Preface.
51. Edwin Morgan, 'Old Gorbals', *Scotsman*, S2, 25 March 2004, 14.
52. Morgan, *Collected Poems*, 83 ('From a City Balcony').
53. Fred Urquhart, 'Forty Three Years: A Benediction', in A. L. Kennedy and Hamish Whyte,

ed., *The Ghost of Liberace* (Aberdeen: Association for Scottish Literary Studies, 1993), 135–46; Christopher Whyte, ed., *Gendering the Nation* (Edinburgh: Polygon, 1995).

54. *PBSV*, 472; Morgan, *Collected Poems*, 248.

55. Tom Gordon, 'Holyrood Poet Morgan Signs Up', *Herald*, 7 October 2004, 3.

56. *PBSV*, 476; Morgan, *Collected Poems*, 433 ('Cinquevalli').

57. Brown, *For the Islands I Sing*, 161.

58. Finlay quoted in Ken Cockburn, 'Early works from the Wild Hawthorn Press', *Scottish Poetry Library Newsletter* 45, July 2005, 5.

59. Ian Hamilton Finlay, 'The Boy and the Guess' (1958), rpt in Yves Abrioux, *Ian Hamilton Finlay: A Visual Primer*, 2nd edn (London: Reaktion Books, 1992), 72.

60. Ian Hamilton Finlay, *The Dancers Inherit the Party and Glasgow Beasts* (Edinburgh: Polygon, 1996), 61.

61. Illustrated in Abrioux, *Ian Hamilton Finlay*, 67, 46–7.

62. *PBSV*, 483 (Abrioux, 94)

63. See Robert Crawford, 'Poetry and Academia: The Instance of Informationism' in Andrew Michael Roberts and Jonathan Allison, ed., *Poetry and Contemporary Culture* (Edinburgh: Edinburgh University Press, 2002) and Robert Crawford, ed., *Contemporary Poetry and Contemporary Science* (Oxford: Oxford University Press, 2006).

64. *The Personal World: John Macmurray on Self and Society*, ed. Philip Conford (Edinburgh: Floris Books, 1996), 72.

65. M. M. Bakhtin, *Speech Genres and Other Late Essays*, ed. Caryl Emerson and Michael Holquist, tr. Vern W. McGee (Austin: University of Texas Press, 1986), 7; see Robert Crawford, *Identifying Poets: Self and Territory in Twentieth-century Poetry* (Edinburgh: Edinburgh University Press, 1993), Introduction.

66. See, e.g., Kenneth White, *On Scottish Ground* (Edinburgh: Polygon, 1998).

67. David Daiches, *Two Worlds* (1956; new edn Edinburgh: Canongate Classics, 1987), Foreword and 129.

68. Muriel Spark, *Curriculum Vitae* (London: Constable, 1992), 53, 21, 22.

69. Ibid., 67, 66; MacDiarmid, *Complete Poems*, I, 32.

70. Spark, *Curriculum Vitae*, 69, 113.

71. Bateman et al., ed., *Scottish Religious Poetry*, 259; Muriel Spark, *All the Poems* (Manchester: Carcanet, 2004), 71.

72. Spark, *Curriculum Vitae*, 148.

73. Muriel Spark, *The Go-Away Bird and Other Stories* (1958; Harmondsworth: Penguin, 1963), 161.

74. T. S. Eliot, *Collected Poems* (London: Faber and Faber, 1974), 65 (*The Waste Land*), 190 ('Burnt Norton').

75. Muriel Spark, *The Prime of Miss Jean Brodie* (1961; rpt Harmondsworth: Penguin, 1965), 5, 6.

76. Ibid., 88, 21.

77. Ibid., 120, 127.

78. Ibid., 108.

79. Spark in Karl Miller, ed., *Memoirs of a Modern Scotland* (London: Faber and Faber, 1970), 151–2.

80. Muriel Spark, *The Abbess of Crewe* (1974; London: Penguin, 1975), 27.

81. Spark, *Curriculum Vitae*, 119.

82. Spark, 'What Images', 152.

83. James Allan Ford, *The Brave White Flag* (1961; rpt Glasgow: Richard Drew, 1985), 143, 187, 282.

84. Alastair Reid, 'Digging up Scotland' in *Whereabouts* (Edinburgh: Canongate, 1987), 29.

85. Elspeth Davie, *Providings* (London: John Calder, 1965), 47.

86. Ruaraidh MacThòmais/Derick Thomson, *Creachadh na Clàrsaich/Plundering the Harp*

(Edinburgh: Macdonald, 1982), 88–9; *PBSV*, 478–9 ('The Herring Girls'); tr. by the poet.

87. *PBSV*, 487 ('The Herring Girls' from Iain Crichton Smith, *Collected Poems* (Manchester: Carcanet, 1992), 222).

88. *PBSV*, 486 ('Two Girls Singing' from Smith, *Collected Poems*, 48).

89. Iain Crichton Smith, *Towards the Human* (Edinburgh: MacDonald Publishers, 1986), 20.

90. Iain Crichton Smith, 'The Double Man' in R. P. Draper, ed., *The Literature of Region and Nation* (London: Macmillan, 1989), 140; Smith, *Collected Poems*, 54 ('The Law and the Grace').

91. Alasdair Maclean, *Night Falls on Ardnamurchan* (Harmondsworth: Penguin, 1984), 114, 192, 167.

92. Bateman et al., ed., *Scottish Religious Poetry*, 280–81 (tr. by the poet), and 320.

93. Robin Jenkins, *Fergus Lamont* (Edinburgh: Canongate, 1979), 136.

94. Robin Jenkins, *Dust on the Paw* (1961; rpt Glasgow: Richard Drew, 1986), 300.

95. Robin Jenkins, *The Cone-Gatherers* (1955; rpt Harmondsworth: Penguin, 1983), 67, 4.

96. Jenkins, *Fergus Lamont*, 138.

97. Archie Hind, *The Dear Green Place* (1966; rpt Edinburgh: Polygon, 1984), 65, 226; Gordon Williams, *From Scenes Like These* (1968; rpt London: Allison and Busby, 1980), 82 and 115.

98. Alan Sharp, *A Green Tree in Gedde* (1965; rpt Glasgow: Richard Drew, 1985), 168.

99. William McIlvanney, *Laidlaw* (1977; rpt London: Coronet, 1985), 154.

100. Donald Campbell, *The Jesuit* (1976) in Bill Findlay, ed., *Scots Plays of the Seventies* (Edinburgh: Scottish Cultural Press, 2001), 207.

101. John Byrne, *Your Cheatin' Heart* in Craig and Wallace, ed., *Twentieth-Century Scottish Drama*, 574, 589, 531–2.

102. Hector MacMillan, *The Rising* (1973) in Findlay, ed., *Scots Plays of the Seventies*, 82.

103. John McGrath, *Six-Pack* (Edinburgh: Polygon, 1986), 177.

104. Alasdair Gray, 'Museum', *Scotlands* 1 (1994), 110; Gray, *Ten Tales Tall and True* (London: Bloomsbury, 1993), 154.

105. Alasdair Gray, 'The Wise Mouse', *Whitehill School Magazine*, Summer 1949, 10; for more on this story see Robert Crawford and Thom Nairn, ed., *The Arts of Alasdair Gray* (Edinburgh: Edinburgh University Press, 1991), Introduction.

106. Alasdair Gray, quoted in Sian Holding, 'Hidden Treasure', *Scotland on Sunday*, *At Home* magazine supplement, 14 September 2003, 4 (where Gray's restored Jonah mural is reproduced).

107. Alasdair Gray, *Lanark* (1981; rpt London: Granada, 1982), 485.

108. Edwin Morgan, *Essays* (Manchester: Carcanet, 1974), 158.

109. Alasdair Gray, ed., *The Book of Prefaces* (London: Bloomsbury, 2000), 631.

110. Elspeth Barker, *O Caledonia!* (Harmondsworth: Penguin, 1991), 84.

111. Shena Mackay, *Babies in Rhinestones* (London: Heinemann, 1983), 73.

112. Douglas Dunn, quoted on front cover of Allan Massie, *The Hanging Tree* (1990; rpt London: Mandarin, 1992); Muriel Spark, quoted on inside front jacket flap of Allan Massie, *Shadows of Empire* (London: Sinclair-Stevenson, 1997).

113. Allan Massie, 'Has Amis gone to the dogs?' *Scotsman*, *Weekend* supplement, 6 September 2003, 7.

114. Karl Miller, *Dark Horses* (London: Picador, 1998), 221, 232.

115. *PBSV*, 503 ('Unrelated Incidents, 3' from Tom Leonard, *Intimate Voices* (Newcastle: Galloping Dog Press, 1984), 88).

116. Tom Leonard, ed., *Radical Renfrew* (Edinburgh: Polygon, 1990), xvii.

117. *PBSV*, 496–7; original from Aonghas MacNeacail, *An Seachnadh agus dàin eile/The Avoiding and other poems* (Loanhead: Macdonald, 1986), 98–9.

118. *PBSV*, 499; Douglas Dunn, *St Kilda's Parliament* (London: Faber and Faber, 1981), 14.

119. *PBSV*, 498; Douglas Dunn, *Terry Street* (London: Faber and Faber, 1969), 55.
120. *PBSV*, 501; 'Land Love' from Douglas Dunn, *Elegies* (London: Faber and Faber, 1985), 47.
121. Douglas Dunn, *Selected Poems* (London: Faber and Faber, 1986), 9.
122. Douglas Dunn, *Northlight* (1988), 26 ('Here and There'); *Selected Poems*, 126.

12 Globalization and a Smirr of Rain

1. J. K. Rowling, introduction to Alexander McCall Smith et al., *One City* (Edinburgh: Polygon, 2005), 7.
2. Salman Rushdie, quoted in Andrew Downie, 'Tears of Shalimar the Clown', *Scotsman*, 27 August 2005, Festival 5.
3. James Kelman, *Some Recent Attacks* (Stirling: AK Press, 1992), 18.
4. Pink Floyd, *The Wall* (London: EMI, 1979).
5. James Kelman, *Not Not While the Giro* (Edinburgh: Polygon, 1983), 13.
6. James Kelman, *The Busconductor Hines* (Edinburgh: Polygon, 1984), 64.
7. Kelman, *Attacks*, 22.
8. Kelman in Sarah Lyall, 'Novelist Speaks Up for his Language', *New York Times*, 29 November 1994, C, 20.
9. Kelman, *Busconductor*, 30.
10. James Kelman, *How Late It Was, How Late* (London: Secker and Warburg, 1994), 107.
11. Kelman in *New York Times*, as note 8 above, C15-20.
12. Tom Leonard, *Intimate Voices* (Newcastle: Galloping Dog Press, 1984), 120.
13. James Kelman, *Translated Accounts* (London: Secker and Warburg, 2001), 300, 139.
14. Irvine Welsh, quoted in David Robinson, 'Sins and Needles', *Scotsman*, 3 December 2005, Critique, 4; and in Carl MacDougall, *Writing Scotland* (Edinburgh: Polygon, 2004), 127.
15. Irvine Welsh, 'The First Day of the Edinburgh Festival' in Hamish Whyte and Janice Galloway, ed., *Scream, if You Want to Go Faster* (Aberdeen: Association for Scottish Literary Studies, 1991), 145.
16. Irvine Welsh, *Trainspotting* (1993; rpt London: Minerva, 1994), 14-15.
17. Ibid., 55, 310.
18. Irvine Welsh, *Porno* (London: Cape, 2002), 323.
19. Welsh, *Trainspotting*, 30.
20. Alan Warner, 'Biography of the Poet', *Verse*, 11.1 (1994), 69.
21. Alan Warner, *These Demented Lands* (London: Cape, 1997), 49.
22. Frank Kermode, 'Lager and Pernod', *London Review of Books*, 22 August 2002, 29.
23. See review quotations in prelims and rear jacket of the Futura paperback editions of *The Wasp Factory* (1987) and *Walking on Glass* (1986).
24. Iain Banks, *Espedair Street* (1987; rpt London: Futura, 1988), 195.
25. Ibid., 138.
26. Ibid., 52, 24.
27. Ibid., 12.
28. Ian Rankin, 'Back on the Beach' in Robert Crawford, ed., *The Book of St Andrews* (Edinburgh: Polygon, 2005), 39.
29. Ian Rankin, 'The Deliberate Cunning of Muriel Spark' in Gavin Wallace and Randall Stevenson, ed., *The Scottish Novel since the Seventies* (Edinburgh: Edinburgh University Press, 1993), 43, 49.
30. Ian J. Rankin, 'An Afternoon' in Alexander Scott and James Aitchison, ed., *New Writing Scotland* 2 (Aberdeen: Association for Scottish Literary Studies, 1984), 121.
31. Rankin, 'The Deliberate Cunning', 46.
32. Ian Rankin, *Set in Darkness* (London: Orion, 2000), 10.
33. *PBSV*, 484.
34. Spark in Rankin, 'The Deliberate Cunning', 51.

NOTES

35. J. K. Rowling, 'Harry and me', *Scotsman*, 9 December 2002, Weekend, 1.
36. Ibid. and J. K. Rowling, 'Introduction' to Alexander McCall Smith et al., *One City* (Edinburgh: Polygon, 2005), 7–9.
37. J. K. Rowling, *Harry Potter and the Prisoner of Azkaban* (London: Bloomsbury, 1999), 66.
38. Rowling, quoted in Stephen McGinty, 'Life after Harry', *Scotsman*, 11 January 2006, 10.
39. P. D. James, *The Lighthouse* (London: Faber and Faber, 2005), 93.
40. Val McDermid, *Clean Break* (1995; rpt London: HarperCollins, 1996), 171.
41. Alan Spence, *The Magic Flute* (1990; rpt London: Black Swan, 1991), 147.
42. Brian McCabe, 'Buddha', *Body Parts* (Edinburgh: Canongate, 1999), 42.
43. Welsh, quoted on front cover of Ron Butlin, *Night Visits* (Edinburgh: Scottish Cultural Press, 1997).
44. Ronald Frame, *Winter Journey* (London: Bodley Head, 1984), 15; *Sandmouth People* (London: Bodley Head, 1987), 169.
45. Frame, *Sandmouth People*, 467.
46. Ronald Frame, *Bluette* (1990; rpt London: Sceptre, 1991), 96, 109, 85.
47. William Boyd, *School Ties* (London: Hamish Hamilton, 1985), 17–18.
48. William Boyd, *Armadillo* (London: Hamish Hamilton, 1998), 33.
49. McWilliam, quoted in MacDougall, *Writing Scotland*, 218; introduction to Spark, *The Prime of Miss Jean Brodie* (London: Penguin, 2000), xii–xiii.
50. Candia McWilliam, *A Case of Knives* (1988; rpt London: Abacus, 1992), 76, 64, 83.
51. McWilliam, introduction to Spark, v.
52. McWilliam, *A Case*, 151.
53. Candia McWilliam, *A Little Stranger* (1989; rpt London: Picador, 1990), 44, 98.
54. Candia McWilliam, *Debatable Land* (1994; rpt London: Picador, 1995), 26, 77, 103, 85, 135.
55. Liz Lochhead, 'A Protestant Girlhood' in Trevor Royle, ed., *Jock Tamson's Bairns* (London: Hamish Hamilton, 1977), 116, 117, 121.
56. *PBSV*, 505 (Lochhead, *Dreaming Frankenstein* (Edinburgh: Polygon, 1984), 139).
57. Liz Lochhead, *Mary Queen of Scots Got Her Head Chopped Off* (London: Penguin, 1989), 11.
58. Liz Lochhead, *Tartuffe* (Edinburgh: Polygon, 1985), Introduction and 11.
59. Sue Glover, *Bondagers*, in Cairns Craig and Randall Stevenson, ed., *Twentieth-century Scottish Drama* (Edinburgh: Canongate, 2001), 689.
60. David Greig, *'Europe' & 'The Architect'* (London: Methuen, 1996), 187, 161, 49, 72.
61. David Greig interviewed by Joan Bakewell for BBC Radio 3's 'Belief' series, 27 December 2005. Earlier quotations are taken from this same interview.
62. Gregory Burke, *Gagarin Way* (London: Faber and Faber, 2001), 61.
63. Janice Galloway, *The Trick is to Keep Breathing* (Edinburgh: Polygon, 1989), 52.
64. Galloway in Peter Mason, 'Treatment Needed by Psychiatric Hospitals', *Glasgow Herald*, 22 October 1991, 16.
65. Galloway, *Trick*, 223.
66. Janice Galloway, *Foreign Parts* (London: Cape, 1994), 13, 35.
67. Galloway interviewed by Cristie L. March, *Rewriting Scotland* (Manchester: Manchester University Press, 2002), 129.
68. Janice Galloway, *Clara* (London: Cape, 2002), 135, 150.
69. Andrew O'Hagan, *Our Fathers* (London: Faber and Faber, 1999), 144.
70. A. L. Kennedy, *Paradise* (London: Cape, 2004), 105, 19.
71. A. L. Kennedy, *Night Geometry and the Garscadden Trains* (1990; rpt London: Phoenix 1993), 110, 115, 119, 121.
72. A. L. Kennedy, *Now That You're Back* (London: Cape, 1994), 221.
73. Kennedy in March, *Rewriting*, 145.
74. A. L. Kennedy, 'Love Composition: The Solitary Vice' in Robert Crawford, ed., *Robert Burns and Cultural Authority* (Edinburgh: Edinburgh University Press, 1997), 38.

75. A. L. Kennedy, 'Avoid the spinning plates', *Herald* (Glasgow), 1 November 1996, 18.
76. A. L. Kennedy, *Indelible Acts* (London: Cape, 2002), 3.
77. Kennedy, *Night Geometry*, 118.
78. Alison Smith, 'Four Success Stories', *Chapman*, 74–5 (1993), 177–92.
79. Ali Smith, *Hotel World* (London: Hamish Hamilton, 2001), 39.
80. Ali Smith, *The Accidental* (London: Hamish Hamilton, 2005), 174, 15.
81. Smith, *Hotel World*, 51.
82. Heaney's letter is reproduced in Srikanth Reddy, ed., *From Poetry to Verse* (Chicago: University of Chicago Library, 2005), Plate 15.
83. See Robert Crawford, *The Modern Poet* (Oxford: Oxford University Press, 2001).
84. Carol Ann Duffy, *Selling Manhattan* (London: Anvil, 1987), 19.
85. Carol Ann Duffy, *Rapture* (London: Picador, 2005), 3.
86. *PBSV*, 509; Duffy, *Selling Manhattan*, 58.
87. *PBSV*, 510; Carol Ann Duffy, *Mean Time* (London: Anvil, 1993), 52.
88. John Burnside, conversation with Robert Crawford, Kathleen Jamie and Don Paterson, recorded by Dave Batchelor at Dundee Contemporary Arts in 2005 in preparation for the making of the BBC Radio Scotland's 2005 series *The Panoramic Pen*; unsourced remarks by John Burnside, Kathleen Jamie and Don Paterson quoted in the present chapter are from the same four-way interview-cum-conversation.
89. John Burnside, *Living Nowhere* (London: Cape, 2003), 134.
90. Burnside in Lawrence Wareing, 'Here, There and Everywhere', *Herald* (Glasgow), 5 February 2005, Books, 4.
91. John Burnside, *The Hoop* (Manchester: Carcanet, 1988), 17.
92. John Burnside, *Common Knowledge* (London: Cape, 1991), 36; *The Asylum Dance* (London: Cape, 2000), 6.
93. John Burnside in Hugh Macpherson, 'Scottish Writers', *Scottish Book Collector*, 11 (1989), 11; Burnside, *Swimming in the Flood* (London: Cape, 1995), 3.
94. *PBSV*, 511; Robin Robertson, *A Painted Field* (London: Picador, 1997), 18.
95. *PBSV*, 514; Robert Crawford and W. N. Herbert, *Sharawaggi* (Edinburgh: Polygon, 1990), 38.
96. Kinloch in Robert Crawford, ed., *Other Tongues* (St Andrews: Verse, 1990), 28.
97. The term was first used in print by Richard Price, 'The Informationists', *Interference* 1 (Oxford: Michael Gardiner, 1991), 11.
98. David Kinloch, *In My Father's House* (Manchester: Carcanet, 2005), 87.
99. *PBSV*, 512–13; Meg Bateman, *Aotromachd* (Edinburgh: Polygon, 1997), 48–9.
100. Kathleen Jamie, *Black Spiders* (Edinburgh: Salamander, 1982), 27.
101. Kathleen Jamie, *The Way We Live* (Newcastle: Bloodaxe, 1987), 11.
102. Kathleen Jamie and Sean Mayne Smith, *The Autonomous Region* (Newcastle: Bloodaxe, 1993), 67, 78.
103. *PBSV*, 515–17; Kathleen Jamie, *Mr and Mrs Scotland are Dead* (Newcastle: Bloodaxe, 2002), 111–13.
104. Ibid., 137, 129.
105. Kathleen Jamie, *Jizzen* (London: Picador, 1999), 19, 26–7, 34, 37; *PBSV*, 517–19.
106. See note 88 above.
107. Kathleen Jamie, *The Tree House* (London: Picador 2004), 3–4.
108. Don Paterson, *Nil Nil* (London: Faber and Faber, 1993), 4, 7.
109. Ibid., 21.
110. Don Paterson, *The Book of Shadows* (London: Picador, 2004), 41.
111. Don Paterson, *God's Gift to Women* (London: Faber and Faber, 1997), 53, 37.
112. Ibid., 15, 16, 17; *PBSV*, 520–22.
113. Don Paterson, *The Eyes* (London: Faber and Faber, 1999), 55, 38.
114. Don Paterson, *Landing Light* (London: Faber and Faber, 2003), 72, 74, 5.

Index

Bible – *cont.*
  Joshua, 366
  King James Bible or Authorized Version,
    161
  New Testament, 8, 118, 308
  Old Testament, 25, 118, 392
'Birks of Invermay', 262
Birlinn (publishing group), 662
Birmingham, 545
Bishop, Isabella Bird, 478
Bisset, Baldred, 58
Bisset, Robert, 401–2
  Douglas, 401–2
  Sketch of Democracy, 346
Bizerta, Tunisia, 603
Black, Joseph, 296
Black, William, 516
  Macleod of Dare, 515
  Wise Women of Inverness, The, 515
Blackford, Mrs, *see* Stoddart, Isabella
  Wellwood
Blackie, John (publisher)
  Library for Boys and Girls, 479
Blacklock, Thomas, 272
  'Happy Marriage', 352
Black Watch regiment, 300, 448
Blackwell, Thomas, 286
  *Enquiry into the Life and Writings of
    Homer, An*, 310
Blackwood, William, 293, 388, 390, 440,
    454, 484
Blackwood's Edinburgh Magazine, 293,
    388, 391, 427, 432, 436, 438, 440,
    445, 446, 447, 450, 456, 478, 485,
    521
  'Noctes Ambrosianae', 428–9
Blaeu, John, 185
Blair, Hugh, 13, 15, 16, 235, 251, 261,
    269, 281, 290–91, 295, 297, 299,
    306, 310, 311, 312, 317, 331, 338,
    371, 380, 416, 422
  British Poets, The, 331
  *Critical Dissertation on the Poems of
    Ossian, A*, 312
  Lectures on Rhetoric and Belles Lettres,
    290
  Sermons, 290
Blair, Robert
  Grave, The, 260–61
Blair, Tony, 574, 662
Blake, George, 643

Clyde Built, 592
Down to the Sea, 592
Mince Collop Close, 591–2
Shipbuilders, The, 592, 593
Blake, William, 312, 366
  illustrations for *The Grave* (Blair), 261
Blamire, Susanna, 372
Blantyre, Lanarkshire, 476
Blantyre, Malawi, 476
Blenheim, Battle of, 230
Bliesblituth, 35
Blind Hary, 7, 15, 82, 100
  Wallace, 79–81, 84, 254–5
Bloodaxe, Eric, King of the Norse, 38
Bloomsbury (publisher), 683
Blyton, Enid, 480, 683, 695
Boadicea, 177
Boccaccio, Giovanni, 202
  Genealogy of the Gods, 102
Bochanan, Dughall, *see* Buchanan, Dugald
Boece, Hector, 94, 104, 165
  Scotorum Historiae, 96
Boethius, 73
  De Consolatione Philosophiae (On
    the Consolation of Philosophy), 70,
    76
Bohemia, 115, 690
Boileau Despréaux, Nicolas, 338
Bologna University, 44, 45, 58, 177
Bolton, 400
Bonar, Horatius, 469
Boniface VIII (pope), 58
Bonnie Prince Charlie, *see* Stuart, Prince
  Charles Edward
Booker Prize, 667–8
Book of Deer, 36
Book of Discipline, 120–22, 124, 134,
    138, 144, 200
Book of Durrow, 24
Book of Kells, 24–5
Book of the Dean of Lismore, 52, 104–6,
    146, 311
Bordeaux, 125, 130
Borges, Jorge Luis, 2, 3, 224, 499, 647
Borneo, 688
Boswell, James, 4, 18, 272, 274, 292, 293,
    311, 329, 330, 335–6, 362, 364, 367,
    379–83, 407, 444, 456, 460
  Account of Corsica, An, 61, 379
  *Journal of a Tour to the Hebrides with
    Samuel Johnson*, 381, 498

Church of Scotland – *cont.*
  *Translations and Paraphrases, in Verse,
    of Several Passages of Sacred
    Scripture*, 369
Cicero, 241
Clanchy, Kate, 713, 725
Clancy, Thomas, 35
Clan Donald, 82
Clan Grant, 321
Clan Ranald, 106
Clarinda, *see* McLehose, Agnes
Clark, Jacqui, 699
Clark, Rev. T., *see* Galt, John ('Rev. T.
  Clark')
Claverhouse, Earl of, *see* Graham, John,
  Earl of Claverhouse
Clearances, Highland, 303, 447, 448, 467,
  575, 578, 582
Clerk, Archibald
  Poems of Ossian in the original Gaelic,
    475
Clerk, John, of Penicuik, 259
Clerke, William
  Marciano, 201–2
Clients of God, *see* Céli Dé
Clifford, John
  Faust, 698
  Losing Venice, 698
Clocktower Press (publisher), 670
Clough, Arthur Hugh, 471
  Bothie of Toper-na-fuosich, 454
Clyde, Firth of, 22, 42, 640
Clyde, River, 47, 361, 389, 504
Clyde, River, Canada, 169
Clydebank, 606
Clydeside, 313, 489, 592, 597, 618, 637,
  640, 643, 654
Cockburn, Alison, 284–5
  'The Flowers o' the Forest', 284, 306
Cockburn, Catherine
  Works, 285
Cockburn, Lord Henry, 407, 456, 484, 492
  Circuit Journeys, 385
  Journal, 385
  Selected Letters, 385, 387
Cocker, W. D., 543
Coimbra University, Portugal, 125
Colburn, Henry (publisher), 390–91
Cold War, 620
Coleridge, Samuel Taylor, 174, 312, 339,
  366, 428, 440

'Colkelbie's Sow', 107
Coll, 447
College of William and Mary, Virginia,
  296
Collins, William (poet), 310
Collins, William (publisher), 388
Colm Cille, *see* Columba, Saint
Cologne, 54, 94
  Minoritenkirche, 54
Colorado, 490
Columba, Saint, 7, 13, 23–7, 29–30, 33,
  36, 51, 60, 64, 177, 368
Colvin, Sidney, 502
Comines, Philipe Des, 418
common sense philosophy, 201, 269, 286,
  351, 371, 400
Communist Party of Great Britain, 549
Comnena, Anna, 418
Congregational Church, 480
conjectural history, 269
Conn, Stewart, 643
  Burning, The, 645
  I Didn't Always Live Here, 643
Connacht, 51
Connell, John
  David Go Back, 569
Connolly, Billy
  Great Northern Welly Boot Show, The,
    645
Conrad, Joseph, 502, 544
  Heart of Darkness, 477, 522
  Secret Agent, The, 501
Conservative Party, 388, 389, 411, 444,
  460, 650, 658, 662, 668
Constable (publisher), 291, 391, 420
Constable, Archibald, 293, 387
Constable, Thomas, 478
Constantinople, 418
Cooper, James Fenimore, 18, 312, 417,
  495
  Leatherstocking Tales, 406
Cope, John, 309
Cope's Tobacco Plant, 491
Corby, 715
Cornwall, 524, 617
Corpus Christi plays, 111
Corrie, Joe, 548–9
  In Time o' Strife, 549
Corsica, 379
Country and Western music, 665
Covenanters and Scottish National

Donaldson, Alexander, 330–31
Donaldson, William, 482
Donaldson v. Becket, 330–31
Donizetti, Gaetano, 4
Donn, Rob, *see* Mackay, Robert (Rob Donn MacAoidh)
Donne, John, 182, 184
Donovan, Ann
  Buddha Da, 688
Dostoevsky, Fyodor, 548
  Crime and Punishment, 501
Douglas, Elizabeth, 153
Douglas, Gavin, 79, 95, 97–104, 108, 110, 116, 237, 245, 247, 256, 257
  'Conscience', 102
  Eneados, 97, 99–103, 196, 238, 243
  Palice of Honour, The, 98–9, 106, 144, 165
Douglas, James, 66, 85
Douglas, James, Lord Queensberry, 211, 231
Douglas, Margaret, 286
Douglas, Norman
  South Wind, 536
Douglas, O., *see* Buchan, Anna
Doyle, Arthur Conan, 454, 519–21, 522, 526, 678
  Adventures of Shelock Holmes, The, 519
  Casebook of Sherlock Holmes, The, 521
  Firm of Girdlestone, The, 519
  Hound of the Baskervilles, The, 521
  Lost World, The, 519
  'Mr Stevenson's Methods in Fiction', 519
  Return of Sherlock Holmes, The, 521
  Sherlock Holmes Stories, 1, 492, 520–21, 683
  Study in Scarlet, A, 520
  White Company, The, 519
'Dream of the Rood', 31–2, 34, 35, 36
Drinan, Adam (Joseph Macleod), 581
Drostán, 36
dr-ttkv3/4tt, 39, 47, 48
Drummond, William, of Hawthornden, 10, 154, 165, 166, 167, 176, 177, 181–5, 186, 189, 190, 198, 200, 201, 203, 238, 239, 244, 426, 601
  Cypresse Grove, A, 183, 185
  Flowres of Sion, 182
  Poems, Amorous, Funerall, Diuine, Pastoral, in Sonnets, Songs, Sextains, Madrigals, 182

'Polemo-Middinia', 185
Skiamachia (Shadow-fighting), 192
'Sleepe, Silence Child, sweet father of soft Rest', 183
'The Angels for the natiuitie of our Lord', 184
'The Oister', 184
Dryburgh Abbey, 9, 44
Dryden, John, 419
Duan Albanach, 42
Duart Castle, Mull, 209
Du Bartas, Guillaume de Salluste, 152
  Historie of Judith, 151
Du Bellay, Joachim, 182
Dublin, 37, 206, 241, 406, 719
  Trinity College, 24
Duff, Mary, 392
Duff, William
  Essay on Original Genius, 277
  History of Rhedi, The, 277
Duffy, Carol Ann, 705, 621, 697, 713, 714–15, 725
  'Ash Wednesday 1984', 714
  Feminine Gospels, 714
  Mean Time, 715
  'Mrs Faust', 715
  'Mrs Freud', 715
  'Mrs Midas', 715
  'Originality', 714
  Other Country, The, 714
  'Poet for Our Times', 715
  'Prayer', 715
  'Queen Kong', 715
  Rapture, 714
  'The Laughter of Stafford Girls' High', 714
  'Warming Her Pearls', 714
  World's Wife, The, 715
Dulwich College, 603
Dumbarton, 313
Dumfries, 360, 386, 392, 450, 507
Dumfries-shire, 30–31, 310, 424, 457, 459
Dumourier, Charles François, 366
Dunbar, 52
Dunbar, James
  Essays on the History of Mankind in Rude and Cultivated Ages, 295
Dunbar, John, 167
Dunbar, William, 1, 86–93, 94, 95, 96, 97, 108, 129, 134, 135, 139, 143, 179, 221, 239, 247, 332, 426, 557, 619, 621

INDEX

Scotstarvit, 186

Scots-Yiddish, 625

Scott, Alexander (c. 1515–83), 143–4,
145, 154, 247
'Ane New Yeir Gift to the Quene Mary,
quhen scho come first Hame', 139

Scott, Alexander (1920–89), 636

Scott, Andrew, 371

Scott, Francis George, 567

Scott, John, 620

Scott, Michael, 430, 446
Cruise of the Midge, The, 446
'Davy Jones and a Yankee Privateer',
446
'Heat and Thirst: A Scene in Jamaica',
446
Tom Cringle's Log, 438, 446

Scott, Patrick
Tillage of Light, The, 180

Scott, Tom
Penguin Book of Scottish Verse, The
(old), 653
Seevin Poems o Maister Francis Villon,
608

Scott, W. R., 269

Scott, Walter, 2, 3, 9, 13, 18, 46, 47, 123,
200, 218, 224, 251, 252, 269, 270,
271, 274, 284, 285, 291, 298, 321,
325, 337, 339, 340, 350–51, 361,
365, 377, 383, 386, 387, 389,
390–91, 392, 394, 395, 396, 398,
399, 400, 403, 404–22, 412, 423,
428, 429, 439, 440, 449, 456, 458,
470, 478, 483, 486, 503, 504, 524,
528, 561, 563, 597, 662, 670, 691
Abbot, The, 408, 417
Anne of Geierstein, 408
Antiquary, The, 408, 419
Betrothed, The, 408
Black Dwarf, The, 408
Bride of Lammermoor, The, 408, 413
Castle Dangerous, 408
Chase, and William and Helen, Two
Ballads, The, 410
Chronicles of the Canongate, 406, 408,
416, 421–2
Count Robert of Paris, 408, 418
Fair Maid of Perth, The, 408, 411
Fortunes of Nigel, The, 408
Götz von Berlichingen (Goethe)
translation, 410, 412

Guy Mannering, 408, 409, 413, 415,
417, 450
Halidon Hill, 412
Harold the Dauntless, 411
Heart of Midlothian, The, 406, 408,
419, 420
Introductions and Notes from the
'Magnum Opus' edition of 1829–33,
408
Ivanhoe, 408, 418, 489
Journal, 420–21, 486
Kenilworth, 406, 408, 418
Lady of the Lake, The, 405, 411
Lay of the Last Minstrel, The, 410, 425,
430
Legend of Montrose, A, 408, 417, 430
Life and Works of John Dryden, The,
407
Life of Napoleon, 460
Lord of the Isles, The, 411
Marmion, A Tale of Flodden Field, 411
'Memoirs', 444
Minstrelsy of the Scottish Border, The,
410–11
Monastery, The, 408, 417, 419
Peveril of the Peak, 408
Pirate, The, 408, 413, 419
plays, 449
Quentin Durward, 408, 418
Redgauntlet, 408, 424
Rob Roy, 406, 408, 420, 450
Rokeby, 411
Saint Ronan's Well, 408, 413, 500–501
Stories from 'The Keepsake', 408
Tale of Old Mortality, The, 408, 417,
429, 433, 443
'Tales of my Landlord', 422
Talisman, The, 406, 408
'The Highland Widow', 421
'The Surgeon's Daughter', 416, 421–2
'The Two Drovers', 421
Waverley, 236, 252, 314, 322, 393, 400,
401, 402, 405, 406, 408, 412–13,
414–16, 417, 418–19, 420, 431, 440,
448, 562, 650
Waverley novels, 280, 405, 406–8, 413,
419
Woodstock, 406, 408

Scott, William Bell, 72
Albrecht Dürer monograph, 470
Iron and Coal, 470

Vikings, 24, 36, 37, 38, 47
'village poets' (Gaelic), 303
Villiers de l'Isle Adam, Auguste, 516
Villon, François, 608
Virago (publisher), 700
Virgil, 76, 152, 197, 241, 252, 272, 367
    Aeneid, 95, 98–9, 100, 101, 103, 190,
        251, 355
    Georgics, 362
Virginia, 371
Virgin Mary, 28, 54, 64, 67, 88, 101, 116,
    139, 286
Voltaire, François Marie Arouet, 276, 278,
    282, 379
    Le Caffe, ou l'Ecossaise, 323
    Shakespeare translations, 339
Volusenus, see Wilson, Florence
Votadini, 34
Vox, 554, 555

Waddell, P. Hately
    Ossian and the Clyde, 475
Walcott, Derek
    Omeros, 363
Waldegrave, Robert, 154
Wales and Welsh, 14, 28, 33, 35, 230, 316,
    541, 593, 725
Walker, Patrick, 261
Wallace, Randall
    Braveheart, 81
Wallace, Robert
    'The Commerce of the 2 Sexes', 323
Wallace, William, 7, 18, 19, 57, 79–81,
    82, 102, 126, 229, 254–5, 260, 313,
    336, 341, 399, 461, 611
Waller, Edmund, 244
Wallyford, 484
Walpole, Horace, 299, 316
'Waly, Waly', 283
Wandering Wull, see Nicholson, William
Ward, Mrs Sarah, 288, 290
Wardlaw, Elizabeth
    'Hardyknute', 248
Wardlaw, Bishop Henry, 69
Wareing, Alfred, 586
Wariston, see Johnston, Archibald, of
    Wariston
Warner, Alan, 673–4, 675, 690
    Morvern Callar, 673–4
    Sopranos, The, 674
    These Demented Lands, 674

Worms Can Carry Me to Heaven, The,
    674
Warner, Marina, 206
Warsaw, 399
Wars of Independence, 57
Warwick University, 707
Washington
    Folger Library, 288
Washington, George, 255
Watergate affair, 632
Waterloo, Battle of, 396
Watson, David, 271
Watson, James, 166, 238–9, 243, 247, 264
    Choice Collection of Comic and Serious
        Scots Poems, A, 238, 239, 244, 247
    Scotland's Grievance regarding Darien,
        238
Watson, John ('Ian Maclaren'), 512, 530
    Beside the Bonnie Briar Bush, 512, 514
    Days of Auld Lang Syne, The, 512
    Kate Carnegie, 514
Watson, Robert, 277, 368
Watson, Roderick
    Literature of Scotland, The, 662
Watt, A. P., 513
Watt, James, 296
Watts, D. E. R., 68
Waugh, Evelyn, 628
Weber, Carl Maria von
    Burns song arrangements, 349
Weber, Henry
    Tales of the East, 422
Wedderburn, David, 186, 187
Wedderburn, James, 136, 363
    Dionysius the Tyrant, 136
Wedderburn, John, 136
Wedderburn, Robert, 136
    Complaynt of Scotland, The, 143
Wedderburn, Robert, son of James
    Wedderburn of Inveresk
    Horrors of Slavery, 363
Weekly Magazine or Edinburgh
    Amusement, 336
Weldon, Fay, 400
Welsh, Irvine, 16, 591, 645, 658, 659, 661,
    669–72, 673, 675, 676, 679, 680,
    685, 687, 717
    Acid House, The, 671
    Bedroom Secrets of the Masterchefs, 671
    Marabou Stork Nightmares, 671
    Porno, 671